THE NAVY OF THE NUCLEAR AGE
1947–2007

THE U.S. NAVY WARSHIP SERIES

The Sailing Navy, 1775–1854
Civil War Navies, 1855–1883
The New Navy, 1883–1922
The Navy of World War II, 1922–1947
The Navy of the Nuclear Age, 1947–2007

THE NAVY OF THE NUCLEAR AGE
1947–2007

Paul H. Silverstone

Routledge
Taylor & Francis Group
NEW YORK AND LONDON

First published 2009
by Routledge
270 Madison Avenue
New York, NY 10016

Simultaneously published in the UK
by Routledge
2 Park Square
Milton Park, Abingdon
Oxon OX14 4RN

Routledge is an imprint of the Taylor & Francis Group, an informa business

© 2009 Paul H. Silverstone

Typeset in New Baskerville by
RefineCatch Limited, Bungay, Suffolk
Printed and bound in the United States of America on acid-free paper by
Edwards Brothers, Inc.

ISBN10: 0–415–97899–8 (hbk)
ISBN10: 0–203–87773–X (ebk)

ISBN13: 978–0–415–97899–6 (hbk)
ISBN13: 978–0–203–87773–9 (ebk)

All rights reserved. No part of this book may be reprinted or reproduced or utilized in any form or by any electronic, mechanical or other means, now known or hereafter invented, including photocopying and recording, or in any information storage or retrieval system, without permission in writing from the publishers.

Trademark Notice: Product or corporate names may be trademarks or registered trademarks, and are used only for identification and explanation without intent to infringe.

Library of Congress Cataloging-in-Publication Data

Silverstone, Paul H.
    The Navy of the Nuclear Age, 1947–2007 / Paul H. Silverstone.
       p. cm.—(U.S. Navy warship series)
    Includes bibliographical references and index.
    ISBN13: 978–0–415–97899–6 (hardback : alk. paper)
       ISBN10: 0–415–97899–8 (hardback : alk. paper) 1. Warships—United States—History—20th century. 2. Warships—United States—History—21st century. 3. United States. Navy—Lists of vessels. I. Title.

VA61.S546 2008
359.8′3097309045—dc22
                                                                                 2008015307

CONTENTS

Introduction	vii
Explanation of Data	xi
Abbreviations	xiii
United States Navy Type Designations	xv
U.S. Naval Ordnance, 1947–2007 by William J. Jurens	xix
Biography – William J. Jurens	xxix
Chronology, 1947–2007	xxxi

1	Aircraft Carriers	1
2	Submarines	13
3	Battleships	37
4	Cruisers	39
5	Destroyers	53
6	Escorts/Frigates	79
7	Amphibious Ships	97
8	Patrol Combatants	127
9	Mine Warfare Ships	141
10	Tenders	163
11	Transports and Supply Ships	195
12	Fleet Tugs	229
13	Sealift Ships	235
14	United States Coast Guard	255
15	National Oceanic and Atmospheric Administration (NOAA)	277

List of Principal Shipbuilders	283
Selected Bibliography	287
Index	289

INTRODUCTION

The sixty years after World War II were a period of world peace punctuated by a series of brutal local wars. The United States Navy was aggressively active throughout the period. In between the routine peacetime cruises and training, wars in Korea, Vietnam, and the Middle East occurred, and during most of the period the cold war with the Soviet Union was omnipresent.

After 1945 the United States demobilized most of the huge armed forces built up for combat operations. For the Navy this meant decommissioning a large percentage of its ships, many finding their way laid up into reserve fleets, while the older and acquired ships were taken off the Navy List.

With the outbreak of war in Korea in 1950, many of the laid-up ships were brought back into service. The war lasted about three years; the Navy actively supporting the ground troops with air operations and coastal bombardments. The Navy was not unscathed, suffering casualties of 505 killed, 1,576 wounded, and 286 prisoners-of-war. Seven Medals of Honor were awarded to Navy personnel, five posthumously. Several ships were sunk and more were damaged.

The tension between the Soviet Union and its allied countries resulted in a competition for superiority at sea. In 1949, the North Atlantic Treaty Organization (NATO) was established to counter Soviet threats. At sea, trouble points appeared in the Mediterranean, Arctic, and the waters off China. The Soviet Union built a large fleet of both submarines and surface warships, which soon appeared in all parts of the world. American and Soviet Navies played a cat-and-mouse game in the North Atlantic between their submarines and our anti-submarine forces. The climax occurred with a crisis in Cuba when Soviet missiles were positioned in that country and American forces challenged the Soviets. Through diplomacy a dangerous situation was defused.

In the Far East, the cold war became hot as military operations expanded in Vietnam. After the truce settlement between north and south in 1954, guerrillas from the north threatened the stability of the government in South Vietnam. Gradually, the United States became involved in ground operations. The falsely-reported Gulf of Tonkin incident in 1962 led to the introduction of large American military forces into what was essentially a civil war. As the enemy, North Vietnam and the Viet Cong, had no navy to fight, the U.S. Navy was involved in carrier operations, coastal bombardments, and riverine operations. Despite the Navy's vital but peripheral role in the war, casualties amounted to 1,631 killed, 4,178 wounded, and 401 missing, plus about 150 taken as POWs. Navy personnel were awarded eleven Medals of Honor, five posthumously. The tragic outcome after ten long years of fighting led to a rethinking of American military strategy.

After Vietnam, incidents at sea involving American sea power continued to occur. Both sides sent out intelligence collectors to learn about the opposing fleets. On many occasions Soviet vessels intruded into American fleet operations, leading in a few instances to actual physical contact between ships at sea. American submarines carried out highly secret operations in or near to Soviet harbors.

In the Middle East, there was continuous tension among the various parties, alternately hot or cold. The U.S. Navy was a continuing presence in the Mediterranean and Indian Oceans. American forces became involved to safeguard American citizens when fighting broke out in Lebanon, Israel, Iran and Iraq. In 1991 after Iraq invaded Kuwait the United States led a multi-national group which forced Iraq forces to withdraw and then invaded Iraq itself. The situation in the Persian Gulf smoldered on for a decade.

After the terrorist attacks on New York and Washington in September 2001, the American government took an aggressive stance first in Afghanistan, and then culminating in the decision to invade Iraq and depose the dictator Saddam Hussein. This in turn led to a long drawn-out war in the area. Navy casualties (to February 2008) total 92 killed and 600 wounded.

During these turbulent years, many drastic changes took place in the Navy. Unparalleled technological advances occurred in ships and weapons resulting in major changes in overall strategy and tactics. Faced with major innovations such as nuclear weapons and guided missiles, the early postwar years saw the first steps in using and defending against these weapons.

A major event at this time was the unification of the armed forces. The traditional armed services were unhappy with the proposal which finally led to them being joined together in a new Department of Defense in 1947. The Army Air Force (formerly Air Corps) became an independent arm as the United States Air Force, and a struggle took place over which service was to take the lead in guided missiles. Long range missiles went to the Air Force, while short range (tactical) missiles were developed by the Army. The Navy lost the first round in developing a new aircraft carrier with the cancellation of the *United States* in 1949 immediately after construction started.

The Navy's first postwar program showed the new priorities calling for construction of one attack aircraft carrier (CVB, *United States*), two hunter-killer cruisers (CLK, *Norfolk*), three hunter-killer submarines, six high-speed submarines (*Tang*), and four high-speed destroyers. Existing and unfinished ships were converted to new plans, two *Essex*-class carriers, two CVL for ASW, twelve destroyers to escort destroyers (DDE), six destroyers for ASW, two DEs to radar pickets, one cargo submarine (SSA), one oiler submarine (SSO), one radar-picket submarine (SSR), and one submarine, one cargo ship and two LSDs for polar exploration.

The development of guided missiles caused great changes in the development of ships. Initial research used war-built German rockets and developments proceeded from these early weapons. In 1947 the submarine *Cusk* fired a Loon missile, the first time a guided missile was fired from a ship. Rapid advances were made. By 1950 several submarines had been adapted to fire missiles. By the end of the 1950s, missile-armed ships had replaced gun-armed ships. The destroyer *Gyatt* was refitted to carry missiles in 1956 and a number of World War II cruisers were rearmed with missiles. In 1961 the cruiser *Long Beach* was completed armed only with missiles. By the 1960s guided missiles had become the main armament of surface warships.

With the cruisers gone, the only big-gun ships left were the *Iowa*-class battleships. At the beginning of the Korean War only the *Missouri* remained in commission. Her three sisters were recommissioned for Korea, but by 1958 all were laid up. The *New Jersey* was used again in Vietnam. They were the subject of controversy, with arguments made for the retention of their 16-inch guns, and they remained on the Navy list. The only big-gun ships remaining, two were reactivated for the Gulf War in 1991. Despite a last-ditch stand by their advocates, they were finally stricken from the list by the 2006.

During the decades after World War II a divergence occurred in the nomenclature of ships as the Navy built a new larger destroyer type which was designated a frigate. At the same time the number of ships in the category designated cruisers was declining. Other navies used a different nomenclature, with the result that the U.S. Navy seemed inferior to the Soviet Navy in the cruiser type, although its frigates were of similar size and power. In 1975, the U.S. Navy revised its nomenclature, so that ships in the frigate category (DL/DLG) were redesignated as cruisers (CG) or destroyers (DDG) according to size. The *Leahy* and *Belknap* classes, and the nuclear *Bainbridge*, *Truxtun* and *California* and *Virginia* classes were reclassified as cruisers, while the smaller *Farragut* class ships were reclassified as guided missile destroyers. Ocean escorts (DE) were also redesignated as frigates (FF), which corresponded to foreign practice for a type smaller than destroyers.

The resulting cruiser classes were a odd mixture of World War II type cruisers and the new former destroyer types. At the same time attack carriers (CVA/CVAN) became multimission carriers (CV/CVN).

The use of nuclear power to fuel surface ships was first tried with the cruiser *Long Beach*, and then extended to aircraft carriers with the revolutionary USS *Enterprise*, completed in 1961. A few other nuclear cruisers were built but for surface ships nuclear power was retained only for the giant *Nimitz*-class aircraft carriers of which ten were built.

The change in the submarine fleet was most dramatic. With the introduction of nuclear powered submarines, the changeover from diesel was rapid. The last diesel submarines were built in 1959 and by 1980 almost all active submarines were nuclear-powered. The combination of nuclear power and ballistic missiles produced the SSBN. These ships could remain at sea submerged for weeks on end with their nuclear-armed long range missiles providing a major deterrent to an enemy during the cold war.

Huge new amphibious assault ships, some larger than World War II aircraft carriers enable the United States to deliver combat-ready units with their equipment, including armor, directly to the point of assault. These ships combine the attributes of transport, helicopter carrier, floating dock and supply ship.

The rise of electronic warfare is evidenced by the tangle of masts and radars which has grown on all types of ships. Starting with the early radar and sonar of World War II for detection of the enemy, new equipment was developed for intelligence, countermeasures, fire control, and navigation.

In 1949 the Military Sea Transportation Service (MSTS) was established to operate transports and supply ships. The similar ships operated by the Army were transferred to this service in 1950. In 1970 it was renamed the Military Sealift Command (MSC). Starting in the 1980s large ships were acquired which were filled with military equipment and supplies and positioned at overseas points to be ready in case of an emergency.

A large number of cargo ships are owned or chartered by the Navy as a Rapid Reserve Force to be used to bring supplies overseas when needed. Most of these are manned by civilians and are unarmed. Both the prepositioning ships and the Sealift ships have been used to great advantage during the wars in the Persian Gulf area starting in 1991. In addition the Navy has gradually decommissioned its large number of auxiliaries and replaced their Navy crews with civilians which are more economic and efficient.

The size of the Navy has changed dramatically. Reaching a peak of 550 ships in 1990, the number declined to 450 in 1994 and only 300 in 2001. New ships are increasingly automated so as to greatly reduce crew size. New designs are streamlined into stealth designs to reduce recognition by enemy radar.

This fifth volume of the U.S. Navy Warships Series brings the compilation of the ships of the U.S. Navy up to the present. The Navy system of nomenclature has simplified the task of listing all the ships of the period, but changes have made it more complicated. In addition the Navy has not followed its own system at times, skipping numbers, and sometimes using numbers wholly out of sequence, such as with the *Seawolf* class submarines. The accounting numbers assigned to the Sealift ships are included mainly to distinguish the many ships from each other.

The pictures used in this volume are predominantly official U.S. Navy photographs. Again, despite the number of photographs included, it has been impossible to illustrate every type and every change made during the period.

I appreciate the assistance of Ernest Arroyo, James Flynn, the late Martin Holbrook, William Jurens, Norman Polmar, the late William Rau, William A. Schell, the late Ted Stone, Chris Wright, and the resources of the Naval Photo Club, International Naval Research Organization (INRO), the U.S. Navy History Division, the U.S. Ship Cancellation Society, the World Ship Society.

EXPLANATION OF DATA

The ships of the Navy for this period are listed according to the type of vessel as designated by the Navy. Combatant vessels are listed first, with auxiliaries following. Listings are also given for some other government departments, the Coast Guard, and the National Oceanic and Atmospheric Administration (NOAA) (formerly the Coast and Geodetic Survey). In most cases, a ship is listed only once under its initial classification and later changes are noted.

In this book, information for ships built or acquired before 1947 is provided only where it pertains to the period after that year. Full particulars and earlier history may be found in the fourth volume of this series on the World War II Navy.[1]

Particulars are given for each ship as follows.

Number. The official Navy number according to the official nomenclature.

Name. Navy name as completed with former names (naval or merchant) given below. Further changes of name, if any, are indicated in the Service Record with new Navy names in **bold** type.

Builder. The builder's abbreviated name. The full name and location of most builders are given in the appendix.

Construction Dates. For Navy-built ships dates given are for laying down of the keel, launching and commissioning. For acquired vessels, dates given are date of launching, acquisition by the Navy and commissioning. For ships of the MSTS/MSC and Sealift ships, as these ships were not commissioned, the final date is the date the ship was placed in service. If the ship was completed as converted or for a foreign navy, the date is in *italics*.

Tonnage. For Navy built ships, tonnage is light displacement, and/or full load displacement. For acquired ships it is gross tonnage (grt), actually a measurement of volume rather than weight.

Dimensions. Standard dimensions given in feet (') and inches (") are length × beam × draft. Where known, length is specified as overall (oa), between perpendiculars (bp)—that is between foreside of stem and aftside of rudder post, or on the waterline (wl). Where no type of length is given, registered dimensions are provided.

Machinery. Number of propellers, mode of propulsion, type and maker of engines and number and type of boilers where known, horsepower and speed. For submarines the surface and submerged figures are separated by a slash (/).

Endurance. Maximum distance a ship could steam at the speed indicated.

Complement. Normal figure for officers and crew. For some ships, where sources vary, a range (50/75) is given. There was often a large variance between peacetime and wartime complements.

Armament. Original number and type of guns or missiles is given first. Later significant changes are given with date, either by listing the entire complement of armament, or by indicating modifications as additions or subtractions from the previous data shown. The date reflects the date of survey rather than when changes were actually made. Minor variations are not necessarily given. Guns are described by size of bore in inches and caliber. Missiles are described by number of launchers.

Armor. Thickness of armor for the areas noted.

Notes. Additional information pertaining to design, construction or later modifications, acquisition, or earlier historical notes of interest, not included in other categories. Changes in Navy type are denoted as reclassified ("Rec").

Service Record. A capsule history of each ship's naval service showing assignment and war service including participation in engagements or operations, major damage to vessel or loss. Casualties are given in parentheses. Changes in Navy name are given here in **bold** type. Also final disposition by the Navy, loss, sale, or transfer to another agency or a foreign country. The term "returned" means returned to previous owner, often WSA or MC.

Battle stars (★) were awarded for the conflicts in Korea and Vietnam. The number of stars is indicated for each ship together with the time periods involved. For the Korean War these are

---

[1] Paul H. Silverstone, *The Navy of World War II, 1922–1947* (New York: Routledge, 2008).

shown as numbers for which the time period is shown in the Chronology. Where no number is given, that ship received only one star.

For the Vietnam War these are shown as time periods which can be aligned with the time periods shown in the Chronology. It has not been possible to find a complete list of stars awarded for Vietnam so no number appears for some ships.

In general, dates for deployments to foreign areas are shown only where ships and crew were entitled to wear campaign ribbons for deployments involving actual or possible combat; these are indicated by a diamond (◆). Areas of the world where deployments were made are indicated as follows, although the operations may have been more widespread. Cuba, Taiwan Straits/Quemoy-Matsu, Korea, Indian Ocean/Iran, Libya, Lebanon, Somalia.

Later history. Brief details of the ship's career after leaving Naval service including later merchant names, service in other government departments or in foreign navies. The name in the foreign navy is followed by the pendant number or numbers if changed, separated by a slash (E12/F12). In some cases where the transliteration of foreign characters has changed over the years, both styles of the name are given.

Ultimate fate is given where known, or the year the ship disappeared from shipping registers (RR). Occasionally a date is given for the last published reference (SE = still existing). The notation NDRF.SE means the ship was laid up in the reserve fleet at time of writing.

The traditional term Navy Yard was discontinued and the yards were redesignated Naval Shipyards on 30 Nov 1945. The naval districts were also realigned.[2] The word "vessel" discontinued in the nomenclature, 25 Aug 1960.

---

[2] In 1948 they were:
1st Me, Vt, NH, Mass, RI; 2nd abolished; 3rd NY, Ct, NJ; 4th Pa, NJ, Del; 5th Md, Va, WV; 6th NC, SC, Ga, Ala, Miss, Tenn; 7th abolished; 8th Tex, La, Ark, Okla; 9th Great Lakes—Mich, Ohio, Minn, Ind, Ill, Ky, Wis, ND, SD, Neb, Kans, Colo, Wyo; 10th PR, Caribbean; 11th NM, Ariz, S Cal; 12th N Cal, Nev, Utah; 13th Wash, Ore, Ida, Mont; 14th Hawaii; 15th CZ; 16th Alaska

ABBREVIATIONS

★	battle stars (Korea, Vietnam)	GUPPY	greater underwater propulsive power
◆	campaigns/expeditions	h/c	helicopter
AAW	anti-air warfare	HMS	Her Majesty's Canadian Ship
AC	Allis-Chalmers	HMS	Her Majesty's Ship
ARG	Amphibious Ready Group	IPDMS	Improved Point Defense Missile System
ASDS	Advanced SEAL Delivery System	IS	in service
ASROC	anti-submarine rocket	L	launched
ASW	anti-submarine warfare	LAMPS	light airborne multi-purpose system
B&W	Babcock & Wilcox	LASH	Lighter aboard ship
bbls	barrels	lchr	launcher
BG	Battle Group	LD	laid down
BHP	brake horsepower	LU	laid up
bp	length between perpendiculars	m/v	merchant vessel
BPDMS	basic point defense missile system	MAP	Military Assistance Program
BU	broken up, breaking up	Marad	Maritime Administration
CE	combustion engineering (boilers)	MC	U.S. Maritime Commission
CODOG	combination diesel or gas turbine	MG	machine guns
comm	commissioned, commission	MPF	Maritime Prepositioning Force
CT	conning tower	MPS	Maritime Prepositioning Ship
CTL	constructive total loss	MSC	Military Sea Command
DASH	drone anti-submarine helicopter	MSP	Mutual Security Program
decomm	decommissioned	MSTS	Military Sea Transportation Service
DET	diesel-electric trandem motor drive (*Cannon* class DEs)	MV	motor vessel
		NASA	National Aeronautics and Space Administration
DTRC	David Taylor Research Center	NATO	North Atlantic Treaty Organization
EPA	Environmental Protection Agency	ND	Naval District
evac	evacuation	NDRF	National Defense Reserve Fleet
FBM	fleet ballistic missile	NECPA	National Emergency Command Post Afloat
f/l	full load	NFAF	Naval Fleet Auxiliary Force
FFU	further fate unknown	NOAA	National Oceanic and Atmospheric Administration
FM	Fairbanks-Morse		
FMR	geared diesel, Fairbanks-Morse reverse gear drive (*Edsall* class DEs)	NYd	Navy Yard
		NRF	Naval Reserve Force
FRAM	fleet rehabilitation and modernization	NRT	naval reserve training
f/v	fishing vessel	NSP	non-self-propelled
grt	gross registered tons	NSYd	Naval Shipyard
GT	geared turbines	oa	length overall

OPDS	Offshore Petroleum Discharge System	SS2007	Strategic Sealift, active Apr 2007
o/s, OS	out of service	SSM	surface-to-surface missile
OSP	Offshore Procurement Program	ST	steam turbines
pdr	pounder	SURTASS	Surveillance Towed Array Sonar System
PPF	Prepositioning Force	SWATH	Small Waterplane-Area Twin Hull
PPS	Prepositioning Ships	SWPS	Stabilized Weapons Platform System
PRC	People's Republic of China	TACAN	Tactical Air Navigation
PUC	Presidential Unit Citation	TE	turbo-electric drive (*Buckley* class DEs)
R(year)	stricken from foreign navy	TEV	turbo-electric drive (DEs)
reacq	reacquired	tkr	tanker
RDF	Rapid Deployment Force	trfd	transferred
rec	reclassified	TS	training ship
recomm	recommissioned	TT	torpedo tubes
RO/RO	roll-off/roll-on	USA	U.S. Army
ROS	Reduced Operational Status	USAF	U.S. Air Force
RR(year)	removed from merchant register	USAHS	U.S. Army Hospital Ship
RRF	Ready Reserve Force	USAT	U.S. Army Transport
SAM	surface-to-air missile	USC&GS	U.S. Coast and Geodetic Survey
SCAJAP	Shipping Control Administration Japan	USCG	U.S. Coast Guard
schr	schooner	USCGC	U.S. Coast Guard Cutter
SE(year)	still existing	USMA	U.S. Military Academy
SEAL	Sea-Air-Land (team)	USMG	U.S. Military Government
SF	Sea Frontier	USN	U.S. Navy
SHP	shaft horsepower	VLS	vertical launch system
SLEP	Service Life Extension Program	VTE	vertical triple expansion
SOSUS	Sound Surveillance System	WGT	geared-turbine drive (*John C. Butler* class DEs)
SS	steam ship	wl	length on waterline

U.S. NAVY TYPE DESIGNATIONS

Aircraft Carriers

AVT	aircraft transport/training carrier
CV	aircraft carrier/multipurpose carrier
CVA	attack aircraft carrier
CVAN	nuclear attack aircraft carrier
CVB	large carrier
CVE	escort carrier
CVHA	assault helicopter aircraft carrier
CVHE	escort helicopter aircraft carrier
CVL	small aircraft carrier
CVN	nuclear carrier
CVS	support aircraft carrier (ASW)
CVT	training carrier
CVU	utility aircraft carrier

Battleships

BB	battleship
BBG	guided missile capital ship (proposed)

Cruisers

CA	heavy cruiser
CAG	guided missile heavy cruiser
CB	large cruiser
CBC	large tactical command ship
CC	command ship
CG	guided missile cruiser (xDLG)
CGN	nuclear guided missile cruiser
CL	light cruiser
CLAA	anti-aircraft cruiser
CLC	tactical command ship
CLG	guided missile light cruiser
CLGN	nuclear guided missile cruiser
CLK	hunter-killer cruiser

Destroyer Types

DD	destroyer
DDE	escort destroyer
DDG	guided missile destroyer
DDK	hunter-killer desetroyer
DDR	radar picket destroyer
DE	escort
DEC	escort, control
DEG	guided missile escort
DER	radar picket escort
DL	frigate
DLG	guided missile frigate
DLGN	nuclear guided missile frigate
FF	frigate (xDE) (30 Jun 1975)
FFG	guided missile frigate (xDEG)
FFT	frigate (reserve training)

Submarines

AGSS	auxiliary research submarine
APSS (LPSS) (SSP)(ASSP)	transport submarine
ASSA	cargo submarine
IXSS	unclassified submarine
SS	submarine
SSAG	auxiliary submarine
SSBN	ballistic missile submarine
SSG	guided missile submarine
SSGN	nuclear guided missile submarine
SSK	anti-submarine submarine
SSN	nuclear submarine
SSO (AOSS)	oiler submarine
SSR	radar picket submarine
SSRN	nuclear radar picket submarine
SST	target & training submarine
X	submersible craft

Large Amphibious Vessels (old)

AGC	amphibious force flagship/
AGF	flagship
AKA	amphibious cargo ship
APA	amphibious transport
APD/LPR	high speed transport
IFS	inshore fire support ship
LSD	landing ship, dock
LS(FF)	landing ship, flotilla-flagship
LSI(G)	landing ship, infantry (gunboat)
LSI(L)	landing ship, infantry (large)
LSI(M)	landing ship, infantry (mortar)
LSM	landing ship, medium
LSM(R)	landing ship, medium (rocket)
LSS(L)	landing ship, support (large)
LST	landing ship, tank
LST(H)	landing ship, tank (evacuation)
LSU	landing ship, utility
LSV	landing ship, vehicle

Large Amphibious Vessels (new)

LCC	amphibious command ship
LCS	littoral combat ship
LFR	inshore fire support ship
LKA	amphibious cargo ship
LHA	amphibious assault ship (general)
LHD	amphibious assault ship (multipurpose)
LPA	amphibious transport
LPD	amphibious transport dock
LPH	amphibious assault ship (helicopter)
LPR	amphibious transport,/small
LCAC	air cushion landing craft
LCU	utility landing craft

Patrol Vessels

PC	submarine chaser (steel)
PCC	submarine chaser (control)
PCE	submarine chaser escort
PCEC	submarine chaser escort (control)
PCER	submarine chaser escort (rescue)
PCF	patrol craft (fast)
PCG	patrol chaser (missile)
PCH	submarine chaser hydrofoil
PCS	submarine chaser sweeper
PF	frigate
PG	gunboat
PGG	patrol gunboat (missile)
PGH	gunboat (hydrofoil)
PGM	motor gunboat
PHM	patrol combatant missile (hydrofoil)
PT	motor torpedo boat
PTF	fast patrol craft
SC	submarine chaser (wood)

Mine Vessels (old)

CM	minelayer
DM	destroyer minelayer
DMS	destroyer minesweeper
ACM	auxiliary minelayer
AM	fleet minesweeper
AMCU	coastal minehunter
AMS (ex-YMS)	coastal minesweeper

Mine Vessels (new) (7 Feb 1955)

MCM	mine countermeasures ship
MM	fleet minelayer
MMA	auxiliary minelayer
MMC	coastal minelayer
MMD	destroyer minelayer
MMF	fleet minelayer
MCS	mine warfare command & support ship
MHC	coastal minehunter
MSB	minesweeping boat
MSC(O)	coastal minesweeper, old
MSC	coastal minesweeper
MSF	fleet minesweeper
MSH	mine hunter
MSI	minesweeper, inshore
MSO	ocean minesweeper
MSS	minesweeper, special (device)

Auxiliaries

AB	crane ship
ACS	crane ship
AD	destroyer tender
ADG	degaussing ship
AE	ammunition ship
AF	store ship
AFS	combat store ship
AG	miscellaneous auxiliary
AGB	ice breaker
AGDE	escort research ship
AGDS	deep submergence support ship
AGEH	hydrofoil research ship
AOE	fast combat support ship
AGER	environmental research ship
AGF	command flagship
AGI	intelligence collector (unofficial)
AGL	lighthouse tender
AGM	missile range instrumentation ship
AGMR	major communications relay ship
AGOR	oceanographic research ship
AGOS	oceanographic surveillance ship
AGP	patrol craft tender
AGR	radar picket ship
AGS	surveying ship
AGSc	coastal surveying ship
AGSL	satellite launching ship (not used)
AGTR	technical research ship
AH	hospital ship

AK	cargo ship		YCK	open cargo lighter
AKD	cargo ship, dock		YCV	Aircraft Transport Lighter
AKE	dry cargo/ammunition ship		YD	Floating Derrick (Crane)
AKL	light cargo ship		YDG	Degaussing Vessel
AKN	net cargo ship		YDT	Diving Tender
AKR	vehicle cargo ship		YF	Covered Lighter
AKR	large medium-speed RO/RO ship		YFD	Yard floating dry dock
AKS	stores issue ship		YFN	Covered Lighter (NSP)
AKV	cargo ship & aircraft ferry		YFNB	large covered lighter
AL	lightship		YFND	dry dock companion craft
AN/ANL	net laying ship		YFNX	lighter (special purpose)
AO	fleet oiler; tanker		YFP	Floating Power Barge
AOG	gasoline tanker		YFB	ferry boat or launch
AOR	replenishment fleet tanker		YFR	covered lighter, reefer
AOT	transport oiler		YFRN	covered lighter, reefer (NSP)
AP	transport		YFRT	covered lighter, range tender
APB	self-propelled barracks ship		YFT	Torpedo Transport Lighter
APC	small coastal transport		YFU	harbor utility craft (1957)
APH	evacuation transport		YG	Garbage Lighter
AR	repair ship		YGN	Garbage Lighter (NSP)
ARB	battle damage repair ship		YHB	house boat
ARC	cable repairing or laying ship		YM	Dredge
ARG	internal combustion engine repair ship		YMP	Mine Planter
ARH	heavy hull repair ship		YMS	motor minesweeper
ARL	landing craft repair ship		YNg	gate vessel
ARSD	salvage lifting ship		YNT	net tender
ARST	salvage craft tender		YO	fuel oil barge
ARS	salvage vessel		YON	fuel oil barge (NSP)
ARV	aircraft repair ship		YOG	gasoline barge
ARVA	aircraft repair ship (aircraft)		YOGN	gasoline barge (NSP)
ARVE	aircraft repair ship (engine)		YOS	oil storage barge
ARVH	helicopter maintenance ship		YP	district patrol vessel
AS	submarine tender		YPD	Pile Driver (floating)
ASR	submarine rescue vessel		YPK	pontoon stowage barge
ATA	auxiliary ocean tug		YR	floating workshop
ATF	fleet ocean tug		YRB	submarine berthing barge
ATR	ocean tug, rescue		YRBM	repair-berthing-messing barge
ATS	salvage & rescue ship		YRD(H)	floating workshop, drycock (hull)
AV	seaplane tender		YRD(M)	floating workshop, drydock (machinery)
AVB	advance aviation base ship (1957)		YRR	radiological repair ship
AVP	small seaplane tender		YS	stevedoring barge
AVS	aviation supply ship		YSD	seaplane wrecking derrick
AVT	auxiliary aircraft transport		YSP	salvage pontoon
AW	distilling ship		YSR	sludge removal barge
IX	unclassified vessel		YTB	harbor tug, big
			YTL	harbor tug, little
			YTM	harbor tug, medium
			YTT	torpedo testing barge
			YV	drone aircraft catapult/control craft
			YW	water barge
			YWN	water barge (NSP)

Floating Dry Docks

AFDB	floating dry dock, big
AFDL	floating dry dock, little
AFDM	floating dry dock, medium
ARD	auxiliary repair dry dock
ARDM	medium auxiliary repair dry dock

Service Craft

YAG	District Auxiliary Miscellaneous
YC	Open Lighter
YCF	car float, railroad

Small Amphibious Vessels

LCC	landing craft, control
LCM	landing craft, mechanized
LCP(L)	landing craft, personnel (large)
LCP(N)	landing craft, personnel (nested)
LCP(R)	landing craft, personnel (ramp)

LCR(L)	landing craft, rubber (large)	WSC	patrol boat
LCR(S)	landing craft, rubber (small)	WSES	surface effect ship
LCS(S)	landing craft, support (small)	WTGB	icebreaking tug
LCV	landing craft, vehicle	WTR	training ship
LCVP	landing craft, vehicle-personnel	WYT	harbor tug
LVT	landing vehicle, tracked	WYTL	small harbor tug
LVT(A)	landing vehicle, tracked (armored)		

U.S. Coast Guard

WAGB	icebreaker
WAGL	lighthouse tender
WAGO	oceanographic cutter
WAGW	weather ship
WAK	cargo cutter
WARC	cable ship
WAT	tug
WAVP	tender type cutter
WAVR	air rescue boat
WDE	destroyer escort
WIX	training cutter
WLB	offshore buoy tender
WLI	inshore buoy tender
WLIC	inland construction tender
WLM	coastal buoy tender
WLR	river buoy tender
WLV	light vessel
WHEC	high endurance cutter
WMEC	medium endurance cutter
WMEH	medium endurance cutter, hydrofoil
WMSL	maritime security cutter (large) 2004
WMSM	maritime security cutter (medium) 2004
WOLE	offshore law enforcement vessel
WPB	maritime patrol boat 2004
WPBH	patrol boat, hydrofoil
WPC	maritime patrol coastal cutter 2004
WPC	patrol craft
WPG	gunboat

NOAA

R	research
S	survey

Prefix E	experimental
Suffix N	nuclear
Prefix T	MSTS/MSC (civilian manned) parentheses not used after 1968 Word "vessel" not used after 1960

Maritime Administration Classification

First letter (ship type) (number indicates size)

C	cargo
P	passenger
R	refrigerator
S	special type
T	tanker
V	tug
VC	victory ship
EC	liberty ship

Second letter (propulsion) (number indicates shafts)

M	motor (diesel)
MET	diesel-electric
S	steam
SE	turbo-electric

U.S. NAVAL ORDNANCE, 1947–2007

William J. Jurens

Ordnance development in the U.S. Navy since the end of the Second World War has been characterized by a) the successive replacement of relatively short ranged large caliber gun-type systems with rocket propelled terminally-guided weapons of greatly extended range and equivalent accuracy, b) the replacement of relatively large, high-cost, high-maintenance manned aircraft with disposable missiles having a much lower impact on the delivery platform, and c) the introduction and deployment of nuclear weapons. Overall, the trend in weapons might be characterized as "fewer, but better"; current weapons are individually much more capable than their predecessors, but there are far fewer of them.

Although reliable data on many older weapons is easy to obtain, it is difficult to obtain and/or publish similar information on more recently deployed weapons, many details of which remain security classified. Precise evaluation of more modern weapon performance is also inhibited by the fact that the practical efficiency of many modern weapons is largely dependent upon electronic systems and computer software which, can (and is) modified without having an impact on exterior appearance. In that regard, information on weapons currently in service must be considered approximate and subject to continuous revision.

The sheer number of weapons that have been developed and deployed over the sixty-year span of this volume means that details of many low-production air-to-air missiles, bombs, and other items, including weapons primarily employed by the Marine Corps, have necessarily been omitted from this analysis.

GUNS

Although some smaller warships continued to mount light weapons intended to interdict unarmed or lightly armed vessels, by the late 1970s almost all guns with a caliber exceeding six inches had been retired from the fleet. Most of the light (six-inch) cruisers were gone by 1965; though some—partially converted to carry missiles—lasted until the early 1970s. Some of the heavy (eight-inch) cruisers, again partially or fully converted to carry missiles, lasted until the late 1970s. One 8″ cruiser, using special ammunition, achieved gun ranges of about 70,000 yards in tests conducted during the Vietnam War. The last post-war designed large-caliber gun appears to have been the 8″/55 Mk 71, unsuccessfully mounted aboard destroyer *Hull* from 1975–79.

The 16″/50 mounted on the *Iowa* class was retired and resurrected several times, notably during the Korean War, the Vietnam War, and the Gulf War. Although a special Gunnery Improvement Program in the 1980s greatly improved the capability of the 16″/50 gun, the ships—and the guns—were finally retired in 1991 after a tragic explosion aboard USS *Iowa* two years before. The last of the old 5″/38s, representing a design then 66 years old, were retired at the turn of the twenty-first century, although some ships continued to mount single multipurpose 5″ caliber weapons—in mounts of considerably greater complexity and capability—thereafter. Although missiles remained the weapon of choice for engaging air targets at long ranges, their size and complexity meant that saturation attacks, i.e. simultaneous attacks by multiple aircraft approaching from various bearings, coupled with the inability of missiles to activate and maneuver in time to engage targets at close range mean that many U.S. Navy warships continue to mount small-caliber (under 3″) weapons for close-in defense against missiles and small attack craft. The most notable of these is the 20 mm "Phalanx" CIWS "SeaWhiz" (Close-in Weapons System). Available in several models, this relatively light (14,500 lb) weapon is capable of engaging closing—i.e. potentially dangerous—targets entirely without human intervention, using onboard radar and computers to correct the stream of depleted uranium or tungsten bullets so long as the target continues to close. At 30,000 or 4,500 rounds per miniute, however, the 1,500 round magazine is depleted quite rapidly. Phalanx deployed in 1977 and remains in front-line service today (2008). The rapid development of missiles and aircraft meant that the old 20 mm and 40 mm guns installed on ships built during World War II did not last long; most of the 40 mm twin and quad mounts had been retired to the "mothball" fleet or had been replaced with 3″ weapons by 1955. By 1975 the only 20 mm guns left remained aboard auxiliaries. Guns had disappeared completely from submarines by about 1960 as their conventionally-powered platforms disappeared.

The conflict in Vietnam, which lasted roughly from 1965 to 1975, saw a brief period of extensive installation and application of automatic small-caliber weapons aboard riverine craft, some adopted from Army and Marine inventories.

The emphasis on missiles and terminal guidance meant there were few really major developments in large-caliber gunnery fire control during the period; in fact the Mk 8 rangekeepers introduced during World War II were retained—and used—aboard the *Iowa* class ships until the 1990s. Fire control for anti-aircraft gun systems fared much better. Radars were, of course, greatly enhanced during this period, although their relatively poor resolution in azimuth and their inability to positively discriminate targets meant that they never completely replaced optical spotting. During the 1980s, unmanned remote piloted vehicles (RPVs), which essentially replaced the aircraft and helicopters previously used for such purposes, permitted battleship spotters to spot fall of shot visually from very close range. The first of these, basically remotely controlled model airplanes, have slowly morphed into the "Predator" type vehicles that are so popular and useful today.

A summary of the most important gun-type weapons of the period is given in Table 1.

ANTI-SUBMARINE WEAPONS

Post-war anti-submarine weapons began with trainable and and stabilized versions of Hedgehog. Mk 15 was mounted on old 40 mm quad mounts. "Weapon Alfa," never really very successful, was introduced in about 1949. It employed a single 12.5″ rocket launcher to deliver a number of 250 lb fast-sinking charges to a range of about 750 yards, mimicking the pattern of Hedgehog. Weapon Alpha was the last variant of the Hedgehog gun-type weapons that shot "dumb" depth charges; subsequent weapons employed homing torpedoes instead. The rocket assisted torpedo (RAT) debuted about 1957; early versions carried a Mk 43 torpedo out to about 5,000 yards (with problematical accuracy); later versions, e.g. RAT C, could take a 30 knot Mk 44 out to 10,000 yards. RAT eventually evolved into "ASROC," which used a Talos booster and a JATO second-stage to deliver a Mk 46 homing torpedo out to about eight nautical miles. ASROC became operational about 1958; early versions used a "pepperbox" launcher; later versions used vertical launchers instead. "SUBROC," similar to ASROC, but launched from submarines, carried a 1–5 Kt warhead out to a range of about 30 nautical miles. Many destroyers retained above-water torpedo tubes in the form of new mounts designed for anti-submarine rather than anti-surface ship engagements.

The diminutive Drone Anti-Submarine Helicopter (DASH), represented an interesting (though basically unsuccessful) innovation which used an unmanned remote-controlled miniature helicopter to deliver an anti-submarine homing torpedo to ranges much greater than ASROC could reach. After 1983 DASH was replaced by the much larger, heavier (and much more capable) Light Airborne MultiPurpose System (LAMPS) which uses a manned SH-60 "Seahawk" helicopter equipped with MAD (Magnetic Anomaly Detector), dipping sonar, sonobuoys, and Mk 46 or Mk 60 homing torpedoes to deliver weapons out to ranges exceeding 200 miles.

As before, torpedoes could be launched from aircraft, surface ships, or submarines. Although anti-ship capability was maintained, the vast majority of post-World War II weapons were intended for use in anti-submarine roles.

TORPEDOES

The end of World War II saw seven weapons in common use, Mk 13, Mk 14, Mk 15, Mk 18, Mk 27, Mk 28, and (mine) Mk 24. Of the 15 types in development in 1945, only only three saw actual service; navol-powered submarine-launched Mk 16, aircraft or destroyer-launched active-homing anti-submarine torpedo Mk 32, and Mk 34, an aircraft-launched passive homer. Torpedoes Mks 27, 32, and 34 were largely seen as "interim" weapons, released for immediate use while newer torpedoes were being developed. Mk 32, a small destroyer-launched active-homer, was replaced by Mk 43. Mk 35 was an active/passive homer, originally intended for delivery by aircraft, ships and submarines (the aircraft delivery requirement was deleted in 1948). Mk 41, a stripped down aircraft-launched version of the old Mk 35 developed in 1944, was unsuccessful, and was quickly replaced by Mk 37 and Mk 43. Mk 37, also a variant of Mk 35, and also an active-homer, became the standard submarine weapon post-war, and was for a time, also issued to destroyers.

Old torpedoes were retired regularly. By 1955, the Navy employed Mk 14, Mk 16, and Mk 37 torpedoes aboard submarines, Mk 37 and Mk 43 aboard destroyers, and Mk 43 aboard aircraft. These were good weapons; Mk 16 was not retired until the mid-1970s, and Mk 14 remained in service until about 1980. Mk 37 began as an electrically-powered two-speed active homer, and retired about 1967. Commencing about 1973, some of the old Mk 37s were refitted with wire guidance and 90 hp thermochemical rotary piston engines, re-emerging as the NT 37 series.

Limitations on the weight that could be carried by aircraft meant that aircraft-launched torpedoes tended to be smaller and much less capable than their submarine- and surface-launched counterparts. The best example was was Mk 43, an electrically-powered active-homer which weighed only 250 lbs and was capable of being carried by virtually any aircraft in the fleet.

Work on Mk 44, an inexpensive 445 lb battery-powered active-homer began about 1952, but it did not reach the fleet until ten years later. Development of Mk 46, intended to replace the old battery-powered Mk 44s, commenced in the late 1950s. Mk 46 Mod 0 used a solid fuel motor that was unsuccessful; later mods were equipped with a 5-cylinder monopropellant cam engine. Mk 46, the successor to Mk 44, went in to production about 1963, with the first units employing a swash-plate engine powered by a solid propellant grain for propulsion. This did not work well, and after some experimentation with a seawater activated battery system, Mk 46 emerged with a liquid-fueled monopropellant cam engine.

In the mid-1950s some old Mk 27 torpedoes, then near retirement, were converted to Mk 39, and used to investigate the use of wire guidance. Wire guidance was formally introduced in torpedo Mk 45, a high-speed, long-range submarine launched weapon capable of carrying a nuclear warhead (which required positive control all the way to the target). Mk 45 was also the first successful submarine-launched weapon to employ a seawater activated battery propulsion system.

Wire-guided torpedo Mk 48 wire, a long-range anti-submarine and anti-ship torpedo, entered service in 1972. Powered by a 500 hp axial-flow liquid-propellant swashplate pump-jet engine, Mk 48 can reach a speed of 55 knots and depths of about 2,500 feet. The ADCAP (ADvanced CAPability) verson, with all digital electronics, has greater speed, range, and target tracking and detection capabilities. Mk 48 Mod 3 allowed two-way communication with the torpedo while it was running.

Torpedo Mk 50, specifically designed to similar dimensions to Mk 46, is designed for deployment from aircraft and surface ships. Propulsion is reportedly via a Rankine-cycle engine using lithium and sulfur-hexaflouride to generate steam.

The most common torpedoes employed during the post-World War II period are described in Table 2.

MINES

The delivery of mines via surface ships was largely abandoned after World War II, with almost all mines now laid via submarines or aircraft. Most newer mines are equipped with multiple activation features, making them very difficult to sweep using older conventional methods.

Mine Mk 52, a modified 1,000 lb aircraft bomb, carrying a 595 lb HBX warhead, first deployed in 1961. It could detect targets passing at less than 5 knots, and, in order to engage passing submarines, could cover depths up to about 600 feet. Mine Mk 55, is similar, but carries a 1,270 lb warhead. Mines Mks 56 and 57 are moored mines specifically designed to attack submerged submarines down to 1,200 feet.

Mine Mk 60, a.k.a. "Captor," specifically designed as an anti-submarine weapon, is basically a moored mine which automatically deploys a modified Mk 46 homing torpedo carrying a 98 lb warhead instead of simply exploding when activated. Development of Captor began in 1961, with the first units entering service in 1979. It is capable of operating at depths up to about 3,000 feet.

Mines Mks 62, 63, and 64—the "Quickstrike" series—were basically modified 500, 1,000, and 2,000 lb bombs, and would appear to be capable of operation at depths up to about 600 feet. Warhead weight is 192, 450, and approximately 1,000 lbs respectively. Mk 65, first deployed in 1983, weighs about 2,400 lbs and probably carries about a 1,000 lb warhead.

The Mk 67 Submarine Launched Mobile Mine (SLMM), introduced to the fleet in 1992, uses a small torpedo-like submarine to carry a Mk 37 torpedo (fused as a mine) into locations that would otherwise be inaccessible to conventional submarines or aircraft.

The most common mines employed during the post-World War II period are described in Table 2.

MISSILES

The first real U.S. naval missile, Loon, arguably the world's first cruise missile as well, was a slightly modified version of the German V-1 "buzzbomb." Built in the United States during the latter months of World War II, Loon was originally manufactured to support the planned landings on the Japanese homeland in 1945. The missile could be launched from submarines and surface ships, and—unlike the original—could be actively controlled all the way to the target, when a radio signal from the firing ship sheared off the wings and put the vehicle into a terminal dive. Although range was nominally 150 miles, the radar horizon from submarines rarely allowed tracking to that distance. Too small to carry nuclear payloads, and never more than experimental, Loon was soon superseded by "Regulus," a much larger and more capable weapon which could still be launched from submarines or large surface ships. Regulus, first deployed in 1953,

Figure 0.1: USS *Mississippi* (EAG 128), the old battleship now a gunnery training ship firing a Terrier missile during at-sea tests, about 1954.

Figure 0.2: A Terrier missile being fired from forward launcher on the cruiser *Long Beach*.

represented the Navy's primary nuclear deterrent prior to Polaris, and eventually morphed into Harpoon and Tomahawk.

The 1960s were dominated by members of the so-called "3-T" program, Tartar, Terrier, and Talos, all introduced about 1959. These three formed a complimentary anti-aircraft group, Tartar (RIM 24) (essentially Terrier without the booster) reaching 9 nautical miles, Terrier (RIM2) reaching 17 nautical miles, and Talos (RIM8) reaching 55. The latter two, i.e. Terrier and Tartar, were capable of carrying a nuclear warhead. Although policy required that nuclear-tipped variants remain under positive control at all times, versions with conventional warheads were granted much more autonomous flight regimes.

The first version of Talos, 6b, was designed to intercept incoming aircraft at ranges up to 70,000 yards. Within a few years the slightly larger "6b1" model effectively doubled this range. Version 6c1, the "unified Talos", was introduced about 1962 and could carry either nuclear or conventional warheads interchangeably. Unfortunately each Talos required the continuous attention of a dedicated guidance radar during flight, making the simultaneous engagement of multiple targets somewhat problematical. Further difficulties lay in the relatively large size of the missile, and its inability to respond quickly enough to protect against short ranged threats, e.g. missiles fired from nearby submarines, destroyers or small craft. Talos was powered by a ram-jet engine which took over after an initial launch by a solid rocket booster.

Terrier, a compact (and by most accounts relatively unreliable) variant of Talos, entered service about 1952. Although it also required full-time radar attention during flight, its small size made it much easier to install on missile frigates or destroyers—Talos generally required a cruiser. The first models, BW-0 and BW-1 were effective out to 20,000 yards; BT-3A, which debuted about 1956, had an improved control system, a 40,000 yard range and could be used as a surface to surface missile as well. Terrier was a two-stage weapon, with booster and sustainer motors.

Tartar, which entered service about 1961, was seen as a short-ranged single-stage version of Terrier, sharing many components, and with shipboard requirements and impact about equivalent to a 5″ twin gun mount. Early versions could reach about 15,000 yards, later versions more than twice this range. All could be used in either surface to air or surface to surface modes.

It was always recognized that the 3-T systems (arguably less Tartar), which required dedicated illuminators for each missile in the air, were vulnerable to being overloaded by saturation attacks "Typhon", a new missile with Talos performance squeezed into a Terrier-sized platform, was an early attempt to replace individual missile beam-riding and illumination with transponders, an idea which would in principle allow less directional radars to control a much larger number of missiles, much as an air traffic controller currently controls airplanes. Development of Typhon was abandoned in 1964 when the giant SPG-59 radar that would be required to control it—an item which would have consumed some 10,000 horsepower—proved too expensive and difficult to build. Funds were thereafter re-directed towards improving Tartar, Terrier, and Talos.

Commencing about 1967, the 3-T missiles were slowly replaced by successively improved (and enlarged) variants of the Standard missile (RIM66), which started out using basically the same airframe as Tartar. Early units had ranges of 16 to 25 nautical miles. SM-2 (RIM-67) which replaced Terrier, deployed about 1981 and could reach 90 nautical miles. Newer versions, e.g. RIM-156, are still in service, and can reach 200 nautical miles.

"Harpoon"—the current version of "Loon"—introduced in various models from 1977 to 1981, is an active-homing turbojet-propelled sea-skimming short range cruise missile that can be launched from aircraft, surface ships and submarines (aircraft-launched versions dispense with the rocket booster used on the surface ship and submarine variants). Surface ship deployment is from Mk 140 or Mk 141 canister launchers, or older Mk 112 ASROC, or Mk 26 (standard) launchers. Block 1B variants deployed in 1982, fly a slightly different profile. Block 1C versions, deployed in 1985 used improved fuel for longer range. Block 1E, the Stand-off Land Attack Missile (SLAM), amounted to an entirely new design and became operational in 1988–1990, just in time for the First Gulf War. Block 1D, represents a larger variant which cannot be launched by submarines; Block 1Gs are Block 1C missiles upgraded to Block ID. Block 1H is an improved Block 1E.

The "Tomahawk" Sea Launched Cruise Missile (SLCM), first deployed in 1980, entered full service in 1983. The vehicle can be launched from both submarines and surface ships, and can carry a variety of conventional and nuclear warheads out to ranges exceeding 1,300 nautical miles. Block 1 came in two variants, BGM-109A Tomahawk Land Attack Missile—Nuclear (TLAM-N), carrying a 5–200 kT W-80-0 nuclear warhead, and BGM-109B Tomahawk Anti-Ship Missile (TASM), with a 100 lb conventional warhead. Tomahawks can be launched from conventional box-launchers or vertical launch systems (VLS). The launch sequence utilizes a rocket booster to attain initial speed, after which a turbofan cruise engine takes over and powers the vehicle on the remainder of its flight. Missiles used against land targets use sophisticated guidance systems to lead them directly to the intended target(s); missiles used against surface ships use a Harpoon-like radar seeker to approach in sea-skimming mode, and may be programmed to attack from above using a terminal "pop-up" mode. Many variants are now in service, with upgrading typically done at three- to four-year intervals. The latest variant as of this writing (2006) is RGM-109E, the Tactical Tomahawk, an economical three-fin version using a cheaper engine and a lighter structure which deployed in 2004; earlier variants, if not expended in combat or testing, were retired in the early 1990s.

Many naval units have been equipped with extremely low-impact "Stinger" missiles for close-in defence. These small missiles, which can be shoulder-fired by one or two men, employ an infrared homing system to deliver a 6.6 lb warhead to vertical ranges exceeding 15,000 feet. "Stinger"—manufactured in a number of variants over the years, first deployed about 1976.

Commencing with "Polaris" in 1962 the U.S. deployed—and continues to deploy—nuclear-tipped ballistic missiles aboard submarines, although numbers were considerably reduced after the fall of the USSR. In a natural evolution, Polaris was replaced by Poseidon in 1972, which was in turn superseded by Trident in 1979 and Trident II in 1989, each missile bigger and more capable than the last. Polaris and its successors were intended as strategic, rather than tactical weapons, primarily intended to deter the possibility of nuclear warfare with the Soviet Union. Commencing about 1990, i.e. with the end of the cold war, many submarines were equipped with vertically-launched land attack missiles which have been subsequently employed in tactical roles.

A summary of the most important missile type weapons is given in Table 3.

NUCLEAR WEAPONS

Many nuclear weapons have been deployed by the Navy during the period covered by this volume. These were intended to be delivered as bombs or depth charges by aircraft, in torpedo warheads from surface ships and submarines, in missiles launched from submarines, aircraft, and surface craft, and, in one case, via a conventional gun. As might be expected, interchangeability and flexibility was much sought after; the A3D "Skywarrior" aircraft for example, was certified to carry no fewer than 13 discrete types of nuclear ordnance.

The early 1950s marked a period of rapid development in nuclear weapons as the Army, Navy, and Air Force battled for design control of these new and powerful devices. The first real "Navy" weapon was the Mk 8 "Elsie" (for "Light Case"), a 3,500-lb gun-type earth penetrator designed to destroy buried fortified structures at depths up to about 100 feet. Mk 8 came in two versions, one for internal and one for external stowage aboard AJ and A4D aircraft. Only about 40 were made. "BOAR" The Bureau of Ordnance Atomic Rocket (BOAR), introduced in 1956, was basically a modified Mk 7 bomb equipped with a rocket motor, one of the first air-to-surface stand-off missiles. BOAR, equipped with a 15,000 lb thrust motor could reach Mach 1, and—in versions designed to explode amongst enemy bomber formations—reach altitudes of 40,000 feet. About 225 were produced. The same Mk 7 warhead used in BOAR was installed aboard "Betty", a half-ton depth charge deployed in 1953. "Betty" was replaced by "Lulu," a much smaller weapon, with a much smaller yield, in 1959.

Nuclear weapons installed aboard missiles included the W-30 warhead which was used in Talos and Terrier. The first Submarine Launched Ballistic Missile (SLBM) weapons deployed aboard submarines were cursed with reliability problems. Polaris, which deployed in 1960 armed with a single (and fairly unreliable) W-47 warhead, and later equipped with three (slightly more reliable) independently targetable 200 Kt W-58 warheads, had a C.E.P. (Circular Error Probable) of about 6,100 feet. Poseidon could deliver anywhere between 6 and 14 independently-targetable W-68 warheads, each with a yield of about 45 Kt, to within about 600 feet, but again reliability was a problem. Trident I could deliver about eight 95 Kt W-76 warheads to within about 500 yards, and Trident II can deliver 8–15 475 Kt W-88 warheads within about 500 feet. It has been reported that the accuracy of nuclear weapons delivery systems (and warhead yields) were, at times, deliberately degraded in order to reassure potential enemies—i.e. the Russians—that they could not be effectively used in first-strike attacks against buried missile silos.

A summary of the most important nuclear weapons deployed by the Navy is given in Table 4.

AIRCRAFT

The development of aircraft over this period saw the more-or-less complete replacement of propeller-driven combat aircraft with jets, although piston-engined aircraft continued—and continue—to serve remarkably well in supportive roles or in situations where endurance is critical. The spotter/scout float-planes mounted aboard cruisers and battleships of World War II were at first replaced with helicopters, then—as carrier-based air became increasingly capable—abandoned altogether. Most propeller-driven fighters were gone by 1955, by then either worn-out or considered obsolete (a notable exception being the AD-1 "Skyraider," which deployed until near the end of the Vietnam War). The twin piston-engined AJ "Savage," produced only in small numbers, was the first aircraft capable of deploying nuclear weapons from carriers. After brief service in that role, most were converted to tankers.

The 1950s and 1960s marked a period of rapid development of jet aircraft, characterized by the sequential introduction of large numbers of usually rather short-lived aircraft, each in turn quickly superseded by a more capable successor. In later years the number of new aircraft introduced decreased in both type and absolute quantity ("fewer, but better"). This, coupled with the ability to upgrade weapons systems without rebuilding the airframe, meant that longevity increased by almost an order of magnitude over aircraft deployed during World War II. Over the years, aircraft armament evolved from the installation of machine guns and "dumb" bombs during the early 1950s to the current (and almost ubiquitous) employment of missiles and so-called "smart bombs" which in their later incarnations have essentially blurred the distinction between unmanned aircraft and missiles. In that context, it is interesting to note that the conventional gun—albeit in much improved form—continues in regular service, with even the most modern fighters continue to mount rapid fire 20 mm cannon.

A summary of the most important aircraft deployed is given in Table 5.

ARMOR

A general shift towards active rather than passive defensive postures—a feeling it was better not to get hit in the first place rather than to minimize damage after a hit had been received—meant that conventional armor in substantive thicknesses was hardly ever mounted aboard ships designed after 1945. As the likelihood of attack by large-caliber kinetic energy penetrators disappeared—to be replaced by the threat of very high speed fragments—thick conventional steel armors were in turn replaced by thin flexible membranes such as Kevlar, and lightweight (though relatively voluminous) ceramic and composite armors similar to those employed in armoured fighting vehicles.

Table 1 U.S. Naval Guns, 1945–2006

Gun	Weight (lbs)	Length (inches)	Initial Velocity (ft/sec)	Projectile Weight (lbs)	Charge Weight (lbs)	Range (yds) at Elevation (deg)	Dates in Service
16″/50 Mk 7	267,900	816	2,690 2,500	1,900 HC 2,700 AP	664 664	41,600@45 42,350@45	1942–1991
16″/45 Mk 6	192,300	736	2,625 2,520 2,300	1,900 HC 2,240 AP 2,700 AP	544 544 544	40,180@45 40,200@45 36,900@45	1940–1958
8″/55 Mk 9–14	67,200	449	2,800 2,800	260 HE 260 AP	90 90	31,860@41 31,860@41	1930–1947
8″/55 Mks 12, 15, 16	38,500	449	2,700 2,500	260 HE 335 AP	86 86	29,800@41 30,050@41	1939–1980
6″/47 Mk 16	9,632	232.3	2,500 2,800	130 AP 105 HE	32 32	26,100@47 23,500@47	1948–1958
5″/38 Mk 12	7,170	224.0	2,500	55.0	15.5	17,300@45	1934–1990
5″/54 Mk 16	5,360	249.0	2,650	69.3	18.5	25,800@45	1945–1980
5″/54 Mk 42	5,662	c.280	2,650	c.70	18.3	25,900@45	1954–1985
5″/62 Mk 45 Mod 4	unk	310	2,725–3,450	64–110*	18–26	26,000–100,000+*	2000–2007+
5″/62 Mk 45 Mod 0–2	3,560	310	c.2,700	c.68	18.25	25,300 @47	1971–2000
3″/50 Mks 22, 27, 33, 34	1,760	160	2,700	13	3.7	14,600@45	1948–1990
76.2 mm/62	1,686	unk	3,000	c.14.0	7.85	c.20,100@45	1964–2007+
57 mm/70	unk	unk	3,120–3,360	c.14.0	2.60	15,000–19,000@45	1968–2007+
40 mm/56	1,150	98.4	2,890	2.00	0.70	c.10,500@45	1942–1960
20 mm/70	150	87	2,750	0.27	0.06	c.4,800@45	1941–1960
M-61 20 mm "Vulcan Phalanx"	13,000 (complete mount)	74	c.3,500	0.22	c.0.08	c.6,000@45 c.1,625@5	1980–2006
0.50 cal. machine gun BMG M2 GAU-18	c.90	c.63	2,850	0.11	0.03	c.7,500@45	1920–2007†
0.50 cal. machine gun GAU-19	139	47	2,910	0.11	0.03	c.7,500@45	1885–2007†

Notes: Only the most significant guns are listed; guns with short service lives or low procurements are generally omitted.
* Lower range refers to conventional munitions, upper range to extended range rocket-assisted projectiles.
† Still in service 2007.

Table 2 U.S. Naval Torpedoes and Mines, 1945–2006

Model	Diameter (inches)	Length (inches)	Weight (lbs)	Charge Weight (lbs)	Speed (knts) at Range (yds)	Dates in Service
Mk 13 (aircraft)	22.5	161	2,216	600	6,300@33.5	1936–1950
Mk 14 (submarine)	21.0	246	3,209	643	9,000@31 4,500@46	1931–1975
Mk 15 (surface)	21.0	288	3,841	825	15,000@26 10,000@33 6,000@45	1935–1975
Mk 18 (submarine)	21.0	245	3,154	575	4,000@29	1943–1950
Mk 23 (submarine)	21.0	246	3,209	643	4,500@46	1931–1980
Mk 24 "Fido" (aircraft)	19.0	84	680	92	4,000@12	1942–1948
Mk 28 (submarine)	21	246	2,800	585	4,000@20	1945–1960
Mk 32 (surface)	19	23	700	107	9,600@12	1950–1955
Mk 34 (aircraft)	21	125	1,150	116	3,600@17 12,000@11	1948–1958
Mk 35 (submarine/surface)	21	162	1,770	270	15,000@27	1949–1960
Mk 37 (submarine/surface)	19	135	1,430	330	10,000@26 23,500@17	1957–1970
Mk 37 NT (submarine/surface)	19	135	1,430	330	15,000@36	1975–1984
Mk 43 Mod 1 (aircraft)	10	91.5	260	54	4,500@15	1951–1960
Mk 43 Mod 3 (aircraft)	10	91.5	265	54	4,500@21	1951–1960
Mk 44 (ASROC) (surface)	12.75	112	425	75	6,000@30	1960–?
Mk 45 "Astor" (submarine)	19	226	c.2,250	Nuclear	15,000@40	1963–1976
Mk 46 (multi-platform)	12.75	102	517	98	8,000@28+	1966–present
Mk 48 (submarine)	21	228	3,430	650	35,000@55	1972–c.1990
Mk 48 "ADCAP" (submarine)	21	228	3,700	650	35,000@63?	1988–present
Mk 50 ALWT "Barracuda" (air/surface)	12.75	112	750	100	17,000@46(?)	1981–present
Mine Mk 52	19	61	c.1,200	595	–	1961–present(?)
Mine Mk 55	23.5	79	c.2,075	1,270	–	1961–present(?)
Mine Mk 56	23.4	113	2,135	357	–	1964
Mine Mk 57	21	128	2,060	340	–	1966
Mine Mk 60 "Captor"	21	145	2,320	98	See Mk 46 Torpedo	1979–present
Mine Mk 62	10.8	49	c.560	192	–	1980–present
Mine Mk 63	14	113	c.1,000	450	–	1981
Mine Mk 64	18	152	c.2,000	1,000(?)	–	1983(?)
Mine Mk 65	20.9	110	2,400	1,000(?)	–	1983
Mine Mk 67 (SLMM)	21	161	1,760	529	?	1992

Note: Weapons are listed by Mark number. Missing Mark numbers represent unsuccessful weapons or weapons which did not see extensive service. Performance details of currently operational torpedoes have been estimated from unclassified sources.

Table 3 U.S. Missiles, 1945–2006

Designation	Weight (lbs)	Diameter (inches)	Length (inches)	Range (naut miles)	Payload Weight (lbs)	Dates in Service
JB-2 "Loon"	5,000	34	325	140	2,000	1946–1952
SSM-N-8 "Regulus"	13,700	56.5	386	500	3,000c W5 or W27 Nuc	1955–1964
SAM-N-7 RIM 2 "Terrier"	2,350–3,000	13.5	162–177	10–40	218c W45 Nuc	1956–1988
SAM-N-6 RIM-8 "Talos"	c.7,800	28	456	50–100	300c W30 Nuc	1959–1979
RIM-24 "Tartar"	c.1,300	13.5	181–186	7–18	c.125c	1962–1990
RIM-66 "Standard"	1,100–1,400	13.5	175	17–25	137c	1970–2004
RIM-67 "Standard"	2,980	13.5	315	65–100	250c	1981–present
RIM-7 "Sea Sparrow"	c.500	8	144	8	86	1976–present
AGM-84 "Harpoon"	1,470	13.5	180	60+	488c	1977–present
FIM-2 "Stinger"	22	3	60	3.5	6.6	1970–present
RUR–5 ASROC	c.1,000	13.25	177	5.0–8.7	Mk 44 or Mk 46 Torpedo or W44 Nuc	1960–present
RUM139 ASROC	c.1,400	16.6	193	7.5	Mk 46 or Mk 48 Torpedo	1962–present
UUM-44 SUBROC	4,000	21	252	30	W55 Nuc	1965–1992
BGM/UGM/RGM-109 "Tomahawk"	4,200	20.5	219–246	250–1,350	1,000c W80 Nuc	1978–present
UGM-27 "Polaris"	35,000	54	388	1,200–2,500	3 × W80 nuc	1962–1974
UGM-73 "Poseidon"	65,000	74	408	2,500–3,200	10–14 MIRV Nuc	1971–1979
UGM-96 "Trident"	70,000	74	408	4,350	8 MIRV Nuc	1979–2002
UGM133 "Trident II"	130,000	83	528	6,000	7 MIRV Nuc	1990–present

1st symbol		2nd symbol		3rd symbol	
A	air	G	surface attack	M	missile
B	multiple	I	air intercept	R	rocket
M	mobile	U	underwater attack		
R	ship				
U	underwater				

Table 4 U.S. Naval Nuclear Weapons, 1945–2006

Model	Diameter (inches)	Length (inches)	Weight (lbs)	Yield	Deployed in
W-5	c.42	76	c.2,500	6–120 Kt	Regulus missile
W-7	30.25	55	983	32 Kt	Mk 90 "Betty" depth charge + Mk 7 bombs
W-23	16	64	c.1,700	c.15 Kt	"Katie" 16″ gun round
W-27	30.25	75	2,800	2Mt	Regulus missile, Mk 27 bomb
W-30	22	48	c.450	300–500 t	Talos missile
W-34	17	32	c.315	10–15 Kt	"Lulu" depth charge, Mk 44 "Astor" torpedo
W-44	13.75	25.5	170	10 Kt	Asroc missile
W-45	11.5	27	150	500 t–15 Kt	Terrier missile
W47	18	46.5	c.730	600 Kt–1.2Mt	Polaris missile
W-55	13	39.4	470	1–5 Kt	SUBROC missile
W-58	15.6 conical	40.3	260	200 Kt	Polaris A-3 missile
W-68	12.5 (?) conical	60(?)	367	c.45 Kt	Poseiden Mk-3 missile*
W-76	c.12.5 conical	48–60	363	100 Kt	Trident missile*
W-80	11.8	31.4	290	c.180 Kt	Tomahawk missile
W-88	21.8	68.9	750 (?)	475 Kt	Trident II missile*
Bomb Mk-4	60	128	10,300	1–31 Kt	B-29, AJ
Bomb Mk-5	44	129–132	3,100	6–120 Kt	Many aircraft
Bomb Mk-7	30.5	183	c.1,675	8–61 Kt	FJ-4, F2H, F-84, A4D-1 aircraft
Bomb Mk-8 "Elsie"	14.5	116–132	3,250	25–30 Kt	AJ & A4D aircraft
Bomb Mk-12	22	155	c.1,150	c.15 Kt	Many aircraft
Bomb Mk-15	34.7	139	7,600	c.1.8 Mt	A3D
Bomb Mk-28	20	170	1,885	70 Kt–1.5 Mt	A3J (A-5) "Vigilante" aircraft
Mk 1 Rocket "BOAR"	30.5	189	2,070	c.32 Kt	Many aircraft
Mk 90 "Betty" Nuclear depth charge	31.5	122	1,250	c.32 Kt	Many aircraft
Mk 101 "Lulu" Nuclear depth charge	18	92.4	1,200	10–15 Kt	Many aircraft

Table 5 U.S. Naval Aircraft, 1945–2006

Name	Type	Number Procured	Gross Wt (lbs)	Span (ft) Length (ft)	Range (naut miles)	Speed (knots)	Dates in use
Douglas AD-1 "Skyraider"	Bomber	3,180	18,250	50'–0" 38'–2"	800	280	1945–1972
Gyrodyne DSN-1 (QH-50) DASH	Drone Helicopter	c.700	885–2,300	rotor dia 20'–0"	26–40	67–92	1962–1970
Lockheed P2V "Neptune"	Patrol	1,036	61,000–75,000	100'–0" 77'–10"	c.4,000	300	1947–1982
Grumman F9F-2 "Panther"	Fighter	1,388	18,800	38'–0" 35'–10"	1,128	502	1949–1962
North American FJ-4 "Fury"	Fighter	1,115	23,700	39'–1" 36'–4"	1,750	465	1953–1962
Grumman F9F-6 "Cougar"	Fighter	1,985	19,750	34'–6" 41'–9"	561	1,050	1954–1969
McDonnell Douglas A4D "Skyhawk"	Fighter	2,876	24,500	27'–6" 40'–4"	450	580	1956–1994
Vought F-8 "Crusader"	Fighter	1,264	34,100	35'–8" 54'–3"	985	1,250	1957–1982
McDonnell-Douglas F-4 "Phantom II"	Fighter	4,261	56,000	38'–5" 58'–4"	1,900	1,230	1960–1989
Grumman E-2C "Hawkeye"	Patrol	215	51,200	81'–0" 58'–0"	1,525	270	1966–present
Bell UH-1N "Huey"	Helicopter		5,550	45'–10"	250	110	1967–present
Grumman EA-6B "Prowler"	Patrol	890	65,000	53'–0" 60'–0"	2,085	565	1971–present
Grumman F-14 "Tomcat"	Fighter	700	74,000	64'–2" 62'–8"	1,800	1340	1973–2006
McDonnell Douglas F/A18A "Hornet"	Fighter	750	36,000	37'5" 56'–0"	2,100	1,180	1983–present
McDonnell Douglas F/A18E "Super Hornet"	Fighter	350+	66,000	44'–9" 60'–1"	600	1,180	1999–present
Sikorsky SH-60 "Seahawk"	Helicopter	204	22,500	64'–8"	200	135	1986–present
Douglas A3D "Skywarrior"	Bomber	c.280	82,000	72'–6" 76'–4"	c.700	2,100	1956–1989

Notes: Aircraft are listed in order of introduction. Generally only aircraft of particular significance or aircraft procured in numbers exceeding 1,000 are listed. Aircraft primarily produced for or used by other services, e.g. those employed exclusively by the Marine Corps, are generally omitted. Many aircraft with similar/identical designations went through a number of model changes and, particularly with more recent aircraft, significant variations in dimensions and capabilities are common. Dates of withdrawal from service are approximate, as aircraft were often retired to training or expended as drones long after they were in active service. For aircraft procured before c.1990, the best general reference remains the third edition of Swanborough and Bowers *United States Navy Aircraft Since 1911*. The Naval Historical Center website contains valuable information as well.

BIOGRAPHY

William J. Jurens

William Jurens has been an associate editor and staff draftsman of the Journal *Warship International* since 1986, and is a Silver Member of the United States Naval Institute. He has been a member of the Society of Naval Architects and Marine Engineers (SNAME), Marine Forensics Panel (SD-7) since 1995, and has published several papers on the loss and wreck examination of various warships, including "The Loss of HMS *Hood*—A Reexamination" (1987), and "A Marine Forensic Analysis of HMS *Hood* and DKM *Bismarck*" (2002). He has, to date, acted as a consultant and contributor in the production of four television programs concerning the loss of HMS *Hood*, DKM *Bismarck*, and the British battle-cruisers sunk at Jutland, and participated in the investigation into the explosion aboard USS *Iowa* in 1989. He has also published a number of papers on ordnance and ballistics, most notably "The Evolution of Battleship Gunnery in the U.S. Navy, 1920–1945" (1991). He regularly collaborates with well-known authors on the production of full-length books dealing with historical naval technology.

He currently teaches Engineering Graphics at Winnipeg Technical College in Winnipeg, Manitoba.

CHRONOLOGY, 1947–2007

Figure 0.3: *USS St. Francis River* (LSMR 525) serving as mother ship for small craft in the Mekong Delta during Operation Deckhouse, Jan 1967. Coast Guard cutter *Point Kennedy* (WPB 82320) and PCF-98 are alongside.

Figure 0.5: LSTs beached after the landings at Inchon, Korea, 15 Sep 1950. Right to left are LST-715, LST-845, and LST-611.

Figure 0.4: *USS Tutuila* (ARG 4), with a floating drydock alongside, serving as tender for fast coastal patrol boats, Vietnam, November 1967. Notice the PCF boats clustered at left.

Figure 0.6: The heavy cruiser *Helena* (CA 75) bombarding targets at Chong-Ji, Korea, Oct 1950.

Figure 0.7: Interior of docking well of USS *Shreveport* (LPD 12), March 1972, with mechanized landing craft preparing for an assault landing.

Figure 0.8: LCU-1643 with American citizens on board enters the docking well of USS *Coronado* (LPD 11) during the evacuation from Beirut, Lebanon, 27 July 1976.

	1946	Dec–4 Mar 1947	*Operation High Jump*, exploration of Antarctica
	1947	18 Feb	Submarine *Cusk* is the first U.S. Navy (USN) ship to launch a guided missile, a Loon
		18 Sep	National Military Establishment (later Defense Department) becomes effective, unifying the armed services
	1948	24 Jun	Soviet forces blockade Berlin; Berlin Airlift begins; blockade ends 9 May 1949, but airlift continues until 30 Sep 1949
	1949	4 Apr	NATO established, becomes effective 24 Aug 1949
		18 Apr	Keel laid for aircraft carrier *United States*, canceled 23 Apr by Secretary of Defense Johnson
		25 Aug	Soviet Union detonates an atomic bomb
		26 Aug	Submarine *Cochino* sinks in Arctic north of Norway
		1 Oct	Military Sea Transportation Service (MSTS) is established with ships of the Naval Ocean Transport Service; Army Transportation Corps ships are transferred in 1950
		8 Dec	Chinese Nationalist government of Chiang Kai-shek moves to Taiwan, abandoning mainland China
Korea	1950	25 Jun	**Korea**: North Korea invades South Korea; U.S. armed forces ordered to support South Korea, 27 Jun, under auspices of the United Nations
Inchon		13–14 Sep	**Korea**: Landings at Inchon; Seoul captured 24 Sep
Wonsan		15 Oct	**Korea**: Landings at Wonsan
		24 Nov	**Korea**: Chinese armed forces start offensive operations in Korea
		1 Dec	**Korea**: Evacuation of Chosan 3–7 Dec 1950; evacaution of Wonsan
		10–24 Dec	**Korea**: Evacuation of Hungnam; 338,000 troops and 91,000 refugees and equipment were transported
	1951	7 Apr	**Korea**: General MacArthur relieved of command by President Truman
		10 Jul	**Korea**: Cease-fire talks at Kaesong begin, moved 8 Oct to Panmunjom
	1952	1 Nov	First U.S. thermonuclear bomb is detonated at Eniwetok
	1953	27 Jul	**Korea**: Armistice signed at Panmunjom, ending Korean War hostilities
	1954	21 Jan	The *Nautilus*, first nuclear-powered submarine is launched
Op.Castle		Feb–May	*Operation Castle*—high yield thermonuclear devices are tested at Bikini
		25–26 Jul	**Taiwan Straits**: U.S. carrier aircraft attacked by PRC aircraft off Hainan
		Aug	**Taiwan Straits**: 1st Taiwan Straits crisis, Quemoy-Matsu Passage to Freedom
		16 Aug	**Vietnam**: Transfer of Vietnamese from north to south starts 293,002 civilians and 17,846 military personnel are transported until 18 May 1955 (*Operation Passage to Freedom*)
		30 Sep	USS *Nautilus*, first nuclear powered submarine, commissioned
	1955	1 Feb	*Operation Deep Freeze*, Antarctica
		6–13 Feb	**Taiwan Straits**: USN evacuates troops and civilians from Tachen Islands off Chinese coast
	1956	29 Oct	Suez Canal nationalized. British & French troops land in Egypt
	1958	Apr	Atmospheric nuclear tests (*Operation Hardtack*)
Lebanon 1958		14 Jul	**Lebanon**: U.S. forces sent to Lebanon (to 30 Sep 1958)
Quemoy-Matsu		23 Jul–1 Jun 1962	**Taiwan Straits**: Seventh Fleet operations off Quemoy and Matsu and in the Taiwan Straits
	1959	30 Dec	*George Washington*, first ballistic missile submarine, commissioned
	1960	10 May	Submarine *Triton* completes circumnavigation of the world submerged
	1961	17 Apr	**Cuba**: Landing at Bay of Pigs, Cuba
		5 May	First man in space—Alan Shepard is launched in Mercury capsule
		1 Jun	2nd fleet ordered off southern Dominican Republic
		13 Aug	Berlin Wall erected
		9 Sep	*Long Beach*, first nuclear surface warship, commissioned.
	1962	Feb–Oct	**Cuba**: Patrol operations off Cuba

CHRONOLOGY, 1947–2007 xxxiii

Cuban missile crisis	1962	4 Oct	**Cuba**: Cuban missile crisis; nuclear warheads arrive in Cuba; quarantine of Cuba by USN forces, 24 Oct
	1963	10 Apr	Nuclear submarine *Thresher* lost with all hands east of Cape Cod
		Oct	Relief operations in Haiti after Hurricane Flora
	1964	2 Aug	**Vietnam**: Destroyer *Maddox* attacked by North Vietnamese torpedo gunboats in Gulf of Tonkin; a second incident is reported on 4 Aug
	1965	11 Mar	**Vietnam**: *Operation Market Time* begins; U.S. Navy operation to stop troops and supplies from flowing by sea to South Vietnam from the north
		27 Apr	Marines land in Dominican Republic to evacuate U.S. citizens, withdraw
		26 May	Dominican Rep.; operations to prevent a government friendly to Cuba from regaining power (*Operation Powerpack*)
	1967	1 Apr	Coast Guard incorporated into new Department of Transportation
		8 Jun	Israeli forces attack USS *Liberty* north of Sinai Peninsula
	1968	21 Jan	**Vietnam**: Siege of Khe Sanh, lasts until April 14
		22 Jan	USS *Pueblo* seized by North Koreans off east coast
		30 Jan	**Vietnam**: Tet Offensive
		22 May	Nuclear submarine *Scorpion* is lost in North Atlantic
		8 Oct	**Vietnam**: Operation Sealords—intended to disrupt North Vietnamese supply lines in and around the Mekong Delta (to 1970)
		1 Nov	**Vietnam**: President Johnson orders cessation of hostilities in North Vietnam (later resumed 6 Apr 1972 until 30 Dec 1972)
	1969	1 Jan	Amphibious ships are reclassified to new L-series designations
		13 Jan	**Vietnam**: *Operation Bold Mariner*—largest amphibious assault of Vietnam War
		14 Apr	**Korea**: U.S. Navy EC-121 plane shot down by North Koreans; TF 71 demonstrates 20–26 Apr 1969
	1970	29 Apr	**Vietnam**: U.S. and South Vietnamese forces invade Cambodia
		1 Aug	MSTS renamed Military Sealift Command (MSC)
	1972	6 May	**Vietnam**: Mining campaign against North Vietnam ports, *Operation Pocket Money*
	1973	27 Jan	**Vietnam**: U.S.–North Vietnam cease fire goes into effect; POWs released
		27 Feb	**Vietnam**: U.S. begins minesweeping operations off Haiphong
		15 Aug	**Vietnam**: U.S. offensive operations in South East Asia end
		6 Oct	War between Syria and Egypt and Israel: Yom Kippur War
	1974	22 Jul	U.S. and British evacuate civilians from Cyprus: Turks land on Cyprus
Evac of Cambodia	1975	12 Apr	**Vietnam**: *Operation Eagle Pull*—evacuation of U.S. personnel from Cambodia
		21 Apr	**Vietnam**: Pres. Nguyen Van Thieu resigns.
Evac of Vietnam		22–30 Apr	**Vietnam**: *Operation Frequent Wind*—evacuation of 1,500 U.S. personnel from Saigon; 26,000 refugees reach the Philippines, also numerous ships of South Vietnam Navy
Mayaguez Op.		12 May	**Vietnam**: U.S. merchant ship *Mayaguez* seized by Cambodian gunboat, ship and crew recovered by U.S. forces on 15 May (41 killed)
		30 Jun	Reclassification of DLG to cruisers, DE to frigates
Beirut Evac	1976	20 Jun–27 Jul	**Lebanon**: Beirut evacuation—263 Americans
	1979	16 Jan	**Southwest Asia**: Revolution in Iran overthrows government of the Shah who flees
		21 Feb	**Southwest Asia**: Navy helps evacuate people from Iranian ports
		8 Mar	**Southwest Asia**: Navy deploys to support North Yemen in its fight with South Yemen
		23 Jul	**Vietnam**: Navy starts rescuing Vietnamese "boat people"
		30 Sep	Panama Canal Zone turned over to the Republic of Panama
		4 Nov	**Southwest Asia**: Iranian militants seize U.S. embassy in Teheran, take hostages (released 20 Jan 1981)
		27 Dec	Soviet forces invade Afghanistan
	1980	24 Apr	**Southwest Asia**: Operation to rescue hostages in Teheran fails—*Operation Eagle Claw*
			Southwest Asia: Tanker escorting operations 1980
Liberia 1980	1980	5 Aug	Liberia (*Operation Sharp Edge*) (to 21 Feb 1991)
	1981	19 Aug	**Libya**: Libyan fighters engage U.S. planes—two Libyan fighters shot down Gulf of Sidra
	1982	2 Apr	Argentine forces land in Falkland Islands
		6 Jun	**Lebanon**: Israeli forces occupy southern Lebanon
Lebanon 1982		23 Jun	**Lebanon**: Evacuation of Beirut embassy
		25 Aug	**Lebanon**: Marines land in Lebanon to provide security for evacuation of PLO
		20 Sep	**Lebanon**: Marines land in Lebanon again following assassination of president Gemayel
	1983	1 Feb	Counter-insurgency operations in Honduras
		18 Apr	**Lebanon**: Terrorists blow up U.S. embassy in Beirut, 61 killed
		1 Sep	Soviet fighters shoot down Korean airliner off Kamchatka
		23 Oct	**Lebanon**: Terrorists destroy Marine barracks in Beirut, 241 killed
Grenada		23 Oct	Invasion of Grenada (*Operation Urgent Fury*)
	1984	21 Feb	**Lebanon**: Marines evacuate Lebanon
Libya/El Dorado	1986	20 Jan	**Libya**: Operations in Gulf of Sidra to demonstrate freedom of the seas to Libya
		24 Mar	**Libya**: Libyan aircraft attack U.S. forces
		12–17 Apr	**Libya**: U.S. carrier aircraft bomb Libya (*Operation Eldorado Canyon*)
	1987	17 May	**Southwest Asia**: Frigate *Stark* damaged by Iraqi missiles in Persian Gulf
		25 May	**Southwest Asia**: U.S. Navy starts escorting reflagged Kuwaiti tankers in Persian Gulf (*Operation Earnest Will*)
		19 Oct	**Southwest Asia**: Two Iranian oil platforms destroyed by U.S. surface warships
	1988	14 Apr	**Southwest Asia**: Frigate *Samuel B. Roberts* damaged by a mine in Persian Gulf
		18 Apr	**Southwest Asia**: Iranian frigates *Sahand* and *Sabalan* attacked by U.S. ships in Gulf, one sunk
		3 Jul	**Southwest Asia**: Cruiser *Vincennes* shoots down Iranian airliner in error, 290 killed
Panama	1989	20 Dec	Invasion of Panama (*Operation Just Cause*)

Liberia 1990	1990	5 Aug	U.S. forces evacuate civilians from civil war in Liberia (thru Nov 1990) (*Operation Sharp Edge*); 1,700 are evacuated from Monrovia
	1990	2 Aug	**Southwest Asia**: Iraqi troops invade Kuwait; U.S. moves to protect Saudi Arabia with massive movement of troops and supplies by ship (*Operation Desert Shield*)
Desert Storm/SW Asia	1991	17 Jan	**Southwest Asia**: *Operation Desert Storm*; coalition forces attack on Iraq and Kuwait, ground war starts on 23 Feb, cease fire ordered 28 Feb
	1991	4 Jan	U.S. starts evacuating civilians from Somalia
		30 Dec	Soviet Union defunct, cold war ends
	1992	Jan	**Southwest Asia**: *Operation Northern Watch/Southern Watch*—Maritime intercept operations and enforcement of no-fly zone in Iraq & Arabian Gulf (to Mar 2003)
Somalia 1992–95	1992	5 Dec	*Operation Restore Hope*, to deliver food and restore security in Somalia (to 31 Mar 1995)
	1993	17 Jan	**Southwest Asia**: Attack on Iraqi installations
	1994	Aug	U.S. Navy operations to halt Cuban refugees coming to U.S. (*Operation Able Vigil*)
Haiti 1994	1994	16 Sep	Haiti (*Operation Uphold Democracy*)—blockade of Haiti (to 31 Mar 1995)
	1995	30 Aug	Strikes on Bosnia, also 5 Sep & 10 Sep (*Operation Deliberate Force*)
		1 Dec	**Southwest Asia**: Iraq (*Operation Maritime Intercept*)
	1996	May	**Taiwan Straits**: 3rd Taiwan Strait Crisis—PRC missile tests Chinese naval exercises in Taiwan area
		3–4 Sep	**Southwest Asia**: Attacks on Iraqi targets
		20 Dec	Operations in Kosovo (*Operation Joint Guard*) (to 20 Jun 1998)
	1998	21 Jun	Bosnia (*Operation Joint Forge*)
			Kosovo (*Operation Noble Anvil*)
		Aug	Terrorist bombings of U.S. embassies in Kenya and Tanzania
		Aug	Attacks on Al Qaeda Afghan camps & Sudan
Desert Fox		16–22 Dec	**Southwest Asia**: U.S. forces launch cruise missile attacks against military targets in Iraq (*Operation Desert Fox*)
	2001	11 Sep	Terrorist attacks on New York and Washington
Afghanistan 2001		7 Oct	U.S. forces commence combat action in Afghanistan against Al Qaeda terrorists and their Taliban supporters (*Operation Enduring Freedom*)
	2003	25 Feb	Coast Guard transferred to Department of Homeland Security
Iraq War 2003	2003	20 Mar	**Southwest Asia**: United States-led coalition including Britain invades Iraq with the stated goal of eliminating Iraqi weapons of mass destruction; by 1 May 2003, President Bush declares "mission accomplished"; occupation of Iraq by foreign military forces continues through 2008 (*Operation Iraqi Freedom*)
Tsunami relief	2004	26 Dec	Earthquake and tsunami devastate Sumatra and neighboring countries killing about 230,000 people
	2006	17–19 Jul	**Lebanon:** Evacuation of Beirut

PHASES OF THE KOREAN WAR

K-1	North Korean Aggression	27 Jun–2 Nov 1950
K-2	Communist China Aggression	3 Nov 1950–24 Jan 1951
K-3	Inchon Landing	13–17 Sep 1950
K-4	1st UN counteroffensive	25 Jan–21 Apr 1951
K-5	Communist China Spring Offensive	22 Apr–8 Jul 1951
K-6	UN Summer Offensive	9 Jul–27 Nov 1951
K-7	2nd Korean Winter	28 Nov 1951–30 Apr 1952
K-8	Korean Defense	1 May–30 Nov 1952
K-9	3rd Korean Winter	1 Dec 1952–30 Apr 1953
K-10	Korea Summer-Fall 53	1 May–17 Jul 1953

PHASES OF THE VIETNAM WAR

Vietnam Advisory Campaign	15 Mar 1962–7 Mar 1965
Vietnam Defense Campaign	8 Mar 1965–24 Dec 1965
Vietnam Counter-offensive	25 Dec 1965–30 Jun 1966
Vietnam Counter-offensive II	1 Jul 1966–31 May 1967
Vietnam Counter-offensive III	1 Jun 1967–29 Jan 1968
Tet Counter-offensive	30 Jan 1968–1 Apr 1968
Vietnam Counter-offensive IV	2 Apr 1968–30 Jun 1968
Vietnam Counter-offensive V	1 Jul 1968–1 Nov 1968
Vietnam Counter-offensive VI	2 Nov 1968–22 Feb 1969
Tet 69 Counter-offensive	23 Feb 1969–8 Jun 1969
Vietnam, Summer–Fall 1969	9 Jun 1969–31 Oct 1969
Vietnam, Winter–Spring 1970	1 Nov 1969–30 Apr 1970
Sanctuary Counter-offensive	1 May 1970–30 Jun 1970
Vietnam Counter-offensive VII	1 Jul 1970–30 Jun 1971
Consolidation I	1 Jul 1971–30 Nov 1971
Consolidation II	1 Dec 1971–29 Mar 1972
Vietnam Ceasefire Campaign	30 Mar 1972–28 Jan 1973

OPERATIONS DESERT SHIELD AND DESERT STORM (GULF WAR)

1. Defense of Saudi Arabia	2 Aug 1990–16 Jan 1991	Desert Shield
2. Liberation and Defense of Kuwait	17 Jan 1991–11 Apr 1991	Desert Storm
3. Southwest Asia Ceasefire Campaign	12 Apr 1991–30 Nov 1995	

1
AIRCRAFT CARRIERS

After World War II those aircraft carriers under construction were completed, so that by 1947 the Navy had on the list three large *Midway* Class carriers (designated CVB) twenty-four standard size *Essex* Class units (designated CV) and nine light carriers (designated CVL). Sixty-six escort carriers (CVE) were also retained, in reserve or employed as auxiliary units.

The introduction of jet aircraft soon showed that many of the smaller carriers were inadequate, the jets needing stronger decks and more room for flight operations than the CVEs and CVLs could provide. The *Essex* class units were large enough to warrant upgrading. In 1952 *Antietam* was fitted with an angled flight deck enabling both takeoffs and landings from different runways. Most of the existing *Essex* class, less *Boxer*, *Princeton*, *Valley Forge*, *Leyte*, and *Tarawa*, and all three of the *Midway* class carriers were subsequently fitted with angled flight decks, enclosed bows, and more powerful steam catapults to assist the heavier jets in their takeoffs. *Oriskany* was completed in 1949 with some of these modifications built right in. *Franklin*, heavily damaged in World War II, was repaired but never recommissioned. *Bunker Hill*, also damaged and repaired, saw only very limited post-war service.

The Navy's first attempt at building a "super-carrier" was aborted when Secretary of Defense Louis Johnson cancelled construction of *United States* immediately after it was laid down in 1949. Carriers larger than the *Midway* class were clearly needed, however, and by 1952 *Forrestal* was laid down, the first of eight near-sisters.

The surviving smaller escort carriers, too small for the new planes, were used principally to transport aircraft, some remaining in service until the Vietnam war. Two, *Tinian* and *Palau*, completed after the war, were never commissioned. Two *Independence*-class light carriers were converted for anti-submarine warfare. By 1959 none of these remained in service, and the two *Saipan* class had been converted for other duties.

The first nuclear-powered carrier made its appearance in 1960. *Enterprise*, named after the most famous carrier of World War II,

was a very successful ship, and succeeding carriers, albeit of somewhat different design, have all been nuclear-powered. Ten similar units have been built, all at Newport News. The first ship, *Nimitz*, was completed in 1975 and the last of the class, *George H.W. Bush*, will commission in 2009. These nuclear powered carriers are the largest warships ever built and are able to remain at sea for long periods without refuelling.

Although the first carriers were named after historic naval vessels and battles, in recent years they have been named after historic persons, mostly presidents of the United States and a famous admiral. Politics has reared its ugly head with carriers named after a senator and a congressman, both of whom were helpful in legislating for the Navy.

All CV and CVB rec CVA, attack carriers, to reflect mission rather than size, a designation discontinued in 1975.

Figure 1.1: *USS Hornet* (CVS 12) prepares to recover the *Apollo 12* command module following its splashdown southeast of Samoa in the South Pacific, 24 Nov 1969.

Figure 1.2: The aircraft carrier *Antietam* (CV 36) was the first to receive an angled flight deck. Here she is underway following the experimental conversion, 5 Jan 1953.

Figure 1.3: USS *Hancock* (CVA 19) at sea refuelling destroyers *Maddox* (DD 731) and *Samuel N. Moore* (DD 747), 12 Mar 1957. Notice the angled flight deck fitted in 1956 and new enclosed bow.

AIRCRAFT CARRIERS ON THE NAVY LIST, 1947

CV 6   *Enterprise*   Decomm 17 Feb 1947. Rec **CVA 6**, 1 Oct 1952. Rec **CVS 6**, 8 Aug 1953. Stricken 20 Oct 1956. Sold 2 Jul 1958, BU Kearny.

CV 9   *Essex*   Out of comm 9 Jan 1947–15 Jan 1951. Modernized (27A), Puget Sd NSYd Feb 1949–Jan 1951. Damaged by aircraft crash landing, off Korea, 16 Sep 1951 (8 killed). Rec **CVA 9**, 1 Oct 1952. Angled flight deck, 1955–56. Rec **CVS 9**, 8 Mar 1960. FRAM 1962. Rammed in collision by submerged submarine *Nautilus* off North Carolina, 10 Nov 1966. Ran aground off Puerto Rico, 21 Jan 1967. Recovered space craft *Apollo 7* and crew of three after a 10-day flight, south of Bermuda, 11 Oct 1968. Decomm 30 Jun 1969. Stricken 1 Jun 1973. Sold 14 May 1975, BU Kearny, NJ.
4★Korea K-6 K-7 K-8 K-9; ◆Lebanon Jul–Aug 1958, Taiwan Straits Sep 1958, Cuba Apr 1961, Jan 1962, Cuban missile crisis Oct–Nov 1962.

CV 10   *Yorktown*   Out of comm 9 Jan 1947–20 Feb 1953. Modernized (27A), Puget Sd NSYd, Mar 1951–Feb 1953. Rec **CVA 10**, 1 Oct 1952. Angled flight deck, 1955. Rec **CVS 10**, 1 Sep 1957. Collided with destroyer *Brush* off San Diego, 23 Oct 1959. FRAM 1966. Recovery ship for spacecraft *Apollo 8*, in Pacific, 27 Dec 1968. Decomm 27 Jun 1970. Stricken 1 Jun 1973.
Later history: museum at Charleston, SC, 1975.
4★Vietnam Jan 1959, Mar–Jun 1960, May 1963, Feb–Apr 1965, Feb–Jul 1966, Mar–Jun 1968; ◆Taiwan Straits 31 Dec 1958, Quemoy-Matsu Jan 1959, Korea Jan–Mar 1968.

CV 11   *Intrepid*   Out of comm 22 Mar 1947–9 Feb 1952. Modernized (27C), Newport News, Apr 1952–Jun 1954. Rec **CVA 11**, 1 Oct 1952. Angled flight deck, 1956–57. Damaged by boiler explosion off Virginia, 25 Apr 1961. Rec **CVS 11**, 31 Mar 1962. Retrieved Scott Carpenter from space capsule *Aurora 7*, 24 May 1962. Recovery ship for Gemini space capsule (Virgil Grissom & John Young) in Atlantic, 23 Mar 1965. FRAM 1965. Ran aground off Jamestown, RI, 7 Sep 1969. Decomm 15 Mar 1974. Stricken 23 Feb 1982 and trfd to museum.
Later history: Museum at New York, NY.
★Vietnam May–Oct 1966, Jun–Nov 1967, Jul–Aug, Oct–Dec 1968; ◆Cuba Jun 1961.

CV 12   *Hornet*   Out of comm 15 Jan 1947–20 Mar 1951. Modernized (27A), New York NSYd, Jul 1951–Sep 1953. Rec **CVA 12**, 1 Oct 1952. Planes shot down two Chinese fighters in South China Sea, 25 Jul 1954. Angled flight deck 1956. Rec **CVS 12**, 27 Jun 1958. FRAM 1965. In collision with destroyer *Epperson* southeast of Tokyo Bay, 20 Sep 1965. Recovered unmanned Apollo spacecraft, 25 Aug 1966. Recovery ship for moon landing craft *Apollo 11* in South Pacific, 24 Jul 1969. Decomm 26 Jun 1970. Stricken 25 Jul 1989. Sold for BU 14 Apr 1993, but trfd to museum assn, 26 May 1998.
Later history: Museum at Alameda, Cal.
★Vietnam Oct–Nov 1965, Jan–Feb 1966, May–Oct 1967, Nov 1968–Apr 1969; ◆Quemoy-Matsu Jul 1959, Oct–Nov 1962, Korea Apr 1969.

CV 13   *Franklin*   Repaired. Decomm 17 Feb 1947. Rec **CVA 13**, 1 Oct 1952. Rec **CVS 13**, 8 Aug 1953. Rec **AVT 8**, 15 May 1959. Stricken 1 Oct 1964. Sold Jul 1966, BU Portsmouth, Va.

CV 14   *Ticonderoga*   Out of comm 9 Jan 1947–11 Sep 1954. Modernized (27C), New York NSYd, Apr 1952–Sep 1954. Angled flight deck, 1956–57. In collision with destroyer *Picking* in South China Sea, 15 Oct 1961. Rec **CVA 14**, 1 Oct 1952. Rec **CVS 14**, 21 Oct 1969. Recovery ship for fifth lunar landing craft *Apollo 16*, in Pacific, 27 Apr 1972, and for sixth and last lunar landing craft *Apollo 17*, 19 Dec 1972. Recovery vessel for the *Skylab 2* space craft, in Pacific, 22 Jun 1973. Decomm and stricken 16 Nov 1973. Sold 15 Aug 1974, BU Portland, Ore.
12★Vietnam Sep–Oct 1961, Apr–May 1963, Aug–Nov 1964, Nov 1965–Apr 1966, Nov 1966–Apr 1967, Jan–Jul 1968, Mar–Jul 1969, Apr–May 1971, Jun 1972; ◆Taiwan Straits Nov–Dec 1958, Quemoy-Matsu Oct 1961, Korea Mar–Apr, Aug 1969.

CV 15   *Randolph*   Out of comm 25 Feb 1948–1 Jul 1953. Modernized (27C), Newport News, Jun 1951–Jul 1953. Rec **CVA 15**, 1 Oct 1952. Angled flight deck, 1955–56. Rec **CVS 15**, 31 Mar 1959. Damaged in collision with m/v *Viscountess* off Charleston, SC, 15 Oct 1961. FRAM 1961. Damaged by elevator accident at sea in Atlantic Ocean, 1 Apr 1964 (2 killed). Decomm 13 Feb 1969. Stricken 1 Jun 1973. Sold 14 May 1975, BU.
◆Lebanon Sep 1958, Cuba Apr–Jul 1961, Nov 1961–Feb 1962, Cuban missile crisis Oct–Nov 1962.

CV 16 *Lexington* Out of comm 23 Apr 1947–15 Aug 1955. Rec **CVA 16**, 1 Oct 1952. Modernized (27) and angled flight deck, Puget Sd NSYd, Sep 1953–Aug 1955. Collided with oiler *Kawishiwi* south of Oahu, May 1959. Modernized at Puget Sd NSYd. Rec **CVS 16**, 1 Oct 1962. Rec **CVT 16**, 1 Jan 1969. Damaged by boiler room fire in drydock at Boston, 7 Sep 1969. Rec **AVT 16** (landing training ship), 1 Jul 1978. Damaged by crash of T2 trainer on flight deck off Pensacola, 29 Oct 1989 (5 killed). Decomm 26 Nov 1991. Stricken 30 Nov 1991.
Later history: To Corpus Christi, Tex., as museum, 23 Jan 1992.
★Vietnam Dec 1960–Jan 1961; ◆Taiwan Straits Aug–Oct 1958, Quemoy-Matsu Oct 1958, Jun–Jul, Oct 1959, Dec 1961, Cuba 8 Sep 1962.

CV 17 *Bunker Hill* Decomm 9 Jan 1947. Rec **CVA 17**, 1 Oct 1952. Rec **CVS 17**, 8 Aug 1953. Rec **AVT 9**, 15 May 1959. Stricken 1 Nov 1966. Used as electronic test platform. Sold 7 Jun 1973, BU Tacoma. Damaged in collision with m/v *Sidney Spiro* off Point Reyes, Cal., 25 Jul 1973 while in tow to BU.

CV 18 *Wasp* Out of comm 17 Feb 1947–10 Sep 1951. Modernized (27A), New York NSYd, May 1949–Sep 1951. Damaged in collision with destroyer minesweeper *Hobson* in North Atlantic 26 Apr 1952. Rec **CVA 18**, 1 Oct 1952. Angled flight deck, 1955. Rec **CVS 18**, 1 Nov 1956. Damaged by explosion of explosives and fire, off Virginia, 19 Aug 1959 (2 killed). Collided with destroyer *Holder* off Cuba, 14 Nov 1962. FRAM Oct 1963. Recovery ship for space capsules *Gemini 6* and *Gemini 7* near Puerto Rico, 16 & 18 Dec 1965. Damaged by heavy seas off Boston, 24 Jan 1966. Recovery ship for space capsule *Gemini 9* east of Cape Kennedy, 6 Jun 1966. Recovery ship for space craft *Gemini 12*, 11 Nov 1966. Damaged in collision with oiler *Salamonie* off San Juan, 24 Mar 1967. Damaged in collision with oiler *Truckee* off U.S. east coast, 12 Jun 1968. Collided with oiler *Chukawan* southwest of Bermuda, 20 Jan 1971. Decomm and stricken 1 Jul 1972. Sold 21 May 1973, BU Kearny, NJ.
◆Lebanon Jul–Sep 1958, Cuban missile crisis Nov 1962.

CV 19 *Hancock* Out of comm 9 May 1947–15 Feb 1954 and 13 Apr 1956–15 Nov 1956. Rec **CVA 19**, 1 Oct 1952. Modernized, Puget Sd NSYd, Dec 1951–Feb 1954. Angled flight deck, 1956. Rec **CVS 19**, 30 Jun 1956. In collision with replenishment oiler *Camden* off Vietnam, 26 Nov 1968. Rec **CV 19**, 1 Jul 1975. Stricken 31 Jan 1976. Sold 1 Sep 1976, BU.
13★Vietnam Mar–May 1962, Nov 1963, Dec 1964–May 1965, Dec 1965–Jul 1966, Feb–Jun 1967, Aug 1968–Feb 1969, Aug 1969–Mar 1970, Nov 1970–May 1971, Feb–Sep 1972; ◆Taiwan Straits Aug–Sep 1958, Quemoy-Matsu Sep 1959, Korea Dec 1968, 30 Oct 1969, Jan–Feb 1970, Evac of Cambodia 11–13 Apr 1975, Evac of Vietnam 29–30 Apr 1975.

CV 20 *Bennington* Out of comm 8 Nov 1946–13 Nov 1952. Modernized (27A), New York NSYd, Dec 1950–Nov 1952. Rec **CVA 20**, 1 Oct 1952. Damaged by boiler room explosion off Guantanamo, 27 Apr 1953 (11 killed). Damaged by explosion in port catapult off Narragansett Bay, 26 May 1954 (103 killed). Angled flight deck, 1954–55. Rec **CVS 20**, 30 Jun 1959. Collided with destroyer *Richard S. Edwards* off California coast, 10 Aug 1960. FRAM 1963. Recovered unmanned *Apollo 4* space craft northwest of Hawaii, 9 Nov 1967. Decomm 15 Jan 1970. Stricken 20 Sep 1989. Sold 12 Jan 1994, BU Port Angeles, Wash., and Alang, India.
5★Vietnam Dec 1960–Jan 1961, Mar–Apr 1961, Apr–May 1962, May, Jul–Sep 1965, Dec 1966–Apr 1967, Jun–Oct 1968; ◆Taiwan Straits Oct–Dec 1958.

CV 21 *Boxer* Damaged by aircraft explosion and fire on hangar deck off Korea, 5 Aug 1952 (9 killed). Rec **CVA 21**, 1 Oct 1952. Rec **CVS 21**, 15 Nov 1955. Converted to amphibious assault ship; rec **LPH 4**, 30 Jan 1959. Decomm and stricken 1 Dec 1969. Sold Feb 1971, BU Kearny, NJ.
8★Korea K-1 K-3 K-4 K-5 K-6 K-7 K-8 K-9 K-10; (as LPH) 2★Vietnam Sep 1965, May–Jun 1966; ◆Cuba Jan–Mar 1961, Jul–Aug 1961, Mar–Jul 1962, Cuban missile crisis Oct–Dec 1962, Dominican Rep Apr–May 1965.

CV 31 *Bon Homme Richard* Out of comm 9 Jan 1947–15 Jan 1951 and 15 May 1953–6 Sep 1955. Rec **CVA 31**, 1 Oct 1952. Modernized (27C), angled flight deck, San Fran NSYd, May 1953–Sep 1955. Decomm 30 Jul 1971. Stricken 20 Sep 1989. Sold 4 Feb 1992, BU Terminal I.
5★Korea K-5 K-6 K-7 K-8 K-9; ★Vietnam Apr 1960, May 1961, Mar–Jun, Sep–Dec 1964, Jul–Dec 1965, Feb–Jul 1967, Feb–Sep 1968, Apr–Oct 1969, May–Oct 1970, ◆Korea May 1968, Jun–Sep 1969. PUC 26 Feb 1967–30 Jul 1967.

CV 32 *Leyte* Rec **CVA 32**, 1 Oct 1952. Rec **CVS 32**, 8 Aug 1953. Damaged by explosion of catapult fuel at Boston NSYd while under conversion, 16 Oct 1953 (37 killed). Recomm Jan 1954. Decomm and rec **AVT 10**, 15 May 1959. Stricken 1 Jun 1969. BU 1971 Portsmouth, Va.
2★Korea 1, 2

CV 33 *Kearsarge* Out of comm 16 Jun 1950–15 Feb 1952. Modernized (27A), Puget Sd NSYd, Feb 1950–Feb 1952. Rec **CVA 33**, 1 Oct 1952. Angled flight deck, 1956–57. Rec **CVS 33**, 1 Oct 1958. FRAM 1962. Retrieved Walter Schirra from spacecraft *Sigma 7* northeast of Midway Island, 3 Oct 1962. Collided with oiler *Mattaponi* off California coast, 5 Nov 1962. In collision with m/v *Oriana* off Los Angeles, 3 Dec 1962. Recovery ship for *Faith 7* capsule (Gordon Cooper) southeast of Midway Island, 15 May 1963. Decomm 13 Feb 1970. Stricken 1 May 1973. Sold 18 Jul 1974, BU 1975.
2★Korea K-8 K-9; 5★Vietnam Jan, Mar–May 1961, Aug–Nov 1964, Aug–Nov 1966, Oct 1967–Feb 1968, May 1969–Aug 1969; ◆Laos May 1961, Korea Jan–Mar 1968.

CV 34 *Oriskany* Construction suspended when 40% complete, 12 Aug 1945. Reordered 8 Aug 1947; completed to modified design (27A). Comm 25 Sep 1950. Rec **CVA 34**, 1 Oct 1952. Damaged by exploding bomb from landing aircraft off Korea, 6 Mar 1953 (2 killed). Out of comm 2 Jan 1957–7 Mar 1959, angled flight deck. Severely damaged by fire on hangar deck off Vietnam, 26 Oct 1966 (44 killed). Collided with ammunition ship *Nitro* in South China Sea, 28 Jun 1972. Rec **CV 34**, 1 Jul 1975. Decomm 30 Sep 1976. In collision with destroyer *McKean* in gale at Bremerton, 14 Nov 1981. Stricken 25 Jul 1989. Repossessed by USN 1997. Towed from Mare Island to Beaumont, Tex., Aug 1999. Sunk as artificial reef off Pensacola, 17 May 2006.
2★Korea K-8 K-9; 5★+Vietnam Sep–Nov 1963, May–Nov 1965, Jun–Oct 1966, Jul 1967–Jan 1968, May–Oct 1969, Jun–Nov 1970, Jun–Nov 1971, Jun 1972–Mar 1973; ◆Quemoy-Matsu Sep–Oct 1959, Oct 1960, Korea Sep–Oct 1969.

CV 36 *Antietam* Out of comm 21 Jun 1949–17 Jan 1951. Damaged by aircraft crash landing off Korea, 4 Nov 1951 (4 killed). Rec **CVA 36**, 1 Oct 1952. Rec **CVS 36**, 8 Jul 1953. First conversion to angled flight deck, Oct 1952. Aviation training ship 1957–62. Decomm 8 May 1963. Stricken 1 May 1973. Sold 28 Feb 1974, BU.
2★Korea K-6 K-7.

CV 37 *Princeton* Out of comm 20 Jun 1948–28 Aug 1950. Collided with oiler *Navasota* off San Diego, 28 Feb 1952. Rec **CVA 37**, 1 Oct 1952. Rec **CVS 37**, Jan 1954. Converted to amphibious assault ship; rec **LPH 5**, 2 Mar 1959. Recovered lunar orbit spacecraft *Apollo 10*, 26 May 1969. Decomm and stricken 30 Jan 1970. Sold 20 May 1971, BU.
8★Korea K-2 K-4 K-5 K-6 K-7 K-8 K-9 K-10; ◆Taiwan Straits Aug–Oct 1958; (as LPH) 5★Vietnam Jan–Apr 1962, Apr–May 1963, Aug–Sep 1963, Oct 1964–May 1965, Sep 1965, Mar–Aug 1966, Mar–May 1967, Jun–Nov 1968; ◆Quemoy-Matsu Mar–Apr 1960, Mar 1963.

CV 38 *Shangri-La* Out of comm 7 Nov 1947–10 May 1951 and 14 Nov 1952–10 Jan 1955. Rec **CVA 38**, 1 Oct 1952. Modernized (27C), angled flight deck, Puget Sd NSYd, Oct 1952–Jan 1955. Collided with destroyer *Newman K. Perry* southwest of Naples, 27 Aug 1965. Rec **CVS 38**, 30 Jun 1969. Decomm 30 Jul 1971. Stricken 15 Jul 1982. Sold 9 Aug 1988, BU Taiwan.
3★Vietnam Apr–Nov 1970; ◆Taiwan Straits Aug–Oct 1958, Cuba Jun 1961.

CV 39 *Lake Champlain* Out of comm 17 Feb 1947–19 Sep 1952. Rec **CVA 39**, 1 Oct 1952. Rec **CVS 39**, 1 Aug 1957. Modernized (27A), Norfolk NYSD, Aug 1950–Sep 1952. Prime recovery ship for first manned space flight, *Mercury* capsule, 5 May 1961. In collision with destroyer *Decatur* off Cape Henry, Va., 6 May 1964. Damaged in collision with m/v *Skauvaag* in Chesapeake Bay, 3 Jun 1964. Recovery ship for *Gemini V* capsule in Atlantic, 29 Aug 1965. Decomm 2 May 1966. Stricken 1 Dec 1969. Sold 28 Apr 1972, BU 1988 Taiwan.
1★Korea K-10; ◆Cuban missile crisis Nov–Dec 1962.

CV 40 *Tarawa* Out of comm 30 Jun 1949–3 Feb 1951. Rec **CVA 40**, 1 Oct 1952. Rec **CVS 40**, 10 Jan 1955. Decomm 13 May 1960. Rec **AVT 12**, 1 May 1961. Stricken 1 Jun 1967. Sold 3 Oct 1968, BU Baltimore.

CV 45 *Valley Forge* Damaged by explosion at Philadelphia, 11 Jun 1947. Rec **CVA 45**, 1 Oct 1952. Rec **CVS 45**, 1 Jan 1954. Converted to amphibious assault ship; rec **LPH 8**, 1 Jul 1961. FRAM Jul 1963. Decomm and stricken 15 Jan 1970. Sold 29 Oct 1971, BU.
8★Korea K-1 K-2 K-3 K-4 K-7 K-8 K-9 K-10; (as LPH) 9★Vietnam May–Jul 1962, Jun, Aug–Oct 1964, Oct 1965–Mar, Sep–Nov 1966, Nov 1967–Jul 1968, Mar–Sep 1969.

Note: 1951: 28,200 tons, 40,600 f/l; 819' × 101'6" × 29'8" (ext beam 151'10"), armor replaced; 8-5"/38, 14 twin 3"/50 guns; 70 a/c 1956: 30,800 tons, 41,200 f/l; 824'6" (oa) × 101' × 30'2" (ext beam 196'); 7-5"/38, 4 twin 3"/50 guns; 50 a/c as CVS.

CV 47 *Philippine Sea* Rec **CVA 47**, 1 Oct 1952. Rec **CVS 47**, 15 Nov 1955. Decomm 28 Dec 1958. Rec **AVT 11**, 15 May 1959. Stricken 1 Dec 1969. Sold Aug 1970, BU.
9★Korea K-1 K-2 K-3 K-4 K-5 K-7 K-8 K-9 K-10; ◆Antarctic Jan 1946–Feb 1947.

Notes: Modernized in several stages. 27A steam catapults, 27C hydraulic catapults. Angled flight deck (SCB-125). All 27 conversions had hurricane bows, revamped islands, new deck edge elevators aft of island, doubled fuel capacity. 27C changes: 40,000 tons f/l, 898' (oa) 101'4" (extreme beam 151'11"), 72 aircraft, 8-5"/38, 14 twin 3"/50 guns. After SCB-125: 43,060 tons f/l, 894'6 (oa) × 103' (extreme beam 166'10"), armament reduced. Various units were downgraded from attack carriers (CVA) to ASW carriers (CVS) as they aged.

Figure 1.4: The aircraft carrier *Midway* (CVB 41) in January 1954. She was completed just after the end of World War II. Notice the changes to the island, bow, and removal of forward 5-inch guns.

Figure 1.6: USS *Coral Sea* (CVA 43) after modernization in 1960. Notice new island structures and masts.

Midway Class

CVB 41 *Midway* Out of comm 14 Oct 1955–30 Sep 1957 for modernization, and 15 Feb 1966–31 Jan 1970 for 2nd modernization. Fired V-2 missile from flight deck, 6 Sep 1947. Rec **CVA 41**, 1 Oct 1952. Rec **CV 41**, 30 Jun 1975. Damaged in collision with m/v tkr *Cactus* southwest of Subic Bay, 29 Jul 1980. Had fire in store room off Japan, 20 Jun 1990. Decomm 11 Apr 1992. Stricken 17 Mar 1997. **Later history:** Museum at San Diego, 29 Aug 2003.
5★Vietnam Mar–Apr 1961, Apr–Nov 1965, May–Oct 1971, May 1972–Feb 1973; ◆Taiwan Straits Sep–Dec 1958, Korea Oct 1971, Evac of Vietnam 29–30 Apr 1975, Iran/Indian Ocean Apr–Jun, Nov 1979–Feb 1980, Aug–Nov 1980, Mar–May 1981, Libya Nov 1987–Feb 1988, Sep–Nov 1989, Gulf War Nov 1990–Mar 1991.
PUC 30 Apr 1972–9 Feb 1973.

CVB 42 *Franklin D. Roosevelt* Rec **CVA 42**, 1 Oct 1952. Out of comm 24 Apr 1954–6 Apr 1956, conversion, angled flight deck. In collision with unknown submarine off Florida, 5 May 1957. Collided with oiler *Pawcatuck* off Virginia coast, 4 Oct 1959. Damaged in collision with m/v *Charles Le Borgne* southeast of Marseille, 13 Oct 1965. Damaged by fire in storage compartment, in South China Sea, 4 Nov 1966 (7 killed). Rec **CV 42**, 30 Jun 1975. Collided with m/v *Oceanus* in Straits of Messina, 11 Jan 1977. Decomm and stricken 1 Oct 1977. Sold 1 Apr 1978, BU Kearny, NJ.

Figure 1.5: USS *Midway* (CVA 41) showing the changes made in 1957 with angled flight deck and new deck-edge elevators.

1★Vietnam Aug 1966–Jan 1967; ◆Cuba Jan–Feb, Nov 1961, Jul–Aug 1962.

CVB 43 *Coral Sea*   Commissioned 1 Oct 1947. Rec **CVA 43**, 1 Oct 1952. Out of comm 24 May 1957–15 Mar 1960 for modernization, angled flight deck. Collided with amphibious ship *Iwo Jima* at San Diego, 20 May 1966. Collided with ammunition ship *Mount Katmai* off Vietnam, 18 Oct 1967. Rec **CV 43**, 30 Jun 1975. In collision with m/v tanker *Napo* southeast of Guantanamo, 11 Apr 1985. Decomm 30 Apr 1990 and stricken. Sold 30 Mar 1993, BU Baltimore & Alang, India. ★Vietnam Apr–May 1961, Jan 1962, Feb–Oct 1965, Sep 1966–Jan 1967, Aug 1967–Feb 1968, Oct 1968–Mar 1969, Oct 1969–Jun 1970, Dec 1971–Jul 1972; ◆Korea Jan–Mar 1968, 10 Dec 1969, Mayaguez Op 15 May 1975, Eagle Claw 1980, Iran/Indian Ocean Feb–May 1980, Oct 1981, Libya/El Dorado Canyon Jan–May 1986.

Notes: First modernization, reconfigured island, starboard elevators, steam catapult. Conical mast, except *Midway*, pole mast. 4–5″ guns removed 1950. All received angled flight deck, enclosed bow 1956–7. Elevators rearranged. *Roosevelt* had limited refit, centerline elevator replaced by deck edge elevators. Second modernization for CV 42 canceled.
Guns removed. Armament: 1975: 3–5″/54. 1984: CV 41 2-BPDMS Mk 25, 2 Phalanx; CV 43: 3 Phalanx.

Independence Class

CVL 22 *Independence*   Decomm 25 Aug 1946. Sunk as target off California, 29 Jan 1951.

CVL 24 *Belleau Wood*   Decomm 13 Jan 1947. Loan to France 5 Sep 1953.
Later history: renamed *Bois Belleau* (R 97). Returned 12 Sep 1960, Stricken 1 Oct 1960. Sold 21 Nov 1960, BU Chester, Pa.

CVL 25 *Cowpens*   Decomm 13 Jan 1947. Rec **AVT 1**, 15 May 1959. Stricken 1 Nov 1959. BU 1960.

CVL 26 *Monterey*   Out of comm 11 Feb 1947–15 Sep 1950. In collision with m/v *Hartismere* in mouth of Mississippi River, 2 Jan 1955. Decomm 16 Jan 1956. Rec **AVT 2**, 15 May 1959. Stricken 1 Jun 1970. Sold May 1971, BU.

CVL 27 *Langley*   Decomm 11 Feb 1947. Loan to France 6 Jun 1951.
Later history: renamed *La Fayette* (R 96). Returned 20 Mar 1963, BU 1963 Baltimore.

CVL 28 *Cabot*   Out of comm 11 Feb 1947–27 Oct 1948. NRT. Decomm 21 Jan 1955. Rec **AVT 3**, 15 May 1959. Trfd to Spain 30 Aug 1967.
Later history: renamed *Dédalo* (R 01). Returned 1989, for museum at New Orleans. BU Brownsville, Tex. 2000.

CVL 29 *Bataan*   Out of comm 11 Feb 1947–13 May 1950. Damaged by rocket accident on flight deck, 22 May 1953. Decomm 9 Apr 1954. Rec **AVT 4**, 15 May 1959. Stricken 1 Sep 1959. Sold 27 Apr 1961, BU. 7★Korea K-2 K-4 K-5 K-7 K-8 K-9 K-10.

CVL 30 *San Jacinto*   Decomm 1 Mar 1947. Rec **AVT 5**, 15 May 1959. Stricken 1 Jun 1970. Sold 15 Dec 1971, BU.

Notes: *Cabot* and *Bataan* modernized for ASW, 1950–51.

Saipan Class

CVL 48 *Saipan*   Decomm 3 Oct 1957. Rec **AVT 6**, 15 May 1959. Rec **CC 3**, 1 Jan 1964, conversion canceled. Rec **AGMR 2**, 1 Sep 1964 and renamed *Arlington*. Recomm 27 Aug 1966. Decomm 14 Jan 1970. Stricken 15 Aug 1975. Sold 1 Jun 1976, BU.
◆Korea Jan–Mar 1968, (as AGMR) 7★Vietnam Aug 1967–Jul 1969.

CVL 49 *Wright*   Decomm 15 Mar 1956. Rec **AVT 7**, 15 May 1959. Rec **CC 2**, 1 Sep 1962, converted to command ship. Recomm 11 May 1963. Decomm 27 May 1970. Stricken 1 Dec 1977. Sold 1 Aug 1980, BU Kearny. (as CC) ★Vietnam Oct 1965.

Notes: *Wright* had one stack removed, late 1940s. Conversion of *Saipan* to command ship canceled and became communications relay ship instead.

Figure 1.7: *USS Saipan* (CVL 48). Completed after the war she remained in commission until 1957 and was then used as a communications ship and renamed *Arlington*.

Figure 1.8: The keel of the *United States* (CVA 58) being laid down at Newport News on 18 Apr 1949. Construction was canceled five days later.

United States

No.	Name	Builder	Keel Laid	Launched	Comm.
CVA 58	*United States*	Newport News	18 Apr 1949	—	—
Displacement	66,000 tons; 79,300 f/l				
Dimensions	1,090′ (oa); 1030′ (wl) × 130′ (extreme beam 190′)				
Machinery	4 screws; ST; 280,000 SHP; 33+ knots				
Complement	5,500				
Armament	8-5″/54, 6-3″/37 guns				

Notes: Heavy aircraft carrier (CVA). Canceled 23 Apr 1949. Four elevators, four catapults, small retractable island. Would have been largest warship ever built.

Figure 1.9: Aircraft carrier *Saratoga* (CVA 60)

Forrestal Class

No.	Name	Builder	Keel Laid	Launched	Comm.
CVA 59	*Forrestal*	Newport News	14 Jul 1952	11 Dec 1954	1 Oct 1955
CVA 60	*Saratoga*	New York NSYd	16 Dec 1952	8 Oct 1955	14 Apr 1956
CVA 61	*Ranger*	Newport News	2 Aug 1954	29 Sep 1956	10 Aug 1957
CVA 62	*Independence*	New York NSYd	1 Jul 1955	6 Jun 1958	10 Jan 1959
Displacement	60,000 tons; 79,200 f/l; *Forrestal*: 56,000 tons; 78,200 f/l				
Dimensions	1,046′ (oa); 990′ (wl) × 130′ × 37′				
Machinery	4 screws; ST; 8 boilers; 280,000 SHP; 34 knots				
Endurance	12,000/20				
Complement	4,600				
Armament	8-5″/54. *1980s*: 2 or 3 Sea Sparrow SAM lchrs, 3 Phalanx.				
—	1984: 59, 60: 2 IPDMS Mk 29 (59, 60, 62; 2 in 61), 3 Phalanx (all except 61)				
Aircraft	85				

Notes: Originally designed with axial decks, modified to angled flight deck. *Saratoga* had engineering problems. SLEP modifications. 59 and 60 ordered as CVB, rec CVA 1 Oct 1952. Open fantails on CV 59, 60.

Service Records:

CVA 59 *Forrestal* In collision with minesweeper *Pinnacle* at Norfolk, Va., 20 Jan 1956. Severely damaged by fire and explosion in Gulf of Tonkin, 29 Jul 1967 (134 killed, 26 aircraft destroyed). Rec **CV 59**, 30 Jun 1975. Collided with replenishment oiler *Savannah* in Caribbean, 9 May 1979. SLEP modernization 1983–85. Rec **AVT 59**, 4 Feb 1992. Was to be training carrier at Pensacola. Decomm and stricken 11 Sep 1993.
★Vietnam Jul–Aug 1967; ◆Cuba Jan–Mar 1962, Lebanon Sep–Nov 1982, Libya May–Jul 1988.

CVA 60 *Saratoga* Collided with m/v *Bernd Leonhardt* off Cape Henry, Va., 25 May 1960. Damaged by fire in eastern Mediterranean, 23 Jan 1961. Rec **CV 60**, 30 Jun 1972. Damaged by fire at Singapore, 29 Oct 1972. Damaged by fire at Norfolk, 22 Sep 1973. In collision with oiler *Mississinewa* off Florida, 15 Dec 1975. Collided with m/v *Ville d'Orient* in Strait of Messina, 6 Oct 1977. Collided with oiler *Waccamaw* south of Crete, 21 Nov 1978. Decomm 1 Oct 1980 for SLEP, recomm 1 Sep 1981. Decomm and stricken 20 Aug 1994.

Figure 1.10: *USS Forrestal* (CVA 59) on fire after an aircraft accident in the Gulf of Tonkin, 29 Jul 1967. She was the first of the super-carriers, and lost 134 men killed and 26 aircraft destroyed. The destroyer *Rupertus* (DD 851) is coming in to assist.

Figure 1.11: The aircraft carrier *John F. Kennedy* (CVA 67) in October 1976. Notice the funnel is at an angle, which distinguishes this ship from others of the class.

1★Vietnam May 1972–Jan 1973; ◆Lebanon Jul–Sep 1958, Cuba Jul–Aug 1961, Cuban missile crisis Dec 1962, Libya Jan–Mar 1986, Gulf War Aug 1990–Mar 1991.

CVA 61 *Ranger* Damaged by boiler room explosion near Japan, 5 Apr 1963. Rec **CV 61**, 30 Jun 1975. In collision with m/v tanker *Fortune* northeast of Singapore, 5 Apr 1979. In collision with replenishment oiler *Wichita* off San Diego, 17 Jul 1983. Fire in engine room in Indian Ocean, 1 Nov 1983. Decomm 10 Jul 1993. Stricken 8 Mar 2004.
13★Vietnam May 1963, Sep 1964–Apr 1965, Jan–Aug 1966, Dec 1967–Jan, Mar–May 1968, Jan–Apr 1969, Nov 1969–May 1970, Nov 1970–May 1971, Dec 1972–Feb 1973; ◆Quemoy-Matsu 24 Jun 1960, Korea Jan–Mar 1968, Mar–Apr 1969, Jan, Apr 1970, Iran/Indian Ocean Oct 1980–Mar 1981, Libya Aug–Nov 1987, Apr–May 1989, Gulf War Jan–Apr 1991, Liberia Dec 1992, Indian Ocean 1992–93.

CVA 62 *Independence* Collided with ammunition ship *Diamond Head* in Caribbean, 27 Apr 1961. In collision with ammunition ship *Wrangell* off South Carolina, 11 Apr 1968. Rec **CV 62**, 28 Feb 1973. Collided with storeship *Denebola* in Mediterranean, 20 Nov 1975. Collided with oiler *Truckee* in Tyrrhenian Sea, 20 Apr 1977. SLEP at Phila NSYd, Apr 1985–Aug 1987. Decomm 30 Sep 1998. Stricken 8 Mar 2004.

Figure 1.12: *USS Constellation* (CVA 64) fitting out at the navy yard in Brooklyn, NY, 1961, following the fire which delayed completion in December 1960. In the foreground is the destroyer *Charles R. Ware* (DD 865) undergoing FRAM modernization.

1★Vietnam Jun–Nov 1965; ◆Cuba Apr 1961, Cuban missile crisis Oct–Nov 1962, Iran/Indian Ocean Dec 1980–May 1981, Grenada Oct–Nov 1983, Lebanon Aug–Dec 1982, Nov 1983–Mar 1984, Gulf War Aug–Nov 1990, Dec 1993–Feb 1994, Indian Ocean Feb–May 1998.

Kitty Hawk Class

No.	Name	Builder	Keel Laid	Launched	Comm.
CVA 63	Kitty Hawk	NY Sbdg	27 Dec 1956	21 May 1960	29 Apr 1961
CVA 64	Constellation	New York NSYd	14 Sep 1957	8 Oct 1960	27 Oct 1961
CVA 66	America	Newport News	9 Jan 1961	1 Feb 1964	23 Jan 1965
CVA 67	John F. Kennedy	Newport News	22 Oct 1964	27 May 1967	7 Sep 1968
Displacement	56,300 tons; 80,940 f/l *2004*: 61,107 tons; 81,953 f/l				
Dimensions	1,047′6″ (oa); 990′(wl) × 129′4″ × 37′ (extreme beam 252′)				
Machinery	4 screws; ST; 8 boilers; 280,000 SHP; 34 knots				
Endurance	12,000/20				
Complement	4,860.				
Armament	63,64,66: Terrier lchrs. *1980s*: 3 Sea Sparrow SAM lchrs, 3 Phalanx. Later 2 8-cell NATO lchrs				
—	1984: 3 IPDMS, 3 Phalanx (64, 66, 67); 2 IPDMS, 3 Phalanx, 3–20 mm (63)				
Aircraft	85				

Notes: *Kennedy* is a separate class, angled funnel. Three steam catapults, four deck edge elevators.

Service Records:

CVA 63 *Kitty Hawk* Collided with oiler *Platte* off San Francisco, 16 Jun 1967. Rec **CV 63**, 29 Apr 1973. Fire in machinery room 700 miles east of Philippines, 11 Dec 1973 (2 dead). Collided with Canadian frigate *Yukon* off Cape Flattery, Wash., 19 Jan 1983. Collided with replenishment oiler *Wabash* at Alameda, Cal., 27 Nov 1983. In collision with Soviet Victor I class submarine in Sea of Japan, 21 Mar 1984. SLEP Jan 1988–1990.

★Vietnam 20 Dec 1962, May–Jun 1964, Nov 1965–May 1966, Dec 1966–May 1967, Dec 1967–Jun 1968, Jan–Aug 1969, Dec 1970–Jun 1971, Mar–Oct 1972; ◆Quemoy-Matsu 15 Nov 1962, Feb–Jul 1987, Korea May–Jun 1969, Iran/Indian Ocean Nov 1979–Jan 1980, May–Sep 1981, Liberia Dec 1992, Mar 1993, Gulf War Jan–Mar 1993, Indian Ocean Jan–Feb 1997, Apr–Jul 1999, Iraq War 2003. PUC 23 Dec 1967–1 Jun 1968.

CVA 64 *Constellation* Damaged by fire while fitting out at Brooklyn, 19 Dec 1960 (50 dead). Fire at sea, 6 Nov 1961 (4 killed). Rec **CV 64**, 30 Jun 1975. Collided with m/v *Banglar Joy* in Arabian Sea, 26 Jun 1980. Decomm 6 Aug 2003. Stricken 2 Dec 2003.

11★Vietnam Jun–Nov 1964, Jun–Nov 1966, Jun–Nov 1967, Jun–Nov 1968, Jan 1969, Sep 1969–Apr 1970, Nov 1971–Jun 1972, Feb–Mar 1973; ◆Cuba Mar–May 1962, Jul–Aug 1962, Korea Oct 1969, Mar 1970, Iran/Indian Ocean Mar–Apr 1979, Persian Gulf Jun–Jul 1987, Libya Jul–Aug 1987, Indian Ocean Apr–Jun 1997, Aug–Sep 1999, Jul–Aug 2001, Apr–Aug 1980, Iraq War 2003. PUC 22 Oct 1971–13 Jun 1972.

CVA 66 *America* Rec **CV 66**, 30 Jun 1975. In collision with oiler *Caloosahatchee* off Charleston, SC, 3 Dec 1980. Damaged by fire in fuel room off North Carolina, 13 May 1989 (2 killed). Decomm 9 Sep 1996. Stricken 20 Oct 1998. Sunk as target off North Carolina, 20 Apr–14 May 2005.

5★Vietnam May–Oct 1968, May–Nov 1970, Jul 1972–Feb 1973; ◆Korea 24–26 Sep 1970, Beirut Evac Jun–Jul 1976, Iran/Indian Ocean May–Oct 1981, Lebanon Jan, May 1983, Libya Mar–Jun 1986, Libya Jul 1989, Gulf War Jan–Apr 1991, Liberia Nov–Dec 1993, Haiti Sep–Oct 1994, Indian Ocean Dec 1995.

CVA 67 *John F. Kennedy* Rec **CV 67**, 1 Dec 1974. Damaged in collision with cruiser *Belknap* in Ionian Sea, 22 Nov 1975 (1 killed). Collided with destroyer *Bordelon* north of Scotland, 14 Sep 1976. To NRF 1 Oct 1994–1 Oct 1999. Decomm 23 Mar 2007.

◆Lebanon Nov 1983–Feb 1984, Gulf War Sep 1990–Mar 1991, Indian Ocean Nov 1999–Mar 2000.

Figure 1.13: The devastation caused by fire and explosions on the flight deck of the *Enterprise* (CVAN 65) southwest of Hawaii, 14 Jan 1969. View looking forward with the remains of several aircraft. The forward section appears untouched.

Figure 1.14: The first nuclear-powered aircraft carrier, *Enterprise* (CVAN 65) showing her characteristic square island structure.

Figure 1.15: The aircraft carrier *Ronald Reagan* (CVN 76) refueling at sea from the oiler *Yukon* (T-AO 202) in the Western Pacific, 28 Jan 2007.

Enterprise

No.	Name	Builder	Keel Laid	Launched	Comm.
CVAN 65	Enterprise	Newport News	4 Feb 1958	24 Sep 1960	25 Nov 1961
Displacement	74,700 tons; 90,970 f/l				
Dimensions	1,123′(oa); 1,040′(wl) × 133′ × 39′; *1985*: 1,101′4″(oa); *2004*: 1,088′ (oa) (extreme beam 252′)				
Machinery	4 screws; ST; 8 reactors; 280,000 SHP; 30+ knots				
Complement	5,688				
Armament	None. 2 Sea Sparrow SAM lchrs, 3 Phalanx added 1981.				

Notes: First nuclear powered aircraft carrier. Four steam catapults, four deck edge elevators. Distinctive island superstructure with eight fixed array radars and no funnel.

Service Record: Overhauled Nov 1964–Jul 1965. Severely damaged by fire and explosion off Hawaii, 14 Jan 1969 (27 killed). Rec **CVN 65**, 1 Jul 1975. ★Vietnam Dec 1965–Jun 1966, Dec 1966–Jun 1967, Feb–Jun 1968, Mar–Jun 1969, Jul–Sep 1971, Jan, Oct 1972—ar 1973; ◆Cuban missile crisis Oct–Dec 1962, Evac of Vietnam 29–30 Apr 1975, Korea Jan–Mar 1968, Apr–May 1969, Libya/El Dorado Canyon Apr–Jun 1986, Libya Feb–Apr 1988, Jan 1990, Desert Fox Dec 1998, Indian Ocean Nov 1998–Jan 1999.

Nimitz Class

No.	Name	Builder	Keel Laid	Launched	Comm.
CVN 68	Nimitz	Newport News	22 Jun 1968	13 May 1972	3 May 1975
CVN 69	Dwight D. Eisenhower ex-*Eisenhower* (25 May 1970)	Newport News	14 Aug 1970	11 Oct 1975	18 Oct 1977
CVN 70	Carl Vinson	Newport News	11 Oct 1975	15 Mar 1980	13 Mar 1982
CVN 71	Theodore Roosevelt	Newport News	31 Oct 1981	27 Oct 1984	25 Oct 1986
CVN 72	Abraham Lincoln	Newport News	3 Nov 1984	13 Feb 1988	11 Nov 1989
CVN 73	George Washington	Newport News	25 Aug 1986	21 Jul 1990	4 Jul 1992
CVN 74	John C. Stennis	Newport News	13 Mar 1991	13 Nov 1993	9 Dec 1995
CVN 75	Harry S. Truman ex-*United States* (2 Feb 1995)	Newport News	29 Nov 1993	7 Sep 1996	25 Jul 1998
CVN 76	Ronald Reagan	Newport News	12 Feb 1998	5 Mar 2001	12 Jul 2003
CVN 77	George H.W. Bush	Newport News	19 May 2003	9 Oct 2006	10 Jan 2009
Displacement	varies, 77,264 to 81,451 tons; 100,020 to 103,877 f/l				
—	81,600 tons; 96,700 f/l				
—	68–70: 91,700 f/l; 72: 104,112 f/l				
Dimensions	1,115′ (oa); 1,040′(wl) × 134′ × 37′ (252′ beam (oa))				
Machinery	4 screws; ST; 2 reactors; SHP 280,000; 30+ knots				
Complement	6,275				
Armament	3 Sea Sparrow SAM lchrs, 3 or 4 Phalanx				
—	2 8-cell NATO Sea Sparrow, 2 RAM missile launchers or 3/4 Phalanx				
—	1984: 3 IPDMS (69, 70), 2 IPDMS (68), 3 Phalanx (68), 4 Phalanx (70)				

Notes: CVAN 68 and 69 rec CVN, 30 Jun 1975. World's largest warships. Four steam catapults, four deck-edge elevators. Gaps in laying down dates caused for political and financial reasons.

Service Records:

CVN 68 *Nimitz*   Aircraft landing on flight deck crashed, east of Florida, 26 May 1981 (14 killed). Refit Jun 1983–Sep 1984 and 1993–94. 3-year nuclear reactor overhaul, 1998–2001, upgrade to island, new antenna mast.
◆Iran/Indian Ocean Jan–May 1980, Eagle Claw, 24–25 Apr 1980, Lebanon Dec 1982–Apr 1983, Libya Nov–Dec 1988, Nov–Dec 1989, Gulf War Apr 1991, Indian Ocean Jan–Mar 1996, Oct 1997–Feb 1998.

Figure 1.16: *USS Nimitz* (CVN 68), May 21, 1975, shortly after being commissioned.

Figure 1.17: *USS George Washington* (CVN 73) in 1995. Notice the flight deck crowded with several types of aircraft. The small white object near the port bow is a Phalanx. CIWS.

CVN 69   *Dwight D. Eisenhower*   Damaged in collision with m/v *Urduliz* anchored in Chesapeake Bay, 29 Aug 1988. 3-year refueling, May 2001–Mar 2005.
    ◆Iran/Indian Ocean Apr–Dec 1980, Lebanon May–Nov 1983, Gulf War Aug 1990, Oct 1991–Feb 1992, Haiti Sep 1994.

CVN 70   *Carl Vinson*   3-year refueling, Nov 2005–.
    ◆Libya May 1990, Gulf War Apr–Jun 1994, Desert Fox Dec 1998, Indian Ocean Dec 1998–Mar 1999.

CVN 71   *Theodore Roosevelt*   Damaged in collision with cruiser *Leyte Gulf* off Cape Hatteras, 14 Oct 1996.
    ◆Gulf War Jan–Apr 1991, Iraq missile strikes Jun 1993, Indian Ocean Mar–Jun 1997, Jul–Sep 1999, Iraq War 2003.

CVN 72   *Abraham Lincoln*   Collided with storeship *Sacramento* in Persian Gulf, 5 Jun 1995.
    ◆Liberia Oct–Nov 1993, Indian Ocean Jul–Oct 1998, Sep 2000–Jan 2001, Iraq War 2003, Tsunami relief 2005.

CVN 73   *George Washington*
    ◆Indian Ocean Nov–Dec 1997.

Figure 1.18: The aircraft carrier *George H.W. Bush* (CVN 77) under construction at Newport News, Sep 2006.

CVN 74   *John C. Stennis*
    ◆Indian Ocean Mar–Jul 1998, Feb–May 2000.

CVN 75   *Harry S. Truman*
    ◆Indian Ocean Dec 2000–Mar 2001, Iraq War 2003.

CVN 76   *Ronald Reagan*

CVN 77   *George H.W. Bush*

Gerald R. Ford

No.	Name	Builder	Keel Laid	Launched	Comm.
CVN 78	*Gerald R. Ford*	Newport News	2008	—	2014

Displacement	100,000 tons
Dimensions	1,092′ (oa); 1,040′ (wl) × 134′ × 39′ (Extreme beam 254′)
Machinery	4 screws; nuclear reactors; 30+ knots
Complement	4,297
Armament	Sea Sparrow, CIWS

Notes: Will replace CVN 65 *Enterprise*. To be comm in 2014. Two additional units planned.

ESCORT CARRIERS

Figure 1.19: The escort carrier *Card* (T-AKV 40) as a civilian-manned aircraft transport operated by the MSTS, 1960s.

ESCORT CARRIERS ON THE NAVY LIST, 1947

Bogue Class

CVE 9   *Bogue*   Decomm 30 Nov 1946. Rec **CVHE 9**, 12 Jun 1955. Stricken 1 Mar 1959. Sold 20 Jun 1960, BU Japan.

CVE 11 *Card*   Decomm 13 May 1946. Rec **CVHE 11**, 12 Jun 1955. Rec **CVU 11**, 1 Jul 1958, MSTS. Rec **AKV 40**, 7 May 1959. Sunk by explosion at pier at Saigon by Vietcong guerrillas, 1 May 1964 (5 killed), salved. Stricken 15 Sep 1970. Sold 14 May 1971. BU Clatskanie, Ore.

CVE 12 *Copahee*   Decomm 5 Jul 1946. Rec **CVHE 12**, 12 Jun 1955. Stricken 1 Mar 1959, sold 25 Jan 1961, BU Japan.

CVE 13 *Core*   Decomm 4 Oct 1946. Rec **CVHE 13**, 12 Jun 1955. Rec **CVU 13**, 1 Jul 1958, MSTS. Rec **AKV 41**, 7 May 1959. Stricken 15 Sep 1970. Sold 28 Apr 1971, BU.

CVE 16 *Nassau*   Decomm 28 Oct 1946. Rec **CVHE 16**, 12 Jun 1955. Stricken 1 Mar 1959. BU Japan 1961.

CVE 18 *Altamaha*   Decomm 27 Sep 1946. Rec **CVHE 18**, 12 Jun 1955. Stricken 1 Mar 1959. Sold 17 Apr 1961, BU Japan.

CVE 20 *Barnes*   Decomm 29 Aug 1946. Rec **CVHE 20**, 12 Jun 1955. Stricken 1 Mar 1959, BU 1960 Japan.

CVE 23 *Breton*   Decomm 30 Aug 1946. Rec **CVHE 23**, 12 Jun 1955. Rec **CVU 23**, 1 Jul 1958, MSTS. Rec **AKV 42**, 7 May 1959. Stricken 6 Aug 1971. BU 1972 Portland, Ore.

CVE 25 *Croatan*   Decomm 20 May 1946. Rec **CVHE 25**, 12 Jun 1955. In svc with MSTS, 16 Jun 1958. Rec **CVU 25**, 1 Jul 1958, MSTS. Rec **AKV 43**, 7 May 1959. Experimental ship for NASA, firing small rockets, Oct 1964–May 1965. Stricken 22 Jun 1971, BU New Orleans.

CVE 31 *Prince William*   Decomm 29 Aug 1946. Rec **CVHE 31**, 12 Jun 1955. Stricken 1 Mar 1959. BU 1961 Japan.

Notes: *Card*, *Core*, *Breton*, and *Croatan* in service with MSTS to support war in Vietnam, 1960s.

Sangamon Class

CVE 27 *Suwannee*   Decomm 8 Jan 1947. Rec **CVHE 27**, 12 Jun 1955. Stricken 1 Mar 1959. Conv to merchant ship canceled 1959. BU 1962 Bilbao.

CVE 28 *Chenango*   Decomm 14 Aug 1946. Rec **CVHE 28**, 12 Jun 1955. Stricken 1 Mar 1959. Sold 12 Feb 1960, BU 1962 Bilbao.

CVE 29 *Santee*   Decomm 21 Oct 1946. Rec **CVHE 29**, 12 Jun 1955. Stricken 1 Mar 1959. BU 1960 Hamburg.

Casablanca Class

CVE 57 *Anzio*   Decomm 5 Aug 1946. Rec **CVHE 57**, 12 Jun 1955. Stricken 1 Mar 1959. Sold 24 Nov 1959, BU Hamburg 1960.

CVE 58 *Corregidor*   Out of comm 30 Jul 1946–19 May 1951. Rec **CVU 58**, 12 Jun 1955, MSTS. Decomm 4 Sep 1958. Stricken 1 Oct 1958. Sold 28 Apr 1959, BU New Orleans.
★Korea K-8; ◆Lebanon 22 Jul 1958.

CVE 59 *Mission Bay*   Decomm 21 Feb 1947. Rec **CVU 59**, 12 Jun 1955. Stricken 1 Sep 1958. Sold 30 Apr 1959, BU Japan 1960.

CVE 60 *Guadalcanal*   Decomm 15 Jul 1946. Rec **CVU 60**, 12 Jun 1955. Stricken 27 May 1958. Sold 30 Apr 1959, BU Japan 1960.

CVE 61 *Manila Bay*   Decomm 31 Jul 1946. Damaged by fire at Boston, 13 Jun 1956. Rec **CVU 61**, 12 Jun 1955. Stricken 27 May 1958. Sold 2 Sep 1959, BU 1960 Japan.

CVE 62 *Natoma Bay*   Decomm 20 May 1946. Rec **CVU 62**, 12 Jun 1955. Stricken 1 Sep 1958. Sold 30 Jul 1959, BU Japan 1960.

CVE 64 *Tripoli*   Out of comm 22 May 1946–5 Jan 1952. Rec **CVU 64**, 12 Jun 1955, MSTS. Decomm 25 Nov 1958. Stricken 1 Feb 1959. Sold 30 Jul 1959, BU 1960 Japan.
★Korea 1952; ◆Lebanon 15 Oct 1958.

CVE 66 *White Plains*   Decomm 10 Jul 1946. Rec **CVU 66**, 12 Jun 1955. Stricken 1 Jul 1958. Sold 29 Jul 1958, BU 1959 Boston.

CVE 69 *Kasaan Bay*   Decomm 6 Jul 1946. Rec **CVU 69**, 12 Jun 1955. Stricken 1 Mar 1959. Sold 2 Feb 1960, BU Hamburg.

CVE 70 *Fanshaw Bay*   Decomm 14 Aug 1946. Rec **CVHE 70**, 12 Jun 1955. Stricken 1 Mar 1959. Sold 26 Sep 1959, BU Portland, Ore.

CVE 74 *Nehenta Bay*   Decomm 15 May 1946. Damaged by crane falling in hurricane at Boston, 31 Aug 1954. Rec **CVU 74**, 12 Jun 1955. Rec **AKV 24**, 7 May 1959. Stricken 1 Aug 1959. Sold 29 Jun 1960, BU Hong Kong.

CVE 75 *Hoggatt Bay*   Decomm 20 Jul 1946 Rec **CVU 75**, 12 Jun 1955. Rec **AKV 25**, 7 May 1959. Stricken 1 Sep 1959. Sold 31 Mar 1960, BU Bilbao.

CVE 76 *Kadashan Bay*   Decomm 14 Jun 1946. Rec **CVU 76**, 12 Jun 1955. Rec **AKV 26**, 7 May 1959. Stricken 1 Aug 1959. BU 1960 Hong Kong.

CVE 77 *Marcus Island*   Decomm 12 Dec 1946. Rec **CVHE 77**, 12 Jun 1955. Rec **AKV 27**, 7 May 1959. Stricken 1 Sep 1959. BU 1960 Osaka.

CVE 78 *Savo Island*   Decomm 12 Dec 1946. Rec **CVU 78**, 12 Jun 1955. Rec **AKV 28**, 7 May 1959. Stricken 1 Sep 1959. BU 1960 Hong Kong.

CVE 80 *Petrof Bay*   Decomm 31 Jul 1946. Rec **CVU 80**, 12 Jun 1955. Stricken 27 Jun 1958. Sold 30 Jul 1959, BU Antwerp.

CVE 81 *Rudyerd Bay*   Decomm 11 Jun 1946. Rec **CVU 81**, 12 Jun 1955. Rec **AKV 29**, 7 May 1959. Stricken 1 Aug 1959. BU 1960 Genoa.

CVE 82 *Saginaw Bay*   Decomm 19 Jun 1946. Rec **CVHE 82**, 12 Jun 1955. Stricken 1 Mar 1959. BU 1960 Rotterdam.

CVE 83 *Sargent Bay*   Decomm 23 Jul 1946. Rec **CVU 83**, 12 Jun 1955. Stricken 27 Jun 1958. BU 1959 Antwerp.

CVE 84 *Shamrock Bay*   Decomm 6 Jul 1946. Rec **CVU 84**, 12 Jun 1955. Stricken 27 Jun 1958. BU 1959 Hong Kong.

CVE 85 *Shipley Bay*   Decomm 28 Jun 1946. Rec **CVHE 85**, 12 Jun 1955. Stricken 1 Mar 1959. BU 1961 Japan.

CVE 86 *Sitkoh Bay*   Out of comm 30 Nov 1946–29 Jul 1950. Damaged in collision with m/v *Seafort* off Point Loma, Cal., 10 Dec 1952. Decomm 27 Jul 1954. Rec **CVU 86**, 12 Jun 1955, MSTS. Rec **AKV 30**, 7 May 1959. Stricken 1 Apr 1960. Sold 19 Aug 1960, BU Japan.
1★Korea 1950–53.

CVE 87 *Steamer Bay*   Out of commission Jan 1947–5 Aug 1950. Rec **CVHE 87**, 12 Jun 1955. Decomm 15 Jan 1959. Stricken 1 Mar 1959. BU Portland, Ore.

CVE 88 *Cape Esperance*   Out of comm 22 Aug 1946–5 Aug 1950. Rec **CVU 88**, 12 Jun 1955, MSTS. Decomm 15 Jan 1959. Stricken 1 Mar 1959. Sold 14 May 1959, BU 1961 Japan.
★Korea 1950–53.

CVE 89 *Takanis Bay*   Decomm 1 May 1946. Rec **CVU 89**, 12 Jun 1955. Rec **AKV 31**, 7 May 1959. Stricken 1 Aug 1959. Sold 29 Jun 1960, BU Japan.

CVE 90 *Thetis Bay*   Out of comm 7 Aug 1946–20 Jul 1956. Rec **CVU 90**, 12 Jun 1955. Rec **CVHA 1**, 1 Jul 1955, flight deck cut down at stern, elevator aft. Rec **LPH 6**, 28 May 1959. Decomm 6 Jan 1964. Stricken 1 Mar 1964. Sold Dec 1964. BU 1967 Portsmouth, Va.
(as LPH) ★Vietnam Sep–Oct 1959, 25 Apr 1961; ◆Quemoy-Matsu Aug, Oct 1959, Aug 1961, Cuban missile crisis Oct–1962.

CVE 91 *Makassar Strait*   Decomm 9 Aug 1946. Rec **CVU 91**, 12 Jun 1955. Stricken 1 Sep 1958. Sunk as target off Point Mugu, Cal., 1958.

CVE 92 *Windham Bay*   Out of comm 23 Aug 1946–28 Oct 1950. Rec **CVU 92**, 12 Jun 1955, MSTS. Decomm 15 Jan 1959. Stricken 1 Feb 1959. BU 1961 Japan.
★Korea 1951–53.

CVE 94 *Lunga Point*   Decomm 24 Oct 1946. Rec **CVU 94**, 12 Jun 1955. Rec **AKV 32**, 7 May 1959. Stricken 1 Apr 1960. Sold 25 Jul 1960, BU 1960 Japan

CVE 97 *Hollandia*   Decomm 17 Jan 1947. Rec **CVU 97**, 12 Jun 1955. Rec **AKV 33**, 7 May 1959. Stricken 1 Apr 1960. Sold 29 Jul 1960, BU Japan.

CVE 98 *Kwajalein*   Decomm 16 Aug 1946. Rec **CVU 98**, 12 Jun 1955. Rec **AKV 34**, 7 May 1959. Stricken 1 Apr 1960. Sold 5 Aug 1960, BU 1961 Japan.

CVE 100 *Bougainville*   Decomm 3 Nov 1946. Rec **CVU 100**, 12 Jun 1955. Rec **AKV 35**, 7 May 1959. Stricken 1 Jun 1960. Sold 29 Aug 1960, BU Japan.

CVE 101 *Matanikau*   Decomm 11 Oct 1946. Rec **CVU 101**, 12 Jun 1955. Rec **AKV 36**, 7 May 1959. Stricken 1 Jun 1960. Sold 27 Jul 1960, BU 1961 Japan.

CVE 104 *Munda*   Decomm 13 Sep 1946. Rec **CVU 104**, 12 Jun 1955. Stricken 1 Sep 1958. Sold 17 Jun 1960, BU Japan.

Figure 1.20: *USS Badoeng Strait* (CVE 116), 19 Jan 1952.

Commencement Bay Class

CVE 105 *Commencement Bay*   Decomm 30 Nov 1946. Rec **CVHE 105**, 12 Jun 1955. Rec **AKV 37**, 7 May 1959. Stricken 1 Apr 1971. BU

CVE 106 *Block Island*   Decomm 28 May 1946–28 Apr 1951. Annapolis training ship May 1946. Decomm 27 Aug 1954. Rec **CVU 106**, 12 Jun 1955. Conversion to LPH 1, Jun 1958 canceled. Rec **AKV 38**, 7 May 1959. Stricken 1 Jul 1959. BU 1960 Japan.

CVE 107 *Gilbert Islands*   Out of comm 21 May 1946–7 Sep 1951. Decomm 15 Jan 1955. Rec **CVU 107**, 12 Jun 1955. Rec **AKV 39**, 7 May 1959. Rec **AGMR 1**, 1 Jun 1963; converted to communications relay ship. Renamed *Annapolis*, 22 Jun 1963. Recomm 7 Mar 1964. Decomm 20 Dec 1969. Stricken 15 Oct 1976. Sold 1 Nov 1979.
★Korea 1952; (as AGMR) 8★Vietnam Sep 1965–Jun 1966, Aug–Dec 1966, Feb 1967–Aug 1968, Mar 1969.

CVE 108 *Kula Gulf*   Out of comm 3 Jul 1946–15 Feb 1951. Rec **CVU 108**, 12 Jun 1955. Decomm 15 Dec 1955. Rec **AKV 8**, 7 May 1959. In service with MSTS, 30 Jun 1965. Stricken 15 Sep 1970. BU 1971.

CVE 109 *Cape Gloucester*   Decomm 5 Nov 1946. Rec **CVHE 109**, 12 Jun 1955. Rec **AKV 9**, 7 May 1959. Stricken 1 Apr 1971. BU 1972.

CVE 110 *Salerno Bay*   Out of comm 4 Oct 1947–20 Jun 1951. Decomm 16 Feb 1954. Rec **CVU 110**, 12 Jun 1955. Rec **AKV 10**, 7 May 1959. Stricken 1 Jun 1961. Sold 30 Oct 1961, BU Bilbao.

CVE 111 *Vella Gulf*   Decomm 9 Aug 1946. Rec **CVHE 111**, 12 Jun 1955. Rec **AKV 11**, 7 May 1959. Stricken 1 Jun 1960; Reinstated 1 Nov 1960. Stricken 1 Dec 1970. Sold 22 Oct 1971, BU Portland, Ore.

CVE 112 *Siboney*   Out of comm 6 Dec 1949–22 Nov 1950. Decomm 31 Jul 1956. Rec **CVU 112**, 12 Jun 1955. Rec **AKV 12**, 7 May 1959. Conversion to AGMR 2 canceled 1963. Stricken 1 Jun 1970. Sold 1971, BU.

CVE 113 *Puget Sound*   Decomm 18 Oct 1946. Rec **CVHE 113**, 12 Jun 1955. Rec **AKV 13**, 7 May 1959. Stricken 1 Jun 1960. Sold 10 Jan 1962, BU Hong Kong.

CVE 114 *Rendova*   Out of comm 27 Jan 1950–3 Jan 1951. Decomm 30 Jun 1955. Rec **CVU 114**, 12 Jun 1955, Rec **AKV 14**, 7 May 1959. Stricken 1 Apr 1971. Sold 1972, BU.
2★Korea K-6 K-7.

CVE 115 *Bairoko*   Out of comm 14 Apr 1950–12 Sep 1950. Damaged by fire and explosion off Japan, 9 May 1951 (5 dead). Decomm 18 Feb 1955. Rec **CVU 115**, 12 Jun 1955. Rec **AKV 15**, 7 May 1959. Stricken 1 Apr 1960. Sold 10 Aug 1960, BU 1961 Hong Kong.
3★Korea K-7 K-8 K-10; ◆OpCastle 1954.

CVE 116 *Badoeng Strait*   Out of comm 20 Apr 1946–6 Jan 1947. Rec **CVU 116**, 12 Jun 1955. Decomm 17 May 1957. Rec **AKV 16**, 7 May 1959. Stricken 1 Dec 1970. Sold 1972, BU.
6★Korea K-1 K-2 K-3 K-7 K-8 K-9.

CVE 117 *Saidor*   Decomm 12 Sep 1947. Rec **CVHE 117**, 12 Jun 1955. Rec **AKV 17**, 7 May 1959. Stricken 1 Dec 1970. Sold 22 Oct 1971, BU Portland, Ore.

CVE 118 *Sicily*   Decomm 5 Jul 1954. Rec **CVU 118**, 12 Jun 1955. Rec **AKV 18**, 7 May 1959. Stricken 1 Jul 1960. Sold 31 Oct 1960, BU 1961 Hong Kong.
5★Korea K-1 K-2 K-3 K-5 K-6.

CVE 119 *Point Cruz*   Out of comm 30 Jun 1947–26 Jul 1951. Rec **CVU 119**, 12 Jun 1955. Decomm 31 Aug 1956. Rec **AKV 19**, 7 May 1959. In service, MSTS 23 Aug 1965. Stricken 15 Sep 1970. BU.
★Korea; ◆Passage to Freedom 1954.

CVE 120 *Mindoro*   Rec **CVU 120**, 12 Jun 1955. Decomm 4 Aug 1955. Rec **AKV 20**, 7 May 1959. Stricken 1 Dec 1959. BU 1960.

CVE 121 *Rabaul*   Never commissioned. Rec **CVHE 121**, 12 Jun 1955. Rec **AKV 21**, 7 May 1959. Stricken 1 Sep 1971. BU

CVE 122 *Palau*   Decomm 15 Jun 1954. Rec **CVU 122**, 12 Jun 1955. Rec **AKV 22**, 7 May 1959. Stricken 1 Apr 1960, sold 13 Jul 1960, BU.
★Korea 1953+.

CVE 123 *Tinian*   Never commissioned. Rec **CVU 123**, 12 Jun 1955. Rec **AKV 23**, 7 May 1959. Stricken 1 Jun 1970, sold 15 Dec 1971 sold, BU.

Note: *Kula Gulf* and *Point Cruz* in service with MSTS with civilian crews 1960s.

2
SUBMARINES

The post World War II transition from conventional to nuclear powerplants completely transformed the capabilities of the submarine. A huge surplus of World War II built "Fleet Boats" meant that all of the older submarines were discarded immediately after World War II, except 26 boats retained as immobilized dockside trainers.

Following the great success of the American submarine war in the Pacific, and faced with a significant threat from submarines of the Soviet Union, the U.S. Navy paid close attention to submarine developments. A careful study of captured Axis units revealed that although big, Japanese submarines were not highly advanced. The newer German submarines, which had evolved to survive in very high-risk environments, were both tougher and considerably faster than contemporary American units. German innovations in propulsion technology were not pursued, probably because it was (correctly) felt that nuclear power held more promise, but a good deal could still be gained in conventional boats by increasing battery power and streamlining the hull. The result was the GUPPY program (Greater Underwater Propulsive Power), in which all deck guns were removed, cleats and bitts were recessed, the bow was rounded, and the conning tower streamlined. One diesel engine was often removed and sonar upgraded. The result was an increase in underwater speed from 9 to 16 knots; 52 boats were converted. Another innovation adopted was the "snorkel" underwater breathing device invented by the Dutch and used by the Germans during the war, which enabled operation of diesel engines at periscope death. A number of older fleet boats were converted into special types, adapted for carrying cargo or troops. Others were converted to oilers, radar pickets, to fire guided missiles, or for anti-submarine warfare. The first new units built after the war, the *Tang* class, were designed as fast-attack boats, with streamlining and snorkels built in.

Three small hunter-killer submarines were built to counter the large Soviet submarine force; a fleet of hundreds was envisioned, but it soon became apparent that larger multi-purpose submarines were more practical.

Construction of the conventionally-powered test submarine *Albacore* in 1953 led to many advances in submarine design, including adoption of the teardrop shape subsequently used in virtually all nuclear submarines. *Albacore* reached an underwater speed of 37 knots.

In 1952, under the leadership of Admiral Hyman G. Rickover, the Navy started the revolution in submarine warfare by ordering a submarine driven by nuclear power using a water-cooled reactor. The first unit, *Nautilus*, was commissioned in 1955. The benefits of safe nuclear power were soon realized; though hardly trouble-free, *Nautilus* was both fast and reliable, and her virtually unlimited submerged endurance enabled her to be the first ship to cruise under the North Pole. The second nuclear submarine, *Seawolf*, was equipped with an unsuccessful sodium-cooled reactor, which the Navy soon replaced with the more reliable water-cooled version. The endurance of nuclear submarines was proved by the submerged round-the-world voyage of the *Triton*. The success of the *Nautilus* led the Navy to discontinue construction of diesel submarines in 1956. Nevertheless some diesel units, which could mimic enemy conventional submarines in exercises, remained in commission until 1990.

In 1958 a crash program to construct ballistic missile submarines capable of launching intercontinental ballistic missiles underwater was started. The first five units were converted from conventional attack submarines and armed with Polaris missiles. They were named after famous Americans, the first being christened *George Washington*. During the next ten years, 41 of these submarines, larger than any predecessor, were built. These ships deployed submerged on sixty-day patrols, each manned with two crews, blue and gold, which went out on alternate missions. At this period, during the height of the cold war, they started carrying pre-targeted missiles. The Polaris missiles were significantly superior to previous missiles and the superior design of the submarines enabled most of them to be upgraded to fire the improved Polaris, Poseidon, and Trident missiles if and as they became available.

By 1965, the Navy had 29 nuclear attack submarines under construction and 22 in commission. The *Thresher* class was a combined hunter-killer and attack submarine, operating quietly, deep-diving, and with a new sonar in the bow. After *Thresher*'s accidental loss in 1963, significant safety improvements were made, although another, *Scorpion*, was later lost to accident as well.

The *Los Angeles* class of 1976 was the largest group of nuclear submarines constructed to a similar design. Amid controversy over the design, in which diving depth was sacrificed to extra speed, 62 submarines were built. Also in 1976 the *Ohio*, the first of a new class of strategic missile submarines was laid down. These ships, of which 18 were built, were the largest submarines built in the United States. They were built to use the new Trident SLBM, to be fired from 24 tubes. That these submarines were given the names of states, previously given to battleships, indicated the importance of this type to the nation.

The *Seawolf* of 1989 was designed for anti-submarine warfare against advanced Soviet submarines, but the end of the cold war, together with the high cost of the ships, led to the program being cut back from the initial plan of 30 ships to three. Of these, the third, *Jimmy Carter*, was redesigned and lengthened for use in special missions. Four of the *Ohio* class SSBNs were later converted for special missions and equipped with cruise missiles.

The newest attack submarines, the *Virginia* class, represent a lower cost and smaller submarine than previous classes. They use masts with high-resolution cameras and fiber-optic data transmission links instead of periscopes.

The practice of naming U.S. submarines for fish and sea creatures continued until 1974, when three were named for legislators who had been helpful to the Navy, as was SSBN 730. The succeeding *Los Angeles* class were named for cities. The strategic missile submarines were named for famous Americans. *Seawolf* followed the old procedure but the next two were named for a state and a former president. Since then both SSBNs and SSNs have been named for states. The logical numbering system was also interrupted with the *Seawolf* class which were given numbers SSN 21 through 23.

SUBMARINES ON THE NAVY LIST, 1947

SS 172 *Porpoise* Decomm Dec 1945. NRT; Dockside trainer 8th ND, 8 May 1947. Stricken 13 Aug 1956. Sold 13 May 1957, BU New Orleans.

SS 173 *Pike* Decomm 15 Nov 1945. NRT; Dockside trainer 5th ND, Sep 1946. Stricken 17 Feb 1956. Sold 14 Jan 1957, BU.

SS 175 *Tarpon* Decomm 15 Nov 1945. NRT; Dockside trainer 8th ND, 9 Apr 1947. Stricken 5 Sep 1956. Lost in tow off Cape Hatteras en route to BU, 26 Aug 1957.

SS 178 *Permit* Decomm 15 Nov 1945. NRT; Dockside trainer 4th ND. Stricken 26 Jul 1956. Sold 27 Jun 1957, BU.

SS 179 *Plunger* Decomm 15 Nov 1945. NRT; Dockside trainer 3rd ND, May 1946. Stricken 6 Jul 1956. Sold 22 Apr 1957, BU.

SS 183 *Seal* Decomm 15 Nov 1945. NRT; Dockside trainer 1st ND, 19 Nov 1947. Stricken 1 May 1956. Sold 25 Apr 1957, BU.

SS 198 *Tambor* Decomm 10 Dec 1945. NRT, Dockside trainer 9th ND. Stricken 1 Sep 1959. 1960 BU.

SS 199 *Tautog* Decomm 8 Dec 1945. NRT; Dockside trainer 9th ND. Stricken 1 Sep 1959. Sold 15 Nov 1959, BU, Manistee, Mich.

SS 206 *Gar* Decomm 11 Dec 1945. NRT; Dockside trainer 9th ND,

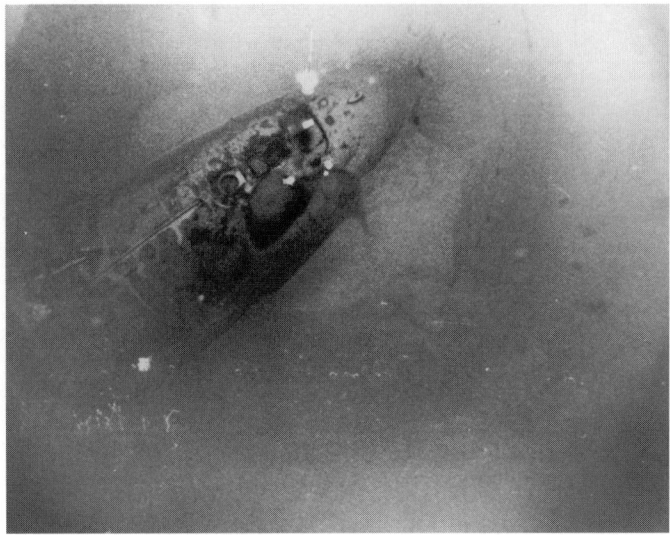

Figure 2.1: The bow section of the wrecked nuclear attack submarine *Scorpion* (SSN 589) on the bottom southwest of the Azores Islands, Jan 1969.

Cleveland, Nov 1948–May 1959. Stricken 1 Aug 1959. Sold 18 Nov 1959, BU.

SS 212 *Gato* Decomm 16 Mar 1946. NRT; Dockside trainer 3rd ND, 1952–1960. Stricken 1 Mar 1960. Sold 25 Jul 1960, BU Philadelphia.

SS 213 *Greenling* Decomm 16 Oct 1946. NRT; Dockside trainer 1st ND, Dec 1946–18 Mar 1960. Stricken 1 Mar 1960. Sold 16 Jun 1960, BU Chelsea, Mass.

SS 214 *Grouper* Rec **SSK 214**, 2 Jan 1951, and converted to hunter-killer submarine, 15 May 1950–29 Jun 1951. Rec **AGSS 214**, 17 May 1958. Research vessel on underwater sound. Again modified 1966. Decomm and stricken 2 Dec 1968. Sold 11 Aug 1970, BU.

SS 217 *Guardfish* Decomm 25 May 1946. NRT; Dockside trainer 3rd ND, 18 Jun 1948. Stricken 1 Jun 1960. Sunk as target off New London, Conn., 18 Oct 1961.

SS 220 *Barb* Out of comm 12 Feb 1947–3 Dec 1951. Decomm 5 Feb 1954 for conv to GUPPY. Recomm 3 Aug 1954. Trfd to Italy 31 Jan 1955.
Later history: renamed *Enrico Tazzoli* (S 511). BU 1974 Livorno.

SS 221 *Blackfish* Decomm 11 May 1946. NRT; Dockside trainer 6th ND, May 1949–54. Stricken 1 Sep 1958. Sold 4 May 1959, BU.

SS 222 *Bluefish* Out of comm 12 Feb 1947–7 Jan 1952. Decomm 20 Nov 1953. Stricken 1 Jun 1959. Sold 8 Jun 1960, BU.

SS 224 *Cod* Decomm 22 Jun 1946. Rec **AGSS 224**, 1 Dec 1962. Rec **IXSS 224**, 30 Jun 1971. Decomm and stricken 15 Dec 1971.
Later history: Museum at Cleveland, Ohio, 1976.

SS 225 *Cero* Out of comm 8 Jun 1946–4 Feb 1952. Decomm 23 Dec 1953. Rec **AGSS 225** 1 Dec 1962. NRT, Detroit, Mich. Stricken 30 Jun 1967. Sold, Oct 1970, BU.

SS 228 *Drum* Decomm 16 Feb 1946. NRT; Dockside trainer DC ND. Rec **AGSS 228**, 1 Dec 1962. Stricken 30 Jun 1968.
Later history: Museum at Mobile, Ala., 1969.

SS 229 *Flying Fish* Rec **AGSS 229**, 29 Nov 1950, underwater sound laboratory. Decomm 28 May 1954. Stricken 1 Aug 1958. Sold 1 May 1959, BU. (Fitted with a circular conning tower with experimental sonar equipment, 1951.)

SS 230 *Finback* Decomm 21 Apr 1950. Stricken 1 Sep 1958. Sold 15 Jul 1959, BU.

SS 231 *Haddock* Decomm 12 Feb 1947. NRT, Dockside trainer 6th ND, Aug 1948–May 1952, Jun 1956–60. Stricken 1 Jun 1960. Sold 23 Aug 1960, BU.

SS 234 *Kingfish* Decomm 9 Mar 1946. NRT, Dockside trainer 1st ND. Stricken 1 Mar 1960. Sold 6 Oct 1960, BU Boston.

SS 235 *Shad* Decomm 24 Apr 1946. NRT, Dockside trainer 1st ND. Stricken 1 Apr 1960. Sold 11 Jul 1960, BU, Kearny, NJ.

SS 236 *Silversides* Decomm 17 Apr 1946. NRT, Dockside trainer 9th ND, Oct 1947. Rec **AGSS 236**, 1 Dec 1962. Stricken 30 Jun 1969.
Later history: Museum at Muskegon, Mich. May 1973.

SS 239 *Whale* Decomm 5 Jan 1947–22 Oct 1956. NRT. Decomm 15 Sep 1957. Stricken 1 Mar 1960. Sold 14 Oct 1960, BU New Orleans.

SS 240 *Angler* Out of comm 12 Feb 1947–2 Apr 1951 and 11 Oct 1952–10 Sep 1953 for conversion to hunter-killer submarine. Rec **SSK 240**, 21 Aug 1951 and recomm 18 Feb 1953. Rec **SS 240**, 15 Aug 1959. In collision with m/v *Export Adventurer* off Block Island, NY, 21 Jul 1961. Rec **AGSS 240**, 28 Jun 1963, training ship. Decomm 1 Apr 1967. Rec **IXSS 240**, 30 Jun 1971. NRT. Stricken 15 Dec 1971. Sold 1 Feb 1974, BU.

SS 241 *Bashaw* Out of comm 20 Jun 1949–3 Apr 1951, converted to hunter-killer submarine. Rec **SSK 241**, 21 Aug 1951. Recomm 28 Mar 1953. Rec **SS 241**, 15 Aug 1959. Rec **AGSS 241**, 1 Sep 1962. Decomm and stricken 13 Sep 1969. Sunk as target, Jul 1972.
3★Vietnam Jun–Aug 1964, Aug–Sep 1965, Mar, May–Jun 1967; ◆Quemoy-Matsu Jun, Sep 1961.

SS 242 *Bluegill* Out of comm 1 Mar 1946–3 May 1951. Out of comm 7 Jul 1952–2 May 1953, converted to hunter-killer submarine. Rec **SSK 242**, 21 Aug 1951. Rec **AGSS 242**, 15 Aug 1959. Decomm and stricken 28 Jun 1969. Scuttled at Lahaina, Maui, Hawaii, 3 Dec 1970 as salvage trainer. Raised and sunk at sea Nov 1983.
★Vietnam Mar–Apr 1962, Feb–Mar, May–Jun 1963, May, Oct–Nov 1966, Feb–Apr 1968; ◆Quemoy-Matsu Jul 1959, Dec 1961–Feb 1962.

SS 243 *Bream* Out of comm 31 Jan 1946–5 Jun 1951. Out of comm 10 Sep 1952–20 Jun 1953, converted to hunter-killer submarine. Rec **SSK 243**, 21 Aug 1951. Rec **SS 243**, 15 Aug 1959. Rec **AGSS 243**, 15 Apr 1965. Stricken 28 Jun 1969. Sunk as target 7 Nov 1969.
★Vietnam Dec 1965–Jan 1966, Aug–Nov 1967, Nov 1968–Feb 1969; ◆Quemoy-Matsu May 1959, Apr 1961, Jan 1963.

SS 244 *Cavalla* Out of comm 16 Mar 1946–10 Apr 1951. Out of comm 3 Sep 1952–15 Jul 1953 for conversion to hunter-killer submarine. Rec **SSK 244**, 18 Feb 1953. Rec **SS 244**, 15 Aug 1959. Rec **AGSS 244**, 1 Jul 1963. Decomm 3 Jul 1968. Stricken 30 Dec 1969.
Later history: Museum at Galveston, Tex., 1971.

SS 245 *Cobia* Out of comm 22 May 1946–6 Jul 1951. Decomm 19 Mar 1954. Rec **AGSS 245**, 1 Dec 1962. Stricken 1 Jul 1970.
Later history: Museum at Manitowoc, Wis., 1986.

SS 246 *Croaker* Out of comm 15 May 1946–7 May 1951 and 18 Mar 1953–11 Dec 1953, for conversion to hunter-killer submarine. Rec **SSK 246**, 9 Apr 1953. In collision with store ship *Alstede* at Cannes, France, 23 Mar 1956. Rec **SS 246**, 15 Aug 1959. Rec **AGSS 246**, 1 May 1967. Decomm 2 Apr 1968. Rec **IXSS 246**, 30 Jun 1971. Stricken 20 Dec 1971. To Groton, Conn., as memorial, 7 Jul 1976, not used & rtnd to USN.
Later history: tfrd to Buffalo, NY, as memorial museum, 22 Jun 1987.

SS 247 *Dace* Out of comm 12 Feb 1947–8 Aug 1951. Decomm 15 Jan 1954. Trfd to Italy 31 Jan 1955.
Later history: Italian *Leonardo da Vinci* (S 510). BU 1975 Livorno.

SS 249 *Flasher* Decomm 16 Mar 1946. Stricken 1 Jun 1959. Sold 31 May 1963, BU Roebling, NJ.
(CT preserved at Groton, Conn.)

SS 251 *Flounder* Decomm 12 Feb 1947. Stricken 1 Jun 1959. Sold 22 Dec 1959, BU.

SS 252 *Gabilan* Decomm 23 Feb 1946. Stricken 1 Jun 1959. Sold 15 Dec 1959, BU.

SS 253 *Gunnel* Decomm 18 May 1946. Stricken 1 Sep 1958. Sold 17 Jul 1959, BU.

SS 254 *Gurnard* Decomm 27 Nov 1945. NRT; Dockside trainer 14th ND, Jul 1949–Jun 1960. Stricken 1 May 1961. Sold 26 Sep 1961, BU Terminal I.

SS 255 *Haddo* Decomm 16 Feb 1946. Stricken 1 Aug 1958. Sold 9 Apr 1959, BU Philadelphia.

SS 256 *Hake* Decomm 13 Jul 1946. NRT Oct 1956. Rec **AGSS 256**, 1 Dec 1962. Stricken 19 Apr 1968. Sold 5 Dec 1972, BU 1973.

SS 258 *Hoe* Decomm 7 Aug 1946. NRT 3rd ND, Sep 1956. Stricken 1 May 1960. Sold 23 Aug 1960, BU Boston, Mass. Prob.

SS 259 *Jack* Decomm 8 Jun 1946. Trfd to Greece 21 Apr 1958.
Later history: renamed *Amfitriti* (Y-17/S-78/S-117). R1967, Returned and sunk as target 5 Sep1967.

SS 260 *Lapon* Out of comm 25 Jul 1946–13 Apr 1957. Decomm and trfd to Greece 18 Aug 1957.
Later history: renamed *Poseidon* (Y-16/S 09). R1976.

SS 261 *Mingo* Out of comm 1 Jan 1947–20 May 1955. Trfd to Japan 15 Aug 1955.
Later history: renamed *Kuroshio* (SS 501). R 1966. Sunk as target 1973.

SS 262 *Muskallunge* Out of comm 29 Jan 1947–31 Aug 1956. Trfd to Brazil 19 Jan 1957
Later history: renamed *Humaitá* (S 14). R1967, sunk as target 9 Jul 1968.

SS 263 *Paddle* Decomm 1 Feb 1946. Trfd to Brazil 18 Jan 1957.
Later history: renamed *Riachuelo* (S 15). Sunk as target Jun 1968.

SS 264 *Pargo* Decomm 12 Jun 1946. NRT, Dockside trainer 13th ND. Stricken 1 Dec 1960. Foundered at wharf, 13 Apr 1961, BU 1961.

SS 265 *Peto* Decomm 25 Jun 1946. NRT, 8th ND, Nov 1956. Stricken 1 Aug 1960. Sold 10 Nov 1960, BU.

SS 266 *Pogy* Decomm 20 Jul 1946. Stricken 1 Sep 1958. Sold 1 May 1959, BU.

SS 267 *Pompon* Out of comm 11 May 1946–15 Jun 1953. Rec **SSR 267**, 1 Mar 1951, converted to radar picket submarine. Recomm 15 Jun 1953. Decomm 2 Feb 1959. Stricken 1 Apr 1960. Sold 25 Nov 1960, BU.
◆Lebanon Jul–Sep 1958.

SS 268 *Puffer* Decomm 28 Jun 1946. NRT, Dockside trainer 13th ND, Jan 1947. Stricken 1 Jul 1960. Sold 4 Nov 1960, BU Portland, Ore.

SS 269 *Rasher* Decomm 22 Jun 1946–14 Dec 1951 and 28 May 1952–22 Jul 1953. Rec **SSR 269**, 14 Mar 1951, converted to radar picket submarine. In collision with destroyer *George K. Mackenzie* in Pacific, 9 Apr 1959. Rec **AGSS 269**, 1 Jul 1960. Decomm 27 May 1967. NRT. Rec **IXSS 269**, 30 Jun 1971. Stricken 20 Dec 1971. Sold 2 Aug 1974, BU Portland, Ore.
2★Vietnam Oct–Dec 1964, May–Jun 1966.

SS 270 *Raton* Out of comm 11 Mar 1949–21 Sep 1953. Rec **SSR 270**, 14 Mar 1951, converted to radar picket submarine. Rec **AGSS 270**, 1 Jul 1960. Decomm and stricken 28 Jun 1969. Used as target 1969. Sold 10 Dec 1973, BU.
★Vietnam Aug 1964, May–Jul 1966.

SS 271 *Ray* Out of comm 12 Feb 1947–13 Aug 1952. Rec **SSR 271**, 14 Mar 1951, converted to radar picket submarine. Decomm 30 Sep 1958. Stricken 1 Aug 1960. Sold 18 Dec 1960, BU.

SS 272 *Redfin* Out of comm 1 Nov 1946–9 Jan 1953. Rec **SSR 272**, 14 Mar 1951, converted to radar picket submarine. Rec **SS 272**, 15 Aug 1959. Rec **AGSS 272**, 28 Jun 1963. Decomm 15 May 1967. NRT. Stricken 1 Jul 1970. Sold 31 Mar 1971, BU.

SS 274 *Rock* Out of comm 1 May 1946–12 Oct 1953. Rec **SSR 274**, 18 Jul 1952, converted to radar picket submarine. Rec **AGSS 274**, 31 Dec 1959. Decomm and stricken 13 Sep 1969. Sunk as target.
★Vietnam Apr 1965, Nov 1966, May 1968.

SS 276 *Sawfish* Decomm 26 Jun 1946. NRT; Dockside trainer 11th ND, May 1947. Stricken 1 Apr 1960. Sold 2 Dec 1960. BU.

SS 280 *Steelhead* Decomm 29 Jun 1946. NRT; Dockside trainer 11th ND. Stricken 1 Apr 1960. Sold 21 Jul 1961.

SS 281 *Sunfish* Decomm 26 Dec 1945. NRT; Dockside trainer 12th ND. Stricken 1 May 1960. Sold 15 Dec 1960, BU.

Figure 2.2: *USS Redfin* (SSR 272), as radar picket submarine, about 1960.

SS 282 *Tunny* Out of comm 13 Dec 1945–6 Mar 1953. Rec **SSG 282**, 6 Mar 1953; converted to Regulus missile test ship. Rec **SS 282**, 15 May 1965. Converted to transport submarine, rec **APSS 282**, 1 Oct 1966. Rec **LPSS 282**, 1 Jan 1968. Decomm 28 Jun 1969. Stricken 30 Jun 1969. Sunk as target 19 Jun 1970.
5★Vietnam Mar–Jun 1967, Oct–Nov 1967, Apr–Aug, Nov 1968.

SS 283 *Tinosa* Out of comm 19 Jun 1949–4 Jan 1952. Decomm 2 Dec 1953. Stricken 1 Sep 1958, used as training hulk. Foundered off Hawaii 1961.

SS 285 *Balao* Out of comm 20 Aug 1946–4 Mar 1952. Rec **AGSS 285**, 1 Apr 1960. Collided while submerged with m/v *Torrent IV* off Florida, 20 Feb 1962. Decomm 11 Jul 1963. Stricken 1 Aug 1963. Sunk as target off Charleston, SC, 4 Sep 1963.
Later history: conning tower on display at Washington NYd museum.

SS 286 *Billfish* Decomm 1 Nov 1946. NRT Boston, Jan 1960. Rec **AGSS 286** 1 Dec 1962. Stricken 1 Apr 1968. Sold 17 Mar 1971, BU.

SS 287 *Bowfin* Out of comm 12 Feb 1947–27 Jul 1951. Decomm 22 Apr 1954. Rec **AGSS 287**, 1 Dec 1962. Rec **IXSS 287**, 30 Jun 1971. Stricken 1 Dec 1971.
Later history: Museum at Pearl Harbor 1979.

SS 288 *Cabrilla* Decomm 7 Aug 1946. Rec **AGSS 288**, 1 Dec 1961. Decomm and stricken 30 Jun 1968.
Later history: Museum at Galveston, Tex. BU 1972 New Orleans.

SS 291 *Crevalle* Out of comm 20 Jul 1946–6 Sep 1951 and 19 Aug 1955–11 Apr 1957. Rec **AGSS 291**, 1 Apr 1960. Decomm 1 Jan 1968. Stricken 15 Apr 1968. Sold 17 Mar 1971, BU.

SS 292 *Devilfish* Decomm 30 Sep 1946. Rec **AGSS 292**, 1 Dec 1962. Stricken 1 Mar 1967. Sunk as target off San Francisco, 14 Aug 1968.

SS 293 *Dragonet* Decomm 16 Apr 1946. Stricken 1 Jun 1961. Sunk as target in Chesapeake Bay, 17 Sep 1961.

SS 295 *Hackleback* Decomm 20 Mar 1946. Rec **AGSS 295**, 1 Dec 1962. Stricken 1 Mar 1967. Sold 4 Dec 1968, BU Portland, Ore.

SS 296 *Lancetfish* Stricken 2 Jun 1958. Sold 20 Aug 1959, BU.

SS 297 *Ling* Decomm 26 Oct 1946. NRT, Mar 1960. Rec **AGSS 297**, 1 Dec 1962. Rec **IXSS 297**, 30 Jun 1971. Stricken 1 Dec 1971.
Later history: Museum at Hackensack, NJ, 1972.

SS 298 *Lionfish* Out of comm 16 Jan 1946–31 Jan 1951. Decomm 5 Dec 1953. NRT; Dockside trainer Mar 1960. Rec **AGSS 298**, 1 Dec 1962. Stricken 20 Dec 1971.
Later history: Museum at Fall River, Mass., 1972.

SS 299 *Manta* Out of comm 10 Jun 1946–2 Aug 1949. Rec **AGSS 299**, 15 Aug 1949. Target ship for experimental ASW projects. Decomm 6 Dec 1955. Dockside trainer 3rd ND, Apr 1960. Stricken 30 Jun 1967. Sunk as target off Norfolk, Va., 16 Jul 1969.

SS 300 *Moray* Decomm 12 Apr 1946. Rec **AGSS 300**, 1 Dec 1962. Stricken 1 Apr 1967. Sunk as target off San Clemente, Cal., 18 Jun 1970.

SS 301 *Roncador* Decomm 7 Aug 1946. NRT, 11th ND. Rec **AGSS 301**, 1 Dec 1962. Rec **IXSS 301**, 29 Jun 1969. Stricken 1 Dec 1971. Sold, BU. [CT on display at San Diego, Cal.]

SS 302 *Sabalo* Out of comm 7 Aug 1946–1 Jun 1951. Decomm and stricken 1 Jul 1971. Sunk as target off San Diego Feb 1973.
★Korea 1953; ★Vietnam Sep–Oct 1964, Jan–Feb 1965, Sep–Dec 1967, Feb–Apr 1969, Jul–Aug 1970.

SS 303 *Sablefish* Rec **AGSS 303**, 30 Mar 1969. Decomm and stricken 1 Nov 1969. Sold 29 Jul 1971, BU.
◆Cuba Mar 1962.

SS 304 *Seahorse* Decomm 2 Mar 1946. Rec **AGSS 304**, 1 Dec 1962. Name canceled 4 Aug 1966. Stricken 1 Mar 1967. Sold 4 Dec 1968, BU Portland, Ore.

SS 307 *Tilefish* Decomm 12 Oct 1959–30 Jan 1960. Trfd to Venezuela, 4 May 1960.
Later history: renamed *Carite* (S 11). R1977.
1★Korea 1950–51.

SS 309 *Aspro* Out of comm 30 Jan 1946–6 Jul 1951 and 30 Apr 1954–3 May 1957. Rec **AGSS 309**, 1 Jul 1960. Decomm 1 Sep 1962. Stricken 9 Oct 1962. Sunk as target off San Diego, Cal., 16 Nov 1962.

SS 310 *Batfish* Out of comm 6 Apr 1946–7 Mar 1952. Rec **AGSS 310**, 1 Dec 1962. Decomm 1 Nov 1969. Stricken 28 Feb 1972.
Later history: On land as museum at Muskogee, Okla.

SS 311 *Archerfish* Out of comm 12 Jun 1946–7 Mar 1952. Damaged by fire off San Diego, 28 Mar 1952. Out of comm 21 Oct 1955–1 Aug 1957. Rec **AGSS 311**, 1 Feb 1960, to study marine weather conditions. Decomm and stricken 1 May 1968. Sunk as target off San Diego 16 Oct 1968.

SS 312 *Burrfish* Out of comm 10 Oct 1946–2 Nov 1948. Rec **SSR 312**, 20 Jan 1948, converted to radar picket submarine. Decomm 17 Dec 1956. Rec **SS 312**, Mar 1961. Trfd to Canada 11 May 1961.
Later history: renamed *Grilse* (SS 71). Returned and stricken 31 Jul 1969. Sunk as target off Can Clemente I., Cal., 19 Nov 1969.

SS 313 *Perch* Out of comm 15 Jan 1947–20 May 1948. Rec **SSP 313**, 19 Jan 1948, converted to transport submarine. Collided with destroyer *Orleck* off San Diego, 2 Mar 1949. Rec **ASSP 313**, 31 Jan 1950. Rec **APSS 313**, 24 Oct 1956. Out of comm 31 Mar 1960–11 Nov 1961. Rec **LPSS 313**, 22 Aug 1968. Rec **IXSS 313**, 30 Jun 1971. Stricken 1 Dec 1971. Sold 15 Jan 1973, BU.
1★Korea K-1; ★Vietnam Jun–Jul 1963, Aug–Sep, Nov–Dec 1965.

SS 315 *Sealion* Out of comm 2 Feb 1946–2 Nov 1948. Rec **SSP 315**, 31 Mar 1948, converted to transport submarine. Rec **ASSP 315**, 31 Jan 1950. Rec **APSS 315**, 24 Oct 1956. Out of comm 30 Jun 1960–20 Oct

Figure 2.3: *USS Burrfish* (SSR 312), radar picket submarine, May 1951. Two radars have been added but there is no streamlining to the hull.

Figure 2.4: *USS Sealion* (ASSP 315), as a submarine transport. Closeup of the conning tower showing the clutter of periscopes and snorkel.

Figure 2.5: *USS Barbero* (SSG 317), guided missile submarine after 1955, showing hangar and launcher for the Regulus missile.

Figure 2.6: *USS Becuna* (SS 319), an early GUPPY type with streamlined conning tower.

Figure 2.7: *USS Baya* (SS 318). Notice the unusually-shaped conning tower and launching racks on the bow.

	1961. Rec **LPSS 315**, 22 Aug 1968. Decomm 20 Feb 1970. Stricken 15 Mar 1977. Sunk as target off Newport, RI, 8 Jul 1978. ◆Cuba Missile Crisis Nov 1962.	
SS 317	*Barbero*	Out of comm 25 Apr 1946–26 Jul 1948. Rec **ASSA 317**, 31 Mar 1948, converted to cargo submarine. Out of comm 30 Jun 1950–28 Oct 1955. Rec **SSG 317**, 27 Oct 1955, cylindrical hangar fitted on hull and launcher for Regulus missiles. . Decomm 30 Jun 1964. Stricken 1 Jul 1964. Sunk as target off Pearl Harbor, 7 Oct 1964.
SS 318	*Baya*	Out of comm 14 May 1946–10 Feb 1948. Rec **AGSS 318**, 15 Aug 1949. Stricken 30 Oct 1972. Sold 26 Sep 1973, BU Terminal I. ★Vietnam May–Jun 1966, Jul 1969.
SS 319	*Becuna*	GUPPY Ia. Rec **AGSS 319**, 1 Oct 1969. Rec **SS 319**, 30 Jun 1971. Decomm 7 Nov 1969. Stricken 15 Aug 1973. **Later history:** Museum at Philadelphia 1976.
SS 320	*Bergall*	Fitted with new sail, 1951–52. Damaged in collision with destroyer *Norris* 230 miles east of Norfolk, Va., 31 Oct 1954. Decomm and trfd to Turkey 17 Oct 1958. **Later history:** renamed *Turgut Reis* (S-24/S-342). R1983; BU 2000.
SS 321	*Besugo*	Out of comm 21 Mar 1958–15 Jun 1965. Rec **AGSS 321**, 1 Dec 1962. Trfd to Italy 31 Mar 1966. **Later history:** renamed *Francesco Morosini* (S 514). R1976. BU Naples. ★Korea 1950–51.

SS 322 *Blackfin* GUPPY Ia. Out of comm 19 Nov 1948–15 May 1951. Stricken 15 Dec 1972. Sunk as target 13 May 1973.
★Korea 1952; ★Vietnam Mar–Jul 1965, Jan–Apr 1967, Jul 1968; ◆Quemoy-Matsu Jan, Apr 1959.

SS 323 *Caiman* NRT, training 1947–51. GUPPY Ia. Decomm and stricken 30 Jun 1972. Trfd to Turkey, 30 Jun 1972.
Later history: renamed *Dumlupinar* (S-339). R1983.
★Korea 1952; ★Vietnam Apr 1959, Sep 1965, Mar 1968, Mar 1969, Feb, Apr 1971; ◆Korea spring 1968.

SS 324 *Blenny* GUPPY Ia. Rec **AGSS 324**, 1 Oct 1969. Decomm 7 Nov 1969. Rec **SS 324**, 30 Jun 1972. Stricken 15 Aug 1973. Trfd to Ocean City, Md., sunk as artificial reef, 10 Nov 1988.
★Korea 1952.

SS 325 *Blower* Decomm 16 Nov 1950. Trfd to Turkey, 16 Nov 1950.
Later history: renamed *Dumlupinar* (D-6). Sunk in collision with Swedish m/v *Naboland* in Dardanelles, 4 Apr 1953.

SS 326 *Blueback* Decomm 23 May 1948 and trfd. to Turkey, 23 May 1948.
Later history: renamed *Ikinci Inönü* (D-2/S-18/S-331). R1973.

SS 327 *Boarfish* Decomm and trfd to Turkey 28 May 1948.
Later history: renamed *Sakarya* (D-3/S-19/S-332). R1975.

SS 328 *Charr* Rec **AGSS 328**, 1 Jul 1966. Decomm 28 Jun 1969. Rec **IXSS 328**, 1 Jun 1971. Stricken 20 Dec 1971. Sold 17 Aug 1972, BU
★Korea 1952; ★Vietnam Feb–May 1965; ◆Quemoy-Matsu Jul–Aug 1959.

SS 329 *Chub* Decomm 23 May, and trfd to Turkey, 25 May 1948.
Later history: renamed *Gür* (D-4/S-20/S-334). R1975.

SS 330 *Brill* Decomm and trfd to Turkey 25 May 1948.
Later history: renamed *Birinci Inönü* (D-1/S-17/S-330). R1972.

SS 331 *Bugara* Rec **AGSS 331**, 30 Jun 1969. Rec **SS 331**, 1 Oct 1969. Stricken 1 Oct 1970. Foundered in tow off Cape Flattery, Wash., 1 Jun 1971.
★Korea 1950–51; ★Vietnam Aug–Sep 1964, Dec 1965–Mar 1966, Jan–Apr 1968, Mar–Apr, Jun 1969.

SS 333 *Bumper* Decomm 1950. Trfd to Turkey 21 Feb 1950.
Later history: renamed *Canakkale* (D-5/S-21/S-333). R1972.

SS 334 *Cabezon* Decomm 24 Oct 1953. Rec **AGSS 334**, 1 Dec 1962. Stricken 15 May 1970. Sold 28 Dec 1971, BU.
★Korea 1950, 1952.

SS 335 *Dentuda* Decomm 11 Dec 1946. NRT; Dockside trainer 12th ND. Rec **AGSS 335**, 1 Dec 1962. Stricken 30 Jun 1967. Stricken 12 Feb 1969. Sold 1969, BU Portland, Ore.

SS 336 *Capitaine* Out of comm 10 Feb 1950–23 Feb 1957. Rec **AGSS 336**, 1 Jul 1960. Decomm 4 Mar 1966. Trfd to Italy 31 Mar 1966.
Later history: renamed *Alfredo Cappellini* (S 513). R1977.
★Vietnam Mar–Apr 1963, Mar 1964; ◆Quemoy-Matsu Mar, May 1963.

SS 337 *Carbonero* Fitted to launch Regulus guided missiles, as test boat, May 1949. Rec **AGSS 337**, 30 Jun 1969. Rec **SS 337**, 1 Oct 1969. Stricken 1 Dec 1970. Sunk as target off Pearl Harbor, 27 Apr 1975.
★Vietnam Jul–Aug 1965, Dec 1966–Jan 1967, Mar–Apr 1967.

SS 338 *Carp* GUPPY, Feb 1952. Rec **AGSS 338**, 1 May 1968. Rec **IXSS 338**, Jun 1971. Stricken 20 Dec 1971. Sold 11 Jul 1973, BU.
★Korea 1952–53.

SS 339 *Catfish* Out of comm 10 Dec 1948–24 Oct 1950, GUPPY II. Stricken 1 Jul 1971 and trfd to Argentina.
Later history: renamed *Santa Fe* (S 21). Beached at South Georgia after being damaged by British aircraft, 25 Apr 1982. Scuttled by British 1982.
★Korea 1950; ★Vietnam May 1962, Jul–Oct 1965, Sep–Oct 1968; ◆Quemoy-Matsu Jan 1960.

SS 340 *Entemedor* Out of comm 10 Dec 1948–24 Oct 1950. GUPPY IIa. Decomm and trfd to Turkey 31 Jul 1972.
Later history: renamed *Preveze* (S-345). R1986.

SS 341 *Chivo* GUPPY Ia. Decomm and stricken 1 Jul 1971, and trfd to Argentina.
Later history: renamed *Santiago del Estero* (S 22). R1981

SS 342 *Chopper* GUPPY Ia. Rec **AGSS 342**, 15 Sep 1969. Decomm 27 Aug 1969. Rec **IXSS 342**, 1 Jul 1971, salvage, Stricken 1 Oct 1971. Training hulk. Foundered while being rigged as a target off Florida, 21 Jul 1976.
◆Cuba Jan–Mar 1962.

SS 343 *Clamagore* GUPPY II. Collided with catamaran m/v *Mango* at San Juan, PR, 4 Feb 1967. Decomm 12 Jun 1975. Stricken 27 Jun 1975.
Later history: Museum at Patriots Point, SC, 1979.
◆Cuba Jan–Feb 1962.

SS 344 *Cobbler* Underwater collision with submarine *Tusk* off New Jersey, 7 Aug 1947. GUPPY II. Stricken 28 Nov 1973. Trfd to Turkey 21 Nov 1973.
Later history: renamed *Çanakkale* (S-341). R1998.
◆Cuba Apr 1961.

SS 345 *Cochino* GUPPY II. Sunk by fire and explosion north of Norway, 26 Aug 1949 (2 dead).

SS 346 *Corporal* GUPPY II. Collided with racing sloop *Medea IV* off Block Island, NY, 3 Sep 1967. Decomm and stricken 21 Nov 1973 and trfd to Turkey.
Later history: renamed *Ikinci Inönü* (S-333). R 1996.

SS 347 *Cubera* GUPPY II. Rec **AGSS 347**, 30 Jun 1969. Decomm and trfd to Venezuela 5 Jan 1972.
Later history: renamed *Tiburon*. R1979.

Figure 2.8: USS *Cubera* (SS 347), another early GUPPY type. She was transferred to Venezuela in 1972.

Figure 2.9: USS *Cusk* (SSG 348), with guided missile hangar and launcher aft, September 1947. She was the first submarine to fire a guided missile.

SS 348 *Cusk*   Rec **SSG 348**, 20 Jan 1948. First submarine to fire a missile from the deck; launching ramp and hangar aft. Rec **SS 348**, 1 Jul 1954. Collided with submarine *Skate* in North Atlantic, 28 Jan 1959. Rec **AGSS 348**, 30 Jun 1969. Decomm and stricken 24 Sep 1969. Sold 26 Jun 1972, BU Portland, Ore.
★Vietnam Aug–Oct 1964, Sep–Nov 1965, Jul–Aug 1967, Nov 1968, Jan 1969.

SS 349 *Diodon*   GUPPY II. Decomm and stricken 15 Jan 1971. Sold 12 May 1972, BU.
★Korea 1950–51; ★Vietnam Jan–Mar 1966, Sep 1969, Sep 1970; ◆Taiwan Straits Nov 1958, Korea Spring 1969.

SS 350 *Dogfish*   GUPPY II. Decomm and stricken 28 Jul 1972, and trfd to Brazil.
Later history: renamed *Guanabara* (S 10). R1983.

SS 351 *Greenfish*   GUPPY II. 1961. Decomm and stricken 19 Dec 1973 and trfd to Brazil.
Later history: renamed *Amazonas*. (S 16). R1992. BU 2004 Niteroi.
★Korea 1951–1952; ★Vietnam May–Jun 1965, Feb 1966, Jul, Nov 1968, Oct 1969; ◆Korea Summer 1969.

SS 352 *Halfbeak*   GUPPY II. In collision with Canadian destroyer *Micmac* at New York, 22 Aug 1955. Decomm and stricken 1 Jul 1971. Sold 1 Jul 1972, BU Wilmington, Del.

SS 362 *Guavina*   Out of comm 8 Jun 1946–1 Feb 1950. Rec **SSO 362**, 13 Aug 1948, converted to submarine oiler (beam increased to 37′). Rec **AGSS 362**, 11 Dec 1951. Rec **AOSS 362**, 22 Jun 1957. Went aground on San Salvador Island, Bahamas, 14 Feb 1958. Decomm 27 Mar 1959. NRT, 5th ND. Stricken 30 Jun 1967. Sunk as target off Cape Henry, 17 Nov 1967.

SS 363 *Guitarro*   Out of comm 6 Dec 1946–6 Feb 1952 and 22 Sep 1953–15 May 1954. Decomm and trfd to Turkey 7 Aug 1954.
Later history: renamed *Preveze* (D-7/S-22/S-340). Returned 1 Jan 1972, BU.

SS 364 *Hammerhead*   Out of comm 9 Feb 1946–6 Feb 1952 and 21 Aug 1953–16 Jul 1954. Decomm 23 Oct 1954. Trfd to Turkey 7 Aug 1954.
Later history: renamed *Çerbe* ((D-8/S-23/S-341). R1972, BU.

SS 365 *Hardhead*   Out of comm 10 May 1946–24 Mar 1953. GUPPY IIa. Stricken 26 Jul 1972, and trfd to Greece.
Later history: renamed *Papanikolis* (S-114). R1993.

SS 366 *Hawkbill*   Out of comm 21 Jun 1946–5 May 1952. GUPPY Ia. Trfd to Netherlands 21 Apr 1953.
Later history: renamed *Zeeleeuw* (S 803). BU 1970.

SS 367 *Icefish*   Out of comm 21 Jun 1946–5 Jun 1952 and 29 Jul 1952–10 Dec 1952. GUPPY Ia. Decomm and trfd to Netherlands 21 Feb 1953.
Later history: renamed *Walrus* (S 802). BU 1971.

SS 368 *Jallao*   Out of comm 30 Sep 1946–4 Dec 1953. GUPPY IIa. Decomm 26 Jun 1974 and trfd to Spain.
Later history: renamed *Narciso Monturiol*.

SS 370 *Kraken*   Decomm 4 May 1946. Trfd to Spain 24 Oct 1959.
Later history: renamed *Almirante Garcia de los Reyes* (S 31). R1982.

SS 372 *Lamprey*   Decomm 3 Jun 1946. Trfd to Argentina 21 Jul 1960.
Later history: renamed *Santiago del Estero* (S 12), 1971, then *S-12*. BU 1971.

SS 373 *Lizardfish*   Decomm 24 Jun 1946. Trfd to Italy 9 Jan 1960.
Later history: renamed *Evangelista Torricelli* (S 512). R1976.

SS 374 *Loggerhead*   Decomm 16 Jun 1946. Rec **AGSS 374**, 1 Dec 1962. NRT. Recomm 6 May 1960. Stricken 30 Jun 1967. Sold 29 Aug 1969, BU 1969 Portland, Ore.

SS 375 *Macabi*   Decomm 16 Jun 1946. Trfd to Argentina 11 Aug 1960.
Later history: renamed *Salta* (S 11), 1971 *S-11*. BU 1971.

SS 376 *Mapiro*   Decomm 16 Mar 1946. Trfd to Turkey 18 Mar 1960.
Later history: renamed *Piri Reis* (S-343). R1973.

SS 377 *Menhaden*   Out of comm 31 May 1946–7 Aug 1951. GUPPY IIa conversion 1952–53. Decomm 13 Aug 1971. Stricken 15 Aug 1973. Used as target, BU 1988.
★Vietnam Apr 1965, Jan–Feb 1967, Jul 1968.

SS 378 *Mero*   Decomm 15 Jun 1946. Trfd to Turkey 26 Apr 1960.
Later history: renamed *Hizir Reis* (S-344). R1980.

SS 381 *Sand Lance*   Decomm 14 Feb 1946–6 Apr 1963. Trfd to Brazil 7 Sep 1963.
Later history: renamed *Rio Grande do Sul* (S 11). R1972.

SS 382 *Picuda*   Out of comm 25 Sep 1946–19 Jun 1953. GUPPY IIa. Conversion to submarine minelayer canceled. Trfd to Spain 1 Oct 1972.
Later history: renamed *Narciso Monturiel* (S 33). R1977.
◆Cuba Feb–Mar 1961, Feb–Jun 1962.

SS 383 *Pampanito*   Decomm 15 Dec 1945. NRT. Apr 1960. Rec **AGSS 383**, 1 Dec 1962. Stricken 20 Dec 1971.
Later history: Museum at San Francisco 1976.

SS 384 *Parche*   Decomm 11 Dec 1946. NRT; Dockside trainer 12th ND. Rec **AGSS 384**, 1 Dec 1962. Stricken 8 Nov 1969. Sold 18 Jun 1970, BU Portland, Ore.

SS 385 *Bang*   Out of comm 12 Feb 1947–4 Oct 1952. GUPPY IIa. Decomm 28 Sep 1972. Trfd to Spain 1 Oct 1972.
Later history: renamed *Cosme Garcia* (S 34). R1983.

SS 387 *Pintado*   Decomm 6 Mar 1946. Rec **AGSS 387**, 1 Dec 1962. Name canceled 25 Oct 1966. Stricken 1 Mar 1967. Sold 20 Jan 1969, BU Portland, Ore.

SS 388 *Pipefish*   Decomm 19 Mar 1946. Rec **AGSS 388**, 1 Dec 1962. Stricken 1 Mar 1967. Sold 20 Jan 1969, BU Portland, Ore. (CT preserved at museum at Fredericksburg, Tex.)

SS 389 *Piranha*   Decomm 31 May 1946. Rec **AGSS 389**, 1 Dec 1962. Stricken 1 Mar 1967. Sold 20 Jun 1970, BU Portland, Ore.

SS 390 *Plaice*   Decomm 11 Nov 1947. Trfd to Brazil 7 Sep 1963.
Later history: renamed *Bahia* (S 12). R1978.

SS 391 *Pomfret*   Decomm Apr 1952–5 Dec 1952. GUPPY IIa. Trfd to Turkey 1 Jul 1971.
Later history: renamed *Oruç Reis* (S-337). R1986.
★Korea 1951, 1952; ★Vietnam May–Jun 1966, Nov–Dec 1967; ◆Korea spring 1969.

SS 392 *Sterlet*   Out of comm 18 Sep 1948–26 Aug 1950. Decomm 30 Sep 1968. Stricken 1 Oct 1968. Sunk as target 31 Jan 1969.
★Korea 1953; ★Vietnam Aug–Sep, Nov–Dec 1964, Aug 1966.

SS 393 *Queenfish*   Rec **AGSS 393**, 1 Jul 1960. Decomm and stricken 1 Mar 1963. Sunk as target 14 Aug 1963.
★Korea 1951, 1953; ◆Quemoy-Matsu Jan–Feb 1961, Aug–Oct 1962, Mar, Jun 1968.

SS 394 *Razorback*   Out of comm Aug 1952–Jan 1954. GUPPY IIa. Decomm and stricken 30 Nov 1970. Trfd to Turkey

Figure 2.10: *USS Pomfret* (SS 391), a GUPPY IIa conversion

Later history: renamed *Murat Reis* (S-336). R2001. Museum at Little Rock, Ark. 2004.

4★Vietnam May 1963, Nov–Dec 1965, Apr 1967, Jan 1969, Jun 1970; ◆Quemoy-Matsu Nov 1959–Jan 1960, May 1963.

SS 395 *Redfish* Rec **AGSS 395**, 1 Jul 1960. Decomm 27 Jun and stricken 30 Jun 1968. Sunk as target off San Diego, 6 Feb 1969.

★Korea 1951; ★Vietnam May 1967, May 1968.

SS 396 *Ronquil* Out of comm 1 May 1952–16 Jan 1953. GUPPY IIa. Trfd to Spain 1 Jul 1971.

Later history: renamed *Isaac Peral* (S 32). R1984.

★Korea 1951, 1953.

SS 397 *Scabbardfish* Decomm Feb 1948–31 Jan 1951. Decomm 15 Aug 1954. Trfd to Greece 26 Feb 1965

Later history: renamed *Traiana* (S 86). R1982.

★Korea 1952.

SS 398 *Segundo* Decomm and stricken 8 Aug 1970. Sunk as target. 1★Korea 1952–53; ★Vietnam Sep, Dec 1964–Jan 1965, May–Aug 1966, Sep 1967–Feb 1968, Jul 1969; ◆Quemoy-Matsu Dec 1958, Jan 1959.

SS 399 *Sea Cat* Rec **AGSS 399**, 15 Aug 1949. Rec **SS 399**, 11 Dec 1953. Rec **AGSS 399**, 29 Jun 1968. Decomm and Stricken 2 Dec 1968. Sold 18 May 1973, BU.

◆Cuba Mar–Oct 1962, Cuba Missile Crisis Nov 1962.

SS 400 *Sea Devil* Out of comm 10 Sep 1948–2 Mar 1951 and 19 Feb 1954–17 Aug 1957. Rec **AGSS 400**, 1 Jul 1960. Decomm 17 Feb 1964. Stricken 1 Apr 1964. Sunk as target by *Volador*, 24 Nov 1964.

★Korea 1952, 1953; ◆Taiwan Straits Dec 1958.

SS 401 *Sea Dog* Damaged in collision with destroyer *Furse* off Tsingtao, 2 Mar 1948. Decomm 27 Jun 1956. Rec **AGSS 401**, 1 Dec 1962. Stricken 2 Dec 1968. Sold 18 May 1973, BU.

SS 402 *Sea Fox* Out of comm 15 Oct 1952–5 Jun 1953. GUPPY IIa. Decomm and stricken 14 Dec 1970, and trfd to Turkey.

Later history: renamed *Burak Reis* (S-335). R1996.

★Korea 1951, 1952; 4★Vietnam May, Jul–Aug 1964.

SS 403 *Atule* Out of comm 8 Sep 1947–8 Mar 1951. GUPPY Ia. Damaged by fire off U.S. east coast, Oct 1953. Rec **AGSS 403**, 1 Oct 1969. Decomm 6 Apr 1970. Rec **SS 403**, 30 Jun 1971. Stricken 15 Aug 1973, Trfd to Peru 1 Sep 1974

Later history: renamed *Pacocha* (SS 50). Sunk in collision with fishing boat northwest of Lima, Peru, 26 Aug 1988.

★Cuba May 1961–Mar 1962, May–Jul, Sep–Oct 1962.

SS 404 *Spikefish* Rec **AGSS 404**, 1 Jul 1962. Decomm 2 Apr 1963. Stricken 1 May 1963. Sunk as target off Long Island, NY, Aug 1964.

◆Cuba Jan–May 1961, Jan–May, Jul 1962.

SS 405 *Sea Owl* Rec **AGSS 405**, 30 Jun 1969. Decomm and Stricken 15 Nov 1969. Sold 3 Jun 1971, BU

SS 406 *Sea Poacher* GUPPY Ia. Rec **AGSS 406**, 1 Nov 1969. Decomm 15 Nov 1969. Rec **SS 406**, 30 Jun 1971. Stricken 15 Aug 1973. Trfd to Peru 1 Jul 1974.

Later history: renamed *La Pedrera* (SS 49). TS1995.

★Cuba Missile Crisis Nov–Dec 1962.

SS 407 *Sea Robin* GUPPY Ia. Decomm and stricken 1 Oct 1970. Sold 3 Jun 1971, BU.

SS 408 *Sennet* Decomm and stricken 2 Dec 1968. Sold 18 May 1973, BU New Orleans.

★Antarctic Dec 1946–Feb 1947.

SS 409 *Piper* Rec **AGSS 409**, 15 Jun 1967. NRT, 16 Jun 1967. Stricken 1 Jul 1970. Sold Jun 1971, BU.

SS 410 *Threadfin* Out of comm 10 Dec 1952–7 Aug 1953. GUPPY IIa. In collision with m/v *Nikolas Mikhalos* in Gulf of Suez, 6 Nov 1959. Decomm 18 Aug 1972 and trfd to Turkey.

Later history: renamed *Birinci İnönü* (S-346). R1998.

◆Cuba Apr 1961.

SS 411 *Spadefish* Decomm 3 May 1946. Rec **AGSS 411**, 1 Dec 1962. Name canceled 4 Aug 1966. Stricken 1 Apr 1967, BU 1969.

SS 412 *Trepang* Decomm 27 Jun 1946. Rec **AGSS 412**, 1 Dec 1962. Stricken 30 Jun 1967. Sunk as target 16 Sep 1969.

SS 413 *Spot* Decomm 19 Jun 1946. Trfd to Chile 12 Jan 1962.

Later history: renamed *Simpson* (SS 21). R1982.

SS 414 *Springer* Decomm 14 Sep 1946–24 Sep 1960. Trfd to Chile 23 Jan 1961.

Later history: renamed *Thomson* (SS 20). R1972.

SS 415 *Stickleback* Out of comm 26 Jun 1946–6 Sep 1951. GUPPY IIa. Sunk in collision with DE *Silverstein* southwest of Pearl Harbor, 30 May 1958.

SS 416 *Tiru* First comm 1 Sep 1948. GUPPY II. FRAM May 1959, lengthened 12′. Ran aground on Frederick Reef, northwest Australia, 4 Nov 1966. Decomm and stricken 1 Jul 1975. Sunk as target off Norfolk, Va., 19 Jul 1979.

★Korea 1951, 1953; ★Vietnam Apr–Jul 1965, Aug 1968, Apr 1970; ◆Quemoy-Matsu 7 Feb 1961, Korea Dec 1969–Jan 1970.

SS 417 *Tench* Out of comm Mar 1946–1 Oct 1950. GUPPY IIa, conv Oct 1950. Rec **AGSS 417**, 1 Oct 1969. Decomm 8 May 1970. Rec **SS 417**, 30 Jun 1971. Stricken 15 Aug 1973. Transfer to Peru for parts canceled. Sold, BU.

SS 418 *Thornback* Our of comm 6 Apr 1946–2 Oct 1953. GUPPY IIa. Decomm 1 Jul 1971 and trfd to Turkey.

Later history: renamed *Uluç Ali Reis* (S-338). R2000, museum at Istanbul.

◆Lebanon Jul–Sep 1958.

SS 419 *Tigrone* Out of comm 30 Mar 1946–1 Nov 1948. Rec **SSR 419** 31 Mar 1948, converted to radar picket submarine.
Out of comm 1 Nov 1957–10 Mar 1962. Rec **SS 419**, 15 Aug 1959. Rec **AGSS 419**, 1 Dec 1963. Experimental sonar ship 1965. Decomm and stricken 27 Jun 1975. Sunk as target 25 Oct 1976.

SS 420 *Tirante* Out of comm 6 Jul 1946–26 Nov 1952. GUPPY IIa. Decomm and stricken 1 Oct 1973. Sold 11 Apr 1974, BU.

SS 421 *Trutta* Out of comm 2 Feb 1946–1 Mar 1951. GUPPY IIa. Out of comm 4 May 1952–2 Jan 1953. Decomm and stricken 1 Jul 1972 and trfd to Turkey.

Later history: renamed *Çerbe* (S-340). R1999.

◆Lebanon Jul–Sep 1958.

SS 422 *Toro* Out of comm 7 Feb 1946–13 May 1947. Rec **AGSS 422**, 1 Jul 1962. Decomm 11 Mar 1963. Stricken 1 Apr 1963. Sold 1965, BU Bordentown, NJ.

SS 423 *Torsk* In collision with destroyer *Johnston* in Long Island Sound, 26 May 1947. Decomm 4 Mar 1968. NRT. Rec **AGSS 423**, 1 May 1968. Stricken 15 Dec 1971.

Later history: Museum at Baltimore, 26 Sep 1972.

SS 424 *Quillback* Out of comm 8 May 1952–27 Feb 1953. GUPPY IIa. Decomm and stricken 23 Mar 1973. Sold 26 Feb 1974, BU.

◆Cuba May–Jun 1961, Cuba Missile Crisis Oct–Nov 1962.

Figure 2.11: USS *Tigrone* (SS 419), with cutdown superstructure and hull for use as an experimental sonar ship, 1960s.

SS 425 *Trumpetfish* GUPPY III conv 1961. Decomm and stricken 15 Oct 1973 and trfd to Brazil.
Later history: renamed *Goias* (S 15). R1990.

SS 426 *Tusk* GUPPY II Oct 1947. Rescued survivors of damaged submarine *Cochino* in Barents Sea, 26 Aug 1949 (6 killed). Rammed in gale by storeship *Aldebaran* when surfacing off Labrador, 9 Nov 1949. Underwater collision with submarine *Cobbler* off New Jersey, 7 Aug 1957. Decomm and trfd to Taiwan, 18 Oct 1973.
Later history: renamed *Hai Pao* (SS 92/794/792). SE2001.

SS 435 *Corsair* Fitted with new sound gear 1947. Rec **AGSS 435**, 1 Apr 1960. Decomm and stricken 1 Feb 1963. Sold 21 Oct 1963, BU.

SS 436 *Unicorn* Canceled 7 Jan 1946. Reinstated for partial completion 26 Feb 1946. Stricken 29 Jul 1958. BU 1959.

SS 437 *Walrus* Canceled 7 Jan 1946. Stricken 9 Jun 1958. BU 1959.

SS 475 *Argonaut* Jul 1952 GUPPY. Conv to SSG, Jul 1955, Regulus I missiles, 1955–60. Decomm and stricken 2 Dec 1968, and. sold to Canada.
Later history: renamed *Rainbow* (SS 75). R1974, BU Portland, Ore., 1977.

SS 476 *Runner* Decomm 25 Jan 1969. Rec **AGSS 476**, 1 Feb 1969. **IXSS 476**, 30 Jun 1971. NRT. Stricken 15 Dec 1971. Sold 15 Jun 1973, BU.

SS 477 *Conger* Rec **AGSS 477**, 9 Mar 1962. Decomm 29 Jul 1963. Stricken 1 Aug 1963. Sold May 1964, BU.

SS 478 *Cutlass* GUPPY II. Decomm and stricken 15 Dec 1971. Trfd to Taiwan 12 Apr 1973
Later history: renamed *Hai Shih* (SS 91/736/791) SE2006.
◆Cuba Jan–Feb 1962, Oct 1962.

SS 479 *Diablo* Rec **AGSS 479**, 1 Jul 1962. Decomm and trfd to Pakistan 1 Jun 1964.
Later history: renamed *Ghazi* (S 130). Blew up while minelaying or sunk by Indian surface craft off Vishakhapatnam, India, 5 Dec 1971.

SS 480 *Medregal* In collision with m/v *The Rodos* south of Hainan, China, 13 Jul 1965. Rec **AGSS 480**, 1 May 1967. Rec **SS 480**, 1 Oct 1969. Decomm and stricken 1 Aug 1970. Sold 13 Jun 1972, BU.
★Vietnam Jun–Jul 1965, Nov 1966, Jun–Jul 1968, Jul–Aug, Nov 1969.

SS 481 *Requin* Rec **SSR 481**, 19 Jan 1948, converted to radar picket submarine. Rec **SS 481**, 15 Aug 1959. Rec **AGSS 481**, 29 Jun 1968. Decomm 3 Dec 1968, NRT. Stricken 20 Dec 1971.
Later history: Museum at Tampa, Fla., 1972, then moved to Pittsburgh, 1990.

SS 482 *Irex* Rec **AGSS 482**, 30 Jun 1969. Decomm and stricken 17 Nov 1969. Sold 13 Sep 1971, BU.

SS 483 *Sea Leopard* GUPPY II. Decomm and stricken 27 Mar 1973 and trfd to Brazil
Later history: renamed *Bahia* (S 12). R1998.
◆Cuba Oct 1962.

SS 484 *Odax* GUPPY II. Decomm and stricken 8 Jul 1972, and trfd to Brazil.
Later history: renamed *Rio de Janeiro* (S 13). R1978

SS 485 *Sirago* GUPPY II. Damaged by explosion at Portsmouth NSYd, 2 Jun 1954. Decomm and stricken 1 Jun 1972. Sold 27 Apr 1973, BU Chesapeake, Va.
◆Cuba Apr 1961.

SS 486 *Pomodon* First GUPPY conversion, Jul 1947. GUPPY II, 1951. Decomm and stricken 1 Aug 1970. Sold 28 Dec 1971, BU.
★Korea 1951–52; ★Vietnam May 1965, Aug–Sep 1966, Aug 1968.

SS 487 *Remora* GUPPY II. 1947. GUPPY III 1963 & lengthened 15 feet. Decomm and stricken 29 Oct 1973, and trfd to Greece
Later history: renamed *Katsonis* (S-115). R1993.
★Korea 1950, 1953; ★Vietnam Dec 1965, May 1966.

SS 488 *Sarda* Rec **AGSS 488**, 1 Jul 1962. Decomm and stricken 1 Jun 1964. Sold Mar 1965, BU Bordentown, NJ.

SS 489 *Spinax* Rec **SSR 489**, 19 Jan 1948. Rec **SS 489**, 15 Aug 1959. Rec **AGSS 489**, 30 Jun 1969. Decomm and stricken 11 Oct 1969. Sold 13 Jun 1972, BU Portland, Ore.
★Vietnam Jul–Aug 1959, Oct–Nov 1965, Mar, May–Jun 1969; ◆Taiwan Straits 28 Oct 1958, Korea Jul 1969.

SS 490 *Volador* Construction suspended 30 Jan 1946; resumed Aug 1947. First comm 1 Oct 1948. GUPPY II. In collision with m/v *Miyahime Maru* off Uraga, Japan, 17 Jan 1970. Decomm 18 Aug 1972, and trfd to Italy.
Later history: renamed *Gianfranco Priaroggia Gazzano* (S 502). R1981.
★Korea 1951; 3★Vietnam May 1960, Sep–Oct 1966, Dec 1967–Jan 1968, Dec 1969; ◆Quemoy-Matsu Feb–Apr 1960, Korea Oct–Nov 1969.

SS 522 *Amberjack* GUPPY II, 1948. Decomm and stricken 17 Oct 1973, and trfd to Brazil.
Later history: renamed *Ceará* (S 12). R1990.

SS 523 *Grampus* First comm 26 Oct 1949. GUPPY II. Decomm and stricken 13 May 1972, and trfd to Brazil.
Later history: renamed *Rio Grande do Sul* (S 11). R1978.

SS 524 *Pickerel* First comm 4 Apr 1949. GUPPY II. Decomm 18 Aug 1972 and trfd to Italy.
Later history: renamed *Primo Longobardo* (S 501). R1981.
★Korea 1950; ★Vietnam Mar 1965, May 1968, May 1969.

SS 525 *Grenadier* First comm 10 Feb 1951. GUPPY II. Decomm and stricken 15 May 1973 and trfd to Venezuela
Later history: renamed *Picua* (S 13/S 22). R1991.
◆Cuba Jul–Aug 1961, Cuba Missile Crisis Oct–Nov 1962.

Notes: 26 old submarines were used as dockside trainers for Naval Reserve with batteries and propellers removed, ballast tanks welded shut, 1946. *Tiru* completed as GUPPY.
302 *Sabalo*, 303 *Sablefish*, 320 *Bergall*, 328 *Charr*, 331 *Bugara*, 337 *Carbonero*, 338 *Carp*, 348 *Cusk*, 392 *Sterlet*, 398 *Segundo*, 399 *Sea Cat*, 405 *Sea Owl*, 408 *Sennet*, 409 *Piper*, 423 *Torsk*, 475 *Argonaut*, 476 *Runner*, 480 *Medregal*, 482 *Irex* fitted with GUPPY sail on fleet hull and snorkel, 1950–1952.

GUPPY (Greater Underwater Propulsive Power project) conversions

Type IA

319 *Becuna*, 322 *Blackfin*, 323 *Caiman*, 324 *Blenny*, 341 *Chivo*, 342 *Chopper*, 366 *Hawkbill*, 367 *Icefish*, 403 *Atule*, 406 *Sea Poacher*, 407 *Sea Robin*, 417 *Tench*.

Type II

339 *Catfish*, 343 *Clamagore*, 344 *Cobbler*, 345 *Cochino*, 346 *Corporal*, 347 *Cubera*, 349 *Diodon*, 350 *Dogfish*, 351 *Greenfish*, 352 *Halfbeak*, 416 *Tiru*, 425 *Trumpetfish*, 426 *Tusk*, 478 *Cutlass*, 483 *Sea Leopard*, 484 *Odax*, 485 *Sirago*, 486 *Pomodon*, 487 *Remora*, 490 *Volador*, 522 *Amberjack*, 523 *Grampus*, 524 *Pickerel*, 525 *Grenadier*.

Type IIA

340 *Entemedor*, 365 *Hardhead*, 368 *Jallao*, 377 *Menhaden*, 382 *Picuda*, 385 *Bang*, 391 *Pomfret*, 394 *Razorback*, 396 *Ronquil*, 402 *Sea Fox*, 410 *Threadfin*, 415 *Stickleback*, 418 *Thornback*, 420 *Tirante*, 421 *Trutta*, 424 *Quillback*.

No.	Name	Explanation	—
SS 551	*Bass*	SSK 2	15 Aug 1959
SS 552	*Bonita*	SSK 3	15 Aug 1959
SS 553	—	OSP Norway—*Kinn*	—
SS 554	—	OSP Denmark—*Springeren*	—
SS 556–562	—	not used	—
SS 570	—	completed as SST 1	—

Figure 2.12: *USS Wahoo* (SS 565), *Tang* class, February 1961. The first postwar designed submarine class.

Tang Class

No.	Name	Builder	Keel Laid	Launched	Comm.
SS 563	*Tang*	Portsmouth NSYd	18 Apr 1949	19 Jun 1951	25 Oct 1951
SS 564	*Trigger*	Electric Boat	24 Feb 1949	14 Jun 1951	31 Mar 1952
SS 565	*Wahoo*	Portsmouth NSYd	24 Oct 1949	16 Oct 1951	30 May 1952
SS 566	*Trout*	Electric Boat	1 Dec 1949	21 Aug 1951	27 Jun 1952
SS 567	*Gudgeon*	Portsmouth NSYd	20 May 1950	11 Jun 1952	21 Nov 1952
SS 568	*Harder*	Electric Boat	30 Jun 1950	3 Dec 1951	19 Aug 1952
Displacement	1,560/2,260 tons; *1957*: 2,100/2,700 tons				
Dimensions	269'2" (oa) × 27'3" × 19'; 563–566: *1957*: 278' (oa). 1967 all 287'				
Machinery	2 screws; diesel; 4,500 BHP; 16 knots electric; 5,600 SHP; 18 knots				
Endurance	Depth 700'				
Complement	83				
Armament	8–21"TT				

Notes: First postwar submarines with features of German type XXI type. Fast attack submarines, short hulls, snorkel, diesel-electric machinery with GUPPY features. *Tang, Trigger, Wahoo,* and *Trout* had radial diesels, re-engined and lengthened 1957–66. *Tang* converted for acoustic research 1975–76. Transfer of *Tang, Wahoo,* and *Trout* to Iran canceled, 1978.

Service Records:

SS 563   *Tang*   Set new USN diving depth record (713'), 1952. Rec **AGSS 563**, 30 Jun 1975. Rec **SS 563**, 15 Aug 1978. Tfr to Iran as *Dolfin* canceled. Decomm and trfd to Turkey 8 Feb 1980. Stricken 6 Aug 1987.
   Later history: renamed *Piri Reis* (S-343) R2004.
   4★Vietnam Sep 1964, Jan–Feb 1965, Mar–Apr 1966, Jul–Nov 1968, May 1969, Jan 1971.

SS 564   *Trigger*   Decomm and stricken 2 Jul 1973. Trfd to Italy 10 Jul 1973.
   Later history: renamed *Livio Piomarta*. R1986.
   ★Vietnam Jan 1973.

SS 565   *Wahoo*   Tfr to Iran as *Nahang* canceled. Decomm 27 Jun 1980. Stricken 15 Jul 1983. Sold Nov 1984, BU.
   3★Vietnam Mar–Apr 1965, Jul 1969, Aug 1970.

SS 566   *Trout*   Decomm 2 Jan 1977. Stricken 19 Dec 1978 and trfd to Iran as *Kousseh* but abandoned by Iranian crew Mar 1979. Rtnd to USN 1992, experimental ship 1994 and target. Stricken 3 Jan 2007.

SS 567   *Gudgeon*   Rec **AGSS 567**, 1 Apr 1979. Rec **SSAG 567**, 5 Nov 1979. Decomm 30 Sep 1983 and trfd to Turkey.
   Later history: renamed *Hizir Reis* (S-342). R2004. Museum at Istanbul, 2005.
   ★Vietnam May–Jun 1968, Mar 1969; ◆ Korea spring 1968.

SS 568   *Harder*   Decomm 10 Jul 1973. Stricken and trfd to Italy, 29 Feb 1974.
   Later history: renamed *Romeo Romei* (S 516). R1988.
   ★Vietnam Jan 1970, Jan 1972, Mar 1973; ◆Korea Nov 1969.

Albacore

No.	Name	Builder	Keel Laid	Launched	Comm.
AGSS 569	*Albacore*	Portsmouth NSYd	15 Mar 1952	1 Aug 1953	6 Dec 1953
Displacement	1,517/1,847 tons				
Dimensions	203'9" (oa) × 27'4" × 18'6"; later 210'6"				
Machinery	1 screw; diesel; 1,500 BHP; 25 knots electric; 15,000 SHP; 35 knots				
Complement	52				
Armament	none				

Notes: Authorized 1950. Research submarine with revolutionary "teardrop" hull. Served as test vehicle; hull modified several times. Major modifications 1960.

Service Record: Decomm 9 Dec 1972. Stricken 1 May 1980.
   Later history: Museum at Portsmouth, NH. 1985.

Figure 2.13: *USS Albacore* (AGSS 569). Experimental submarine with new "teardrop" hull design.

X-1

No.	Builder	Keel Laid	Launched	Completed
X-1	Jakobson	1 May 1952	7 Sep 1955	7 Oct 1955

Displacement	31.5 tons/36.3 tons
Dimensions	49′7″ × 12′2″ × 6′2″
Machinery	1 screw; hydrogen peroxide/diesel engine; 90 hp; 10/10.5 knots
Complement	4

Notes: Depth limit 400′. Experimental submarine.

Service Record: OS 2 Dec 1957. In service 1964, 1965, 1966. Stricken 16 Feb 1973.
    Later history: On display at Submarine Force Museum, Groton, Conn.

Darter

No.	Name	Builder	Keel Laid	Launched	Comm.
SS 576	Darter	Electric Boat	10 Nov 1954	28 May 1956	26 Oct 1956

Displacement	1,870/2,388 tons
Dimensions	268′7″ (oa) × 27′2″ × 19′
Machinery	2 screws; diesel; 4,500 BHP; 19.5 knots electric, 4,500 SHP; 14 knots
Complement	85
Armament	8–21″TT

Notes: Authorized 1954. Improved *Tang* class. Depth 700′ Introduced snorkel mast used in all later submarines.

Service Record: Flooded while surfacing in western Pacific, 14 May 1978. In collision with tanker m/v *Kansas Getty* off Pusan, Korea, 19 Sep 1985. Decomm 1 Dec 1989. Stricken 17 Jan 1990. Sunk as target off Pearl Harbor, 7 Jan 1992.

Figure 2.14: *USS Blueback* (SS 581). The last diesel combat submarine in the Navy.

Barbel Class

No.	Name	Builder	Keel Laid	Launched	Comm.
SS 580	Barbel	Portsmouth NSYd	18 May 1956	19 Jul 1958	17 Jan 1959
SS 581	Blueback	Ingalls	15 Apr 1957	16 May 1959	15 Oct 1959
SS 582	Bonefish	New York Sbdg	3 Jun 1957	22 Nov 1958	9 Jul 1959

Displacement	2,155/2,895 tons
Dimensions	219′6″ (oa) × 29′ × 27′11″
Machinery	1 screw; 3 diesel; 4,800 BHP; 15 knots 2 electric; 3,150 SHP; 25 knots
Endurance	19,000 miles
Complement	78
Armament	6–21″TT

Notes: Authorized 1955–56. Built with bow-mounted diving planes, later shifted to sails. Last diesel combat submarines built for USN. Tear-drop hull.

Service Record:

SS 580   *Barbel*   Damaged when accidentally rammed and sank a North Korean m/v in Gulf of Tonkin Mar 1966. Damaged in diving accident, 1 May 1989 (2 lost), not repaired. Decomm 4 Dec 1989. Stricken 17 Jan 1990. Sunk as target 30 Jan 2001.
    ★Vietnam 21 Mar 1966, 13 May 1967, 28 Nov 1969, 21 Jan 1971.

SS 581   *Blueback*   Decomm 1 Oct 1990. Stricken 30 Oct 1990.
    Later history: Museum at Portland, Ore. 1994.
    ★Vietnam May 1965, Jun 1967, Sep 1971, Korea Apr–May 1967.

SS 582   *Bonefish*   Damaged by fire 160 m. east of Cape Canaveral, 24 Apr 1988 (3 killed). Decomm 28 Sep 1988. Stricken 28 Feb 1989. Sold 17 Aug 1989, BU New Orleans.
    ★Vietnam Aug–Oct 1966, Nov–Dec 1966, Nov–Dec 1967, Mar 1970, Jun–Jul 1971; ◆Korea spring 1968.

Dolphin

No.	Name	Builder	Keel Laid	Launched	Comm.
AGSS 555	Dolphin	Portsmouth NSYd	9 Nov 1962	8 Jun 1968	17 Aug 1968

Displacement	860/950 tons
Dimensions	165′ (oa); 152′ (wl) × 19′4″ × 16′
Machinery	1 screw; diesel; 15 knots electric; 1,650 SHP; 7.5 knots
Complement	22
Armament	1–21″TT removed 1970.

Notes: Authorized 1960. Experimental deep-diving submarine. Small size needed in order to achieve required strength. Built with high yield strength steel. Special experimental TT, later removed.

Service Record: Abandoned by crew after catching fire 100 miles west of San Diego, 21 May 2002, towed back. O/s 22 Sep 2006. Decomm and stricken 15 Jan 2007.

KILLER SUBMARINES

SSK 214 *Grouper*
SSK 240 *Angler*
SSK 241 *Bashaw*
SSK 242 *Bluegill*
SSK 243 *Bream*
SSK 244 *Cavalla*
SSK 246 *Croaker*

Figure 2.15: *USS K-3* (SSK 3), submarine killer, in May 1952, later renamed *Bonita*.

Figure 2.16: *USS Grayback* (SSG 574), built to carry the Regulus missile which can be seen forward, at her commissioning ceremony, March 1958.

K Class

No.	Name	Builder	Keel Laid	Launched	Comm.
SSK 1	K-1	Electric Boat	1 Jul 1949	2 Mar 1951	10 Nov 1951
SSK 2	K-2	Mare I NSYd	23 Feb 1950	2 May 1951	16 Nov 1952
SSK 3	K-3	Mare I NSYd	19 May 1950	21 Jun 1951	11 Jan 1952

Displacement	890/1,160 tons
Dimensions	196′1″ (oa) × 24′7″ × 16′
Machinery	2 screws; diesel-electric; 13/8.5 knots
Complement	37
Armament	4–21″TT

Notes: Authorized 1948. Sonar bow dome in *Barracuda* removed 1959.

Service Record:

SSK 1 K-1 renamed **Barracuda**, 15 Dec 1955. Rec **SST 3**, 15 Aug 1959. Decomm 1 Aug 1972. Stricken 1 Oct 1973. Sold 26 Feb 1974, BU near Charleston, SC.

SSK 2 K-2 renamed **Bass**, 15 Dec 1955. Decomm 1 Oct 1957. Rec **SS 551**, 15 Aug 1959. Stricken 1 Apr 1965, BU.

SSK 3 K-3 renamed **Bonita** 15 Dec 1955. Decomm 7 Nov 1958. Rec **SS 552**, 15 Aug 1959. Stricken 1 Apr 1965, BU.

GUIDED MISSILE SUBMARINES

SSG 282 *Tunny*
SSG 317 *Barbero*
  Armed with two Regulus I missiles.
SSG 348 *Cusk*

Grayback

No.	Name	Builder	Keel Laid	Launched	Comm.
SS 574	Grayback	Mare I NSYd	1 Jul 1954	2 Jul 1957	7 Mar 1958

Displacement	2,671/3,652 tons
Dimensions	322′4″ (oa) × 30′ × 19′ (*1969:* 334′ (oa))
Machinery	2 screws; diesel; 4,500 BHP; 20 knots electric; 5,600 SHP; 12 knots
Complement	88
Armament	4 Regulus I SSM, 8–21″TT

Notes: Started as *Darter* class and converted to missile submarine during construction. As LPSS carried 67 troops. Converted to transport at Mare I NSYd, Nov 1967–May 1969, lengthened. Missile hangars refitted for swimmers.

Service Record: Rec **SSG 574**, 26 Jul 1956. Damaged by fire in northern Pacific, 27 Aug 1963. Decomm 25 May 1964. Rec **APSS 574**, 1 Dec 1964 (conversion deferred). Rec **LPSS 574**, 30 Aug 1968. Recomm 9 May 1969. Rec **SS 574**, 30 Jun 1975. Decomm and stricken 16 Jan 1984. Sunk as target off Subic Bay, 13 Apr 1986.

★Vietnam May 1971.

Growler

No.	Name	Builder	Keel Laid	Launched	Comm.
SSG 577	Growler	Portsmouth NSYd	15 Feb 1955	5 Apr 1958	30 Aug 1958

Displacement	2,543/3,515 tons
Dimensions	317′7″ (oa) × 27′2″ × 19′
Machinery	2 screws; diesels; 4,600 BHP; 20 knots electric; 5,600 SHP; 12 knots
Complement	95
Armament	2 Regulus II SSM, 6–21″TT

Notes: Authorized 1954. Reordered 1956 as missile submarine with longer hull. Conversion to LPSS canceled.

Service Record: Developed leak during deepwater dive off Portsmouth, NH, 5 Nov 1958. Damaged by running into ice floe near Petropavlovsk, about 1960. Decomm 25 May 1964. Stricken 30 Sep 1980.

Later history: Museum at New York, NY. 1988.

TRANSPORT SUBMARINES

APSS 282 *Tunny*
SSP 313 *Perch*
SSP 315 *Sealion*
APSS 574 *Grayback*

CARGO SUBMARINE

ASSA 317 *Barbero*

SUBMARINE OILER

SSO 362 *Guavina*

RADAR PICKET SUBMARINES

Note: Radar picket program abandoned late 1950s.

SSR 267 *Pompon*
SSR 269 *Rasher*
SSR 270 *Raton*
SSR 271 *Ray*
SSR 272 *Redfin*
SSR 274 *Rock*
SSR 312 *Burrfish*
SSR 419 *Tigrone*
SSR 481 *Requin*
SSR 489 *Spinax*

Sailfish Class

No.	Name	Builder	Keel Laid	Launched	Comm.
SSR 572	*Sailfish*	Portsmouth NSYd	8 Dec 1953	7 Sep 1955	14 Apr 1956
SSR 573	*Salmon*	Portsmouth NSYd	10 Mar 1954	25 Feb 1956	25 Aug 1956
Displacement	2,485/3,170 tons				
Dimensions	350'6" (oa) × 30' × 18'				
Machinery	2 screws; diesel; 6,000 BHP; 19.5 knots; electric; 8,200 SHP; 14 knots				
Complement	95				
Armament	2–21"TT; 1966 6–21" TT				

Notes: Authorized 1952. Built as radar picket submarines with large radars aft of sail, removed 1961.

Service Records:
SSR 572 *Sailfish*   Rec **SS 572**, 1 Mar 1961. FRAM 1965–66. Decomm and stricken 30 Sep 1978. Sunk as target 23 May 2007.
SSR 573 *Salmon*   Rec **SS 573**, 1 Mar 1961. FRAM 1964–65. Rec **AGSS 573**, 29 Jun 1968. Rec **SS 573**, 30 Jun 1969. Decomm 1 Oct 1977. Stricken 14 Jan 1985. Sunk as target, 5 Jun 1993.
★Vietnam Oct–Nov 1965, Mar 1966, Jul–Aug 1967, Dec 1968–Jan 1969, Apr–Jun 1970; ◆Quemoy-Matsu Sep–Oct 1959, Jan 1960, Oct 1962.

TRAINING SUBMARINES

T Class

No.	Name	Builder	Keel Laid	Launched	Comm.
SST 1	*T-1*	Electric Boat	1 Apr 1952	17 Jul 1953	9 Oct 1953
SST 2	*T-2*	Electric Boat	1 May 1952	14 Oct 1953	20 Nov 1953
Displacement	303/347 tons				
Dimensions	131'3" (oa) × 13'7" × 11'				
Machinery	1 screw; diesel-electric; 10/10.5 knots				
Complement	14				
Armament	1–21"TT				

Notes: Authorized 1951.

Service Records:
SST 1   *T-1*   ex-AGSS 570. Renamed **Mackerel**, 15 Jul 1956. Stricken 31 Jan 1973. Sunk as target off Puerto Rico, 18 Oct 1978.
SST 2   *T-2*   Renamed **Marlin**, 15 Jul 1956. Decomm and stricken 31 Jan 1973.
    Later history: museum at Omaha, Nebraska, 1974. (On land.)
SST 3   *Barracuda*   see SSK 1

Note: In 2005 the Swedish submarine **Gotland** was acquired by lease for one year to aid in ASW training against diesel submarines.

NUCLEAR ATTACK SUBMARINES

Nautilus

No.	Name	Builder	Keel Laid	Launched	Comm.
SSN 571	*Nautilus*	Electric Boat	14 Jun 1952	21 Jan 1954	30 Sep 1954
Displacement	3,533/4,092 tons				
Dimensions	323'9" (oa) × 27'8" × 22'				
Machinery	2 screws; ST; 1 reactor; 13,400 SHP; 18/23 knots				
Complement	109				
Armament	6–21"TT				

Notes: Authorized 1951. World's first nuclear submarine. Crossed the Arctic Ocean fully submerged, 1958. Overhauled and modified 1972–74.

Service Record: Damaged in collision with carrier *Essex* while submerged, off Morehead City, NC, 10 Nov 1966. Decomm and stricken 3 Mar 1980, rec as floating equipment (nuclear fuel removed).
    Later history: museum at New London 1982.
    ◆PUC 22 Jul 1958–5 Aug 1958.

Figure 2.17: *USS Nautilus* (SSN 569). The first nuclear submarine at Portland, England, 13 Aug 1958.

Seawolf

No.	Name	Builder	Keel Laid	Launched	Comm.
SSN 575	Seawolf	Electric Boat	15 Sep 1953	21 Jul 1955	30 Mar 1957

Displacement	3,741/4,287 tons
Dimensions	337′6″ (oa) × 27′8″ × 21′6″
Machinery	2 screws; ST; 1 reactor; 15,000 SHP; 19/20+ knots
Complement	151
Armament	6–21″TT

Notes: Competitive prototype to *Nautilus* with alternative sodium reactor, which was replaced in 1959.

Service Record: Out of comm 12 Dec 1958–30 Sep 1960 for new reactor. Ran aground while submerged off Cape Cod, 30 Jan 1968. Rammed undersea mountain in Gulf of Maine, 1967. Decomm 30 Mar 1987. Stricken 10 Jul 1987. BU 1997.

Skate Class

No.	Name	Builder	Keel Laid	Launched	Comm.
SSN 578	Skate	Electric Boat	21 Jul 1955	16 May 1957	23 Dec 1957
SSN 579	Swordfish	Portsmouth NSYd	25 Jan 1956	27 Aug 1957	15 Sep 1958
SSN 583	Sargo	Mare I NSYd	21 Feb 1956	10 Oct 1957	1 Oct 1958
SSN 584	Seadragon	Portsmouth NSYd	20 Jun 1956	16 Aug 1958	5 Dec 1959

Displacement	2,570/2,861 tons
Dimensions	267′7″ (oa) × 25′ × 21′
Machinery	2 screws; ST; 1 reactor; 15,000 SHP; 23/20+ knots
Complement	83
Armament	8–21″TT

Notes: First class of nuclear submarines. Similar to *Nautilus*.

Service Record:

SSN 578 *Skate* — Collided with tender *Fulton* at New London, 24 Jul 1958. Collided with submarine *Cubera* in North Atlantic, 28 Jan 1959. First submarine to surface at the North Pole, 17 Mar 1959. Decomm 12 Sep 1986. Stricken 30 Oct 1986. BU 1995.

SSN 579 *Swordfish* — Ran aground near Lanai, Hawaii, 16 Feb 1975. Decomm 2 Jun 1989. Stricken 17 Jan 1990. BU 1996
★Vietnam Mar–Apr 1968, Jun–Jul 1971; ◆Korea spring 1968.

SSN 583 *Sargo* — Damaged by explosion and fire at Pearl Harbor, 14 Jun 1960 (1 killed). Damaged in collision with submarine *Barb* off Oahu, 14 Oct 1965. Decomm 26 Feb 1988. Stricken 21 Apr 1988. BU 1995.
★Vietnam Aug–Sep 1964, Feb 1970; ◆Korea fall 1969.

SSN 584 *Seadragon* — Decomm 12 Jun 1984. Stricken 30 Apr 1986. BU.
★Vietnam Aug–Sep 1964, Sep, Dec 1966, Feb 1967, Jan 1968, Jan–Mar 1972.

Triton

No.	Name	Builder	Keel Laid	Launched	Comm.
SSRN 586	Triton	Electric Boat	29 May 1956	19 Aug 1958	10 Nov 1959

Displacement	5,939/7,773 tons
Dimensions	447′5″ × 36′11″ × 24′
Machinery	2 screws; ST; 2 reactors; 34,000 SHP; 27/27+ knots
Complement	177; 159 (SSN)
Armament	6–21″TT

Notes: Authorized 1956. Designed as radar picket submarine with retractable radar in sail. Only submarine with two reactors. Largest submarine ever built at the time. Made first submerged circumnavigation of the world, 16 Feb–10 May 1960.

Service Record: Rec **SSN 586**, 1 Mar 1961. Decomm 3 May 1969. Stricken 30 Apr 1986.
◆PUC 16 Feb 1960–10 May 1960.

Skipjack Class

No.	Name	Builder	Keel Laid	Launched	Comm.
SSN 585	Skipjack	Electric Boat	29 May 1956	26 May 1958	15 Apr 1959
SSN 588	Scamp	Mare I NSYd	23 Jan 1959	8 Oct 1960	5 Jun 1961
SSN 589	Scorpion	Electric Boat	20 Aug 1958	19 Dec 1959	29 Jul 1960
SSN 590	Sculpin	Ingalls	3 Feb 1958	31 Mar 1960	1 Jun 1961
SSN 591	Shark	Newport News	24 Feb 1958	16 Mar 1960	9 Feb 1961
SSN 592	Snook	Ingalls	7 Apr 1958	31 Oct 1960	24 Oct 1961

Displacement	3,075/3,500 tons
Dimensions	251′9″ (oa) × 31′7″ × 28′
Machinery	1 screw, ST, 1 reactor, 15,000 SHP, 15/30+ knots
Complement	93
Armament	6–21″TT

Notes: Authorized 1956–57. Highly successful. New hull form with larger diameter. Test depth 700′.

Service Record:

SSN 585 *Skipjack* — Struck uncharted sea mountain in Mediterranean, 6 Jun 1973. Decomm and stricken 19 Apr 1990. BU 1998.

SSN 588 *Scamp* — Decomm and stricken 28 Apr 1988. BU 1991.
3★Vietnam Aug–Sep 1967, Oct 1971, Jun 1972.

SSN 589 *Scorpion* — Collided with a barge during storm at Naples, 15 Apr 1968. Lost in North Atlantic near Azores (probable torpedo explosion), 22 May 1968 (99 lost).

SSN 590 *Sculpin* — Decomm and stricken 3 Aug 1990. BU 2001.
★Vietnam Apr 1972.

SSN 591 *Shark* — Decomm and stricken 15 Sep 1990. BU 1996.
★Vietnam Jul 1968.

SSN 592 *Snook* — Became entangled in Soviet trawler fishing net off California, 23 Apr 1975. Decomm 16 Oct 1986. Stricken 14 Nov 1986. BU 1997.
★Vietnam Jun 1966, Jun 1971; ◆Korea summer 1969.

Figure 2.18: USS *Skate* (SSN 578) was the first submarine to surface at the North Pole, 17 Mar 1959.

Halibut

No.	Name	Builder	Keel Laid	Launched	Comm.
SSGN 587	*Halibut*	Mare I NSYd	11 Apr 1957	9 Jan 1959	4 Jan 1960

Displacement	3,850/4,895 tons
Dimensions	350′ (oa) × 29′7″ × 20′
Machinery	2 screws; ST; 1 reactor; 6,000 SHP; 15.5/15+ knots
Complement	119, then 97
Armament	4–21″TT, 5 Regulus I (later 2 Regulus II) SSM; *1965* 6–21″TT.

Note: Authorized 1956. Similar to *Skate* with missile hangar forward. Hangar built for storage of two Regulus II missiles was later used for research equipment. Missiles removed 1965. Became attack submarine on termination of Regulus program. Converted to deep submergence search vessel; refitted as carrier for DSSV.

Service Record: Made seven patrols before cancellation of Regulus. Rec **SSN 587**, 25 Jul 1965. Searched for and found lost Soviet missile submarine *K-129*, Sep 1958. Tapped Soviet underwater cable in Sea of Okhotsk, 1972. Decomm 30 Jun 1976. Stricken 30 Apr 1986. BU 1994 Bremerton.
◆PUC 1968, 1972

Tullibee

No.	Name	Builder	Keel Laid	Launched	Comm.
SSN 597	*Tullibee*	Electric Boat	26 May 1958	27 Apr 1960	9 Nov 1960

Displacement	2,317/2,640 tons
Dimensions	273′ (oa) × 23′4″ × 21′
Machinery	1 screw; turbo-electric & ST; 1 reactor; 2,500 SHP; 15/20 knots
Complement	87
Armament	4–21″TT

Notes: Authorized 1958. Small hunter-killer boat designed to operate off enemy ports. First submarine with bow-mounted sonar. Depth 700′.

Service Record: Damaged in collision with m/v *Hagen* off Cape Hatteras, 6 Oct 1972. Disabled by propeller shaft failure in Mediterranean, 16 Jun 1978. Decomm and stricken 18 Jun 1988. BU 1996.
◆Libya Feb–Apr 1986.

Figure 2.19: *USS Tullibee* (SSN 597) was built as a small hunter-killer submarine.

Thresher (Permit) Class

No.	Name	Builder	Keel Laid	Launched	Comm.
SSN 593	*Thresher*	Portsmouth NSYd	28 May 1958	9 Jul 1960	3 Aug 1961
SSN 594	*Permit* ex-SSGN 594 (1 May 62)	Mare I NSYd	16 Jul 1959	1 Jul 1961	29 May 1962
SSN 595	*Plunger* ex-SSGN 595 (1 May 1962)	Mare I NSYd	2 Mar 1960	9 Dec 1961	21 Nov 1962
SSN 596	*Barb* ex-SSGN 596 (1 May 1962) ex-*Pollack* (23 Jul 1959), ex-*Plunger* (28 Apr 1959)	Ingalls	9 Nov 1959	12 Feb 1962	24 Aug 1963
SSN 603	*Pollack* ex-*Barb* (23 Jul 1959)	New York Sbdg	14 Mar 1960	17 Mar 1962	26 May 1964
SSN 604	*Haddo*	New York Sbdg	9 Sep 1960	18 Aug 1962	16 Dec 1964
SSN 605	*Jack*	Portsmouth NSYd	16 Sep 1960	24 Apr 1963	31 Mar 1967
SSN 606	*Tinosa*	Portsmouth NSYd	24 Nov 1959	9 Dec 1961	17 Oct 1964
SSN 607	*Dace* ex-SSGN 607 (1 May 1962)	Ingalls	6 Jun 1960	18 Aug 1962	4 Apr 1964
SSN 612	*Guardfish*	New York Sbdg	28 Feb 1961	15 May 1965	20 Dec 1966
SSN 613	*Flasher*	Beth; Quincy	14 Apr 1961	22 Jun 1963	22 Jul 1966
SSN 614	*Greenling*	Electric Boat	15 Aug 1961	4 Apr 1964	3 Nov 1967
SSN 615	*Gato*	Electric Boat	15 Dec 1961	14 May 1964	25 Jan 1968
SSN 621	*Haddock*	Ingalls	24 Apr 1961	21 May 1966	22 Dec 1967

Displacement	3,700/4,300 tons
Dimensions	278′6″ (oa) × 31′9″ × 25′2″; SSN 605: 296′9″ (oa); 613–615: 292′2″ (oa)
Machinery	1 screw; ST; 1 reactor; 15,000 SHP; 20/30 knots
Complement	120
Armament	4–21″TT, Subroc. Harpoon added later.

Notes: Designed to combine best features of *Skipjack* and *Tullibee*. Depth 1,300′. Completion of later units delayed by modifications after loss of *Thresher*, 1963, after which class was renamed. *Flasher*, *Greenling*, and *Gato* completed with additional safety features. *Jack* had modified noise-reducing propellers, necessitating longer engine space. SSN 594–596 and 607 planned as missile submarines armed with four Regulus II.

Service Records:

SSN 593 *Thresher* — In collision with tug at Port Canaveral, Fla., 3 Jun 1962. Lost during deep diving tests off Portsmouth, NH, 10 Apr 1963 (129 lost).

SSN 594 *Permit* — In collision with m/v *Hawaiian Citizen* near Farallon Islands, 10 May 1962. Damaged in collision with submarine *La Jolla* off San Francisco, 31 Dec 1982. Decomm and stricken 23 Jul 1991. BU 1993.

SSN 595 *Plunger* — Decomm 3 Jan 1990. Stricken 2 Feb 1990. BU 1996.
★Vietnam Apr 1969, Nov 1970.

SSN 596 *Barb* — In collision with submarine *Sargo* west of Oahu, 13 Oct 1965. Decomm and stricken 20 Dec 1989. BU 1996.
★Vietnam May 1967, Apr 1971.

SSN 603 *Pollack* — Decomm and stricken 1 Mar 1989. BU 1995.

SSN 604 *Haddo* — Decomm 12 Jun 1991. Stricken 30 Aug 1991. BU 1992.
◆Iran/Indian Ocean Dec 1980.

SSN 605 *Jack* — Collided with amphibious assault ship *Trenton* at Alexandria, Egypt, 27 Apr 1981. Decomm and stricken 11 Jul 1990. BU 1992.
◆Libya Jan–May 1986.

SSN 606 *Tinosa* Collided with submarine *John Adams* at Portsmouth, NH, 7 Jun 1963. Decomm and stricken 15 Jan 1992. BU 1992.
◆Lebanon Jun 1986.
SSN 607 *Dace* In collision with a fishing vessel in Narragansett Bay, RI, 24 Mar 1975. Decomm 2 Dec 1988. Stricken 1 Mar 1989. BU 1997.
◆Libya Mar–Jun 1986.
SSN 612 *Guardfish* Ran aground in Pearl Harbor, 24 Dec 1967. Decomm and stricken 4 Feb 1992. BU 1992
★Vietnam Aug–Oct 1968; ◆Iran/Indian Ocean Mar–May 1980,
SSN 613 *Flasher* Damaged by fire while fitting out at Groton, Conn., 7 May 1963 (3 killed). Decomm and stricken 14 Sep 1992. BU 1992
★Vietnam Jun 1969; ◆Iran/Indian Ocean Dec 1979–Feb 1980, Sep–Oct 1981; PUC Spring 1970.
SSN 614 *Greenling* Completed at Quincy. Decomm and stricken 18 Apr 1994. BU 1994
SSN 615 *Gato* Completed at Quincy. In collision with Soviet submarine *K-19* (Hotel class) in Barents Sea, 15 Nov 1969. Decomm and stricken 26 Apr 1996. BU
SSN 621 *Haddock* Developed a leak and floods during a deep dive near Hawaii, 6 Dec 1975. Refit Oct 1984–Sep 1987. Decomm and stricken 7 Apr 1993. BU 2001.
★Vietnam Feb–Mar 1969; ◆Korea spring 1969, Iran/Indian Ocean Jan–Mar 1980, Jun–Jul 1981.

Figure 2.21: The nuclear attack submarine *Parche* (SSN 683) in Sep 2004. She won a record eight citations for intelligence operations tapping Soviet underwater cables from 1979 to 1986. Notice the extra structure aft of the sail.

Figure 2.20: USS *Lapon* (SSN 661) won a commendation for tracking a *Soviet Yankee*-class submarine continuously for a record 47 days in 1968. (Mike Lennon)

Figure 2.22: USS *Richard B. Russell* (SSN 687), Sturgeon class, in San Francisco Bay.

Sturgeon Class

No.	Name	Builder	Keel Laid	Launched	Comm.
SSN 637	*Sturgeon*	Electric Boat	10 Aug 1963	26 Feb 1966	3 Mar 1967
SSN 638	*Whale*	Beth; Quincy	27 May 1964	14 Oct 1966	12 Oct 1968
SSN 639	*Tautog*	Ingalls	27 Jan 1964	15 Apr 1967	17 Aug 1968
SSN 646	*Grayling*	Portsmouth NSYd	12 May 1964	22 Jun 1967	11 Oct 1969
SSN 647	*Pogy*	New York Sbdg	5 May 1964	3 Jun 1967	15 May 1971
SSN 648	*Aspro*	Ingalls	23 Nov 1964	29 Nov 1967	20 Feb 1969
SSN 649	*Sunfish*	Beth; Quincy	15 Jan 1965	14 Oct 1966	15 Mar 1969
SSN 650	*Pargo*	Electric Boat	3 Jun 1964	17 Sep 1966	5 Jan 1968
SSN 651	*Queenfish*	Newport News	11 May 1964	25 Feb 1966	6 Dec 1966
SSN 652	*Puffer*	Ingalls	8 Feb 1965	30 Mar 1968	9 Aug 1969
SSN 653	*Ray*	Newport News	4 Jan 1965	21 Jun 1966	12 Apr 1967
SSN 660	*Sand Lance*	Portsmouth NSYd	15 Jan 1965	11 Nov 1969	25 Sep 1971
SSN 661	*Lapon*	Newport News	26 Jul 1965	16 Dec 1966	14 Dec 1967
SSN 662	*Gurnard*	Mare I NSYd	22 Dec 1964	20 May 1967	6 Dec 1968
SSN 663	*Hammerhead*	Newport News	29 Nov 1965	14 Apr 1967	28 Jun 1968
SSN 664	*Sea Devil*	Newport News	12 Apr 1966	5 Oct 1967	30 Jan 1969
SSN 665	*Guitarro*	Mare I NSYd	9 Dec 1965	27 Jul 1968	9 Sep 1972
SSN 666	*Hawkbill*	Mare I NSYd	12 Sep 1966	12 Apr 1969	4 Feb 1971
SSN 667	*Bergall*	Electric Boat	16 Apr 1966	17 Feb 1968	13 Jun 1969
SSN 668	*Spadefish*	Newport News	21 Dec 1966	15 May 1968	14 Aug 1969
SSN 669	*Seahorse*	Electric Boat	13 Aug 1966	15 Jun 1968	19 Sep 1969
SSN 670	*Finback*	Newport News	26 Jun 1967	7 Dec 1968	4 Feb 1970
SSN 672	*Pintado*	Mare I NSYd	27 Oct 1967	16 Aug 1969	11 Sep 1971
SSN 673	*Flying Fish*	Electric Boat	30 Jun 1967	17 May 1969	29 Apr 1970
SSN 674	*Trepang*	Electric Boat	28 Oct 1967	27 Sep 1969	14 Aug 1970
SSN 675	*Bluefish*	Electric Boat	13 Mar 1968	10 Jan 1970	8 Jan 1971

SSN 676	*Billfish*	Electric Boat	20 Sep 1968	1 May 1970	12 Mar 1971
SSN 677	*Drum*	Mare I NSYd	20 Aug 1968	23 May 1970	15 Apr 1972
SSN 678	*Archerfish*	Electric Boat	19 Jun 1969	16 Jan 1971	17 Dec 1971
SSN 679	*Silversides*	Electric Boat	13 Oct 1969	4 Jun 1971	5 May 1972
SSN 680	*William H. Bates* ex-*Redfish* (25 Jun 1971)	Ingalls	4 Aug 1969	11 Dec 1971	12 May 1973
SSN 681	*Batfish*	Electric Boat	9 Feb 1970	9 Oct 1971	1 Sep 1972
SSN 682	*Tunny*	Ingalls	22 May 1970	10 Jun 1972	26 Jan 1974
SSN 683	*Parche*	Ingalls	10 Dec 1970	13 Jan 1973	17 Aug 1974
SSN 684	*Cavalla*	Electric Boat	4 Jun 1970	19 Feb 1972	9 Feb 1973
SSN 686	*L. Mendel Rivers*	Newport News	26 Jun 1971	2 Jun 1973	1 Feb 1975
SSN 687	*Richard B. Russell*	Newport News	19 Oct 1971	12 Jan 1974	16 Aug 1975
Displacement	3,860/4,630 tons				
Dimensions	292′2″ (oa) × 31′8″ × 29′5″; 678–687: 302′ (oa); *Parche*: 1991: 401′6″ (oa).				
Machinery	1 screw; ST; 1 reactor; 15,000 SHP; 120 knots				
Complement	129				
Armament	4–21″TT, Subroc, Harpoon, Tomahawk				

Notes: Improved *Permit* class. Diving planes on sail rotated to vertical for breaking through polar ice. Depth 1300′. *Cavalla* modified in 1983 to support commando swimmers. *Guitarro* was trials ship for submarine-launched Tomahawk. *Parche* modified and lengthened, 1987–91, for underwater operations.

Service Records:

SSN 637 *Sturgeon*   Ran aground while submerged in deep water off Virgin Islands, 21 May 1973. Decomm and stricken, 1 Aug 1994. BU 1995.

SSN 638 *Whale*   Decomm and stricken 25 Jun 1996. BU 1997.

SSN 639 *Tautog*   Collided with Soviet Echo II-class submarine *K-108*, Jun 1970. Decomm and stricken 31 Mar 1997. BU 2004.
★Vietnam Jan 1971; ◆Iran/Indian Ocean Apr–Aug 1980.

SSN 646 *Grayling*   Collided underwater with Soviet Delta-III-class SSN, 20 Mar 1993. Decomm and stricken 18 Jul 1997. BU 1998.

SSN 647 *Pogy*   Completed by Ingalls. Decomm and stricken 11 Jun 1999. BU 2000.
★Vietnam Oct–Nov 1972.

SSN 648 *Aspro*   Decomm and stricken 3 Mar 1995. BU 2000.
★Vietnam Dec 1970, 24 Aug 1972; ◆Iran/Indian Ocean Oct 1981.

SSN 649 *Sunfish*   Decomm and stricken 28 Mar 1997. BU 1997.

SSN 650 *Pargo*   Decomm and stricken 14 Apr 1995. BU 1996.

SSN 651 *Queenfish*   Decomm and stricken 14 Apr 1992. BU 1993.
◆Korea spring 1968.

SSN 652 *Puffer*   Decomm and stricken 12 Jul 1996. BU 1997.
★Vietnam Sep 1971, 1 Jan 1973; ◆Iran/Indian Ocean May–Jul 1980.

SSN 653 *Ray*   Struck bottom damaging bow in Mediterranean, 20 Sep 1977. Decomm and stricken 16 Mar 1993. BU 2003.

SSN 660 *Sand Lance*   Decomm and stricken, 7 Aug 1998. BU 1999.

SSN 661 *Lapon*   Tracked Soviet Yankee-class submarine for record 47 days, 1968. Decomm and stricken 8 Aug 1992. BU 2004. ◆PUC 1969

SSN 662 *Gurnard*   Ran aground while submerged off San Diego, 23 May 1989. Decomm and stricken 28 Apr 1995. BU 1996.
★Vietnam summer 1970, Oct 1971, 9 Aug 1972; ◆Iran/Indian Ocean Dec 1980–feb 1981.

SSN 663 *Hammerhead*   Decomm and stricken 5 Apr 1995.
◆Iran/Indian Ocean Jun–Aug 1981.

SSN 664 *Sea Devil*   In collision with frigate *Miller* in Pacific, 13 Apr 1989. Decomm and stricken 16 Oct 1991. BU 1999.

SSN 665 *Guitarro*   Sank at dock by workers' error while fitting out at Vallejo, 15 May 1969. Refloated 18 May 1969. Damaged by fire northwest of San Diego 17 May 1984. Decomm and stricken 29 May 1992. BU 1994.

SSN 666 *Hawkbill*   Decomm and stricken 15 Mar 2000. BU 2000.

SSN 667 *Bergall*   Collided with submarine rescue vessel *Kittiwake* at Norfolk, Va., 23 Apr 1984. Decomm and stricken 6 Jun 1996. BU 1997.

SSN 668 *Spadefish*   In collision with French m/v *Le Nohic* in English Channel, . . Nov 1991. Decomm and stricken 11 Apr 1997. BU 1997.
◆Grenada Oct–Nov 1983, Libya/El Dorado Canyon Apr–Jun 1986, Gulf War Aug–Sep 1990.

SSN 669 *Seahorse*   Ran aground at Charleston, SC, 24 Jan 1972. Decomm and stricken, 17 Aug 1995. BU 1996.

SSN 670 *Finback*   In collision with submarine rescue vessel *Kittiwake* at Norfolk, Va., 8 Jan 1974. Decomm and stricken 28 Mar 1997. BU 1997.

SSN 672 *Pintado*   Damaged in submerged head-on collision with a Soviet Yankee-class submarine off Kamchatka, 2 May 1974. Decomm and stricken 26 Feb 1998. BU 1998.
◆Iran/Indian Ocean Nov 1979–Jan 1980, Mar–May 1981.

SSN 673 *Flying Fish*   Decomm and stricken, 16 May 1996. BU

SSN 674 *Trepang*   Decomm and stricken 1 Jun 1999. BU 2000.

SSN 675 *Bluefish*   Decomm and stricken 31 May 1996. BU 2000.
◆Iran/Indian Ocean Jan–Jun 1981.

SSN 676 *Billfish*   Decomm and stricken 1 Jul 1999.

SSN 677 *Drum*   In collision with m/v *Sea Bright* in Hong Kong harbor, 16 Mar 1995. Decomm and stricken 30 Oct 1995.
◆Iran/Indian Ocean Dec 1980–Jan 1981.

SSN 678 *Archerfish*   In collision with submarine *Philadelphia* at New London, 28 Sep 1977. Decomm and stricken 31 Mar 1998. BU 1998.

SSN 679 *Silversides*   Decomm and stricken 22 Jul 1994. BU 2001.
◆Grenada Oct–Nov 1983.

SSN 680 *William H. Bates*   Decomm and stricken 11 Feb 2000. BU 2002.
◆Iran/Indian Ocean Dec 1978–Jan 1979.

SSN 681 *Batfish*   Ran aground at Charleston, SC, 22 Jan 1973. Decomm and stricken 17 Mar 1999. BU 2002.
◆Indian Ocean May–Jun 1998.

SSN 682 *Tunny*   Decomm and stricken 13 Mar 1998. BU 1998.
◆Iran/Indian Ocean Mar–Apr 1979.

SSN 683 *Parche*   Modified for ocean-engineering missions 1976. Tapped Soviet underwater cable in Sea of Okhotsk, 1979–93. Decomm 19 Oct 2004. Stricken 18 Jul 2005.
PUC 1979, 1980, 1981, 1982, 1986, 1 May–1 Aug 1993, 1994, 1998 (Sail is on display at Puget Sound Navy Museum, Bremerton, Wash.)

SSN 684 *Cavalla*   Decomm and stricken 30 Mar 1998. BU 2000.
◆Iran/Indian Ocean Feb–Mar 1981.

SSN 686 *L. Mendel Rivers*   Decomm and stricken 10 May 2001. BU 2002
◆Indian Ocean Dec 1997–Jan 1998.

SSN 687 *Richard B. Russell*   Decomm and stricken 24 Jun 1994. BU 2003

Narwhal

No.	Name	Builder	Keel Laid	Launched	Comm.
SSN 671	*Narwhal*	Electric Boat	17 Jan 1966	9 Jun 1967	12 Jul 1969
Displacement	4,450/5,350 tons				
Dimensions	314′ (oa) × 38′ × 26′				
Machinery	1 screw; ST; 1 reactor; 17,000 SHP; 20/30 knots				
Complement	120				
Armament	4–21″TT, Subroc				

Notes: Similar to *Sturgeon* class with different reactor. Built to evaluate natural-circulation S5G reactor plant.

Service Record: Decomm 1 Jul 1999. To be a museum at Newport, Ky. 2007
◆Libya Jan 1986.

Glenard P. Lipscomb

No.	Name	Builder	Keel Laid	Launched	Comm.
SSN 685	Glenard P. Lipscomb	Electric Bt	5 Jun 1971	4 Aug 1973	21 Dec 1974

Displacement	5,800/6,480 tons
Dimensions	365′ (oa) × 31′9″ × 28′10″
Machinery	1 screw; turbine-electric; 1 reactor; 25+ knots
Complement	120
Armament	4–21″TT, Subroc

Notes: Built to evaluate turbine-electric drive, sacrificing speed for quiet machinery. Fully operational, but design not further utilized

Service Record: Decomm and stricken 11 Jul 1990. BU 1997.

Los Angeles Class

No.	Name	Builder	Keel Laid	Launched	Comm.
SSN 688	Los Angeles	Newport News	8 Jan 1972	6 Apr 1974	13 Nov 1976
SSN 689	Baton Rouge	Newport News	18 Nov 1972	26 Apr 1975	25 Jun 1977
SSN 690	Philadelphia	Electric Boat	12 Aug 1972	19 Oct 1974	25 Jun 1977
SSN 691	Memphis	Newport News	23 Jun 1973	3 Apr 1976	17 Dec 1977
SSN 692	Omaha	Electric Boat	27 Jan 1973	21 Feb 1976	11 Mar 1978
SSN 693	Cincinnati	Newport News	6 Apr 1974	19 Feb 1977	10 Jun 1978
SSN 694	Groton	Electric Boat	3 Aug 1973	9 Oct 1976	8 Jul 1978
SSN 695	Birmingham	Newport News	26 Apr 1975	29 Oct 1977	16 Dec 1978
SSN 696	New York City	Electric Boat	15 Dec 1973	18 Jun 1977	3 Mar 1979
SSN 697	Indianapolis	Electric Boat	19 Oct 1974	30 Jul 1977	5 Jan 1980
SSN 698	Bremerton	Electric Boat	8 May 1976	22 Jul 1978	28 Mar 1981
SSN 699	Jacksonville	Electric Boat	21 Feb 1976	18 Nov 1978	16 May 1981
SSN 700	Dallas	Electric Boat	9 Oct 1976	28 Apr 1979	18 Jul 1981
SSN 701	La Jolla	Electric Boat	16 Oct 1976	11 Nov 1979	24 Oct 1981
SSN 702	Phoenix	Electric Boat	30 Jul 1977	8 Dec 1979	19 Dec 1981
SSN 703	Boston	Electric Boat	11 Aug 1978	19 Apr 1980	30 Jan 1982
SSN 704	Baltimore	Electric Boat	21 May 1979	13 Dec 1980	24 Jul 1982
SSN 705	City of Corpus Christi ex-Corpus Christi (1983), ex-Chicago	Electric Boat	4 Sep 1979	25 Apr 1981	8 Jan 1983
SSN 706	Albuquerque	Electric Boat	27 Dec 1979	13 Mar 1982	21 May 1983
SSN 707	Portsmouth	Electric Boat	8 May 1980	18 Sep 1982	1 Oct 1983
SSN 708	Minneapolis-Saint Paul	Electric Boat	20 Jan 1981	19 Mar 1983	17 Mar 1984
SSN 709	Hyman G. Rickover	Electric Boat	24 Jul 1981	17 Aug 1983	21 Jul 1984
SSN 710	Augusta	Electric Boat	1 Apr 1982	21 Jan 1984	19 Jan 1985
SSN 711	San Francisco	Newport News	26 May 1977	27 Oct 1979	24 Apr 1981
SSN 712	Atlanta	Newport News	17 Aug 1978	16 Aug 1980	6 Mar 1982
SSN 713	Houston	Newport News	29 Jan 1979	21 Mar 1981	25 Sep 1982
SSN 714	Norfolk	Newport News	1 Aug 1979	31 Oct 1981	21 May 1983
SSN 715	Buffalo	Newport News	25 Jan 1980	8 May 1982	5 Nov 1983
SSN 716	Salt Lake City	Newport News	26 Aug 1980	16 Oct 1982	12 May 1984
SSN 717	Olympia	Newport News	31 Mar 1981	30 Apr 1983	17 Nov 1984
SSN 718	Honolulu	Newport News	10 Nov 1981	24 Sep 1983	6 Jul 1985
SSN 719	Providence	Electric Boat	14 Oct 1982	4 Aug 1984	27 Jul 1985
SSN 720	Pittsburgh	Electric Boat	15 Apr 1983	8 Dec 1984	23 Nov 1985
SSN 721	Chicago	Newport News	5 Jan 1983	13 Oct 1984	27 Sep 1986
SSN 722	Key West	Newport News	6 Jul 1983	20 Jul 1985	12 Sep 1987
SSN 723	Oklahoma City	Newport News	4 Jan 1984	2 Nov 1985	9 Jul 1988
SSN 724	Louisville	Electric Boat	16 Sep 1984	14 Dec 1985	8 Nov 1986
SSN 725	Helena	Electric Boat	28 Mar 1985	28 Jun 1986	11 Jul 1987
SSN 750	Newport News	Newport News	3 Mar 1984	15 Mar 1986	3 Jun 1989

Displacement	6,000/6,900 tons
Dimensions	360′ (oa) × 33′ × 32′6″
Machinery	1 screw; ST; 1 reactor; 30,000 SHP; 25/30 knots
Complement	141
Armament	4–21″TT, Subroc, Harpoon, Tomahawk

Notes: High-speed attack submarines designed to oppose new Soviet submarines. Larger than previous designs to accommodate larger nuclear propulsion plant and improved sonar capability. Harpoon and Tomahawk missiles could be fired through torpedo tubes. This group lacked under-ice and minelaying capability. Refitted with Tomahawk and extra quieting from 1984. SSN 719 and later vessels have VLS tubes for Tomahawk. *Buffalo*, *Los Angeles* and *La Jolla* fitted for special operations capability with drydock shelter, 2005. SSN 744–759 not used.

Figure 2.23: The *Los Angeles*-class submarine *Chicago* (SSN 721) arriving at the Kitsap Naval Base, Bangor, Wash., 4 Feb 2005.

Service Records:

SSN 688 *Los Angeles*   Cruised with President Carter on board off Cape Canaveral, Fla., 27 May 1977.
◆Iran/Indian Ocean Apr–Jun 1979, Jan–Apr 1980, May–Jun 1981.

SSN 689 *Baton Rouge*   Damaged in underwater collision with Russian submarine *Barracuda* (Sierra class) off Kola Inlet, 11 Feb 1992. Decomm and stricken 13 Jan 1995. BU 1997.
◆Iran/Indian Ocean Mar–Aug 1980, Sep–Oct 1981.

SSN 690 *Philadelphia*   In collision with submarine *Archerfish* at New London, 28 Sep 1977. Rammed in collision with m/v *Yaso Aysen* in Persian Gulf, 5 Sep 2005.
◆Iran/Indian Ocean Aug 1980–Jan 1981, Gulf War Jan–Mar 1991.

SSN 691 *Memphis*   used as R&D platform Aug 1989.
◆Iran/Indian Ocean Nov 1980–Feb 1981.

SSN 692 *Omaha*   Decomm and stricken 5 Oct 1995.
◆Iran/Indian Ocean Aug–Nov 1980.

SSN 693 *Cincinnati*   Decomm and stricken 29 Jul 1995.
◆Iran/Indian Ocean Feb–Jun 1981.

SSN 694 *Groton*   Decomm and stricken 7 Nov 1997.
◆Iran/Indian Ocean Apr–Sep 1980.

SSN 695 *Birmingham*   Decomm and stricken 22 Dec 1997.

SSN 696 *New York City*   Decomm and stricken 30 Apr 1997.
◆Iran/Indian Ocean Jul–Sep 1981.

SSN 697 *Indianapolis*   Decomm and stricken 22 Dec 1998.

SSN 698 *Bremerton*
◆Iran/Indian Ocean Aug–Sep 1981, Iraq War 2003.

SSN 699 *Jacksonville*   Slightly damaged in collision with m/v *General Z. Dogan* off Cape Charles, Va., 22 Mar 1982. In collision with m/v *Saudi Makkah* off Cape Henry, Va., 17 May 1996.

SSN 700 *Dallas*   Damaged by grounding near Andros, Bahamas, 27 Aug 1981.
◆Libya Feb–Apr 1986.

SSN 701 *La Jolla*   In collision with submarine *Permit* off San Francisco, 31 Dec 1982. Sank fishing vessel *Yong Chang* in collision off Chinhae, South Korea, 11 Feb 1998.

SSN 702 *Phoenix*   Decomm and stricken 29 Jul 1998.
◆Libya Feb 1986.

SSN 703 *Boston*   Decomm and stricken 19 Nov 1999. BU 2003.

SSN 704 *Baltimore*   Decomm and stricken 10 Jul 1998.

SSN 705 *City of Corpus Christi*   Collided underwater with a Soviet nuclear submarine, 21 Jan 1989.
◆Libya May–Jun 1986.

SSN 706 *Albuquerque*

SSN 707 *Portsmouth*   Decomm and stricken 18 Aug 2005.
◆Grenada Oct 1983, Indian Ocean Jan–Mar 1996.

SSN 708 *Minneapolis-Saint Paul*   Decomm and stricken, 1 Nov 2007.
◆Gulf War Sep 1990–Jan 1991.

SSN 709 *Hyman G. Rickover*
◆Libya Jan–Mar 1986.

SSN 710 *Augusta*   Damaged in underwater collision with Soviet Delta class submarine in North Atlantic, Oct 1986.
◆Iraq War 2003.

SSN 711 *San Francisco*   Severely damaged running into an undersea mountain south of Guam, 8 Jan 2005 (1 killed). Repaired with bow of decommissioned *Honolulu*, 2005.

SSN 712 *Atlanta*   Ran aground near Gibraltar, 29 Apr 1986. Decomm and stricken 16 Dec 1999.

SSN 713 *Houston*   Sank m/v tug *Barcona* by snagging its tow cablell, off Long Beach, Cal., 14 Jun 1989. Decomm canceled 2001.

SSN 714 *Norfolk*   Collided with storeship *San Diego* in Chesapeake Bay, 16 Jan 1989. Decomm canceled 2001.

SSN 715 *Buffalo*

SSN 716 *Salt Lake City*   Underwater collision with soviet nuclear submarine, 10 Jan 1989. Decomm 15 Jan 2006.

SSN 717 *Olympia*
◆Indian Ocean Oct 1997–Jan 1998, Aug–Sep 1999.

SSN 718 *Honolulu*   Bow used to repair damaged *San Francisco*, 2005. Decomm 30 Sep 2007.
Iraq War 2003.

SSN 719 *Providence*
◆Indian Ocean Feb–May 1998, Iraq War 2003.

SSN 720 *Pittsburgh*
◆Gulf War Jan–Feb 1991, Indian Ocean Dec 1998–Mar 1999, Jul–Sep 2000, Iraq War 2003.

SSN 721 *Chicago*
◆Gulf War Feb–Mar 1991.

SSN 722 *Key West*
◆Indian Ocean May–Jun 1997.

SSN 723 *Oklahoma City*
◆Indian Ocean Dec 1995.

SSN 724 *Louisville*   Fired first submarine-launched Tomahawk cruise missile in combat, 19 Jan 1991.
◆Gulf War Jan 1991.

SSN 725 *Helena*
◆Indian Ocean May–Jun 1997.

SSN 750 *Newport News*   Damaged in collision while submerged with m/v *Mogamigawa* in Strait of Hormuz, 8 Jan 2007.
◆Gulf War Feb–Mar 1991, Indian Ocean Oct–Nov 1998, Iraq War 2003.

Improved Los Angeles Class

No.	Name	Builder	Keel Laid	Launched	Comm.
SSN 751	*San Juan*	Electric Boat	16 Aug 1985	6 Dec 1986	6 Aug 1988
SSN 752	*Pasadena*	Electric Boat	20 Dec 1985	12 Sep 1987	11 Feb 1989
SSN 753	*Albany*	Newport News	22 Apr 1985	13 Jun 1987	7 Apr 1990
SSN 754	*Topeka*	Electric Boat	13 May 1986	23 Jan 1988	21 Oct 1989
SSN 755	*Miami*	Electric Boat	24 Oct 1986	12 Nov 1988	30 Jun 1990
SSN 756	*Scranton*	Newport News	29 Aug 1986	3 Jul 1989	26 Jan 1991
SSN 757	*Alexandria*	Electric Boat	19 Jun 1987	23 Feb 1990	29 Jun 1991
SSN 758	*Asheville*	Newport News	9 Jan 1987	24 Feb 1990	28 Sep 1991
SSN 759	*Jefferson City*	Newport News	21 Sep 1987	17 Aug 1990	29 Feb 1992
SSN 760	*Annapolis*	Electric Boat	15 Jun 1988	18 May 1991	11 Apr 1992
SSN 761	*Springfield*	Electric Boat	29 Jan 1990	4 Jan 1992	9 Jan 1993
SSN 762	*Columbus*	Electric Boat	9 Jan 1991	1 Aug 1992	24 Jul 1993
SSN 763	*Santa Fe*	Electric Boat	9 Jul 1991	12 Dec 1992	8 Jan 1994
SSN 764	*Boise*	Newport News	25 Aug 1988	23 Mar 1991	7 Nov 1992
SSN 765	*Montpelier*	Newport News	19 May 1989	23 Aug 1991	13 Mar 1993
SSN 766	*Charlotte*	Newport News	17 Aug 1990	3 Oct 1992	16 Sep 1994
SSN 767	*Hampton*	Newport News	2 Mar 1990	3 Apr 1992	6 Nov 1993
SSN 768	*Hartford*	Electric Boat	22 Feb 1992	4 Dec 1993	10 Dec 1994
SSN 769	*Toledo*	Newport News	6 May 1991	28 Aug 1993	24 Feb 1995
SSN 770	*Tucson*	Newport News	15 Aug 1991	20 Mar 1994	18 Aug 1995
SSN 771	*Columbia*	Electric Boat	21 Apr 1993	24 Sep 1994	9 Oct 1995
SSN 772	*Greeneville*	Newport News	28 Feb 1992	17 Sep 1994	16 Feb 1996
SSN 773	*Cheyenne*	Newport News	6 Jul 1992	16 Apr 1995	13 Sep 1996

Displacement	6,300/7,147 tons
Dimensions	362′ (oa) × 33′ × 32′6″
Machinery	1 screw; ST; 1 reactor; 30,000 SHP; 22/33 knots
Complement	141
Armament	4–21″TT, Subroc; Harpoon & Tomahawk VLS

Notes: VLS tubes. *Charlotte* and *Greeneville* modified to deploy Advanced SEAL Delivery System (ASDS) 2003. The ASDS vehicle is 55 tons, 65′ × 6′9″, with its own propulsion and can carry eight SEALs. Under-ice capable.

Service Record:

SSN 751 *San Juan*
  ◆Iraq War 2003
SSN 752 *Pasadena*
  ◆Indian Ocean Dec 1998–Mar 1999.
SSN 753 *Albany*
SSN 754 *Topeka*
  ◆Gulf War Nov 1992.
SSN 755 *Miami*
  ◆Indian Ocean Nov 1998–Jan 1999, Desert Fox 1998.
SSN 756 *Scranton*
  ◆Indian Ocean Oct 1999–Mar 2000.
SSN 757 *Alexandria*
  ◆Indian Ocean Dec 2000–Mar 2001.
SSN 758 *Asheville*
  ◆Indian Ocean Feb–May 2000.
SSN 759 *Jefferson City* Attacks on Iraq, 3–4 Sep 1996.
  ◆Indian Ocean Aug–Nov 1998, Feb–May 2000.
SSN 760 *Annapolis*
  ◆Indian Ocean Nov 1997–Mar 1998.
SSN 761 *Springfield*
  ◆Indian Ocean Feb–Jul 2000.
SSN 762 *Columbus*
  ◆Indian Ocean Dec 1998–Mar 1999.
SSN 763 *Santa Fe*
  ◆Indian Ocean Aug–Sep 1999.
SSN 764 *Boise*
  ◆Iraq War 2003
SSN 765 *Montpelier*
  ◆Indian Ocean Mar–Jun 1997, Iraq War 2003.
SSN 766 *Charlotte*
  ◆Indian Ocean Feb–Mar 1998.
SSN 767 *Hampton*
SSN 768 *Hartford* Ran aground off La Maddalena, Italy, 23 Oct 2003.
SSN 769 *Toledo*
  ◆Iraq War 2003.
SSN 770 *Tucson* Damaged in collision with USNS *Gilliland* at Newport News, Jun 1996.
  ◆Indian Ocean Mar–May 1998.
SSN 771 *Columbia* Attack on Al Quaeda camps in Afghanistan, 20 Aug 1998.
  ◆Indian Ocean Jul–Aug 1998, Iraq War 2003.
SSN 772 *Greeneville* Sank Japanese fishery training ship *Ehime Maru* while surfacing off Honolulu, 9 Feb 2001.
SSN 773 *Cheyenne*
  ◆Indian Ocean Dec 1998–Mar 1999, Sep 2000–Jan 2001, Iraq War 2003.

Seawolf Class

No.	Name	Builder	Keel Laid	Launched	Comm.
SSN 21	*Seawolf*	Electric Boat	21 Aug 1992	24 Jun 1995	19 Jul 1997
SSN 22	*Connecticut*	Electric Boat	8 Mar 1994	1 Sep 1997	11 Dec 1998
Displacement	7,460/9,137 tons				
Dimensions	353′ (oa) × 40′ × 36′				
Machinery	1 screw; ST; 1 reactor; SHP 40,000; 15/35 knots				
Complement	134				
Armament	Tomahawk (fired from TT); 8-angled 26.5″TT				

Notes: Designed as advanced *Los Angeles* class to oppose advanced Soviet types. About 30 were planned. The designation SSN 21 indicated an attack submarine for the 21st century and the designation was kept although out of the numbering sequence. Can carry 50 Tomahawk or Harpoon missiles.

Figure 2.24: The attack submarine *Connecticut* (SSN 22) at New London, Conn., 25 Jul 2007.

Service Record:

SSN 21 *Seawolf*
SSN 22 *Connecticut*

No.	Name	Builder	Keel Laid	Launched	Comm.
SSN 23	*Jimmy Carter*	Electric Boat	12 Dec 1995	13 May 2004	19 Feb 2005
Displacement	10,460/12,158 tons				
Dimensions	453′ (oa) × 40′ × 35′				
Machinery	1 screw; ST; 1 reactor; 40,000 SHP; 15/30 knots				
Complement	144				
Armament	8 angled 26.5″ TT, Harpoon, Tomahawk (fired from TT)				

Notes: *Seawolf* class with extra amidships section to accommodate special missions and ASDS. Reported to be equipped to tap undersea cables. Accommodates 50 SEALs.

Figure 2.25: USS *Jimmy Carter* (SSN 23), the third unit of the *Seawolf* class, underway during sea trials. She was modified while under construction with an extra section amidships for use on special operations, 3 Feb 2005.

Figure 2.26: USS *Texas* (SSN 775), 25 Aug 2006, arriving at Port Canaveral, Fla.

Virginia Class

No.	Name	Builder	Keel Laid	Launched	Comm.
SSN 774	*Virginia*	Electric Boat	2 Sep 1999	16 Aug 2003	23 Oct 2004
SSN 775	*Texas*	Newport News	12 Jul 2002	9 Apr 2005	9 Sep 2006
SSN 776	*Hawaii*	Electric Boat	27 Aug 2004	17 Jun 2006	5 May 2007
SSN 777	*North Carolina*	Newport News	22 May 2004	21 Apr 2007	3 May 2008
SSN 778	*New Hampshire*	Electric Boat	30 Apr 2007	21 Feb 2008	25 Oct 2008
SSN 779	*New Mexico*	Newport News	12 Apr 2008	—	—
SSN 780	*Missouri*	Electric Boat	—	—	—
SSN 781	*California*	Newport News	—	—	—
SSN 782	*Mississippi*	Electric Boat	—	—	—
SSN 783	*Minnesota*	Newport News	—	—	—
SSN 784	*North Dakota*	Newport News	—	—	—
Displacement	6,950/7,800 tons				
Dimensions	377′ (oa) × 34′ × 30′6″				
Machinery	1 screw; GT; 1 reactor; 25/32 knots				
Complement	134				
Armament	4–21″TT, 12 vertical tubes for Tomahawk LAM, Harpoon				

Notes: Jointly built by Newport News and General Dynamics. A lower cost submarine, smaller than previous classes. They will be able to conduct covert long-term surveillance of land areas, littoral waters or other naval forces and to support special forces. They are armed with new highly accurate Tomahawk cruise missiles. They have extendable masts containing high-resolution cameras and infared laser rangefinders transmitted by fiberoptic data links instead of periscopes.

Service Record:

774 *Virginia*
775 *Texas*
776 *Hawaii*
777 *North Carolina*
778 *New Hampshire*
779 *New Mexico*

STRATEGIC MISSILE SUBMARINES

Used to operate deterrent patrols. Always at sea with alternating (blue and gold) crews. Units were decommissioned as newer *Ohio* class ships came on line to stay within SALT I treaty limits. Under SALT limitations older units could be replaced with same number of larger more powerful units. Each FBM submarine is assigned two crews, "Blue" and "Gold," which alternate on patrols. For capability of missiles, see U.S. Naval Ordnance introduction.

George Washington Class

No.	Name	Builder	Keel Laid	Launched	Comm.
SSBN 598	*George Washington*	Electric Boat	1 Nov 1957	9 Jun 1959	31 Dec 1959
SSBN 599	*Patrick Henry*	Electric Boat	27 May 1958	22 Sep 1959	9 Jun 1960
SSBN 600	*Theodore Roosevelt*	Mare I NSYd	20 May 1958	3 Oct 1959	13 Feb 1961
SSBN 601	*Robert E. Lee*	Newport News	28 Aug 1958	18 Dec 1959	16 Sep 1960
SSBN 602	*Abraham Lincoln*	Portsmouth NSYd	1 Nov 1958	14 May 1960	11 Mar 1961
Displacement	6,000/6,700 tons				
Dimensions	381′8″ (oa) × 33′ × 29′				
Machinery	1 screw; ST; 1 reactor; 15,000 SHP; 20/30 knots				
Complement	140				
Armament	16 Polaris A-2 (later A-3) SLBM, 6-21″TT				

Notes: Redesign of *Skipjack* type, converted after being ordered. First ballistic missile submarines in the West. Modified for Polaris A-3, 1964–66.

Service Records:

SSBN 598 *George Washington*   First underwater launching of ballistic missile (Polaris A1) off Cape Canaveral, Fla., 20 Jul 1960. Sank Japanese m/v *Nissho Maru* in collision while surfacing southwest of Sasebo, 9 Apr 1981. Rec **SSN 598**, 20 Nov 1981. Decomm 24 Jan 1985. Stricken 30 Apr 1986. BU 1998.

Figure 2.27: USS *George Washington* (SSBN 598), the first ballistic missile submarine

SSBN 599 *Patrick Henry*   Rec **SSN 599**, 24 Oct 1981. Decomm 25 May 1984. Stricken 16 Dec 1985. BU 1997.

SSBN 600 *Theodore Roosevelt*   Ran aground while submerged off Scotland, 18 Mar 1968. Decomm 28 Feb 1981. Stricken 1 Dec 1982. BU 1995.

SSBN 601 *Robert E. Lee*   In collision with m/v *Transindiana*, 11 Oct 1978. Rec **SSN 601**, 1 Mar 1982. Decomm 1 Dec 1983. Stricken 30 Apr 1986. BU 1991.

SSBN 602 *Abraham Lincoln*   Decomm 28 Feb 1981. Stricken 1 Dec 1982. BU 1994.

Ethan Allen Class

No.	Name	Builder	Keel Laid	Launched	Comm.
SSBN 608	*Ethan Allen*	Electric Boat	14 Sep 1959	22 Nov 1960	8 Aug 1961
SSBN 609	*Sam Houston*	Newport News	28 Dec 1959	2 Feb 1961	6 Mar 1962
SSBN 610	*Thomas A. Edison*	Electric Boat	15 Mar 1960	15 Jun 1961	10 Mar 1962
SSBN 611	*John Marshall*	Newport News	4 Apr 1960	15 Jul 1961	21 May 1962
SSBN 618	*Thomas Jefferson*	Newport News	3 Feb 1961	24 Feb 1962	4 Jan 1963

Displacement	6,955/7,900 tons
Dimensions	410′6″ (oa) × 33′ × 30′
Machinery	1 screw; ST; 1 reactor; 15,000 SHP; 20/30 knots
Complement	140
Armament	16 Polaris A-2 (later A-3) SLBM, 4-21″TT

Notes: First SSBN design. All modified to carry A-3 Polaris; could not carry Poseidon missiles. *Sam Houston* and *John Marshall* converted to special-mission submarines 1984–86.

Service Records:

SSBN 608 *Ethan Allen*   Fired Polaris A2 missile with nuclear warhead in South Central Pacific (Operation Dominic Phase I), 6 May 1962. Damaged in collision with m/v *Octavian* in eastern Mediterranean, 9 Jan 1965. Rec **SSN 608**, 1 Sep 1980. Decomm 31 Mar 1983. Stricken 2 Apr 1983. BU 1999.

SSBN 609 *Sam Houston*   Rec **SSN 609**, 10 Nov 1980. Ran aground in Carr Inlet, Wash., 29 Apr 1988. Decomm and stricken 6 Sep 1991. BU 1992.

SSBN 610 *Thomas A. Edison*   In collision with destroyer *Wadleigh* during exercises off Norfolk, Va., 9 Apr 1962. Rec **SSN 610**, 6 Oct 1980. Slightly damaged in collision with destroyer *Leftwich* off Subic Bay in South China Sea, 29 Nov 1982. Decomm 1 Dec 1983. Stricken 30 Apr 1986. BU 1997.

SSBN 611 *John Marshall*   Collided with Soviet submarine in Mediterranean, Dec 1967. Rec **SSN 611**, 20 Jun 1981, recomm 1 May 1981. Decomm and stricken 22 Jul 1992. BU 1993.
◆Cuba Jun 1962.

SSBN 618 *Thomas Jefferson*   Rec **SSN 618**, 20 Nov 1980, 11 Mar 1981. Decomm 24 Jan 1985. Stricken 30 Apr 1986. BU 1998.

Figure 2.29: *USS Mariano G. Vallejo* (SSBN 658), *Lafayette* class, 1968, underway. Notice enormous length.

Figure 2.28: *USS Thomas A. Edison* (SSBN 610), Ethan Allen class.

Figure 2.30: *USS Stonewall Jackson* (SSBN 634), *Lafayette* class. The flat area aft of the sail contains the missile launching tubes.

					1964
					c 1963
					23 Nov 1963
				3	27 Dec 1963
				1962	20 Feb 1964
SSB.				Apr 1963	9 Apr 1964
SSBN 627	*James Madison*			15 Mar 1963	28 Jul 1964
SSBN 628	*Tecumseh*	Electric Boat	62	22 Jun 1963	29 May 1964
SSBN 629	*Daniel Boone*	Mare I NSYd	6 1962	22 Jun 1963	23 Apr 1964
SSBN 630	*John C. Calhoun*	Newport News	14 Jun 1962	22 Jun 1963	15 Sep 1964
SSBN 631	*Ulysses S. Grant*	Electric Boat	18 Aug 1962	2 Nov 1963	17 Jul 1964
SSBN 632	*Von Steuben*	Newport News	4 Sep 1962	18 Oct 1963	30 Sep 1964
SSBN 633	*Casimir Pulaski*	Electric Boat	12 Jan 1963	1 Feb 1964	14 Aug 1964
SSBN 634	*Stonewall Jackson*	Mare I NSYd	4 Jul 1962	30 Nov 1963	26 Aug 1964
SSBN 635	*Sam Rayburn*	Newport News	3 Dec 1962	20 Dec 1963	2 Dec 1964
SSBN 636	*Nathanael Greene*	Portsmouth NSYd	21 May 1962	12 May 1964	19 Dec 1964
SSBN 640	*Benjamin Franklin*	Electric Bt	25 May 1963	5 Dec 1964	22 Oct 1965
SSBN 641	*Simon Bolivar*	Newport News	17 Apr 1963	22 Aug 1964	29 Oct 1965
SSBN 642	*Kamehameha*	Mare I NSYd	2 May 1963	16 Jan 1965	10 Dec 1965
SSBN 643	*George Bancroft*	Electric Boat	24 Aug 1963	20 Mar 1965	22 Jan 1966
SSBN 644	*Lewis and Clark*	Newport News	29 Jul 1963	21 Nov 1964	22 Dec 1965
SSBN 645	*James K. Polk*	Electric Boat	23 Nov 1963	22 May 1965	16 Apr 1966
SSBN 654	*George C. Marshall*	Newport News	2 Mar 1964	21 May 1965	29 Apr 1966
SSBN 655	*Henry L. Stimson*	Electric Boat	4 Apr 1964	13 Nov 1965	20 Aug 1966
SSBN 656	*George Washington Carver*	Newport News	24 Aug 1964	14 Aug 1965	15 Jun 1966
SSBN 657	*Francis Scott Key*	Electric Boat	5 Dec 1964	23 Apr 1966	3 Dec 1966
SSBN 658	*Mariano G. Vallejo*	Mare I NSYd	7 Jul 1964	23 Oct 1965	16 Dec 1966
SSBN 659	*Will Rogers*	Electric Boat	20 Mar 1965	21 Jul 1966	1 Apr 1967

Displacement	7,250/8,250 tons
Dimensions	425′ (oa) × 33′ × 31′6″
Machinery	1 screw; ST; 1 reactor; 15,000 SHP; 20/30 knots
Complement	145
Armament	18 Polaris A-2 or A-3 missiles, 4–21″TT. *1970–77*: 18 Poseidon C-3 missiles

Notes: Enlarged *Ethan Allen* type. *Daniel Webster* had diving planes mounted on the bow. 640–659 had quieter engines. 616–625 had Polaris A-2, remainder A-3; all converted to Poseidon 1971–77. Four additional units not built. *Kamehamema* and *Henry L. Stimson* converted for special operations.

Service Records:

SSBN 616 *Lafayette*   Decomm 15 Aug 1991. Decomm and stricken 12 Aug 1991. BU 1992

SSBN 617 *Alexander Hamilton*   Decomm and stricken 23 Feb 1993. BU 1994

SSBN 619 *Andrew Jackson*   Launched first Polaris A-3 missile from a submarine, 26 Oct 1963. Decomm and stricken 31 Aug 1989. BU 1999.

SSBN 620 *John Adams*   Collided with submarine *Tinosa* at Portsmouth, NH, 7 Jun 1963. Decomm and stricken 24 Mar 1989. BU 1996.

SSBN 622 *James Monroe*   Decomm and stricken 25 Sep 1990. BU 1995.

SSBN 623 *Nathan Hale*   Decomm 3 Nov 1986. Stricken 31 Dec 1986. BU 1994.

SSBN 624 *Woodrow Wilson*   Damaged by fire while building at Mare Island, 8 May 1963. Ran aground near New London, Conn., 4 Jun 1979. Decomm and stricken 1 Sep 1994. BU 1998.

SSBN 625 *Henry Clay*   Ran aground in James River, 1 Jul 1964. Decomm and stricken 5 Nov 1990. BU 1997.

SSBN 626 *Daniel Webster*   Decomm and stricken 30 Aug 1990.

SSBN 627 *James Madison*   Collided underwater with Soviet submarine in North Sea, 3 Nov 1974. Decomm and stricken 20 Nov 1992. BU 1997.

SSBN 628 *Tecumseh*   Decomm and stricken 23 Jul 1993. BU 1994.

SSBN 629 *Daniel Boone*   Damaged in collision with m/v *President Quezon* off Cape Henry, Va., 28 May 1970. Went aground in James River, Va., 27 Apr 1987. Decomm and stricken 18 Feb 1994. BU 1994.

SSBN 630 *John C. Calhoun*   Decomm and stricken 28 Mar 1994. BU 1994.

SSBN 631 *Ulysses S. Grant*   Decomm and stricken 12 Jun 1992. BU 1993.

SSBN 632 *Von Steuben*   Damaged in collision with m/v *Sealady* which sank, off Cadiz, Spain, 9 Aug 1968. Decomm and stricken 26 Feb 1994. BU 2001.

SSBN 633 *Casimir Pulaski*   Decomm and stricken 7 Mar 1994. BU 1994.

SSBN 634 *Stonewall Jackson*   Decomm and stricken 9 Feb 1995. BU 1995.

SSBN 635 *Sam Rayburn*   Stricken 28 Aug 1989, dockside trainer Decomm and Stricken 31 Jul 1989.

SSBN 636 *Nathanael Greene*   Ran aground in Charleston harbor, 29 Jan 1970. Lost propeller at sea and was towed in for repair, 11 Aug 1984. Ran aground in Irish Sea, 13 Mar 1986. Decomm 15 Dec 1986. Stricken 31 Jan 1987. BU 2000.

SSBN 640 *Benjamin Franklin*   Sank tug in collision at Groton, Conn., 11 Apr 1972. Decomm and stricken 23 Nov 1993. BU 1995.

SSBN 641 *Simon Bolivar*   Damaged in collision with cargo ship *Betelgeuse* southeast of Charleston, SC, 31 Aug 1967. Decomm and stricken 8 Feb 1995. BU 1995.

SSBN 642 *Kamehameha*   Slightly damaged by hitting submerged object in Mediterranean, 14 Dec 1974. Rec **SSN 642**, 31 Aug 1992. Decomm 4 Aug 2001. Stricken 2 Apr 2002. BU 2003.
◆Indian Ocean Jul–Sep 1999.

SSBN 643 *George Bancroft*   Decomm and stricken 21 Sep 1993. BU 1998.

SSBN 644 *Lewis and Clark*   Decomm and stricken 1 Aug 1992. BU 1996.

SSBN 645 *James K. Polk*   Rec **SSN 645**, 1 Oct 1993. Decomm and stricken 8 Jul 1999. BU 2000.

SSBN 654 *George C. Marshall*   Collided with a Soviet submarine in Mediterranean, Dec 1967. Decomm and stricken 24 Sep 1992. BU 1994.

SSBN 655 *Henry L. Stimson*   Decomm and stricken 5 May 1993. BU 1994.
SSBN 656 *George Washington Carver*   Decomm and stricken 18 Mar 1993. BU 1994.
SSBN 657 *Francis Scott Key*   Decomm and stricken 2 Sep 1993. BU 1995.
SSBN 658 *Mariano G. Vallejo*   Decomm and stricken 10 Mar 1995. BU 1995.
SSBN 659 *Will Rogers*   Collided with trawler *New Dawn* in Firth of Clyde, 3 Jan 1989. Decomm and stricken 12 Apr 1993. BU 1994.

Figure 2.31: The ballistic missile submarine *Pennsylvania* (SSBN 735) arriving at Kitsap, Wash., 20 Jul 2005, after completing her fiftieth patrol at sea.

Figure 2.32: The guided missile submarine *Florida* (SSGN 728) arriving in Cumberland Sound, 11 Apr 2006, following her conversion from a ballistic missile submarine.

Ohio Class

No.	Name	Builder	Keel Laid	Launched	Comm.
SSBN 726	*Ohio*	Electric Boat	10 Apr 1976	7 Apr 1979	11 Nov 1981
SSBN 727	*Michigan*	Electric Boat	4 Apr 1977	26 Apr 1980	11 Sep 1982
SSBN 728	*Florida*	Electric Boat	9 Jun 1977	14 Nov 1981	18 Jun 1983
SSBN 729	*Georgia*	Electric Boat	7 Apr 1979	6 Nov 1982	11 Feb 1984
SSBN 730	*Henry M. Jackson* ex-*Rhode Island* (1984)	Electric Boat	7 Apr 1980	15 Oct 1983	6 Oct 1984
SSBN 731	*Alabama*	Electric Boat	27 Aug 1981	19 May 1984	25 May 1985
SSBN 732	*Alaska*	Electric Boat	9 Mar 1983	12 Jan 1985	25 Jan 1986
SSBN 733	*Nevada*	Electric Boat	8 Aug 1983	14 Sep 1985	16 Aug 1986
SSBN 734	*Tennessee*	Electric Boat	9 Jun 1986	13 Dec 1986	17 Dec 1988
SSBN 735	*Pennsylvania*	Electric Boat	2 Mar 1987	23 Apr 1988	9 Sep 1989
SSBN 736	*West Virginia*	Electric Boat	18 Dec 1987	14 Oct 1989	20 Oct 1990
SSBN 737	*Kentucky*	Electric Boat	18 Dec 1987	11 Aug 1990	13 Jul 1991
SSBN 738	*Maryland*	Electric Boat	18 Dec 1987	10 Aug 1991	13 Jun 1992
SSBN 739	*Nebraska*	Electric Boat	18 Dec 1987	15 Aug 1992	10 Jul 1993
SSBN 740	*Rhode Island*	Electric Boat	23 Apr 1988	17 Jul 1993	9 Jul 1994
SSBN 741	*Maine*	Electric Boat	4 Apr 1989	16 Jul 1994	29 Jul 1995
SSBN 742	*Wyoming*	Electric Boat	27 Jan 1990	22 Jul 1995	13 Jul 1996
SSBN 743	*Louisiana*	Electric Boat	15 May 1991	27 Jul 1996	6 Sep 1997

Displacement	16,764/18,750 tons
Dimensions	560′ (oa) × 42′ × 36′3″
Machinery	1 screw; 2 ST; 1 reactor; 28/? knots
Complement	172
Armament	24 Trident tubes: 726–733 Trident I/C-4. 730–733 rearmed with D-5, and 734 in 2006. 735–743 D-5.

Notes: Largest undersea vessels built in the United States. SSBN 726–729 were converted to be used for special operations and to fire cruise missiles starting in 2002. Rec SSGN, to carry up to 154 Tomahawk missiles, ASDS, and drydock shelters for special operations. 726 and 727 converted at Puget Sd NSYd and 728 and 729 at Norfolk NSYd, 2004–07.

Service Records:

726   *Ohio*   Rec **SSGN 726**, 1 Oct 2002. Out of comm 29 Oct 2002–9 Jan 2006 for conversion. Recomm 7 Feb 2006.
727   *Michigan*   Rec **SSGN 727**, 1 Jan 2004. Out of comm 2002–13 Dec 2006, for conversion. Recomm 12 Jun 2007.
728   *Florida*   Rec **SSGN 728**, 1 Oct 2002. Out of comm 2002–29 May 2006, for conversion.
729   *Georgia*   Sank Navy tug *Secota* in collision off Midway, 22 Mar 1986. Rec **SSGN 729**, 1 Mar 2004. Recomm 28 Mar 2008.
730   *Henry M. Jackson*
731   *Alabama*
732   *Alaska*
733   *Nevada*   Disabled by power system breakdown, Jun 1987.
734   *Tennessee*
735   *Pennsylvania*   Ran aground off Port Canaveral, Fla., 29 Sep 1989.
736   *West Virginia*
737   *Kentucky*   Collided with submarine *San Juan* off Long Island, NY, 19 Mar 1998.
738   *Maryland*
739   *Nebraska*
740   *Rhode Island*
741   *Maine*
742   *Wyoming*
743   *Louisiana*

3
BATTLESHIPS

The four units of the *Iowa* class marked the end of the line for U.S. Navy battleship construction, the planned *Montana* class units having been abandoned whilst still on the drawing board. The two *North Carolina* class and four *South Dakota* class units, unable to keep up with the fast carriers, were placed in reserve shortly after World War II, and were scrapped or turned into museum ships. Units of the *Iowa* class, pronounced dead several times, were resurrected to serve in Korea, Vietnam, and in the First Gulf War, and were finally retired only in the early 1990s.

BATTLESHIPS ON THE NAVY LIST, 1947

BB 41　*Mississippi*　Rec **AG 126**, 15 Feb 1946, converted to experimental gunnery ship. Decomm 17 Sep 1956. Stricken 30 Jul 1956. Sold 28 Nov 1956, BU.

Tennessee Class

BB 43　*Tennessee*　Decomm 14 Feb 1947. Stricken 1 Mar 1959. Sold 10 Jul 1959, BU Baltimore.

BB 44　*California*　Decomm 14 Feb 1947. Stricken 1 Mar 1959. Sold 10 Jul 1959, BU Baltimore.

Colorado Class

BB 45　*Colorado*　Decomm 7 Jan 1947. Stricken 1 Mar 1959. Sold 22 Jun 1959, BU Baltimore.
　　　Plan to replace *Mississippi* as training ship canceled, too costly.

BB 46　*Maryland*　Decomm 3 Apr 1947. Stricken 1 Mar 1959. Sold 8 Jul 1959, BU San Francisco.

BB 48　*West Virginia*　Decomm 9 Jan 1947. Stricken 1 Mar 1959. Sold 24 Aug 1959, BU Tacoma.

North Carolina Class

BB 55　*North Carolina*　Decomm 27 Jun 1947. Stricken 1 Jun 1960.
　　　Later history: Museum at Wilmington, NC, 6 Sep 1961.

BB 56　*Washington*　Decomm 27 Jun 1947. Stricken 1 Jun 1960. Sold 24 May 1961, BU Kearny, NJ.

South Dakota Class

BB 57　*South Dakota*　Decomm 31 Jan 1947. Stricken 1 Jun 1962. Sold 25 Oct 1962, BU Kearny, NJ.

BB 58　*Indiana*　Decomm 11 Sep 1947. Stricken 1 Jun 1962. Sold 6 Sep 1963, BU Richmond, Cal.

BB 59　*Massachusetts*　Decomm 27 Mar 1947. Stricken 1 Jun 1962.
　　　Later history: Museum at Fall River, Mass., 8 Jun 1965

BB 60　*Alabama*　Decomm 9 Jan 1947. Stricken 1 Jun 1962.
　　　Later history: Museum at Mobile, Ala., 1964.

Iowa Class

BB 61　*Iowa*　Out of comm 24 Mar 1949–25 Aug 1951 and 24 Feb 1958–28 Apr 1984. Bombarded shore targets in Korea, 8 Apr–16 Oct 1952. Mediterranean 1955. Explosion in B turret on maneuvers off Puerto Rico, 19 Apr 1989 (47 killed); turret remained inoperative. Decomm 26 Oct 1990. Stricken 12 Jan 1995. Reinstated 4 Jan 1999. Towed from Newport, RI, to Suisun Bay, Cal., Mar 2001. Stricken 17 Mar 2006.
　　　Later history: LU at Bremerton; to be museum at Stockton, Cal. 2★Korea K-7 K-8; ◆Libya Dec 1987–Feb 1988.

BB 62　*New Jersey*　Out of comm 30 Jun 1948–21 Nov 1950. Damaged by shore battery off Wonsan, Korea, 20 May 1951 (1 killed). Bombarded targets in area of Wonsan, then Kansong and Chongjin, May–Nov 1951. Again bombarded targets in east coast of Korea, May–Oct 1952. Mediterranean 1955. Out of comm 21 Aug 1957–6 Apr 1968 and 17 Dec 1969–28 Dec 1982. Bombarded targets near DMZ, Vietnam, Sep–Mar 1969. Decomm 28 Feb 1991. Stricken 12 Jan 1995. Reinstated 12 Feb 1998, but stricken 4 Jan 1999. Trfd to museum assn, 27 Jul 2000.

Figure 3.1: *USS New Jersey* (BB 62) in 1968 after being recommissioned for service in Vietnam. The smaller anti-aircraft guns have been removed. The superstructure shows prominent additions of radar and communications masts.

Later history: Museum at Camden, NJ, 2000.
4★Korea K-5 K-6 K-9 K-10; 2★Vietnam Sep 1968–Mar 1969; ◆Lebanon Sep 1983–Apr 1984, Libya Dec 1989.

BB 63 *Missouri* Carried President Truman from Rio de Janeiro to U.S., 7–19 Sep 1947. Went aground in Chesapeake Bay near Old Point Comfort, Va., 17 Jan 1950, refloated 1 Feb. Bombarded Samchok, Korea, 15 Sep 1950, and then in area of Wonsan and Hungnam, Oct–Dec 1950, through Mar 1951. Attacked targets at Chongjin and other east coast areas, Oct 1951–Apr 1952. Out of comm 26 Feb 1955–10 May 1986. Escorted carriers and bombarded shore targets in Iraq, 1991. Decomm 31 Mar 1992. Stricken 12 Jan 1995. Trfd to memorial assn in Hawaii, 4 May 1998.
Later history: Museum at Pearl Harbor, Jun 1998.
5★Korea K-1 K-2 K-4 K-8 K-9; ◆Libya Sep–Nov 1987, Gulf War Jan–Mar 1991.

BB 64 *Wisconsin* Out of comm 1 Jul 1948–3 Mar 1951. Bombarded targets in areas of Kaesong and east coast, Nov–Dec 1951 and Jan 1952. Hit by coastal gunfire off Songjin, Korea, 15 Mar 1952. Damaged in collision with destroyer *Eaton* off Virginia Capes, 6 May 1955. Repaired with bow section of incomplete *Kentucky*. Out of comm 8 Mar 1958–22 Oct 1988. Decomm 30 Sep 1991. Stricken 12 Jan 1995. Reinstated 12 Feb 1998. Stricken 17 Mar 2006.
Later history: Museum at Norfolk, Va. 2000.
1★Korea K-7; ◆Gulf War Aug 1990–Mar 1991.

BB 66 *Kentucky* Canceled, 17 Feb 1947, 72% complete. Floated out of building dock, 20 Jan 1950. Section of bow used to repair *Wisconsin*, May 1956. Stricken 9 Jun 1958. Sold 31 Oct 1958, BU 1958 Baltimore.

Notes: Stern catapults removed early 1950s. Plans to complete *Kentucky* as missile ship canceled; engines used in AOE 1 & 2. *New Jersey* recomm for Vietnam, 1968, with 40 mm guns removed, helicopter landing pad added. All four recomm in 1980s, modernized with new radar, four 5-inch mounts replaced by Harpoon and Tomahawk launchers. 1991: Harpoon, Tomahawk and Phalanx added.
Displacement: 45,231 tons lt; 57,271 f/l
Armament: (1977) 9-16″/50, 20-5″/38 and 2-6pdr (*Iowa*, *Wisconsin*), 2-40 mm (*New Jersey*), 20-quad 40 mm (*Missouri*).

4 CRUISERS

Although the Navy had many cruisers on the Navy List in 1947, within little more than a decade, this category had been mostly phased out. Although their medium-size guns proved useful during the Korean War for shore bombardment, their conventional armament was soon supplanted by guided missiles which could be used at greater distances. The pre-World War II treaty-based distinction between light and heavy cruisers based on gun caliber lost its significance and the last true cruisers were converted to guided missile carriers. Guns virtually disappeared; the first nuclear-powered cruiser, *Long Beach*, carried an armament of guided missiles later supplemented by a pair of 5″ guns. Other nuclear-powered cruisers, all now retired, followed.

Intermediate types, i.e. ships larger than destroyers but smaller than the old cruisers were first designated as frigates, a usage that differed from other navies. In 1975 the nomenclature was revised, so that the *Leahy* and *Belknap* classes of frigates (DL), and the nuclear-powered *Bainbridge, Truxtun,* and *California* and *Virginia* classes (DLGN) were redesignated cruisers (CG or CGN). In 1980 the new modified *Spruance* class destroyers (DDG) were reclassified as cruisers (CG), becoming the *Ticonderoga* class. The last of the type, *Port Royal*, commissioned in 1994, and no further cruiser types have been built since that time.

LARGE CRUISERS ON THE NAVY LIST, 1947

CB 1   *Alaska*   Decomm 17 Feb 1947. Stricken 1 Jun 1960. Sold 24 May 1961, BU Kearny, NJ.

CB 2   *Guam*   Decomm 17 Feb 1947. Stricken 1 Jun 1960. Sold 24 May 1961, BU Baltimore.

CB 3   *Hawaii*   Construction suspended, 17 Feb 1947, 84% complete. Planned conversion to guided missile ship abandoned. Rec **CBC 1**, 26 Feb 1952, large command ship, but conversion canceled, and rec **CB 3**, 9 Oct 1954. Stricken 9 Jun 1958. Sold 15 Apr 1959, BU Baltimore.

CRUISERS ON THE NAVY LIST, 1947

Northampton Class

CA 27   *Chester*   Decomm 10 Jun 1946. Stricken 1 Mar 1959. Sold 11 Aug 1959, BU Panama City, Fla.

CA 28   *Louisville*   Decomm 17 Jun 1946. Stricken 1 Mar 1959. Sold 14 Sep 1959, BU Panama City, Fla.

CA 31   *Augusta*   Decomm 16 Jul 1946. Stricken 1 Mar 1959. Sold 9 Nov 1959, BU Kearny, NJ.

CA 33   *Portland*   Decomm 12 Jul 1946. Stricken 1 Mar 1959. Sold 30 Sep 1959, BU Panama City, Fla.

New Orleans Class

CA 32   *New Orleans*   Decomm 10 Feb 1947. Stricken 1 Mar 1959. Sold 22 Sep 1959, BU Baltimore.

CA 36   *Minneapolis*   Decomm 10 Feb 1947. Stricken 1 Mar 1959. Sold 14 Aug 1959, BU Chester.

CA 37   *Tuscaloosa*   Decomm 13 Feb 1946. Stricken 1 Mar 1959. Sold 25 Jun 1959, BU Baltimore.

CA 38   *San Francisco*   Decomm 10 Feb 1946. Stricken 1 Mar 1959. Sold 9 Sep 1959, BU Panama City, Fla.

CA 45   *Wichita*   Decomm 3 Feb 1947. Stricken 1 Mar 1959. Sold 14 Aug 1959, BU Panama City, Fla.

Baltimore Class

CA 68   *Baltimore*   Out of comm 8 Jul 1946–28 Nov 1951. Mediterranean 1952, 1953, and 1954. Decomm 31 May 1956. Stricken 15 Feb 1971. Sold May 1972, BU Portland, Ore.

CA 69   *Boston*   Out of comm 12 Mar 1946–1 Nov 1955. Rec **CAG 1**, 4 Jan 1952. (See below.)

CA 70   *Canberra*   Out of comm 7 Mar 1947–15 Jun 1956. Rec **CAG 2**, 4 Jan 1952. (See below.)

CA 71   *Quincy*   Out of comm 19 Oct 1946–31 Jan 1952. Decomm 2 Jul 1954. Stricken 1 Oct 1973. Sold 31 Jul 1974, BU Tacoma. ★Korea 1953

CA 72 *Pittsburgh* Out of comm 7 Mar 1947–25 Sep 1951. Mediterranean 1953. Decomm 28 Aug 1956. Stricken 1 Jul 1973. Sold 11 or 22 Jul 1974, BU Tacoma.

CA 73 *Saint Paul* Bombarded targets off northeast coast of Korea, Nov–Dec 1950, and north of Inchon Jan 1951. Active in area of Wonsan and Chongjin, Nov 1951–Apr 1952. Damaged by fire in 8-inch turret off Wonsan, Korea, 21 Apr 1952 (30 killed). Bombarded east coast of Korea, Feb–Jul 1953. Carried President Eisenhower on visit to Taiwan, Jun 1960. Made five deployments to Vietnam providing gunfire support, May 1961–Sep 1970. Hit by enemy shellfire, 2 Sep 1967. Decomm 30 Apr 1971. Stricken 31 Jul 1978. Sold Jan 1980, BU.
8★Korea K-2 K-4 K-5 K-6 K-7 K-8 K-9 K-10; 8★Vietnam Oct 1960, May 1961, Jun–Oct 1966, Jun–Oct 1967, Apr–Oct 1968, Apr–Sep 1969, May–Sep 1970; ◆Quemoy-Matsu Aug–Nov 1959, Mar–Apr, Jun, Oct 1960, Nov 1961, Korea Apr 1969.

CA 74 *Columbus* In collision with destroyer *Floyd B. Parks* off Luzon, 11 Mar 1956. Decomm 8 May 1959 for conversion. Rec **CG 12**, 30 Sep 1959. (See below.)

CA 75 *Helena* Bombarded Tanchon, Korea, 7 Aug 1950 and later other areas. Returned to bombarding targets in Korea, Apr–Nov 1951. Damaged by shore battery at Wonsan, Korea, 31 Jul 1951. Damaged again off Hungnam, 23 Oct 1951. Bombarded targets in Korea, Jun–Nov 1952. Decomm 29 Jun 1963. Stricken 1 Jan 1974. Sold 13 Nov 1974, BU.
4★K-1 K-5 K-6 K-8. ◆Taiwan Straits Aug–Nov 1958.

CA 122 *Oregon City* Decomm 15 Dec 1947. Stricken 1 Nov 1970. Sold 2 Aug 1973, BU Portsmouth, Va.

CA 123 *Albany* Decomm for conversion to CG, 30 Jun 1958. Rec **CG 10**, 1 Nov 1958. (See below.)

CA 124 *Rochester* Mediterranean Mar–Jun 1948. Landings at Pohang, Korea, Jul 1950 and Inchon, 13 Sep 1950. Gunfire support for troops ashore Oct–Dec 1950. Bombarded targets in northeast Korea, Nov 1951–Apr 1952. Decomm 10/15 Aug 1961. Stricken 1 Oct 1973. Sold 31 Jul 1974, BU Portland, Ore.
7★Korea K-1 K-2 K-3 K-6 K-7 K-8 K-9.

CA 130 *Bremerton* Out of comm 9 Apr 1948–23 Nov 1951. Bombarded targets in Korea at Wonsan and Chongjin, 1952, and other targets 1953. Decomm 29 Jul 1960. Stricken 1 Oct 1973. Sold 11 Jul 1974, BU Tacoma.
★Korea K-8 K-10.

CA 131 *Fall River* Decomm 31 Oct 1947. Damaged in collision with pier at San Francisco, 29 Jan 1953. Conversion to **CG 12** canceled, 1 Nov 1958. Stricken 19 Feb 1971. Sold 28 Aug 1972, BU Portland, Ore.
Later history: Bow is on display at Fall River, Mass.

CA 132 *Macon* Out of comm 12 Apr 1950–16 Oct 1950. Mediterranean 1956. Decomm 10 Mar 1961. Stricken 1 Nov 1969. Sold 22 Jun or 5 Jul 1973, BU.

CA 133 *Toledo* Bombarded enemy shore installations Jul–Aug 1950. Landings at Inchon, Sep 1950, and Wonsan, Oct 1950. Provided fire support near Inchon, then Wonsan, Apr–Nov 1951, and Jan–Mar 1953. Decomm 21 May 1960. Stricken 1 Jan 1974. Sold 30 Oct 1974, BU Terminal I.
6★Korea K-1 K-3 K-5 K-6 K-8 K-9; ★Vietnam Oct 1959; ◆Quemoy-Matsu Sep 1959.

CA 135 *Los Angeles* Out of comm 9 Apr 1948–27 Jan 1951. Bombarded enemy positions on east coast of Korea, Jun–Nov 1951, and again Oct 1952–Apr 1953. Slight damage by shore gunfire off Wonsan, 2 Apr 1953. Decomm 15 Nov 1963. Name canceled 5 May 1971. Stricken 1 Jan 1974. Sold 16 May 1975, BU Terminal I.
5★Korea K-5 K-6 K-7 K-8 K-9; ◆Taiwan Straits Sep–Oct 1958, Quemoy-Matsu Sep–Oct 1958.

CA 136 *Chicago* Out of comm 6 Jun 1947–2 May 1964. Rec **CG 11**, 1 Nov 1958. (See below.)

Notes: *Helena, Macon, Toledo,* and *Los Angeles* could carry 3 Regulus I or 2 Regulus II in hangars aft; canceled 1958.
Armament: *1977:* CA 70: 6–8″/55, 10–5″/38, 4–30″/50, 2–40 mm; CA 73: 9–8″/55, 10–5″/38, 12–3″/50, 2–40 mm. Catapults removed 1948–50.

Des Moines Class

CA 134 *Des Moines* Comm 16 Nov 1948. Annual deployments to Mediterranean, 1949 to 1957 and 1958–61. Decomm 14 Jul 1961. Stricken 9 Jul 1991. Sold 22 Aug 2006, BU Brownsville, Tex.
◆Lebanon Jul–Aug 1958.

CA 139 *Salem* Comm 14 May 1949. Annual deployments to Mediterranean 1950–1957. Damaged in collision with cargo ship *Whitley* off New Jersey, 2 Nov 1950. Decomm 30 Jan 1959. Stricken 12 Jul 1991. Trfd to U.S. Naval Shipbuilding Museum, Quincy, Mass. as museum 13 Oct 1994.
Later history: Museum at Quincy, Mass. 1995.

CA 148 *Newport News* Comm 29 Jan 1949. Annual deployments to Mediterranean 1950–1961. Bombarded shore targets in DMZ area, Vietnam Oct 1967–Apr 1968. Damaged by turret explosion off DMZ, Vietnam, 30 Sep 1972 (20 killed). Turret not repaired, center barrel

Figure 4.1: *USS Macon* (CA 132), 10 Jun 1951, Baltimore class.

Figure 4.2: *USS Newport News* (CA 148), Feb 1960. The last traditional cruiser class built for the Navy. Notice the prominent director towers forward and aft, massive funnel, and masts cluttered with radars.

removed. Decomm 27 Jun 1975. Stricken 31 Jul 1978. Sold 25 Feb 1993, BU New Orleans.
★Vietnam Oct 1967–Apr 1968, Dec 1968–Jun 1969, May–Nov 1972;
◆Lebanon Sep 1958, Cuba Feb–Mar, Jun 1961, Dominican Rep May 1965.

Notes: Armament: *1977*: CA 134: 9–8″/55, 12–5″/38, 20–3″/50, 2–6 pdr; CA 139: 9–8″/55, 12–5″/38, 22–3″/50, 2–6 pdr; CA 148: 8–8″/55, 12–5″/38, 4–3″/50, 2–40 mm.

Brooklyn Class

CL 40 *Brooklyn* Decomm 3 Jan 1947. To Chile 9 Jan 1951.
Later history: renamed *O'Higgins* (CL 02). R1992. Sank in tow en route to India for BU, 3 Nov 1992.

CL 41 *Philadelphia* Decomm 3 Feb 1947. To Brazil 29 Jan 1951.
Later history: renamed *Barroso* (C 11). BU 1974 Sao Paulo.

CL 42 *Savannah* Decomm 3 Feb 1947. Stricken 1 Mar 1959. Sold 6 Jan 1960, BU.

CL 43 *Nashville* Decomm 24 Jun 1946. To Chile 9 Jan 1951.
Later history: renamed *Prat* (CL 03), renamed *Chacabuco* 1982. R1982. BU 1985, Taiwan.

CL 46 *Phoenix* Decomm 3 Jul 1946. To Argentina 12 Apr 1951.
Later history: renamed *17 de Octubre* (C 4), renamed *General Belgrano* 1956.
Torpedoed and sunk by British submarine *Conqueror* off the Falkland Islands, 2 May 1982.

CL 47 *Boise* Decomm 1 Jul 1946. To Argentina 12 Apr 1951.
Later history: renamed *9 de Julio* (C 5). R1978. BU 1983, Brownsville, Tex.

CL 48 *Honolulu* Decomm 3 Feb 1947. Stricken 1 Mar 1959. Sold 10 Dec 1959, BU Baltimore.

CL 49 *St. Louis* Decomm 20 Jun 1946. To Brazil 29 Jan 1951.
Later history: renamed *Tamandaré* (C 12). Capsized and sank off South Africa en route to BU, Sep 1986.

Atlanta Class (Rec CLAA 18 Mar 1949)

CL 53 *San Diego* Decomm 4 Nov 1946. Stricken 1955. Sold 25 Jan 1960, BU.

CL 54 *San Juan* Decomm 9 Nov 1946. Stricken 1 Mar 1959. Sold 31 Oct 1961, BU Terminal I.

CL 95 *Oakland* Decomm 1 Jul 1949. Stricken 1 Mar 1959. Sold 24 Nov 1959, BU.

CL 96 *Reno* Decomm 4 Nov 1946. Stricken 1 Mar 1959. hull used for tests. Sold 26 Mar 1962. BU.

CL 97 *Flint* Decomm 6 May 1947. Stricken 1 Sep 1965. Sold Oct 1966, BU Terminal I.

CL 98 *Tucson* Decomm 11 Jun 1949. Stricken 1 Jun 1966. Experimental hulk. Sold 24 Feb 1971, BU Terminal I.

CL 119 *Juneau* Mediterranean 1947–49. Bombarded targets in Korea, Jun–Jul 1950. Sank three torpedo boats near Chumonchin Chan, 2 Jul 1950. Decomm 23 Jul 1956. Stricken 1 Nov 1959. Sold 25 Apr 1960, BU.
5★Korea K-1 K-2 K-4 K-7 K-8.

CL 120 *Spokane* Mediterranean 1949. Decomm 27 Feb 1950. Rec **AG 191**, 1 Apr 1966; conversion to sonar test ship canceled. Stricken 15 Apr 1972. Sold 2 or 17 May 1973, BU.

CL 121 *Fresno* Decomm 17 May 1949. Stricken 1 Apr 1965. Sold 17 Jun 1966, BU Kearny, NJ.

Cleveland Class

CL 55 *Cleveland* Decomm 7 Feb 1947. Stricken 1 Mar 1959. Sold 1 Feb 1960, BU.

Figure 4.3: The anti-aircraft cruiser *USS Spokane* (CLAA 120). Notice that two of the three turrets forward and aft are on the main deck unlike previous units of the class.

CL 56 *Columbia* Decomm 30 Nov 1946. Stricken 1 Mar 1959. Sold 18 Dec 1959, BU Baltimore.

CL 57 *Montpelier* Decomm 24 Jan 1947. Stricken 1 Mar 1959. Sold 22 Jan 1960, BU.

CL 58 *Denver* Decomm 7 Feb 1947. Stricken 1 Mar 1959. Sold 29 Jan 1960, BU.

CL 60 *Santa Fe* Decomm 19 Oct 1946. Stricken 1 Mar 1959. Sold 5 Nov 1959, BU Portland, Ore.

CL 62 *Birmingham* Decomm 2 Jan 1947. Stricken 1 Mar 1959. Sold 13 Oct 1959, BU.

CL 63 *Mobile* Decomm 9 May 1947. Stricken 1 Mar 1959. Sold 16 Dec 1959, BU Portland, Ore.

CL 64 *Vincennes* Decomm 10 Sep 1946. Stricken 1 Apr 1966. Sunk as target off southern California, 28 Oct 1969.

CL 65 *Pasadena* Decomm 12 Jan 1950. Stricken 1 Dec 1970. Sold 5 Jan 1972, BU Portland, Ore.

CL 66 *Springfield* Decomm . . Jan 1950. Rec **CLG 7**, 23 May 1957. (See below.)

CL 67 *Topeka* Decomm 18 Jun 1949–26 Mar 1960. Rec **CLG 8**, 23 May 1957. (See below.)

CL 80 *Biloxi* Decomm 29 Oct 1946. Stricken 1 Sep 1961. Sold 28 Feb 1962. BU Portland, Ore.

CL 81 *Houston* Decomm 15 Dec 1947. Stricken 1 Mar 1959. Sold 31 May 1961, BU.

CL 82 *Providence* Decomm 14 Jun 1949. Rec **CLG 6**, 23 May 1957. (See below.)

CL 83 *Manchester* Slightly damaged by fire off Oahu, 3 Aug 1950. Conducted shore bombardments, Sep–Oct 1950. Landings at Inchon and Wonsan. Evacuated crew from wrecked Thai corvette *Prasae* on enemy coast, 8 Jan 1951. Bombarded enemy positions at Wonsan and Songjin, Jan–May 1951. Again bombarded enemy positions on east coast, Dec 1951–May 1952, and Feb–Jul 1953. Decomm 27 Jun 1956. Stricken 1 Apr 1960. Sold 31 Oct 1960, BU.
9★Korea K-1 K-2 K-3 K-4 K-5 K-7 K-8 K-9 K-10.

CL 86 *Vicksburg* Decomm 30 Jun 1947. Stricken 1 Oct 1962. Sold 25 Aug 1964, BU Terminal I.

CL 87 *Duluth* Decomm 25 Jun 1949. Stricken 1 Jan 1960. Sold 14 Nov 1960, BU.

CL 89 *Miami* Decomm 30 Jun 1947. Stricken 1 Sep 1961. Sold 26 Jul 1962, BU.

CL 90 *Astoria* Decomm 1 Jul 1949. Stricken 1 Nov 1969. Sold 12 Jan 1971, BU.

CL 91 *Oklahoma City* Decomm 30 Jun 1947–7 Sep 1960. Rec **CLG 5**, 23 May 1957. (See below.)

CL 92 *Little Rock* Decomm 24 Jun 1949–3 Jun 1960. Rec **CLG 4**, 23 May 1957. (See below.)

CL 93   *Galveston*   laid up incomplete 1947. Rec **CLG 93**, 4 Feb 1956. (See below.)
CL 101 *Amsterdam*   Decomm 30 Jun 1947. Stricken 2 Jan 1971. Sold 11 Feb 1972, BU Terminal I.
CL 102 *Portsmouth* Decomm 15 Jun 1949. Stricken 1 Dec 1970. Sold 26 Feb 21 Mar 1974, BU.
CL 103 *Wilkes-Barre* Decomm 6 Sep 1947. Stricken 15 Jan 1971. Sunk off Key West as breakwater, 12 May 1972.
CL 104 *Atlanta*   Decomm 1 Jul 1949. Stricken 1 Oct 1962. Reinstated as **IX 304**, 15 May 1964; converted to weapons effects test ship. Explosive tests early 1965. Stricken 1 Apr 1970. Sunk as target off San Clemente, Cal., 1 Oct 1970.
CL 105 *Dayton*   Decomm 1 Mar 1949. Stricken 1 Sep 1961. Sold 3 Apr 1962, BU Baltimore.
CL 106 *Fargo*   Decomm 14 Feb 1960. Stricken 1 Mar 1970. Sold 18 Aug 1971, BU.
CL 107 *Huntington* Decomm 15 Jun 1949. Stricken 1 Sep 1961. Sold 30 Apr 1962, BU Kearny, NJ.

Notes: *Atlanta* converted to target ship 1964. Hull cut down to main deck and two DLG superstructures erected to test for durability and high energy air explosions. *Fargo* and *Huntington* were a separate class with one funnel.

Figure 4.4: *USS Worcester* (CL 144), 1950. Notice that two of the three turrets forward and aft are on the main deck.

Worcester Class

CL 144 *Worcester* Comm 26 Jun 1948. Mediterranean 1949 and 1950. Landings at Inchon. Bombarded targets near Wonsan, Oct 1950. Mediterranean 1951. Decomm 19 Dec 1958. Stricken 1 Dec 1970. Sold 5 Jul 1972, BU Portland, Ore.
2★Korea K-1 K-3.
CL 145 *Roanoke*   Comm 4 Apr 1949. Mediterranean 1950, 1952, 1955. Decomm 31 Oct 1958. Stricken 1 Dec 1970. Sold 22 Feb 1972, BU Richmond, Cal.

Notes: Automatic 6″ guns, no TT.

GUIDED MISSILE CRUISERS

Long Beach

No.	Name	Builder	Keel Laid	Launched	Comm.
CGN 9	Long Beach	Beth; Quincy	2 Dec 1957	14 Jul 1959	9 Sep 1961
	ex-CGN 160 (1 Jul 1957), ex-CLGN 160 (6 Dec 1956)				
Displacement	14,200 tons; 17,100 f/l				
Dimensions	721′3″(oa) × 73′3″ × 29′8″				
Machinery	2 screws; ST; 2 reactors; 80,000 SHP; 30+ knots				
Endurance	360000/20				
Complement	958				
Armament	1 twin Talos lchr (removed 1979), 2 twin Terrier/Standard-ER SAM lchrs, 2 Harpoon lchrs, 2 Tomahawk lchrs, 2-5″/38, 2 Phalanx, ASROC, 2-triple TT				

Notes: First nuclear-powered surface warship, and first warship with guided missiles as main battery. Designed with no guns, 2–5″ guns added. Originally designed for Regulus, then Polaris, missiles. Construction delayed by five-month strike. Original planned name *Brooklyn*. Carried 40 Talos and 240 Terrier missiles. Modernized Oct 1980 to Mar 1983.

Service Record: Overhaul and refueling Aug 1965–Feb 1966. Transferred to Pacific Feb 1966. Shot down two enemy aircraft off North Vietnam with Talos

Figure 4.5: The guided missile cruiser *Long Beach* (CGN 9), July 1961. The first nuclear powered surface warship and first with a main battery of guided missiles. Terrier launchers are forward, and Talos aft.

missiles, May–Jun 1968. Collided with m/v *David Salman* at San Francisco, 2 Jul 1974. Decomm and stricken 1 May 1995. BU Bremerton.
★Vietnam Nov 1966–Jun 1967, May–Oct 1968, Sep 1969–Jan 1970, Apr–Nov 1972; ◆ Laos Sep 1987, Libya Sep–Nov 1987, Jan 1990, Gulf War Jul–Oct 1991.

No.	Name	ex-	Converted by	Recommissioned
CAG 1	*Boston*	CA 69	NY Sbdg	1 Nov 1955
CAG 2	*Canberra*	CA 70	NY Sbdg	15 Jun 1956

Notes: Former *Baltimore* class heavy cruisers. After turret replaced with Terrier missile launchers. Superstructure modified, single funnel, trellis masts added. Armament: 6–8″/55, 8–3″/50 guns, twin Terrier lchrs. Terrier removed 1968.

CLG 3	*Galveston*	CL 93	Phila. NSYd	25 May 1958
CLG 4	*Little Rock*	CL 92	NY Sbdg	3 Jun 1960
CLG 5	*Oklahoma City*	CL 91	Beth; S.Fran.	7 Sep 1960

Notes: Former *Cleveland* class light cruisers. Two trellis masts, aft tower superstructure rebuilt. Armament: 1 twin Talos lchr (all), 3–6″/47, 2–5″/38 guns (CLG 4–5), 6–6″/47, 6–5″/38 guns (CLG 3).

Figure 4.6: The guided missile cruiser *Canberra* (CAG 2), converted from a Baltimore class heavy cruiser, with the aft turret removed and superstructure rebuilt.

Figure 4.8: *USS Topeka* (CLG 8) retains two turrets forward, with Terrier launcher aft.

Figure 4.7: *USS Little Rock* (CLG 4), flagship, 6th Fleet, about 1961. Compare with the original layout of a *Cleveland* class cruiser, enlarged superstructure, trellis masts. Missile launchers have been added, while retaining one 6-inch turret.

CLG 6	*Providence*	CL 82	Boston NSYd	17 Sep 1959
CLG 7	*Springfield*	CL 66	Beth; Quincy	2 Jul 1960
CLG 8	*Topeka*	CL 67	New York NSYd	26 Mar 1960

Notes: Former *Cleveland* class light cruisers. Partial conversions, original superstructure and forward guns retained. Armament: 1 twin Terrier lchr (all), 3-6″/47, 2-5″/38 guns (6–7), 6-6″/47, 6-5″/38 guns (8) *Oklahoma City 1977*: 2 Phalanx, 3-6″/47, 2-5″/38, 2-40mm, RBOC.

Service Records:

CAG 1   *Boston*   Rec **CA 69**, 1 May 1968. Decomm 5 May 1970. Stricken 1 Nov 1973. Sold 28 Mar 1975, BU New Orleans.
5★Vietnam Apr–Oct 1967, Apr–Sep 1968, Jun–Oct 1969; ◆Lebanon Jul–Sep 1958, Cuba Apr 1961.

CAG 2   *Canberra*   Carried President Eisenhower to Bermuda conference, Mar 1957. Ceremonial flagship for selection of the unknown servicemen of World War II and Korea, May 1958. Rec **CA 70**, 1 May 1968. Decomm 2 Feb 1970.
Stricken 31 Jul 1978. Sold 15 Jul 1980, BU Terminal I.
★Vietnam Feb–Jun 1965, Feb–May 1966, Dec 1966–Apr 1967, Oct 1967–Apr 1968, Oct–Dec 1968; ◆Cuba Oct–Nov 1961, Cuban missile crisis Oct–Nov 1962, Korea Jan–Mar 1968.

CLG 3   *Galveston*   Rec **CLG 3**, 23 May 1957. Gunfire support at Chu Lai and Van Tuong Peninsula, 1965. Decomm 25 May 1970. Stricken 21 Dec 1973. Sold 16 May 1975, BU Terminal I.
★Vietnam Jun–Nov 1965, Nov 1968–Jan 1969; ◆Cuba Mar 1961.

CLG 4   *Little Rock*   Annual deployments to Mediterranean 1961 to 1965. Damaged in collision with Greek destroyer *Lonkhi* in Gulf of Lakonia, Greece, 13 Jun 1970. Rec **CG 4**, 1 Jul 1975.
Stricken 22 Nov 1976. To Buffalo, NY, memorial 1 Jun 1977.
Later history: Museum at Buffalo, NY.
◆Cuba Jan 1962.

CLG 5   *Oklahoma City*   7th Fleet flagship off Vietnam 1965–66. Rec **CG 5**, 1 Jul 1975. Decomm and stricken 15 Dec 1979. Sunk as target by Korean submarine *Lee Chun*, 25 Mar 1999.
★Vietnam Jul–Nov 1964, Mar, May 1965–Mar 1966, May–Nov 1966, Dec 1968–Dec 1969; ◆Quemoy-Matsu Apr 1962, Korea Apr 1969, Jan 1970–Jul 1972, Sep–Dec 1972, Feb 1973, Evac of Vietnam 29–30 Apr 1975.

CLG 6   *Providence*   Bombarded shore positions in Vietnam, 1 Apr and 25 May 1967, and south of Da Nang, 10 Oct 1967. Continued gunfire support in 1968. Decomm 31 Aug 1973. Rec **CG 6**, 1 Jul 1975. Stricken 31 Jul 1978. Sold 1 Feb or 31 Jul 1980, BU.
★Vietnam Apr 1963, Jan 1964, Dec 1966–Nov 1968, Apr–Nov 1972; ◆Korea Jan–Mar 1968.

CLG 7   *Springfield*   Mediterranean 1960–67 and 1970–73. Decomm 15 Jun May 1974. Rec **CG 7**, 1 Jul 1975. Stricken 31 Jul 1978. Sold 1 Mar 1980, BU.

CLG 8   *Topeka*   Decomm 5 Jun 1969. Stricken 1 Dec 1973. Sold 28 Mar 1975, BU New Orleans.
3★Vietnam Jun–Sep 1964, Dec 1965–May 1966.

No.	Name	ex-	Converted at	Recomm
CG 10	*Albany*	CA 123	Boston NSYd	3 Nov 1962
CG 11	*Chicago*	CA 136	San Fran NSYd	2 May 1964
CG 12	*Columbus*	CA 74	Puget Sd NSYd	1 Dec 1962

Notes: All upperworks removed to main deck, replaced by new superstructure with two large "mack" structures (105′ above deck). Conversion of *Chicago* and *Fall River* to CG 11–12 canceled Jun 1958, funds used for SSBN. Reordered 1959 for *Chicago* and *Columbus*. Originally converted without guns, but 5″ guns added later. Plan to install Poseidon ballistic missiles abandoned. Carried 92 Talos and 80 Tartar missiles. *Albany* and *Chicago* modernized 1970. Armament: 2 twin Talos (fore and aft), 2 twin Tartar lchrs (amidships), ASROC, 6 ASW TT; 2-5″/38 added.

Figure 4.9: *USS Chicago* (CG 11), 3 Mar 1964, shortly after recommissioning as a missile cruiser. A dramatic change from her earlier appearance, with tall "macks" (combination funnel and stack), missile launchers forward and aft. ASROC can be seen between the macks.

Figure 4.10: *USS Northampton* (CLC 1), flagship of the Second Fleet, 1950s. *Baltimore* class cruiser completed as command ship.

Service Records:

- CG 10   *Albany*   Out of comm for conversion 30 Jun 1958–3 Nov 1962. Out of comm 1 Mar 1967–9 Nov 1968, modernized. Decomm 29 Aug 1980. Stricken 30 Jun 1985. Sold 12 Aug 1990, BU.
- CG 11   *Chicago*   Primary air defense for mining of Haiphong harbor, 1972, shot down one aircraft with Talos. Collided with frigate *Bradley* off San Diego, Jun 1973. Decomm 1 Mar 1980. Stricken 31 Jan 1984. Sold 9 Dec 1991. BU Terminal I.
  ★Korea Jan–Mar 1968, Apr 1969, ★Vietnam Jun–Nov 1966, Nov 1967–Apr 1968, May–Aug 1969, Oct 1970–Feb 1971, Dec 1971–Jun 1972.
- CG 12   *Columbus*   Out of comm for conversion 8 May 1959–1 Dec 1962. Decomm 31 Jan 1975. Stricken 9 Aug 1976. Sold 3 Oct 1977, BU Portland, Ore.
  ★Vietnam Sep–Oct 1964; ◆Taiwan Straits Aug–Dec 1958, Quemoy-Matsu Apr 1962.
- CG 13   *Rochester*   CA 124 conversion canceled.
- CG 14   *Bremerton*   CA 130 conversion canceled.
- CG 15   not used.

COMMAND SHIPS

Northampton

No.	Name	Builder	Keel Laid	Launched	Comm.
CLC 1	*Northampton* ex-CA 125 (1 Nov 1947)	Beth; Quincy	31 Aug 1944	27 Jan 1951	7 Mar 1953
Displacement	14,700 tons; 17,200 f/l				
Dimensions	677′(oa); 664′ (wl) × 71′ × 29′				
Machinery	4 screws; ST; 120,000 SHP; 32 knots				
Complement	1,675				
Armament	4–5″/54, 8–3″/50 replaced by twin 3″/70; removed 1962; *1970*: 1–5″/54′; *1977*: 2–40 mm				
Armor	6″ side, 3″ & 2″ decks				

Notes: Incomplete hull of *Baltimore* Class heavy cruiser built one deck higher as task force command ship, later tactical command ship. Forward guns off center to clear foremast on bow which was 125′ high; had largest radar afloat when built. Converted to serve as emergency national command post for the president (NECPA).

Figure 4.11: *USS Wright* (CC 2), the former light carrier, converted to a headquarters ship 1962.

Service Record: Rec **CC 1**, 15 Sep 1961, command ship. Decomm 8 Apr 1970. Stricken 1 Dec 1977. Sold 1 Mar 1980, BU.
◆Cuba Apr, Jun, Dec 1961–Jan 1962.

No.	Name	former	Date
CC 2	*Wright*	CVL 49	1 Sep 1962
CC 3	*Saipan*	CVL 48	1 Jan 1964, canceled

Notes: *Wright* converted 1962. Fitted with command and communication facilities. Antenna masts placed on flight deck.

FRIGATES

Note: USN designation of this type as frigates was abandoned and all ships were reclassified in 1975 as either destroyers or cruisers. The term frigate (FF) was assigned to former escorts (DE).

Norfolk Class

No.	Name	Builder	Keel Laid	Launched	Comm.
DL 1	*Norfolk* ex-CLK 1 (9 Feb 1951)	NY Sbdg	1 Sep 1949	29 Dec 1951	4 Mar 1953
CLK 2	*New Haven*	Phila. NSYd			

Displacement	5,600 tons; 7,041 f/l
Dimensions	540′ (oa) × 54′3″ × 27′
Machinery	2 screws; ST; 80,000 SHP; 32.5 knots
Endurance	6,000/20
Complement	540
Armament	4 twin 3″/50, 8–20 mm guns, 4 weapon Alfa; new 3″/70 fitted, 20 mm removed. Weapon Alfa removed, replaced aft by ASROC.

Notes: First major U.S. warship built after World War II, based on *Atlanta*-class hull. Designed as hunter-killer cruiser able to operate in rough weather but was too expensive to produce in large numbers. Originally classified as hunter-killer cruiser. Uneven stacks, clipper bow. Used as ASW test ship.

Service Record:

1 *Norfolk* Middle East Apr–Oct 1968. Decomm 15 Jan 1970. Stricken 1 Nov 1973. Sold 13 or 22 Aug 1974, BU Brownsville, Tex. ◆Cuban missile crisis Oct–Nov 1962.

2 *New Haven* deferred 2 Mar 1949. Canceled 9 Feb 1951.

Mitscher Class

No.	Name	Builder	Keel Laid	Launched	Comm.
DL 2	*Mitscher*	Bath	3 Oct 1949	26 Jan 1952	16 May 1953
DL 3	*John S. McCain*	Bath	24 Oct 1949	12 Jul 1952	12 Oct 1953
DL 4	*Willis A. Lee*	Beth;Quincy	1 Nov 1949	26 Jan 1952	28 Sep 1954
DL 5	*Wilkinson*	Beth;Quincy	1 Feb 1950	23 Apr 1952	29 Jul 1954

Displacement	3,500 tons; 4,730 f/l
Dimensions	493′ (oa) 450′ (wl) × 50′ × 21′
Machinery	2 screws; ST; 80,000 SHP; 35 knots
Endurance	4,500/20
Complement	440
Armament	2–5″/54, 2-twin 3″/50, 4 TT, 2 triple ASW torpedo lchrs, 2 weapon Alfa; new 3″/70 fitted, later removed.

Notes: ex-DD 927–930, 9 Feb 1951. Authorized 1948. Two raked stacks, vertical mast. DASH/ASW refit 1960–62. *Mitscher* and *John S. McCain* converted to missile destroyers with single Standard/Tartar SAM launcher aft, two trellis masts, ASROC forward. Conversion of second pair canceled.

Service Record:

DL 2 *Mitscher* Out of comm 18 Mar 1966–29 Jun 1968, for conversion to guided missile destroyer; rec **DDG 35**, 15 Mar 1967. Decomm and stricken 1 Jun 1978. Sold 1 Aug 1980, BU.

DL 3 *John S. McCain* Out of comm 14 Jun 1966–6 Sep 1969, for conversion to guided missile destroyer; rec **DDG 36**, 15 Mar 1967. Decomm and stricken 29 Apr 1978. Sold 13 Dec 1979, BU. ★Vietnam Oct–Nov 1965; ◆Taiwan Straits Sep–Nov 1958, Quemoy-Matsu Jan 1960, (as DDG) ★Vietnam Apr–May 1971, Apr–Oct 1972.

DL 4 *Willis A. Lee* Cruised in Great Lakes 1959. Rec **DDG 37** canceled. Decomm 20 Dec 1969. Stricken 15 May 1972. Sold 1 Jun 1973, BU. ◆Cuban missile crisis Oct–Nov 1962.

DL 5 *Wilkinson* Rec **DDG 38** canceled. Decomm 19 Dec 1969. Stricken 1 May 1974. Sold 13 Jun 1975, BU. ★Vietnam Mar–May 1961; ◆Taiwan Straits Dec 1958, Quemoy-Matsu Oct–Dec 1959.

Figure 4.12: USS *Norfolk* (DL 1) Designed as a hunter-killer cruiser with new twin 3-inch guns. Weapon Alfa can be seen just forward of the bridge, and ASROC is aft forward of the gun turrets.

Figure 4.13: USS *John S. McCain* (DL 3), 22 Mar 1965. After DASH refit, one 3-inch mount and Weapon Alfa removed.

Coontz Class

No.	Name	Builder	Keel Laid	Launched	Comm.
DLG 6	*Farragut*	Beth; Quincy	3 Jun 1957	18 Jul 1958	10 Dec 1960
DLG 7	*Luce* ex-*Dewey* (12 Feb 1957)	Beth; Quincy	1 Oct 1957	11 Dec 1958	20 May 1961
DLG 8	*MacDonough*	Beth; Quincy	15 Apr 1958	9 Jul 1959	4 Nov 1961
DLG 9	*Coontz*	Puget Sd NSYd	2 Mar 1957	6 Dec 1958	15 Jul 1960
DLG 10	*King*	Puget Sd NSYd	2 Mar 1957	6 Dec 1958	17 Nov 1960
DLG 11	*Mahan*	San Fran NSYd	31 Jul 1957	7 Oct 1959	25 Aug 1960
DLG 12	*Dahlgren*	Phila NSYd	1 Mar 1958	16 Mar 1960	8 Apr 1961

Figure 4.14: USS *Preble* (DLG 15), 8 Jun 1970, *Coontz* class, after ASW modifications.

DLG 13	William V. Pratt	Phila NSYd	1 Mar 1958	16 Mar 1960	4 Nov 1961
DLG 14	Dewey	Bath	10 Aug 1957	30 Nov 1958	7 Dec 1959
DLG 15	Preble	Bath	16 Dec 1957	23 May 1959	9 May 1960

Displacement	4,150 tons; 5,350 f/l
Dimensions	512′6″(oa) × 52′6″ × 25′
Machinery	2 screws; ST; 4 boilers; 85,000 SHP; 34 knots
Endurance	4,000/20
Complement	392
Armament	1–5″/54, 2 twin 3″/50 guns; 1 twin Terrier launcher, ASROC; 6–21″TT AAW mod: 3″ removed.

Notes: Authorized 1956–57. DL 6–8 rec DLG, 14 Nov 1956. Two raked stacks, vertical trellis masts. Modified for AAW, 1968–71. *King* fitted with Phalanx as test ship 1973–74. All reclassified as guided missile destroyers (DDG) 1975.

Service Records:

DLG 6 *Farragut* Out of comm 1 May 1968–13 Sep 1969. Rec **DDG 37**, 30 Jun 1975. Decomm 31 Oct 1989. Stricken 20 Nov 1992. Sold 15 Dec 2006, BU.
◆Cuba Mar–Jun 1961, (as DDG) Iran/Indian Ocean Nov 1980–Jan 1981, Lebanon Dec 1982–May 1983, Libya Mar–Jun 1986.

DLG 7 *Luce* Out of comm 27 Feb 1970–22 May 1971. Rec **DDG 38**, 30 Jun 1975. Decomm 1 Apr 1991. Stricken 20 Nov 1992. Sold 17 Jun 2005, BU Philadelphia.
◆Dominican Rep Apr–May 1965.

DLG 8 *MacDonough* Out of comm 6 Apr 1973–4 May 1974. Rec **DDG 39**, 30 Jun 1975. Damaged by fire, 22 Feb 1992, not repaired. Decomm 23 Oct 1992. Stricken 30 Nov 1992. Sold 15 Dec 2004, BU 2005 Philadelphia.
◆Cuba Apr–Jun 1962, Cuban missile Crisis Oct–Nov 1962, (as DDG) Iran/Indian Ocean Jul–Oct 1981, Aug 1982, Gulf War Oct 1990–Feb 1991.

DLG 9 *Coontz* Out of comm 23 Feb 1971–18 Mar 1972. Rec **DDG 40**, 30 Jun 1975. Decomm 4 Oct 1989. Stricken 26 Jan 1990. Sold 4 Apr 2003, BU Philadelphia 2003.
★Vietnam 20 Dec 1962, Sep 1964–Jan 1965, Feb–Jul 1966, Sep–Dec 1967, Dec 1968–Mar 1969, Jun–Aug 1970; ◆Korea Mar 1968, Mar–Apr 1969, Apr–May 1970, (as DDG) Grenada Oct–Nov 1983.

DLG 10 *King* Damaged by fire in Gulf of Tonkin, 23 May 1969. Out of comm 30 Apr 1974–17 Sep 1977. Rec **DDG 41**, 30 Jun 1975. Decomm 28 Mar 1991. Stricken 20 Nov 1992. Sold 15 Apr 1994. BU 1995 Wilmington, NC.
★Vietnam Sep, Nov 1963, May–Oct 1965, Jun–Dec 1966, Oct 1967–Feb 1968, Apr–Aug 1969, Aug–Oct 1970, Nov 1971–Jan 1972, Oct 1972–Mar 1973; ◆Korea Mar 1969, Sep–Nov 1970, Sep–Oct 1971, (as DDG) Libya Mar–Jun 1986.

DLG 11 *Mahan* Out of comm 15 Aug 1973–1 Apr 1975. Rec **DDG 42**, 30 Jun 1975. Decomm and Stricken 15 Jun 1993. Sold 31 Aug 1995, repossessed. Sold 15 May 2004, BU Philadelphia 2004.
12★Vietnam Oct 1962, Sep, Nov 1963, Nov 1965–Mar 1966, Dec 1966–May 1967, Sep–Nov 1968, Jan–Mar, May 1970, Jan–Jul 1972; ◆Quemoy-Matsu Aug, Oct 1962, Korea Dec 1968, Apr, Aug–Nov 1969, Jan–Feb, Apr, Jun–Sep 1970, (as DDG) Lebanon Jun–Oct 1983, May 1983, Libya Jan–Mar 1986, Gulf War Oct 1991–Feb 1992.

DLG 12 *Dahlgren* Out of comm 24 Feb 1972–17 Mar 1973. Rec **DDG 43**, 30 Jun 1975. Decomm 31 Jul 1992. Stricken 20 Nov 1992. Sold 15 Apr 1994, repossessed. Sold 28 Mar 2006, BU 2008 Brownsville, Tex.
★Vietnam Apr–Jul 1967; ◆Cuba Sep–Oct 1961, Quemoy-Matsu Oct–Nov 1962, (as DDG) Libya May–Jul 1988, Mar–Aug 1990.

DLG 13 *William V. Pratt* Out of comm 5 Oct 1972–6 Oct 1973 for modernization. Rec **DDG 44**, 30 Jun 1975. Decomm 30 Sep 1991. Stricken 20 Nov 1992. Sold 14 Sep 1995. BU Brownsville, Tex. 1995.
1★Vietnam Aug–Dec 1967; ◆Cuba Apr–May 1962, (as DDG) Lebanon Aug–Dec 1982, Gulf War Jan–Apr 1991.

DLG 14 *Dewey* Damaged by boiler explosion at Toulon, France, 4 Sep 1969. Out of comm 21 Nov 1969–13 Mar 1971. Rec **DDG 45**, 30 Jun 1975. Decomm 31 Aug 1990. Stricken 20 Nov 1992. Sold 15 Apr 1994. BU 1994 Wilmington, NC.
★Vietnam Jan, Mar–May 1968, Jul–Aug 1972; ◆Cuban missile crisis Oct–Nov 1962, Korea Jan–Mar 1968.

DLG 15 *Preble* Out of comm 31 Jan 1969–23 Mar 1970. Rec **DDG 46**, 30 Jun 1975. Decomm 15 Nov 1991. Stricken 20 Nov 1992. Sold 15 Apr 1994, repossessed. Sold 10 Feb 2003, BU Philadelphia 2003.
★Vietnam 28 Mar 1961, Jun 1964, Jun–Oct 1965, Nov 1966–Feb 1967, Feb–Jun 1968, Jun–Sep 1971, Aug 1972–Feb 1973; ◆Korea Jan–Mar 1968, Apr–May 1971, (as DDG) Iran/Indian Ocean May–Oct 1981, Gulf War Jan–Mar 1991.

Leahy Class

No.	Name	Builder	Keel Laid	Launched	Comm.
DLG 16	Leahy	Bath	3 Dec 1959	1 Jul 1961	4 Aug 1962
DLG 17	Harry E. Yarnell	Bath	31 May 1960	9 Dec 1961	2 Feb 1963
DLG 18	Worden	Bath	19 Sep 1960	2 Jun 1962	3 Aug 1963
DLG 19	Dale	NY Sbdg	6 Sep 1960	28 Jul 1962	23 Nov 1963
DLG 20	Richmond K. Turner	NY Sbdg	9 Jan 1961	6 Apr 1963	13 Jun 1964
DLG 21	Gridley	Puget Sd.Brdg	15 Jul 1960	31 Jul 1961	25 May 1963
DLG 22	England	Todd; S.Pedro	4 Oct 1960	6 Mar 1962	7 Dec 1963
DLG 23	Halsey	San Fran.NSYd	26 Aug 1960	15 Jan 1962	20 Jul 1963
DLG 24	Reeves	Puget Sd NSYd	1 Jul 1960	12 May 1962	15 May 1964

Displacement	4,650 tons; 7,630 f/l 8,200 f/l (1985)
Dimensions	533′ (oa) × 54′10″ × 24′6″
Machinery	2 screws; ST; 4 boilers; 85,000 SHP; 34 knots
Endurance	8,000/20
Complement	379 423 (1987)
Armament	2-twin 3″/50 guns, 2 twin Terrier launchers, ASROC; 2 triple torpedo launchers. *1980s*: 2 twin Terrier/Standard-ER SAM, 8 Harpoon SSM, 2 Phalanx, ASROC, 6–12.75″ASW TT.

Notes: Authorized 1958–59. Introduced the "Mack" combined mast and exhaust stacks. 80 missiles carried. Modified for AAW 1967–72. Reclassified Cruisers (CG) 1975.

Service Records:

DLG 16 *Leahy* Out of comm 18 Feb 1967–4 May 1968 for modernization. Rec **CG 16**, 30 Jun 1975. Decomm and stricken, 1 Oct 1993. Sold 6 Jul 2005, BU Brownsville, Tex.
◆Dominican Rep Apr–May 1965, (as CG) Iran/Indian Ocean Aug–Nov 1980, Libya Sep–Dec 1989, Gulf War Apr–Jul 1991, Liberia Feb–Mar 1993.

DLG 17 *Harry E. Yarnell* Out of comm 9 Feb 1968–12 Jul 1969 for modernization. Rec **CG 17**, 30 Jun 1975. Decomm and stricken 29 Oct 1993. Sold 16 Feb 1995, canceled. Sold 17 Apr 2002, BU.
◆Beirut Evac Jun–Jul 1976, Iran/Indian Ocean Dec 1980–Mar 1981, Lebanon Nov 1983–Mar 1984.

DLG 18 *Worden* Rammed by Greek m/v in Hong Kong harbor, 13 Aug 1967. Out of comm 10 Nov 1969–16 Jan 1971 for modernization. Damaged by two U.S. missiles off North Vietnam, 16 Apr 1972 (1 killed). Rec **CG 18**, 30 Jun 1975. Decomm and stricken 1 Oct 1993. Sunk as target 17 Jun 2000.
9★Vietnam Sep–Dec 1964, Feb–Jun 1966, May–Sep 1967, Nov 1968–Apr 1969, Feb 1972–Feb 1973, Evac of Vietnam 29–30 Apr 1975; ◆Korea Nov 1971–Jan 1972, (as CG) Iran/Indian Ocean Apr–Jul 1980, Persian Gulf Jun–Jul 1987, Gulf War Oct 1990–Feb 1991.

DLG 19 *Dale* Out of comm 10 Nov 1970–11 Dec 1971. Rec **CG 19**, 30 Jun 1975. In collision with British frigate *Ambuscade* in Indian Ocean, 27 Apr 1983. Decomm and stricken 27 Sep 1994. Sunk as target 6 Apr 2000.
★Vietnam Feb–May 1965, Jun–Oct 1966, Dec 1967–Apr 1968, Mar–Apr, Jul 1969, May–Jun 1970; ◆Korea Apr–Jun 1969, (as CG) Lebanon Jan 1983, Libya Mar–Jun 1986, Libya Jul–Dec 1989, Gulf War Jun–Jul 1991.

DLG 20 *Richmond K. Turner* Out of comm 5 May 1971–27 May 1972. Rec **CG 20**, 30 Jun 1975. Decomm 13 Apr 1995. Stricken 30 Jun 1995. Sunk as target off Puerto Rico, 9 Aug 1998.
8★Vietnam Jun–Nov 1965, Nov 1966–Mar 1967, Jul–Nov 1968, Jun–Jul 1970; ◆Korea Mar–Jun 1970, (as CG) Grenada Oct–Nov 1983, Lebanon Nov 1983–Feb 1984, Jan–Mar 1986, Libya Oct 1987–Feb 1988, Gulf War Jan–Apr 1991.

DLG 21 *Gridley* Out of comm 10 Sep 1968–17 Jan 1970. Rec **CG 21**, 30 Jun 1975. Decomm and stricken 21 Jan 1994. Sold 31 Mar 2005, BU.
★Vietnam Jun–Sep 1964, Aug 1965–Jan 1966, Mar–May 1968, Dec 1970–Jan 1971, Mar–Apr 1971, Jun–Nov 1972; ◆Korea Jan–Mar 1971, Evac of Vietnam 29–30 Apr 1975, Mayaguez Op 15 May 1975, (as CG) Iran/Indian Ocean May 1980, Oct 1981, Libya Aug–Nov 1987, Gulf War Jun–Sep 1992.

DLG 22 *England* Damaged by explosion and fire during construction at San Pedro, 30 Mar 1962. Out of comm 10 Apr 1970–26 Jun 1971. Rec **CG 22**,. 30 Jun 1975. Decomm and stricken 21 Jan 1994. Sold 20 Oct 2004, BU Brownsville.
★Vietnam Jan–Mar 1965, Jan–May 1966, Mar–Jun 1967, Jul–Dec 1968, Jun–Nov 1972; ◆(as CG) Iran/Indian Ocean Apr–Jun 1979, Gulf War Aug–Nov 1990.

DLG 23 *Halsey* Out of comm 4 Nov 1971–16 Dec 1972. Rec **CG 23**, 30 Jun 1975. Decomm and stricken 28 Jan 1994. Sold 1 Nov 2002 30 Nov 2003, BU Brownsville, Tex.
★Vietnam Feb–Jul 1965, Aug–Oct 1966, Jan–Jul 1968, Jul–Dec 1969, Jan–Mar 1971; ◆Korea Jun–Oct 1969, (as CG) Nov 1979–Jan 1971, Iran/Indian Ocean Feb 1980, May–Sep 1981, Persian Gulf Feb–Jul 1987, Libya Jun–Sep 1988, Gulf War Dec 1991–Mar 1992.

DLG 24 *Reeves* Out of comm 10 Apr 1969–29 Aug 1970. Rec **CG 24**, 30 Jun 1975. Slightly damaged by bomb dropped in error by U.S. plane in Indian Ocean, 30 Oct 1989. Decomm and stricken 12 Nov 1993. Sunk as target off Australia, 31 May 2001.
3★Vietnam May–Oct 1965, Jul 1966–Jun 1968, Jan–Jun 1968, Jul–Dec 1971, Oct 1972–Mar 1973; ◆(as CG) Iran/Indian Ocean Feb–May 1980, Mar–May 1981, Jul 1987, Libya Jul–Sep 1987, Sep–Oct 1989.

Bainbridge

No.	Name	Builder	Keel Laid	Launched	Comm.
DLGN 25	*Bainbridge*	Beth; Quincy	15 May 1959	15 Apr 1961	6 Oct 1962

Displacement	7,850 tons; 8,580 f/l
Dimensions	565′ (oa); 550′ (wl) × 57′10″ × 24′6″
Machinery	2 screws; ST; 2 reactors; 60,000 SHP; 30 knots
Endurance	90,000/20
Complement	497 558
Armament	2 twin 3″/50 guns; 2 twin Terrier launchers; ASROC, 2-triple torpedo launchers; *1976*: 2–20 mm replaced 2–3″. *1980s*: 2 twin Terrier/Standard-ER SAM lchrs, 8 Harpoon SSM, 2 Phalanx, ASROC, 2-triple 12.75″ASW TT.

Notes: Authorized 1959. A nuclear-powered *Leahy*. Two lattice masts. 80 missiles carried.

Figure 4.15: *USS Reeves* (DLG 24), *Leahy* class. This class introduced the "mack," a combination of mast and stack. There are twin Terrier launchers fore and aft, and ASROC forward.

Figure 4.16: *USS Bainbridge* (DLGN 25, later CGN 25), similar to *Leahy* class with nuclear power.

Figure 4.17: *USS Jouett* (CG 29) with twin Terrier launcher forward and Phalanx CIWS amidships.

Figure 4.18: The guided missile frigate *Belknap* (DLG 26), lead ship of her class, later designated as cruisers.

Figure 4.19: *USS Belknap* (DLG 26) after the fire which resulted from her collision with the aircraft carrier *John F. Kennedy* in the Mediterranean, 22 Nov 1975. Here she is under tow on the 29th.

Service Record: Rec **CGN 25**, 30 Jun 1975. Ran aground off Den Helder, Netherlands, 28 Jun 1989. Decomm and stricken 13 Sep 1996. Sold 1 Nov 1999, BU Bremerton.

★Vietnam Dec 1965–Jun 1966, Dec 1966–Jun 1967, Jan–Jun 1969, Jul–Nov 1971, Oct 1972–Mar 1973; ◆Korea Jun–Jul 1971, (as CGN) Iran/Indian Ocean Nov 1979–Feb 1980, Mar–Apr 1981, Gulf War Oct 1991–Apr 1992.

Belknap Class

No.	Name	Builder	Keel Laid	Launched	Comm.
DLG 26	Belknap	Bath	5 Feb 1962	20 Jul 1963	7 Nov 1964
DLG 27	Josephus Daniels	Bath	23 Apr 1962	2 Dec 1963	8 May 1965
DLG 28	Wainwright	Bath	2 Jul 1962	25 Apr 1964	8 Jan 1966
DLG 29	Jouett	Puget Sd NSYd	25 Sep 1962	30 Jun 1964	3 Dec 1966
DLG 30	Horne	San Fran.NSYd	12 Dec 1962	30 Oct 1964	15 Apr 1967
DLG 31	Sterett	Puget Sd NSYd	25 Sep 1962	30 Jun 1964	8 Apr 1967
DLG 32	William H. Standley	Bath	29 Jul 1963	19 Dec 1964	9 Jul 1966
DLG 33	Fox	Todd; S.Pedro	15 Jan 1963	21 Nov 1964	28 May 1966
DLG 34	Biddle	Bath	9 Dec 1963	2 Jul 1965	21 Jan 1967
Displacement	5,340 tons; 7,900 f/l				
Dimensions	547′ (oa); 530′ (wl) × 54′10″ × 29′				
Machinery	2 screws; ST; 4 boilers; 85,000 SHP; 33 knots				
Endurance	7,100/20				
Complement	477				
Armament	1–5″/54, 2–3″/50 guns; 1 twin Terrier/ASROC, launcher, 2–21″ TT (removed), 2 triple ASW torpedo launchers. *1980s*: 1 twin Terrier/Standard-ER SAM lchr, 8 Harpoon SSM, 1–5″/54 gun, 2 Phalanx, ASROC, 6–12.75″ASW TT.				

Notes: Authorized 1961–62. Single missile launcher forward, allowing missile stowage in bow section. Two "macks" combining masts and stacks.

Service Records:

DLG 26 *Belknap*   Rec **CG 26**, 30 Jun 1975. Severely damaged in collision with carrier *John F. Kennedy* in Ionian Sea, 22 Nov 1975 (7 killed). Out of comm 20 Dec 1975–10 May 1980. Hosted President G.H.W. Bush during meeting with Soviet President Gorbachev at Malta, 2 Dec 1989. Decomm and stricken 15 Feb 1995. Sunk as target 24 Sep 1998.

★Vietnam Oct 1967–Feb 1968, Jan–Feb 1970, ◆Korea Dec 1969–Jan 1970, (as CG) Lebanon Jun–Sep 1983.

DLG 27 *Josephus Daniels*   Rec **CG 27**, 30 Jun 1975. In collision with cruiser *Conyngham* in Greek waters, 2 Aug 1976. In collision with tanker *Omnium Mariner* in Palma de Majorca harbor, 31 Jan 1978. Decomm and stricken 21 Jan 1994. Sold 8 Nov 1999, BU Brownsville, Tex.

★Vietnam Apr–Sep 1970; ◆ (as CG) Libya 1988–Jan 1989.

DLG 28 *Wainwright*   Rec **CG 28**, 30 Jun 1975. Went aground in Charleston harbor, 14 Mar 1979. Decomm and stricken 10 Nov 1993. Sold 16 Dec 1994. Sunk as target 13 Jun 2002.

4★Vietnam Jun–Sep 1967, Jul 1968–Jan 1969, Nov 1970–Feb 1971; ◆Korea Sep–Oct 1970, (as CG) Lebanon Sep–Oct 1982, Libya Feb–Jun 1988.

DLG 29 *Jouett*   Rec **CG 29**, 30 Jun 1975. Decomm and stricken 28 Jan 1994. Sunk as target, 10 Aug 2007.

★Vietnam Feb–Jul 1968, Sep 1969–Jan 1970, Oct 1970–Mar 1971, Sep 1972–Feb 1973; ◆Korea Oct 1969, (as CG) Iran/Indian Ocean Nov 1979–Jan 1980, Gulf War Aug–Nov 1990.

DLG 30 *Horne* Rec **CG 30**, 30 Jun 1975. Decomm and stricken 4 Feb 1994.
★Vietnam Jun–Nov 1968, Feb–Jun 1970, Jul–Nov 1971, Nov 1972–Mar 1973; ◆(as CG) Libya Nov–Dec 1987, Jan–Feb 1988, Liberia Mar–May 1993, Gulf War Jan–Apr 1991.

DLG 31 *Sterett* Rec **CG 31**, 30 Jun 1975. Decomm and stricken 24 Mar 1994. Sold 29 Jul 2005, BU Brownsville, Tex.
9★Vietnam Jul 1968–Mar 1969, May–Sep 1969, Jan–May 1970, Feb–Jul 1972; ◆Korea Mar–May, Jul, Oct–Dec 1969, Mar, Jun–Jul 1970, (as CG) Iran/Indian Ocean Dec 1978–Jan 1979, Mar–Apr 1979, Libya Dec 1989.

DLG 32 *William H. Standley* Rec **CG 32**, 30 Jun 1975. Decomm and stricken 11 Feb 1994. Sunk as target off Australia, 22 Jul 2005.
4★Vietnam Jan–Jun 1969, Feb–Jun 1971; ◆Korea Mar–Apr 1971, (as CG) Iran/Indian Ocean Feb–May 1980, Liberia Dec 1992, Feb–Mar 1993.

DLG 33 *Fox* Rec **CG 33**, 30 Jun 1975. Decomm and stricken 15 Apr 1994. Sold 28 Oct 2007, BU Brownsville, Tex.
★Vietnam Nov 1968–Feb 1969, Jun–Oct 1970, Sep 1971–Jan 1972, Feb–Mar 1973; ◆(as CG) Iran/Indian Ocean Nov 1980–Mar 1981, Quemoy-Matsu Jun–Jul 1987, Libya Jul–Aug 1987, Gulf War Dec 1991–Mar 1992.

DLG 34 *Biddle* Rec **CG 34**, 30 Jun 1975. Collided with amphibious assault ship *Raleigh* at Norfolk, Va., 10 Jan 1981. Decomm and stricken 30 Nov 1993. Sold 2 Jan 2002, BU Philadelphia.
★Vietnam Mar–Jul 1968, Jun–Nov 1969, May–Sep 1972; ◆(as CG) Lebanon May–Jun 1984, Aug–Oct 1982, Libya/El Dorado Jan–Jun 1986, Gulf War Aug 1990–Mar 1991.

Truxtun

No.	Name	Builder	Keel Laid	Launched	Comm.
DLGN 35	*Truxtun*	NY Sbdg	17 Jun 1963	19 Dec 1964	27 May 1967

Displacement	8,250 tons; 9,050 f/l
Dimensions	565' (oa) × 58' × 30'
Machinery	2 screws; ST; 2 reactors; 60,000 SHP; 30+ knots
Complement	479 591
Armament	1–5"/54, 2–3"/50 guns; 1 twin Terrier/ASROC launcher, 2–21"TT, 6–12"A/S TT; LAMPS h/c. *1980s*: 1 twin Terrier/Standard-ER SAM lchr, 8 Harpoon, 1–5"/54, 2 Phalanx, ASROC, 4–12.75"ASW TT.

Notes: Authorized 1962. Modification of *Belknap* design with armament reversed. Trellis masts. A third DLGN, designed to carry Typhon missiles, canceled 7 Jan 1964.

Service Record: Rec **CGN 35**, 30 Jun 1975. Decomm and stricken 11 Sep 1995. BU Bremerton 1999.
7★Vietnam Feb–Jul 1968, Oct–Dec 1969, Mar–Jul 1971, Aug 1972–Jan 1973; ◆Korea Jan–Mar 1968, Feb 1970, Apr 1971, (as CGN) Iran/Indian Ocean Apr–Aug 1980, Libya Feb–Apr 1988, May–Jun 1990, Gulf War Sep 1991.

California Class

No.	Name	Builder	Keel Laid	Launched	Comm.
DLGN 36	*California*	Newport News	23 Jan 1970	22 Sep 1971	16 Feb 1974
DLGN 37	*South Carolina*	Newport News	1 Dec 1970	1 Jul 1972	25 Jan 1975

Displacement	10,530 tons f/l
Dimensions	596' (oa) × 61' × 31'6"
Machinery	2 screws, ST, 2 reactors, 60,000 SHP; 30+ knots
Complement	603
Armament	*1980s*: 2 Terrier/Standard-ER SAN lchrs, 8 Harpoon, 2–5"/54, 2 Phalanx, ASROC, 4–12.75"ASW TT

Notes: Authorized 1967. Planned to produce new surface vessels to screen nuclear carriers. No h/c hangar.

Service Record:

DLGN 36 *California* Rec **CGN 36**, 30 Jun 1975. Decomm and stricken 9 Jul 1999. BU 2000 Bremerton.
◆Iran/Indian Ocean Jan–May 1980, May–Oct 1981, Eagle Claw 1980, Persian Gulf Feb–Jun 1987, Libya Nov–Dec 1988, Gulf War 31 Jul 1991.

DLGN 37 *South Carolina* Rec **CGN 37**, 30 Jun 1975. Decomm and stricken 30 Jul 1999. BU Bremerton
◆Iran/Indian Ocean Apr–Dec 1980, Eagle Claw 1980, Gulf War Oct–Dec 1990.

Figure 4.20: The nuclear guided missile frigate *Truxtun* (DLGN 35), later reclassified cruiser, 12 Jun 1970.

Figure 4.21: *USS South Carolina* (CGN 37). Visible are the two 5-inch guns, ASROC, and two unarmed launchers fore and aft.

Virginia Class

No.	Name	Builder	Keel Laid	Launched	Comm.
CGN 38	*Virginia*	Newport News	19 Aug 1972	14 Dec 1974	11 Sep 1976
CGN 39	*Texas*	Newport News	18 Aug 1973	9 Aug 1975	10 Sep 1977
CGN 40	*Mississippi*	Newport News	22 Feb 1975	31 Jul 1976	5 Aug 1978
CGN 41	*Arkansas*	Newport News	17 Jan 1977	21 Oct 1978	18 Oct 1980
CGN 42	—	—	—	—	—

Displacement	11,300 tons f/l
Dimensions	585′ (oa) × 63′ × 29′6″
Machinery	2 screws; ST; 2 reactors; 60,000 SHP; 30+ knots
Complement	520–579
Armament	*1980s*: 2 twin Tartar/Standard-MR SAM, 8 Harpoon. *1984*: 8 Tomahawk, 2–5″/54, 2 Phalanx, ASROC, 6–12.75″ASW TT

Notes: DLGN 38–40 rec CGN 38–40, 30 Jun 1975. Improved *California* class. Originally planned with LAMPS h/c.

Service Record:

CGN 38 *Virginia* Decomm and stricken 10 Nov 1994. BU 2002 Bremerton.
◆Iran/Indian Ocean Apr–Dec 1980, Lebanon May, Jun–Aug 1983, Gulf War Jan–Apr 1991.

CGN 39 *Texas* Hit quay and was holed at Brisbane, 19 Jul 1983. Decomm and stricken 16 Jul 1993. BU 2001 Bremerton.
◆Iran/Indian Ocean Jan–May 1980, Eagle Claw 1980, Libya Jul–Sep 1988, Gulf War Apr–Jul 1991.

CGN 40 *Mississippi* Decomm and stricken 28 Jul 1997.
◆Lebanon Dec 1982–Apr 1983, Gulf War Sep 1990–Mar 1991.

CGN 41 *Arkansas* In collision with m/v *Megara Ilea* off Messina, Sicily, 3 Jan 1983. Decomm and stricken 7 Jul 1998. BU 1999 Bremerton.
◆Lebanon Dec 1982–May 1983, Libya Apr–Jun 1986, Gulf War Jul–Oct 1991.

CGN 42 canceled 1979, never authorized

Figure 4.22: Guided missile cruiser *Chosin* (CG 65) during an exercise off Guam, 1 May 2007.

Figure 4.23: USS *Leyte Gulf* (CG 55) underway in the Atlantic Ocean, 22 Feb 2004.

Figure 4.24: USS *Cape St. George* (CG 71) firing a missile.

Ticonderoga Class

No.	Name	Builder	Keel Laid	Launched	Comm.
CG 47	*Ticonderoga*	Ingalls	21 Jan 1980	24 Apr 1981	22 Jan 1983
CG 48	*Yorktown*	Ingalls	19 Oct 1980	17 Jan 1983	4 Jul 1984
CG 49	*Vincennes*	Ingalls	20 Oct 1982	14 Jan 1984	6 Jul 1985
CG 50	*Valley Forge*	Ingalls	14 Apr 1983	23 Jun 1984	18 Jan 1986
CG 51	*Thomas S. Gates*	Bath	31 Aug 1984	14 Dec 1985	22 Aug 1987
CG 52	*Bunker Hill*	Ingalls	11 Jan 1984	11 Mar 1985	20 Sep 1986
CG 53	*Mobile Bay*	Ingalls	6 Jun 1984	22 Aug 1985	21 Feb 1987
CG 54	*Antietam*	Ingalls	15 Nov 1984	14 Feb 1986	6 Jun 1987
CG 55	*Leyte Gulf*	Ingalls	18 Mar 1985	20 Jun 1986	5 Sep 1987
CG 56	*San Jacinto*	Ingalls	24 Jul 1985	14 Nov 1986	23 Jan 1988
CG 57	*Lake Champlain*	Ingalls	3 Mar 1986	3 Apr 1987	12 Aug 1988
CG 58	*Philippine Sea*	Bath	8 May 1986	12 Jul 1987	18 Mar 1989
CG 59	*Princeton*	Ingalls	15 Oct 1986	25 Sep 1987	11 Feb 1989
CG 60	*Normandy*	Bath	7 Apr 1986	19 Mar 1988	9 Dec 1989
CG 61	*Monterey*	Bath	19 Aug 1987	23 Oct 1988	16 Jun 1990
CG 62	*Chancellorsville*	Ingalls	24 Jun 1987	15 Jul 1988	4 Nov 1989

CG 63	*Cowpens*	Bath	23 Dec 1987	11 Mar 1989	13 Feb 1991
CG 64	*Gettysburg*	Bath	17 Aug 1988	22 Jul 1989	22 Jun 1991
CG 65	*Chosin*	Ingalls	22 Jul 1988	1 Sep 1989	12 Jan 1991
CG 66	*Hué City*	Ingalls	20 Feb 1989	1 Jun 1990	14 Sep 1991
CG 67	*Shiloh*	Bath	1 Aug 1989	8 Sep 1990	18 Jul 1992
CG 68	*Anzio*	Ingalls	21 Aug 1989	2 Nov 1990	2 May 1992
CG 69	*Vicksburg* ex-*Port Royal*	Ingalls	30 May 1990	2 Aug 1991	14 Nov 1992
CG 70	*Lake Erie*	Bath	6 Mar 1990	13 Jul 1991	24 Jul 1993
CG 71	*Cape St. George*	Ingalls	19 Nov 1990	10 Jan 1992	12 Jun 1993
CG 72	*Vella Gulf*	Ingalls	22 Apr 1991	30 May 1992	18 Sep 1993
CG 73	*Port Royal*	Ingalls	20 Nov 1991	20 Nov 1992	9 Jul 1994

Displacement	9,530 tons f/l
Dimensions	565′10″ (oa); 532′8″ (wl) × 55′ × 31′6″
Machinery	2 screws; GT; 80,000 SHP; 30+ knots
Endurance	6,000/20
Complement	364
Armament	2 twin Standard-MR lchrs (47–51), 2 61-cell VLS (others), 2 Seahawk h/c, 8 Harpoon, 2–5″/54, 2 Phalanx, ASROC, 6–12.75″ASW TT

Notes: 47 and 48 ex-DDG 47–48, 1 Jan 1980. Built around Aegis system, designed to automatically detect, track and attack multiple targets. *Spruance* class hulls, more heavily armed. Aluminum armor. The first five units were armed with older missile launchers.

Service Record:

CG 47 *Ticonderoga* Had fire in exhaust vent in Atlantic, 10 Sep 1984. Decomm and stricken 30 Sep 2004.
◆Lebanon Nov 1983–Feb 1984, Libya Mar–Jun 1986, Gulf War Aug 1990.

CG 48 *Yorktown* In collision with Soviet frigate *Bezzavetniy* in Black Sea, 12 Feb 1988. Decomm and stricken 10 Dec 2004.
◆Libya Jan–Mar 1986.

CG 49 *Vincennes* Shot down Iranian airliner in error over Persian Gulf causing 290 deaths, 3 Jul 1988. Decomm 29 Jun 2005.
◆Libya May–Aug 1988, May–Jun 1990.

CG 50 *Valley Forge* Decomm and stricken 30 Aug 2004. Sunk as target off Kauai, Hawaii, 2 Nov 2006.
◆Persian Gulf Jun–Jul 1987, Gulf War Jan–Apr 1991, Liberia Dec 1992, Indian Ocean Jul–Nov 1998, Iraq War 2003.

CG 51 *Thomas S. Gates* Decomm & stricken 16 Dec 2005.
◆Gulf War Sep 1990–Mar 1991.

CG 52 *Bunker Hill*
◆Libya Sep–Nov 1987, Sep–Nov 1989, Gulf War Oct 1990–Mar 1991, Indian Ocean Feb–May 1998, Sep 2000–Jan 2001, Iraq War 2003.

CG 53 *Mobile Bay*
◆Libya Jul–Aug 1989, Gulf War Oct 1990–Mar 1991, Iraq War 2003.

CG 54 *Antietam* Had fire in forward engine room at San Diego, 13 Dec 2002.
◆Libya Nov–Dec 1988, Gulf War Aug–Nov 1990, Indian Ocean Jan–Feb 1997, Dec 1998–Mar 1999.

CG 55 *Leyte Gulf* Damaged in collision with carrier *Theodore Roosevelt* off Cape Hatteras, 14 Oct 1996.
◆Gulf War Jan–Apr 1991, Indian Ocean Jul–Sep 1999.

CG 56 *San Jacinto*
◆Gulf War Sep 1990–Mar 1991, Indian Ocean Mar–Jul 1998, Dec 2000–Mar 2001, Iraq War 2003.

CG 57 *Lake Champlain* Not damaged by fire while undergoing repairs at San Diego, 10 Nov 2007.
◆Libya Dec 1989, Gulf War Jul–Oct 1991, Indian Ocean Oct 1997–Jan 1998, Feb–May 2000.

CG 58 *Philippine Sea*
◆Gulf War Aug 1990–Feb 1991.

CG 59 *Princeton* Damaged by mine in Persian Gulf, 18 Feb 1991.
◆Gulf War Jan–Apr 1991, Desert Fox 1998, Indian Ocean Dec 1998–Mar 1999.

CG 60 *Normandy*
◆Gulf War Jan–Apr 1991, Indian Ocean Nov 1997–Mar 1998, Jul–Sep 2000.

CG 61 *Monterey* In collision with AFS *Spica* in Persian Gulf, 17 Mar 2005.
◆Indian Ocean Dec 1995, Oct 1999–Mar 2000.

CG 62 *Chancellorsville*
◆Gulf War Apr–Jul 1991, Iraq missile strikes Jun 1993. Indian Ocean Apr–Jul 1999, Iraq War 2003.

CG 63 *Cowpens* Attacked Iraqi installations, 17 Jan 1993. Attack on Al Quaeda camps in Afghanistan, 20 Aug 1998.
◆Indian Ocean Jan–Feb 1997, Iraq War 2003.

CG 64 *Gettysburg* In collision with Iranian frigate *Bayandor* in Persian Gulf, 13 Oct 1996.
◆Haiti 1994, Desert Fox 1998, Indian Ocean Nov 1998–Jan 1999.

CG 65 *Chosin*
◆Gulf War Sep 1992, Indian Ocean May–Jun 1997, Aug–Sep 1999, Jul–Aug 2001.

CG 66 *Hué City*

CG 67 *Shiloh* Attacks on Iraq, 3–4 Sep 1996. Attack on Al Quaeda camps in Afghanistan, 20 Aug 1998.
◆Indian Ocean Jul–Oct 1998, Sep 2000–Jan 2001, Iraq War 2003, Tsunami relief 2005.

CG 68 *Anzio*
◆Indian Ocean Oct–Nov 1998, Iraq War 2003.

CG 69 *Vicksburg*
◆Haiti Sep 1994, Indian Ocean Dec 1995–Feb 1996.

CG 70 *Lake Erie* Destroyed a non-functioning satellite 133 miles over the Pacific Ocean, 21 Feb 2008.
◆Indian Ocean May–Jun 1997, Aug–Sep 1999.

CG 71 *Cape St. George*
◆Indian Ocean Sep–Nov 1998, Feb–May 2000, Iraq War 2003.

CG 72 *Vella Gulf*
◆Indian Ocean Mar–Jun 1997.

CG 73 *Port Royal*
◆Indian Ocean Jan–Mar 1996, Oct 1997–Jan 1998, Feb–May

5
DESTROYERS

Destroyers still under construction at the end of World War II were completed incorporating the lessons of war experience, including innovations in machinery, radar, sonar, and anti-submarine weapons. Destroyers older than the *Benson* class were quickly scrapped after World War II. The large *Fletcher* class were modified for continued service and continued to serve into the 1960s. In order to extend their service lives, many *Sumner* and *Gearing* class ships were overhauled and modified under the Fleet Rehabilitation and Modernization (FRAM) program of the 1960s, though most were gone—or transferred to other nations—by 1978.

Post World War II destroyer nomenclature can be confusing even to the initiate. The first new ships to be ordered post World War II were the *Mitscher* class which were given a new category, frigate (DL). They were followed by the smaller *Forrest Sherman* class, which were given DD numbers. The *Charles F. Adams* class, designed as a missile version of the *Forrest Sherman* class were given numbers in a new category, DDG. Another class, the *Farragut* class, was built at the same time with the designation DLG.

For ease of design and mass production the new *Spruance* class of the 1970s, also given DD numbers, was built at a single new shipyard built by Ingalls at Pascagoula, Mississippi. They were the first major U.S. warships built with gas turbines. The last unit of this class was decommissioned in 2005.

This confusing assortment of destroyer designations was swept away in 1975 when the Navy revised its nomenclature again. The frigate category of DL/DLG was eliminated and most of the ships were reclassified as cruisers (CG/CGN), while the smaller *Farraguts* were given new DDG numbers. The term frigate was reassigned to the smaller destroyer escorts and the symbol DE was replaced by FF. In 1980 the latter units of the *Spruance* class were reclassified as cruisers, becoming known as the *Ticonderoga* class.

The mission of destroyers changed as well as their size. Destroyers, today divided into DD and DDG categories, operate to support carrier battle groups, amphibious and replenishment groups, and combine the functions of anti-submarine warfare and multi-mission surface combatants. The wide array of missiles now available, including cruise missiles, has expanded the capability of the destroyer. This, coupled with the large expense of building heavier surface combatants has increased the attractiveness of destroyer types.

The *Arleigh Burke* class DDGs are the largest destroyers yet built and also the most powerful. The class will include sixty-two ships. Their principal capability is anti-air warfare with the ability to counter both enemy aircraft and missiles. The later ships of the class (DDG 79–112) are slightly larger, have more missile launching cells, and can operate two helicopters.

The proposed new *Zumwalt* class (DDG 1000), which will be significantly larger than previous ships, incorporates a completely new hull configuration free of angled surfaces and projections, resulting in a stark (and much more stealthy) hull form. This includes a wave-piercing tumblehome hull and single integrated superstructure without the usual projecting masts, resembling the sail of a submarine. They will be able to provide all-weather fire support in littoral areas, as well as anti-submarine and surface warfare capability. The new AGS guns will provide long-range precision naval fire to support fast moving expeditionary forces far inland, up to 83 miles. Greater automation permits a much smaller crew than previous units.

Unfortunately, by starting the new *Zumwalt* class with the number DDG 1000, the Navy has again violated its singular and practical numbering system by confusing the DD and DDG series. In reality the first *Zumwalt* should have been numbered either DD 998 or DDG 113.

Destroyers continue to be named after distinguished Naval and Marine Corps officers and enlisted personnel and civilians with naval connections. DDG 81 was named for Sir Winston Churchill, England's great wartime leader, and DDG 80 *Roosevelt* was named for both Franklin D. and Eleanor Roosevelt. DDG 70 was the second destroyer named for a woman, Rear Admiral Grace D. Hopper.

DESTROYERS ON THE NAVY LIST, 1947

Benson and Livermore Classes

DD 421 *Benson*   Decomm 18 Mar 1946. Trfd to Taiwan, 26 Feb 1954.
Later history: renamed *Lo Yang* (14). BU 1974.

DD 422 *Mayo*   Decomm 18 Mar 1946. Stricken 1 Dec 1970. Sold 8 May 1972, BU New Orleans.

DD 423 *Gleaves*   Decomm 8 May 1946. NRT 1947. Stricken 1 Nov 1969. Sold 1972, BU New Orleans.

DD 424 *Niblack*   Decomm 25 Apr 1946. NRT 1947. Stricken 31 Jul 1968. Sold 31 Jul 1973, BU.

DD 425 *Madison*   Decomm 13 Mar 1946. Stricken 1 Jun 1968. Sunk as target off Florida, 14 Oct 1969.

DD 427 *Hilary P. Jones*   Decomm 6 Feb 1947. Trfd to Taiwan, 26 Feb 1954.
Later history: renamed *Han Yang* (15). BU 1974.

DD 428 *Charles F. Hughes*   Decomm 18 Mar 1946. Stricken 1 Jun 1968. Sunk as target off Virginia, 26 Mar 1969.

DD 429 *Livermore*   Decomm 24 Jan 1947. NRT 1947–50. Ran aground off Cape Cod, 30 Jul 1949. Decomm (O/S) 15 May 1950. Stricken 19 Jul 1956. Hull used for experimental purposes, Indian Head, Md., 1956–58. Sold 3 Mar 1961, BU Popes Creek, Md.

DD 430 *Eberle*   Out of comm 3 Jun 1946–19 May 1950. NRT 1947. Decomm 22 Jan 1951. Trfd to Greece, 22 Jan 1951.
Later history: renamed *Niki* (D-63). R1972.

DD 431 *Plunkett*   Decomm 3 May 1946. NRT 1947. Trfd to Taiwan 16 Feb 1959.
Later history: renamed *Nan Yang* (17). R1974.

DD 432 *Kearny*   Decomm 7 Mar 1946. Stricken 1 Jun 1971. Sold 6 Oct 1972, BU.

DD 435 *Grayson*   Decomm 4 Feb 1947. Stricken 1 Jun 1971. Sold 22 Nov 1972, BU New Orleans.

DD 437 *Woolsey*   Decomm 6 Feb 1947. Stricken 1 Jul 1971. Sold 18 May 1974, BU Brownsville, Tex.

DD 438 *Ludlow*   Out of comm 20 May 1946–21 Nov 1950. NRT 1947. Decomm 22 Jan 1951. Trfd to Greece 18 Apr 1951.
Later history: renamed *Doxa* (D-20). R1971.

DD 439 *Edison*   Decomm 18 May 1946. Stricken 1 Apr 1966. Sold 29 Dec 1966, BU Kearny, NJ.

DD 440 *Ericsson*   Decomm 15 Mar 1946. Stricken 1 Jun 1970. Sunk as target 17 Nov 1970.

DD 441 *Wilkes*   Decomm 4 Mar 1946. Name canceled 16 Jul 1968. Stricken 1 Mar 1971. Sold 29 Jun 1972, BU New Orleans.

DD 442 *Nicholson*   Out of comm 26 Feb 1946–17 Jul 1950. Recomm 15 Jan 1951. Trfd to Italy, 11 Jun 1951.
Later history: renamed *Aviere* (D 554). SE1972.

DD 443 *Swanson*   Decomm 10 Dec 1945. Stricken 1 Mar 1971. Sold 29 Jun 1972, BU New Orleans.

DD 454 *Ellyson*   (see DMS 19).

DD 455 *Hambleton*   (see DMS 20).

DD 456 *Rodman*   (see DMS 21).

DD 458 *Macomb*   (see DMS 23).

DD 460 *Woodworth*   Out of comm 11 Apr 1946–14 Jan 1951. NRT 30 Jan 1947. Recomm 21 Nov 1950. Trfd to Italy, 11 Jun 1951.
Later history: renamed *Artigliere* (D 553). R1971, sunk as target 27 May 1983.

DD 462 *Fitch*   (see DMS 25).

DD 464 *Hobson*   (see DMS 26).

DD 484 *Buchanan*   Out of comm 21 May 1946–11 Dec 1948. Trfd to Turkey, 29 Apr 1949.
Later history: renamed *Gelibolu* (G-1/D-23/D-345). R1977.

DD 486 *Lansdowne*   Decomm 2 May 1946. Trfd to Turkey, 10 Jun 1949.
Later history: renamed *Gaziantep* (G-3/D-22/D-344/D-348). Sunk as target 13 Mar 1979.

DD 487 *Lardner*   Decomm 16 May 1946. Trfd to Turkey, 10 Jun 1949.
Later history: renamed *Gemlik* (G-4/D-21/D-247). R1979; sunk as target 1 Nov 1982.

DD 488 *McCalla*   Out of comm 17 May 1946–11 Dec 1948. Trfd to Turkey 29 Apr 1949.
Later history: renamed *Giresun* (G-2/D-23/D-345). R1975.

DD 489 *Mervine*   (see DMS 31).

DD 490 *Quick*   (see DMS 32).

DD 491 *Farenholt*   Decomm 26 Apr 1946. Stricken 1 Jun 1971. Sold 22 Nov 1972. BU 1972 Kearny, NJ.

DD 492 *Bailey*   Decomm 2 May 1946. Stricken 1 Jun 1968. Sunk as target off Florida, 4 Nov 1969.

DD 493 *Carmick*   (see DMS 33).

DD 494 *Doyle*   (see DMS 34).

DD 495 *Endicott*   (see DMS 35).

DD 496 *McCook*   (see DMS 36).

DD 497 *Frankford*   Decomm 4 Mar 1946. Stricken 1 Jun 1971. Sunk as target 4 Dec 1973.

DD 598 *Bancroft*   Decomm 1 Feb 1946. Stricken 1 Jun 1971. Sold 16 Mar 1973, BU.

DD 600 *Boyle*   Decomm 29 Mar 1946. Stricken 1 Jun 1971. Sunk as target 3 May 1973.

DD 601 *Champlin*   Decomm 31 Jan 1947. Stricken 2 Jan 1971. Sold 8 May 1972, BU Houston, Tex.

DD 602 *Meade*   Decomm 17 Jun 1946. Stricken 1 Jun 1971. Sunk as target 19 Jun 1973.

DD 603 *Murphy*   Decomm 9 Mar 1946. Stricken 1 Nov 1970. Sold 6 Oct 1972, BU.

DD 604 *Parker*   Decomm 31 Jan 1947. Stricken 1 Jul 1971. Sold 25 May 1973, BU New Orleans.

DD 605 *Caldwell*   Decomm 24 Apr 1946. Stricken 1 May 1965. Sold 4 Nov 1966, BU Baltimore.

DD 606 *Coghlan*   Decomm 31 Mar 1947. Stricken 1 Jul 1971. Sold 29 May 1974, BU Camden, NJ.

DD 607 *Frazier*   Decomm 15 Apr 1946. Stricken 1 Jul 1971. Sold 6 Oct 1972, BU.

DD 608 *Gansevoort*   Decomm 1 Feb 1946. Stricken 1 Jul 1971. Sunk as target off Florida, 23 Mar 1972.

DD 609 *Gillespie*   Decomm 17 Apr 1946. Stricken 1 Jul 1971. Sunk as target off Puerto Rico, 16 Jul 1973.

DD 610 *Hobby*   Decomm 1 Feb 1946. Stricken 1 Jul 1971. Sunk as target off South Carolina, 28 Jun 1972.

DD 611 *Kalk*   Decomm 3 May 1946. Stricken 1 Jun 1968. Sunk as target off Florida, 20 Mar 1969.

DD 612 *Kendrick*   Decomm 31 Mar 1947. Stricken 1 May 1966. Sunk as target off Key West, 2 Mar 1968.

DD 613 *Laub*   Decomm 2 Feb 1946. Stricken 1 Jul 1971. Sold 12 Jun 1975, BU Baltimore.

DD 614 *Mackenzie*   Decomm 4 Feb 1946. Stricken 1 Jul 1971. Sunk as target off Florida, 6 May 1974.

DD 615 *McLanahan*   Decomm 2 Feb 1946. Stricken 1 Jul 1971. Sold 29 May 1974, BU Brownsville, Tex.

DD 616 *Nields*   Decomm 25 Mar 1946. Stricken 15 Sep 1970. Sold 8 May 1972, BU New Orleans.

DD 617 *Ordronaux*   Decomm Jan 1947. Stricken 1 Jul 1971. Sold 16 Mar 1973, BU.

DD 618 *Davison*   (see DMS 37).

DD 619 *Edwards*   Decomm 11 Apr 1946. Stricken 1 Jul 1971. Sold 25 May 1973, BU New Orleans.

DD 621 *Jeffers*   (see DMS 27).

DD 623 *Nelson*   Decomm 6 May 1946. Stricken 1 Mar 1968. Sold 18 Jul 1969, BU.

DD 624 *Baldwin*   Decomm 20 Jun 1946. Stricken 1 Jun 1961. Went aground on Montauk Point, NY, 16 Apr 1961. Scuttled off Long Island, 5 Jun 1961.

DD 626 *Satterlee*   Decomm 16 Mar 1946. Stricken 1 Dec 1970. Sold 8 May 1972, BU New Orleans.

DD 627 *Thompson*   (see DMS 38).

DD 628 *Welles*   Decomm 4 Feb 1946. Stricken 1 Mar 1968. Sold 18 Jul 1969, BU.

DD 632 *Cowie*   (see DMS 39).

DD 633 *Knight*   (see DMS 40).

DD 634 *Doran*   (see DMS 41).

DD 635 *Earle*   (see DMS 42).

DD 637 *Gherardi*   (see DMS 30).

DD 638 *Herndon*   Decomm 8 May 1946. Stricken 1 Jul 1971. Sunk as target off Florida, 23 May 1974.

DD 641 *Tillman*   Decomm 6 Feb 1947. Stricken 1 Jun 1970. Sold 8 May 1972, BU New Orleans.

DD 645 *Stevenson*   Decomm 27 Apr 1946. Stricken 1 Jun 1968. Sold 2 Jun 1970, BU Portsmouth, Va.

DD 646 *Stockton*   Decomm 16 May 1946. Stricken 1 Jul 1971. Sold 25 May 1973, BU New Orleans.

DD 647 *Thorn*   Decomm 6 May 1946. Stricken 1 Jul 1971. Sunk as target off Florida, 26 Aug 1974.

Notes: A proposal to convert two *Benson* class to corvettes (DDC) for use as convoy escorts as prototypes for the entire class was dropped in 1955.

Fletcher Class

DD 445 *Fletcher*   Out of comm 15 Jan 1947–3 Oct 1949. Rec **DDE 445**, 26 Mar 1949. Ran aground off Yangdo, Korea, 31 May 1952. Rec **DD 445**, 1 Jul 1962. Decomm 1 Aug 1969. Stricken 1 Aug 1969. Sold 22 Feb 1972, BU Taiwan.
5★Korea K-1 K-3 K-7 K-8 K-10; ★Vietnam Jan 1961, Nov 1965, Jan–Feb 1966, Dec 1966–Apr 1967, Mar–Aug 1968, Dec 1968–Apr 1969; ◆Quemoy-Matsu 21 Sep 1959.

DD 446 *Radford*   Out of comm 17 Jan 1946–17 Oct 1949. Rec **DDE 446**, 26 Mar 1949. FRAM II Nov 1960 Pearl Hbr NSYd. Rec **DD 446**, 1 Jul 1962. Decomm and stricken 10 Nov 1969. Sold Oct 1970, BU, Portland, Ore.
5★Korea K-1 K-3 K-7 K-8; 5★Vietnam Mar 1962, Mar–May, Jul–Aug 1965, Aug–Nov 1966, Sep 1967–Jan 1968, Apr–Jun 1969; ◆Taiwan Straits Aug–Sep 1958, Quemoy-Matsu Sep–Nov 1959, Mar, May 1962, Korea Mar–Apr 1969, Jun–Jul 1969.

DD 447 *Jenkins*   Out of comm 1 May 1946–2 Nov 1951. Rec **DDE 447**, 2 Jan 1951. FRAM II Jan 1961 Pearl Hbr NSYd. Rec **DD 447**, 1 Jul 1962. In collision with New Zealand frigate *Otago* at Pearl Harbor, 31 Aug 1964. Decomm and stricken 2 Jul 1969. Sold 17 Feb 1971, BU Taiwan.
1★Korea K-8; 5★Vietnam Feb–Apr 1965, Feb–Apr 1966, May–Oct 1967, Sep 1968–Jan 1969; ◆Taiwan Straits 14 Oct 1958.

DD 448 *La Vallette*   Decomm 16 Apr 1946. Stricken 1 Feb 1974. Sold to Peru for parts, 26 Jul 1974, BU.

DD 449 *Nicholas*   Out of comm 12 Jun 1946–19 Feb 1951. Rec **DDE 449**, 26 Mar 1949. FRAM II Jul 1960 Pearl Hbr NSYd. Rec **DD 449**, 1 Jul 1962. Decomm and stricken 30 Jan 1970. Sold Oct 1970, BU Portland, Ore.
5★Korea K-5 K-6 K-8 K-9 K-10; 9★Vietnam Mar–Apr 1961, May 1964, Apr 1965, Oct 1965–Feb 1966, Dec 1966–Jan 1967, Mar–Apr 1967, Mar–Aug 1968, Aug–Nov 1969; ◆OpCastle; Korea Jul 1969.

DD 450 *O'Bannon*   Out of comm 21 May 1946–19 Feb 1951. Rec **DDE 450**, 26 Mar 1949. Rec **DD 450**, 1 Jul 1962. Stricken 30 Jan 1970. Sold 6 Jun 1970, BU.
3★Korea K-7 K-8 K-10; ★Vietnam Jan–Mar 1965, Feb–Jun 1966, Oct 1967–Mar 1968, May–Oct 1969; ◆Taiwan Straits Aug–Sep 1958, Quemoy-Matsu Jan, Mar 1960, Korea Jan–Mar 1968, May–Sep 1969.

DD 465 *Saufley*   Out of comm 12 Jun 1946–15 Dec 1949. Rec **DDE 465**, 26 Mar 1949. Rec **EDDE 465**, 1 Jan 1951. Rec **EDD 465**, 1 Jul 1962. Decomm 29 Jan 1965. Stricken 1 Sep 1966. Sunk as target off Key West, 20 Feb 1968.
◆Cuba Mar–Oct 1962, Cuba Missile Crisis Oct–Nov 1962.

DD 466 *Waller*   Out of comm 10 Jun 1946–5 Jul 1950. Rec **DDE 466**, 26 Mar 1949. Rec **DD 466**, 1 Jul 1962. Collided with Soviet destroyer *Bessledniy* in Sea of Japan, 10 May 1967, and with DDGS O25, 11 May 1967. Decomm and stricken 15 Jul 1969. Sunk as target off Newport, RI, 17 Jun 1970.
2★Korea K-5 K-6; 2★Vietnam Oct–Nov 1968; ◆Cuba Apr 1961, Apr–Jun 1962, Cuba Missile Crisis Oct–Nov 1962.

DD 468 *Taylor*   Out of comm 31 May 1946–3 Dec 1951. Rec **DDE 468**, 2 Jan 1951. Rec **DD 468**, 1 Jul 1962. Decomm 3 Jun 1969. Stricken 2 Jul 1969. Trfd to Italy.
Later history: renamed *Lanciere* (D 560). R1971.
2★Korea K-8 K-10; 6★Vietnam Feb–Apr 1965, Mar–Apr 1966, May–Oct 1967, Aug 1968–Jan 1969; ◆Taiwan Straits Oct 1958, Quemoy-Matsu Jan 1959.

DD 470 *Bache*   Out of comm 4 Feb 1946–1 Oct 1951. Rec **DDE 470**, 2 Jan 1951. Rec **DD 470**, 1 Jul 1962. Wrecked in gale off Rhodes, Greece, 6 Feb 1968. Stricken 1 Mar 1968, BU.
2★Vietnam Nov 1965–Feb 1966; ◆Cuba Apr 1961, Jun–Aug 1962, Cuba Missile Crisis, Oct–Nov 1962, Dominican Rep. May 1965.

DD 471 *Beale*   Out of comm 11 Apr 1946–1 Nov 1951. Rec **DDE 471**, 2 Jan 1951. Rec **DD 471**, 1 Jul 1962. Stricken 1 Oct 1968. Sunk as target off Virginia, 24 Jun 1969.
1★Vietnam Jul–Nov 1966; ◆Cuba Apr 1961, Jun–Aug 1962, Cuba Missile Crisis Oct–Nov 1962.

DD 472 *Guest*   Decomm 4 Jun 1946. Trfd to Brazil, 5 Jun 1959.
Later history: renamed *Pará* (D 27). R1978.

DD 473 *Bennett*   Decomm 18 Apr 1946. Trfd to Brazil 15 Dec 1959.
Later history: renamed *Paraíba* (D28). R1978.

DD 474 *Fullam*   Decomm 15 Jan 1947. Used in nuclear tests 1958. Stricken 1 Jun 1962. Sunk as target off Cape Henry, Va., 7 Jul 1962

DD 475 *Hudson*   Decomm 31 May 1946. Stricken 1 Dec 1972. Sold 9 Nov 1973, BU Portland, Ore.

DD 478 *Stanly*   Decomm 15 Jan 1947. Stricken 1 Dec 1970. Sold 16 Dec 1971, BU Taiwan.

DD 479 *Stevens*   Decomm 2 Jul 1946. Stricken 1 Dec 1972. Sold 9 Nov 1973, BU Portland, Ore.

Figure 5.1: *Fletcher* class destroyer *Bache* (DD 470) was blown aground by gale force winds outside harbor in Rhodes, Greece, 6 Feb 1968.

DD 480	*Halford*	Decomm 15 May 1946. Stricken 1 May 1968. Sold 2 Apr 1970, BU 1970 Terminal I.	
DD 498	*Philip*	Out of comm Jan 1947–30 Jun 1950. Rec **DDE 498**, 26 Mar 1949. Bombarded targets in Wonsan harbor, 5 Dec 1952. Rec **DD 498**, 1 Jul 1962. Decomm 30 Sep 1968. Stricken 1 Oct 1968. Sold 15 Dec 1971. Foundered in tow in Pacific en route to BU, 2 Feb 1972. 5★Korea K-5 K-6 K-8 K-9 K-10; ★Vietnam Feb 1964, Jul–Sep 1965, Aug–Nov 1966, Sep 1967–Jan 1968; ◆OpCastle 1954.	
DD 499	*Renshaw*	Out of comm Feb 1947–2 Jun 1950. Rec **DDE 499**, 26 Mar 1949. Damaged by shore gunfire off Kojo, Korea, 11 Oct 1951. Rec **DD 499**, 1 Jul 1962. Decomm 14 Feb 1969. Stricken 14 Feb 1970. Sold 9 Sep 1970, BU Portland, Ore. 5★Korea K-5 K-6 K-8 K-9 K-10; 6★Vietnam Apr–Sep 1965, Aug–Nov 1966, Apr–Sep 1968, Jul 1969; ◆OpCastle 1954, Korea Aug 1969.	
DD 500	*Ringgold*	Decomm 23 Mar 1946. Trfd to West Germany 14 Jul 1959. **Later history:** renamed *Z-2* (D 171). Sold to Greece, 18 Sep 1981, renamed *Kimon* (D-65). R1987 BU 1993.	
DD 501	*Schroeder*	Decomm 29 Apr 1946. Stricken 1 Oct 1972. Sold 5 Dec 1973, BU New Orleans.	
DD 502	*Sigsbee*	Decomm 1 May 1946. Stricken 1 Dec 1974. Sold 29 Jul 1975, BU.	
DD 507	*Conway*	Out of comm 25 Jun 1946–48 Nov 1950. Rec **DDE 507**, 26 Mar 1949. Rec **DD 507**, 1 Jul 1962. Decomm and stricken 15 Nov 1969. Sunk as target off Chesapeake Bay, 26 Jun 1970. 1★Korea K-6; ★Vietnam Jul–Oct 1966; ◆Cuba Apr 1961, Apr–Jun 1962, Cuba Missile Crisis Oct–Nov 1962.	
DD 508	*Cony*	Out of comm 18 Jun 1946–17 Nov 1949. Rec **DDE 508**, 26 Mar 1949. Rec **DD 508**, 1 Jul 1962. Decomm and stricken 2 Jul 1969. Sunk as target off Puerto Rico, 20 Mar 1970. 2★Korea K-5 K-6; ★Vietnam Aug–Dec 1967; ◆Cuba Apr 1961, Apr–Jun 1962, Cuba Missile Crisis Oct–Nov 1962.	
DD 509	*Converse*	Decomm 23 Apr 1946. Trfd to Spain, 1 Jul 1959. **Later history:** renamed *Almirante Valdés* (D 23). R1986.	
DD 510	*Eaton*	Out of comm 21 Jun 1946–11 Dec 1951. Rec **DDE 510**, 2 Jan 1951. Damaged in collision with battleship *Wisconsin* off Virginia Capes, 7 May 1956. Rec **DD 510**, 1 Jul 1962. Decomm and stricken 2 Jul 1969. Sunk as target off Puerto Rico, 27 Mar 1970. ★Vietnam Jun 1967–Jan 1968; ◆Cuba Apr 1961, Jun–Jul 1961, Cuba Missile Crisis Oct–Nov 1962.	
DD 511	*Foote*	Decomm 18 Apr 1946. Stricken 1 Oct 1972. Sold 5 Dec 1973, BU New Orleans.	
DD 513	*Terry*	Decomm Jan 1947. Stricken 1 Apr 1974. Sold to Peru for parts, 26 Jul 1974, BU.	
DD 515	*Anthony*	Decomm 17 Apr 1946. Trfd to West Germany 17 Jan 1958. **Later history:** renamed *Z-1* (D 170). Sold to Greece for parts 1979, BU.	
DD 516	*Wadsworth*	Decomm 18 Apr 1946. Trfd to West Germany, 6 Oct 1959. **Later history:** renamed *Z-3* (D 172). To Greece, 30 Oct 1980, renamed *Nearchos* (D 65). BU 1993.	
DD 517	*Walker*	Out of comm 31 May 1946–15 Sep 1950. Rec **DDE 517**, 28 Mar 1949. Rec **DD 517**, 1 Jul 1962. Damaged in collision with Soviet destroyer off Hawaii, 11 May 1957. In collision with New Zealand frigate *Otago* at Pearl Harbor, 31 Aug 1964. Decomm and stricken 2 Jul 1969. Trfd to Italy 1969. **Later history:** renamed *Fante* (D 561). SE1978. 2★Korea K-7 K-8; 3★Vietnam Feb–Apr 1965, Feb–Jun 1966, May–Oct 1967, Aug 1968–Jan 1969.	
DD 519	*Daly*	Out of comm 18 Apr 1946–6 Jul 1951. Decomm 2 May 1960. Stricken 1 Dec 1974. Sold 22 Apr 1976, BU. 1★Korea K-10.	
DD 520	*Isherwood*	Out of comm 1 Feb 1946–5 Apr 1951. Decomm 11 Sep 1961. Trfd to Peru 8 Oct 1961. **Later history:** renamed *Guise* (DD 72). R1981. ◆Taiwan Straits Aug–Oct 1958, Quemoy-Matsu Nov 1960–Jan 1961.	
DD 521	*Kimberly*	Out of comm 5 Feb 1947–8 Feb 1951. Decomm 16 Jan 1954. Trfd to Taiwan 1 Jun 1967. **Later history:** renamed *An Yang* (997/918). R1999. Sunk as target SW of Ryukyu Is., 14 Oct 2003. 1★Korea K-7.	
DD 527	*Ammen*	Out of comm 15 Apr 1946–5 Apr 1951. Damaged in collision with destroyer *Collett* off San Diego, 19 Jul 1960, CTL (11 killed). Decomm 15 Sep 1960. Stricken 1 Oct 1960. Sold 20 Apr 1961, BU Terminal I. ◆Taiwan Straits Aug–Nov 1958.	
DD 528	*Mullany*	Out of comm 14 Feb 1946–8 Mar 1951. Decomm and stricken, 6 Oct 1971. Trfd to Taiwan. **Later history:** renamed *Chiang Yang* (947/909). R1999. ★Vietnam Jun–Aug 1965, Oct–Nov 1965, Nov 1966–Mar 1967, Mar–Jul 1968; ◆Taiwan Straits Aug–Nov 1958, Quemoy-Matsu Nov 1960–Jan 1961, Apr–May 1962.	
DD 530	*Trathen*	Out of comm 18 Jan 1946–1 Aug 1951. Decomm 11 May 1965. Stricken 1 Nov 1972. Used as target, BU Nov 1973. 1★Korea K-9; ★Vietnam Sep 1964; ◆Taiwan Straits Sep 1958–Jan 1959, Quemoy-Matsu Oct–Dec 1959, Jul–Aug 1962.	
DD 531	*Hazelwood*	Out of comm 18 Jan 1946–12 Sep 1951. Test ship for DASH system 1958–1963. Decomm 19 Mar 1965. Stricken 1 Dec 1974. Sold 14 Apr 1976, BU. ◆Cuba Jan–Feb 1962, Cuba Missile Crisis Oct–Nov 1962.	
DD 532	*Heermann*	Out of comm 12 Jun 1946–12 Sep 1951. Decomm 20 Dec 1957. Trfd to Argentina.14 Aug 1961. **Later history:** renamed *Brown* (D 20). R1982.	
DD 534	*McCord*	Out of comm 15 Apr 1947–1 Aug 1951. Decomm 9 Jun 1954. Stricken 1 Oct 1972. 2 Jan 1974, BU New Orleans. 2★Korea K-9 K-10.	
DD 535	*Miller*	Out of comm 19 Dec 1945–19 May 1951. NRT 1959–64. Decomm 30 Jun 1964. Renamed ***James Miller***, 5 Aug 1971. Stricken 1 Dec 1974. Sold 31 Jul 1975, BU. 2★Korea K-8 K-9; ◆Lebanon Jul–Sep 1958, Cuba Jan–Mar 1961.	
DD 536	*Owen*	Out of comm 10 Dec 1946–17 Aug 1951. Decomm 27 May 1958. Stricken 15 Apr 1973. Sold 27 Nov 1973, BU Portland, Ore. 2★Korea K-9 K-10.	
DD 537	*The Sullivans*	Out of comm 10 Jan 1946–6 Jul 1951. Decomm 7 Jan 1965. Stricken 1 Dec 1974. Trfd to City of Buffalo, NY, 21 Jun 1977. **Later history:** museum at Buffalo, NY. 2★Korea K-8 K-9; ◆Lebanon Jul–Sep 1958, Cuba Feb–Apr 1962, Cuba Missile Crisis Oct–Nov 1962.	
DD 538	*Stephen Potter*	Out of comm 21 Sep 1945–29 Mar 1951. Decomm 21 Apr 1958. Stricken 1 Dec 1972. Sold 9 Nov 1973, BU Portland, Ore. 1★Korea K-10.	
DD 539	*Tingey*	Out of comm Mar 1946–27 Jan 1951. Damaged in collision with DE *Vammen* off southern California, 1 Aug 1963. Decomm 30 Nov 1963. Stricken 1 Nov 1965. Sunk as target off San Francisco, 22 Apr 1966. 5★Korea K-5 K-6 K-7 K-8 K-9; ★Vietnam Mar 1962.	
DD 540	*Twining*	Out of comm 14 Jun 1946–10 Jun 1950. NRT 1947. Decomm 1 Jul 1971 and stricken. Trfd to Taiwan 16 Aug 1971. **Later history:** renamed *Kwei Yang* (956/908) (*Kuei Yang*) (DD 8). R1999. 5★Korea K-6 K-7 K-8 K-9 K-10; ◆Taiwan Straits Aug–Sep 1958, 14 Dec 1958, Quemoy-Matsu Feb–Mar 1961.	
DD 541	*Yarnall*	Out of comm 15 Jan 1947–28 Feb 1951. Decomm 30 Sep 1958. Trfd to Taiwan. 10 Jun 1968. **Later history:** renamed *Kun Yang* (934/919) (*Kuen Yang*) (DD 8). R1999. 5★Korea K-5 K-6 K-7 K-8 K-9.	

Figure 5.2: The *Fletcher* class destroyer *Bradford* (DD 545), still mounting five 5-inch guns. A tripod mast has been installed.

DD 544 *Boyd* Out of comm 15 Jan 1947–24 Nov 1950. Damaged in collision with m/v *Tamon Maru* off San Diego, 9 Nov 1955. Decomm 1 Oct 1969. Trfd to Turkey 1 Oct 1969.
Later history: renamed *Iskenderun* (D 343). R1982; BU 1984.
5★Korea K-5 K-6 K-7 K-8 K-9; ★Vietnam Feb–Jul 1965, Jun–Jul 1966, Apr–Jul 1968; ◆Taiwan Straits Aug 1958, Quemoy-Matsu Sep 1959, Aug–Oct 1960, Korea May 1968.

DD 545 *Bradford* Out of comm 11 Jul 1946–27 Oct 1950. Sank friendly small boat in error off Yangdo, Korea, 20 May 1953. Decomm 28 Sep 1962. Trfd to Greece 18 Oct 1962.
Later history: renamed *Thyella* (D-28). R1981.
6★Korea K-4 K-5 K-6 K-7 K-8 K-10; ◆Quemoy-Matsu May 1959, Aug–Oct 1960.

DD 546 *Brown* Out of comm 1 Aug 1946–27 Oct 1950. Decomm and trfd to Greece 18 Oct 1962.
Later history: renamed *Navarinon* (D-63). R1981.
5★Korea K-4 K-5 K-6 K-8 K-9; ◆Quemoy-Matsu May 1959, Oct–Nov 1960, 6 Jan 1961.

DD 547 *Cowell* Out of comm 22 Jul 1946–21 Sep 1951. Decomm and trfd to Argentina 17 Aug 1971.
Later history: renamed *Almirante Storni* (D 24). BU 1982.
2★Korea K-9 K-10; ★Vietnam Sep–Oct 1964; ◆Taiwan Straits Sep 1958, Quemoy-Matsu Dec 1959–Jan 1960, Mar–May 1961, Jul–Aug 1962.

DD 550 *Capps* Decomm 15 Jan 1947. Trfd to Spain, 15 May 1957.
Later history: renamed *Lepanto* (D 21). R1985.

DD 551 *David W. Taylor* Decomm 17 Aug 1946. Trfd to Spain 15 May 1957.
Later history: renamed *Almirante Ferrandiz* (D 22). R1980s.

DD 553 *John D. Henley* Decomm 30 Apr 1946. Stricken 1 May 1968. Sold May 1970, BU Portland, Ore.

DD 554 *Franks* Decomm 31 May 1946. Stricken 1 Dec 1972. Sold 7 Aug 1973, BU Portland, Ore.

DD 556 *Hailey* Out of comm 27 Jan 1946–27 Apr 1951. Recomm 3 Nov 1960. Trfd to Brazil 20 Jul 1961.
Later history: renamed *Pernambuco* (D 30). SE1972.
2★Korea K-8 K-9; ◆Lebanon Jul–Sep 1958.

DD 558 *Laws* Out of comm 10 Dec 1946–2 Nov 1951. NRT 1958. Decomm 30 Mar 1964. Stricken 15 Apr 1973. Sold 3 Dec 1973, BU Portland, Ore.
2★Korea K-9 K-10; ★Vietnam Apr 1962.

DD 561 *Prichett* Out of comm 14 Mar 1946–17 Aug 1951. Damaged in collision with destroyer *Cushing* off Korea, 19 Feb 1953. Decomm and stricken 10 Jan 1970. Trfd to Italy, 17 Jan 1970.
Later history: renamed *Geniere* (D 555). BU 1975.
2★Korea K-9 K-10; 6★Vietnam Aug–Oct 1964, Jun–Sep 1965, Aug–Nov 1966, Dec 1967–May 1968, Jul–Aug, Oct 1969; ◆Taiwan Straits Sep–Dec 1958, Quemoy-Matsu Nov 1959–Jan 1960, Mar–Jun 1961, Jul–Sep 1962, Korea Jun–Jul 1969.

DD 562 *Robinson* Out of comm 12 Jun 1946–3 Aug 1951. Decomm 1 Jun 1964. Stricken 1 Dec 1974. Sunk as target off Puerto Rico, 12 Apr 1982.

DD 563 *Ross* Out of comm 4 Jun 1946–27 Oct 1951. Decomm 6 Nov 1959. Stricken 1 Dec 1974. Sunk as target off Puerto Rico, 28 Jan 1975.

DD 564 *Rowe* Out of comm 31 Jan 1947–5 Oct 1951. Decomm 6 Nov 1959. Stricken 1 Dec 1974. Sunk as target off Puerto Rico, 23 Feb 1978.

DD 565 *Smalley* Out of comm Jan 1947–3 Jul 1951. Decomm 30 Sep 1957. Stricken 1 Apr 1965. Sold 4 Jan 1966, BU Portsmouth, Va.
1★Korea K-10.

DD 566 *Stoddard* Out of comm. Jan 1947–9 Mar 1951. Decomm 26 Sep 1969. Stricken 1 Jun 1975. Used as test platform, Pacific Missile Range. Sunk northwest of Hawaii off Kauai, 22 Jul 1997.
3★Vietnam Jul–Nov 1965, Dec 1966–Apr 1967, Jul–Nov 1968; ◆Taiwan Straits Aug–Oct 1958, Quemoy-Matsu Mar–Apr 1962.

DD 567 *Watts* Out of comm 12 Apr 1946–6 Jul 1951. NRT 1958–1962. Decomm 26 Sep 1969. Stricken 1 Feb 1974. Sold 16 Aug 1974, BU Tacoma, Wash.

DD 568 *Wren* Out of comm 13 Jul 1946–7 Sep 1951. Decomm Oct 1963. Stricken 1 Dec 1974. Sold 22 Oct 1975, BU Camden, NJ.
◆Cuba Dec 1961.

DD 569 *Aulick* Decomm 18 Apr 1946. Trfd to Greece 21 Aug 1959.
Later history: renamed *Sfendoni* (D-85) (*Sphendoni*). R1992. SE1993.

DD 570 *Charles Ausburne* Decomm 18 Apr 1946. Trfd to West Germany 12 Apr 1960.
Later history: renamed *Z-6* (D 180). R1969. BU.

DD 571 *Claxton* Decomm 18 Apr 1946. Trfd to West Germany 15 Dec 1959.
Later history: renamed *Z-4* (D 178) Sold to Greece for parts, 26 Feb 1981, BU.

DD 572 *Dyson* Decomm 31 Mar 1947. Trfd to West Germany 17 Feb 1960.
Later history: renamed *Z-5* (D 179). To Greece for parts 1982, BU.

DD 573 *Harrison* Decomm 1 Apr 1946. Stricken 1 May 1968. Trfd to Mexico 19 Aug 1970.
Later history: renamed *Cuauhtemoc* (E 02). R1982.

DD 574 *John Rodgers* Decomm 25 May 1946. Stricken 1 May 1968. Trfd to Mexico 19 Aug 1970.
Later history: renamed *Cuitlahuac* (E 01). R2002. To be returned to Mobile for restoration as museum, 2008.

DD 575 *McKee* Decomm 25 Feb 1946. Stricken 1 Oct 1972. Sold 5 Dec 1972, BU New Orleans.

DD 576 *Murray* Out of comm 27 Mar 1946–15 Nov 1951. Rec **DDE 576**, 2 Jan 1951. Rec **DD 576**, 1 Jul 1962, Decomm May 1965. Stricken 1 Jun 1965. Sold 16 Aug 1966, BU Baltimore.
◆Cuba Apr 1961, Jun–Jul 1962, Cuba Missile Crisis Oct–Nov 1962.

DD 577 *Sproston* Out of comm 18 Jan 1946–15 Sep 1950. Rec **DDE 577**, 28 Mar 1949. Rec **DD 577**, 1 Jul 1962. Decomm 30 Sep 1968. Stricken 1 Oct 1968. Sold 1971, BU Kaohsiung, Taiwan.
1★Korea K-8; 3★Vietnam Dec 1960–Jan 1961, Mar 1961, Jan–May 1966, Apr–Jul 1967; ◆Taiwan Straits Aug–Sep 1958, Quemoy-Matsu Sep–Oct 1959, Nov 1960.

DD 578 *Wickes* Decomm 20 Dec 1945. Stricken 1 Nov 1972. Sunk as target off Santa Rosa, Cal., 8 Apr 1974.

DD 580 *Young* Decomm Jan 1947. Stricken 1 May 1968. Sunk as target off Atlantic coast, 16 Apr 1970.

DD 581 *Charrette* Decomm 15 Jan 1947. Trfd to Greece 16 Jun 1959.
Later history: renamed *Velos* (D-16). R1991. Museum at Poros, Greece.

DD 582 *Conner* Decomm 5 Jul 1946. Trfd to Greece 15 Apr 1959.
Later history: renamed *Aspis* (D-06). R1991. BU 1998.

DD 583 *Hall* Decomm 10 Dec 1946. Trfd to Greece 9 Feb 1960.
Later history: renamed *Lonkhi* (D-56). R1990. BU 1997.

DD 585 *Haraden* Decomm 2 Jul 1946. Stricken 1 Nov 1972. Sunk as target off Point Mugu, Cal., Nov 1973.

DD 587 *Bell* Decomm 14 Jun 1946. Stricken 1 Nov 1972. Sunk as target, 11 May 1975.

DD 588 *Burns* Decomm 25 Jun 1946. Stricken 1 Nov 1972. Sunk as target, 20 Jun 1974.

DD 589 *Izard* Decomm 31 May 1946. Stricken 1 May 1968. Sold 2 Apr 1970, BU Terminal I.

DD 590 *Paul Hamilton* Decomm 24 Sep 1945. Stricken 1 May 1968. Sold 2 Apr 1970, BU Terminal I.

DD 592 *Howorth* Decomm 30 Apr 1946. Stricken 1 Jun 1961. Sunk as target off San Diego, 8 Mar 1962.

DD 593 *Killen* Decomm 9 Jul 1946. Stricken 1 Jan 1963. Used as target off Puerto Rico. Hulk sold 15 Apr 1975, BU.

DD 594 *Hart* Decomm 31 May 1946. Stricken 15 Apr 1973. Sold 14 Nov 1973, BU Portland, Ore.

DD 595 *Metcalfe* Decomm Mar 1946. Stricken 2 Jan 1971. Sold 6 Jun 1972, BU.

DD 596 *Shields* Out of comm 14 Jun 1946–15 Jul 1950. NRT 1947–49, 1963–72. Decomm 1 Jul 1972. Trfd to Brazil 1 Jul 1972.
Later history: renamed *Maranhão* (D 33). BU 1990.
3★Korea K-6 K-7 K-9; ◆Taiwan Straits Aug–Dec 1958, Quemoy-Matsu Feb–Mar 1961.

DD 597 *Wiley* Decomm 15 May 1946. Stricken 1 May 1968. Sold 2 Apr 1970, BU Terminal I.

DD 629 *Abbot* Out of comm 21 May 1946–26 Feb 1951. NRT 1964. Decomm 26 Mar 1965. Stricken 1 Dec 1974. Sold 1 Aug 1975, BU Baltimore.
◆Lebanon Aug–Sep 1958, Cuba Jul–Aug, Nov 1962.

DD 630 *Braine* Out of comm 26 Jul 1946–6 Apr 1951. Decomm and stricken, 17 Aug 1971 and trfd to Argentina.
Later history: renamed *Almirante Domecq Garcia* (D 23). Sunk as target 7 Oct 1983.
8★Vietnam Dec 1960–Jan 1961, Mar–Apr 1961, Mar 1964, Jun–Oct 1965, Oct–Dec 1966, Aug–Nov 1968, Apr 1969; ◆Taiwan Straits Aug–Nov 1958, Quemoy-Matsu Mar–Apr 1962.

DD 631 *Erben* Out of comm 31 May 1946–19 May 1951. Damaged by grounding near Kojo, Korea, 6 Jan 1952. Decomm 27 Jun 1958. To South Korea 1 May 1963.
Later history: renamed *Chung Mu* (DD 91/DD 911). R1988.
5★Korea K-6 K-7 K-8 K-9 K-10.

DD 642 *Hale* Out of comm 15 Jan 1947–24 Mar 1951. Decomm 30 Jul 1960. Trfd to Colombia 23 Jan 1961.
Later history: renamed *Antioquia* (DD 01). SE1972.
◆Lebanon Aug 1958, Taiwan Straits 22 Sep 1958.

DD 643 *Sigourney* Out of comm 20 Mar 1946–7 Sep 1951. Decomm 1 May 1960. Stricken 1 Dec 1974. Sold 31 Jul 1975, BU.

DD 644 *Stembel* Out of comm 31 May 1946–9 Nov 1951. Decomm 27 May 1958. Trfd to Argentina 7 Aug 1961.
Later history: renamed *Rosales* (D 22). SE1972.
2★Korea K-8 K-10.

DD 649 *Albert W. Grant* Decomm 16 Jul 1946. Stricken 14 Apr 1971. Sold 30 May 1972, BU.

DD 650 *Caperton* Out of comm 6 Jul 1949–6 Apr 1951. Decomm 27 Apr 1960. Stricken 1 Dec 1974. Sunk as target, 1980s.
1★Korea K-10.

DD 651 *Cogswell* Out of comm 30 Apr 1946–7 Jan 1951. Stricken 1 Oct 1968. Trfd to Turkey 1 Oct 1969.
Later history: renamed *Izmit* (D 342). R1980; BU 1984.
★Vietnam Dec 1960–Jan, Mar–Apr 1961, May 1962, Jun–Nov 1965, Dec 1966–Mar 1967; ◆Taiwan Straits Oct–Nov 1958, Quemoy-Matsu Mar–Apr 1962.

Figure 5.3: USS *Ingersoll* (DD 652), *Fletcher* class, 15 Aug 1955. The number 3 5-inch mount has been removed and the 40mm guns replaced by twin 3-inch guns. The pole foremast has been replaced by a tripod mast.

DD 652 *Ingersoll* Out of comm 19 Jul 1946–4 May 1951. Decomm and stricken 20 Jan 1970. Sunk as target.19 May 1974.
3★Vietnam Dec 1960–Apr 1961, May 1962, Feb–Mar 1964, Jul–Nov 1965, Dec 1966–Mar 1967, Jul–Nov 1968. ◆Taiwan Straits Sep–Nov 1958.

DD 653 *Knapp* Out of comm 5 Jul 1946–3 May 1951. Decomm 4 Mar 1957. Stricken 6 Mar 1972. Sold 27 Aug 1973, BU, Portland, Ore. Bridge on display at museum, Astoria, Ore.

DD 654 *Bearss* Out of comm 31 Jan 1947–7 Sep 1951. Decomm 30 Dec 1963. Stricken 1 Dec 1974. Sold 14 Apr 1976, BU.
◆Cuba Dec 1961–Jan 1962, Cuba Missile Crisis Oct–Nov 1962.

DD 655 *John Hood* Out of comm 3 Jul 1946–3 Aug 1951. Decomm 1964. Stricken 1 Dec 1974. Sold 12 Apr 1976, BU.

DD 656 *Van Valkenburgh* Out of comm 12 Apr 1946–8 Mar 1951. Decomm 26 Feb 1954. Trfd to Turkey 28 Feb 1967.
Later history: renamed *Izmir* (D-340). BU 1987.
1★Korea K-10.

DD 657 *Charles J. Badger* Out of comm 21 May 1946–10 Sep 1951. Decomm 20 Dec 1957. Stricken 1 Feb 1974. Sold to Chile for parts 17 May 1974, BU.

DD 658 *Colahan* Out of comm 14 Jun 1946–16 Dec 1950. NRT 1947. Decomm and stricken 1 Aug 1966. Sunk as target off San Diego, 18 Dec 1966.
5★Korea K-6 K-7 K-8 K-9 K-10; ★Vietnam Apr 1962.

DD 659 *Dashiell* Out of comm 30 Mar 1946–3 May 1951. Decomm 29 Apr 1960. Stricken 1 Dec 1974. Sold 21 Sep 1975. BU Wilmington, Del.
★Korea K-10.

DD 660 *Bullard* Decomm 20 Dec 1946. Stricken 1 Dec 1972. Sold 14 Nov 1973, BU New Orleans.

DD 661 *Kidd* Out of comm 10 Dec 1946–28 Mar 1951. Damaged in collision with m/v *Hainan* in Long Beach harbor, 21 Apr 1953. Decomm 19 Jun 1964. Stricken 1 Dec 1974.
Later history: Museum at Baton Rouge, La.
4★Korea K-6 K-7 K-8 K-9; ◆Taiwan Straits Aug–Sep 1958, Cuba Oct 1961–Jan 1962.

DD 662 *Bennion* Decomm 20 Jun 1946. Stricken 15 Apr 1971. Sold 30 May 1973, BU.

DD 663 *Heywood L. Edwards* Decomm 1 Jul 1946. Trfd to Japan 10 Mar 1959.
Later history: renamed *Ariake* (DD 183). Returned 9 Mar 1974. Sold to South Korea for parts 1975, BU.

DD 664 *Richard P. Leary* Decomm 10 Dec 1946. To Japan 10 Mar 1959.
Later history: renamed *Yugure* (DD 184). Returned 9 Mar 1974. Sold to South Korea for parts 1975, BU.

DD 665 *Bryant* Decomm 15 Jan 1947. Stricken 1 Jun 1969. Sunk as target off California, 24 Aug 1969.

DD 666 *Black* Out of comm 5 Aug 1946–18 Jul 1951. Sank South Korean intelligence boat in collision off Nando, 7 Mar 1953. Decomm 21 Sep 1969. Stricken 21 Sep 1969. Sold 17 Feb 1971, BU Taiwan.
2★Korea K-9 K-10; 3★Vietnam Jul 1958, May–Jun 1964, Feb–Jul 1965, Jul–Sep 1966, Sep 1967–Jan 1968; ◆Taiwan Straits Aug–Sep 1958, Quemoy-Matsu Jul–Oct 1959, Mar–Apr 1961, Aug 1962, Korea Feb–May 1969.

DD 667 *Chauncey* Out of comm 19 Dec 1945–18 Jul 1950. Decomm 14 May 1954. Stricken 1 Oct 1972. Sold 2 Jan 1974, BU New Orleans.
2★Korea K-9, K-10.

DD 668 *Clarence K. Bronson* Out of comm 16 Jul 1946–7 Jun 1951. Decomm 29 Jun 1960. Trfd to Turkey 14 Jan 1967
Later history: renamed *Istanbul* (D-340). BU 1987.
1★Korea K-10.

DD 669 *Cotten* Out of comm 15 Jul 1946–3 Jul 1951. Decomm 2 May 1960. Stricken 1 Dec 1974. Sold 31 Jul 1975, BU.
1★Korea K-10.

DD 670 *Dortch* Out of comm 19 Jul 1946–4 May 1951. Decomm 13 Dec 1957. Trfd to Argentina 14 Aug 1961
Later history: renamed *Espora* (D 21). BU 1977.
1★Korea K-10.

DD 671 *Gatling* Out of comm 16 Jul 1946–4 Jun 1951. Decomm 2 May 1960. Stricken 1 Dec 1974. Sold 22 Feb 1977, BU.
1★Korea K-10.

DD 672 *Healy* Out of comm 11 Jul 1946–3 Aug 1951. Decomm 11 Mar 1958. Stricken 1 Dec 1974. Sold 12 Apr 1976, BU.

DD 673 *Hickox* Out of comm 10 Dec 1946–19 May 1951. Decomm 20 Dec 1957. Trfd to South Korea 15 Nov 1968.
Later history: renamed *Pusan* (DD 93/DD 913). R1988. BU 1989.
2★Korea K-8 K-9.

DD 674 *Hunt* Out of comm 15 Dec 1945–31 Oct 1951. Decomm 30 Dec 1963. Stricken 1 Dec 1974. Sold 14 Aug 1975, BU Brownsville, Tex.
◆Lebanon Aug 1958.

DD 675 *Lewis Hancock* Out of comm 10 Jan 1946–19 May 1951. Decomm 18 Dec 1957. Trfd to Brazil 2 Aug 1967.
Later history: renamed *Piaui* (D 31). R1989.
2★Korea K-8 K-9.

DD 676 *Marshall* Out of comm Dec 1945–27 Apr 1951. In collision with destroyer *Gregory* off San Diego, 14 Apr 1952. Decomm and stricken 19 Jul 1969. Sold Jun 1970, BU Puget Sd NSYd.
4★Korea K-6 K-7 K-8 K-9; ◆Taiwan Straits Sep 1958, Quemoy-Matsu Jan–Feb 1961.

DD 677 *McDermut* Out of comm 15 Jan 1947–29 Dec 1950. In collision with destroyer *Gregory* off southern California, 10 Sep 1963. Decomm 16 Dec 1963. Stricken 1 Apr 1965. Sold 4 Jan 1966, BU Terminal I.
5★Korea K-5 K-6 K-7 K-8 K-9; ★Vietnam Feb–Mar 1962; ◆Taiwan Straits Aug–Sep 1958, Quemoy-Matsu Jul, Sep 1959, Sep–Oct 1960, May 1962.

DD 678 *McGowan* Out of comm 30 Apr 1946–6 Jul 1951. Decomm 30 Nov 1960. Trfd to Spain.
Later history: renamed *Jorge Juan* (D 25). R1988.
2★Korea K-8 K-9; ◆Lebanon Jul–Sep 1958.

DD 679 *McNair* Out of comm 28 May 1946–6 Jul 1951. Decomm 30 Dec 1963. Stricken 1 Dec 1974. Sold 10 Jun 1976. BU Camden, NJ.
2★Korea K-8 K-9; ◆Lebanon Jul–Sep 1958, Cuba May 1961, Oct 1961–Feb 1962.

DD 680 *Melvin* Out of comm 31 May 1946–26 Feb 1951. Decomm 13 Jan 1954. Stricken 1 Dec 1974. Sold 29 Aug 1975, BU Camden, NJ.

DD 681 *Hopewell* Out of comm 15 Jan 1947–28 Mar 1951. Damaged when aircraft crashed into superstructure off California, 11 Nov 1955 (5 killed). Decomm and stricken, 2 Jan 1970. Sunk as target off southern California, 11 Feb 1972.
4★Korea K-6 K-7 K-8 K-9; ★Vietnam Aug 1964–Jan 1965, Apr–Jul 1966, Jul–Nov 1967, Dec 1968–Apr 1969; ◆Taiwan Straits Aug–Sep 195K-8 Quemoy-Matsu Oct–Nov 1960.

DD 682 *Porterfield* Out of comm 15 Jul 1946–27 Apr 1951. Hit by shore battery near Chodo Island, Korea, 3 Feb 1952. Decomm 7 Nov 1969. Stricken 1 Mar 1975. Sunk as target off west coast, 18 Jul 1982.
4★Korea K-6 K-7 K-8 K-9; ★Vietnam Oct–Dec 1958, Jan 1961, Apr 1963, Sep 1964–Jan 1965; ◆Taiwan Straits Aug–Dec 1958, Quemoy-Matsu Oct–Dec 1958, Nov 1959–Jan 1960, Jan–Mar 1961, Dec 1962–Feb 1963.

DD 683 *Stockham* Out of comm Nov 1947–14 Nov 1951. Decomm 2 Sep 1957. Stricken 1 Dec 1974. Sunk as target off Puerto Rico, 15 Feb 1977.

DD 684 *Wedderburn* Out of comm 4 Apr 1946–21 Nov 1950. NRT Aug 1946–1950. Decomm and stricken 1 Oct 1969. Sold 25 Jan 1972, BU Taiwan.
4★Korea K-6 K-7 K-8 K-9; 6★Vietnam Sep–Nov 1964, Jan 1965, Feb–May 1966, May–Sep 1967, Dec 1968–Apr 1969; ◆Taiwan Straits Aug–Sep 1958, Aug–Oct 1960, Apr–May 1963.

DD 685 *Picking* Out of comm 20 Dec 1945–26 Jan 1951. Damaged in collision with carrier *Ticonderoga* in South China Sea, 15 Oct 1961. Decomm 6 Sep 1969. Stricken 1 Mar 1975. Sunk as target off Point Mugu, Cal. 27 Feb 1997.
1★Korea K-10; ★Vietnam Sep 1964, Aug–Sep, Nov–Dec 1965, Jan–May 1967, Mar–Jul 1968; ◆Taiwan Straits Nov 1958, Quemoy-Matsu Jan 1959, Feb–Mar 1960, Oct, Dec 1961–Jan 1962.

DD 686 *Halsey Powell* Out of comm 10 Dec 1946–27 Apr 1951. Decomm 27 Apr 1968. Trfd to South Korea.
Later history: renamed *Seoul* (DD 92). SE1972.
4★Korea K-6 K-7 K-8 K-9; ◆Taiwan Straits Aug–Nov 1958, Quemoy-Matsu Sep 1958, Jan–Feb 1961.

DD 687 *Uhlmann* Out of comm 14 Jun 1946–23 May 1950. NRT 1947. Damaged by shore gunfire off Chaho, Korea, 3 Nov 1952. Damaged by grounding in Pescadores Is., 3 Mar 1954, while assisting a grounded m/v. Decomm and stricken 15 Jul 1972. Sold 21 Mar 1974, BU Portland, Ore.
4★Korea K-6 K-7 K-8 K-9; 5★Vietnam May–Sep 1965, Sep 1966–Jan 1967, Feb–Jul 1968; ◆Quemoy-Matsu Jul–Aug 1959, Oct–Nov 1960, Korea Aug–Sep 1968.

DD 688 *Remey* Out of comm 10 Dec 1946–14 Nov 1951. Decomm 30 Dec 1963. Stricken 1 Dec 1974. Sold 29 Aug 1975, BU Camden, NJ.

DD 689 *Wadleigh* Out of comm Jan 1947–3 Oct 1951. Collided with submarine *Thomas Edison* off Virginia Capes, 9 Apr 1962. Decomm 28 Jun 1962. Trfd to Chile 26 Jul 1962.
Later history: renamed *Blanco Encalada* (DD 14). BU 1983.
◆Lebanon Jul–Sep 1958.

DD 690 *Norman Scott* Decomm 30 Apr 1946. Stricken 15 Apr 1973. Sold 14 Nov 1973, BU Portland, Ore.

DD 691 *Mertz* Decomm 23 Apr 1946. Stricken 1 Oct 1970. Sold 16 Dec 1971. BU Taiwan.

DD 793 *Cassin Young* Out of comm 28 May 1946–8 Sep 1951. Decomm 29 Apr 1960. Stricken 1 Dec 1974.
Later history: Museum at Boston, Mass.

DD 794 *Irwin* Out of comm 21 May 1946–26 Feb 1951. Decomm 10 Jan 1958. Trfd to Brazil 10 May 1968
Later history: renamed *Santa Catarina* (D 32). R1989.
1★Korea K-10.

DD 795 *Preston* Out of comm 24 Apr 1946–26 Jan 1951. Decomm and stricken and trfd to Turkey 15 Nov 1969.
Later history: renamed *Içel* (D-344). BU 1981.
1★Korea K-10; ★Vietnam Jun–Aug 1964, Aug 1965–Jan 1966, May–Aug 1967, Sep–Dec 1968; ◆Taiwan Straits Nov 1958, Quemoy-Matsu Nov 1958.

DD 796 *Benham* Out of comm 18 Oct 1946–24 Mar 1951. Decomm and trfd to Peru 15 Dec 1960.
Later history: renamed *Villar* (D 71). R1980.
◆Lebanon Aug, Oct 1968.

DD 797 *Cushing* Out of comm 3 Feb 1947–17 Aug 1951. Damaged in collision with destroyer *Prichett* off Korea, 19 Feb 1953. Decomm 8 Nov 1960. Trfd to Brazil 20 Jul 1961.
Later history: renamed *Paraná* (D 29). BU 1982.
2★Korea K-9 K-10; ◆Taiwan Straits Sep, Dec 1958, Quemoy-Matsu Nov 1959–Jan 1960.

DD 798 *Monssen* Out of comm 30 Apr 1946–31 Oct 1951. Decomm 11 Dec 1957. Went aground in tow near Beach Haven, NJ, 6 Mar 1962; refloated 19 Apr 1962. Stricken 1 Feb 1963. Sold 21 Oct 1963, BU.

DD 799 *Jarvis* Out of comm 29 Jun 1946–8 Feb 1951. Decomm 24 Oct 1960. Trfd to Spain 3 Nov 1960.
Later history: renamed *Alcalá Galiano* (D 24). BU 1988.
1★Korea K-8; ◆Taiwan Straits Sep–Oct 1958, Dec 1958, Quemoy-Matsu Oct–Nov 1959.

DD 800 *Porter* Out of comm 3 Jul 1946–9 Feb 1951. Collided with destroyer *Picking* off Virginia coast, 16 Nov 1952. Decomm 10 Aug 1953. Stricken 1 Oct 1972. Sold 21 Mar 1974, BU.
1★Korea K-8.

DD 802 *Gregory* Out of comm 15 Jan 1947–27 Apr 1951. In collision with destroyer *Marshall* off San Diego, 14 Apr 1952. Damaged in collision with destroyer *Benner* off California, 18 Feb 1963. In collision with destroyer *McDermut* off southern California, 10 Sep 1963. Decomm 1 Feb 1964. Stricken 1 May 1966. Used as non-seagoing training ship *Indoctrinator* at San Diego. Grounded as target on San Clemente I., 4 Mar 1971.
4★Korea K-6 K-7 K-8 K-9; ★Vietnam Feb–Mar 1962; ◆Taiwan Straits Aug–Nov 1958, Quemoy-Matsu Nov 1959, Nov–Dec 1960, Jan–May 1962.

DD 804 *Rooks* Out of comm 11 Jun 1946–19 May 1951. Decomm and trfd to Chile 26 Jul 1962.
Later history: renamed *Cochrane* (DD 15). SE1972.
2★Korea K-8 K-9; ◆Lebanon Jul–Aug 1958.

Notes: 18 converted to DDE: 445, 446, 449, 450, 465, 507, 508, 517, 577 in 1948; 466, 498, 499 in 1949; 447, 468, 470, 471, 510, 576 in 1950. In remaining units, one 5″ gun and 5 TT removed; 40 mm guns replaced by 3″. Many had pole foremasts replaced by tripods. Also, number 3 5-inch mount was removed and 40 mm guns replaced by 3 twin 3-inch guns. *Hazelwood* was modified to serve as test ship for DASH program with helicopter hangar and platform fitted amidships.

Sumner Class

DD 692 *Allen M. Sumner* FRAM II Dec 1961 Charleston NSYd. Went aground off French Riviera, 8 Jun 1962. Decomm and stricken 15 Aug 1973. Sold 13 Nov 1974, BU Philadelphia.
1★Korea K-10; 2★Vietnam Feb–Aug 1967; ◆Cuba Feb 1962, Cuba Missile Crisis Oct–Nov 1962, Dominican Rep Apr–May, Aug–Sep 1965.

DD 693 *Moale* FRAM II Dec 1961 Charleston NSYd. Decomm and stricken 2 Jul 1973. Sold 13 Nov 1974, BU Brownsville, Tex.
1★Korea K-10; ◆Cuba Mar–Apr 1962.

DD 694 *Ingraham* FRAM II Dec 1961 Norfolk NSYd. Decomm 16 Jun 1971. Trfd to Greece 16 Jul 1971.
Later history: renamed *Miaoulis* (D-211). R1992. Sunk as target, 2 Oct 2001.
1★Korea K-10; ★Vietnam Nov 1965–Feb 1966; ◆Cuba Jan 1962, Cuba Missile Crisis Oct–Nov 1962.

DD 696 *English* Lost bow in collision with destroyer *Wallace L. Lind* in N. Atlantic, 31 Oct 1953. Decomm and stricken 15 May 1970. Trfd to Taiwan, 11 Aug 1970.

Figure 5.4: *USS Ault* (DD 698), *Sumner* class, June 1956. (T. Rayner) Notice twin 3-inch guns replacing aft bank of torpedo tubes.

Later history: renamed *Huei Yang* (972/906). R1999. Sunk as target, 14 Oct 2003.
4★Korea K-1 K-2 K-4 K-5; ◆Cuba Apr–Jun 1961, Cuba Missile Crisis Oct–Nov 1962.

DD 697 *Charles S. Sperry* Out of comm 15 Mar 1948–1 Jul 1950. Damaged by coastal batteries off Songjin, Korea, 23 Dec 1950. FRAM II Jun 1960 Norfolk NSYd. Decomm and stricken 15 Dec 1973. Trfd to Chile 8 Jan 1974.
Later history: renamed *Ministro Zenteno*. R1990.
4★Korea K-1 K-2 K-4 K-5; ★Vietnam Dec 1965–Feb 1966; ◆Cuba Jul–Aug 1961, Cuba Missile Crisis Oct–Nov 1962.

DD 698 *Ault* Out of comm 31 May 1950–15 Nov 1950. Damaged in collision with destroyer *Haynsworth* in Sea of Japan, lost bow, 20 Dec 1953. FRAM II Dec 1962 Boston NSYd. NRT 1970. Decomm 16 Jul 1973. Stricken 16 or 1 Sep 1973. Sold 9 May 1974, BU Baltimore.
2★Vietnam Mar–Aug 1967; ◆Lebanon Oct 1958, Cuba Mar–May 1961.

DD 699 *Waldron* Out of comm 17 May 1950–20 Nov 1950. FRAM II Dec 1962 Norfolk NSYd. In collision with tug *Kiowa* in Atlantic, 13 Jun 1968. Decomm and stricken 30 Oct 1973. Trfd to Colombia 30 Oct 1973.
Later history: renamed *Santander* (DD 03). R1984.
1★Vietnam Aug–Dec 1967; ◆Cuba Apr–May 1961.

DD 700 *Haynsworth* Out of comm 19 May 1950–22 Sep 1950. Damaged in collision with destroyer *Ault* off Japan, 20 Dec 1953. Decomm and stricken 30 Jan 1970. Trfd to Taiwan 12 May 1970.
Later history: renamed *Yuen Yang* (944/905). R1999.
◆Lebanon Oct 1958, Cuba Apr–May 1961, May–Jun 1962, Cuba Missile Crisis Oct–Nov 1962.

DD 701 *John W. Weeks* NRT 26 Apr 1946. Out of comm 31 May 1950–24 Oct 1950. Decomm and stricken 12 Aug 1970. Sunk as target off Virginia, 19 Nov 1970.
★Vietnam Mar–Jul 1969; ◆Cuba Mar–May 1961, Cuba Missile Crisis Oct–Nov 1962, Korea Apr 1969.

DD 702 *Hank* Decomm and stricken 1 Jul 1972, and trfd to Argentina.
Later history: renamed *Segui* (D 25). R1982.
4★Korea K-1 K-2 K-4 K-5; ◆Cuba Apr–Jun 1961, Cuba Missile Crisis Oct–Nov 1962.

DD 703 *Wallace L. Lind* Damaged in collision with destroyer *English* in North Atlantic, 31 Oct 1953. FRAM II Jul 1962 Norfolk NSYd. Decomm and stricken 4 Dec 1973 and trfd to South Korea.
Later history: renamed *Dae Gu/ Daegu* (DD 917). SE1993.
4★Korea K-1 K-2 K-4 K-5; 3★Vietnam May–Oct 1968, Sep 1970–Feb 1971; ◆Cuba Sep–Oct 1962, Cuba Missile Crisis Oct–Nov 1962, Korea Sep 1970.

DD 704 *Borie* Out of comm 11 Dec 1948–19 Sep 1949. FRAM II Jun 1962 Norfolk NSYd. Decomm and stricken 1 Jul 1972 and trfd to Argentina.
Later history: renamed *Hipolito Bouchard* (D 26). R1984; BU 1992.
4★Korea K-1 K-2 K-4 K-5; ★Vietnam May–Oct 1968; ◆Cuba Aug–Oct 1962, Cuba Missile Crisis Oct–Dec 1962.

DD 705 *Compton* Decomm and stricken 27 Sep 1972 and trfd to Brazil.
Later history: renamed *Mato Grosso* (D 34). BU 1990.

DD 706 *Gainard* Decomm and stricken 26 Feb 1971. Transfer to Iran canceled. Sold 26 Mar 1974, BU Baltimore.
◆Cuba Jul–Sep 1961, Cuba Missile Crisis Oct–Nov 1962.

DD 707 *Soley* Out of comm 15 Apr 1947–29 Jan 1949. Lost by grounding, Jan 1970. Decomm 13 Feb 1970. Stricken 1 Jul 1970. Sunk as target off Norfolk, 18 Sep 1970.
1★Korea K-7; ◆Cuba Missile Crisis Oct–Nov 1962.

DD 708 *Harlan R. Dickson* Ran aground in Cape Cod Canal, 27 Jul 1970. Decomm and stricken 1 Jul 1972. Sold 27 Apr 1973, BU Baltimore.
★Cuba Aug 1961, Cuba Missile Crisis Oct–Dec 1962.

DD 709 *Hugh Purvis* FRAM II Oct 1960 Boston NSYd. Decomm 15 Jun 1972. Trfd to Turkey 1 Jul 1972.
Later history: renamed *Zafer* (D-356). R1993; BU 1994.
★Vietnam Oct 1968–Feb 1969; ◆Cuba Sep 1962, Cuba Missile Crisis Oct–Nov 1962.

DD 722 *Barton* Out of comm 22 Jan 1947–11 Apr 1949. Slightly damaged by shore gunfire off east coast of Korea, 10 Aug 1952. Damaged by mine east of Wonsan, Korea, 16 Sep 1952 (5 killed). Decomm and stricken 1 Oct 1968. Sunk as target off Virginia, 8 Oct 1969.
2★Korea K-7 K-8; ◆Cuba Jun–Jul 1961, Cuba Missile Crisis Oct–Nov 1962.

DD 723 *Walke* Out of comm 30 Jun 1947–5 Oct 1950. Severely damaged by mine off North Korea, 12 Jun 1951 (26 killed). FRAM II Oct 1961 Mare I NSYd. Damaged by fire and ran aground at Long Beach, Cal., 9 Jun 1966. Decomm 30 Nov 1970. Stricken 1 Feb 1974. Sold 19 Mar 1975, BU Tacoma.
4★Korea K-4 K-5 K-8 K-9; 7★Vietnam Aug–Sep 1965, May–Jun, Aug–Oct 1966, May 1967–Feb 1968, May–Oct 1969; ◆Korea Jan–Mar 1968, Oct 1969.

DD 724 *Laffey* Out of comm 30 Jun 1947–26 Jan 1951. FRAM II Sep 1962 Norfolk NSYd. Decomm and stricken 29 Mar 1975.
Later history: museum at Patriots Point, SC.
2★Korea K-7 K-8.

DD 725 *O'Brien* Out of comm 4 Oct 1947–5 Oct 1950. FRAM II Oct 1961 Mare I NSYd. Damaged by shore gunfire off Dong Hoi, Vietnam, 23 Dec 1966 (2 killed). Decomm and stricken 18 Feb 1972. Sunk as target off southern California, 13 Jul 1972.
5★Korea K-4 K-5 K-6 K-8; 8★Vietnam Nov 1965, Jan–Feb 1966, Dec 1966–Apr 1967, Jun–Oct 1968, Dec 1969–Mar 1970, Dec 1970–Apr 1971; ◆Korea Jan 1970, Iran/Indian Ocean Apr–Aug 1980.

DD 727 *De Haven* FRAM II Aug 1960 San Fran NSYd. Decomm 3 Dec 1973. Trfd to South Korea 5 Dec 1973.
Later history: renamed *Inchon* (D 918). BU 1993.
6★Korea K-1 K-3 K-6 K-7 K-8 K-9; ★Vietnam Aug–Sep, Nov 1963, Jun 1964, Jul–Nov 1965, Aug–Nov 1966, Jan–May 1967, Aug 1967–Jul 1968, Oct–Nov 1969, Jan–Feb 1970, Dec 1970–Apr 1971; ◆Taiwan Straits Sep–Oct 1958, Quemoy-Matsu Sep–Oct 1959, Oct–Dec 1961, 19 Jul 1962.

DD 728 *Mansfield* Damaged by mine and lost bow off Chongjin, Korea, 30 Sep 1950 (5 killed). FRAM II Sep 1960 Long Bch NSYd. Decomm and stricken 1 Feb 1974. Trfd to Argentina for parts 4 Jun 1974.
★Korea K-1 K-3 K-6 K-7; ★Vietnam Jan 1962, Sep–Dec 1965, Aug–Nov 1966, Jan, Mar–Jul, Sep 1967–Jun 1968, Oct 1969–Feb 1970; ◆Taiwan Straits Aug–Oct 1958, Quemoy-Matsu Sep–Oct 1959, 16 Jul 1962, Korea 30 Oct 1969.

DD 729 *Lyman K. Swenson* FRAM II Jan 1961 Mare I NSYd. Decomm 12 Feb 1971. Stricken 1 Feb 1974. Sold 6 May 1974, BU.
6★Korea K-1 K-3 K-6 K-7 K-8 K-9; ★Vietnam May 1963, Aug–Nov 1963, Apr–May 1964, Oct 1965–Jan 1966, May–Sep 1967, Jan–Apr 1969, Apr–Aug 1970; ◆Taiwan Straits Aug–Sep 1958, Quemoy-Matsu Aug–Sep 1959, Aug–Sep 1962, Korea Mar–Apr 1969.

DD 730 *Collett* Damaged by shore gunfire off Inchon, 13 Sep 1950. Damaged in collision with destroyer *Ammen* off Long Beach, Cal, 19 Jul 1960. Bow replaced from incomplete *Seaman*. FRAM II Aug 1960 Long Bch NSYd. Decomm 18 Dec 1970. Stricken 1 Feb 1974 and trfd to Argentina.
Later history: renamed *Piedrabuena* (D 29). R1984. BU 1992. Sunk as target 1988.
6★Korea K-1 K-3 K-6 K-7 K-8 K-9; ★Vietnam Apr–May 1962, May 1963, Jun–Aug 1965, Aug–Nov 1966, Jan–Dec 1967, Mar–Jul 1968, Oct 1969–Feb 1970; ◆Taiwan Straits Sep–Oct 1958, Quemoy-Matsu Sep–Oct 1959, Aug–Sep 1962, Korea Jan–Mar 1968, 10 Dec 1969.

DD 731 *Maddox* Attacked by North Vietnam torpedo boats off coast of Vietnam, 2–4 Aug 1964; Gulf of Tonkin incident, 2–5 Aug 1964. Decomm 1 Jul 1972. Stricken 6 Jul 1972 and trfd to Taiwan.
Later history: renamed *Po Yang* (928/910). R1985.
6★Korea K-1 K-2 K-7 K-8 K-9 K-10; ★Vietnam Aug–Sep 1964, Aug–Nov 1965, Oct 1966–Aug 1967, Aug–Dec 1968.

DD 732 *Hyman* Slightly damaged by shore batteries off Kalma-Gak, Korea, 23 Nov 1951. Decomm and stricken 16 Nov 1969. Sold 13 Oct 1970, BU New Orleans.
2★Korea K-6 K-7; ◆Cuba Oct–Dec 1961.

DD 734 *Purdy* Sank British m/v *British Columbian* in collision off Dutch coast, 22 Sep 1957. Decomm and stricken 2 Jul 1973. Sold 11 Jun 1974, BU Baltimore.
3★Korea K-6 K-7 K-10; ◆Cuba Oct–Dec 1961, Cuba Missile Crisis Oct–Nov 1962.

DD 744 *Blue* Out of comm 14 Feb 1947–14 May 1949 and 12 Dec 1949–15 Sep 1950. FRAM II Jan 1961 S.Fran NSYd. Minor damage from shore fire off North Vietnam, 16 Jul 1968. Decomm 27 Jan 1971. Stricken 1 Feb 1974. Sunk as target off southern California, 28 Apr 1977.
6★Korea K-4 K-5 K-6 K-7 K-8 K-10; ★Vietnam May–Jun 1964, Jul–Aug 1965, Jul 1966–Jan 1967, Mar–Aug 1967, Oct 1967–Mar 1968, Jun–Jul 1968, Oct–Dec 1969; ◆Quemoy-Matsu Aug 1959, Nov 1962–Feb 1963, Korea Feb 1968, 10 Dec 1969.

DD 745 *Brush* Damaged by mine off Tanchon, North Korea, 26 Sep 1950 (13 killed). Damaged by shore gunfire off Wonsan, 15 May 1953. Decomm and stricken 27 Oct 1969. Trfd to Taiwan 9 Dec 1969.
Later history: renamed *Hsiang Yang* (986/901). R1984.
5★Korea K-1 K-7 K-8 K-9 K-10; ★Vietnam May 1960, Jul–Aug 1964, Dec 1965–Apr 1966, May–Sep 1967, Jan–Feb 1969.

DD 746 *Taussig* In collision with DE *Marsh* in Pacific, 28 Feb 1949. FRAM II Sep 1962 Long Bch NSYd. Decomm 1 Dec 1970. Stricken 1 Sep 1973. Trfd to Taiwan 6 May 1974.
Later history: renamed *Lo Yang* (949/914). R2000.
8★Korea K-1 K-2 K-3 K-4 K-6 K-7 K-9 K-10; 6★Vietnam Feb–Apr 1965, May–Sep 1966, Mar–May 1968, Jun–Oct 1969; ◆Taiwan Straits Oct–Nov 1958, Quemoy-Matsu Jan–Feb 1960, Korea Jan–Mar 1968, Aug 1969.

DD 747 *Samuel N. Moore* Damaged by shore gunfire off Hungnam, Korea, 17 Oct 1951, and again off Wonsan, 8 Apr 1953. Decomm and stricken 24 Oct 1969. Trfd to Taiwan 10 Dec 1969.
Later history: renamed *Heng Yang* (976/902). R1995
6★Korea K-1 K-2 K-7 K-8 K-9 K-10; 7★Vietnam May–Aug 1964, Nov 1965–Mar 1966, Apr–Aug 1967, Aug 1968–Jan 1969; ◆Korea 2–4 Dec 1968.

DD 748 *Harry E. Hubbard* Out of comm 15 Jan 1947–14 May 1949, 12 Dec 1949–27 Oct 1950. Decomm and stricken 17 Oct 1969. Sold Jun 1970, BU Portland, Ore.

DD 752 *Alfred A. Cunningham* Out of comm 12 May 1947–5 Oct 1950. Damaged by shore gunfire off Songjin, Korea, 19 Sep 1952 (none killed). FRAM II Sep 1961 Long Bch NSYd. Decomm 24 Feb 1971. Stricken 1 Feb 1974. Sunk as target off Point Mugu, Cal., 12 Oct 1979.
6★Korea K-4 K-5 K-6 K-7 K-8 K-10; 7★Vietnam Oct 1965, Jan–Feb 1966, Jan–Feb 1967, Jan, Mar–Apr, Jul–Oct 1968, Nov 1969–Mar 1970; ◆Laos Jan 1970.

5★Korea K-4 K-5 K-6 K-8 K-9; ★Vietnam Mar–Apr 1962, Sep–Oct 1964, Nov 1965–Mar 1966, Apr–Aug 1967, Aug 1968–Jan 1969; ◆Quemoy-Matsu Jul–Aug 1960, May–Jun 1962.

DD 753 *John R. Pierce* Out of comm 24 Jan 1947–11 Apr 1949. Slightly damaged by shore gunfire off Songjin, Korea, 6 Aug 1952. Decomm and stricken 2 Jul 1973. Sold 6 Nov 1974, BU Chester, Pa.
1★Korea K-8; ◆Cuba Missile Crisis Oct–Nov 1962.

DD 754 *Frank E. Evans* Out of comm 14 Dec 1949–15 Sep 1950. Damaged by coastal gunfire off Wonsan, 18 Jun 1951. FRAM II Oct 1961 Long Bch NSYd. Cut in two in collision with Australian carrier *Melbourne* in South China Sea, 2 Jun 1969, bow sank (74 killed). Stricken 1 Jul 1969. Stern sunk as target off Subic Bay, 10 Oct 1969.
6★Korea K-4 K-5 K-6 K-7 K-8 K-9 K-10; ★Vietnam Jul–Sep 1965, Aug–Nov 1966, Oct 1967–Feb 1968, May 1969; ◆Korea Jan–Mar 1968.

DD 755 *John A. Bole* FRAM II Aug 1962 S.Fran NSYd. Decomm 6 Nov 1970. Stricken 1 Feb 1974. Trfd to Taiwan for parts, 6 May 1974, BU.
7★Korea K-2 K-4 K-5 K-7 K-8 K-9 K-10; ★Vietnam Feb–Apr 1965, Apr–Aug 1966, Mar–Jun 1968, Feb–May 1970.
◆Taiwan Straits 13 Oct 1958, 19–21 Nov 1958, Quemoy-Matsu Jan 1960, Korea Jan–Mar 1968, 12 Apr 1970.

DD 756 *Beatty* Severely damaged in collision with CV *Intrepid* in English Channel, 7 Jul 1958. Decomm 14 Jul 1972. Stricken 1 Aug 1972. Trfd to Venezuela 14 Jul 1972.
Later history: renamed *Carabobo* (D 21). R1981
2★Korea K-6 K-7; ◆Cuba Oct–Dec 1961, Nov 1962.

DD 757 *Putnam* Out of comm 4 Mar 1950–23 Oct 1950. FRAM II Mar 1963 NY NSYd. Decomm and stricken 6 Aug 1973. Sold 24 Jun 1974, BU.
◆Cuba Mar–Apr 1961.

DD 758 *Strong* Out of comm 9 May 1947–14 May 1949. FRAM II Nov 1962 Charleston NSYd. Decomm and stricken 30 Sep 1973. Trfd to Brazil 31 Oct 1973.
Later history: renamed *Rio Grande do Norte* (D 37). R1996. Foundered en route to BU off Durban, South Africa, 1996.
1★Korea K-8; 3★Vietnam Dec 1967–May 1968; ◆Dominican Rep Jul–Aug 1965, Korea Jan–Mar 1968,

DD 759 *Lofberg* FRAM II Jul 1962 S.Fran NSYd. Decomm 15 Jan 1971. Stricken 1 Feb 1974. Sold to Taiwan for parts 6 May 1974, BU.
7★Korea K-2 K-4 K-5 K-7 K-8 K-9 K-10; ★Vietnam Feb–Apr 1965, Apr–Jul 1966, Sep 1967–Feb 1968, Dec 1968–Apr 1969, Apr–Jul 1970, Korea Jan–Mar 1968, Apr 1969, Apr–May 1970; ◆Taiwan Straits Oct–Nov 1958, Persian Gulf 7 May 1961.

DD 760 *John W. Thomason* Damaged in collision with destroyer *Buck* off Korea, 11 Nov 1950. FRAM II Jan 1960 Long Bch NSYd. Decomm 8 Dec 1970. Trfd to Taiwan 6 May 1974.
Later history: renamed *Nan Yang* (954/917). R2000.
6★Korea K-2 K-4 K-5 K-7 K-9 K-10; ★3+Vietnam Feb–Apr 1965, Apr–Jun, Aug 1966, Oct 1967–Feb 1968, May–Oct 1969; ◆Taiwan Straits Oct–Nov 1958, Korea Mar–Apr 1965, Jan–Mar 1968, Sep 1969.

DD 761 *Buck* Damaged in collision with destroyer *John W. Thomason* off Korea, 11 Nov 1950. FRAM Jul 1962 Long Bch NSYd. Decomm 16 Jul 1973 and trfd to Brazil.
Later history: renamed *Alagoas* (D 36) R1995.
6★Korea K-2 K-5 K-7 K-8 K-9 K-10; ★Vietnam Apr–May 1961, Sep 1963, Feb–Jun 1965, Jul–Nov 1966, Dec 1967–Jan 1968, May–Sep 1969, Aug 1970–Jan 1971; ◆Taiwan Straits Oct–Nov 1958, Korea Jan–Mar 1968, 15 May 1969, Sep–Oct 1969.

DD 762 *Henley* Out of comm 15 Mar 1950–23 Sep 1950. Decomm and stricken 1 Jul 1973. Sold 24 Jun 1974, BU.
◆Cuba Mar–Apr 1961, Cuba Missile Crisis Oct–Nov 1962.

DD 770 *Lowry* Out of comm 30 Jun 1947–27 Dec 1950. FRAM II Dec 1960 Norfolk NSYd. Decomm 29 Oct 1973. Trfd to Brazil.
Later history: renamed *Espirito Santo* (D 38). R1996.
2★Korea K-7 K-8; ★Vietnam Apr–Nov 1968; ◆Cuba Jan–Mar 1961, Cuba Missile Crisis Oct–Nov 1962.

DD 775 *Willard Keith* Out of comm Jun 1947–23 Oct 1950. NRT 1963–72. Decomm and stricken 1 Jul 1972. Trfd to Colombia.
Later history: renamed *Caldas* (D 41). R1982.
◆Cuba Mar–Apr 1961, Cuba Missile Crisis Oct–Nov 1962.

DD 776 *James C. Owens* Out of comm 3 Apr 1950–20 Sep 1950. Damaged by shore batteries, Songjin, North Korea, 7 May 1952. FRAM II Oct 1962 Charleston NSYd. Decomm and stricken 15 Jul 1973 and trfd to Brazil.
Later history: renamed *Sergipe* (D 35). R1995.
2★Korea K-7 K-8; ◆Cuba Dec 1962, Korea Jan–Mar 1968, Nov 1967, Jan–Jun 1968, Jun–Nov 1970.

DD 777 *Zellars* FRAM II May 1960 Norfolk NSYd. Decomm and stricken 19 Mar 1971. Trfd to Iran 12 Oct 1973.
Later history: renamed *Babr* (DDG 7). R1994.
4★Korea K-2 K-4 K-5 K-6; ◆Cuba Missile Crisis Oct–Nov 1962.

DD 778 *Massey* FRAM II Jul 1960 Norfolk NSYd. Decomm and stricken 17 Sep 1973. Sold 13 Nov 1974, BU.
4★Korea K-1 K-2 K-4 K-5; ★Vietnam Mar–Jul 1966; ◆Cuba Jul–Aug 1961.

DD 779 *Douglas H. Fox* Damaged by mine off Trieste, 29 Aug 1947 (3 killed). Out of comm 21 Apr 1950–15 Nov 1950. Damaged by shore gunfire off Hungnam, Korea, 14 May 1952 (3 killed). FRAM II Oct 1962 Norfolk NSYd. Decomm and stricken 15 Dec 1973. Trfd to Chile 8 Jan 1974.
Later history: renamed *Ministro Portales* (DD 17). Sunk as target 11 Nov 1998.
1★Korea K-7; ★Vietnam Mar–Jul 1969; ◆Cuba Missile Crisis Dec 1962, Korea Jun 1969.

DD 780 *Stormes* Out of comm Aug 1950–23 Oct 1950. FRAM II Jan 1961 Norfolk NSYd. Decomm 5 Dec 1970. Stricken 16 Feb 1972. Trfd to Iran 16 Feb 1972.
Later history: renamed *Palang* (DDG 9). R1994.
2★Korea K-5 K-6; 1★Vietnam Jul–Nov 1966; ◆Cuba Jan–Mar 1961, Cuba Missile Crisis Nov 1962, Dominican Rep May 1965.

DD 781 *Robert K. Huntington* FRAM II Sep 1960 Norfolk NSYd. Decomm and stricken 31 Oct 1973 and trfd to Venezuela
Later history: renamed *Falcon* (D 22), R 1981.
2★Vietnam Nov 1968–Mar 1969.

Figure 5.5: *USS Douglas H. Fox* (DD 779), *Sumner* class, after her FRAM conversion. Notice remodeled superstructure, small radar mainmast, helicopter landing pad.

DD 857 *Bristol* In collision with m/v *Italia Fassio* in fog off Nantucket I, 29 Sep 1959. Decomm and stricken 21 Nov 1969. Trfd to Taiwan 9 Dec 1969.
Later history: renamed *Hua Yang* (988/903). R1995.
2★Korea K-6 K-7; ◆Cuba Oct–Nov 1961, Jan–Feb 1962, Cuba Missile Crisis Nov–Dec 1962.

Notes: Tripod mast replaced pole foremast. After torpedo tubes replaced by quad 40 mm mount, and 20 mm guns removed. In early 1950s most had 40 mm guns replaced by 2 twin and 2 single 3″AA guns. Most were modernized under FRAM program in early 1960s, others had remaining TT removed and two triple ASW torpedo launchers installed. Most as indicated had FRAM refits, with new ASW TT, hedgehog, variable depth sonar, helicopter landing pad, radar mainmast.

Gearing Class

DD 710 *Gearing* In collision with m/v in Chesapeake Bay, 11 Jun 1959. FRAM I Oct 1962 Boston NSYd. Decomm and stricken 1 Jul 1973. Sold 6 Nov 1974, BU Chester, Pa.
◆Congo Feb 1961, Cuba Jul 1961, Cuba Missile Crisis Oct–Nov 1962, Dominican Rep May–Jun 1965.

DD 711 *Eugene A. Greene* Out of comm 1 Apr–1 Dec 1952. Rec **DDR 711**, 18 Jul 1952. Rec **DD 711**, 25 Mar 1963. FRAM I Oct 1962 Boston NSYd. Damaged in collision with oiler *Waccamaw* in E. Mediterranean, 16 Jun 1970. Decomm and trfd to Spain 31 Aug 1972.
Later history: renamed *Churruca* (D 61). R1989. Sunk as target 12 Dec 1991.
★Vietnam Jul–Sep 1966; ◆Cuba, Aug 1962, Cuba Missile Crisis Oct–Nov 1962, Dominican Rep May 1965.

DD 712 *Gyatt* Out of comm 31 Oct 1955–3 Dec 1956. Rec **DDG 712**, 3 Dec 1956. Terrier launcher fitted aft. Rec **DDG 1**, 23 Apr 1957. Rec **DD 712**, 1 Oct 1962. Decomm and stricken 22 Oct 1969. Sunk as target off Virginia, 11 Jun 1970.

DD 713 *Kenneth D. Bailey* Out of comm 22 Dec 1952–29 Aug 1953. Rec **DDR 713**, 9 Apr 1953. Damaged in collision with USNS *Haiti Victory* in Straits of Gibraltar, 4 Mar 1959. Rec **DD 713**, 1 Jan 1969. FRAM II Oct 1960 Charleston NSYd. Decomm 2 Apr 1970. Stricken 1 Feb 1974. Trfd to Iran for parts, 13 Jan 1975, BU.
◆Lebanon Sep 1958.

DD 714 *William R. Rush* Out of comm 21 Dec 1951–3 Sep 1952. Rec **DDR 714**, 18 Jul 1952. FRAM I NY NSYd Jun 1964/Apr 1965. Rec **DD 714**, 1 Jul 1964. Decomm and stricken 1 Jul 1978 and trfd to South Korea.
Later history: renamed *Kang Won* (DD 922). Museum in Korea, 2000.
2★Korea K-4 K-5; ◆Cuba Missile Crisis Oct–Nov 1962.

DD 715 *William M. Wood* Out of comm 30 Sep 1952–6 Jun 1953. Rec **DDR 715**, 2 Oct 1952. Rec **DD 715**, 1 Jul 1964. FRAM I NY NSYd, May 1964/Mar 1965. Decomm and stricken 1 Dec 1976. Sunk as target off Puerto Rico, 8 Mar 1983.
◆Lebanon Jul–Sep 1958, Cuba Apr, Dec 1961, Cuba Missile Crisis Oct–Dec 1962, Dominican Rep Apr–May 1965.

DD 716 *Wiltsie* Hit by coastal gunfire off Tanchon, 11 Jun 1953, and again near Chabo, 8 Jul 1953. FRAM I Pearl Hbr NSYd, Nov 1961/Sep 1962. Decomm and stricken, 23 Jan 1976. Trfd to Pakistan 29 Apr 1977.
Later history: renamed *Tariq* (D 165), renamed *Nazim* 1990.
8★Korea K-1 K-2 K-3 K-4 K-6 K-7 K-9 K-10; 7★Vietnam Feb–Jun 1965, Jul–Oct 1966, Oct 1967–Feb 1968, May, Jul–Oct 1969, Aug–Oct 1970, Jan 1971, Aug 1972–Jan 1973; ◆Taiwan Straits Dec 1958, Quemoy-Matsu Jan–Feb 1959, Korea Jun–Jul, Sep 1969, Nov–Dec 1970.

DD 717 *Theodore E. Chandler* Damaged in collision with destroyer *Ozbourn* off Tsingtao, Yellow Sea, 24 Nov 1948. FRAM I San Fran NSYd, Feb 1961/Jan 1962. Damaged by shore gunfire off Vietnam, 6 May 1968. Decomm and stricken 1 Apr 1975.
Sold 1 Dec 1975, BU Tacoma, Wash.

9★Korea K-1 K-2 K-3 K-4 K-6 K-7 K-8 K-9 K-10; 8★Vietnam Jul 1962, Aug–Sep, Nov 1964, Oct 1965–Jan 1966, Aug, Oct–Nov 1966, Jan–Feb, Apr–Oct 1967, Dec 1967–Jun 1968, Oct 1969–Jan 1970, Dec 1970–Apr 1971, Feb–Mar 1973; ◆Quemoy-Matsu Dec 1958–Feb 1959, May–Jun 1960, Korea Feb 1970.

DD 718 *Hamner* FRAM I San Fran NSYd, Nov 1962. Collided with replenishment oiler *Camden* in Gulf of Tonkin, 24 Jan 1971. Decomm and stricken 1 Oct 1979. Trfd to Taiwan 17 Dec 1980.
Later history: renamed *Yun Yang* (912/927). SE2001.
8★Korea K-1 K-2 K-3 K-4 K-6 K-7 K-9 K-10; ★Vietnam Feb–May 1965, Jul 1965, Jul–Nov 1966, Oct 1967–Feb 1968, Jun–Jul, Sep–Oct 1969, Oct 1970–Feb 1971, Mar–Sep 1972; ◆Quemoy-Matsu Dec 1958–Feb 1959, May–Jun 1961, Korea 4 Aug 1969; PUC Korea.

DD 719 *Epperson* Rec **DDE 719**, 28 Jan 1948. Comm 19 Mar 1949. Rec **DD 719**, 30 Jun 1962. FRAM I Pearl Hbr NSYd Dec 1964. Collided with carrier *Hornet* southeast of Tokyo, 20 Sep 1965. Decomm and stricken 1 Dec 1975. Trfd to Pakistan. 29 Apr 1977.
Later history: renamed *Taimur* (D166). R1999. Sunk as target Mar 2000.
5★Korea K-5 K-6 K-8 K-9 K-10; ★Vietnam May 1962, Oct–Dec 1965, Feb–Apr 1967, Mar–Aug 1968, Jul–Nov 1969, Sep–Nov 1970, Oct 1971–Jan 1972, Dec 1972–Mar 1973; ◆OpCastle 1954, Korea Jul, Oct 1969, Aug 1970, Oct–Nov 1971.

DD 720 *Castle* construction suspended 11 Feb 1946. Stricken 2 Nov 1954. Sold 29 Aug 1955, BU.

DD 721 *Woodrow R. Thompson* construction suspended 11 Feb 1946. Stricken 2 Nov 1954. Sold 29 Aug 1955, BU.

DD 742 *Frank Knox* Rec **DDR 742**. 18 Mar 1949. FRAM II May 1961 Mare I NSYd. Ran aground on reef in South China Sea, 18 Jul 1965; refloated 25 Aug. Rec **DD 742**, 1 Jan 1969. Decomm and stricken 30 Jan 1971 and trfd to Greece.
Later history: renamed *Themistocles* (D-210). R1992. Sunk as target off Crete, 11 Sep 2001.
5★Korea K-1 K-2 K-3 K-4 K-8; ★Vietnam Jan 1962, Mar–Jun 1964, Jun–Jul 1965, Aug–Dec 1967, Feb–Jun 1969, Jun–Oct 1970; ◆Quemoy-Matsu Mar–Apr 1960, Nov–Dec 1961, 19 Jul 1962, Korea May 1969.

DD 743 *Southerland* Rec **DDR 743**, 18 Mar 1949. Damaged by shore gunfire off Kojo, Korea, 14 Jul 1952. Rec **DD 743**, 1 Apr 1964. FRAM I Mare I NSYd Oct 1964. Planned transfer to Ecuador canceled, Jan 1981. Decomm and stricken 23 Feb 1981. Hulk used as target, sunk 2 Aug 1997.
8★Korea K-1 K-2 K-3 K-4 K-7 K-8 K-9 K-10; 10★Vietnam Apr–Jul 1965, Jul–Nov 1966, Jan–May 1968, Apr–May 1969, Sep–Nov 1970, Jul–Nov 1971; ◆Quemoy-Matsu Apr 1960, Korea May–Jul 1969, Jul 1970.

DD 763 *William C. Lawe* FRAM I Nov 1961 Charleston NSYd. Sank tug in collision at Jacksonville, Fla., 22 Jul 1963. Decomm and stricken 1 Oct 1983. Sunk as target 14 Jul 1999.
2★Vietnam; ◆Lebanon Sep–Oct 1958, Cuba Dec 1961, Cuba Missile Crisis Oct–Nov 1962, Dominican Rep Apr–May, Aug–Sep 1965, Korea Mar 1971, Feb–Jun 1971, Dec 1972–Mar 1973.

DD 764 *Lloyd Thomas* Completed as DDK, comm 21 Mar 1947. Rec **DDE 764**, 4 Mar 1950. FRAM II NY NSYd Nov 1961. Rec **DD 764**, 30 Jun 1962. Damaged by gun turret explosion off S.Vietnam, 11 Sep 1970. Decomm and stricken 12 Oct 1972. To Taiwan.
Later history: renamed *Dang Yang* (911). R1999. Sunk off Taiwan, 30 Oct 2002. Fu Yang (907).
★Vietnam Sep–Dec 1970, Feb–Jun 1972; ◆Cuba Jan–Feb 1962.

DD 765 *Keppler* Completed as DDK, comm 23 May 1947. Rec **DDE 765**, 4 Mar 1950. In collision with destroyer *Johnston* off North Carolina, 14 Jan 1961. FRAM II, NY NSYd Sep 1961. Rec **DD 765**, 30 Jun 1962. Decomm and stricken and trfd to Turkey 1 Jul 1972.
Later history: renamed *Tinaztepe* (D-355). R1984.
2★Korea K-2 K-4; ★Vietnam Nov 1966–Mar 1967, Sep 1970–Feb 1971, Sep–Dec 1971; ◆Cuba Missile Crisis Oct–Nov 1962.

DD 766 *Lansdale* Construction suspended, 7 Jan 1946. Bow used to repair damaged DD 884, May 1956. Stricken 8 Jun 1958. Sold 23 Mar 1959, BU incomplete, Terminal I.

DD 767 *Seymour D. Owens* Construction suspended, 7 Jan 1946. Bow used to repair damaged DD 838, Oct 1951. Stricken 8 Jun 1950. Sold 23 Mar 1959, BU incomplete. Terminal I.

DD 782 *Rowan* Damaged by shore gunfire off Wonsan, Korea, 22 Feb 1952, and on 17 Jun 1953. FRAM I Phila NSYd May 1964. Collided with Soviet m/v *Kapitan Vislobokov* in Sea of Japan, 1 Feb 1968. Decomm and stricken 18 Dec 1975. Trfd to Taiwan 10 Jun 1977.
Later history: renamed *Chao Yang* (916). Went aground and sank in tow en route to Taiwan, 22 Aug 1977.
3★Korea K-8 K-9 K-10; 11★Vietnam Feb–Jun 1965, Dec 1967–Jan 1968, Jun–Aug 1969, Oct 1970–Feb 1971, Dec 1971–Mar 1972, Jun 1972–Jan 1973; ◆Quemoy-Matsu Jun–Jul 1961, Korea Jan–Mar 1968, Apr–Jun 1969, Dec 1971–Jan 1972, Evac of Vietnam 29–30 Apr 1975.

DD 783 *Gurke* FRAM I, Puget Sd NSYd May 1964. Decomm and stricken 20 Jan 1976. Trfd to Greece 17 Mar 1977.
Later history: renamed *Tompazis* (D-215) (*Toumbazis*). SE1993. R1997.
4★Korea K-7 K-8 K-9 K-10; ★Vietnam May 1964, Dec 1964–Apr 1965, Jun–Oct 1966, Dec 1967—May 1968, Mar–Aug 1969, Aug–Dec 1970, Jan–Jul 1972; ◆Quemoy-Matsu Jul 1961, Korea Jan–Mar 1968, Apr, Jun–Jul 1969, Nov–Dec 1971, Evac of Vietnam 29–30 Apr 1975.

DD 784 *McKean* Rec **DDR 784**, 18 Jul 1952. Rec **DD 784**, 1 Dec 1963. FRAM I, Long Bch NSYd, Nov 1964. Collided with oiler *Cacapon* off Okinawa, 20 Mar 1970. Damaged in collision with carrier *Oriskany* in gale at Bremerton, 14 Nov 1981. Decomm 1 Oct 1981. Trfd to Turkey for parts, 25 Nov 1982, BU.
★Vietnam Jun–Jul 1960, Aug–Dec 1965, Dec 1966–Apr 1967, Jun–Oct 1968, Mar–Jul 1970, Oct 1971–Jan 1972; ◆Quemoy-Matsu May–Jun 1962, Korea Mar 1970.

DD 785 *Henderson* FRAM I, Mare I NSYd Apr 1962. Decomm and stricken 30 Sep 1980. Trfd to Pakistan 30 Sep 1980.
Later history: renamed *Tughril* (D 167), renamed *Nazim* (D 156), 1998. SE2001.
4★Korea K-7 K-8 K-9 K-10; ★Vietnam May 1963, Aug–Nov 1964, Aug–Dec 1965, Feb–May 1967, Apr–Aug 1968, Jan–Apr 1970, Feb–Jun 1971, Dec 1972–Mar 1973; ◆Antarctic Dec 1946–Mar 1947, Quemoy-Matsu Feb–Mar 1959, May–Jul 1960, Korea May 1968, Dec 1969–Jan 1970.

DD 786 *Richard B. Anderson* FRAM I, Puget Sd NSYd Jul 1961. Decomm and stricken 20 Dec 1975. Trfd to Taiwan 10 Jun 1977.
Later history: renamed *Kai Yang* (924) (915). R1999.
4★Korea K-4 K-5 K-6 K-8; 11★Vietnam Nov 1964–Jan 196K-5 Feb–Jun 1966, May–Sep 1967, Nov 1968–Feb 1969, Aug–Sep 1970–Jan 1971, May–Dec 1972, Feb 1973; ◆Quemoy-Matsu Jun–Jul 1959, Korea Apr 1969, Evac of Vietnam 29–30 Apr 1975.

DD 787 *James E. Kyes* FRAM I, Puget Sd NSYd Jan 1963. Decomm 31 Mar 1973. Trfd to Taiwan 26 Apr 1973.
Later history: renamed *Chien Yang* (912). SE2001.
6★Korea K-1 K-2 K-6 K-7 K-9 K-10; ★Vietnam Jul–Sep 1965, Aug–Nov 1966, Oct 1967–Jan 1968, May–Aug 1969, Apr–May 1971, Jun–Dec 1972; ◆Passage to Freedom, Quemoy-Matsu Apr–May 1959, Jun–Jul 1960, Jul–Aug 1961, Jan–Feb 1962, Korea Jan–Mar 1968, Oct 1969.

DD 788 *Hollister* Damaged by gun explosion, southwest of Pearl Harbor, 14 Apr 1949. FRAM I, Puget Sd NSYd Dec 1961. Decomm 31 Aug 1979. Stricken 1 Oct 1979. Trfd to Taiwan 13 Mar 1983.
Later history: renamed *Shao Yang* (929). SE2001.
5★Korea K-1 K-2 K-3 K-4 K-8; ★Vietnam Apr 1959, Oct–Dec 1965, Aug–Oct 1966, Jan–Aug 1967, Nov 1967–Jun 1968, Oct–Dec 1969, Jan–Apr 1971, Jul–Dec 1972; ◆Quemoy-Matsu Mar–Apr 1960, Sep–Oct 1962, Korea Jan 1970, Dec 1970–Jan 1971.

DD 789 *Eversole* FRAM I, Puget Sd NSYd Feb 1963. Decomm and trfd to Turkey 11 Jul 1973.
Later history: renamed *Gayret* (D-352) R1995 Museum at Izmit, 1997.
7★Korea K-1 K-2 K-3 K-6 K-7 K-9 K-10; ★Vietnam Oct–Nov 1965, Jun–Oct 1968, Nov 1969–Mar 1970, Feb–May 1971, Apr–Jun, Aug–Oct 1972; ◆Quemoy-Matsu Apr–May 1959, Jun–Jul 1960, Jul–Aug 1961, Korea Jan 1970.

DD 790 *Shelton* Damaged by shore gunfire at Wonsan, Korea, 27 Feb 1952. FRAM I, Long Bch NSYd Jun 1961. Decomm and stricken 31 Mar 1973. Trfd to Taiwan 18 Apr 1973.
Later history: renamed *Lao Yang* (920). R1999.
6★Korea K-1 K-2 K-6 K-7 K-9 K-10; 8★Vietnam Apr–Jun 1964, Oct 1965–Feb 1966, Feb–Apr 1967, Nov 1968–Apr 1969, Apr–Aug 1970, May–Aug 1971, Jul–Dec 1972; ◆Quemoy-Matsu Apr–May 1959, Mar–May, Sep, Nov–Dec 1962, Feb 1963, Korea Apr 1969.

DD 791 *Seaman* Construction suspended 11 Feb 1946. Delivered incomplete, 25 Jun 1946. Bow used to repair damaged DD 730, 1960. Stricken 1 Mar 1961. Sold 12 Sep 1961, BU incomplete.

DD 805 *Chevalier* Rec **DDR 805**, 18 Mar 1949. Rec **DD 805**, 13 Jul 1962. FRAM II, Long Bch NSYd Aug 1962. Decomm 1 Jul 1972. Trfd to South Korea 5 Jul 1972.
Later history: renamed *Chung Buk* (DD 915). SE2001.
9★Korea K-1 K-2 K-3 K-4 K-6 K-7 K-8 K-9 K-10; ★Vietnam Nov 1963, Apr–Jul 1965, Jun–Oct 1966, Sep 1967–Feb 1968, Feb–Jul 1969, Aug–Nov 1970, Dec 1971–Mar 1972; ◆Quemoy-Matsu Dec 1958–Feb 1959, Mar–May 1960, Korea Aug 1969.

DD 806 *Higbee* Rec **DDR 806**, 18 Mar 1949. Rec **DD 806**, 1 Jun 1963. FRAM I, San Fran NSYd Feb 1964. Damaged by aircraft bomb off Vietnam, 19 Apr 1972. Decomm and stricken 15 Jul 1979. Sunk as target Jun 1983.
7★Korea K-1 K-2 K-3 K-6 K-7 K-9 K-10; ★Vietnam Feb–Mar 1962, Aug, Oct–Dec 1964, Feb–May 1965, Jul–Sep 1965, Jan–Apr 1966, Jan–Mar 1968, Jan–Jun 1969, May–Aug 1970, Feb–Jul 1972, Feb 1973; ◆Quemoy-Matsu Apr–May 1959, Jun 1960, Jan–Feb 1962.

DD 807 *Benner* Rec **DDR 807**, 18 Mar 1949. Rec **DD 807**, 15 Nov 1962. FRAM II, Long Bch NSYd Feb 1963. Damaged in collision with destroyer *Gregory* off California, 18 Feb 1963. Decomm 20 Nov 1970. Stricken 1 Feb 1974. Sold 18 Apr 1975, BU Tacoma.
5★Vietnam Oct–Nov 1965, Dec 1966–Mar 1967, Jun–Oct 1968, Nov 1969–Mar 1970; ◆Taiwan Straits Aug–Oct 1958, Quemoy-Matsu Sep–Oct 1959, Korea Jan 1970.

DD 808 *Dennis J. Buckley* Rec **DDR 808**, 18 Mar 1949. Rec **DD 808**, 1 Dec 1963. FRAM I, Puget Sd NSYd Oct 1964. Decomm and stricken 2 Jul 1973. Sold 28 Mar 1974, BU.
★Vietnam May–Oct 1965, Sep 1966–Jan 1967, Feb–Jul 1968, Aug–Oct 1969, Dec 1969–Jan 1970, Mar, May–Jul 1971, Apr–Oct 1972; ◆Taiwan Straits Sep–Dec 1958, Quemoy-Matsu Nov–Dec 1959, Korea 30 Oct 1969.

DD 817 *Corry* Out of comm 1 Apr 1953–9 Jan 1954. Rec **DDR 817**, 9 Apr 1953. Rec **DD 817**, 1 Jan 1964. FRAM I, Norfolk NSYd Sep 1964. In collision with m/v *Normannis* in Delaware River, 8 May 1976. Decomm 27 Feb 1981 and trfd to Greece, 8 Jul 1981.
Later history: renamed *Kriezis* (D-217). R1993.
★Vietnam Oct 1968–Mar 1969, Jan–Feb 1973; ◆Cuba Oct 1961 Cuba Missile Crisis Oct–Nov 1962, Dominican Rep May 1965.

DD 818 *New* Rec **DDE 818**, 4 Mar 1950. Rec **DD 818**, 30 Jun 1962. FRAM I, Norfolk NSYd Dec 1963. Decomm and stricken 1 Jul 1976. Trfd to South Korea 23 Feb 1977.
Later history: renamed *Taejon/Daejeon* (DD 919). SE2001.
★Vietnam Aug 1967–Jan 1968; ◆Lebanon Jul–Aug 1958, Cuba Missile Crisis Nov 1962.

DD 819 *Holder* Rec **DDE 819**, 4 Mar 1950. Rec **DD 819**, 30 Jun 1962. Collided with carrier *Wasp* off Cuba, 14 Nov 1962. FRAM I, Norfolk NSYd Oct 1963. Decomm and stricken 1 Oct 1976. Trfd to Ecuador 1 Sep 1978.
Later history: renamed *Presidente Eloy Alfaro* (DD 01). R1991.
★Vietnam Jul–Nov 1966; ◆Cuba Missile Crisis Nov 1962, Dominican Rep May 1965.

Figure 5.6: *USS Rich* (DDE 820), *Gearing* class, converted to escort destroyer.

DD 820 *Rich* Out of comm 15 Jun 1947–30 Apr 1948. Rec **DDE 820**, 4 Mar 1950. Rec **DD 820**, 30 Jun 1962. FRAM I, NY NSYd Nov 1963. Collided with oiler *Caloosahatchee* north of Virgin Is., 12 Jul 1977. Decomm and stricken 15 Dec 1977. Sold Dec 1979, BU.
3★Vietnam May–Oct 1968, Nov 1972–Feb 1973; ◆Lebanon Jul–Aug 1958, Cuba Missile Crisis Nov 1962.

DD 821 *Johnston* Damaged in collision with submarine *Torsk* in Long Island Sound, 26 May 1947. Collided with destroyer *Keppler* off North Carolina, 14 Jan 1961. FRAM I, Boston NSYd Nov 1962. Decomm and trfd to Taiwan 27 Feb 1981.
Later history: renamed *Chen Yang* (928). SE2001.
★Vietnam Jan–May 1968; ◆Cuba Missile Crisis Dec 1962.

DD 822 *Robert H. McCard* FRAM I, Boston NSYd Dec 1962. Decomm 5 Jun 1980. Trfd to Turkey 9 Jun 1980.
Later history: renamed *Kiliç Ali Paşa* (D-349). R1998.
★Vietnam Jan–May 1968.

DD 823 *Samuel B. Roberts* FRAM I, Phila NSYd Feb 1962. Decomm and stricken 2 Nov 1970. Sunk as target off Puerto Rico, 14 Nov 1971.
★Vietnam Nov 1965–Feb 1966; ◆Lebanon Aug–Sep 1958, Cuba Apr 1962, Cuba Missile Crisis Oct–Nov 1962.

DD 824 *Basilone* Rec **DDE 824**, 28 Jan 1948. Completed as DDE, comm 26 Jul 1949. Went aground in Hampton Roads, 5 Jan 1956. Rec **DD 824**, 30 Jun 1962. FRAM I, Phila NSYd Apr 1964. Damaged by boiler explosion south of Newport, RI, 5 Feb 1973. Decomm and stricken 1 Nov 1977. Sunk as target off Florida, 9 Apr 1982.
3★Vietnam Mar–Jul 1966, Jul–Aug 1972; ◆Lebanon Jul–Aug 1958, Cuba Missile Crisis Oct–Nov 1962.

DD 825 *Carpenter* Cpl by Newport News as DDK, comm 15 Dec 1949. Rec **DDK 825**, 28 Jan 1948. Rec **DDE 825**, 4 Mar 1950. Rec **DD 825**, 30 Jun 1962. FRAM I, Pearl Hbr NSYd Mar 1965. Decomm and stricken 20 Feb 1981. Trfd to Turkey 27 Feb 1981.
Later history: renamed *Anittepe* (D-347). R1997.
1★Korea K-10; 5★Vietnam Dec 1960–Jan 1961, Apr 1961, Jan–May 1966, Mar–Jul 1967, Oct 1968–Feb 1969, Jul–Nov 1970, Sep 1971–Feb 1972; ◆Taiwan Straits Aug–Sep 1958, Quemoy-Matsu Sep–Dec 1959, Oct–Nov 1962, Korea Sep 1970.

DD 826 *Agerholm* Slight damage by coastal battery, 1952. FRAM I, Mar 1961 Mare I NSYd. Fired live ASROC missile with 1-kiloton nuclear warhead southwest of San Diego (Operation Dominic), 11 May 1962. Damaged by engine room fire off San Diego, 7 Feb 1973. Decomm and stricken 1 Dec 1978. Sunk as target off San Diego, 18 Jul 1982.
4★Korea K-4 K-5 K-6 K-8; 8★Vietnam Nov 1964–Jan 1965, Feb 1966–Jun1966, Jun–Oct 1967, Jan–Jun 1969, Jul–Nov 1970, Aug–Nov 1971; ◆Korea Sep 1970, Oct 1971.

DD 827 *Robert A. Owens* cpl by Newport News as DDK, comm 5 Nov 1949. Rec **DDK 827**, 28 Jan 1948. Rec **DDE 827**, 4 Mar 1950. Rec **DD 827**, 30 Jun 1962. FRAM I Nov 1964 Norfolk NSYd. Collided with tender *Yellowstone* off Florida, 19 Mar 1981. Decomm 22 Feb 1982 and trfd to Turkey.
Later history: renamed *Alçitepe* (D-346). R1998.
◆Cuba Missile Crisis Oct–Nov 1962.

DD 828 *Timmerman* construction suspended 1946–51. Experimental unit, new light-weight machinery, comm 26 Sep 1952. Rec **EAG 152**, 11 Dec 1953. Rec **AG 152**, 11 Jan 1954. Decomm 27 Jul 1956. Stricken 4 Apr 1958. Sold 21 Apr 1959, BU.

DD 829 *Myles C. Fox* Rec **DDR 829**, 18 Mar 1949. Rec **DD 829**, 1 Apr 1964. FRAM I Oct 1964 Puget Sd NSYd. Decomm and stricken 1 Oct 1979. Trfd to Greece for parts 2 Aug 1980, BU.
3★Vietnam Nov 1966–Feb 1967, Apr–Jun 1972; ◆Cuba Apr–Jun 1962, Dominican Rep May–Jun 1965.

DD 830 *Everett F. Larson* Rec **DDR 830**, 18 Mar 1949. Rec **DD 830**, 1 Dec 1962. FRAM II Jan 1963 Long Bch NSYd. Decomm and trfd to South Korea 30 Oct 1972.
Later history: renamed *Jeong Buk/Jeonbuk* (DD 916). SE2001.
★Vietnam Aug–Sep 1965, Aug–Oct 1966, Oct 1967–Jan 1968, May–Sep 1969, Jan–Jun 1971, Mar–Jul 1972; ◆Taiwan Straits Sep 1958, Quemoy-Matsu Jul–Sep 1959, Korea Jan–Mar 1968.

DD 831 *Goodrich* Rec **DDR 831**, 18 Mar 1949. FRAM II Sep 1960 Norfolk NSYd. Rec **DD 831**, 1 Jan 1969. Decomm 30 Nov 1969. Stricken 1 Feb 1974. Sold 16 Aug 1977, BU Kearny, NJ.

DD 832 *Hanson* Rec **DDR 832**, 18 Mar 1949. Rec **DD 832**, 1 Dec 1963. FRAM I Dec 1964 San Fran. NSYd. Decomm 31 Mar 1973. Trfd to Taiwan 18 Apr 1973.
Later history: renamed *Liao Yang* (921). SE2001.
8★Korea K-1 K-2 K-3 K-4 K-6 K-9 K-10; ★Vietnam May 1961, May–Oct 1965, Sep 1966–Jan 1967, Jun–Sep 1968, Aug–Dec 1969, Mar–Jul 1971, May–Oct 1972; ◆Taiwan Straits Oct–Nov 1958, Quemoy-Matsu Jan 1960, Korea May 1968, Oct–Nov 1969, Apr–May 1971.

DD 833 *Herbert J. Thomas* Rec **DDR 833**, 18 Mar 1949. Rec **DD 833**, 1 Dec 1963. FRAM I Aug 1965 Mare I NSYd. Decomm 4 Dec 1970. Trfd to Taiwan 6 May 1974.
Later history: renamed *Han Yang* (915). R1999
6★Korea K-1 K-2 K-7 K-8 K-9 K-10; ★Vietnam Oct 1966–Feb 1967, Mar–Jun 1968, Jul–Nov 1969; ◆Quemoy-Matsu Mar 1960, Korea Jan–Mar 1968, Aug 1969.

DD 834 *Turner* Rec **DDR 834**, 18 Mar 1949. 1960 FRAM II Aug 1960 NY NSYd. Rec **DD 834**, 1 Jan 1969. Decomm and stricken 26 Sep 1969. Sold 13 Oct 1970, BU New Orleans.
◆Lebanon Sep–Oct 1958, Dominican Rep May 1965.

DD 835 *Charles P. Cecil* Rec **DDR 835**, 18 Mar 1949. Rec **DD 835**, 1 Jun 1963. FRAM I May 1964 NY NSYd. Decomm and stricken 1 Oct 1979. Trfd to Greece 2 Aug 1980.
Later history: renamed *Apostolis* (D-216). SE1993. R1992
★Vietnam Nov 1966–Mar 1967, Apr–Jul 1972; ◆Lebanon Apr 1958, Cuba Aug–Dec 1961, Cuba Missile Crisis Oct–Nov 1962.

DD 836 *George K. Mackenzie* FRAM I Dec 1963 NY NSYd. Decomm and stricken 1 Oct 1976. Sunk as target off California, 15 Oct 1976.
8★Korea K-1 K-2 K-3 K-4 K-6 K-7 K-9 K-10; ★Vietnam 24 Mar 1961, Jun–Jul 1962, Aug–Nov 1964, Jan–Feb, Apr–Jun 1965, Nov 1965, Jan–Jul 1966, Aug–Nov 1967, Jul 1968–Jun 1970, Jan–Apr 1972; ◆Quemoy-Matsu Feb–Mar 1962, Korea Aug, Oct 1969, Mar 1970.

DD 837 *Sarsfield* Served as experimental destroyer from 1945. Out of comm Aug 1962–30 Apr 1963. FRAM I May 1963 Boston NSYd. Decomm and stricken and trfd to Taiwan 1 Oct 1977.
Later history: renamed *Te Yang* (925). SE2001.
1★Vietnam May–Sep 1972; ◆Cuba Jan–Mar 1961, Dec 1961–Jan 1962, Apr 1962.

DD 838 *Ernest G. Small* Went aground on Block Island, NY, 3 Apr 1947. Damaged by mine off Hungnam, Korea, 7 Oct 1951 (9 killed) and lost

Figure 5.7: *USS Sarsfield* (DD 837), *Gearing* class. FRAM conversion, she lost one forward turret.

bow in heavy seas, 11 Oct. Repaired with bow of incomplete *Seymour D. Owens*. Out of comm 15 Jan 1952–2 Dec 1952. Rec **DDR 838**, 18 Jul 1952. FRAM II Dec 1960–Aug 1961 San Fran NSYd. Rec **DD 838**, 1 Jan 1969. Decomm and stricken 13 Nov 1970. Trfd to Taiwan 19 Feb 1971.
Later history: renamed *Fu Yang* (962/907). Sunk as target 8 Oct 2003.
4★Korea K-1 K-2 K-3 K-6; ★Vietnam Jun–Oct 1964, Jan–Jul 1965, Sep–Dec 1965, Apr–May 1966, Sep–Oct 1967, Nov 1968–Apr 1969, Mar–Aug 1970; ◆Korea Apr 1969.

DD 839 *Power* Collided with destroyer *Warrington* off Puerto Rico, 12 Jan 1955. FRAM I Jan 1962 Charleston NSYd. Decomm and stricken, trfd to Taiwan 1 Oct 1977.
Later history: renamed *Shen Yang* (923). SE2001
★Vietnam Oct 1968–Feb 1969; ◆Lebanon Sep 1958, Cuba Feb–Apr 1962.

DD 840 *Glennon* FRAM I Jul 1963 Boston NSYd. Decomm and stricken 1 Oct 1976. Sunk as target off Puerto Rico, 26 Feb 1981.
★Vietnam Jun–Sep 1972.

DD 841 *Noa* FRAM I May 1961 Phila NSYd. Decomm and trfd to Spain 31 Oct 1973.
Later history: renamed *Blas de Lezo* (D 65). R1991.
★Vietnam Mar–Apr 1968, Apr–Aug 1969; ◆Lebanon Jul 1958.

DD 842 *Fiske* Out of comm 1 Apr 1952–25 Nov 1952. Rec **DDR 842**, 18 Jul 1952. Rec **DD 842**, 1 Dec 1963. FRAM I Jan 1965 NY NSYd. Decomm and trfd to Turkey 5 Jun 1980.
Later history: renamed *Piyale Paşa* (D-350). R1999.
2★Korea K-4 K-5; ★Vietnam Mar–Jul 1966; ◆Cuba Jun–Jul 1962, Cuba Missile Crisis Oct–Nov 1962, Dominican Rep May 1965.

DD 843 *Warrington* Collided with destroyer *Power* off Puerto Rico, 12 Jan 1955. FRAM I May 1962 NY NSYd. Severely damaged by U.S. mines off Vietnam, 17 Jul 1972, CTL. Decomm 30 Sep 1972. Stricken 1 Oct 1972. Sold 24 Apr 1973, BU Taiwan.
2★Vietnam Nov 1966–Mar 1967, Jul 1972; ◆Cuba Mar 1961, Jul–Oct 1962, Cuba Missile Crisis Oct–Nov 1962.

DD 844 *Perry* FRAM I May 1960 Boston NSYd. Damaged in collision with carrier *Shangri-La* off Leghorn, 28 Aug 1965 (1 killed). Decomm 30 Jun 1973. Stricken 2 Jul 1973. Sold 11 Jun 1974, BU.
★Vietnam Jan–Aug 1969, Nov–Dec 1972; ◆Cuba Apr 1961, Dominican Rep May 1965, Korea Apr–May 1969.

DD 845 *Bausell* FRAM I Jun 1961 Puget Sd NSYd. Decomm and stricken, 30 May 1978. Sunk as target 13 Jul 1987.
4★Korea K-4 K-5 K-6 K-8; ★Vietnam Sep–Dec 1964, Feb–Jun 1966, Jun–Sep 1967, Oct 1968–Feb 1969, Jun–Nov 1970, Dec 1971–Nov 1972, Jan–Feb 1973; ◆Evac of Vietnam 29–30 Apr 1975, Mayaguez Op 15 May 1975.

DD 846 *Ozbourn* Lost bow in collision with destroyer *Theodore E. Chandler* in Yellow Sea, 2 Nov 1948 (2 killed). Damaged by shore gunfire off Wonsan, Korea, 18 Feb 1951. FRAM I Dec 1961 Puget Sd NSYd. Decomm and stricken 1 Jun 1975. Sold 1 Dec 1975, BU Tacoma, Wash.
5★Korea K-1 K-2 K-3 K-4 K-8; ★Vietnam Aug–Nov 1964, Sep–Dec 1965, Aug–Oct 1966, Jan–May 1967, Aug–Dec 1967, Mar–Jul 1968, Oct–Nov 1969, Jan–Feb 1970, Dec 1970–Apr 1971, Apr–Sep 1972; ◆Korea Dec 1969, Feb 1970.

DD 847 *Robert L. Wilson* Rec **DDE 847**, 4 Mar 1950. Rec **DD 847**, 1 Aug 1962. FRAM I Nov 1963 Phila NSYd. Decomm and stricken 30 Sep 1974. Sunk as target off Puerto Rico, 25 Jan 1980.
3★Vietnam Oct 1968–Mar 1969; ◆Lebanon Jul–Aug 1958, Cuba Sep–Oct 1962, Cuba Missile Crisis Oct–Nov 1962, Dominican Rep May 1965.

DD 848 *Witek* Rec **EDD 848**, Jul 1946, experimental vessel. Decomm 19 Aug 1968. Stricken 17 Sep 1968. Sunk as target off Virginia, 4 Jun 1969.
◆Cuba Jul–Sep 1961, Cuba Missile Crisis Oct–Nov 1962.

DD 849 *Richard E. Kraus* Rec **EAG 151**, 25 Aug 1949. Rec **DD 849**, 11 Dec 1953. FRAM I May 1964 Boston NSYd. Decomm and stricken 1 Jul 1976. Trfd to South Korea 23 Feb 1977.
Later history: renamed *Kuang Ju/Kwangju* (DD 921). SE2001.
2★Vietnam Mar–Jul 1966, Dec 1972–Feb 1973; ◆Cuba Missile Crisis Oct–Nov 1962.

DD 850 *Joseph P. Kennedy Jr.* FRAM I May 1962 NY NSYd. Decomm 2 Jul 1973. Stricken 2 Nov 1976.
Later history: Museum at Fall River, Mass.
2★Korea K-4 K-5; ◆Cuba Jun–Aug 1962, Cuba Missile Crisis Oct–Nov 1962.

DD 851 *Rupertus* Damaged by grounding in Straits of Shimonoseki, 23 Mar 1952. FRAM I Nov 1963 San Fran NSYd. Decomm and stricken 10 Jul 1973 and trfd to Greece.
Later history: renamed *Koundouriotis* (D-213). R1995.
7★Korea K-2 K-4 K-5 K-6 K-7 K-8 K-10; ★Vietnam Mar–Apr 1961, Aug–Nov 1964, Jan–Apr, Jun 1965, Jan–Jul 1966, Jul–Nov 1967, Aug–Nov 1968, Jan–Jul 1969, Oct–Nov 1969, Jan–Feb, Apr–Jun 1970, Jul–Nov 1971, Jul 1972–Jan 1973; ◆Quemoy-Matsu Aug–Sep 1961, Feb–Mar 1962, Korea Dec 1968, Sep–Dec 1969, Feb–Apr, Jul–Sep 1970.

DD 852 *Leonard F. Mason* Damaged in collision with destroyer *Fechteler* southeast of Oahu, 22 Apr 1949. FRAM I Jan 1964 Boston NSYd. Decomm and stricken 2 Nov 1976. Trfd to Taiwan 10 Mar 1978.
Later history: renamed *Sui Yang* (926). SE2001.
7★Korea K-2 K-4 K-5 K-6 K-7 K-8 K-10; ★Vietnam Aug, Oct–Dec 1964, Mar–May, Jul–Nov 1965, Jan–May 1966, Oct 1967–Feb 1968, Sep 1968–Jan 1969, Mar–May, Aug, Oct–Nov 1969, Feb, May–Jun 1970, Nov 1971–Mar 1972, Dec 1972–Jan 1973; ◆Quemoy-Matsu Feb–Mar 1962, Korea Jul 1969, Sep–Oct 1969, Dec 1969–Apr 1970.

DD 853 *Charles H. Roan* Severely damaged in collision with destroyer *Brownson* off North Carolina, 8 Nov 1950. FRAM I Jun 1962 NY NSYd. Decomm and stricken and trfd to Turkey 21 Sep 1973.
Later history: renamed *Maresal Fevzi Çakmak* (D-351). R1994
★Vietnam Sep 1972; ◆Lebanon Aug 1958, Taiwan Straits Sep 1958, Cuba Missile Crisis Oct–Nov 1962, Dominican Rep Apr–May 1965.

DD 858 *Fred T. Berry* Conv to DDK. Rec **DDE 858**, 4 Mar 1950. FRAM II Oct 1961 Boston NSYd. Rec **DD 858**, 30 Jun 1962. Decomm and stricken 15 Sep 1970. Scuttled as reef off Key West, 4 May 1972.
2★Korea K-2 K-4; ★Vietnam Mar, May–Jul 1966; ◆Cuba Dec 1961–62.

DD 859 *Norris* Conv to DDK. Rec **DDE 859**, 4 Mar 1950. Damaged in collision with submarine *Bergall* at Norfolk, Va., 31 Oct 1954. FRAM II Oct 1961 Phila NSYd. Rec **DD 859**, 30 Jun 1962. Decomm 4 Dec 1970. Trfd to Turkey 1 Feb 1974.

Later history: renamed *Kocatepe* (D-354). SE1993.
2★Korea K-2 K-4; ★Vietnam Nov 1966–Feb 1967; ◆Cuba Dec 1961–Jan 1962, Cuba Missile Crisis Oct–Nov 1962.

DD 860 *McCaffery* Conv to DDK. Rec **DDE 860**, 4 Mar 1950. FRAM II Nov 1961 NY NSYd. Rec **DD 860**, 30 Jun 1962. Decomm 1970. Stricken 30 Sep 1973. Sold 29 May 1974, BU.
2★Korea K-2 K-4; ★Vietnam Mar–Aug 1967, Dec 1972–Mar 1973; ◆Cuba Feb 1962, Cuba Missile Crisis Oct–Nov 1962.

DD 861 *Harwood* Conv to DDK. Rec **DDE 861**, 4 Mar 1950. FRAM II Dec 1961 NY NSYd. Rec **DD 861**, 30 Jun 1962. Decomm 17 Dec 1971 and trfd to Turkey.
Later history: renamed *Kocatepe* (D-354). Sunk in error by Turkish aircraft off Cyprus, 22 Jul 1974.
★Vietnam May–Oct 1968; ◆Cuba Feb–Apr 1962, Cuba Missile Crisis Oct–Nov 1962.

DD 862 *Vogelgesang* FRAM I Mar 1962–Jan 1963 Boston NSYd. Decomm 23 Feb and trfd to Mexico 24 Feb 1982.
Later history: renamed *Quetzalcoatl* (E 03), renamed *Ilhuicamina* (E 10), 1973. SE2001.
2★Vietnam Jun–Nov 1966; ◆Cuba Jul 1961, Dominican Rep May 1965.

DD 863 *Steinaker* Rec **DDR 863**, 1 Jul 1952. Rec **DD 863**, 1 Jul 1964. FRAM I Mar 1965 Boston NSYd. Out of comm 2 Jul 1952–28 Feb 1953. Decomm 23 Feb and trfd to Mexico 24 Feb 1982.
Later history: renamed *Netzahualcoyotl* (E 04/E 11). SE2001.
★Vietnam May–Oct 1968; ◆Lebanon Jul–Sep 1958, Cuba Dec 1961, Cuba Missile Crisis Oct–Nov 1962.

DD 864 *Harold J. Ellison* FRAM I Jan 1963 NY NSYd. Decomm and stricken 1 Oct 1983 and trfd to Pakistan.
Later history: renamed *Shah Jehan* (D 164). SE1993.
★Vietnam Nov 1965–Feb 1966; ◆Lebanon Jul–Aug 1958.

DD 865 *Charles R. Ware* FRAM I Jan 1962 NY NSYd. Decomm and stricken 12 Dec 1974. Sunk as target 15 Nov 1981.
★Vietnam Apr–Aug 1967; ◆Cuba Mar–Apr 1962, Cuba Missile Crisis Oct–Nov 1962.

DD 866 *Cone* FRAM I Jan 1963 NY NSYd. Decomm and trfd to Pakistan 1 Oct 1982.
Later history: renamed *Alamgir* (D 160). SE1993.
★Vietnam Jan–May 1968, Dec 1972–Feb 1973; ◆Lebanon Jul–Sep 1958.

DD 867 *Stribling* FRAM I May 1961 Charleston NSYd. Decomm and stricken 1 Jul 1976. Sunk as target off Puerto Rico, 27 Jul 1980.
2★Vietnam Mar–Aug 1969; ◆Lebanon Jul 1958, Cuba Jul–Aug 1961, Korea 25 Jun 1968, Jul–Aug 1961.

DD 868 *Brownson* Severely damaged in collision with destroyer *Charles H. Roan* off Bermuda/North Carolina, 8 Nov 1950. FRAM I May 1964 Boston NSYd. Collided with Polish trawler in North Sea, 11 Jul 1958. Decomm and stricken 30 Sep 1976. Sold May 1977, BU.
★Vietnam Nov 1966–Mar 1967; ◆Antarctic Dec 1946–Mar 1947, Cuba Apr–May 1962, Cuba Missile Crisis Oct–Nov 1962.

DD 869 *Arnold J. Isbell* FRAM I Jun 1961–May 1962 Puget Sd NSYd. Decomm and trfd to Greece 4 Dec 1973.
Later history: renamed *Sakhtouris* (D-214). R1992.
6★Korea K-2 K-4 K-5 K-6 K-7 K-8; 2★Vietnam May 1963, Mar 1964, Nov 1965–Apr 1966, Feb–Jun 1967, Aug 1968, Dec 1968–Jan 1969, Mar–Jul 1970, Oct 1971–Feb 1972.

DD 870 *Fechteler* Damaged in collision with destroyer *Leonard F. Mason* southeast of Oahu, 22 Apr 1949. Out of comm 1 Apr–1 Dec 1953. Rec **DDR 870**, 9 Apr 1953. Rec **DD 870**, 25 Mar 1963. FRAM I Dec 1963 Long Beach NSYd. Decomm and stricken 11 Sep 1970. Sold 28 Jun 1972, BU Portland, Ore.
1★Korea K-8; ★Vietnam Oct 1961, Jun–Sep 1964, Aug–Dec 1965, Mar–Aug 1967, Aug–Dec 1968, Feb–Apr 1970; ◆Taiwan Straits Nov 1958, Quemoy-Matsu Jan 1959, Feb–Mar 1960, Sep–Oct 1961.

DD 871 *Damato* Rec **DDE 871**, 4 Mar 1950. Rec **DD 871** 30 Jun 1962. FRAM I Feb 1964 Norfolk NSYd. (Tr to Egypt canc.) Decomm 30 Sep 1980. Stricken 1 Oct 1980. Trfd to Pakistan 30 Sep 1980.
Later history: renamed *Tippu Sultan* (D 168), renamed *Nazim* (D156), 1993. R1998.
★Vietnam Jul 1967–Jan 1968; ◆Lebanon Aug 1958, Cuba Sep–Oct 1962, Cuba Missile Crisis Oct–Nov 1962, Dominican Rep Aug 1965.

DD 872 *Forrest Royal* FRAM I Apr 1962 Boston NSYd. Decomm and trfd to Turkey 27 Mar 1971.
Later history: renamed *Adatepe* (D-353). R1993.
4★Korea K-1 K-2 K-4 K-5; ★Vietnam Apr–Aug 1967; ◆Lebanon Aug 1958, Taiwan Straits Sep 1958, Cuba Jun–Jul 1962, Quemoy-Matsu Oct–Nov 1962.

DD 873 *Hawkins* Rec **DDR 873**, 18 Mar 1949. Rec **DD 873**, 1 Dec 1973. FRAM I Jan 1965 Boston NSYd. Decomm and stricken 1 Oct 1979. Trfd to Taiwan 17 Mar 1983.
Later history: renamed *Tsu Yang* (930). R1998. Superstructure removed for training.
2★Korea K-4 K-5; ★Vietnam Dec 1965; ◆Cuba Jun–Jul 1962, Cuba Missile Crisis Oct–Nov 1962.

DD 874 *Duncan* Damaged by internal explosion off San Pedro, Cal., 1 Mar 1948. Rec **DDR 874**, 18 Mar 1949. FRAM II Jun 1961 Long Bch NSYd. Rec **DD 874**, 1 Jan 1969. Decomm 15 Jan 1971. Stricken 1 Sep 1973. Sunk as target off southern California, 31 Jul 1980.
7★Korea K-2 K-4 K-5 K-6 K-7 K-8 K-10; ★Vietnam Nov 1963, Apr–May 1964, Sep–Dec 1965, Jan–May 1967, Dec 1968–Mar 1969, May–Jun 1970; ◆Quemoy-Matsu May 1959, May–Jun 1960, Oct–Dec 1961, Nov 1962, May–Jun 1963, Korea Mar–Apr 1969, Mar–Apr 1970.

DD 875 *Henry W. Tucker* Rec **DDR 875**, 18 Mar 1949. Damaged by shore gunfire at Wonsan, Korea, 28 Jun 1951. Rec **DD 875**, 25 Mar 1963. FRAM I Dec 1963 Boston NSYd. Decomm and trfd to Brazil 3 Dec 1973.
Later history: renamed *Marcilio Dias* (D 25). SE1993.
7★Korea K-2 K-4 K-5 K-6 K-7 8, K-10; ★Vietnam Mar–May 1961, Aug–Nov 1964, Feb–Jun 1965, Aug–Nov 1965, Jan–Jul 1966, Jul–Nov 1967, Aug–Sep, Nov 1968–Mar 1969, May–Sep, Nov 1969–Feb 1970, Apr–Jun 1970, Jul–Aug 1971, Jul 1972–Jan 1973; ◆Quemoy-Matsu Jun–Sep 1960, Korea Apr–Jun, Oct–Nov 1969, Mar–Apr 1970.

DD 876 *Rogers* Rec **DDR 876**, 18 Mar 1949. Rec **DD 876**, 30 Jul 1963. FRAM I Jun 1964 Charleston NSYd. Decomm 19 Feb 1981. Stricken 1 Oct 1980. Trfd to South Korea 25 Jul 1981.
Later history: renamed *Jeong Ju/ Jeonju* (DD 925). SE2001.
5★Korea K-4 K-5 K-6 K-8 K-9; 3★Vietnam Jan–Apr 1965, Mar–Jul 1966, Oct 1967–Feb 1968, Feb–Jun 1969, Aug–Nov 1970, Jul–Nov

Figure 5.8: *USS Henry W. Tucker* (DDR 875), *Gearing* class radar picket destroyer, February 1964, with radar mast aft.

DD 877 *Perkins*   1971, Jan–Feb 1973; ◆Quemoy-Matsu Jun–Aug 1959, Sep 1960, Mar–Jun 1962, Korea Jan–Mar 1968, May 1969, Sep 1970.

DD 877 *Perkins*   Rec **DDR 877**, 18 Mar 1949. Damaged by shore gunfire, Korea, 16 Sep 1951. Rec **DD 877**, 30 Sep 1962. FRAM Nov 1962 Long Bch NSYd. Decomm and trfd to Argentina 15 Jan 1973.
Later history: renamed *Comodoro Py* (D27). R1984.
4★Korea K-4 K-5 K-6 K-8; ★Vietnam Nov 1963, Apr–Jul 1965, Aug 1966–Jan 1967, Oct–Dec 1967, Feb 1968, May–Sep 1969, Aug 1970–Jan 1971; ◆Korea Jan–Mar 1968, Sep–Oct 1969.

DD 878 *Vesole*   Rec **DDR 878**, 18 Mar 1949. Rec **DD 878**, 1 Dec 1963. FRAM I Oct 1964 Phila NSYd. Collided with tug off Singapore, 4 Aug 1970. Decomm and stricken 1 Dec 1976. Sunk as target 14 Apr 1983.
2★Vietnam Dec 1965; ◆Lebanon Jul–Sep 1958, Cuba Apr 1961, Cuba Missile Crisis Sep–Dec 1962.

DD 879 *Leary*   Rec **DDR 879**, 18 Mar 1949. Rec **DD 879**, 1 Dec 1963. FRAM I Jan 1965 Phila NSYd. Decomm and trfd to Spain 31 Oct 1973.
Later history: renamed *Langara* (D 65). R1992.
★Vietnam Jun, Aug–Dec 1967, Mar–Aug 1969; ◆Lebanon Aug 1958, Cuba Apr, Dec 1961, Cuba Missile Crisis Oct–Nov 1962, Dominican Rep Aug 1965.

DD 880 *Dyess*   Rec **DDR 880**, 18 Mar 1949. Rec **DD 880**, 1 Dec 1963. FRAM I Feb 1965 Boston NSYd. Decomm and stricken 27 Feb 1981. Sold to Greece for parts 18 Jul 1981, BU.
★Vietnam Mar–Jul 1966; ◆Cuba Apr 1961–Apr 1962, Cuba Missile Crisis Oct–Nov 1962.

DD 881 *Bordelon*   Out of comm 11 Dec 1948–19 Sep 1949. Rec **DDR 881**, 18 Mar 1949. Rec **DD 881**, 25 Mar 1963. FRAM I Dec 1963 Charleston NSYd. Damaged in collision with carrier *John F. Kennedy* off Scotland, 14 Sep 1976. Decomm 1 Jul 1972. Stricken 1 Feb 1977. Trfd to Iran for spare parts, Jul 1977, BU.
★Vietnam Dec 1967–May 1968, Nov 1972–Feb 1973; ◆Cuba Aug 1962, Cuba Missile Crisis Oct–Dec 1962, Dominican Rep Jul–Aug 1965.

DD 882 *Furse*   Rec **DDR 882**, 18 Mar 1949. Rec **DD 882**, 25 Mar 1963. FRAM I Oct 1963 Phila NSYd. Decomm and trfd to Spain 31 Aug 1972.
Later history: renamed *Gravina* (D62). R1991.
★Vietnam Apr–Jun 1968; ◆Cuba Aug 1962, Cuba Missile Crisis Oct–Nov 1962.

DD 883 *Newman K. Perry*   Rec **DDR 883**, 18 Mar 1949. Rec **DD 883**, 1 Dec 1963. FRAM I Feb 1965 Boston NSYd. Damaged in collision with carrier *Shangri-La* southwest of Naples, 27 Aug 1965 (1 killed). Decomm and trfd to South Korea 27 Feb 1981.
Later history: renamed *Kyungki* (DD 923). R1998.

★Vietnam Nov 1966–Mar 1967; ◆Lebanon Sep 1958, Cuba Mar–Apr 1961, Cuba Missile Crisis Oct–Nov 1962.

DD 884 *Floyd B. Parks*   Damaged in collision with cruiser *Columbus* in South China Sea, 11 Mar 1956 (2 killed); lost bow. Repaired with bow of incomplete *Lansdale*. FRAM I May 1963 Puget Sd NSYd. Stricken 2 Jul 1973. Sold 28 Mar 1974, BU.
4★Korea K-4 K-5 K-6 K-8; ★Vietnam Jun–Oct 1965, Nov 1966–Feb 1967, Feb–Jul 1968, Sep 1969–Jan 1970, Feb–Jul 1971, Jul–Dec 1972; ◆Quemoy-Matsu Sep–Oct 1960, Sep–Oct 1961.

DD 885 *John R. Craig*   FRAM I Feb 1963 San Fran NSYd. Damaged by shore gunfire off N. Vietnam, 10 Apr 1972. Decomm and stricken 27 Jul 1979. Sunk as target off southern California, 6 Jun 1980.
4★Korea K-4 K-5 K-6 K-8; ★Vietnam Apr–Aug 1965, Jan–Dec 1966, Mar–Jun 1968, Jun–Oct 1969, Apr 1971, Dec 1971–Jun 1972, Feb–Mar 1973; ◆Quemoy-Matsu Sep–Oct 1960, Sep–Nov 1961, Korea Jan–Mar 1968, Sep 1969, Jan–Feb 1971.

DD 886 *Orleck*   Damaged in collision with submarine *Perch* off Point Loma, Cal., 22 Mar 1949. Damaged by shore gunfire off Taejo, Korea, 19 Jul 1952. FRAM I Nov 1963 Long Bch NSYd. Collided with oiler *Neches* off Vietnam, 19 Mar 1970. Decomm and trfd to Turkey 1 Oct 1982.
Later history: renamed *Yücetepe* (D-345). R1998. Trfd to Southwest Texas War Memorial, Orange, Tex., by Turkey, 12 Aug 2000.
4★Korea K-4 K-5 K-6 K-8; ★Vietnam Oct–Dec 1964, Mar–Apr, Jul–Sep 1965, Nov 1965–May 1966, Oct 1967–Feb 1968, Sep 1968–Jan 1969, Mar–May, Jul, Oct–Dec 1969, Feb–May 1970, Nov 1971–Jan 1972, Dec 1972–Feb 1973; ◆Quemoy-Matsu Jun–Jul 1960, Jul–Aug 1961, Korea Feb, Aug–Oct 1969, Jan, Jun 1970.

DD 887 *Brinkley Bass*   Damaged by shore gunfire at Wonsan, Korea, 20 May 1951 (1 killed), and again off Hodo Pando, 24 Mar 1952. FRAM I May 1962 Puget Sd NSYd. Damaged in collision with destroyer *Waddell* in Gulf of Tonkin, 5 Feb 1966. Decomm and stricken and trfd to Brazil 3 Dec 1973.
Later history: renamed *Mariz e Barros* (D 26). SE1993.
7★Korea K-2 K-4 K-5 K-6 K-7 K-8 K-10; ★Vietnam Nov 1965–Feb 1966, Feb–Apr 1967, Aug 1968–Jan 1969, Feb–Jun 1970, Jun–Sep 1971; ◆Quemoy-Matsu May–Jun 1960.

DD 888 *Stickell*   Rec **DDR 888**, 3 Dec 1951. Out of comm 13 Dec 1952–2 Sep 1953. FRAM I Mar 1964 Phila NSYd. Rec **DD 888**, 1963. Decomm and stricken 1 Jul 1972, and trfd to Greece.
Later history: renamed *Kanaris* (D-212). SE1993. R1993.
6★Korea K-2 K-4 K-5 K-6 K-7 K-8; 1★Vietnam Mar–Jun 1966; ◆Cuba Oct 1961, Cuba Missile Crisis Oct–Nov 1962, Dominican Rep Jun–Jul 1965.

DD 889 *O'Hare*   Out of comm 3 Jan 1953–1 Sep 1963. Rec **DDR 889**, 4 Apr 1953. Rec **DD 889**, 23 Mar 1963. FRAM I Dec 1963 Norfolk NSYd. Decomm 31 Oct 1973 and trfd to Spain.
Later history: renamed *Mendez Nuñez* (D 63). R1992.
★Vietnam Jul–Nov 1966, Jan 1973; ◆Cuba Oct 1961, Cuba Missile Crisis Oct–Nov 196K-2 Dominican Rep May 1965.

DD 890 *Meredith*   FRAM I Jun 1961 Phila NSYd. Decomm and stricken 29 Jun 1979. Trfd to Turkey 7 Dec 1979.
Later history: renamed *Savaştepe* (D-348). R1994; BU 1995.
★Vietnam Mar–Aug 1969; ◆Lebanon Aug–Sep 1958, Congo Oct–Nov 1961, Korea Apr–May 1969.

Notes: DD 818, 819, 820, 848 and 871 were completed as hunter-killer destroyers (DDK), armed with 4–5″/38 guns. DD 827 had 6–3″/50, weapon Alfa. All fitted with tripod masts, 1950s, and rearmed with 3-inch guns replacing 40 mm. FRAM modernizations were carried out starting 1960. FRAM I extended service life 8 years: 6–5″/38, 6–3″/50, 5 TT, 2 Hedgehog; FRAM II extended service life 5 years. Ex-DDE: 4–5″/38, 2–3″/50, ASROC, 6 TT, 1 hedgehog. Ex-DDR: 6–5″/38, 2–3″/50, 8 TT, 2 hedgehog; DD 713, 831 and 874 retained TACAN tripod mast aft after reversion to DD. DD 712 had 4–5″/38, 4–3″/50, 6 TT; DD 848 4–5″, 4–3″/50, 8–40 mm, 5 TT. All had new taller stacks.

Figure 5.9: *USS Bordelon* (DD 881), *Gearing* class FRAM 1 conversion, 20 Jul 1964.

Figure 5.10: USS *Conway* (DDE 507) coming alongside for refuelling during the 1960s. She was one of eighteen units converted to escort destroyers, retaining only two 5-inch guns, weapon Alfa added forward, and torpedo tubes replaced by ASW launchers.

ESCORT DESTROYERS

DDE 445	*Fletcher*
DDE 446	*Radford*
DDE 447	*Jenkins*
DDE 449	*Nicholas*
DDE 450	*O'Bannon*
DDE 465	*Saufley*
DDE 466	*Waller*
DDE 468	*Taylor*
DDE 470	*Bache*
DDE 471	*Beale*
DDE 498	*Philip*
DDE 499	*Renshaw*
DDE 507	*Conway*
DDE 508	*Cony*
DDE 515	*Anthony*
DDE 517	*Walker*
DDE 576	*Murray*
DDE 577	*Sproston*

Notes: *Fletcher* class destroyers converted 1950 and rec DDE. Armament: 2–5″, 4–3″/50 guns, weapon Alfa, TT replaced by 4 ASW launchers. All rec DD, 1 Jul 1962.

DDE 719	*Epperson*	—
DDE 764	*Lloyd Thomas*	DDK
DDE 765	*Keppler*	DDK
DDE 818	*New*	—
DDE 819	*Holder*	—
DDE 820	*Rich*	—
DDE 824	*Basilone*	—
DDE 825	*Carpenter*	DDK
DDE 827	*Robert A. Owens*	DDK
DDE 847	*Robert L. Wilson*	—
DDE 858	*Fred T. Berry*	DDK
DDE 859	*Norris*	DDK
DDE 860	*McCaffery*	—
DDE 861	*Harwood*	—
DDE 871	*Damato*	—

Notes: Gearing class destroyers, some originally converted as hunter-killer destroyers (DDK). DDE designation eliminated 1962.

Figure 5.11: USS *Carpenter* (DDK 825), 26 Jun 1950, was completed as a "hunter-killer" destroyer, later reclassified DDE. Notice different armament from standard units.

Figure 5.12: USS *Robert A. Owens* (DDE 827), *Gearing* class completed to a modified design as an escort destroyer, June 1958, with only two turrets and two Weapon Alfa mounts.

RADAR PICKET DESTROYERS

DD 711 *Eugene A. Greene*   Rec **DDR 711**, 18 Jul 1952. Rec **DD 711**, 25 Mar 1963.
DD 713 *Kenneth D. Bailey*   Rec **DDR 713**, 9 Apr 1953. Rec **DD 713**, 1 Jan 1969.
DD 714 *William R. Rush*   Rec **DDR 714**, 18 Jul 1952. Rec **DD 714**, Apr 1965.
DD 715 *William M. Wood*   Rec **DDR 715**, 2 Oct 1952. Rec **DD 715**, 1 Jul 1964.
DD 742 *Frank Knox*   Rec **DDR 742**, 18 Mar 1949. Rec **DD 742**, 1 Jan 1969.
DD 743 *Southerland*   Rec **DDR 743**, 18 Mar 1949. Rec **DD 743**, 1 Apr 1964.
DD 784 *McKean*   Rec **DDR 784**, 18 Jul 1952. Rec **DD 784**, 1 Dec 1963.
DD 805 *Chevalier*   Rec **DDR 805**, 13 Mar 1949. Rec **DD 805**, 13 Jul 1962.
DD 806 *Higbee*   Rec **DDR 806**, 18 Mar 1949. Rec **DD 806**, 1 Jun 1963.
DD 807 *Benner*   Rec **DDR 807**, 18 Mar 1949. Rec **DD 807**, 15 Nov 1962.
DD 808 *Dennis J. Buckley*   Rec **DDR 808**, 18 Mar 1949. Rec **DD 808**, 1 Dec 1963.
DD 817 *Corry*   Rec **DDR 817**, 9 Apr 1953. Rec **DD 817**, 1 Jan 1964.
DD 829 *Myles C. Fox*   Rec **DDR 829**, 18 Mar 1949. Rec **DD 829**, 1 Apr 1964.
DD 830 *Everett F. Larson*   Rec **DDR 830**, 18 Mar 1949. Rec **DD 830**, 1 Dec 1962.
DD 831 *Goodrich*   Rec **DDR 831**, 18 Mar 1949. Rec **DD 831**, 1 Jan 1969.
DD 832 *Hanson*   Rec **DDR 832**, 18 Mar 1949. Rec **DD 832** 1 Dec 1963.
DD 833 *Herbert J. Thomas*   Rec **DDR 833**, 18 Mar 1949. Rec **DD 833**, 1 Dec 1963.
DD 834 *Turner*   Rec **DDR 834**, 18 Mar 1949. Rec **DD 834**, 1 Jan 1969.
DD 835 *Charles P. Cecil*   Rec **DDR 835**, 18 Mar 1949. Rec **DD 835**, 1 Jun 1963.
DD 838 *Ernest G. Small*   Rec **DDR 838**, 18 Jul 1952. Rec **DD 838**, 1 Jan 1969.
DD 842 *Fiske*   Rec **DDR 842**, 18 Jul 1952. Rec **DD 842**, 1 Dec 1963.
DD 863 *Steinaker*   Rec **DDR 863**, 1 Jul 1952. Rec **DD 863**, 1 Jul 1964.

No.	Name				
DD 870	Fechteler		Rec **DDR 870**, 9 Apr 1953. Rec **DD 870**, 25 Mar 1963.		
DD 873	Hawkins		Rec **DDR 873**, 18 Mar 1949. Rec **DD 873**, 1 Dec 1973.		
DD 874	Duncan		Rec **DDR 874**, 18 Mar 1949. Rec **DD 874**, 1 Jan 1969.		
DD 875	Henry W. Tucker		Rec **DDR 875**, 18 Mar 1949. Rec **DD 875**, 25 Mar 1963.		
DD 876	Rogers		Rec **DDR 876**, 18 Mar 1949. Rec **DD 876**, 30 Jul 1963.		
DD 877	Perkins		Rec **DDR 877**, 18 Mar 1949. Rec **DD 877**, 30 Sep 1962.		
DD 878	Vesole		Rec **DDR 878**, 18 Mar 1949. Rec **DD 878**, 1 Dec 1963.		
DD 879	Leary		Rec **DDR 879**, 18 Mar 1949. Rec **DD 879**, 1 Dec 1963.		
DD 880	Dyess		Rec **DDR 880**, 18 Mar 1949. Rec **DD 880**, 1 Dec 1963.		
DD 881	Bordelon		Rec **DDR 881**, 18 Mar 1949. Rec **DD 881**, 25 Mar 1963.		
DD 882	Furse		Rec **DDR 882**, 18 Mar 1949. Rec **DD 882**, 25 Mar 1963.		
DD 883	Newman K. Perry		Rec **DDR 883**, 18 Mar 1949. Rec **DD 883**, 1 Dec 1963.		
DD 888	Stickell		Rec **DDR 888**, 3 Dec 1951. Rec **DD 888**, 1963.		
DD 889	O'Hare		Rec **DDR 889** 4 Apr 1953. Rec **DD 889** 23 Mar 1963.		

Notes: Some converted but not reclassified until later, tripod mainmast, additional 40 mm guns, no TT. Conversion of *Orleck* canceled.

Forrest Sherman Class

No.	Name	Builder	Keel Laid	Launched	Comm.
DD 931	Forrest Sherman	Bath	27 Oct 1953	5 Feb 1955	9 Nov 1955
DD 932	John Paul Jones	Bath	18 Jan 1954	7 May 1955	5 Apr 1956
DD 933	Barry	Bath	15 Mar 1954	1 Oct 1955	9 Jul 1956
DD 936	Decatur	Beth;Quincy	13 Sep 1954	15 Dec 1955	7 Dec 1956
DD 937	Davis	Beth;Quincy	1 Feb 1955	28 Mar 1956	6 Mar 1957
DD 938	Jonas Ingram	Beth;Quincy	15 Jun 1955	7 Aug 1956	19 Jul 1957
DD 940	Manley	Bath	10 Feb 1955	12 Apr 1956	1 Feb 1957
DD 941	DuPont	Bath	11 May 1955	8 Sep 1956	1 Jul 1957
DD 942	Bigelow	Bath	6 Jul 1955	2 Feb 1957	8 Nov 1957
DD 943	Blandy	Beth;Quincy	29 Dec 1955	19 Dec 1956	26 Nov 1957
DD 944	Mullinix	Beth;Quincy	5 Apr 1956	18 Mar 1957	7 Mar 1958
DD 945	Hull	Bath	12 Sep 1956	10 Aug 1957	3 Jul 1958
DD 946	Edson	Bath	3 Dec 1956	4 Jan 1958	7 Nov 1958
DD 947	Somers	Bath	4 Mar 1957	30 May 1958	3 Apr 1959
DD 948	Morton	Ingalls	4 Mar 1957	23 May 1958	26 May 1959
DD 949	Parsons	Ingalls	17 Jun 1957	19 Aug 1958	29 Oct 1959
DD 950	Richard S. Edwards	Puget Sd Brdg	20 Dec 56	24 Sep 1957	5 Feb 1959
DD 951	Turner Joy ex-*Joy* (26 Jul 1957)	Puget Sd.Brdg	30 Sep 1957	5 May 1958	3 Aug 1959

Displacement	2,850 tons, 4,050 f/l
Dimensions	418'5" (oa); 407' (wl) × 45' × 15'
Machinery	2 screws; ST; 4 boilers; 70,000 SHP; 33 knots
Endurance	4,500/20
Complement	337
Armament	3–5"/54, 2 twin 3"/70 guns, 4–21"TT, 6–12.75"ASWTT, 2 hedgehog. ASW mod: 2–5"/54, ASROC, 2 triple torpedo launchers. As DDG: 1 Tartar launcher, 1–5"/54 gun, 1 ASROC, 2 triple torpedo launchers.

Notes: Two raked stacks, two upright tripod masts. First postwar destroyers built for USN.
DD 933, 937, 938, 940, 941, 943, 948, 950 modified for ASW service, 1967–72. DD 932, 936, 947, 949 converted to missile destroyers (DDG), lattice masts replaced tripods, 1966–67. Conversion of DD 951 canceled. *Hull* used as test ship for Mk 71 8" gun 1975, later canceled.

Figure 5.13: USS *Hull* (DD 945), *Forrest Sherman* class, as built.

Service Records:

DD 931 *Forrest Sherman* Out of comm 20 Dec 1965–23 Sep 1967. Decomm 5 Nov 1982. Stricken 27 Jul 1990. Sold 11 Dec 1992, resold 8 Jun 1994, repossessed.
  ◆Lebanon Aug 1958, Taiwan Straits Sep 1958, Cuba Apr 1961, Iran/Indian Ocean Apr–Jul 1980.

DD 932 *John Paul Jones* Rec **DDG 32**, 15 Mar 1967. Out of comm 2 Dec 1965–23 Sep 1967. Decomm 15 Dec 1982. Stricken 30 Nov 1985. Sunk as target off southern California, 31 Jan 2001.
  ★Vietnam Nov 1968–Mar 1969, Mar–Jul 1970, Apr–Jun 1972; ◆Cuba Feb–Mar 1962, Cuba Missile Crisis Oct–Nov 1962, (as DDG) Evac of Vietnam 29–30 Apr 1975, Iran/Indian Ocean Feb–Mar 1980.

DD 933 *Barry* Out of comm Apr 1967–19 Apr 1968. Decomm 5 Nov 1982. Stricken 31 Jan 1983.
  Later history: Museum at Washington DC.
  ★Vietnam Nov–Dec 1965; ◆Lebanon Jul–Aug 1958, Cuba Dec 1961, Cuba Missile Crisis Oct–Nov 1962.

DD 936 *Decatur* Damaged in collision with carrier *Lake Champlain* off Cape Henry, Va., 6 May 1964. Rec **DDG 31**, 15 Sep 1966. Out of comm 15 Jun 1966–29 Apr 1967. Decomm 30 Jun 1983. Stricken 16 Mar 1988. Self-defense test ship 1994–2003. Sunk as target in Pacific, 21 Jul 2004.
  ★Vietnam Aug 1968–Jan 1969, Mar–Jul 1970, Nov 1971–Feb 1972, Feb–Mar 1973; ◆Cuba Missile Crisis Oct–Nov 1962, (as DDG) Korea Dec 1968, Iran/Indian Ocean Jan–Mar 1979.

DD 937 *Davis* Out of comm 31 Oct 1969–17 Oct 1970. Decomm 20 Dec 1982. Stricken 27 Jul 1990. Sold 11 Dec 1992, resold 8 Jun 1994, BU Baltimore.
  ★Vietnam Mar–Jul 1966, Oct 1968–Feb 1969, Jul–Nov 1972; ◆Cuba Aug 1961, Cuba Missile Crisis Oct–Nov 1962. Dominican Rep Jun–Jul 1965, Iran/Indian Ocean Mar–Jun 1979, Oct 1981.

DD 938 *Jonas Ingram* Out of comm 29 Apr 1969–1 Aug 1970. Decomm 4 Mar 1983. Stricken 15 Jun 1983. Sunk as target 23 Jul 1988.
  ◆Lebanon Sep 1958, Oct–Nov 1982, Iran/Indian Ocean Feb–Apr 1981.

DD 940 *Manley* Damaged by heavy seas in eastern Atlantic, 12 Dec 1957. Damaged by small explosion off Vietnam, 7 Dec 1966. Damaged by shell explosion off Da Nang, 17 Mar 1967. Out of comm 30 Jan 1970–17 Apr 1971. Damaged by fire at Mayport, Fla., Feb 1979 (1 killed). Decomm 4 Mar 1983. Stricken 1 Jun 1990. Sold 11 Dec 1992, resold 8 Jun 1994, BU Baltimore.
  ★Vietnam Nov 1966–Mar 1967, Dec 1967–May 1968; ◆Cuba Missile Crisis Oct–Nov 1962, Lebanon Aug–Sep 1982.

DD 941 *DuPont* Out of comm 23 May 1969–9 May 1970. Decomm 4 Mar 1983. Stricken 1 Jun 1990. Sold 14 Jan 1993, BU.

Destroyers 71

★Vietnam Aug–Dec 1967, Oct 1968–Feb 1969; ◆Cuba Mar–Apr 1961, Cuba Missile Crisis Oct–Nov 1962, Dominican Rep Sep 1965, Iran/Indian Ocean Apr–Oct 1981, Lebanon Aug–Oct 1982.

DD 942 *Bigelow* Explosion in gun mount off Vietnam, 20 Apr 1967. Decomm 5 Nov 1982. Stricken 1 Jun 1990. Sold 11 Dec 1992, resold 8 Jun 1994, sale canceled. Sunk as target, 2 Apr 2003.
★Vietnam Mar–Aug 1967; ◆Cuba Missile Crisis Oct–Nov 1962, Dominican Rep May 1965, Iran/Indian Ocean May–Aug 1981.

DD 943 *Blandy* Out of comm 15 Jan 1969–2 May 1970. Decomm 5 Nov 1982. Stricken 27 Jul 1990. Sold 11 Dec 1992, resold 30 Jun 1994, BU Baltimore.
★Vietnam May–Oct 1968, Oct 1972–Feb 1973; ◆Cuba Missile Crisis Oct–Nov 1962, Iran/Indian Ocean Dec 1978–May 1979.

DD 944 *Mullinix* Decomm 11 Aug 1983. Stricken 26 Jul 1990. Sunk as target by *Iowa*, 22 Aug 1992.
★Vietnam Aug–Nov 1966, Feb–Jul 1969, May, Aug–Sep 1972; ◆Cuba Missile Crisis Oct–Nov 1962, Iran/Indian Ocean Dec 1978, Apr–Jul 1980, Lebanon Dec 1982–Jan 1983.

DD 945 *Hull* Decomm 11 Jul 1983. Stricken 15 Nov 1983. Sunk as target off southern California, 7 Apr 1998.
★Vietnam Jun–Sep 1965, Sep 1966–Jan 1967, Feb–Jun 1968, Jul 1969–Jan 1970, Apr–Aug 1971, May–Oct 1972; ◆Quemoy-Matsu Sep–Oct 1960, Sep–Oct 1961.

DD 946 *Edson* Damaged by fire off Hawaii, 12 Dec 1974. Decomm 15 Dec 1988. Stricken 31 Jan 1989. To *Intrepid* museum 30 Jun 1989
Later history: museum at New York, NY. 1989–2003. To be moved to Sheboygan, Wis.
★Vietnam Jul–Sep 1964, Nov 1965–Mar 1966, Feb–Mar, May–Jul 1967, Apr–Sep 1968, Apr–Aug 1970, May–Sep 1971; ◆Quemoy-Matsu Mar 1960, Dec 1962–Jan 1962, Evac of Cambodia Apr 1975, Evac of Vietnam 29–30 Apr 1975.

DD 947 *Somers* Rec **DDG 34**, 15 Mar 1967. Out of comm 11 Apr 1966–10 Feb 1968. Decomm 19 Nov 1982. Stricken 26 Apr 1988. Sunk as target off Kauai, 22 Jul 1998.
5★Vietnam May 1960, Feb–May 1965, (as DDG) Dec 1968, Jan–Apr 1970, Dec 1970–May 1971, May–Oct 1972; ◆Quemoy-Matsu Jun–Jul 1961, Korea Feb 1970.

DD 948 *Morton* Out of comm 26 Sep 1969–15 Aug 1970. Decomm 22 Nov 1982. Stricken 7 Feb 1990. Sold 4 Mar 1992, BU.
★Vietnam Apr 1960, Sep–Nov 1964, Apr–Aug 1966, May–Oct 1967, Dec 1968–Mar 1969, Oct 1971–Feb 1972, Oct 1972–Feb 1973; ◆Quemoy-Matsu May–Jun 1961.

DD 949 *Parsons* Rec **DDG 33**, 15 Mar 1967. Out of comm 19 Jan 1966–3 Nov 1967. Sank f/v *Orient* in collision off southern California, 12 Dec 1969. Collided with salvage vessel *Grasp* southwest of Tokyo, 5 May 1977. Decomm 19 Nov 1982. Stricken 1 Dec 1984. Sunk as target, 25 Apr 1989.
★Vietnam Dec 1960, Sep–Dec 1964, (as DDG) Nov 1968–Apr 1969, Apr–Jul 1970, Dec 1971–Nov 1972; ◆Quemoy-Matsu Jan–Feb 1961, Apr–May 1963, (as DDG) Korea Apr 1969, Iran/Indian Ocean Nov 1979–Feb 1980, Aug–Oct 1980.

DD 950 *Richard S. Edwards* Damaged in collision with carrier *Bennington* off California, 10 Aug 1960. Out of comm 27 Feb 1970–15 Jan 1971. Decomm 15 Dec 1982. Stricken 7 Feb 1990. Sunk as target, Pacific Missile Range, 3 Sep 1991.
6★Vietnam Apr–May 1961, Apr 1963, Sep 1964–Jan 1965, Mar–Jul 1966, Sep 1967–Feb 1968, Feb–Jun 1969, Apr–Oct 1972. ◆Quemoy-Matsu Mar–Apr 1963.

DD 951 *Turner Joy* Gulf of Tonkin Incident, 4 Aug 1964. Explosion in 5-inch gun mount off Vietnam, 26 Oct 1965 (3 killed). Decomm 22 Nov 1982. Stricken 13 Feb 1990.
Later history: museum at Bremerton, Wash., 10 Apr 1991.
9★Vietnam Jun–Sep 1964, Aug 1965–Apr 1967, Apr–Sep 1968, Dec 1969–May 1970, Mar–Jun 1971, Jan–Mar 1973; ◆Quemoy-Matsu Jul–Aug 1960, Korea Feb 1970.

No.	Former	date	Rec	date
DD 927–930	—	—	DL 2–5	9 Feb 1951
DD 934	*Hanazuki* (Japanese)	—	—	—
DD 935	*T-35* (German)	—	—	—
DD 939	*Z-39* (German)	—	—	—
DD 952–959	—	—	DDG 2–9	23 Apr 1957

No.	Builder	Completed	Built for	Name	Fate
DD 960	Mitsubishi	13 Feb 1960	Japan	*Akizuki* (DD 161)	SE1972
DD 961	SMJ, Kobe	29 Feb 1960	Japan	*Teruzuki* (DD 162)	SE1972
DD 962		16 Dec 1958	Pakistan	*Shah Jahan* (164)	SE1972

ex-HMS *Charity* (acq 4 Oct 1957, stricken 16 Dec 1958)

Spruance Class

No.	Name	Builder	Keel Laid	Launched	Comm.
DD 963	*Spruance*	Ingalls	27 Nov 1972	10 Nov 1973	20 Sep 1975
DD 964	*Paul F. Foster*	Ingalls	6 Feb 1973	23 Feb 1974	21 Feb 1976
DD 965	*Kinkaid*	Ingalls	19 Apr 1973	25 May 1974	10 Jul 1976
DD 966	*Hewitt*	Ingalls	23 Jul 1973	24 Aug 1974	25 Sep 1976
DD 967	*Elliot*	Ingalls	15 Oct 1973	19 Dec 1974	22 Jan 1977
DD 968	*Arthur W. Radford*	Ingalls	24 Jan 1974	1 Mar 1975	16 Apr 1977
DD 969	*Peterson*	Ingalls	29 Apr 1974	21 Jun 1975	9 Jul 1977
DD 970	*Caron*	Ingalls	1 Jul 1974	24 Jun 1975	1 Oct 1977
DD 971	*David R. Ray*	Ingalls	23 Sep 1974	23 Aug 1975	19 Nov 1977
DD 972	*Oldendorf*	Ingalls	27 Dec 1974	21 Oct 1975	4 Mar 1978
DD 973	*John Young*	Ingalls	17 Feb 1975	7 Feb 1976	20 May 1978
DD 974	*Comte de Grasse*	Ingalls	4 Apr 1975	26 Mar 1976	5 Aug 1978
DD 975	*O'Brien*	Ingalls	9 May 1975	8 Jul 1976	3 Dec 1977
DD 976	*Merrill*	Ingalls	16 Jun 1975	1 Sep 1976	11 Mar 1978
DD 977	*Briscoe*	Ingalls	21 Jul 1975	15 Dec 1976	3 Jun 1978
DD 978	*Stump*	Ingalls	22 Aug 1975	30 Apr 1977	19 Aug 1978
DD 979	*Conolly*	Ingalls	29 Sep 1975	25 Jun 1977	14 Oct 1978
DD 980	*Moosbrugger*	Ingalls	3 Nov 1975	20 Aug 1977	16 Dec 1978
DD 981	*John Hancock*	Ingalls	16 Jan 1976	28 Sep 1977	10 Mar 1979
DD 982	*Nicholson*	Ingalls	20 Feb 1976	29 Nov 1977	12 May 1979

Figure 5.14: *USS Arthur W. Radford* (DD 968) fitted with Advanced Enclosed Mast/Sensor (AEM/S) in place of the mainmast 1997.

72   The Navy of the Nuclear Age, 1947–2007

DD 983	John Rodgers	Ingalls	12 Aug 1976	25 Feb 1978	14 Jul 1979
DD 984	Leftwich	Ingalls	12 Nov 1976	8 Apr 1978	25 Aug 1979
DD 985	Cushing	Ingalls	2 Feb 1977	17 Jun 1978	21 Sep 1979
DD 986	Harry W. Hill	Ingalls	1 Apr 1977	10 Aug 1978	15 Nov 1979
DD 987	O'Bannon	Ingalls	24 Jun 1977	25 Sep 1978	15 Dec 1979
DD 988	Thorn	Ingalls	29 Aug 1977	22 Nov 1978	16 Feb 1980
DD 989	Deyo	Ingalls	14 Oct 1977	20 Jan 1979	22 Mar 1980
DD 990	Ingersoll	Ingalls	16 Dec 1977	10 Mar 1979	12 Apr 1980
DD 991	Fife	Ingalls	6 Mar 1978	1 May 1979	31 May 1980
DD 992	Fletcher	Ingalls	24 Apr 1978	16 Jun 1979	12 Jul 1980
DD 997	Hayler	Ingalls	20 Oct 1980	27 Mar 1982	5 Mar 1983

Displacement	7,410 tons; 9,250 f/l
Dimensions	563′4″ (oa); 528′10″(wl) × 55′ × 29′
Machinery	2 screws; gas turbines; 86,000 SHP; 32.5 knots
Endurance	6,000/20
Complement	325
Armament	1–8 cell NATO Sea Sparrow, 1–21 cell RAM lchr, 8 Harpoon SSM, 30-cell VLS Tomahawk Built: 2–5″/54, 1 ASROC, 1 Sea Sparrow, 6–12.75″TT; 2 LAMPS h/c

Notes: Primarily ASW destroyers. First major warships powered by gas turbines. Same hulls and machinery as *Ticonderoga* class cruisers. Two LAMPS helicopters planned. First ships fitted with Harpoon. *Arthur W. Radford* fitted with Advanced Enclosed Mast/Sensor (AEM/S) in place of mainmast 1997; test platform for DD(X) program 2004; superstructure removed, new power plants.

Figure 5.15: Destroyer *Hayler* (DD 997) in the Atlantic Ocean, 18 Jun 2001.

Service Records:

DD 963 *Spruance* Damaged by grounding on reef off Andros, Bahamas, 15 Jan 1989. In collision with m/v *Matsumi Maru No. 7* in Malacca Straits, 20 Jun 1992. Decomm 23 Mar 2005. Stricken 18 Mar 2005. Sunk as target off Virginia Capes, 6 Dec 2006.
◆Libya May–Jul 1988, Gulf War Feb–Mar 1991.

DD 964 *Paul F. Foster* Decomm 27 Mar 2003. Stricken 6 Apr 2004. Converted to self-defense test ship, rec **EDD 964**, 16 Mar 2005.
◆Iran/Indian Ocean Mar 1980, Libya Apr–Jun 1989, Gulf War Jan–Apr 1991, Indian Ocean Apr–Jun 1997, Apr–Jul 1999.

DD 965 *Kinkaid* Damaged in collision with m/v *Kota Petoni* in Malacca Straits, 12 Nov 1989 (1 killed). Decomm 7 Jan 2003. Stricken 6 Apr 2004. Sunk as target, 14 Jul 2004.
◆Iran/Indian Ocean Jan–Mar 1979, Indian Ocean Oct 1997–Jan 1998, Aug–Sep 1999, Jul–Aug 2001.

DD 966 *Hewitt* Attacked Iraqi installations, 17 Jan 1993. Attacks on Iraq, 3–4 Sep 1996. Decomm 19 Jul 2001. Stricken 5 Jun 2002. BU 2002, Brownsville, Tex.
◆Iran/Indian Ocean Jun–Aug 1980, Libya Jan 1990, Gulf War Jun–Sep 1991, Indian Ocean Apr–Jul 1999, Dec 2000–Mar 2001.

DD 967 *Elliot* Attack on Al Quaeda camps in Afghanistan, 20 Aug 1998. Decomm 2 Dec 2003. Stricken 6 Apr 2004. Sunk as target off Australia, 23 Jul 2005.
◆Iran/Indian Ocean Apr–Jun 1979, Libya May–Jun 1990, Gulf War Sep–Dec 1991, Indian Ocean Jul–Oct 1998, Feb–May 2000.

DD 968 *Arthur W. Radford* Damaged in collision with m/v *Saudi Riyadh* off Virginia Beach, 4 Feb 1999. Decomm and stricken 6 Apr 2004. Loan to Northrup Grumman as DD(X) trials ship, civilian crew.
◆Lebanon Jun–Jul, Sep 1983, Gulf War Oct 1991–Mar 1992, Indian Ocean May–Jul 2000.

DD 969 *Peterson* Decomm 4 Oct 2002. Stricken 6 Nov 2002. Sunk as target, 16 Feb 2004.
◆Iran/Indian Ocean Oct 1980–Feb 1981, Lebanon Jun–Jul 1984, Libya/El Dorado Mar–Jun 1986, Liberia Aug 1990–Feb 1991, Iraq missile strikes Jun 1993.

DD 970 *Caron* In collision with Soviet frigate *SKR-6* (Mirka II class) in

Figure 5.16: USS *Caron* (DD 970), *Spruance* class destroyer. Notice 5-inch gun and ASROC forward, Phalanx CIWS above bridge, heavy vertical tripod masts.

Black Sea, 12 Feb 1988. Attacked Iraqi installations, 17 Jan 1993. Decomm 15 Oct 2001. Stricken 5 Jun 2002. Used as target, sank accidentally as result of explosions south of Puerto Rico, 4 Dec 2002.
◆Grenada Oct–Nov 1983, Lebanon Nov 1983–Feb 1984, Libya/El Dorado Jan–Mar 1986, Gulf War Jan–May 1991, Indian Ocean Feb–Jun 1996. Haiti 1994.

DD 971 *David R. Ray* Sank with gunfire hulk of m/v tkr *New Carissa* leaking oil off Oregon, 11 Mar 1999. Decomm 26 Feb 2002. Stricken 6 Nov 2002.
◆Iran/Indian Ocean Nov 1979–Feb 1980, May–Oct 1981, Gulf War Aug–Sep 1990, Indian Ocean Jul–Oct 1997, Apr–Jul 1999.

DD 972 *Oldendorf* Decomm 20 Jun 2003. Stricken 6 Apr 2004. Sunk as target off Hawaii, 22 Aug 2005.
◆Libya Nov 1987–Feb 1988, Gulf War Nov–Mar 1991, Indian Ocean Jan–Mar 1996, Dec 1998–Mar 1999, Jul 2000–Jan 2001.

DD 973 *John Young* Destroyed Iranian oil platforms, 19 Oct 1987. Decomm 30 Sep 2002. Stricken 6 Nov 2002. Sunk as target off Hawaii, 13 Apr 2004.

◆Libya Aug–Nov 1987, Gulf War Feb–Jun 1992, Indian Ocean Mar–Jul 1996, Dec 1997–May 1998, Oct 1999–Mar 2000.

DD 974 *Comte de Grasse* Decomm and stricken 5 Jun 1998. Sunk as target off Virginia, 7 Jun 2006.
◆Iran/Indian Ocean Jul–Sep 1980, Libya Jul 1989, Gulf War Sep 1992, Haiti Sep–Oct 1994.

DD 975 *O'Brien* Decomm and stricken 24 Sep 2004. Sunk as target off Hawaii, 9 Feb 2006.
◆Libya Apr–Jul 1988, Gulf War Aug–Dec 1990, Indian Ocean Mar–Jul 1998, Iraq War 2003.

DD 976 *Merrill* Decomm and stricken 26 Mar 1998. Sunk as target 1 Aug 2003.
◆Libya Feb–Apr 1988, Dec 1989–Mar 1990, Gulf War Jul–Oct 1991, Indian Ocean May–Jun 1997.

DD 977 *Briscoe* Attack on Al Quaeda camps in Sudan, 20 Aug 1998. Decomm 2 Oct 2003. Stricken 6 Apr 2004. Sunk as target off North Carolina, 25 Aug 2005.
◆Iran/Indian Ocean Jul–Sep 1980, Grenada Nov 1983, Lebanon Apr–May, Jul–Aug 1984, Gulf War Aug–Oct 1992, Indian Ocean Apr–Aug 1998, Iraq War 2003.

DD 978 *Stump* Attacked Iraqi installations, 17 Jan 1993. Decomm and stricken 22 Oct 2004. Sunk as target off Virginia, 7 Jun 2006.
◆Libya May–Jun 1988, Indian Ocean Jan 1997, Dec 2000–Mar 2001.

DD 979 *Conolly* Decomm and stricken 18 Sep 1998.
◆Iran/Indian Ocean Sep–Nov 1980, Libya Apr–Aug 1989, Gulf War Apr–Aug 1992.

DD 980 *Moosbrugger* Collided with frigate *W.S. Sims* at Guantanamo, 22 Nov 1985. Decomm 15 Dec 2000. BU 2006, Brownsville, Tex.
◆Grenada Oct–Nov 1983, Lebanon Nov 1983–Feb 1984, Gulf War Oct 1990–Mar 1991.

DD 981 *John Hancock* Decomm 16 Oct 2003. Stricken 10 July 2006. Sold 12 May 2006, BU Brownsville, Tex.
◆Gulf War Jan–May 1992.

DD 982 *Nicholson* Damaged in collision with support ship *Detroit* east of Norfolk, Va., 27 Aug 2000. Decomm 20 Sep 2000. Stricken 6 Apr 2004. Sunk as target, 30 Jul 2004.
◆Libya Mar–Aug 1990, Indian Ocean Jan–May 1997, Nov 1998–Jan 1999, Desert Fox 1998.

DD 983 *John Rodgers* Decomm and stricken 4 Sep 1998. Sold 9 Sep 2005, BU Brownsville, Tex.
◆Lebanon May–Oct 1983, Gulf War Aug 1990.

DD 984 *Leftwich* Collided with submarine *Thomas Edison* off Subic Bay, 29 Nov 1982. Destroyed Iranian oil platforms, 19 Oct 1987. Decomm and stricken 27 Mar 1998. Sunk as target off Hawaii, 1 Aug 2003.
◆Iran/Indian Ocean Jul–Sep 1981, Libya Sep–Nov 1987, Gulf War Dec 1990–Mar 1991, Indian Ocean Jan–Apr 1997.

DD 985 *Cushing* Decomm and stricken, 21 Sep 2005. Sunk as target Jul 2008.
◆Iran/Indian Ocean Jul–Sep 1981, Indian Ocean Jan–Feb 1997, Oct 1999–Mar 2000, Iraq War 2003.

DD 986 *Harry W. Hill* Damaged in collision with replenishment ship *Kansas City* in Gulf of Oman, 14 Jan 1991. Decomm and stricken 29 May 1998. Sunk as target, 15 Jul 2004.
◆Libya Jan 1989, Gulf War Jan–Mar 1991, Indian Ocean Oct 1997–Jan 1998.

DD 987 *O'Bannon* Decomm and stricken 19 Aug 2005. To be trfd to Turkey.
◆Libya Jan–Apr 1989, Haiti Sep–Oct 1994, Indian Ocean Aug–Dec 1997.

DD 988 *Thorn* Decomm 25 Aug 2004. Sunk as target off U.S. east coast, 22 Jul 2006.
◆Lebanon Oct–Nov 1982, Indian Ocean Apr–Sep 1997.

DD 989 *Deyo* Damaged when struck by cargo ship *Gilliland* which broke loose during storm while converting at Newport News, Jun 1996. Decomm 7 Nov 2003. Stricken 6 Apr 2004. Sunk as target off North Carolina, 25 Aug 2005.
◆Iran/Indian Ocean Jul–Oct 1981, Libya Dec 1987–Feb 1988, Aug–Dec 1989, Iraq War 2003.

DD 990 *Ingersoll* Collided with Canadian replenishment ship *Provider* as Esquimault, BC, 29 Jan 1986. Damaged in collision with m/v tanker *Matsumi Maru No. 7* in Strait of Malacca, 20 Jun 1992. Decomm and stricken 24 Jul 1998. Sunk as target 29 Jul 2003.
◆Libya Mar–Jun 1990, Gulf War Apr–Jul 1991, Indian Ocean Dec 1995–Mar 1996, Dec 1997.

DD 991 *Fife* In collision with Soviet destroyer *Razyashchyy* in Indian Ocean, 17 Nov 1983. Decomm 28 Feb 2003. Stricken 6 Apr 2004. Sunk as target in Pacific, 23 Aug 2005.
◆Libya Sep–Nov 1989, Gulf War Oct 1990–Mar 1991, Indian Ocean Feb–May 2000.

DD 992 *Fletcher* In collision with destroyer *Towers* and frigate *Francis Hammond* in Subic Bay, 22 May 1982. Decomm and stricken 1 Oct 2004. Sunk as target off Hawaii, 16 Jul 2008.
◆Indian Ocean Jan–Apr 1997, Desert Fox 1998, Sep 2000–Jan 2001, Iraq War 2003.

DD 997 *Hayler* Damaged in collision with German oiler *Rhon* off Norway, 23 Oct 1988. Attack on Al Quaeda camps in Sudan, 20 Aug 1998. Decomm 25 Aug 2003. Stricken 6 Apr 2004. Sunk as target off North Carolina, 14 Nov 2004.
◆Desert Fox 1998.

GUIDED MISSILE DESTROYERS

DDG 1   *Gyatt*   ex-DD 712 (23 Apr 1957)

Charles F. Adams Class

No.	Name	Builder	Keel Laid	Launched	Comm.
DDG 2	Charles F. Adams	Bath	16 Jun 1958	8 Sep 1959	10 Sep 1960
DDG 3	John King	Bath	25 Aug 1958	30 Jan 1960	4 Feb 1961
DDG 4	Lawrence	NY Sbdg	27 Oct 1958	27 Feb 1960	6 Jan 1962
DDG 5	Biddle	NY Sbdg	18 May 1959	4 Jun 1960	5 May 1962
DDG 6	Barney	NY Sbdg	10 Aug 1959	10 Dec 1960	11 Aug 1962
DDG 7	Henry B. Wilson	Defoe	28 Feb 1958	22 Apr 1959	17 Dec 1960
DDG 8	Lynde McCormick	Defoe	4 Apr 1958	28 Jul 1959	3 Jun 1961
DDG 9	Towers	Todd; Seattle	1 Apr 1958	23 Apr 1959	6 Jun 1961
DDG 10	Sampson	Bath	2 Mar 1959	21 May 1960	24 Jun 1961
DDG 11	Sellers	Bath	3 Aug 1959	9 Sep 1960	28 Oct 1961
DDG 12	Robison	Defoe	28 Apr 1959	27 Apr 1960	9 Dec 1961
DDG 13	Hoel	Defoe	3 Aug 1959	4 Aug 1960	16 Jun 1962
DDG 14	Buchanan	Todd; Seattle	23 Apr 1959	11 May 1960	7 Feb 1962
DDG 15	Berkeley	NY Sbdg	29 Aug 1960	29 Jul 1961	15 Dec 1962
DDG 16	Joseph Strauss	NY Sbdg	27 Dec 1960	9 Dec 1961	20 Apr 1963
DDG 17	Conyngham	NY Sbdg	5 Jan 1961	19 May 1962	13 Jul 1963
DDG 18	Semmes	Avondale	18 Aug 1960	20 May 1961	10 Dec 1962
DDG 19	Tattnall	Avondale	14 Nov 1960	26 Aug 1961	13 Apr 1963
DDG 20	Goldsborough	Puget Sd Brdg	3 Jan 1961	15 Dec 1961	9 Nov 1963
DDG 21	Cochrane	Puget Sd Brdg	31 Jul 1961	18 Jul 1962	21 Mar 1964
DDG 22	Benjamin Stoddert	Pugt Sd Brdg	11 Jun 1962	8 Jan 1963	12 Sep 1964

DDG 23	*Richard E. Byrd*	Todd; Seattle	12 Apr 1961	6 Feb 1962	7 Mar 1964
DDG 24	*Waddell*	Todd; Seattle	6 Feb 1962	26 Feb 1963	28 Aug 1964
DDG 25	—	Defoe	21 Sep 1962	26 Sep 1963	—
DDG 26	—	Defoe	16 Oct 1962	9 Jan 1964	—
DDG 27	—	Defoe	16 Feb 1965	5 May 1966	—
DDG 28	—	Bath	1 Mar 1966	11 Aug 1967	—
DDG 29	—	Bath	12 Apr 1966	13 Apr 1968	—
DDG 30	—	Bath	3 Apr 1967	1 Feb 1969	—

Displacement	3,370 tons, 4,500 f/l
Dimensions	432′(oa); 420′(wl) × 47′ × 20′
Machinery	2 screws; ST; SHP 80,000; 35 knots
Endurance	4,500/20
Complement	354
Armament	2–5″/54, twin Tartar, ASROC, 6–21″TT

Notes: Improved *Forrest Sherman* class with missiles. Three each built for Australia and West Germany. DD 952–959 rec DDG 952–959, 16 Aug 1956 and DDG 2–9, 26 Jun 1957.

Service Record:

DDG 2 *Charles F. Adams* Decomm 1 Aug 1990. Stricken 20 Nov 1992. ◆Cuba Feb–Mar 1961, Cuba Missile Crisis Oct–Nov 1962, Iran/Indian Ocean Dec 1980–Mar 1981.

DDG 3 *John King* Decomm 30 Mar 1990. Stricken 12 Jan 1993. BU Brownsville, Tex. 1999.
★Vietnam Jan–Mar 1973; ◆Cuba Jul–Aug 1962, Iran/Indian Ocean Nov–Dec 1962. Dominican Rep Jun–Jul 1966, Lebanon Aug–Oct 1982.

DDG 4 *Lawrence* Decomm 30 Mar 1990. Stricken 16 May 1990. Sold 15 Apr 1994 & 10 Feb 1999, canceled. Sold 4 Oct 2003, BU Philadelphia.
★Vietnam Aug–Dec 1972; ◆Cuba Apr–May 1962, Cuba Missile Crisis Oct–Nov 1962, Iran/Indian Ocean Sep–Nov 1980, Libya Jul–Aug 1989.

DDG 5 *Biddle* Renamed **Claude V. Ricketts**, 28 Jul 1964. Decomm 31 Oct 1989. Stricken 1 Jun 1990. Sold 15 Apr 1994, canceled. Sold 8 Nov 2002, BU Philadelphia.
◆Cuba Aug–Sep 1962, Cuba Missile Crisis Oct–Nov 1962, Iran/Indian Ocean Nov 1979–Feb 1980, Lebanon Nov 1983–Feb 1984.

DDG 6 *Barney* Decomm 17 Dec 1990. Stricken 20 Nov 1992. Sold 15 Apr 1994, canceled. Sold 22 Feb 2006, BU Norfolk, Va.
★Vietnam Apr–Aug 1967, ◆Iran/Indian Ocean Dec 1980–Mar 1981.

DDG 7 *Henry B. Wilson* Collided with New Zealand frigate *Inverell* in Coral Sea, 1 Aug 1968. Damaged by premature explosion of 5″ shell off Vietnam, 5 Jan 1973. Collided with replenishment ship *Kansas City* in Subic Bay, 24 Feb 1975. Decomm 2 Oct 1989. Stricken 26 Jan 1990. Sold 20 Jun 1994, Conv to power-generating barge. Sunk as target off California, 15 Aug 2003.
★Vietnam Jul–Oct 1965, Jan–Apr 1967, Mar–Jul 1968, Nov 1969–Mar 1970, Sep–Nov 1971, Jul 1972–Jan 1973; ◆Evac of Cambodia 11–13 Apr 1975, Evac of Vietnam 29–30 Apr 1975, Mayaguez Op 15 May 1975, Korea 10–13 Jan 1970, Jul–Sep 1971.

DDG 8 *Lynde McCormick* Decomm 1 Oct 1991. Stricken 20 Nov 1992. Sold 20 Jun 1994, conv to power-generating barge. Sunk as target off California, 24 Feb 2001.
★Vietnam Apr–May 1963, Aug–Dec 1964, Apr, Jun–Aug 1966, Oct 1967–Mar 1968, Feb–Jun 1969, Aug 1970–Jan 1971, Nov 1971–Feb 1972; ◆Korea Jan–Mar 1968, Apr–Jun 1969, Libya Feb–May 1988, Dec 1989.

DDG 9 *Towers* Collided with destroyer *Fletcher* and frigate *Francis Hammond* in Subic Bay, 22 May 1982. Decomm 1 Oct 1990. Stricken 27 May 1992. Sold 20 Jun 1994, conv to power-generating barge. Sunk as target 9 Oct 2002.

Figure 5.17: *USS Berkeley* (DDG 15), *Charles F. Adams* class guided missile destroyer.

4★Vietnam Jun–Jul 1962, Feb–May 1965, Jul–Nov 1966, Dec 1968–Feb 1969, Feb–Jun 1971, Jul–Dec 1972; ◆Iran/Indian Ocean Mar–May 1981, Libya Nov 1987–Jan 1988, Sep–Oct 1989.

DDG 10 *Sampson* Damaged by electrical fire in North Atlantic, 14 Jan 1965. Ran aground at San Juan, PR, 29 May 1977. Decomm 24 Jun 1991. Stricken 20 Nov 1992. Sold 15 Oct 2003, BU Philadelphia.
◆Cuba Sep–Oct 1961, Lebanon Feb–Apr 1983, Feb–Mar 1987, Grenada Nov 1983, Gulf War Aug–Sep, Nov–Dec 1990.

DDG 11 *Sellers* Decomm 31 Oct 1989. Stricken 20 Nov 1992. Sold 15 Sep 2004, BU Philadelphia.
◆Cuba Missile Crisis Oct–Nov 1962, Iran/Indian Ocean May–Jul 1981, Lebanon Apr 1984.

DDG 12 *Robison* Decomm 1 Oct 1991. Stricken 20 Nov 1992. Sold 20 Jun 1994, conv to power-generating barge. BU 1996.
7★Vietnam Dec 1964–Jan 1965, Feb–Jun 1966, Aug 1967–Jan 1968, Jan–May 1969, Aug–Nov 1970, Jul–Nov 1971, Jun–Nov 1972; ◆Korea Jun 1969, Sep 1970, Oct–Nov 1971, Iran/Indian Ocean Apr–Jun 1979, Libya Jul–Sep 1988, May 1990.

DDG 13 *Hoel* Destroyed Iranian oil platforms, 19 Oct 1987. Decomm 1 Oct 1990. Stricken 20 Nov 1992. Sold 20 Jun 1994, conv to power-generating barge.
★Vietnam Apr–Jul 1965, Aug 1966–Jan 1967, Jan–Jun 1968, Oct 1969–Mar 1970, Dec 1970–Mar 1971, Jul–Dec 1972; ◆Korea 10 Dec 1969, Jan, Apr 1971, Iran/Indian Ocean Jan–Mar 1979, May–Sep 1981, Libya Sep–Nov 1987.

DDG 14 *Buchanan* Damaged by coast batteries off Vietnam, 17 Apr 1972. Decomm 1 Oct 1991. Stricken 20 Nov 1992. Sunk as target in Pacific, 14 Jun 2000.
★Vietnam Nov 1963, Feb–Jul 1965, Jul–Nov 1966, Feb–Jul 1968, Apr–Jul 1969, Aug–Nov 1970, Mar–Aug 1972; ◆Korea Apr, Jun, Aug 1969, Libya Aug–Nov 1987, May–Jun 1989.

DDG 15 *Berkeley* In collision with m/v *Coralita* at Cairns, Queensland, 3 Sep 1988. Decomm 1 May 1992. Stricken and trfd to Greece 1 Oct 1992.
Later history: renamed *Themistoklis* (D-221). R2002.
★Vietnam Apr–Oct 1964, Dec 1965–Apr 1966, May–Oct 1967, Aug–Nov 1968, Mar–Jul 1970, May–Aug 1971, May–Oct 1972; ◆Korea Mar 1970, May–Jun 1971, Iran/Indian Ocean Nov 1979–Jan 1980, May–Jul 1981, Libya Jan 1990.

DDG 16 *Joseph Strauss*   Decomm 1 Feb 1990. Trfd to Greece 1 Oct 1991.
Later history: renamed *Formion* (D-220). R2002.
★Vietnam Aug 1964, Oct 1964–Jul 1965, Sep–Nov 1965, Feb–Jun 1966, Feb–May 1967, Aug 1968–Jan 1969, Apr–Jun 1970, Feb–Aug 1972; ◆Libya Feb–Apr 1988.

DDG 17 *Conyngham*   In collision with cruiser *Josephus Daniels* in Greece, 2 Aug 1976. Damaged by engine room fire off Cape Hatteras, 8 May 1990 (1 killed). Decomm 29 Oct 1990. Stricken 30 May 1991. Sold 15 Apr 1994, canceled. Sold 5 Feb 2001, BU Philadelphia.
◆Evac of Beirut Jun–Jul 1976, Lebanon Jun–Jul 1983, Persian Gulf Apr–Jul 1987.

DDG 18 *Semmes*   Damaged when struck by Greek m/v *Mantric* in Naples harbor, 11 Feb 1970. Decomm 12 Sep 1991. Trfd to Greece 1 Oct 1991.
Later history: renamed *Kimon* (D-218). R2004.
◆Dominican Rep May–Jun 1965, Iran/Indian Ocean Aug–Oct 1981, Lebanon May 1984, Libya May–Jul 1988.

DDG 19 *Tattnall*   Decomm 18 Jan 1991. Stricken 12 Jan 1993. Sold 15 Apr 1994, canceled; sold 10 Feb 1999, BU Brownsville.
◆Iran/Indian Ocean Feb–Apr 1980, Feb–May 1981, Lebanon Nov 1983–Jan 1984, Gulf War Aug 1990.

DDG 20 *Goldsborough*   Damaged by boiler explosion northwest of Taiwan, 4 Nov 1970 (2 killed). Damaged by shore gunfire off North Vietnam, 19 Dec 1972 (3 killed). Decomm and stricken 29 Apr 1993, trfd to Australia for parts. BU 1994, Goa, India.
★Vietnam Feb–Apr 1965, Feb–Jul 1966, Sep, Nov 1967, Dec 1968–Apr 1969, Aug–Sep, Nov 1970–Jan 1971, Sep 1971–Feb 1972, Nov 1972–Mar 1973; ◆Korea Sep–Oct 1970, Iran/Indian Ocean 1980–Mar 1981, Libya Jul–Sep 1988, Gulf War Aug–Nov 1990.

DDG 21 *Cochrane*   Decomm 1 Oct 1990. Stricken 20 Nov 1992. Sold 19 Sep 2001, BU Brownsville.
★Vietnam Mar–Jun 1963, Aug–Sep 1965, Aug–Nov 1966, Mar–Aug 1968, Jul–Dec 1969, Feb–Jul 1971, Aug–Dec 1972; ◆Evac of Cambodia 29–30 Apr 1975, Korea Jul, Oct 1969, Apr 1971, Persian Gulf Jun–Jul 1987, Libya Jul–Aug 1987, Sep–Nov 1989, Iran/Indian Ocean Oct 1980–Jan 1981.

DDG 22 *Benjamin Stoddert*   Slight damage by coast batteries off Vietnam, 17 Apr 1972. Explosion in 5-inch mount, 26 Jun 1972 (4 killed). Decomm 20 Dec 1991. Stricken 20 Nov 1992. Foundered in tow from Pearl Harbor en route to BU in Brownsville, 3 Feb 2001.

★Vietnam Dec 1965–Apr 1966, Apr–Sep 1967, Jul 1968, May–Sep 1969, Aug 1970–Jan 1971, Apr–Sep 1972; ◆Evac of Vietnam 29–30 Apr 1975, Korea Apr–Oct 1969.

DDG 23 *Richard E. Byrd*   Decomm 27 Apr 1990. Stricken 1 Oct 1992. Trfd to Greece for parts. Sunk as target off Crete, 19 Jun 2003.
◆Iran/Indian Ocean Mar–Jul 1980.

DDG 24 *Waddell*   Collided with destroyer *Brinkley Bass* in Gulf of Tonkin, 5 Feb 1966. Decomm 1 Oct 1992 and trfd to Greece.
Later history: renamed *Nearchos* (D-219). SE2001. R2003.
11★Vietnam Nov 1965–Mar 1966, Mar–Apr 1967, Aug 1968–Aug 1969, Oct–Nov 1969, Feb–Mar, May–Jun 1970, Dec 1971–Jun 1972, Feb–Mar 1973; ◆Korea Apr, Sep 1969, Jun–Jul 1970, Iran/Indian Ocean Dec 1978–Jan 1979, Mar–Apr 1979, Persian Gulf Apr–Jun 1987, Libya Nov–Dec 1988.

DDG 25   Trfd to Australia 22 May 1965 as *Perth* (DDG 38). R 1999. Scuttled as dive wreck at Albany, WA.

DDG 26   Trfd to Australia 18 Dec 1965 as *Hobart* (DDG 39). R2000.

DDG 27   Trfd to Australia 24 Jun 1968 as *Brisbane* (DDG 41). Sunk as target off Queensland as diving reef, 31 Jul 2005.

DDG 28   Trfd to West Germany 22 Mar 1969 as *Lütjens* (D 185) R2003.

DDG 29   Trfd to West Germany 20 Sep 1969 as *Mölders* (D 186) R2003: museum ship at Wilhelmshaven.

DDG 30   Trfd to West Germany 2 May 1970 as *Rommel*. (D 187). R1999. BU Aliaga, Turkey, 2004.

Conversions:

DDG 31 *Decatur* (ex-DD 936)   Decomm 30 Jun 1983. Stricken 16 Mar 1988. Self-defense test ship, Pacific Missile Range, 2 Feb 1996–Sep 2003. Sunk as target 21 Jul 2004.

DDG 32 *John Paul Jones* (ex-DD 932)   Decomm 15 Dec 1982. Stricken 30 Apr 1986. Sunk as target 31 Jan 2001.

DDG 33 *Parsons* (ex-DD 949)   Sank m/v *Orient* in collision off southern California, 12 Dec 1969. Decomm 19 Nov 1982. Stricken 1 Dec 1984. Sunk as target 25 Apr 1989.

DDG 34 *Somers* (ex-DD 947)   Decomm 19 Nov 1982. Stricken 26 Apr 1988. Sunk as target 22 Jul 1998.

Notes: *Forrest Sherman* class conversions. 1 Tartar SAM launcher, 1–5″/54 gun, 1 ASROC, 2 triple torpedo launchers. Two trellis masts replaced original pole masts. Conversion of *Turner Joy* canceled.

DDG 35 *Mitscher* (ex-DL 2)   Decomm and stricken 1 Jun 1978. Sold 1 Aug 1980, BU.

DDG 36 *John S. McCain* (ex-DL 3)   Decomm 30 Apr 1978. Stricken 29 Apr 1978. Sold 13 Dec 1979, BU.

Notes: *Mitscher* class conversions. 1 Tartar SAM launcher, 2–5″/54 guns, 1 ASROC, 2 triple torpedo launchers. Two tripod trellis masts replaced original masts.

DDG 37 *Farragut*   Decomm 31 Oct 1989. Stricken 20 Nov 1992.

DDG 38 *Luce*   Decomm 1 Apr 1991. Stricken 20 Nov 1992. Sold 17 Jun 2005, BU Philadelphia.

DDG 39 *MacDonough*   Damaged by fire, 22 Feb 1992, not repaired. Decomm 23 Oct 1992. Stricken 30 Nov 1992. Sold 15 Sep 2004, BU Philadelphia.

DDG 40 *Coontz*   Decomm 4 Oct 1989. Stricken 26 Jan 1990. Sold 15 Apr 1994, canceled. BU Philadelphia 2002.

DDG 41 *King*   Decomm 28 Mar 1991. Stricken 20 Nov 1992. Sold 15 Apr 1994, BU Wilmington, NC.

DDG 42 *Mahan*   Decomm and stricken 15 Jun 1993. Sold 31 Aug 1995, canceled. Sold 18 May 2004, BU Brownsville, Tex.

DDG 43 *Dahlgren*   In collision with tanker *Egeria* off Virginia Capes, 21 Mar 1974. Collided with m/v *Eurybates* off Colon, Panama, 7 Aug 1975. Had engine room fire off North Carolina coast, 22 Feb 1992 (2 killed). Decomm 31 Jul 1992. Stricken 20 Nov 1992. Sold 15 Apr 1994, canceled. Sold 28 Mar 2006, BU Brownsville, Tex.

Figure 5.18: *USS Parsons* (DDG 33), *Forrest Sherman* class conversion to guided missile destroyer. Notice trellis masts, helicopter landing pad aft.

Figure 5.19: *USS Mahan* (DDG 42), *Coontz* class conversion to guided missile destroyer.

Figure 5.20: *USS William V. Pratt* (DDG 44), *Coontz* class, in New York harbor, 1976.

DDG 44 *William V. Pratt* Decomm 30 Sep 1991. Stricken 20 Nov 1992. Sold 14 Sep 1995. BU Brownsville, Tex.

DDG 45 *Dewey* Decomm 31 Aug 1990. Stricken 20 Nov 1992. Sold 15 Apr 1994. BU Wilmington, NC.

DDG 46 *Preble* Decomm 15 Nov 1991. Stricken 20 Nov 1992. Sold 15 Apr 1994, canceled. Sold 10 Feb 2003, BU Philadelphia.

Notes: *Coontz* class frigates, DLG 6–15, rec 30 Jun 1975.

DDG 47/48   rec CG 47/48
DDG 49/50   not used

Kidd Class

No.	Name	Builder	Keel Laid	Launched	Comm.
DDG 993	*Kidd*	Ingalls	26 Jun 1978	13 Oct 1979	27 Jul 1981
DDG 994	*Callaghan*	Ingalls	23 Oct 1978	19 Jan 1980	29 Aug 1981
DDG 995	*Scott*	Ingalls	12 Feb 1979	29 Mar 1980	24 Oct 1981
	ex-DD 996 (23 Apr 1978)				
DDG 996	*Chandler*	Ingalls	12 May 1979	24 May 1980	13 Mar 1982
	ex-DD 998 (23 Apr 1978)				

Displacement	6,950 tons; 9,574 tons f/l
Dimensions	563′4″ (oa); 529′ (wl) × 55′ × 30′
Machinery	2 screws; 4 gas turbines; SHP 86,000; 30+ knots
Endurance	6,000/20
Complement	331
Armament	2 twin launchers Standard-ER SM-2 SAM/ASROC; 8 Harpoon SSM, 2–5″/54, 2–20 mm Phalanx; 6 TT

Notes: Originally ordered for Iran. Acquired 25 Jul 1979. Original DD 995 (*Ardeshir*) and 997 (*Shapour*) canceled Jun 1976. Rec DD to DDG, 8 Aug 1979. Original Iranian names were *Khouroush, Daryush, Nader* and *Anoushirvan*. *Spruance*-class hulls and propulsion. Planned to include LAMPS helicopters.

Service Records:

DDG 993 *Kidd* Destroyed Iranian oil platforms, 19 Oct 1987. Decomm and stricken 12 Mar 1998. Trfd to Taiwan 25 Aug 2006.
  Later history: renamed *Tso Ying* (DDG 1803).
  ◆Lebanon Jan–May 1983, Libya Jul–Nov 1987, Persian Gulf Jul 1987, Gulf War Feb–Jun 1991.

DDG 994 *Callaghan* Decomm and stricken 31 Mar 1998. Trfd to Taiwan, 29 Oct 2005.
  Later history: renamed *Suao* (DDG 1802).
  ◆Libya Sep–Dec 1988, Persian Gulf Feb–Jul 1987, Gulf War Feb–Jun 1992, Indian Ocean Jan–Mar 1996.

DDG 995 *Scott* Decomm and stricken 11 Dec 1998. Trfd to Taiwan, 29 Oct 2005.
  Later history: renamed *Keelung* (DDG 1801).
  ◆Libya/ El Dorado Canyon Jan–Mar 1986, Gulf War Aug 1990.

DDG 996 *Chandler* Decomm and stricken 23 Sep 1999. Trfd to Taiwan 25 Aug 2006.
  Later history: renamed *Ma Kong* (DDG 1805).
  ◆Libya Nov 1987–Mar 1988, Oct 1993, Gulf War Dec 1991–Mar 1992.

Arleigh Burke Class

No.	Name	Builder	Keel Laid	Launched	Comm.
DDG 51	*Arleigh Burke*	Bath	6 Dec 1988	16 Sep 1989	4 Jul 1991
DDG 52	*Barry*	Bath	26 Feb 1990	10 May 1991	12 Dec 1992
	ex-*John Barry* (8 Dec 1989), ex-*Barry* (9 May 1989)				
	ex-*John Barry* (1 Feb 1988)				
DDG 53	*John Paul Jones*	Bath	8 Aug 1990	26 Oct 1991	18 Dec 1993
DDG 54	*Curtis Wilbur*	Bath	12 Mar 1991	16 May 1992	19 Mar 1994
DDG 55	*Stout*	Ingalls	12 Aug 1991	16 Oct 1992	13 Aug 1994
DDG 56	*John S. McCain*	Bath	3 Sep 1991	26 Sep 1992	2 Jul 1994
DDG 57	*Mitscher*	Ingalls	12 Feb 1992	7 May 1993	10 Dec 1994
DDG 58	*Laboon*	Bath	24 Mar 1992	20 Feb 1993	18 Mar 1995
DDG 59	*Russell*	Ingalls	24 Jul 1992	20 Oct 1993	20 May 1995
DDG 60	*Paul Hamilton*	Bath	24 Aug 1992	24 Jul 1993	27 May 1995
DDG 61	*Ramage*	Ingalls	4 Jan 1993	11 Feb 1994	22 Jul 1995
DDG 62	*Fitzgerald*	Bath	9 Feb 1993	29 Jan 1994	14 Oct 1995
DDG 63	*Stetham*	Ingalls	11 May 1993	17 Jun 1994	21 Oct 1995
DDG 64	*Carney*	Bath	3 Aug 1993	23 Jul 1994	13 Apr 1996
DDG 65	*Benfold*	Ingalls	27 Sep 1993	9 Nov 1994	30 Mar 1996
DDG 66	*Gonzalez*	Bath	3 Feb 1994	18 Feb 1995	12 Oct 1996
DDG 67	*Cole*	Ingalls	28 Feb 1994	10 Feb 1995	8 Jun 1996

DDG 68	*The Sullivans*	Bath	27 Jul 1994	12 Aug 1995	19 Apr 1997
DDG 69	*Milius*	Ingalls	8 Aug 1994	1 Aug 1995	23 Nov 1996
DDG 70	*Hopper*	Bath	23 Feb 1995	6 Jan 1996	6 Sep 1997
DDG 71	*Ross*	Ingalls	10 Apr 1995	22 Mar 1996	28 Jun 1997
DDG 72	*Mahan*	Bath	17 Aug 1995	29 Jun 1996	14 Feb 1998
DDG 73	*Decatur*	Bath	15 Jan 1996	10 Nov 1996	29 Aug 1998
DDG 74	*McFaul*	Ingalls	26 Jan 1996	18 Jan 1997	25 Apr 1998
DDG 75	*Donald Cook*	Bath	7 Jul 1996	3 May 1997	21 Aug 1998
DDG 76	*Higgins*	Bath	14 Nov 1996	4 Oct 1997	24 Apr 1999
DDG 77	*O'Kane*	Bath	8 May 1997	28 Mar 1998	23 Oct 1999
DDG 78	*Porter*	Ingalls	2 Dec 1996	12 Nov 1997	20 Mar 1999

Displacement	6,682 tons; 8,373 fl (5l: 6,624 tons, 8,315 fl)
Dimensions	504′4″ (oa); 465′10″ (wl) × 66′11″ × 30′7″
Machinery	2 screws; gas turbines; SHP 100,000; 31 knots
Endurance	4,400/20
Complement	316
Armament	90-cell VLS Standard-MR SM-2/Tomahawk/VLA ASROC, 8 Harpoon SSM, 1–5″/54, 2–20 mm Phalanx; 6 ASW TT

Notes: Similar hull to CG 47 class. First destroyers since World War II to have steel superstructures. Helicopter landing pad but no hangar. Two squat funnels and sharply raked mast.

Service Records:

DDG 51 *Arleigh Burke*
 ◆Indian Ocean Oct–Nov 1998, Dec 2000–Mar 2001, Iraq War 2003.
DDG 52 *Barry*
 ◆Indian Ocean Dec 1997–Apr 1998, Feb–May 2000, Beirut Evac, 17–19 Jul 2006.
DDG 53 *John Paul Jones*
 ◆Indian Ocean May–Jun 1997, Oct 1999–Mar 2000.
DDG 54 *Curtis Wilbur*
 ◆Indian Ocean Dec 1995, Apr–Jul 1999.
DDG 55 *Stout*
 ◆Indian Ocean Nov 1998–Jan 1999, Desert Fox 1998.
DDG 56 *John S. McCain*
 ◆Indian Ocean Dec 1995–Mar 1996, Feb–May 1998, Oct 1999–Mar 2000, Iraq War 2003.
DDG 57 *Mitscher*
 ◆Iraq War 2003.
DDG 58 *Laboon*   Attacks on Iraq, 3–4 Sep 1996.
 ◆Indian Ocean Feb–May 2000.
DDG 59 *Russell*   Attacks on Iraq, 3–4 Sep 1996.
 ◆Indian Ocean Mar–Jul 1998, Feb–May 2000.
DDG 60 *Paul Hamilton*   Damaged in collision with Iranian m/v in Persian Gulf, 6 Dec 2002.
 ◆Indian Ocean Jan–Apr 1997, Sep 2000–Jan 2001, Desert Fox 1998, Iraq War 2003.
DDG 61 *Ramage*
DDG 62 *Fitzgerald*
 ◆Indian Ocean Apr–Jun 1997, Dec 1998–Mar 1999, Desert Fox 1998. Dec 2000–Mar 2001.
DDG 63 *Stetham*
 ◆Indian Ocean Jul–Oct 1997, Apr–Jul 1999.
DDG 64 *Carney*
 ◆Indian Ocean Nov 1997–Mar 1998.
DDG 65 *Benfold*
 ◆Indian Ocean Oct 1997–Jan 1998, Aug–Sep 1999, Jul–Aug 2001, Tsunami relief 2005.
DDG 66 *Gonzalez*   Struck reef off St. Martin and extensively damaged underside, 12 Nov 1996.
 ◆Beirut Evac, 17–19 Jul 2006.
DDG 67 *Cole*   Severely damaged by terrorist bomb attack in Aden harbor, 12 Oct 2000 (17 killed). In service 19 Apr 2002.
 ◆Indian Ocean Mar–Jul 1998.
DDG 68 *The Sullivans*
 ◆Indian Ocean Oct 1999–Mar 2000.
DDG 69 *Milius*   Attack on Al Quaeda camps in Afghanistan, 20 Aug 1998.
 ◆Indian Ocean Jul–Dec 2000, Jul–Oct 1998, Iraq War 2003.
DDG 70 *Hopper*
 ◆Desert Fox 1998, Indian Ocean Feb–May 2000.
DDG 71 *Ross*
DDG 72 *Mahan*
DDG 73 *Decatur*
DDG 74 *McFaul*   Collided with destroyer *Winston S. Churchill* off Jacksonville, 22 Aug 2005.
DDG 75 *Donald Cook*
 ◆Indian Ocean Jul–Sep 2000, Iraq War 2003
DDG 76 *Higgins*
 ◆Indian Ocean Dec 2000–Mar 2001, Iraq War 2003.
DDG 77 *O'Kane*
DDG 78 *Porter*   Sank two pirate skiffs off Indian Ocean, 28 Oct 2007.
 ◆Iraq War 2003.

Figure 5.21: *USS Winston S. Churchill* (DDG 81) in the English Channel, 22 Aug 2001.

Figure 5.22: *USS Oscar Austin* (DDG 79), in 2000.

Improved Arleigh Burke Class

No.	Name	Builder	Keel Laid	Launched	Comm.
DDG 79	Oscar Austin	Bath	9 Oct 1997	7 Nov 1998	19 Aug 2000
DDG 80	Roosevelt	Ingalls	15 Dec 1997	10 Jan 1999	14 Oct 2000
DDG 81	Winston S. Churchill	Bath	7 May 1998	17 Apr 1999	10 Mar 2001
	ex-Winston Churchill (3 Aug 1998)				
DDG 82	Lassen	Ingalls	24 Aug 1998	15 Oct 1999	21 Apr 2001
DDG 83	Howard	Bath	9 Dec 1998	20 Nov 1999	20 Oct 2001
DDG 84	Bulkeley	Ingalls	10 May 1999	21 Jun 2000	8 Dec 2001
DDG 85	McCampbell	Bath	5 Jul 1999	2 Jul 2000	17 Aug 2002
DDG 86	Shoup	Ingalls	13 Dec 1999	22 Nov 2000	22 Jun 2002
DDG 87	Mason	Bath	20 Jan 2000	23 Jun 2001	12 Apr 2003
DDG 88	Preble	Ingalls	22 Jun 2000	1 Jun 2001	9 Nov 2002
DDG 89	Mustin	Ingalls	15 Jan 2001	12 Dec 2001	26 Jul 2003
DDG 90	Chafee	Bath	12 Apr 2001	2 Nov 2002	18 Oct 2003
DDG 91	Pinckney	Ingalls	16 Jul 2001	26 Jun 2002	29 May 2004
DDG 92	Momsen	Bath	16 Nov 2001	19 Jul 2003	28 Aug 2004
DDG 93	Chung-Hoon	Ingalls	14 Jan 2002	15 Dec 2002	18 Sep 2004
DDG 94	Nitze	Bath	20 Sep 2002	3 Apr 2004	5 Mar 2005
DDG 95	James E. Williams	Ingalls	15 Jul 2002	25 Jun 2003	11 Dec 2004
DDG 96	Bainbridge	Bath	7 May 2003	30 Oct 2004	12 Nov 2005
DDG 97	Halsey	Ingalls	24 Feb 2003	9 Jan 2004	30 Jul 2005
DDG 98	Forrest Sherman	Ingalls	12 Aug 2003	30 Jun 2004	28 Jan 2006
DDG 99	Farragut	Bath	7 Jan 2004	9 Jul 2005	4 May 2006
DDG 100	Kidd	Ingalls	1 Mar 2004	15 Dec 2004	30 May 2007
DDG 101	Gridley	Bath	30 Jul 2004	28 Dec 2005	10 Feb 2007
DDG 102	Sampson	Bath	14 Mar 2005	17 Sep 2006	3 Nov 2007
DDG 103	Truxtun	Ingalls	11 Apr 2005	17 Apr 2007	—
DDG 104	Sterett	Bath	17 Nov 2005	20 May 2007	9 Aug 2008
DDG 105	Dewey	Ingalls	4 Oct 2006	18 Jan 2008	—
DDG 106	Stockdale	Bath	10 Aug 2006	24 Feb 2008	—
DDG 107	Gravely	Ingalls	26 Nov 2007	—	—
DDG 108	Wayne E. Meyer	Bath	18 May 2007	—	—
DDG 109	Jason Dunham	Bath	11 Apr 2008	—	—
DDG 110	William P. Lawrence	Ingalls	—	—	—
DDG 111	Spruance	Bath	—	—	—
DDG 112	Michael Murphy	Bath	—	—	—

Displacement	6,600 tons; 9,217 fl
Dimensions	508'6" (oa); 471' (wl) × 66'11 × 30'7
Machinery	2 shafts; gas turbines; SHP 100,000; 31 knots
Endurance	4400/20
Complement	316
Armament	96-cell VLS Standard-MR SM-2/Tomahawk/VLA ASROC, 2 LAMPS helicopters. 1–5"/62, (1–5"/54 DD 79–80), 2–20mm Phalanx; 6 ASW TT

Notes: Flight IIA type, with 6 additional VLS cells, no Harpoon canisters and two helicopter hangars. Able to support two Seahawk helicopters. *Mason* (DDG 87) was the last major warship to be launched on an inclined building way. A number of units of this class suffered significant structural hull damage in rough seas.

Service Records:
DDG 79 *Oscar Austin*
◆Iraq War 2003.
DDG 80 *Roosevelt*
DDG 81 *Winston S. Churchill*   In collision with destroyer *McFaul* off Jacksonville, 22 Aug 2005.
◆Iraq War 2003.
DDG 82 *Lassen*
DDG 83 *Howard*
DDG 84 *Bulkeley*
DDG 85 *McCampbell*   Damaged in collision with m/v *Rokya I* in northern Persian Gulf, 25 Mar 2006.
DDG 86 *Shoup*
◆Tsunami relief 2005.
DDG 87 *Mason*
DDG 88 *Preble*
DDG 89 *Mustin*
DDG 90 *Chafee*
DDG 91 *Pinckney*
DDG 92 *Momsen*
DDG 93 *Chung-Hoon*
DDG 94 *Paul H. Nitze*
DDG 95 *James E. Williams*
DDG 96 *Bainbridge*
DDG 97 *Halsey*
DDG 98 *Forrest Sherman*
DDG 99 *Farragut*
DDG 100 *Kidd*   Damaged incomplete by hurricane Katrina, 29 Aug 2005.
DDG 101 *Gridley*
DDG 102 *Sampson*
DDG 103 *Truxtun*   Damaged by fire while incomplete, 20 May 2006.
DDG 104 *Sterett*
DDG 105 *Dewey*
DDG 106 *Stockdale*
DDG 107 *Gravely*
DDG 108 *Wayne E. Meyer*
DDG 109 *Jason Dunham*
DDG 110 *William P. Lawrence*
DDG 111 *Spruance*
DDG 112 *Michael Murphy*

DD 21   *Zumwalt*   class "Land-attack" destroyer, program canceled 1 Nov 2001.

Zumwalt Class

No.	Name	Builder	Keel Laid	Launched	Comm.
DDG 1000	Zumwalt	Bath	—	—	—
DDG 1001	—	Ingalls	—	—	—

Displacement	14,564 tons
Dimensions	600' × 80'7" × 27'7"
Machinery	2 main and 2 auxiliary turbine generator sets; 30 knots
Complement	142
Armament	80-cell VLS for Tomahawk, Standard, ASROC; 2–155mm (AGS), 2–57mm guns

Notes: Planned as the next-generation multimission destroyer. Cost is estimated at twice that of the *Arleigh Burke* units. The original thirty units was cut to seven, and then in August 2008 to two.

6
ESCORTS/FRIGATES

DESTROYER ESCORTS ON THE NAVY LIST, 1947

Buckley Class (type TE)

DE 51   *Buckley*   Decomm 3 Jul 1946. Rec **DER 51**, 26 Apr 1949. Rec **DE 51**, 29 Sep 1954. Stricken 1 Jun 1968. Sold 1969.

DE 57   *Fogg*   Decomm 27 Oct 1947. Rec **DER 57**, 18 Mar 1949. Rec **DE 57**, 29 Sep 1954. Stricken 1 Apr 1965. Sold Jan 1966, BU Portsmouth, Va.

DE 59   *Foss*   Decomm 30 Oct 1957. Stricken 1 Nov 1965. Sunk as target by submarine *Sabalo* off San Diego, 6 Sep 1966.
1★Korea K-2.

DE 153   *Reuben James*   Converted to radar picket, Oct 1945. Decomm 11 Oct 1947. Rec **DER 153**, 18 Mar 1949. Rec **DE 153**, 28 Sep 1954. Stricken 30 Jun 1968. Sunk as target 1 Mar 1971.

DE 198   *Lovelace*   Decomm 22 May 1946. Stricken 1 Jul 1967. Sunk as target off California, 25 Apr 1968.

DE 199   *Manning*   Decomm 15 Jan 1947. Stricken 31 Jul 1968. Sold 27 Oct 1969, BU.

DE 200   *Neuendorf*   Decomm 14 May 1946. Stricken 1 Jul 1967. Sunk as target off California, 30 Nov 1967.

DE 201   *James E. Craig*   Decomm 2 Jul 1946. Stricken 30 Jun 1968. Sunk as target off California, Feb 1969.

DE 202   *Eichenberger*   Decomm 14 May 1946. Stricken 1 Dec 1972. Sold 9 Nov 1973, BU.

DE 203   *Thomason*   Decomm 22 May 1946. Stricken 30 Jun 1968. Sold 30 Jun 1969, BU Terminal I.

DE 210   *Otter*   Decomm Jan 1947. Stricken 1 Nov 1969. Sunk as target off Puerto Rico, 6 Jul 1970.

DE 213   *William T. Powell*   Rec **DER 213**, 18 Mar 1949. Out of comm 9 Dec 1949–28 Nov 1950. Rec **DE 213**, 1 Dec 1954. Decomm 17 Jan 1958. BU 1966, Wilmington, Del.

DE 214   *Scott*   Decomm 3 Mar 1947. Stricken 1 Jul 1965. Sold 20 Jan 1967, BU New Orleans.

DE 217   *Coolbaugh*   Decomm 21 Feb 1960. Stricken 1 Jul 1972. Sold 27 Jul 1973, BU Portsmouth, Va.

DE 218   *Darby*   Out of comm 28 Apr 1947–24 Oct 1950, 23 Feb 1959–2

Figure 6.1: *USS J. Douglas Blackwood* (DE 219), *Buckley* class, August 1958, as naval reserve training ship.

Oct 1961. NRT. Damaged in collision with m/v *Soya Atlantic* in Chesapeake Bay, 19 Mar 1960 (2 killed). Decomm 1 Aug 1962. Stricken 23 Sep 1968. Sunk as target 24 May 1970.
◆Cuba Mar–Apr 1962.

DE 219   *J. Douglas Blackwood*   Out of comm 20 Apr 1947–5 Feb 1951, 1 Aug 1958–2 Oct 1961. NRT 1957–1970. Decomm 1 Aug 1962. Stricken 30 Jan 1970. Sunk as target 20 Aug 1971.
◆Cuba Mar–Apr 1962.

DE 220   *Francis M. Robinson*   Decomm 20 Jun 1960. Stricken 1 Jul 1972. Sold 29 Jun 1973, BU.

DE 222   *Fowler*   Decomm 28 Jun 1946. Stricken 1 Jul 1965. Sold 29 Dec 1966, BU.

DE 223   *Spangenberg*   Decomm 18 Jul 1947. Rec **DER 223**, 18 Mar 1949. Rec **DE 223**, 1 Dec 1954. Stricken 1 Nov 1965. Sold 3 Oct 1966, BU Bordentown, NJ.

DE 575   *Ahrens*   Decomm 24 Jun 1946. Stricken 1 Apr 1965. Sold 20 Jan 1967, BU New Orleans, La.

DE 577   *Alexander J. Luke*   Converted to DER 1946. Rec **DER 577**, 18 Mar 1949. Decomm 18 Oct 1947. Rec **DE 577**, 28 Sep 1954. Stricken 1 May 1970. Sunk as target off Newport, RI, 22 Oct 1970.

Figure 6.2: *USS Vammen* (DE 644), *Buckley* class.

DE 578 *Robert I. Paine* Decomm 21 Nov 1947. Rec **DER 578**, 18 Mar 1949. Rec **DE 578**, 1 Dec 1954. Stricken 1 Jun 1968. Sold 18 Jul 1969, BU.

DE 633 *Foreman* Decomm 28 Jun 1946. Stricken 1 Apr 1965, BU Baltimore.

DE 634 *Whitehurst* Out of comm 27 Nov 1946–1 Sep 1950. NRT. 6 Dec 1958/2 Oct 1961. NRT 1 Aug 1962. Damaged in collision with merchant m/v *Hoyanger* in Strait of Juan de Fuca, 17 Jan 1965. Decomm and stricken 12 Jul 1969. Sunk as target by submarine *Trigger*, 28 Apr 1971.
3★Korea K-4 K-5 K-6; ★Vietnam Mar–Apr 1962.

DE 638 *Willmarth* Decomm 26 Apr 1946. Stricken 1 Dec 1966. Sold 1 Jul 1968, BU, Wilmington, Del.

DE 639 *Gendreau* Decomm 13 Mar 1948. Stricken 1 Dec 1972. Sold 6 Sep 1973, BU Terminal I.

DE 640 *Fieberling* Decomm 13 Mar 1948. Stricken 1 Mar 1972. Sold 1972, BU Portland, Ore.

DE 641 *William C. Cole* Decomm 28 Apr 1948. Stricken 1 Mar 1972. Sold 20 Nov 1972, BU Portland, Ore.

DE 642 *Paul G. Baker* Decomm 3 Feb 1947. Stricken 1 Dec 1969. Sold Oct 1970, BU Terminal I.

DE 643 *Damon M. Cummings* Decomm 3 Feb 1947. Stricken 1 Mar 1972. Sold 15 May 1973, BU Seattle.

DE 644 *Vammen* Out of comm 3 Feb 1947–15 Feb 1952 and 18 Jun 1960–2 Oct 1961. Collided with destroyer *Tingey* off southern California, 2 Aug 1963. Decomm 1 Aug 1962. Stricken 12 Jul 1969. Sunk as target 18 Feb 1971.
1★Korea K-8; ★Vietnam Mar–May 1962.

DE 665 *Jenks* Decomm 26 Jun 1946. Stricken 1 Feb 1966. Sold 5 Mar 1968, BU New Orleans.

DE 666 *Durik* Decomm 15 Jun 1946. Stricken 1 Jun 1965. Sold 30 Jun 1967, BU New Orleans.

DE 667 *Wiseman* Out of comm 31 May 1946–11 Sep 1950 and 16 May 1959–2 Oct 1961; NRT. Damaged by submerged rock off Korea, 23 Dec 1952. Decomm 1 Aug 1962, NRT. Stricken 15 Apr 1973. Sold 28 Mar 1974, BU.
6★Korea K-2 K-4 K-5 K-6 K-8, K-9; ★Vietnam Apr–May 1962.

DE 678 *Harmon* Decomm 25 Mar 1947. Stricken 1 Aug 1965. Sold 30 Jan 1967, BU Wilmington, Del.

DE 679 *Greenwood* Out of comm 2 Sep 1958–2 Oct 1961. Decomm 1 Aug 1962. Stricken 20 Feb 1967. Sold 6 Sep 1967, BU Kearny, NJ.
◆Cuba Aug, Oct 1961–Jul 1962.

DE 680 *Loeser* Out of comm 28 Mar 1947–9 Mar 1951 and 1 Dec 1958–2 Oct 1961. NRT. Decomm 1 Aug 1962. Reserve training. Stricken 23 Sep 1968. Sunk as target 1969.
◆Cuba Jan–Mar 1962.

DE 681 *Gillette* Decomm 3 Feb 1947. Stricken 1 Dec 1972. Sold 6 Sep 1973, BU Terminal I.

DE 683 *Harry R. Kenyon* Decomm 3 Feb 1947. Stricken 1 Dec 1969. Sold 13 Oct 1970, BU Terminal I.

DE 696 *Spangler* Out of comm 30 Jun 1948–5 Jul 1951. Decomm 8 Oct 1958. Stricken 1 Mar 1972. Sold 20 Nov 1972, BU Portland, Ore.

DE 697 *George* Decomm 8 Oct 1958. Stricken 1 Nov 1969. Sold 15 Oct 1970, BU Terminal I.

DE 698 *Raby* Rec **DEC 698**, 2 Nov 1949. Decomm 22 Dec 1953. Rec **DE 698**, 27 Dec 1957. Stricken 1 Jun 1968. Sold 18 Jul 1969, BU.

DE 699 *Marsh* Damaged in collision with destroyer *Taussig* 500 m. west of San Francisco, 22 Feb 1949. Out of comm 16 Aug 1958–15 Dec 1961. NRT 1 Aug 1962. Decomm, in service, 12 Aug 1962. OS 30 Jun 1969. Stricken 15 Apr 1973. Sold 23 Jan 1974, BU.
4★Korea K-1 K-2 K-4 K-8; ★Vietnam Mar–May 1962.

DE 700 *Currier* Decomm 4 Apr 1960. Stricken 1 Dec 1966. Sunk as target off San Clemente I., Cal., 11 Jul 1967.
1★Korea K-8 +.

DE 701 *Osmus* Decomm 15 Mar 1947. Stricken 1 Dec 1972. Sold 9 Nov 1973, BU.

DE 702 *Earl V. Johnson* Decomm 18 Jun 1946. Stricken 1 May 1967. Sold 3 Sep 1968, BU New Orleans.

DE 703 *Holton* Decomm 31 May 1946. Stricken 1 Nov 1972. Sold 9 May 1974, BU.

DE 704 *Cronin* Out of comm 31 May 1946–9 Feb 1951. Rec **DEC 704**, 13 Sep 1950. Decomm 4 Dec 1953. Rec **DE 704**, 27 Dec 1957. Stricken 1 Jun 1970. Sunk as target off Florida, 16 Dec 1971.

DE 705 *Frybarger* Out of comm 30 Jun 1947–6 Oct 1950. Rec **DEC 705**, 13 Sep 1950. Decomm 9 Dec 1954. Rec **DE 705**, 27 Dec 1957. Stricken 1 Dec 1972. Sold 9 Nov 1973, BU.
1★Korea 1952.

DE 790 *Borum* Decomm 15 Jun 1946. Stricken 1 Aug 1965. Sold 1967 sold, BU.

DE 791 *Maloy* Rec **EDE 791**, 14 Aug 1946. Decomm 28 May 1965. Stricken 1 Jun 1965. Sold 11 Mar 1966, BU.
◆Cuba Apr–Jun 1961, Cuba Missile Crisis Nov 1962.

DE 795 *Gunason* Decomm 13 Mar 1948. Stricken 1 Sep 1973. Sunk as target 28 Jul 1974.

DE 796 *Major* Decomm 13 Mar 1948. Stricken 1 Dec 1972. Sold 9 Nov 1973, BU.

DE 797 *Weeden* Out of comm 9 May 1946–26 May 1950. NRT Nov 1946. Decomm 26 Feb 1958. Stricken 30 Jun 1968. Sold 27 Oct 1969, BU, Portland, Ore.

DE 798 *Varian* Decomm 15 Mar 1946. Stricken 1 Dec 1972. Sold 12 Jan 1974, BU, New Orleans.

DE 799 *Scroggins* Decomm 15 Jun 1946. Stricken 1 Jul 1965. Sold 5 Apr 1967, BU.

DE 800 *Jack W. Wilke* Rec EDE 800, 1946. ASW experimental ship Decomm 24 May 1960. Stricken 1 Aug 1972. Sold 9 Jan 1974, BU.

Notes: DE 217–219, 678–680, 696–698, 700–701 had 2–5″ guns. DE 51, 57, 153, 213, 223, 577, 578 converted to DER, with 2–5″ guns, no TT. DE 698, 704, and 705 converted to direct amphibious landings (DEC).

Cannon Class (type DET)

DE 102 *Thomas* Decomm 13 Mar 1946. Trfd to China, 29 Oct 1948.
Later history: renamed *Tai Ho* (23). R1972.

DE 103 *Bostwick* Decomm 30 Apr 1946. Trfd to China, 14 Dec 1948.
Later history: renamed *Tai Tsang* (24). R1975.

DE 104 *Breeman* Decomm 26 Apr 1946. Trfd to China, 29 Oct 1948.
Later history: renamed *Tai Hu* (25). R1972.

DE 105 *Burrows* Decomm 14 Jun 1946. Trfd to Netherlands 1 Jun 1950.
Later history: renamed *Van Amstel* (F 806). R1967.

DE 112 *Carter* Decomm 10 Apr 1946. Trfd to China, 14 Dec 1948.
Later history: renamed *Tai Chao* (26). R1973.

Escorts/Frigates 81

DE 113 *Clarence L. Evans* Decomm 29 May 1947. Trfd to France 29 Mar 1952.
  Later history: renamed *Berbère* (F 723). R1963.
DE 162 *Levy* Decomm 4 Apr 1947. Stricken 1 Aug 1973. Sold 18 Jun 1974, BU.
DE 163 *McConnell* Decomm 29 Jun 1946. Stricken 1 Oct 1972. Sold 26 Feb 1974, BU.
DE 164 *Osterhaus* Decomm 26 Jun 1946. Stricken 1 Nov 1972. Sold 9 May 1974, BU.
DE 165 *Parks* Decomm Mar 1946. Stricken 1 Jul 1972. Sold 28 Sep 1973, BU Baltimore.
DE 166 *Baron* Decomm 26 Apr 1946. Trfd to Uruguay 3 May 1952.
  Later history: renamed *Uruguay* (1). R1990.
DE 167 *Acree* Decomm 1 Apr 1946. Stricken 1 Jul 1972. Sold 19 Jun 1973, BU Baltimore.
DE 168 *Amick* Decomm 16 May 1947. Trfd to Japan 14 Jun 1955.
  Later history: renamed *Asahi* (DE 262). Trfd to Philippines 13 Sep 1976, renamed *Datu Sikatuna*. (PF 77). R1989.
DE 169 *Atherton* Decomm 10 Dec 1945. Trfd to Japan 14 Jun 1955.
  Later history: renamed *Hatsuhi* (DE 263). Trfd to Philippines 13 Sep 1976, renamed *Rajah Humabon* (PF 78/PF 6). R1993, recomm.
DE 170 *Booth* Decomm 4 Mar 1946. Trfd to Philippines 15 Dec 1967.
  Later history: renamed *Datu Kaliantiaw* (PS 76). Wrecked in typhoon, 21 Sep 1981.
DE 171 *Carroll* Decomm 19 Jun 1946. Stricken 1 Aug 1965. Sold 30 May 1967, BU.
DE 172 *Cooner* Decomm 25 Jun 1946. Stricken 1 Jul 1972. Sold 19 Oct 1973, BU Baltimore.
DE 173 *Eldridge* Decomm 17 Jun 1946. Trfd to Greece 15 Jan 1951.
  Later history: renamed *Leon* (D 54/D 217). R1992.
DE 176 *Micka* Decomm 14 Jun 1946. Stricken 1 Aug 1965. Sold 15 May 1967, BU.
DE 180 *Trumpeter* Decomm 14 Jun 1946. Stricken 1 Aug 1973. Sold 18 Jun 1974, BU.
DE 181 *Straub* Decomm 17 Oct 1947. Stricken 1 Aug 1973. Sold 18 Jun 1974, BU.
DE 182 *Gustafson* Decomm 26 Jun 1946. Trfd to Netherlands 23 Oct 1950.
  Later history: renamed *Van Ewijck* (F 808). R1967. BU.
DE 183 *Samuel S. Miles* Decomm 28 Mar 1946. Trfd to France 12 Aug 1950.
  Later history: renamed *Arabe* (F 717). R1963.
DE 184 *Wesson* Decomm 24 Jun 1946. Trfd to Italy 10 Jan 1951.
  Later history: renamed *Andromeda* (F 592). R1972 BU 1976.
DE 185 *Riddle* Decomm 8 Jun 1946. Trfd to France 12 Aug 1950.
  Later history: renamed *Kabyle* (F 718). R1964, BU Italy.
DE 186 *Swearer* Decomm 25 Feb 1946. Trfd to France 16 Sep 1950.
  Later history: renamed *Bambara* (F 719). R1964, BU Italy.
DE 187 *Stern* Decomm 26 Apr 1946. Trfd to Netherlands 3 May 1951.
  Later history: renamed *Van Zijll* (F 811). R1967, BU.
DE 188 *O'Neill* Decomm 2 May 1946. Trfd to Netherlands 23 Oct 1950.
  Later history: renamed *Dubois* (F 809). R1967, BU.
DE 189 *Bronstein* Decomm 5 Nov 1945. Trfd to Uruguay 3 May 1952.
  Later history: renamed *Artigas* (2). R1988.
DE 190 *Baker* Decomm 4 Mar 1946. Trfd to France, 29 Mar 1952.
  Later history: renamed *Malgache* (F 724). R1970, BU.
DE 191 *Coffman* Decomm 30 Apr 1946. Stricken 1 Jul 1972. Sold 27 Jul 1973, BU Baltimore.
DE 192 *Eisner* Decomm 5 Jul 1946. Trfd to Netherlands 3 May 1951.
  Later history: renamed *De Zeeuw* (F 810). R1967.
DE 193 *Garfield Thomas* Decomm 27 Mar 1947. Trfd to Greece 19 Jan 1951.
  Later history: renamed *Panthir* (D 67/D 227). R1992.
DE 194 *Wingfield* Decomm 15 Jun 1946. Trfd to France 10 Sep 1950.
  Later history: renamed *Sakalave* (F 760). R1963, BU 1964.
DE 195 *Thornhill* Decomm 17 Jun 1946. Trfd to Italy 10 Jan 1951.
  Later history: renamed *Aldebaran* (F 590). R. 1976.

DE 196 *Rinehart* Decomm 17 Jul 1946. Trfd to Netherlands 1 Jun 1950.
  Later history: renamed *De Bitter* (F 807). R1967.
DE 739 *Bangust* Decomm 17 Nov 1946. Trfd to Peru 21 Feb 1952.
  Later history: renamed *Castilla* (61). R 1979.
DE 740 *Waterman* Decomm 31 May 1946. Trfd to Peru 21 Feb 1952.
  Later history: renamed *Aguirre* (62). R1974.
DE 741 *Weaver* Decomm 29 May 1947. Trfd to Peru 21 Feb 1952.
  Later history: renamed *Rodriguez* (63/AMS 163). SE 1987.
DE 742 *Hilbert* Decomm 19 Jun 1946. Stricken 1 Aug 1972. Sold 28 Sep 1973, BU.
DE 743 *Lamons* Decomm 14 Jun 1946. Stricken 1 Aug 1972. Sold 28 Sep 1973, BU.
DE 744 *Kyne* Out of comm 14 Jun 1946–21 Nov 1950. NRT 1947. Decomm 17 Jun 1960. Stricken 1 Aug 1972. Sold 19 Oct 1973, BU Wilmington, Del.
DE 745 *Snyder* Out of comm 1946–14 May 1950. NRT 1947. Decomm 5 May 1960. Stricken 1 Aug 1972. Sold 19 Oct 1973, BU Wilmington, Del.
DE 746 *Hemminger* Out of comm 17 Jun 1946–1 Dec 1950. NRT 1947. Decomm 21 Feb 1958. Trfd to Thailand 22 Jul 1959.
  Later history: renamed *Pin Klao* (3/1/413). SE2001.
DE 747 *Bright* Decomm 19 Apr 1946. Trfd to France 11 Nov 1950.
  Later history: renamed *Touareg* (F 721). R1964, BU Italy.
DE 748 *Tills* Out of comm 14 Jun 1946–21 Nov 1950 and 18 Oct 1959–1 Oct 1961. NRT 1947. Decomm 1 Aug 1962. Stricken 23 Sep 1968. Sunk as target off Virginia, 3 Apr 1969.
  ◆Cuba Apr–Jun 1962.
DE 749 *Roberts* Out of comm (in service) 3 Mar 1947–13 Aug 1950. NRT 1947. Recomm 2 Oct 1961. Collided with m/v *Luossa* at Baltimore, 24 Oct 1963. Decomm 1 Oct 1964, IS. OS 21 Sep 1968. Stricken 23 Sep 1968. Sunk as target Nov 1971.
  ◆Cuba Apr–May 1962.
DE 750 *McClelland* Decomm 15 May 1946–14 Jul 1950. NRT 1946–50. Decomm 12 Sep 1960. Stricken 1 Aug 1972. Sold 19 Oct 1973, BU Baltimore.
DE 763 *Cates* Decomm 28 Mar 1947. Trfd to France 11 Nov 1950.
  Later history: renamed *Soudanais* (F 722). R1963, BU Italy.
DE 764 *Gandy* Decomm 17 Jun 1946. Trfd to Italy 10 Jan 1951.
  Later history: renamed *Altair* (F 591). R1972.
DE 765 *Earl K. Olsen* Decomm 17 Jun 1946–21 Nov 1950. NRT 1947. Decomm 25 Feb 1958. Stricken 1 Aug 1972. Sold 28 Sep 1973, BU.
DE 766 *Slater* Decomm 26 Sep 1947. Trfd to Greece 15 Mar 1951.
  Later history: renamed *Aetos* (D 01/D 212). Museum at New York 1995, later Albany, NY.
DE 767 *Oswald* Decomm 30 Apr 1946. Stricken 1 Aug 1972. Sold 19 Oct 1973, BU Baltimore.
DE 768 *Ebert* Decomm 14 Jun 1946. Trfd to Greece 15 Mar 1951.
  Later history: renamed *Ierax* (D 31/D 213). SE1993.
DE 769 *Neal A. Scott* Decomm 30 Apr 1946. Stricken 1 Jun 1968. Sold 1969, BU.
DE 770 *Muir* Decomm Sep 1947. Trfd to South Korea 2 Feb 1956.
  Later history: renamed *Kyong Ki* (DE 71). R 1977.
DE 771 *Sutton* Decomm Sep 1947. Trfd to South Korea 2 Feb 1956.
  Later history: renamed *Kang Won* (DE 72). R 1977.

Notes: TT removed.

Edsall Class (Type FMR)

DE 129 *Edsall* Decomm 11 Jun 1946. Stricken 1 Jun 1968. Sold Jul 1969, BU.
DE 130 *Jacob Jones* Decomm 26 Jul 1946. Stricken 2 Jan 1971. Sold 17 Jul 1973, BU.
DE 131 *Hammann* Decomm 24 Oct 1945. Stricken 1 Oct 1972. Sold 13 Dec 1973, BU.

Figure 6.3: *USS Huse* (DE 145), *Edsall* class

DE 132 *Robert E. Peary* Decomm 13 Jun 1947. Stricken 1 Jul 1966. Sold 6 Sep 1967, BU Kearny, NJ.

DE 133 *Pillsbury* Out of comm 1947–15 Mar 1955. Rec **DER 133**, Aug 1954. Decomm 20 Jun 1960. Stricken 1 Jul 1965. Sold 1966, BU Baltimore.

DE 134 *Pope* Decomm 17 May 1946. Stricken 2 Jan 1972. Sold 17 Jul 1973, BU Brownsville, Tex.

DE 135 *Flaherty* Decomm 17 Jun 1946. Stricken 1 Apr 1965. Sold 13 Oct 1966, BU Baltimore.

DE 137 *Herbert C. Jones* Decomm 2 May 1947. Stricken 1 Jul 1972. Sold 29 Jun 1973, BU.

DE 138 *Douglas L. Howard* Decomm 17 Jun 1946. Stricken 1 Oct 1972. Sold 9 May 1974, BU.

DE 139 *Farquhar* Decomm 14 Jun 1946. Stricken 1 Oct 1972. Sold 26 Feb 1974, BU.

DE 140 *J.R.Y. Blakely* Decomm 14 Jun 1946. Stricken 2 Jan 1971. Sold 17 Jul 1973, BU Brownsville, Tex.

DE 141 *Hill* Decomm 7 Jun 1946. Stricken 1 Oct 1972. Sold 13 Dec 1973, BU.

DE 142 *Fessenden* Out of comm 24 Jun 1946–4 Mar 1952. Rec **DER 142**, 1 Oct 1951. Decomm 30 Jun 1960. Stricken 1 Sep 1966. Sunk as target off Pearl Harbor, 20 Dec 1967.

DE 144 *Frost* Decomm 18 Jun 1946. Stricken 1 Apr 1965. Sold 29 Dec 1966.

DE 145 *Huse* Out of comm 27 Mar 1946–3 Aug 1951. Decomm 30 Jun 1965. Stricken 1 Aug 1973. Sold 11 Jun 1974, BU.
◆Cuba Oct 1961–Jul 1962.

DE 146 *Inch* Decomm 17 May 1946. Stricken 1 Oct 1972. Sold 26 Feb 1974, BU.

DE 147 *Blair* Out of comm 28 Jun 1946–5 Oct 1951 and 13 Nov 1956–2 Dec 1957. Rec **DER 147**, 2 Dec 1957. Decomm 1 Apr 1960. Stricken 1 Dec 1972. Sold 13 Aug 1974, BU Seattle.

DE 148 *Brough* Out of comm 22 Mar 1946–7 Sep 1951. Decomm Jun 1965. Stricken 1 Nov 1965. Sold 13 Oct 1966, BU Baltimore.
◆Antarctic Oct 1956–Feb 1957, Sep 1957–Feb 1958, Sep 1958–Jan 1959, Cuba Sep–Oct 1962, Cuba Missile Crisis Oct–Nov 1962.

DE 149 *Chatelain* Decomm 14 Jun 1946. Stricken 1 Aug 1973. Sold 11 Jun 1974, BU.

DE 150 *Neunzer* Decomm Jan 1947. Stricken 1 Jul 1972. Sold 11 Oct 1973, BU Hillsaide, NJ.

DE 151 *Poole* Decomm Jan 1947. Stricken 2 Jan 1971. Sold 23 Jan 1974, BU.

DE 152 *Peterson* Out of comm 1 May 1946–2 May 1952. Decomm Jun 1965. Stricken 1 Aug 1973. Sold 11 Jun 1974, BU.
◆Antarctic Sep 1959–Feb 1960, Cuba Apr–May 1961, Cuba Missile Crisis Oct–Nov 1962.

DE 238 *Stewart* Decomm 27 Mar 1946. Stricken 1 Oct 1972.
Later history: Museum at Galveston, Tex., 1974.

DE 239 *Sturtevant* Out of comm 24 Mar 1946–3 Aug 1951 and 11 Nov 1956–5 Oct 1957. Rec **DER 239**, 1 Nov 1956. Decomm 30 Jun 1960. Stricken 1 Dec 1972. Sold 6 Sep 1973, BU Terminal I.

DE 240 *Moore* Decomm 30 Jun 1947. Stricken 1 Aug 1973. Sunk as target off Virginia, 13 Jun 1975.

DE 241 *Keith* Decomm 20 Sep 1946. Stricken 1 Nov 1972. Sold 13 Dec 1973, BU.

DE 242 *Tomich* Decomm 20 Sep 1946. Stricken 1 Nov 1972. Sold 13 Dec 1973, BU.

DE 243 *J. Richard Ward* Decomm 13 Jun 1946. Stricken 2 Jan 1971. Sold 10 Apr 1972, BU Port Lavaca, Tex.

DE 244 *Otterstetter* Out of comm 21 Sep 1946–6 Jun 1952. Rec **DER 244**, 1 Oct 1951. Decomm 20 Jun 1960. Stricken 1 Aug 1974. Sunk as target off Puerto Rico, 15 Feb 1976.

DE 245 *Sloat* Decomm 6 Aug 1947. Stricken 2 Jan 1971. Sold 5 Apr 1972, BU Portsmouth, Va.

DE 246 *Snowden* Out of comm 29 Mar 1946–6 Jun 1951 and Aug 1960–2 Aug 1961. NRT. Decomm 1 Aug 1962. Stricken 23 Sep 1968. Sunk as target off Newport, RI, 27 Jun 1969.
◆Cuba Oct 1961–Jul 1962.

DE 247 *Stanton* Decomm 2 Jun 1947. Stricken 1 Dec 1970. Sunk as target off Puerto Rico, 16 Oct 1972.

DE 248 *Swasey* Decomm 15 Jan 1946. Stricken 1 Nov 1972. Sold 26 Feb 1973, BU.

DE 249 *Marchand* Decomm 25 Apr 1947. Stricken 2 Jan 1971. Sold 23 Jan 1974, BU.

DE 250 *Hurst* Decomm 1 May 1946. Stricken 1 Dec 1972. Trfd to Mexico 1 Oct 1973.
Later history: renamed *Manuel Azueta* (A 06), renamed *Comodoro Manuel Azueta Perillos* (E 30). SE2001.

DE 251 *Camp* Out of comm 1 May 1946–31 Jul 1956. Rec **DER 251**, 7 Dec 1955. Decomm 13 Feb 1971. Trfd to Vietnam 13 Feb 1971.
Later history: renamed *Tran Hung Dao* (HQ 1). Recovered, May 1975. Trfd to Philippines 5 Apr 1976, renamed *Rajah Lakandula* (PF 4). R 1988.
★Vietnam Sep 1965–Feb 1966, Aug 1966–Jan 1967, Jul–Aug, Oct 1967–Feb 1968, Aug–Sep, Nov 1968–Feb 1969, Jan–Feb 1970; ◆Cuba Sep–Oct 1961, Jun–Aug 1962.

DE 252 *Howard D. Crow* Out of comm 22 May 1946–6 Jul 1951. Decomm and stricken 23 Sep 1968. Sold Oct 1970, BU Beaumont, Tex.
◆Cuba Oct 1961–Jul 1962.

DE 253 *Pettit* Decomm 6 May 1946. Stricken 1 Aug 1973. Sunk as target off Puerto Rico, 30 Sep 1974.

DE 254 *Ricketts* Decomm 17 Apr 1946. Stricken 1 Nov 1972. Sold 18 Jan 1974, BU, Brownsville, Tex.

DE 255 *Sellstrom* Out of comm 13 Jun 1946–1 Oct 1956. Rec **DER 255**, 21 Oct 1955. Decomm Jun 1960. Stricken 1 Nov 1965. Sold Apr 1967, BU. Portsmouth, Va.

DE 316 *Harveson* Out of comm 9 May 1947–12 Feb 1951. Rec **DER 316**, 12 Feb 1951. Decomm 30 Jun 1960. Stricken 1 Dec 1966. Sunk as target off San Diego, 10 Oct 1967.

DE 317 *Joyce* Out of comm 1 May 1946–28 Feb 1951. Rec **DER 317**, 13 Sep 1950. Decomm 17 Jun 1960. Stricken 1 Dec 1972. Sold 6 Sep 1973, BU Terminal I.

DE 318 *Kirkpatrick* Out of comm 1 May 1946–23 Feb 1952. Rec **DER 318**, 1 Oct 1951. Decomm 24 Jun 1960. Stricken 1 Aug 1974. Sold 12 Mar 1975, BU.

DE 320 *Menges* Decomm Jan 1947. Stricken 2 Jan 1971. Sold 10 Apr 1972, BU Portsmouth, Va.

DE 321 *Mosley* Decomm 15 Mar 1946. Stricken 2 Jan 1971. Sold 17 Jul 1973, BU Brownsville, Tex.

Escorts/Frigates 83

DE 322 *Newell* Decomm 20 Nov 1945. To USCG 20 Jul 1951–31 Mar 1954, WDE 422. Rec **DER 322**, 1 Nov 1956. Recomm 20 Aug 1957. Decomm 21 Sep 1968. Stricken 23 Sep 1968. BU 1972.
★Vietnam Jun–Dec 1965, Jun–Dec 1966, Dec 1967–Jan 1968.

DE 323 *Pride* Decomm 26 Apr 1946. Stricken 2 Jan 1971. Sold 23 Jan 1974, BU.

DE 324 *Falgout* Decomm 18 Apr 1947. To USCG 24 Aug 1951–21 May 1954, WDE 424. Rec **DER 324**, 28 Oct 1954. Recomm 30 Jun 1955. Decomm 30 Jun 1969. Stricken 1 Jun 1975. Sunk as target off California, 12 Jan 1977.
★Vietnam Apr–Aug 1965, Jan–Jun 1966, Nov 1966–Jun 1967, Jan–Jun 1968, Dec 1968–Jan, Mar–Apr 1969.

DE 325 *Lowe* Decomm 1 May 1946. To USCG, 20 Jul 1951–1 Jun 1954, WDE 425. Rec **DER 325**, 28 Oct 1954. Recomm, 15 Jan 1956. Decomm 20 Sep and stricken 23 Sep 1968. Sold 3 Sep 1969, BU.
★Vietnam Aug–Sep, Dec 1965, Oct 1966–Apr 1967, Oct 1967–Feb 1968.

DE 326 *Thomas J. Gary* Out of comm 7 Mar 1947–2 Aug 1957. Rec **DER 326**, 1 Nov 1956. Decomm and stricken 22 Oct 1973, and trfd to Tunisia
Later history: renamed *President Habib Bourguiba*, renamed *Indakh* (E 7). SE2001
◆Cuba Feb–Mar 1961, Feb–Jun 1962, Cuba Missile Crisis Nov 1962, Antarctic Oct 1965–Mar 1966, Oct–Dec 1966.

DE 327 *Brister* Out of comm 4 Oct 1946–21 Jul 1956. Rec **DER 327**, 21 Oct 1955. Decomm and stricken 23 Sep 1968. Sold 15 Dec 1971, BU 1972 Kaohsiung.
★Vietnam Apr–Sep 1965, Jan–Jun 1966, Nov 1966–May 1967, Feb–May 1968; ◆Cuba Missile Crisis Nov–Dec 1962.

DE 328 *Finch* Decomm 4 Oct 1946. To USCG 24 Aug 1951–23 Apr 1954, WDE 428. Rec **DER 328**, 21 Oct 1955. Recomm 17 Aug 1956. Decomm 1 Oct 1973. Stricken 1 Feb 1974. Sold 24 Jul 1974, BU.
★Vietnam Jul–Sep 1965, Dec 1965–May 1966, Oct 1966–Jan 1967, Sep–Dec 1967, Jun–Jul 1968.

DE 329 *Kretchmer* Out of comm 20 Sep 1946–22 Sep 1956. Rec **DER 329**, 21 Oct 1955. Decomm 1 Oct 1973. Stricken 30 Sep 1973. Sold 9 May 1974, BU.
★Vietnam Sep–Dec 1965, Mar–Sep 1966, Jan–Aug 1967, Jul–Aug 1968, Mar–May 1969; ◆Cuba Missile Crisis Nov–Dec 1962.

DE 330 *O'Reilly* Decomm 15 Jun 1946. Stricken 15 Jan 1971. Sold 10 Apr 1972, BU Portsmouth, Va.

DE 331 *Koiner* Decomm 4 Oct 1946. To USCG, 20 Jun 1951–19 May 1954, WDE 431. Rec **DER 331**, 28 Oct 1954. Recomm 26 Aug 1955. Decomm 21 Sep 1968. Stricken 23 Sep 1968. Sold 3 Sep 1969, BU.
★Vietnam Aug–Dec 1965, Feb–Sep 1966, Jan–Jul 1967, Feb–Jun 1968.

DE 332 *Price* Out of comm 16 May 1947–1 Aug 1956. Rec **DER 332**, 21 Oct 1955. Decomm 30 Jun 1960. Stricken 1 Aug 1974. Sold 12 Mar 1975, BU.

DE 333 *Strickland* Out of comm 15 Jun 1946–2 Feb 1952. Rec **DER 333**, 1 Oct 1951. Decomm 17 Jun 1958. Stricken 1 Dec 1972. Sold 13 Aug 1974, BU Seattle.

DE 334 *Forster* Decomm 15 Jun 1946. To USCG 20 Jun 1951–25 May 1954, WDE 434. Rec **DER 334**, 21 Oct 1955. Recomm 23 Oct 1956. Decomm 1 Oct 1971. Trfd to Vietnam 25 Sep 1971.
Later history: renamed *Tran Khanh Du* (HQ 04), renamed *Dai Ky* (HQ 03). Captured by North Vietnam after fall of Saigon, 30 Apr 1975. Hulked <1998.
★Vietnam Apr–Aug 1965, Jan–Aug 1966, Feb–Apr 1967, Feb–May 1968, Jan–Mar 1969; ◆Quemoy-Matsu Jan, May 1961, Antarctic Jan–Mar 1963.

DE 335 *Daniel* Decomm 12 Apr 1946. Stricken 15 Jan 1971. Sold 23 Jan 1974, BU.

DE 336 *Roy O. Hale* Out of comm 11 Jul 1946–29 Jan 1957. Rec **DER 336**, 21 Oct 1955. Decomm 15 Jul 1963. Stricken 1 Aug 1974. Sold 12 Mar 1975, BU.
◆Cuba Mar–Apr 1961, Cuba Missile Crisis Nov 1962.

DE 337 *Dale W. Peterson* Decomm 27 Mar 1946. Stricken 2 Jan 1971. Sold 10 Apr 1972, BU Portsmouth, Va.

DE 338 *Martin H. Ray* Decomm Mar 1946. Stricken 1 May 1966. Sold 30 Mar 1967, BU New Orleans.

DE 382 *Ramsden* Decomm 13 Jun 1946. To USCG, 28 Mar 1952–10 Apr 1954, WDE 482. Rec **DER 382**, 1 Nov 1956. Recomm 10 Dec 1957. Decomm 23 Jun 1960. Stricken 1 Aug 1974. Reported sunk as target.

DE 383 *Mills* Out of comm 14 Jun 1946–3 Oct 1957. Rec **DER 383**, 1 Nov 1956. Decomm 27 Oct 1970. Stricken 1 Aug 1974. Sold 12 Mar 1975, BU.
◆Cuba Missile Crisis Oct 1962, Antarctic Sep 1964–Mar 1965.

DE 384 *Rhodes* Out of comm 13 Jun 1946–1 Aug 1955. Rec **DER 384**, 1 Dec 1954. Decomm 10 Jul 1963. Stricken 1 Aug 1974. Sold 12 Mar 1975, BU.
◆Cuba Feb–Oct 1961, Mar–Oct 1962, Cuba Missile Crisis Oct–Dec 1962.

DE 385 *Richey* Decomm Mar 1950. To USCG 28 Mar 1952–14 May 1954, WDE 485. Stricken 30 Jun 1968. Sunk as target off California, Jul 1969.

DE 386 *Savage* Decomm 13 Jun 1946. Rec **DER 386**, 28 Oct 1954. Recomm 18 Jun 1955. Decomm 17 Oct 1969. Stricken 1 Jun 1975. Sunk as target off California, 25 Oct 1982.
6★Vietnam Jun–Nov 1965, Jun–Nov 1966, Aug–Sep 1967, Aug–Oct, Dec 1968.

DE 387 *Vance* Decomm 27 Feb 1946. To USCG, 15 May 1952–16 Jun 1954, WDE 487. Rec **DER 387**, 1 Nov 1956 Recomm 5 Oct 1956. Decomm 10 Oct 1969. Stricken 1 Jun 1975. Sunk as target 1985.
7★Vietnam May–Sep 1965, Jan–Aug 1966, Jan–May 1967, Mar–Aug 1968, Feb–May 1969; ◆Antarctic Sep 1961–Feb 1962.

DE 388 *Lansing* Decomm 25 Apr 1946. To USCG, 15 Jun 1952–29 Mar 1954, WDE 488. Rec **DER 388**, 21 Oct 1955. Recomm 18 Dec 1956. Decomm 21 May 1965. Stricken 1 Feb 1974. Sold 24 Jul 1974, BU.

DE 389 *Durant* Decomm 27 Feb 1946. To USCG, 15 May 1952–16 Jun 1954, WDE 489. Rec **DER 389**, 7 Dec 1955. Recomm 8 Dec 1956. Decomm 1 Mar 1969. Stricken 1 Apr 1974. Sold 24 Jul 1974, BU.
◆Antarctic Sep 1962–Feb 1963.

DE 390 *Calcaterra* Out of comm 1 May 1946–12 Sep 1955. Rec **DER 390**, 28 Oct 1954. Stricken 2 Jul 1973. Sold 9 May 1974, BU.
◆Cuba Missile Crisis Oct–Nov 1962, Antarctic Sep 1965–Feb 1966.

DE 391 *Chambers* Decomm 22 Apr 1946. To USCG 11 Jun 1952–30 Jul 1954, WDE 491. Rec **DER 391**, 28 Oct 1954. Recomm 1 Jun 1955. Decomm 20 Jun 1960. Stricken 1 Mar 1975. Sold 24 Sep 1975, BU Camden, NJ.

DE 392 *Merrill* Decomm 1 May 1946. Stricken 2 Apr 1972. Sold 23 Jan 1974, BU.

DE 393 *Haverfield* Out of comm 30 Jun 1947–4 Jan 1955. Rec **DER 393**, 2 Sep 1954. Decomm and stricken 2 Jun 1969. Sold 15 Dec 1971, BU Kaohsiung.
★Vietnam Jul 1965–Jan 1966, Jun–Nov 1966, May–Jul, Sep–Oct 1967, Jul–Aug, Nov 1968; ◆Quemoy-Matsu Oct, Dec 1961–Jan 1962.

DE 394 *Swenning* Decomm 18 Jun 1946. Stricken 1 Jul 1972. Sold 9 Jan 1974, BU Philadelphia.

DE 395 *Willis* Decomm 14 Jun 1946. Stricken 1 Jul 1972. Sold 17 Aug 1973, BU New Bedford, Mass.

DE 396 *Janssen* Decomm 12 Apr 1946. Stricken 1 Jul 1972. Sold 28 Sep 1973, BU Baltimore.

DE 397 *Wilhoite* Out of comm 19 Jun 1946–29 Jan 1955. Rec **DER 397**, 2 Sep 1954. Decomm and stricken 2 Jul 1969. Sold 19 Jul 1972, BU, Tacoma.
6★Vietnam Jun 1965–Jan 1966, Jun 1966–Jan 1967, Jun–Oct 1967, Aug 1968–Jan 1969; ◆Antarctic Sep 1960–Mar 1961.

DE 398 *Cockrill* Decomm 21 Jun 1946. Stricken 1 Aug 1973. Sunk as target off Florida, 19 Nov 1974.

84 The Navy of the Nuclear Age, 1947–2007

DE 399 *Stockdale* Decomm 15 Jun 1946. Stricken 1 Jul 1972. Sunk as target off Florida, 20 May 1974.

DE 400 *Hissem* Out of comm 15 Jun 1946–31 Aug 1956. Rec **DER 400**, 21 Oct 1955. Decomm 15 May 1970. Stricken 1 Jun 1975. Sunk as target off San Diego, 24 Feb 1987.
★Vietnam Sep 1965–Feb 1966, Sep 1966–May 1967, Jan, Mar–Apr 1968, Feb–May 1969; ◆Cuba Missile Crisis Oct–Nov 1962, Antarctic Sep 1963–Feb 1964.

Notes: DE 152 refitted for ASW, 1951–52, with two hedgehogs replacing 1–3″ gun. TT removed in some ships. Planned rearmament with 5″ guns not carried out.

Rudderow Class (type TEV)

DE 224 *Rudderow* Decomm 15 Jan 1947. Stricken 1 Nov 1969. Sold 1970, BU Terminal I.

DE 225 *Day* Decomm 16 May 1946. Stricken 30 Jun 1968. Sunk as target off California, Mar 1969.

DE 231 *Hodges* Decomm 22 Jun 1946. Stricken 1 Dec 1972. Sold 28 Aug 1973, BU Terminal I.

DE 579 *Riley* Decomm 15 Jan 1947. Trfd to Taiwan 10 Jul 1968.
Later history: renamed *Tai Yuan* (959/827). R 1996

DE 580 *Leslie L.B. Knox* Decomm 15 Jun 1946. Stricken 15 Jan 1972. Sold 15 May 1973, BU.

DE 581 *McNulty* Decomm 2 Jul 1946. Stricken 1 Mar 1972. Sunk as target off southern California, 16 Nov 1972.

DE 582 *Metivier* Decomm 1 Jun 1946. Stricken 30 Jun 1968. Sold 1969, BU Portland, Ore.

DE 583 *George A. Johnson* Out of comm 31 May 1946–16 Dec 1950. NRT 1947. Decomm 30 Sep 1957. Stricken 1 Nov 1965. Ran aground south of San Francisco en route to BU, 12 Oct 1966. BU 1966.

DE 584 *Charles J. Kimmel* Decomm 15 Jan 1947. Stricken 30 Jun 1968. Sunk as target off southern California, 13 Nov 1969.

DE 585 *Daniel A. Joy* Out of comm 7 Feb 1949–11 Dec 1949. NRT 1947, Great Lakes. Decomm 14 May 1965. Stricken 15 May 1965. Sold 11 Mar 1966, BU Wilmington, Del.
◆Cuba Feb–Mar 1962.

DE 586 *Lough* Decomm 24 Jun 1946. Stricken 1 Nov 1969. Sold Oct 1970, BU Terminal I.

DE 587 *Thomas F. Nickel* Out of comm 31 May 1946–22 Sep 1950. NRT 1947. Decomm 26 Feb 1958. Stricken 1 Dec 1972. Sold 9 Jun 1973, BU.

DE 588 *Peiffer* Decomm 1 Jun 1946. Stricken 1 Dec 1966. Sunk as target off southern California, 16 May 1967.

DE 589 *Tinsman* Decomm 11 May 1946. Stricken 15 May 1972. Sold 14 Sep 1973, BU.

DE 684 *De Long* Out of comm 25 Apr 1947–7 Feb 1951, 16 Jul 1958–Oct 1961. Decomm 1 Aug 1962. Stricken 8 Aug 1969. Sunk as target off Puerto Rico, 19 Feb 1970.
◆Cuba Feb–Mar 1962.

DE 685 *Coates* Out of commission 16 Apr 1946–7 Feb 1951. NRT. Decomm and stricken 30 Jan 1970. Sunk as target, 19 Sep 1971.
◆Cuba Jan–Mar 1962.

DE 686 *Eugene E. Elmore* Decomm 31 May 1946. Stricken 30 Jun 1968. Sold Jun 1969 Portland, Ore.

DE 706 *Holt* Decomm 2 Jul 1946. Trfd to South Korea 19 Jun 1963.
Later history: renamed *Chung Nam* (DE 73). R 1984.

DE 707 *Jobb* Decomm 13 May 1946. Stricken 1 Nov 1969. Sold Oct 1970, BU New Orleans.

DE 708 *Parle* Out of comm 10 Jul 1946–2 Mar 1951. IS, NRT 1959. Recomm Oct 1961. Decomm Aug 1962. OS and stricken 1 Jul 1970. Sunk as target off Florida, 27 Oct 1970.
◆Cuba Dec 1961, Mar–Apr 1962.

Figure 6.4: *USS Parle* (DE 708), *Rudderow* class.

John C. Butler Class (type WGT)

DE 339 *John C. Butler* Out of comm 26 Jun 1946–27 Dec 1950. Decomm 18 Dec 1957. Stricken 1 Jun 1970. Sunk as target off California, Nov 1971.

DE 340 *O'Flaherty* Decomm Jan 1947. Stricken 1 Dec 1972. Sold 9 Nov 1973, BU.

DE 341 *Raymond* Out of comm 24 Jan 1947–27 Apr 1951. Decomm 22 Sep 1958. IS 22 Sep 1958–31 May 1960. Stricken 1 Jul 1972. Sunk as target off Florida, 22 Jan 1974.

DE 342 *Richard W. Suesens* Decomm 15 Jan 1947. Stricken 15 Mar 1972. Sold 15 Jun 1973, BU, Terminal I.

DE 343 *Abercrombie* Decomm 15 Jun 1946. Stricken 1 May 1967. Sunk as target off San Diego, 7 Jan 1968.

DE 345 *Robert Brazier* Decomm 16 Sep 1946. Stricken 1 Jan 1968. Sunk as target off California, 9 Jan 1969.

DE 346 *Edwin A. Howard* Decomm 25 Sep 1946. Stricken 1 Dec 1972. Sold 27 Aug 1973, BU Terminal I.

DE 347 *Jesse Rutherford* Decomm 21 Jun 1946. Stricken 1 Jan 1968. Sunk as target off California, 8 Dec 1968.

DE 348 *Key* Decomm 9 Jul 1946. Stricken 1 Mar 1972. Sold 19 Dec 1972.

DE 349 *Gentry* Decomm 2 Jul 1946. Stricken 15 Jan 1972. Sold 15 Jan 1973.

DE 350 *Traw* Decomm 7 Jun 1946. Stricken 1 Aug 1967. Sunk as target off Baja California, 17 Aug 1968.

DE 351 *Maurice J. Manuel* Out of comm 20 May 1946–27 Apr 1951. Decomm 30 Oct 1957. Stricken 1 May 1966. Sunk as target, Aug 1966.

DE 352 *Naifeh* Out of comm 27 Jun 1946–26 Jan 1951. Decomm 17 Jun 1960. Stricken 1 Jan 1966. Sunk as target off San Clemente I, 11 Jul 1966.
2★Korea K-6 K-8.

DE 353 *Doyle C. Barnes* Decomm 15 Jan 1947. Stricken 1 Dec 1972. Sold 27 Aug 1973, BU Terminal I.

DE 354 *Kenneth M. Willett* Out of comm 24 Oct 1946–25 May 1951. Decomm 26 Feb 1959. Stricken 1 Jul 1972. Sunk as target off Puerto Rico, 5 Mar 1974.

DE 355 *Jaccard* Decomm 30 Sep 1946. Stricken 1 Nov 1967. Sunk as target, 4 Oct 1968.

DE 356 *Lloyd E. Acree* Decomm 10 Oct 1946. Stricken 15 Jan 1972. Sold 15 May 1973, BU.

DE 357 *George E. Davis* Out of comm 26 Aug 1946–11 Jul 1951. Decomm 11 Nov 1954. Stricken 1 Dec 1972. Sold 5 Dec 1973, BU.

DE 358 *Mack* Decomm 11 Dec 1946. Stricken 15 Mar 1972. Sold 15 May 1973, BU.

DE 359 *Woodson* Out of comm 15 Jan 1947–19 May 1951. Decomm 11 Aug 1962. Stricken 1 Jul 1965. Sold 16 Aug 1966, BU, Baltimore. ◆Cuba Apr–Jun 1962.

DE 360 *Johnnie Hutchins* Out of comm 14 May 1946–22 Nov 1950. NRT 1950. Decomm 25 Feb 1958. Stricken 1 Jul 1972. Sold 9 Jan 1974, BU Camden, NJ.

DE 361 *Walton* Out of comm 31 May 1946–26 Jan 1951. Decomm 20 Sep and stricken 23 Sep 1968. Sunk as target off California, 7 Aug 1969.
2★Korea K-8 K-10; 2★Vietnam Apr 1962.

DE 362 *Rolf* Decomm 3 Jun 1946. Stricken 1 Dec 1972. Sold 6 Sep 1973, BU.

DE 363 *Pratt* Decomm 14 May 1946. Stricken 15 Mar 1972. Sold 15 Jan 1973.

DE 364 *Rombach* NRT 1947. Decomm 9 Jan 1958. Stricken 1 Mar 1972. Sold 19 Dec 1972, BU.

DE 365 *McGinty* Out of comm 15 Jan 1947–28 Mar 1951 and 19 Sep 1959–2 Oct 1961. NRT. Decomm 1 Aug 1962. Stricken 23 Sep 1968. Sold 27 Oct 1969.
3★Korea K-6 K-7 K-10; ★Vietnam Apr 1962; ◆Taiwan Straits Sep–Oct 1958.

DE 366 *Alvin C. Cockrell* Out of comm 2 Jul 1946–27 Jun 1951 and 17 Jan 1959–1 Oct 1961. Decomm 1 Aug 1962 and OS 20 Sep 1968. Stricken 23 Sep 1968. Sunk as target off San Clemente I., Cal., 19 Sep 1969.
★Vietnam Mar–May 1962.

DE 367 *French* Decomm 29 May 1946. Stricken 15 May 1972. Sold 30 Aug 1973, BU Tacoma, Wash.

DE 368 *Cecil J. Doyle* Decomm 2 Jul 1946. Stricken 1 Jul 1967. Sunk as target off California, 2 Dec 1968.

DE 369 *Thaddeus Parker* Out of comm 31 May 1946–21 Sep 1951. Decomm and stricken 1 Sep 1967. Sold 9 Jul 1968, BU Portsmouth, Va. ◆Cuba Jun–Jul 1962.

DE 370 *John L. Williamson* Decomm 14 Jun 1946. Stricken 15 Sep 1970. Sold 15 May 1973, BU.

DE 371 *Presley* Decomm 20 Jun 1946. Stricken 30 Jun 1968. Sold 2 Apr 1970, BU Terminal I.

DE 372 *Williams* Decomm 4 Jun 1946. Stricken 1 Jul 1967. Sunk as target off San Diego, 29 Jun 1968.

DE 402 *Richard S. Bull* Decomm Mar 1946. Stricken 30 Jun 1968. Sunk as target off southern California, 24 Jun 1969.

DE 403 *Richard M. Rowell* Decomm 2 Jul 1946. Stricken 30 Jun 1968. Sold Jun 1969, BU Portland, Ore.

DE 405 *Dennis* Decomm 31 May 1946. Stricken 1 Dec 1972. Sold 27 Aug 1973, BU Terminal I.

DE 406 *Edmonds* Out of comm 31 May 1946–28 Feb 1951. Decomm Apr 1965. Stricken 15 May 1972. Sold 30 Aug 1973, BU Tacoma, Wash.
2★Korea K-6 L-7; ★Vietnam Feb–Apr 1962; ◆Taiwan Straits Sep 1958–Jan 1959.

DE 408 *Straus* Decomm 15 Jan 1947. Stricken 1 May 1966. Sunk as target off San Diego, 1 Aug 1973.

DE 409 *La Prade* Decomm 11 May 1946. Stricken 15 Jan 1972. Sold 15 Jan 1973, BU.

DE 410 *Jack Miller* Decomm 1 Jun 1946. Stricken 30 Jun 1968. Sold Jul 1969, BU.

DE 411 *Stafford* Decomm 16 May 1946. Stricken 15 Mar 1972. Sold 15 May 1973, BU.

DE 412 *Walter C. Wann* Decomm 31 May 1946. Stricken 30 Jun 1968. Sold Jun 1969, BU Terminal I.

DE 414 *Le Ray Wilson* Out of comm 15 Jan 1947–28 Mar 1951. Decomm 30 Jan 1959. Stricken 15 May 1972. Sold 30 Aug 1973, BU.

DE 415 *Lawrence C. Taylor* Decomm 23 Apr 1946. Stricken 1 Dec 1972. Sold 23 Aug 1973, BU Terminal I.

DE 416 *Melvin R. Nawman* Out of comm 23 Apr 1946–28 Mar 1951. Decomm 30 Aug 1960. Stricken 1 Jul 1972. Sold 28 Sep 1973, BU.

DE 417 *Oliver Mitchell* Decomm 24 Apr 1946. Stricken 15 Mar 1972. Sold 15 Jan 1973, BU.

DE 418 *Tabberer* Out of comm 24 Apr 1946–7 Apr 1951. Decomm May 1960. Stricken 1 Jul 1972. Sold 3 Oct 1973, BU Camden, NJ.

DE 419 *Robert F. Keller* Decomm 24 Apr 1946–2 Oct 1961. NRT 1946–1959. Decomm Jan 1965. NRT 1965–72. Stricken 1 Jul 1972. Sold 9 Jan 1974, BU Philadelphia.
◆Cuba Dec 1961.

DE 420 *Leland E. Thomas* Decomm 3 May 1946. Stricken 1 Dec 1972. Sold 6 Sep 1973, BU.

DE 421 *Chester T. O'Brien* Out of comm 2 Jul 1946–28 Mar 1951. Decomm 21 Feb 1959. NRT. Stricken 1 Jul 1972. Sold 28 Mar 1974, BU.

DE 422 *Douglas A. Munro* Out of comm 15 Jan 1947–28 Feb 1951. Decomm 24 Jun 1960. Stricken 1 Dec 1965. Sunk as target Jan 1966.
3★Korea K-6 K-7 K-10; ◆Taiwan Straits Sep, Nov–Dec 1958, Quemoy-Matsu Dec 1958–Jan 1959.

DE 423 *Dufilho* Decomm 14 May 1946. Stricken 1 Dec 1972. Sold 23 Aug 1973, BU Terminal I.

DE 424 *Haas* Out of comm 31 May 1946–19 May 1951. Decomm 24 Jan 1958. Stricken 1 Jul 1966. Sold 6 Sep 1967, BU.

DE 438 *Corbesier* Decomm 2 Jul 1946. Stricken 1 Dec 1972. Sold 14 Nov 1973, BU.

DE 439 *Conklin* Decomm 17 Jan 1946. Stricken 1 Oct 1970. Sold 12 May 1972, BU.

DE 440 *McCoy Reynolds* Out of comm 31 May 1946–28 Mar 1951. Decomm and trfd to Portugal 7 Feb 1957.
Later history: renamed *Corte Real* (F 334). R1968, BU.
1★Korea K-8.

DE 441 *William Seiverling* Out of comm 21 Mar 1947–27 Dec 1950. Damaged by coastal gunfire off Wonsan, Korea, 8 Sep 1951. Decomm 27 Sep 1957. Stricken 1 Dec 1972. Sold 20 Sep 1973, BU.
5★Korea K-5 K-6 K-8 K-9 K-10.

DE 442 *Ulvert M. Moore* Out of comm 24 May 1946–27 Jan 1951. Hit by shore gunfire off Hungnam, Korea, 17 Oct 1951. Decomm 10 Oct 1958. Stricken 1 Dec 1965. Sunk as target off San Nicolas I., Calif., 13 Jul 1966.
3★Korea K-6 K-8 K-9.

DE 443 *Kendall C. Campbell* Decomm 31 May 1946. Stricken 15 Jan 1972. Sold 15 Jan 1973.

DE 444 *Goss* Out of comm 15 Jun 1946–27 Dec 1950. Decomm 10 Oct 1958. Stricken 1 Mar 1972. Sold 20 Nov 1972 BU Seattle.

DE 445 *Grady* Out of comm 2 Jul 1946–21 Nov 1950. NRT 1947. Decomm 18 Dec 1957. Stricken 30 Jun 1968. Sold 1969 BU Portland, Ore.

Figure 6.5: *USS Chester T. O'Brien* (DE 421), *John C. Butler* class.

DE 446 *Charles E. Brannon* Out of comm 21 May 1946–21 Nov 1950. NRT 1947. Decomm 18 Jun 1960. Stricken 23 Sep 1968. Sold 27 Oct 1969, BU.
★Vietnam Mar–May 1962.

DE 447 *Albert T. Harris* Out of comm 26 Jul 1946–27 Apr 1951. NRT 1946–50, 1957. Decomm 21 Sep 1968. Stricken 23 Sep 1968. Sunk as target off Virginia Capes, 9 Apr 1969.
◆Antarctic Jun–Jul 1962.

DE 448 *Cross* Out of comm 14 Jun 1946–6 Jun 1951. Damaged by fire at sea off Cape May, NJ, 25 Mar 1953. Decomm 2 Jan 1958. Stricken 1 Jul 1966. Sold 5 Mar 1968, BU New Orleans.

DE 449 *Hanna* Out of comm 31 May 1946–27 Dec 1950. Damaged by shore gunfire at Songjin, Korea, 24 Dec 1952. Decomm 11 Dec 1959. Stricken 1 Dec 1972. Sold 14 Nov 1973, BU.
5★Korea K-5 K-6 K-8 K-9 K-10.

DE 450 *Joseph E. Connolly* Decomm 20 Jun 1946. Stricken 1 Jun 1970. Sunk as target 24 Feb 1973.

DE 508 *Gilligan* Out of comm 2 Jul 1946–15 Jul 1950. NRT 1947. Decomm 31 Mar 1959. Stricken 1 Mar 1972. Sold 1972, BU Portland, Ore.

DE 509 *Formoe* Out of comm 27 May 1946–27 Jun 1951. Decomm 7 Feb 1957. Trfd to Portugal 1957.
Later history: renamed *Diogo Cão* (F 333). R1968. BU.

DE 510 *Heyliger* Out of comm 20 Jun 1946–28 Mar 1951. Decomm 2 Jan 1958. Stricken 1 May 1966. Sunk as target 1969

DE 531 *Edward H. Allen* Out of comm 10 May 1946–26 Feb 1951. Decomm 9 Jan 1958. Stricken 1 Jul 1972, sold 9 Jan 1974, BU.

DE 532 *Tweedy* Out of comm 10 May 1946–2 Apr 1952 and 20 Jun 1959–2 Oct 1961. NRT. Decomm 29 May 1968. Stricken 30 Jun 1968. Sunk as target off Florida, May 1970.
◆Cuba Apr–May 1962.

DE 533 *Howard F. Clark* Decomm 15 Jul 1946. Stricken 15 May 1972. Sold 30 Aug 1973, BU.

DE 534 *Silverstein* Out of comm 15 Jan 1947–28 Feb 1951. Damaged in collision with submarine *Stickleback*, which sank, off Hawaii, 30 May 1958. Decomm 30 Jan 1959. Stricken 1 Dec 1972. Sold 14 Nov 1973, BU.
3★Korea K-6 K-7 K-10.

DE 535 *Lewis* Out of comm 31 May 1946–28 Mar 1952. Damaged by shore gunfire at Wonsan, Korea, 21 Oct 1952 (7 killed). Decomm 27 May 1960. Stricken 1 Jan 1966. Sunk as target 21 Apr 1966.
1★Korea K-8.

DE 536 *Bivin* Decomm 15 Jan 1947. Stricken 30 Jun 1968. Sunk as target off southern California, 17 Jul 1969.

DE 537 *Rizzi* Out of comm 18 Jun 1946–28 Mar 1951. Decomm 28 Feb 1958. Stricken 1 Aug 1972. Sold 9 Jan 1974, BU.

DE 538 *Osberg* Out of commission 25 Sep 1957–25 Feb 1951. Decomm 25 Feb 1958. Stricken 1 Aug 1972. Sold 5 Feb 1974, BU.

DE 539 *Wagner* Construction suspended, 61.5% complete, 17 Feb 1947. Ordered completed as radar picket ship, 1 Jul 1954. Rec **DER 539**, 2 Sep 1954. First comm 22 Nov 1955. Decomm Jun 1960. Stricken 1 Nov 1974. Sold Aug 1977. BU Kearny, NJ.

DE 540 *Vandivier* Construction suspended, 17 Feb 1947. Ordered completed as radar picket ship, 1 Jul 1954. Rec **DER 540**, 2 Sep 1954. First comm 11 Oct 1955. Decomm 30 Jun 1960. Stricken 1 Nov 1974. Sunk as target off Florida, 7 Feb 1975.

Notes: DER 539–540 completed to new design. 1,745 tons; two tripod masts.

RADAR PICKET DESTROYER ESCORTS

DE 51 *Buckley* Rec **DER 51**, 26 Apr 1949. Rec **DE 51**, 29 Sep 1954.
DE 57 *Fogg* Rec **DER 57**, 18 Mar 1949. Rec **DE 57**, 29 Sep 1954.
DE 153 *Reuben James* Rec **DER 153**, 18 Mar 1949. Rec **DE 153**, 28 Sep 1954.
DE 213 *William T. Powell* Rec **DER 213**, 18 Mar 1949. Rec **DE 213**, 1 Dec 1954.
DE 223 *Spangenberg* Rec **DER 223**, 18 Mar 1949. Rec **DE 223**, 1 Dec 1954.
DE 577 *Alexander J. Luke* Rec **DER 577**, 18 Mar 1949. Rec **DE 577**, 28 Sep 1954.
DE 578 *Robert I. Paine* Rec **DER 578**, 18 Mar 1949. Rec **DE 578**, 1 Dec 1954.

Note: These DEs were converted to radar pickets in 1945–46, but not reclassified until 1949.

DE 133 *Pillsbury* Rec **DER 133**, Aug 1954. Decomm 20 Jun 1960.
DE 142 *Fessenden* Rec **DER 142**, 1 Oct 1951. Decomm 30 Jun 1960.
DE 147 *Blair* Rec **DER 147**, 2 Dec 1957. Decomm 15 Jun 1960. Stricken 1 Dec 1972.
DE 239 *Sturtevant* Rec **DER 239**, 1 Nov 1956. Decomm Jun 1960. Stricken 1 Dec 1972.
DE 244 *Otterstetter* Rec **DER 244**, 1 Oct 1951. Decomm 20 Jun 1960. Stricken 1 Aug 1974.
DE 251 *Camp* Rec **DER 251**, 7 Dec 1955. **Later history:** Trfd to Vietnam, 13 Feb 1971.
DE 255 *Sellstrom* Rec **DER 255**, 21 Oct 1955. Decomm Jun 1960. Stricken 1 Nov 1965.
DE 316 *Harveson* Rec **DER 316**, 12 Feb 1951. Decomm 30 Jun 1960. Stricken 1 Dec 1966.
DE 317 *Joyce* Rec **DER 317**, 13 Sep 1950. Decomm 17 Jun 1960. Stricken 1 Dec 1972.
DE 318 *Kirkpatrick* Rec **DER 318**, 1 Oct 1951. Decomm 24 Jun 1960. Stricken 1 Aug 1974.
DE 322 *Newell* Rec **DER 322**, 1 Nov 1956. Decomm 21 Sep 1968. Stricken 23 Sep 1968.
DE 324 *Falgout* Rec **DER 324**, 28 Oct 1954. Stricken 1 Jun 1975.
DE 325 *Lowe* Rec **DER 325**, 28 Oct 1954. Decomm 20 Sep and stricken 23 Sep 1968.
DE 326 *Thomas J. Gary* Rec **DER 326**, 1 Nov 1956. Decomm 22 Oct 1973.
DE 327 *Brister* Rec **DER 327**, 21 Oct 1955. Stricken 23 Sep 1968.
DE 328 *Finch* Rec **DER 328**, 21 Oct 1955. Stricken 1 Feb 1974.
DE 329 *Kretchmer* Rec **DER 329**, 21 Oct 1955. Stricken 30 Sep 1973.
DE 331 *Koiner* Rec **DER 331**, 28 Oct 1954. Stricken 23 Sep 1968.
DE 332 *Price* Rec **DER 332**, 21 Oct 1955. Stricken 1 Aug 1974.
DE 333 *Strickland* Rec **DER 333**, 1 Oct 1951. Decomm 17 Jun 1958. Stricken 1 Dec 1972.

Figure 6.6: *USS Harveson* (DER 316) *Edsall* class radar picket conversion at Brooklyn Naval Shipyard, New York.

Figure 6.7: USS *Wagner* (DER 539), completed in 1955 as radar picket, May 1957.

DE 334	Forster	Rec **DER 334**, 21 Oct 1955. **Later history:** Trfd to Vietnam 25 Sep 1971.
DE 336	Roy O. Hale	Rec **DER 336**, 21 Oct 1955. Decomm. 15 Jul 1963. Stricken 1 Aug 1974.
DE 382	Ramsden	Rec **DER 382**, 1 Nov 1956. Decomm 23 Jun 1960. Stricken 1 Aug 1974.
DE 383	Mills	Rec **DER 383**, 1 Nov 1956. Stricken 1 Aug 1974.
DE 384	Rhodes	Rec **DER 384**, 1 Dec 1954. Decomm 10 Jul 1963. Stricken 1 Aug 1974.
DE 386	Savage	Rec **DER 386**, 28 Oct 1954. Decomm 17 Oct 1969. Stricken 1 Jun 1975.
DE 387	Vance	Rec **DER 387**, 1 Nov 1956. Decomm 10 Oct 1969. Stricken 1 Jun 1975.
DE 388	Lansing	Rec **DER 388**, 21 Oct 1955. Decomm 21 May 1965. Stricken 1 Feb 1974.
DE 389	Durant	Rec **DER 389**, 21 Oct 1955. Stricken 1 Apr 1974.
DE 390	Calcaterra	Rec **DER 390**, 28 Oct 1954. Stricken 2 Jul 1973.
DE 391	Chambers	Rec **DER 391**, 28 Oct 1954. Decomm 20 Jun 1960. Stricken 1 Mar 1975.
DE 393	Haverfield	Rec **DER 393**, 2 Sep 1954. Stricken 2 Jun 1969. BU 1971.
DE 397	Wilhoite	Rec **DER 397**, 2 Sep 1954. Decomm 2 Jul 1969 and Stricken.
DE 400	Hissem	Rec **DER 400**, 21 Oct 1955. Stricken 1 Jun 1975.
DE 539	Wagner	Rec **DER 529**, 2 Sep 1954.
DE 540	Vandivier	Rec **DER 530**, 2 Sep 1954.

Note: Conversion to DER included new tripod foremast and pole mainmast, additional radar, and enclosed superstructure above the maindeck. Armament 2–3″/50 guns.

CONTROL ESCORT VESSELS

DE 698	Raby	Rec **DEC 698**, 2 Nov 1949. Rec **DE 698**, 27 Dec 1957.
DE 704	Cronin	Rec **DEC 704**, 13 Sep 1950. Rec **DE 704**, 27 Dec 1957.
DE 705	Frybarger	Rec **DEC 705**, 13 Sep 1950. Rec **DE 705**, 27 Dec 1957.

Note: Rated as amphibious warfare vessels.

ESCORTS

Dealey Class

No.	Name	Builder	Keel Laid	Launched	Comm.
DE 1006	Dealey	Bath	15 Dec 1952	8 Nov 1953	3 Jun 1954
DE 1014	Cromwell	Bath	3 Aug 1953	4 Jun 1954	24 Nov 1954
DE 1015	Hammerberg	Bath	12 Nov 1953	20 Aug 1954	2 Mar 1955
DE 1021	Courtney	Defoe	2 Sep 1954	2 Nov 1955	24 Sep 1956
DE 1022	Lester	Defoe	2 Sep 1954	5 Jan 1956	14 Jun 1957
DE 1023	Evans	Puget Sd Brdg	8 Apr 1955	14 Sep 1955	14 Jun 1957
DE 1024	Bridget	Puget Sd Brdg	19 Sep 1955	25 Apr 1956	24 Oct 1957
DE 1025	Bauer	Beth; S.Fran.	1 Dec 1955	4 Jun 1957	21 Nov 1957
DE 1026	Hooper ex-*Gatch*	Beth; S.Fran.	4 Jan 1956 (19 Jul 1956)	1 Aug 1957	18 Mar 1958
DE 1027	John Willis	NY Sbdg	5 Jul 1955	4 Feb 1956	21 Feb 1957
DE 1028	Van Voorhis	NY Sbdg	29 Aug 1955	28 Jul 1956	22 Apr 1957
DE 1029	Hartley	NY Sbdg	31 Oct 1955	24 Nov 1956	26 Jun 1957
DE 1030	Joseph K. Taussig	NY Sbdg	3 Jan 1956	3 Jan 1957	10 Sep 1957

Displacement	1,340 tons; 1,950 f/l
Dimensions	314′6″ (oa) × 36′9″ × 9′3″
Machinery	1 screw; GT; 20,000 hp; 25 knots
Complement	150
Armament	4–3″/50, Weapon Alfa (except 1006), 2 TT. (Alfa removed in late 1960s.)

Notes: DE 1006, 1014–1015 had upright stack, others raked. All FRAM, except 1006, 1014. *Dealey* had British Squid depth charge launchers in place of weapon Alfa. Aluminum superstructure, lattice masts.

Service Records:

1006 *Dealey* Decomm and stricken 28 Jul 1972 and trfd to Uruguay.
Later history: renamed *18 de Julio* (3). R1995. BU 2000
◆Lebanon Jul–Sep 1958, Cuba May–Jun 1961, Aug–Oct 1962, Dominican Rep May–Jun 1965.

1014 *Cromwell* Decomm and stricken 5 Jul 1972. Sold 15 Jun 1973, BU
◆Lebanon Jul–Sep 1958.

1015 *Hammerberg* Decomm and stricken 14 Dec 1973. Sold 18 Jun 1974, BU
◆Cuba Aug–Sep 1962.

1021 *Courtney* Decomm and stricken 14 Dec 1973. Sold 18 Jun 1974, BU
◆Cuba May–Jun 1961.

1022 *Lester* Decomm and stricken 14 Dec 1973. Sold 18 Jun 1974, BU
◆Lebanon Jul–Sep 1958.

1023 *Evans* Decomm and stricken 3 Dec 1973. Sold 24 Jul 1974, BU.
★Vietnam May 1963, Aug–Sep 1964, Mar–Jul 1966, May–Oct 1967; ◆Quemoy-Matsu Jun 1960, Jul 1961.

1024 *Bridget* Decomm and stricken 12 Nov 1973. Sold 24 Jul 1974, BU.
★Vietnam Aug–Nov 1964, Feb–Jul 1966, May–Oct 1967; ◆Taiwan Straits Sep 1958.

1025 *Bauer* Decomm and stricken 3 Dec 1973. Sold 13 Aug 1974, BU Terminal I.
★Vietnam May 1963, Aug–Oct 1964; ◆Taiwan Straits Aug–Nov 1958, Quemoy-Matsu Nov 1959, Jan 1960, Jun 1961, Feb 1963.

Figure 6.8: USS *Hartley* (DE 1029), *Dealey* class after FRAM conversion 1962 with Weapon Alfa.

1026 *Hooper*   Decomm and stricken 6 Jul 1973. Sold 23 Jan 1974, BU.
★Vietnam May 1963, Aug–Oct 1964, Mar–Jul 1966, May–Oct 1967; ◆Quemoy-Matsu Jan–Mar 1959.

1027 *John Willis*   Decomm and stricken 14 Jul 1972. Sold 24 Apr 1973, BU.
◆Lebanon Jul–Sep 1958.

1028 *Van Voorhis*   Decomm and stricken 1 Jul 1972. Sold 30 May 1973, BU.
◆Lebanon Jul–Sep 1958.

1029 *Hartley*   Damaged in collision with m/v *Blue Master* near Cape Henry, Va., 16 Jun 1965. Decomm and stricken 8 Jul 1972 and trfd to Colombia.
Later history: renamed *Boyaca* (16). Museum at Guatape, Colombia, 1995.
◆Lebanon Aug–Sep 1958.

1030 *Joseph K. Taussig*   Decomm and stricken 1 Jul 1972. Sold 30 May 1973, BU.
◆Lebanon Jul–Aug 1958.

Off Shore Procurement (OSP)

No.	Builder	Completed	Built for	Name	Fate
DE 1007	Mediteranée	3 Nov 1956	France	Le Normand (F 765)	R1983
DE 1008	Mediteranée	1 Jan 1957	France	Le Lorrain (F 768)	R1976
DE 1009	Loire	20 Sep 1956	France	Le Picard (F 766)	R1983
DE 1010	Loire	29 Mar 1957	France	Le Gascon (F 767)	R1980
DE 1011	Loire	1 Jun 1957	France	Le Champenois (F 770)	R1976
DE 1012	Mediteranée	14 Jun 1956	France	Le Savoyard (F 771)	R1980
DE 1013	Penhoët	11 Jul 1957	France	Le Bourguignon (F 769)	R1976
DE 1016	Lorient	15 Apr 1955	France	Le Corse (F 761)	R1976
DE 1017	Lorient	19 Jan 1956	France	Le Brestois (F 762)	R1976
DE 1018	Loire	5 Aug 1955	France	Le Boulonnais (F 763)	R1977
DE 1019	Mediteranée	7 Apr 1955	France	Le Bordelais (F 764)	R1976, BU 1981
DE 1020	Taranto	7 Mar 1957	Italy	Cigno (D 572/F 555)	R1983
DE 1031	Taranto	14 Jul 1957	Italy	Castore (D 573/F 553)	R1984
DE 1032	Castellammare	1 Jul 1957	Portugal	Pero Escobar (F 335)	R1976

Figure 6.9: USS *McMorris* (DE 1036), *Claud Jones* class, May 1962. Notice ASW launcher forward, ASW torpedoes amidships.

DE 1039	Lisnave	10 Dec 1966	Portugal	Almirante Pereira da Silva (F 472)	R1992
DE 1042	Lisnave	1 Aug 1967	Portugal	Almirante Gago Coutinho (F 473)	R1992
DE 1046	Viana do Castelo	1 Dec 1967	Portugal	Almirante Magalhães Correia (F 474)	R1992

Claud Jones Class

No.	Name	Builder	Keel Laid	Launched	Comm.
DE 1033	Claud Jones	Avondale	1 Jun 1957	27 May 1958	10 Feb 1959
DE 1034	John R. Perry	Avondale	1 Oct 1957	29 Jul 1958	5 May 1959
DE 1035	Charles Berry	Amer; Lorain	29 Oct 1958	17 Mar 1959	25 Nov 1959
DE 1036	McMorris	Amer; Lorain	5 Nov 1958	26 May 1959	4 Mar 1960

Displacement	1,284 tons. 1,777 f/l
Dimensions	312′ (oa) × 37′ × 17′2″
Machinery	1 screw, geared diesel, 20,000 hp, 23 knots
Endurance	7,000/12
Complement	150
Armament	2–3″/50, 2 hedgehog, 2 triple ASW TT.

Notes: Unable to carry modern sonar and ASW. DE 1035–1036 completed by Avondale. Hedgehogs replaced in 1035–1036 by Terne III ASW missile launcher. TT replaced in all by torpedo launchers. 1033–1034 had after 3″ gun removed.

Service Records:

DE 1033 *Claud Jones*   Decomm and stricken 16 Dec 1974 and trfd to Indonesia.
Later history: renamed *Mongisidi* (343). SE2001.
★Vietnam May–Aug 1971, Aug–Sep 1972; ◆Cuba Jan–Apr 1962, Cuba Missile Crisis Oct–Nov 1962.

DE 1034 *John R. Perry*   Decomm and stricken 20 Feb 1973 and trfd to Indonesia.
Later history: renamed *Samadikun* (341). SE2001.
★Vietnam Jun–Jul 1968, Aug 1971; ◆Cuba May–Aug 1962, Cuba Missile Crisis Oct–Nov 1962.

DE 1035 *Charles Berry*   Decomm and stricken 31 Jan 1974 and trfd to Indonesia.
Later history: renamed *Martadinata* (342). SE2001.
★Vietnam Dec 1971–Mar 1972.

DE 1036 *McMorris*   Damaged in collision with gasoline tanker *Tombigbee* 75 miles southeast of Honolulu, 31 Jan 1967. Decomm and stricken 16 Dec 1974 and trfd to Indonesia.
Later history: renamed *Ngurah Rai* (344). SE2001.
★Vietnam Jun–Aug 1965, Aug 1968, Jan 1970, Apr–Jul 1972; ◆Korea Dec 1969.

FRIGATES

Bronstein Class

No.	Name	Builder	Keel Laid	Launched	Comm.
DE 1037	*Bronstein*	Avondale	16 May 1961	31 Mar 1962	16 Jun 1963
DE 1038	*McCloy*	Avondale	15 Sep 1961	9 Jun 1962	21 Oct 1963
Displacement	2,360 tons				
Dimensions	371'6" (oa) × 40'5" × 23'				
Machinery	1 screw; ST; 2 boilers; 20,000 SHP; 24 knots				
Endurance	3,000/20				
Complement	199				
Armament	1 twin and 1 single 3"/50AA, 1ASROC, 6–12.75" TT,				

Notes: Rec **FF**, 1 Jul 1975. Completely new and larger design. Mast and stacks combined in "mack" structure. Helicopter deck, no hangar.

Service Records:

FF 1037 *Bronstein*   Decomm 13 Dec 1990. Stricken 4 Oct 1991. Trfd to Mexico 16 Nov 1993.
Later history: renamed *Hermenegildo Galeana* (E 42). SE 2001.
★Vietnam Feb–Mar, May–Jul 1966, May–Oct 1967, Jun–Jul 1969, Apr–May 1971, Sep 1972–Jan 1973.

FF 1038 *McCloy*   Towed array probably disabled a Soviet Victor III class submarine off South Carolina, 31 Oct 1983. Decomm 14 Dec 1990. Stricken 4 Oct 1991. Trfd to Mexico 16 Nov 1993.
Later history: renamed *Nicolas Bravo* (E 40). SE2001.
◆Beirut evac Jun–Jul 1976, Lebanon Aug–Sep 1982.

Figure 6.10: *USS Voge* (DE 1047), *Garcia* class, about 1970.

Garcia Class

No.	Name	Builder	Keel Laid	Launched	Comm.
DE 1040	*Garcia*	Beth; S.Fran.	16 Oct 1962	31 Oct 1963	21 Dec 1964
DE 1041	*Bradley*	Beth; S.Fran.	17 Jan 1963	26 Mar 1964	15 May 1965
DE 1043	*Edward McDonnell*	Avondale	1 Apr 1963	15 Feb 1964	15 Feb 1965
DE 1044	*Brumby*	Avondale	1 Aug 1963	6 Jun 1964	15 Aug 1965
DE 1045	*Davidson*	Avondale	30 Sep 1963	2 Oct 1964	7 Dec 1965
DE 1047	*Voge*	Defoe	21 Nov 1963	4 Feb 1965	25 Nov 1966
DE 1048	*Sample*	Lockheed	19 Jul 1963	28 Apr 1964	23 Mar 1968
DE 1049	*Koelsch*	Defoe	19 Feb 1964	8 Jun 1965	10 Jun 1967
DE 1050	*Albert David*	Lockheed	29 Apr 1964	19 Dec 1964	19 Oct 1968
DE 1051	*O'Callahan*	Defoe	19 Feb 1964	2 Oct 1965	13 Jul 1968
Displacement	2,620 tons; 3,400 f/l				
Dimensions	414'6" (oa) × 44'3" × 14'5"				
Machinery	1 screw; ST; 2 boilers; 35,000 SHP; 27 knots				
Endurance	4,000/20				
Complement	247				
Armament	2–5"/38 guns, 1 ASROC, 6–12.75"TT				

Notes: Rec **FF**, 1 Jul 1975. Enlarged *Bronstein* design. *Bradley* mounted Sea Sparrow BPDMS 1967–68. The experimental frigate *Glover* (AGDE 1) was similar.

Service Records:

FF 1040 *Garcia*   Damaged by explosion at Boston, 20 Apr 1982. Decomm 10 Nov 1988. Trfd to Pakistan 31 Jan 1989.
Later history: renamed *Saif* (F 264). Returned and stricken 13 Jan 1994. Sold, BU Singapore.
◆Lebanon Nov 1983, Jan 1984, Libya Jan–Mar 1986.

FF 1041 *Bradley*   Collided with cruiser *Chicago* off San Diego, Jun 1973. In collision with oiler *Pecos* at Terminal Island, Cal., 4 Jan 1980. Decomm 30 Sep 1988. Trfd to Brazil 15 Apr 1989.
Later history: renamed *Pernambuco* (D 30). SE2001
★Vietnam Jul–Nov 1966, Feb–Mar, May–Jun 1970, Mar–Aug 1971, Dec 1972; ◆Korea Jan–Mar 1968, Iran/Indian Ocean Dec 1978–Jan 1979.

FF 1043 *Edward McDonnell*   Damaged by collision with a Finnish m/v at Hamburg, 5 Mar 1975. Decomm 30 Sep 1988. Stricken 15 Dec 1992. Sold 7 Dec 2001, BU Philadelphia.
◆Lebanon Dec 1982–May 1983.

FF 1044 *Brumby*   Decomm 31 Mar 1989. Trfd to Pakistan 31 Mar 1989.
Later history: renamed *Harbah* (F 266). Returned 19 Aug 1994. Sold, BU Singapore.
◆Iran/Indian Ocean Mar–Jul 1980, Lebanon Jan, Mar–Apr 1983.

FF 1045 *Davidson*   Damaged by boiler room fire while refueling at sea off Diego Garcia, Jun 1980. Decomm 8 Dec 1988. Trfd to Brazil 25 Jul 1989.
Later history: renamed *Paraíba* (D 28). R2002. Sank in tow off Rio de Janeiro en route to BU in India, 18 Dec 2004.
★Vietnam May–Oct 1967, Nov 1968–Apr 1969, Jun–Oct 1970, Jul–Nov 1971, Apr–Oct 1972; ◆ Korea Apr 1969, Sep–Oct 1971, Iran/Indian Ocean Apr–Aug 1980.

FF 1047 *Voge*   Damaged in collision with Soviet Echo II class submarine in Ionian Sea, 28 Aug 1976. Decomm 1 Aug 1989. Stricken 15 Dec 1992. Sold 26 May 2000, BU Chester, Pa.
◆Beirut evac Jun–Jul 1976, Iran/Indian Ocean Jun–Oct 1980, Oct 1981.

FF 1048 *Sample*   Decomm 23 Sep 1988. Trfd to Brazil 24 Aug 1989.
Later history: renamed *Paraná* (D 29). R2002. BU Aliaga, India, 2005.
5★Vietnam May 1967, Aug–Sep 1970, Feb–Aug 1972, Korea Oct–Nov 1970; ◆Iran/Indian Ocean Aug–Nov 1980.

FF 1049 *Koelsch* Decomm 31 May 1989, Trfd to Pakistan 31 May 1989.
Later history: renamed *Siqqat* (F 267). Returned and stricken 19 Aug 1994. Sold, BU Singapore.
◆Iran/Indian Ocean Feb–Apr 1980, Dec 1980–Mar 1981, Beirut evac Jun–Jul 1976.

FF 1050 *Albert David* Collided with a North Vietnamese junk, 16 Jan 1972. Decomm 18 Sep 1989, Trfd to Brazil 18 Sep 1989.
Later history: renamed *Pará* (D 27). SE2001
3★Vietnam Nov 1969–Mar 1970, Dec 1971, Feb–Jun 1972, Jan–Feb 1973.

FF 1051 *O'Callahan* Decomm 20 Dec 1988. Trfd to Pakistan 8 Feb 1989.
Later history: renamed *Aslat* (F 265). Returned to U.S., stricken 14 Nov 1993. Sold, BU Singapore.
★Vietnam Apr–Aug 1970, May–Jul, Sep 1971; ◆Korea May–Jun 1970, May–Jun 1971.

Knox Class

No.	Name	Builder	Keel Laid	Launched	Comm.
DE 1052	Knox	Todd;Seattle	5 Oct 1965	19 Nov 1966	12 Apr 1969
DE 1053	Roark	Todd;Seattle	2 Feb 1966	24 Apr 1967	22 Nov 1969
DE 1054	Gray	Todd;Seattle	19 Nov 1966	3 Nov 1967	4 Apr 1970
DE 1055	Hepburn	Todd;Seattle	1 Jun 1966	25 Mar 1967	3 Jul 1969
DE 1056	Connole	Avondale	23 Mar 1967	20 Jul 1968	30 Aug 1969
DE 1057	Rathburne	Lockheed	8 Jan 1968	2 May 1969	16 May 1970
DE 1058	Meyerkord	Todd; S.Pedro	1 Sep 1966	15 Jul 1967	28 Nov 1969
DE 1059	W.S. Sims	Avondale	10 Apr 1967	4 Jan 1969	3 Jan 1970
DE 1060	Lang	Todd; S.Pedro	25 Mar 1967	17 Feb 1968	28 Mar 1970
DE 1061	Patterson	Avondale	12 Oct 1967	3 May 1969	14 Mar 1970
DE 1062	Whipple	Todd;Seattle	24 Apr 1967	12 Apr 1968	22 Aug 1970
DE 1063	Reasoner	Todd;Seattle	6 Jan 1969	1 Aug 1970	22 Jun 1971
DE 1064	Lockwood	Todd;Seattle	3 Nov 1967	5 Sep 1968	5 Dec 1970
DE 1065	Stein	Lockheed	1 Jun 1970	19 Dec 1970	8 Jan 1972
DE 1066	Marvin Shields	Todd;Seattle	12 Apr 1968	23 Oct 1969	10 Apr 1971
DE 1067	Francis Hammond	Todd; S.Pedro	15 Jul 1967	11 May 1968	25 Jul 1970
DE 1068	Vreeland	Avondale	20 Mar 1968	14 Jun 1969	13 Jun 1970
DE 1069	Bagley	Lockheed	22 Sep 1970	24 Apr 1971	6 May 1972
DE 1070	Downes	Todd; Seattle	5 Sep 1968	13 Dec 1969	28 Aug 1971
DE 1071	Badger	Todd; S.Pedro	17 Feb 1968	7 Dec 1968	1 Dec 1970
DE 1072	Blakely	Avondale	3 Jun 1968	23 Aug 1969	28 Jul 1970
DE 1073	Robert E. Peary ex-*Conolly* (12 May 1971)	Lockheed	20 Dec 1970	23 Jun 1971	23 Sep 1972
DE 1074	Harold E. Holt	Todd; S.Pedro	11 May 1968	3 May 1969	26 Mar 1971
DE 1075	Trippe	Avondale	29 Jul 1968	1 Nov 1969	19 Sep 1970
DE 1076	Fanning	Todd; S.Pedro	7 Dec 1968	24 Jan 1970	23 Jul 1971
DE 1077	Ouellet	Avondale	15 Jan 1969	17 Jan 1970	12 Dec 1970
DE 1078	Joseph Hewes	Avondale	15 May 1969	7 Mar 1970	24 Apr 1971
DE 1079	Bowen	Avondale	11 Jul 1969	2 May 1970	22 May 1971
DE 1080	Paul	Avondale	12 Sep 1969	20 Jun 1970	14 Aug 1971
DE 1081	Aylwin	Avondale	13 Nov 1969	29 Aug 1970	18 Sep 1971
DE 1082	Elmer Montgomery	Avondale	23 Jan 1970	21 Nov 1970	30 Oct 1971
DE 1083	Cook	Avondale	20 Mar 1970	23 Jan 1971	31 Dec 1971
DE 1084	McCandless	Avondale	4 Jun 1970	20 Mar 1971	18 Mar 1972
DE 1085	Donald B.Beary	Avondale	24 Jul 1970	22 May 1971	22 Jul 1972
DE 1086	Brewton	Avondale	2 Oct 1970	24 Jul 1971	8 Jul 1972
DE 1087	Kirk	Avondale	4 Dec 1970	28 Sep 1971	8 Sep 1972
DE 1088	Barbey	Avondale	5 Feb 1971	4 Dec 1971	11 Nov 1972
DE 1089	Jesse L. Brown	Avondale	8 Apr 1971	18 Mar 1972	17 Feb 1973
DE 1090	Ainsworth	Avondale	11 Jun 1971	15 Apr 1972	31 Mar 1973
DE 1091	Miller	Avondale	6 Aug 1971	2 Jun 1972	30 Jun 1973
DE 1092	Thomas C. Hart	Avondale	8 Oct 1971	12 Aug 1972	28 Jul 1973
DE 1093	Capodanno	Avondale	25 Feb 1972	21 Oct 1972	17 Nov 1973
DE 1094	Pharris	Avondale	22 Mar 1972	16 Dec 1972	26 Jan 1974
DE 1095	Truett	Avondale	27 Apr 1972	17 Feb 1973	1 Jun 1974
DE 1096	Valdez	Avondale	30 Jun 1972	24 Mar 1973	27 Jul 1974
DE 1097	Moinester	Avondale	25 Aug 1972	12 May 1973	2 Nov 1974
DE 1098/1101	—	—	—	—	—
DE 1102/1107	—	—	—	—	—

Figure 6.11: USS *Donald B. Beary* (DE 1085), *Knox* class, with "mack." Notice helicopter flight deck aft built for DASH, adapted for LAMPS.

Displacement	3,011 tons, 4,100 f/l
Dimensions	438′ (oa) × 46′9″ × 24′9″
Machinery	1 screw; ST; 2 boilers; 35,000 SHP; 27+ knots
Endurance	4,500/20
Complement	217
Armament	1 Sea Sparrow launcher Mk 25, 1–5″/54 gun, 1 ASROC, 4–12.75″TT

Notes: Conceived as ASW ships, with large sonar dome on bow. Helicopter flight deck for DASH. Distinctive "Mack" combination of mast and stack. Rec **FF**, 1 Jul 1975. Built to carry DASH, canceled; later adapted to carry LAMPS. Ten ships authorized not built (1098–1107). Fitted with SQR-18 towed array in 1985. *Downes* was test ship for NATO Sea Sparrow (Mk 29).

Service Records:

FF 1052 *Knox* Decomm 14 Feb 1992. Stricken 11 Jan 1995. Sunk as target off Guam, 7 Aug 2007.
★Vietnam Oct 1970–Feb 1971, Oct–Dec 1971; ◆Evac of Cambodia 11–13 Apr 1975, Evac of Vietnam 29–30 Apr 1975, Libya Nov 1987–Jan 1988, May–Jun 1990, Iran/Indian Ocean Nov 1979–Feb 1980.

FF 1053 *Roark* Damaged by engine room fire off Midway, 19 Jan 1971. Decomm 14 Dec 1991. Stricken 11 Jan 1995. Sold 13 Oct 2004, BU Brownsville, Tex.

Figure 6.12: *USS Ainsworth* (FF 1090), *Knox* class.

3★Vietnam May–Jun 1971, Mar–Aug 1972; ◆Iran/Indian Ocean Oct 1981.

FF 1054 *Gray* Decomm 29 Sep 1991. Stricken 11 Jan 1995. Sold 26 May 2000, BU San Francisco.
★Vietnam May–Aug 1971, Jul–Dec 1972; ◆Korea Mar–Apr 1971, Iran/Indian Ocean Mar 1981.

FF 1055 *Hepburn* Damaged by fire off San Diego, 18 Mar 1977. Decomm 20 Dec 1991. Stricken 11 Jan 1995. Sunk as target 4 Jun 2002.
★Vietnam Jan–May 1971, Jun–Nov 1972; ◆Korea Feb–Mar 1971, Iran/Indian Ocean May–Jul 1981, Persian Gulf Feb–Apr 1987.

FF 1056 *Connole* Decomm 14 Aug 1992, Trfd to Greece 30 Aug 1992.
Later history: renamed *Epirous* (*Ipiros*) (F-456). R2002.
◆Beirut evac Jun–Jul 1976, Lebanon Jan–Mar 1983.

FF 1057 *Rathburne* Decomm 14 Feb 1992. Stricken 11 Jan 1995. Sunk as target 5 Jul 2002.
★Vietnam May–Sep 1971, Aug–Dec 1972; ◆Libya Jan 1990.

FF 1058 *Meyerkord* Decomm 14 Dec 1991. Stricken 11 Jan 1995. Sold 15 Dec 2000, BU San Francisco.
★Vietnam Apr–May 1971, Aug 1972–Jan 1973; ◆Evac of Vietnam 29–30 Apr 1975.

FF 1059 *W.S. Sims* Collided with destroyer *Moosbrugger* at Guantanamo, 22 Nov 1985. Decomm 6 Sep 1991. Stricken 11 Jan 1995. Trfd to Turkey for spares 1999, BU.
◆Grenada Oct–Nov 1983, Lebanon Nov 1983–Feb 1984.

FF 1060 *Lang* Decomm 12 Dec 1991. Stricken 11 Jan 1995. Sold 17 Jan 2001, BU San Francisco.
★Vietnam May–Sep 1971, Aug 1972–Jan 1973; ◆Korea Jun–Jul 1971, Evac of Vietnam 29–30 Apr 1975, Op Mayaguez 15 May 1975, Iran/Indian Ocean Mar 1981.

FF 1061 *Patterson* Decomm 30 Sep 1991. Stricken 11 Jan 1995. Sold 29 Sep 1999, BU Baltimore.
◆Iran/Indian Ocean Nov 1980–Jan 1981.

FF 1062 *Whipple* Decomm 14 Feb 1992. Stricken 11 Jan 1995. Trfd to Mexico, 14 Dec 2001.
Later history: renamed *Almirante Francisco Javier Mina.* (F-140)
2★Vietnam Feb–Jul 1972; ◆Gulf War Apr–Jul 1991.

FF 1063 *Reasoner* Decomm and trfd to Turkey 28 Aug 1993.
Later history: renamed *Koçatepe* (F 252). SE2001.
◆Evac of Vietnam 29–30 Apr 1975, Iran/Indian Ocean Apr–Jun 1980, Lebanon Apr–Jun 1986, Libya Mar–May 1988, Gulf War Aug–Nov 1990.

FF 1064 *Lockwood* Damaged in collision with m/v *Santo Nino-R* off Yokosuka, Japan, 20 Dec 1985. Stricken 30 Sep 1993. Sold 29 Sep 1999, BU Baltimore.
★Vietnam Mar–Aug 1972; ◆Iran/Indian Ocean Mar–May 1981, Libya Dec 1988.

FF 1065 *Stein* In collision with m/v at Kobe, Japan, 28 May 1973. Rec **FFT** 15 Dec 1991. Decomm 19 Mar 1992. Stricken 11 Jan 1995. Trfd to Mexico 29 Jan 1998.
Later history: renamed *Ignacio Allende* (E 50). SE 2001.
◆Iran/Indian Ocean Nov 1979–Jan 1980, Persian Gulf Feb–Jul 1987, Libya Dec 1989, Gulf War Apr–Jul 1991.

FF 1066 *Marvin Shields* Decomm 2 Jul 1992. Stricken 11 Jan 1995. Trfd to Mexico 29 Jan 1997.
Later history: renamed *Mariano Abasolo* (E 51) SE 2001.
★Vietnam Jun–Nov 1972; ◆Gulf War Oct 1990–Feb 1991.

FF 1067 *Francis Hammond* Collided with destroyers *Fletcher* and *Towers* in Subic Bay, 22 May 1982. Decomm 2 Jul 1992. Stricken 11 Jan 1995. Sold Nov 2001, BU Brownsville, Tex.
★Vietnam Mar–Jul 1972; ◆Iran/Indian Ocean Mar–May 1980, Aug–Nov 1980, Libya Nov 1987–Feb 1988, Gulf War Jan–Apr 1991.

FF 1068 *Vreeland* Decomm 30 Jun 1992 and stricken 11 Jan 1995. Trfd to Greece 25 Jul 1992.
Later history: renamed *Makedonia* (F-458). SE2002.
◆Iran/Indian Ocean Dec 1978, Lebanon Aug–Oct 1982, Libya/El Dorado Canyon Mar–Jun 1986, Panama Dec 1989–Jan 1990, Gulf War Jan–Jun 1991.

FF 1069 *Bagley* Decomm 26 Sep 1991. Stricken 11 Jan 1995. Sold 29 Sep 1999, BU Baltimore.
◆Iran/Indian Ocean Apr–Aug 1980, Libya/El Dorado Canyon Apr–Jun 1986, Libya Feb–Apr 1988, Jan 1990.

FF 1070 *Downes* Decomm 5 Jun 1992. Stricken 11 Jan 1995. Sunk as target off California, 15 Aug 2003.
◆Iran/Indian Ocean Apr–Jun 1979, Dec 1980–Feb 1981.

FF 1071 *Badger* Decomm 20 Dec 1991. Stricken 11 Jan 1995. Sunk as target 22 Jul 1998.
1★Vietnam Apr–Sep 1972; ◆Iran/Indian Ocean Oct 1980–Mar 1981.

FF 1072 *Blakely* Decomm 15 Nov 1991. Stricken 11 Jan 1995. Sold 29 Sep 1999, BU Baltimore.
★Vietnam Jan–Feb 1973; ◆Iran/Indian Ocean Feb–May 1981.

FF 1073 *Robert E. Peary* Decomm 7 Aug 1992. Stricken 11 Jan 1995. Trfd to Taiwan 7 Aug 1992.
Later history: renamed *Chi Yang.* (932). SE2001
◆Iran/Indian Ocean Aug–Nov 1980, Libya Sep 1987, Gulf War Sep–Dec 1991.

FF 1074 *Harold E. Holt* Boarded seized m/v *Mayaguez* off Cambodia, 14 May 1975. Decomm 2 Jul 1992. Stricken 11 Jan 1995. Sunk as target 10 Jul 2002.
★Vietnam Jun–Nov 1972; ◆Evac of Vietnam 29–30 Apr 1975, Mayaguez Op, 15 May 1975, Iran/Indian Ocean Apr–Aug 1980, Libya Sep 1987, Gulf War Apr–Jul 1991.

FF 1075 *Trippe* Damaged in collision with oiler *Platte* north of Puerto Rico, 19 Apr 1989. Decomm 30 Jul 1992. Stricken 11 Jan 1995. Trfd to Greece 30 Jul 1992.
Later history: renamed *Thraki* (F-457). R2002; sunk as target off Crete, 18 Jun 2003.
1★Vietnam Jul–Aug 1972.

FF 1076 *Fanning* Decomm 30 Jul 1993. Trfd to Turkey 31 Jul 1993.
Later history: renamed *Adatepe* (F 251). R2001.
★Vietnam Jan–Mar 1973; ◆Iran/Indian Ocean Nov 1979–Feb 1980, May–Oct 1981, Libya Jul–Sep 1988.

FF 1077 *Ouellet* Collided with frigate *John A. Moore* at Pearl Harbor, 26 Oct 1984. Decomm 6 Aug 1993. Stricken 11 Jan 1995. Trfd to Thailand 19 Aug 1995.
Later history: renamed *Phuttha Loetla Naphalai* (462). SE2001.
★Vietnam Feb–Jul 1972; ◆Iran/Indian Ocean Oct 1980–Mar 1981, Persian Gulf Jun–Jul 1987, Libya Jul–Aug 1987.

FF 1078 *Joseph Hewes* Rec **FFT 1078**, 15 Dec 1991. Decomm 30 Jun 1994, stricken 11 Jan 1995. Trfd to Taiwan 1995.
Later history: renamed *Lan Yang* (935). SE2001.
★Vietnam Jul–Nov 1972, ◆Lebanon May–Jul, Oct–Nov 1983, Libya Jul–Aug 1989.

FF 1079 *Bowen* Rec **FFT 1079**, 15 Dec 1991. Decomm and trfd to Turkey 3 Jun 1994.
Later history: renamed *Akdeniz* (F 257). SE2001.
◆Lebanon Aug–Oct 1983.

FF 1080 *Paul* Decomm 14 Aug 1992. Stricken 11 Jan 1995. Sold to Turkey for parts, 9 Jan 2000, BU.
★Vietnam Nov 1972, Jan–Feb 1973; ◆Lebanon Nov 1983–Feb 1984, Libya Jan–Mar 1986.

FF 1081 *Aylwin* Collided with replenishment ship *Seattle* in Atlantic, 11 Jun 1982. Damaged in collision with anchored m/v tanker *Pluto* in Boston harbor, 17 Jan 1990. Decomm 15 May 1992. Stricken 11 Jan 1995. Trfd to Taiwan 29 Apr 1998.
Later history: renamed *Ning Yang* (938). SE2001.
◆Iran/Indian Ocean Nov–Dec 1979, Lebanon Aug–Nov 1982, Libya Mar–Jun 1986.

FF 1082 *Elmer Montgomery* Decomm 30 Jun 1993 and stricken. Trfd to Turkey for parts, 13 Dec 1993, BU.
◆Iran/Indian Ocean May–Jun 1979, Libya May–Jul 1988, Gulf War Aug 1990–Jan 1991.

FF 1083 *Cook* Damaged in collision with storeship *Mars* in fog off Point Loma, Cal., 14 May 1979. Decomm 30 Apr 1992. Stricken 11 Jan 1995. Trfd to Taiwan 31 May 1994.
Later history: renamed *Hae Yang* (936). SE2001.
◆Evac of Cambodia Apr 1975, Evac of Vietnam 29–30 Apr 1975, Iran/Indian Ocean Mar–May 1980, Oct 1981, Quemoy-Matsu Jun–Jul 1987, Libya Jul–Aug 1987, May 1989.

FF 1084 *McCandless* Rec **FFT 1084**, 31 Dec 1991. Decomm and trfd to Turkey, 6 May 1994.
Later history: renamed *Trakya* (F 254). SE2001.
◆Beirut evac Jun–Jul 1976, Gulf War Jul–Oct 1991.

FF 1085 *Donald B. Beary* Rec **FFT 1085**, 15 Dec 1991. Decomm and trfd to Turkey 20 May 1994.
Later history: renamed *Karadeniz* (F 255). SE2001.
◆Iran/Indian Ocean Mar–Apr 1979, Libya Feb–Mar 1986.

FF 1086 *Brewton* Decomm 2 Jul 1992 and stricken 11 Jan 1995. Trfd to Taiwan 23 Jul 1992.
Later history: renamed *Fong Yang* (936).
◆Gulf War Aug–Nov 1990.

FF 1087 *Kirk* Decomm and trfd to Taiwan 6 Aug 1993.
Later history: renamed *Fen Yang* (934). SE2001.
◆Evac of Cambodia Apr 1975, Iran/Indian Ocean Aug–Nov 1980, Mar–May 1981, Gulf War Sep–Oct 1992.

FF 1088 *Barbey* Decomm 19 Mar 1992. Stricken 11 Jan 1995. Trfd to Taiwan 21 Jun 1994.
Later history: renamed *Hwai Yang* (937). SE2001.
◆Persian Gulf Feb–Jul 1987, Iran/Indian Ocean Mar–May 1980, Oct 1981, Gulf War Jul–Nov 1990.

FF 1089 *Jesse L. Brown* Rec **FFT 1089**, 31 Dec 1991. Decomm and t rfd to Egypt 27 Jul 1994. Stricken 11 Jan 1995.
Later history: renamed *Damiyat* (961). SE2001.
◆Libya Jan–May 1986, Iran/Indian Ocean Oct–Dec 1990.

FF 1090 *Ainsworth* Rec **FFT 1090**, 15 Dec 1991. Decomm and trfd to Turkey 27 May 1994.
Later history: renamed *Ege* (F 256). SE2001.
◆Iran/Indian Ocean Dec 1979–Mar 1980, Apr–Oct 1981, Lebanon Jan 1983, Libya Jan–Mar 1986.

FF 1091 *Miller* Collided with submarine *Sea Devil* in Pacific, 13 Apr 1989. Decomm 15 Oct 1991. Stricken 11 Jan 1995. Trfd to Turkey for parts, 19 Jul 1999, BU.
◆Iran/Indian Ocean Nov 1979–Mar 1980.

FF 1092 *Thomas C. Hart* Decomm and trfd to Turkey, 30 Aug 1993.
Later history: renamed *Zafer* (F 253). SE2001.
◆Iran/Indian Ocean Jun–Oct 1980, Gulf War Aug 1990–Mar 1991.

FF 1093 *Capodanno* Stricken and trfd to Turkey 30 Jul 1993.
Later history: renamed *Mauvenet* (F 250). SE2001.
◆Lebanon Dec 1982–Feb 1983, Libya/El Dorado Canyon Jan–May 1986, Gulf War Oct–Nov 1992.

FF 1094 *Pharris* Decomm 15 Apr 1992. Stricken 11 Jan 1995. Trfd to Mexico, 2 Feb 2000.
Later history: renamed *Guadalupe Victoria*. (F 213)
◆Lebanon May–Jul, Oct 1983, Iran/Indian Ocean Aug–Oct 1981, Libya/El Dorado Jan–Jun 1986, Libya May–Jul 1988.

FF 1095 *Truett* Rec **FFT 1095**, 31 Dec 1991. Decomm 30 Jul 1994 and trfd to Thailand.
Later history: renamed *Phuttha Yotfa Chulalok* (461). SE2001.
◆Lebanon Aug–Oct 1982, Gulf War Jul–Oct 1991.

FF 1096 *Valdez* Decomm 16 Dec 1991. Stricken 11 Jan 1995. Trfd to Taiwan 29 Apr 1998.
Later history: renamed *Yi Yang* (939). SE2001.

FF 1097 *Moinester* Rec **FFT 1097**, 31 Dec 1991. Decomm and trfd to Egypt 28 Jul 1994.
Later history: renamed *Rasheed* (966). SE2001.
◆Beirut evac Jun–Jul 1976, Lebanon Jul 1983.

FF 1098/1101 Deferred 1968–69
FF 1102/1107 Deferred 1968–69
FF 1098 *Glover* see AGDE 1
◆Iran/Indian Ocean Nov 1979–Feb 1980, Lebanon Dec 1982–Feb 1983

MISSILE FRIGATES

Brooke Class

No.	Name	Builder	Keel Laid	Launched	Comm.
DEG 1	*Brooke*	Lockheed	19 Dec 1962	19 Jul 1963	12 Mar 1966
DEG 2	*Ramsey*	Lockheed	4 Feb 1963	15 Oct 1963	3 Jun 1967
DEG 3	*Schofield*	Lockheed	15 Apr 1963	7 Dec 1963	11 May 1968
DEG 4	*Talbot*	Bath	4 May 1964	6 Jan 1966	22 Apr 1967
DEG 5	*Richard L. Page*	Bath	4 Jan 1965	4 Apr 1966	5 Aug 1967
DEG 6	*Julius A. Furer* ex-Furer (5 Apr 1966)	Bath	12 Jul 1965	22 Jul 1966	11 Nov 1967

Displacement	2,640 tons, 3,245 f/l
Dimensions	414′6″(oa) × 44′3″ × 14′6″
Machinery	1 screw; ST; 2 boilers; 35,000 SHP; 27 knots
Endurance	4,000/20
Complement	236
Armament	1 Tartar/Standard-MR SAM launcher, 1–5″/38 gun, 1 ASROC, 6–12.75″TT

Notes: Rec **FFG**, 1 Jul 1975. Missile version of *Garcia* class. ASW TT removed.

Service Records:

FFG 1 *Brooke* Decomm 17 Sep 1988. Trfd to Pakistan 8 Feb 1989.
Later history: renamed *Khaibar* (D 162). Returned to U.S. 14 Nov 1993, Stricken 2 Jan 1994. Sold, BU Singapore.
★Vietnam Mar–Jun 1968, Feb–Mar, May 1970, Sep–Oct 1971, Nov 1972–Mar 1973; ◆Korea Jan–Mar 1968, Jul–Oct 1971.

FFG 2 *Ramsey* Decomm 1 Sep 1988. Stricken 25 Jan 1992. Hulk sunk as target 15 Jun 2000.
5★Vietnam Jun–Dec 1969, Mar 1970, Jun–Jul, Sep, Oct 1971, Sep 1972–Feb 1973; ◆Korea Jan 1970.

Figure 6.13: USS Brooke (DEG 1), as built 1966.

Figure 6.14: USS Clark (FFG 11), Perry class, April 1989.

FFG 3   *Schofield*   Decomm 8 Sep 1988. Stricken 25 Jan 1992. Sunk as target, 2 Nov 1999.
4★Vietnam Jun–Jul 1969, Apr–May 1971, Oct 1972–Feb 1973.

FFG 4   *Talbot*   Decomm 30 Sep 1988. Trfd to Pakistan 31 May 1989.
Later history: renamed *Hunain* (D 169). Returned to U.S. 11 Dec 1993, Stricken. Sold, BU Singapore.
◆Iran/Indian Ocean Dec 1978–May 1979.

FFG 5   *Richard L. Page*   Sank f/v *Chickadee* in collision off Virginia, 21 Apr 1987. Decomm 30 Sep 1988. Trfd to Pakistan 31 Mar 1989.
Later history: renamed *Tabuk* (D 163). Returned 15 Jan 1994, stricken. Sold 29 Mar 1994, BU Singapore.
◆Iran/Indian Ocean Mar–Apr 1979, Lebanon Nov 1983–Mar 1984.

FFG 6   *Julius A. Furer*   31 Jan 1989 decomm and trfd to Pakistan.
Later history: renamed *Badr* (D 161). Returned to U.S. 11 Dec 1993, Stricken Sold, BU Singapore.
◆Iran/Indian Ocean Nov 1979, Lebanon Aug–Nov 1982.

Offshore Procurement (OSP)

No.	Builder	Completed	Built for	Name
DEG 7	Bazan	24 Sep 1973	Spain	*Baleares* (F 71)
DEG 8	Bazan	23 May 1974	Spain	*Andalucia* (F 72)
DEG 9	Bazan	16 Jan 1975	Spain	*Cataluña* (F 73)
DEG 10	Bazan	2 Dec 1975	Spain	*Asturias* (F 74)
DEG 11	Bazan	10 Nov 1976	Spain	*Extremadura* (F 75)

Figure 6.15: USS Estocin (FFG 15).

Oliver Hazard Perry Class

No.	Name	Builder	Keel Laid	Launched	Comm.
FFG 7	Oliver Hazard Perry	Bath	31 Jul 1975	25 Sep 1976	17 Dec 1977
FFG 8	McInerney	Bath	16 Jan 1978	4 Nov 1978	15 Dec 1979
FFG 9	Wadsworth	Todd; S.Pedro	13 Jul 1977	29 Jul 1978	28 Feb 1980
FFG 10	Duncan	Todd; Seattle	29 Apr 1977	1 Mar 1978	15 May 1980
FFG 11	Clark	Bath	17 Jul 1978	24 Mar 1979	17 May 1980
FFG 12	George Phillip	Todd; S.Pedro	14 Dec 1977	16 Dec 1978	18 Nov 1980
FFG 13	Samuel Eliot Morison ex-*Samuel E. Morison* (17 Aug 1979)	Bath	4 Dec 1978	14 Jul 1979	11 Oct 1980
FFG 14	Sides	Todd; S.Pedro	7 Aug 1978	19 May 1979	11 Dec 1980
FFG 15	Estocin	Bath	2 Apr 1979	3 Nov 1979	10 Jan 1981
FFG 16	Clifton Sprague	Bath	30 Jul 1979	16 Feb 1980	21 Mar 1981
FFG 17	—	Todd; Seattle	29 Jul 1977	21 Jun 1978	*15 Nov 1980*
FFG 18	—	Todd; Seattle	1 Mar 1978	1 Dec 1978	*21 Mar 1981*
FFG 19	John A. Moore	Todd; S.Pedro	19 Dec 1978	20 Oct 1979	14 Nov 1981
FFG 20	Antrim	Todd; Seattle	21 Jun 1978	27 Mar 1979	26 Sep 1981
FFG 21	Flatley	Bath	13 Nov 1979	15 May 1980	20 Jun 1981
FFG 22	Fahrion	Todd; Seattle	1 Dec 1978	24 Aug 1979	16 Jan 1982
FFG 23	Lewis B. Puller	Todd; S.Pedro	23 May 1979	15 Mar 1980	17 Apr 1982
FFG 24	Jack Williams	Bath	25 Feb 1980	30 Aug 1980	19 Sep 1981
FFG 25	Copeland	Todd; S.Pedro	24 Oct 1979	26 Jul 1980	7 Aug 1982
FFG 26	Gallery	Bath	17 May 1980	20 Dec 1980	5 Dec 1981
FFG 27	Mahlon S. Tisdale	Todd; S.Pedro	19 Mar 1980	7 Feb 1981	13 Nov 1982

FFG 28	*Boone*	Todd; Seattle	27 Mar 1979	16 Jan 1980	13 Nov 1982
FFG 29	*Stephen W. Groves*	Bath	16 Sep 1980	4 Apr 1981	17 Apr 1982
FFG 30	*Reid*	Todd; S.Pedro	8 Oct 1980	27 Jun 1981	19 Feb 1983
FFG 31	*Stark*	Todd; Seattle	24 Aug 1979	30 May 1980	23 Oct 1982
FFG 32	*John L. Hall*	Bath	5 Jan 1981	24 Jul 1981	26 Jun 1982
FFG 33	*Jarrett*	Todd; S.Pedro	11 Feb 1981	17 Oct 1981	2 Jul 1983
FFG 34	*Aubrey Fitch*	Bath	10 Apr 1981	17 Oct 1981	9 Oct 1982
FFG 35	—	Todd; Seattle	16 Jan 1980	26 Sep 1980	*29 Jan 1983*
FFG 36	*Underwood*	Bath	3 Aug 1981	6 Feb 1982	29 Jan 1983
FFG 37	*Crommelin*	Todd; Seattle	30 May 1980	1 Jul 1981	18 Jun 1983
FFG 38	*Curts*	Todd; S.Pedro	1 Jul 1981	6 Mar 1982	8 Oct 1983
FFG 39	*Doyle*	Bath	23 Oct 1981	22 May 1982	21 May 1983
FFG 40	*Halyburton*	Todd; Seattle	26 Sep 1980	13 Oct 1981	7 Jan 1984
FFG 41	*McClusky*	Todd; S.Pedro	21 Oct 1981	18 Sep 1982	12 Oct 1983
FFG 42	*Klakring*	Bath	19 Feb 1982	18 Sep 1982	20 Aug 1983
FFG 43	*Thach*	Todd; S.Pedro	6 Mar 1982	18 Dec 1982	17 Mar 1984
FFG 44	—	Todd; Seattle	3 Jul 1981	26 Mar 1982	*21 Jul 1984*
FFG 45	*De Wert*	Bath	14 Jun 1982	18 Dec 1982	19 Nov 1983
FFG 46	*Rentz*	Todd; S.Pedro	18 Sep 1982	16 Jul 1983	30 Jun 1984
FFG 47	*Nicholas*	Bath	27 Sep 1982	23 Apr 1983	10 Mar 1984
FFG 48	*Vandegrift*	Todd; Seattle	13 Oct 1981	15 Oct 1982	24 Nov 1984
FFG 49	*Robert G. Bradley*	Bath	28 Dec 1982	13 Aug 1983	11 Aug 1984
FFG 50	*Jesse L. Taylor*	Bath	5 May 1983	5 Nov 1983	1 Dec 1984
FFG 51	*Gary*	Todd; S.Pedro	18 Dec 1982	19 Nov 1983	17 Nov 1984
FFG 52	*Carr*	Todd; Seattle	26 Mar 1982	26 Feb 1983	27 Jul 1985
FFG 53	*Hawes*	Bath	22 Aug 1983	17 Feb 1984	2 Sep 1985
FFG 54	*Ford*	Todd; S.Pedro	16 Jul 1983	23 Jun 1984	29 Jun 1985
FFG 55	*Elrod*	Bath	14 Nov 1983	12 May 1984	6 Jul 1985
FFG 56	*Simpson*	Bath	27 Feb 1984	31 Aug 1984	9 Nov 1985
FFG 57	*Reuben James*	Todd; S.Pedro	19 Nov 1983	8 Feb 1985	22 Mar 1986
FFG 58	*Samuel B. Roberts*	Bath	21 May 1984	8 Dec 1984	12 Apr 1986
FFG 59	*Kauffman*	Bath	8 Apr 1985	29 Mar 1986	28 Feb 1987
FFG 60	*Rodney M. Davis*	Todd; S.Pedro	8 Feb 1985	11 Jan 1986	9 May 1987
FFG 61	*Ingraham*	Todd; S.Pedro	30 Mar 1987	25 Jun 1988	5 Aug 1989

Displacement	2,750 tons; 3,650 tons f/l; 4,100 f/l (FFG 8, 28, 29, 32, 33, 36–61)
Dimensions	445′ (oa) × 45′ × 24′6″
	453′ (oa) (FFG 8, 28, 29, 32, 33, 36–61)
Machinery	1 screw; gas turbines; 40,000 SHP; 29 knots
Endurance	4,500/20
Complement	219
Armament	1 Standard-MR SAM launcher, 1–76 mm gun, 1 Phalanx, 6–12.75″TT

Notes: *Perry* originally designated PF 109, rec FFG 7, 30 Jun 1975. Lightly armed, built to be cheap, but costs rose during construction. Largest class of combatants built since World War II. Later units were "long-hull" with improved LAMPS III helicopter. Limited armament and single screw viewed as defects in design. Four built for Australia, and two others built in Australia.

Service Records:

FFG 7   *Oliver Hazard Perry*   Decomm 20 Feb 1997. Stricken 3 May 1999. Sold 9 Sep 2005, BU Philadelphia.
  ◆Haiti Sep 1994.

FFG 8   *McInerney*
  ◆Lebanon Jan 1983, Gulf War Feb–Jun 1990.

FFG 9   *Wadsworth*   Decomm and trfd to Poland 28 Jun 2002.
  Later history: renamed *Generał Thadeusz Kołciuszko* (273).

FFG 10   *Duncan*   Decomm 17 Dec 1994. Stricken 5 Jan 1998. Trfd to Turkey for parts, 5 Apr 1999, BU

FFG 11   *Clark*   Decomm and stricken 15 Mar 2000 and trfd to Poland
  Later history: renamed *Generał Kazimierz Pułaski* (272).
  ◆Beirut evac Jun 1982, Lebanon Dec 1983–Jan 1984.

FFG 12   *George Philip*   Decomm 28 Mar 2003.

FFG 13   *Samuel Eliot Morison*   Decomm and trfd to Turkey 10 Apr 2002. Stricken 23 Jul 2002.
  Later history: renamed *Gorkova* (F 496).
  ◆Grenada Nov 1983, Haiti Sep–Oct 1994.

FFG 14   *Sides*   Decomm 28 Feb 2003. Stricken 24 May 2004.

FFG 15   *Estocin*   Decomm 30 Sep 2000. Stricken 3 Apr 2003 and trfd to Turkey.
  Later history: renamed *Göksu* (F 497).
  ◆Lebanon Oct–Nov 1982.

FFG 16   *Clifton Sprague*   Decomm 2 Jun 1995. Stricken 4 Sep 1997. Trfd to Turkey 27 Aug 1997.
  Later history: renamed *Gaziantep* (F 490). SE2001.
  ◆Lebanon Apr 1983, Grenada Oct–Nov 1983, Haiti Sep 1994.

FFG 17   Completed for Australia 15 Nov 1980 as *Adelaide* (FFG 01). R2008.

FFG 18   Completed for Australia 21 Mar 1981 as *Canberra* (FFG 02). R2005.

FFG 19   *John A. Moore*   Collided with frigate *Ouellet* at Pearl Harbor, 26 Oct 1984. Decomm and stricken 1 Sep 2000 and trfd to Turkey.
  Later history: renamed *Gediz* (F 495). SE2001.
  ◆Libya Jan–Apr 1988.

FFG 20   *Antrim*   Hit by radio-controlled drone off Virginia, 10 Feb 1983 (1 killed). In collision with frigate *Flatley* north of Puerto Rico, 16 Mar 1983. Decomm 8 May 1996. Stricken 4 Sep 1997. Trfd to Turkey 27 Aug 1997.
  Later history: renamed *Giresun* (F 491). SE2001.
  ◆Lebanon Jun–Jul 1983.

FFG 21   *Flatley*   In collision with frigate *Antrim* north of Puerto Rico, 16 Mar 1983. Decomm 8 May 1996. Trfd to Turkey 27 Aug 1997.
  Later history: renamed *Gemlik* (F 492). SE2001.
  ◆Lebanon Jun–Jul 1983, Persian Gulf Jul 1987, Libya Jul–Nov 1987.

FFG 22   *Fahrion*   Decomm and stricken 31 Mar 1998 and trfd to Egypt.
  Later history: renamed *Sharm El-Sheikh* (901). SE2001.
  ◆Lebanon Nov 1983–Feb 1984, Libya Jun–Sep 1988.

FFG 23   *Lewis B. Puller*   Decomm and stricken 18 Sep 1998 and trfd to Egypt.
  Later history: renamed *Toushka* (902). SE2001.

FFG 24   *Jack Williams*   Decomm 27 Oct 1995. Stricken and trfd to Bahrain 13 Sep 1996.
  Later history: renamed *Sabha* (90). SE2001.
  ◆Lebanon Oct–Nov 1983, Libya/El Dorado Feb–May 1986, Libya Feb–Jun 1988, Aug–Dec 1989, Haiti 1990, Gulf War May–Oct 1992.

Escorts/Frigates

FFG 25 *Copeland*   Decomm and stricken 18 Sep 1996, and tfrd to Egypt 18 Sep 1996.
Later history: renamed *Sharm El-Sheikh*, renamed *Mubarak* (911), 1997. SE2001.
◆Libya Mar–Apr 1988.

FFG 26 *Gallery*   Decomm and stricken 14 Jun 1996. Trfd to Egypt 25 Sep 1996.
Later history: renamed *Taba* (916). SE2001.
◆Lebanon Dec 1983–Jan 1984, Libya Oct 1987–Feb 1988, Apr–Aug 1989, Gulf War Jun–Nov 1991.

FFG 27 *Mahlon S. Tisdale*   Decomm 27 Sep 1996. Stricken 20 Feb 1998. Trfd to Turkey 5 Apr 1999.
Later history: renamed *Gökçeada* (F 494). SE2001.

FFG 28 *Boone*
◆Libya Aug–Dec 1989, Gulf War Dec 1991–Apr 1992.

FFG 29 *Stephen W. Groves*
◆Lebanon Nov 1983–Feb 1984, Gulf War Jun–Oct 1992, Indian Ocean Jan 1997.

FFG 30 *Reid*   Decomm 25 Sep 1998. Trfd to Turkey 5 Jan 1999.
Later history: renamed *Gelibolu* (F 493). SE2001.
◆Persian Gulf Apr–Jun 1987, Libya Oct–Nov 1988, Gulf War Apr–Sep 1990, Indian Ocean Jan–Feb 1997.

FFG 31 *Stark*   Damaged by two Exocet missiles fired by Iraqi aircraft and fire in Persian Gulf, 17 May 1987 (37 killed). Decomm 7 May 1999. Sold 7 Oct 2005, BU Philadelphia.
◆Persian Gulf Apr–Jul 1987, Gulf War Sep–Dec 1991.

FFG 32 *John L. Hall*
◆Gulf War Aug 1990.

FFG 33 *Jarrett*
◆Libya Jul–Sep 1987, Gulf War Jan–Apr 1991, Indian Ocean Aug–Nov 1998, Feb–May 2000.

FFG 34 *Aubrey Fitch*   Decomm 12 Dec 1997. Stricken 3 May 1999. Sold 11 Mar 2004, BU 2005 Philadelphia.
◆Grenada Nov 1983, Gulf War Sep–Dec 1991, Haiti Sep 1994.

FFG 35   Completed for Australia 29 Jan 1983 as *Sydney* (FFG 03). SE001.

FFG 36 *Underwood*   Went aground at Alexandria, Egypt, 20 Oct 1999.
◆Gulf War May–Sep 1991, Indian Ocean Feb–Jun 1996.

FFG 37 *Crommelin*
◆Persian Gulf Jun–Jul 1987, Libya Apr–Jul 1989, Indian Ocean Mar–Jul 1998, Sep 2000–Jan 2001.

FFG 38 *Curts*
◆Libya Sep–Oct 1987, Gulf War Nov 1990–Mar 1991.

FFG 39 *Doyle*
◆Libya Sep 1988–Jan 1989.

FFG 40 *Halyburton*
◆Libya/El Dorado Mar–Jun 1986, Libya Jun–Sep 1988, Gulf War Jan–Apr 1991, Indian Ocean Jan–May 1997, Apr–Jul 1999.

FFG 41 *McClusky*
◆Libya Nov 1987–Mar 1988, Gulf War Jul–Oct 1991, Indian Ocean Dec 1998–Mar 1999.

FFG 42 *Klakring*
◆Libya Jul–Nov 1987, Gulf War Dec 1991–May 1992, Haiti 1994, Indian Ocean Apr–Jul 1999.

FFG 43 *Thach*
◆Gulf War May–Sep 1992, Indian Ocean Mar–Jul 1996, Jul–Oct 1998, Jul–Aug 2001, Iraq War 2003.

FFG 44   Completed for Australia 21 Jul 1984 as *Darwin* (FFG 04). SE2001.

FFG 45 *De Wert*
◆Libya Jan–May 1986, Libya Jan–Apr 1989, Gulf War Oct–Nov 1991.

FFG 46 *Rentz*
◆Libya Aug–Nov 1987, Jul–Nov 1989, Gulf War Apr–Jul 1991, Liberia Sep–Oct 1993, Indian Ocean Jul–Oct 1997, Feb–May 2000.

FFG 47 *Nicholas*   Engaged Iraqi patrol boats, 1 Feb 1991.
◆Libya Jun–Sep 1988, Gulf War Oct 1990–Feb 1991, Indian Ocean Apr–Sep 1997, Apr–Jul 1999, Jun–Aug 2001.

FFG 48 *Vandegrift*   Damaged in collision with cargo ship *Yano* at San Diego, 25 Feb 1996.
◆Libya Jul–Nov 1988, Gulf War Aug–Sep 1990, Iraq War 2003.

FFG 49 *Robert G. Bradley*
◆Libya Jun–Sep 1988, Gulf War Jul–Nov 1990.

FFG 50 *Jesse L. Taylor*
◆Libya Sep 1988–Jan 1989, Gulf War Jul–Nov 1990, Indian Ocean Oct 1999–Mar 2000.

FFG 51 *Gary*
◆Libya Mar–Jun 1988, Gulf War Jul–Oct 1991, Indian Ocean Dec 1995, Oct 1997–Jan 1998, Oct 1999–Mar 2000, Iraq War 2003.

FFG 52 *Carr*
◆Libya Nov 1989–Apr 1990, Gulf War Jan–Apr 1992, Desert Fox 1998, Iraq War 2003.

FFG 53 *Hawes*
◆Libya Aug–Oct 1987, Jan–Apr 1989, Gulf War Jan–Apr 1991, Indian Ocean Jul–Sep 2000, Iraq War 2003.

FFG 54 *Ford*
◆Libya Sep 1987–Jan 1998, Gulf War Jan–Mar 1991, Indian Ocean Jan–Mar 1996, Oct 1997–Jan 1998, Oct 1999–Mar 2000.

FFG 55 *Elrod*
◆Libya Oct 1997–Feb 1988, Apr–Aug 1989, Gulf War Oct 1991–Feb 1992, Indian Ocean Dec 1995–Feb 1996, Oct–Dec 1997.

FFG 56 *Simpson*
◆Libya Nov 1989–Apr 1990, Gulf War Feb–May 1991, Liberia Nov–Dec 1993, Indian Ocean Sep 2000–Mar 2001.

FFG 57 *Reuben James*
◆Libya Jan–Apr 1988, Indian Ocean Dec 1995–Mar 1996, Dec 1997, Iraq War 2003.

FFG 58 *Samuel B. Roberts*   Severely damaged by Iranian mine in Persian Gulf, 14 Apr 1988 (none dead).
◆Libya Apr 1988, Gulf War Sep 1990–Mar 1991, Nov 1992, Indian Ocean Nov–Dec 1997, Jan–Apr 1998, Feb–May 2000.

FFG 59 *Kauffman*
◆Gulf War May–Sep 1991.

FFG 60 *Rodney M. Davis*
◆Libya Sep–Dec 1988.

FFG 61 *Ingraham*
◆Liberia Oct–Nov 1993, Gulf War Jul–Oct 1991, Indian Ocean Apr–Jun 1997, Apr–Jul 1999.

7
AMPHIBIOUS SHIPS

AMPHIBIOUS ASSAULT SHIPS

Figure 7.1: *USS Belleau Wood* (LHA 3), *Tarawa* class assault ship, sailing alongside destroyer *John Young* (DD 873).

No.	Name	Former	Date	
LPH 1	Block Island	CVE 105	1 Jun 1958	conversion canceled
LPH 4	Boxer	CV 21	30 Jan 1959	—
LPH 5	Princeton	CV 37	2 Mar 1959	—
LPH 6	Thetis Bay	CVE 90	28 May 1959	—
LPH 8	Valley Forge	CV 45	1 Jul 1961	—

Three converted *Essex* class carriers without angled flight deck, and one former escort carrier.

Figure 7.2: *USS Thetis Bay* (LPH 6), a former *Casablanca* class escort carrier, converted to helicopter carrier.

Iwo Jima Class

No.	Name	Builder	Keel Laid	Launched	Comm.
LPH 2	Iwo Jima	Puget Sd NSYd	13 Feb 1959	17 Sep 1960	26 Aug 1961
LPH 3	Okinawa	Phila.NSYd	1 Apr 1960	19 Aug 1961	14 Apr 1962
LPH 7	Guadalcanal	Phila.NSYd	1 Sep 1961	16 Mar 1963	20 Jul 1963
LPH 9	Guam	Phila.NSYd	15 Nov 1962	22 Aug 1964	16 Jan 1965
LPH 10	Tripoli	Ingalls	15 Jun 1964	31 Jul 1965	6 Aug 1966
LPH 11	New Orleans	Phila.NSYd	1 Mar 1966	3 Feb 1968	16 Nov 1968
LPH 12	Inchon	Ingalls	8 Apr 1968	24 May 1969	20 Jun 1970

Displacement	11,000 tons, 18,300 f/l
Dimensions	602'3"(oa) 556' (wl) × 83'8" × 26'
Machinery	1 screw; ST; 2 boilers; 22,000 SHP; 22 knots
Endurance	10000/20
Complement	685
Armament	4 twin 3"/50AA guns; later 2 Sea Sparrow SAM lchrs, 2 twin 3"/50AA, 2 Phalanx. 25 helicopters

Notes: Can accommodate 2,000 troops, or one Marine battalion. First ships built to operate helicopters. Did not carry landing craft.

Figure 7.3: *USS Princeton* (LPH 5), one of four former *Essex* class aircraft carriers converted to carry helicopters.

Figure 7.4: *USS Okinawa* (LPH 3) of the *Iwo Jima* class, first built to operate helicopters.

Service Record:

LPH 2   *Iwo Jima*   In collision with carrier *Coral Sea* at San Diego, 20 May 1966. Recovery ship for failed lunar landing craft *Apollo 13*, 16 Apr 1970. In collision with LPD *Nashville* southwest of Azores, 3 Mar 1975. Damaged by fire set by arsonist at Norfolk NSYd, 3 Jul 1979. Steam valve ruptured off Bahrain, 30 Oct 1990 (10 killed). Decomm 14 Jul 1993. Stricken 24 Sep 1993. Sold 18 Dec 1995, BU Brownsville, Tex.
    8★Vietnam Nov 1963, Apr–Oct 1965, Aug 1966–Mar 1967, Nov 1967–May 1968, May–Oct 1969, Dec 1970–May 1971; ◆Cuban Missile Crisis Nov–Dec 1962, Beirut Evac Jul 1976, Lebanon Jun–Nov 1983, May 1983, Gulf War Sep 1990–Mar 1991.

LPH 3   *Okinawa*   Recovered unmanned space craft *Apollo 6* north of Hawaii, 4 Apr 1968. Recovery ship for fourth lunar landing craft *Apollo 15* in Pacific, 7 Aug 1971. Decomm and stricken 17 Dec 1992, NDRF. Sunk as target off southern California, 6 Jun 2002.
    7★Vietnam Apr–Nov 1967, Dec 1968–May 1969, Jun–Nov 1970, May 1971, Apr–Nov 1972; ◆Cuban Missile Crisis Oct–Dec 1962, Dominican Rep May 1965, evac of Cambodia Apr 1975, evac of Vietnam 29–30 Apr 1975, Iran/Indian Ocean Mar–Jun 1980, Aug–Oct 1981, Eagle Claw 1980, Libya Nov 1987–Feb 1988, Gulf War Sep–Nov 1990, Jan–Mar 1991.

LPH 7   *Guadalcanal*   Recovery ship for space capsule *Gemini 10*, east of Cape Kennedy, 21 Jul 1966. Recovery ship for spacecraft *Apollo 9*, 13 Mar 1969. Collided with oiler *Waccamaw* south of Sardinia, 24 Sep 1981. Decomm 31 Aug 1994. Stricken 15 Sep 1994. Sunk as target off Virginia, 19 May 2005.
    ◆Dominican Rep May, Oct 1965, Beirut evac Jun 1976, Iran/Indian Ocean Jul–Aug 1980, Lebanon Feb–May 1983, Sep 1983, Libya/El Dorado Canyon Mar–Apr 1986, Libya Aug–Nov 1987, Liberia Oct–Nov 1993.

LPH 9   *Guam*   Recovery ship for space craft *Gemini 11*, southeast of Cape Kennedy, 15 Sep 1966. Decomm 25 Aug 1998. Stricken 28 Aug 1998. Sunk as target off North Carolina, 16 Oct 2001.
    ◆Dominican Rep Feb 1966, Beirut evac Jun 1982, Feb 1984, Lebanon Aug–Nov 1982, Grenada Oct–Nov 1983, Lebanon Nov 1983–Nov 1984, Gulf War Sep 1990–Mar 1991, Liberia Jul 1994, Apr–Aug 1996, Indian Ocean Feb–Mar 1998.

LPH 10   *Tripoli*   Severely damaged by mine in Persian Gulf, 18 Feb 1991 (none killed). Decomm and stricken 16 Sep 1995. Trfd to Army as test platform 27 Jun 1997.
    9★Vietnam May, Aug–Dec 1967, Jul 1968–Feb 1969, Nov 1969–Jun 1970, Oct–Nov 1971, Feb, Apr–Jul 1972; ◆Gulf War Jan–Jun 1991, Indian Ocean 1992–93, Liberia Dec 1992–Feb 1993, Jul–Oct 1994. Vigilant support 1994.

LPH 11   *New Orleans*   Recovery ship for third lunar landing craft *Apollo 14* in South Pacific, 7 Feb 1970. Recovery vessel for *Skylab 4* after a 84-day orbital flight, Feb 1974. Recovery vessel for *Apollo 18* after rendezvous in space with Soviet *Soyuz 19*, 24 Jul 1975. Decomm 31 Oct 1997. Stricken 23 Oct 1998, NDRF. To be sunk as target 2006.
    ★Vietnam Aug 1969–Mar 1970, May–Jul 1971, Aug 1972–Mar 1973; ◆Lebanon Aug–Oct 1980, Gulf War Jan–Jul 1991, Liberia Oct–Dec 1993.

LPH 12   *Inchon*   In collision with oiler *Caloosahatchee* in western Mediterranean, 16 Dec 1975. Collided with LSD *Spiegel Grove* in Atlantic, 5 Feb 1980. Converted to mine countermeasures support ship (Ingalls), and rec **MCS 12**, 6 Mar 1995. Damaged by fire in engine room during overhaul, 30 Oct 2001. Decomm 20 Jun 2002. Stricken 24 May 2004. Sunk as target off Virginia Beach, Va., 5 Dec 2004.
    1 ★Vietnam Nov 1972–Mar 1973; ◆Lebanon Oct 1982–Feb 1983, Liberia Aug 1990–Feb 1991, Feb–Apr 1994.

Figure 7.5: The assault ship *Peleliu* (LHA 5) showing off her stern docking well, 8 Jan 2002.

Figure 7.6: USS *Peleliu* (LHA 5). Notice the deck edge and stern elevators, helicopters on deck.

Tarawa Class

No.	Name	Builder	Keel Laid	Launched	Comm.
LHA 1	*Tarawa*	Ingalls	15 Nov 1971	1 Dec 1973	29 May 1976
LHA 2	*Saipan*	Ingalls	21 Jul 1972	28 Jul 1974	15 Oct 1977
LHA 3	*Belleau Wood* ex-*Philippine Sea*	Ingalls	5 Mar 1973	11 Apr 1977	23 Sep 1978
LHA 4	*Nassau* ex-*Leyte Gulf*	Ingalls	13 Aug 1973	28 Jan 1978	28 Jul 1979
LHA 5	*Peleliu* ex-*Da Nang* (15 Feb 1978), ex-*Khe Sanh*	Ingalls	12 Nov 1976	6 Jan 1979	3 May 1980
Displacement	25,120 tons; 39,400 f/l				
Dimensions	833'9" (oa); 777'10" (wl) × 106' (132') × 26'				
Machinery	2 screws; ST; 2 boilers; 70,000 SHP; 24 knots				
Endurance	10000/20				
Complement	1103				
Armament	2 Sea Sparrow SAM lchrs, 3–5"/54 guns; *1985*: 1 Phalanx added; 35 Harrier/helicopters *1992*: 2 RAM lchrs replaced Sea Sparrow; *2004*: 2 RAM lchrs, 4 Bushmaster, 2 Phalanx.				

Notes: Can accommodate 1,900 troops. Large docking well in stern. 9 ships planned, LHA 6–9 not built 1971. One deck-edge and one stern elevators.

Service Records:

LHA 1 *Tarawa*
◆Iran/Indian Ocean Jan–Feb 1981, Lebanon Sep–Oct 1983, Gulf War Jan 1991–Sep 1992, Indian Ocean Mar–Jun 1998, Oct–Dec 2000, Iraq War 2003.

LHA 2 *Saipan*   Decomm and stricken 24 Apr 2007.
◆Iran/Indian Ocean Oct–Dec 1980, Grenada Nov 1983, Liberia 1990, Gulf War Oct 1991–Feb 1992, Iraq War 2003.

LHA 3 *Belleau Wood*   Decomm 28 Oct 2005. Sunk as target near Hawaii, 12–13 Jul 2006.
◆Iran/Indian Ocean Apr–Jun 1981, Desert Fox Dec 1998, Indian Ocean Nov 1998–Feb 1999.

LHA 4 *Nassau*   In collision with carrier *Nimitz* at Norfolk, Va., 14 Apr 1986.
◆Lebanon Apr–Jul 1984, Gulf War Sep 1990–Mar 1991, Iraq War 2003.

LHA 5 *Peleliu*   Minor fire at Long Beach, Cal., Jun 1989.
◆Gulf War Oct–Nov 1990, Jul–Oct 1991, Liberia Mar–Jun 1994, Indian Ocean Dec 1995–Mar 1996, Oct 1997–Jan 1998.

No.	Name	Builder	Keel Laid	Launched	Comm.
LHA 6	*America*	Ingalls	—	—	2012
Displacement	44,971 tons f/l				
Dimensions	844' × 106'				
Machinery	2 shafts, 2 gas turbines, 70,000 bhp, 20+ knots				
Complement	1,204				
Armament	2 RAM launchers, 2 Sea Sparrow, 2 Phalanx				

Notes: ordered 2 Jun 2007. Has no well deck to increase space for aircraft. Will support a Marine Expeditionary Brigade (1,687 men).

Wasp Class

No.	Name	Builder	Keel Laid	Launched	Comm.
LHD 1	*Wasp*	Ingalls	30 May 1985	19 Sep 1987	6 Jul 1989
LHD 2	*Essex*	Ingalls	20 Mar 1989	2 Mar 1991	17 Oct 1992
LHD 3	*Kearsarge*	Ingalls	6 Feb 1990	26 Mar 1992	16 Oct 1993
LHD 4	*Boxer*	Ingalls	18 Apr 1991	7 Aug 1993	11 Feb 1995
LHD 5	*Bataan*	Ingalls	22 Jun 1994	15 Mar 1996	20 Sep 1997
LHD 6	*Bonhomme Richard*	Ingalls	18 Apr 1995	14 Mar 1997	15 Aug 1998
LHD 7	*Iwo Jima*	Ingalls	12 Dec 1997	4 Feb 2000	30 Jun 2001
LHD 8	*Makin Island*	Ingalls	14 Feb 2004	22 Sep 2006	—
Displacement	28,233 tons; 40,535 f/l				
Dimensions	844' (oa); 777'10" (wl) × 106' × 26'8" (extreme beam 140')				
Machinery	2 screws; ST; 2 boilers; 77,000 SHP; 24 knots; *Makin Island*: gas turbines & electric drive				
Endurance	9500/20				
Complement	1142				
Armament	2 Sea Sparrow SAM launchers, 3 Phalanx, 40 helicopters/Harriers *Makin Island*: 2 Sea Sparrow missile launchers, 2 Phalanx, 2 RAM systems				

Notes: Can accommodate 1,875 troops. Similar to *Tarawa* class with more aircraft. *Makin Island*, new engines.

Service Records:

LHD 1 *Wasp*   In collision with support ship *Seattle*, 29 Mar 1995.
◆Liberia Mar–Apr, Jun–Jul 1993, Haiti Sep–Oct 1994.

LHD 2 *Essex*
◆Indian Ocean Jan–Feb 1997, Aug–Nov 1998, Tsunami relief 2005.

LHD 3 *Kearsarge*
◆Iraq War 2003.

LHD 4 *Boxer*
◆Indian Ocean May–Jun 1997, Jan–Apr 1999, Jul 2001, Iraq War 2003.

LHD 5 *Bataan*
◆Iraq War 2003.

LHD 6 *Bonhomme Richard*
◆Indian Ocean Mar–Jun 2000, Iraq War 2003, Tsunami relief 2005.

LHD 7 *Iwo Jima*
◆Beirut Evac, 17–19 Jul 2006.

LHD 8 *Makin Island*   Damaged during hurricane Katrina, 2006.

Figure 7.7: The amphibious assault ship *Essex* (LHD 2) leaving Busan, Korea, 8 Apr 2007.

Figure 7.8: *USS Bataan* (LHD 5) in the Arabian Sea, 21 Feb 2007. A CH-53E Super Stallion helicopter is lifting cargo from the flight deck.

Figure 7.9: *USS Bonhomme Richard* (LHD 6) off Guam, 1 May 2007.

AMPHIBIOUS TRANSPORT DOCKS

No.	Name	Builder	Keel Laid	Launched	Comm.
LPD 1	*Raleigh*	New York NSYd	23 Jun 1960	17 Mar 1962	8 Sep 1962
LPD 2	*Vancouver*	New York NSYd	19 Nov 1960	15 Sep 1962	11 May 1963
LPD 3	*La Salle*	New York NSYd	2 Apr 1962	3 Aug 1963	22 Feb 1964

Displacement	8,275 tons, 14,650 f/l
Dimensions	521′6″(oa); 500′ (wl) × 84′ × 21′7″
Machinery	2 screws; ST; 2 boilers; 24,000 SHP; 21.6 knots
Endurance	16,500/10
Complement	490
Armament	4 twin 3″/50 guns. *1980s*: 2 twin 3″/50, 2 Phalanx.

Notes: As AGF, *La Salle* fitted with command and communication facilities, h/c hangar; painted white. Improved LSD with helicopter deck over docking well. 930 troops.

Service Records:

LPD 1   *Raleigh*   Collided with liner m/v *France* in New York harbor, 19 Aug 1966. In collision with cruiser *Biddle* at Norfolk, Va., 10 Jan 1981. Collided with oiler *Waccamaw* in Mediterranean, 13 Oct 1981. Decomm 13 Dec 1991. Stricken 25 Jan 1992. Sunk as target, 4 Dec 1994.
◆Dominican Rep Apr–Jun 1965, Beirut evac Jun 1976, Lebanon Feb–May 1983, Libya Aug–Nov 1987, Gulf War Sep 1990–Mar 1991.

LPD 2   *Vancouver*   Decomm 31 Mar 1992. Stricken 8 Apr 1997. NDRF. SE. 10★Vietnam Feb–Apr, Aug 1965, Aug 1966–Mar 1967, Feb–Aug 1968, Aug 1969–Mar, Jul–Aug 1970, May–Sep 1971, Jul 1972; ◆Evac of Cambodia Apr 1975, evac of Vietnam 29–30 Apr 1975, Iran/Indian Ocean Aug–Oct 1980, Gulf War Jan–May 1991.

LPD 3   *La Salle*   In collision with m/v *Deganya* off Cape Henry, Va., 21 Mar 1967. Rec **AGF 3**, 1 Jul 1972. Damaged by fire at Norfolk NSYd, 21 Apr 1983. Decomm 27 May 2005. Sunk as target, 11 Apr 2007.
◆Dominican Rep May 1965, (as AGF) Iran/Indian Ocean Dec 1978–May 1979, Nov 1979–Nov 1980, Persian Gulf Feb–Jul 1987, Libya Jul 1987–Mar 1988, Jul 1989–Aug 1990, Gulf War.

Figure 7.10: *USS Raleigh* (LPD 1). An improved LSD with landing pad over the docking well.

Figure 7.11: USS *Nashville* (LPD 13), *Austin* class.

Figure 7.12: USS *Duluth* (LPD 6), 1971. Aerial view shows large helicopter deck and hangar, covering docking well.

No.	Name	Builder	Keel Laid	Launched	Comm.
LPD 4	Austin	New York NSYd	4 Feb 1963	27 Jun 1964	6 Feb 1965
LPD 5	Ogden	New York NSYd	4 Feb 1963	27 Jun 1964	19 Jun 1965
LPD 6	Duluth	New York NSYd	18 Dec 1963	14 Aug 1965	18 Dec 1965
LPD 7	Cleveland	Ingalls	30 Nov 1964	7 May 1966	21 Apr 1967
LPD 8	Dubuque	Ingalls	25 Jan 1965	6 Aug 1966	1 Sep 1967
LPD 9	Denver	Lockheed	7 Feb 1964	23 Jan 1965	26 Oct 1968
LPD 10	Juneau	Lockheed	23 Jan 1965	12 Feb 1966	12 Jul 1969
LPD 11	Coronado	Lockheed	3 May 1965	30 Jul 1966	23 May 1970
LPD 12	Shreveport	Lockheed	27 Dec 1965	22 Oct 1966	12 Dec 1970
LPD 13	Nashville	Lockheed	14 Mar 1966	7 Oct 1967	14 Feb 1970
LPD 14	Trenton	Lockheed	8 Aug 1966	3 Aug 1968	6 Mar 1971
LPD 15	Ponce	Lockheed	31 Oct 1966	20 May 1970	10 Jul 1971
LPD 16	Feb 1969 canceled				

Displacement	10,000 tons, 16,900 f/l
Dimensions	568′9″ (oa) × 84′ × 23′
Machinery	2 screws; ST; 2 boilers; 24,000 SHP; 20 knots
Endurance	7700/20
Complement	425
Armament	4 twin 3″/50. *1980s*: 2 twin 3″/50, 2 Phalanx. 1 helicopter

Notes: Enlarged *Raleigh* class. Small docking well. *Austin* had no hangar. *Coronado* converted to flagship 1980. 930/840 troops.

Service Records:

LPD 4   *Austin*   Decomm and stricken 27 Sep 2006.
◆Dominican Rep Jul–Aug 1966, Lebanon May–Jun–Sep 1983, Liberia Jul 1994, Iraq War 2003.

LPD 5   *Ogden*   Decomm 21 Feb 2007.
9★Vietnam Feb–Mar, Jun 1966, Mar–Sep 1967, Aug 1968–Feb 1969, Dec 1969–Jan, Mar–Oct 1970, May 1971, Oct 1972–Mar 1973; ◆Gulf War Sep–Nov 1990, Jan–Mar 1991, Indian Ocean 1997.

LPD 6   *Duluth*   Completed by Phila.NSYd. Decomm and stricken, 28 Sep 2005.
8★Vietnam May–Nov 1967, Dec 1968–May 1969, Oct–Nov 1970, Mar, Oct–Dec 1971, Feb–Jul 1972; ◆Evac of Vietnam 29–30 Apr 1975, Lebanon Sep–Oct 1983, Gulf War Feb–Mar 1992, Liberia Mar–Jun 1994, Indian Ocean Aug–Nov 1998, Oct–Dec 2000, Iraq War 2003, Tsunami relief 2005.

LPD 7   *Cleveland*   In collision with oiler *Ashtabula* off Thailand, 12 Jun 1982. Collided with ammunition ship *Shasta* off Long Beach, Cal., 26 Sep 1984.
9★Vietnam Nov 1967–May 1968, May–Nov 1969, Jul 1970, Dec 1970–Apr 1971, Aug 1972–Mar 1973. ◆Gulf War Jul–Oct 1991, Liberia Jul–Oct 1994, Indian Ocean Jan–Feb 1997, Jan–Apr 1999, Jul 2001, Iraq War 2003.

LPD 8   *Dubuque*
8★Vietnam May–Nov 1968, Oct 1969–Mar 1970, Apr–Jul, Sep 1971, Dec 1972–Feb 1973; ◆Evac of Cambodia Apr 1975, evac of Vietnam 29–30 Apr 1975, Libya Jun–Nov 1988, Gulf War Sep–Oct 1990, Indian Ocean Nov 1998–Feb 1999, Iraq War 2003.

LPD 9   *Denver*   Collided with LPH *New Orleans* off San Diego, 4 Dec 1984. Damaged in collision with oiler *Yukon* 180 miles west of Hawaii, 13 Jul 2000.
6★Vietnam Feb–Aug 1970, Mar, May–Jun, Nov 1971, Jan–Jul 1972; ◆Evac of Vietnam 29–30 Apr 1975, Iran/Indian Ocean Aug–Oct 1981, Gulf War Jan–Jul 1991, Liberia Oct 1993–Feb 1994, Indian Ocean Mar–Jun 1998, Mar–Jun 2000.

LPD 10   *Juneau*
2★Vietnam Aug, Oct 1970, Dec 1970–Mar 1971, Jun–Nov 1972; ◆Gulf War Jan–May 1991, Liberia Dec 1992–Feb 1993, Indian Ocean Oct 1997–Jan 1998.

LPD 11   *Coronado*   Converted to command ship, rec **AGF 11**, 1 Oct 1980. Out of comm 14 Nov 2003–18 Feb 2004. Decomm 25 Feb 2005, to MCS. Stricken 30 Sep 2006.
◆Beirut evac Jul 1976, Iran/Indian Ocean Nov 1980–Oct 1981, Libya/El Dorado Canyon Jan–Apr 1986, Libya Feb–Apr 1988.

LPD 12   *Shreveport*   In collision with LPD *Nashville* in Caribbean, 23 Feb 1972. Damaged propellers in Suez Canal, 16 Feb 2000. Decomm 28 Sep 2007.
◆Lebanon Oct 1982–Feb 1983, Gulf War Sep 1990–Mar 1991, Liberia Oct–Nov 1993, Indian Ocean Feb–Mar 1998, Jan–Feb 2000.

LPD 13   *Nashville*   In collision with LPD *Shreveport* in Caribbean, 23 Feb 1972. Collided with LPH *Iwo Jima* southwest of Azores, 3 Mar 1975.
◆Iran/Indian Ocean Jul–Aug 1980, Lebanon Aug–Nov 1982, Beirut evac Jun 1982, Gulf War Oct 1991–Feb 1992, Liberia Mar–Apr, Jun–Jul 1993, Haiti Sep–Oct 1994, Beirut Evac, 17–19 Jul 2006.

LPD 14   *Trenton*   Collided with submarine *Jack* at Alexandria, Egypt, 27 Apr 1981. Decomm 7 Dec 2006. Trfd to India 17 Jan 2007.
Later history: renamed *Jalashwa* (L 41).

◆Grenada Oct–Nov 1983, Lebanon Sep 1983, Nov 1983–Apr 1984, Beirut evac Feb 1984, Libya Feb–Jun 1988, Gulf War Sep 1990–Mar 1991, Liberia Feb–Apr 1994, Beirut Evac, 17–19 Jul 2006.

LPD 15 *Ponce* Collided with LSD *Fort Snelling* in Atlantic, 2 Feb 1982.
◆Beirut evac Jul 1976, Lebanon Apr–Jul 1984, Liberia 1990, Apr–Aug 1996, Gulf War Sep 1990–Nov 1991, Iraq War 2003.

LPD 16 canceled Feb 1969

No.	Name	Builder	Keel Laid	Launched	Comm.
LPD 17	*San Antonio*	Avondale	9 Dec 2000	12 Jul 2003	14 Jan 2006
LPD 18	*New Orleans*	Avondale	14 Oct 2002	11 Dec 2004	10 Mar 2007
LPD 19	*Mesa Verde*	Avondale	25 Feb 2003	19 Nov 2005	15 Dec 2007
LPD 20	*Green Bay*	Avondale	11 Aug 2003	11 Aug 2006	—
LPD 21	*New York*	Avondale	10 Sep 2004	19 Dec 2007	—
LPD 22	*San Diego*	Ingalls	23 May 2007	—	—
LPD 23	*Anchorage*	Avondale	24 Sep 2007	—	—
LPD 24	*Arlington*	Ingalls	—	—	—
LPD 25	*Somerset*	Avondale	—	—	—

Displacement	24,900 tons f/l
Dimensions	684′ (oa) × 105′ × 23′
Machinery	2 screws; diesel; 41,600 SHP; 25 knots
Complement	381
Armament	2 RAM launchers, 2 Bushmaster, 2 Phalanx. 1 or 2 helicopters

Notes: 720 troops. LPD 26–28 canceled. Carry 2 LCAC or 1 LCU.

LPD 17 *San Antonio* Completed by Ingalls.
LPD 18 *New Orleans*
LPD 19 *Mesa Verde*
LPD 20 *Green Bay*
LPD 21 *New York*
LPD 22 *San Diego*
LPD 23 *Anchorage*
LPD 24 *Arlington*
LPD 25 *Somerset*

Figure 7.13: *USS San Antonio* (LPD 17), lead ship of a new class, entering New York harbor, 24 May 2006. A new stealth design with less protruding or angled surfaces.

LITTORAL COMBAT SHIPS

Note: Despite its type designation LCS starting with the letter L, the Navy classes these ships as Surface Combatants rather than amphibious vessels.

No.	Name	Builder	Keel Laid	Launched	Comm.
LCS 1	*Freedom*	Marinette	2 Jun 2005	23 Sep 2006	Sep 2008
LCS 3	—	Bollinger	—	—	—

Displacement	2,176 tons; 2,784 f/l
Dimensions	379′ (oa) × 59″ × 13′
Machinery	2 screws; 2 gas turbines; 2 diesels; 2 waterjets; 47 knots
Complement	26
Armament	RAM lchr, 1–57 mm gun, 2 MH-60 h/c

Notes: Built as fast inexpensive ships able to conduct various duties. Became too costly.

LCS 1 *Freedom* Damaged by fire at shipyard while fitting out, 25 Apr 2007.
LCS 3 Canceled 12 Apr 2007.

No.	Name	Builder	Keel Laid	Launched	Comm.
LCS 2	*Independence*	Austal	19 Jan 2006	29 Apr 2008	Jan 2009
LCS 4	—	Austal	—	—	—

Displacement	2,794 f/l
Dimensions	418′ (oa) × 104′ × 12′11″
Machinery	2 screws; 2 gas turbines; 2 diesels; 4 waterjets; 45 knots+
Endurance	3550/18; 1150/45
Complement	est 50
Armament	1–57 mm gun, 2 VLS, 2 Harpoon lchrs, 2 Phalanx, 3 ASW TT, 2 SH-60 h/c

Notes: Fast inexpensive ships able to conduct various duties. Trimaran hull.

LCS 2 *Independence*
LCS 4 Canceled 1 Nov 2007

DOCK LANDING SHIPS

Dock Landing Ships on the Navy List, 1947

LSD 1 *Ashland* Out of comm 30 Aug 1946–27 Dec 1950. Converted to seaplane tender, Jul 1957. Out of comm 14 Sep 1957–29 Nov 1961. Decomm 22 Nov 1969. Stricken 25 Nov 1969, sold 15 May 1970, BU 1971.
◆Cuba Jan–Feb 1962.

Figure 7.14: *USS Rushmore* (LSD 14).

LSD 2 *Belle Grove* Out of comm 30 Aug 1946–27 Dec 1950. FRAM Dec 1961. Decomm and stricken 12 Nov 1969. Sold 24 Jul 1970, BU.
7★Vietnam May–Oct 1965, Feb–Apr 1966, Oct–Nov 1966, Sep 1967–Feb 1968, Mar–Aug 1969; ◆Op Castle 1954, Cuban Missile Crisis Nov–Dec 1962.

LSD 3 *Carter Hall* Out of comm 12 Feb 1947–27 Jan 1957. FRAM Oct 1961 S.Fran NSYd. Decomm and stricken 31 Oct 1969. Sold 28 Aug 1970, BU.
★Vietnam Jul–Aug 1962, Feb–Mar 1964, Jul 1965–Jan 1966, Dec 1966–May 1967, May–Aug 1968; ◆Cuban Missile Crisis Nov–Dec 1962.

LSD 4 *Epping Forest* Out of comm 25 Mar 1947–1 Dec 1950. Converted to mine countermeasures support ship, rec **MCS 7**, 30 Nov 1962. Stricken 1 Nov 1968. Sold 30 Oct 1969, BU.
5★Korea K-6 K-7 K-8 K-9 K-10; ★Vietnam Nov 1961–Jan 1962, Jul, Oct 1964, Mar–Oct 1965, Mar, May–Jun, Sep–Oct 1966, Mar–Apr, Jun 1967, Apr–May, Aug 1968; ◆Passage to Freedom 1954.

LSD 5 *Gunston Hall* Out of comm 7 Jul 1947–5 Mar 1949, conv for polar operations. Decomm 1 May 1970. Trfd to Argentina 25 May 1970.
Later history: renamed *Candido de Lasala* (Q 43). R1981.
7★Korea K-1, K-2 K-3 K-6 K-7 K-9 K-10; 7★Vietnam Dec 1964–May 1965, Jun–Dec 1966, Mar–Jul 1968, Sep 1969–Feb 1970; ◆Passage to Freedom, Cuban Missile Crisis Nov–Dec 1962.

LSD 6 *Lindenwald* Out of comm 5 Apr 1947–18 Feb 1949. Converted for polar operations. Decomm 12 Dec 1956, to MSTS. Recomm 1 Jul 1960. Decomm 30 Nov 1967. Stricken 1 Dec 1967. Sold 26 Sep 1968, BU.
◆Cuban Missile Crisis Oct–Dec 1962, Dominican Rep May–Jun 1965.

LSD 7 *Oak Hill* Out of comm 17 Mar 1947–26 Jan 1951. FRAM May 1960 S.Fran NSYd. Decomm 26 Oct and stricken 31 Oct 1969. BU 1973 Kaohsiung.
6★Vietnam Oct 1965, Jan–Apr 1966, Mar–Aug 1967, Sep 1968–Feb 1969; ◆Quemoy–Matsu Aug–Nov 1958, Jan 1961, Sep 1962.

LSD 8 *White Marsh* Out of comm Mar 1946–8 Nov 1950. Decomm Sep 1956, trfd to MSTS. Stricken 15 Apr 1976. Trfd to Taiwan 17 Nov 1960.
Later history: renamed *Tung Hai*, renamed *Chung Cheng* (191), 1976. R1985, BU.

LSD 13 *Casa Grande* Out of comm 23 Oct 1946–1 Nov 1950. FRAM Dec 1961 Charleston NSYd. Decomm 6 Feb 1970. Stricken 1 Nov 1976. Sold 6 Apr 1992, BU.
◆Cuban Missile Crisis Oct–Dec 1962, Dominican Rep May–Jun 1965.

LSD 14 *Rushmore* Out of comm 16 Aug 1946–21 Sep 1950. FRAM Dec 1962 Long Bch NSYd. Decomm 30 Sep 1970. Stricken 1 Nov 1976. Reacq 30 Apr 1986 for experimental use; stricken 2 Oct 1986. Sunk as target 29 Apr 1993.
◆Cuba Jun 1961.

LSD 15 *Shadwell* Out of comm 10 Jul 1947–20 Sep 1950. FRAM Nov 1961. In collision with transport *Cambria* off Malta, 8 Jul 1969. Decomm 9 Mar 1970. Stricken 1 Nov 1976, trfd to Energy Research and Development Admin. Stricken 15 Jul 1985.
◆Cuba Jan–Mar 1962, Cuban Missile Crisis Oct–Dec 1962, Dominican Rep May–Jun 1965.

LSD 16 *Cabildo* Out of comm 15 Jan 1947–5 Oct 1950. Damaged by shore gunfire off Hodo Pando, Korea, 26 Apr 1952. FRAM Jan 1962. Decomm 31 Mar 1970. Stricken 15 Oct 1976. Sunk as target off San Nicolas Island, Cal., Sep 1985.
2★Korea K-7 K-8; 7★Vietnam Jun–Oct 1965, Apr–Jun 1966, Jan–Apr 1967, May–Nov 1968; ◆Cuban Missile Crisis Nov–Dec 1962.

LSD 17 *Catamount* FRAM Mar 1962 Long Bch NSYd. Decomm 7 Apr 1970. Stricken 31 Oct 1974, sold 4 Dec 1975.
Later history: Merchant *Wareship Two*.
7★Korea K-1 K-2 K-4 K-5 K-7 K-8 9; 7★Vietnam Jul–Aug 1958, Apr 1961, Oct–Nov 1962, Dec 1965–May 1966, Apr–Nov 1967, Nov 1968–May 1969. ◆Taiwan Straits Sep–Oct 1958.

LSD 18 *Colonial* FRAM Jan 1961. Decomm 30 Jun 1970. Stricken 15 Oct 1976. Sold 8 Sep 1993, BU Shanghai.
7★Korea K-1 K-2 K-4 K-5 K-6 K-7 K-8; 6★Vietnam Aug–Nov 1965, Jul 1965, Mar–Aug 1966, Dec 1967–May 1968; ◆Cuban Missile Crisis Nov–Dec 1962.

LSD 19 *Comstock* FRAM 1963. Decomm Jan 1970. Stricken 30 Jun 1976. Sold for BU, but resold to Taiwan Navy 1985.
Later history: renamed *Chung Cheng* (191). SE2004.
10★Korea K-1 K-2 K-3 K-4 K-5 K-6 K-7 K-8 K-9 K-10; 5★Vietnam Sep 1963, Jan–May 1965, Aug–Sep 1965, Aug 1966–Jan 1967, Nov 1967–Mar 1968, Jun–Oct 1969; ◆Passage to Freedom, Quemoy–Matsu Jun–Jul 1959, Mar 1962, May 1963.

LSD 20 *Donner* Out of comm 12 Aug 1949–15 Sep 1950. FRAM Dec 1960 Norfolk NSYd. Decomm 23 Dec 1970. Stricken 1 Nov 1976, trfd to Energy Research and Development Admin. NDRF. BU 2005 Brownsville, Tex.
★Korea K-1 K-2 K-3 K-4 K-8; ◆Dominican Rep May 1965.

LSD 21 *Fort Mandan* Out of comm 16 Jan 1948–25 Oct 1950. FRAM Feb 1961. Decomm and trfd to Greece, 23 Jan 1971.
Later history: renamed *Nafkratoussa* (L 153). R2000, BU 2001.

LSD 22 *Fort Marion* FRAM Apr 1960 Long Bch NSYd. Decomm 13 Feb 1970. Stricken 31 Oct 1974. Trfd to Taiwan 15 Apr 1977.
Later history: renamed *Chen Hai* (618/192). R1999, sunk as artificial reef 9 Dec 2000.
5★Korea K-1 K-2 K-3 K-4 K-8; 5★Vietnam Apr 1961, Oct 1965–Feb, Jun 1966, Sep–Dec 1967, Dec 1968–May 1969; ◆Quemoy-Matsu Sep–Oct 1958, Lebanon Apr–May 1961.

LSD 25 *San Marcos* Out of comm 19 Dec 1947–26 Jan 1951. FRAM Dec 1962. Decomm 1 Jul 1971 and trfd to Spain.
Later history: renamed *Galicia* (TA 31/L 31). R1988, BU.
◆Lebanon Sep–Oct 1958, Cuba Mar–Apr 1961.

LSD 26 *Tortuga* Out of comm 18 Aug 1947–15 Sep 1950. Decomm 26 Jan 1970. Stricken 15 Oct 1976. Used as target and scuttled off San Miguel Island, 21 Aug 1988.
5★Korea K-4 K-5 K-6 K-8 K-9; 8★Vietnam Aug–Sep 1964, Jun–Jul 1965, Apr–Sep 1966, Sep 1967–Feb 1968, Mar–Aug 1969; ◆Passage to Freedom.

LSD 27 *Whetstone* Out of comm 20 Oct 1948–2 Dec 1950. Decomm 2 Apr 1970. Stricken 30 Apr 1976. Sold 17 Feb 1983, BU.
4★Korea K-5 K-6 K-9 K-10; 8★Vietnam Aug–Sep 1964, Jul 1965, Mar–Aug 1966, Dec 1967–May 1968, May–Sep 1969; ◆Passage to Freedom, Cuban Missile Crisis Nov–Dec 1962.

No.	Name	Builder	Keel Laid	Launched	Comm.
LSD 28	*Thomaston*	Ingalls	3 Mar 1953	9 Feb 1954	17 Sep 1954
LSD 29	*Plymouth Rock*	Ingalls	5 May 1953	7 May 1954	29 Nov 1954
LSD 30	*Fort Snelling*	Ingalls	17 Aug 1953	16 Jul 1954	24 Jan 1955
LSD 31	*Point Defiance*	Ingalls	23 Nov 1953	28 Sep 1954	31 Mar 1955
LSD 32	*Spiegel Grove*	Ingalls	7 Sep 1954	10 Nov 1955	8 Jun 1956
LSD 33	*Alamo*	Ingalls	11 Oct 1954	20 Jan 1956	24 Aug 1956
LSD 34	*Hermitage*	Ingalls	11 Apr 1955	12 Jun 1956	14 Dec 1956
LSD 35	*Monticello*	Ingalls	6 Jun 1955	10 Aug 1956	29 Mar 1957

Displacement	6,880 tons, 11,270 f/l; 32–34: 12,150 f/l
Dimensions	510′ (oa) × 84′ × 19′
Machinery	2 screws; ST; 2 boilers; 24,000 SHP; 22.5 knots
Endurance	10000/20
Complement	348
Armament	8 twin 3″/50, 12–20 mm guns. 1985: 3 twin 3″/

Notes: 341 troops. Removable helicopter deck above docking well.

Figure 7.15: *USS Fort Snelling* (LSD 30), in the 1950s. Notice twin 3-inch guns along the hull.

Service Records:

LSD 28 *Thomaston*   Decomm 28 Sep 1984. Stricken 24 Feb 1992. Sold 29 Sep 1995, canceled. NDRF. SE.
11★Vietnam Apr–May, Aug–Sep 1963, Dec 1964–May 1965, Aug–Sep 1965, Feb–Mar, Aug–Nov 1966, Jan–Mar 1967, Mar–Aug 1968, Aug 1969–Mar 1970, Apr–Oct 1971, Jun 1972; ◆Cuban Missile Crisis Nov–Dec 1962, evac of Cambodia Apr 1975, evac of Vietnam 29–30 Apr 1975, Iran/Indian Ocean Apr–Jun 1981.

LSD 29 *Plymouth Rock*   Decomm 30 Sep 1983. Stricken 24 Feb 1992. Sold 25 Aug 1995, BU.
◆Lebanon Jul–Sep 1958, Cuba Dec 1961–Jan 1962, Cuban Missile Crisis Oct–Dec 1962, Dominican Rep Oct 1965.

LSD 30 *Fort Snelling*   In collision with oiler *Waccamaw* north of Corsica, 3 Apr 1978. Collided with LPD *Ponce* in North Atlantic, 2 Feb 1982. Sank m/v *Diana D.* in collision off Brest, France, 23 Nov 1983. Decomm 5 Sep 1984. Stricken 24 Feb 1992. Sold 25 Aug 1995, BU.
◆Lebanon Jul–Oct 1958, Cuba Jan–Mar, Jun–Aug, Nov–Dec 1961, Cuban Missile Crisis Oct–Dec 1962, Dominican Rep Apr–Jun 1965, Sep 1966, Beirut evac Jun 1982, Lebanon Oct 1982–Feb 1983, Grenada Oct–Nov 1983, Lebanon Nov 1983–Apr 1984.

LSD 31 *Point Defiance*   Damaged in collision with oiler *Ponchatoula* north of Hawaii, 13 Feb 1970. In collision with LPH *Inchon* in North Atlantic, 5 Feb 1980. Decomm 30 Sep 1983. Stricken 24 Feb 1992. Sold 29 Sep 1995, canceled. NDRF. SE.
10★Vietnam Nov 1963, May–Oct 1965, Apr–May, Nov 1966–Jun 1967, Jun–Nov 1968, Nov 1969–Mar 1970, Jun 1970, Apr–Oct 1972; ◆Cuban Missile Crisis Nov–Dec 1962.

LSD 32 *Spiegel Grove*   Collided with m/v *Honesty* at Augusta, Sicily, 27 Jan 1976. Collided with assault ship Inchon in North Atlantic, 5 Feb 1980. Decomm 2 Oct 1989. Stricken 13 Dec 1989. NDRF. Sunk as artificial reef off Key Largo, Fla., 17 May 2002.
◆Lebanon Jul–Sep 1958, Cuba Jan–Mar 1961, Feb–Mar, Jul 1962, Cuban Missile Crisis Oct–Nov 1962, Dominican Rep Jul 1965, Aug–Sep 1966, Beirut evac Jun 1976 and Jun 1982.

LSD 33 *Alamo*   Collided with oiler *Kawishiwi*, 5 Apr 1966. Collided with oiler *Guadalupe* north of Danang, Vietnam, 6 Jul 1972. Decomm 28 Sep 1990. Trfd to Brazil 12 Nov 1990.
Later history: renamed *Rio de Janeiro* (G 31). SE2001.
11★Vietnam Mar 1963, Aug–Nov 1964, Jul 1965, Mar–Aug 1966, Aug, Oct–Dec 1970, Apr–Oct 1972; ◆Taiwan Straits Nov–Dec 1958, Quemoy-Matsu Nov–Dec 1959, Mar 1960, Mar 1963, Iran/Indian Ocean Mar–Jun 1980, Aug–Oct 1981.

LSD 34 *Hermitage*   In collision with LST *Lamoure County* off Georgia, 29 Apr 1987. Decomm 2 Oct 1989. Trfd to Brazil 28 Nov 1989.
Later history: renamed *Ceará* (G 30). SE2001.
★Vietnam Jun–Nov 1967; ◆Cuba Jun 1961, Jun 1962, Cuban Missile Crisis Dec 1962, Dominican Rep Jun–Jul 1965, Beirut evac Jun 1982, Lebanon Aug–Nov 1982.

LSD 35 *Monticello*   Decomm 1 Oct 1985. Stricken 24 Feb 1992. Sold 29 Sep 1995, canceled. NDRF. SE.
11★Vietnam Dec 1960–Jan, Mar–Apr 1961, Aug–Sep 1964, Sep 1965–Mar 1966, Feb–Sep 1967, Mar, Aug 1968–Feb 1969, Feb–Sep 1970, Mar, Nov 1971, Oct 1972–Jan 1973.

No.	Name	Builder	Keel Laid	Launched	Comm.
LSD 36	Anchorage	Ingalls	13 Mar 1967	5 May 1968	15 Mar 1969
LSD 37	Portland	Beth; Quincy	21 Sep 1967	20 Dec 1969	3 Oct 1970
LSD 38	Pensacola	Beth; Quincy	12 Mar 1969	11 Jul 1970	27 Mar 1971
LSD 39	Mount Vernon	Beth; Quincy	29 Jan 1970	17 Apr 1971	13 May 1972
LSD 40	Fort Fisher	Beth; Quincy	15 Jul 1970	22 Apr 1972	9 Dec 1972

Displacement	8,600 tons; 14,000 f/l.
Dimensions	553′3″(oa); 534′(wl) × 85′ × 18′6″
Machinery	2 screws; ST; 2 boilers; 24,000 SHP; 22 knots
Endurance	14,000/12
Complement	358
Armament	4 twin 3″/50. *1980s*: 2 twin 3″/50, 2 Phalanx.

Notes: 376 troops. Removable helicopter deck above docking well; no hangar.

Service Record:

LSD 36 *Anchorage*   Decomm 1 Oct 2003. Stricken 8 Mar 2004.
6★Vietnam Feb, Jun–Nov 1970, Apr, Oct 1971–Jul 1972; ◆Evac of Vietnam 29–30 Apr 1975, Iran/Indian Ocean Feb–Mar 1980, Gulf War Jan–May 1991, Liberia Mar–Jun 1994, Indian Ocean Dec 1995–Mar 1996, Aug–Nov 1998, Sep 2000–Jan 2001, Iraq War 2003.

LSD 37 *Portland*   Damaged by fire in Persian Gulf, 2003. Decomm 30 Aug 2003. Stricken 8 Mar 2004. Sunk as target off Virginia coast, 25 Apr 2004.
◆Beirut evac Jul 1976, Lebanon May–Jun–Nov 1983, Libya Jan–Mar 1988, Gulf War Sep 1990–Mar 1991, Liberia Feb–Apr 1994, Iraq War 2003.

LSD 38 *Pensacola*   Ran aground off North Carolina, Nov 1994. Decomm and stricken 30 Sep 1999 and tfrd to Taiwan.
Later history: renamed *Tan Hai*, renamed *Hso Hai*, (LSD 193) 2000.
◆Iran/Indian Ocean Jul–Aug 1980, Lebanon Feb–May 1983, Gulf War Sep 1990–Mar 1991.

LSD 39 *Mount Vernon*   Decomm 25 Jul 2003. Stricken 8 Mar 2004. Sunk as target off Kauai, Hawaii, 16 Jun 2005.
◆Evac of Vietnam 29–30 Apr 1975, Libya Oct 1987–Feb 1988, Gulf War Jan–May 1991, Indian Ocean Mar–Jun 1998.

LSD 40 *Fort Fisher*   Decomm and stricken 27 Feb 1998. NDRF. SE.
◆Gulf War Jul–Sep 1992, Indian Ocean May–Jun 1997.

No.	Name	Builder	Keel Laid	Launched	Comm.
LSD 41	Whidbey Island	Lockheed	4 Aug 1981	10 Jun 1983	9 Feb 1985
LSD 42	Germantown	Lockheed	5 Aug 1982	29 Jun 1984	8 Feb 1986
LSD 43	Fort McHenry	Lockheed	10 Jun 1983	1 Feb 1986	8 Aug 1987
LSD 44	Gunston Hall	Avondale	26 May 1986	27 Jun 1987	22 Apr 1989
LSD 45	Comstock	Avondale	27 Oct 1986	16 Jan 1988	3 Feb 1990

LSD 46	*Tortuga*	Avondale	23 Mar 1987	15 Sep 1988	17 Nov 1990
LSD 47	*Rushmore*	Avondale	9 Nov 1987	6 May 1989	1 Jun 1991
LSD 48	*Ashland*	Avondale	4 Apr 1988	11 Nov 1988	9 May 1992

Displacement	12,434 tons; 15,745 f/l
Dimensions	609′7″ (oa); 580′ (wl) × 84′ × 20′
Machinery	2 screws; diesels; 41,600 BHP; 20+ knots
Endurance	8,000/20
Complement	342
Armament	2 Phalanx. Later: 2 RAM launchers, 2 Bushmaster 2 h/c.

Notes: 560 troops. First LSD to operate LCACs. Can carry 4 LCAC.

Service Record:

LSD 41 *Whidbey Island*
◆Liberia Aug 1990–Feb 1991, Haiti Sep 1994, Indian Ocean Jan–Feb 2000, Beirut Evac, 17–19 Jul 2006.

LSD 42 *Germantown*
◆Gulf War Jan–Jul 1991, Indian Ocean Nov 1998–Feb 1999, Desert Fox 1998.

LSD 43 *Fort McHenry*
◆Gulf War Sep–Nov 1990, Jan–Mar 1991, Liberia Sep–Oct 1994, Tsunami relief 2005.

LSD 44 *Gunston Hall*
◆Gulf War Sep 1990–Mar 1991, Iraq War 2003.

LSD 45 *Comstock*
◆Gulf War Jul–Oct 1991, Liberia Oct 1993–Jan 1994, Indian Ocean Oct 1997–Jan 1998, Iraq War 2003.

LSD 46 *Tortuga*   Ran aground near Morehead City, NC, 6 Jun 2002.
◆Liberia Jul 1994, Iraq War 2003.

LSD 47 *Rushmore*
◆Liberia Dec 1992–Feb 1993, Aug 1994, Iraq War 2003.

LSD 48 *Ashland*
◆Liberia Oct–Nov 1993, Haiti Sep–Oct 1994, Indian Ocean Feb–Mar 1998, Iraq War 2003.

No.	Name	Builder	Laid down	Launched	Comm.
LSD 49	*Harpers Ferry*	Avondale	15 Apr 1991	16 Jan 1993	7 Jan 1995
LSD 50	*Carter Hall*	Avondale	11 Nov 1991	2 Oct 1993	30 Sep 1995
LSD 51	*Oak Hill*	Avondale	21 Sep 1992	11 Jun 1994	8 Jun 1996
LSD 52	*Pearl Harbor*	Avondale	27 Jan 1995	24 Feb 1996	30 May 1998

Displacement	11,894 tons; 16,695 f/l
Dimensions	609′5″(oa); 579′11(wl) × 84′ × 20′
Machinery	2 screws; diesels; 41,600 BHP; 22 knots
Endurance	8,000/20
Complement	333
Armament	2 RAM launchers, 2 Phalanx, 2 Bushmaster.

Notes: 400 troops. Similar to *Whidbey Island* class with smaller docking well, but increased troop and cargo capacity. Can carry 2 LCAC.
LSD 53 and 54 canceled.

Service Records:

LSD 49 *Harpers Ferry*
◆Indian Ocean Jan–Feb 1997, Jan–Apr 1999, Jul 2001.

LSD 50 *Carter Hall*

LSD 51 *Oak Hill*   Ran aground off Morehead City, NC, 18 Feb 2000.
◆Indian Ocean Feb–Mar 1998.

LSD 52 *Pearl Harbor*
◆Indian Ocean Mar–Jun 2000, Iraq War 2003.

Figure 7.16: *USS Fort McHenry* (LSD 43) during a training exercise, 9 Mar 2002.

Figure 7.17: The dock landing ship *Harpers Ferry* (LSD 49) in the Gulf of Thailand, 29 May 2006. An MH-60S Seahawk lands on the flight deck.

TANK LANDING SHIPS

Tank Landing Ships on the Navy List, 1947

Note: Names assigned 1 Jul 1955 (except MSTS ships).

LST 17   Decomm 15 Jan 1946. SCAJAP, Q015. Sunk as target 15 Aug 1956.

LST 31 *Addison County*   Decomm 8 Jan 1946. SCAJAP, Q005. Stricken 11 Aug 1955. Sunk as target.

LST 32 *Alameda County*   Out of comm Jul 1946–7 Mar 1951. Converted to advance aviation base ship and rec **AVB 1**, 28 Sep 1957. Decomm 25 Jun 1962. Stricken 30 Jun 1962. Trfd to Italy 20 Nov 1962.
Later history: renamed *Anteo* (A 5306). R1988.
◆Lebanon Jul–Oct 1958.

LST 47   Decomm 11 Jan 1946. SCAJAP, Q007. U.S. Army, MSTS, 1952. Stricken 30 Jun 1975. Trfd to Philippines 13 Sep 1976.
Later history: renamed *Tarlac* (LT 500). R1991.
◆Passage to Freedom.

LST 50   Decomm 6 Feb 1946. SCAJAP, Q046. Converted to battle damage repair ship, rec **ARB 13**, 14 Nov 1951. Trfd to Norway 14 Nov 1952.
Later history: renamed *Ellida* (A534). Trfd to Greece, 16 Sep 1960, renamed *Sakipis* (A 329). R1977.

LST 53   Decomm early 1946. SCAJAP, Q021. Decomm May 1955. Rec **APL 59**, Sep 1954. Trfd to South Korea May 1955.
Later history: renamed *Chang Su* (811).

LST 57 *Armstrong County*   Decomm 24 Jan 1946. SCAJAP, Q028. Rtnd 1950. Stricken 21 Sep 1955; sunk as target 1956.

LST 60 *Atchison County*   Decomm 27 Jun 1946. Stricken 1 Nov 1958. Sold.
Later history: Merchant *Elmer*. BU 1973.

LSTH 117   Decomm 16 Feb 1946. SCAJAP, Q063. Rec **LST 117**, 6 Mar 1952. MSTS, 1952. Stricken 10 Jun 1973. Trfd to Singapore 27 Jun 1974, but sold commercial.

LST 176   Decomm 6 Jan 1946. SCAJAP, Q002. MSTS, 1952. Stricken 1 Nov 1973.
◆Passage to Freedom.

LST 209 *Bamberg County*   Decomm 28 Jun 1946. MSTS, 1951. Recomm 24 Aug 1951. Decomm 10 Dec 1956. Stricken 1 Nov 1958. Sold for use as drydock at Baton Rouge 1961.

LST 218   Decomm 19 Jan 1946. SCAJAP, Q020. Trfd to South Korea, 30 May 1955.
Later history: renamed *Bibong* (218/LST 673). R1999.

LSTH 222   Decomm Feb 1946. SCAJAP, Q044. MSTS, 1952. Trfd to Philippines 15 Jul 1972.
Later history: renamed *Mindoro Occidental* (LT 93). R1991.

LST 227   Decomm 22 Jan 1946. SCAJAP, Q025 Trfd to South Korea, 29 Mar 1955.
Later history: renamed *Tukbong* (*Duk Bong*) (808/LST 672). R1989.

LST 230   Decomm 4 Mar 1946. SCAJAP, Q082. MSTS Stricken 30 Jun 1975. Trfd to Philippines 13 Sep 1976.
Later history: renamed *Laguna* (LT 501). SE2001.

LST 263 *Benton County*   Decomm 29 May 1946. Stricken 1 Nov 1958. Sold 1960.
Later history: Merchant barge *TMT Puerto Rico*.

LST 266 *Benzie County*   Decomm 25 Jun 1947. Stricken 1 Nov 1958. Sold 4 Aug 1959, BU.

LST 270   Decomm NRT 1947. Sold 12 May 1950.
Later history: Merchant barge *U-303*, renamed *Margaret C*.

LST 276   Decomm 15 Feb 1946. SCAJAP, Q079. MSTS. Stricken 10 Jun 1973. Trfd to Singapore 27 Jun 1974, but sold commercial.

LST 277   Decomm 12 Feb 1946. SCAJAP, Q055. MSTS, 1952. Stricken and trfd to Chile 2 Feb 1973.
Later history: renamed *Comandante Toro* (AP 97).

LST 279 *Berkeley County*   Decomm 14 Jun 1955. Trfd to Taiwan 30 Jun 1955.
Later history: renamed *Chung Chi* (218). SE2001.

LST 281   Decomm 9 Mar 1946. SCAJAP, Q092. MSTS, 1952. Stricken 19 May 1954.

LST 287   MSTS, 1951. Stricken; reinstated 9 Dec 1965. Stricken 30 Jun 1975. Trfd to Philippines 13 Sep 1976.
Later history: renamed *Samar Oriental* (LT 502). R>1901.

LST 288 *Berkshire County*   Decomm 6 Mar 1946. SCAJAP, Q085. Laid up 1950. Trfd to South Korea 5 Mar 1956.
Later history: renamed *Gaebong* (*Kae Bong*) (810/LST 675). SE2001.

LST 291   Decomm 18 Jun 1947. Went aground on submerged reef off Eleuthera, Bahamas, 1954. Stricken 17 May 1954. Sunk as target Jul 1954.

LST 306 *Bernalillo County*   Decomm 13 Jun 1946. Sank f/v in collision in Puget Sound, 11 Mar 1955. Stricken 1 Feb 1959. Sold 22 Oct 1959.
Later history: Merchant barge *Turkey Island*.

LST 325   Decomm 2 Jul 1946. MSTS, 1951. Stricken 1 Sep 1961. Trfd to Greece 1 Sep 1964.
Later history: renamed *Syros* (L 144). Returned to U.S. 10 Jan 2001 for use as museum at Mobile, Ala., now at Evansville, Ind.

LST 344 *Blanco County*   Out of comm 7 Jun 1946–5 Jan 1952 and 28 Feb 1956–9 Jun 1966. Decomm 3 Oct 1969. Stricken 15 Sep 1974. Sold 1 Jul 1975.
Later history: Merchant *Olmeca*. Went aground, 24 Dec 1983, CTL BU 1984.
5★Vietnam Nov 1966–Jan, Mar–Aug, Oct–Dec 1967, Apr–Jul, Oct–Dec 1968.

LST 356 *Bledsoe County*   Decomm 2 Jul 1946. Stricken 1 Sep 1960. Sold 8 Mar 1961.
Later history: Merchant *Brunal*, renamed *Inagua Crest* 1962, to Indonesian Navy, renamed *Teluk Tomini* (508) 1968. SE2001.

LST 389 *Boone County*   Decomm 12 Mar 1946. Stricken 1 Jun 1959. Trfd to Greece 9 Aug 1960.
Later history: renamed *Lesbos* (L 172). BU Aliaga, Turkey, 2000.

LST 391 *Bowman County*   Decomm. Trfd to Greece 9 Aug 1960.
Later history: renamed *Rodos* (L 391). R1997.

LST 399   Decomm 8 Dec 1945. SCAJAP, Q088. MSTS 1952. Stricken 1 Nov 1973. Reacq as support ship, Pacific Missile Range, 25 Nov 1980. Rec **IX 511**, 30 Sep 1982. Stricken 15 Jun 1985.

LST 400 *Bradley County*   Decomm. To Taiwan 30 Sep 1958.
Later history: renamed *Chung Suo* (217). SE2001.

LST 456   Decomm 1946. SCAJAP, Q043. MSTS 1952. Stricken 15 Jun 1973. Sold 27 Sep 1973.
Later history: Merchant *Karkas*, renamed *Bshair* 1999. SE2003.

LST 482 *Branch County*   Decomm 23 Feb 1946. SCAJAP, Q072. Stricken 11 Aug 1955. Sunk as target off San Diego, 22 Feb 1956.

LST 483 *Brewster County*   Decomm 10 Feb 1946. SCAJAP, Q050. Stricken 11 Aug 1955. Sunk as target.

LST 488   Decomm 11 Jan 1946. SCAJAP, Q009. MSTS 1952. Trfd to Philippines 15 Jul 1972.
Later history: renamed *Surigao del Norte* (LT 94). R1991.

LST 491   Decomm 12 Jan 1946. SCAJAP, Q010. MSTS. Stricken 30 Jun 1975. Trfd to Philippines 13 Sep 1976.
Later history: renamed *Lanao del Sur* (LT 503). R1991.

LST 503   Out of comm 11 Jun 1946–Oct 1950. Decomm and trfd to Taiwan 4 Apr 1955.
Later history: renamed *Chung Kuang* (216). SE2001.

LST 504 *Buchanan County*   Decomm 22 Jan 1946. SCAJAP, Q016. Stricken 11 Aug 1955. Sunk as target Feb 1956.

LST 509 *Bulloch County*   Decomm and trfd to Vietnam 8 Apr 1970.
Later history: renamed *Qui Nhon* (HQ 502). Captured by North Vietnam, Apr 1975. SE2001.
6★Vietnam Mar–Apr, Jun–Jul, Sep–Dec 1967, Feb–Jun 1968, Mar–May 1969.

LST 510 *Buncombe County*   Decomm 1 Jul 1946. Stricken 1 Nov 1958. Sold 1959.
Later history: Merchant *Virginia Beach*, renamed *Cape Henlopen* 1964. SE2003.

LST 512 *Burnett County*   Decomm 28 Mar 1947. Stricken 18 Feb 1957. Trfd to Peru 11 Oct 1957.
Later history: renamed *Paita* (141). SE1981.

LST 515 *Caddo Parish*   NRT 1947. Out of comm 10 Oct 1955–2 Aug 1963. Decomm 26 Nov 1969. Trfd to Philippines 26 Nov 1969.
Later history: renamed *Bataan* (LT 85). *Maquindanao* (LT 96). R1991.
9★Vietnam May 1966–Jun 1967, Aug–Nov 1967, Mar 1968–Oct 1969; ◆Dominican Rep Jun–Jul, Oct–Nov 1965.

LST 516 *Calaveras County*   Out of comm 28 Feb 1947–22 Sep 1950. Decomm 21 Dec 1955. Stricken 1 Oct 1958.
4★Korea K-6 K-7 K-9 K-10; ◆Passage to Freedom.

LST 519 *Calhoun County*   Decomm and stricken 8 Nov 1962. Sunk as target 1963.

LST 520   Decomm 13 Jan 1946. SCAJAP, Q013. MSTS 1952. Stricken and trfd to Taiwan 1 Oct 1958.
Later history: renamed *Chung Shu* (228). SE2001.
◆Passage to Freedom.

LST 521 *Cape May County*   Decomm 21 Oct 1945. MSTS, 1950. Stricken 1 Nov 1959.
  Later history: Merchant *Cal-Agro*, renamed *Terry P.* 1965, *Banten* 1966, *Teluk Banten* 1969.
LST 525 *Caroline County*   Out of comm 25 Jun 1946–Oct 1950 and 15 Sep 1954–mid 1965. Decomm early 1970. Stricken 15 Sep 1974. Sold 1 Aug 1975, BU.
  4★Vietnam Jan–Jun, Aug–Nov 1967, Jan–Mar, Aug–Nov 1968, Feb 1969.
LST 527 *Cassia County*   Out of comm 28 Feb 1946–21 Sep 1950. Decomm 21 Dec 1956. Stricken 1 Oct 1958; sunk as target 3 Mar 1959.
  2★Korea K-7 K-10.
LST 528 *Catahoula County*   Decomm Mar 1954. Stricken 21 Nov 1960.
  Later history: Merchant *Noramar*, renamed *J.E. Poole* 1973, *Tsimenteus II* 1976.
LST 529 *Cayuga County*   Out of comm 7 Jun 1946–22 Sep 1950. Decomm 17 Dec 1963 and trfd to Vietnam 16 Dec 1963.
  Later history: renamed *Thi Nai* (HQ 502). Escaped to Philippines, Apr 1975. Trfd to Philippines 17 Nov 1975, renamed *Cotabato del Sur* (LT 87). R2003, BU.
  3★Korea K-6 K-7 K-10.
LST 530   Decomm Jan 1946. SCAJAP, Q017. MSTS 1952. Stricken 15 Jun 1973. Sold 21 Aug 1973, BU.
LST 532 *Chase County*   Out of comm 8 Jun 1955–29 May 1963. Decomm 30 Jun 1967. MSTS Stricken 10 Jun 1973. Trfd to Singapore 27 Jun 1974, but sold commercial.
  Later history: Merchant *Constructors* 1976.
  ★Vietnam Apr–Oct 1966 Jan–Mar 1967; ◆Dominican Rep May, Jul 1965.
LST 533 *Cheboygan County*   Out of comm 1 Dec 1955–18 Nov 1961. Decomm May 1969. Stricken 15 Sep 1974; Sold 17 Nov 1975, BU Wilmington, NC.
  ◆Cuban Missile Crisis Oct–Dec 1962.
LST 535   Decomm 14 Jan 1946. SCAJAP, Q014. MSTS 1952. Stricken 1 Oct 1958 and trfd to Taiwan.
  Later history: renamed *Chung Wan* (229). R1993.
  ◆Passage to Freedom.
LST 542 *Chelan County*   Decomm 1956. Stricken 1 Nov 1959. Sold 28 Apr 1961.
  Later history: Merchant barge *ZB-108A*.
LST 546   Decomm Jan 1946. SCAJAP, Q076. MSTS 31 Mar 1952. Stricken and trfd to Philippines 15 Jul 1972.
  ◆Passage to Freedom.
  Later history: renamed *Surigao del Sur* (LT 95). R1991.
LST 548   Decomm 15 Feb 1946. SCAJAP, Q067. MSTS 1952. Stricken 1 Jan 1960; Sold 1960, BU.
  ◆Passage to Freedom.
LST 550   Decomm 13 Jan 1946. SCAJAP, Q012. MSTS 1952. Stricken 1 Nov 1973, BU.
LST 551 *Chesterfield County*   Out of comm 10 Jun 1955–21 Dec 1965. Decomm and stricken 1 Jun 1970. Sold Feb 1971 BU Japan.
  2★Vietnam Mar, May–Aug, Oct, Dec 1966–Jan 1967; ◆OpCastle 1954, Dominican Rep May–Jun, Oct 1965.
LST 561 *Chittenden County*   Out of comm 30 Apr 1946–18 Sep 1950. Went aground on Kauai I., 2 Jun 1958. Decomm 2 Jun 1958. Stricken 27 Jun 1958; sunk as target off Oahu, Hawaii, 21 Oct 1958.
  2★Korea K-7 K-8.
LST 566   Decomm 11 Mar 1946. SCAJAP, Q094. MSTS 1952. Stricken 1 Nov 1973. Trfd to Philippines 13 Sep 1976.
  Later history: renamed *Lanao del Norte* (LT 504). SE2001.
LST 572   Decomm 8 Mar 1946. SCAJAP, Q090. MSTS 1952. Stricken 15 Jun 1973. Sold 19 Nov 1973.
LST 578   Decomm 22 Mar 1946. SCAJAP, Q099. MSTS 1952. Trfd to Taiwan 16 Sep 1958.
  ◆Passage to Freedom.
  Later history: renamed *Chung Pang* (230). SE2001.
LST 579   Decomm 24 Feb 1946. SCAJAP, Q073. MSTS 1952. Stricken 30 Jun 1975. Trfd to Singapore 4 Jun 1976.
  Later history: renamed *Intrepid* (L 203). SE2001.
LST 581   Decomm 28 Jan 1946. SCAJAP, Q030. MSTS 1952. Stricken 1 Jun 1972. Sold 25 May 1973, BU.
LST 583 *Churchill County*   Decomm Mar 1946–1 Nov 1960. Decomm 11 Dec 1968. Stricken 15 Sep 1974. Sold Jun 1975.
  Later history: merchant *Petrola 131*.
  ◆Dominican Rep Jun 1966.
LST 587   Decomm Feb 1946. SCAJAP, Q042. MSTS 1952. Grounded in storm off Okinawa, 23 Dec 1968. Stricken 15 Jun 1973. Sold 21 Aug 1973. BU.
LST 590   Decomm 2 Feb 1946. SCAJAP, Q036. MSTS 1952. Stricken 15 Jun 1973. Sold 17 Sep 1973.
  1★Vietnam.
LST 600   Decomm 31 Mar 1952, MSTS. Lost by grounding in storm off Okinawa, 23 Dec 1968. Stricken 1 Jun 1969. Sold 1970.
LST 601 *Clarke County*   Decomm 1946. SCAJAP, Q074. Out of comm 23 Nov 1955–28 Jul 1966. Decomm 1970. Trfd to Indonesia 15 Jul 1970.
  Later history: renamed *Teluk Saleh* (510). SE2001.
  6★Vietnam Jan–Feb, Apr–May, Jul–Aug, Oct–Dec 1967, Mar, Jun–Jul, Sep–Oct 1969, Jan–May 1970.
LST 602 *Clearwater County*   Out of comm Dec 1946–1950. USAF 1957–1969. Decomm 1969. Stricken 1 May 1972. Trfd to Mexico 30 May 1972.
  Later history: renamed *Manzanillo*, renamed *Papaloapan* (A 02) 1993.
  2★Korea K-7 K-10.
LST 603 *Coconino County*   Out of comm 12 May 1955–8 Jun 1966. Decomm 4 Apr 1969 and trfd to Vietnam.
  Later history: renamed *Vung Tau* (HQ 503). Capt by North Vietnam, Apr 1975. SE2001.
  6★Vietnam Dec 1966–Jan, Apr–Jul 1967, Dec 1967, Mar–Jun, Aug–Dec 1968, Feb–Mar 1969.
LST 607   Decomm 11 Jan 1946. SCAJAP, Q008. MSTS 1952. Stricken 30 Jun 1975. Trfd to Philippines 13 Sep 1976.
  Later history: renamed *Leyte del Sur* (LT 505). R1991.
LST 611 *Crook County*   Decomm 26 Oct 1956. Stricken 1 Jul 1958.
  3★Korea K-1 K-3 K-6.
LST 613   Decomm 6 Jan 1946. SCAJAP, Q038. MSTS 1952. Stricken 30 Jun 1975. Trfd to Singapore 4 Jun 1976.
  Later history: renamed *Persistence* (L 205). R1998.
LST 616   Decomm 19 Jan 1946. SCAJAP, Q019. MSTS 1952. Stricken 1 May 1961. Trfd to Indonesia 17 Jun 1951.
  Later history: renamed *Teluk Baier* (502). SE2001.
LST 623   Decomm Feb 1946. SCAJAP, Q075. MSTS 1952. Damaged by grounding at Sokcho-ri, Korea, 18 Mar 1953. Stricken 30 Jun 1975. Trfd to Singapore 4 Jun 1976.
  Later history: renamed *Perseverance* (L 206).
LST 625   Decomm 11 Feb 1946. SCAJAP, Q052. MSTS 1952. Stricken 19 May 1954. FFU.
LST 626   Decomm 2 Mar 1946. MSTS 1952. Stricken 1 Jun 1972. Sold 10 May 1973.
LST 629   Decomm 4 Mar 1946. SCAJAP, Q083. MSTS 1952. Stricken 30 Jun 1975. Trfd to Singapore 4 Jun 1976.
  Later history: renamed *Excellence* (L 202). SE2001.
  ◆Passage to Freedom.
LST 630   Decomm 13 Feb 1946. SCAJAP, Q059. MSTS 1952. Stricken 15 Jun 1973. Sold 10 Oct 1973.
LST 643   Decomm Jan 1946. SCAJAP, Q018. MSTS 1952. Stricken 15 Jun 1973. Sold 15 Aug 1973.
LST 649   Decomm Mar 1946. MSTS 1952. Stricken 30 Jun 1975. Trfd to Singapore 4 Jun 1976.
  Later history: renamed *Resolution* (A 84/L 204). R1993.

Figure 7.18: *USNS LST-629* (T-LST 629), operated by the MSTS with civilian crew. Notice goal post mast, and merchant-style name on bow.

LST 652   Decomm 5 Mar 1946. SCAJAP, Q086. MSTS 1952. Stricken 1 May 1961. Trfd to Indonesia 17 Jun 1961.
Later history: renamed *Teluk Kau* (504). SE2001.

LST 657   Decomm Feb 1946. SCAJAP, Q071. MSTS 1952. Stricken 1 May 1961. Trfd to Indonesia 17 Jun 1961.
Later history: renamed *Teluk Menado*. R1983.

LST 664   Decomm 19 Apr 1955, MSTS. Stricken 15 Jun 1973. Sold 10 Oct 1973.
Later history: merchant *Kargadan* se03.

LST 685 *Curry County*   Decomm 22 Jul 1946. NRT 1947–50. Stricken 1 Nov 1958. Sold 1959.
Later history: Merchant *Sulmar*. BU 1973 Argentina.

LST 689 *Daggett County*   Decomm Mar 1946. Stricken 1 Oct 1959. Trfd to Japan 1 Apr 1961.
Later history: renamed *Oosumi* (4001). Trfd to Philippines 1978, renamed *Davao Oriental* (LT 506). R1991.

LST 692 *Daviess County*   Out of comm Dec 1946–1951. MSTS. Decomm and stricken 1 Jun 1964; reinstated 27 Dec 1965. Stricken 30 Jun 1975. Trfd to Philippines 13 Sep 1976.
Later history: renamed *Benguet* (LT 507). SE2001.
2★Korea K-7 K-8; ◆Passage to Freedom.

LST 694   Decomm 1 Dec 1947. To Army 22 Apr 1948–1 Mar 1950, MSTS Stricken 4 Feb 1958. Sold 1959.
Later history: Merchant *Maria Laris*. BU 1962.

LST 715 *De Kalb County*   Decomm 17 Apr 1946. To Army 28 Jun 1946–25 Jul 1950 Recomm 30 Aug 1950. MSTS Dec 1965. Stricken 1 Nov 1973. Sold 30 Apr 1984, BU.
6★Korea K-1 K-2 K-3 K-4 K-7 K-8.

LST 722 *Dodge County*   Out of comm 13 Jul 1946–16 Nov 1951 and 3 Jan 1956–27 Dec 1961. NRT 1947. Decomm Nov 1969. Stricken 15 Sep 1974. Trfd to Thailand 17 Dec 1975.
Later history: renamed *Prathong* (LST 5/715). SE2001.
◆Cuban Missile Crisis Oct–Dec 1962.

LST 731 *Douglas County*   Decomm 2 Jun 1950. Rec **LST 731**, 6 Mar 1952. Stricken 1 Nov 1958. FFU.

LST 735 *Dukes County*   Out of comm 18 Jul 1946–3 Nov 1950. Minesweeper support ship. Decomm 1957. Trfd to Taiwan May 1957.
Later history: renamed *Chung Hsi, Kaohsiung* (AGC 219), 1964. SE1987.
3★Korea K-8 K-9 K-10.

LST 742 *Dunn County*   Out of comm 25 Apr 1946–1 Sep 1950. To Army 28 Jun 1946–1 Jul 1950, MSTS. Decomm and stricken 1 Feb 1961. Sold 6 Sep 1961.

Later history: Merchant barge *ZB-101A*.
5★Korea K-1 K-2 K-3 K-4 K-7.

LST 758 *Duval County*   Out of comm 13 Jul 1946–3 Nov 1950. Decomm 28 Oct 1969. Stricken 1 Nov 1976. Sold 18 Aug 1981.
4★Korea K-6 K-8 K-9 K-10; ◆Passage to Freedom, Cuban Missile Crisis Oct–Dec 1962.

LST 759 *Eddy County*   Decomm 29 Mar 1946. Stricken 1 Oct 1958. FFU.

LST 761 *Esmeraldo County*   Decomm 16 Jul 1946. Stricken 1959. Sunk as target 1959.

LST 762 *Floyd County*   Out of comm Dec 1946–3 Nov 1950. Decomm 3 Sep 1969. Stricken 1 Apr 1975. Sold 4 Dec 1975.
Later history: Merchant *LST-1*, renamed *Petrola 141* 1978. BU 1988.
1★Korea K-7; 3★Vietnam; ◆OpCastle 1954.

LST 772 *Ford County*   Out of comm 3 Jul 1946–3 Nov 1950. Decomm 1957 and stricken 19 Mar 1958. Destroyed as target.
★Korea K-5 K-6 K-7 K-8 K-9 K-10; ★Vietnam Jul–Sep 1965, Apr–Sep 1966, Apr–Sep 1968; ◆Passage to Freedom.

LST 783   Decomm 22 Aug 1946. NRT 1947. Stricken 16 Jun 1950. Sold 27 Jun 1950, BU Philadelphia.

LST 784 *Garfield County*   Decomm 29 Mar 1946. Stricken 1959; sunk as target.

LST 786 *Garrett County*   Out of comm 9 Jul 1946–15 Oct 1966. Converted to patrol craft tender, rec **AGP 786**, 25 Sep 1970. Trfd to Vietnam 24 Apr 1971.
Later history: renamed *Can Tho* (HQ 801). Escaped to Philippines, Apr 1975. Trfd to Philippines 13 Sep 1977, renamed *Kalinga Apayo* (LT 516). SE2001.
7★Vietnam Mar–Oct 1967, Dec 1968–Sep 1969, Jan–Jul 1970, Nov 1970, Jan–Feb 1971; PUC 31 Jan 1968–29 Feb 1968.

LST 794 *Gibson County*   Decomm 9 Jul 1946. Stricken 1 Nov 1958; sunk as target 22 May 1959.

LST 799 *Greer County*   Out of comm 22 Apr 1946–30 Aug 1950. To Army 6 May 1946–26 Aug 1950. Decomm 18 Jan 1960. Stricken 1 Nov 1960; Sold to West Germany 1960.
Later history: renamed *Bamberg* (A 1403/N 122). Conversion to minelayer canc. BU 1968.
9★Korea K-1 K-2 K-3 K-4 K-5 K-6 K-7 K-8 K-10.

LST 802 *Hamilton County*   Out of comm 21 Jul 1946–30 Aug 1950. To Army 21 Jul 1946–1 Jul 1950, MSTS. Decomm and trfd to Japan 30 Jun 1960.
Later history: renamed *Hayatomo* (MST 461). SE1972.
7★Korea K-1 K-2 K-3 K-4 K-6 K-7 K-8; ◆Taiwan Straits Sep–Oct 1958.

LST 803 *Hampden County*   Out of comm 15 Jun 1949–15 Nov 1950. Decomm 2 Jan 1958. Stricken 17 Apr 1958; sunk as target off California, 26 Sep 1958.
5★Korea K-5 K-6 K-7 K-9 K-10; ◆Passage to Freedom.

LST 819 *Hampshire County*   Out of comm 15 Nov 1946–8 Sep 1950 and 24 Jun 1955–9 Jul 1966. Decomm 19 Dec 1970. Stricken 1 Apr 1975, Sold 4 Dec 1975.
Later history: Merchant *LST-2*, renamed *Petrola 142* 1979. BU 1996, Aliaga, Turkey.
4★Korea K-4 K-5 K-7 K-8; 10★Vietnam Nov 1966–Aug 1967, Nov 1967–Jan 1968, Mar–Apr, Jun–Jul 1968, Feb–May, Jun–Aug, Oct–Nov 1969, Apr–Jun 1970; PUC 25 Jan 1969–19 Apr 1969.

LST 821 *Harnett County*   Out of comm 8 Jul 1946–20 Aug 1966. Converted to patrol craft tender, rec **AGP 821**, 25 Sep 1970. Decomm and trfd to Vietnam 12 Oct 1970.
Later history: renamed *My Tho* (HQ 800). Escaped to Philippines 1975. Trfd to Philippines 15 Nov 1975, renamed *Dumagat* (AL 57), then *Sierra Madre* 1989. SE2001.
9★Vietnam Jan 1967–Feb 1968, Apr 1968–May 1969, Aug 1969–Jul 1970; PUC 31 Jan 1968–29 Feb 1968.

LST 822 *Harris County*   Out of comm 27 Jul 1946–23 Nov 1950. Decomm 21 Feb 1956, MSTS. Stricken 30 Jun 1975; Trfd to Philippines 13 Sep 1976.

Later history: renamed *Aurora* (LT 508). R1991.

4★Korea K-4 K-5 K-8 K-9; ◆Passage to Freedom.

LST 824 *Henry County*   Out of comm 15 May 1946–5 Sep 1959. Decomm and stricken 1 Apr 1975. Trfd to Malaysia 7 Oct 1976.

Later history: renamed *Sri Banggi* (A 1501). SE2001.

4★Vietnam Sep–Nov 1965, Feb–Jul 1966, Nov 1967–Jan 1968.

LST 825 *Hickman County*   Out of comm 22 May 1946–3 Nov 1950 and 20 Sep 1955–22 Mar 1963. Decomm 26 Nov 1969 and trfd to Philippines.

Later history: renamed *Cagayan* (LT 97). R1991.

2★Korea K-8 K-9; 10★Vietnam May–Dec 1966, Mar–Aug, Oct–Dec 1967, Feb–Aug 1968, Dec 1968–Nov 1969; ◆Passage to Freedom, Dominican Rep May–Jun, Aug–Dec 1965.

LST 827 *Hillsborough County*   Out of comm 7 Jun 1949–3 Nov 1950. Decomm 28 Jan 1958. Stricken 28 Mar 1958; sunk as target in Gulf of California, 15 Aug 1958.

3★Korea K-2 K-4 K-7.

LST 835 *Hillsdale County*   Decomm Mar 1946. Stricken Oct 1959. Trfd to Japan 1 Apr 1961.

Later history: renamed *Shimokita* (4002). Trfd to Philippines 1978, renamed *Cavite* (LT 509). R1985c.

LST 836 *Holmes County*   Out of comm 25 Jul 1946–3 Nov 1950. Decomm 1 Jul 1971 and trfd to Singapore.

Later history: renamed *Endurance* (L201). R1998.

3★Korea K-5 K-6 K-10; 12★Vietnam Nov 1965–Mar 1966, Apr, Jun–Aug 1967, Oct 1968–Feb, May–Sep, Dec 1969, Feb–Mar, Jun, Sep–Nov 1970, Jan–May 1971; ◆Taiwan Straits Sep 1958.

LST 838 *Hunterdon County*   Out of comm 7 Aug 1946–10 Sep 1966. Converted to patrol craft tender, rec **AGP 838**, 25 Sep 1970. Decomm 30 Jun 1971. Trfd to Malaysia 1 Jul 1971.

Later history: renamed *Sri Langkawi* (A 1500).

7★Vietnam Mar–Dec 1967, Feb–Mar 1968, Nov 1968–Oct 1969, Jan 1970–Mar 1971; PUC 20–29 Feb 1968.

LST 839 *Iredell County*   Out of comm 24 Jul 1946–18 Jun 1966. Decomm Jul 1970 and trfd to Indonesia 15 Jul 1970.

Later history: renamed *Teluk Bone* (511). SE2001.

11★Vietnam Oct 1966–Feb 1967, May–Nov 1967, Jan–Apr 1968, Dec 1968–May 1970; PUC 25 Jan–15 Feb 1969.

LST 840 *Iron County*   Out of comm 1 Jun 1946–3 Nov 1950. Decomm 1 Jul 1958 and trfd to Taiwan.

Later history: renamed *Chung Fu* (223). R1997.

3★Korea K-5 K-6 K-9 K-10; ◆Passage to Freedom.

LST 845 *Jefferson County*   Decomm 28 Nov 1960. Stricken 1 Feb 1961; Sold 22 Aug 1961.

Later history: Merchant barge *ZB-107F*.

6★Korea K-1 K-2 K-3 K-4 K-8 K-9; ◆ Passage to Freedom.

LST 846 *Jennings County*   Out of comm 14 Oct 1949–3 Nov 1950 and 7 Dec 1953–11 Jun 1966. Damaged by fire in Vietnam Decomm and stricken 25 Sep 1970. FFU.

1★Korea K-6; 8★Vietnam Nov–Dec 1966, Mar–Aug, Oct 1967–Jun 1968, May 1969–Mar 1970, Jun–Aug 1970; ◆Passage to Freedom; 2 PUC 31 Jan–29 Feb 1968, 18 Oct–5 Dec 1968.

LST 848 *Jerome County*   Out of comm 10 Aug 1946–7 Dec 1959. Decomm 1 Apr 1970 and trfd to Vietnam.

Later history: renamed *Nha Trang* (HQ 505). Escaped to Philippines 1975. Trfd to Philippines 1976, renamed *Agusan del Sur* (LT 54). R1992.

5★Vietnam Sep–Oct 1965, Apr–Jun 1966, Dec 1967–Apr 1968; PUC 29 Jan–18 Feb 1968.

LST 849 *Johnson County*   Decomm 13 Jun 1946. Stricken and trfd to South Korea 13 Jan 1959.

Later history: renamed *Weebong* (*Wi Pong*) (812/LST 676). SE2001.

LST 850 *Juniata County*   Decomm 17 May 1946. Stricken 1 Nov 1958; sunk as target.

LST 853 *Kane County*   Decomm 24 Jul 1946. Trfd to Korea 22 Dec 1958.

Later history: renamed *Suyeong* (*Su Yong*) (813/LST 677). SE2001.

LST 854 *Kemper County*   Out of comm 21 Oct 1949–20 Nov 1950. Decomm 24 May 1969. Stricken 1 Apr 1975. Trfd to Barbados 6 Jan 1976.

Later history: renamed *Northpoint*. Sold to Panama 1980s, renamed *El Gato Blanco*.

★Korea K-5 K-6 K-7 K-9 K-10; 5★Vietnam Nov 1965–Apr 1966, Feb–Jun 1967, Jul–Dec 1968.

LST 855 *Kent County*   Out of comm 15 Feb 1950–3 Nov 1950. Decomm 22 Jan 1958. Stricken 19 Mar 1958; sunk as target 19 Mar 1958.

6★Korea K-5 K-6 K-7 K-8 K-9 K-10; ◆Passage to Freedom.

LST 857 *King County*   Converted to experimental guided missile test ship, rec **EAG 157**, 17 May 1958. Decomm 28 Jul 1960. Stricken 1 Aug 1960. Sold 25 Apr 1961, BU Portland, Ore.

7★Korea K-1 K-3 K-6 K-7 K-8 K-9 K-10.

LST 859 *Lafayette County*   Decomm, stricken and trfd to Taiwan 15 Aug 1958.

Later history: renamed *Chung Cheng* (224). R1989.

6★Korea K-1 K-3 K-7 K-8 K-9 K-10.

LST 880 *Lake County*   Out of comm 1 Oct 1946–20 Aug 1951. MSTS 1950–51. Decomm 25 Nov 1958. Stricken 1959; sunk as target.

LST 883 *La Moure County*   Out of comm 20 Apr 1946–26 Aug 1950. Trfd to Army 18 Aug 1946–1 Jul 1950, MSTS. Decomm 7 Dec 1959. Stricken 1 Jan 1960. Sold 30 Nov 1960, BU Portland, Ore.

7★Korea K-1 K-2 K-3 K-4 K-7 K-8 K-10.

LST 887 *Lawrence County*   Out of comm 23 Jul 1946–3 Nov 1950. Decomm 22 Mar 1960. Stricken 1 Nov 1960. Trfd to Indonesia Dec 1960.

Later history: renamed *Tandjung Nusanive*. R1974.

3★Korea K-6 K-7 K-9; ◆Passage to Freedom.

LST 888 *Lee County*   Decomm 2 Sep 1946. NRT 1947. Stricken 1 Jun 1959. Sold 18 Apr 1961.

Later history: Merchant barge *Barge No. 20*.

LST 898 *Lincoln County*   Out of comm 9 May 1946–28 Aug 1950. To Army 25 Jun 1946–1 Jul 1950, MSTS. Decomm 24 Mar 1961. Stricken 1 Jun 1962. Trfd to Thailand 31 Aug 1962.

Later history: renamed *Chang* (LST 2/712). SE2006.

6★Korea K-1 K-2 K-3 K-4 K-7 K-8.

LST 900 *Linn County*   Decomm 15 May 1946. Trfd to Korea 2 Dec 1958.

Later history: renamed *Bukhan* (815/LST 678). SE2001.

LST 901 *Litchfield County*   Out of comm 9 Aug 1946–30 Nov 1951 and 20 Dec 1955–5 Mar 1966. Decomm 6 Dec 1969. Stricken 1 Apr 1975; Sold 14 Jan 1977.

Later history: merchant *Petrola 132*. BU 1996 Aliaga, Turkey.

2★Korea K-8 K-9; 6★Vietnam Jul–Nov 1966, Jan–Feb, Apr–May, Aug–Sep 1967, Jan–Mar, May–Oct 1968, Jul 1969; ◆Passage to Freedom.

LST 902 *Luzerne County*   Out of comm 3 Aug 1946–18 Jan 1952 and 30 Nov 1955–29 Mar 1963. Decomm 1970. Stricken 12 Aug 1970.

Later history: Merchant barge *ZB Fontana*, renamed *Katmai*.

2★Korea K-8 K-9; 12★Vietnam Apr–May, Jul–Nov 1966, Jan–Apr, Jun 1967–May 1968, Sep 1968–Jan, May–Dec 1969, Mar–May 1970, Feb 1972; ◆Passage to Freedom, Dominican Rep May–Jul 1965.

LST 903 *Lyman County*   Decomm 10 Sep 1946. Stricken 1 Nov 1958. Sunk as target off Baja California, 29 Mar 1958.

LST 904 *Lyon County*   Decomm 15 Nov 1946. Stricken 1 Nov 1958. Sunk as target off coast of Washington, 13 May 1959.

LST 905 *Madera County*   Out of comm 11 Sep 1946–30 Mar 1963. Decomm and trfd to Philippines 26 Nov 1969.

Later history: renamed *Ilocos Norte* (LT 98). R1992.

9★Vietnam May–Nov 1966, Jan–Jun, Aug–Dec 1967, Jan–Feb, Jun 1968–Nov 1969; ◆Dominican Rep Jun, Aug–Sep 1965.

LST 912 *Mahnomen County*   Out of comm 25 Aug 1955–27 Mar 1963. Lost by grounding in typhoon at Chulai, Vietnam, 30 Dec 1966. Decomm 31 Jan 1967. Stricken 31 Jul 1967.

2★Vietnam May–Jul, Sep 1966–Feb 1967.

LST 914 *Mahoning County*   Out of comm 28 Jun 1946–26 Aug 1950. To Army 28 Jun 1946–26 Aug 1950. Stricken 1 Oct 1959. Sold 22 Jun 1960, BU Portland, Ore.
6★Korea K-1 K-2 K-3 K-4 K-7 K-8.

LST 938 *Maricopa County*   NRT 1947. Out of comm Dec 1949–14 Dec 1951. Decomm 29 Feb 1956. Stricken 1 Jun 1962. Trfd to Vietnam 12 Jul 1962.
Later history: renamed *Da Nang* (HQ 501). Captured by North Vietnam 29 Apr 1975, *Tran Khanh Du.* SE2005.

LST 953 *Marinette County*   Decomm 12 Nov 1946. NRT 1947–1950. Stricken 1 Nov 1958. Sold.
Later history: Merchant barge *TMT Florida.*

LST 973   Out of comm 24 May 1946–6 Sep 1950. To Army 2 Aug 1946–6 Sep 1950. Decomm 7 Nov 1951 and trfd to France 7 Nov 1951.
Later history: renamed *Golo* (L-9008). R1960.
4★Korea K-1 K-2 K-3 K-4.

LST 975 *Marion County*   Decomm 16 Apr 1946. To Army 28 Apr 1946–1 Jul 1950, MSTS. Stricken 1 Jun 1962. Trfd to Vietnam 12 Jul 1962.
Later history: renamed *Camranh* (HQ 500). Escaped to Philippines, 29 Apr 1975. Trfd to Philippines, 15 Oct 1976, renamed *Zamboanga del Sur* (LT 86). SE2001.
6★Korea K-1 K-2 K-3 K-4 K-7 K-8.

LST 980 *Meeker County*   Out of comm 16 Dec 1955–23 Sep 1966. Decomm 15 Dec 1970. Stricken 1 Apr 1975. Sold 4 Dec 1975.
Later history: Merchant *LST 3*, renamed *Petrola 143* 1979.
9★Vietnam Apr–Jun, Sep–Dec 1967, Feb–May, Jul–Oct, Dec 1968–Jan 1969, Mar–Apr 1969, Jan–Mar, Jun–Jul 1970.

LST 983 *Middlesex County*   Out of comm 10 Jan 1956–27 Sep 1961. Decomm 15 Oct 1969. Stricken 15 Sep 1974. Trfd to Indonesia 1974.
Later history: renamed *Teluk Tomani*, merchant *Alimos* 19.

LST 987 *Millard County*   Decomm 3 Sep 1946. NRT 1947–1950. Stricken 1 Jun 1960. Sold to West Germany 18 Aug 1961. Not converted and sold 1968.
Later history: Merchant *Esperance III* 1973, dredge *Columbus* 1986, *Colombia* 2000, *Columbia* 2001. SE2003.

LST 988 *Mineral County*   NRT 1947. Out of comm 13 Jun 1950–7 Jun 1951. Decomm and stricken 27 Sep 1957; sunk as target.

LST 993   Decomm 1 Jun 1946. Trfd to China 7 Feb 1948 (31 May 1946).
Later history: renamed *Chung Hsun* (208). Probably lost 1959.

LST 1010   Decomm 24 Apr 1947. To Army 24 Apr 1947–1 Mar 1950, MSTS. Trfd to Korea 22 Mar 1955.
Later history: renamed *Unbong* (807/LST 671). SE2001.

LST 1032 *Monmouth County*   Out of comm 14 Oct 1955–21 Dec 1965. Decomm and stricken 12 Aug 1970.
11★Vietnam May–Nov 1966, Jan–Aug 1967, Dec 1967–May 1970. ◆Dominican Rep Jun–Jul, Oct 1965.

LST 1038 *Monroe County*   Decomm Jun 1949. Stricken 1 Nov 1958. Sold.
Later history: Merchant *Jose P.*, renamed *Adri XXIX* 1968.

LST 1041 *Montgomery County*   Decomm 31 Jun 1956. Stricken 1 Jun 1960. Trfd to West Germany 28 Aug 1961. Not converted and BU 1968.

LST 1048 *Morgan County*   Decomm 14 May 1946–26 Aug 1950. To Army 2 Aug 1946–1 Jul 1950, MSTS. Decomm 10 May 1956. Stricken 1 Aug 1959. Sold 10 Jun 1960, BU.
3★Korea K-8.

LST 1064 *Nansemond County*   Decomm 21 Aug 1946. Stricken 1 Oct 1959. Trfd to Japan 1 Apr 1961.
Later history: renamed *Shiretoko* (4003). Trfd to Philippines 24 Sep 1976 and renamed *Samar del Norte* (LT 510). R>2001.

LST 1066 *New London County*   Out of comm Mar 1946–21 Dec 1965. Decomm 27 Dec 1967, MSTS. Stricken 10 Jun 1973. Trfd to Chile 29 Aug 1973.
Later history: renamed *Comandante Hemmerdinger* (AP 88). R1983. Merchant *Maquiserv*, 1984.
2★Vietnam Apr–Jun, Aug 1966–Jan 1967; ◆Dominican Rep May–Sep 1965.

Figure 7.19: *USS Middlesex County* (LST 983) in the 1960s. Notice deckload of Army trucks, tripod mast.

Figure 7.20: *USS Monmouth County* (LST 1032). A standard war-built LST

LST 1067 *Nye County*   Out of comm 13 Aug 1946–21 Dec 1965. Decomm 27 Mar 1967, MSTS. Stricken 10 Jun 1973. Trfd to Chile 29 Aug 1973.
Later history: renamed *Comandante Araya* (AP 89). R1981.
2★Vietnam Mar 1966–Feb 1967; ◆Dominican Rep Jun, Nov 1965.

LST 1068 *Orange County*   Out of comm 9 Aug 1946–8 Sep 1950. Decomm and stricken 27 Sep 1957. Sunk as target 18 Jun 1958.
4★Korea K-4 K-5 K-7 K-8.

LST 1069 *Orleans Parish*   Out of comm 6 Aug 1946–11 Jan 1952. NRT 1947. Out of comm 16 Dec 1957–19 Dec 1958, converted to mine support vessel. Rec **MCS 6**, 19 Jan 1959. Decomm 20 May 1966, MSTS. Rec **LST 1069**, 1 Jun 1966. Stricken 30 Jun 1975. Trfd to Philippines, 13 Sep 1976.
Later history: renamed *Cotabato del Norte* (LT 511). R1991.

LST 1070   Rec **AG 146**, renamed *Electron*, 27 Jan 1949. Rec **AKS 27**, 18 Aug 1951. Stricken 1 Apr 1960; Sold Dec 1960.
Later history: Merchant barge *Foss 209*. SE1980.

LST 1071 *Ouachita County*   Out of comm 10 Jun 1946–3 Jan 1951. Decomm 5 Feb 1956. Stricken 1 Nov 1959.
Later history: Merchant barge *Foss 210.* SE1980.

LST 1072   Decomm 2 Apr 1951, MSTS. To USAF Sep 1966. Returned Stricken 30 Jun 1975. Trfd to Philippines 13 Sep 1976.
Later history: renamed *Tawi Tawi* (LT 512). R>2001.

LST 1073 *Outagamie County*   Out of comm 5 Aug 1946–3 Nov 1950. Decomm 3 Nov 1960 and trfd to Brazil.
Later history: renamed *Garcia d'Avila* (G 28). R1990, BU.
5★Korea K-4 K-5 K-6 K-9 K-10; 8★Vietnam Jan–Jun 1966, Dec 1968–Jan, Mar, Aug–Dec 1969, May–Aug 1970; ◆Korea Apr 1970.

Amphibious Ships   111

LST 1074 *Overton County*   Decomm 4 Sep 1946. Stricken 1 Nov 1958.
  Later history: Merchant barge *Foss 201*. SE1980.
LST 1076 *Page County*   Out of comm 13 Jun 1946–28 Nov 1960. Decomm 5 Mar 1971 and trfd to Greece.
  Later history: renamed *Kriti* (L 171). R1996.
  6★Vietnam Jun 1968–Jan 1970, May–Oct 1970; ◆Cuban Missile Crisis Nov–Dec 1962.
LST 1077 *Park County*   Out of comm 31 Jul 1946–6 Sep 1950 and 12 May 1955–9 Apr 1966. Decomm and trfd to Mexico 20 Sep 1971.
  Later history: renamed *Rio Panuco* (A 01).
  5★Korea K-2 K-4 K-5 K-7 K-8; 11★Vietnam Aug 1966–Mar 1967, May–Jun 1967, Jan–Apr, Jun–Nov 1968, Jun–Nov 1969, Feb–Mar, May, Aug–Nov 1970, Jan–Jun 1971.
LST 1078   Rec **AG 147**, renamed ***Proton***, 27 Jan 1949. Rec **AKS 28**, 18 Aug 1951. Stricken 1 Jan 1959.
  Later history: Merchant barge *Foss 200*.
LST 1079 *Payette County*   Out of comm Mar 1946–Oct 1950. Stricken 1 Nov 1959. Sold 18 May 1961.
  Later history: Merchant barge *557*.
LST 1080 *Pender County*   Out of comm 29 Aug 1946–3 Oct 1950. Decomm 2 Jan 1958. Trfd to Korea 30 Oct 1958.
  Later history: renamed *Hwasan* (816/LST 679). SE2001.
  5★Korea K-4 K-5 K-8 K-9; ◆Passage to Freedom.
LST 1081 *Pima County*   Out of comm 30 Jul 1946–7 Aug 1950. Decomm 12 Dec 1956. Stricken 1 Nov 1958; Sold Jun 1960
  Later history: Merchant barge *518N*, renamed merchant *Baltic Ferry* 1966, *Sable Ferry* 1972, *Nickel Ferry* 1977. Destroyed by fire at La Union, El Salvador, 1 Dec 1979.
LST 1082 *Pitkin County*   Out of comm 5 Aug 1946–6 Sep 1950 and 1 Sep 1955–9 Jul 1966. Decomm 1 Sep 1971. Stricken 1 Apr 1975. Sold 4 Dec 1975.
  Later history: Merchant *LST-4* 1976, renamed *Petrola 144* 1979. BU 1988 Gadani, Pakistan.
  4★Korea K-4 K-5 K-7 K-8; 10★Vietnam Nov–Dec 1966, Feb–Apr, Jun–Jul, Sep–Oct 1967, Dec 1967–Feb 1968, Apr 1968–Jan 1969, Jul–Nov 1969, Feb, Jun 1970, Nov 1970–Mar 1971.
LST 1083 *Plumas County*   Out of comm Aug 1946–8 Sep 1950. Decomm 22 Aug 1961. MSTS 1965–72. Stricken 1 Jun 1972. Sold 10 May 1973.
  3★Korea K-4 K-5 K-8.
LST 1084 *Polk County*   Out of comm 13 Aug 1946–3 Nov 1950. Decomm 30 Oct 1969. Stricken 15 Sep 1974. Sold 1 Dec 1975.
  Later history: Merchant *Grigoroussa* 1977. BU 1985 Perama, Greece.
  3★Korea K-6 K-9 K-10; 4★Vietnam Jan–Mar 1966, Jul–Sep 1967, Dec 1968–Apr 1969.
LST 1085   Rec **AG 148**, renamed ***Colington***, 27 Jan 1949. Rec **AKS 29**, 18 Aug 1951. Stricken 1 Apr 1960. Sold 26 May 1961.
  Later history: Merchant barge *ZB-104F*, renamed *Tuny* 1968.
LST 1086 *Potter County*   Decomm 7 Aug 1946. Stricken 1 Jun 1959. Trfd to Greece 9 Aug 1960.
  Later history: renamed *Ikaria* (L 154). R1999.
LST 1087   Decomm 11 Aug 1947. To USA 19 Apr 1948. Stricken 29 Sep 1947. To USAF.
  Later history: Merchant *Coos Bay*. BU 1979 Pakistan.
LST 1088 *Pulaski County*   Out of comm 29 Aug 1946–21 May 1963. Decomm Jul 1967, MSTS. Stricken 1 Nov 1973. Sold Jan 1975.
  2★Vietnam Apr 1966–Mar 1967; ◆Dominican Rep May–Aug 1965.
LST 1089 *Rice County*   Out of comm 16 Aug 1946–6 Sep 1950. Decomm 9 Mar 1960. Trfd to West Germany 7 Oct 1960.
  Later history: renamed *Bochum* (A 1404/N 120), converted to minelayer. Trfd to Turkey 12 Dec 1972, renamed *Sancaktar* (L-404/A-580/N-112/NL-121). SE2001.
  4★Korea K-4 K-5 K-7 K-8; ◆Taiwan Straits Sep–Oct 1958.
LST 1090 *Russell County*   Out of comm 22 Jul 1946–3 Nov 1950. Decomm 5 Apr 1960. Stricken 1 Nov 1960. Trfd to Indonesia 27 Dec 1960.
  Later history: renamed *Tandjung Radja*. Lost by grounding 1963.
  5★Korea K-4 K-5 K-6.
LST 1091 *Sagadahoc County*   Decomm 5 Jul 1946. Trfd to Taiwan 21 Oct 1958.
  Later history: renamed *Chung Chih* (226). SE2001.
LST 1096 *St. Clair County*   Out of comm 24 Aug 1946–3 Oct 1950. Decomm 26 Sep 1969. Stricken 1 Apr 1975. Sold 4 Dec 1975.
  Later history: Merchant *LST-5* 1976, renamed *Petrola 145* 1979. BU 1988.
  5★Korea K-8 K-9 10; 3★Vietnam Feb–Jul 1966, Jul–Aug, Nov–Dec 1968; ◆Passage to Freedom, Quemoy-Matsu Mar, May 1960.
LST 1097   Decomm 19 Dec 1946. Rec **AG 149**, renamed ***League Island***, 27 Jan 1949. Rec **AKS 30**, 18 Aug 1951. Stricken 1 Apr 1960; Sold 3 Mar 1961.
  Later history: Merchant *Magellan*.
LST 1101 *Saline County*   Out of comm 6 Jun 1946–3 Nov 1950. Decomm 9 Mar 1960. Trfd to West Germany 1 Oct 1960.
  Later history: renamed *Bottrop* (A 1405/N 121), converted to minelayer. Trfd to Turkey 13 Dec 1972, renamed *Bayraktar* (L- 403/A-579/N-111/NL-120). SE2001.
  5★Korea K-4 K-5 K-6 K-9 K-10.
LST 1102   Decomm 21 Nov 1947. Rec **AG 150**, renamed ***Chimon***, 27 Jan 1949. Rec **AKS 31**, 18 Aug 1951. Stricken 2 Nov 1959.
  Later history: Merchant barge *Julia I.*, renamed *567*.
LST 1110 *San Bernardino County*   Decomm 15 Aug 1958. Trfd to Taiwan 16 Sep 1958.
  Later history: renamed *Chung Chiang* (225). R1993.
LST 1120   Decomm 14 Jan 1948. Stricken 19 Feb 1948. Sold 20 Aug 1948, BU Seattle.
LST 1122 *San Joaquin County*   Out of comm 15 Jun 1949–8 Nov 1950. Decomm 26 Sep 1969. Stricken 1 May 1972. Sold 5 Sep 1974.
  Later history: Merchant barge *50*.
  5★Korea K-4 K-5 K-6 K-9 K-10; 1★Vietnam Jan–Feb 1967.
LST 1123 *Sedgwick County*   Out of comm 9 Sep 1955–4 Jun 1966. Decomm 6 Dec 1969. Stricken 15 May 1975. Trfd to Malaysia 7 Oct 1976.
  Later history: renamed *Rajah Jarom* (S 1502). R1999.
  6★Korea K-1 K-2 K-3 K-4 K-8 K-9; 7★Vietnam Dec 1966–Jan, Mar–Apr, Jun–Oct 1967, Jan–Mar 1968, Aug–Dec 1968, Apr–Aug 1969; PUC 23 Apr 1969–6 May 1969.
LST 1126 *Snohomish County*   Decomm and stricken 1 Jul 1970; Sold Jan 1971, BU Taiwan.
  8★Vietnam Apr–Aug 1965, Feb–Jul 1966, Feb–Jun 1967, Nov 1968–Feb, May–Sep 1969, Feb–Mar 1970.
LST 1128 *Solano County*   Decomm 29 Jul 1946. Stricken 1 Nov 1958. Trfd to Indonesia 31 Mar 1960.
  Later history: renamed *Teluk Langsa* (501). SE2001.
LST 1129 *Somervell County*   Decomm 31 Jul 1946. Stricken 1 Nov 1958. FFU.
LST 1130   Damaged by grounding at Yap, 12 Mar 1948. Stricken 12 Mar 1948. Destroyed 24 Mar 1948.
LST 1134 *Stark County*   Decomm and trfd to Thailand 16 May 1966.
  Later history: renamed *Pangan*. (LST 3/713). SE2001.
  3★Korea K-1 K-2 K-3.
LST 1135   Decomm 28 Apr 1948. Stricken 12 Aug 1948; Sold 29 Jun 1948, BU.
LST 1138 *Steuben County*   Decomm. Stricken 1 Feb 1961. Sold 11 Aug 1961. BU 1962 Portland, Ore.
  5★Korea K-1 K-2 K-3 K-7 K-10.
LST 1140   Decomm 3 Jun 1949. Stricken 15 Aug 1949; Sold 26 Jan 1950.
  Later history: Merchant barge *Foss 206*.
LST 1141 *Stone County*   Out of comm 24 Aug 1949–3 Nov 1950. Decomm and trfd to Thailand 12 Mar 1970.
  Later history: renamed *Lanta* (LST 4/714). SE2001.
  4★Korea K-6 K-7 K-9 K-10; 5★Vietnam Sep 1965, Jun–Oct 1966, Apr–Sep 1968.

LST 1142 *Stafford County* Decomm 15 Nov 1946. Stricken 1 Nov 1958. Sold 1963.
  Later history: Merchant barge *Foss 202*.
LST 1144 *Sublette County* Decomm 11 Feb 1955. Stricken 1 Jun 1960. Trfd to Taiwan 21 Sep 1961.
  Later history: renamed *Chung Yeh* (231). SE2001.
LST 1146 *Summit County* Decomm Dec 1969. Stricken 1 Nov 1976; Trfd to Ecuador 14 Feb 1977.
  Later history: renamed *Hualcopo* (T 55/TR 61). SE2001.
  1★Korea K-7; 4★Vietnam Jan–Jul 1966, Nov 1967–Mar 1968.
LST 1148 *Sumner County* Out of comm 11 May 1946–3 Oct 1950. Decomm 9 Oct 1969. Stricken 15 Sep 1974; Sold Jun 1975.
  2★Korea K-9 K-10; ★Vietnam Jul 1965–Jan 1966, Sep–Oct 1966, Mar 1968–Feb, May–Jun, Sep–Dec 1969.
  ◆Passage to Freedom.
LST 1150 *Sutter County* Out of comm 13 Sep 1946–16 Apr 1966. Decomm 12 Mar 1971. Stricken 15 Sep 1974.
  Later history: Merchant *Marland II*, renamed *Amal* 1979. Broke moorings, drifted aground at Jeddah broke in two, 10 Nov 1986 and forepart sank 2 Jan 1987.
  8★Vietnam Oct, Dec 1966–Mar, May–Dec 1967, Apr–Aug, Oct 1968, Apr–May, Nov 1969–Feb, Jul–Aug 1970.
LST 1152 *Sweetwater County* Decomm 1 Jul 1946. Trfd to Taiwan 21 Oct 1958.
  Later history: renamed *Chung Ming* (227). SE2001.

Notes: Names assigned to 158 survivors, 1 Jul 1955, except for 36 Japanese-manned ships. Many had pole mast replaced by tripod to support radar.

No.	Name	Builder	Launched	Comm.
LST 1153	*Talbot County*	Boston NSYd	24 Apr 1947	3 Sep 1947
LST 1154	*Tallahatchie County*	Boston NSYd	19 Jul 1946	24 May 1949
LST 1155	—	Boston NSYd	—	—
Displacement	2,324 tons			
Dimensions	382′ (oa) × 54′ × 14′5″			
Machinery	2 screws; GT, 6,000 SHP; 14 knots			
Complement	272			
Armament	2–5″/38, 2-twin 40 mm, 2–20 mm guns			

Notes: Names assigned 1 Jul 1955.

LST 1153 Decomm 3 Apr 1970. Stricken 1 May 1973; Sold 9 Apr 1974, BU.
  ◆Cuban Missile Crisis Oct–Dec 1962, Dominican Rep Jul 1966.

LST 1154 Out of comm 9 Dec 1960–3 Feb 1962. Converted to advance aviation base ship; rec **AVB 2**, 3 Feb 1962. Decomm and stricken 15 Jan 1970. BU
LST 1155 Canceled 7 Jun 1946

No.	Name	Builder	Launched	Comm.
LST 1156	*Terrebonne Parish*	Bath IW	9 Aug 1952	21 Nov 1952
LST 1157	*Terrell County*	Bath IW	6 Dec 1952	14 Mar 1953
LST 1158	*Tioga County*	Bath IW	11 Apr 1953	20 Jun 1953
LST 1159	*Tom Green County*	Bath IW	2 Jul 1953	12 Sep 1953
LST 1160	*Traverse County*	Bath IW	3 Oct 1953	19 Dec 1953
LST 1161	*Vernon County*	Ingalls	25 Nov 1952	18 May 1953
LST 1162	*Wahkiakum County*	Ingalls	23 Jan 1953	13 Aug 1953
LST 1163	*Waldo County*	Ingalls	17 Mar 1953	17 Sep 1953
LST 1164	*Walworth County*	Ingalls	15 May 1953	26 Oct 1953
LST 1165	*Washoe County*	Ingalls	14 Jul 1953	30 Nov 1953
LST 1166	*Washtenaw County*	Christy	22 Nov 1952	29 Oct 1953
LST 1167	*Westchester County*	Christy	18 Apr 1953	10 Mar 1954
LST 1168	*Wexford County*	Christy	28 Nov 1953	15 Jun 1954
LST 1169	*Whitfield County*	Christy	22 Aug 1953	14 Sep 1954
LST 1170	*Windham County*	Christy	22 May 1954	15 Dec 1954
Displacement	2,590 tons; 5,800 f/l			
Dimensions	384′ (oa); 370′ (wl) × 55′ × 17′			
Machinery	2 screws; diesels; 6,000 BHP; 14 knots			
Endurance	10000/10			
Complement	115			
Armament	3 twin 3″/50			

Notes: Named 1 Jul 1955. 392 troops. Names assigned 1 Jul 1955.

Service Record:

LST 1156 *Terrebonne Parish* Decomm and trfd to Spain, 29 Oct 1971.
  Later history: renamed *Velasco* (L 11). SE1993.
  ◆Cuban Missile Crisis Nov–Dec 1962, Dominican Rep Mar, May–Jun, Aug–Sep 1966.
LST 1157 *Terrell County* Decomm 25 Mar 1971. Stricken 1 Nov 1976. Trfd to Greece 17 Mar 1977.
  Later history: renamed *Oinoussai* (*Inouse*) (L 104). R2003.
  12★Vietnam Nov 1961, Mar, Jul–Aug, Oct–Dec 1965, Mar–Dec 1966, Feb, May, Jul–Sep 1967, Mar–Jun 1968, Dec 1968–Feb, May–Jun, Sep–Dec 1969, Mar–May, Oct 1970; ◆OpCastle 1954, Quemoy-Matsu May–Jun, Aug–Sep 1959, Apr–May, Aug–Sep, Nov 1961, Mar, Jul 1962, Mar–May 1963; PUC 1 Jan–4 Feb 1969.

Figure 7.21: *USS Tallahatchie County* (LST 1154).

Figure 7.22: *USS Wahkiakum County* (LST 1162).

Amphibious Ships 113

LST 1158 *Tioga County* First shipboard test of Sea Sparrow missile, 10 May 1965. Decomm 23 Dec 1970. MSTS, 1972. Stricken 1 Nov 1973. NDRF. Sold 17Aug 2005, BU.
3★Vietnam Jan–Mar 1966, Apr–Sep 1967; ◆Taiwan Straits 26 Dec 1958.

LST 1159 *Tom Green County* Decomm and trfd to Spain 5 Jan 1972.
Later history: renamed *Conde del Venadito* (L 13). R1990.
12★Vietnam Mar–May 1965, Jul 1965–Feb 1966, Apr–Jun, Aug 1966–Jan, Mar, May–Jul 1967, Feb–Jun 1968, Sep–Oct, Dec 1968–Jan 1969, Jul–Aug, Nov 1969, Apr–May, Oct–Dec 1970, Apr–May 1971; ◆Passage to Freedom, Taiwan Straits Sep 1958.

LST 1160 *Traverse County* Decomm 1 Dec 1970. MSTS Stricken 1 Nov 1973. Trfd to Peru 7 Aug 1984.
Later history: renamed *Eten* (DT 144). SE2001.
◆Lebanon Jul–Oct 1958, Cuban Missile Crisis Oct–Dec 1962.

LST 1161 *Vernon County* Decomm 14 Jun 1973. Trfd to Venezuela 29 Jun 1973.
Later history: renamed *Amazonas* (T21/T51). Sunk as target 2004.
14★Vietnam Jul–Oct 1958, Aug–Sep 1964, Feb–May 1965, Jul–Aug, Oct 1965–Feb 1966, Apr–May, Jul–Nov 1966, Jun–Aug 1967, Dec 1967–Feb, May–Jun, Aug–Oct 1968, Jan 1969, Jul–Aug, Nov 1969–Feb, Sep–Nov 1970, Apr–May, Sep–Nov 1971, Jan–May, Oct–Nov 1972; ◆Quemoy-Matsu Mar, May, Dec 1962, Mar 1963; PUC 28 Feb 1969–25 Mar 1969.

LST 1162 *Wahkiakum County* Decomm 16 Oct 1970. MSTS 1972 Stricken 1 Nov 1973. NDRF. BU 2005 Brownsville, Tex.
◆Cuban Missile Crisis Oct–Dec 1962, Dominican Rep May 1965.

LST 1163 *Waldo County* Decomm 21 Dec 1970. MSTS Stricken 1 Nov 1973. Trfd to Peru 7 Aug 1984.
Later history: renamed *Pisco* (DT 142). SE2001.
◆Cuba Nov–Dec 1961, Dominican Rep May–Jun 1965.

LST 1164 *Walworth County* Decomm 2 Apr 1971. MSTS Stricken 1 Nov 1973. Trfd to Peru 7 Aug 1984.
Later history: renamed *Paita* (DT 141). SE2001.
◆Lebanon Jul–Oct 1958, Cuba Jan–Mar 1962, Cuban Missile Crisis Nov–Dec 1962.

LST 1165 *Washoe County* Decomm 25 Mar 1971, MSTS. Stricken 1 Nov 1973. Trfd to Peru 7 Aug 1984.
Later history: renamed *Callao* (DT 143). SE2001.
12★Vietnam Aug–Sep 1964, Mar–Sep 1965, Feb–May, Jul, Sep–Oct 1966, Jan–Jul, Sep–Dec 1967, Mar–Apr, Jun–Sep, Nov 1969–Aug, Oct 1970; PUC 18 Oct 1968–5 Dec 1968.

LST 1166 *Washtenaw County* Decomm 6 Feb 1973, IS. Converted to minesweeper support ship, rec **MSS 2**, 9 Feb 1973. Stricken 30 Aug 1973. Sold 1 Oct 1974.
Later history: Merchant *Al Manhal*, renamed *El Centroamericano*. CTL Jan 1984. Being restored for museum at Portland, Ore. 2005.
15★Vietnam Jun 1962, Mar–May 1965, Jul–Sep, Nov 1965–Jan 1966, Jun 1966–Jan, Apr, Jul, Oct 1967–Mar 1968, Jun, Oct–Dec 1968, Feb, Sep–Nov 1969, Feb, May, Sep 1970, Feb–Apr, Aug, Oct–Dec 1971; ◆Quemoy-Matsu Sep 1958, Jun, Nov–Dec 1961, Mar 1962, Lebanon Jun 1962; 2 PUC 29 Jan 1968–4 Mar 1968. PUC 5 Feb 1969–23 Feb 1969, 1 Mar 1969–31 Mar 1969.

LST 1167 *Westchester County* Damaged by underwater explosion in Mytho River, 1 Nov 1968. Decomm 30 Nov 1973. Trfd to Turkey 27 Aug 1974.
Later history: renamed *Serdar* (L-402). R2005.
15★Vietnam Jul–Aug 1962, Aug–Sep 1964, Mar–May 1965, Jul–Aug, Oct 1965–Mar 1966, May–Oct 1966, Feb, Aug 1967–Jan 1968, Mar–Jun, Sep–Nov 1968, Mar–May, Jul–Aug, Oct 1969–Feb 1970, Jul–Oct 1970, Feb–Mar, Jun–Aug 1971, Apr–May, Jul–Sep 1972; ◆Taiwan Straits Aug 1958, Quemoy-Matsu 22 Jul 1961.

LST 1168 *Wexford County* Decomm and trfd to Spain 29 Oct 1971.
Later history: renamed *Martin Alvarez* (L 12). R1995.
5★Vietnam Sep–Nov 1965, Dec 1967–May 1968, Jul–Aug, Nov 1970.

LST 1169 *Whitfield County* Decomm 15 Mar 1973. Trfd to Greece 17 Mar 1977.
Later history: renamed *Kos* (L 116). R2000. Sunk as target 24 Jun 2004.
12★Vietnam Aug–Sep 1964, Mar–Sep 1965, Nov 1965–Mar 1966, Sep 1966–Feb, Apr–Jun 1967, Aug 1967–Mar 1968, May, Jul–Feb 1969, May–Jul 1969, Feb, Dec 1970–Jan 1971, May–Jun 1971, Jan, Jul–Sep 1972; ◆Lebanon Jun–Jul 1962; PUC 8 May 1969–5 Jul 1969.

LST 1170 *Windham County* Decomm 1 Jun 1973 and trfd to Turkey
Later history: renamed *Ertugrul* (L 401). SE2001.
14★Vietnam Aug–Sep 1964, Mar–May 1965, Jul–Aug, Oct 1965–Mar 1966, May 1966, Feb–Apr, Jun–Jul, Nov–Dec 1967, Jun–Aug 1968, May, Aug–Nov 1969, Dec 1970–Feb, Jul–Sep 1971, Feb–May, Aug–Nov 1969, Dec 1970–Feb, Jul–Sep 1971, Feb–May, Sep–Nov 1972; ◆Lebanon Jun 1962; PUC 25 Mar 1969–10 May 1969.

No.	Name	Builder	Launched	Comm.
LST 1171	*De Soto County*	Avondale	28 Feb 1957	10 Jun 1958
LST 1172	—	—	—	—
LST 1173	*Suffolk County*	Boston NSYd	5 Sep 1956	15 Aug 1957
LST 1174	*Grant County*	Avondale	12 Oct 1956	17 Dec 1957
LST 1175	*York County*	Newport News	5 Mar 1957	8 Nov 1957
LST 1176	*Graham County*	Newport News	9 Sep 1957	17 Apr 1958
LST 1177	*Lorain County*	Amer; Lorain	22 Jun 1957	3 Oct 1958
LST 1178	*Wood County*	Amer; Lorain	14 Dec 1957	5 Aug 1959

Displacement	4,164 tons; 8,000 f/l
Dimensions	445′ (oa); 426′ (wl) × 62′ × 16′8″
Machinery	2 screws; diesels; 13,700 BHP; 17.5 knots
Endurance	9000/15
Complement	184
Armament	3 twin 3″/50

Notes: *Graham County* converted to gunboat support ship (AGP); 575 troops; *Wood County* conversion to support ship for Pegasus-class PHMs canceled, 1977.

Service Records:

LST 1171 *De Soto County* Decomm 17 Jul 1972 and trfd to Italy.
Later history: renamed *Grado* (L 9890). R1989.
1★Vietnam Sep 1969; ◆Cuban Missile Crisis Oct–Dec 1962.

LST 1172 not built, canceled 1955.

LST 1173 *Suffolk County* Decomm 25 Aug 1972. Stricken 16 Feb 1989. NDRF. Sold 26 Feb 1999, BU Brownsville, Tex.
◆Lebanon Sep–Oct 1958, Cuban Missile Crisis Oct–Dec 1962, Dominican Rep Feb 1966.

Figure 7.23: *USS Grant County* (LST 1174) with sectional pontoons hung on the side.

Figure 7.24: *USS Wood County* (LST 1178), 13 May 1966.

Figure 7.25: Stern view of *USS Boulder* (LST 1190) fitting out at San Diego, August 1970, showing stern port, and twin funnels.

Figure 7.26: *USS Newport* (LST 1179), August 1969. This class abandoned the bow doors for bow horns to support the landing ramp.

LST 1174 *Grant County*   Decomm 27 Jul 1972. Trfd to Brazil 15 Jan 1973.
  Later history: renamed *Duque de Caxias* (G 26). R2000
  ◆Cuba Jan–Mar 1962, Cuban Missile Crisis Oct–Dec 1962, Dominican Rep Jun 1965.

LST 1175 *York County*   Decomm 17 Jul 1972. Stricken 8 May 1992. Trfd to Italy 17 Jul 1972.
  Later history: renamed *Caorle* (L 9891). BU Naples.
  1★Vietnam; ◆Lebanon Sep–Oct 1958, Cuban Missile Crisis Oct–Dec 1962, Dominican Rep May–Jun, Oct 1965.

LST 1176 *Graham County*   Converted to patrol craft tender, rec **AGP 1176**, 1 Aug 1972. Decomm 1 Mar 1977. Stricken 1 Mar 1977, BU.
  ◆Dominican Rep Feb 1966.

LST 1177 *Lorain County*   Decomm 1 Sep 1972. Stricken 16 Feb 1989. NDRF. BU 2002 Brownsville, Tex.
  ◆Cuba Aug 1961, May, Aug 1962, Cuban Missile Crisis Oct–Dec 1962.

LST 1178 *Wood County*   Decomm 1 May 1972. Conversion to AGHS (hydrofoil support ship) canc 1977. Stricken 16 Feb 1989. NDRF. Sold 2002, BU Brownsville, Tex.
  ◆Cuban Missile Crisis Oct–Dec 1962, Dominican Rep Apr–Jun 1965.

No.	Name	Builder	Keel Laid	Launched	Comm.
LST 1179	Newport	Phila.NSYd	1 Nov 1966	3 Feb 1968	7 Jun 1969
LST 1180	Manitowoc	Phila.NSYd	27 Feb 1967	4 Jan 1969	24 Jan 1970
LST 1181	Sumter	Phila.NSYd	14 Nov 1967	13 Dec 1969	20 Jun 1970
LST 1182	Fresno	National Stl	16 Dec 1967	28 Sep 1968	22 Nov 1969
LST 1183	Peoria	National Stl	22 Feb 1968	23 Nov 1968	21 Feb 1970
LST 1184	Frederick	National Stl	13 Apr 1968	8 Mar 1969	25 Mar 1970
LST 1185	Schenectady	National Stl	2 Aug 1968	24 May 1969	13 Jun 1970
LST 1186	Cayuga	National Stl	28 Sep 1968	12 Jul 1969	8 Aug 1970
LST 1187	Tuscaloosa	National Stl	23 Jan 1969	6 Sep 1969	24 Oct 1970
LST 1188	Saginaw	National Stl	24 May 1969	7 Feb 1970	23 Jan 1971
LST 1189	San Bernardino	National Stl	12 Jul 1969	28 Mar 1970	27 Mar 1971
LST 1190	Boulder	National Stl	6 Sep 1969	22 May 1970	4 Jun 1971
LST 1191	Racine	National Stl	11 Dec 1969	15 Aug 1970	9 Jul 1971
LST 1192	Spartanburg County	National Stl	7 Feb 1970	7 Nov 1970	1 Sep 1971
LST 1193	Fairfax County	National Stl	28 Mar 1970	18 Dec 1970	16 Oct 1971
LST 1194	La Moure County	National Stl	22 May 1970	13 Feb 1971	18 Dec 1971
LST 1195	Barbour County	National Stl	15 Aug 1970	15 May 1971	12 Feb 1972
LST 1196	Harlan County	National Stl	7 Nov 1970	24 Jul 1971	8 Apr 1972
LST 1197	Barnstable County	National Stl	19 Dec 1970	2 Oct 1971	27 May 1972
LST 1198	Bristol County	National Stl	13 Feb 1971	4 Dec 1971	5 Aug 1972

Displacement	4,793 tons, 8,450 f/l
Dimensions	522′2″(oa) × 69′6″ × 17′6″
Machinery	2 screws, diesels, 16,500 BHP, 22 knots
Complement	253
Armament	2 twin 3″/50. repl by 2 Phalanx 1980s.

Notes: Bow horns to support bow ramp instead of doors, bow and stern ramps. 386 troops.

Service Record:

LST 1179 *Newport*   Collided with hydrofoil *Pegasus* north of Cuba, 30 Sep 1981. Decomm 1 Oct 1992. Stricken 13 Jul 2001 and trfd to Mexico, 23 May 2001.

Later history: renamed *Sonora*, renamed *Papaloapan* (A 411), 2001.
◆Beirut evac 27 Jul 1976, Iran/Indian Ocean Oct–Dec 1980.

LST 1180 *Manitowoc* Decomm 30 Jun 1993. Trfd to Taiwan.10 Jul 1996
Later history: renamed *Chung Ho* (232). SE2001.
2★Vietnam Mar, Jun 1971, Apr–Oct 1972; ◆Beirut evac Jun 1982, Feb 1984, Grenada Oct–Nov 1983, Lebanon Aug–Nov 1982, Nov 1983–Apr 1984, Gulf War Sep 1990–Mar 1991.

LST 1181 *Sumter* Decomm 30 Sep 1993. Trfd to Taiwan 14 Jul 1995.
Later history: renamed *Chung Ping* (233). SE2001.
2★Vietnam May 1971, May–Sep 1972; ◆Lebanon Oct 1982–Feb 1983, Liberia 1990.

LST 1182 *Fresno* Decomm 8 Apr 1993. Stricken 2003.
2★Vietnam Feb–Apr 1971, Jan–Feb 1973.

LST 1183 *Peoria* Decomm 28 Jan 1994. Trfd to Venezuela 31 Dec 1995
Later history: renamed *Golfo de Venezuela*, never delivered and lease terminated 31 May 1996. Stricken 6 Nov 2002. Sunk as target, 12 Jul 2004.
2★Vietnam Apr–Jun, Aug–Sep 1971; ◆Evac of Cambodia Apr 1975, evac of Vietnam 29–30 Apr 1975, Gulf War Jan–Jul 1991.

LST 1184 *Frederick* Decomm and stricken 5 Nov 2002 and trfd to Mexico.
Later history: renamed *Usumacinta* (A 412).
3★Vietnam Oct 1970, Apr–Jun, Aug, Oct 1971, Apr–May 1972; ◆Evac of Cambodia Apr 1975, evac of Vietnam 29–30 Apr 1975, Iran/Indian Ocean Aug–Oct 1980, Lebanon Sep–Oct 1983, Gulf War Jan–May 1991, Liberia Mar–Jun 1994.

LST 1185 *Schenectady* Decomm 10 Dec 1993. Stricken 13 Jul 2001. Sunk as target west of Hawaii, 22 Nov 2004.
3★Vietnam May, Dec 1971–Jul 1972; ◆Iran/Indian Ocean Aug–Oct 1981, Gulf War Sep–Oct 1990.

LST 1186 *Cayuga* Decomm 29 Jul 1994. Trfd to Brazil 26 Aug 1994
Later history: renamed *Mattoso Maia* (G 28). SE2001.
2★Vietnam Mar 1971, May 1972; ◆Gulf War Sep–Nov 1990, Jan–Mar 1991, Liberia Oct 1993–Feb 1994.

LST 1187 *Tuscaloosa* Decomm 18 Feb 1994. Stricken 2003.
4★Vietnam Jun, Oct 1971, Feb, Apr–Jun 1972; ◆Evac of Vietnam 29–30 Apr 1975, Iran/Indian Ocean Apr–Jun 1981, Gulf War Feb–Mar 1992.

LST 1188 *Saginaw* Decomm and stricken 28 Jun 1994. Trfd to Australia 24 Aug 1994.
Later history: renamed *Kanimbla* (L 51). SE2001.
◆Beirut evac Jun 1982, Lebanon Aug–Nov 1982, Apr–Jul 1984, Gulf War Sep 1990–Mar 1991.

LST 1189 *San Bernardino* Decomm and stricken 30 Sep 1995. Trfd to Chile 8 Dec 1995.
Later history: renamed *Valdivia* (R 93) SE2001.
1★Vietnam Oct 1972–Feb 1973; ◆Iran/Indian Ocean Mar–Jun 1980, Gulf War Sep–Oct 1990.

LST 1190 *Boulder* Went aground off Norway, 12 Sep 1988. Decomm 28 Feb 1994. Stricken 2003

LST 1191 *Racine* Decomm 2 Oct 1993. Stricken 2003
1★Vietnam Nov 1972, Feb 1973, ◆Iran/Indian Ocean Aug–Oct 1980.

LST 1192 *Spartanburg County* Decomm, stricken and trfd to Malaysia, 16 Dec 1994.
Later history: renamed *Sri Indera Putera* (1505). SE2001
◆Lebanon Feb–May 1983, Gulf War Sep 1990–Mar 1991, Liberia Feb–Apr 1994.

LST 1193 *Fairfax County* Damaged by fire in engine room in Mediterranean, 29 Sep 1978. Decomm and stricken 17 Aug 1994. Trfd to Australia 27 Sep 1994.
Later history: renamed *Manoora* (L 52). SE2001.
◆Lebanon Feb–May 1983.

LST 1194 *La Moure County* Collided with LSD *Hermitage* off Georgia, 29 Apr 1987. Ran aground off Chile during exercises, 12 Sep 2000, not repaired. Decomm and stricken 17 Nov 2000. Sunk as target 10 Jul 2001.
◆Iran/Indian Ocean Jul–Aug 1980, Lebanon Oct 1982–Feb 1983, Gulf War Sep 1990–Mar 1991.

LST 1195 *Barbour County* Ran aground off San Diego, 25 Apr 1984. In collision with minesweeper *Conquest* off Pearl Harbor, 11 Sep 1987. Decomm 30 Mar 1992. Stricken 13 Jul 2001. Sunk as target off Hawaii, 6 Apr 2004.
◆Evac of Vietnam 29–30 Apr 1975, Iran/Indian Ocean Jan–Feb 1981, Libya Oct–Nov 1987, Gulf War Jan–May 1991.

LST 1196 *Harlan County* Decomm 14 Apr 1995 and trfd to Spain.
Later history: renamed *Pizarro* (L 42). SE2001
◆Lebanon May–Nov 1983, Gulf War Oct 1991–Feb 1992, Liberia Jul 1994.

LST 1197 *Barnstable County* In collision with m/v *Pounetes* at Curacao, 11 Feb 1977. Decomm 29 Jun 1994. Trfd to Spain 26 Aug 1994.
Later history: renamed *Hernán Cortes* (L 41). SE2001.
◆Beirut evac Jun 1976, Feb 1984, Grenada Oct–Nov 1983, Lebanon Nov 1983–Apr 1984, Iran/Indian Ocean Jul–Aug 1990, Liberia Aug 1990–Feb 1991, Mar–Apr, Jun–Jul 1993.

LST 1198 *Bristol County* Stricken 29 Jul 1994. Trfd to Morocco 16 Aug 1994.
Later history: renamed *Sidi Mohammed Ben Abdallah* (407). SE2001.
◆Gulf War Jul–Oct 1991.

LANDING SHIPS, MEDIUM

161 landing ships, medium (LSM) were on the Navy List, 1 Jan 1950.

Those remaining were named, 14 Oct 1959: 161 *Kodiak*, 175 *Oceanside*, 373 *Lakeland*, 540 *Raritan*.

Figure 7.27: *USS LSM-557*, June 1958.

ROCKET SHIPS

Rocket Ships on the Navy List, 1947

Names assigned, 1 Oct 1955

LSMR 401 *Big Black River* Decomm 15 Feb 1954. Rec **LFR 401**, 1 Jan 1969. Stricken 1 May 1973; Sold 9 Jul 1974.
7★Korea K-1 K-2 K-3 K-4 K-6 K-7 K-8.

LSMR 402 *Big Horn River* Decomm 16 Jan 1948. Stricken 1 Oct 1958. Sold 1959.
Later history: Merchant barge *P.T. and S. 402.*

LSMR 403 *Blackstone River*   Decomm 13 May 1955. Stricken 1955. Sold 1959.
   Later history: Merchant barge *204*. SE80
   7★Korea K-1 K-2 K-3 K-4 K-6 K-7 K-8.
LSMR 404 *Black Warrior River*   Decomm 10 Nov 1954. Rec **LFR 404**, 1 Jan 1969. Stricken 1 Oct 1958. Sold 1959.
   Later history: Merchant barge *Cape Flattery I*. BU 1994.
   7★Korea K-1 K-2 K-3 K-4 K-6 K-7 K-8.
LSMR 405 *Broadkill River*   Out of comm 10 Feb 1947–28 Mar 1951. Rec **LFR 405**, 1 Jan 1969. Decomm 16 Nov 1955. Stricken 1 May 1973. Sold 22 May 1974.
LSMR 406 *Canadian River*   Decomm 10 Feb 1947. Stricken 1 Feb 1960. Sold 21 Jul 1960.
   Later history: Merchant barge *205*. BU 1990.
LSMR 407 *Chariton River*   Decomm 10 Feb 1947. Stricken 1959. Sold 1960.
   Later history: Merchant barge *T.T. and B.Co. No.16*, 19.. *O and H 55*, 19.. *Skookum No.1*.
LSMR 408 *Charles River*   Decomm 16 Jan 1948. Stricken 1959. Sold 1960.
   Later history: Merchant barge *T.T. and B.Co. No.17*, 19.. *O and H 65*.
LSMR 409 *Clarion River*   Out of comm 6 Feb 1947–5 Oct 1950. Damaged by shore gunfire at Wolsari, Korea, 4 Jun 1953.
   Rec **LFR 409**, 1 Jan 1969. Out of comm 26 Oct 1955–18 Sep 1965. Decomm 8 May 1970. Stricken 8 May 1970. Sold Nov 1970.
   4★Korea K-5 K-6 K-9 K-10; 8★Vietnam May–Nov 1966, Jan–Mar, Jun–Aug, Oct 1967–Feb 1968, Jul–Sep, Nov–Dec 1968, Mar, May–Oct 1969, Jun–Oct 1970.
LSMR 410 *Clark Fork River*   Decomm 6 Feb 1947. Stricken 1 Feb 1960. Sold 21 Jul 1960.
   Later history: Merchant barge *252*.
LSMR 411 *Cumberland River*   Out of comm 6 Feb 1947–26 Jan 1951. Decomm 12 Oct 1954. Stricken 1 Feb 1960. Sold 5 Jul 1960, BU.
LSMR 412 *Des Plaines River*   Out of comm 3 May 1950–30 Aug 1950. Decomm 20 Sep 1955. Rec **LFR 412**, 1 Jan 1969. Stricken 1 Sep 1972. Sold 14 Dec 1973.
   3★Korea K-5 K-6 K-8 K-9.
LSMR 501 *Elk River*   Decomm 1 Aug 1946. Rec **IX 501**, 1 Apr 1967. Converted to deep submergence support ship. In service Jan 1969. Sunk as target 24 Feb 2001.
LSMR 502 *Escalante River*   Decomm 4 May 1946. Stricken 1958. Stricken 1959.
   Later history: Merchant barge *544*. SE80
LSMR 503 *Flambeau River*   Decomm 3 May 1946. Stricken 1958. Sold 1959.
LSMR 504 *Gila River*   Decomm 11 May 1946. Stricken 1 Feb 1960; sold 7 Jul 1960.
   Later history: Merchant barge *Barge 504*, renamed *Cape Cleare*.
LSMR 505 *Grand River*   Decomm 20 May 1946. Stricken 1 Oct 1958. Sold 1959.
   Later history: Merchant barge *Foss 157*, 1959, *Bell 157*. SE80
LSMR 506 *Green River*   Decomm 20 May 1946. Stricken 1 Oct 1958. Sold 1959.
   Later history: Merchant barge *545*.
LSMR 507 *Greenbriar River*   Decomm 5 Feb 1947. Stricken 1 Oct 1958. Sold 1959.
   Later history: Merchant barge *Barge 507*. SE80
LSMR 508 *Gunnison River*   Decomm 5 Feb 1947. Converted to drone aircraft catapult control ship and rec **YV 3**, 9 May 1960; named *Targeteer*, 26 Jun 1960. Recomm 7 Apr 1961; decomm 13 Dec 1968. Stricken 1 Jan 1969; Sold Dec 1969
LSMR 509 *Holston River*   Decomm 5 Feb 1947. Stricken 1 Oct 1958. Sold 1959.
   Later history: Merchant barge *O & H 85*. BU 1991.
LSMR 510 *James River*   Decomm 5 Feb 1947. Stricken 1 Feb 1960; Sold 12 Apr 1961. Struck submerged object and sank off Miami, Fla., 18 May 1970.

LSMR 511 *John Day River*   Decomm 21 May 1947. Stricken 1 Feb 1960; Sold 5 Jul 1960, BU.
LSMR 512 *Lamoille River*   Decomm 5 Dec 1955. Rec **LFR 512**, 1 Jan 1969. Stricken 1 May 1973; Sold 22 May 1974, BU.
   Later history: Merchant *Uhod*.
LSMR 513 *Laramie River*   Decomm 12 Apr 1948. Rec **LFR 513**, 1 Jan 1969. Stricken 1 May 1973; Sold 9 Apr 1974, BU Baltimore.
LSMR 514 *Maurice River*   Decomm 30 Jul 1954. Stricken 1 Feb 1960. Sold 5 Jul 1960.
   Later history: Merchant barge *JFK 1*.
LSMR 515 *Owyhee River*   Decomm 16 Nov 1955. Rec **LFR 515**, 1 Jan 1969. Stricken 1 May 1973; sold 22 May 1974.
   Later history: Merchant *Najram*, renamed *Bilal II* 1983.
LSMR 516 *Pearl River*   Decomm 23 Apr 1948. Stricken 1 Oct 1958. Sold 1961, BU.
LSMR 517 *Pee Dee River*   Decomm 13 Apr 1955. Stricken 1 Feb 1960; Sold 22 Jun 1960.
   Later history: Merchant *Petromar Salvor*, renamed *Offshore Salvor* 1964, *Goldrill 4* 1968, *Yukon Bleu* 1979, *Western Sea* 1980.
LSMR 518 *Pit River*   Decomm 21 May 1947. Stricken 1 Oct 1958; sold Jun 1959.
LSMR 519 *Powder River*   Decomm 21 May 1947. Stricken 1 Oct 1958. Sold 1959.
   Later history: Merchant barge *J.S. 21*.
LSMR 520 *Raccoon River*   Out of comm 15 May 1946–2 Feb 1951. Decomm 8 Apr 1955. Stricken 1 Feb 1960. Sold 22 Jun 1960.
   Later history: Merchant barge *LSMR 520*
LSMR 521 *Rainy River*   Decomm 20 Jun 1946. Stricken 1 Oct 1958. Sold 4 Aug 1959.
   Later history: Merchant barge *P-102*.
LSMR 522 *Red River*   Out of comm 19 Apr 1946–2 Apr 1951. Decomm 15 May 1955. Rec **LFR 522**, 1 Jan 1969. Stricken 1 May 1973; sold 22 May 1974.
   Later history: Merchant *Bilal* 1976.
LSMR 523 *Republican River*   Decomm 2 Jul 1946. Stricken 1 Feb 1960. Sold 21 Oct 1960.
LSMR 524 *St. Croix River*   Decomm 21 May 1946. Stricken 1 Oct 1958. Sold 1961.
LSMR 525 *St. Francis River*   Out of comm 28 Mar 1946–16 Sep 1950 and 21 Nov 1955–18 Sep 1965. Rec **LFR 525**, 1 Jan 1969. Stricken 17 Apr 1970; sold Nov 1970, BU Sasebo, Japan.

Figure 7.28: *USS St. Francis River* (LSMR 525), 1966. Rocket launchers range the deck forward of the 5-inch gun.

3★Korea K-6 K-9 K-10; 10★Vietnam Apr–May, Aug–Oct 1966, Dec 1966–Feb, Apr–Jun, Aug–Nov 1967, Apr–Jun, Aug–Nov 1968, Jan–Mar, May–Aug, Oct 1969–Jan 1970.

LSMR 526 *St. Johns River* Decomm 28 May 1946. Stricken 1 Oct 1958; sold 4 Aug 1959.

LSMR 527 *St. Joseph River* Out of comm 28 Mar 1946–14 Oct 1950. Decomm 5 Aug 1955. Trfd to South Korea 15 Sep 1960.
Later history: renamed *Si Hung* (311). R1982.
2★Korea K-8 K-9.

LSMR 528 *St. Mary's River* Decomm 30 Apr 1946. Stricken 1 Oct 1958. Sold 4 Aug 1959.
Later history: Merchant barge *David-T.* BU 1989.

LSMR 529 *St. Regis River* Decomm 31 Mar 1946. Stricken 1 Feb 1960; Sold 5 Jul 1960.

LSMR 530 *Salmon Falls River* Decomm 25 Jun 1946. Stricken 1 Oct 1958. Sold 1959.
Later history: Merchant barge *P-101*.

LSMR 531 *Smoky Hill River* Decomm 29 May 1946. Rec **LFR 531**, 1 Jan 1969. Stricken 1 May 1973; Sold 9 Apr 1974, sold to Panama 14 Mar 1975.
Later history: renamed *Tiburon* (GC 10). R1989.

LSMR 532 *Smyrna River* Decomm 17 Jun 1946. Trfd to West Germany 5 Sep 1958.
Later history: renamed *Otter* (L754). R1967.

LSMR 533 *Snake River* Decomm 10 Jul 1946. Stricken 1 Oct 1958. Sold 1959.
Later history: Merchant *Narragansett*, renamed *Carolinian II.* SE80.

LSMR 534 *Thames River* Decomm 25 Apr 1946. Trfd to West Germany 5 Sep 1958.
Later history: renamed *Natter* (L 755). R1967.

LSMR 535 *Trinity River* Decomm 10 Jun 1946. Stricken 1958. Sold 7 Jul 1959.

LSMR 536 *White River* Out of comm 31 Jul 1946–16 Sep 1950 and 7 Sep 1956–2 Oct 1965. Rec **LFR 536**, 1 Jan 1969. Decomm and stricken 22 May 1971. Sold Nov 1970.
2★Korea K-8 K-9 K-10; ★Vietnam May–Jul, Oct–Dec 1966, Feb–Mar, Jun–Aug, Oct 1967–Apr 1968, Jun–Jul, Nov–Dec 1968, Jan–Feb, Apr–Jun, Oct 1969–Mar 1970.

Displacement	1,084 tons f/l
Dimensions	203′6″ (oa); 197′3″ (wl) × 34′6″ × 6′8″ (501–536: 206′3″(oa); 204′6″(wl))
Machinery	2 screws; diesel; SHP 2,800; 12.6 knots
Complement	138
Armament	1–5″/38, 4–4.2″ mortars, 4–40 mmAA, 10 rocket launchers

Notes: named 1 Oct 1955   LSMR rec LFR 1 Jan 1969

INSHORE FIRE SUPPORT SHIP

No.	Name	Builder	Keel Laid	Launched	Comm.
IFS 1	*Carronade*	Puget Sd.Brdg	19 Nov 1952	26 May 1953	25 May 1955

Displacement	1,500 tons
Dimensions	245′ × 39′ × 10′
Machinery	2 screws; diesel; 3,100 SHP; 15 knots
Complement	162
Armament	1–5″/38, 8 rocket launchers, 2–40 mm guns

Notes: Built to provide inshore naval gunfire support for amphibious landings.
Service Record: Rec **LFR 1**, 1 Jan 1969. Out of comm 31 May 1960–1965. Decomm 1969. Stricken 1 May 1973. Sold 13 Aug 1974, BU Seattle.
10★Vietnam Apr–May, Jul–Oct 1966, Mar–Jun, Aug–Dec 1967, Feb–Mar, May–Nov 1968, Mar 1969–Jan 1970.

Figure 7.29: USS *LCS(L)-6*, a support landing ship.

INFANTRY LANDING SHIPS

All LCI types rec LSI, 28 Feb 1949.
74 LSI(L), 6 LSI(M), 25 LS(FF), and 106 LSS(L) remained on the Navy List, 1 Jan 1950.
Many trfd to foreign countries including 53 LSS(L) to Japan 1952.

UTILITY LANDING CRAFT

LCU 1610–1681

Displacement	190 tons; 390 fl
Dimensions	134′9″ (oa) × 29′9″ × 6′11″
Machinery	2 screws; diesels; 1700 BHP; 11 knots
Complement	6

Built 1959–60 (1610–1624), 1967–1976 (1625–1679), 1986 (1680–1681) LCU 1637 was an experimental type of all-aluminum construction.

Notes: Surviving units of the LCT (5) 1–500 and LCT (6) 501–1465 types rec LSU in 1949 and again rec LCU 15 Apr 1952. LCU 1466–1609 type were built in 1954–1957. 1594–1601 were built in Japan for Taiwan and 1602–1607 for Japan under OSP.

AMPHIBIOUS COMMAND SHIPS

Formerly Amphibious Force Flagships (AGC); survivors reclassified **LCC**, 1 Jan 1969.

Command Ships on the Navy List, 1947

AGC 1 *Appalachian* Decomm 21 Mar 1947. Stricken 1 Mar 1959, BU 1960.

AGC 2 *Blue Ridge* Decomm 14 Mar 1947. Stricken 1 Jan 1960. Sold, 26 Aug 1960; BU 1961, Portland, Ore.

AGC 3 *Rocky Mount* Decomm 22 Mar 1947. Stricken 1 Jul 1960, BU 1973 Portland, Ore.

Figure 7.30: *USS Pocono* (AGC 16), headquarters ship, refitted with large radar mast and landing pad.

AGC 5 *Catoctin* Decomm 26 Feb 1947. Stricken 1 Mar 1959, BU South Portland, Me. .
AGC 7 *Mount McKinley* Rec **LCC 7**, 1 Jan 1969. Decomm 26 Mar 1970. Stricken 30 Jul 1976. Sold 22 Sep 1977, BU.
  8★Korea K-1 K-2 K-3 K-4 K-5 K-7 K-8 K-9; 3★Vietnam Sep 1964–Jan 1965, Mar–Apr 1965, Jun–Jul 1966, Jul 1967–Feb 1968, Feb–Jul 1969; ◆Lebanon Jul 1958, Cuba Missile Crisis Oct–Dec 1962.
AGC 8 *Mount Olympus* Decomm 4 Apr 1956. Stricken 1 Jun 1961. Sold 22 Jan 1973, BU.
  ◆Antarctic Dec 1946–Mar 1947.
AGC 9 *Wasatch* Decomm 30 Aug 1946. Stricken 1 Jan 1960. BU 1961, Terminal I.
AGC 10 *Auburn* Decomm 7 May 1947. Stricken 1 Jul 1960. Sold 17 Feb 1961, BU 1961 Baltimore.
AGC 11 *Eldorado* Collided with transport *George Clymer* in storm off Okinawa, 26 Jul 1964. Rec **LCC 11**, 1 Jan 1969. Decomm 8 Nov 1972. Stricken 16 Nov 1972. Sold 10 Aug 1973, BU.
  8★Korea K-1 K-2 K-3 K-4 K-5 K-6 K-9 K-10; 10★Vietnam Jun–Jul 1962, Aug–Sep 1964, Nov–Dec 1965, Mar–Apr 1966, Feb–Jul 1967, Aug, Oct 1968–Jan 1969, Mar–Jul 1970, Aug 1971–Jan 1972; ◆Cuban Missile Crisis Nov–Dec 1962.

Figure 7.31: *USS Blue Ridge* (LCC 19), amphibious command ship. The flat top design accommodates a large landing pad for helicopters and can accommodate a large array of electronic equipment, antennas, and transmitters.

AGC 12 *Estes* Out of comm 30 Jun 1949–31 Jan 1951. Rec **LCC 12**, 1 Jan 1969. Decomm 31 Oct 1969. Stricken 30 Jul 1976. BU Portland, Ore.
  2★Korea 1952–52; 6★Vietnam Mar–Apr 1961, Jun–Oct 1965, Aug 1966–Jan 1967, Feb–Jul 1968, Aug–Sep 1969; ◆OpCastle 1954; Passage to Freedom.
AGC 13 *Panamint* Decomm . . Jan 1947. Stricken 1 Jul 1960, sold 17 Feb 1961, BU 1961 Baltimore.
AGC 14 *Teton* Decomm 30 Aug 1946. Stricken 1 Jun 1961. Sold Mar 1962, BU.
AGC 15 *Adirondack* Out of comm 1 Feb 1950–4 Apr 1951. Decomm 9 Nov 1955. Stricken 1 Jun 1961. Sold 7 Nov 1972, BU.
AGC 16 *Pocono* Out of comm 19 Jun 1949–18 Aug 1951. Rec **LCC 16**, 1 Jan 1969. Damaged in collision with USCGC *Courier*, Jun 1970. Decomm 16 Sep 1971. Stricken 1 Dec 1976. Sold 9 Dec 1981, BU 1982.
  ◆Lebanon Jul–Oct 1958, Cuba Feb–May 1961, Cuban Missile Crisis Nov–Dec 1962, Dominican Rep May–Jun 1965.
AGC 17 *Taconic* Rec **LCC 17**, 1 Jan 1969. Decomm 17 Dec 1969. Stricken 1 Dec 1976.
  ◆Lebanon Jul–Oct 1958, Cuba Jun 1961, Dominican Rep May–Jun 1965.

Notes: Helicopter landing pad added in 1950s.

No.	Name	Former	Date
AGC 396	*Williamsburg*	ex-PG 56	10 Nov 1945
Displacement	1,870 tons f/l		
Dimensions	244′ × 26′ ×		
Machinery	2-screws; diesel; 2,200 hp; 16 knots.		

Notes: Presidential yacht (General Communications Vessel). Decomm 30 Jun 1953. Stricken 1 Apr 1962.

Later history: Research ship *Anton Bruun* 1962. Damaged when drydock sank, 1968. Sold, renamed *Williamsburg*.

No.	Name	Builder	Keel Laid	Launched	Comm.
LCC 19	*Blue Ridge*	Phila NSYd.	27 Feb 1967	4 Jan 1969	14 Nov 1970
LCC 20	*Mount Whitney*	Newport News	8 Jan 1969	8 Jan 1970	16 Jan 1971
Displacement	11,500 tons; 19,290 f/l				
Dimensions	636′5″(oa); 579′11″(wl) × 82′ × 28′10″; 108′ extreme beam				
Machinery	1 screw; ST; 2 boilers; 22,000 SHP; 22 knots				
Endurance	13,500/16				
Complement	800				
Armament	2 twin 3″/50. *1974*: 2 Sea Sparrow BPDMS added. *1985*: 2 Phalanx. later 2 Bushmaster				

Notes: AGC rec LCC, 1 Jan 1969. AGC 21 canceled. Hull and propulsion similar to *Iwo Jima* class LPH, large helicopter flight deck. Flat top design in order to accommodate large array of electronic equipment, antennas and transmitters. Armament removed 1992.

Service Record:

LCC 19 *Blue Ridge*
  2★Vietnam Feb–Jun 1972; ◆Evac of Cambodia Apr 1975, evac of Vietnam 29–30 Apr 1975, Gulf War Aug 1990–Apr 1991.
LCC 20 *Mount Whitney* Command ship, NATO striking fleet, 1975–2005.
  ◆Iraq War 2003, Haiti Sep–Oct 1994, Beirut evac, 17–19 Jul 2006.

COMMAND FLAGSHIPS

No.	Name	Former	Date	Decomm
AGF 1	*Valcour*	AVP 55	15 Dec 1965	15 Jan 1973
AGF 3	*La Salle*	LPD 3	1 Jul 1972	27 May 2005

Armament: 1977: 4-twin 30″/50, 2–40 mm. *1995*: 2 Bushmaster, 2 Phalanx. Guns removed 1990s; complement 493.

AGF 11	*Coronado*	LPD 11	1 Oct 1980	25 Feb 2005

Notes: Complement 481, later 117 Navy and 153 civilians. Armament: 2 Phalanx, 2 twin 3″/50 guns; removed 1990s.

AMPHIBIOUS CARGO SHIPS

Amphibious Cargo Ships on the Navy List, 1947

AKA 3 *Bellatrix*   Reacq 27 Aug 1951. Recomm 15 May 1952. Decomm 3 Jun 1955. Stricken 1 Jul 1960. Reacq 15 Mar 1963. Trfd to Peru 30 Mar 1964.
   Later history: renamed *Independencia* (D 130). R1991. Abandoned at sea 2000 m. west of Hawaii en rte to BU in China 11 Dec 1991.
   1★Korea K-8.

AKA 4 *Electra*   Reacq 16 Oct 1951. Recomm 3 May 1952. Decomm 13 May 1955. Stricken 1 Jul 1961.

Note: Type C2-T.

AKA 12 *Libra*   Out of comm 19 Apr 1948–28 Aug 1950. Decomm 6 Oct 1955. Rec **LKA 12**, 1 Jan 1969. Stricken 1 Jan 1977. Sold 27 Sep 1984, BU 1985.

AKA 13 *Titania*   MSTS, 1 Oct 1949. Decomm 19 Jul 1955. Stricken 1 Jul 1961. BU 1974.
   7★Korea K-1 K-2 K-5 K-6 K-7 K-8 K-9.

AKA 14 *Oberon*   MSTS, 1 Oct 1949. Decomm 27 Jun 1955. Stricken 1 Jul 1960. BU 1970 Seattle.
   5★Korea K-4 K-5 K-6 K-7 K-8.

Note: Type C2-F.

AKA 15 *Andromeda*   MSTS, 1 Oct 1949. Decomm 1 May 1956. Stricken 1 Jul 1960. Sold 12 Mar 1971, BU 1971 Seattle.
   5★Korea K-4 K-5 K-6 K-9 +1953; ◆Passage to Freedom.

AKA 19 *Thuban*   Out of comm 30 Aug 1949–10 Apr 1951. MSTS, 1 Oct 1949. Decomm 31 Oct 1967. Rec **LKA 19**, 1 Jan 1969. Stricken 1 Sep 1977. Lost in tow en route to BU in Spain, 6 Dec 1985.
   3★Korea K-1 K-2 K-3; ★Vietnam Feb–Jun 1961, Apr–May 1962; ◆Cuban Missile Crisis Nov–Dec 1962.

AKA 20 *Virgo*   MSTS, 1 Oct 1949. Decomm 8 May 1958. Stricken 1 Jul 1961. Reacq 19 Aug 1965. Rec **AE 20**, 1 Nov 1965. Recomm 19 Aug 1966. Decomm 18 Feb 1971. Stricken 1 Jan 1971. Sold 19 Nov 1973, BU Taiwan.
   9★Korea K-1 K-3 K-4 K-5 K-6 K-7 K-8 K-9 K-10, (as AE 20) 9★Vietnam Feb–Apr 1966, May–Aug 1967, Apr–Oct 1968, May–Nov 1969, Jun–Nov 1970.

AKA 53 *Achernar*   MSTS, 1 Oct 1949. In collision with m/v *Captain Theo* off Lewes, Del., 28 Dec 1953. Out of comm 18 Feb 1956–1 Sep 1961. Decomm 1 Jul 1963. Trfd to Spain 2 Feb 1965.
   Later history: renamed *Castilla*. R1980. BU 1987.
   3★Korea K-1 K-2 K-3.

AKA 54 *Algol*   Out of comm 26 Nov 1947–18 Feb 1948 and 2 Jan 1958–17 Nov 1961. Rec **LKA 54**, 1 Jan 1969. Decomm 23 Jul 1970. Stricken 1 Jan 1977. Scuttled as fishing reef off New Jersey, 22 Nov 1991.
   5★Korea K-1 K-2 K-4 K-5 K-8; ◆Passage to Freedom, Cuban Missile Crisis Oct–Dec 1962.

Figure 7.32: *USS Valcour* (AGF 1), as command ship, in white paint for Middle East service, about 1970.

AKA 55 *Alshain*   MSTS, 1 Oct 1949. In collision with AGC *Mount Olympus* near Guantanamo, 13 May 1952. Decomm 14 Jan 1956. Stricken 1 Jul 1960. BU 1978 Brownsville, Tex.
   3★Korea 1953, Inchon.

AKA 56 *Arneb*   Out of comm 16 Mar 1948–19 Mar 1949. Damaged by ice in Antarctic, 18 Nov 1956, 31 Dec 1956 and again 30 Jan 1957. Rec **LKA 56**, 1 Jan 1969. Decomm 12 Aug and stricken 13 Aug 1971. Sold 1 Mar 1973, BU Brownsville, Tex.
   ◆Antarctic Dec 1955–Feb 1956, Dec 1956–Feb 1957, Jan–Feb 1958, Jan–Feb 1959, Dec 1959–Feb 1960, Feb–Mar 1961, Dec 1961–Mar 1962, Dec 1962–Mar 1963, Dominican Rep May 1965.

AKA 57 *Capricornus*   Out of comm 30 Mar 1948–12 Oct 1950. Rec **LKA 57**, 1 Jan 1969. Decomm 10 Feb 1970. Stricken 1 Jan 1977.
   ◆Lebanon Jul–Oct 1958, Cuban Missile Crisis Oct–Dec 1962, Dominican Rep May–Jun, Oct 1965.

AKA 58 *Chara*   MSTS, 1 Oct 1949. Out of comm 1 Oct 1949–Jun 1950. Decomm 21 Apr 1959. Stricken 1 Jul 1960. Reacq 23 Aug 1965. Rec **AE 31**, 1 Nov 1965. Recomm 25 Jan 1966. Decomm and stricken 10 Mar 1972. BU Portland, Ore.
   7★Korea K-1 K-2 K-4 K-6 K-7 K-8 K-9; ★Vietnam Nov 1966–Mar 1967, Oct 1967–Jan 1968, Nov 1968–Apr 1969, Feb–Jul 1970, May–Nov 1971; ◆Taiwan Straits Aug–Sep 1958, (as AE 31) Korea Jan–Mar 1968.

AKA 59 *Diphda*   MSTS, 1 Oct 1949. Out of comm 5 Feb 1952–11 Nov 1952, MSTS. Decomm 11 May 1956. Stricken 1 Jul 1961. BU 1976 Richmond, Cal.
   6★Korea K-1 K-2 K-4 K-5 K-6 K-8 1953.

AKA 60 *Leo*   MSTS, 1 Oct 1949. Decomm 11 Feb 1955. Stricken 1 Jul 1960. BU 1976 Terminal I, Cal.
   5★Korea K-4 K-5 K-6 K-7 K-9.

AKA 61 *Muliphen*   MSTS, 1 Oct 1949. Rec **LKA 61**, 1 Jan 1969. Decomm 31 Aug 1970. Stricken 1 Jan 1977. Sold 28 Oct 1988. Sunk as artificial reef off Port St. Lucie, Fla., Jan 1989.
   ◆Lebanon Jul–Sep 1958.

AKA 88 *Uvalde*   Out of comm 9 Nov 1946–31 Mar 1951, 2 Jan 1958–18 Nov 1961. Stricken 1 Jul 1960. Reacq 1 Sep 1961. Recomm 18 Nov 1961. Decomm and stricken 1 Dec 1968. Sold 26 Jun 1969, BU Portsmouth, Va.
   3★Korea K-2 K-7 K-10; ◆Passage to Freedom, Cuban Missile Crisis Oct–Dec 1962, Dominican Rep Jun 1965.

AKA 89 *Warrick*   Decomm 3 Dec 1957. Stricken 1 Jul 1961. Sunk as target by submarine *Trigger* off Cape Flattery, 28 May 1971.
   2★Korea K-1 1951, 1952, 1953.

AKA 90 *Whiteside*   Decomm 30 Jan 1958. Stricken 1 Jul 1961. Sunk as target 1971.
   4★Korea K-1 K-2 K-3 K-8 1952, 1953.

AKA 91 *Whitley*   Damaged in collision with cruiser *Salem* off New Jersey, 2 Nov 1950. Decomm 16 Aug 1955. Stricken 1 Jul 1960. Reacq 1 Dec 1961. To Italy 1 Feb 1962.
  Later history: renamed *Etna* (A 5328). BU 1979 Naples.
AKA 92 *Wyandot*   Decomm 10 Jul 1959. Stricken 1 Jul 1960. Reacq 1 Sep 1961. Recomm Nov 1961. Decomm Sep 1962. Trfd to MSTS, **T-AKA 92**, Mar 1963. Rec **AK 283**, 1 Jan 1969. In collision with m/v *Sacramento Venture* off Keelung, Taiwan, 7 Apr 1974. Out of service, 31 Oct 1975. Stricken 31 Mar 1986. Sold 9 Jan 1988, BU Taiwan.
  ◆Antarctic 1955, 1957, 1958, 1959, Jan–Feb 1970.
AKA 93 *Yancey*   Out of comm 1 Mar 1958–17 Nov 1961. Rec **LKA 93**, 1 Jan 1969. Damaged in collision with Chesapeake Bay Bridge in gale, 21 Jan 1970. Decomm 20 Jan 1971. Stricken 1 Sep 1977. Sunk as artificial reef off Morehead City, NC, 1990.
  3★Korea K-1 K-4 K-10; ◆Antarctic Dec 1946–Feb 1947, Cuban Missile Crisis Oct–Dec 1962, Dominican Rep Apr–May 1965, Feb–Mar, Aug 1966.
AKA 94 *Winston*   OC 1947–48. Decomm 1 Feb 1957. Stricken 1 Jul 1960. Reacq 1 Sep 1961. Recomm 24 Nov 1961. Rec **LKA 94**, 1 Jan 1969. Decomm Nov 1969. Stricken 1 Sep 1976. BU 1980 Taiwan.
  6★Korea K-1 K-2 K-4 K-5 K-9 K-10; 6★Vietnam Oct 1962–May 1963, Jun–Dec 1964, May–Aug 1965, Apr–Aug 1966, Sep–Oct 1967, Nov 1968–May 1969.
AKA 95 *Marquette*   Decomm 19 Jul 1955. Stricken 1 Jul 1960. BU 1972.
AKA 96 *Mathews*   Reacq . . . 1951. Recomm 16 Feb 1952. Decomm 31 Oct 1968. Stricken 1 Nov 1968. BU 1969 Oakland, Cal.
  ★Korea 1953; 4★Vietnam Jun 1962, May–Aug 1965, Oct 1965, May–Jun 1966, Aug 1967–Feb 1968; ◆Cuban Missile Crisis Nov–Dec 1962.
AKA 97 *Merrick*   Reacq 1951. Recomm 19 Jan 1952. Rec **LKA** 97, 1 Jan 1969. Decomm 17 Sep 1969. Stricken 1 Sep 1976. BU 1980 Taiwan.
  ★Korea 1952, 1953; 7★Vietnam May–Oct 1965, Feb–Apr 1966, Dec 1966–Jun 1967, Jun–Nov 1968; ◆Antarctic Dec 1946–Feb 1947, Cuban Missile Crisis Nov–Dec 1962.
AKA 98 *Montague*   Decomm 22 Nov 1955. Stricken 1 Jul 1960. BU 1971 Seattle.
  4★Korea K-1 K-2 K-4 K-7; ◆Passage to Freedom.
AKA 99 *Rolette*   Reacq 13 Aug 1951. Recomm 23 Feb 1952. Decomm 1 May 1956. Stricken 1 Jul 1960. BU 1978 Portland, Ore.
AKA 100 *Oglethorpe*   MSTS, 1 Oct 1949. Decomm and stricken 1 Nov 1968. BU 1969 Portsmouth, Va.
  2★Korea K-1 K-3; ◆Lebanon Sep–Oct 1958, Cuba Feb–Mar 1962, Cuban Missile Crisis Oct–Nov 1962, Dominican Rep Jun–Sep 1965.

Notes: Type C2-S-B1.

AKA 103 *Rankin*   Out of comm 21 May 1947–22 Mar 1952. Rec **LKA 103**, 1 Jan 1969. Decomm 11 May 1971. Stricken 1 Jan 1977. Sunk as an artificial reef off Stuart, Fla., May 1988.
  ◆Cuba Feb, Jun 1961–Mar 1962, Jul–Aug 1962, Cuban Missile Crisis Oct–Dec 1962, Dominican Rep Apr–Jun 1965.
AKA 104 *Seminole*   Rec **LKA 104** 1 Jan 1969. Went aground in Puget Sound, 14 Jul 1969. Decomm 23 Dec 1970. Stricken 1 Sep 1976. Sold 16 Nov 1977. BU.
  6★Korea K-1 K-2 K-3 K-4 K-9 K-10; 7★Vietnam Jul–Aug 1962, Mar, Oct 1966, Mar–Jul 1967, Sep 1968–Feb 1969, Jan–May 1970.
AKA 105 *Skagit*   Out of comm 30 Jun 1949–26 Aug 1950. Rec **LKA 105**, 1 Jan 1969. Decomm and stricken 1 Jul 1969.
  1★Korea 8; 3★Vietnam Nov 1965–Apr 1966, Jun, Sep 1967; ◆Passage to Freedom, Taiwan Straits 1 Sep 1958.
AKA 106 *Union*   Rec **LKA 106**, 1 Jan 1969. Decomm 5 Jun 1970. Stricken 1 Sep 1976. Sold Sep 1977, BU Terminal I.
  2★Korea K-7 K-8; 6★Vietnam Mar–May 1965, Aug–Nov 1966, Jan 1967, Mar–Aug 1968, Sep–Nov 1969; ◆Cuban Missile Crisis Nov–Dec 1962.

Figure 7.33: *USS Wyandot* (AKA 92), 1950s, in Japan.

Figure 7.34: *USS Union* (AKA 106), March 1959.

AKA 107 *Vermilion*   Out of comm 26 Aug 1949–16 Oct 1950. Rec **LKA 107**, 1 Jan 1969. Decomm 13 Apr 1971. Stricken 1 Sep 1977. Sunk as artificial reef off Myrtle Beach, SC, 4 Mar 1988.
  ◆Lebanon Jul–Oct 1958, Cuban Missile Crisis Oct–Dec 1962, Dominican Rep May–Jun 1965.
AKA 108 *Washburn*   Rec **LKA 108**, 1 Jan 1969. Decomm 16 May 1970. Stricken 1 Sep 1976. BU 1980.
  5★Korea K-1 K-2 K-3 K-6 K-10; 7★Vietnam Dec 1964–May 1965, Aug 1965, Sep 1966–Feb 1967, Feb–Aug 1968, May–Oct 1969; ◆Quemoy-Matsu 12 Jan 1962, Cuban Missile Crisis Nov–Dec 1962.

Notes: Type C2-S-AJ3.

No.	Name	Builder	Launched	Acquired	Comm.
AKA 112	*Tulare* ex-*Evergreen Mariner*	Beth; S.Fran.	22 Dec 1953	1955	12 Jan 1956
Displacement		9,050 tons; 17,500 f/l			
Dimensions		564′(oa); 528′6″(wl) × 76′ × 28′			
Machinery		1 screw; ST; 22,000 SHP; 22 knots			
Complement		425			
Armament		6-twin 3″/50. *1975*: 3-twin 3″/50			

Notes: Type C4-S-1b. 319 troops. Helicopter landing deck aft.

Service Record: Rec **LKA 112**, 1 Jan 1969. Decomm 15 Feb 1980. Stricken 1 Aug 1981. Reacq May 1984. Decomm 31 Mar 1986. Stricken 31 Aug 1992. NDRF. SE.
    Later history: Training ship *Bay State* (tfr canc).
    10★Vietnam Aug–Sep 1964, Jul 1965, Mar, May–Aug 1966, Dec 1967–May 1968, Mar–Aug 1969, Jan 1970, Dec 1970–Jan 1971 May 1971, Dec 1972–Feb 1973; ◆Quemoy-Matsu Mar 1960.

No.	Name	Builder	Keel Laid	Launched	Comm.
LKA 113	*Charleston*	Newport News	5 Dec 1966	2 Dec 1967	14 Dec 1968
LKA 114	*Durham*	Newport News	10 Jul 1967	29 Mar 1968	24 May 1969
LKA 115	*Mobile*	Newport News	15 Jan 1968	19 Oct 1968	20 Sep 1969
LKA 116	*St. Louis*	Newport News	3 Apr 1968	4 Jan 1969	22 Nov 1969
LKA 117	*El Paso*	Newport News	22 Oct 1968	17 May 1969	17 Jan 1970

Displacement	10,000 tons; 20,700 tons f/l
Dimensions	575′6″(oa); 549′9″ (wl) × 82′ × 25′5″
Machinery	1 screw; ST; 2 boilers; 22,000 SHP; 20+ knots
Endurance	9600/16
Complement	360
Armament	4 twin 3″/50 guns. *1980s*: 2 Phalanx repl. 2–3″

Notes: AKA 113 rec LKA 14 Dec 1968, and 114–117, 1 Jan 1969. 226 troops. Helicopter deck.

Service Record:

AKA 113 *Charleston*   Decomm 27 Apr 1992.
    1★Vietnam Apr 1971; ◆Beirut Evac Jun 1976.
AKA 114 *Durham*   Decomm 25 Feb 1994.
    ★Vietnam Mar, Jun–Sep 1970, Apr 1971; ◆Evac of Cambodia Apr 1975, Evac of Vietnam 29–30 Apr 1975, Gulf War Sep–Nov 1990, Jan–Mar 1991.
AKA 115 *Mobile*   Decomm 4 Feb 1994. Conversion to training ship canceled; OS 1 Nov 1996.
    4★Vietnam Jul–Sep 1970, Apr, Oct–Nov 1971, Jan–Jul 1972. ◆Evac of Vietnam 29–30 Apr 1975, Iran/Indian Ocean Mar–Jun 1980, Gulf War Jan–Apr 1991.
AKA 116 *St. Louis*   Decomm 2 Nov 1992.
    2★Vietnam Aug, Oct 1970, Dec 1970–Mar 1971, Apr–Oct 1972; ◆Iran/Indian Ocean Jan/Feb 1981.
AKA 117 *El Paso*   Decomm 21 Apr 1994. Conversion to training ship canceled; OS 23 Oct 1996.
    ◆Iran/Indian Ocean Oct–Dec 1980, Lebanon May–Nov 1983, Liberia Mar–Jul 1993.

ATTACK TRANSPORTS

Attack Transports on the Navy List, 1947

APA 18   *President Jackson*   MSTS, 1 Oct 1949. Decomm 6 Jul 1955. Stricken 1 Oct 1958. Sold 23 Apr 1973, BU Kaohsiung.
    3★Korea K-1 K-2 K-3.
APA 19   *President Adams*   MSTS, 1 Oct 1949. Decomm 14 Jun 1950. Stricken 1 Oct 1958. Sold 22 Jan 1973, BU Taiwan.
APA 20   *President Hayes*   Decomm 30 Jun 1949. Stricken 1 Oct 1958. Sold 8 May 1975, BU.
APA 30   *Thomas Jefferson*   MSTS, 1 Oct 1949. Decomm 18 Jul 1955. Stricken 1 Oct 1958. Sold 1 Mar 1973, BU Portland, Ore.
    2★Korea K-1 K-2 1951.

Notes: Type C3-A.

APA 25   *Arthur Middleton*   Decomm 21 Oct 1946. Stricken 1 Oct 1958. Sold 9 May 1973, BU Brownsville, Tex.

Figure 7.35: *USS Charleston* (LKA 113), April 1969. A built for the purpose amphibious cargo ship.

Figure 7.36: *USS George Clymer* (APA 27), November 1960.

APA 26   *Samuel Chase*   Decomm 26 Feb 1947. Stricken 1 Oct 1958. Sold 9 May 1973, BU Brownsville, Tex.
APA 27   *George Clymer*   Collided with AGC *Eldorado* in storm off Okinawa, 26 Jul 1964. Stricken 1 Nov 1967. Sold 1968, BU Terminal I.
    7★Korea K-1 K-3 K-5 K-6 K-7 K-9 K-10; 3★Vietnam Jan 1963, Sep 1964, Jul 1965, Mar–Jul 1966; ◆Quemoy-Matsu Jan, Mar 1960, Sep 1961.

Notes: Type C3-P.

APA 21   *Crescent City*   Decomm 30 Apr 1948. Stricken 1 Oct 1958.
    Later history: training ship *Golden Bear* 1971. To Marad 17 Jul 1995. NDRF. Trfd to Artship Foundation, Oakland, Cal., as museum, 6 Aug 1999. Sold Feb 2004.
APA 28   *Charles Carroll*   Decomm 27 Dec 1946. Stricken 1 Oct 1958. Sold 1 Apr 1977.
APA 31   *Monrovia*   Out of comm 26 Feb 1947–30 Nov 1950. Decomm 31 Oct and stricken 1 Nov 1968. BU Portsmouth, Va. ◆Lebanon Jul–Oct 1958, Cuban Missile Crisis Oct–Dec 1962, Dominican Rep May–Jun 1965.
APA 32   *Calvert*   Out of comm 26 Feb 1947–18 Oct 1950. Decomm 30 Jun 1966. Stricken 1 Aug 1966. Cargo training hulk.
    1★Korea K-9 1953; 2★Vietnam Apr 1961, Oct 1965–Jan 1966, Laos Apr–May 1961; ◆Passage to Freedom, Taiwan Straits Aug–Sep 1958, Quemoy-Matsu Feb–Mar 1961.

Notes: Type C3-Delta.

Figure 7.37: *USS Cambria* (APA 36).

APA 33 *Bayfield* Decomm 30 Sep 1968. Stricken 1 Oct 1968. BU 1969, San Pedro, Cal..
4★Korea K-1 K-2 K-4 K-8; 2★Vietnam May–Oct 1965, Feb–May 1967; ◆Passage to Freedom, Taiwan Straits Dec 1958, Quemoy-Matsu Nov 1959, Mar 1960, Mar–Apr 1962, Cuban Missile Crisis Nov–Dec 1962,

APA 36 *Cambria* Out of comm 30 Jun 1949–11 Sep 1950. In collision with LSD *Shadwell* off Malta, 8 Jul 1969. Stricken 14 Sep 1970. BU 1972.
Later history: merchant *Jean Claude Duvalier* 1971. BU 1972 Portsmouth, Va.
◆Lebanon Sep–Oct 1958, Cuba Jan–Mar 1962, Cuban Missile Crisis Oct–Dec 1962.

APA 37 *Cavalier* Decomm and stricken 1 Oct 1968. BU 1969.
2★Korea K-1 K-3; 5★Vietnam Aug–Nov 1964, Mar, Jun–Aug 1966, Jan–May 1968.

APA 38 *Chilton* Rec **LPA 38**, 1 Jan 1969. Decomm and stricken 1 Jul 1972. BU 1974 Camden, NJ.
◆Lebanon Jul–Oct 1958, Cuba Apr–Jun 1961, Cuban Missile Crisis Oct–Nov 1962, Dominican Rep May–Jun 1965.

APA 44 *Fremont* Rec **LPA 44**, 1 Jan 1969. Decomm 2 Sep 1969. Stricken 1 Jun 1973. BU 1974.
◆Lebanon Jul–Sep 1958, Cuba Jan 1962.

APA 45 *Henrico* Decomm 14 Feb 1968. Rec **LPA 45**, 1 Jan 1969. Stricken 1 Jun 1973. BU 1977 Richmond, Cal.
9★Korea K-1 K-2 K-3 K-4 K-6 K-7 K-8 K-9 K-10; 1★Vietnam Jun–Jul 1959, Jan–May 1965, Aug 1966–Mar 1967; ◆Cuban Missile Crisis Nov–Dec 1962.

Notes: Type C3-S-A2.

APA 67 *Burleson* Decomm 9 Nov 1946. Static training ship. Rec **IX 67**, 5 Oct 1956. Stricken 1 Sep 1968, BU.

Notes: Type S4-SE-BD1.

APA 128 *Arenac* Decomm 10 Jul 1946. Stricken 1 Oct 1958. Sold 14 Aug 1974, BU Brownsville, Tex.

APA 132 *Barnwell* Decomm 1 Feb 1947. Stricken 1 Oct 1958. Reacq 9 Sep 1983. Sunk as target, Mar 1986.

APA 136 *Botetourt* Out of comm 5 Jun 1946–23 Sep 1950. Decomm 27 Apr 1956. Stricken 1 Jul 1961. Sold 14 Aug 1974, BU.

APA 140 *Brookings* Decomm 25 Jul 1946. Stricken 1 Oct 1958. BU 1984.

APA 144 *Clinton* Decomm 2 May 1946. Stricken 1 Oct 1958. Reacq 9 Nov 1983 for target practice. Sunk as target Aug 1984.

APA 148 *Crockett* Decomm 15 Oct 1946. Stricken 1 Oct 1958. BU.

APA 152 *Latimer* Out of comm 26 Feb 1947–23 Sep 1950. Decomm 15 May 1956. Stricken 1 Jul 1960. Sold 28 Oct 1971, BU Panama City, Fla.

APA 156 *Mellette* Out of comm 3 Feb 1946–18 Oct 1950. Decomm 18 Jun 1955. Stricken 1 Jul 1960. BU 1988 Kaohsiung.

APA 160 *Deuel* Out of comm 17 May 1946–23 Oct 1950. Decomm 27 Jun 1956. Stricken 1 Dec 1958. BU 1974.
★Korea 1953.

APA 164 *Edgecombe* Decomm 31 Jan 1947. Stricken 1 Oct 1958. BU 1987 Taiwan.

APA 168 *Gage* Decomm 26 Feb 1947. Stricken 1 Oct 1958. NDRF. SE.

APA 172 *Grimes* Decomm 26 Feb 1947. Stricken 1 Oct 1958. Sold 14 Aug 1974, BU.

APA 176 *Kershaw* Decomm 20 Dec 1946. Stricken 1 Oct 1958. Sold 8 Jun 1982, BU.

APA 180 *Lavaca* Decomm 31 Jan 1947. Stricken 1 Oct 1958. Sold 14 Oct 1992, BU.

APA 188 *Olmsted* Out of comm 21 Feb 1947–2 Feb 1952. Decomm 27 Feb 1959. Stricken 1 Jul 1960. BU 1986, Spain.
◆Lebanon Jul–Sep 1958.

APA 192 *Rutland* Decomm 26 Feb 1947. Stricken 1 Oct 1958. Sold Jun 1982, BU.

APA 193 *Sanborn* Out of comm 14 Aug 1946–6 Jan 1951. Decomm 11 May 1956. Stricken 1 Jul 1960. Sold 28 Oct 1971, BU Panama City, Fla.

APA 194 *Sandoval* Out of comm 19 Jul 1946–22 Sep 1951. Decomm 22 Jun 1955. Stricken 1 Jul 1960. Reinstated 1 Sep 1961. Recomm 20 Nov 1961. Rec **LPA 194**, 1 Jan 1969. Decomm 3 Mar 1970. Stricken 1 Dec 1976. BU 1983.
2★Korea K-7 K-8; ◆Cuba Feb 1962, Cuban Missile Crisis Oct–Nov 1962.

APA 195 *Lenawee* Out of comm 3 Aug 1946–30 Sep 1950. Collided with high speed transport *Wantuck* in Pacific, 25 Aug 1957. Decomm 20 Jun 1967. Stricken 30 Jun 1968. Sold 17 Jul 1975, BU.
3★Korea K-5 K-6 10, 1953; 1★Vietnam Sep 1963, Dec 1964–Jan 1965, Apr–May 1965, Aug 1965, Oct–Dec 1966.

APA 196 *Logan* Out of comm 27 Nov 1946–10 Nov 1951. Decomm 14 Jun 1955. Stricken 1 Jul 1960. BU 1979, Nissho, Japan.
1★Korea K-8.

APA 197 *Lubbock* Decomm 14 Dec 1946. Stricken 1 Oct 1958. Sold 18 Apr 1975, BU.

APA 198 *McCracken* Decomm 10 Oct 1946. Stricken 1 Oct 1958. Sold 9 May 1975, BU Portland, Ore.

APA 199 *Magoffin* Out of comm 14 Aug 1946–4 Oct 1950. Decomm 10 Apr 1968. Stricken 31 Oct 1968. Sold 1 Dec 1976, BU.
2★Korea K-5 K-8; 4★Vietnam Jul–Aug 1958, Aug–Sep 1964, Oct 1965–Feb 1966, May–Nov 1967; ◆Passage to Freedom, Taiwan Straits Aug–Sep 1958, Quemoy-Matsu Dec 1960, Mar 1961, Sep 1962.

APA 201 *Menard* Out of comm 14 Jun 1948–2 Dec 1950. Decomm 18 Oct 1955. Stricken 1 Sep 1961. Sold 17 Jul 1975, BU Portland, Ore.
3★Korea K-5 K-6 K-8; ◆Passage to Freedom.

APA 202 *Menifee* Out of comm 31 Jul 1946–2 Dec 1950. Decomm 29 Jun 1955. Stricken 1 Oct 1958. Sold 8 May 1975, BU Portland, Ore.
★Korea 1951, 1952.

APA 203 *Meriwether* Decomm 14 Aug 1946. Stricken 1 Oct 1958. Sold 8 May 1975, BU.

APA 204 *Sarasota* Out of comm 1 Aug 1946–3 Feb 1951. Decomm 2 Sep 1955. Stricken 1 Jul 1960. BU 1983, Spain.

APA 205 *Sherburne* Decomm 3 Aug 1946. Stricken 1 Oct 1958. Reinstated as **AGM 22**, 16 Apr 1969. Renamed **Range Sentinel**, 26 Apr 1971. IS 21 Oct 1971. (See p. 182)

APA 206 *Sibley* Decomm 27 Nov 1946. Stricken 1 Oct 1958. Sold 18 Apr 1975, BU.

APA 207 *Mifflin* Decomm 5 Jul 1946. Stricken 1 Oct 1958. Sold 17 Jul 1975. BU Seattle.

APA 208 *Talladega*   Out of comm 27 Dec 1946–8 Dec 1951. Rec **LPA 208**, 1 Jan 1969. Decomm 20 Oct 1969. Stricken 1 Dec 1976. Sold, BU.
  2★Korea K-9 K-10; 3★Vietnam May–Oct 1965, Feb–Mar 1966, Oct 1967. ◆Quemoy-Matsu Mar 1959, Mar–Apr 1960, Mar, Jun 1962.
APA 209 *Tazewell*   Decomm 27 Dec 1946. Stricken 1 Oct 1958. Sold 11 Dec 1972, BU Portland, Ore.
APA 210 *Telfair*   Out of comm 20 Jul 1946–12 Sep 1950. Decomm 29 Feb 1958. Stricken 1 Jul 1960. Reinstated 24 Aug 1961. Recomm 22 Nov 1961. Decomm 31 Oct 1968. Stricken 1 Nov 1968. Sold 26 Jun 1969, BU Baltimore.
  3★Korea K-4 K-5 K-9 1953; ◆Passage to Freedom.
APA 211 *Missoula*   Decomm 13 Sep 1946. Stricken 1 Oct 1958. Sold 5 Mar 1975, BU Portland, Ore.
APA 212 *Montrose*   Out of comm 26 Oct 1946–12 Sep 1950. Rec **LPA 212**, 1 Jan 1969. Decomm and stricken 2 Nov 1969. BU 1970 Portland, Ore.
  3★Korea K-4 K-5 K-6; 6★Vietnam Nov 1965–Mar 1966, Mar–Jun 1967, Aug–Sep, Nov 1968–Jan 1969; ◆Passage to Freedom, Taiwan Straits Sep, Nov 1958.
APA 213 *Mountrail*   Out of comm 12 Jul 1946–9 Sep 1950 and 1 Oct 1955–22 Nov 1961. Rec **LPA 213**, 1 Jan 1969. Decomm 13 Aug 1970. Stricken 1 Dec 1976, BU.
  3★Korea K-4 K-5 K-8; ◆Passage to Freedom, Cuba Feb 1962, Cuban Missile Crisis Oct, Dec 1962.
APA 214 *Natrona*   Decomm 29 Jul 1946. Stricken 1 Oct 1958. Sold 5 Mar 1975, BU.
APA 215 *Navarro*   Out of comm 15 Mar 1946–2 Dec 1950. Rec **LPA 215**, 1 Jan 1969. Decomm 20 Aug 1970. Stricken 1 Dec 1976, sold, BU.
  6★Vietnam May 1962, May 1965–Feb 1966, Aug 1967–Feb 1968.
APA 216 *Neshoba*   Decomm 4 Dec 1946. Stricken 1 Oct 1958. Sold 5 Mar 1975, BU Portland, Ore.
APA 217 *New Kent*   Out of comm 29 Jul 1949–10 Oct 1951. Decomm 12 Jul 1954. Stricken 1 Oct 1958. Sold 28 Oct 1971, BU.
APA 218 *Noble*   Decomm 1 Jul 1964. Trfd to Spain 19 Dec 1964.
  Later history: renamed *Aragon*. R1982.
  2★Korea K-6 K-7; ★Vietnam Apr–May, Aug–Sep, Nov 1963; ◆Quemoy-Matsu Aug, Oct–Nov 1960, Mar 1962, Cuban Missile Crisis Nov–Dec 1962.
APA 219 *Okaloosa*   Decomm 21 Jul 1949. Stricken 1 Oct 1958. Sold 28 Oct 1971, BU.
APA 220 *Okanogan*   Rec **LPA 220**, 1 Jan 1969. Decomm 5 Feb 1970. Stricken 5 Feb 1970. Sold 2 Oct 1979, BU.
  1★Korea K-8; 5★Vietnam Jun 1960, Nov 1963, May–Oct 1965, Jul, Nov 1966–Mar 1967, Jun–Nov 1968.
  ◆Taiwan Straits Aug–Sep 1958, Quemoy-Matsu Mar 1960, Cuban Missile Crisis Nov–Dec 1962.
APA 221 *Oneida*   Decomm 27 Dec 1946. Stricken 1 Oct 1958. Sold 8 May 1975, BU Tacoma.
APA 222 *Pickaway*   Rec **LPA 222**, 1 Jan 1969. Decomm 25 Jun 1970. Stricken 1 Dec 1976. Sold, BU.
  6★Korea K-1 K-3 K-6 K-7 K-9 K-10; 4★Vietnam Jan 1963, Aug–Nov 1964, Jul 1965, Mar–Aug 1966, Jun–Oct 1967.
APA 224 *Randall*   Decomm 6 Apr 1956. Returned 1 Jul 1960. Sold 28 Oct 1971, BU.
APA 226 *Rawlins*   Decomm 15 Nov 1946. Stricken 1 Oct 1958. BU 1988 Taiwan.
APA 227 *Renville*   Out of comm 30 Jun 1949–5 Jan 1952. Decomm 23 Apr 1968. Stricken 1 Sep 1976.
  2★Korea K-9 K-10; 3★Vietnam Aug–Oct 1964, Jul 1965, May–Sep 1966; ◆Quemoy-Matsu Dec 1958, Taiwan Straits Dec 1958, Cuban Missile Crisis Nov–Dec 1962.

Figure 7.38: *USS Renville* (APA 227), a Victory-ship attack transport.

Figure 7.39: *USS Navarro* (APA 215). Notice NV identifying marking on her landing craft.

APA 228 *Rockbridge*   Out of comm 8 Mar 1947–23 Dec 1950. Decomm 29 Nov 1968. Stricken 1 Dec 1968. BU 1969, Baltimore.
  ◆Lebanon Jul–Oct 1958, Cuban Missile Crisis Oct–Dec 1962.
APA 229 *Rockingham*   Decomm 17 Mar 1947. Stricken 1 Oct 1958. Sold 2 Oct 1979.
APA 230 *Rockwall*   Out of comm 15 Mar 1947–3 Mar 1951. Decomm 28 Sep 1955. Stricken 1 Dec 1958. BU 1975.
APA 232 *San Saba*   Decomm 17 Dec 1946. Stricken 1 Oct 1958. Sold 8 May 1975, BU Portland, Ore.
APA 234 *Bollinger*   Decomm 1 Apr 1947. Stricken 15 Dec 1974.
APA 235 *Bottineau*   Out of comm 8 Mar 1947–24 Mar 1951. Decomm 31 Aug 1955. Stricken 1 Jul 1961. BU 1983.
APA 236 *Bronx*   Decomm 30 Jun 1949. Stricken 1 Oct 1958.
APA 237 *Bexar*   Rec **LPA 237**, 1 Jan 1969. Decomm 7 Aug 1970. Stricken 1 Sep 1976, sold, BU.
  4★Korea K-1 K-2 K-6 K-7; 5★Vietnam Nov 1964–May 1965, Feb–Mar, Aug 1966–Jan 1967, Feb–Sep 1969; ◆Cuban Missile Crisis Nov–Dec 1962.
APA 238 *Dane*   Decomm 20 Dec 1946. Stricken 1 Oct 1958. Sold 5 Mar 1975, BU.
APA 239 *Glynn*   Out of comm 12 Dec 1946–3 Mar 1951. Decomm 9 Sep 1955. Stricken 1 Jul 1960. BU 1985.

Notes: Type VC2-S-AP5.

Figure 7.40: *USS Francis Marion* (APA 249). Mariner-type cargo ship converted to attack transport.

Figure 7.41: *USS Cook* (APD 130), high speed transport, 1961. One of the last of many destroyer escorts converted to high speed transports.

No.	Name	Builder	Launched	Acquired	Comm.
APA 248	Paul Revere ex-*Diamond Mariner*	NY Sbdg	15 May 1952	11 Apr 1953	3 Sep 1958
APA 249	Francis Marion ex-*Prairie Mariner*	NY Sbdg	30 Mar 1953	13 Feb 1954	6 Jul 1961
Displacement	10,709 tons; 16,838 f/l				
Dimensions	563'6" (oa); 528' (wl) × 76' × 28'				
Machinery	1 screw; ST; 2 boilers; 19,250 SHP; 22 knots				
Complement	414				
Armament	4 twin 3"/50 guns				

Notes: Type C4-S-1a. 1,657 troops. *Paul Revere* converted by Todd, San Pedro. APA to LPA, 1 Jan 1969.

Service Record:

APA 248 *Paul Revere* Decomm 1 Oct 1979. Stricken 1 Jan 1980. Trfd to Spain 17 Jan 1980.
 Later history: renamed *Castilla* (L 21). R1998.
 ★Vietnam Dec 1960–Jan, Mar–May 1961, May 1964, Oct–Nov 1965, Jan–Mar 1966, Jun, Aug–Nov 1967, Mar–Aug 1969, Sep–Oct, Dec 1970–Mar 1971, Aug 1972–Feb 1973; ◆Quemoy-Matsu Oct, Dec 1962.

APA 249 *Francis Marion* Damaged in collision with m/v *Starlight* off Cape Henry, Va., 4 Mar 1979. Decomm and stricken 14 Sep 1979. Trfd to Spain 11 Jul 1980.
 Later history: renamed *Aragon* (L 22). R2000.
 ◆Cuban Missile Crisis Oct–Dec 1962.

HIGH SPEED TRANSPORTS

Reclassified **LPR**, 1 Jan 1969.

High Speed Transports on the Navy List, 1947

APD 37 *Charles Lawrence* Decomm 21 Jun 1946. Stricken 1 Sep 1964. Sold 28 Jan 1966, BU New Orleans.

APD 38 *Daniel T. Griffin* Decomm 30 May 1946. Stricken 1 Dec 1966. Trfd to Chile 17 Jan 1967.
 Later history: renamed *Virglio Uribe* (DE 29). R1995, BU.

APD 39 *Barr* Decomm 12 Jul 1946. Stricken 1 Jun 1960. Sunk as target off Puerto Rico, 23 Mar 1963.

APD 40 *Bowers* Out of comm 10 Feb 1947–6 Feb 1951. Decomm 18 Dec 1958. Trfd to Philippines, 31 Oct 1960.
 Later history: renamed *Rajah Soliman* (D 66). Sunk in typhoon in Bataan Shipyard, Jun 1964; refloated Jan 1965 and rtnd. Sold Dec 1965, BU.

APD 42 *Gantner* Decomm 2 Aug 1949. Stricken 15 Jan 1966. Trfd to Taiwan 22 Feb 1966.
 Later history: renamed *Wen Shan* (34/ 834). R1992.

APD 43 *George W. Ingram* Decomm 15 Jan 1947. Stricken 1 Jan 1967. Trfd to Taiwan 17 May 1967.
 Later history: renamed *Kang Shan* (43). R1978.

APD 44 *Ira Jeffery* Decomm 18 Jun 1946. Stricken 1 Jun 1960. Sunk as target off Charleston, SC, 31 Jul 1962.

APD 45 *Lee Fox* Decomm 13 May 1946. Stricken 1 Sep 1964. Sold 31 Jan 1966, BU New Orleans.

APD 46 *Amesbury* Decomm 3 Jul 1946. Stricken 1 Jun 1960. Sold 24 Oct 1962, BU.

APD 48 *Blessman* Decomm 28 Aug 1946 or 15 Jan 1947. Stricken 1 Jun 1967. Trfd to Taiwan 17 May 1967.
 Later history: renamed *Chung Shan* (44/ 845). R1995.

APD 49 *Joseph E. Campbell* Decomm 15 Nov 1946. Stricken 1 Dec 1966. Trfd to Chile 15 Nov 1966.
 Later history: renamed *Riquelme* (DE 28), used for spare parts, BU.

APD 50 *Sims* Decomm 24 Apr 1946. Stricken 1 Jun 1960. Sold 14 Apr 1961, BU.

APD 51 *Hopping* Decomm 5 May 1947. Stricken 1 Sep 1964. Sold 15 Aug 1966, BU, Baltimore.

APD 52 *Reeves* Decomm 30 Jul 1946. Stricken 1 Jun 1960. hulk sold to Ecuador as Floating power plant.

APD 53 *Hubbard* Decomm 15 Mar 1946. Stricken 1 May 1966. Sold 1 Jul 1968, BU.

APD 55 *Laning* Out of comm 28 Jun 1946–6 Apr 1951. Decomm 13 Sep 1957. Rec **LPR 55**, 1 Jan 1969. Stricken 1 Mar 1975. Sold 30 Sep 1975, BU Camden, NJ.

APD 56 *Loy* Decomm 21 Feb 1947. Stricken 1 Sep 1964. Sold 15 Aug 1966, BU Baltimore.

APD 57 *Barber* Decomm 22 May 1946. Stricken 27 Nov 1968. Trfd to Mexico 17 Feb 1969.
 Later history: renamed *Chihuahua* (B 08), renamed *José Maria Morelos y Pavon* (E 22), 1993. R2002.

APD 59 *Newman* Decomm 18 Feb 1946. Stricken 1 Sep 1964. Sold 15 Aug 1966, BU Baltimore.

APD 60 *Liddle* Out of comm 18 Jun 1946–27 Oct 1950 and 2 Feb 1959–29 Nov 1961. Decomm 18 Mar 1967. Stricken 5 Apr 1967. Sold 25 Jan 1968, BU.
◆Cuban Missile Crisis Oct–Dec 1962, Dominican Rep May–Jun 1965.

APD 61 *Kephart* Decomm 21 Jun 1946. Stricken 1 May 1967. Trfd to South Korea 23 Jul 1967.
Later history: renamed *Kyong Buk* (*Kyong Puk*). (PG 85/DE 826). R1985.

APD 62 *Cofer* Decomm 28 Jun 1946. Stricken 1 Apr 1966. Sold 5 Mar 1968, BU New Orleans.

APD 63 *Lloyd* Out of comm 1 Jul 1946–3 Jan 1951. Decomm 18 Feb 1958. Stricken 1 Jun 1966. Sold 5 Mar 1968, BU New Orleans.

APD 65 *Burke* Decomm 22 Jun 1949. Stricken 1 Jun 1968, Trfd to Colombia 1968.
Later history: renamed *Almirante Brion* (DT 07). R1974, BU.

APD 66 *Enright* Decomm 21 Jun 1946. Trfd to Ecuador 14 Jul 1967.
Later history: renamed *25 de Julio* (E 12), renamed *Moran Valverde* (DD 03) 1967. R1989.

APD 69 *Yokes* Decomm 19 Aug 1946. Stricken 1 Apr 1964. Sold Apr 1965, BU Terminal I.

APD 70 *Pavlic* Decomm 15 Nov 1946. Stricken 1 Apr 1967. Sold 1 Jul 1968, BU.

APD 71 *Odum* Decomm 15 Nov 1946. Stricken 1 Dec 1966. Trfd to Chile 15 Nov 1966.
Later history: renamed *Serrano* (DE 26). R1984, BU.

APD 72 *Jack C. Robinson* Decomm 13 Dec 1946. Stricken 1 Dec 1966. Trfd to Chile 15 Nov 1966.
Later history: renamed *Orella* (DE 27). R1984.

APD 73 *Bassett* Out of comm 29 Apr 1946–7 Dec 1950. Decomm 26 Nov 1957. Stricken 1 May 1967. Trfd to Colombia 6 Sep 1968.
Later history: renamed *Almirante Tono* (DT 04). R1977.

APD 74 *John P. Gray* Decomm 29 Apr 1946. Stricken 1 Mar 1967. Sold 3 Sep 1968, BU New Orleans.

APD 75 *Weber* Decomm 6 Jun 1947. Stricken 1 Jun 1960. Sunk as target, 15 Jul 1962.

APD 76 *Schmitt* Decomm 28 Jun 1949. Stricken 1 May 1967. Trfd to Taiwan 18 Feb 1969.
Later history: renamed *Lung Shan* (44). R1978.

APD 77 *Frament* Decomm 30 May 1946. Stricken 1 Jun 1960. Sold to Ecuador as Floating power plant.

APD 78 *Bull* Decomm 5 Jun 1947. Stricken 15 Jun 1966. Trfd to Taiwan 13 Jun 1966.
Later history: renamed *Lu Shan* (36/ 821). R1995, BU.

APD 79 *Bunch* Decomm 31 May 1946. Stricken 1 Apr 1964. BU.

APD 80 *Hayter* Decomm 19 Mar 1946. Stricken 1 Dec 1966. Trfd to South Korea 23 Jul 1967.
Later history: renamed *Chun Nam* (*Jon Nam*) (PG 86/DE 827). R1986.

APD 81 *Tatum* Decomm 15 Nov 1946. Stricken 1 Jun 1960. Sold 8 May 1961, BU.

APD 84 *Haines* Decomm 29 Apr 1946. Stricken 1 Jun 1960. Sold 19 May 1961, BU.

APD 85 *Runels* Decomm 10 Feb 1947. Stricken 1 Jun 1968. Sold 15 Jun 1961, BU Portsmouth, Va.

APD 86 *Hollis* Out of comm 5 May 1947–6 Apr 1951. Decomm 16 Oct 1956. Rec **LPR 86**, 1 Jan 1969. Stricken 15 Sep 1974. Sold 1 Jul 1975, BU.

APD 87 *Crosley* Decomm 15 Nov 1946. Stricken 1 Jun 1960. Hulk sold to Ecuador as floating power plant.

APD 88 *Cread* Decomm 2 Mar 1946. Stricken 1 Jun 1960. Sold 21 Feb 1961, BU New Orleans.

APD 89 *Ruchamkin* Out of comm 27 Feb 1946–9 Mar 1951. Damaged in collision with tkr m/v *Washington* off Virginia Capes, 14 Nov 1952 (7 dead). Out of comm 13 Aug 1957–18 Nov 1961. FRAM 1963. Rec **LPR 89**, 1 Jan 1969. Decomm and trfd to Colombia 24 Nov 1969.
Later history: renamed *Cordoba* (DT 15). R1980. Museum at Bogota 1980.
◆Cuba Dec 1961–Jan 1962, Dominican Rep Apr–Jun 1965.

APD 90 *Kirwin* Out of comm 6 Apr 1946–15 Jan 1965. Decomm 20 Dec 1968. Rec **LPR 90**, 1 Jan 1969. Stricken 15 Sep 1974. Sold 11 Aug 1975, BU.

APD 91 *Kinzer* Decomm 18 Dec 1946. Stricken 1 Mar 1965. Trfd to Taiwan 21 Apr 1965.
Later history: renamed *Yu Shan* (44/826/832). R1997.

APD 92 *Register* Decomm 31 Mar 1946. Stricken 1 Sep 1966. Trfd to Taiwan 11 Jul 1966.
Later history: renamed *Tai Shan* (38/878). R1992.

APD 93 *Brock* Decomm 5 May 1946. Sold 1 Jun 1960. Hulk sold to Colombia as floating power plant.

APD 94 *John Q. Roberts* Decomm 30 May 1946. Stricken 1 Jun 1960. Sold 16 Dec 1961, BU Savannah, Ga.

APD 95 *William M. Hobby* Decomm 6 Apr 1946. Stricken 1 May 1967. Trfd to South Korea, 23 Jul 1967.
Later history: renamed *Chi Ju* (*Cheju*) (PG 87/APD 822). R1989.

APD 96 *Ray K. Edwards* Decomm 30 Aug 1946. Stricken 1 Jun 1960. Sold 15 Jun 1961, BU.

APD 97 *Arthur L. Bristol* Decomm 29 Apr 1946. Stricken 1 Jun 1964. Sold 4 Aug 1965, BU Baltimore.

APD 98 *Truxtun* Decomm 15 Mar 1946. Name canceled 24 Jun 1963. Stricken 15 Jan 1966. Trfd to Taiwan 22 Nov 1965.
Later history: renamed *Fu Shan* (35/ 838). R1996, BU.

APD 99 *Upham* Decomm 25 Apr 1946. Stricken 1 Jun 1960. Hulk sold to Colombia as floating power plant.

APD 100 *Ringness* Decomm Apr 1946. Rec **LPR 100**, 1 Jan 1969. Stricken 15 Sep 1974. Sold Jun 1975, BU.

APD 101 *Knudson* Out of comm 4 Nov 1946–6 Aug 1953. Decomm 2 Jan 1958. Rec **LPR 101**, 1 Jan 1969. Stricken 15 Jul 1972. Sold 10 Jan 1975, BU Tacoma, Wash.
◆Passage to Freedom.

APD 102 *Rednour* Decomm 24 Jul 1946. Stricken 1 Mar 1967. Trfd to Mexico 17 Feb 1969.
Later history: renamed *Coahuila* (B 07), renamed *Vicente Guerrero* (E 21), 1993. SE2001.

APD 103 *Tollberg* Decomm 20 Dec 1946. Stricken 1 Nov 1964. Trfd to Colombia 14 Aug 1965.
Later history: renamed *Almirante Padilla* (DT 12). R1973.

APD 104 *William J. Pattison* Decomm 5 Jul 1946. Stricken 1 Jun 1960. Sold 18 Jan 1962, BU.

APD 105 *Myers* Decomm 31 Jan 1947. Stricken 1 Jun 1960. Hulk sold to Colombia as floating power plant.

APD 106 *Walter B. Cobb* Out of comm 29 Mar 1946– 6 Feb 1951. Decomm 15 May 1957. Stricken 15 Jan 1966. Trfd to Taiwan, 22 Feb 1966.
Later history: Sank after collision with ex-*Gantner* off California on 17 Apr while in tow to Taiwan, 21 Apr 1966.

APD 107 *Earle B. Hall* Out of comm 27 Sep 1946–7 Dec 1950 and 13 Sep 1957–29 Nov 1961. Decomm 12 Jan 1965. Stricken 1 Feb 1965. Sold 28 Jan 1966, BU Wilmington, Del.
◆Cuban Missile Crisis Oct–Dec 1962.

APD 108 *Harry L. Corl* Decomm 21 Jun 1946. Stricken 15 Jan 1966. Trfd to South Korea, 1 Jun 1966.
Later history: renamed *Ah San* (APD 82). R1984.

APD 109 *Belet* Decomm 22 May 1946. Stricken 12 Dec 1963. Trfd to Mexico.
Later history: renamed *California* (H 3/B 03). Lost by grounding off Baja California, 16 Jan 1972.

APD 110 *Julius A. Raven* Decomm 31 May 1946. Stricken 15 Jan 1966. Trfd to South Korea, 1 Jun 1966.
Later history: renamed *Ung Po* (APD 83). R1984.

APD 111 *Walsh* Decomm 26 Apr 1946. Stricken 1 May 1966. Sold 1 Jul 1968, BU.

APD 112 *Hunter Marshall* Decomm 30 May 1946. Stricken 1 Jun 1960. Hulk sold to Ecuador as floating power plant.

APD 113 *Earheart* Decomm 29 Apr 1946. Stricken 12 Dec 1963. Trfd to Mexico.
Later history: renamed *Papaloapan* (H 4/B 04). Ran aground 1976, BU.

APD 114 *Walter S. Gorka* Decomm 20 Mar 1947. Stricken 1 Jun 1960. Hulk sold to Ecuador as floating power plant.

APD 115 *Rogers Blood* Decomm 19 Mar 1946. Stricken 1 Jun 1960. Sold 14 Dec 1961, BU New Orleans.

APD 116 *Francovich* Decomm 29 Apr 1946. Stricken 1 Apr 1964. Sold May 1965, BU.

APD 117 *Joseph M. Auman* Decomm 10 Jul 1946. Stricken 12 Dec 1963. Trfd to Mexico.
Later history: renamed *Tehuantepec* (H 5/B 05), renamed *Zacatacas*. R1989.

APD 118 *Don O. Woods* Decomm 18 Jun 1946. Stricken 12 Dec 1963. Trfd to Mexico Dec 1963.
Later history: renamed *Usumacinta* (H 6/B 06), renamed *Miguel Hidalgo* (E 20), 1993. R2002.

APD 119 *Beverly W. Reid* Decomm 5 May 1947–18 Mar 1967. Rec **LPR 119**, 1 Jan 1969. Decomm 19 Nov 1969. Stricken 15 Sep 1974. Sold 18 Aug 1975, BU.

APD 120 *Kline* Decomm 10 Mar 1947. Stricken 15 Jan 1966. Trfd to Taiwan 22 Feb 1966.
Later history: renamed *Shou Shan* (37/ 893/837). R1997. Sunk as target 18 Oct 2000.

APD 121 *Raymon W. Herndon* Decomm 15 Nov 1946. Stricken 1 Sep 1966. Trfd to Taiwan 11 Jul 1966.
Later history: renamed *Heng Shan* (39). R1976.

APD 122 *Scribner* Decomm 15 Nov 1946. Stricken 1 Aug 1966. Sold 6 Sep 1967, BU.

APD 123 *Diachenko* Decomm 30 Jun 1959–8 Jun 1962. Rec **LPR 123**, 1 Jan 1969. Decomm 31 Oct 1969. Stricken 15 Sep 1974. Sold 1 Jun 1975, BU.
6★Korea K-1, K-2 K-3 K-4 K-7 K-8; 5★Vietnam Jul 1958, Nov 1963, Jun–Nov 1965, Aug–Sep 1966, Mar–Aug 1968; ◆Taiwan Straits Sep 1958.

APD 124 *Horace A. Bass* Rec **LPR 124**, 1 Jan 1969. Decomm 9 Feb 1959. Stricken 15 Sep 1974. Sold 11 Aug 1975.
6★Korea K-1, K-2 K-3 K-6 K-7 K-8.

APD 125 *Wantuck* In collision with transport *Lenawee* in Pacific, 25 Aug 1957. Decomm 15 Nov 1957. Stricken 4 Mar 1958. Sold 27 Oct 1958, BU.
5★Korea K-1, K-2 K-3 K-9 K-10; ◆Passage to Freedom.

APD 126 *Gosselin* Decomm 11 Jul 1949. Stricken 1 Apr 1964. Sold 23 Mar 1965, BU Terminal I.

APD 127 *Begor* Out of comm 20 Jul 1959–20 Nov 1961. Decomm 11 May 1962. Rec **LPR 127**, 1 Jan 1969. Stricken 15 May 1975. Sold 6 Dec 1976, BU Terminal I.
6★Korea K-2 K-4 K-5 K-6 K-9 K-10; ◆Passage to Freedom.

APD 128 *Cavallaro* Out of comm 17 May 1946–4 Sep 1953. Decomm 15 Oct 1959 and trfd to South Korea.
Later history: renamed *Kyung Nam* (APD 81/DE 822). R2000. Sunk as target Feb 2003.
★Passage to Freedom.

APD 129 *Donald W. Wolf* Decomm 15 May 1946. Stricken 1 Mar 1965. Trfd to Taiwan, 3 Apr 1965.
Later history: renamed *Hwa Shan* (33/ 854). SE1987.

APD 130 *Cook* Out of comm 31 May 1946–6 Oct 1953. Rec **LPR 130**, 1 Jan 1969. Decomm and stricken 15 Nov 1969. Sold 24 Jul 1970, BU Terminal I.
7★Vietnam Jan–Feb 1960, Jan 1962, Sep 1963, Dec 1964–May 1965, Jul–Aug 1966, Sep 1967–Feb, Jun–Jul 1968, Mar–Aug 1969; ◆Passage to Freedom, Quemoy-Matsu Jan, Mar 1960.

APD 131 *Walter X. Young* Decomm 2 Jul 1946. Stricken 1 May 1962. Used as test hulk, sunk as target, 11 Apr 1967.

APD 132 *Balduck* Out of comm 31 May 1946–5 Nov 1953. Decomm 28 Feb 1958. Rec **LPR 132**, 1 Jan 1969. Stricken 15 Jul 1975. Sold 16 Nov 1976, BU Terminal I.
◆Passage to Freedom.

APD 133 *Burdo* Decomm 28 Feb 1958. Stricken 1 Apr 1966. Sold 30 Mar 1967, BU New Orleans.

APD 134 *Kleinsmith* Decomm 16 May 1960. Trfd to Taiwan, 16 May 1960.
Later history: renamed *Tien Shan* (615). R1993.

APD 135 *Weiss* Out of comm 2 May 1949–14 Oct 1950 and 2 Mar 1958–20 Nov 1961. FRAM Jan 1964. Ran aground in typhoon at Okinawa, 27 Jul 1964. Rec **LPR 135**, 1 Jan 1969. Decomm Jan 1970. Stricken 15 Sep 1974. Sold 24 Jun 1975, BU.
3★Korea K-6 K-8 K-9; 6★Vietnam Feb–Mar 1963, Aug–Sep 1964, Nov 1965–Jan, Mar–Apr 1966, May–Aug 1967, Sep 1968–Feb 1969.

APD 136 *Carpellotti* Decomm 21 Apr 1958. Stricken 1 Dec 1959, Sold 20 Jun 1960. BU 1966, Baltimore.

APD 139 *Bray* Decomm 10 May 1946. Stricken 1 Jun 1960. Sunk as target, 26 Mar 1963.

8
PATROL COMBATANTS

GUNBOATS

Asheville Class

No.	Name	Builder	Keel Laid	Launched	Comm.
PG 84	Asheville	Tacoma	15 Apr 1964	1 May 1965	6 Aug 1966
PG 85	Gallup	Tacoma	27 Apr 1964	15 Jun 1965	22 Oct 1966
PG 86	Antelope	Tacoma	10 May 1965	18 Jun 1966	4 Nov 1967
PG 87	Ready	Tacoma	10 Jun 1965	12 May 1967	6 Jan 1968
PG 88	Crockett	Tacoma	18 Jun 1965	4 Jun 1966	24 Jun 1967
PG 89	Marathon	Tacoma	21 Jun 1966	22 Apr 1967	11 May 1968
PG 90	Canon	Tacoma	28 Jun 1966	22 Jul 1967	26 Jul 1968
PG 92	Tacoma	Tacoma	24 Jul 1967	13 Apr 1968	14 Jul 1969
PG 93	Welch	Petersen	8 Aug 1967	25 Jul 1968	8 Sep 1969
PG 94	Chehalis	Tacoma	15 Aug 1967	6 Aug 1968	8 Nov 1969
PG 95	Defiance	Petersen	3 Oct 1967	24 Aug 1968	24 Sep 1969
PG 96	Benicia	Tacoma	14 Apr 1969	20 Dec 1969	25 Apr 1970
PG 97	Surprise	Petersen	24 May 1968	7 Dec 1968	17 Oct 1969
PG 98	Grand Rapids	Tacoma	20 May 1969	10 Jan 1970	5 Sep 1970
PG 99	Beacon	Petersen	15 Jul 1968	17 May 1969	22 Nov 1969
PG 100	Douglas	Tacoma	8 Aug 1969	19 Jun 1970	6 Feb 1971
PG 101	Green Bay	Petersen	4 Nov 1968	14 Jun 1969	5 Dec 1969

Displacement	225 tons, 245 f/l
Dimensions	164′6″(oa) × 23′8″ × 9′6″
Machinery	2 screws; diesels; 1,750 BHP; 16 knots gas turbine; 14,000 SHP; 40+ knots
Complement	29
Armament	1–3″/50, 1–40mm guns.
—	1975 (86, 87, 98, 100) 2 Standard-ARM SSM launchers.

Notes: Rec PGM to **PG**, 1 Apr 1967. Aluminum hulls, aluminum-fiberglass superstructure, with diesels for cruising and gas turbines for high speed. Could attain a speed of 40 knots from full stop in one minute. PG 96, 98 and 100 destroyed by fire at shipyard Aug 1968, and new hulls were built. Built for coastal patrol and blockading; used off Cuba and in Vietnam. *Benicia* fitted with launcher for Standard-ARM SSM 1971; 86, 87, 98, and 100 fitted with 2 launchers.

Service Records:

PG 84 *Asheville* Decomm and stricken 31 Jan 1977.
   Later history: to Mass. Maritime Academy 11 Apr 1977. BU 1985, Brownsville, Tex.

Figure 8.1: *USS Welch* (PG 93), *Asheville* class gunboat built with aluminum hull and superstructure.

   14★Vietnam May 1967–Jul 1968, Nov 1968–Feb 1969, May–Oct 1969, Feb–Jun 1970, Jan–May, Nov–Dec 1971, Oct–Dec 1972.

PG 85 *Gallup* Stricken 31 Jan 1977. Reinstated 17 Jul 1981. Stricken 9 Oct 1984. Sold 13 May 2007, BU Brownsville, Tex.
   ★Vietnam Apr–Dec 1967, Nov–Dec 1968, May–Sep 1969, Dec 1969–Feb 1970, Jul–Oct 1970, Apr–Aug 1971.

PG 86 *Antelope* Decomm Stricken 1 Oct 1977.
   Later history: to EPA 17 Jan 1978, renamed *Peter W. Anderson*.
   ★Vietnam Jan–Jul 1970, Jan–Apr 1971.

PG 87 *Ready* Stricken 1 Oct 1977. to Massachusetts Maritime Academy, 1 Mar 1978.
   Later history: Training ship. BU.
   2★Vietnam Jan–Jul 1970.

PG 88 *Crockett* Stricken 15 Dec 1976.
   Later history: to EPA 18 Apr 1977, renamed *Rachel Carson*. Museum at Muskegon, Mich., 1982. BU 1994.
   ★Vietnam Mar–Dec 1969, Oct 1970–Feb 1971, Aug–Dec 1971, Jun 1972.

PG 89 *Marathon* Stricken 31 Jan 1977. To Massachusetts Maritime Academy, 18 Apr 1977
   Later history: Training ship *Marathon*. BU.

PG 90   *Canon*   Damaged by Vietcong fire in Vietnam, 14 Jul 1970. Stricken 15 Dec 1976. Reinstated 17 Jul 1981. Stricken 9 Oct 1984.
★Vietnam Jun–Aug 1970, Apr–Aug 1971, Mar–Jul 1972.

PG 92   *Tacoma*   Decomm 30 Sep 1981. Trfd to Colombia 16 May 1983.
Later history: renamed *Quitasueño* (GC 112). SE2001.
2★Vietnam Sep 1970–Jan 1971, Oct–Dec 1972.

PG 93   *Welch*   Decomm 30 Sep 1981. Trfd to Colombia 16 May 1983
Later history: renamed *Albuquerque* (GC 111). SE2001.
2★Vietnam Oct–Dec 1970, Jun–Sep 1972.

PG 94   *Chehalis*   Stricken 1 Aug 1976. To DTRC, renamed *Athena I*, 21 Aug 1975.

PG 95   *Defiance*   Decomm and trfd to Turkey 11 Jun 1973.
Later history: renamed *Yildirim* (P 338). Damaged by explosion near Lesbos, Greece, 11 Apr 1985; BU Aliaga, Turkey.

PG 96   *Benicia*   Decomm 2 Oct 1971. Trfd to South Korea 15 Oct 1971.
Later history: renamed *Paek Ku 51* (PGM 351). R1991. BU Korea 1998.

PG 97   *Surprise*   Decomm 25 Feb and trfd to Turkey 28 Feb 1973.
Later history: renamed *Bora* (P 339). SE2001.

PG 98   *Grand Rapids*   Stricken 1 Oct 1977. to DTRC, renamed *Athena II*, 3 Oct 1977.

PG 99   *Beacon*   Collided with m/v *Suriname* off Cuba, 25 Feb 1972. Decomm 10 Apr 1977. Trfd to Greece 22 Nov 1989.
Later history: renamed *Ormi* (P 230). SE2001.

PG 100   *Douglas*   Stricken 1 Oct 1977. to DTRC 1990, renamed *Lauren*. Stricken 2000. Sunk as target on NC coast, 30 Apr 2008.

PG 101   *Green Bay*   Decomm 10 Apr 1977. Trfd to Greece 22 Nov 1989.
Later history: renamed *Tolmi* (P 229). SE2001.

FRIGATES

Frigates on the Navy List, 1947

PF 3   *Tacoma*   To USSR, 17 Aug 1945–17 Oct 1949, renamed *EK-11*. Recomm 1 Dec 1950. Decomm and trfd to South Korea 9 Oct 1951.
Later history: renamed *Taedong* (PF 63). R1973 as a museum.
3★Korea K-4 K-5 K-6.

PF 4   *Sausalito*   To USSR, 17 Aug 1945–1 Nov 1949, renamed *EK-16*. Recomm 15 Sep 1950. Decomm 9 Jun 1952. Trfd to South Korea 3 Sep 1952.
Later history: renamed *Imchin* (PF 66). R1973.
4★Korea K-2 K-4 K-7 K-8.

PF 5   *Hoquiam*   To USSR, 17 Aug 1945–1 Nov 1949, renamed *EK-13*. Recomm 27 Sep 1950. Hit by shore gunfire at Songjin, Korea, 7 May 1951. Decomm 5 Oct 1951 and trfd to South Korea.
Later history: renamed *Naktong* (PF 65). R1973.
5★Korea K-1 K-2 K-4 K-5 K-6.

PF 6   *Pasco*   To USSR, 17 Aug 1945–15 Jul 1950, renamed *EK-12*. Trfd to Japan 14 Jan 1953.
Later history: renamed *Kashi* (PF 283), renamed *YAC-12*. BU 1969.

PF 7   *Albuquerque*   To USSR, 17 Aug 1945–15 Nov 1949, renamed *EK-14*. Recomm 3 Oct 1950. Hit by shore gunfire in Wonsan harbor, Korea, 12 Jun 1952. Decomm 28 Feb 1953. Trfd to Japan 30 Nov 1953.
Later history: renamed *Tochi* (PF 296), renamed *YAC-15* 1965. BU 1973.
3★Korea K-6 K-8 K-9.

PF 8   *Everett*   To USSR, 17 Aug 1945–15 Nov 1949, renamed *EK-15*. Recomm 26 Jul 1950. Damaged by coastal gunfire off Wonsan, 3 Jul 1951. Decomm 10 Mar 1953. Trfd to Japan 29 Aug 1953.
Later history: renamed *Kiri* (PF 291), renamed *YAC-20*, 1970. R1975.
4★Korea K-5 K-6 K-7 K-8.

Figure 8.2: *USS Glendale* (PF 36), patrol frigate in service during Korean War after her return from Russia, June 1951.

PF 21   *Bayonne*   To USSR, 2 Sep 1945–14 Nov 1949, renamed *EK-25*. Recomm 28 Jul 1950. Decomm 31 Jan 1953. Trfd to Japan 31 Oct 1953.
Later history: renamed *Buna* (PF 294), renamed *YAC-11*, 1966. R1967, BU 1973.
6★Korea K-1 K-3 K-6 K-7 K-8 K-9.

PF 22   *Gloucester*   To USSR, 4 Sep 1945–31 Oct 1949, renamed *EK-26*. Recomm 11 Oct 1950. Damaged by coastal gunfire off Kojo, Korea, 11 Nov 1951. Decomm 15 Sep 1952. Trfd to Japan 30 Sep 1953.
Later history: renamed *Tsuge* (PF 292). BU 1969.
7★Korea K-1 K-2 K-4 K-5 K-6, K-7 K-8.

PF 25   *Charlottesville*   To USSR, 13 Jul 1945–17 Oct 1949, renamed *EK-1*. Trfd to Japan 14 Jan 1953.
Later history: renamed *Matsu* (PF 286), renamed *YTE-09* 1966. R1973.

PF 26   *Poughkeepsie*   To USSR, 2 Sep 1945–31 Oct 1949, renamed *EK-27*. Trfd to Japan 14 Jan 1953.
Later history: Japanese *Momi* (PF 284), renamed *YAC-13* 1965. R1970.

PF 27   *Newport*   To USSR, 4 Sep 1945–14 Nov 1949, renamed *EK-28*. Recomm 27 Jul 1950. Decomm 30 Apr 1952. Trfd to Japan 30 Sep 1953.
Later history: renamed *Kaede* (PF 293), renamed *YAC-17* 1966. R1975.
4★Korea K-1 K-3 K-6 K-7.

PF 34   *Long Beach*   To USSR, 13 Jul 1945–17 Oct 1949, renamed *EK-2*. Trfd to Japan 30 Nov 1953.
Later history: renamed *Shii* (PF 297), renamed *YAS-44* 1967. R1970.

PF 36   *Glendale*   To USSR, 12 Jun 1945–16 Nov 1949, renamed *EK-6*. Recomm 11 Oct 1950. Decomm 29 Oct 1951 and trfd to Thailand.
Later history: renamed *Tachin* (1/411) Preserved as memorial at Sattahib, <2001.
4★Korea K-2 K-4 K-5 K-6.

PF 37   *San Pedro*   To USSR, 13 Jul 1945–17 Oct 1949, renamed *EK-5*. Trfd to Japan 30 Mar 1953.
Later history: renamed *Kaya* (PF 288), renamed *YAC-23* 1972. R1977.

PF 38   *Coronado*   To USSR, 13 Jul 1945–16 Oct 1949, renamed *EK-8*. Trfd to Japan 14 Jan 1953.
Later history: renamed *Sugi* (PF 298). R1971.

PF 39   *Ogden*   To USSR, 13 Jul 1945–17 Oct 1949, renamed *EK-10*. Trfd to Japan 14 Jan 1953.
Later history: renamed *Kusu* (PF 281), renamed *YAS-50* 1970, *YAC-22* 1971. R1973.

PF 46   *Bisbee*   To USSR, 27 Aug 1945–1 Nov 1949, renamed *EK-17*. Recomm 18 Oct 1950. Decomm 13 Feb 1952 (21 Oct 1951). Trfd to Colombia.
Later history: renamed *Capitan Tono* (FG 12). R1962.
3★Korea K-2 K-4 K-6.

PF 47   *Gallup*   To USSR, 27 Aug 1945–14 Nov 1949, renamed *EK-22*. Recomm 18 Oct 1950. Decomm 29 Oct 1951 and trfd to Thailand.
Later history: renamed *Prasae* (2/412). R2000. Preserved as memorial at Sattahib.
1★Korea K-5.

PF 48   *Rockford*   To USSR, 27 Aug 1945–1 Nov 1949, renamed *EK-18*. Trfd to South Korea 5 Nov 1950.
Later history: renamed *Apnok* (62). Irreparably damaged in collision, 21 May 1952. Returned 3 Sep 1952. Sunk as target 30 Sep 1953.

PF 49   *Muskogee*   To USSR, 27 Aug 1945–1 Nov 1949, renamed *EK-19*. Trfd to South Korea 23 Oct 1950.
Later history: renamed *Duman* (PF 61). R1973.

PF 50   *Carson City*   To USSR, 29 Aug 1945–31 Oct 1949, renamed *EK-20*. Trfd to Japan 30 Apr 1953.
Later history: renamed *Sakura* (PF 290), renamed *YAC-16* 1966. R1973.

PF 51   *Burlington*   To USSR, 13 Jul 1945–14 Nov 1949, renamed *EK-21*. Recomm 5 Jan 1951. Decomm 15 Sep 1952. Trfd to Colombia 26 Jun 1953.
Later history: renamed *Almirante Brión* (FG 14). R1968.
5★Korea K-4 K-5 K-6 K-7 K-8.

PF 52   *Allentown*   To USSR, 13 Jul 1945–15 Oct 1949 renamed *EK-9*. Trfd to Japan 24 Mar 1953.
Later history: renamed *Ume* (PF 289), renamed *YAC-14* 1965. BU 1971 Taiwan.

PF 53   *Machias*   To USSR, 13 Jul 1945–17 Oct 1949, renamed *EK-4*. Trfd to Japan 28 Jan 1953.
Later history: renamed *Nara* (PF 282), renamed *YTE-08* 1966. BU 1973.

PF 54   *Sandusky*   To USSR, 13 Jul 1945–17 Oct 1949, renamed *EK-7*. Trfd to Japan 16 Feb 1953.
Later history: renamed *Nire* (PF 287), renamed *YAC-19* 1969. R1970.

PF 55   *Bath*   To USSR, 13 Jul 1945–15 Nov 1949, renamed *EK-29*. Trfd to Japan 23 Dec 1953.
Later history: renamed *Maki* (PF 298), renamed *YAS-36* 1966. BU 1973.

PF 70   *Evansville*   To USSR, 4 Sep 1945-Oct/Nov 1949. Recomm 29 Jul 1950. Decomm 28 Feb 1953. Trfd to Japan 4 Dec 1953.
Later history: renamed *Keyaki* (PF 295). R1976.
6★Korea K-1 K-3 K-6 K-7 K-8 K-9.

Notes: 26 frigates on loan to USSR during World War II were returned in 1949 and 13 were returned to service during the Korean War.

HYDROFOILS

Note: see also *Plainview* (AGEH 1) (p. 179)

No.	Name	Builder	Keel Laid	Launched	Comm.
PCH 1	*High Point*	Martinac	27 Feb 1961	17 Aug 1962	3 Sep 1963
Displacement	120 tons f/l				
Dimensions	115′ (oa) × 31′ × 6′/17′				
Machinery	diesel; 600 BHP; 12 knots 2 gas turbines; 6,200 SHP; 48 knots (foilborne)				
Endurance	2,000/12 & 500/45				
Complement	13				
Armament	MG, 4–12.75″ ASW TT. Harpoon SSM for testing.				

Notes: First hydrofoil in USN. Aluminum hull and superstructure. Designed by Boeing. Turbine broke down 1975, cost of repairs was prohibitive.

Service Record: On loan to USCG as WMEH 1, 2 Mar 1977–30 Sep 1978. Sold Feb 2002.

No.	Name	Builder	Keel Laid	Launched	Comm.
PGH 1	*Flagstaff*	Grumman	1 Jun 1966	15 Jul 1966	14 Sep 1968
Displacement	67 tons				
Dimensions	82′ (oa) 74′4″ (wl) × 21′6″ × 4′4″ (18′ foils extended)				
Machinery	(foilborne) Rolls Royce gas turbine; 3,620 hp; 45 knots; (hull-borne) GM diesel; 2 waterjets; 8 knots,				
Complement	12				
Armament	1–40 mm gun, 1–81 mm mortar				

Notes: Competitive with *Tucumcari*. Thirty per cent of weight supported by stern foil. 36 PGH were planned.

Service Record: To USCG 29 Sep 1976, as WPBH 1. Decomm 30 Sep 1978. BU 1978.

No.	Name	Builder	Keel Laid	Launched	Comm.
PGH 2	*Tucumcari*	Boeing	1 Sep 1966	15 Jul 1967	7 Mar 1968
Displacement	57 tons				
Dimensions	71′9″ (oa) × 19′6″ × 14′ (foils down)				
Machinery	(foilborne) Proteus gas turbine, 3,040 hp, 50 knots; (hull borne) 1 diesel, 150 SHP				
Complement	13				
Armament	1–40 mm gun, 1–81 mm mortar				

Notes: Competitive with *Flagstaff*. Aluminum construction. Seventy per cent of weight supported by aft foils.

Service Record: Vietnam 1969. Wrecked on reef off Puerto Rico, 16 Nov 1972. Stricken 7 Nov 1973. Used as test hulk. BU 1973.

No.	Builder	Keel Laid	Launched	Completed	Built for	Name (No.)	Fate
PF 103	Levingston	20 Aug 1962	7 Jul 1963	18 May 1964	Iran	*Bayandor* (81)	SE2001.
PF 104	Levingston	12 Sep 1962	Oct 1963	22 Jul 1964	Iran	*Naghdi* (82)	SE2001
PF 105	Levingston	1 May 1967	4 Jan 1968	11 Feb 1969	Iran	*Milanian* (83).	Sunk 1982
PF 106	Levingston	12 Jun 1967	4 Apr 1968	13 Feb 1969	Iran	*Khanamvie* (84).	Sunk 1982
PF 107	Amer; Toledo	1 Apr 1970	17 Oct 1970	1 Nov 1971	Thailand	*Tapi* (431)	SE2001
PF 108	Norfolk SB	18 Feb 1972	2 Jun 1973	10 Aug 1974	Thailand	*Khirirat* (432)	SE2001
Displacement	900 tons, 1,135 f/l			Endurance	2400/18		
Dimensions	275′6″(oa) × 33′2″ × 10′3″			Complement	140		
Machinery	2 screws; diesels; 5,800 hp; 20 knots			Armament	2–3″/50, 2–40mm		

Notes: MAP for Iran & Thailand. Similar to Indonesian *Pattimura* class built in Italy. PF 105 and 106 were sunk by Iraqi forces in 1982–83.

PF 109–112   rec FFG 7–10

Figure 8.3: *USS High Point* (PCH 1) firing a Harpoon missile in 1974. She was classified as a submarine chaser.

Figure 8.4: The hydrofoil gunboat *Flagstaff* (PGH 1), built to be competitive with *Tucumcari*. She was supposed to make 50 knots foilborne.

Figure 8.5: *USS Tucumcari* (PGH 2), hydrofoil gunboat, at rest, with foils retracted.

HYDROFOIL MISSILE SHIPS

No.	Name	Builder	Keel Laid	Launched	Comm.
PHM 1	*Pegasus*	Boeing	9 May 1972	9 Nov 1974	9 Jul 1977
	ex-*Delphinus* (26 Apr 1974)				
PHM 2 (i)	*Hercules*	Boeing	30 May 1974		
PHM 3/6					
PHM 2	*Hercules*	Boeing	12 Sep 1980	13 Apr 1982	12 Mar 1983
PHM 3	*Taurus*	Boeing	30 Jan 1979	8 May 1981	7 Oct 1981
PHM 4	*Aquila*	Boeing	10 Jul 1979	16 Sep 1981	26 Jun 1982
PHM 5	*Aries*	Boeing	7 Jan 1980	5 Nov 1981	18 Sep 1982
PHM 6	*Gemini*	Boeing	13 May 1980	17 Feb 1982	13 Nov 1982

Displacement	198 tons; 285 f/l
Dimensions	132′8″ (oa); 116′ (wl) × 28′2″ × 6′2″/23′2″
Machinery	2 waterjets; diesels; 1,630 BHP; 12 knots
	1 waterjet, gas turbine, 16,767 SHP, 51 knots (foilborne)
Endurance	1,225/11 or 600/40
Complement	23
Armament	8 Harpoon SSM, 1–76 mm

Notes: Originally 30 ships were planned but program was canceled in 1975, then reinstated 1976. Originally a Joint program with West Germany and Italy, but those nations withdrew after U.S. cancellation of the program. Heavily armed with high speed designed for sea control operations; aluminum hulls. Much improved over previous designs, but too expensive. Used principally for interdiction of drug smuggling.

Service Records:

PHM 1 *Pegasus*   Collided with LST *Newport* north of Cuba, 30 Sep 1981. Decomm and stricken 30 Jul 1993. Sold 19 Aug 1996, BU.
PHM 2 (i)   canceled Aug 1975, 40.9% complete
PHM 3/6 (i)   canceled 6 Apr 1977; reordered 20 Oct 1977.
PHM 2 *Hercules*   Decomm and stricken 30 Jul 1993. Sold 19 Aug 1996, BU.
PHM 3 *Taurus*   Decomm and stricken 30 Jul 1993. Sold 19 Aug 1996, BU.
◆Grenada.

Figure 8.6: *USS Pegasus* (PHM 1), hydrofoil missile ship, foilborne. This class had a troubled start and proved too expensive.

PHM 4 *Aquila*   Decomm and stricken 30 Jul 1993. Sold 19 Aug 1996, BU.
◆Grenada.
PHM 5 *Aries*   Decomm and stricken 30 Jul 1993. Sold 19 Aug 1996.
Later history: museum at Brunswick, Mo.
PHM 6 *Gemini*   Decomm and stricken 30 Jul 1993. Sold 19 Aug 1996, BU.

PATROL CHASERS (MISSILE)

(MISSILE CORVETTES)

No.	Builder	Keel Laid	Launched	Completed	Saudi Name (No.)	—
PCG 1	Tacoma	30 May 1979	26 Jan 1980	20 Sep 1981	*Badr* (612)	SE2001
PCG 2	Tacoma	13 Dec 1979	13 May 1980	May 1982	*Al-Yarmook* (614)	SE2001
PCG 3	Tacoma	19 May 1980	5 Sep 1980	Oct 1982	*Hitteen* (616)	SE2001
PCG 4	Tacoma	22 Sep 1980	18 Jun 1981	Jan 1983	*Tabuk* (618)	SE2001

Displacement	870 tons, 1,038 f/l
Dimensions	246′(oa) × 31′6″ × 8′10″
Machinery	2 screws; CODOG; gas turbines; 23,000 BHP; 30 knots diesel; 4,000 hp; 20 knots
Endurance	4,000/20
Complement	58
Armament	8 Harpoon SSM launchers, 1–3″/62, 1 Phalanx, 1–81″ mortar, 2–40 mm grenade lchrs, 6–12.75″ASW TT

Notes: OSP for Saudi Arabia.

No.	Builder	Keel Laid	Launched	Completed	Thai Name (No.)	Fate
PCG 5	Tacoma	6 Feb 1984	11 Mar 1986	26 Sep 1986	*Ratanakosin* (1)	SE1993
PCG 6	Tacoma	26 Mar 1984	20 Jul 1986	19 Feb 1987	*Sukhothai* (2)	SE1993

Displacement	890 tons; 960 f/l
Dimensions	76.82 × 9.55 × 2.44 meters
Machinery	2 screws; diesel; 16,000 hp,
Endurance	3,000/16
Complement	87
Armament	8 Harpoon SSM launchers, Albatross SAM, 1–76 mm/62, 2–40 mm/70 guns, 5 ASW TT

Notes: OSP for Thailand.

PATROL GUNBOATS (MISSILE)

No.	Builder	Keel Laid	Launched	Completed	Saudi Name (No.)	—
PGG 1	Peterson	15 Sep 1978	22 Sep 1979	15 Dec 1980	*Al-Siddiq* (511)	SE2001
PGG 2	Peterson	12 Mar 1979	17 May 1980	22 Jun 1981	*Al-Farooq* (513)	SE2001
PGG 3	Peterson	19 Oct 1979	23 Aug 1980	3 Sep 1981	*Abdul Aziz* (515)	SE2001
PGG 4	Peterson	4 Mar 1980	15 Nov 1980	23 Nov 1981	*Faisal* (517)	SE2001
PGG 5	Peterson	27 Jun 1980	28 Mar 1981	11 Jan 1982	*Khalid* (519)	SE2001
PGG 6	Peterson	21 Oct 1980	13 Jun 1981	21 Jun 1982	*Amr* (521)	SE2001
PGG 7	Peterson	10 Feb 1981	23 Sep 1981	11 Aug 1982	*Tariq* (523)	SE2001
PGG 8	Peterson	8 May 1981	12 Dec 1981	18 Oct 1982	*Oqbah* (525)	SE2001
PGG 9	Peterson	4 Sep 1981	3 Apr 1982	6 Dec 1982	*Abu Obaidah* (527)	SE2001

Displacement	425 tons, 478 f/l
Dimensions	190′6″(oa) × 26′6″ × 6′7″
Machinery	2 screws; gas turbine and diesel, 23,000 BHP and 6116 hp; 38 and 25 knots
Endurance	2,900/14
Complement	38
Armament	4 Harpoon SSM launchers, 1–3″/62 gun, 1 Phalanx.

Notes: Built for Saudi Arabia. A development of *Asheville* class.

PATROL VESSELS

Submarine Chasers on the Navy List, 1947

[Remaining ships named 15 Feb 1956]

PC-461 *Bluffton*   Decomm 15 Aug 1946. Stricken 5 Sep 1957. Sold 5 Aug 1958.
PCC-463   Decomm 16 Aug 1946. Stricken 20 Jul 1953. Sunk as target off Key West, 10 Jul 1953.
PC-465 *Paragould*   Stricken 1 Jul 1960. Trfd to Venezuela, 11 Apr 1961.
Later history: renamed *Pulpo* (P 07). R1978.
PCC-466 *Carmi*   Decomm Mar 1947. Stricken 1 Jul 1960.
PCC-469   Decomm Dec 1946. Stricken 1949. Sunk as target Jun 1949.
PC-470 *Antigo*   Decomm <1950. Stricken 1 Jul 1960.
PC-483 *Rolla*   Decomm 18 Jun 1946. Stricken 1 Jul 1960. Trfd to Venezuela 11 Apr 1961.
Later history: renamed *Camaron* (P 08). R1978.
PC-484 *Cooperstown* Decomm Mar 1947. Stricken 1 Jul 1960. Trfd to Venezuela 11 Apr 1961.
Later history: renamed *Togogo* (P 09). R1978.
PC-485   Decomm 9 Feb 1946. Stricken. Trfd to South Korea Jan 1952.
Later history: renamed *Han Rasan* (PC 705). Lost in typhoon at Guam, 24 Nov 1962, BU
PC-486 *Jasper*   Decomm 30 Apr 1959. Stricken 1 May 1959.
PC-487 *Larchmont*   Decomm <1950. Stricken 1 Jul 1960. Trfd to Venezuela, 24 Jul 1961.
Later history: renamed *Mejillon* (P 01).
PC-490   Decomm 12 Mar 1946. Stricken 12 Dec 1946. Trfd to China 27 Aug 1948.
Later history: renamed *Wu Seng*. R1952.
PC-492   Decomm 13 Feb 1946. Stricken Trfd to China, 30 Jun 1948.
Later history: renamed *Hwangpu*, then *Fu Kiang* (P 105). SE1972.
PC-553 *Malone*   Decomm 9 Jul 1946. Stricken 5 Sep 1957. Sold 1 Jul 1958; BU Baltimore.
PC-560 *Oberlin*   Decomm 28 Jan 1947. Stricken 5 Sep 1957. BU.
PC-564 *Chadron*   Out of comm 1946–1950. Stricken 1 Nov 1962. Trfd to South Korea 22 Jan 1964.
Later history: renamed *Sol Ak* (PC 709). R1974.
PC-565 *Gilmer*   Decomm 26 Apr 1946. Stricken 1 Jul 1960. Trfd to Venezuela 1 Jun 1962.
Later history: renamed *Alcatraz* (P 03). SE1972.

Figure 8.7: *USS Chadron* (PC 564), submarine chaser, sometime in the late 1950s, little changed from her wartime appearance.

PC-566 *Honesdale* Decomm 8 Jan 1947. NRT 1947. Stricken 1 Jul 1960. Trfd to Venezuela Jul 1961.
Later history: renamed *Calamar* (P 02). R1978.

PC-567 *Riverhead* Decomm 12 Jul 1946. Stricken 15 Mar 1963, to USAF.

PC-568 *Altus* Decomm 30 Apr 1946. Stricken 15 Mar 1963, to USAF. Trfd to Philippines 2 Mar 1968.
Later history: renamed *Nueva Viscaya* (PS 80). Sunk in typhoon at Cebu, 13 Nov 1993.

PC-569 *Petoskey* Decomm 25 Mar 1947. Stricken 1 Jul 1960.

PC-570 Stricken 3 Jul 1946. Trfd to Thailand Dec 1952.
Later history: renamed *Longlom* (PC 8). R1994.

PC-571 *Anoka* Decomm 15 Nov 1946. Stricken 1 Nov 1959. Sold 9 May 1960.

PC-572 *Tooele* Decomm 9 Dec 1959. Stricken 1 Jul 1960. Sold to Venezuela Oct 1960, and discarded.

PC-579 *Wapakoneta* Decomm 17 Dec 1955. Stricken 1 Jul 1960.
Later history: Merchant *Hydra*.

PC-580 *Malvern* Decomm 27 Mar 1958. Stricken 1 Apr 1960. Trfd to Indonesia.
Later history: renamed *Hui* (318/805). SE1987.

PC-581 *Manville* Decomm 27 Mar 1959. Stricken 1 Apr 1960. Trfd to Indonesia.
Later history: renamed *Torani* (317). SE1962.

PCC-582 *Lenoir* Out of commission 1 Feb 1950–3 Oct 1952. Decomm 15 Jan 1955 Rec **PC 582**, 27 Oct 1955. Stricken 1 Jul 1960. Trfd to Venezuela Jun 1962.
Later history: renamed *Albatros* (P 04). R 1978.

PC-586 *Patchogue* NRT 1947. Decomm Jan 1950. Stricken 1 Apr 1959. Sold, BU.

PC-587 Stricken. To MC 12 Apr 1948. Trfd to Dominican Republic 14 Apr 1948.
Later history: renamed *18 de Diciembre* (BA 101). R1960.

PC-588 *Houghton* Decomm 29 Jul 1946. Stricken 1 Apr 1959. Sold 11 May 1960.

PCC-589 *Metropolis* Decomm Mar 1946. Rec **PC 589**, 27 Oct 1955. Stricken 1 Apr 1959. Sold 1 Dec 1959.

PC-592 *Towanda* NRT 1947. Decomm Jan 1950. Stricken 1 Apr 1959.

PC-595 Stricken <1950. Trfd to China 30 Jun 1948.
Later history: renamed *PG-502*. BU.

PC-597 *Kerrville* Decomm 30 Apr 1947. Stricken 5 Sep 1957. BU Baltimore.

PC-600 Stricken <1950. Trfd to South Korea 21 Jan 1952.
Later history: renamed *Myo Hyang San* (PC-706) BU 1968.

PC-601 *Arcata* Decomm 27 Jul 1946. Stricken 1 Jul 1960. Sold Apr 1961.

PC-602 *Alturas* Decomm Jan 1947. Stricken 1 Jul 1960. Sold Apr 1961.

PC-603 *Solvay* Decomm 8 Jan 1947. NRT 1947–56. Stricken 1 Jul 1960.

PC-606 *Andrews* Decomm 24 Mar 1947. Stricken 5 Sep 1957. BU Baltimore.

PC-608 Decomm 21 May 1946. Stricken 1 Jul 1948. Sold to Mexico 1952.
Later history: renamed *GC-31*. R1964.

PC-610 Decomm Dec 1945. NRT. Beached at Hen and Chickens Reef, RI, as bombing target, 7 Jun 1950 and destroyed.

PC-612 Stricken 25 Mar 1948.

PC-614 Sold. Trfd to Mexico 1952.
Later history: renamed *GC-32*. R1964.

PC-616 Decomm <1950. Sold Trfd to Thailand Jun 1952.
Later history: renamed *Tongpliu* (PC 6). R1993.

PC-617 *Beeville* Decomm 30 Jun 1947. Stricken 5 Sep 1957. Sold 5 Aug 1958, BU.

PC-618 *Weatherford* Rec **EPC 618**, Apr 1947. [Given tripod mast] Decomm and stricken 1 Nov 1965. Salvage training hulk. Sunk as target, 1 Nov 1968.

PC-619 *Dalhart* Decomm 28 Apr 1947. Stricken Trfd to Venezuela 5 Jul 1961.
Later history: renamed *Gaviota* (P 10). R1979.

PC-620 *Bethany* Decomm Jan 1947. Stricken 5 Sep 1957. Sold, BU 1958 Baltimore.

PC-776 *Pikeville* Decomm 21 May 1946. NRT 1946. Stricken 1 Apr 1959. Sold 14 Sep 1960, BU.

PC-777 *Waynesburg* Decomm 28 Apr 1946. NRT 1946–59. Stricken 1 Apr 1959.

PC-778 *Gallipolis* NRT 1947. Decomm Oct 1949. Stricken 1 Apr 1959; Sold 15 Sep 1959.

PC-779 *Mechanicsburg* Decomm 20 Mar 1950. Stricken 1 Apr 1959.

PC-780 *Maynard* Decomm 14 Aug 1946. Stricken 1 Apr 1959. Sold 16 Sep 1959.

PC-781 *Metuchen* Decomm 14 Aug 1946. NRT 1947–1949. Stricken 1 Nov 1959. Sold 14 Aug 1959, BU.

PC-782 *Glenolden* Decomm Jan 1947. NRT 1947. Stricken 1 Apr 1959. Sold 14 Sep 1959.

PC-785 *Frostburg* NRT 1947. Decomm <1950. Stricken 1 Apr 1958.

PC-786 Decomm 22 Jun 1946. NRT 1947. Stricken Trfd to Taiwan 3 Apr 1954.
Later history: renamed *Hsiang Kiang* (118). SE1962.

PC-808 *Ripley* NRT 1947. Decomm 10 Mar 1949. Stricken 1 Apr 1959. Sold 17 Aug 1959.

PC-817 *Welch* Decomm 22 Jul 1946. NRT 1946–50. Stricken 1 Apr 1959. Sold.

PC-822 *Asheboro* Decomm 12 Jul 1946. NRT 1946–50. Stricken 1 Apr 1959. Sold 1959.

PC 1077 *Edenton* Decomm <1950. Stricken Trfd to Venezuela 11 Jan 1961.
Later history: renamed *Caracol* (P 06). SE1972.

PC 1078 NRT 1947. Decomm and trfd to Taiwan 19 May 1954.
Later history: renamed *?Tzu Chiang* PC 109.

PCC 1079 *Ludington* Decomm Mar 1946. Stricken 1 Jul 1960. Sold 13 Mar 1961.

PCC 1081 *Cadiz* Decomm 31 Dec 1946. Rec **PC 1081**, 27 Oct 1955. Stricken 1 Jul 1960.

PC 1086 Decomm 2 Mar 1951. Stricken Trfd to France 2 Mar 1951.
Later history: renamed *Flamberge* (P631). Trfd to Cambodia 1956, renamed *E-311*. Recovered May 1975.

PC 1087 *Placerville* Decomm 20 Feb 1947. Stricken 15 Apr 1976. Trfd to Taiwan 16 Jul 1957.
Later history: renamed *Tung Kiang* (*Tung Chang*) (119). SE1972.

PC 1119 *Greencastle* Decomm 9 Jan 1947. Stricken 1957 Sold 1 Jul 1958, BU Baltimore.
PC 1120 *Carlinville* Decomm Jan 1947. Stricken 1 Apr 1959. Sold 1975.
   Later history: merchant *Island Transport*, renamed *Ohana Kai* 1977 (Greenpeace). BU 1991.
PCC 1125 *Cordele* Decomm <1950. Stricken 1 Apr 1959.
PC 1130 Decomm 2 Nov 1946. Trfd to France 28 Sep 1950.
   Later history: renamed *L'Intrépide* (P 630). Trfd to Vietnam 1954, renamed *Van Kiep* (HQ 02). R1965.
PC 1135 *Canastota* Decomm <1950. Stricken 1 Apr 1959.
PCC 1136 *Galena* Decomm 28 Jul 1946. Rec **PC 1136**, 27 Oct 1955. Stricken 1 Apr 1959. Sold 11 Mar 1960.
PCC 1137 *Worthington* Decomm 10 Aug 1946. Stricken 1 Apr 1959.
   Later history: Merchant *Widgeon*.
PC 1138 *Lapeer* Decomm 13 Sep 1946. Stricken 1 Apr 1959.
   Later history: Merchant *Knick Bay* 1977, renamed *Mister B.*, *Duenas* 1987. SE1998.
PC 1139 Decomm 23 Jul 1946. Trfd to France 28 Sep 1950.
   Later history: renamed *L'Impétueux* (P 629). Trfd to Cambodia 1954. Returned to U.S. 1956.
PC 1140 *Glenwood* Decomm Jan 1947. Stricken 1 Jul 1960. Sold Mar 1961.
   Later history: merchant *Daniel L. Harris III*. SE1983.
PC 1141 *Pierre* NRT. Decomm 28 Oct 1958 and trfd to Indonesia 25 Oct 1958.
   Later history: renamed *Tjakalang* (313). SE1962.
PC 1142 *Hanford* Decomm Oct 1946. Trfd to Taiwan 15 Jul 1957.
   Later history: renamed *Pei Kiang* (*Pei Chang*) (P122). SE1972.
PC 1143 Decomm <1950. Trfd to France 1951.
   Later history: renamed *Glaive* (P-632). Trfd to Vietnam 1954, renamed *Tayket* (HQ 05). R1965.
PC 1144 Decomm <1950. Trfd to France 1951.
   Later history: renamed *Mousquet* (P-633). Trfd to Vietnam 1955, renamed *Chi Lang*. R1962.
PC 1145 *Winnemucca* Out of comm 15 Feb 1946–1950. Stricken 1 Jun 1960. Trfd to South Korea 1 Nov 1960.
   Later history: renamed *O Tae San* (PC 707). SE1962.
PC 1146 Decomm <1950. Trfd to France 1951.
   Later history: renamed *Trident* (P 634). Trfd to Vietnam 1956, renamed *Tuy Dong* (HQ 04). R1965.
PC 1149 *Susanville* Decomm 20 Feb 1947. Trfd to Taiwan 16 Jul 1957.
   Later history: renamed *Hsi Kiang* (*Hsi Chang*) (P 120). Trfd to Taiwan Customs Svc 1972.
PC 1167 Decomm <1950. Trfd to France 1951.
   Later history: renamed *L'Ardent*. (P 635). Trfd to Vietnam 1956, renamed *Dong Da*. R1961.
PCC 1168 Decomm 31 Dec 1946. Stricken Trfd to China 1954.
   Later history: renamed *Ching Kiang* (116). SE1962.
PCC 1169 *Escondido* Decomm 1950. Stricken Trfd to Taiwan 15 Jul 1957.
   Later history: renamed *Liu Kiang* (*Liu Chang*) (123). SE1962.
PC 1170 *Kelso* Decomm 5 Aug 1955. Stricken 1 Jul 1960. Sold 25 Apr 1961, BU.
PC 1171 Decomm 4 Dec 1946. Trfd to France 1951.
   Later history: renamed *L'Inconstant* (P636). Trfd to Cambodia 1956, renamed *E-312*. Fled to Philippines and trfd 1976, renamed *Negros Oriental* (PS 29). R1991.
PC 1172 *Olney* Decomm Feb 1955. Stricken 1 Jul 1960. Sold 20 May 1961.
   Later history: Merchant *Gleaner*. SE1976.
PC 1173 *Andalusia* Decomm Mar 1946. Stricken 1 Jul 1960. Sunk as target off Cape Charles, Va., 23 Nov 1965.
PC 1174 *Fredonia* Decomm 28 Jun 1946. Stricken 1957. Sunk as artificial reef off Boynton Beach, Fla., 1968.
PC 1175 *Vandalia* Decomm 16 Aug 1946. Stricken. Trfd to Taiwan 15 Jul 1957.
   Later history: renamed *Han Kiang* (*Han Chang*) (124). Wrecked 1969.

PC 1176 *Minden* Decomm 23 May 1946. Stricken 1 Jul 1960. Trfd to Venezuela Jun 1962.
   Later history: renamed *Petrel* (P 05). R1978.
PCC 1177 *Guymon* Decomm 27 Jul 1946. Stricken 1 Jul 1960. Sold 25 Apr 1961. BU Seattle.
PCC 1178 *Kewaunee* Decomm 4 Sep 1946. Rec **PC 1178**, 27 Oct 1955. Stricken 1 Nov 1959. BU 1960, Portland, Ore.
PC 1179 *Morris* Decomm 13 May 1946. Stricken 1 Jul 1960; Sold May 1961, BU Portland, Ore.
PCC 1180 *Woodstock* Decomm 15 Nov 1946. Stricken 1 Jul 1960. BU 1961.
PC 1181 *Wildwood* Decomm 18 Aug 1946. Stricken 1 Apr 1959.
PC 1182 Decomm 9 Aug 1946. NRT 1947. Trfd to Taiwan 26 Jul 1954.
   Later history: renamed *Yuan Kiang* (110). SE1962.
PC 1186 *Ipswich* Decomm 22 Jul 1946. NRT 1947. Stricken 1 Apr 1959. Sold.
PC 1191 *Bel Air* Decomm 12 Jul 1946. NRT 1947. Stricken 1 Apr 1959.
PC 1193 *Ridgway* NRT 1947. Decomm 2 Mar 1950. Stricken 1 Apr 1959. Sold 16 Sep 1959, BU.
PC 1196 *Mayfield* Decomm Jul 1946. NRT 1947–1949. Stricken 1 Apr 1959. Sold, BU.
PC 1198 *Westerly* Decomm 15 Mar 1950. Stricken 1 Apr 1959.
PC 1201 *Kittery* Decomm 30 Jul 1946. NRT 1947–1950. Stricken 1 Apr 1959. Sold 9 Oct 1959, BU.
PC 1208 Decomm 9 Aug 1946. NRT 1947. Trfd to Taiwan 26 Jul 1954.
   Later history: renamed *Li Kiang* (P 111). SE1972.
PC 1209 *Medina* NRT 1947. Decomm Jan 1950. Stricken 1 Apr 1959. Sold 9 Oct 1959, BU.
PC 1212 *Laurinburg* Decomm 23 Aug 1946. NRT 1946–49. Stricken 1 Apr 1959.
PC 1213 *Louden* Decomm 20 Jul 1946. NRT 1946–. Stricken 1 Apr 1959. Sold 14 Dec 1959, BU Portland, Me.
PC 1216 *Elkins* Decomm 10 May 1946. NRT 1946. Stricken 1 Apr 1959.
PC 1225 *Waverly* Decomm 18 Jul 1946. Stricken 5 Sep 1957. BU 1958.
PC 1228 *Munising* Decomm 19 Jul 1946. Stricken 7 Sep 1957. Sold 1 Jul 1958, BU Baltimore.
PC 1229 *Wauseon* Decomm 7 Aug 1946. Stricken 5 Sep 1957. BU 1958 Baltimore.
PCC 1230 *Grinnell* Decomm Mar 1946. Rec **PC 1230**, 27 Oct 1955. Stricken 1 Apr 1959. Sold 1960s.
   Later history: merchant *Grinnell*, renamed *Bolivar* 1971. SE1976.
PCC 1231 *Tipton* Decomm 28 Jun 1946. Rec **PC 1231**, 27 Oct 1955. Stricken 1 Jul 1960.
PC 1232 Decomm 15 Aug 1946. Stricken. Trfd to Taiwan Jun 1954.
   Later history: renamed *Chang Kiang* (118). Sunk by PRC warships south of Quemoy, 6 Aug 1965.
PC 1233 Decomm 20 Sep 1946. NRT 1947. Trfd to Taiwan 26 Jul 1954.
   Later history: renamed *Kung Kiang* (P 113). R1970.
PC 1237 *Abingdon* NRT 1947. Decomm Oct 1949. Stricken 1 Apr 1959.
PC 1240 *Culpeper* NRT 1947. Decomm 15 Feb 1956. Stricken 1 Apr 1959.
PC 1242 *Port Clinton* Decomm 1 Jul 1947. Stricken 1 Dec 1959.
PCC 1244 *Martinez* Decomm 15 Feb 1950. Rec **PC 1244**, 27 Oct 1955. Stricken 1 Jul 1960. Sold 19 May 1961, BU Astoria, Ore.
PC 1246 *Canandaigua* Decomm Jan 1947. Stricken 1 Feb 1957.
PCC 1251 *Ukiah* Decomm 3 Aug 1946. Stricken 1 Jul 1960. Sold 1 Jul 1960.
PC 1252 *Tarrytown* Decomm 28 Jun 1946. Stricken 1 Jul 1960. Trfd to Venezuela, discarded, BU.
PC 1253 Decomm <1950. Stricken Trfd to Thailand 1952.
   Later history: renamed *Liulom* (PC 7). R1994.
PC 1254 Decomm <1950. Stricken. Trfd to Taiwan May 1954.
   Later history: renamed *Po Kiang* (P114). R1970.

PCC 1260 *Durango* Decomm 12 Apr 1946. Rec **PC 1260**, 27 Oct 1955. Stricken 1 Nov 1959.

PC 1262 Decomm <1950. Trfd to Taiwan Jan 1954.
Later history: renamed *Chung Kiang* (115). R1972.

PC 1263 *Milledgeville* Decomm 16 Feb 1959. Trfd to Taiwan 1 Jul 1959.
Later history: renamed *To Kiang* (125). R1971.

PC 1546 *Grosse-Pointe* Decomm 12 Aug 1955. Trfd to South Korea 21 Nov 1960.
Later history: renamed *Kum Chong San* (PC 708). SE1962.
◆OpCastle.

PC 1547 *Corinth* Decomm <1950. Stricken 1958.

PC 1569 *Anacortes* Decomm 9 Aug 1946. Stricken 1 Jun 1960. Trfd to Vietnam 23 Nov 1960.
Later history: renamed *Van Don* (HQ 06). SE1972.

PC 1590 Out of comm 19 Jun 1946–20 Mar 1951. NRT 1947. Decomm 21 Oct 1954. Stricken 17 Sep 1954. Sunk as target.

PATROL CRAFT, ESCORT

PCE-842 *Marfa* Decomm 7 Nov 1947. NRT 1947–55. Stricken 1 Sep 1961. Trfd to South Korea 11 Dec 1961.
Later history: renamed *Tang Po* (PCE 56). Sunk by North Korean batteries in Sea of Japan, 19 Jan 1967.

PCE-843 *Skowhegan* NRT 1947. Decomm Mar 1955. Stricken 1 Feb 1960. Sold 1961.
Later history: Merchant *893*.

PCE-845 *Worland* Out of commission 22 Dec 1947–11 Dec 1950. Decomm 25 May 1964. Stricken 1 Jun 1964.
Later history: Merchant *S.S.Advance II*, 1964. Sunk as artificial reef off Kitty Hawk, NC, 1994.

PCE-846 *Eunice* Decomm 11 Jun 1946. Trfd to Ecuador 29 Nov 1960.
Later history: renamed *Esmeraldas* (E03/E22). SE1972.

PCER-849 *Somersworth* NRT 1947. Decomm Sep 1965. Rec **EPCER 849**, 1959. Stricken 1 Apr 1966. Sold 28 Feb 1967.

PCER-850 *Fairview* Rec **EPCER 850**, 1959. Stricken 1 May 1968. Sold 1969.

PCER-851 *Rockville* NRT 1947. Rec **EPCER 851**, 15 Oct 1951. Stricken 21 Dec 1968. Trfd to Colombia 5 Jun 1969.
Later history: renamed *San Andres* (BO 151). (AGS) R1980s.

PCER-852 *Brattleboro* Rec **EPCER 852**, 1959. Stricken 1 Nov 1965. Trfd to Vietnam 21 Apr 1966.
Later history: renamed *Ngoc Hoi* (HQ 12). Recovered May 1975. Trfd to Philippines, Nov 1975, renamed *Miguel Malvar* (PS 19). SE2001.

PCER-853 *Amherst* Out of commission Oct 1945–28 Nov 1950. NRT 1947. Rec **EPCER 853**, 1959. Great Lakes. Decomm 6 Feb 1970. Trfd to Vietnam 3 Jun 1970.
Later history: renamed *Van Kiep II* (HQ 14). Recovered May 1975. Trfd to Philippines, 5 Apr 1976, renamed *Datu Marikudo* (PS 23). SE2001.

PCER-855 *Rexburg* Rec **EPCER 855**, 7 Jun 1946. Decomm and stricken 2 Mar 1970. Sold 28 Oct 1970.
Later history: Merchant *Excalibur*, renamed *Atlantic Breeze* 1979. SE1998.

PCER-856 *Whitehall* Out of commission 23 Jun 1946–18 Nov 1950. NRT 1947. Rec **PCE 856**, 15 Mar 1962. Decomm and stricken 1 Jul 1970. Sold 15 May 1973.
Later history: Merchant *Donna Marie*, renamed *Atlantic Surf* 1979, *Atlantic Shore* 1981. SE1998.

PCER-857 *Marysville* Rec **EPCER 857**, 22 Mar 1947. Stricken 15 Jul 1970.
Later history: Merchant *Marysville*.

PCE-870 *Dania* Decomm 18 Oct 1946. Trfd to South Korea 9 Dec 1961.
Later history: renamed *Pyok Pa* (PCE 57). SE1962.

Figure 8.8: *USS Marysville* (EPCER 857) used for experimental purposes, has been disarmed.

Figure 8.9: *USS PCE-842*, in service for naval reserve training, was later named *Marfa*. Notice the protective bubbles covering some of her aft guns.

PCEC-873 Decomm 1947. Rec **PCE 873**, 1955. Stricken Trfd to South Korea 1 Nov 1954.
Later history: renamed *Hansan* (PCEC 53). SE1962.

PCE-874 *Pascagoula* Out of commission 25 Nov 1946–1 May 1959. NRT. Decomm 30 Apr 1959. Stricken 1 May 1959. Trfd to Ecuador 5 Dec 1960.
Later history: renamed *Manabi* (E02/E23). R1970.

PCEC-877 *Havre* NRT. Rec **PCE 877**, 27 Oct 1955. Decomm 1970. Stricken 1 Jul 1970.

PCE-880 *Ely* NRT. Stricken 1 Jul 1970. Trfd to State of Maine.
Later history: Merchant *Aqualab II*, renamed *Atlantic Mist* 1978. SE1998.

PCE-882 Decomm 1948. Rec **PCE 882**, 27 Oct 1955. Trfd to South Korea 14 Feb 1955.
Later history: renamed *Ro Ryang* (PCEC 51). SE1967.
★Korea K-2 K-4 K-8 K-9.

PCEC-886 *Banning* Rec **PCE 886**, 27 Oct 1955. Stricken 1 May 1961. Sold Dec 1969.
Later history: Merchant *Growler*.
★Korea K-8 K-9.

PCE-892 *Somerset* Decomm Oct 1947. NRT 1947–Mar 1955. Stricken 1 Jun 1961. Trfd to South Korea 9 Dec 1961.
Later history: renamed *Ryul Ro* (PCE 58). SE1962.

PCE-894 *Farmington* Decomm 19 Dec 1947. Stricken 1 Dec 1964. Trfd to Burma 18 Jun 1965.
  Later history: renamed *Yan Taing Aung* (41). SE2001.
PCE-895 *Crestview* Decomm 1958. Trfd to Vietnam 29 Nov 1961.
  Later history: renamed *Dong Da II* (HQ 07). Recovered May 1975. Trfd to Philippines, Nov 1975, renamed *Sultan Kudarat* (PS 22). SE2001.
PCEC-896 Decomm 2 Aug 1953. Stricken Trfd to South Korea 14 Feb 1955.
  Later history: renamed *Myong Ryang* (PCEC 52). SE1962. 6★Korea K-1 K-2 K-3 K-7 K-8 K-9.
PCEC-898 Decomm 4 Nov 1950. Stricken Trfd to South Korea 2 Sep 1955.
  Later history: renamed *Okpo* (PCEC 55). SE1962. 3★Korea K-7 K-9 K-10.
PCE-899 *Lamar* Out of comm 16 Dec 1949–13 Dec 1950. Decomm 25 May 1964. Trfd to USCG 29 Jul 1964.
  Later history: USCGC *Lamar*. Stricken 8 Nov 1971 and sold.
PCE-900 *Groton* Decomm 19 Aug 1955. Stricken 1 Feb 1960.
  Later history: Merchant *Atlantic Beach*. SE1998.
PCE-902 *Portage* Decomm 1950. NRT Stricken 1 Jul 1970. Sold 14 Dec 1973.
  Later history: Merchant *Atlantic Venture*. SE1998.
PCE-903 *Batesburg* Decomm 1960. Stricken Trfd to South Korea 9 Dec 1961.
  Later history: renamed *Sa Chon* (PCE 59). SE1962.
PCE-904 *Gettysburg* Out of commission 5 Jan 1950–21 Nov 1950. Decomm 2 Sep 1955. Stricken. Sold 1960, BU Baltimore.

Note: 16 PCS remained on the Navy List in 1950 and the nine remaining in 1956 were named.
1376 *Winder*, 1385 *Hollidaysburg*, 1386 *Hampton*, 1387 *Beaufort*, 1401 *McMinnville*, 1413 *Elsmere*, 1423 *Prescott*, 1431 *Grafton*, and 1444 *Conneaut*.

No.	Builder	Keel Laid	Launched	Completed	Dutch Name (No.)	—
PCE 1604	General; Boston	18 Dec 1952	30 Jul 1953	4 May 1954	*Fret* (F 818)	BU 1988
PCE 1605	General; Boston	2 Mar 1953	6 Mar 1954	5 Aug 1954	*Hermelijn* (F 819)	BU 1987
PCE 1606	General; Boston	3 Aug 1953	1 May 1954	2 Dec 1954	*Vos* (F 820)	BU1988
PCE 1607	Avondale	15 Nov 1952	2 Jan 1954	26 Mar 1954	*Wolf* (F 817)	BU1985
PCE 1608	Avondale	1 Dec 1952	30 Jan 1954	11 Jun 1954	*Panter* (F 821)	BU1987
PCE 1609	Avondale	10 Dec 1952	20 Mar 1954	11 Jun 1954	*Jaguar* (F 822)	BU1988

Displacement	805 tons; 975 f/l
Dimensions	184′6″ (oa); 180′ (bp) × 33′ × 9′5″
Machinery	2 screws; diesel; SHP 1,600; 15 knots
Complement	96
Armament	1–3″/, 6–40 mm, 8–20 mm guns

Notes: MAP for Netherlands.

No.	Builder	Completed	Built for	Name (No.)	Fate
PC 1610	Dubigeon	21 Jul 1955	France	*Le Fougueux* (P641)	(See below)
PC 1611	Mediteranée	3 Nov 1955	France	*L'Opiniâtre* (P642)	Sold 1978
PC 1612	Provence	10 Sep 1955	France	*L'Agile* (P643)	Sold 1978
PC 1613	Dubigeon	27 Sep 1954*	Portugal	*Funchal* (P587), renamed *Maio*, 1957	R1975
PC 1614	Normand	9 Feb 1955*	Portugal	*Porto Santo* (P588)	R1974
PC 1615	Mediteranée	1 Jun 1956*	Yugoslavia	*PBR-581, Udarnik*	R1988
PC 1616	Dubigeon	23 Aug 1955	Ethiopia	*Belay Deress*	To Italy, 3 Feb 1959
—	—	—	Italy	*Vedetta* (F597)	R1977
PC 1617	Normand	7 Jun 1955	Portugal	*S. Nicolau* (P589)	R1975
PC 1618	Dubigeon	12 Mar 1957	West Germany	*UW-12* (W51)	R Dec 1969
—	—	—	Tunisia	*Sakiet Sidi Youssef* (P303)	R1988 Dec 1969

*launched

Displacement	366 tons; 400 f/l
Dimensions	173′8″ (oa); 170′ (bp) × 23′ × 10′
Machinery	2 screws; diesel; 3,240 BHP; 17.5 knots
Complement	62
Armament	2–40 mm, 2–20 mm guns, ASW

Notes: OSP for foreign countries, built in France. *Le Fougueux* was sold 1978 as a Boy Scout training ship. Preserved and restored in 1999. PC 1616 intended for West Germany, but delivered to Ethiopia instead; shortly afterwards returned and transferred to Italy.

No.	Builder	Completed	Built for	Name (No.)	Fate
PCE 1619	Castellammare	1 Jun 1955	Italy	*Albatros* (F 541)	R1989
PCE 1620	Castellammare	23 Oct 1955	Italy	*Alcione* (F 544)	R1991
PCE 1621	Castellammare	29 Dec 1955	Italy	*Airone* (F 545)	R1991
PCE 1622	Castellammare	31 Jan 1957	Denmark	*Bellona* (F 344)	R1981
PCE 1623	Tirreno	30 Jul 1955	Denmark	*Diana* (F 345)	R1974
PCE 1624	Tirreno	28 Aug 1956	Denmark	*Flora* (F 346)	R1988
PCE 1625	Taranto	10 Aug 1955	Denmark	*Triton* (F 347)	R1981
PCE 1626	Breda	2 Oct 1956	Netherlands	*Lynx* (F823)	Trfd to Italy 19 Oct 1961
—	—	—	Italy	*Aquila* (F542)	R1991

Displacement	800 tons; 950 f/l
Dimensions	250′4″ (oa) × 31′6″ × 9′3″
Machinery	2 screws; diesels; 5,200 BHP; 19 knots
Endurance	2,400/18
Complement	109
Armament	2–3″ guns, replaced by 4–40 mm guns

Notes: MDAP for various countries, built in Italy.

No.	Builder	Completed	Built for	Name (No.)	Fate
SC 1627	Willemsoord	6 Aug 1954	Netherlands	*Balder* (P 802)	R1985
SC 1628	Willemsoord	9 Aug 1954	Netherlands	*Bulgia* (P 803/A880)	SE1993
SC 1629	Willemsoord	1 Dec 1954	Netherlands	*Freyr* (P 804)	R1986 = mv
SC 1630	Willemsoord	3 Feb 1955	Netherlands	*Hadda* (P805)	R1986
SC 1631	Willemsoord	23 Mar 1955	Netherlands	*Hefring* (P 806)	R1986

Displacement	149 tons; 225 f/l
Dimensions	119'2" (oa); 114'10" (bp) × 20'3" × 5'10"
Machinery	2 screws; diesel; 1,050 SHP; 15.5 knots
Complement	27
Armament	1–40 mm, 3–20 mm guns, ASW

Notes: OSP for Netherlands, built in Netherlands.

No.	Builder	Completed	Built for	Name	Fate
SC 1632	South Coast	1955	Thailand	*SC-31*, renamed *SC-7*	R1973
SC 1633	South Coast	1955	Thailand	*SC-32*, renamed *SC-8*	R1976
SC 1634	South Coast	1955	Thailand	*SC-33*	BU 8 Mar 1962

Displacement	110 tons; 169 f/l
Dimensions	119' × 17' × 6'2"
Machinery	2 screws; diesel; 15.5 knots
Complement	27
Armament	1–40 mm, 3–20 mm guns

Notes: MDAP for Thailand. Wooden hull. *SC-33* was beached after an explosion at Bangkok, 26 Dec 1961.

No.	Builder	Launched	Completed	Built for	Name (No.)	Fate
PC 1635	Viana do Castelho	2 May 1956	27 Dec 1956	Portugal	*Brava* (P590)	R1976
PC 1636	Viana do Castelho	2 May 1956	11 Apr 1957	Portugal	*Fogo* (P591)	R1974
PC 1637	Mondego	10 Jul 1956	17 May 1957	Portugal	*Boavista* (P 592)	R1976
PC 1638	Gunderson	1964	24 Sep 1964	Turkey	*Sultan Hisar* (P 111)	R2001
PC 1639	Gunderson	9 Jul 1964	22 Apr 1965	Turkey	*Demir Hisar* (P 112)	R2000
PC 1640	Gunderson	14 May 1964	22 Apr 1965	Turkey	*Yar Hisar* (P 113)	SE2005
PC 1641	Gunderson	14 May 1964	3 Dec 1965	Turkey	*Ak Hisar* (P 114)	SE2005
PC 1642	Gunderson	5 Nov 1964	20 May 1964	Turkey	*Sivri Hisar* (P 115)	R2001
PC 1643	Gunderson	Dec 1964	Jul 1965	Turkey	*Koç Hisar* (P 116)	R2001
PC 1646	ASMAR	7 Jan 1970	27 Nov 1971	Chile	*Papudo* (P 37)	SE1993
PC 1647	ASMAR	—	—	Chile	*Pisagua* (P 38)	Canceled

Displacement	280 tons; 366 tons
Dimensions	173'9" (oa); 170' (wl) × 23' × 10'3"
Machinery	2 screws; 2 diesels; 2,800 BHP; 19 knots
Endurance	5,000/10
Complement	69
Armament	1–3", 1–40 mm, 4–20 mm

Notes: OSP for Portugal, built there. MAP for Turkey. PC 1643 built in sections by Gunderson and assembled at Golcük DY. Two additional units for Chile, *Abtao* (P36) and *Pisagua* (P38) were canceled.

No.	Builder	Completed	Built for	Name (No.)	Fate
PC 1644	Helsingor	25 May 1966	Denmark	*Peder Skram* (D320/F352)	R 1991. Museum
PC 1645	Helsingor	16 Apr 1967	Denmark	*Herluf Trolle* (D321/F353)	R 1991. BU 1995

Displacement	2,030 tons
Dimensions	396'6" (oa) × 39'6" × 11'9"
Machinery	2 screws; CODOG; diesel; 4,800 hp; 13 knots gas turbines; 44,000 hp; 32.5 knots
Complement	191
Armament	2 quad Harpoon launchers, Sea Sparrow SAM, 2–5"/38, 4–40 mm, 4–21"TT

Notes: OSP for Denmark, built in Denmark

PATROL VESSELS

Cyclone Class

No.	Name	Builder	Keel Laid	Launched	Comm.
PC 1	*Cyclone*	Bollinger	22 Jun 1991	1 Feb 1992	7 Aug 1993
PC 2	*Tempest*	Bollinger	30 Sep 1991	4 Apr 1992	21 Aug 1993
PC 3	*Hurricane*	Bollinger	20 Nov 1991	6 Jun 1992	15 Oct 1993
PC 4	*Monsoon*	Bollinger	15 Feb 1992	10 Oct 1992	22 Jan 1994
PC 5	*Typhoon*	Bollinger	15 May 1992	3 Mar 1993	12 Feb 1994
PC 6	*Sirocco*	Bollinger	20 Jun 1992	29 May 1993	11 Jun 1994
PC 7	*Squall*	Bollinger	17 Feb 1993	28 Aug 1993	4 Jul 1994
PC 8	*Zephyr*	Bollinger	6 Mar 1993	3 Dec 1993	15 Oct 1994
PC 9	*Chinook*	Bollinger	16 Jun 1993	6 Feb 1994	28 Jan 1995
PC 10	*Firebolt*	Bollinger	17 Sep 1993	19 Jun 1994	10 Jun 1995
PC 11	*Whirlwind*	Bollinger	4 Mar 1994	9 Sep 1994	1 Jul 1995
PC 12	*Thunderbolt*	Bollinger	9 Jun 1994	2 Dec 1994	7 Oct 1995
PC 13	*Shamal*	Bollinger	22 Sep 1994	3 Mar 1995	27 Jan 1996
PC 14	*Tornado*	Bollinger	25 Aug 1998	7 Jun 1999	24 Jun 2000

Displacement	354 tons f/l; 386 tons (with stern ramp)
Dimensions	170'6" (oa); 157'5" (wl) × 25' × 7'10"; 179' with stern ramp
Machinery	4 screws; 4 diesels; 13,400 BHP; 35 knots
Endurance	2,000/12
Complement	39
Armament	2–25 mm, 2 MG, Stinger missiles

Notes: Intended for coastal interdiction and support of special operations. Considered too small for their mission. Outdated design, non-stealth. Were to be armed with SWPS and 2 Bushmaster. (For appearance, see *Shamal*, p. 267). *Tornado* built with stern ramp for special warfare boats. *Tempest*, *Monsoon*, *Zephyr*, and *Shamal* converted in 2000; *Hurricane*, *Squall*, *Whirlwind*, and *Thunderbolt* in 2005. The class was to be transferred to the Coast Guard starting in 1998, but this was canceled because of lack of funds in 2001. After Sep 2001, they were used for coastal patrols. Five units loaned to Coast Guard in 2004–5, *Monsoon* and *Tempest* returned 22 Aug 2008.

Service Record:

PC 1 *Cyclone* To USCG, 28 Feb 2000, not comm. Stricken 28 Feb 2000. Trfd to Philippines 6 Mar 2003.
Later history: renamed *Mariano Alvarez*.

PC 2 *Tempest* Decomm 1 Oct 2005. To USCG 1 Oct 2005–22 Aug 2008.
◆Indian Ocean Jul–Sep 1999.

PC 3 *Hurricane*
◆Haiti Sep–Oct 1994.

PC 4 *Monsoon* Ran aground off Haiti, 1994. Decomm 1 Oct 2004. To USCG 8 Oct 2004–22 Aug 2008.
Later history: renamed USCGC *Monsoon* (WPC 4).
◆Haiti Sep–Oct 1994.

PC 5 *Typhoon* Persian Gulf Apr 2004–.
PC 6 *Sirocco* Persian Gulf Apr 2004–.
PC 7 *Squall*

PC 8 *Zephyr* Decomm 1 Oct 2004. To USCG 8 Oct 2004.
Later history: USCGC *Zephyr* (WPC 8).

PC 9 *Chinook*
◆Iraq War 2003.

PC 10 *Firebolt* Damaged by striking a buoy off Iraqi coast, 16 Feb 2004. Investigated unidentified dhow which blew up in Arabian Gulf, 24 Apr 2004 (3 killed).
◆Iraq War 2003.

PC 11 *Whirlwind*
◆Indian Ocean Jul–Sep 2000.

PC 12 *Thunderbolt* Trfd to USCG as *Thunderbolt* (WPC 12), 5 Mar 1998–17 Jul 1998.

PC 13 *Shamal* Decomm 1 Oct 2004. To USCG 6 Dec 2004.
Later history: USCGC *Shamal* (WPC 13).

PC 14 *Tornado* Decomm 1 Oct 2004. To USCG 6 Dec 2004.
Later history: USCGC *Tornado* (WPC 14).

PATROL MOTOR GUNBOATS

PGM 31 **Later history:** To Taiwan Jul 1954, renamed *Chu Kiang*.

No.	Builder	Launched	Completed/tfrd	Built for	Name (No.)	Fate
PGM 33	Georgia Sbdg	—	15 Sep 1954	Philippines	*Camarines Sur* (G48)	R1974
PGM 34	Georgia Sbdg	—	22 Nov 1954	Philippines	*Sulu* (G49)	R1974
PGM 35	Georgia Sbdg	—	3 Jan 1955	Philippines	*La Union* (G50)	R1974
PGM 36	Georgia Sbdg	—	18 May 1955	Philippines	*Antique* (G51)	R1974
PGM 37	Georgia Sbdg	29 May 1954	2 Mar 1956	Philippines	*Masbate* (G52)	R1965
PGM 38	Georgia Sbdg	—	3 May 1956	Philippines	*Misamis Occidental* (G53)	R1974
PGM 39	Tacoma	—	29 Nov 1959	Philippines	*Agusan* (G61)	SE2001
PGM 40	Tacoma	—	9 Jan 1960	Philippines	*Catanduanes* (G62)	SE2001
PGM 41	Tacoma	—	9 Feb 1960	Philippines	*Romblon* (G63)	SE2001
PGM 42	Tacoma	—	9 Mar 1960	Philippines	*Palawan* (G64)	SE2001
PGM 43	Marinette	1959	29 Aug 1959	Burma	*PGM 401*	—
PGM 44	Marinette	—	29 Aug 1959	Burma	*PGM 402*	—
PGM 45	Marinette	—	19 Sep 1959	Burma	*PGM 403*	—
PGM 46	Marinette	—	19 Sep 1959	Burma	*PGM 404*	—
PGM 51	Peterson	1959	26 May 1961	Burma	*PGM 405*	—
PGM 52	Peterson	—	28 May 1961	Burma	*PGM 406*	trfd to Ethiopia
—	—	—	—	Ethiopia	*PC 11*	lost Apr 1977
PGM 53	Peterson	—	24 Aug 1961	Ethiopia	*PC 13*	R1984
PGM 54	Peterson	—	24 Aug 1961	Ethiopia,	*PC 14*	R1984
PGM 55	Marinette	—	10 Nov 1961	Indonesia	*Silungkang* (P572)	1
PGM 56	Marinete	—	10 Nov 1961	Indonesia	*Waitatiri* (P571)	2
PGM 57	Marinette	—	10 Nov 1961	Indonesia	*Kalukuang* (P570)	3
PGM 58	Marinette	—	14 May 1962	Ethiopia	*PC 15*	SE1987
PGM 59	Martinac	—	20 Mar 1963	Vietnam	*Kim Qui* (HQ605)	SE1972
PGM 60	Martinac	—	11 Mar 1963	Vietnam	*May Rut* (HQ606)	SE1972
PGM 61	Martinac	—	9 Apr 1963	Vietnam	*Nam Du* (HQ607)	SE1972
PGM 62	Martinac	—	1 May 1963	Vietnam	*Hoa Lu* (HQ608)	SE1972
PGM 63	Martinac	—	21 May 1963	Vietnam	*To Yen.* (HQ609)	SE1972
PGM 64	Marinette	—	17 Sep 1962	Vietnam	*Phu Du* (HQ600)	SE1972
PGM 65	Marinette	—	26 Sep 1962	Vietnam	*Tien Moi* (HQ601)	SE1972
PGM 66	Marinette	—	15 Oct 1962	Vietnam	*Minh Hoa* (HQ602)	SE1972
PGM 67	Marinette	—	12 Sep 1962	Vietnam	*Kien Vang* (HQ603)	SE1972
PGM 68	Marinette	—	5 Sep 1962	Vietnam	*Keo Ngua* (HQ604)	Scuttled 2 May 1975
PGM 69	Marinette	—	7 May 1963	Vietnam	*Dinh Hai* (HQ610)	SE1972
PGM 70	Marinette	—	14 May 1963	Vietnam	*Truong Sa* (HQ611)	SE1972
PGM 71	Peterson	14 Sep 1964	5 May 1965	Thailand	*T-11*	SE2001
PGM 72	Peterson	12 Oct 1964	26 Jun 1965	Vietnam	*Thai Binh* (HQ612)	SE1972

No.	Builder	Launched	Completed/tfrd	Built for	Name	Fate
PGM 73	Peterson	9 Nov 1964	16 Jul 1965	Vietnam,	*Thi Tu* (HQ613)	SE1972
PGM 74	Peterson	7 Dec 1964	29 Jul 1965	Vietnam	*Song Tu* (HQ614)	SE1972
PGM 75	Peterson	11 Jan 1965	16 Oct 1965	Ecuador	*Quito* (LG 31)	4
PGM 76	Peterson	10 Mar 1965	16 Oct 1965	Ecuador	*Guayaquil* (LG 32)	5
PGM 77	Peterson	14 May 1965	14 Jan 1966	Dominican Rep	*Betelgeuse* (GC 102)	SE2001
PGM 78	Peterson	5 Jun 1965	19 Nov 1965	Peru	*Rio Sama* (PC 222)	R>2001
PGM 79	Peterson	24 Aug 1965	28 Dec 1965	Thailand	*T-12*	SE2001
PGM 80	Marinette	21 Mar 1966	17 May 1966	Vietnam	*Taysa* (HQ 615)	—
PGM 81	Marinette	18 May 1966	21 Jul 1966	Vietnam	*Phu Qui* (HQ 617)	—
PGM 82	Marinette	16 Feb 1966	29 Aug 1966	Vietnam	*Hong Sa* (HQ 616)	—
PGM 83	Marinette	8 Mar 1966	30 Sep 1967	Vietnam	*Hon Troc* (HQ 618)	6
PGM 91	Tacoma	7 Jun 1966	3 Nov 1966	Vietnam	*Tho Chau* (HQ 619)	—
PGM 102	Peterson	19 Oct 1966	21 Nov 1966	Liberia	*Alert*	R1981
PGM 103	Peterson	21 Aug 1967	3 Nov 1967	Iran	*Parvin* (211)	SE2001
PGM 104	Peterson	4 May 1967	9 Aug 1967	Turkey	*AB 21* (P 121)	SE2001
PGM 105	Peterson	25 May 1967	22 Sep 1967	Turkey	*AB 22* (P 122)	SE2001
PGM 106	Peterson	7 Jul 1967	3 Nov 1967	Turkey	*AB 23* (P 123)	SE2001
PGM 107	Peterson	13 Apr 1967	28 Aug 1967	Thailand	*T-13*	SE2001
PGM 108	Peterson	14 Sep 1967	22 Jan 1968	Turkey	*AB 24* (P 124)	SE2001

Displacement	130 tons
Dimensions	101′ (oa) 98′ (bp) × 21′ × 6′8″
Machinery	2 screws; diesels; BHP 1,800; 18.5 knots
Endurance	1,000/15
Complement	15 to 26
Armament	1–40 mm, 2–20 mm

Notes: For PGM 84–101 see *Asheville* Class. Armament varied

[1] PGM 55 — trfd to Philippines, renamed *Yachi* (G 57).
[2] PGM 56 — trfd to Philippines, renamed *Yanga* (G 58).
[3] PGM 57 — trfd to Philippines, renamed *Yundi* (G 59).
[4] PGM 75 — renamed *Veinticinco de Julio* 1975. SE2001.
[5] PGM 76 — renamed *Diez de Agosto* 1975. Sunk in collision with m/v *Dole Ecuador*, 29 Aug 1995.
[6] PGM 83 — escaped to Philippines, & trfd Nov 1975, renamed *Basilan* (PG 60). R1989.

No.	Builder	Launched	Completed/tfrd	Built for	Name	Fate
PGM 47	Copenhagen	10 Nov 1960	19 Dec 1961	Denmark	*Daphne* (P530)	R1992
PGM 48	Copenhagen	16 May 1961	30 Aug 1962	Denmark	*Havmanden* (P532)	R1978
PGM 49	Copenhagen	20 Jun 1962	26 Apr 1963	Denmark	*Najaden* (P534)	R1992
PGM 50	Copenhagen	29 May 1963	18 Dec 1963	Denmark	*Neptun* (P536)	R1992

Displacement	150 tons; 170 f/l
Dimensions	124′8″ × 22′ × 6′6″
Machinery	3 screws; diesels 2600 hp; 29 knots
Complement	23
Armament	1–40 mm, ASW

Notes: Others built without U.S. support. Danish version of World War II German R-boats.

No.	Builder	Launched	Completed/tfrd	Built for	Name	Fate
PGM 109	Rio de Janeiro	—	30 Nov 1970	Brazil	*Piratini* (P 10)	SE2001
PGM 110	Rio de Janeiro	—	Mar 1971	Brazil	*Pirajá* (P 11)	SE2001
PGM 111	SIMA, Callao	—	30 Jun 1972	Peru	*Rio Chira* (PC 223)	SE2001
PGM 112	Peterson	1 Jul 1968	24 Apr 1969	Iran	*Bahram* (212)	SE2001
PGM 113	Peterson	12 Aug 1968	4 Apr 1969	Thailand	*T-14*	SE2001
PGM 114	Peterson	29 Apr 1969	17 Jun 1969	Thailand	*T-15*	SE2001
PGM 115	Peterson	24 Apr 1969	12 Feb 1970	Thailand	*T-16*	SE2001
PGM 116	Peterson	10 May 1969	12 Feb 1970	Thailand	*T-17*	SE2001
PGM 117	Peterson	9 Jun 1969	12 Feb 1970	Thailand	*T-18*	SE2001
PGM 118	Rio de Janeiro	—	Jun 1971	Brazil	*Pampeiro* (P12)	SE2001

PGM 119	Rio de Janeiro	—	29 Jul 1971	Brazil	*Parati* (P 13)	SE2001
PGM 120	Rio de Janeiro	—	30 Sep 1971	Brazil	*Penedo* (P14)	SE2001
PGM 121	Rio de Janeiro	—	29 Oct 1971	Brazil	*Poti* (P15)	SE2001
PGM 122	Peterson	—	1970	Iran	*Nahid* (213)	SE2001
PGM 123	Peterson	5 Apr 1970	25 Dec 1970	Thailand	*T-19*	SE2001
PGM 124	Peterson	22 Jun 1970	Oct 1970	Thailand	*T-20*	SE2001

Displacement	105 tons
Dimensions	95′ × 19′ × 6′6″
Machinery	2 screws; diesels; 1,100 BHP; 17 knots
Endurance	1,700/12
Complement	16
Armament	3–12.7 mm MG

Notes: OSP for various foreign countries. Same design as 95-foot Coast Guard cutters.

FAST PATROL BOATS

PT-613, 616, 619, 620 were still existing in 1950. Transferred to Korea, Jan 1952. Four motor torpedo boats were built after the war in 1951.

Figure 8.10: USS *PT 810* built with aluminum hull in 1951, shortly after completion.

No.	Builder	Displacement	Dimensions
PT 809	Electric Boat	95 tons	98′6″ × 26′6″ × 5′6″.
PT 810	Bath	90 tons	89′6″ × 24′1″ × 5′9″
PT 811	Trumpy	90 tons	94′11″ × 24′11″ × 4′2″
PT 812	Phila. NSYd	102 tons	105′ × 22′5″ × 5′5″

Notes: Aluminum hulls, 4 screws, Packard gasoline engines, 42 knots. All rec as service craft 13 Apr 1951. Later used for drone recovery, 1975.

PT 809	used to screen presidential yacht, unofficially named *Guardian*. Renamed *Retriever*, DR-1, 1 Jul 1975. BU 1990s.
PT 810	rec **PTF 1**, 21 Dec 1962. Stricken 1 Aug 1965, sunk as target in Vietnam.
PT 811	rec **PTF 2**, 21 Dec 1962. Stricken 1 Aug 1965, sunk as target in Vietnam.
PT 812	re-engined with an early form of gas turbine, not successful. BU Korea 1968.

Nasty Class

No.	Builder	—
PTF 3/16	Boatservice	1962–65
PTF 17/22	Trumpy	1968–70

Displacement	85 tons f/l
Dimensions	80′4″ (oa) × 24′6″ × 6′9″
Machinery	2 screws; diesels; 6,200 BHP; 45 knots
Complement	19
Armament	1–40 mmAA, 2–20 mmAA guns, 1–81 mm mortar /or 2–40 mm, 2–20 mm

Notes: "Nasty" class, PTF 3–16 built in Norway. PTF 5 ex-*Knurr*, 6 ex-*Lyr*, 7 ex-*Skrei*, 8 ex-*Delfin*. Mahogany hulls.

Service Record:

PTF 4	Lost by grounding, Vietnam, 4 Nov 1965.
PTF 8	Went aground on reef, Vietnam, 16 Jun 1966.
PTF 9	Went aground on reef, 7 Mar 1966.
PTF 14	Went aground on reef and destroyed by USN aircraft, Vietnam, 22 Apr 1966.
PTF 15	Went aground on reef attempting to rescue *PTF-14*, Vietnam, 22 Apr 1966.
PTF 16	Sunk by enemy action, Vietnam, 19 Aug 1966.

No.	Builder	—
PTF 23/26	Sewart Seacraft	1968

Displacement	72 tons; 111 f/l
Dimensions	94′9″ (oa) × 23′2″ × 7′
Machinery	2 screws; diesels; 6,200 BHP; 40 knots
Complement	19
Armament	1–40 mmAA, 2–20 mmAA, 1–81 mm mortar

Notes: "Osprey" class, improved Nasty type. Aluminum hulls. In service 1968. All discarded by 1986.

Note: *Hiddensee*, a Soviet *Tarentul I* class missile craft, formerly in the East German Navy, was acquired in 1992 for tests. Transferred to Battleship Cove, Fall River, Mass., as a museum, 20 Oct 1996.

Figure 8.11: Fast patrol boat *PCF-71* in Vietnam, July 1969. These craft were known as *Swift Boats*.

Figure 8.12: *USS PCF-43*, on patrol in the Cua Lon River, Vietnam, Jan 1969.

Fast Patrol Craft (Swift Boats)

125 built, 104 trfd to South Vietnam 1968–70.
22.2 tons fl; 51;′5:″ × 14′11″ × 3′6″; 2 shafts, diesels, 960 bhp, 28 knots, complement 6; 1–81 mm mortar

War Losses

PCF-4   Damaged by detonated mine in Gulf of Thailand, 14 Feb 1966 (4 killed). CTL, BU.
PCF-8   Capsized and sank in Bodega Bay, Cal., 18 Dec 1969.
PCF-10 Damaged by enemy fire and sank while being repaired, in Song Bo De River, 3 Sep 1969; salvaged.
PCF-14 Foundered in heavy seas in Cua Viet River, 30 Nov 1967.
PCF-19 Attacked in error by U.S. aircraft off DMZ, 17 Jun 1968 (5 killed).
PCF-41 Sunk by gunfire in Song Dinh Ba River, 22 May 1966 (1 killed).
PCF-43 Hit by enemy rocket fire and destroyed by explosion in Rach Duong Keo Canal, 12 Apr 1969 (1 killed).
PCF-70 Swept ashore in typhoon and lost near Chu Lai, 1971.
PCF-76 Foundered in heavy seas in Cua Viet bay, 6 Nov 1967.
PCF-77 Foundered in monsoon at mouth of Hue River, 15 Nov 1966 (3 lost).
PCF-97 Sunk by weapons fire off Ca Mau Peninsula, Vietnam, 25 Jun 1967; salvaged and repaired.

9
MINE WARFARE SHIPS

MINELAYERS

Minelayers on the Navy List, 1947

CM 5　*Terror*　Decomm 1 Sep 1947. In service 1950. Rec **MM 5**, 7 Feb 1955. Rec **MMF 5**, 27 Oct 1955. Decomm 6 Aug 1956. Stricken 1 Nov 1970, BU 1971.

DM 23　*Robert H. Smith*　Decomm 29 Jan 1947. Stricken 26 Feb 1971. Sold 14 Nov 1973, BU. Formerly DD 735.

DM 24　*Thomas E. Fraser*　Decomm 12 Sep 1955. Stricken 1 Nov 1970. Sold 29 May 1974, BU Philadelphia. Formerly DD 736.

DM 25　*Shannon*　Decomm 24 Oct 1955. Stricken 1 Nov 1970. Sold 27 Apr 1973, BU Baltimore. Formerly DD 737.

DM 26　*Harry F. Bauer*　Decomm 12 Mar 1956. Stricken 15 Aug 1971. Sold 29 May 1974, BU. Formerly DD 738.

DM 27　*Adams*　Decomm 19 Jan 1947. Stricken 1 Dec 1970. Sold 16 Dec 1971, BU Taiwan. Formerly DD 739.

DM 28　*Tolman*　Decomm 29 Jan 1947. Stricken 1 Dec 1970. Sunk as target 25 Jan 1997. Formerly DD 740.

DM 29　*Henry A. Wiley*　Decomm 29 Jan 1947. Stricken 15 Oct 1970. Sold 30 May 1972, BU. Formerly DD 749.

DM 30　*Shea*　Decomm 9 Apr. 1958. Stricken 1 Sep 1973. Sold 24 Jul 1974, BU Tacoma. Formerly DD 750.
　　　◆OpCastle 1954.

DM 32　*Lindsey*　Decomm 25 May 1946. Stricken 1 Oct 1970. Sunk as target, 1 May 1972. Formerly DD 771.

DM 33　*Gwin*　Out of comm 3 Sep 1946–8 Jul 1952. Decomm 3 Apr. 1958. Stricken 15 Aug 1971. Formerly DD 772.
　　　Trfd to Turkey 22 Oct 1971.
　　　Later history: renamed *Muavenet* (DM 357). Damaged beyond repair by Sea Sparrow missile fired in error by U.S. carrier *Saratoga*, 2 Oct 1991. BU 1993.

Note: *Sumner* class destroyers converted while under construction. All rec **MMD**, 7 Feb 1955.

AUXILIARY MINELAYERS

No.	Name	Builder	Launched	Acquired
ACM 11	*Camanche*　　　　　　　　　　　ex-*Brig. Gen. Royal T. Frank* (MP 12)	Marietta	31 Oct 1942	2 Dec 1949
ACM 12	*Canonicus*　　　　　　　　　　　ex-*Maj. Gen. Erasmus Weaver* (MP 10)	Marietta	7 Sep 1942	20 Dec 1949
ACM 13	*Miantonomah*　　　　　　　　　ex-*Col. Horace F. Spurgin* (MP 14)	Marietta	24 Dec 1941	25 Jan 1950
ACM 14	*Monadnock*　　　　　　　　　　ex-*Maj. Samuel Ringgold* (MP 11)	Marietta	6 Oct 1942	Mar 1951
ACM 15	*Nausett*　　　　　　　　　　　　ex-*Maj. Gen. Wallace P. Randolph* (MP 7)	Marietta	2 Jun 1942	21 Mar 1951
ACM 16	*Puritan*　　　　　　　　　　　　ex-*Col. Alfred A. Maybach* (MP 13)	Marietta	5 Dec 1942	27 Mar 1951
Displacement	910 tons; 1,315 f.l			
Dimensions	189′ (oa) × 37′ × 12′			
Machinery	2 screws; reciprocating; 1,200 SHP; 12 knots			
Complement	125			
Armament	none			

Notes: Acquired from U.S. Army, never in naval service. All rec **MMA**, 7 Feb 1955. Names assigned 1 May 1955. None saw active service in the Navy.

ACM 11　*Camanche*　Stricken 1 Jul 1960.
　　　Later history: Merchant *Pilgrim* 1963, renamed *Cape Cod*.

ACM 12　*Canonicus*　Stricken 1 Jul 1960.
　　　Later history: Merchant *Ocean Star* 1961, renamed *Kipman*, *Zodiac*, *Golden Crest*, *New Jersey* 1969.

ACM 13　*Miantonomah*　Decomm 10 Jul 1955. Stricken 1 Jul 1960.
　　　Later history: Merchant *Nautilus* 1963, renamed *Aleutian Mist*, *New Star* 1991. SE1998.

ACM 14　*Monadnock*　Stricken 1 Jul 1960.
　　　Later history: Merchant *Tahiti* 1964, renamed *Amazonia* 1968, *Dear* 1982, *Maxim's des Mers* 1986, *Majestic* 1989, *Maxim's des Mers* 1990.

ACM 15　*Nausett*　Stricken 1 Jul 1960. Sold 17 May 1961.
　　　Later history: merchant *Sea Searcher*, renamed *Thunderbolt*. Sank at dock in Miami, raised and sunk as artificial reef off Marathon, Fla., 3 Mar 1986.

ACM 16 *Puritan*   Stricken 1 Nov 1959. Sold 1961.
   Later history: Merchant *Puritan* 1962, renamed *White Star*.

COASTAL MINELAYERS

No.	Formerly	Trfd	To	New name	Fate
MMC 1	MSF 117	1 Oct 1959	Norway	*Gor* (N 48)	SE1972
MMC 2	MSF 119	1 Oct 1959	Norway	*Tyr* (N 47)	SE1972
MMC 3	MSF 323	27 Jan 1961	Norway	*Brage* (N 49)	SE1972
MMC 5	MSF 112	15 Dec 1962	Norway	*Uller* (N 50)	SE1972
MMC 6	LSM 301	1 Dec 1953	Greece	*Aktion* (N 04)	R2000
MMC 7	LSM 303	1 Dec 1953	Greece	*Amvrakia* (N 05)	R2002
MMC 8	LSM 390	13 May 1954	Denmark	*Beskytteren*	R1965
MMC 9	LSM 392	8 Jun 1954	Denmark	*Vindhunden*	R1964
MMC 10	LSM 481	Sep 1952	Turkey	*Marmaris* (N 100/N 103)	R1990
MMC 11	LSM 484	Sep 1952	Turkey	*Mordo_an* (N 101)	R1993
MMC 12	LSM 490	6 Oct 1952	Turkey	*Meriç* (N 102)	R1988
MMC 13	LSM 492	6 Oct 1952	Norway	*Vale* (N 45)	Trfd to Turkey 1960
—	—	1 Nov 1960	Turkey	*Mürefte* (N104/N105)	R1993
MMC 14	LSM 493	6 Oct 1952	Norway	*Vidar* (N 46)	Trfd to Turkey, 1960
—	—	1 Nov 1960	Turkey	*Mersin* (N103/N104)	R1993

OSP:

No.	Builder	Cpl	for	New name	Fate
MMC 4	Nakskov	7 Nov 1963	Denmark	*Falster* (N 80)	SE1993
MMC 15	Frederikshavn	29 Apr 1964	Denmark	*Møen* (N 82)	SE1993
MMC 16	Frederikshavn	16 Sep 1964	Turkey	*Nusret* (N108/N110)	SE2001

MINE COUNTERMEASURES SUPPORT SHIPS

MCS 1 *Catskill*   Out of comm 30 Aug 1946–6 Oct 1967. Decomm 1 Dec 1970. Stricken 20 Nov 1970. Sold 19 Nov 1973. Formerly LSV 1. 5★Vietnam May–Jun 1969, Mar–Apr, Jun 1970.

MCS 2 *Ozark*   Out of comm 29 Jun 1946–24 Jun 1966. Decomm 6 Feb 1970. Stricken 1 Apr 1974. Sunk as target 1 Sep 1975. Formerly LSV 2.

MCS 3 *Osage*   Decomm 16 May 1947. Stricken 1 Sep 1961. Sold 11 Dec 1974, BU. Formerly LSV 3.

MCS 4 *Saugus*   Decomm 24 Mar 1947. Stricken 1 Sep 1961. BU Terminal I, 1975. Formerly LSV 4.

MCS 5 *Monitor*   Decomm 22 May 1947. Stricken 1 Sep 1961. Formerly LSV 5.

MCS 6 *Orleans Parish*   Rec LST 1069, 1 Jun 1966. Formerly LST 1069.

MCS 7 *Epping Forest*   Stricken 1 Nov 1968. Formerly LSD 4.

MCS 12 *Inchon*   conv cpl 28 May 1996. Formerly LPH 12.

Notes: LSV 1–5 rec MCS 1–5, 18 Oct 1956. *Catskill* and *Ozark* converted to mine countermeasures support ships, others never recomm. *Ozark* was able to carry 20 36-foot minesweeping launches and two minesweeping helicopters, and provide support functions for minesweepers. Also could be fitted for minelaying. MCS 6, 7, and 12 converted as indicated.

Figure 9.1: *USS Ozark* (MCS 2), mine countermeasures ship, about 1968, built as a landing ship, vehicle. She could carry minesweeping launches, but her davits are empty here.

Figure 9.2: *USS Orleans Parish* (MCS 6), former tank landing ship, converted to provide support for minesweepers. Notice two minesweeping boats on the deck.

Figure 9.3: The former landing ship dock *Epping Forest* (MCS 7) converted to support minesweepers.

MINESWEEPERS

Minesweepers on the Navy List, 1947

ex-Destroyers

DMS 19 *Ellyson*   Rec **DD 454**, 4 May 1954. Decomm 19 Oct 1954. Trfd to Japan 20 Oct 1954.
Later history: renamed *Asakaze*. R1969. Trfd to Taiwan for spare parts, 1 Aug 1970. Comm as *Hsuen Yang* (DD 16) 1970. Sunk as part of making a movie, 1976.

DMS 20 *Hambleton*   Rec **DD 455**, 15 Jan 1955. Decomm 15 Jan 1955. Stricken 1 Jun 1971. Sold 22 Nov 1972, BU New Orleans.

DMS 21 *Rodman*   Rec **DD 456**, 15 Jan 1955. Decomm 28 Jul 1955. Trfd to Taiwan 28 Jul 1955.
Later history: renamed *Hsuen Yang* (16). Damaged by grounding on Matsu Island, 22 May 1970 and BU Taiwan.

DMS 23 *Macomb*   Rec **DD 458**, 4 May 1954. Decomm 19 Oct 1954. Trfd to Japan, 19 Oct 1954.
Later history: renamed *Hatakaze*. Trfd to Taiwan, 6 Aug 1970, renamed *Hsien Yang*, stationary training ship 1973.

DMS 25 *Fitch*   Rec **DD 462**, 15 Jul 1955. Decomm 24 Feb 1956. Stricken 1 Jul 1971, sunk as target, 1 Nov 1973.

DMS 26 *Hobson*   Sunk in collision with carrier *Wasp* 700 miles west of Azores, 27 Apr 1952 (176 killed).

DMS 27 *Jeffers*   Rec **DD 621**, 15 Jan 1955. Decomm 23 May 1955. Stricken 1 Jul 1971. BU.

DMS 30 *Gherardi*   Decomm 17 Dec 1955. Rec **DD 637**, 15 Jul 1955. Stricken 1 Jun 1971. Sunk as target off Puerto Rico, 3 Jun 1973.

DMS 31 *Mervine*   Decomm 27 May 1949. Rec **DD 489**, 15 Jul 1955. Stricken 31 Jul 1968. Sold 27 Oct 1969, BU.

DMS 32 *Quick*   Decomm 28 May 1949. Rec **DD 490**, 15 Jul 1955. Stricken 15 Jan 1972. Sold 27 Aug 1973, BU Portland, Ore.

DMS 33 *Carmick*   Decomm 13 Feb 1954. Rec **DD 493**, 15 Jul 1955. Stricken 1 Jul 1971. Sold 7 Aug 1972, BU Portland, Ore.
6★Korea K-1 K-2 K-4 K-6 K-8 K-9

DMS 34 *Doyle*   Rec **DD 494**, 15 Jan 1955. Decomm 19 May 1955. Stricken 1 Dec 1970. Sold 6 Oct 1972, BU.
6★Korea K-1 K-2 K-4 K-6 K-7 K-8

DMS 35 *Endicott*   Hit by shore batteries off Kojo, Korea, 4 Feb 1952, and again off Songjin, 19 Apr 1952. Decomm 17 Aug 1954. Rec **DD 495**, 15 Jul 1955. Stricken 1 Nov 1969. Sold 6 Oct 1970, BU Terminal I.
5★Korea K-1 K-2 K-4 K-9 K-10.

DMS 36 *McCook*   Decomm 27 May 1949. Rec **DD 496**, 15 Jul 1955. Stricken 15 Jan 1972, sold 27 Aug 1973, BU Portland, Ore.

DMS 37 *Davison*   Decomm 24 Jun 1949. Rec **DD 618**, 15 Jul 1955. Stricken 15 Jan 1972. Sold 27 Aug 1973 sold, BU Portland, Ore.

DMS 38 *Thompson*   Damaged by gunfire off Songjin, Korea (3 killed), 14 Jun 1951 and 20 Aug 1952. Damaged again off Songjin, 20 Aug 1952 (3 killed). Decomm 18 May 1954. Rec **DD 627**, 15 Jul 1955. Stricken 1 Jul 1971. Sold 7 Aug 1972 BU Portland, Ore.
7★Korea K-1 K-2 K-4 K-5 K-6 K-8 K-9.

DMS 39 *Cowie*   Decomm 21 Apr 1947. Rec **DD 632**, 15 Jul 1955. Stricken 1 Dec 1970. Sold 22 Feb 1972, BU Taiwan.

DMS 40 *Knight*   Decomm 19 Mar 1947. Rec **DD 633**, 15 Jul 1955. Stricken 1 Dec 1966. Sunk as target off southern California, 27 Oct 1967.

DMS 41 *Doran*   Decomm 29 Jan 1947. Rec **DD 634**, 15 Jul 1955. Stricken 15 Jan 1972. Sold 27 Aug 1973, BU Portland, Ore.

DMS 42 *Earle*   Decomm 17 May 1947. Rec **DD 635**, 15 Jul 1955. Stricken 1 Dec 1969. Sold 9 Sep 1970, BU Terminal I.

Notes: *Benson*-class destroyers converted for minesweeping.

Raven-Auk Classes [AM rec MSF, 7 Feb 1955]

AM 55 *Raven*   Decomm 31 May 1946. Stricken 1 May 1967. Sunk as target off California 30 Jul 1969.

AM 57 *Auk*   Decomm 1 Jul 1946. Stricken 1 Aug 1956.

AM 58 *Broadbill*   Out of comm 3 Jun 1946–19 Mar 1952. Decomm 25 Jan 1954. Stricken 1 Jul 1972. Sold 1 Dec 1973.

AM 59 *Chickadee*   Decomm 15 May 1946. Stricken 15 Aug 1976. Trfd to Uruguay, 18 Aug 1966.
Later history: renamed *Comandante Pedro Campbell* (4/24). R2003

AM 60 *Nuthatch*   Decomm 3 Jun 1946. Stricken 1 Dec 1966. Sunk as target off southern California, 14 Oct 1967.

AM 61 *Pheasant*   Decomm 15 Jan 1947. Stricken 1 Dec 1966. Sunk as target.

AM 62 *Sheldrake*   Out of comm 31 May 1946–14 Apr 1952. Converted to surveying ship, rec **AGS 19**, 1 Apr 1952. Decomm 1 Aug 1968. Stricken 30 Jun 1968. Sold 2 Nov 1971, BU.
★Vietnam Jan, Oct 1967–Mar 1968.

AM 64 *Starling*   Decomm 15 May 1946. Stricken 1 Jul 1972. Trfd to Mexico, 16 Feb 1973.
Later history: renamed *Valentin Gomez Farias* (G 11/C 79). SE2001.

AM 100 *Heed*   Out of comm 15 Jan 1947–5 Mar 1952. Decomm 27 Jan 1954. Stricken 1 Mar 1967. Sold 1969.

AM 101 *Herald*   Out of comm 31 May 1946–5 Mar 1952. Decomm 15 Apr 1955. Stricken 1 Jul 1972. Trfd to Mexico, 11 Apr 1973
Later history: renamed *Mariano Matamoros* (G 17/H 01). SE1987.

Figure 9.4: *USS Gherardi* (DMS 30), high speed minesweeper, converted destroyer. Notice minesweeping gear on stern replacing aft 5-inch gun.

Figure 9.5: Minesweeper *USS Ruddy* (MSF 380) in service about 1950.

AM 102 *Motive* Decomm 15 Jun 1946. Stricken 1 Dec 1966. Sunk as target 1 Nov 1967.

AM 103 *Oracle* Decomm 29 May 1946. Stricken 1 Dec 1966. Sunk as target 1967.

AM 104 *Pilot* Out of comm 15 Jan 1947–5 Mar 1952. Decomm Oct 1954. Stricken 1 Jul 1972. Trfd to Mexico 1 Feb 1973.
Later history: renamed *Juan Aldama* (G 18/C 85). SE2001.

AM 105 *Pioneer* Decomm 8 Jul 1946. Stricken 1 Jul 1972. Trfd to Mexico 19 Sep 1972.
Later history: renamed *Leandro Valle* (G 01/C 70). SE2001

AM 107 *Prevail* Out of comm 31 May 1946–1 Apr 1952. Converted to survey ship and rec **AGS 20**, 1 Apr 1952. Decomm and stricken 10 Jan 1964. Sold 13 Oct 1964, BU.
◆Cuba Apr–Aug 1962.

AM 108 *Pursuit* Out of comm 30 Apr 1947–15 Feb 1950. Converted to survey ship and rec **AGS 17**, 18 Aug 1952. Decomm 30 Jun and stricken 1 Jul 1960.

AM 109 *Requisite* Out of comm 23 Dec 1947–15 Feb 1950. Converted to survey ship and rec **AGS 18**, 18 Aug 1952. Decomm 23 Dec 1963. Stricken 1 Apr 1964. Sold 3 Feb 1965.
◆Cuba May 1962.

AM 110 *Revenge* Out of comm 18 Mar 1947–14 Feb 1951. Decomm 9 Mar 1955. Stricken 1 Nov 1966. Sold 6 Oct 1967, BU 1968 New Orleans.

AM 111 *Sage* Out of comm Feb 1947–16 Mar 1951. Decomm 19 Apr 1955. Stricken 1 Jul 1972. Trfd to Mexico, 1 Feb 1973.
Later history: renamed *Hermenegildo Galeana* (G 19), renamed *Mariano Matamoros* (C 86), 1993. SE2001.

AM 112 *Seer* Out of comm 26 Apr 1947–8 Nov 1950. Decomm 11 Mar 1955. Converted to coastal minelayer and rec **MMC 5**, 1 Oct 1955. Trfd to Norway, 15 Dec 1962.
Later history: renamed *Uller* (N 50). SE1972.

AM 114 *Staff* Out of comm 15 Jan 1947–14 Jan 1952. Decomm 15 Aug 1955. Stricken 1 Mar 1967. Sold 17 Nov 1967, BU New Orleans.

AM 116 *Speed* Decomm 7 Jun 1946. Stricken 1 Jun 1966. Trfd to South Korea, 17 Nov 1967.
Later history: renamed *Sunchon* (PCE 1002). SE1972.

AM 117 *Strive* Out of comm 6 Jun 1946–1 Jan 1952. Decomm 8 Jan 1955. Converted to coastal minelayer and rec **MMC 1**, 25 Jan 1958. Trfd to Norway, 1 Oct 1959.
Later history: renamed *Gor* (N 48). SE1978.

AM 118 *Steady* Decomm 18 Jun 1946. Stricken 1 Feb 1968. Trfd to Taiwan, 15 Aug 1967.
Later history: renamed *Ping Ching* (*Ping Jin*) (867). R1998.

AM 119 *Sustain* Out of comm 17 Jun 1946–14 Jan 1952. Decomm 2 Feb 1955. Converted to coastal minelayer and rec **MMC 2**, 25 Jan 1958. Trfd to Norway, 1 Oct 1959.
Later history: renamed *Tyr* (N 47). SE1972.

AM 120 *Sway* Decomm 15 Jan 1947. Stricken 1 Jul 1972. Trfd to Mexico, 16 Feb 1973.
Later history: renamed *Ignacio Manuel Altamirano* (G 12/C 80). SE2001.

AM 122 *Swift* Out of comm 4 Jun 1946–19 Dec 1951. Decomm 13 Dec 1955. Stricken 1 Jul 1972. Sold 26 Mar 1974, BU.
2★Korea K-9 K-10.

AM 123 *Symbol* Out of comm 31 May 1946–28 Oct 1950. Decomm 27 Jul 1956. Stricken 1 Jul 1972. Trfd to Mexico, 19 Sep 1972.
Later history: renamed *Guillermo Prieto* (G 02/C 71). SE2001.
2★Korea K-7 K-8.

AM 124 *Threat* Decomm 31 May 1946. Stricken 1 Jul 1972. Trfd to Mexico, 16 Feb 1973.
Later history: renamed *Francisco Zarco* (G 13/C 81). SE2001.

AM 126 *Token* Out of comm 6 Jan 1948–12 Apr 1951. Decomm 16 Apr 1954. Stricken 1 Dec 1966. Sold 17 Nov 1967, BU.

AM 127 *Tumult* Decomm 21 Sep 1954. Stricken 1 May 1967. Sold 1969, BU New Orleans.

AM 128 *Velocity* Decomm 7 Oct 1946. Stricken 1 Jul 1972. Trfd to Mexico, 2 Jul 1973.
Later history: renamed *Ignacio L. Vallarta* (G 14/C 82). SE2001.

AM 131 *Zeal* Out of comm 4 Jun 1946–19 Dec 1951. Decomm 6 Jul 1956. Stricken 1 Dec 1966. Sunk as target 9 Jan 1967.
1★Korea K-8.

AM 314 *Champion* Decomm 30 Jan 1947. Stricken 1 Jul 1972. Trfd to Mexico, 16 Sep 1972.
Later history: renamed *Mariano Escobedo* (G 03/C 72). SE2001.

AM 315 *Chief* Out of comm 17 Mar 1947–28 Feb 1952. Decomm 15 Mar 1955. Stricken 1 Jul 1972. Trfd to Mexico 16 Feb 1973.
Later history: renamed *Jésus Gonzalez Ortega* (G 15/C 83). SE2001.
2★Korea K-8 K-9.

AM 316 *Competent* Out of comm 30 Jan 1947–29 Feb 1952. Decomm 15 Apr 1955. Stricken 1 Jul 1972. Trfd to Mexico, 19 Sep 1972.
Later history: renamed *Ponciano Arriaga* (G 04). R1988
2★Korea K-8 K-9.

AM 317 *Defense* Out of comm 31 May 1946–16 Feb 1952. Decomm 15 Apr 1955. Stricken 1 Jul 1972. Trfd to Mexico 19 Sep 1972.
Later history: renamed *Manuel Doblado* (G 05/C 73). SE2001.
2★Korea K-8 K-9.

AM 318 *Devastator* Out of comm 30 Jan 1947–26 Feb 1952. Decomm 15 Apr 1955. Stricken 1 Jul 1972. Trfd to Mexico 19 Sep 1972.
Later history: renamed *Sebastian Lerdo de Tejada* (G 06/C 74). SE2001.
2★Korea K-8 K-9.

AM 319 *Gladiator* Out of comm 2 Oct 1946–29 Feb 1952. Decomm 15 Mar 1955. Stricken 1 Jul 1972. Trfd to Mexico, 19 Sep 1972
Later history: renamed *Santos Degollado* (G 07/C 75). SE2001.
2★Korea K-8 K-9.

AM 320 *Impeccable* Out of comm 27 Mar 1947–12 Mar 1952. Decomm 14 Oct 1955. Stricken 1 Jul 1972. Sold 26 Mar 1974, BU.
2★Korea K-8 K-9.

AM 322 *Spear* Decomm Aug 1946. Stricken 1 Jul 1972. Trfd to Mexico, 19 Sep 1972.
Later history: renamed *Ignacio de la Llave* (G 08/C 76). SE2001.

AM 323 *Triumph* Out of comm 30 Jan 1947–28 Feb 1952. Decomm 29 Aug 1955. Converted to coastal minelayer and rec **MMC 3**, 4 Dec 1959. Trfd to Norway, 27 Jan 1961.
Later history: renamed *Brage* (N 49). BU 1978.

AM 324 *Vigilance* Decomm 30 Jan 1947. Stricken 1 Dec 1966. Trfd to Philippines, 19 Aug 1967.
Later history: renamed *Quezon* (PS 70). SE2001.

AM 340 *Ardent* Decomm 30 Jan 1947. Stricken 1 Jul 1972. Trfd to Mexico, 19 Sep 1972.
Later history: renamed *Juan N. Alvarez* (G 09/C 77). SE2001.

AM 341 *Dextrous* Out of comm 5 Jun 1946–1 Dec 1950. Hit by shore batteries at Wonsan, 11 Aug 1951 (1 killed), and again near Hodo Pando, 11 Jan 1952. Decomm 31 Oct 1956. Stricken 1 Jun 1967. Trfd to South Korea, 15 Dec 1967.
Later history: renamed *Koje* (PCE 1003). SE1972.
5★Korea K-5 K-6 K-7 K-9 K-10.

AM 372 *Murrelet* Out of comm 20 Jun 1946–28 Oct 1950. Hit by shore gunfire in Songjin harbor, Korea, 25 May 1952. Decomm 14 Mar 1957. Stricken 1 Dec 1964. Trfd to Philippines, 12 Jun 1965.
Later history: renamed *Rizal* (PS 69/PS 74). R1994, recomm. SE2001.
5★Korea K-5 K-6 K-7 K-8 K-10.

AM 373 *Peregrine* Rec **AG 176**, 25 Feb 1964, experimental test ship. Decomm 31 Jan 1969. Stricken 1 Feb 1969. Sold 1970, BU Oakland.
◆Cuba Jun 1962, Cuba missile crisis Oct–Nov 1962.

AM 374 *Pigeon* Out of comm 10 Jul 1946–30 Nov 1950. Decomm 14 Jan 1955. Stricken 1 Dec 1966. Sold 6 Oct 1967, BU.

AM 375 *Pochard* Out of comm 15 Jan 1947–27 Feb 1952. Decomm 3 Aug 1955. Stricken 1 Dec 1966. Sold 17 Nov 1967, BU New Orleans.

AM 376 *Ptarmigan* Out of comm 3 Jun 1946–28 Oct 1950. Decomm 17 May 1957. Trfd to South Korea, 25 Jul 1963.

Mine Warfare Ships 145

Later history: renamed *Shin Song* (PCE 1001). SE1972.
4★Korea K-5 K-6 K-7 K-10.

AM 377 *Quail* Out of comm 27 Jan 1947-about 1951. Decomm 12 Aug 1955. Stricken 1 Dec 1966. Sold 17 Nov 1967, BU New Orleans.

AM 378 *Redstart* Out of comm 26 Nov 1946–1 Dec 1950. Decomm 15 Mar 1957. Stricken 1 Apr 1965. Trfd to Taiwan, 22 Jul 1965
Later history: renamed *Wu Sheng* (884/866). R1998.
5★Korea K-5 K-6 K-7 K-9 K-10.

AM 379 *Roselle* Decomm 20 Jun 1946. Stricken 1 Jul 1972. Trfd to Mexico, 16 Feb 1973.
Later history: renamed *Melchior Ocampo* (G 10), renamed *Manuel Gutierrez Zamora* (C 78), 1993. SE2001.

AM 380 *Ruddy* Out of comm 15 Jan 1947–12 Mar 1952. Decomm 31 Aug 1956. Trfd to Peru, 1 Nov 1960.
Later history: renamed *Galvez* (68). R1981.
2★Korea K-9 K-10.

AM 381 *Scoter* Decomm 16 Apr 1947. Stricken 1 Jul 1972. Trfd to Mexico, 19 Sep 1972.
Later history: renamed *Gutierrez Zamora*, renamed *Melchior Ocampo* (G 16/C 84), 1993. SE2001

AM 382 *Shoveler* Out of comm 5 Nov 1946–24 Jul 1951. Decomm 28 Sep 1956. Trfd to Peru 1 Nov 1960.
Later history: renamed *Diez Canseco* (69). R1981.
1★Korea K-8.

AM 383 *Surfbird* Out of comm 5 Jun 1946–12 Mar 1952. Converted to degaussing ship and rec **ADG 383**, 15 Jun 1957. Decomm 18 Dec 1970. Stricken 21 Feb 1975. Sold 4 Nov 1975.
Later history: Merchant *Helenka B.* SE1980.
2★Korea K-9 K-10, (as ADG) 8★Vietnam Aug 1963, Apr–May 1965, Aug–Oct 1966, Sep–Nov 1967, Mar–Jun 1968, Dec 1968, Mar, Aug–Oct 1969; ◆Taiwan Straits Sep–Oct 1958.

AM 384 *Sprig* Decomm Jun 1954. Stricken 1 Jul 1972. Sold 14 Dec 1973, BU New Orleans.

AM 385 *Tanager* Decomm 10 Dec 1954. Trfd to USCG, 4 Oct 1963.
Later history: USCGC *Tanager* (WTR 885). Stricken 3 Nov 1972. Sold 1972. Merchant *Tanager.*

AM 386 *Tercel* Decomm 10 Nov 1954. Stricken 1 Jul 1972. Salvage training hulk.

AM 387 *Toucan* Out of comm 1 Jul 1946–27 Oct 1951. Decomm 1 May 1957. Trfd to Taiwan, 15 Dec 1964.
Later history: renamed *Chien Men* (45). Sunk by PRC forces south of Quemoy, 6 Aug 1965.
2★Korea K-7 K-10.

AM 388 *Towhee* Decomm Mar 1954. Converted to survey vessel and rec **AGS 28**, recomm 1 Apr 1964. Decomm 30 Apr 1969. Stricken 1 May 1969. Sold 6 Mar 1970, BU Oakland.
★Vietnam Dec 1966, Oct 1967–Mar 1968.

AM 389 *Waxwing* Out of comm 12 May 1947–19 Mar 1952. Decomm 12 May 1957. Stricken 1 Apr 1965. Trfd to Taiwan, 14 Oct 1965.
Later history: renamed *Chu Yung* (896/870). R1998.

AM 390 *Wheatear* Decomm 17 Nov 1954. Stricken 1 Jul 1972. Sold 20 Dec 1973, BU New Orleans.

Admirable Class [AM rec MSF, 7 Feb 1955]

AM 159 *Change* Decomm 3 Jul 1946. Stricken 1 Apr 1960. Sold 24 Oct 1960.

AM 160 *Clamour* Decomm 12 Jun 1946. Stricken 1 Dec 1959, BU.

AM 161 *Climax* Decomm 31 May 1946. Stricken 1 Dec 1959.

AM 162 *Compel* Decomm 12 Jun 1946. Stricken 1 Dec 1959, sold 26 Aug 1960.

AM 163 *Concise* Decomm 31 May 1946. Stricken 1 Dec 1959.

AM 164 *Control* Decomm 6 Jun 1946. Stricken 18 Mar 1958, sold 30 Mar 1959.

AM 165 *Counsel* Decomm 15 Jan 1947. Stricken 1 Jul 1972, sold 1 Sep 1973.

AM 214 *Crag* Decomm 19 Mar 1948. Trfd to Mexico, 1 Oct 1962.
Later history: renamed *DM-15*, renamed *General Pedro Maria Anaya* (C58/A 08), 1993. SE2001.

AM 215 *Cruise* Decomm 5 Sep 1946. Stricken 1 Jul 1972, sold 1 Mar 1973.
Later history: Merchant *Gregory Poole.* SE1980.

AM 216 *Deft* Decomm 9 Nov 1946. Trfd to China, 27 Aug 1948, BU 1959.

AM 218 *Density* Decomm 3 Mar 1947. Stricken 1 Apr 1960. Sold 24 Oct 1960.
Later history: Merchant *Manoula* 1955, renamed *Galaxy* (offshore radio station) 1964. BU 1970.

AM 219 *Design* Decomm 24 Aug 1946. Stricken 1 Apr 1960. Sold 24 Oct 1960.

AM 220 *Device* Out of comm 24 Aug 1946–16 Mar 1950. Decomm 4 Feb 1954. Trfd to Mexico, 1 Oct 1962.
Later history: renamed *DM-11*, renamed *Cadete Augustin Melgar* (C 54), 1993. SE2001.

AM 221 *Diploma* Decomm 3 Sep 1946. Trfd to Mexico, 1 Oct 1962.
Later history: renamed *DM-17*, renamed *Cadete Francisco Marquez* (C 59), 1993. SE2001.

AM 223 *Dour* Decomm 15 Mar 1947. Trfd to Mexico, 1 Oct 1962.
Later history: renamed *DM-16*. R1986.

AM 224 *Eager* Decomm 27 Sep 1946. Trfd to Mexico, 1 Oct 1962.
Later history: renamed *DM-06*. R1986.

AM 232 *Execute* Decomm 6 Aug 1946. Stricken 1 May 1962. Trfd to Mexico, 1 Oct 1962.
Later history: renamed *DM-03*, renamed *General Juan N. Mendez* (C 51), 1993. SE2001.

AM 233 *Facility* Decomm 11 Sep 1946. Stricken 1 May 1962. Trfd to Mexico 1 Oct 1962.
Later history: renamed *DM-04*. R1972.

AM 238 *Garland* Decomm 2 Aug 1946. Stricken 1 Apr 1960. Sold 24 Oct 1960.

AM 239 *Gayety* Out of comm 7 Jun 1946–11 May 1951. Decomm 1 Mar 1954. Trfd to South Vietnam, 17 Apr 1962.
Later history: renamed *Chi Lang II* (HQ 08), 1975. Escaped to Philippines, 1975. Trfd to Philippines, Nov 1975, renamed *Magat Salamat* (PS 20). SE2001.

AM 240 *Hazard* Decomm 27 Jul 1946. Stricken 1 Nov 1967. Sold 22 Oct 1968.
Later history: Museum at Omaha, Neb.

AM 241 *Hilarity* Decomm 26 Aug 1946. Trfd to Mexico 1 Oct 1962.
Later history: renamed *DM-02*. R1986.

AM 242 *Inaugural* Decomm 9 Sep 1946. Stricken 1 Mar 1967. Sold 11 Mar 1968.
Later history: museum at St. Louis 1968. Capsized and sunk by flooding river, 1 Sep 1993.

AM 246 *Implicit* Decomm 16 Nov 1946. Trfd to China 15 Jun 1948.
Later history: renamed *Yung Chia.* (47). SE1972.

AM 249 *Incredible* Decomm 6 Nov 1946. In svc 28 Nov 1947–28 Sep 1949. Recomm 14 Aug 1950. Decomm 21 Sep 1954. Stricken 1 Dec 1959. Sold 8 Aug 1960, BU Terminal I.
4★Korea K-1 K-2 K-4 K-5; PUC 10 Oct-24 Oct 1950.

AM 252 *Instill* Out of comm 26 Feb 1947–16 May 1951. Decomm and stricken 1 May 1962. Trfd to Mexico 1 Oct 1962.
Later history: renamed *DM-10*. R1986.

AM 253 *Intrigue* Decomm 31 May 1946. Trfd to Mexico 1 Oct 1962.
Later history: renamed *DM-19*, renamed *Cadete Vicente Suarez* (C 61), 1993. SE2001.

AM 254 *Invade* Decomm 7 Aug 1946. Stricken 1 May 1962. Trfd to Mexico 1 Oct 1962.

Later history: renamed *DM-18*, renamed *General Ignacio Zaragoza* (C 60), 1993. SE2001.

AM 255 *Jubilant* Out of comm 18 May 1946–11 May 1951. Decomm 27 Apr 1954. Stricken 1 May 1962. Trfd to Mexico 1 Oct 1962.
Later history: renamed *DM-01*, renamed *General Miguel Negrete* (C 50) 1993. SE2001.

[**Note:** name also given as *Riva Palacio*, sunk as artificial reef off Veracruz, Aug 2001]

AM 256 *Knave* Decomm 1 May 1946. Trfd to Mexico 1 Oct 1962.
Later history: renamed *DM-13*, renamed *Cadete Juan Escutia* (C 56), 1993. SE2001.

AM 261 *Mainstay* Out of comm 6 Nov 1946–1 Mar 1949 and 10 Jan 1950–12 Dec 1950. Decomm 21 Sep 1954. Stricken 1 Dec 1959. Sold 8 Aug 1960, BU Terminal I.
★Korea 1950–51.

AM 266 *Nimble* Decomm 10 Oct 1946. Trfd to China 30 Jun 1948, BU 1951.

AM 269 *Opponent* Decomm 27 Aug 1946. Stricken 1 Apr 1960. Sold 3 Feb 1961.

AM 273 *Phantom* Decomm 10 Oct 1946. Trfd to China 15 Jun 1948.
Later history: renamed *Yung Ming*. R1949.

AM 274 *Pinnacle* Decomm 9 Oct 1946. Trfd to China 15 Jun 1948.
Later history: renamed *Yung Hsiu* (48). SE1972.

AM 275 *Pirate* Out of comm 6 Nov 1946–14 Aug 1950. Sunk by mine off Wonsan, Korea, 12 Oct 1950 (6 killed).
1★Korea K-1; PUC 11–12 Oct 1950.

AM 276 *Pivot* Decomm 6 Nov 1946. Trfd to China 27 Aug 1948.
Later history: renamed *Yung Shou* (49). R1970

AM 277 *Pledge* Out of comm 6 Nov 1946–28 Nov 1947. Sunk by mine off Wonsan, Korea, 12 Oct 1950 (7 killed).
2★Korea K-1, K-3; PUC 10–12 Oct 1950.

AM 280 *Prowess* Out of comm Dec 1945–1 Sep 1965. Rec **IX 305**, 1 Mar 1966. Stricken 3 Jun 1970. Trfd to South Vietnam 4 Jun 1970.
Later history: renamed *Ha Hoi* (HQ 07). Captured by North Vietnam, 30 Apr 1975. Hulked <1998.

AM 283 *Ransom* Out of comm 3 Mar 1947–16 Mar 1951. Decomm Jun 1953. Trfd to Mexico 1 Oct 1962.
Later history: renamed *DM-12*, renamed *Teniente Juan de la Barrera* (C 55), 1993. SE2001.

AM 284 *Rebel* Decomm 12 Jun 1946. Trfd to Mexico 1 Oct 1962.
Later history: renamed *DM-14*, renamed *Cadete Fernando Montes de Oca* (C 57), 1993. SE2001.

AM 285 *Recruit* Decomm 15 Aug 1946. Trfd to Mexico 1 Oct 1962.
Later history: renamed *DM-07*

AM 286 *Reform* Decomm 9 Nov 1946. Trfd to China 15 Jun 1948. BU 1950 (reported lost 1948).

AM 287 *Refresh* Decomm 9 Nov 1946. Trfd to China 30 Jun 1948.
Later history: renamed *Yung Chang* (51). Sunk by PRC gunboat off South China, 14 Nov 1965.

AM 288 *Reign* never commissioned. Stricken 1 Dec 1959.

AM 289 *Report* never commissioned. Stricken 1 Apr 1963. Loan to War Dept as mtb tender 1963–1967. Trfd to Korea Apr 1967.
Later history: renamed *Kojin*. R1973.

AM 296 *Scout* Out of comm 26 Feb 1947–11 May 1951. Decomm 1 Mar 1954. Stricken 1 May 1962. Trfd to Mexico 1 Oct 1962.
Later history: renamed *DM-09*. R1971.

AM 297 *Scrimmage* Decomm 22 Jun 1946. Stricken 1 Apr 1960.
Later history: Merchant *Giant II*, renamed *Mahi* 1968. Sunk as artificial reef off Hawaii, 1982.

AM 298 *Scuffle* Decomm 19 Jun 1946. Trfd to Mexico 1 Oct 1962.
Later history: renamed *DM-05*, renamed *General Felipe Xicotencatl* (C 53), 1993. Sunk as target 2000.

AM 299 *Sentry* Decomm 19 Jun 1946. Stricken 1 Feb 1962. Trfd to South Vietnam 13 Jul 1962.
Later history: renamed *Ky Hoa* (HQ 09). SE1972.

AM 300 *Serene* Decomm 19 Jul 1946. Stricken 1 Aug 1963. Trfd to South Vietnam 24 Jan 1964.
Later history: renamed *Nhut Tao* (HQ 10). Sunk by Chinese warships off Paracel Islands, 20 Jan 1974.

AM 301 *Shelter* Decomm 7 Jun 1946. Stricken 1 Aug 1963. Trfd to South Vietnam 24 Jan 1964.
Later history: renamed *Chi Linh* (HQ 11). Escaped to Philippines May 1975. Trfd to Philippines, renamed *Datu Tupas*, 1975.

AM 302 *Signet* Decomm 18 Jul 1946. Stricken 1 Jan 1965. Trfd to Dominican Republic 13 Jan 1965.
Later history: renamed *Separación* (BM 454/C 454), renamed *Prestol Botello* 1976. R1999.

AM 303 *Skirmish* Decomm . . Dec 1945. Stricken 1 Jan 1965. Trfd to Dominican Republic 13 Jan 1965.
Later history: renamed *Tortuguero* (BM 455/C 455). R1997.

AM 304 *Scurry* Decomm 29 Jun 1946. Stricken 1 May 1967. Training hulk. Sunk as target off Virginia, 14 Aug 1973.

AM 306 *Specter* Decomm 2 Jul 1946. Stricken 1 Jul 1972. Trfd to Mexico 11 Apr 1973.
Later history: renamed *DM-04*, renamed *General Manuel E. Rincon* (C 52), 1993. SE2001.

AM 307 *Staunch* Decomm 29 Jun 1946. Stricken 1 Apr 1967. Sold 9 Oct 1969, BU.

AM 308 *Strategy* Decomm 14 May 1946. Stricken 1 Oct 1967, BU 1969.

AM 309 *Strength* Decomm 19 Jul 1946. Stricken 1 Apr 1967. Salvage training hulk, Washington, DC. Sunk as artificial reef off Panama City, Fla., 1987.

AM 310 *Success* Decomm 9 Jul 1946. Stricken 1 May 1962. Trfd to Mexico 1 Oct 1962.
Later history: renamed *DM-08*. R1971.

AM 311 *Superior* Decomm 22 May 1946. Stricken 1 Jul 1972. Sold Jun 1975.

AM 356 *Creddock* Decomm 26 Mar 1946. Stricken 1 Feb 1966. Trfd to Burma 17 Feb 1967.
Later history: renamed *Yan Gyi Aung* (42). SE2001.

AM 357 *Dipper* Decomm 15 Jan 1947. Stricken 1 Dec 1959. Sold 5 Jan 1961.
Later history: Merchant *Mermaid II*.

AM 362 *Gadwall* Decomm 14 Jun 1946. Stricken 1 Nov 1966. Sold 11 Mar 1968.

AM 364 *Graylag* Decomm 12 Aug 1946. Stricken 1 Oct 1967. Sold, BU.

AM 365 *Harlequin* Decomm 27 May 1946. Stricken 1 May 1962. Trfd to Mexico 1973.

Figure 9.6: *USS Prowess* (AM 280), *Admirable* class minesweeper. She was transferred to Vietnam in 1970 and remained in service until the 1990s.

Later history: renamed *DM-20, Oceanografico* 1976, *Aldebaran* (H 02), 1993. SE2001.

AM 366 *Harrier* Decomm 28 Mar 1946. Stricken 1 Dec 1959.
Later history: Merchant *Sea Scope*, renamed *Atlantic Coast*. SE1998.

Agile Class

No.	Name	Builder	Keel Laid	Launched	Comm.
MSO 421	*Agile*	Luders	22 Feb 1954	19 Nov 1955	21 Jun 1956
MSO 422	*Aggressive*	Luders	25 May 1951	4 Oct 1952	25 Nov 1953
MSO 423	*Avenge*	Luders	1 Aug 1951	15 Mar 1953	13 May 1954
MSO 424	*Bold*	Norfolk NYd	12 Dec 1951	14 Mar 1953	25 Sep 1953
MSO 425	*Bulwark*	Norfolk NYd	12 Dec 1951	14 Mar 1953	12 Nov 1953
MSO 426	*Conflict*	Fulton	13 Aug 1951	16 Dec 1952	23 Mar 1954
MSO 427	*Constant*	Fulton	16 Aug 1951	14 Feb 1953	8 Sep 1954
MSO 428	*Dash*	Astoria	2 Jul 1951	20 Sep 1952	14 Aug 1953
MSO 429	*Detector*	Astoria	1 Oct 1951	5 Dec 1952	26 Jan 1954
MSO 430	*Direct*	Hiltebrant	2 Feb 1952	27 May 1953	9 Jul 1954
MSO 431	*Dominant*	Hiltebrant	23 Apr 1952	5 Nov 1953	8 Nov 1954
MSO 432	*Dynamic*	Colberg	31 Oct 1951	17 Dec 1952	15 Dec 1953
MSO 433	*Engage* ex-*Elusive* (6 Mar 1953)	Colberg	7 Nov 1951	18 Jun 1953	29 Jun 1954
MSO 434	*Embattle*	Colberg	14 Nov 1951	27 Aug 1953	16 Nov 1954
MSO 435	*Endurance*	Martinac	28 Jan 1952	9 Aug 1952	19 Mar 1954
MSO 436	*Energy*	Martinac	3 Mar 1952	13 Feb 1953	16 Jul 1954
MSO 437	*Enhance*	Martinolich	12 Jul 1952	11 Oct 1952	16 Apr 1955
MSO 438	*Esteem*	Martinolich	1 Sep 1952	20 Dec 1952	10 Sep 1955
MSO 439	*Excel*	Higgins	9 Feb 1953	25 Sep 1953	24 Feb 1955
MSO 440	*Exploit*	Higgins	28 Dec 1951	10 Apr 1953	31 Mar 1954
MSO 441	*Exultant*	Higgins	22 May 1952	6 Jun 1953	22 Jun 1954
MSO 442	*Fearless*	Higgins	23 Jul 1952	17 Jul 1953	22 Sep 1954
MSO 443	*Fidelity*	Higgins	15 Dec 1952	21 Aug 1953	19 Jan 1955
MSO 444	*Firm*	Martinac	16 Apr 1952	15 Apr 1953	12 Oct 1954
MSO 445	*Force*	Martinac	26 Aug 1952	26 Jun 1953	4 Jan 1955
MSO 446	*Fortify*	Seattle Sbdg	30 Nov 1951	14 Feb 1953	16 Jul 1954
MSO 447	*Guide*	Seattle Sbdg	20 Feb 1952	17 Apr 1954	13 May 1955
MSO 448	*Illusive*	Martinolich	23 Oct 1951	12 Jul 1952	14 Nov 1953
MSO 449	*Impervious*	Martinolich	18 Nov 1951	29 Aug 1952	15 Jul 1954
MSO 450	—	Bellingham	16 Jan 1952	25 Oct 1952	*19 Jan 1954*
MSO 451	—	Bellingham	21 Mar 1952	10 Jan 1953	*16 Mar 1954*
MSO 452	—	Bellingham	15 Aug 1952	20 Aug 1953	*19 May 1954*
MSO 453	—	Bellingham	1 Nov 1952	11 Apr 1953	*16 Jul 1954*
MSO 454	—	Bellingham	15 Jan 1953	5 Jun 1953	*1 Sep 1954*
MSO 455	*Implicit*	Wilmington Bt	29 Oct 1951	5 Jun 1953	10 Mar 1954
MSO 456	*Inflict*	Wilmington Bt	29 Oct 1951	16 Oct 1953	11 May 1954
MSO 457	*Loyalty*	Wilmington Bt	9 Nov 1951	22 Nov 1953	11 Jun 1954
MSO 458	*Lucid*	Higgins	16 Mar 1953	14 Nov 1953	4 May 1955
MSO 459	*Nimble*	Higgins	27 Apr 1953	6 Aug 1954	11 May 1955
MSO 460	*Notable*	Higgins	8 Jun 1953	15 Oct 1954	8 Jun 1955
MSO 461	*Observer*	Higgins	20 Jul 1953	19 Oct 1954	31 Aug 1955
MSO 462	*Pinnacle*	Higgins	24 Aug 1953	3 Jan 1955	21 Oct 1955
MSO 463	*Pivot*	Wilmington Bt	31 Mar 1952	9 Jan 1954	12 Jul 1954
MSO 464	*Pluck*	Wilmington Bt	31 Mar 1952	6 Feb 1954	11 Aug 1954
MSO 465	*Prestige*	Wilmington Bt	15 Apr 1952	30 Apr 1954	11 Sep 1954
MSO 466	*Prime*	Wilmington Bt	30 Dec 1952	27 May 1954	11 Oct 1954
MSO 467	*Reaper*	Wilmington Bt	15 May 1952	25 Jun 1954	10 Nov 1954
MSO 468	*Rival*	Luders	1 Feb 1952	15 Aug 1953	3 Sep 1954
MSO 469	*Sagacity*	Luders	6 Oct 1952	20 Feb 1954	20 Jan 1955
MSO 470	*Salute*	Luders	15 Mar 1954	14 Aug 1954	4 May 1955
MSO 471	*Skill*	Luders	17 Aug 1953	3 Apr 1955	7 Nov 1955

Figure 9.7: *USS Constant* (MSO 427). *Agile* class non-magnetic minesweeper with plywood hulls, she was in service from 1954 to 1992.

Figure 9.8: *USS Leader* (MSO 490), Sep 1982. One of the *Agile* class modernized with new engines in 1965.

MSO 472	*Valor*	Burger	28 Apr 1952	13 May 1953	29 Jul 1954
MSO 473	*Vigor*	Burger	16 Jun 1952	24 Jun 1953	8 Nov 1954
MSO 474	*Vital*	Burger	31 Oct 1952	12 Aug 1953	9 Jun 1955
MSO 475	—	Bellingham	3 Mar 1953	25 Sep 1953	*20 Oct 1954*
MSO 476	—	Bellingham	15 Apr 1953	26 Sep 1953	*16 Feb 1955*
MSO 477	—	Bellingham	10 Jun 1953	2 Feb 1954	*14 Apr 1955*
MSO 478	—	Bellingham	26 Aug 1953	25 Apr 1954	*24 Apr 1955*
MSO 479	—	Bellingham	1 Oct 1953	22 Jun 1954	*1 Jun 1955*
MSO 480	—	Astoria	24 Sep 1952	11 Apr 1953	*27 May 1954*
MSO 481	—	Astoria	8 Dec 1952	7 Nov 1953	*21 Sep 1954*
MSO 482	—	Astoria	11 Apr 1953	6 Mar 1954	*31 Jan 1955*
MSO 483	—	Peterson	19 Feb 1952	2 May 1953	*22 Jul 1954*
MSO 484	—	Peterson	27 Feb 1952	2 May 1953	*23 Sep 1954*
MSO 485	—	Peterson	17 Feb 1952	23 Aug 1953	*22 Nov 1954*
MSO 486	—	Burger	16 May 1953	19 Nov 1953	*15 Aug 1955*
MSO 487	—	Burger	18 Aug 1953	1 Apr 1954	*23 Nov 1955*
MSO 488	*Conquest*	Martinac	26 Mar 1953	20 May 1954	20 Jul 1955
MSO 489	*Gallant*	Martinac	21 May 1953	4 Jun 1954	14 Sep 1955
MSO 490	*Leader*	Martinac	22 Sep 1953	15 Sep 1954	16 Nov 1955
MSO 491	*Persistent*	Martinac	17 Jun 1954	23 Apr 1955	3 Feb 1956
MSO 492	*Pledge*	Martinac	24 Jun 1954	20 Jul 1955	20 Apr 1956
MSO 493	*Stalwart*	Broward	22 Jun 1954	3 Dec 1955	23 Apr 1957
MSO 494	*Sturdy*	Broward	15 Oct 1954	28 Jan 1956	23 Oct 1957
MSO 495	*Swerve*	Broward	20 Dec 1954	1 Nov 1955	27 Jul 1957

MSO 496	Venture	Broward	11 Jan 1955	27 Nov 1956	3 Feb 1958	
AM 497	—	—	—	—	—	
MSO 498	—	Bellingham	11 Feb 1954	13 Aug 1954	*27 Sep 1955*	
MSO 499	—	Bellingham	25 Apr 1954	15 Oct 1954	*1 Nov 1955*	
MSO 500	—	Bellingham	23 Jun 1954	7 Jan 1955	*30 Jan 1956*	
MSO 501	—	Bellingham	17 Aug 1954	25 Feb 1955	*14 Feb 1956*	
MSO 502	—	Bellingham	15 Oct 1954	6 May 1955	*4 Apr 1956*	
MSO 503	—	Tacoma Boat	15 Oct 1953	19 Jun 1954	*16 Dec 1955*	
MSO 504	—	Tacoma Boat	25 Nov 1953	25 Mar 1955	*15 Feb 1956*	
MSO 505	—	Tacoma Boat	25 Jun 1954	6 Aug 1955	*4 Apr 1956*	
MSO 506	—	Martinolich	18 Aug 1953	13 Nov 1954	*23 Feb 1956*	
MSO 507	—	Martinolich	16 Sep 1953	19 Feb 1954	*15 Jun 1956*	

Displacement	716 tons; 853 f/l
Dimensions	172' (oa); 165' (wl) × 35' × 14'
Machinery	2 screws; diesels; 2,280 BHP; 15.5 knots
Endurance	3300/10
Complement	78
Armament	1–40 mmAA; 1 twin 20 mm in modernized units

Notes: AM rec MSO, 7 Feb 1955. Non-magnetic minesweepers, plywood hulls. Design based on experience in Korean War. 13 fully modernized 1965, including new engines, *Engage, Enhance, Esteem, Exultant, Fearless, Fidelity, Force, Fortify, Illusive, Impervious, Inflict, Conquest*, and *Leader*, after which conversion program was canceled. 36 units transferred to foreign navies on completion.

Service Records:

MSO 421 *Agile* Decomm 28 Jul 1972. Stricken 1 Sep 1977. Sold Feb 1980, BU.
◆Cuba Sep–Oct 1962.

MSO 422 *Aggressive* Decomm 2 Jul 1971. Stricken 28 Feb 1975. Sold 1 May 1980, BU.
◆Lebanon Aug–Sep 1958, Cuba Sep–Oct 1962, Cuba missile crisis Oct–Nov 1962

MSO 423 *Avenge* Damaged by fire in drydock at Baltimore, 6 Oct 1969. Decomm 31 Jan 1970. Stricken 1 Feb 1970.
◆Taiwan Straits 9 Sep 1958.

MSO 424 *Bold* Decomm Jul 1971. Stricken 28 Feb 1975. Sold 1 Jun 1981, BU.
◆Cuba Aug–Sep 1962.

MSO 425 *Bulwark* Stricken 28 Feb 1975. Sold May 1980, BU.
◆Cuba Aug–Sep 1962.

MSO 426 *Conflict* Decomm 1 Apr 1972. Stricken 9 Jun 1972; sold 14 Dec 1973, BU.
★Vietnam Apr–Juln 1962, Nov 1965–Jun 1966, Oct 1967–Mar 1968, Apr–May 1969, Sep 1971–Jan 1972; ◆Quemoy-Matsu Mar 1960.

MSO 427 *Constant* Decomm 30 Sep 1992. Stricken 9 Mar 1994. Sold 17 Aug 1998, BU Long Beach, Cal. 2001.
★Vietnam Feb–Apr 1965, Jul 1966–Feb 1967, Nov 1968–Feb 1969, Dec 1970–Jan 1971, Mar–May 1971; ◆Taiwan Straits Sep–Nov 1958, Quemoy-Matsu Oct–Dec 1960.

MSO 428 *Dash* Decomm and stricken 1 Oct 1982. Sold 26 Jan 1984, BU.
◆Dominican Rep Oct 1965.

MSO 429 *Detector* Decomm and stricken 1 Oct 1982. Sold 26 Jan 1984, BU.
◆Dominican Rep Oct–Nov 1966.

MSO 430 *Direct* Damaged by fire en route to Boston, 20 Jul 1977. Stricken 1 Oct 1982. Sold 26 Jan 1984, BU.
◆Dominican Rep Oct 1965.

MSO 431 *Dominant* Decomm and stricken 1 Oct 1982. Sold 26 Jan 1984, BU.
◆Dominican Rep Oct–Nov 1965.

MSO 432 *Dynamic* Decomm 8 Jun 1971. Trfd to Spain 1 Jul 1971.
Later history: renamed *Guadalete* (PVZ 41/M 41). R1998.
★Vietnam Feb–Jun 1962, Nov 1965–Jan 1966, Mar–Jul 1966.

MSO 433 *Engage* Decomm 30 Dec 1991. Stricken 20 Apr 1992. Sold 15 Apr 1994, canceled. Sold 4 Dec 2000, BU Baltimore 2001.
★Vietnam Jul–Aug 1962, Sep 1964, Apr–May 1966, Jan 1971–Jan 1973; ◆Quemoy-Matsu Aug–Sep 1960, May–Jun, Aug 1962.

MSO 434 *Embattle* Decomm 24 Jul 1972. Stricken 15 May 1976. Sold, hulked SE 1992.
★Vietnam Mar–Jul 1965, May–Aug 1968, Jan–Mar 1970.

MSO 435 *Endurance* Collided with British submarine *Rorqual* in Subic Bay, 13 Jun 1969. Stricken 1 Jul 1972; sold 14 Dec 1973.
★Vietnam Apr–Jul 1962, Nov 1965–Jun 1966, Mar–Jul 1969, Aug–Dec 1970.

MSO 436 *Energy* Decomm and trfd to Philippines 5 Jul 1972.
Later history: renamed *Davao del Norte.* R1977, BU.
★Vietnam Feb–Apr 1965, Jul 1966–Feb 1967, Nov 1968–Mar 1969, Jan–Apr 1971; ◆Taiwan Straits Sep 1958.

MSO 437 *Enhance* Damaged by fire 43 m. south of San Diego, 5 Jan 1975. Decomm 13 Dec 1991. Stricken 21 Feb 1992. Sold 6 Mar 2000, BU Long Beach, Cal.
★Vietnam May–Sep 1965, Feb–Sep 1967, Oct 1968–Feb 1969; ◆Earnest Will.

MSO 438 *Esteem* Decomm and stricken 20 Sep 1991. Sold 6 Mar 2000, BU Long Beach, Cal.
★Vietnam Dec 1961–Feb 1961, Oct–Dec 1965, Jun–Jul 1967, Mar–Jun 1969; ◆Libya Oct 1987–Apr 1988, Earnest Will.

MSO 439 *Excel* Decomm 30 Sep 1992. Stricken 28 Mar 1994. Sold 17 Aug 1998, BU Long Beach, Cal. 1999.
★Vietnam May–Jul 1965, Sep–Oct 1965, Feb–Jun 1967, Aug, Oct–Dec 1969, May–Jun 1971.

MSO 440 *Exploit* Decomm 16 Dec 1993. Stricken 28 Mar 1994. Sold 4 Dec 2000, BU Baltimore.
◆Dominican Rep Apr–Jun 1965.

MSO 441 *Exultant* Damaged by engine-room fire off Savannah, 12 Aug 1960 (5 killed). Decomm 30 Jun 1993. Stricken 9 Mar 1994. Sold 4 Dec 2000, BU Baltimore.

MSO 442 *Fearless* Decomm 23 Oct 1990. Stricken 28 Oct 1990. Sold Dec 1992, BU.
◆Libya Oct 1987–Apr 1988, Earnest Will.

MSO 443 *Fidelity* Decomm 19 May 1989. Stricken 16 Jun 1989. Sold 10 Sep 1990, BU.
◆Lebanon Aug–Sep 1958.

MSO 444 *Firm* Trfd to Philippines 5 Jul 1972.
Later history: renamed *Davao del Sur.* R1977, BU.
★Vietnam Apr–Jul 1965, Jan–May 1967, May–Sep 1968, Sep–Dec 1969, Dec 1970–Apr 1971.

MSO 445 *Force* Burned and sank west of Guam, 24 Apr 1973 (none killed).
★Vietnam Mar–Jul 1965, Nov 1966–May 1967, Feb–May 1972.

MSO 446 *Fortify* Decomm 31 Aug 1992. Stricken 9 Mar 1994. Sold 4 Dec 2000, BU Baltimore.
★Vietnam Jul–Aug 1962, Sep 1964, Apr–Oct 1966, Aug–Dec 1971, Jun, Nov 1972, Jan–Mar 1973, ◆Taiwan Straits 11 Sep 1958.

MSO 447 *Guide* Decomm 1 Apr 1972. Stricken 9 Jun 1972. Sold 14 Dec 1973, BU.
★Vietnam Jun–Oct 1965, Feb–Sep 1967, May–Aug 1970, Sep–Dec 1971.

MSO 448 *Illusive* Out of comm 29 Nov 1970–2 Mar 1972. Decomm 30 Mar 1990. Stricken 1 Jun 1990. Sold 9 Feb 1993, BU Baltimore.
★Vietnam Jan 1962, Oct 1965–Mar 1966, Jun–Dec 1967, Oct–Nov 1968, Jan–Feb 1969, ◆Libya Oct 1987–Apr 1988, Earnest Will.

MSO 449 *Impervious* Decomm 12 Dec 1991. Stricken 18 Mar 1992. Sold 15 Apr 1994. Sold 4 Dec 2000, BU Baltimore.
★Vietnam Jul 1962, Sep 1964, Apr–Nov 1966, Jan–Apr 1968, Jan–Jun 1972, Feb–Mar 1973, ◆Gulf War Sep 1990–Sep 1991.

MSO 450 Trfd to France 19 Jan 1954, as *Berneval* (M 613). R1987.

MSO 451 Trfd to France 16 Mar 1954, as *Bir Hakeim* (M 614). Returned 4 Sep 1970; trfd to Uruguay, 1970 renamed *Maldonado* (MS 33). R1979.

Mine Warfare Ships   149

MSO 452   Trfd to France 19 May 1954, as *Garigliano*.(M 617). R1988.
MSO 453   Trfd to France 16 Jul 1954, as *Alençon* (M 612). SE1993.
MSO 454   Trfd to France 1 Sep 1954, as *Dompaire*. (M 616). R1987.
MSO 455 *Implicit*   Decomm 30 Sep 1994. Stricken 29 Nov 1994. Trfd to Taiwan, 30 Sep 1994.
   Later history: renamed *Yung Yang.* (1306). SE2001.
   ★Vietnam Feb–Jun 1962, Jan–Jun 1966, Apr–Jun 1969, Aug–Dec 1970.
MSO 456 *Inflict*   Decomm 30 Mar 1990. Stricken 23 May 1990. Sold 4 Dec 1992, BU Baltimore.
   ★Vietnam Sep 1964, Apr–Nov 1966, Jan 1972, Libya Oct 1987–Apr 1988; ◆Earnest Will.
MSO 457 *Loyalty*   Stricken 1 Jul 1972; sold 14 Dec 1973.
   ★Vietnam Sep 1964, Apr–Oct 1966, May–Aug 1968, Aug–Dec 1969, Jan–May 1971.
MSO 458 *Lucid*   Decomm 23 Dec 1970. Stricken 15 May 1976. Sold 30 Dec 1976. Hulk SE near San Francisco, 2002.
   ★Vietnam Jul, Sep–Oct 1965, Feb–Jun, Aug–Sep 1967, Jun–Oct 1968, Apr–Jul 1970.
MSO 459 *Nimble*   Decomm 24 Nov 1970. Stricken 1 Nov 1976. Sold 6 Sep 1981, BU.
   ★Vietnam Jan–Feb 1966; ◆Lebanon Jul–Oct 1958.
MSO 460 *Notable*   Stricken 1 Feb 1971; Sold 30 Aug 1971, BU 1971.
   ◆Cuba Jan–Feb 1962, Cuba missile crisis Nov–Dec 1962.
MSO 461 *Observer*   Decomm 1 Jul 1972. Stricken 1 Sep 1977. Sold 1 Apr 1979, BU.
   ◆Dominican Rep May 1965.
MSO 462 *Pinnacle*   In collision with carrier *Forrestal* at Norfolk, Va., 20 Jan 1956. Decomm 24 Nov 1970. Stricken 1 Sep 1977. Sold Feb 1978, BU.
   ◆Lebanon Aug–Oct 1958.
MSO 463 *Pivot*   Went aground in Naruto Strait, Japan, 23 Aug 1958. Trfd to Spain 1 Jul 1971.
   Later history: renamed *Guadalmedina* (M 42). SE2001.
   ★Vietnam Feb–Apr 1965, Jul 1966–Jan 1967, Nov 1968–Mar 1969, Apr–Jul 1970; ◆Taiwan Straits Oct 1958.
MSO 464 *Pluck*   Decomm 29 Nov 1990. Stricken 16 Jan 1991. Sold 2 Sep 1992, BU.
   ★Vietnam Feb–Apr 1965, Jul 1966–Feb 1967, Mar–Jul 1969, Apr–Aug 1971; ◆Taiwan Straits Sep–Oct 1958.
MSO 465 *Prestige*   Lost by grounding in Nasuto Strait, Japan, 23 Aug 1958.
MSO 466 *Prime*   Decomm 6 Nov 1970. Stricken 28 Feb 1975. Sold 7 Jan 1977, BU.
   ★Vietnam Apr–Jul 1965, Jan–May 1967, Jun–Oct 1968, Dec 1969–Apr 1970.
MSO 467 *Reaper*   Decomm 24 Jul 1972. Stricken 28 Feb 1975. Sold 7 Jan 1977, BU.
   ★Vietnam Apr–Jul 1965, Jan–Jul 1967, Jul–Oct 1968, Jan–Feb 1970.
MSO 468 *Rival*   Stricken 1 Feb 1971; sold 30 Aug 1971.
   ◆Cuba Jan–Feb 1962, Cuba missile crisis Nov–Dec 1962.
MSO 469 *Sagacity*   Damaged by grounding in Charleston harbor, Mar 1970. Decomm and stricken 1 Oct 1970. BU 1971.
   ◆Lebanon Jul–Oct 1958.
MSO 470 *Salute*   Decomm 15 May 1970. Stricken 1 Feb 1971; sold 30 Aug 1971, BU 1973
   ◆Cuba Jan–Feb 1962, Cuba missile crisis Nov–Dec 1962.
MSO 471 *Skill*   Decomm 15 Dec 1970. Stricken 1 Sep 1977. Sold Apr 1979, BU.
   ◆Lebanon Jul–Oct 1958.
MSO 472 *Valor*   Decomm Jul 1970. Stricken 1 Feb 1971. Sold 30 Aug 1971.
MSO 473 *Vigor*   Decomm 4 Apr 1972. Trfd to Spain 5 Apr 1972.
   Later history: renamed *Guadiana* (M 44). R1999.
   ◆Cuba Jul–Dec 1961, Aug 1962.

MSO 474 *Vital*   Decomm 24 Jul 1972. Stricken 1 Sep 1977. Sold 21 Jul 1979, BU.
MSO 475   Trfd to France 20 Oct 1954, as *Mytho* (M 618). R1987.
MSO 476   Trfd to France 16 Feb 1955, as *Cantho* (M 615). R1989.
MSO 477   Trfd to France 14 Apr 1955, as *Vinh Long.* (M 619). BU 1992.
MSO 478   Trfd to Portugal 24 Apr 1955, as *S. Jorge* (M 415). BU 1974.
MSO 479   Trfd to Portugal 1 Jun 1955, as *Pico* (M 416).
   Later history: Trfd to Belgium for spare parts 1973; Sea Cadet ship 1985. Burned at Oostend, 1997.
MSO 480   Trfd to Netherlands 27 May 1954 as *Onversaagd* M 884/A 854). R1979.
MSO 481   Trfd to Netherlands 21 Sep 1954 as *Onbevreesd*. (M 885/A 855). R1989.
MSO 482   Trfd to Netherlands 31 Jan 1955 as *Onvervaard*. (M 888/A 858). SE1982
MSO 483   Trfd to Netherlands 22 Jul 1954 as *Onvershrokken* (M 886/A 856), renamed *Merkur* 1973. Museum at Scheveningen 1993.
MSO 484   Trfd to Netherlands 23 Sep 1954 as *Onvermoeid* (M 887/A 857). R1975.
MSO 485   Trfd to Netherlands 22 Nov 1954 as *Onverdroten* (M 889/A 859). SE1982.
MSO 486   Trfd to Portugal 15 Aug 1955 as *Graciosa* (M417). R1974.
MSO 487   Trfd to Portugal 23 Nov 1955 as *Corvo* (M 418). R1974.
MSO 488 *Conquest*   Decomm 29 Oct 1970. Damaged in collision with LST *Barbour County* in Pacific, 11 Sep 1987. Decomm and stricken 29 Jun 1994. Trfd to Taiwan, 3 Aug 1994.
   Later history: renamed *Yung Tzu* (1307). SE2001.
   ★Vietnam Jan 1960, Nov 1961–Feb 1962, Oct 1965–Mar 1966, Jun–Dec 1967, Oct–Nov 1968, Jan–Feb 1969; ◆Quemoy-Matsu Dec 1959, Nov 1961, Libya Nov 1987–Aug 1990, Nov–Dec 1988, Earnest Will.
MSO 489 *Gallant*   Decomm and stricken 29 Apr 1994. Trfd to Taiwan.3 Aug 1994.
   Later history: renamed *Yung Ku* (1308). SE2001.
   ★Vietnam Dec 1961–Feb 1962, Oct–Dec 1965, Jun–Dec 1967, Aug–Dec 1969, May–Sep 1971.
MSO 490 *Leader*   Out of comm 29 Nov 1970–11 Feb 1972. Out of comm 12 Dec 1991–11 Feb 1972. Stricken 18 Mar 1992. Sold 15 Apr 1994, BU Wilmington, NC.
   ★Vietnam May–Oct 1965, Oct 1968–Feb 1969, Mar 1973; ◆Quemoy-Matsu Jun–Jul 1959, Jul 1961, Gulf War Sep 1990–Sep 1991. PUC 18 Oct–5 Dec 1968.
MSO 491 *Persistent*   Decomm 26 Apr 1971. Trfd to Spain 1 Jul 1971.
   Later history: renamed *Guadalquivir* (M 43). SE2001.
   ★Vietnam Apr–Jun 1962, Nov 1965–May 1966, Oct 1967–Mar 1968, Apr, Jun 1969, Aug–Dec 1970.
MSO 492 *Pledge*   Decomm and Stricken 31 Jan 1994. Trfd to Taiwan 3 Aug 1994.
   Later history: renamed *Yung The* (1309). SE2001.
   ★Vietnam Dec 1961–Feb 1962, Oct–Dec 1965, Oct 1966, Jun–Jul 1967, Sep–Dec 1967, Apr–Jun 1969.
MSO 493 *Stalwart*   Sunk by explosion and fire in San Juan harbor, 25 Jun 1966. Stricken 1 Jul 1967. Sold 15 Nov 1968, BU.
   ◆Lebanon Aug–Sep 1958.
MSO 494 *Sturdy*   Stricken 1 Sep 1977. Sold 1 May 1978, BU.
MSO 495 *Swerve*   Decomm 1 Jul 1971. Stricken 1 Sep 1977. Sold 1 Feb 1978, BU.
MSO 496 *Venture*   Decomm 2 Aug 1971. Stricken 1 Sep 1977. Sold 1 May 1978, BU.
MSO 497   not awarded.

MSO 498   Trfd to Norway 27 Sep 1955 as *Lagen* (M 950). Trfd to Belgium, 14 Apr 1966, renamed *A.F. Dufour* (M 903). BU 2007.
MSO 499   Trfd to Norway 1 Nov 1955 as *Namsen* (M951). Trfd to Belgium, 14 Apr 1966, renamed *De Brouwer* (M 904). BU 2007.
MSO 500   Trfd to France 30 Jan 1956 as *Berlaimont* (M520). R1989.
MSO 501   Trfd to France 14 Feb 1956 as *Origny* (M 621). R1985.
MSO 502   Trfd to France 4 Apr 1956 as *Autun* (M 622). R1985.
MSO 503   Trfd to Belgium 16 Dec 1955 as *Artevelde* (M 907). R1985.
MSO 504   Trfd to Belgium 15 Feb 1956 as *Breydel* (M 906). R 1993, to be a museum.
MSO 505   Trfd to France 4 Apr 1956 as *Baccarat* (M 623). R1993.
MSO 506   Trfd to Italy 23 Feb 1956 as *Storione* (P 5431). R1997. SE2001.
MSO 507   Trfd to Italy 15 Jun 1956 as *Salmone* (P 5430). R1996.

MSO 509 *Adroit*   Decomm 12 Dec 1991. Stricken 8 May 1992. Sold 15 Apr 1994, BU Baltimore.
◆Lebanon Aug–Sep 1958, Gulf War Sep 1990–Sep 1991.
MSO 510 *Advance* Decomm 23 Dec 1970. Stricken 15 May 1976. Sold 6 Jan 1977. Still hulked in 2002.
5★Vietnam Feb–Mar 1965, Jul–Nov 1966, Nov 1968–Mar 1969, May–Aug 1970.
MSO 511 *Affray*   Decomm 20 Dec 1992. Stricken 28 Jun 1993. Sold 4 Dec 2000, BU Baltimore 2001.
◆Dominican Rep Apr–Jun 1965.
MSO 512   Trfd to France 23 Jul 1956 as *Narvik* (M609/A769). R1989.
MSO 513   Trfd to France 21 Sep 1956 as *Ouistreham* (M 610). R1994.
MSO 514   Trfd to France 21 Nov 1956 as *Colmar* (M 624). R1985.
MSO 515   Trfd to Belgium 12 Oct 1956 as *Georges Truffaut* (M 908). SE2001.
MSO 516   Trfd to Belgium 25 Jan 1957 as *François Bovesse* (M 909) R1993. SE2001.
MSO 517   Trfd to Italy 12 Mar 1957 as *Sgombro* (P 5432). R2000.
MSO 518   Trfd to Italy 20 Jun 1957 as *Squalo* (P 5433). R2000. SE2001.

Acme Class

No.	Name	Builder	Keel Laid	Launched	Comm.
MSO 508	*Acme*	Sample	16 Nov 1954	23 Jun 1955	27 Sep 1956
MSO 509	*Adroit*	Sample	18 Nov 1954	20 Aug 1955	4 Mar 1957
MSO 510	*Advance*	Sample	28 Jun 1955	12 Jul 1956	16 Jun 1958
MSO 511	*Affray*	Sample	24 Aug 1955	18 Dec 1956	8 Dec 1958
MSO 512	—	Peterson	1 Sep 1954	23 Apr 1955	*23 Jul 1956*
MSO 513	—	Peterson	21 Oct 1954	30 Jul 1955	*21 Sep 1956*
MSO 514	—	Peterson	30 Apr 1955	29 Oct 1955	*21 Nov 1956*
MSO 515	—	Tampa Marine	1 Feb 1955	1 Nov 1955	*12 Oct 1956*
MSO 516	—	Tampa Marine	1 Apr 1955	8 Feb 1956	*25 Jan 1957*
MSO 517	—	Tampa Marine	15 Jun 1955	21 Jun 1956	*12 Mar 1957*
MSO 518	—	Tampa Marine	15 Jun 1955	3 Dec 1956	*20 Jun 1957*
Displacement	720 tons, 780 f/l				
Dimensions	173′ (oa) × 36′ × 14′				
Machinery	2 screws, diesels, 2,800 BHP, 14 knots				
Endurance	3,300/10				
Complement	57				
Armament	1–20 mmAA gun				

Notes: Improved *Agile* class. Fitted as mine division flagships.

Service Record:

MSO 508 *Acme*   Decomm 6 Nov 1970. Stricken 15 May 1976. Sold 6 Jan 1977, BU.
★Vietnam Jun–Sep 1968, Jan–Mar 1970.

Ability Class

No.	Name	Builder	Keel Laid	Launched	Comm.
MSO 519	*Ability*	Peterson	5 Mar 1956	29 Dec 1956	4 Aug 1958
MSO 520	*Alacrity*	Peterson	3 May 1956	8 Jun 1957	1 Oct 1958
MSO 521	*Assurance*	Peterson	28 Jan 1957	31 Aug 1957	21 Nov 1958
MSO 522	—	Peterson	2 Mar 1959	29 Oct 1959	*12 Dec 1960*
Displacement	801 tons, 950 f/l				
Dimensions	189′ (oa); 173″ (bp) × 36′ × 12′				
Machinery	2 screws; diesel; 2,700 hp; 15 knots				
Endurance	3,200/12				
Complement	75				
Armament	1–40 mm gun				

Notes: Fitted as mine division flagships. Tripod mast.

Figure 9.9: *USS Advance* (MSO 510). Improved *Agile* class.

Figure 9.10: *USS Ability* (MSO 519). Notice tripod mast.

Mine Warfare Ships 151

Service Record:

MSO 519 *Ability* Decomm Jun 1970. Stricken 1 Feb 1971, BU 1972.
- ◆Cuba Jan–Feb 1962, Cuba missile crisis Nov–Dec 1962.

MSO 520 *Alacrity* rec **AG 520** 1 Jun 1973. Decomm and stricken 30 Sep 1977. Sold 28 Dec 1979 BU.
- ◆Dominican Rep May 1965.

MSO 521 *Assurance* rec **AG 521** 1 Mar 1973. Decomm and stricken 30 Sep 1977. Sold 1 Jul 1978, BU.

MSO 522 Trfd to Belgium 12 Dec 1960 as *J.E. van Haverbeke* (M 902). SE2001

MSO 523–528 Canceled 1968

MINE COUNTERMEASURES SHIPS

Avenger Class

No.	Name	Builder	Keel Laid	Launched	Comm.
MCM 1	*Avenger*	Peterson	3 Jun 1983	15 Jun 1985	12 Sep 1987
MCM 2	*Defender*	Marinette	1 Dec 1983	4 Apr 1987	30 Sep 1989
MCM 3	*Sentry*	Peterson	8 Oct 1984	20 Sep 1986	6 Oct 1989
MCM 4	*Champion*	Marinette	28 Jun 1984	15 Apr 1987	8 Feb 1991
MCM 5	*Guardian*	Peterson	8 May 1985	20 Jun 1987	16 Dec 1989
MCM 6	*Devastator*	Peterson	9 Feb 1987	11 Jun 1988	6 Oct 1990
MCM 7	*Patriot*	Marinette	31 Mar 1987	15 May 1990	18 Oct 1991
MCM 8	*Scout*	Peterson	8 Jun 1987	20 May 1989	15 Dec 1990
MCM 9	*Pioneer*	Peterson	5 Jun 1989	25 Aug 1990	7 Dec 1992
MCM 10	*Warrior*	Peterson	25 Sep 1989	8 Dec 1990	30 Dec 1992
MCM 11	*Gladiator*	Peterson	7 May 1990	29 Jun 1991	4 Jun 1993
MCM 12	*Ardent*	Peterson	22 Oct 1990	16 Nov 1991	18 Feb 1994
MCM 13	*Dextrous*	Peterson	11 Mar 1991	20 Jun 1992	9 Jul 1994
MCM 14	*Chief*	Peterson	19 Aug 1991	12 Jun 1993	5 Nov 1994

Displacement	1,195 tons; 1,312 tons fl
Dimensions	224′4″ (oa); 212′10″ (wl) × 39′ × 11′6″
Machinery	2 screws; 4 diesel; 2,600 BHP; 13.5 knots
Endurance	2,500/10
Complement	81
Armament	2 MG

Notes: Fiberglass-sheathed wood hull. Designed to locate and destroy mines in deep waters not found by conventional techniques.

Service Record:

MCM 1 *Avenger*
- ◆Gulf War Sep 1990–Jun 1991.

MCM 2 *Defender*
MCM 3 *Sentry*
MCM 4 *Champion*
MCM 5 *Guardian*
- ◆Gulf War May 1991–Jan 1992.

MCM 6 *Devastator*
MCM 7 *Patriot*
- ◆Gulf War Jan 1992.

MCM 8 *Scout*
MCM 9 *Pioneer*
MCM 10 *Warrior*
MCM 11 *Gladiator*
MCM 12 *Ardent*
- ◆Indian Ocean Mar 1996, Jan–Mar, Jul–Dec 1997, Jan–Mar 1998, Jun–Sep 2000, Desert Fox Dec 1998, Iraq War 2003.

MCM 13 *Dextrous*
- ◆Indian Ocean Mar 1966, Jan–Mar, Jul–Dec 1997, Jan–Mar 1998, Jun–Sep 2000, Desert Fox Dec 1998, Iraq War 2003.

MCM 14 *Chief*

COASTAL MINESWEEPERS

No.	Name	ex-YMS	No.	Name	ex-YMS
AMS 1	*Albatross*	80	AMS 31	*Partridge*	437
AMS 2	*Bobolink*	164	AMS 32	*Pelican*	441
AMS 3	*Bunting*	170	AMS 33	*Plover*	442
AMS 4	*Cardinal*	179	AMS 34	*Redhead*	443
AMS 5	*Condor*	192	AMS 35	*Sanderling*	446
AMS 6	*Courser*	201	AMS 36	*Swallow*	461
AMS 7	*Crow*	215	AMS 37	*Swan*	470
AMS 8	*Curlew*	218	AMS 38	*Verdin*	471
AMS 9	*Flicker*	219	AMS 39	*Waxbill*	479
AMS 10	*Firecrest*	231	AMS 40	*Chatterer*	415
AMS 11	*Flamingo*	238	AMS 41	*Barbet*	45
AMS 12	*Goldfinch*	306	AMS 42	*Brambling*	109
AMS 13	*Grackle*	312	AMS 43	*Brant*	113
AMS 14	*Grosbeak*	317	AMS 44	*Courlan*	114
AMS 15	*Grouse*	321	AMS 45	*Crossbill*	120
AMS 16	*Gull*	324	AMS 46	*Egret*	136
AMS 17	*Hawk*	362	AMS 47	*Fulmar*	193
AMS 18	*Heron*	369	AMS 48	*Lapwing*	268
AMS 19	*Hornbill*	371	AMS 49	*Lorikeet*	271
AMS 20	*Hummer*	372	AMS 50	*Nightingale*	290
AMS 21	*Jackdaw*	373	AMS 51	*Reedbird*	291
AMS 22	*Kite*	374	AMS 52	*Rhea*	299
AMS 23	*Lark*	376	AMS 53	*Robin*	311
AMS 24	*Linnet*	395	AMS 54	*Ruff*	327
AMS 25	*Magpie*	400	AMS 55	*Seagull*	402
AMS 26	*Merganser*	417	AMS 56	*Turkey*	444
AMS 27	*Mocking Bird*	419	AMS 57	*Redpoll*	294
AMS 28	*Osprey*	422	AMS 58	*Siskin*	425
AMS 29	*Ostrich*	430	AMS 59		451
AMS 30	*Parrakeet*	434			

Notes: 58 YMS retained postwar were named and rec AMS 17 Feb 1947 (1–40) and 1 Sep 1947 (41–56). AMS rec MSC(O), 7 Feb 1955.

AMS 1 *Albatross* Rec **EAMS 1**, 7 Feb 1955. Rec **EMSC(O) 1**, 10 Feb 1955. Decomm and stricken 20 Mar 1958. Sold 19 Feb 1959.
Later history: merchant *Dorado*.

AMS 2 *Bobolink* rec **MHC 44**, 7 Feb 1955. Stricken 1 Jan 1960.

AMS 3 *Bunting* rec **MHC 45**, 7 Feb 1955. Decomm 30 Jun 1958. Stricken 1 Jun 1960.

AMS 4 *Cardinal* Decomm 18 Nov 1957. Stricken 1 Nov 1959. Trfd to Brazil 15 Aug 1960.
Later history: renamed *Javari* (M 11). R1970.

Figure 9.11: *USS Avenger* (MCM 1), mine countermeasures ship with fiberglass hull, 1998.

Figure 9.12: *USS Crow* (AMS 7) was one of 58 former YMS boats retained after World War II, reclassified and named, shown in 1950.

AMS 5   *Condor*   Trfd to Japan, Mar 1955.
Later history: renamed *Ujishima* (MSC 658). Rtnd and sunk as target, Aug 1968.
6★Korea K-5 K-6 K-7 K-8 K-9 K-10.
AMS 6   *Courser*   Stricken 1 Nov 1959.
AMS 7   *Crow*   Stricken 1 Nov 1959.
AMS 8   *Curlew*   Trfd to South Korea, 6 Jan 1956.
Later history: renamed *Kum Hwa.* (519). R1977.
8★Korea K-2 K-4, K-5 K-6 K-7 K-8 K-9 K-10.
AMS 9   *Flicker*   Decomm Oct 1953. Stricken 1 Jan 1960.
AMS 10   *Firecrest*   Damaged by shore gunfire at Hungnam, Korea, 5 Oct 1951. Trfd to Japan, 15 Mar 1955.
Later history: renamed *Etajima* (MSC 656). R1969.
7★Korea K-3 K-4 K-6 K-7 K-8 K-9 K-10.
AMS 11   *Flamingo*   Stricken 1 Nov 1959.
AMS 12   *Goldfinch*   Decomm 11 Oct 1957. Stricken 2 Nov 1957. Sold 2 Jun 1960.
AMS 13   *Grackle*   Decomm 11 Oct 1957. Stricken 1 Mar 1963. Trfd to Brazil 19 Apr 1963.
Later history: renamed *Juruena* (M 14). SE1972.
AMS 14   *Grosbeak*   Decomm 7 Dec 1955. Stricken 1 Nov 1959.
AMS 15   *Grouse*   Went aground off Rockport, Me., 21 Sep 1963. Destroyed 28 Sep 1963.
AMS 16   *Gull*   Damaged by shore gunfire off Songjin, 16 Mar 1953. Rec **MHC 46**, 7 Feb 1955. Decomm 14 Jan 1958. Stricken Mar 1959.
9★Korea K-1 K-2 K-4 K-5 K-6 K-7 K-8 K-9 K-10.
AMS 17   *Hawk*   Stricken 17 Oct 1957.
AMS 18   *Heron*   Decomm 21 Mar 1955. Trfd to Japan.
Later history: renamed *Nuwajima* (MSC 657). R1967. Sunk as target 1 Aug 1969.
8★Korea K-2 K-4 K-5 K-6 K-7 K-8 K-9 K-10.
AMS 19   *Hornbill*   Decomm 1955. Stricken 1 Nov 1959. Sold 30 Jun 1960.
Later history: merchant *Los Buscaderos*, renamed *Peacock* 1968, *Spirit of America*. Sunk off Santa Cruz Is, Calif.
AMS 20   *Hummer*   Out of comm 23 Jun 1946–3 Nov 1950. Decomm 13 Nov 1953. Trfd to Japan 16 Mar 1959.
Later history: renamed *Moroshima* (MSC 612). SE1962.
AMS 21   *Jackdaw*   Stricken 1 Jan 1960. Trfd to Brazil, 18 Jan 1960.
Later history: renamed *Jurua* (M 13). SE1972.
AMS 22   *Kite*   Decomm 6 Jan 1956. Trfd to South Korea.
Later history: reanmed *Kim Po* (520). SE1972.

10★Korea K-1 K-2 K-3 K-4 K-5 K-6 K-7 K-8 K-9 K-10; PUC 10–24 Oct 1950.
AMS 23   *Lark*   Decomm 13 Nov 1953. Trfd to Japan 14 Feb 1955.
Later history: renamed *Ninoshima* (MSC 613).
AMS 24   *Linnet*   Decomm 13 Sep 1957. NRT. Stricken 1 Oct 1968.
AMS 25   *Magpie*   Sunk by mine off Chusan, east coast of Korea, 1 Oct 1950 (21 killed).
1★Korea K-1.
AMS 26   *Merganser*   Rec **MHC 47**, 7 Feb 1955. Stricken 1 May 1959.
Later history: merchant yacht *Miss Juanita*.
9★Korea K-1 K-2 K-4 K-5 K-6 K-7 K-8 K-9 K-10; PUC 11–24 Oct 1950.
AMS 27   *Mockingbird*   Decomm 6 Jan 1956. Trfd to South Korea.
Later history: renamed *Ko Chang* (521). SE1972.
10★Korea K-1 K-2 K-3 K-4 K-5 K-6 K-7 K-8 K-9 K-10; PUC 10–24 Oct 1950.
AMS 28   *Osprey*   Hit by shore gunfire at Wonsan, 29 Oct 1951, and off Songjin, 24 Apr 1952. Trfd to Japan, 22 Mar 1955.
Later history: renamed *Yakushima* 656). R1969.
10★Korea K-1 K-2 K-3 K-4 K-5 K-6 K-7 K-8 K-9 K-10; PUC 10–24 Oct 1950.
AMS 29   *Ostrich*   Decomm Jan 1958. Stricken 1 Nov 1959. BU 1960.
AMS 30   *Parrakeet*   Decomm 21 May 1947. Stricken 23 Jun 1947. Sold 9 Oct 1947.
Later history: merchant *Dan*. Stranded in Queen Charlotte Sound, BC, 30 Mar 1949.
AMS 31   *Partridge*   Sunk by mine off Wonsan, Korea, 2 Feb 1951 (8 killed).
4★Korea K-1 K-2 K-3 K-4; PUC 10–24 Oct 1950.
AMS 32   *Pelican*   Decomm 16 Apr 1955. Trfd to Japan.
Later history: renamed *Ogishima* (MSC 655). R1968.
9★Korea K-1 K-2 K-4 K-5 K-6 K-7 K-8 K-9 K-10.
AMS 33   *Plover*   Stricken 1 Oct 1968.
AMS 34   *Redhead*   Rec **MHC 48**, 7 Feb 1955. Decomm 6 Dec 1957. Stricken 1 Nov 1959.
10★Korea K-1 K-2 K-3 K-4 K-5 K-6 K-7 K-8 K-9 K-10; PUC 11–24 Oct 1950.
AMS 35   *Sanderling*   Rec **MHC 49**, 7 Feb 1955. Decomm 14 Nov 1957. Stricken 1 Nov 1959.
AMS 36   *Swallow*   Hit by shore gunfire in Songjin harbor, 25 Jun 1952. Decomm 16 Apr 1955, trfd to Japan.
Later history: renamed *Yugeshima* (MSC 660). R1968.
9★Korea K-1 K-2 K-4 K-5 K-6 K-7 K-8 K-9 K-10.
AMS 37   *Swan*   Decomm 6 Oct 1955. Stricken 1 Nov 1959. Sold.
AMS 38   *Verdin*   Decomm 1 Jul 1955. Stricken 1 Nov 1959.
AMS 39   *Waxbill*   Damaged by shore gunfire off Wonsan, Korea, 27 Apr 1952. Rec **MHC 50**, 7 Feb 1955. Decomm 30 Jun 1958. Stricken 1 Nov 1959.
6★Korea K-5 K-6 K-7 K-8 K-9 K-10.
AMS 40   *Chatterer*   Trfd to Japan, 16 Apr 1955.
Later history: renamed *Yurishima* (MSC 661). R1967.
10★Korea K-1 K-2 K-3 K-4 K-5 K-6 K-7 K-8 K-9 K-10; PUC 10–24 Oct 1950.
AMS 41   *Barbet*   Decomm 17 Jun 1955. Stricken 1 Nov 1960.
AMS 42   *Brambling*   Stricken 1 Nov 1959.
AMS 43   *Brant*   Stricken 1 Nov 1959.
AMS 44   *Courlan*   Stricken 1 Nov 1959.
AMS 45   *Crossbill*   Stricken 1 Nov 1959.
AMS 46   *Egret*   Stricken 1 Nov 1959. Trfd to Brazil 15 Aug 1960.
Later history: renamed *Jutai*. (M 12). SE1972.
AMS 47   *Fulmar*   Stricken 1 Oct 1968.
AMS 48   *Lapwing*   Decomm 17 Nov 1957. Stricken 1 Nov 1959.
Later history: merchant *Weems*.
AMS 49   *Lorikeet*   Decomm 18 Sep 1957. Stricken 1 Oct 1968.
AMS 50   *Nightingale*   Stricken 1 Nov 1959.
AMS 51   *Reedbird*   Decomm 16 Dec 1957. Stricken 1 Oct 1968.

AMS 52 *Rhea*   Decomm 23 Dec 1957. Stricken 1 Nov 1959. Sold 1960. BU 1997.
AMS 53 *Robin*   Decomm 7 Dec 1957. Stricken 1 Aug 1961.
AMS 54 *Ruff*   Decomm 13 Dec 1947. Stricken 14 Nov 1969.
AMS 55 *Seagull*   Decomm 11 Oct 1957. Stricken 1 Nov 1959.
AMS 56 *Turkey*   Decomm 23 Nov 1956. Stricken 1 Oct 1968.
AMS 57 *Redpoll*   Decomm 8 Nov 1957. Stricken 1 Jul 1959. **Later history:** oceanographic research vessel, merchant *Sir Horace Lamb*. BU 1976.
AMS 58 *Siskin*   Decomm 14 Oct 1957. Stricken 1 Oct 1968.
AMS 59   canceled, not converted. Retained as PCS-1400.

Adjutant Class

No.	Name	Builder	Completed	Built for	Name	Fate
MSC 60	*Adjutant*	Consolidated	23 Mar 1953	Portugal	*Ponta Delgada* (M405)	R1974
MSC 61	—	Consolidated	30 Jun 1953	Portugal	*Horta* (M406)	R1976
MSC 62	—	Consolidated	12 Aug 1953	Portugal	*Angra do Heroísmo* (M 407)	R1974.
MSC 63	—	Nevins	22 Jul 1953	Belgium	*Lier* (M912)	[1]
MSC 64	—	Nevins	3 Feb 1954	Belgium	*St. Niklaas* (M918)	[2]
MSC 65	—	Nevins	30 Mar 1954	Belgium	*Diksmuide* (M920)	[3]
MSC 66	—	Harbor	16 Mar 1953	France	*Aconit* (M640), renamed *Marjolaine* 1967	[4]
MSC 67	—	Harbor	1 Jun 1953	France	*Azalée* (M668)	R1985
MSC 68	—	Harbor	10 Aug 1953	France	*Camélia* (M671)	R1980
MSC 69	*Bittern*	Sample	11 Mar 1953	France	*Acacia* (M638)	R1983
MSC 70	*Chukor*	Sample	19 May 1953	France	*Acanthe* (M639)	R1981
MSC 71	—	Sample	31 Aug 1953	France	*Ajonc* (M667/A701)	R1989
MSC 72	*Dotterel*	Burger	13 Jan 1953	Italy	*Abete* (M5501)	R1977
MSC 73	—	Burger	13 Jan 1953	Italy	*Betulla* (M5503)	Sold 7 Apr 1976.
MSC 74	—	Grebe	6 Jul 1953	Italy	*Castagno* (M5504)	[5]
MSC 75	—	Grebe	2 Feb 1954	Italy	*Gelso* (M5509)	[6]
MSC 76	—	Grebe	26 Oct 1954	Italy	*Ontano* (M5513)	R 1993
MSC 77	*Macaw*	Quincy Adams	9 May 1953	Belgium.	*Diest* (M910)	[7]
MSC 78	—	Quincy Adams	24 Jul 1953	Belgium	*Maaseik* (M913)	[8]
MSC 79	—	Lake Union	4 Aug 1953	Italy	*Acacia* (M5502)	Sold 9 Apr 1976.
MSC 80	—	Lake Union	15 Sep 1953	Italy	*Ciliegio* (M5506)	Sold 9 Apr 1976.
MSC 81	—	Lake Union	23 Oct 1953	Italy	*Faggio* (M5507)	R1980
MSC 82	—	Lake Union	29 Dec 1953	Italy	*Larice* (M5510)	R1988
MSC 83	—	Stephen Bros	22 Jul 1953	France	*Bégonia* (M669)	R1974
MSC 84	—	Stephen Bros	5 Oct 1953	France	*Coquelicot* (M673)	[9]
MSC 85	—	Stephen Bros	30 Nov 1953	France	*Giroflée* (M677)	R1981
MSC 86	—	Stephen Bros	24 Jan 1954	France	*Laurier* (M681)	R1980
MSC 87	—	Stephen Bros	26 Mar 1954	France	*Magnolia* (M685/A770)	R1988
MSC 88	—	Berg	21 Oct 1953	Italy	*Cedro* (M5505)	R1982
MSC 89	—	Berg	28 Jan 1954	Italy	*Frassino* (M5508)	R1991
MSC 90	—	Berg	6 May 1954	Italy	*Noce* (M5511)	R1982
MSC 91	—	M.M.Davis	20 Sep 1953	Portugal	*Vila do Porto* (M408)	R1976
MSC 92	—	M.M.Davis	13 Feb 1954	Portugal	*Santa Cruz* (M409)	R1976
MSC 93	—	National Stl	3 Feb 1954	France	*Lilas* (M682)	R1981. BU 1986
MSC 94	—	National Stl	5 Mar 1954	France	*Marguerite* (M686)	[10]
MSC 95	—	National Stl	7 May 1954	France	*Narcisse*, renamed *Alysse* (M690) 1954	[11]
MSC 96	—	Tacoma	1 Jun 1954	France	*Lobelia* (M684)	R1985
MSC 97	—	Tacoma	30 Jun 1954	France	*Muguet* (M688)	R1981
MSC 98	—	Tacoma	23 Jun 1954	France	*Liseron* (M683/A723)	R1987
MSC 99	—	Tacoma	12 Aug 1954	France	*Mimosa* (M687)	R1985
MSC 100	—	Tampa Marine	31 Jan 1954	Netherlands	*Breukelen* (M852)	R1972
MSC 101	—	Hodgdon	21 May 1953	Belgium	*Eeklo* (M911)	[12]
MSC 102	—	Hodgdon	23 Jul 1953	Norway	*Sauda* (M311)	R1986
MSC 103	—	Hodgdon	22 Sep 1953	Belgium	*Roeselaere* (M914)	[13]
MSC 104	—	Hodgdon	30 Oct 1953	Belgium	*Arlon* (M915)	[14]
MSC 105	—	Tampa Marine	3 Jul 1953	Netherlands	*Beemster* (M845)	SE1972
MSC 106	—	Tampa Marine	10 Aug 1953	Netherlands	*Berta* (M847), renamed *Bedum* 1953	R1976
MSC 107	—	Tampa Marine	8 Oct 1953	Netherlands	*Borculo* (M849)	SE1972
MSC 108	—	Tampa Marine	23 Nov 1953	Netherlands	*Borne* (M850)	R1975

MSC 109	Broward	26 Oct 1953	Netherlands	*Bolsward* (M846)	SE1972
MSC 110	Broward	9 Apr 1954	Netherlands	*Beilen* (M848)	R1975
MSC 111	Broward	4 Feb 1954	Netherlands	*Brummen* (M851)	R1974
MSC 112	Broward	21 May 1954	Netherlands	*Blaricum* (M853)	R1976
MSC 113	Tacoma	4 Nov 1953	France	*Chrysanthème* (M672)	R1983
MSC 114	Tacoma	4 Feb 1954	France	*Gardénia* (M676/A711)	R1989
MSC 115	Tacoma	17 Mar 1954	France	*Jacinthe* (M680/A680)	R1982
MSC 116	Pacific	10 Nov 1953	France	*Bleuet* (M670)	R1983
MSC 117	Pacific	16 Feb 1954	France	*Églantine* (M675)	BU1985
MSC 118	Pacific	7 Apr 1954	France	*Glycine* (M679)	R1985
MSC 119	National Stl	5 Oct 1953	France	*Cyclamen* (M674)	R1983
MSC 120	National Stl	25 Oct 1953	France	*Glaïeul* (M678)	R1974
MSC 123	Stephen Bros	1 May 1954	France	*Myosotis* (M689)	[15]
MSC 124	Stephen Bros	12 Jun 1954	France	*Pavot* (M693/M631)	[16]
MSC 125	Stephen Bros	28 Aug 1954	France	*Pivoine* (M695/M633)	R1984
MSC 126	Stephen Bros	6 Nov 1954	France	*Réséda* (M697/M635)	R1984
MSC 127	Hiltebrant	10 Jan 1955	Denmark	*Aarøsund* (M 571)	R1981
MSC 128	Hiltebrant	27 Mar 1955	Denmark	*Alssund* (M 572)	R1988
MSC 129	Hiltebrant	19 Jul 1955	Denmark	*Egernsund* (M 573)	R1988
MSC 130	Hiltebrant	18 May 1955	Spain	*Turia* (M24/P52)	R1999
MSC 131	Hiltebrant	7 Feb 1955	Belgium	*De Panne* (M925)	[17]
MSC 132	Hiltebrant	14 Nov 1955	Norway	*Sira* (M 312)	R1992
MSC 133	Bellingham	30 Mar 1954	Italy.	*Olmo* (M5512)	R1980
MSC 134	Bellingham	13 May 1954	Italy	*Pino.* (M5514)	R1980
MSC 135	Bellingham	30 Jun 1954	Italy	*Pioppo* (M5515/A5307)	R1980
MSC 136	Bellingham	9 Sep 1954	Italy	*Platano* (M5516)	R1990
MSC 137	Bellingham	4 Nov 1954	Italy	*Quercia.* (M5517)	R1981
MSC 138	Bellingham	6 Feb 1955	Pakistan	*Muhafiz* (M163)	[18]
MSC 139	South Coast	1 Feb 1954	Spain	*Nalón* (M21/P51)	R1999[19]
MSC 140	South Coast	1 Apr 1954	France	*Paquerette* (M692)	[20]
MSC 141	South Coast	1 Jun 1954	France	*Pervenche.* (M694/M632)	R1980
MSC 142	South Coast	2 Aug 1954	France	*Renoncule* (M696/M634)	[21]
MSC 143	South Coast	1 Oct 1954	Spain	*Llobregat* (M 22)	R1979[22]
MSC 144	South Coast	1 Dec 1954	Japan	*Yashima* (MSC 651).	[23]
MSC 145	Stowman	26 May 1954	Portugal	*Velas* (M410)	R1976
MSC 146	Stowman	13 Aug 1954	Portugal	*Lajes* (M411)	R1976
MSC 147	Stowman	17 Nov 1954	Portugal	*S.Pedro* (M412)	R1974
MSC 148	Kneass	7 Apr 1954	Netherlands	*Breskens* (M855)	R1976
MSC 149	Kneass	24 Jul 1954	Netherlands	*Boxtel* (M857)	R1976
MSC 150	Kneass	30 Oct 1954	Netherlands	*Brouwershaven* (M858)	R 1976[24]
MSC 151	Hodgdon	15 Dec 1953	Belgium	*Bastogne* (M916)	[25]
MSC 152	Hodgdon	2 Feb 1954	Belgium	*Charleroi* (M917)	[26]
MSC 153	Hodgdon	31 Mar 1954	Belgium	*Herve* (M921)	[27]
MSC 154	Hodgdon	15 May 1954	Belgium	*Malmedy* (M922)	[28]
MSC 155/166	—	—	Germany	—	[29]
MSC 167	Puget Sd NYd	11 Dec 1953	Netherlands	*Brielle* (M854).	R 1975
MSC 168	Puget Sd NYd	8 Jan 1954	Netherlands	*Bruinisse* (M856)	R1972
MSC 169	Consolidated	10 Feb 1954	Belgium	*St. Truiden* (M919)	[30]
MSC 170	Consolidated	26 May 1954	Belgium	*Blankenberghe* (M913)	[31]
MSC 171	Consolidated	11 Aug 1954	Belgium	*Laroche* (M924)	[32]
MSC 214	CRDA	8 Nov 1956	Italy	*Bambu* (M5521/P495)	SE2001
MSC 215	CRDA	8 Nov 1956	Italy	*Ebano* (M5522)	R1990
MSC 216	CRDA	5 Dec 1956	Italy	*Mango* (M5523/P496)	R1997
MSC 217	CRDA	9 Jan 1957	Italy	*Mogano* (M5524/P497)	R1999
MSC 238	CRDA	28 Feb 1957	Italy	*Palma* (M5525/P498)	SE2001
MSC 239	CRDA	28 Feb 1957	Italy	*Rovere* (M5526)	R1974
MSC 240	CRDA	15 Apr 1957	Italy	*Sandalo* (M5527)	R1988

Displacement	405 tons
Dimensions	144′ (oa); 138′ (pp) × 27′ × 9′
Machinery	2 screws; diesel; SHP 900; 14 knots
Complement	40
Armament	2–20 mmAA guns

Notes: Rec AMS To MSC, 7 Feb 1955.

[1] MSC 63 — Trfd to Taiwan 30 Oct 1969 renamed *Yung Shan* (476/165). R1995.
[2] MSC 64 — Trfd to Taiwan 30 Oct 1969 renamed *Yung Jen* (485/163). R1995.
[3] MSC 65 — Trfd to Taiwan, 30 Oct 1969 renamed *Yung Sui* (462/164). R1994.
[4] MSC 66 — Trfd to Tunisia Jul 1977 renamed *Sousse*. R1988.
[5] MSC 74 — Trfd to Greece, 10 Oct 1995, renamed *Erato* (M 60). R2006.
[6] MSC 75 — Trfd to Greece, 10 Oct 1995, renamed *Euniki* (M 61). SE2001.
[7] MSC 77 — Trfd to Taiwan 30 Oct 1969, renamed *Yung Fu* (482/162). R1995.
[8] MSC 78 — Trfd to Taiwan 30 Oct 1969, renamed *Yung Chen* (441/168). R1995.
[9] MSC 84 — Trfd to Tunisia 21 Jun 1973, renamed *Hannibal*. R1988.
[10] MSC 94 — Trfd to Uruguay 10 Nov 1969 renamed *Rio Negro* (MS 32/13). R1990.
[11] MSC 95 — Trfd to Japan 3 Jun 1955 renamed *Hashima* (MSC 625), renamed *YAS-47*, 1970.
[12] MSC 101 — Trfd to Taiwan, 30 Oct 1969 renamed *Yung Ching* (432/167). SE2001.
[13] MSC 103 — Trfd to Norway Mar 1966 renamed *Tana* (M 313). SE1993.
[14] MSC 104 — Trfd to Norway May 1966 renamed *Alta* (M 314). SE1993.
[15] MSC 123 — Trfd to Taiwan 4 Jun 1955 renamed *Yung An* (449). SE1993.
[16] MSC 124 — Trfd to Turkey 24 Mar 1970 renamed *Selçuk* (M 508). R2001.
[17] MSC 131 — Trfd to Turkey 19 Nov 1970 renamed *Seymen* (M 507). R1994.
[18] MSC 138 — Sunk by Indian missile off Karachi, 4 Dec 1971.
[19] MSC 139 — Tfr to France as *Oeillet*, canceled; 1 Feb 1954.
[20] MSC 140 — Trfd to Taiwan 4 Jun 1955 renamed *Yung Ping* (156). R1982.
[21] MSC 142 — Trfd to Turkey 24 Mar 1970 renamed *Seyhan* (M 509). R1998.
[22] MSC 143 — Retired after a fire, 4 Jul 1979. Tfr to France, *Roselys*, canceled 1 Oct 1954.
[23] MSC 144 — Tfr to France, *Tulipe*, canceled 1 Dec 1954.
[24] MSC 150 — Merchant *V.A.Islander*, renamed *Alysse Maru* 1980, *Gigamile* 1980.
[25] MSC 151 — Trfd to Norway Sep 1966 renamed *Glomma* (M317). R1991.
[26] MSC 152 — Trfd to Taiwan Oct 1969 renamed *Yung Chi* (497/166). R<1991.
[27] MSC 153 — Trfd to Greece 25 Jul 1969 renamed *Antiopi* (M 205). R1995.
[28] MSC 154 — Trfd to Greece 26 Sep 1969 renamed (*Faedra*) *Phedra*. (M 206). SE1987.
[29] MSC 155/166 — canceled (for Germany).
[30] MSC 169 — Trfd to Greece 25 Jul 1969 renamed *Atalanti* (M 202) SE1987.
[31] MSC 170 — Trfd to Greece 11 Sep 1969 renamed *Thalia* (M 210) SE1987.
[32] MSC 171 — Trfd to Greece 11 Sep 1969 renamed *Niovi* (M 254) SE1987.

MSC-172 Class

No.	Builder	Launched	Completed	Built for	Name	Fate
MSC 172	Wilton	12 Oct 1954	20 Jul 1955	Netherlands	*Dokkum* (M801)	1
MSC 173	Gusto	22 Mar 1955	28 Oct 1955	Netherlands	*Hoogezand* (M802)	R1992
MSC 174	Wilton	13 Aug 1955	20 Dec 1955	Netherlands	*Roermond* (M806)	R1987
MSC 175	De Noord	1 Feb 1955	5 Nov 1955	Netherlands	*Naaldwijk* (M809)	R1993
MSC 176	Gusto	2 Sep 1955	21 Apr 1956	Netherlands	*Abcoude* (M810)	2
MSC 177	Wilton	24 Mar 1955	4 Jan 1956	Netherlands	*Drachten* (M812)	R1993
MSC 178	Smit	5 Apr 1955	20 Mar 1956	Netherlands	*Ommen* (M813)	R1993
MSC 179	Smit	30 Mar 1955	15 Mar 1956	Netherlands	*Giethoorn* (M815)	R1993
MSC 180	Arnhem	21 May 1955	1 Apr 1956	Netherlands	*Venlo* (M817)	R1992
MSC 181	Gusto	24 Mar 1956	3 Aug 1956	Netherlands	*Drunen* (M818)	R1984
MSC 182	Haarlemse	28 Nov 1956	10 Mar 1957	Netherlands	*Woerden* (A882/M820)	R1991
MSC 183	Wilton	27 Jan 1956	10 May 1956	Netherlands	*Naarden* (M823)	R1997
MSC 184	De Noord	8 May 1956	15 Oct 1956	Netherlands	*Hoogeveen* (M827)	R1992
MSC 185	Gusto	21 Jul 1956	20 Dec 1956	Netherlands	*Staphorst* (M828)	R1984
MSC 186	Niestern	26 Apr 1956	25 Oct 1956	Netherlands	*Sittard* (M830)	R1997
MSC 187	Smits	13 Mar 1956	18 Aug 1956	Netherlands	*Gemert* (M841)	R1992
MSC 188	Smit	9 Feb 1956	20 Aug 1956	Netherlands	*Veere* (M842)	R1984
MSC 189	Arnhemse	31 May 1956	25 Nov 1956	Netherlands	*Rhenen* (M844)	R1986
MSC 210	DTCN	6 Oct 1952	23 Apr 1954	France	*Sirius* (M701)	—
MSC 211	Normand	15 Apr 1953	4 Jul 1953	France	*Algol* (M704)	R1976

No.	Builder	Keel Laid	Launched		Name		Fate
MSC 212	Normand	27 Jun 1953	30 Oct 1953	France	*Aldébaran* (M705)		R1978. BU 1980
MSC 213	Normand	18 Nov 1952	29 Jun 1953	France	*Régulus* (M706)		—
MSC 222	Normand	21 Jun 1955	24 Aug 1955	France	*Pégase* (M710)		—
MSC 223	Normand	21 Jul 1955	29 Dec 1955	France	*Bellatrix* (M750)		R1972
MSC 224	Amyot	23 May 1955	9 Aug 1955	France	*Persée* (M748)		—
MSC 225	Amyot	12 Jul 1956	2 Aug 1956	France	*Dénébola* (M751)		R1972
MSC 226	Penhoet	8 Mar 1955	25 Oct 1955	France	*Centaure* (M752)		R1971
MSC 227	Penhoet	23 Apr 1955	26 Mar 1956	France	*Fomalhaut* (M753)		R1970
MSC 228	Normand	31 Dec 1955	21 Feb 1956	France	*Canopus* (M754)		R1986
MSC 229	Normand	27 Feb 1956	23 Apr 1956	Yugoslavia	*Hrabri* (M151)		3
MSC 230	Normand	26 May 1956	26 Jul 1956	Yugoslavia	*Slobodni* (M153)		4
MSC 231	Normand	26 Jun 1956	4 Oct 1956	Yugoslavia	*Smeli* (M152)		5
MSC 232	Amyot	23 May 1955	15 Sep 1955	France	*Phénix* (M749)		renamed *P-749*
MSC 233	Amyot	6 Oct 1955	16 Oct 1955	France	*Capella* (M755)		6
MSC 234	Amyot	3 Jan 1956	26 Jan 1956	France	*Céphée* (M756)		R1988
MSC 235	Amyot	3 Jan 1956	30 Apr 1956	France	*Verseau* (M757)		R1988
MSC 236	Penhoët	3 May 1956	25 Jul 1956	France	*Lyre* (M759)		—
MSC 237	Penhoët	13 Mar 1956	28 Nov 1956	France	*Aries* (M758)		7
MSC 241	CUF SY (Lisbon)	5 Sep 1955	4 Jun 1956	Portugal	*Sao Roque* (M401)		R1992
MSC 242	CUF SY (Lisbon)	15 Sep 1955	10 Aug 1956	Portugal	*Lagoa* (M403)		R1992
MSC 243	DTCN	13 May 1953	7 Feb 1955	France	*Rigel* (M702)		—
MSC 244	DTCN	21 Jan 1953	26 Feb 1955	France	*Antarés* (M703)		R1981
MSC 245	Penhoët	14 Jan 1953	27 Oct 1953	France	*Véga* (M707)		R1981
MSC 246	Penhoët	16 Nov 1953	27 Feb 1954	France	*Cassiopée* (M740)		R1976
MSC 247	Penhoët	18 May 1954	28 Mar 1955	France	*Eridan* (M741)		8
MSC 248	Normand	19 Nov 1953	9 Feb 1954	France	*Castor* (M708)		R1973
MSC 249	Normand	16 Jul 1954	24 Sep 1954	France	*Pollux* (M709)		R1970
MSC 250	Seine	10 Nov 1953	14 Apr 1954	France	*Orion* (M742)		R1970
MSC 251	Seine	12 Jan 1955	29 Mar 1955	France	*Sagittaire* (M743)		R1979
MSC 252	Normandie	12 Aug 1954	5 Oct 1954	France	*Achernar* (M744)		R1970
MSC 253	Normandie	12 Dec 1954	10 Jan 1955	France	*Procyon* (M745)		R1970
MSC 254	Amyot	21 Dec 1957	9 May 1958	France	*Mercure* (M765)		R1990

Displacement	373 tons; 417 tons f/l
Dimensions	149′8″ (oa) × 28′ × 9′
Machinery	2 screws; diesel; 2,500 SHP; 16 knots
Complement	38
Armament	2–40 mm guns

Notes: OSP. Based on British "Ton" class. MSC 253 was a modified type.

[1] MSC 172 renamed *Van Speijk* (Y 8001), 1986.
[2] MSC 176 Tfrd to Peru, renamed *Carasco* (AH 171), 1994. SE2001.
[3] MSC 229 renamed *Vukov Klanac*. Damaged, Sep 1991, captured by Croatia, R<1999.
[4] MSC 230 renamed *Blitvenica*.
[5] MSC 231 renamed *Podgora*.
[6] MSC 233 Damaged in collision with a Guatemalan m/v off Zeebrugge, 28 Feb 1987; not repaired, BU.
[7] MSC 237 Tfrd to Morocco 28 Nov 1974, renamed *Tawfic*. R1985.
[8] MSC 247 renamed *Aldébaran* 1977. R1981.

No.	Name	Builder	Keel Laid	Launched	Comm.
MSC 121	*Bluebird*	Mare I NSYd	5 Feb 1952	11 May 1953	24 Jul 1953
MSC 122	*Cormorant*	Mare I NSYd	5 Feb 1952	8 Jun 1953	14 Aug 1953
MSC 190	*Falcon*	Quincy Adams	7 May 1953	21 Sep 1953	24 Nov 1954
MSC 191	*Frigate Bird*	Quincy Adams	20 Jul 1953	24 Oct 1953	13 Jan 1955
MSC 192	*Hummingbird*	Quincy Adams	24 Oct 1953	25 Dec 1954	9 Feb 1955
MSC 193	*Jacana*	Quincy Adams	26 Feb 1954	25 Feb 1955	10 Mar 1955
MSC 194	*Kingbird*	Quincy Adams	26 Feb 1954	21 May 1955	27 Apr 1955
MSC 195	*Limpkin*	Broward	17 Apr 1953	21 May 1954	26 Mar 1955
MSC 196	*Meadowlark*	Broward	18 May 1953	28 Aug 1954	14 May 1955
MSC 197	*Parrot*	Broward	23 Dec 1953	27 Nov 1954	28 Jun 1955
MSC 198	*Peacock*	Harbor	29 Jan 1953	19 Jun 1954	16 Mar 1955
MSC 199	*Phoebe*	Harbor	26 Feb 1953	21 Aug 1954	29 Apr 1955
MSC 200	*Redwing*	Tampa Marine	1 Jul 1953	29 Apr 1954	7 Jan 1955

MSC 201	Shrike	Tampa Marine	1 Sep 1953	21 Jul 1954	21 Mar 1955
MSC 202	Spoonbill	Tampa Marine	2 Nov 1953	3 Aug 1954	14 Jun 1955
MSC 203	Thrasher	Tampa Marine	1 Apr 1954	6 Oct 1954	16 Aug 1955
MSC 204	Thrush	Tampa Marine	7 May 1954	5 Jan 1955	8 Nov 1955
MSC 205	Vireo	Bellingham	14 Sep 1953	30 Apr 1954	7 Jun 1955
MSC 206	Warbler	Bellingham	15 Oct 1953	18 Jun 1954	23 Jul 1955
MSC 207	Whippoorwill	Bellingham	7 Jan 1954	13 Aug 1954	20 Oct 1955
MSC 208	Widgeon	Bellingham	3 May 1954	15 Oct 1954	28 Nov 1955
MSC 209	Woodpecker	Bellingham	23 Jun 1954	7 Jan 1955	3 Feb 1956

Displacement	362 tons; 370 f/l
Dimensions	144′3″ (oa) × 27′2″ × 12′
Machinery	2 screws; diesel; SHP 600; 14 knots
Endurance	2,500/10
Complement	39
Armament	1 twin 20 mm

Notes: AMS rec MSC, 7 Feb 1955. Non-magnetic minesweepers, plywood hulls.

Figure 9.13: USS *Limpkin* (MSC 195) was transferred to Indonesia in 1971.

Service Records:

MSC 121 *Bluebird* Stricken 2 Jan 1975. Sold Sep 1979, BU.
   ◆Cuba Jan–Apr 1961, Oct 1961–Jan 1962, Dominican Rep Jul–Oct 1965.
MSC 122 *Cormorant* Stricken 15 Mar 1974.
   Later history: merchant *Pelican* 1974.
MSC 190 *Falcon* Trfd to Indonesia 24 Jun 1971.
   Later history: renamed *Pulau Aru*.
MSC 191 *Frigate* Bird Trfd to Indonesia 11 Aug 1971.
   Later history: renamed *Pulau Antung*.
   ◆Cuba Aug–Oct 1961, Jul–Aug 1962, Dominican Rep Dec 1965–Jan 1966.
MSC 192 *Hummingbird* Trfd to Indonesia 12 Jul 1971.
   Later history: renamed *Pulau Impalasa*.
   ◆Cuba Jan 1961, Dominican Rep Dec 1965–Feb 1966.
MSC 193 *Jacana* Trfd to Indonesia 7 Apr 1971.
   Later history: renamed *Pulau Aruan*.
   ◆Cuba Aug–Oct 1961, Jul–Aug 1962, Dominican Rep Jan–Mar 1966.
MSC 194 *Kingbird* Damaged in collision with m/v at Pensacola, 12 May 1971, CTL. Stricken 1 Jul 1972. Sold 1 Mar 1973.
   ◆Cuba Jan–Apr 1961, Oct 1961–Jan 1962, Dominican Rep Aug–Oct 1965.
MSC 195 *Limpkin* Trfd to Indonesia 24 Jun 1971.
   Later history: renamed *Pulau Anjer*.
   ◆Cuba Jan 1961, Dominican Rep Jan–Mar 1966.
MSC 196 *Meadowlark* Trfd to Indonesia 7 Apr 1971.
   Later history: renamed *Pulau Alau*.
   ◆Cuba Apr–May 1961, Dominican Rep Jun–Aug 1965.
MSC 197 *Parrot* Decomm 26 Sep 1968, NRT. Stricken 1 Aug 1972, Trfd to Sea Cadets 23 Aug 1973. Sold 1 Dec 1976.
   ◆Cuba Apr–May 1961, Dominican Rep Jun–Sep 1965.
MSC 198 *Peacock* Stricken 1 Jul 1975. Sold 1 Sep 1976, BU.
   ★Vietnam Mar–Apr, Jul, Sep–Dec 1965, Feb–Apr, Sep–Nov 1966, Apr–Jun, Oct–Nov 1969, Mar–Jun 1970; ◆Taiwan Straits Sep–Oct 1958.
MSC 199 *Phoebe* Stricken 1 Jul 1975. BU.
   ★Vietnam Jul 1964, Mar–Apr 1965, Sep–Nov 1965, Mar–Apr, Jul–Sep, Nov–Dec 1966, Mar–Apr, Nov–Dec 1967, Sep–Oct 1968, Mar–Jun, Sep–Nov 1969, May 1970.
MSC 200 *Redwing* Decomm and trfd to Spain 16 Jun 1959.
   Later history: renamed *Sil* (M 29/PVZ 55/M27) R2003.
MSC 201 *Shrike* Decomm 27 Sep 1968, NRT. Stricken 1 Jul 1975. BU 1978.
MSC 202 *Spoonbill* Decomm and trfd to Spain 16 Jun 1959.
   Later history: renamed *Duero* (M28/M 23). R1999.
MSC 203 *Thrasher* Decomm 1 Aug 1961, NRT. Stricken 1 Jul 1975. Trfd to Singapore 5 Dec 1975.
   Later history: renamed *Mercury* (M 102). R1990.
MSC 204 *Thrush* Decomm 1 Jul 1975. Leased to Virginia Marine Institute. Stricken 1 Aug 1977, BU 1982.
MSC 205 *Vireo* Decomm 1 Oct 1970, NRT. Stricken 1 Jul 1975. Trfd to Fiji 14 Oct 1975.
   Later history: renamed *Kula* (205). R1985.
   ★Vietnam Jul–Jul 1964, Mar–Jun, Sep–Dec 1965, Apr–Jun, Aug–Dec 1966, Jan–Mar 1969, Nov 1969–Jan 1970; ◆Taiwan Straits Sep–Nov 1958.
MSC 206 *Warbler* Decomm 1 Oct 1970, NRT. Stricken 1 Jul 1975. Trfd to Fiji 14 Jun 1976.
   Later history: renamed *Kiro* (206). R1996. Disposed of by burning, 1996.
   7★Vietnam Jul 1964, Apr–Jun 1965, Jan–Feb, May–Jul, Sep–Oct 1966, Feb–Mar, Oct–Nov 1967, Apr–Jun, Nov 1968–Jan 1969, May–Jun 1969, May–Jul 1970; ◆Taiwan Straits Sep–Nov 1958.
MSC 207 *Whippoorwill* Decomm 15 Dec 1970, NRT. Stricken 1 Jul 1975. Trfd to Singapore 5 Dec 1975.
   Later history: renamed *Jupiter* (M 101). R1995.
   6★Vietnam Jul 1964, Apr–May, Dec 1965–Jan 1966, Mar–Apr, Jul–Aug, Nov–Dec 1966, Jul–Aug 1968, Mar–May 1969, Jul–Aug 1970; ◆Taiwan Straits Sep–Nov 1958.
MSC 208 *Widgeon* Decomm 10 Oct 1969, NRT. Stricken 2 Jul 1973. BU 1974.
   6★Vietnam Jul 1964, Sep–Nov 1965, Feb–Jul, Dec 1966, Jul–Sep 1967, Jun–Jul 1968, May–Sep 1969; ◆Taiwan Straits Sep–Nov 1958, Korea Oct 1967/.
MSC 209 *Woodpecker* Decomm 15 Dec 1970, NRT. Stricken 1 Jul 1975. Trfd to Fiji 14 Oct 1975.
   Later history: renamed *Kikau* (204). Sunk as artificial reef, 1990.
   ★Vietnam Jul 1964, Apr–Jun, Oct–Nov 1965, Mar–Apr, Jul–Aug, Oct–Nov 1966; ◆Taiwan Straits Sep–Nov 1958.

No.	Builder	Launched	Completed	Built for	Name	Fate
MSC 218	Bellingham	—	15 Feb 1956	Philippines	*Zambales* (M55)	R1979
MSC 219	Bellingham	—	23 Apr 1956	Philippines	*Zamboanga del Norte* (M56)	R1979
MSC 220	Bellingham	24 Jun 1955	22 Jun 1956	Spain	*Júcar* (M 23/M 21)	SE 2001
MSC 221	Bellingham	—	23 May 1956	Denmark	*Omøsund* (M 576)	R1982
MSC 255	Stephen Bros	—	1 Jul 1956	Japan	*Tsushima* (MSC 652)	R1978
MSC 256	Stephen Bros	12 Aug 1955	16 Sep 1956	Denmark	*Grønsund* (M 574)	R1999
MSC 257	Stephen Bros	17 Mar 1956	11 Nov 1956	Denmark	*Guldborgsund* (M 575)	R1993
MSC 258	Stephen Bros	—	28 Jan 1957	Japan	*Toshima* (MSC 654)	R1978
MSC 259	Hodgdon	—	4 Jun 1956	Belgium	*Verviers* (M 934)	R1987
MSC 260	Hodgdon	—	23 Aug 1956	Belgium	*Veurne* (M 935)	R1987
MSC 261	Hodgdon	—	24 Oct 1956	Pakistan	*Mujahid* (M164)	R1995, museum
MSC 262	Hodgdon	—	8 Jan 1957	Pakistan	*Murabak* (M162)	R1985
MSC 263	Harbor	22 Dec 1955	30 Aug 1956	Denmark	*Ulvsund* (M 577)	R1989
MSC 264	Harbor	10 Mar 1956	9 Nov 1956	Denmark	*Vilsund* (M 578)	R1995
MSC 265	Quincy Adams	28 Jan 1956	9 Jul 1956	Spain	*Ulla* (M27/P54)	R1993
MSC 266	Quincy Adams	14 Apr 1956	9 Oct 1956	Spain	*Miño* (PVZ53/M25/M28)	R1999
MSC 267	Quincy Adams	—	25 Apr 1957	Pakistan	*Mahmood* (M160)	R1995

Displacement	375 tons
Dimensions	144′ (oa) × 27′ × 8′3″
Machinery	2 screws, diesels, 880 SHP, 14 knots
Complement	39
Armament	1–20 mm gun

MSC 265   Sunk as artificial reef off La Manga del Menor, 14 Oct 1999.

MSC 268 Class

No.	Builder	Launched	Completed	Built for	Name	Fate
MSC 268	Bellingham	6 Sep 1957	28 Sep 1958	Turkey	*Samsun* (M257/M510)	SE2001
MSC 269	Bellingham	8 Nov 1957	18 Dec 1958	Spain	*Ebro* (M26/M22)	R2005
MSC 270	Bellingham	4 Jan 1958	23 Jan 1959	Turkey	*Sinop* (M258/M511)	R2004
MSC 271	Bellingham	1958	13 Mar 1959	Turkey	*Sürmene* (M259/M512)	SE2001
MSC 272	Bellingham	1958	24 Apr 1959	Turkey	*Seddülbahir* (M260/M513)	SE2001
MSC 273	Bellingham	—	12 Jun 1959	Pakistan	*Munsif.* (M166)	R1979
MSC 274	Bellingham	—	24 Jul 1959	Pakistan	*Mukhtar* (M165)	R1995
MSC 275	Bellingham	22 Nov 1958	4 Sep 1959	Iran	*Shahbaz* (275).	Lost by fire, 1975
MSC 276	Bellingham	—	28 Oct 1959	Iran	*Shahrokh* (301)	SE1993
MSC 277	Tacoma	—	25 May 1959	Taiwan	*Yung Nien* (479)	R1991
MSC 278	Tacoma	—	21 Jun 1959	Taiwan	*Yung Chuan* (423/158)	SE2001
MSC 279	Tacoma	8 Aug 1958	20 Aug 1959	Spain	*Genil* (M31/M25)	R2004
MSC 280	Tacoma	29 Oct 1959	—	Italy	*Mandorlo* (M5519)	R1993
MSC 281	Stephens	26 Jun 1959	—	South Vietnam	*Ham Tu II* (HQ114)	SE1972
MSC 282	Stephens	21 Aug 1959	—	South Vietnam	*Chuong Duong II* (HQ115)	SE1972
MSC 283	Stephens	18 Sep 1959	—	South Vietnam	*Bach Dang* (HQ116)	Ran aground 9 Nov 1970, CTL
MSC 284	Harbor	—	12 Jun 1959	South Korea	*Kum San* (522/MSC 551)	SE2001
MSC 285	Harbor	—	14 Aug 1959	South Korea	*Ko Heung* (523/MSC 552)	SE2001
MSC 286	Harbor	—	30 Aug 1959	South Korea	*Kum Kok* (525/MSC 553)	SE2001
MSC 287	Tampa Marine	1 May 1958	18 May 1959	Spain	*Tajo* (M 30/M 24)	R2002
MSC 288	Tampa Marine	3 Sep 1958	29 Jun 1959	Spain	*Odiel* (M32/M26)	R2004

Displacement	370 tons
Dimensions	152′ (oa) × 28′ × 7′
Machinery	2 screws; diesel; SHP 1,200; 14 knots
Endurance	2,400/10
Complement	38
Armament	2–20 mm guns

MSC 291 Class

No.	Builder	Completed	Built for	Name	Fate
MSC 291	Tacoma	18 Sep 1961	Iran	*Simorgh* (302)	Lost 1981
MSC 292	Peterson	16 May 1962	Iran	*Karkas* (303)	SE1993
MSC 293	Peterson	14 Jul 1962	Pakistan	*Momin* (M 161)	R1985
MSC 294	Peterson	29 Jun 1963	Pakistan	*Moshal* (M 167)	R1985
MSC 295	Peterson	13 Aug 1963	South Korea	*Namyang* (526/MSC 555)	SE2001
MSC 296	Peterson	14 Oct 1963	South Korea	*Hadong* (527/MSC 556)	SE2001
MSC 297	Peterson	21 Nov 1963	Thailand	*Ladya* (5/635)	R1995
MSC 298	Tacoma	9 Nov 1964	Greece	*Doris* (M 245/A 475)	R1995.
MSC 299	Tacoma	4 Jan 1965	Greece	*Aigli* (M 246)	R1996
MSC 300	Tacoma	22 Mar 1965	Taiwan	*Yung Ju* (457/159)	Lost by grounding 1992
MSC 301	Tacoma	17 Aug 1965	Thailand	*Tadindeng* (7)	R1992
MSC 302	Dorchester	21 Dec 1964	Taiwan	*Yung Hsin* (488/160)	R1995
MSC 303	Dorchester	24 Jun 1965	Thailand	*Bangkeo* (6/612)	SE2001
MSC 304	Dorchester	27 Jul 1965	Turkey	*Silifke* (M263/M514)	SE2001
MSC 305	Dorchester	16 Dec 1965	Turkey	*Saros* (M264/M515)	SE2001
MSC 306	Dorchester	11 Apr 1966	Taiwan	*Yung Lo* (469/161)	R1995
MSC 307	Peterson	23 May 1964	Greece	*Dafni* (M 247)	R2004
MSC 308	Peterson	14 Jul 1964	Greece	*Kichli* (M 241)	—
MSC 309	Peterson	1 Sep 1964	Greece	*Kissa* (M 242)	—
MSC 310	Peterson	13 Oct 1964	Greece	*Aedon* (M 248)	—
MSC 311	Peterson	15 May 1965	Turkey	*Sigaçik* (M265/M516)	SE2001
MSC 312	Peterson	19 Jun 1965	Turkey	*Sapanca* (M266/M517)	SE2001
MSC 313	Peterson	28 Aug 1965	Thailand	*Donchedi* (8/613)	SE2001
MSC 314	Peterson	22 Jun 1967	Greece	*Pleias* (M240)	SE1987
MSC 315	Peterson	28 Jul 1967	Turkey	*Sariyer* (M267/M518)	SE2001
MSC 316	Peterson	20 Jun 1968	South Korea	*Samkok* (528/MSC 557)	SE2001
MSC 317	Peterson	7 Aug 1968	Greece	*Argo*, renamed *Klio* (M 213)	R2006
MSC 318	Peterson	3 Oct 1968	Greece	*Avra* (M 214)	—
MSC 319	Peterson	3 Dec 1968	Greece	*Alkyon* (M211)	SE1987
MSC 320	Peterson	2 Oct 1975	South Korea	(*Yong Dong*) *Yeongdong* (MSC 558)	SE2001
MSC 321	Peterson	2 Oct 1975	South Korea	*Ok Cheon* (MSC 559)	SE2001

Displacement	375 tons
Dimensions	145′ 8″ (oa) × 28′ × 8′3″
Machinery	2 screws; diesel; SHP 880; 14 knots
Complement	40
Armament	1–20 mm gun

Albatross Class

No.	Name	Builder	Keel Laid	Launched	Comm.
MSC 289	*Albatross*	Tacoma Boat	26 Feb 1959	26 Mar 1960	20 Apr 1961
MSC 290	*Gannet*	Tacoma Boat	1 May 1959	26 May 1960	14 Jul 1961

Displacement	378 tons
Dimensions	145′ (oa) × 28′ × 13′
Machinery	2 screws; diesel; SHP 1,000; 13 knots
Complement	45
Armament	2 MG

Notes: Originally intended for transfer to Spain.

Service Records:

MSC 289 *Albatross*   Decomm and stricken 1 Apr 1970. Sold, Nov 1970, BU Japan.
★Vietnam Jul 1964, Apr–Jun 1965, Oct–Nov 1965, Jan–Feb, May–Jul, Sep–Nov 1966, Jan–Feb, Sep–Oct 1967, Apr–Jun, Oct–Nov 1968, Mar 1969.

MSC 290 *Gannet*   Stricken 1 Apr 1970.
★Vietnam Jul 1964, Dec 1965–Jan 1966, Apr–Jun, Aug–Sep, Dec 1966–Jan 1967, May–Jun 1967, Mar–Apr, Sep–Oct 1968, Jan–Feb 1970.

160 The Navy of the Nuclear Age, 1947–2007

No.	Builder	Laid Down	Launched	Completed	Built for	Name (No.)
MSC 322	Peterson	12 May 1976	20 Dec 1976	6 Jul 1978	Saudi Arabia	*Addiriyah* (412)
MSC 323	Peterson	24 Aug 1976	26 May 1977	15 Aug 1978	Saudi Arabia	*Al-Quysumah* (414)
MSC 324	Peterson	28 Dec 1976	6 Sep 1977	7 Sep 1978	Saudi Arabia	*Al-Wadeeah* (416)
MSC 325	Peterson	5 Mar 1977	7 Dec 1977	20 Oct 1978	Saudi Arabia	*Safwa* (418)

Displacement 320 tons; 407 f/l
Dimensions 153′ (oa) × 26′9″ × 8′3″
Machinery 2 screws; diesels; 1,200 hp; 13 knots
Complement 39
Armament 1–20 mm

Notes: OSP for Saudi Arabia.

COASTAL MINESWEEPERS (UNDERWATER LOCATOR)

Coastal Minehunters

No.	Name	Formerly
AMC(U) 1/6	—	LCT 843/847, 887/890
AMC(U) 7/10	—	LCIL 589, 400, 409, 513
AMC(U) 11	*Blackbird*	LCIL 515
AMC(U) 12	*Harkness*	YMS 242
AMC(U) 13	*James M. Gilliss*	YMS 262
AMC(U) 14	*Minah*	PCS 1465
	Reclassified **AMC(U)** 7 Mar 1952	
AMC(U) 15	*Accentor*	LSIL 652 /canceled
AMC(U) 16	*Avocet*	LSIL 653
AMC(U) 17	*Blue Jay*	LSIL 654 /not comm
AMC(U) 18	*Chaffinch*	LSIL 694 /not comm
AMC(U) 19	*Chewink*	LSIL 701 /not comm
AMC(U) 20	*Chimango*	LSIL 703 /not comm
AMC(U) 21	*Cockatoo*	LSIL 709
AMC(U) 22	*Cotinga*	LSIL 776 /not comm
AMC(U) 23	*Dunlin*	LSIL 777 /canceled
AMC(U) 24	*Goldcrest*	LSIL 869
AMC(U) 25	*Jacamar*	LSIL 870
AMC(U) 26	*Kestrel*	LSIL 874
AMC(U) 27	*Kildeer*	LSIL 883 /canceled
AMC(U) 28	*Longspur*	LSIL 884 /not comm
AMC(U) 29	*Magpie*	LSIL 944 /not comm
AMC(U) 30	*Mallard*	LSIL 963 /not comm
AMC(U) 31	*Medrick*	LSIL 966 /canceled
AMC(U) 32	*Minivet*	LSIL 969 /canceled
AMC(U) 33	*Oriole*	LSIL 973
AMC(U) 34	*Ortolan*	LSIL 976
AMC(U) 35	*Owl*	LSIL 982
AMC(U) 36	*Partridge*	LSIL 1001 /canceled
AMC(U) 37	*Rail*	LSIL 1022
AMC(U) 38	*Sandpiper*	LSIL 1008
AMC(U) 39	*Sentinel*	LSIL 1052 /not comm
AMC(U) 40	*Shearwater*	LSIL 1053 /canceled
AMC(U) 41	*Skimmer*	LSIL 1093
AMC(U) 42	*Sparrow*	LSIL 1098 /canceled
	Rec **AMC(U)** 1 Sep 1954	
AMC(U) 44	*Bobolink*	AMS 2 / YMS 164
AMC(U) 45	*Bunting*	AMS 3/ YMS 170
AMC(U) 46	*Gull*	AMS 16/ YMS 324
AMC(U) 47	*Merganser*	AMS 26/ YMS 417
AMC(U) 48	*Redhead*	AMS 34/ YMS 443
AMC(U) 49	*Sanderling*	AMS 35/ YMS 446
AMC(U) 50	*Waxbill*	AMS 39/ YMS 479
	All rec **MHC**, 7 Feb 1955	

Figure 9.14: *USS Blackbird* (AMCU 11), was one of five infantry landing craft converted to coastal minesweeper (underwater locator).

Figure 9.15: *USS Bittern* (MHC 43), a prototype minehunter built in 1957.

No.	Name	Builder	Keel Laid	Launched	Comm.
MHC 43	Bittern	Consolidated	18 Aug 1955	4 Mar 1957	26 Aug 1957

Displacement	358 tons
Dimensions	144'5" (oa) × 28' × 8'
Machinery	2 screws; diesels; SHP 1,200; 14 knots
Complement	44
Armament	1–40 mmAA, 2–20 mm gun

Notes: AMCU rec MHC, 7 Feb 1955. Built on MSC hull.

Service Record: Decomm 1 Sep 1965. Stricken 1 Feb 1972. Sold 4 Dec 2000, BU Baltimore.

Cardinal Class

No.	Name	Builder	Keel Laid	Launched	Comm.
MSH 1	Cardinal	Bell-Halter	13 Feb 1986	—	—
MSH 2/5	—	Bell-Halter	—	—	—

Displacement	470 tons
Dimensions	150' × —
Machinery	2 screws; diesels; 1,200 BHP
Complement	45
Armament	none

Notes: Small minehunters, fiberglass hulls. 17 were planned. Failed test and program was canceled 24 Nov 1986. Replaced by *Osprey* class.

Osprey Class

No.	Name	Builder	Keel Laid	Launched	Comm.
MHC 51	Osprey	Intermarine	16 May 1988	23 Mar 1991	20 Nov 1993
MHC 52	Heron	Intermarine	7 Apr 1989	21 Mar 1992	6 Aug 1994
MHC 53	Pelican	Avondale	6 May 1991	27 Feb 1993	18 Nov 1995
MHC 54	Robin	Avondale	28 Jan 1992	11 Sep 1993	11 May 1996
MHC 55	Oriole	Avondale	8 May 1991	22 May 1993	16 Sep 1995
MHC 56	Kingfisher	Avondale	24 Mar 1992	18 Jun 1994	26 Oct 1996
MHC 57	Cormorant	Avondale	8 Apr 1992	21 Oct 1995	5 Apr 1997
MHC 58	Blackhawk	Intermarine	3 Sep 1992	27 Aug 1994	11 May 1996
MHC 59	Falcon	Intermarine	3 Apr 1993	3 Jun 1995	8 Feb 1997
MHC 60	Cardinal	Intermarine	1 Feb 1994	9 Mar 1996	18 Oct 1997
MHC 61	Raven	Intermarine	15 Nov 1994	28 Sep 1996	5 Sep 1998
MHC 62	Shrike	Intermarine	1 Aug 1995	24 May 1997	31 May 1999

Displacement	803 tons; 918 tons f/l
Dimensions	187'9" (oa); 174'2" (wl) × 35'11" × 36'1"
Machinery	2 cycloidal screws; 2 diesels; 1,160 BHP; 15 knots
Endurance	1,500/10
Complement	51
Armament	1/2 MG

Notes: Modified Italian *Lerici* class, glass reinforced plastic hull. Replaced *Cardinal* class.

Service Record:
MHC 51 *Osprey*   Decomm and stricken 15 Jun 2006.
MHC 52 *Heron*   Decomm 1 Oct 2006. Trfd to Greece. 16 Mar 2007.
    Later history: renamed *Kalipso* (M 64).
MHC 53 *Pelican*   Decomm 1 Oct 2006. Trfd to Greece 16 Mar 2007.
    Later history: renamed *Efniki* (M 61).
MHC 54 *Robin*   Decomm and stricken 15 Jun 2006.
MHC 55 *Oriole*   Decomm and stricken 30 Jun 2006.

Figure 9.16: *USS Oriole* (MHC 55), an *Osprey* class minehunter, 10 Mar 2003.

Figure 9.17: The *Osprey* class coastal minehunter *USS Blackhawk* (MHC 58) pulls into her homeport in Ingleside, Texas, after a six-month deployment to the Western Atlantic, 1 Sep 2004.

MHC 56 *Kingfisher*   Decomm and stricken 1 Dec 2007.
MHC 57 *Cormorant*   Decomm and stricken 1 Dec 2007.
MHC 58 *Blackhawk*   Decomm and stricken 1 Dec 2007.
MHC 59 *Falcon*   Decomm and stricken 30 Jun 2006.
MHC 60 *Cardinal*   Decomm 7 Jan 2007, trfd to Egypt.
    Later history: renamed *El Sadeeq* (521).
    ◆Indian Ocean Aug–Sep 2000, Iraq War 2003.
MHC 61 *Raven*   Decomm 7 Jan 2007, trfd to Egypt.
    Later history: renamed *Al Faruq* (524).
    ◆Indian Ocean Aug–Sep 2000, Iraq War 2003.
MHC 62 *Shrike*   Decomm and stricken 1 Dec 2007.

INSHORE MINESWEEPERS

1 *Cove*	2 *Cape*
Displacements	MSI 1–2 120 tons, 248 f/l
Dimensions	112' × 23' × 9'
Machinery	1 screw; diesel; 650 hp; 12 knots complement 20.
MSI 3–10	to Netherlands

MSI 11–12	to Denmark
MSI 13–14	to Iran
MSI 15–18	to Turkey
MSI 19–54	not used
MSI 55–74	to Italy
MSI 75–81	to UK
MSI 82–83	to Belgium
MSI 84–89	to UK
MSI 90–97	to Belgium
MSI 98–101	to Yugoslavia

MINESWEEPING BOATS

MSB 5–54	Built 1952–56
Displacement	30 tons, 39 f/l
Dimensions	57.2′ (oa) × 15.5′ × 4′
Machinery	2 screws; geared diesels; 600 hp; 12 knots, comp 6

(MSB-29: 80 tons f/l; 82′ (oa) × 19′ × 5.5′)

Notes: Unnamed. MSB-24 not built. Used extensively in Vietnam. MSB 1–4 were former Army boats built in 1946. 4 MSB transferred to Panama, 3 Mar 1993.

Losses:

MSB-3	Lost by collision with a dolphin, 20 Jan 1967, salved.
MSB-14	Sunk in collision with m/v *Mui Finn* in Long Tau River, 14 Jan 1967.
MSB-23	Destroyed by fire while under construction, 2 Feb 1955.
MSB-43	Sunk after collision with a dolphin, 20 Jan 1967.
MSB-45	Sunk by mine in Saigon shipping channel, 15 Feb 1967.
MSB-54	Sunk by mine in Long Tau River, 31 Oct 1966 (2 lost).

Figure 9.18: *MSB-21*, in Long Tau River, near Saigon, 1967. Fifty of these boats were built in 1952–54

MINESWEEPERS, SPECIAL (DEVICE)

MSS 1	*Harry L. Glucksman*	Acquired 1 Sep 1970. Comm 16 Jun 1969. Decomm 15 Mar 1973. Sold 2 Sep 1975, BU Brownsville, Tex.
MSS 2	*Washtenaw County*	ex-LST 1166

Notes: MSS 1 was a former Liberty Ship, intended to sweep pressure mines by detonating them with a pressure wave, for use in Vietnam waters. See also YAG 36–39.

10 TENDERS

DESTROYER TENDERS

Destroyer Tenders on the Navy List, 1947

AD 14   *Dixie*   FRAM Jun 1961 Mare I NSYd. Decomm and stricken 15 Jun 1982. Sold 17 Feb 1983, BU Taiwan.
3★Korea K-4 K-7 K-8; 2★Vietnam Nov 1964–Apr 1965; ◆Iran/Indian Ocean Dec 1979–May 1980, Aug–Oct 1981.

AD 15   *Prairie*   FRAM Jan 1962 S.Fran NSYd. Decomm and stricken 26 Mar 1993. Sold 6 Apr 1993, BU India.
★Korea 1951, 1952; 1★Vietnam Mar 1973; ◆Libya Sep–Dec 1988, Gulf War Mar–Jun 1992.

AD 17   *Piedmont*   FRAM Feb 1963 Long Bch NSYd. Decomm and stricken 30 Sep 1982. Trfd to Turkey 2 Nov 1982.
Later history: renamed *Derya* (A 576). R1994, BU.
4★Korea K-1 K-7 K-8 K-9; 1★Vietnam Jul 1964, Jun–Jul 1972; ◆Taiwan Straits Aug–Nov 1958.

AD 18   *Sierra*   FRAM Sep 1962 Norfolk NSYd. Decomm and stricken 29 Oct 1993. Sold 25 Aug 1995, sale canceled.
◆Cuba Oct–Dec 1961, Sep–Oct 1962.

AD 19   *Yosemite*   FRAM Apr 1960 Boston NSYd. Decomm and stricken 27 Jan 1994, NDRF. Sunk as target, 18 Nov 2003.
◆Cuba Feb 1962, Cuba missile crisis Nov–Dec 1962, Gulf War Nov 1991–Feb 1992.

Dixie class; Armament 1977: 2–40 mm, 4–20 mm guns; 40 mm removed 1980. FRAM modernization included adding DASH helicopter platform and hangar at stern.

AD 16   *Cascade*   Out of comm 12 Feb 1947–5 Apr 1951. FRAM Oct 1965 Boston NSYd. Decomm 22 Nov and stricken 23 Nov 1974. Sold 2 Sep 1975, BU.

AD 20   *Hamul*   Decomm 9 Jun 1962. Stricken 1 Jul 1963, sold 16 Oct 1975, BU 1976.
1★Korea K-9, 1952–52; ◆Taiwan Straits Dec 1958.

AD 21   *Markab*   Out of comm 3 Jun 1947–26 Feb 1952 and 31 Jul 1955–1 Jul 1960. Rec **AR 23**, 15 Apr 1960.
Decomm 19 Dec 1969. Stricken 1 Sep 1976.
★Vietnam Nov 1967.

Figure 10.1: *USS Yosemite* (AD 19) in the 1950s, prior to her FRAM refit.

Figure 10.2: *USS Cascade* (AD 16), destroyer tender, September 1962, prior to her FRAM refit.

AD 22 *Klondike* Out of comm 30 Nov 1946–15 Jul 1959. Rec **AR 22**, 20 Feb 1960. Decomm 15 Dec 1970. Stricken 15 Sep 1974. Sold 8 May 1975, BU Portland, Ore.
1★Vietnam Mar–Apr 1969.
AD 23 *Arcadia* Decomm 1947–1 Aug 1951. Decomm 28 Jun 1968. Stricken 1 Jul 1973. Sold 1 Aug 1974, BU 1975, Camden, NJ.
◆Cuba Sep–Oct 1962.
AD 24 *Everglades* First comm.25 May 1951. Decomm 15 Aug 1970. Stricken 24 May 1989.
AD 25 *Frontier* Out of comm 29 Sep 1947–11 Nov 1951. Decomm 28 Jun 1968. Stricken 1 Dec 1972. Sold 18 Apr 1975, BU Portland, Ore.
★Korea 1952–53.
AD 26 *Shenandoah* Decomm and stricken 1 Apr 1980. Sold 1 Mar 1982.
◆Lebanon Jul 1958.
AD 27 *Yellowstone* In collision with Greek m/v *Mautric* at Naples, 10 Feb 1970. Decomm 11 Sep 1974. Stricken 12 Sep 1974. Sold 2 Sep 1975, BU.
◆Cuba Apr 1961.
AD 28 *Grand Canyon* Rec **AR 28**, 12 Mar 1971. Decomm and stricken 1 Sep 1978. Sold Jun 1980, BU.
AD 29 *Isle Royale* First comm 9 Jun 1962. Decomm 30 Jun 1971. Stricken 15 Sep 1976. BU 1977 Wilmington, Cal.
1★Vietnam Jan 1967.
AD 31 *Tidewater* Recomm 2 Oct 1951. Decomm 20 Feb 1971 and trfd.to Indonesia. Stricken 14 Mar 1980.
Later history: renamed *Dumai*. R1984.
AD 36 *Bryce Canyon* First comm 15 Sep 1950. Decomm 1 Jun 1981. Stricken 30 Jun 1981. Sold 6 Apr 1982, BU Terminal I.
1★Korea K-8; ◆Cuba missile crisis Nov 1962.

Armament: *1977* AD 24: 1–3″/50, 2–40 mm; 26: 2–40 mm, 4–20 mm; AD 36: 1–5″/38. DASH Helicopter platform added at stern.

Figure 10.3: *USS Shenandoah* (AD 26), at an Italian port in the 1960s. The Italian destroyer *Indomito* can be seen at right.

No.	Name	Builder	Keel Laid	Launched	Comm.
AD 37	*Samuel Gompers*	Puget Sd NSYd	9 Jul 1964	14 May 1966	1 Jul 1967
AD 38	*Puget Sound*	Puget Sd NSYd	15 Feb 1965	16 Sep 1966	27 Apr 1968
AD 39	—	—	—	—	—
AD 40	—	—	—	—	—
AD 41	*Yellowstone*	National Stl	27 Jun 1977	27 Jan 1979	31 May 1980
AD 42	*Acadia*	National Stl	14 Feb 1978	28 Jul 1979	6 Jun 1981
AD 43	*Cape Cod*	National Stl	27 Jan 1979	2 Aug 1980	17 Apr 1982
AD 44	*Shenandoah*	National Stl	2 Aug 1980	6 Feb 1982	17 Dec 1983

Displacement	13,600 tons, 22,260 f/l; 41–44: 13,318 tons; 20,225 f/l
Dimensions	643′4″ (oa); 620′ (wl) × 85′ × 22′6″
Machinery	1 screw; ST; 2 boilers; 20,000 SHP; 20 knots
Complement	1,360
Armament	1–5″/38 (37–38), later removed. (1977) 37: 2–40 mm, 4–20 mm; 38: also 1–5″/38; (2006) 2–40 mm GL

Notes: Similar to *Spear* class submarine tenders. AD 45, planned, not built. Designed to support surface combatants with guided missiles and gas turbines, or nuclear propulsion. Able to support six DDG alongside simultaneously. Engines aft, helicopter hangar aft.

Service Records:

AD 37 *Samuel Gompers* Decomm 27 Oct 1995. Stricken 7 Apr 1999. Sunk as target 21 Jul 2003.
1★Vietnam Apr 1972, ◆Iran/Indian Ocean Apr–Sep 1981, Gulf War May–Aug 1991.

Figure 10.4: *USS Samuel Gompers* (AD 37), the first postwar destroyer tender, built in 1967. Notice the single 5-inch gun, later removed in 1977.

AD 38 *Puget Sound* Decomm 27 Jan 1996.
◆Lebanon Jan–May 1983, Sep–Oct 1983, Libya Mar–Jun 1989, Gulf War Feb–May 1991.
AD 39 canceled 1969.
AD 40 not built 1973. Canceled 1 Apr 1974.
AD 41 *Yellowstone* Decomm 31 Jan 1996. Stricken 7 Apr 1999. NDRF SE.
◆Gulf War Sep–Oct 1990, Jan–Feb 1991.
AD 42 *Acadia* Decomm 16 Dec 1994.
◆Persian Gulf Jun–Jul 1987, Libya Jul–Aug 1987, Gulf War Oct 1990–Mar 1991, Liberia Dec 1993.

Figure 10.5: *USS Bushnell* (AS 15), submarine tender, during the 1950s.

AD 43   *Cape Cod*   Decomm 29 Sep 1995. Stricken 7 Apr 1999. NDRF SE. ◆Libya Dec 1987–Mar 1988, Gulf War Feb–May 1991.

AD 44   *Shenandoah*   Decomm 13 Sep 1996. Stricken 7 Apr 1999. NDRF SE. ◆Gulf War Jul–Aug 1991.

SUBMARINE TENDERS

Submarine Tenders on the Navy List, 1947

AS 11   *Fulton*   Out of comm 3 Apr 1947–10 Apr 1951. New London, Conn., 1959–1971, 1976–1983. FRAM Dec 1959 Phila NSYd. Damaged by fire, 1984. Decomm 30 Sep 1991. Stricken 20 Dec 1991. Sold 17 Nov 1995, BU Brownsville, Tex.

AS 12   *Sperry*   FRAM Sep 1961 Long Bch NSYd. Decomm and stricken 30 Sep 1982, NDRF SE.

AS 15   *Bushnell*   Out of comm 30 Apr 1948–21 Feb 1952. FRAM Dec 1962 Phila NSYd. Damaged by fire in Gulf of Mexico, 6 Dec 1965. Damaged by fire and explosion, early 1970. Decomm 30 Jun 1970. Stricken 15 Nov 1980. Sunk as target off Virginia, 3 Jun 1983.

AS 16   *Howard W. Gilmore*   FRAM Apr 1962 Charleston NSYd. Decomm 30 Sep 1980. Stricken 1 Dec 1980, NDRF Sold 10 Feb 2006, BU, Chesapeake, Va.

AS 17   *Nereus*   FRAM May 1960 Long Bch NSYd. Decomm 27 Oct 1971. Stricken 13 Jun 1989, NDRF SE.

AS 18   *Orion*   FRAM Feb 1961 Phila NSYd. Decomm and stricken 30 Sep 1993. NDRF. Sold 2 Jun 2006, BU Baltimore.

AS 19   *Proteus*   Out of comm Jan 1959–8 Jul 1960. Converted and lengthened at Charleston NSYd. 1959–60, to service SSBN at Holy Loch, Rota, Guam, then Diego Garcia. Decomm and stricken 30 Sep 1992. Reacq as **IX 518** (unnamed), 1 Feb 1994. OS Sep 1999. Stricken 13 Mar 2001. BU 2008 Brownsville.

Fulton class: Armament: AS 11, 12, 18, 19: 4–20 mm; 15, 17: 2–5″/38, *Proteus* lengthened with section added amidships, new dimensions 573′10″ × 73′4″ × 25′6″, displacement 18,500 f/l; thwartships travelling crane added for Polaris missiles. As IX 518, berthing auxiliary, funnels and most superstructure removed.

AS 13   *Griffin*   Decomm 12 Oct 1945. Stricken 1 Aug 1972. Sold 4 Apr 1973, BU Portland, Ore.

AS 14   *Pelias*   OS 21 Oct 1950. Decomm 14 Jun 1970. Stricken 1 Aug 1971. BU 1973 Portland, Ore.

AS 22   *Euryale*   Decomm 7 Oct 1946. Stricken 1 Dec 1971. Sold 9 Aug 1972, BU Portland, Ore.

AS 23   *Aegir*   Decomm 18 Oct 1946. Stricken 1 Jun 1971. Sold 16 May 1972, BU Terminal I.

Figure 10.6: *USS Holland* (AS 32), the first postwar submarine tender. Her name commemorated one of the first submarine tenders that was named after John P. Holland, builder of the Navy's first submarine.

AS 24   *Anthedon*   Decomm 21 Sep 1946. Stricken 1 Sep 1961. Trfd to Turkey 7 Feb 1969.
    Later history: renamed *Donatan* (A 583). R1985.

AS 25   *Apollo*   Decomm 12 Feb 1947. Stricken 1 Jul 1963. BU 1974.

AS 26   *Clytie*   Decomm 5 Oct 1946. Stricken 1 Sep 1961. Sold 2 Nov 1970, BU Castellon, Spain.

No.	Name	Builder	Keel Laid	Launched	Comm.
AS 31	*Hunley*	Newport News	28 Nov 1960	28 Sep 1961	16 Jun 1962
AS 32	*Holland*	Ingalls	5 Mar 1962	19 Jan 1963	7 Sep 1963

Displacement	10,500 tons; 18,300 f/l
Dimensions	599′ (oa) × 90′3″ × 24′8″
Machinery	1 screw; diesel-electric; BHP 15,000; 19 knots
Endurance	10,000/12
Complement	1,081
Armament	2 twin 3″ AA; *1977*: 4–20 mm

Notes: Built to support FBM submarines. *Hunley* had large hammerhead crane amidships.

Service Records:

AS 31   *Hunley*   Damaged by fire in Atlantic, 6 Aug 1977. Decomm 30 Sep 1994. Stricken 3 May 1995, NDRF. Sold 5 Jan 2007, BU New Orleans.

AS 32   *Holland*   Damaged by fire at Puget Sound NSYd, 26 Mar 1975. Decomm 30 Sep 1996. Stricken 12 May 2000. NDRF SE

No.	Name	Builder	Keel Laid	Launched	Comm.
AS 33	*Simon Lake*	Puget Sd NSYd	7 Jan 1963	8 Feb 1964	7 Nov 1964
AS 34	*Canopus*	Ingalls	2 Mar 1964	12 Feb 1965	4 Nov 1965
AS 35	—	not built	—	—	—

Displacement	12,000 tons; 19,934 f/l
Dimensions	643′9″ (oa) × 85′ × 28′6″
Machinery	1 screw; ST; 2 boilers; SHP 20,000; 18 knots
Endurance	7,600/18
Complement	1,075/612
Armament	2-twin 3″/50; *2003*: 4–20 mm

Notes: Built to service SSBN. Funnel aft.

Figure 10.7: USS *Canopus* (AS 34), submarine tender built to service ballistic missile submarines. Notice the heavy lifting cranes amidships.

Service Records:

AS 33   *Simon Lake*   Holy Loch. Decomm 31 Jul 1999. Stricken 25 Apr 2006. ◆Indian Ocean Apr–Jun 1998.

AS 34   *Canopus*   Decomm 30 Nov 1994. Stricken 3 May 1995. Sold 2003 for BU in UK. NDRF SE.

AS 35   —   not built 1965.

No.	Name	Builder	Keel Laid	Launched	Comm.
AS 36	L.Y. Spear	Beth; Quincy	5 May 1966	7 Sep 1967	28 Feb 1970
AS 37	Dixon	Beth; Quincy	7 Sep 1967	20 Jun 1970	7 Aug 1971
AS 38	—	not built	—	—	—

Displacement	12,770 tons, 22,628 f/l; 38–41: 13,842 tons, 22,650 f/l
Dimensions	645′8″ (oa); 620′ (wl) × 85′ × 25′6
Machinery	1 screw; ST; 2 boilers; SHP 20,000; 18 knots
Endurance	7,600/18
Armament	2–5″/38; *1977*: 4–20 mm; *2003*: 2 twin–20 mm, 2–40 mm GL

Notes: Helicopter platform, no hangar.

Service Records:

AS 36   *L.Y. Spear*   Decomm 30 Sep 1996. Stricken 31 May 1999. ◆Iran/Indian Ocean Apr–Jul 1980, Gulf War Aug–Nov 1991.

AS 37   *Dixon*   Decomm 15 Dec 1995. Stricken 18 Mar 1996. Sunk as target, 21 Jul 2003. ◆Iran/Indian Ocean Feb–May 1981, Gulf War Aug–Nov 1992.

AS 38   authorized but not built 1969.

No.	Name	Builder	Keel Laid	Launched	Comm.
AS 39	Emory S. Land	Lockheed	2 Mar 1976	4 May 1977	7 Jul 1979
AS 40	Frank Cable	Lockheed	2 Mar 1976	14 Jan 1978	29 Oct 1979
AS 41	McKee	Lockheed	14 Jan 1978	16 Feb 1980	15 Aug 1981

Displacement	13,842 tons; 22,650 f/l
Dimensions	645′8″ (oa) 620′ (wl) × 85′ × 25′6
Machinery	1 screw, ST, 2 boilers, SHP 20,000, 18 knots
Endurance	7,600/18
Armament	4–20 mm; later 1–40 mm, 1–20 mm; *2003*: 2 twin–20 mm, 2–40 mm GL

Notes: Modified *L.Y. Spear* class, fitted to support *Los Angeles* class. Helicopter platform, no hangar.

Figure 10.8: The submarine tender *Frank Cable* (AS 40) leaving Pearl Harbor, 25 Apr 2005. *L.Y. Spear* class

AS 39   *Emory S. Land*   ◆Iran/Indian Ocean Oct–Dec 1980, Libya Jun–Sep 1988.

AS 40   *Frank Cable*

AS 41   *McKee*   Decomm 1 Oct 1999. Stricken 25 Apr 2006. ◆Gulf War Mar–May 1991.

SUBMARINE RESCUE VESSELS

ASR on the Navy List, 1947

ASR 7   *Chanticleer*   Decomm 9 Jun 1973. Stricken 1 Jun 1973. Sold 22 May 1974.
★Korea 1951, 1952; 4★Vietnam Feb 1966, Jun, Aug 1969, Apr 1971, Dec 1972, ◆Korea Jun 1971.

ASR 8   *Coucal*   Decomm 14 Sep 1977. Stricken 15 Sep 1977. Sunk as target 19 Jan 1991.
★Korea 1951, 1953; 4★Vietnam Jun–Jul 1966, Nov 1970, May 1972.

ASR 9   *Florikan*   Damaged by fire at Long Beach, Cal., 30 Oct 1972. Decomm 2 Aug 1991. Stricken 3 Sep 1991. NDRF SE.
★Korea 1951–52, 1953; 1★Vietnam Mar–Apr 1969.

ASR 10   *Greenlet*   Decomm and trfd to Turkey 12 Jun 1970.
Later history: renamed *Akin* (A 585). SE2001.
★Korea 1950, 1952; 3★Vietnam Apr 1967, Oct–Nov 1969.

ASR 13   *Kittiwake*   Decomm and stricken 30 Sep 1994. NDRF SE.

ASR 14   *Petrel*   Decomm 30 Sep 1991. Stricken 9 Oct 1991. NDRF Sold 5 Dec 2003, BU 2004 Chesapeake, Va.

ASR 15   *Sunbird*   First comm 23 Jun 1950. Decomm 30 Sep 1993. Stricken 2 Nov 1993. NDRF Sold 8 Jul 2005, BU Chesapeake, Va.

ASR 16   *Tringa*   Decomm and stricken 30 Sep 1977.

Armament: ASR 8, 9, 13–16: 2–20 mm

ASR 12   *Penguin*   Out of comm 4 Sep 1947–3 Apr 1952. Decomm 24 Jun 1970. Stricken 30 Jun 1970.
Later history: Merchant *Percheron*, renamed *Dona Rosa Maria* 1986. SE1998.

ASR 19   *Bluebird*   Decomm 15 Aug 1950 and trfd to Turkey.
Later history: renamed *Kurtaran* (A 584). R2000.

ASR 20   *Skylark*   First comm 1 Mar 1951. Decomm and stricken 30 Jun 1973 and trfd to Brazil.
Later history: renamed *Gastão Moutinho* (K10/A10). SE1993.

Tenders 167

Figure 10.9: *USS Tringa* (ASR 16), submarine rescue vessel, in 1966.

Figure 10.11: Seaplane tender *USS Pine Island* (AV 12) served in the Antarctic, Korea, and Vietnam.

SEAPLANE TENDERS

Seaplane Tenders on the Navy List, 1947

AV 4   *Curtiss*   Decomm 24 Sep 1957. Stricken 1 Jul 1963. Sold 10 Jan 1972, BU.
★Korea 1950; ◆OpCastle 1954, Antarctic Jan–Feb 1957.

AV 5   *Albemarle*   Out of comm 15 Aug 1950–21 Oct 1957. Converted to tend Seamaster flying boats, Feb 1956, fitted with stern ramp. Decomm 21 Oct 1960. Stricken 1 Sep 1962. Reacq and conv to helicopter maintenance ship, 7 Aug 1964. Rec **ARVH 1** and renamed ***Corpus Christi Bay***, 27 Mar 1965. Ramp removed, large helicopter landing pad added aft, MSTS, complement 129. Stricken 31 Dec 1974. Sold 17 Jul 1975, BU Brownsville, Tex.
(As ARVH) ★Vietnam.

AV 7   *Currituck*   Out of comm 7 Aug 1947–1 Aug 1951 and 12 Feb 1958–20 Aug 1960. Modernized 1958–60. Bombarded Vietcong positions in Mekong Delta area, 23 Jun 1965. Decomm 31 Oct 1967. Stricken 1 Apr 1971. Sold 10 Jan 1973, BU.
2★Vietnam Jun 1964, May–Aug 1965, Sep 1966, Nov 1966–Apr 1967.
◆Antarctic Dec 1946–Feb 1947, Quemoy-Matsu 5 Aug 1961.

AV 8   *Tangier*   Decomm 5 Aug 1946. Stricken 1 Jun 1961. Sold 12 Dec 1961.
Later history: Merchant *Detroit*. BU 1975 Valencia, Spain.

AV 9   *Pocomoke*   Decomm 10 Jul 1946. Stricken 1 Jun 1961. Sold 12 Dec 1961, BU 1962.

AV 10   *Chandeleur*   Decomm 12 Feb 1947. Stricken 1 Apr 1971. BU 1972.

AV 11   *Norton Sound*   Converted to mobile missile test ship 1948. Test ship for Loon (V-1), Aerobee, Lark, Regulus I, Terrier, Tartar, Sea Sparrow, and Standard-ER/MR missile systems. Rec **AVM 1**, 8 Aug 1951. Fired missiles with low-yield nuclear warheads (Project Argus), 1968. Out of comm 10 Aug 1962–20 Jun 1964, modernized, new superstructure. Test ship for Aegis system. Decomm 11 Dec 1986. Stricken 26 Jan 1987. Sold 20 Oct 1988, BU 1989 Kaohsiung.

AV 12   *Pine Island*   Out of comm 1 May 1950–7 Oct 1950. Decomm 16 Jun 1967. Stricken 1 Feb 1971. Sold 7 Feb 1972, BU Portland, Ore.
★Korea 1951; 2★Vietnam Dec 1960, Aug–Sep 1964, Oct 1965–Feb, Apr 1966. ◆Antarctic Dec 1946–Mar 1947, Taiwan Straits Aug–Nov 1958.

AV 13   *Salisbury Sound*   Decomm 31 Mar 1967. Stricken 1 Feb 1971. Sold 7 Feb 1972, BU Portland, Ore.
★Korea 1950, 1952; 4★Vietnam May–Jun 1959, Dec 1963, Feb, May–Jun, Oct 1966. ◆Quemoy-Matsu Feb–Mar, May 1959, Mar 1960, Apr 1961, Oct 1962.

Figure 10.10: *USS Ortolan* (ASR 22), submarine rescue vessel built in 1970 on twin catamaran hulls.

No.	Name	Builder	Keel Laid	Launched	Comm.
ASR 21	*Pigeon*	Alabama DD	17 Jul 1968	13 Aug 1969	30 Apr 1973
ASR 22	*Ortolan*	Alabama DD	28 Aug 1968	20 Sep 1970	14 Jul 1973

Displacement	3,411 tons; 4,570 f/l
Dimensions	251′ (oa) × 86′ × 21′3″
Machinery	2 screws; diesels; 6,000 BHP; 15 knots
Endurance	10,000/13
Complement	195
Armament	*Pigeon*: 2–3″/50, removed. *1980s*: 2–20mm guns

Notes: Twin catamaran hulls, providing a large deck working area. Built to carry and support DSRVs.

Service Records:

ASR 21   *Pigeon*   Decomm and stricken 31 Aug 1992. NDRF. Non-operational training ship, San Diego, 23 Mar 2001. NDRF. SE.

ASR 22   *Ortolan*   Decomm and stricken 30 Mar 1995. NDRF. SE.

AV 14 *Kenneth Whiting* Out of comm 29 May 1947–24 Oct 1951. Decomm 30 Sep 1958. Stricken 1 Jul 1961. Sold 21 Feb 1962, BU.
★Korea 1952, 1953.

AV 15 *Hamlin* Decomm 15 Jan 1947. Stricken 1 Jul 1963. BU 1972 Terminal I.

AV 16 *St. George* Decomm 1 Aug 1946. Stricken 1 Jul 1963. Trfd to Italy 10 Dec 1967.
Later history: renamed *Andrea Bafile* (A 5314). R1995.

AV 17 *Cumberland Sound* Decomm 27 May 1947. Stricken 1 Jul 1961. Sold 2 Apr 1962.
Later history: Merchant barge *Big Z*, renamed *Carol I* 1975.

AVP 10 *Barnegat* Decomm 17 May 1946. Stricken 23 May 1958. Sold 1962.
Later history: Merchant *Kentavros*. BU 1986 Eleusis, Greece.

AVP 12 *Casco* Decomm 10 Apr 1947. Loan to USCG 19 Apr 1949.
Later history: USCGC *Casco* (WAVP 370). Returned 21 May 1969, sunk as target 15 May 1969.

AVP 13 *Mackinac* Decomm Jan 1947. Loan to USCG, 19 Apr 1949.
Later history: USCGC *Mackinac* (WAVP 371). Returned 21 Jul 1968. Sunk as target off Virginia, 23 Jul 1968.

AVP 21 *Humboldt* Decomm 19 Mar 1947. Loan to USCG 24 Jan 1949.
Later history: USCGC *Humboldt* (WAVP 372). Returned 22 May 1970. BU 1970, Italy.

AVP 22 *Matagorda* Decomm 20 Feb 1946. Loan to USCG 7 Mar 1949.
Later history: USCGC *Matagorda* (WAVP 373). Returned 30 Oct 1968. Sunk as target off Hawaii, 31 Oct 1969.

AVP 23 *Absecon* Decomm 19 Mar 1947. Loan to USCG 5 Jan 1949.
Later history: USCGC *Absecon* (WAVP 374). Returned 9 May 1972. Trfd to Vietnam 15 Jul 1972, renamed *Tham Pham Ngu Lao* (HQ 15). Captured by North Vietnam, May 1975. SE 2000.

AVP 24 *Chincoteague* Decomm 12 Dec 1946. Loan to USCG 7 Mar 1949.
Later history: USCGC *Chincoteague* (WAVP 375). Trfd to Vietnam 21 Jun 1972, renamed *Ly Thoung Kiet*. Trfd to Philippines Apr 1976, renamed *Andres Bonifacio* (PS 7). R1993.

AVP 25 *Coos Bay* Decomm 30 Apr 1946. Loan to USCG 5 Jan 1949.
Later history: USCGC *Coos Bay* (WAVP 376). Returned 2 Dec 1967. Sunk as target off Virginia 9 Jan 1968.

AVP 26 *Half Moon* Decomm 4 Sep 1946. Loan to USCG 30 Jul 1948.
Later history: USCGC *Half Moon* (WAVP 378). Returned 18 Jun 1970. BU 1970 Italy.

AVP 28 *Oyster Bay* **AGP 6**. Reinstated 3 Jan 1949. Rec **AVP 28**, 16 Mar 1949. Trfd to Italy, 23 Oct 1957.
Later history: renamed *Pietro Cavezzale* (A 5301). R1993.

AVP 29 *Rockaway* Decomm 21 Mar 1946. Loan to USCG 24 Dec 1948.
Later history: USCGC *Rockaway* (WAVP 377), then (WAGO 377). Stricken 25 Oct 1973. BU.

AVP 30 *San Pablo* Out of comm 13 Jan 1947–17 Sep 1948, recomm as surveying vessel. Rec **AGS 30**, 25 Aug 1949. Decomm 29 May 1969. Stricken 1 Jul 1969. Sold 14 Sep 1971, BU.
◆Cuba May–Jun 1962, Cuba missile crisis Oct–Nov 1962.

AVP 31 *Unimak* Decomm 23 Jul 1946. Loan to USCG 14 Sep 1948.
Later history: USCGC *Unimak* (WAVP 379), then (WTR 379), (WHEC 379). Returned 23 Apr 1988.

AVP 32 *Yakutat* Decomm 29 Jul 1946. Loan to USCG 31 Aug 1948.
Later history: USCGC *Yakutat* (WAVP 380). Trfd to Vietnam 1 Jan 1971, renamed *Tran Nhat Duat* (HQ 3). Returned Apr 1975, Trfd to Philippines for BU 1976.

AVP 33 *Barataria* Decomm 24 Jul 1946. Loan to USCG Sep 1948.
Later history: USCGC *Barataria* (WAVP 381). Sold Sep 1970, BU Vancouver, BC.

AVP 34 *Bering Strait* Decomm 21 Jun 1946. Loan to USCG 14 Sep 1948.
Later history: USCGC *Bering Strait* (WAVP 382). Trfd to Vietnam 1 Jan 1971, renamed *Tran Quan Khai* (HQ 2). Trfd to Philippines Apr 1976, renamed *Diego Salang* (PS 9). R1985.
★Korea 1952.

AVP 35 *Castle Rock* Decomm 6 Aug 1946. Loan to USCG 16 Sep 1948.
Later history: USCGC *Castle Rock* (WAVP 383). Trfd to Vietnam 21 Dec 1971, renamed *Tran Vinh Trong* (HQ 06). Trfd to Philippines Apr 1976, renamed *Francisco Dagahoy* (PS 10). R1985.

AVP 36 *Cook Inlet* Decomm 31 Mar 1946. Loan to USCG 20 Sep 1948.
Later history: USCGC *Cook Inlet* (WAVP 384). Trfd to Vietnam 21 Dec 1971, renamed *Tran Quoc Toan* (HQ 05). Trfd to Philippines 1976 for BU.

AVP 37 *Corson* Out of comm 21 Jun 1946–13 Feb 1951. Decomm 9 Mar 1956. Stricken 1 Apr 1966. Sunk as target.
★Korea 1953.

AVP 38 *Duxbury Bay* Decomm 30 Apr 1966. Stricken 1 May 1966. Sold Jul 1967, BU.
◆Cuba missile crisis Oct 1962.

AVP 39 *Gardiners Bay* Decomm 1 Feb 1958. Trfd to Norway 17 May 1958.
Later history: renamed *Haakon VII* (A 537). BU 1975.
4★Korea K-1 K-2 K-4 K-10.

AVP 40 *Floyds Bay* Decomm 26 Feb 1960. Stricken 1 Mar 1960. Sold 20 Jul 1960.
Later history: commercial drilling barge.
1★Korea K-8, 1953.

AVP 41 *Greenwich Bay* Decomm Jun 1966. Stricken 1 Jul 1966. Sold 21 Jun 1967, BU Baltimore.

AVP 48 *Onslow* Out of comm Jun 1947–Jan 1951. Decomm 22 Apr 1960. Stricken 1 Jun 1960. Sold 18 Jun/Oct 1960.
Later history: Merchant *President Quezon*, renamed *Quezon*, *Pioneer Iloilo* 1965, *Galaxy* 1967. Went aground in storm off Cebu and sank, 19 Oct 1971.
1★Korea K-8; ◆Taiwan Straits Aug–Sep 1958.

AVP 49 *Orca* Out of comm 31 Oct 1947–15 Dec 1951. Decomm Mar 1960. Trfd to Ethiopia Jan 1962.
Later history: renamed *Ethiopia* (A 01). Escaped to Yemen during Eritrean revolution, 1991, probably BU locally.

AVP 50 *Rehoboth* Out of comm 30 Jun 1947–2 Sep 1948 recomm as survey ship. Rec **AGS 50**, 1948. Stricken 15 Apr 1970. BU 1970.
2★Vietnam Nov 1965–Feb 1966.

AVP 51 *San Carlos* Decomm 30 Jun 1947. Rec **AGOR 1** and renamed *Josiah Willard Gibbs*, 15 Dec 1958. IS 18 Dec 1958, MSTS. Stricken 15 Feb 1977. Trfd to Greece 7 Dec 1971.
Later history: renamed *Hephaistos*.

AVP 52 *Shelikof* Out of comm 30 Jun 1947–22 Jan 1952. Decomm 18 Jul 1954. Stricken 1 May 1960. Sold 20 Dec 1960.
Later history: Merchant *Kypros*, renamed *Artemis* 1963, *Artemis K.* 1974, *Golden Princess* 1980. Sank in storm while laid up at Piraeus, Jan 1981.

Figure 10.12: *USS Duxbury Bay* (AVP 38), small seaplane tender, painted white for Middle East service, rearmed with 3-inch guns.

AVP 53 *Suisun*   Decomm 5 Aug 1955. Stricken 1 Apr 1966. Sunk as target, Oct 1966.
★Korea 1951–52.
AVP 54 *Timbalier*   Decomm 15 Nov 1954. Stricken 1 May 1960. Sold 20 Dec 1960.
Later history: Merchant *Rodos*. BU 1989.
AVP 55 *Valcour*   Damaged in collision with m/v *Thomas Tracy* off Cape Henry, 14 May 1951. Rec **AGF 1**, 15 Dec 1965, converted to command flagship. Decomm 15 Jan 1973 and stricken. Electromagnetic test ship. Sold May 1977, BU.
◆Cuba Nov–Dec 1962.

ADVANCE AVIATION BASE SHIPS

No.	Name	Former	Date
AVB 1	*Alameda County*	LST 32	28 Sep 1957
AVB 2	*Tallahatchie County*	LST 1154	3 Feb 1962

AVIATION LOGISTICS SHIPS

No.	Name	Builder	Launched	Acquired	In service
T-AVB 3	*Wright* ex-*Young America*, ex-*Mormacsun*	Ingalls	12 Jul 1969	12 Jun 1984	14 May 1986
T-AVB 4	*Curtiss* ex-*Great Republic*, ex-*Mormacsky*	Ingalls	1 Dec 1968	27 Jan 1986	18 Aug 1987

Displacement	14,000 tons; 12,409 lt, 27,580 f/l
Dimensions	600′11″ (oa); 559′10″ (wl) × 90′ × 34′
Machinery	1 screw; ST; 2 boilers; 30,000 SHP; 23.6 knots
Endurance	9,000/23.6
Complement	341
Armament	none

Notes: Type C5-S-78a. Converted RO/RO ships to provide maintenance for Marine helicopters. Converted by Todd; Galveston. Assigned to RRF. Prefix SS.

Figure 10.13: *USS Tallahatchie County* (AVB 2), former landing ship tank converted to advance aviation base ship.

Figure 10.14: *USNS Wright* (AVB 3), assigned to the Ready Reserve Force, served in the 1991 Gulf War.

Service Records:
AVB 3 *Wright*   MSC
◆Gulf War Sep 1990–Apr 1991, Oct 1991.
AVB 4 *Curtiss*   MSC
◆Gulf War Sep 1990–Apr 1991.

AVIATION STORE SHIP

AVS 8 *Jupiter*   Our of comm 23 May 1947–10 Oct 1950. Decomm Jun 1964. Stricken 1 Aug 1965. BU 1971, Portland, Ore.
7★Korea K-4 K-5 K-6 K-7 K-8 K-9 K-10; ★Vietnam Oct–Nov 1963;
◆Taiwan Straits Sep–Oct 1958.

AVIATION TRANSPORTS

No.	Name	Former
AVT 1	*Cowpens*	CVL 25
AVT 2	*Monterey*	CVL 26
AVT 3	*Cabot*	CVL 28
AVT 4	*Bataan*	CVL 29
AVT 5	*San Jacinto*	CVL 30
AVT 6	*Saipan*	CVL 48
AVT 7	*Wright*	CVL 49
AVT 8	*Franklin*	CVS 13
AVT 9	*Bunker Hill*	CVS 17
AVT 10	*Leyte*	CVS 32
AVT 11	*Philippine Sea*	CVS 47
AVT 12	*Tarawa*	CVS 40
AVT 16	*Lexington*	CV 16
AVT 59	*Forrestal*	CV 59

Note: Reclassified as non-combatant ships. AVT 1–11 rec 15 May 1959 (AVT 12, 1 May 1961). *Lexington* and *Forrestal* were training carriers.

Figure 10.15: Repair ship USS *Hector* (AR 7) in 1983. Notice lack of armament.

Figure 10.16: USS *Cadmus* (AR 14), repair ship, was transferred to Taiwan in 1974.

REPAIR SHIPS

REPAIR SHIPS ON THE NAVY LIST, 1947

AR 5   *Vulcan*   Decomm 30 Sep 1991. Stricken 28 Jul 1992, NDRF. Sold 9 Nov 2006, BU Chesapeake, Va.
◆Cuba missile crisis Oct–Nov 1962, Dominican Rep May 1965, Gulf War Jan–Feb 1991.

AR 6   *Ajax*   Decomm 31 Dec 1986. Stricken 16 May 1989. Sold 23 May 1997, BU Brownsville, Tex.
★Korea 1951–53, 5★Vietnam Jun 1968, Sep–Oct 1969, Apr–May 1970, Aug–Nov 1971; ◆Passage to Freedom 1954, Iran/Indian Ocean Jul–Oct 1980.

AR 7   *Hector*   Decomm 31 Mar 1987. Trfd to Pakistan 20 Apr 1989.
Later history: renamed *Maowin* (A 20). Returned and stricken 19 Aug 1994. Sold 9 Sep 1994, BU Alang, India.
1★Korea K-1 1952, 1953; 2★Vietnam Jul–Aug 1970, Feb–Jul 1972, ◆Libya Jan 1982–Jun 1983.

ARH 1   *Jason*   Rec **AR 8**, 9 Sep 1957. Decomm and stricken 24 Jun 1995, NDRF. Sold 9 Nov 2006, BU Brownsville, Tex.
1★Korea K-10, 1950–52; 3★Vietnam Jul–Aug 1968, Dec 1969–Jan 1970, Mar–Apr 1971. ◆Iran/Indian Ocean Dec 1980–Feb 1981, Libya Oct–Dec 1987, Aug 1989, Gulf War Jan–Apr 1991.

AR 9   *Delta*   Out of comm 5 Mar 1947–1 Nov 1950 and 1 Dec 1955–1 Nov 1959. Decomm 20 Jun 1970. Stricken 1 Oct 1977, used as APB at Bremerton. Sold 19 Jul 1983.
1★Korea K-8; 1★Vietnam Jun–Jul 1969.

AR 12   *Briareus*   Out of comm 15 Oct 1946–22 Sep 1951. Decomm 9 Sep 1955. Stricken 1 Jan 1977. Sold 19 Nov 1980, BU Chesapeake, Va.

Armament: 1977: *Vulcan, Ajax, Hector, Jason*: 2–40 mm, 4–20 mm; *Delta*: 2 twin 3″/50.

AR 13   *Amphion*   Comm 30 Jan 1946. Decomm 2 Oct 1971 and trfd to Iran. Stricken 1 Nov 1976.
Later history: renamed *Chah Bahar* (441). Sunk at Bandar Abbas, date unk.
◆Lebanon Aug–Oct 1958, Dominican Rep Jun–Jul 1965.

AR 14   *Cadmus*   Decomm 14 Sep 1971. Stricken 15 Jan and trfd to Taiwan 31 Jan 1974.
Later history: renamed *Yu Tai* (521). SE1993.

AR 19   *Xanthus*   Decomm 3 Sep 1946. Stricken 1 Sep 1962, BU 1974.

AR 20   *Laertes*   Out of comm 15 Jan 1947–19 Dec 1951. Decomm 26 Feb 1954. Stricken 1 Sep 1962. BU 1972 Portland, Ore.
1★Korea K-8.

AR 21   *Dionysus*   Out of comm 31 Jan 1947–13 Feb 1952. Decomm 1 Jul 1955. Stricken 1 Sep 1961. BU 1978.

No.	Name	Former	Date
AR 22	*Klondike*	AD 22	20 Feb 1960
AR 23	*Markab*	AD 21	15 Apr 1960
AR 24	*Grand Canyon*	AD 28	12 Mar 1971

INTERNAL COMBUSTION ENGINE REPAIR SHIPS

ARG 2   *Luzon*   Out of comm 24 Jun 1947–20 Sep 1950 and 15 Mar 1955–3 Nov 1955. Decomm 1 Jul 1960. Stricken 1 Sep 1961. Sold 19 Aug 1974, BU.
1★Korea K-10, 1953; ◆Taiwan Straits Sep–Oct 1958.

ARG 3   *Mindanao*   Decomm 17 May 1947. Stricken 1 Sep 1962. Sunk as artificial reef off Daytona Beach, Fla., 1980.

ARG 4   *Tutuila*   Out of comm 7 Dec 1946–7 May 1951. Decomm 21 Feb 1972, stricken and trfd to Taiwan.
Later history: renamed *Tien Tai*.
13 ★Vietnam Jul 1966–Nov 1968, May 1969–Jul 1970, Sep 1970–Jan 1972. ◆Cuba missile crisis Oct–Nov 1962, Dominican Rep May–Jun 1965.

ARG 5   *Oahu*   Decomm 7 Jan 1947. Stricken 1 Jul 1963. BU 1979 Tacoma.

ARG 6   *Cebu*   Decomm 30 Jun 1947. Stricken 1 Sep 1962. BU 1973 Portland, Ore.

ARG 7   *Culebra Island*   Decomm 15 Jan 1947. Stricken 1 Sep 1962. BU 1973 Portland, Ore.

ARG 8   *Maui*   Decomm 30 Aug 1946. Stricken 1 Sep 1962. BU 1972.

ARG 9   *Mona Island*   Decomm 31 Oct 1947. Stricken 1 Sep 1962. Sunk as artificial reef, 1975.

ARG 10   *Palawan*   Decomm 15 Jan 1947. Stricken 1 Jul 1963. Scuttled as fish reef off Redondo Beach, Cal., 13 Sep 1977.

ARG 11   *Samar*   Decomm 24 Jul 1947. Stricken 1 Sep 1962. BU 1973 Portland, Ore.

ARG 16   *Kermit Roosevelt*   Decomm 31 Oct 1959. Stricken 1 Jan 1960. Sold 25 Aug 1960, BU Portland, Ore.
3★Korea K-1 K-2 K-10.

ARG 17 *Hooper Island* Out of comm 24 Jan 1948–12 Apr 1952. Decomm 15 Jul 1959. Stricken 1 Jul 1960. BU 1970 Portland, Ore. 1★Korea K-9; ◆Passage to Freedom 1954.

ARG 18 *Holland* Decomm 21 Mar 1947. Stricken 18 Jun 1952. Sold 3 Oct 1953, BU.

AIRCRAFT REPAIR SHIPS

ARV 1 *Chourre* Out of comm 28 Nov 1948–21 Feb 1952. Decomm 13 Feb 1955. Stricken 1 Sep 1962. BU 1971. 2★Korea K-8 K-9.

ARV 2 *Webster* Decomm 28 Jun 1946. Stricken 1 Sep 1962. Scuttled off Cape Henry, 1975.

BATTLE DAMAGE REPAIR SHIPS

ARB 1 *Aristaeus* Decomm 15 Jan 1947. Stricken 1 Jul 1961. Sold 14 Mar 1962, BU Oakland.

ARB 2 *Oceanus* Decomm Jan 1947. Stricken 1 Jul 1961.
Later history: merchant barges *ZB-102F* and *ZF-102A*, renamed *630* 1965.

ARB 3 *Phaon* Decomm Jan 1947. Stricken 1 Jul 1961. Sold 8 Jul 1962.
Later history: merchant barges *ZB-103A* and *ZF-103F*, renamed *Delong 103*. SE1980.

ARB 4 *Zeus* Decomm 30 Aug 1946. Stricken 1 Jun 1973. Sold 9 Jul 1974.
Later history: merchant *Cape St. Elias*, renamed *Coastal Star* 1988.

ARB 5 *Midas* Decomm 15 Jan 1947. Stricken 15 Apr 1976. Sold 1980.

ARB 7 *Sarpedon* Decomm 29 Jan 1947. Stricken 15 Apr 1976.
Later history: merchant *Petrola 133*. BU 1989.

ARB 8 *Telamon* Decomm 20 May 1947. Stricken 1 Jun 1973. Sold 1974.

ARB 9 *Ulysses* Decomm 28 Feb 1947. Stricken 1961. Trfd to West Germany 1 Jul 1961.
Later history: renamed *Wotan* (A 513). SE1987.

ARB 10 *Demeter* Decomm 27 May 1947. Sold 3 Sep 1959.
Later history: merchant *Motonave*, renamed *Demeter* 1963. Lost by grounding south of San Lorenzo, Ecuador, 12 Jan 1964.

ARB 11 *Diomedes* Decomm 8 Dec 1946. Stricken 1961. Trfd to West Germany 7 Jun 1961.
Later history: renamed *Odin* (A 512). SE1987.

ARB 12 *Helios* Decomm 3 Dec 1946. Trfd to Brazil 19 Jan 1962.
Later history: renamed *Belmonte* (G 24). R1997. Sunk as target, 19 Mar 2002.

ARB 13 ex-LST 50, 14 Nov 1952. Transferred to Norway 1952.
Later history: renamed *Ellida* (A 534). Returned to U.S. 1 Jul 1960, trfd to Greece 16 Sep 1960. Renamed *Sakipis* (A 329). SE1962.

LANDING CRAFT REPAIR SHIPS

ARL 1 *Achelous* Decomm 16 Jan 1947. Stricken 1 Jun 1973, sold 21 Jan 1974, BU.

ARL 2 *Amycus* Decomm 15 Nov 1946. Stricken 1 Jun 1970, sold 13 Aug 1971.
Later history: merchant barge *Tyonek*.

ARL 3 *Agenor* Decomm 15 Nov 1946. Trfd to France 2 Mar 1951.
Later history: renamed *Vulcain* (A656). Trfd to Taiwan 1957, renamed *Shung Shan/Sung Shan* (ARL 336), renamed *Tai Wu* (AP 520). SE 1987

ARL 4 *Adonis* Decomm 11 Oct 1946. Stricken 1 Jan 1960. Sold 14 Oct 1960.
Later history: merchant barge *Mendocino Woodsman*.

ARL 7 *Atlas* Out of comm 13 Sep 1946–1 Jun 1951. Decomm 13 Apr 1956. Stricken 1 Jun 1972. Sold 18 Sep 1973.
Later history: merchant barge *Whitney*.
★Korea 1951–52; ◆Passage to Freedom 1954.

ARL 8 *Egeria* Decomm 20 May 1947. Stricken 1 Oct 1977. Sold 1980, BU.

ARL 9 *Endymion* Decomm 30 Nov 1946. Stricken 1 Jun 1972. Sold 5 Sep 1973.
Later history: merchant *Petrola 18*, renamed *Sete 58* 1978.

ARL 10 *Coronis* Decomm 29 Jul 1946. Stricken 1 Jul 1961. Sold 31 Oct 1961.
Later history: merchant *Trailer Princess*.

ARL 11 *Creon* Decomm 8 Jun 1949. Stricken 1 Jul 1960. Sold 16 Feb 1961.
Later history: merchant barge *A.T.B. 65*.

ARL 12 *Poseidon* Decomm 30 Nov 1946. Stricken 1 Jul 1961. Sold 3 Nov 1961.
Later history: merchant barge *Navifor II*.

ARL 13 *Menelaus* Out of comm 5 Jun 1947–14 Dec 1950. Decomm 5 Sep 1955. Stricken 1 Jun 1960. Sold 28 Oct 1960.
Later history: merchant *Maryland Clipper*. Sold 1978.

ARL 14 *Minos* Out of comm 18 Jun 1946–22 Sep 1950. Decomm 19 Aug 1955. Stricken 1 Jan 1960. Sold 18 Oct 1960.
Later history: merchant *Kargadan*.

ARL 15 *Minotaur* Out of comm 26 Feb 1947–14 Jun 1951. Decomm 3 Oct 1955 and loan to Korea.
Later history: renamed *Duk Soo* (ARL 1).

ARL 16 *Myrmidon* Decomm 7 Jul 1947. Stricken 1 Apr 1960. Sold 21 Dec 1960, BU.

ARL 17 *Numitor* Decomm 1 Jul 1947. Stricken 1 Apr 1960. Sold 21 Dec 1960, BU.

ARL 18 *Pandemus* Out of comm 23 Sep 1946–14 Dec 1951. Decomm 30 Sep 1968. Stricken 1 Oct 1968. Sunk as target.1969.
◆Cuba missile crisis Dec 1962.

ARL 19 *Patroclus* Decomm 2 Oct 1946. Trfd to Turkey 22 Aug 1952.
Later history: renamed *Basaran* (A 582). R1993.

ARL 20 *Pentheus* Decomm 20 Apr 1946. Stricken 1 Jan 1960. Sold 13 Jun 1960.
Later history: merchant barge *TMT San Juan*.

ARL 21 *Proserpine* Out of comm 18 Jan 1947–27 Oct 1950. Decomm 24 May 1956. Sold 26 Sep 1960.
Later history: merchant barge *McLeod*.

ARL 22 *Romulus* Out of comm 12 May 1947–2 Apr 1952. Decomm 1 Jun 1956. Stricken 1 Oct 1960. Trfd to Philippines Nov 1961.
Later history: renamed *Aklan*, then *Kamagong* (AR 67). R1989.
1★Korea K-10.

ARL 23 *Satyr* Out of comm 1 Aug 1947–8 Sep 1950 and 17 Apr 1956–15 Feb 1968. Decomm and trfd to South Vietnam 30 Sep 1971.
Later history: renamed *Vinh Long*. Trfd to Philippines 24 Jan 1977, renamed *Yakal* (AR 517/AD 617). SE2001.
2★Korea K-5 K-6; 8★Vietnam Jul 1968–Apr 1969, Jan–Sep 1970, Dec 1970, Apr–Sep 1971. PUC 25 Jan–21 Apr 1969.

ARL 24 *Sphinx* Out of comm 26 May 1947–3 Nov 1950, 31 Jan 1956–16 Dec 1967 and 30 Sep 1971–1 Apr 1985. AGI off Central America, 1985–89. Decomm 19 Jun 1989. Trfd for museum at Dunkirk, NY, 2 Dec 2002, but stripped and sold for BU, Chesapeake, Va., 2007.
1★Korea K-7; 8★Vietnam Jun 1968–Jun 1969, Aug 1969–Dec 1970, Mar–Jun 1971. ◆Passage to Freedom 1954. PUC 25 Jan–19 Jun 1969.

ARL 26 *Stentor* Decomm Dec 1947. Stricken 1 Jul 1960. Sold 23 Jan 1961, BU.

ARL 28 *Typhon* Decomm 7 Aug 1947. Stricken 1 Jul 1960. Sold 23 Feb 1961.
Later history: merchant barge *P.T.& S. 28*

Figure 10.17: *USS Krishna* (ARL 38), repair ship for landing craft, in about 1960, was a converted LST. She earned ten battle stars for service in Vietnam.

ARL 29 *Amphitrite*   Decomm 18 Nov 1947. Stricken 1 Jul 1961. Sold 16 Apr 1962.
  Later history: merchant barge *TMT Biscayne*.
ARL 30 *Askari*   Out of comm 21 Mar 1956–13 Aug 1966. Decomm 1 Sep 1971, and trfd to Indonesia 22 Feb 1979.
  Later history: renamed *Jaja Widjaja* (921). SE2001.
  4★Korea K-1 K-2 K-3 K-4; 12★Vietnam Feb 1967–Oct 1968, Jan 1969–Aug 1971. ◆Passage to Freedom 1954. 2 PUC 29 Jan–4 Mar 1968, 6 Dec 1968–31 Mar 1969.
ARL 31 *Bellerophon*   Decomm 26 Mar 1948. Stricken 1 Oct 1977. Sold 29 May 1980.
ARL 33 *Chimaera*   Decomm 8 Mar 1948. Stricken 1 Jul 1961. Sold 30 Mar 1962.
  Later history: merchant *Santa Teresa*.
ARL 35 *Daedalus*   Decomm 23 Oct 1947. Stricken 1 Jan 1960. Sold 15 Sep 1960.
  Later history: merchant *Virginia Clipper*, renamed *Diana D.* 1984. Lost.
ARL 36 *Gordius*   Decomm 21 Dec 1955. Stricken 1 Feb 1961. Trfd to Iran, 7 Sep 1961.
  Later History: renamed *Sohrab*. SE1972.
ARL 37 *Indra*   Decomm 6 Oct 1947–Dec 1967. Decomm May 1970. Stricken 1 Dec 1977, used as APB at Norfolk. Sunk as artificial reef off North Carolina, 4 Aug 1992.
  2★Vietnam May–Oct 1968.
ARL 38 *Krishna*   Decomm, Trfd to Philippines 30 Oct 1971.
  Later history: renamed *Narra* (AR 88). R1992.
  10★Vietnam Aug–Nov 1964, Sep 1965–Jul 1966, Apr 1967–Apr 1968, Sep–Nov 1969, Dec 1970–Mar 1971, May–Oct 1971.
ARL 39 *Quirinus*   Decomm 27 Jun 1947. Trfd to Venezuela Jun 1962.
  Later history: renamed *Guyana* (T 18).

Armament: *1977*: 8, 24, 31, 37: 2-quad 40 mm, 8–20 mm (24, 37 no 20 mm).

SALVAGE LIFTING VESSELS

ARSD 1 *Gypsy*   Out of comm 21 Jan 1948–8 Aug 1951. Decomm 23 Dec 1955. Stricken 1 Jun 1973. Sold 1974, BU.
  2★Korea K-9 K-10, ◆OpCastle 1954.
ARSD 2 *Mender*   Out of comm 21 Jan 1948–12 Sep 1951. Decomm 20 Dec 1955. Stricken 1 Jun 1973. Sold 1974.
  2★Korea K-7 K-8.
ARSD 3 *Salvager*   Decomm 23 Nov 1965. Rec **YMLC 3**, 16 Oct 1967. Stricken 1 Aug 1972.
ARSD 4 *Windlass*   Comm 9 Apr 1946. Decomm 23 Nov 1965. Rec **YMLC 4**, 16 Oct 1967. Stricken 1 Aug 1972. Sold 6 Mar 1973, BU.
  ◆Cuba missile crisis Nov 1962.

SALVAGE CRAFT TENDERS

ARST 1 *Laysan Island*   Decomm 21 Apr 1947. Stricken 1 Jun 1973.
ARST 3 *Palmyra*   Decomm 20 Jun 1947. Stricken 1 Jun 1973. Sold 9 Apr 1974.

AIRCRAFT REPAIR SHIPS

ARVE 3 *Aventinus*   Out of comm 30 Aug 1946–25 Jul 1950. Decomm 4 Apr 1952. Trfd to Chile 23 Aug 1963.
  Later history: renamed *Aguila*. Scuttled after running aground, Aug 1990.
  ★Korea 1950–51.
ARVE 4 *Chloris*   Out of comm 18 Jun 1946–5 Jan 1951. Decomm 9 Dec 1955. Stricken 1 Jun 1973. Sold 9 Apr 1974.
  Later history: merchant *Avlon*. BU 1986 Piraeus.
ARVA 5 *Fabius*   Out of comm 30 Aug 1946–28 Jul 1950. Decomm 4 Apr 1952. Stricken 1 Jun 1973.
  Later history: merchant *Arta*.
  ★Korea 1951.
ARVA 6 *Megara*   Out of comm 3 Jun 1946–5 Jan 1951. Decomm 16 Jan 1956. Trfd to Mexico 1 Oct 1973.
  Later history: renamed *General Vicente Guerrero* (A 05), renamed *Rio Grijalva* (A 03), 1993. SE2001.

AERONAUTICAL MAINTENANCE SHIPS

No.	Name	Former	Date
ARVH 1	*Corpus Christi Bay*	AV 5	27 Mar 1965
	Converted to repair helicopters in Vietnam.		1★Vietnam.
ARVH 2	*Curtiss*	AV 4	conv.canc.
ARVH 3	*Hamlin*	AV 15	conv.canc.
ARVH 4	*St. George*	AV 16	conv.canc.

CABLE REPAIRING SHIPS

ARC 1 *Portunus* Ex-LSM 275. Recomm 2 Jul 1952. Decomm 30 Apr 1959. Stricken 1 May 1959. Trfd to Portugal, 16 Nov 1959, renamed *Medusa* (A 5214), renamed *S.Rafael*, 1965. R1976.
ARC 3 *Aeolus* Ex-AKA 47. ex-*Turandot*. Reacq 4 Nov 1954, comm 14 May 1955. Damaged in collision with tanker, Sep 1962. Decomm 1 Oct 1973, MSTS. Stricken 28 Feb 1985. Sunk as artificial reef off North Carolina, Aug 1988.
ARC 4 *Thor* Ex-AKA 49. ex-*Vanadis*. Reacq 14 Apr 1955, comm 3 Jan 1956. Decomm 2 Jul 1973, MSTS. OS Apr 1974. Stricken 1 Mar 1978.
ARC 5 *Yamacraw* Ex-WARC 333. Stricken 2 Jul 1965.

Notes: *Aeolus* and *Thor* were former attack transports reacq in 1954. *Yamacraw* was a former Army mine planter transferred to the Coast Guard in 1946 and converted for cable laying.

Figure 10.20: *USS Thor* (ARC 4), a former attack cargo ship converted in 1955, as she appeared in 1969.

Figure 10.18: *USNS Corpus Christi Bay* (T-ARVH 1), the former seaplane tender *Albemarle*, was converted to repair helicopters in Vietnam.

Figure 10.21: *USNS Neptune* (ARC 2), cable repair ship, was acquired in 1953.

No.	Name	Builder	Keel Laid	Launched	Comm.
ARC 2	*Neptune* ex-*William H.G. Bullard*	Pusey & Jones	22 Jan 1945	22 Aug 1945	1 Jun 1953
ARC 6	*Albert J. Myer* ex-*Albert J. Myer*	Pusey & Jones	14 Apr 1945	7 Nov 1945	13 May 1963
Displacement	4,410 tons; 7,400 f/l				
Dimensions	370' (oa); 322' (wl) × 47' × 24'11"				
Machinery	2 screws; VTE; 2 boilers; 4,800 SHP; 14 knots *1978–80*: diesel-electric; 4,000 BHP; 13 knots				
Endurance	10,000/13				
Complement	85				
Armament	none				

Figure 10.19: *USS Yamacraw* (ARC 5), cable repair ship, was transferred from the Coast Guard in 1959. She was built as an Army mine planter.

Notes: Type S3-S2-BP1. *Myer* acquired from Army. Modernized and re-engined 1978–82.

Service Records:

ARC 2 *Neptune* to MSC 8 Nov 1973. OS 21 Oct 1991. Stricken 20 Aug 1992, NDRF. Sold 18 Jul 2005, BU Brownsville, Tex.

ARC 6 *Albert J. Myer* to MSC 8 Nov 1973. OS 13 Feb 1994. Stricken 7 Nov 1994, NDRF. Sold 18 Jul 2005, BU Brownsville, Tex.

No.	Name	Builder	Keel Laid	Launched	In service
T-ARC 7	*Zeus*	Natl Steel	1 Jun 1981	30 Oct 1982	19 Mar 1984

Displacement   8,297 tons; 14,225 f/l
Dimensions   502′6″ (oa); 454′ (wl) × 73′2″ × 23′10″
Machinery   2 screws; diesel-electric; 12,500 BHP; 15.8 knots
Endurance   10,000/15
Complement   120/60
Armament   none

Notes: A second ship was planned but never ordered.

Service Record: MSC.

SALVAGE VESSELS

Salvage Vessels on the Navy List, 1947

ARS 1 *Viking* OS 17 Mar 1953. Stricken 19 Apr 1953. Sold 22 Jul 1953, BU.

ARS 5 *Diver* Decomm 27 Jul 1946. Sold 12 Apr 1949.
Later history: Merchant *Rescue*, renamed *Rescue M.* 1976, *Grand Day* 1976, *Rescue M.* 1979.

ARS 6 *Escape* Out of comm 20 Jul 1946–12 Jul 1951. Decomm 1 Sep 1978. To USCG 4 Dec 1980
Later history: USCGC *Escape* (WMEC 6) Returned to USN 12 Jul 1995 and stricken. NDRF. SE.
◆Cuba Dec 1961–Jan 1962, Cuba missile crisis Oct–Nov 1962, Dominican Rep Jul–Oct 1965.

ARS 7 *Grapple* Out of comm 30 Aug 1946–26 Dec 1951. Damaged by coastal gunfire off Wonsan, 12 Aug 1952.
Damaged in error by gunfire of minesweeper *Chief* off Wonsan, 14 Aug 1952 (2 killed). Decomm and stricken 1 Dec 1977, and trfd to Taiwan.
Later history: renamed *Tai Hu*. (324/552). SE2001.
2★Korea K-4 K-8; 5★Vietnam Dec 1966–Jan 1967, Jun–Jul 1968, Aug–Nov 1969, Nov–Dec 1970, Mar 1971. ◆Passage to Freedom 1954, Taiwan Straits Aug–Sep 1958, Earnest Will.

Figure 10.22: *USNS Zeus* (T-ARC 7), fitting out at her builder's yard in September 1983. The destroyer tender *Shenandoah* is alongside.

Figure 10.23: *USS Conserver* (ARS 39), salvage vessel, October 1960, entering Pearl Harbor.

ARS 8 *Preserver* Out of comm 23 Apr 1947–1 Dec 1950 and 30 Sep 1986–25 Sep 1987. Decomm 7 Aug 1992. Stricken 16 Mar 1994, NDRF. Sold 26 Aug 2005, BU Chesapeake, Va.
◆Dominican Rep May–Jun 1965.

ARS 19 *Cable* Decomm 15 Sep 1947 and loaned for commercial service.
Later history: Merchant *Cable*. Stricken 15 Apr 1977. Sunk as target by frigate *Valdez*, 7 Aug 1978.

ARS 20 *Chain* Went aground on Block Island, NY, 29 Mar 1946. Decomm 9 Nov 1946. Rec **AGOR 17**, 1 Apr 1967. MSTS. Stricken 30 Dec 1977. BU 1979.

ARS 21 *Curb* Decomm 20 Dec 1946. Loaned for commercial service, 10 May 1947. Stricken 30 Apr 1981.
Later history: Merchant *Curb* 1947. Sunk as artificial reef off Key West, Fla., 23 Nov 1983.

ARS 22 *Current* Out of comm 9 Feb 1948–10 Oct 1951. Decomm 28 Apr 1972. Stricken 1 Jun 1973, sold Jan 1975.
Later history: Merchant *Grand Day*.
3★Korea K-7 K-8 K-10; 7★Vietnam Jun–Aug 1964, Oct 1965, Oct–Dec 1968, Dec 1969–Jan 1970, Mar–Apr 1970, May–Jun, Aug–Sep 1971. ◆Passage to Freedom 1954, Quemoy-Matsu Dec 1959–Jan 1960.

ARS 23 *Deliver* Decomm and stricken 15 Aug 1979, and trfd to South Korea.
Later history: renamed *Gum I/Gumi* (ARS 27). R1998.
3★Korea K-6 K-7 K-10; 9★Vietnam Jul–Aug 1966, Dec 1967–Jun 1968, Aug 1969, May–Oct 1970, Nov 1971, Jan–Mar 1972; ◆Evac of Vietnam 29–30 Apr 1975.

ARS 24 *Grasp* Out of comm 12 Dec 1946–10 Oct 1950. Decomm 7 Mar 1978. Stricken 31 Mar 1978, and trfd to South Korea.
Later history: renamed *Chang Won* (ARS 26). R1998.
2★Korea K-8, K-9; 5★Vietnam Sep 1963, Jul–Aug 1967, Jun–Sep 1968, Feb–Apr 1969, Aug–Oct 1970, Mar 1971; ◆Korea Apr 1971.

ARS 25 *Safeguard* Out of comm 12 Dec 1947–13 Feb 1952. Stricken 30 Sep 1979; Trfd to Turkey 28 Sep 1979.
Later history: renamed *Işin* (A 589). SE2001.
2★Korea K-8, K-9; 10★Vietnam Aug–Sep 1964, Oct 1965–Feb 1966, Nov–Dec 1967, Oct 1968–Feb 1969, Feb–May, Jun–Jul 1970, Jul–Aug 1971, Nov 1972–Mar 1973.

ARS 27 *Snatch* Decomm 23 Dec 1946. Loaned to Scripps Institute 1960.
Later history: Merchant *Argo*. Rec **AGOR 18**, 1 Apr 1967. Stricken 1 May 1970. Sold 8 Nov 1971, BU Taiwan.

ARS 28 *Valve* Decomm 26 Aug 1946. Stricken 12 Mar 1948. Sold 26 Jul 1948.

ARS 29 *Vent* Decomm 30 Aug 1946. Stricken 12 Mar 1948. Sold 30 Jun 1948.
   Later history: Merchant *Western Pioneer*.
ARS 33 *Clamp* Decomm 6 May 1947. Stricken 1 Jul 1963, NDRF. SE.
ARS 34 *Gear* Decomm 13 Dec 1946. Loaned for commercial service, 24 Feb 1953. Stricken 30 Apr 1981. Sold 1 Jul 1982, BU.
ARS 38 *Bolster* Decomm and stricken 24 Sep 1994, NDRF. SE.
   6★Korea K-1 K-2 K-4, K-7 K-8 K-9; 11★Vietnam Feb 1966, Oct 1967–Feb 1968, Mar–May, Jul–Aug 1969, Apr–Sep 1970, Oct 1971–Sep 1972.
ARS 39 *Conserver* Out of comm 30 Sep 1986–25 Sep 1987. Decomm and stricken 1 Apr 1994. Trfd to Mexico as *Matlalcueye* (A 64) canceled 23 Jul 1998.
   Later history: Sunk as target off Hawaii, 13 Nov 2004.
   8★Korea K-1 K-2 K-3 K-4 K-6 K-7 K-8 K-9 K-10; 6★Vietnam Aug–Sep, Nov 1966–Jan 1967, Mar–Jun 1968, Jun–Oct 1969, Aug–Nov 1970; ◆Taiwan Straits Sep–Oct 1958.
ARS 40 *Hoist* Helped recover H-bomb off Spain, Feb 1966, after USAF aerial collision. Decomm and stricken 30 Sep 1994. BU 2007, Chesapeake, Va.
   ◆Cuba Oct–Nov 1961, Cuba missile crisis Oct–Nov 1962, Lebanon Dec 1983, Mar 1984.
ARS 41 *Opportune* Decomm and stricken 30 Apr 1993. NDRF. BU 2004, Chesapeake, Va.
   1★Vietnam Jan–Feb 1966; ◆Cuba missile crisis Nov–Dec 1962, Lebanon Jun–Jul 1983, Gulf War Nov 1990–Mar 1991 (Mediterranean).
ARS 42 *Reclaimer* Out of comm 23 Jun 1947–1 Dec 1950. Decomm and stricken 16 Sep 1994, NDRF. Sunk as target 2006.
   6★Korea K-5 K-6 K-7 K-8 K-9 K-10; 5★Vietnam May 1964, Mar–May 1965, Feb–Apr, Jun 1966, May–Sep 1967, Jun–Oct 1968, Jan 1971, Mar–Aug 1972; ◆Passage to Freedom 1954.
ARS 43 *Recovery* Decomm and stricken 30 Sep 1994. Trfd to Taiwan 30 Sep 1998.
   Later history: renamed *Da Juen* SE2001 (556).
   ◆Lebanon Feb–Mar 1983, Grenada Oct–Nov 1983.

Armament: ARS 38, 40, 43: 2–20 mm; 39, 41, 42: also 1–40 mm.

No.	Name	Builder	Keel Laid	Launched	Comm.
ARS 50	*Safeguard*	Peterson	8 Nov 1982	12 Nov 1983	17 Aug 1985
ARS 51	*Grasp*	Peterson	30 Mar 1983	21 Apr 1984	14 Dec 1985
ARS 52	*Salvor*	Peterson	24 Oct 1983	28 Jul 1984	12 Aug 1986
ARS 53	*Grapple*	Peterson	25 Apr 1984	8 Dec 1984	15 Nov 1986

Displacement	2,300 tons; 2,880 f/l
Dimensions	254′11″ (oa); 240′ (wl) × 51′ × 15′6″
Machinery	2 screws; geared diesels; 4,200 BHP; 13.5 knots
Endurance	8,000/12
Complement	106
Armament	2 MG

Notes: Built to replace war-built ships.

Service Records:
ARS 50 *Safeguard* Decomm 26 Sep 2007, MSC.
ARS 51 *Grasp* Salvaged wreck of S-3B Viking ASW aircraft off Virginia from a depth of 10,000 ft, Jul 1990. Helped salvage TWA flight 800 off Long Island, 1996. Decomm 19 Jan 2006, MSC.
   ◆Haiti Sep 1994.
ARS 52 *Salvor* Decomm 12 Jan 2007, MSC.
ARS 53 *Grapple* Decomm 13 Jul 2006, MSC.

MISCELLANEOUS AUXILIARIES

MISCELLANEOUS AUXILIARIES ON THE NAVY LIST, 1947

AG 23 *Sequoia* Sold 18 May 1977. Sold 1 Jun 1977.
   Later history: Merchant *Sequoia*. SE
AG 68 *Basilan* Decomm 22 Apr 1946. Stricken 22 May 1947. BU 1972, Portland, Ore.
AG 69 *Burias* Decomm 9 Apr 1946. Stricken 17 Jul 1947. BU 1970, Portland, Ore.
AG 73 *Belle Isle* Decomm 30 Aug 1946. Rec **AKS 21**, 18 Aug 1951. Stricken 1 Apr 1960.
AG 74 *Coasters Harbor* Decomm 3 Jul 1947. Rec **AKS 22**. 18 Aug 1951. Stricken 1 Apr 1960, BU 1961.
AG 75 *Cuttyhunk Island* Decomm 3 May 1946. Rec **AKS 23** 18 Aug 1951. Stricken 1 Apr 1960, BU 1960.
AG 76 *Avery Island* Decomm 26 May 1947. Rec **AKS 24** 18 Aug 1951. Stricken 1 Apr 1960, BU 1961.
AG 77 *Indian Island* Decomm 11 May 1947. Rec **AKS 25** 18 Aug 1951. Stricken 1 Apr 1960, BU 1960.

Figure 10.24: *USS Safeguard* (ARS 50), built for the purpose salvage vessel, as completed, 1985.

Figure 10.25: *USS Mississippi* (AG 128), the old battleship as a gunnery training ship. Notice various gun mounts and missile launchers aft.

Figure 10.26: *USS Whidbey* (AG 141), 1950. A former Army freight ship used as Fleet X-ray ship.

AG 78   *Kent Island*   Decomm 22 Jun 1946. Rec **AKS 26** 18 Aug 1951. Stricken 1 Apr 1960. Sold 2 Nov 1960, BU New Orleans.
AG 126 *McDougal*   ex-DD 358. Decomm 24 Jun 1946. Stricken 15 Aug 1949. Sold 22 Sep 1949, BU.
AG 127 *Winslow*   ex-DD 359. Decomm 28 Jun 1950. Stricken 5 Dec 1957. Sold 23 Feb 1959, BU.
AG 128 *Mississippi*   ex-BB 41. Decomm 17 Sep 1956. Stricken 30 Jul 1956. Sold 28 Nov 1956, BU.
AG 129 *Whitewood*   ex-AN 63. Decomm 1 Apr 1949. Stricken 7 Jun 1949. Sold 3 Mar 1950.
AG 130–140   rec AKL 1–11

No.	Name	Builder	Launched	Acquired	Comm.
AG 141	*Whidbey* ex-FS 395	Ingalls	1944	22 Feb 1947	8 Aug 1947
AG 177	*Shearwater* ex-FS 411	Hickinbotham	1945	10 Apr 1964	
Displacement:	465 tons				
Dimensions	177′ (oa); 165′ (wl) × 32′9″ × 14′3″				
Machinery	2 screws; diesel; HP 1,000; 19 knots				
Complement	24				

Notes: *Whidbey* was fleet x-ray ship. *Shearwater* used as survey support ship. Both acquired from U.S. Army.

AG 141   *Whidbey*   In service 1964. Stricken 1 May 1959.
   Later history: Merchant *Sea Search*. BU 1968 Singapore.
   ★Korea 1952.
AG 177   *Shearwater*   Returned to Army and stricken 24 Jun 1967.

No.	Name	Builder	Launched	Acquired	Comm.
AG 142	*Nashawena* ex-BSP 2,098, *Col William A. Glassford*	Seattle Sbdg	1944	20 Jun 1947	20 Jun 1947
Displacement	602 tons				
Dimensions	154′ (wl) × 36′ × 6′				

Service Record: Acquired from U.S. Army. Rec **YAG 35**, 1 Sep 1947. Sold 1 Jun 1960.
   Later history: Merchant *Omega*.

Figure 10.27: *USS Observation Island* (EAG 154), test ship for Polaris and Poseidon missiles.

No.	Name	Builder	Launched	Acquired	Comm.
EAG 153	*Compass Island* ex-YAG 56 (19 Jun 1956) ex-*Garden Mariner*	NY Sbdg	12 Mar 1953	29 Mar 1956	3 Dec 1956
EAG 154	*Observation Island* ex-YAG 57 (19 Jun 1956) ex-*Empire State Mariner*	NY Sbdg	15 Aug 1953	10 Sep 1956	5 Dec 1958
Displacement	17,600 tons f/l (154); 16,076 f/l (1953); 2004: 154: 13,060 lt, 16,076 f/l				
Dimensions	563′ (oa) × 76′ × 29′				
Machinery	1 screw; ST; 2 boilers; 22,000 SHP; 20 knots				
Complement	350; 126				
Armament	none. *1977*: 153: 4–20 mm				

Notes: Type C4-S-1a. AG 153 completed as test ship for inertial navigation systems. AG 154 acquired before completion as Polaris and Poseidon missile test ship; as AGM fitted with massive missile tracking antennas. Acquisition of AG 155 canceled.

Service Records:

EAG 153   *Compass Island*   Rec **AG 153**, 1 Apr 1968. Decomm 1 May 1980. Stricken 31 Mar 1986, NDRF. Towed to UK for BU 2003.
   ◆Cuba Jun–Sep, Nov–Dec 1961, Mar 1962, Cuba missile crisis Nov 1962.
EAG 154   *Observation Island*   Rec **AG 154**, 1 Apr 1968. Decomm 25 Sep 1972. Converted to AGM, 1977–81, and rec **T-AGM 23**, 1 May 1979, MSC. Used to monitor Soviet tests in Pacific, 1979, and compliance with strategic arms treaties.
   ◆Indian Ocean Apr–Jun 1998.

Figure 10.28: *USNS Phoenix* (T-AG 172), Forward Depot Ship,

Tenders 177

Figure 10.29: *USNS Kingsport* (T-AG 164) served in various capacities, as hydrographic research ship, satellite communications programs support ship, and support of undersea surveillance programs.

No.	Name	Builder	Launched	Acquired	In service
AG 164	*Kingsport*	Calship	29 May 1944	1 Mar 1950	1 Mar 1950
	ex-AK 239 (14 Nov 1961), ex-*Kingsport Victory*				
AG 172	*Phoenix*	Oregon	10 Apr 1945	25 Oct 1962	20 Nov 1962
	ex-*Arizona*, ex-*Capital Victory*				
AG 173	*Provo*	Oregon	17 Jun 1945	2 Mar 1963	1963
	ex-*Utah*, ex-*California*, ex-*Drew Victory*				
AG 174	*Cheyenne*	Oregon	26 Jun 1945	29 Dec 1963	1963
	ex-*Wyoming*, ex-*Middlesex Victory*				
Displacement	7,190 tons; 10,680 f/l				
Dimensions	455′ (oa); 436′ (wl) × 62′ × 22′				
Machinery	1 screw; ST; 2 boilers; 8,500 SHP; 15.2 knots				
Complement	69				
Armament	none				

Notes: Type: VC2-S-AP3. *Kingsport* was Project Advent satellite communications programs support ship 1961–66, then hydrographic research ship; supported undersea surveillance programs 1966. Others were Forward Depot Ships.

Service Record:
AG 164 *Kingsport* OS 22 Nov 1983. Stricken 31 Jan 1984. BU 1992, Alang, India.
AG 172 *Phoenix* Stricken 15 Jun 1973. Sold 31 Aug 1973, BU 1973 Kaohsiung, Taiwan.
AG 173 *Provo* Stricken 15 Jun 1973. Sold 31 Aug 1973, BU 1973 Kaohsiung, Taiwan.
AG 174 *Cheyenne* Stricken 15 Jun 1973. Sold 31 Aug 1973, BU Kaohsiung, Taiwan.

AG 179 *Haverford* ex-*Mercer Victory*
AG 180 *Antioch* ex-*Alfred Victory*
AG 181 *Adelphi* ex-*Adelphi Victory*
AG 182 *Lynn* ex-*Lynn Victory*
AG 183 *Clarksburg* ex-*Clarksburg Victory*
AG 184 *Clemson* ex-*Lindenwood Victory*
AG 185 *Carthage* ex-*American Victory*
AG 186 *Bessemer* ex-*Bessemer Victory*
AG 187 *Milford* ex-*Greeley Victory*
AG 188 *Radcliffe* ex-*Princeton Victory*
AG 189 *Rollins* ex-*High Point Victory*
AG 190 *Webster* ex-*Hobart Victory*

Forward Depot Ships, MSTS. Acquisition canceled 1 Feb 1966.

No.	Name	Builder	Launched	Acquired	In service
AG 175	*Sgt. Curtis E. Shoup*	Kaiser#4	25 May 1945	1 Mar 1963	1 Mar 1963
	ex-*Sgt. Curtis E. Shoup* (USA), ex-*Spindle Eye*				
Displacement	3,805 tons				
Dimensions	378′9″ (oa) × 50′3″ × 16′10″				
Machinery	1 screw; diesel; 1,700 SHP; 10.7 knots				
Complement	62				

Notes: Type CM-1-AV1. Survey Support Ship. Helicopter freighter, with landing platform on bow.

Service Record: OS 20 Dec 1969. Stricken 28 Apr 1970. Sold 9 May 1973, BU 1973 Taiwan.

No.	Name	Builder	Launched	Acquired	In service
AG 178	*Flyer*	Moore	20 Dec 1944	22 Mar 1965	2 Sep 1965
	ex-*American Flyer*, ex-*Water Witch*				
Displacement	7,360 tons; 11,000 f/l				
Dimensions	459′2″ (oa); 435′ (wl) × 63′ × 28′				
Machinery	1 screw; GT; 2 boilers; 6,000 SHP				
Complement	53				

Notes: Type: C2-S-B1. Hydrographic research ship for undersea surveillance. MSC.

Service Record: OS 1975. Stricken 17 Jul 1975. Sold Jul 1976, BU 1976 Portland, Ore.

No.	Name	Former	Date	Reclassified	Date
AG 143	*Mark*	—	—	AKL 12	31 Mar 1949
AG 144	*Tingles*	—	—	AKL 13	31 Mar 1949
AG 145	*Hewell*	—	—	AKL 14	31 Mar 1949
AG 146	*Electron*	LST 1070	27 Jan 1949	AKS 27	18 Aug 1951
AG 147	*Proton*	LST 1078	27 Jan 1949	AKS 28	18 Aug 1951
AG 148	*Colington*	LST 1085	27 Jan 1949	AKS 29	18 Aug 1951
AG 149	*League Island*	LST 1097	27 Jan 1949	AKS 30	18 Aug 1951
AG 150	*Chimon*	LST 1102	27 Jan 1949	AKS 31	18 Aug 1951
EAG 151	*Richard E. Kraus*	DD 849	25 Aug 1949	—	—
EAG 152	*Timmerman*	DD 828	11 Dec 1953	—	—
AG 155	—	—	acquisition canceled	—	—
AG 156	—	LSM 398	acquisition canceled	—	—
AG 157	*King County*	LST 857	17 May 1958	—	—
AG 158	—	(AGER) not built	—	—	—
AG 159	*Oxford*	—	—	AGTR 1	1 Apr 1964
AG 160	*Range Tracker*	—	—	AGM 1	27 Nov 1960
AG 161	*Range Recoverer*	—	—	AGM 2	27 Nov 1960
AG 162	*Mission Capistrano*	AO 112	1 Apr 1961	—	—

No.	Name				
AG 163	Glover	—	—	AGDE 1	1 Jul 1975
AG 165	Georgetown	—	—	AGTR 2	1 Apr 1964
AG 166	Jamestown	—	—	AGTR 3	1 Apr 1964
AG 167	Belmont	—	—	AGTR 4	1 Apr 1964
AG 168	Liberty	—	—	AGTR 5	1 Apr 1964
AG 169	Pvt. Jose F. Valdez	APC 119	1 Dec 1962	(AGI)	—
AG 170	Lt. James E. Robinson	AK 274	1 Dec 1962	—	—
AG 171	Sgt. Joseph E. Muller	APC 118	1 Dec 1962	(AGI)	—
AG 176	Peregrine	MSF 373	25 Feb 1964	—	—
AG 191	Spokane	CL 120	1 Apr 1966	(not converted)	—
AG 192	S.P. Lee	AGS 31	25 Sep 1970	—	—
AG 194	Vanguard	AGM 19	30 Sep 1980	—	—
AG 195	Hayes	AGOR 16	20 Mar 1989	—	—
AG 335	Hunting	LSM 335	1 Jan 1969	to Dept of Interior	21 Dec 1970
AG 520	Alacrity	MSO 520	1 Jun 1973	—	—
AG 521	Assurance	MSO 521	1 Mar 1973	—	—

Figure 10.32: *USS King County* (AG 157), former LST used as guided missile test ship, 1958. A Regulus II missile is readied for launching.

Figure 10.30: *USNS Mission Capistrano* (T-AG 162), former oiler converted to sound testing ship, 1961.

Figure 10.33: The heavy-lift research ship *Glomar Explorer* showing the unusual lifting equipment on this large ship.

No.	Name	Builder	Launched	Acquired	In service
AG 193	Glomar Explorer ex-Hughes Glomar Explorer (1978)	Sun	14 Nov 1972	30 Sep 1976	never
Displacement	63,300 tons f/l; 27,445 grt				
Dimensions	618′9″ (oa); 556′11″ (wl) × 115′8″ × 46′8″				
Machinery	2 screws; diesel-electric; 13,200 BHP; 10.8 knots				
Complement	189				

Notes: Heavy lift ship. Built clandestinely by CIA to salvage Soviet Golf-class ballistic missile submarine *K-129* (Project 629), sunk in 16,500 feet depth in 1968. Only a portion recovered, Aug 1974. Acquired by USN after that operation failed, 30 Sep 1976.

Service Record: Laid up 17 Jan 1977. Loaned to Chevron USA Production Co. 2 Jul 1996.

Figure 10.31: *USS Timmerman* (AG 152), *Gearing* class destroyer constructed as an experimental ship to test advance design engineering equipment, 1954.

ICEBREAKERS

AG 88   *Burton Island*   Rec **AGB 1**, 1 Mar 1949. To USCG, 15 Dec 1966 as USCGC *Burton Island* (WAGB 283).
◆Antarctic Feb 1946–Mar 1947, Dec 1947–Feb 1948, Dec 1957–Mar 1958, Feb–Mar 1960, Nov 1961–Feb 1962, Nov 1963–Mar 1964, Nov 1965–Jan 1966, Dec 1970–Mar 1971.

AG 89   *Edisto*   Rec **AGB 2**, 1 Mar 1949. Decomm and to USCG, 20 Oct 1965 as USCGC *Edisto* (WAGB 284).
◆Antarctic Dec 1947–Feb 1948, Dec 1955–Feb 1956, Jan–Mar 1959, Dec 1960–Apr 1961, Nov 1962–Mar 1963, Jan–Mar 1965, Dec 1969–Mar 1970.

Figure 10.34: The icebreaker USS *Burton Island* (AGB 1), prior to transfer to the Coast Guard in 1966.

Transferred to Coast Guard:

No.	Name	USCG No.	Date
AGB 3	*Atka*	WAGB 280	31 Oct 1966

◆Antarctic Jan–Feb 1955, Dec 1956–Mar 1957, Nov 1957–Feb 1958.

AGB 5	*Staten Island*	WAGB 278	1 Feb 1966

◆Antarctic Jan–Feb 1957, Dec 1958–Mar 1959, Dec 1960–Apr 1961, Nov–Dec 1962, Jan–Mar 1963, Nov 1964–Mar 1965, Dec 1970–Mar 1971.

AGB 6	*Westwind*	WAGB 281	1966

No.	Name	Builder	Keel Laid	Launched	Comm.
AGB 4	*Glacier*	Ingalls	3 Aug 1953	27 Aug 1954	27 May 1955
Displacement	5,100 tons; 8,449 f/l				
Dimensions	309'6" (oa) × 74' × 29'				
Machinery	2 screws; diesel-electric; 21,000 SHP; 17.6 knots				
Complement	248				
Armament	2–5" guns; *1977*: 2–40 mm				

Service Record: To USCG, **WAGB 4**, 30 Jun 1966. Trfd to Glacier Society, Bridgeport, Conn. 30 Oct 2000, as museum.
◆Antarctic Dec 1955–Apr 1956, Oct 1956–Feb 1957, Nov 1957–Mar 1958, Oct 1958–Mar 1959, Dec 1959–Mar 1960, Dec 1960–Mar 1961, Nov–Dec 1961, Jan–Mar 1962, Nov 1962–Mar 1963, Nov 1963–Mar 1964, Nov 1964–Mar 1965, Nov 1965–Apr 1966.

ESCORT RESEARCH SHIP

No.	Name	Builder	Keel Laid	Launched	Comm.
AGDE 1	*Glover* ex-AG 163	Bath	29 Jul 1963 (13 Nov 1965)	17 Apr 1965	13 Nov 1965
Displacement	2,643 tons; 3,426 f/l				
Dimensions	414'6" (oa) × 44'2" × 14'6"				
Machinery	1 screw; ST; 2 boilers; 35,000 SHP; 27 knots				
Complement	236				
Armament	1–5"/38 gun, 1 ASROC, 6–12.75" TT				

Notes: Experimental frigate, similar to *Brooke* class. Sonar trials ship 1990.

Figure 10.35: USS *Glover* (AGDE 1), an experimental ship similar to *Brooke* class guided missile frigates, built in 1965. She served as an operational unit FF 1098 for ten years after 1979.

Figure 10.36: The Deep Submergence Support Ship Tender USS *Point Loma* (AGDS 2) was built as the Dock Cargo Ship *Point Barrow* (AKD 1) and converted in 1974.

Service Record: Rec **AGFF 1**, 1 Jul 1975. Rec **FF 1098**, 1 Oct 1979. Rec **AGFF 1**, 15 Jun 1990, to MSC. Out of service, 28 Sep 1992. Stricken 20 Nov 1992. Sold 15 Apr 1994, BU 1995 Wilmington, NC.

DEEP SUBMERGENCE SUPPORT SHIP TENDERS

No.	Name	Former	Date
AGDS 1	*White Sands*	ARD 20	Sold 1 Sep 1974
AGDS 2	*Point Loma*	AKD 1	28 Feb 1974

HYDROFOIL RESEARCH SHIP

No.	Name	Builder	Keel Laid	Launched	Comm.
AGEH 1	*Plainview*	Lockheed	8 May 1964	28 Jun 1965	3 Mar 1969

Displacement	300 tons
Dimensions	220′ × 40′5″ × 24′4″
Machinery	2 screws; diesel; 1,200 BHP; 12 knots 2 waterjets; gas turbines; 30,000 SHP; ~50 knots
Complement	20
Armament	2 triple ASW TT

Notes: Built to evaluate hydrofoil performance. Aluminum hull with three retractable foils.

Service Record: Stricken 30 Sep 1978. Stripped and aground in Columbia River, 1988.

INTELLIGENCE COLLECTION SHIPS

No.	Name	Former	Date
AGER 1	*Banner*	AKL 25	1 Jun 1967
AGER 2	*Pueblo*	AKL 44	1 Jun 1967
AGER 3	*Palm Beach*	AKL 45	2 May 1967

Note: Officially designated Environmental Research Ships.

No.	Name	Builder	Launched	Acquired	Comm.
AGTR 1	*Oxford* ex-AG 159 (1 Apr 1964) ex-*Samuel R. Aitken*	New England	31 Jul 1945	Oct 1960	8 Jul 1961
AGTR 2	*Georgetown* ex-AG 165 (1 Apr 1964) ex-*Robert W. Hart*	New England	10 Jul 1945	10 Aug 1962	9 Nov 1963
AGTR 3	*Jamestown* ex-AG 166 (1 Apr 1964) ex-*J. Howland Gardner*	New England	10 Jul 1945	10 Aug 1962	13 Dec 1963

Displacement	7,330 tons; 11,365 f/l
Dimensions	441′6″(oa); 417′(wl) × 57′ × 23′
Machinery	1 screw; VTE; 2,500 SHP; 11 knots
Complement	254
Armament	4 MG

Notes: Type EC2-S-C5. Officially designated Technical Research Ships.

Figure 10.37: The hydrofoil research ship USS *Plainview* (AGEH 1), January 1972, with foils retracted.

Figure 10.38: USS *Palm Beach* (AGER 3), intelligence collector. Her sister *Pueblo* was seized by North Korean forces 1968.

Figure 10.39: USS *Jamestown* (AG 166), 1963, former Liberty Ship used for intelligence surveillance.

Service Records:

1	*Oxford*	Decomm and stricken 19 Dec 1969. BU 1970 Taiwan. 10★Vietnam Jun–Dec 1965, Mar 1966–Apr 1967, Sep 1967–Oct 1969.
2	*Georgetown*	Decomm and stricken 19 Dec 1969. BU 1971.
3	*Jamestown*	Decomm and stricken 19 Dec 1969. BU 1970 Portland, Ore. 9★Vietnam Jan 1966–Jan 1967, Apr 1967–Oct 1969

No.	Name	Builder	Launched	Acquired	Comm.
AGTR 4	*Belmont* ex-AG 167 (1 Apr 1964) ex-*Iran Victory*	Oregon	25 Mar 1944	Feb 1963	2 Nov 1964
AGTR 5	*Liberty* ex-AG 168 (1 Apr 1964) ex-*Simmons Victory*	Oregon	6 Apr 1945	Feb 1963	30 Dec 1964

Displacement	4,420 tons; 11,100 f/l
Dimensions	455′3″(oa); 436′(wl) × 62′ × 28′6″
Machinery	1 screw; turbine; 8,500 SHP; 16 knots
Complement	358
Armament	4 MG

Notes: Type VC2-S-AP3. Officially designated Technical Research Ships. Tripod radar tower mounted forward of funnel.

Figure 10.40: USS *Liberty* (AGTR 5), at Malta, 14 June 1967, following Israeli attack off coast of Egypt.

Service Record:

AGTR 4 *Belmont* Decomm and stricken 16 Jan 1970, BU 1970 Baltimore.
◆Dominican Rep Apr–Jul 1965.
AGTR 5 *Liberty* Strafed and torpedoed by Israeli mtb's and aircraft off Sinai, 2 Jun 1967 (34 killed). Decomm 28 Jun 1968. Stricken 1 Jun 1970. BU 1970 Baltimore.
◆PUC 8 Jun 1967.

AG 169 *Pvt. Joseph F. Valdez* ex-APC 119
AG 171 *Sgt Joseph E. Muller* ex-APC 118

MISSILE RANGE INSTRUMENTATION SHIPS

No.	Name	Builder	Launched	Acquired	In service
AGM 1	*Range Tracker* ex-*AG 160* (27 Nov 1960) ex-*Skidmore Victory*, ex-*President Buchanan*, ex-*Skidmore Victory*	Oregon	19 May 1945	1960	1961
AGM 3	*Longview* ex-*AK 238* (27 Nov 1960) ex-*Haiti Victory*	Permanente 2	20 Jul 1944	1 Mar 1950	1960
AGM 4	*Richfield* ex-*AK 253* (27 Nov 1960) ex-*Pvt. Joe E. Mann*, ex-*Owensboro Victory*	Permanente 2	21 Jul 1945	7 Aug 1950	1960
AGM 5	*Sunnyvale* ex-*AK 256* (27 Nov 1960) ex-*Dalton Victory*	Calship	6 Jun 1944	9 Aug 1950	1960
AGM 6	*Watertown* ex-*Niantic Victory*	Oregon	25 Apr 1944	11 Aug 1960	1961
AGM 7	*Huntsville* ex-*Knox Victory*	Oregon	13 Apr 1945	11 Aug 1960	1961
AGM 8	*Wheeling* ex-*Seton Hall Victory*	Oregon	22 May 1945	28 May 1964	1964
AGM 11	*Twin Falls* ex-*Twin Falls Victory*	Oregon	6 Feb 1945	1 Jul 1964	1964
Displacement	7,190 tons; 10,680 f/l				
Dimensions	455′ (oa); 436′ (wl) × 62′ × 24′				
Machinery	1 screw; ST; 2 boilers; 8,500 SHP; 17.7 knots				
Complement	106/81				

Notes: Type: VC2-S-AP2. *Longview, Sunnyvale, Watertown,* and *Huntsville* operated at the Air Force Western Test Range in the Pacific.

Service Records:

AGM 1 *Range Tracker* OS 27 Sep 1969. Stricken 28 Apr 1970. Sold 10 Jul 1970, BU Portland, Ore.
AGM 3 *Longview* Stricken 1 Nov 1974. Sold 27 Apr 1976, BU Kaohsiung.
AGM 4 *Richfield* Stricken 9 Oct 1969. BU 1976 USA.
AGM 5 *Sunnyvale* Stricken 15 Dec 1974. Sold 17 Jul 1975, BU Terminal I, Cal.
AGM 6 *Watertown* Stricken 16 Feb 1972. Sold 23 May 1974, BU Pusan, Korea.
AGM 7 *Huntsville* Stricken 8 Nov 1974. Sold 17 Jul 1975, BU Terminal I.
AGM 8 *Wheeling* Stricken 31 Oct 1980. Sunk as target 12 Jul 1981.
AGM 11 *Twin Falls* Stricken 28 Apr 1970. Reacq 1971 but conversion to **AGS 37** canceled. Stricken 1 Sep 1972. Sold 6 Nov 1972 to New York City.
Later history: Merchant *John W. Brown II*. BU 1982.

No.	Name	Builder	Launched	Acquired	In service
AGM 2	*Range Recoverer* ex-AG 161 (27 Nov 1960) ex-USAF E-42-1834, ex-FS-278 (USA)	Wheeler	Nov 1944	6 Apr 1960	22 Jun 1960
Displacement	550 tons				
Dimensions	176′6 (oa); 165′ (wl) × 32′ × 11′5″				
Machinery	2 screws; diesel; 1,000 hp; 10 knots				
Complement	24				

Notes: Originally built for U.S. Army.

Figure 10.41: USNS *Wheeling* (T-AGM 8), converted Victory Ship.

Figure 10.42: USNS *General Hoyt S. Vandenberg* (T-AGM 10), missile range instrumentation ship with three large radars, converted 1964.

Service Record: Rec **YFRT 524**, name canceled 16 May 1972. Stricken 15 May 1974.

No.	Name	Builder	Launched	Acquired	Comm.
AGM 9	Gen. H.H. Arnold ex-AP 139 Gen. R.E. Callan	Kaiser	23 May 1944	1964	1 Jul 1964
AGM 10	Gen. Hoyt S. Vanderberg ex-AP 145 Gen. Harry Taylor	Kaiser	10 Oct 1943	1964	13 Jul 1964

Displacement	16,600 tons f/l
Dimensions	522′10″ (oa) × 71′6″ × 26′4″
Machinery	1 screw; ST; 2 B&W boilers; 9,000 SHP; 16.5 knots
Complement	203

Notes: Type C4-S-A1. Former transports acquired from Air Force in 1964, MSC. Range instrumentation ships. Three large radar towers amidships.

Service Records:

AGM 9 Gen.Arnold   Stricken 1 Mar 1982. BU 1982.
AGM 10 Gen.Vandenberg   OS 8 Feb 1983. Stricken 29 Apr 1993. NDRF.

No.	Name	Builder	Launched	Acquired
AGM 12	American Mariner ex-American Mariner	Beth; Fair	30 Dec 1941	1 Jul 1964

Displacement	5,080 tons
Dimensions	441′6″ (oa) × 56′11″ × 23′
Machinery	1 screw; VTE; 11 knots

Notes: Type: EC2-S-C1. Used as cadet training ship in World War II.

Service Record: Ran aground off Cape Kennedy, 21 Jan 1965. Stricken 1 Jul 1966. Scuttled in Chesapeake Bay, Oct 1966.

No.	Name	Builder	Launched	Acquired
AGM 13	Sword Knot ex-USAF E-45-1852 (1963) ex-Sword Knot	Cons; Wilm.	14 Mar 1945	1 Jul 1964
AGM 14	Rose Knot ex-USAF E-45-1850 (1963) ex-Rose Knot	Penn. SY	6 Dec 1944	1 Jul 1964
AGM 15	Coastal Sentry ex-USAF E-45-1849 (1963) ex-Coastal Sentry	L.D.Smith	21 Jan 1945	1 Jul 1964
AGM 16	Coastal Crusader ex-USAF E-45-1851 (1963) ex-Coastal Crusader	L.D.Smith	24 Jun 1945	1 Jul 1964
AGM 17	Timber Hitch ex-USAF E-45-1848 (1963) ex-Timber Hitch	Cons; Wilm	12 Oct 1944	1 Jul 1964
AGM 18	Sampan Hitch ex-USAF E-45-1861 (1963) ex-Sampan Hitch	Butler	12 Jul 1945	1 Jul 1964

Displacement	3,666 tons; 6,090 f/l
Dimensions	338′9″ × 50′4″ × 17′7″
Machinery	1 screw; diesel; 1,700 hp; 11.5 knots
Complement	78

Notes: Type: C1-M-AV1.

Service Records:

AGM 13 Sword Knot   Stricken 1 Apr 1972. BU 1973, California.
AGM 14 Rose Knot   Stricken 9 Oct 1969. Sold May 1973. BU 1987, China.
AGM 15 Coastal Sentry   Stricken 9 Oct/7 Nov 1968. BU 1968 Hong Kong.
AGM 16 Coastal Crusader   Conversion to **AGS 36** canceled 1969. Stricken 30 Apr 1976. Sold 12 Apr 1977. BU 1977 Tacoma.

Figure 10.43: *USNS Coastal Crusader* (T-AGM 16), missile range instrumentation ship.

AGM 17 Timber Hitch   Stricken 9 Oct 1969. Sold 27 Jul 1977. BU1977 Brownsville.
AGM 18 Sampan Hitch   Stricken 9 Oct 1969. Sold Apr 1973. BU 1973 Kaohsiung.

No.	Name	Former	Reacquired	In service
AGM 19	Vanguard ex-Muscle Shoals (1 Sep 1965)	AO 122 Mission San Fernando	28 Sep 1964	28 Feb 1966
AGM 20	Redstone ex-Johnstown (1 Sep 1965)	AO 114 Mission De Pala	19 Sep 1964	30 Jun 1966
AGM 21	Mercury ex-Flagstaff (1 Sep 1965)	AO 126 Mission San Juan	28 Oct 1964	16 Sep 1965

Displacement	13,882 tons; 24,761 f/l
Dimensions	595′ (oa) × 75′ × 25′
Machinery	1 screw; TE; 10,000 SHP; 14 knots
Endurance	27,000/16
Complement	196

Notes: Former tankers, converted and lengthened 1965 by Gen. Dynamics, Quincy. Satellite communications ships, Project Apollo. *Vanguard* fitted with new forward deckhouse, 1968.
Vanguard converted to navigation research ship 1980. MSC.

Service Records:

AGM 19 Vanguard   Rec **AG 194**, 30 Sep 1980. OS 30 Mar 1998. Stricken 13 Dec 1999, NDRF. SE.
AGM 20 Redstone   OS 6 Aug 1993. Stricken 7 Dec 1993. Sold 17 Nov 1995, sale canceled.
AGM 21 Mercury   OS 1970. Stricken 28 Apr 1970.
  Later history: Merchant *Kopaa*. BU 1984 Taiwan.

No.	Name	Builder	Launched	Recquired	In service
AGM 22	Range Sentinel ex-Sherburne APA 205 (26 Apr 1971)	Permanente	10 Jul 1944	22 Oct 1969	14 Oct 1971

Displacement	11,860 tons f/l
Dimensions	455′ (oa) × 62′ × 23′
Machinery	1 screw; ST; 2 boilers; 8,500 SHP; 17.7 knots
Endurance	10,000/15
Complement	96
Armament	none

Notes: Type VC2-S-AP5. Reacquired for conversion to support Poseidon FBM program, MSC.

Service Record: OS 9 Jul 1997. Stricken 3 May 1999, NDRF. SE.

Tenders 183

Figure 10.44: *USNS Redstone* (T-AGM 20), satellite communications ship, converted 1966.

Figure 10.45: *USNS Range Sentinel* (T-AGM 22), for support of FBM program.

No.	Name	Former	Date
AGM 23	*Observation Island*	AG 154	1 May 1979
AGM 24	*Invincible*	AGOS 10	4 Apr 2000

MAJOR COMMUNICATIONS RELAY SHIPS

No.	Name	Former	Date	—
AGMR 1	*Annapolis*	CVE 107	1 Jun 1963	Stricken 15 Oct 1976
AGMR 2	*Arlington*	CVL 48	1 Sep 1964	Stricken 15 Aug 1975

OCEANOGRAPHIC SURVEILLANCE SHIPS

No.	Name	Builder	Keel Laid	Launched	In Service
AGOS 1	*Stalwart*	Tacoma	3 May 1982	11 Jul 1983	21 Mar 1984
AGOS 2	*Contender*	Tacoma	10 Jan 1983	20 Dec 1983	30 May 1984
AGOS 3	*Vindicator*	Tacoma	14 Apr 1983	1 Jun 1984	29 Oct 1984
AGOS 4	*Triumph*	Tacoma	13 Jul 1983	7 Sep 1984	19 Feb 1985
AGOS 5	*Assurance*	Tacoma	16 Apr 1984	12 Jan 1985	1 May 1985
AGOS 6	*Persistent*	Tacoma	22 Oct 1984	6 Apr 1985	14 Aug 1985
AGOS 7	*Indomitable*	Tacoma	26 Jan 1985	16 Jul 1985	2 Dec 1985
AGOS 8	*Prevail*	Tacoma	13 Mar 1985	7 Dec 1985	4 Mar 1986
AGOS 9	*Assertive*	Tacoma	30 Jul 1985	20 Jun 1986	12 Sep 1986
AGOS 10	*Invincible*	Tacoma	8 Nov 1985	8 Nov 1986	30 Jan 1987
AGOS 11	*Audacious* ex-*Dauntless* (1985)	Tacoma	29 Feb 1988	28 Jan 1989	12 Jun 1989
AGOS 12	*Bold* ex-*Vigorous* (1985)	Tacoma	13 Jun 1988	22 May 1990	16 Oct 1989
AGOS 13	*Adventurous*	Halter	19 Dec 1985	23 Sep 1987	19 Aug 1988
AGOS 14	*Worthy*	Halter	3 Apr 1986	6 Feb 1988	16 Dec 1988
AGOS 15	*Titan*	Halter	30 Oct 1986	18 Jun 1988	8 Mar 1989
AGOS 16	*Capable*	Halter	2 Jun 1987	28 Oct 1988	9 Jun 1989
AGOS 17	*Tenacious* ex-*Intrepid*	Halter	26 Feb 1988	17 Feb 1989	29 Sep 1989
AGOS 18	*Relentless*	Halter	22 Apr 1988	12 May 1989	12 Jan 1990

Displacement	1,600 tons; 2,285 f/l
Dimensions	224′ (oa); 203′8″ (wl) × 43′ × 15′
Machinery	2 screws; diesel-electric; 3,200 BHP; 11 knots
Endurance	3,000/11
Complement	29

Notes: Fitted with SURTASS. MSC, unarmed. Hulls similar to ATF 166 class. *Stalwart*, *Indomitable* and *Capable* modified as air defense (radar) ships. Six projected for transfer to USCG, but found unfit, too slow. As AGM, *Invincible* has a large radome abaft funnels; *Worthy* has two radomes.

Service Records:
AGOS 1 *Stalwart*   Loan to Naval Surface Warfare Center, 1 Oct 1992–31 Mar 1993. OS 13 Apr 2002. Stricken 2 Dec 2002.
   Later history: State of New York port security research ship.
AGOS 2 *Contender*   OS 1 Oct 1992. Stricken 11 Dec 1992.
   Later history: trfd to U.S. Merchant Marine Academy, Kings Point, NY, renamed *Kings Pointer*.
AGOS 3 *Vindicator*   OS 30 Mar and stricken 30 Jun 1993. To USCG 15 May 1994. To NOAA 30 Oct 2001.
   Later history: renamed *Hi'Ialakai*.
AGOS 4 *Triumph*   OS 20 Jun 1994. Stricken 6 Jan 1995. Reacq.14 Apr 1995. Stricken 6 Jan 1996, NDRF. SE.
AGOS 5 *Assurance*   OS 28 Mar 1994. Stricken 6 Jan 1995. NDRF. Trfd to Portugal 30 Sep 1999.
   Later history: renamed *Almirante Gago Coutinho* (A 523). SE2001.

Figure 10.46: *USNS Invincible* (T-AGM 24), converted 2000. Employed by USAF for surveillance of Chinese and North Korean missile programs.

Figure 10.47: USS *Annapolis* (AGMR 1), 12 Jun 1964, the former escort carrier *Gilbert Islands* (CVE 107), converted to Major Communications Relay Ship in 1963.

Figure 10.49: USNS *Prevail* (T-AGOS 8), oceanographic surveillance ship, about 1990.

Figure 10.48: USS *Arlington* (AGMR 2), converted from the aircraft carrier *Saipan* in 1963, served two years in Vietnam

Figure 10.50: USNS *Effective* (T-AGOS 21), SWATH design Oceanographic Surveillance Ship, 1993.

AGOS 6 *Persistent*   OS 11 Oct 1994, to USCG. Stricken 6 Jan 1995. React 26 Aug 1999. Tfrd to Great Lakes Maritime Academy, Traverse City, Mich., 1 Aug 2002.
    Later history: renamed *State of Michigan*. NDRF. SE.

AGOS 7 *Indomitable*   OS 13 Apr 2002. Stricken 2 Dec 2002. To NOAA 9 Dec 2002.
    Later history: renamed *McArthur II*, 2003.

AGOS 8 *Prevail*   Rec **IX 537**, 17 Oct 2003. Training ship for maritime interdiction operations.

AGOS 9 *Assertive*   Stricken 3 Mar 2004. Tfrd to NOAA 31 Mar 2004.

AGOS 10 *Invincible*   OS 6 Feb 1995. Stricken 9 May 1995. IS 18 Mar 1998 for dual band radar experiments. Reinstated 4 Apr 2000. Rec **AGM 24**, 4 Apr 2000. Employed by USAF for surveillance of Chinese and North Korean missile programs.
    ◆Indian Ocean May–Jul 2000.

AGOS 11 *Audacious*   OS 30 Nov 1995. Stricken 6 Feb 1997. Trfd to Portugal 9 Dec 1996.
    Later history: renamed *Dom Carlos I* (A 522). SE2001.

AGOS 12 *Bold*   Stricken 31 Mar 2004. Trfd to EPA, 31 Mar 2004.
    Later history: IS with EPA as *Bold* (OSV 224).

AGOS 13 *Adventurous*   OS, to NOAA 1 Jun 1992. Stricken 5 Jun 1992. NDRF.
    Later history: renamed *Oscar Elton Sette*, 2003.

AGOS 14 *Worthy*   OS to U.S. Geological Survey 17 Mar 1993 but not used. Stricken 20 May 1993. Tfrd to U.S. Army 1995 as missile range support ship at Kwajalein.

AGOS 15 *Titan*   OS and tfrd to NOAA 31 Aug 1993
    Later history: renamed *Ka'Imimoana*, 25 Apr 1996.

AGOS 16 *Capable*   to NOAA 14 Sep 2004
    Later history: renamed *Okeanos Explorer*, 2006.

AGOS 17 *Tenacious*   OS 3 Feb 1995. Trfd to New Zealand 10 Oct 1996.
    Later history: renamed *Resolution* (A 14). SE2001.

AGOS 18 *Relentless*   OS and trfd to NOAA 17 Mar 1993. Stricken 20 May 1993.
    Later history: renamed *Gordon Gunter*, 1998.

No.	Name	Builder	Keel Laid	Launched	In service
T-AGOS 19	Victorious	McDermott	12 Apr 1988	2 May 1990	21 Mar 1991
T-AGOS 20	Able	McDermott	23 May 1989	16 Feb 1991	22 Jul 1992
T-AGOS 21	Effective	McDermott	18 Feb 1991	26 Sep 1991	15 Jan 1993
T-AGOS 22	Loyal	McDermott	7 Oct 1991	19 Sep 1992	1 Jul 1993

Displacement	2,676 tons; 3,438 f/l
Dimensions	234′6″ (oa); 190′8″ (wl) × 93′6″ × 25′
Machinery	2 screws, diesel-electric, 3,200 SHP, 16 knots
Endurance	3,000/10
Complement	37
Armament	none

Notes: SWATH design. SURTASS.

Service Records:

AGOS 19 *Victorious*   MSC.
AGOS 20 *Able*   MSC. OS 8 Jul 2003.
AGOS 21 *Effective*   MSC.
AGOS 22 *Loyal*   MSC.

No.	Name	Builder	Keel Laid	Launched	In service
T-AGOS 23	Impeccable	Halter	17 Dec 1993	28 Apr 1998	20 Mar 2001
AGOS 24	Integrity	Tampa	—	—	—

Displacement	5,362 f/l
Dimensions	281′6″ (oa); 232′ (wl) × 95′9″ × 26′
Machinery	2 screws; diesel-electric; 5,000 SHP; 12 knots
Endurance	8,000/15
Complement	56
Armament	none

Notes: SWATH design. *Impeccable* originally ordered from American SB, Tampa; hull transferred for completion by Halter. Four were planned.

Service Records:

AGOS 23 *Impeccable*   MCS.
AGOS 24 *Integrity*   canceled 1 Nov 1991.

GUNBOAT SUPPORT SHIPS / PATROL CRAFT TENDERS

AGP 786	*Garnett County*	25 Sep 1970
AGP 821	*Harnett County*	25 Sep 1970
AGP 838	*Hunterdon County*	25 Sep 1970
AGP 1176	*Graham County*	1 Aug 1972

Notes: Converted LSTs.

RADAR PICKET SHIPS

No.	Name	Builder	Launched	Acquired/Comm.
AGR 1	Guardian ex-YAG 41 ex-*James G. Squires*	Jones; P.C.	8 May 1945	1 Feb 1955
AGR 2	Lookout ex-YAG 42 ex-*Claude Kitchin*	Jones; P.C.	24 May 1945	5 Mar 1955
AGR 3	Skywatcher ex-YAG 43 ex-*Rafael R. Rivera*	Jones; P.C.	16 Jan 1945	29 Mar 1955
AGR 4	Searcher ex-YAG 44 ex-*James W. Wheeler*	Jones; P.C.	23 Jan 1945	2 Apr 1955
AGR 5	Scanner ex-*Edwin D. Howard*	Jones; P.C.	27 Feb 1945	30 Jan 1956
AGR 6	Locator ex-*Frank O. Peterson*	Jones; P.C.	23 Mar 1945	21 Jan 1956
AGR 7	Picket ex-*James F. Harrell*	Jones; P.C.	17 May 1945	8 Feb 1956
AGR 8	Interceptor ex-*Edward W. Burton*	Jones; P.C.	12 Sep 1945	15 Feb 1956
AGR 9	Investigator ex-*Charles A. Draper*	Jones; P.C.	9 Jan 1945	16 Jan 1957
AGR 10	Outpost ex-*Francis J. O'Gara*	Jones; P.C.	8 Jun 1945	6 Feb 1957
AGR 11	Protector ex-*Warren P. Marks*	Jones; P.C.	15 Mar 1945	20 Feb 1957
AGR 12	Vigil ex-*Raymond Van Brogan*	Jones; P.C.	27 Jan 1945	5 Mar 1957
AGR 13	Interdictor ex-*Edwin H. Duff*	Jones; P.C.	29 Jun 1945	7 Apr 1958
AGR 14	Interpreter ex-*Dudley H. Thomas*	Jones; P.C.	8 Feb 1945	29 Sep 1958
AGR 15	Interrupter ex-*William J. Riddle*	Jones; P.C.	31 Jan 1945	16 Oct 1958
AGR 16	Watchman ex-*Vernon S. Hood*	Jones; P.C.	20 Feb 1945	12 Jan 1959

Displacement	3,600 tons; 11,365 f/l
Dimensions	441′6″ (oa); 417′ (wl) × 56′11″ × 23′
Machinery	2 screw; VTE; 2,500 hp; 11 knots
Complement	151
Armament	2–3″/50 guns

Notes: Type EC2-S-C1. ex-YAGR (27 Sep 1958). Designed to patrol ocean approaches to United States. Large radar mast mounted aft.

Service Records:

AGR 1   *Guardian*   Decomm 28 Jul 1965. Stricken 1 Sep 1965. BU 1971 Bilbao.
   ◆Cuba Jun–Jul 1961.
AGR 2   *Lookout*   Decomm 12 Jul 1965. Stricken 1 Sep 1965. BU 1970 Bilbao.
   ◆Cuba Jun–Aug 1961.
AGR 3   *Skywatcher*   Decomm 29 Mar 1965. Stricken 1 Apr 1965, BU 1971 Santander, Spain.
   ◆Cuba May–Oct 1961.

Figure 10.51: *USS Interdictor* (AGR 13), 1959. She was one of 16 Liberty Ships converted to radar picket ships to patrol off the U.S. coast.

AGR 4   *Searcher*   Damaged by fire at sea 125 miles southeast of New York, 13 Nov 1955 (1 killed). Decomm and stricken 1 Jul 1965, BU 1970.
◆Cuba Apr–May 1961.
AGR 5   *Scanner*   Decomm 21 Jul 1965. Stricken 1 Sep 1965, BU 1974.
AGR 6   *Locator*   Decomm 9 Aug 1965. Stricken 1 Sep 1965, BU 1974 Portland, Ore.
AGR 7   *Picket*   Stricken 1 Sep 1965. BU 1978 Richmond, Cal.
AGR 8   *Interceptor*   Decomm 7 Jun 1965. Stricken 1 Sep 1965. BU 1978.
AGR 9   *Investigator*   Decomm 29 Mar 1965. Stricken 1 Apr 1965. BU 1971 Santander, Spain.
◆Cuba Aug–Oct 1961.
AGR 10 *Outpost*   Decomm 1 Jul 1965. Stricken 1 Sep 1965. BU 1970 Bilbao.
◆Cuba Aug–Nov 1961, Jul–Oct 1962.
AGR 11 *Protector*   Decomm 28 Jul 1965. Stricken 1 Sep 1965. NDRF. BU 2004 Brownsville.
◆Cuba Apr–May 1961.
AGR 12 *Vigil*   Decomm 3 Mar 1965. Stricken 1 Apr 1965. BU 1970 Bilbao, Spain.
◆Cuba Jul–Aug 1961.
AGR 13 *Interdictor*   Decomm 5 Aug 1965. Stricken 1 Sep 1965. BU 1974 Portland, Ore.
AGR 14 *Interpreter*   Decomm and stricken 1 Jul 1965. BU 1974.
AGR 15 *Interrupter*   Renamed **Tracer** 4 Sep 1959. Decomm Jul 1965. Stricken 1 Sep 1965.
Later history: converted to fish factory, renamed *Unisea*. BU 2000 China.
AGR 16 *Watchman*   Decomm and stricken 1 Sep 1965. BU 1974 Portland, Ore.

SURVEYING SHIPS

Surveying Ships on the Navy List, 1947

AGS 7   *Littlehales*   Formerly PCS 1388. Decomm 12 Oct 1949. Sold 24 Jan 1950.
Later history: merchant *John O*.
AGS 8   *Dutton*   Formerly PCS 1396. Rec **AGSc 8**, 27 Jul 1946. Decomm 26 Aug 1949. Sold 21 Feb 1950.
AGS 9   *Armistead Rust*   Formerly PCS 1404. Decomm 9 Jun 1946. Stricken 21 Oct 1948. Sold 28 Oct 1948.
AGS 10 *John Blish*   Formerly PCS 1457. Rec **AGSc 10**, 27 Jul 1946. Decomm 26 Aug 1949. Sold 10 Feb 1950, BU Baltimore.
AGS 12 *Harkness*   Formerly YMS 242. Rec **AGSc 12**, 27 Jul 1946. Out of comm 22 Sep 1950–5 Sep 1951. Rec **AMCU 12**, 18 Aug 1951, conv to minehunter. Rec **MHC 12**, 7 Feb 1955. Decomm 2 Apr 1958. Stricken 1 Nov 1959. Sold 1960.
AGS 13 *James M. Gilliss*   Formerly YMS 262. Rec **AGSc 13**, 27 Jul 1946. Out of comm 22 Sep 1950–5 Sep 1951. Rec **AMCU 13**, 18 Aug 1951, conv to minehunter. Rec **MHC 13** 1 Feb 1955. Decomm 6 Aug 1958. Stricken 1 Jan 1960. Sold 17 Jun 1960.
AGSc 14 *Simon Newcomb*   Formerly YMS 263. Rec **AGSc 14**, 27 Jul 1946. Ran aground at Mother Burns Cove, Labrador, 9 Aug 1949. Decomm 10 Nov 1949. Stricken 31 Jan 1950. Sold 25 Apr 1950, BU.
AGSc 15 *Littlehales*   Formerly YF 854. 14 Feb 1959. Stricken 20 Feb 1968. Sunk as target 3 Apr 1969.
AGS 15 *Tanner*   Formerly AKA 34, *Pamina*. Decomm 14 Jul 1969. Stricken 1 Aug 1969. BU 1970 Portland, Ore
2★Vietnam Oct–Dec 1967, Feb–Mar 1968.
AGS 16 *Maury*   Formerly AKA 36, *Renate*. Decomm and stricken 19 Dec 1969. BU 1973 Terminal I.
5★Vietnam Apr 1960, Nov 1960–May 1961, Oct 1961–May 1962, Oct 1962–Apr 1963, Dec 1965–Jun 1966, Mar–Aug 1967, Apr–Sep 1968;
◆Quemoy-Matsu 11–13 May 1962, Korea Aug–Sep 1969.

Note: *Tanner* and *Maury* converted from attack cargo ships in 1946.

Figure 10.52: *USS Maury* (AGS 16), former attack cargo ship *Renate*, converted in 1946.

Figure 10.53: *USS Prevail* (AGS 20), a former minesweeper used as a surveying ship.

Figure 10.54: *USS Rehoboth* (AGS 50), former seaplane tender used as a surveying ship, Jul 1954.

AGS 17 *Pursuit*   Formerly AM 108. 18 Aug 1952. Decomm 30 Jun 1960. Stricken 1 Jul 1960.
AGS 18 *Requisite* Formerly AM 109. 8 Aug 1952. Out of comm 23 Dec 1947–15 Feb 1950. Decomm 23 Dec 1968. Stricken 1 Apr 1964.
AGS 19 *Sheldrake* Formerly AM 62. 1 Apr 1952. Out of comm 31 May 1946–14 Apr 1953. Decomm 1 Aug 1968.
AGS 20 *Prevail*   Formerly AM 107. 1 Apr 1952. Out of comm 31 May 1946–1 Apr 1952. Decomm 10 Jan 1964.
AGS 30 *San Pablo* Formerly AVP 30. 25 Aug 1949. Stricken 1 Jun 1969. BU.
AGS 50 *Rehoboth*   Formerly AVP 50. 2 Sep 1948. Stricken 15 Apr 1970. BU.
AGS 24 *Serrano*   Formerly ATF 112. 15 Jun 1960 Out of comm 31 May 1950–30 Jun 1960. Decomm 2 Jan 1970.
AGS 28 *Towhee*   Formerly MSF 388. 1 Apr 1964 Out of comm Mar 1954–1 Apr 1964. Decomm 30 Apr 1969. Stricken 1 May 1969.
AGS 35 *Sgt. George D. Keathley* Formerly APC 117. 1 Dec 1967 OS Dec 1971.
AGS 36 *Coastal Crusader* AGM 16 conversion canceled.
AGS 37 *Twin Falls* Formerly AGM 11 conversion canceled.
AGS 41–44   not used
AGS 46–49   not used
AGS 53–59   not used

No.	Name	Builder	Launched	Acquired	In service
AGS 21	*Bowditch* ex-*South Bend Victory*	Oregon	30 Jun 1945	2 Aug 1957	12 Sep 1958
AGS 22	*Dutton* ex-*Tuskegee Victory*	Oregon	8 May 1945	2 Nov 1957	15 Oct 1958
AGS 23	*Michelson* ex-*Joliet Victory*	Oregon	14 Jun 1944	8 Feb 1958	15 Dec 1958

Displacement	7,190 tons; 13,050 f/l
Dimensions	455′3″ (oa); 436′ (wl) × 62′ × 28′6″
Machinery	1 screw; ST; 2 boilers; 8,500 SHP; 15 knots
Complement	100
Armament	none

Notes: Type VC2-S-AP3. MSTS. Conducted surveys to support FBM program.

Service Records:

AGS 21 *Bowditch* Irreparably damaged in hurricane at Rio de Janeiro, Jan 1987. Stricken 26 May 1987. BU 1987 Kaohsiung.
AGS 22 *Dutton*   Decomm 1 Sep 1989. Stricken 14 Feb 1990, NDRF. BU 2007, Brownsville.
AGS 23 *Michelson* Stricken 15 Apr 1975. Sold 22 Sep 1977. BU.

No.	Name	Builder	Keel Laid	Launched	In service
AGS 25	*Kellar*	Marietta	20 Nov 1962	30 Jul 1964	5 Feb 1969
AGS 31	*S.P. Lee*	Defoe	27 Jun 1966	19 Oct 1967	12 Dec 1968

Displacement	1,200 tons
Dimensions	209′ (oa) 191′6″ (wl) × 39′ × 15′
Machinery	1 screw, diesel, 2,000 hp, 17 knots
Endurance	12,000/12
Complement	34

Notes: MSC. Same design as *Conrad* class AGORs.

Service Records:

AGS 25 *Kellar* Capsized in hurricane before completion at New Orleans, 9 Sep 1965. Trfd to Portugal 21 Jan 1972.
  Later history: renamed *Almeida Carvalho* (A 527). R2002.
AGS 31 *S. P. Lee* Rec **AG 192**, 25 Sep 1970. Loan to U.S. Geological Survey, Feb 1974. Returned 1 Aug 1992, OS. Stricken 1 Oct 1992. Trfd to Mexico 7 Dec 1992.
  Later history: renamed *Antares* (H 06). SE2001.

Figure 10.55: *USNS Dutton* (T-AGS 22), one of three Victory Ships converted to Surveying Ships.

Figure 10.56: *USNS S.P. Lee* (T-AG 192), at Malta, 23 Oct 1970. (Pavia)

No.	Name	Builder	Keel Laid	Launched	In Service
T-AGS 26	*Silas Bent*	Amer; Lorain	2 Mar 1964	16 May 1964	20 Mar 1966
T-AGS 27	*Kane*	Christy	19 Dec 1964	20 Nov 1965	19 May 1967
T-AGS 33	*Wilkes*	Defoe	18 Jul 1968	31 Jul 1969	28 Jun 1971
T-AGS 34	*Wyman*	Defoe	18 Jul 1968	30 Oct 1969	3 Nov 1971

Displacement	1,935 tons; 2,558 f/l
Dimensions	285′3″(oa); 261′4″ (bp) × 48′ × 15′
Machinery	1 screw; diesel–electric; 3,600 BHP; 14 knots
Endurance	6,300/14
Complement	79
Armament	none

Notes: MSC. Differ in appearance.

Service Records:

AGS 26 *Silas Bent* Stricken 28 Oct 1999. Trfd to Turkey 29 Sep 1999.
  Later history: renamed *Çesme* (A 599). SE2001.
AGS 27 *Kane* OS 31 Mar 2001. Trfd to Turkey 14 Mar 2001.
  Later history: renamed *Çanadarli* (A 580). SE2007.
  ★Indian Ocean Jul–Sep 1998, Feb–May 2000.
AGS 33 *Wilkes* Trfd to Tunisia 29 Aug 1995.
  Later history: renamed *Kheireddine*.
AGS 34 *Wyman* OS 10 Mar 1997. Stricken 3 May 1999, NDRF. SE.

Figure 10.57: *USNS Wyman* (T-AGS 34), Surveying Ship.

Figure 10.58: *USNS Harkness* (T-AGS 32), surveying ship, built in England 1971.

No.	Name	Builder	Keel Laid	Launched	In service
T-AGS 29	*Chauvenet*	Fairfield	24 May 1967	13 May 1968	13 Nov 1970
T-AGS 32	*Harkness*	Fairfield	30 Jun 1967	12 Jun 1968	29 Jan 1971
Displacement		3,040 tons; 4,200 f/l			
Dimensions		393′2″ (oa) × 54′ × 16′			
Machinery		1 screw; diesel; 3,600 BHP; 15 knots			
Endurance		12,000/15			
Complement		177			
Armament		none			

Notes: MSC. Largest ships to be built for research. Built in British yard. Helicopter deck and hangar.

Service Records:

AGS 29 *Chauvenet*   OS, 7 Nov 1992.
  Later service: To Texas Maritime Academy 29 May 1996, renamed *Texas Clipper II*. NDRF. Rtnd 2005 and trfd to Missile Defense Agency, renamed *Pacific Collector*. Converted to AGM type, 2006. NDRF. SE.
  ◆Gulf War Sep 1990–Jul 1992.

AGS 32 *Harkness*   OS 15 Mar 1993, NDRF. Tfrd to Maine Maritime Academy.
  Later service: merchant *State of Maine*. Reacq as non-operational TS at NY State Maritime Academy, 8 Jan 2001, then Mass. Maritime Academy, 28 Feb 2001. NDRF. SE.
  ◆Gulf War Feb 1991–Nov 1992.

No.	Name	Builder	Launched	Acquired	In service
T-AGS 38	*H.H. Hess* ex-*Canada Mail*	Natl Steel	30 May 1964	9 Jul 1976	16 Jan 1978
Displacement		13,520 tons; 17,874 f/l			
Dimensions		563′6″(oa) × 76′ × 31′6″			
Machinery		1 screw; ST; 2 boilers; 19,250 SHP; 20 knots			
Endurance		14,000/20			
Complement		48			

Notes: Type C4-S-1a. Unarmed. MCS. Converted by National Steel.

Service Record: OS 5 Feb 1992. Stricken 28 Jul 1992. Was to be trfd to California Maritime Academy, Vallejo, renamed *Golden Bear*. NDRF. SE.

No.	Name	Builder	Keel Laid	Launched	In Service
T-AGS 39	*Maury*	Sparrows Pt	29 Jul 1986	4 Sep 1987	31 Mar 1989
T-AGS 40	*Tanner*	Sparrows Pt	22 Oct 1986	28 Feb 1989	31 Aug 1990
Displacement		8,810 tons; 15,821 f/l			
Dimensions		449′10″(oa) × 72′ × 30′6″			
Machinery		1 screw; diesels; 25,000 BHP; 21 knots			
Endurance		18,000/20			
Complement		104			
Armament		none			

Notes: *Tanner* suffered from major engineering problems.

Service Records:

AGS 39 *Maury*   OS, to California Maritime Academy, 25 Oct 1994. Stricken 1 Oct 1994.
  Later history: To California Maritime Academy 4 May 1996, renamed *Golden Bear*. To RRF 15 Apr 1999. NDRF. SE.

AGS 40 *Tanner*   OS Stricken 1 Oct 1993. To State of Maine, 6 Oct 1997
  Later history: renamed *State of Maine*. NDRF. SE.

No.	Name	Builder	Keel Laid	Launched	In Service
T-AGS 45	*Waters*	Avondale	21 May 1991	6 Jun 1992	26 May 1993
Displacement		12,208 tons f/l			
Dimensions		442′ (oa) × 69′ × 21′2″			
Machinery		2 screws; diesel-electric; SHP 7,400; 13.2 knots			
Complement		89			

Notes Built to replace *Mizar*. Large multifunctional AGS. MCS.

No.	Name	Builder	Keel Laid	Launched	In service
T-AGS 51	*John McDonnell*	Halter	3 Aug 1989	13 Dec 1990	15 Nov 1991
T-AGS 52	*Littlehales*	Halter	25 Oct 1989	14 Feb 1991	10 Jan 1992
Displacement		1,394 tons; 2,238 tons f/l			
Dimensions		208′2″(oa); 190′ (wl) × 45′ × 14′			
Machinery		1 screw; diesel; 16 knots			
Endurance		13,800/16			
Complement		33			

Notes: Coastal survey ships. MCS.

Service Records:

AGS 51 *John McDonnell*
  ◆Gulf War Sep–Nov 1992, Indian Ocean Apr–Jun 1998, May–Jul 2000; Tsunami relief 2005.

AGS 52 *Littlehales*   OS and stricken 27 Feb 2003, to NOAA, 8 Jul 2003.
  Later history: renamed *Thomas Jefferson*.
  ◆Indian Ocean May–Jul 2000.

Figure 10.59: USNS *Pathfinder* (T-AGS 60), 1995. One of six large surveying ships built in the 1990s.

No.	Name	Builder	Keel Laid	Launched	Comm./IS
T-AGS 60	*Pathfinder*	Halter	18 Aug 1992	7 Oct 1993	28 Oct 1994
T-AGS 61	*Sumner*	Halter	18 Nov 1992	19 May 1994	30 May 1995
T-AGS 62	*Bowditch*	Halter	16 Jun 1993	15 Oct 1994	19 Jun 1996
T-AGS 63	*Henson*	Halter	13 Oct 1995	21 Oct 1996	20 Feb 1998
T-AGS 64	*Bruce C. Heezen*	Halter	19 Aug 1997	25 Mar 1999	13 Jan 2000
T-AGS 65	*Mary Sears*	Halter	28 Jul 1999	19 Oct 2000	17 Dec 2001

Displacement	3,019 tons; 4,762 f/l; 2,800 lt; 5,100 f/l
Dimensions	328′ (oa) × 58′ × 19′
Machinery	2 screws; diesel-electric; SHP 8,000; 16 knots
Endurance	12,000/12
Complement	55

Notes: Long range ocean survey and research vessels. MSC.

Service Records:
AGS 60 *Pathfinder*
AGS 61 *Sumner*
AGS 62 *Bowditch*
 ◆Indian Ocean Jul–Sep 1998.
AGS 63 *Henson*
AGS 64 *Bruce C. Heezen*
AGS 65 *Mary Sears*
 ◆Tsunami relief 2005.

OCEANOGRAPHIC RESEARCH SHIPS

AGOR 1 *Josiah Willard Gibbs*   Formerly AVP 51. 15 Dec 1958. Stricken 15 Feb 1977. Trfd to Greece.
AGOR 2   15 Jun 1960. OSP for Norway, named *H.U. Sverdrup*.

No.	Name	Builder	Keel Laid	Launched	In service
AGOR 3	*Robert D. Conrad*	Gibbs	19 Jan 1961	26 May 1962	29 Nov 1962
AGOR 4	*James M. Gilliss*	Christy	31 May 1961	19 May 1962	5 Nov 1962
AGOR 5	*Charles H. Davis*	Christy	15 Jun 1961	30 Jun 1962	25 Jan 1963
AGOR 6	*Sands*	Marietta	23 Aug 1962	14 Sep 1963	13 Nov 1964
AGOR 7	*Lynch*	Marietta	7 Sep 1962	17 Mar 1964	22 Oct 1965
AGOR 9	*Thomas G. Thompson*	Marinette	12 Sep 1963	18 Jul 1964	4 Sep 1965
AGOR 10	*Thomas Washington*	Marinette	12 Sep 1963	1 Aug 1964	17 Sep 1965
AGOR 12	*De Steiguer*	Northwest	12 Nov 1965	21 Mar 1966	28 Feb 1969
AGOR 13	*Bartlett*	Northwest	18 Nov 1965	24 May 1966	15 Apr 1969

Displacement	1,200 tons; 1,380 f/l
Dimensions	208′10″(oa); 191′6″(wl) × 39′ × 15′2″
Machinery	1 screw; diesel-electric; 10,000 BHP; 13.5 knots
Endurance	12,000/9
Complement	47

Notes: Operated by scientific institutions. Civilian manned. Vary in detail with different bridge, mast, and side structure arrangements.

Figure 10.60: USNS *Sands* (T-AGOR 6), oceanographic research ship.

Service Records:
AGOR 3 *Robert D. Conrad*   Lamont Geological Observatory, Columbia University. OS.26 Jul 1989. Stricken 4 Oct 1989, NDRF. BU 2004, Chesapeake, Va.
AGOR 4 *James M. Gilliss*   University of Miami. Trfd to Mexico 15 Jun 1983.
 Later history: renamed *Altair* (H 05). SE2001.
AGOR 5 *Charles H. Davis*   Trfd to New Zealand 10 Aug 1970.
 Later history: renamed *Tui* (A 05). Returned 27 Aug 1998. Scuttled as artificial reef off Tutukaka, New Zealand, 20 Feb 1999.
AGOR 6 *Sands*   OS 1973. Trfd to Brazil 1 Jul 1974.
 Later history: renamed *Almirante Câmara* (H 41). SE2001.
AGOR 7 *Lynch*   OS 24 Sep 1991. Stricken 6 Nov 1991. NDRF. Sold 4 Jun 2001, BU Brownsville.
AGOR 9 *Thomas G. Thompson*   University of Washington. Rec **IX 517**, unnamed 11 Dec 1989. Renamed *Pacific Escort*, 1989, then *Gosport*, 1995. Stricken 27 Feb 2004. Sunk as target in NATO exercise, 14 Nov 2004.
AGOR 10 *Thomas Washington*   Scripps Institute. OS and stricken 1 Aug 1992. Trfd to Chile 28 Sep 1992.
 Later history: renamed *Vidal Gormaz* (AGOR 60). SE2001.
AGOR 12 *De Steiguer*   OS Stricken. Trfd to Tunisia 2 Nov 1992.
 Later history: renamed *Salammbo* (701).
AGOR 13 *Bartlett*   OS. Trfd to Morocco 26 Jul 1993.
 Later history: renamed *Abou el Barakat al Barbari* (702). SE2001.

AGOR 8 *Eltanin*   Formerly AK 270. 15 Nov 1962.
AGOR 11 *Mizar*   Formerly AK 272. 15 Apr 1964.
AGOR 17 *Chain*   Formerly ARS 20. 1 Apr 1967. Woods Hole Oceanographic Inst.
AGOR 18 *Argo*   Formerly ARS 27. 1 Apr 1967.

Figure 10.61: *USNS Knorr* (T-AGOR 15), Nov 1969, as built. Operated by Woods Hole Oceanographic Institute.

No.	Name	Builder	Keel Laid	Launched	In service
AGOR 14	*Melville*	Defoe	12 Jul 1967	10 Jul 1968	27 Aug 1969
AGOR 15	*Knorr*	Defoe	9 Aug 1967	21 Aug 1968	14 Jan 1970
AGOR 19/20	—	—	—	—	—

Displacement	1,915 tons; 2,670 f/l
Dimensions	279' (oa); 244'9" (wl) × 46'4" × 15'
Machinery	3 cycloidal propellers (1 forward); diesel-electric; 2,500 BHP; 12.5 knots
Endurance	10,000/10
Complement	58
Armament	none

Notes: Operated by research institutions. Improved *Conrad* class. Differ in appearance. Re-engined 1988–91.

Service Records:

AGOR 14 *Melville*   To Scripps Institution of Oceanography.
AGOR 15 *Knorr*   To Woods Hole Oceanographic Institute.
AGOR 19/20   canceled Feb 1969.

No.	Name	Builder	Keel Laid	Launched	In Service
T-AGOR 16	*Hayes* ex-*Hudson*	Todd; Seattle	12 Nov 1969	2 Jul 1970	21 Jul 1971

Displacement	2,329 tons; 3,080 f/l (as AG) 3,453 tons; 4,037 f/l
Dimensions	246'10"(oa); 220' (wl) × 75' × 22'4"
Machinery	2 screws; geared diesel-electric; 5,400 BHP; 15 knots
Endurance	6,000/14
Complement	74/49
Armament	none

Notes: Catamaran design to provide greater open-deck work area, each hull 24' beam. MSC. Converted to acoustic research ship 1987–90.

Service Record: Laid up 1983. Rec **T-AG 195**, 20 Mar 1989, in service MSC, 19 Jun 1992.

No.	Name	Builder	Keel Laid	Launched	In Service
AGOR 21	*Gyre*	Halter	9 Oct 1972	25 May 1973	14 Nov 1973
AGOR 22	*Moana Wave*	Halter	10 Oct 1972	23 Jun 1973	16 Jan 1974

Displacement	950 tons f/l
Dimensions	176'(oa) × 36' × 14'6"; *1984*: 22: 204'2"(oa)
Machinery	2 screws; turbo diesels; 1,700 BHP; 13 knots
Endurance	8,000/10
Complement	21
Armament	none

Notes: Operated by research institutions. *Moana Wave* modified to test SURTASS, 1980, lengthened 1984.

Service Records:

AGOR 21 *Gyre*   Texas A&M University. Stricken 17 Aug 1992.
     Later service: merchant *Gyre*.
AGOR 22 *Moana Wave*   Leased to Univ of Hawaii. 1 Jul 1994–30 May 1999. Stricken 30 May 1999.

No.	Name	Builder	Keel Laid	Launched	In Service
AGOR 23	*Thomas G. Thompson* ex-*Ewing*	Halter	23 Mar 1989	27 Jul 1990	8 Jul 1991
AGOR 24	*Roger Revelle* ex-*Revelle*	Halter	9 Dec 1993	20 Apr 1995	11 Jun 1996
AGOR 25	*Atlantis*	Halter	16 Aug 1994	1 Feb 1996	3 Mar 1997

Displacement	2,155 tons; 3,250 f/l
Dimensions	274' (oa); 243' (wl) × 53' × 19'
Machinery	2 screws; diesel-electric; 6,000 HP; 15 knots
Endurance	11,300/12
Complement	60

Notes: A fourth ship, the original AGOR 26, was built for NOAA as *Ronald H. Brown*. *Atlantis* was converted in 1997 to serve as support ship for DSRV *Alvin*.

Service Record:

AGOR 23 *Thomas G. Thompson*   Operated by Univ of Washington, 8 Jul 1991.
AGOR 24 *Roger Revelle*   Operated by Scripps Institution of Oceanography, 11 Jun 1996.
AGOR 25 *Atlantis*   Operated by Woods Hole Oceanographic Institute.

No.	Name	Builder	Keel Laid	Launched	In Service
AGOR 26	*Kilo Moana*	Halter	9 Feb 2001	17 Nov 2001	Oct 2002

Displacement	2,542 tons f/l
Dimensions	186'(oa); 172' (wl) × 88' × 25'
Machinery	2 screws; diesel-electric; 4,880 HP; 15 knots
Endurance	10,000/11
Complement	48

Notes: SWATH design. Operated by School of Ocean & Earth Science, Hawaii.

DEGAUSSING VESSELS

No.	Name	Former	Fate
ADG 8	*Lodestone*	PCE 876	Stricken 21 Feb 1975. Sold 13 Apr 1976, BU Terminal I.
ADG 9	*Magnet*	PCE 879	Stricken 21 Feb 1975. Sunk as target off California, 4 Mar 1976.
ADG 10	*Deperm*	PCE 883	Stricken 21 Feb 1975. Sunk as target, 22 Sep 1982.
ADG 11	*Ampere*	AM 359	Stricken 1 Jul 1961. Sold 21 Jun 1962.
ADG 383	*Surfbird*	MSF 383	Stricken 21 Feb 1975.

Note: ADG 8–11 named 1 Feb 1955. ADG 11: 3★Korea K-8 K-9 K-10.

Figure 10.62: USS *Surfbird* (ADG 383), a former minesweeper converted to degaussing vessel.

Figure 10.63: USS *Catalpa* (AN 10), *Aloe* class net layer.

NET LAYING SHIPS

AN rec ANL, 1 Jan 1969.

Aloe Class

AN 6	*Aloe*	Decomm 3 Aug 1946. Stricken 1 Sep 1962. Sold 14 May 1971, BU.
AN 7	*Ash*	Decomm 13 Dec 1946. Stricken 1 Sep 1962. Sold 14 May 1971, BU.
AN 8	*Boxwood*	Decomm 13 Nov 1946. Stricken 1 Sep 1962.
AN 9	*Butternut*	Stricken 18 Jul 1969. Reacq as **YAG 60**, 28 Oct 1969. Stricken 1 Jul 1971. Training hulk at Pearl Harbor. Destroyed as target, 1977.
		★Korea 1951.
AN 10	*Catalpa*	Out of comm 21 Oct 1946–7 Aug 1950. Decomm 7 Oct 1955. Stricken 1 Sep 1962. BU 1974.
		★Korea 1953.
AN 11	*Chestnut*	Decomm 7 Sep 1946. Stricken 1 Sep 1962.
AN 12	*Cinchona*	Decomm 6 Nov 1946. Stricken 1 Sep 1962.
AN 13	*Buckeye*	Decomm 4 Mar 1947. Stricken 1 Jul 1963. Salvage training hulk 1976.
AN 14	*Buckthorn*	Decomm 20 Aug 1947. Stricken 1 Jul 1963.
AN 15	*Ebony*	Decomm 23 Mar 1946. Stricken 1 Sep 1962. Sold 22 Jan 1976.
AN 16	*Eucalyptus*	Decomm 6 Mar 1946. Stricken 1 Sep 1962.
AN 19	*Holly*	Decomm 7 Jun 1946. Stricken 1 Sep 1962. Sold 10 Aug 1971.
AN 20	*Elder*	Damaged by fire at sea north of Kwajalein, 11 Mar 1950. Decomm 18 Dec 1959. Stricken 1 Sep 1962. ★Korea 1951.
AN 22	*Locust*	Decomm 8 Jul 1946. Stricken 1 Sep 1962. Trfd to France 24 Feb 1966.
		Later history: renamed *Locuste* (A 765). Sank after hitting reef in Fiji Islands, 30 Jul 1978.
AN 24	*Mango*	Decomm 4 Apr 1947. Stricken 1 Sep 1962. Sold 1976.
AN 26	*Mimosa*	Decomm 27 Sep 1946. Stricken 1 Sep 1962. Sold 10 Aug 1971.
AN 27	*Mulberry*	Decomm 11 Apr 1960. Stricken 1 Jul 1963. Trfd to Ecuador Nov 1965.
		Later history: renamed *Orion* (101). BU 1980.
		1★Korea K-10, 1952, 1953.
AN 28	*Palm*	Decomm 1 Jan 1947. Stricken 1 Sep 1962. Sold 22 Jun 1971.
AN 29	*Hazel*	Decomm 11 Feb 1958. Stricken 1 Sep 1962. Sold 23 Jan 1974, BU 1974 Baltimore.
AN 30	*Redwood*	Decomm 6 Jun 1947. Stricken 1 Sep 1962.
AN 31	*Rosewood*	Decomm 10 Jun 1946. Stricken 1 Sep 1962. Trfd to France 15 Jan 1969.
		Later history: renamed *Libellule*. R1981.
AN 32	*Sandalwood*	Decomm 13 Aug 1946. Stricken 1 Sep 1962. Trfd to France 6 Sep 1967.
		Later history: renamed *Luciole* (A 777). R 1981.
AN 33	*Nutmeg*	Decomm Jan 1947. Stricken 1 Sep 1962.
AN 34	*Teaberry*	Out of comm 19 Dec 1946–19 Apr 1952. Decomm 7 Jul 1961. Stricken 1 Aug 1961. Sold 12 Jan 1962.
		Later history: Merchant *Pacific Salvor*. BU 1975.
AN 35	*Teak*	Decomm 30 Aug 1946. Stricken 1 Sep 1962. Sold 16 Mar 1976, BU.

Cohoes Class

AN 78	*Cohoes*	Decomm 3 Sep 1947. Stricken 1 Jul 1963. Reacq May 1967. Rec **ANL 78**, 1 Jan 1969. Stricken 30 Jun 1972. Sold 1 Feb 1973.
		Later history: Merchant *Glacier*.
		9★Vietnam Jul 1968–Mar 1970, Sep–Nov 1970, Feb 1971–Apr 1972.
AN 79	*Etlah*	Out of comm 14 Mar 1947–10 Aug 1951. Decomm 31 May 1960. Stricken 1 Jul 1963. Trfd to Dominican Republic 29 Sep 1976.

Figure 10.64: Net laying ship USS *Cohoes* (ANL 78), recommissioned in 1967.

Later history: renamed *Cambiaso* (P 207). R1994.
★Korea 1952, 1953.

AN 80 *Suncook* Decomm 12 Jun 1947. Stricken 1 Sep 1962, to Bureau of Mines.
Later history: Merchant *Grass Valley*. Returned 18 Jun 1968. Sold 28 Jul 1971, BU.

AN 81 *Manayunk* Decomm 19 Jul 1946. Stricken 1 Sep 1962. Sold 8 Dec 1971.
Later history: Merchant *Heron* 1973. SE1998.

AN 82 *Marietta* Out of comm 19 Mar 1947–14 Feb 1952. Decomm 21 Dec 1959. Trfd to Venezuela 23 Feb 1962.
Later history: renamed *Puerto Santo* (H01/H11). SE1987.

AN 83 *Nahant* Out of comm 31 Jul 1946–14 Feb 1952. Decomm 30 Sep 1968. Stricken 1 Oct 1968. Trfd to Uruguay 15 Oct 1968.
Later history: renamed *Huracán* (BT30/AM25). SE1987.

AN 84 *Naubuc* Decomm 6 Sep 1946. Stricken 1 Sep 1962. Reacq 1 Sep 1967. Rec **YRST 4**, 1 Apr 1968. Stricken 1 Feb 1975. Sold 1975, BU.

AN 85 *Oneota* Decomm 6 Feb 1947. Stricken 1 Jul 1963.

AN 86 *Passaconaway* Decomm . . Dec 1946. Stricken 1 Jul 1963. Trfd to Dominican Republic 29 Sep 1976.
Later history: renamed *Separación* (P 208). SE2001.

AN 87 *Passaic* Decomm . . Mar 1947. Stricken 1 Jul 1963. Trfd to Dominican Republic 29 Sep 1976.
Later history: renamed *Calderas* (P 209). SE2001.

AN 88 *Shakamaxon* Decomm 21 Apr 1947. Stricken 1 Jul 1963. Trfd to Dept of Interior, (Micronesia), 8 Nov 1968.
Later history: Merchant *Hafa Adai*. Foundered at Palau, 21 Dec 1981.

AN 89 *Tonawanda* Out of comm 9 Aug 1946–18 Mar 1952. Decomm 18 Dec 1959. Trfd to Haiti 13 May 1960.
Later history: renamed *Jean Jacques Dessalines*.

AN 90 *Tunxis* Out of comm 30 Jun 1945–20 Feb 1953. Decomm 20 Jul 1955. Trfd to Venezuela 1 Aug 1963.
Later history: renamed *Puerto de Nutrias* (H 02). SE1972.

AN 91 *Waxsaw* Decomm 23 Mar 1960. Trfd to Venezuela 1 Aug 1963.
Later history: renamed *Puerto Miranda* (H 03). R1977.

AN 92 *Yazoo* Decomm 28 Aug 1962. Stricken 1 Jul 1963. BU 1975.

No.	Builder	Launched	Built for	Name	Fate
AN 93	Beth; Staten I.	May 1952	Netherlands	*Cerberus* (A 895)	Trfd to Turkey 17 Sep 1970
—	—	—	Turkey	*AG-6* (P 306)	SE2001
AN 94	Penhoët	21 Nov 1953	France	*Scarabée* (A 764)	R1987
AN 95	Penhoët	18 Feb 1954	France	*Grillon* (A 763)	R1987
AN 96	Seine Maritime	3 Jun 1954	France	*Criquet* (A 761)	R1987
AN 97	Seine Maritime	6 Jul 1954	France	*Fourmi* (A 762)	R1987
AN 98	Rochelle	23 Sep 1954	France	*Cigale* (A 760)	R1987
AN 99	Ansaldo	11 Jul 1954	Italy	*Alicudi* (A 5,304)	SE1987
AN 100	Ansaldo	26 Sep 1954	Italy	*Filicudi* (A 5,305)	SE1972
AN 101	Penhoët	28 Sep 1954	Spain	*CR-1*	—
AN 102	—	—	—	—	—
AN 103	Kroger	1959	Greece	*Thetis* (A 307)	SE2001
AN 104	Kroger	20 Oct 1960	Turkey	*AG-5* (P 305)	SE2001

UNCLASSIFIED VESSELS

Note: The numbers 236 to 299 and 312 to 500 were not used.

IX 15 *Prairie State* Stricken 26 Mar 1956. Sold 18 May 1956 and BU Baltimore.

IX 20 *Constellation* Sail frigate. Decomm 4 Feb 1955. Trfd to private ownership and preserved at Baltimore, Md.

[IX 21] *Constitution* Sail frigate. Preserved at Boston NSYd, Mass. IX designation withdrawn 1975.

IX 25 *Reina Mercedes* Old Spanish cruiser. Annapolis 1912–57. Stricken 6 Sep 1957. Sold, BU Baltimore.

IX 40 *Olympia* Old cruiser. Stricken 11 Sep 1957. Museum at Philadelphia.

IX 43 *Freedom* Stricken 1 Apr 1968.

IX 47 *Vamarie* Stricken 22 Jun 1955. BU Dec 1955.

IX 48 *Highland Light* Stricken 1 Apr 1965. Sold Mar 1966.

IX 49 *Spindrift* Stricken 22 Dec 1952.

IX 87 *Saluda* Rec **YAG 87**, 29 Jun 1968. Sold 15 Apr 1974.

IX 205 *Callao* Decomm 10 May 1950. Sold 30 Sep 1950, BU 1951.

IX 234 *Eastwind* former German yacht. Stricken 27 Oct 1949.

IX 235 *Royono* Stricken 1 Jul 1967. Sold 25 May 1968.

No.	Name	Former	Date	Fate
IX 302/303	—	not used	—	—
IX 304	*Atlanta*	CL 104	15 May 1964	Stricken 1 Apr 1970
IX 305	*Prowess*	MSF 280	1 Mar 1966	Stricken 3 Jun 1970
IX 306	—	FS 221	Jan 1966	Stricken 30 Nov 1988; sold 12 Oct 1989
	Torpedo trials ship			
IX 307	*Brier*	WLI 299	10 Mar 1969	Stricken 15 Aug 1982; sold 2 Jun 1983
	Instrumentation for testing explosives			
IX 308	*New Bedford*	AKL 17	Feb 1969	Stricken 4 Apr 1995; sold 11 Jun 1996
	Torpedo test ship			
IX 309	(Monob I)	YW 87	1969	Rec **YAG 61**, 1 Jul 1970, trfd to Mexico 2 Aug 1996, renamed *Rio Suchiate* (A 27); SE2001
	Mobile Noise Barge			
IX 310	(unnamed floating equipment)	—	1 Jun 1969	—
	undersea warfare center, acoustic research. 1,070 tons; 174′ × 33′			
IX 311	*Benewah*	APB 38	26 Feb 1971	—
IX 501	*Elk River*	LFR 50	11 Apr 1967	Stricken 13 Aug 1999; sunk as target 24 Feb 2001
	Test ship for deep-sea diving and salvage.			
IX 502	*Mercer*	APB 39	1 Nov 1975	Rec **APL 39**, 7 Mar 2001
IX 503	*Nueces*	APB 40	1 Nov 1975	Rec **APL 40**, 7 Mar 2001
IX 504	*Echols*	APB 37	1 Feb 1976	Stricken 22 Dec 1995; sold 12 Jun 2003
IX 505	—	YTM 759	1 Nov 1976	Stricken
IX 506	*Sea Lion*	YFU 82	1 Apr 1978	Stricken 21 Aug 1997
	Research platform, Long Beach, Cal.			

Tenders 193

No.	Name		Launched	
IX 507	Gen. Hugh J. Gaffey	AP 121	1 Nov 1978	Stricken 26 Oct 1993; sunk as target 16 Jun 2000

Stationary berthing ship, Bremerton.

IX 508	Orca	LCU 1618	1 Dec 1979	Stricken 19 Jun 2003; sold 2 Feb 2004
IX 509	(ex-underwater explosive barge no.1)	—	1 Dec 1979	Stricken 18 Dec 1992; BU 2006 Chesapeake, Va.
IX 510	(unnamed)	AP 127	1 Jul 1982	OS 23 Apr 1991; Stricken 26 Oct 1993; BU 2004 Brownsville
IX 511	—	LST 399	30 Sep 1982	Stricken 15 Jun 1985, sunk as target 15 Jun 1985
IX 512	—	BD 6651	1 Sep 1983	Stricken 13 Dec 1995; sold 16 May 1997

Trident missile-firing simulator test barge.

| IX 513 | — | (test barge) | — | Discarded 20 Nov 1997 |

EMPRESS II. Effects of electro-magnetic pulse on communications and weapons systems.

| IX 514 | Bay Lander | YFU 79 | 31 Mar 1986 | — |

Helicopter training craft.

| IX 515 | Sea Flyer | (SES 200) | 11 May 1987 | — |

ex-USCGC *Dorado* (WSES 1)
Converted to Lifting Body Research Ship 2000

| IX 516 | (barge) | — | 15 Apr 1988 | Sunk in hurricane at Charleston, Sep 1989; refloated |

Missile firing simulator

| IX 517 | Gosport | AGOR 9 | 11 Dec 1989 | OS 19 Jun 2003; Stricken 27 Feb 2004; sunk as target 14 Nov 2004 |
| IX 518 | (unnamed) | AS 19 | 1 Feb 1994 | Stricken 13 Mar 2001 |

Berthing and messing barge

| IX 519 | — | YC 1643 | — | Stricken 16 Feb 2002 |

Berthing and working space; welded to USS *LaSalle*

IX 520	—	APL 19	—	Stricken 13 Mar 2001; sunk as target 13 Jun 2002
IX 521	—	ABSD 1D	16 Aug 1996	Stricken 26 Apr 2006
IX 522	—	ABSD 2D	16 Aug 1996	—
IX 523	—	YOG 93	25 Nov 1996	Stricken 26 May 2005
IX 524	—	ABSD 2F	22 Jul 1997	—
IX 525	—	ABSD 1C	2 Mar 1998	—
IX 526	—	YRST 1	26 Mar 1998	Rec **YR 94**, 3 Apr 2000
IX 527	—	YFN 1259	7 Apr 1999	—

Acoustic measurement, Ketchikan

| IX 528 | — | YRDH 1 | 7 Apr 1999 | — |

Acoustic measurement, Ketchikan

IX 529	Sea Shadow	—	15 Mar 2000	(see below.)
IX 530	—	YFND 5	6 Sep 2000	Stricken 2 May 2008
IX 531	—	YP 679	7 Aug 2001	Stricken 21 Mar 2007
IX 532	ex-*Joint Venture* (HSV-X1)	—	(See below.)	—
IX 533	—	YD 222	25 Jun 2002	—

Support vessel, Norfolk

IX 534	—	ABSD 2B	10 Oct 2002	Stricken 17 Sep 2007
IX 535	—	ABSD 2H	10 Oct 2002	Stricken 17 Sep 2007
IX 536	—	YD 253	19 Dec 2002	—
IX 537	Prevail	AGOS 8	6 Sep 2003	TSV 1
IX 538	—	—	17 Oct 2003	—
IX 539	—	YNG 17	19 Apr 2007	—
IX 540	Neodesha	YTB 815	3 Aug 2007	—
IX 541	—	YF 284	—	—
IX 542	White Bush	WLM 542	—	Sunk as target 17 Jun 2004
IX 543	—	YFN 793	17 Oct 2007	—
IX 544	—	YFN 794	17 Oct 2007	—
IX 545	—	YTB 814	3 Aug 2007	ex-*Waxahachie*

No.	Name	Builder	Launched	In service
IX 529	Sea Shadow	Lockheed	1985	1 Mar 1985

Displacement	499 tons; 563 f/l
Dimensions	118'1"(wl); 164'(oa) × 58' × 14'
Machinery	2 screws; diesel-electric; 1,600 SHP; 13–15 knots
Complement	12

Notes: Stealth research ship. On list as IX 529, 15 Mar 2000. Angled fuselage, twin hulls. Stricken 22 Aug 2006. NDRF. SE.

No.	Name	Builder	Launched	In service
IX 532	HSV-X1 ex-*Joint Venture*	Incat, Tasmania	7 Nov 1998	11 Oct 2001

Displacement	971 tons
Dimensions	313' (oa) 282' (wl) × 87'4" × 13'
Machinery	4 water Jet, 4 diesel, 38,600 SHP, 45 knots
Complement	30

Notes: High-speed catamaran. Stricken 15 Mar 2004. All aluminum hull.

◆Iraq War 2003.

No.	Name	Builder	Launched	In service
HSV 2	Swift	Incat, Tasmania	29 Jul 2003	15 Aug 2003

Displacement	1,872 tons
Dimensions	318'11" (oa) 301'9'" (wl) × 87'4" × 11'3"
Machinery	4 water Jet, 4 diesel, 40,000 SHP, 38 knots
Complement	42
Armament	1–25 mm, MG

Notes: High-speed catamaran, developed from HSV-X1 design. Helicopter landing pad. Can carry 970 troops in seats. Achieved 47 knots on trails.

◆Beirut Evac, 17–19 Jul 2006

No.	Name	Builder	Launched	In service
HSV 4676	Westpac Express	Austal (Fremantle)	9 Apr 2001	11 Jul 2001

Displacement	tons
Dimensions	290'11" (wl) × 87' × 14'
Machinery	4 water Jet, 4 diesel, 40,000 BHP, 36 knots
Complement	42
Armament	1–25 mm, MG

Notes: High-speed catamaran, developed from HSV-X1 design. Helicopter landing pad. Can carry 970 troops in seats.

Chartered by MSC to support III Marine Expeditionary Force in the Western Pacific.

Figure 10.65: *Joint Venture* (HSV-XI) (IX 532), 2002. High-speed all-aluminum hull catamaran. (James W. Goss)

Figure 10.66: *HSV-2 Swift*. An experimental high-speed catamaran. She took part in the evacuation of civilians from Beirut in 2006.

Figure 10.67: The Littoral Surface Craft-Experimental (X-Craft), christened *Sea Fighter* (FSF 1).

X-CRAFT

No.	Name	Builder	Launched	In service
FSF-1	*Sea Fighter*	Nichols	Feb 2005	2005
Displacement	950 tons; 1,400 f/l			
Dimensions	265′ (oa) 239′6″ (wl) × 73′ × 11′9″			
Machinery	4 waterjets, CODOG, 2 gas turbines, 67,200 shp + 2 diesel; 50 knots			
Endurance	4,000/20			
Complement	26			

Note: A high-speed aluminum catamaran for testing a variety of technologies to enable operations in near-shore waters, as a Litoral Surface Craft. It evaluates the hydrodynamic performance, structural behavior, mission flexibility, and propulsion system of high-speed vessels. Trials were very successful. Carries two helicopters.

11 TRANSPORTS AND SUPPLY SHIPS

AMMUNITION SHIPS

AE 3   *Lassen*   Decomm 5 Jan 1947. Stricken 1 Jul 1961. BU 1976.

AE 4   *Mount Baker*   Sank m/v *Apnok* in collision off South Korea, 27 Mar 1952. Out of comm 15 Aug 1946–5 Dec 1951. Decomm and stricken 2 Dec 1969. BU 1974.
4★Korea K-7 K-8 K-9 K-10; 7★Vietnam Jan–Feb, May–Jun 1965, Feb–Nov 1966, Oct 1967–Mar 1968, Nov 1968–Jun 1969; ◆Taiwan Straits Sep 1958.

AE 5   *Rainier*   Out of comm 30 Aug 1946–25 May 1951. Decomm and stricken, 7 Aug 1970. BU 1971.
4★Korea K-7 K-8 K-9 K-10; 8★Vietnam Aug–Oct 1964, Jun–Jul, Oct–Dec 1965, Mar–Jul 1967, Jul 1968–Jan 1969, Sep 1969–Mar 1970; ◆Taiwan Straits Nov 1958.

AE 6   *Shasta*   Out of comm 10 Aug 1946–15 Jul 1953. Decomm and stricken 1 Jul 1969. Sold 24 Mar 1970, BU Castellon, Spain.

Figure 11.1: *USS Vesuvius* (AE 15), ammunition ship.

1★Vietnam Nov 1966–Apr 1967, Jan–Mar 1973; ◆Lebanon Jul–Sep 1958, Libya Aug–Nov 1987.

AE 8   *Mauna Loa*   Out of comm 2 Jun 1947–31 Jan 1955 and 16 Dec 1958–27 Nov 1961. Decomm 26 Feb 1971. Stricken 1 Oct 1976. 3★Vietnam Nov 1967–Apr 1968.

AE 9   *Mazama*   Out of comm 3 Aug 1946–24 Apr 1952 and 10 Jun 1957–27 Nov 1961. Decomm 13 Mar 1970. Stricken 1 Sep 1970. Sold 1 Mar 1973, BU Oakland, Cal.
4★Vietnam May–Oct 1966, Apr–Oct 1969; ◆Cuba Feb–Mar 1962, Cuba Missile Crisis Oct–Dec 1962, Dominican Rep May 1965.

AE 10   *Sangay*   Decomm 20 Jul 1947. Stricken 1 Jul 1960. Sold 19 Nov 1980.

AE 12   *Wrangell*   Out of comm 19 Nov 1946–14 Nov 1951. Collided with carrier *Independence* off South Carolina, 11 Apr 1968. Decomm 21 Dec 1970. Stricken 1 Oct 1976. BU 1983.
5★Vietnam Nov 1965–May 1966, Oct 1968–Apr 1969; ◆Lebanon Jul–Sep 1958, Cuba Missile Crisis Oct–Nov 1962.

AE 13   *Akutan*   Decomm 19 Oct 1946. Stricken 1 Jul 1960.

AE 14   *Firedrake*   Out of comm 21 Feb 1946–11 Oct 1951. Decomm 19 Mar 1971. Stricken 15 Jul 1976. Sold 1 Dec 1977.
3★Korea K-7, K-9 K-10; 6★Vietnam Jul 1964, Nov 1965–May 1966, Dec 1967, Feb–Aug 1969, Jul–Sep 1970; ◆Taiwan Straits Oct 1958, Quemoy-Matsu 11 Jul 1959.

AE 15   *Vesuvius*   Out of comm 20 Aug 1946–15 Nov 1951. Decomm and stricken 14 Aug 1973. Sold 5 Apr 1974, BU.
2★Korea K-8, K-10; 13★Vietnam Apr 1963, Mar–Jun, Aug–Nov 1965, Jun–Nov 1966, Aug 1967–Feb 1968, Aug 1968–Mar 1969, Oct 1969–Apr 1970, Feb–Jul 1971, Mar 1972–Jan 1973.

AE 16   *Mount Katmai*   Collided with carrier *Coral Sea* off Vietnam, 18 Oct 1967. Decomm and stricken 14 Aug 1973. Sold 5 Apr 1974. BU 1974.
9★Korea K-1 K-2 K-3 K-4 K-5 K-6 K-8 K-9 K-10; 9★Vietnam May–Nov 1965, Jul 1966–Jan 1967, Sep 1967–Mar 1968, Oct 1968–Mar 1969, Dec 1969–Jun 1970, Feb–Aug 1971, May–Sep 1972, Jan 1973; ◆Quemoy-Matsu 23 Jul 1961.

AE 17   *Great Sitkin*   Decomm and stricken 2 Jul 1973. Sold 12 Mar 1974, BU Camden, NJ.

2★Vietnam May–Jun 1968, Sep–Oct 1968; ◆Cuba Missile Crisis Oct–Dec 1962.

AE 18 *Paricutin* Out of comm 30 Apr 1948–28 Jul 1950. Decomm 23 Apr 1971. Stricken 1 Jun 1973. Sold 16 Oct 1975, BU.
7★Korea K-2 K-4 K-5 K-6 K-7 K-8 K-9; 10★Vietnam Sep 1964, Jul 1965–Feb 1966, Sep 1966–Jan 1967, Mar–Jul 1968, Jun–Oct 1969, May–Oct 1970; ◆Korea Apr 1969.

AE 19 *Diamond Head* Out of comm 23 Aug 1946–9 Aug 1951. Severely damaged in collision with carrier *Independence* in Caribbean, 27 Apr 1961. Decomm and stricken 1 Mar 1973. Sold 3 Oct 1974, BU Camden, NJ.
3★Vietnam May–Dec 1967, Mar 1968; ◆Cuba Apr, Aug 1961, Oct 1962.

No.	Name	Builder	Keel Laid	Launched	Comm.
AE 21	*Suribachi*	Sparrows Pt	31 Jan 1955	2 Nov 1955	17 Nov 1956
AE 22	*Mauna Kea*	Sparrows Pt	16 May 1955	3 May 1956	30 Mar 1957
AE 23	*Nitro*	Sparrows Pt	20 May 1957	25 Jun 1958	1 May 1959
AE 24	*Pyro*	Sparrows Pt	21 Oct 1957	23 Jul 1958	24 Jul 1959
AE 25	*Haleakala*	Sparrows Pt	10 Mar 1958	17 Feb 1959	3 Nov 1959
Displacement	10,000 tons; 17,000 f/l				
Dimensions	512′ (oa) × 72′ × 29′				
Machinery	1 screw; ST; 2 boilers; 16,000 SHP; 20.6 knots				
Endurance	10,000/20				
Complement	316				
Armament	4 twin 3″/50, later 2 twin 3″/50; *1977*: 1 twin 3″/50				

Notes: A 6th ship proposed for 1959 was canceled. Designed for rapid underway replenishment. Modernized in 1960s, fitted to transfer guided missiles (FAST). After 3″ guns replaced by helicopter deck.

Service Record:

AE 21 *Suribachi* Decomm 2 Dec 1994. Stricken 12 Dec 1996. Tfr to MSC canceled. NDRF. SE.
1★Vietnam Jun 1972–Feb 1973, ◆Lebanon Dec 1982–Apr 1983, Grenada Oct–Nov 1983, Libya May–Jul 1988, Gulf War Aug 1990.

AE 22 *Mauna Kea* Decomm 30 Jun 1995. Stricken 12 Dec 1996. Tfr to MSC canceled. NDRF. Sunk as target 12 Jul 2006.
12★Vietnam Apr–May 1962, Apr–Jun 1963, Aug–Nov 1964, Jan–Jul 1967, Mar–Apr, Jun–Sep 1968, Apr–Oct 1969, Jun 1970–Jan 1971, Aug 1971–Jun 1972, Aug 1972–Jan 1973; ◆Taiwan Straits Sep–Oct 1958, Quemoy-Matsu Aug 1959, Apr 1960, May 1963, Libya May–Jun 1990, Gulf War Sep 1992.

AE 23 *Nitro* Collided with carrier *Oriskany* in South China Sea, 28 Jun 1972. Decomm 28 Apr 1995. Stricken 14 Aug 1995. NDRF. SE.
2★Vietnam May 1972–Jan 1973; ◆Cuba Missile Crisis Nov 1962, Lebanon Nov–Dec 1983, Mar 1984, Gulf War Jan–Apr 1991.

AE 24 *Pyro* Decomm 31 May 1994. Stricken 8 Apr 1997. NDRF. SE.
9★Vietnam Feb–Sep 1965, Mar–Sep 1966, Jul–Nov 1967, Nov 1969–May 1970, Dec 1970–May 1971, Feb–Oct 1971; ◆Libya Feb–May 1988, Gulf War Jan–Apr 1991.

AE 25 *Haleakala* Decomm and stricken 10 Dec 1993. Sold 29 Mar 1994, BU Alang, India.
13★Vietnam Dec 1965–Aug 1966, Apr–Oct 1967, May–Nov 1968, Jul–Sep, Nov 1969–Jan 1970, Nov–Dec 1970, Nov 1971–Aug 1972; ◆Evac of Vietnam 29–30 Apr 1975, Gulf War Feb–Mar 1991.

No.	Name	Builder	Keel Laid	Launched	Comm.
AE 26	*Kilauea*	Gen.Dyn. Quincy	12 Mar 1966	9 Aug 1967	10 Aug 1968
AE 27	*Butte*	Gen.Dyn. Quincy	21 Jul 1966	9 Aug 1967	14 Dec 1968
AE 28	*Santa Barbara*	Sparrows Pt	20 Dec 1966	23 Jan 1968	11 Jul 1970
AE 29	*Mount Hood*	Sparrows Pt	8 May 1967	17 Jul 1968	1 May 1971
AE 32	*Flint*	Ingalls	4 Aug 1969	9 Nov 1970	20 Nov 1971
AE 33	*Shasta*	Ingalls	20 Nov 1969	3 Apr 1971	26 Feb 1972
AE 34	*Mount Baker*	Ingalls	5 Oct 1970	23 Oct 1971	22 Jul 1972
AE 35	*Kiska*	Ingalls	8 Apr 1971	11 Mar 1972	16 Dec 1972
Displacement	9,338 tons; 19,937 f/l				
Dimensions	564′ (oa) × 81′ × 25′9″				
Machinery	1 screw; ST; 3 boilers; 22,000 SHP; 22 knots				
Endurance	10,000/20				
Complement	401 / 125 (USNS)				
Armament	26–27, 32–34: 4-twin 3″/50 AA, 2 helicopters; 28–29, 35: 1-twin 30″/50; *1970s*: 4-3″ removed, 2 Phalanx added				

Notes: Funnel aft with helicopter landing area and hangar at stern. Armament removed on transfer to MSC. Underway replenishment for missiles and munitions. FAST.

Service Record:

AE 26 *Kilauea* Decomm, to MSC 1 Oct 1980. Out of service 21 Dec 2003.

Figure 11.2: *USS Mauna Kea* (AE 22), ammunition ship, 1970, in South China Sea.

Figure 11.3: *USS Butte* (AE 27), 1983. Notice helicopter landing pad aft, and lack of armament.

Transports and Supply Ships 197

Figure 11.4: *USS Virgo* (AE 30), attack cargo ship converted to ammunition ship, 1965.

Figure 11.5: *USS Aldebaran* (AF 10), store ship.

Figure 11.6: *USS Hyades* (AF 28), store ship.

		4★Vietnam Aug 1970–Jan 1971, Sep 1971–Jun 1972, ◆Iran/Indian Ocean Feb–Apr 1980, Libya Sep–Oct 1989, Gulf War Sep 1990–Mar 1991, Indian Ocean Jan–May 1998.	
AE 27	*Butte*	Decomm, to MSC 3 Jun 1996. OS 24 May 2004. Sunk as target 30 Jun 2006.	
		1★Vietnam Feb–Mar 1973; ◆Iran/Indian Ocean Feb–Mar 1981, Lebanon Jun–Oct 1983, Indian Ocean Dec 1995.	
AE 28	*Santa Barbara*	Decomm, to MSC 30 Sep 1998. OS, stricken 3 Aug 2005. Sold 31 Oct 2006, BU Brownsville, Tex.	
		1★Vietnam Jul 1972–Jan 1973; ◆Gulf War Jan–May 1991, Indian Ocean Mar–Jun 1998.	
AE 29	*Mount Hood*	Decomm and stricken 13 Aug 1999. NDRF. SE.	
		1★Vietnam May 1972–Jan, Mar 1973; ◆Evac of Vietnam 29–30 Apr 1975, Iran/Indian Ocean Jul–Sep 1981, Persian Gulf Feb–Jul 1987, Gulf War Feb–Mar 1991, Liberia Oct–Nov 1993, Indian Ocean May–Aug 1997.	
AE 32	*Flint*	In collision with replenishment oiler *Wabash* northwest of Hawaii, 9 Jun 1976. Decomm, to MSC 4 Aug 1995.	
		1★Vietnam Nov 1972, Jan–Mar 1973; ◆Evac of Vietnam 29–30 Apr 1975, Iran/Indian Ocean Jun–Aug 1980, Libya Jul–Sep 1988, Gulf War Aug–Nov 1990.	
AE 33	*Shasta*	In collision with LPD *Cleveland* off Long Beach, Cal., 26 Sep 1984. Decomm, to MSC 1 Oct 1997.	
		◆Iran/Indian Ocean Mar–Apr, Jun–Jul 1981, Gulf War Jan–Apr 1991, Indian Ocean Jan–Mar 1996.	
AE 34	*Mount Baker*	Decomm, to MSC 18 Dec 1996.	
		◆Iran/Indian Ocean Apr–Jun 1981, Lebanon Oct 1982–May 1983, Jun, Sep–Oct 1983, Libya Jan–May 1986, Gulf War Oct 1991–Feb 1992, Indian Ocean May–Jul 2000, Dec 2000–Mar 2001, Iraq War 2003.	
AE 35	*Kiska*	Decomm, to MSC 1 Aug 1996.	
		◆Mayaguez Op 15 May 1975, Iran/Indian Ocean Nov 1980–Mar 1981, Libya Nov–Dec 1988, Gulf War Nov 1990–Mar 1991.	
AE 20	*Fomalhaut*	Formerly AK 22. 27 Dec 1948. Stricken Sep 1962.	
AE 30	*Virgo*	Formerly AKA 20. 1 Nov 1965. Stricken 1 Jan 1971. Sold 19 Nov 1973, BU.	
AE 31	*Chara*	Formerly AKA 58. 1 Nov 1965. Stricken 10 Mar 1972. Sold 11 Dec 1972, BU.	

STORE SHIPS

AF 10	*Aldebaran*	Decomm 28 Jun 1968. Stricken 1 Jun 1973. Sold 14 Nov 1974, BU Brownsville, Tex.
		2★Vietnam May–Jun, Oct 1962; ◆Lebanon Aug 1958, Cuba Missile Crisis Oct–Nov 1962.
AF 11	*Polaris*	Decomm 18 Jan 1946. Stricken 7 Feb 1946. Reacq 6 Oct 1948. Recomm 1 Jul 1949 Decomm 12 Jan 1957. Stricken 10 Oct 1957. BU 1974 Oakland, Cal.
		5★Korea K-4 K-5 K-6 K-7 K-10.

Note: Type C2-Cargo

AF 28	*Hyades*	Decomm 31 Dec 1968. Stricken 1 Oct 1976. BU 1983.
		◆Lebanon Aug–Sep 1958, Cuba Missile Crisis Oct–Dec 1962.
AF 29	*Graffias*	Decomm and stricken 19 Dec 1969. BU 1973.
		8★Korea K-1 K-2 K-4 K-5 K-6 K-8 K-9 K-10; 7★Vietnam May 1961, Feb, Aug 1962, Feb–Apr, Nov–Dec 1965, Jun–Jul 1966, Jan–Feb, Sep–Nov 1967, Aug–Nov 1968, Jun–Aug 1969; ◆Taiwan Straits Sep–Nov 1958, Quemoy-Matsu Feb, May 1959, Feb–Apr, Jun, Aug–Nov 1960, Feb–Apr, Jul, Oct–Nov 1961, Jan, Jul 1962, Feb–Mar 1963.

Note: Type C2-S-B1

AF 30	*Adria*	Decomm 16 Jun 1954. Stricken 1 Jul 1960.
AF 31	*Arequipa*	Decomm 25 Aug 1955. Stricken 1 Sep 1961. Sold Dec 1972, BU 1973 Terminal I.
		★Korea 1951.
AF 32	*Corduba*	Decomm 18 Nov 1955. Stricken 1 Jul 1960. Sold 15 Jul 1974, BU Camden, NJ.
AF 33	*Karin*	Decomm 15 Dec 1958. Stricken 1 Sep 1961.
		Later history: merchant *Typhoon* 1969, renamed *Ocean Typhoon* 1975, *Ben Ocean Typhoon* 1976.
		2★Korea 2, 8, 1951, 1952; ◆Passage to Freedom 1954.

AF 34 *Kerstin* Decomm 12 May 1950. Stricken 16 Jun 1950.
  Later history: merchant *Reefer Star* 1973. SE1998 RR1998.
AF 35 *Latona* Decomm 15 Apr 1949. Stricken 28 Apr 1949. BU 1973.
AF 36 *Lioba* Decomm 14 Oct 1955. Stricken 1 Jul 1960. Sold 18 Oct 1973, BU Camden, NJ.
AF 37 *Malabar* Decomm 26 Sep 1955. Stricken 1 Jul 1960. Sold 20 Jul 1977.
AF 38 *Merapi* Decomm 16 Jan 1959. Stricken 1 Jul 1960. Sold 22 Apr 1966, BU 1966.
  2★Korea K-2 K-9 1952–53; ◆OpCastle 1954, Passage to Freedom 1954.
AF 42 *Bondia* Decomm 29 Jul 1946 and returned.
  Later history: Merchant *Flemish Bend*. Reacq as *Bondia*, 27 Jul 1951, MSTS. Stricken 1 May 1973. Sold 19 Nov 1973, BU Kaohsiung.
AF 44 *Laurentia* Decomm 18 Jun 1946.
  Later history: Merchant *Wall and Crown*. Reacq as *Laurentia*, 1 Jul 1950, MSTS. Stricken 28 Apr 1970. Sold 14 Jun 1973, BU Kaohsiung.
AF 47 *Valentine* Decomm 6 Aug 1946. Stricken 8 Oct 1946.
  Later history: Merchant *Pier Bend*. Reacq as *Valentine*, 5 Jul 1951, MSTS. Stricken 16 Apr 1959. Merchant *Northgate* 1967, renamed *All Alaskan* 1977. Wrecked 57N 170W in Gulf of Alaska, 20 Mar 1987.

Note: Type R1-M-AV3

No.	Name	Builder	Launched	Acquired	Comm.
AF 48	*Alstede* ex-*Ocean Chief*	Moore	28 Nov 1944	10 May 1946	17 May 1946
AF 49	*Zelima* ex-*Golden Rocket*	Moore	2 Mar 1945	1946	27 Jul 1946
AF 50	*Bald Eagle*	Moore	7 May 1942	1 Mar 1950	
AF 51	*Blue Jacket*	Moore	14 Feb 1942	1 Mar 1950	
AF 52	*Golden Eagle*	Moore	15 Mar 1942	1 Mar 1950	18 Nov 1961
AF 54	*Pictor* ex-*Great Republic*	Moore	4 Jun 1942	Sep 1950	13 Sep 1950
AF 55	*Aludra* ex-*Matchless*	Moore	14 Oct 1944	1 Jul 1952	7 Jul 1952
AF 60	*Sirius* ex-*Trade Wind*	Moore	11 Apr 1942	18 May 1956	12 Jan 1957
AF 61	*Procyon* ex-*Flying Scud*	Moore	1 Jul 1942	8 Aug 1961	24 Nov 1961
AF 62	*Bellatrix* ex-*Fleetwood*	Moore	4 Dec 1944	Aug 1961	18 Nov 1961
Displacement	6,914 tons; 15,500 f/l				
Dimensions	459'2" (oa); 435' (wl) × 63' × 28'				
Machinery	1 screw; GT; 6000 shp; 16 knots				
Complement	292				
Armament	2 twin 40 mm guns; AF 55: 4 twin 3"/50				

Notes: Type R2-S-BV1/CS-S-BV1. AF 52 *Arcturus* had helicopter landing deck aft.

Service Records:

AF 48 *Alstede* Damaged in collision with submarine *Croaker* at Cannes, France, 23 Mar 1956. Decomm and stricken 31 Oct 1969. Sold 2 Jun 1970, BU Castellon, Spain.
  4★Korea K-7 K-8 K-9 K-10; ◆Dominican Rep May–Jun 1965.
AF 49 *Zelima* Decomm Sep 1969. Stricken 1 Jun 1976. Sold 25 Nov 1981, BU 1981 Taiwan.
  1★Korea 4, 1950–1953; 5★Vietnam Sep 1961, Apr 1963, Sep–Oct 1964, Jun–Aug, Oct 1965, Jan–Mar, Jul–Aug 1966, Oct–Dec 1968, May–Jun 1969; ◆Passage to Freedom 1954, Taiwan Straits Oct–Dec 1958, Quemoy-Matsu Jul–Aug 1959, May–Jun 1960, Jan–Feb, Sep–Oct 1961, Mar–Apr 1963.
AF 50 *Bald Eagle* MSTS. Stricken 19 Oct 1971. Sold 1 Mar 1973, BU Brownsville, Tex.

Figure 11.7: USS *Alstede* (AF 48), a store ship acquired in 1946.

AF 51 *Blue Jacket* MSTS. Sank coaster m/v *Dirk* in collision in North Sea, 9 Feb 1964. Stricken 19 Oct 1971. Sold 1 Mar 1973, BU Brownsville, Tex.
AF 52 *Golden Eagle* MSTS. Renamed *Arcturus*, 13 Oct 1961. Comm 18 Nov 1961. Decomm 16 Mar 1973. Stricken 9 Dec 1985. Sunk as target 24 Jul 1997.
AF 54 *Pictor* Decomm 13 Dec 1969. Stricken 1 Jun 1976. Sold 25 Nov 1981, BU 1987 Taiwan.
  1★Korea K-10, 1951, 1952, 1953; 8★Vietnam Apr 1964, Dec 1964–Jan 1965, Aug–Oct 1965, Apr–Jun 1966, Dec 1966–Jan 1967, Jul–Oct 1967, Jun–Aug 1968, Jan–Feb 1969, Aug–Oct 1969; ◆Taiwan Straits Sep 1958, Quemoy-Matsu 11 May 1961.
AF 55 *Aludra* Decomm 12 Sep 1969. Stricken 1 Jun 1976. Sold 1 Nov 1977.
  Later history: Merchant *Aleutian Monarch* 1978. Gutted by fire at Beaver Inlet, Alaska, 12 Nov and scuttled 19 Nov 1981.
  1★Korea K-9; 8★Vietnam Mar–Apr 1965, Oct–Nov 1965, Aug–Sep 1966, Apr–Jun 1967, Nov 1967–Feb 1968, Sep–Oct 1968. ◆Passage to Freedom 1954, Taiwan Straits Sep 1958, Quemoy-Matsu 23 Jul 1961, Korea Jan–Apr 1968.
AF 60 *Sirius* Decomm 3 Feb 1964. Stricken 1 Aug 1965. Sold 13 Apr 1971, BU Seattle.
AF 61 *Procyon* Decomm 8 Dec 1975. Stricken 1 Jun 1976. Sold 25 Nov 1981, BU 1987 Taiwan.
  10★Vietnam Aug–Sep 1964, Jun–Jul 1965, Dec 1965–Feb 1966, Nov 1966–Jan 1967, Jun–Aug 1967, Mar–Jun 1968, Dec 1968–Mar 1969, Feb–Jun 1970.
AF 62 *Bellatrix* Decomm 30 Sep 1968. Stricken 1 Oct 1968. BU 1969 Portland, Ore.
  5★Vietnam May–Jul 1964, Dec 1964–Mar 1965, Nov 1965–Jan 1966, May–Jun 1966, Nov 1965–Jan 1966, May–Jun 1966, Feb–Apr 1967, Nov 1967–Jan 1968, May–Jun 1968; ◆Quemoy-Matsu May–Jun 1962, Jan 1963.

No.	Name	Builder	Launched	Acquired
AF 53	*Grommet Reefer* ex-*Grommet Reefer* LD as *Kenneth E. Gruennert*	Butler	29 Jul 1944	1 Mar 1950
Displacement	2,382 tons; 6,240 f/l			
Dimensions	338'8" × 50' × 21'			
Machinery	1 screw; diesel; 1,700 SHP; 10.5 knots			
Complement	40			

Notes: Type C1-M-AV1. MSTS, unarmed.

Service Record: Wrecked in gale, broke in half, off Livorno, Italy, 15 Dec 1952.

No.	Name	Builder	Launched	Acquired	Comm/In service
AF 56	*Denebola*	Oregon	10 Jun 1944	1 May 1952	20 Jan 1954
	ex-*Hibbing Victory* (1954)				
AF 57	*Regulus*	Oregon	7 Jun 1944	5 May 1952	3 Feb 1954
	ex-*Escanaba Victory* (1954)				
AF 63	*Asterion*	Calship	27 Jul 1944	12 Nov 1961	Sep 1962
	ex-*Arcadia Victory* (1962)				
AF 64	*Perseus*	Oregon	11 May 1945	1961	Sep 1962
	ex-*Union Victory* (1962)				

Displacement	4,960 tons; 12,130 f/l
Dimensions	455'2" × 62' × 28'6"
Machinery	1 screw; GT; 8,500 SHP; 16 knots
Complement	225
Armament	4 twin 3"/50 guns

Notes: Type: VC2-S-AP3. AF 63–64, MSTS. Helicopter landing deck aft.

Service Records:

AF 56   *Denebola*   In collision with carrier *Independence* in Mediterranean, 20 Nov 1975. Decomm and stricken 30 Apr 1976. BU 1976.
◆Lebanon Sep 1958, Cuba Missile Crisis Nov 1962.

AF 57   *Regulus*   Went aground in typhoon at Hong Kong, 16 Aug 1971, not repaired. Decomm and stricken 10 Sep 1971. BU.
11★Vietnam Apr 1961, Apr–Jun 1965, Mar–Apr, Sep–Nov 1966, May–Jul 1967, Feb–Apr 1968, Nov–Dec 1968, Oct–Dec 1969, Jun–Sep 1970, Apr–Jul 1971.

AF 63   *Asterion*   Damaged in collision with m/v *Kokoku Maru* off San Francisco, 4 Jun 1963. Stricken 15 Jun 1973. Sold 31 Aug 1973, BU Hong Kong.

AF 64   *Perseus*   Stricken 15 Jun 1973. Sold 31 Aug 1973, BU Kaohsiung.

Figure 11.8: *USS Denebola* (AF 56), store ship, with the Sixth Fleet in the Mediterranean, 1962. Notice twin 3-inch guns mounted forward.

No.	Name	Builder	Keel Laid	Launched	Comm.
AF 58	*Rigel*	Ingalls	15 Mar 1954	15 Mar 1955	2 Sep 1955
AF 59	*Vega*	Ingalls	24 May 1954	26 Apr 1955	10 Nov 1955

Displacement	7,950 tons; 15,540 f/l
Dimensions	502' (oa); 475' (wl) × 72' × 29'
Machinery	1 screw; ST; 2 boilers; 16,000 SHP; 20 knots
Endurance	10,000/21
Complement	350/116 (USNS)
Armament	4 twin 3"/50; *1977*: 59: 2-twin 30"/50

Notes: Type R3-S-4A. The only built-for-the-purpose store ships.

Service Records:

AF 58   *Rigel*   Decomm, to MSC **T-AF 58**, 23 Jun 1975. OS 9 Sep 1992. Stricken 16 May 1994, NDRF. BU 2003 Britain.
◆Lebanon 15 Oct 1958, Cuba Missile Crisis Oct–Nov 1962, Dominican Rep May 1965, Iran/Indian Ocean Jan–Mar 1980, Feb–Mar, Jul–Oct 1981, Lebanon Sep–Dec 1982, Apr, Jul–Aug, Oct–Nov 1983, May–Jun 1984, Libya Jan–Feb 1986, Liberia 1990, Gulf War Jan 1991–Jan 1992.

AF 59   *Vega*   Decomm and stricken 29 Apr 1977. BU 1988 Kaohsiung.
10★Vietnam Mar 1961, Dec 1961–Jan 1962, Oct–Dec 1964, Jul–Sep 1965, Feb–Apr, Sep–Oct 1966, Oct–Nov 1966, Aug–Oct 1967, Apr–Aug 1968, May–Jul 1969, Oct 1970–Mar 1971, Apr–Sep 1972;
◆Quemoy-Matsu 2 Apr 1961, 20 Dec 1961, Korea Apr 1969, evac of Cambodia 11–13 Apr 1975, evac of Vietnam 29–30 Apr 1975, Mayaguez Op 15 May 1975.

Figure 11.9: *USS Vega* (AF 59), built for the purpose store ship.

COMBAT STORE SHIPS

No.	Name	Builder	Keel Laid	Launched	Comm.
AFS 1	*Mars*	Natl Steel	5 May 1962	15 Jun 1963	13 Dec 1963
AFS 2	*Sylvania*	Natl Steel	18 Aug 1962	25 Aug 1963	11 Jul 1964
AFS 3	*Niagara Falls*	Natl Steel	22 May 1965	26 Mar 1966	29 Apr 1967
AFS 4	*White Plains*	Natl Steel	2 Oct 1965	23 Jul 1966	12 Oct 1968
AFS 5	*Concord*	Natl Steel	26 Mar 1966	17 Dec 1966	27 Nov 1968
AFS 6	*San Diego*	Natl Steel	11 Mar 1967	13 Apr 1968	24 May 1969
AFS 7	*San Jose*	Natl Steel	8 Mar 1969	13 Dec 1969	23 Oct 1970

Displacement	9,200 tons; 16,500 f/l
Dimensions	581'3" (oa); 529'8" (wl) × 79' × 24'
Machinery	1 screw; ST; 3 B&W boilers; 22,000 SHP; 20 knots
Endurance	10,000/20
Complement	430
Armament	4 twin 3"/50 AA guns, 2 helicopters. *1980s*: 4–3" replaced by 2 Phalanx.

Notes: Underway replenishment ships combining function of AF, AKS and AVS. Armament removed on transfer to MSC. Helicopter landing deck and hangar aft.

Figure 11.10: USS *San Jose* (AFS 7), a new type of underway replenishment ship combining the functions of several other types.

Figure 11.11: Combat store ship *Saturn* (T-AFS 10) with a CH-46 *Sea Knight* helicopter lifting off the deck, in the Southeast Asia area, 9 Feb 2002.

Service Records:

AFS 1   *Mars*   Collided with m/v *Seiwa Maru* in fog in Tokyo Bay, 26 May 1966. In collision with frigate *Cook* in fog off Point Loma, Cal., 14 May 1979. Decomm 1 Feb 1993, to MSC. OS 19 Feb 1998. Sunk as target, Hawaii, 15 Jul 2006.
11★Vietnam Jan–Jul, Sep 1965–Feb 1967, Apr–Dec 1967, Sep 1968–Apr 1969, Jun–Aug, Oct–Dec 1969, Feb–Mar 1970, Dec 1970–May 1971, May–Nov 1972, Korea Jan–Mar 1968, ◆Evac of Vietnam 29–30 Apr 1975, Iran/Indian Ocean Apr–Sep 1980, Persian Gulf Feb–Jul 1987, Libya Nov 1988–Jan 1989, Gulf War Dec 1990–Mar 1991, Liberia Nov 1993–Apr 1994, Aug–Oct 1994.

AFS 2   *Sylvania*   In collision with store ship *Concord* at Rota, Spain, 28 Nov 1970. Collided with AOR *Kalamazoo* off Virginia. Capes, 28 Jan 1981. Decomm 26 May 1994. Stricken 5 Jan 1995. Sold 28 Jul 2001, BU. NDRF. SE.
◆Lebanon Sep–Nov 1982, Mar 1984, Gulf War Oct 1990, Jan–Feb 1991.

AFS 3   *Niagara Falls*   Decomm 23 Sep 1994, to MSC. Went aground in Malakal harbor, Palau, 27 Oct 2005.
10★Vietnam Apr–Sep 1968, Feb 1969–Jan 1970, Apr 1970–Nov 1971, Jul 1972–Mar 1973, ◆Korea 10 Feb 1970, Iran/Indian Ocean Jan 1979, Oct–Nov 1980, Jan–Feb 1981, Jun–Jul 1987, Libya Aug 1987, Dec 1989–Jan 1990, Gulf War Jan 1991–Oct 1992, Liberia Dec 1992–Jan 1993, Indian Ocean Jul–Oct 1998, Tsunami relief 2005.

AFS 4   *White Plains*   Damaged by fire in South China Sea, 9 May 1989 (6 killed). Decomm 17 Apr 1995. Stricken 24 Aug 1995. Sunk as target off southern California, 8 Jul 2002.
5★Vietnam Sep 1969–Feb 1970, Jul–Nov 1970, Dec 1971–Jun 1972, Jan–Mar 1973; ◆Evac of Vietnam 29–30 Apr 1975, Iran/Indian Ocean Apr–May 1979, Dec 1979–Feb 1980, Apr–Jun 1980, Apr–Sep 1981, Gulf War Aug–Oct 1990, Liberia Oct–Nov 1993.

AFS 5   *Concord*   In collision with AFS *Sylvania* at Rota, Spain, 28 Nov 1970. Decomm 15 Oct 1992, to MSC.
◆Lebanon Jun–Oct 1983, May 1983, Gulf War Sep 1990, Tsunami relief 2005.

AFS 6   *San Diego*   In collision with submarine *Norfolk* in Chesapeake Bay, 16 Jan 1989. Decomm 11 Aug 1993, to MSC. OS 10 Dec 1997. Stricken 8 Sep 2003. Sold 14 Apr 2006, BU Brownsville, Tex.
◆Lebanon Jan–Apr 1983, Apr–May 1984, Libya Jan 1986, Gulf War Jan–Apr 1991, Haiti Sep 1994.

AFS 7   *San Jose*   Decomm 2 Nov 1993, to MSC.
3★Vietnam Oct 1971–Feb 1972, Sep 1972–Mar 1973; ◆Iran/Indian Ocean Nov 1979–Feb 1980, Libya Sep–Oct 1989, Gulf War Sep 1990–Mar 1991, Indian Ocean Mar, Jul 1997, Tsunami relief 2005.

No.	Name	Builder	Keel Laid	Launched	In service
T-AFS 8	*Sirius* ex-*Lyness*	Swan Hunter	7 Apr 1965	7 Apr 1966	17 Jan 1981
T-AFS 9	*Spica* ex-*Tarbatness*	Swan Hunter	15 Apr 1966	22 Feb 1967	4 Nov 1981
T-AFS 10	*Saturn* ex-*Stromness*	Swan Hunter	5 Oct 1965	16 Sep 1966	30 Sep 1984
Displacement	9,010 tons; 16,792 f/l				
Dimensions	523'3" (oa); 489'10" (wl) × 72' × 25'6"				
Machinery	1 screw; turbo diesel; 12,700 BHP; 19 knots				
Endurance	11,000/19				
Complement	170				
Armament	none, 2 helicopters (8)				

Notes: Purchased from Britain during Iranian hostage crisis. *Lyness* originally acquired on charter 17 Jan 1981, acquired 1 Mar 1982. *Sirius* has hangar aft. MSC.

Service Record:

AFS 8   *Sirius*   OS and stricken 1 Jul 2005. Tfrd to Texas Maritime Academy.
Later history: renamed *Texas Clipper III*. 2005 NDRF. SE.
◆Lebanon Jan–Feb 1983, Mar 1984, Libya/El Dorado Canyon Feb–May 1986, Gulf War Nov 1990, Feb–Apr 1991, Indian Ocean Feb–Jul 1996, Jan–Mar, Jul–Nov 1997, Iraq War 2003.

AFS 9   *Spica*   In collision with cruiser *Monterey* in Persian Gulf, 17 Mar 2005. OS 26 Jan 2008.
◆Gulf War Oct 1990–Mar 1991, Liberia Mar, Jun–Jul 1993, Apr, Jun, Aug 1994, Indian Ocean Dec 1995–Mar 1996, Nov 1997–Apr 1998, Iraq War 2003.

AFS 10   *Saturn*
◆Gulf War Apr 1991–May 1992, Indian Ocean Mar–Jul 1998.

CARGO SHIPS

AK 22   *Fomalhaut*   Decomm 25 Jun 1946. Rec **AE 20**, 27 Dec 1948. Stricken. Sep 1962. BU 1972 Baltimore.

AK 87   *Sagitta*   ex-USA *Marvin Lyle Thomas*. Reacq as *Sagitta*, 26 Apr 1952, MSTS. Returned 23 Feb 1960, Stricken 1 Jul 1961. Returned to U.S. Army, 25 Apr 1966, renamed *Resource*, stevedore training ship. BU 1977 Brownsville, Tex.

Figure 11.12: USS *Alcona* (AK 157), cargo ship.

AK 89 *Vela* ex-USA *Joe C. Specker*. Reacq as *Vela*, 11 Jun 1952, MSTS. Stricken 3 Apr 1959. Sold 23 Nov 1970, BU 1970, Bilbao.

AKN 6 *Galilea* Stricken 1 Sep 1961. BU 1972.

AK 157 *Alcona* Arctic service 1946. Damaged in collision with m/v *York* south of Norfolk, Va., 24 Oct 1947. Decomm 6 May 1955. Stricken 1 Apr 1960. BU.

AK 162 *Beltrami* Decomm 10 Nov 1955. Stricken 1 Apr 1960. BU 1960.

AK 170 *Chicot* Decomm 24 Jul 1951 and trfd to Dept of Interior.
Later history: Merchant *Chicot*, renamed *San Luis* 1970. BU 1972 Hong Kong.

AK 179 *Faribault* Decomm 20 Jul 1956. Stricken 1 Apr 1960. BU Oakland, Cal.
2★Korea 9, 10; ◆Passage to Freedom 1954.

AK 180 *Fentress* Reacq 1 Jul 1950, MSTS. Stricken 15 Oct 1973. Passage to Freedom 1954.
Later history: Merchant *Fentress*. Went aground in typhoon at Saipan, 15 Nov 1981.

AK 184 *Grainger* Reacq 9 May 1947. Decomm 7 Feb 1956. Stricken 1 Apr 1960. BU 1960.
2★Korea 1, 3.

AK 187 *Hennepin* SCAJAP. Reacq 1 Apr 1950, MSTS. OS 16 Jul 1958. Stricken 1 Jun 1960. BU 1960.
1★Korea 7; ◆Passage to Freedom 1954.

AK 188 *Herkimer* SCAJAP. Reacq 1 Apr 1950, MSTS. Stricken 15 Jun 1973. To Dept of Interior 3 Oct 1973.
Later history: merchant *Herkimer* (Trust Territories of the Pacific). BU 1984 Shodoshima.
◆ Passage to Freedom 1954.

AK 198 *Muskingum* Reacq 1 Apr 1950, MSTS. Stricken 10 Jun 1973. To Dept of Interior 3 Oct 1973.
Later history: merchant *Muskingum* (Trust Territories of the Pacific). BU 1982.
◆Passage to Freedom 1954.

AK 200 *Pembina* SCAJAP. Reacq 28 Jun 1950, MSTS. OS 18 Apr 1957. Stricken 31 Mar 1958.
Later history: To Army, 29 May 1968, renamed *Resolute*, renamed *Kathleen Pearcy* 1989, *Pembina* 1992, Merchant *Spirit of Grace*, 1996.
◆Passage to Freedom 1954.

AK 213 *Sussex* Decomm 5 Dec 1959. Stricken 1 Jan 1960. Sold 27 Jul 1960, BU.
3★Korea K-6 K-7 K-8; ◆Passage to Freedom 1954.

Type C1-M-AV1

No.	Name	Builder	Keel Laid	Launched	In Service
AK 237	*Greenville Victory*	Calship	21 Mar 1944	24 May 1944	1 Mar 1950
AK 238	*Haiti Victory*	Perm.#2	24 Apr 1944	20 Jul 1944	1 Mar 1950
AK 239	*Kingsport Victory*	Calship	4 Apr 1944	29 May 1944	1 Mar 1950
AK 240	*Pvt. John R. Towle* ex-*Appleton Victory*	Oregon	9 Dec 1944	19 Jan 1945	1 Mar 1950
AK 241	*Pvt. Francis X. McGraw* ex-*Wabash Victory*	Calship	14 Apr 1945	9 Jun 1945	1 Mar 1950
AK 242	*Sgt. Andrew Miller* ex-*Radcliffe Victory*	Perm. #2	22 Feb 1945	4 Apr 1945	1 Mar 1950
AK 243	*Sgt. Archer T. Gammon* ex-*Yale Victory*	Perm. #2	13 Dec 1944	31 Jan 1945	1 Mar 1950
AK 244	*Sgt. Morris E. Crain* ex-*Mills Victory*	Perm. #2	14 Feb 1945	28 Mar 1945	1 Mar 1950
AK 251	*Lt. George W.G. Boyce* ex-*Waterville Victory*	Beth-Fair	13 Jul 1945	19 Sep 1945	3 Aug 1950
AK 252	*Lt. Robert Craig* ex-*Bowling Green Victory*	Calship	21 Jun 1945	28 Aug 1945	2 Aug 1950
AK 253	*Pvt. Joe E. Mann* ex-*Owensboro Victory*	Perm. #2	12 Jun 1945	21 Jul 1945	7 Aug 1950
AK 254	*Sgt. Truman Kimbro* ex-*Hastings Victory*	Perm. #1	30 Sep 1944	30 Nov 1944	5 Aug 1950
AK 256	*Dalton Victory*	Calship	8 Apr 1944	6 Jun 1944	9 Aug 1950
AKV 3	*Lt. James E. Robinson* ex-*Czechoslovakia Victory*	Oregon	25 Nov 1943	20 Jan 1944	1 Mar 1950
AKV 4	*Pvt. Joseph F. Merrell* ex-*Grange Victory*	Calship	27 May 1944	17 Jul 1944	1 Mar 1950
AKV 5	*Sgt. Jack J. Pendleton* ex-*Mandan Victory*	Oregon	15 Apr 1944	26 May 1944	1 Mar 1950

No.	Name	Builder	Launched	Acquired	Comm.
AK 257	*Altair* ex-*Aberdeen Victory*	Oregon	30 May 1944	7 Jul 1951	31 Jan 1952
AK 258	*Antares* ex-*Nampa Victory*	Oregon	19 May 1944	23 Jul 1951	12 Feb 1952
AK 259	*Alcor* ex-*Rockland Victory*	Oregon	29 Apr 1944	10 Jul 1951	1 Mar 1952
AK 260	*Betelgeuse* ex-*Colombia Victory*	Calship	10 Apr 1944	3 Aug 1951	15 Apr 1952

Displacement	4,420 tons; 12,450 f/l
Dimensions	455′3″(oa); 436′ (wl) × 62′ × 28′6″
Machinery	1 screw; ST; 2 boilers; 8,500 SHP; 17 knots
Complement	49
Armament	none (257–260: 2 or 4 twin 40 mm guns)

Notes: Type VC2-S-AP2. AK 257–260 were Comm., others MSTS. *Alcor* was supply ship for FBM submarines. *Altair* had helicopter landing pad.

Figure 11.13: *USNS Lt. James E. Robinson* (T-AKV 3), acquired from the Army in 1950.

Figure 11.14: *USNS Pvt. Francis X. McGraw* (T-AK 241), a cargo ship acquired from the Army in 1950 and assigned to MSTS.

Figure 11.15: *USS Betelgeuse* (AK 260), cargo ship acquired and commissioned in 1952.

Service Records:

AK 237 *Greenville Victory* MSTS. Stricken 16 Jan 1981. BU 1983 Brownsville.
★Vietnam, ◆Antarctic 1955–56, 1956–57, 1957–58, 1961; Evac of Vietnam Apr 1975.

AK 238 *Haiti Victory* MSTS. Damaged in collision with destroyer *Kenneth D. Bailey* in Strait of Gibraltar, 5 Mar 1959. First vessel to recover an orbited space vehicle, 11 Aug 1960. Rec **AGM 3** and renamed *Longview*, 27 Nov 1960.

AK 239 *Kingsport Victory* MSTS. Rec **AG 164** and renamed *Kingsport*, 14 Nov 1961. OS 22 Nov 1983. Stricken 31 Jan 1984. BU 1992.

AK 240 *Pvt. John R. Towle* MSTS. OS 25 Aug 1980. Stricken 31 Jul 1982. BU Brownsville.
★Korea K-7, 1952; ◆Antarctic 1956–57, 1958, 1961.

AK 241 *Pvt. Francis X. McGraw* MSTS. Stricken 15 May 1974. Sold 14 Aug 1974, BU.

AK 242 *Sgt. Andrew Miller* MSTS. Stricken 16 Jan 1981. BU 1983.
1★Vietnam; ◆Evac of Vietnam Apr 1975.

AK 243 *Sgt. Archer. T. Gammon* MSTS. Stricken 1 May 1973; BU 1973 Taiwan.
★Korea 1950, 1951, 1952.

AK 244 *Sgt. Morris E. Crain* MSTS. Stricken 1 Apr 1975; BU 1975 Tacoma.

AK 251 *Lt. George W.G. Boyce* MSTS. Stricken 15 Jul 1973. Sold 1 Oct 1974, BU Portland, Ore.
4★Korea K-4 K-5 K-6 K-7.

AK 252 *Lt. Robert Craig* MSTS. Stricken 15 Jun 1973. Sold 26 Dec 1973. BU 1974.
1★Vietnam

AK 253 *Pvt. Joe E. Mann* Rec **AGM 4** and renamed *Richfield*, 27 Oct 1960.

AK 254 *Sgt. Truman Kimbro* Stricken 16 Jan 1981. Sold 26 Dec 1973. BU 1982.
2★Korea K-2 K-4; ◆Evac of Vietnam Apr 1975.

AK 256 *Dalton Victory* Rec **AGM 5** and renamed *Sunnyvale*, 27 Oct 1960.
3★Korea K-7 K-8 K-9 1950–53.

AKV 3 *Lt. James E.Robinson* MSTS. Rec **AK 274**, 7 May 1959. Rec **AG 170**, 1 Dec 1962, cable transport ship. Rec **AK 174**, 1 Jul 1964. Stricken 16 Jan 1981. Sold 17 Feb 1983, BU.

AKV 4 *Pvt. Joseph F.Merrell* MSTS. Rec **AK 275**, 7 May 1959. Damaged in collision with m/v *Pearl Venture* south of Monterey, Cal. 29 Dec 1973, CTL. Stricken 31 Jan 1974. Sold 19 Aug 1974, BU Taiwan.
★Korea; ◆Antarctic 1956–57, 1962, 1963.

AKV 5 *Sgt. Jack J. Pendleton* MSTS. Rec **AK 276**, 7 May 1959. Went aground on Triton I., Paracel Is, 25 Sep 1973; lost when island seized by PRC, Jan 1974. Stricken 15 Feb 1974.
★Korea K-6, 1951.

AK 257 *Altair* Rec **AKS 32**, 12 Aug 1952. Out of comm 5 Jan–15 Dec 1953 for conversion. Decomm 2 May 1969. Stricken 1 Jun 1973. Sold 14 Nov 1974, BU.
◆Cuba Missile Crisis Nov 1962.

AK 258 *Antares* Rec **AKS 33**, 1 Apr 1959. Damaged by fire off North Carolina, 27 Mar 1964. Decomm 18 Dec 1964. Stricken 1 Sep 1965. BU 1975.
◆Lebanon Oct 1958.

AK 259 *Alcor* Decomm 30 Dec 1968. Stricken 31 Dec 1968. BU 1970 La Spezia.
◆Lebanon Aug 1958

AK 260 *Betelgeuse* Collided with submarine *Simon Bolivar* off Charleston, SC, 31 Aug 1967. Decomm 15 Jan 1971. Stricken 1 Feb 1974. Sold 2 Dec 1975. Went aground en route to BU in Taiwan, 17 Jan 1976.

No.	Name	Builder	Keel laid	Launched	In Service
AK 245	*Capt. Arlo L. Olson* ex-*Bell Ringer*	Jones, Brun	2 Mar 1945	8 May 1945	1 Mar 1950
AK 246	*Col. William J. O'Brien* ex-*Maiden's Eye*	Consol; Wilm	17 Jan 1945	13 Feb 1945	1 Mar 1950
AK 247	*Pvt. John F. Thorson* ex-*Becket Bend*	Southeastern	8 Jan 1945	26 Feb 1945	1 Mar 1950
AK 248	*Sgt. George Peterson* ex-*Coastal Guide* ex-AK 218	L.D. Smith	9 Mar 1945	13 May 1945	1 Mar 1950

AK 249	*Short Splice*	Consol; Wilm	15 Jan 1945	3 Mar 1945	1 Mar 1950
AK 250	*Pvt Frank J. Petrarca* ex-*Long Splice*	Consol; Wilm	18 Apr 1945	7 Jun 1945	1 Jul 1950
Displacement	2,382 tons; 6,240 f/l				
Dimensions	338'8 (oa); 321 (wl) × 50 × 21'1				
Machinery	1 screw; diesel; 1,700 hp; 11 knots				
Complement	35				
Armament	none				

Notes: Type: C1-M-AV1. All MSTS. *Short Splice* and *O'Brien* converted to heavy-lift ships.

Service Records:

AK 245 *Capt. Arlo L. Olson*   Returned 22 May 1958. Sold 4 Mar 1971, BU Portland, Ore.
◆Passage to Freedom 1954.

AK 246 *Col. William J. O'Brien*   Stricken 1 Sep 1973. BU 1973 Rotterdam.

AK 247 *Pvt. John F. Thorson*   Returned 1 Oct 1958. Stricken 29 Aug 1960. BU 1960.

AK 248 *Sgt. George Peterson*   Returned 23 Mar 1959. Sold 15 Dec 1971.
Later history: Merchant *Marsha Lynn*, renamed *Al Ind Esk a Sea* 1982. Burned and sank off Everett, Wash., 20 Oct 1982.

AK 249 *Short Splice*   Stricken 15 Jun 1973. Sold 31 Aug 1973, BU 1973 Hong Kong.

AK 250 *Pvt. Frank J. Petrarca*   Stricken 9 Apr 1959; reacq 7 Apr 1960. Stricken 15 Oct 1973. Sold 1 Dec 1977.
Later history: Merchant *Arctic Producer* 1979, renamed *Arctic Enterprise* 1989.

No.	Name	Builder	Keel laid	Launched	In Service
AK 255	*Pvt. Leonard C. Brostrom* ex-*Marine Eagle* (1948)	Sun	5 Dec 1942	10 May 1943	30 Aug 1950
AK 267	*Marine Fiddler*	Sun	15 Dec 1944	15 May 1945	11 Dec 1952
Displacement	11,400 tons; 22,056 f/l				
Dimensions	522'10" (oa) × 71'8" × 33'				
Machinery	1 screw; ST; 2 boilers; 9,000 SHP; 15.8 knots				
Complement	52				
Armament	none				

Notes: Type C4-S-B1. AK 255 fitted with heavy lift cargo booms, could carry locomotives. AK 267 converted to heavy-lift ship 1954.

Figure 11.16: *USNS Short Splice* (T-AK 249), a cargo ship acquired from the Army in 1950 and assigned to MSTS.

Figure 11.17: *USNS Pvt. Leonard F. Brostrom* (T-AK 255), heavy-lift cargo ship. The harbor tugs *Tuscumbia* (YTB 762) and *Kalispell* (YTB 784) are alongside.

Figure 11.18: *USNS Cepheus* (T-AK 265), 1956. One of six small cargo ships acquired in 1951 for loan to South Korea.

Service Records:

AK 255 *Pvt. Leonard C. Brostrom*   OS 29 May 1980. Sold 8 Jun 1982. BU.

AK 267 *Marine Fiddler*   Stricken 31 Mar 1986. NDRF 12/98 BU 2004. Chesapeake, Va.

No.	Name	Builder	Laid Down	Launched	Acquired
AK 261	*Alchiba* ex-*Charles F. Winsor*, ex-*Northern Courier*	Ingalls, Dec	30 Dec 1944	29 May 1945	12 Jun 1951
AK 262	*Algorab* ex-*Elisha Whitney*	Penn SY	6 Sep 1943	31 Oct 1943	12 Jun 1951
AK 263	*Aquarius* ex-*John D. Whidden*	Butler; Dul	5 Oct 1943	24 Nov 1943	12 Jun 1951
AK 264	*Centaurus* ex-*Nat Brown*, ex-*Northern Explorer*	McCloskey	2 Oct 1944	25 Mar 1945	12 Jun 1951
AK 265	*Cepheus* ex-*Richard W. Dixie*	Avondale	13 Nov 1944	21 Feb 1945	12 Jun 1951
AK 266	*Serpens* ex-*William Lester*, ex-*Northern Yeoman*	McCloskey	16 Oct 1944	17 Jun 1945	12 Jun 1951
Displacement	1,677 tons; 5,202 f/l				
Dimensions	269'10" (oa); 250'(wl) × 41'1" × 20'5"				
Machinery	1 screw; turbine; 10 knots				

Notes: Type N3-S-A2. Acquired for loan to Korea.

Service Records:

AK 261 *Alchiba* Trfd to Korea 12 Jun 1951. Stricken 1 Feb 1960. Sold 27 Jun 1960, BU Hong Kong.
AK 262 *Algorab* Trfd to Korea 12 Jun 1951. Stricken 1 Feb 1960. Sold 27 Jun 1960, BU Hong Kong.
AK 263 *Aquarius* Trfd to Korea 12 Jun 1951. Stricken 1 Feb 1960. Sold 27 Jun 1960, BU Hong Kong.
AK 264 *Centaurus* Trfd to Korea 12 Jun 1951. Stricken 1 Feb 1960. BU 1960 Hong Kong.
AK 265 *Cepheus* Trfd to Korea 12 Jun 1951. Stricken 1 Feb 1960. BU 1960 Hong Kong.
AK 266 *Serpens* Trfd to Korea 12 Jun 1951. Stricken 1 Feb 1960. BU 1960 Hong Kong.

No.	Name	Builder	Keel Laid	Launched	In service
AK 269	*Comet*	Sun	15 May 1956	31 Jul 1957	27 Jan 1958
Displacement	7,605 tons; 18,150 f/l				
Dimensions	499′ (oa); 447′9″ (wl) × 78′ × 27′				
Machinery	2 screws; ST; 2 B&W boilers; 13,200 SHP, 18 knots				
Endurance	12000/18				
Complement	56				
Armament	none				

Notes: Type C3-ST-14a. Vehicle cargo ship. Two side ports. MSTS.

Service Record: Collided with tug *Julia C. Moran* in New York harbor, 23 Jun 1961. Rec **LSV 7**, 1 Jun 1963. Rec **AKR 7**, 1 Jan 1969. OS 22 Apr 1984. RRF 1985–2006.
◆Gulf War. Laid up 28 Jul 2006. NDRF. SE.

No.	Name	Builder	Keel Laid	Launched	Comm.
AK 270	*Eltanin*	Avondale	4 Jun 1956	16 Jan 1957	12 Oct 1957
AK 271	*Mirfak*	Avondale	5 Jul 1956	5 Aug 1957	30 Dec 1957
AK 272	*Mizar*	Avondale	21 Jan 1957	7 Oct 1957	7 Mar 1958
Displacement	2,036 tons; 4,942 f/l				
Dimensions	262′ 2″ (oa); 247′9″ (wl) × 51′6″ × 22′9″				
Machinery	2 screws; diesel-electric; 3,200 BHP; 12 knots				
Complement	61				
Armament	none				

Notes: Type C1-ME2-13a. Cargo ships with ice-strengthened hulls. MSC. *Mizar* converted to deep-ocean research ship with a center well for lowering towed instruments.

Figure 11.19: *USNS Eltanin* (T-AGOR 8), oceanographic research ship.

Figure 11.20: *USNS Taurus* (T-AKR 8), was a landing ship dock under construction at the end of World War II and completed as a civilian vessel. Acquired by the Navy in 1959.

Service Records:

AK 270 *Eltanin* Rec **AGOR 8**, 15 Nov 1962. Trfd to Argentina 19 Feb 1974
  Later history: renamed *Islas Orcadas*. Returned 1 Aug 1979. Stricken 19 Apr 1988. Out of service 2 Jul 1990. Sold 5 Feb 1992, BU.
  ◆Antarctic Sep 1963–Apr 1964.
AK 271 *Mirfak* OS 11 Dec 1979. Stricken 21 Feb 1992, NDRF. BU 2003, Brownsville, Tex.
AK 272 *Mizar* Rec **AGOR 11**, 15 Apr 1964. Damaged in collision with icebreaker *Edisto* north of Iceland, 5 Oct 1972. Damaged by engine room explosion and fire west of Sumatra, 19 May 1977. Out of service 17 Jan 1990. Stricken 7 Feb 1992, NDRF. Sold 8 Jul 2005, BU Chesapeake, Va.

No.	Name	Builder	Launched	Acquired	Comm.
AK 273	*Taurus* ex-*TMT Carib Queen* ex-LSD 23 *Fort Snelling*	Gulf	Aug 46	15 Jan 1959	15 May 1959
Displacement	6,000 tons; 9,950 f/l				
Dimensions	457′9″ (oa); 454′ (wl) × 72′2″ × 18′				
Machinery	2 screws; GT; 7,400 SHP; 16 knots				
Complement	69				
Armament	none				

Notes: Laid down as dock landing ship, completed as commercial vessel.

Service Record: Rec **LSV 8**, 1 Jun 1963. Rec **AKR 8**, 14 Aug 1969. Stricken 18 Jun 1971.
  Later history: Merchant *Douglas Carver* 1974, renamed *Inco 109* 1988. BU 1989 Alang, India.

No.	Name	Builder	Keel Laid	Launched	In service
AK 277	*Schuyler Otis Bland*	Ingalls	29 May 1950	30 Jan 1951	15 Sep 1961
Displacement	5,394 tons; 15,910 f/l				
Dimensions	478′2″(oa); 450′10″(wl) × 70′ × 26′				
Machinery	1 screw; ST; 2 boilers; 13,750 SHP; 18.5 knots				
Complement	23				
Armament	none				

Notes: Type C3-S-DX1. Prototype cargo ship, not economically competitive. Acquired 4 Aug 1961, MSC.

Service Record: Stricken 15 Aug 1979. Sold 28 Nov 1979, BU Taiwan.

Transports and Supply Ships   205

Figure 11.21: *USNS Schuyler Otis Bland* (T-AK 277). A prototype cargo ship used by the Navy after it was found to be not economically competitive.

Figure 11.22: *USNS Meteor* (T-AKR 9), built as a RO-RO ship for the Navy named *Sea Lift* in 1965. Seen here in 1975 after being renamed.

No.	Name	Builder	Keel Laid	Launched	In service
AK 278	*Sea Lift*	Puget Sd Brdg	19 May 1964	18 Apr 1965	19 May 1967
Displacement	11,130 tons; 22,150 f/l (1986); 16,467 grt				
Dimensions	540′ (oa); 499′6″ (wl) × 83′8″ × 29′				
Machinery	2 screws; ST; 2 boilers; 19,400 SHP; 20 knots				
Endurance	10000/20				
Complement	47				
Armament	none				

Notes: Type C4-ST-67a. Built as roll on/roll off ship.

Service Record: Rec **LSV 9**, 1 Jun 1963. Rec **AKR 9**, 14 Aug 1969. Renamed *Meteor*, 12 Sep 1975. To RDF, 3 Apr 1980. Out of service 30 Oct 1985. RRF 1986–2005. ◆Gulf War. Laid up 28 Jul 2006. NDRF. SE.

No.	Name	Builder	Launched	Acquired
AK 279	*Norwalk* ex-*Norwalk Victory*	Oregon	10 Jul 1945	30 Dec 1963
AK 280	*Furman* ex-*Furman Victory*	Oregon	6 Mar 1945	18 Sep 1963

Figure 11.23: *USNS Southern Cross* (T-AK 285), acquired as a pre-positioning ship and served with Ready Reserve Force until 1993.

AK 281	*Victoria* ex-*Ethiopia Victory*	Perm. #2	20 Apr 1944	11 Oct 1965
AK 282	*Marshfield* ex-*Marshfield Victory*	Oregon	15 May 1944	28 May 1970
Displacement	6,700 tons; 11,150 f/l			
Dimensions	455′ (oa); 436′ (wl) × 62′ × 24′			
Machinery	1 screw; ST; 2 boilers; 8,500 SHP; 17 knots			
Complement	69			
Armament	none			

Notes: Type VC2-S-AP. FBM resupply ships. Could carry 16 missiles. *Furman* had FBM gear removed, later served as research ship, Sep 1981.

Service Records:

AK 279 *Norwalk* Stricken 1 Aug 1979. Sold 8 Sep 1993, BU India.
AK 280 *Furman* OS 22 Oct 1986. Stricken 13 Apr 1992, NDRF. Sold 30 Oct 2003, BU Brownsville.
AK 281 *Victoria* Damaged by fire at Brooklyn, NY, 3 Aug 1973. OS 7 Nov 1983. Stricken 31 Mar 1986. BU 1988 Taiwan.
AK 282 *Marshfield* OS 23 Oct 1992. Stricken 30 Nov 1992, NDRF. Sold 26 Aug 2005, BU 2006, Chesapeake, Va.
AK 283 *Wyandot* Ex-AKA 92. 1 Jan 1969. Stricken 31 Mar 1986.

No.	Name	Builder	Launched	Acquired	In service
AK 284	*Northern Light* ex-*Cove*, ex-*Mormaccove*	Sun	29 Jun 1961	1980	22 Apr 1980
AK 285	*Southern Cross* ex-*Mormactrade*	Sun	23 Jan 1962	1 Dec 1979	1 May 1980
AK 286	*Vega* ex-*Kingsbay*, ex-*Bay*, ex-*Mormacbay*	Sun	12 May 1960	29 Apr 1981	18 Mar 1983
Displacement	18,365 tons f/l; 9,361 grt				
Dimensions	483′3″ (oa) × 68′ × 31′10″ 284: 487′7″(oa)				
Machinery	1 screw; ST; 2 boilers; 11,000 SHP; 19 knots				
Endurance	14,000/18				
Complement	50 to 70				
Armament	none				

Notes: Type C3-S-33a. MSC. 284–285 acquired as pre-positioning ships, 286 as SSBN supply ship.

Service Records:

AK 284 *Northern Light* OS 26 Apr 1984. RRF 1984–2000. ◆Gulf War. NDRF. SE.

AK 285 *Southern Cross* OS 13 Sep 1984. RRF 1985–1994. NDRF. SE.
AK 286 *Vega* to MSC 4 Mar 1983. OS 28 Apr 1994. Stricken 7 Nov 1998. BU 1999 Brownsville.

CARGO SHIP, DOCK

No.	Name	Builder	Keel Laid	Launched	In service
AKD 1	*Point Barrow*	Maryland Sbdg	18 Sep 1956	25 May 1957	9 May 1958
Displacement	5,562 tons; 12,430 f/l				
Dimensions	492′ (oa); 475′ (wl) × 78′ × 28′; *1987*: 465′6″(oa) × 74′ × 22′6″				
Machinery	2 screws; ST; 2 boilers; 6,000 SHP; 15 knots				
Endurance	8,800/10				
Complement	44 (1987)				
Armament	none				

Notes: Type S2-ST-23a. MSTS. Built as dock cargo ship for supplying Arctic radar installations. Converted 1965 to carry Saturn missile boosters to Cape Kennedy for Project Apollo, with large hangar over the docking well. Overhauled 1982 as support ship for Trident test firings and to support deep submergence vehicles, including *Trieste II*.

Service Record: Rec **AGDS 2** and renamed **Point Loma**, 28 Feb 1974. Decomm 1 Oct 1986, to MCS. Stricken 1 Oct 1993. Sold 29 Sep 1995, sale canceled. NDRF. Sold 15 Dec 2005, BU 2006 Brownsville, Tex.

DRY CARGO SHIPS

No.	Name	Builder	Keel Laid	Launched	In service
T-AKE 1	*Lewis and Clark*	Nat. Steel	26 Jan 2004	21 May 2005	20 Jun 2006
T-AKE 2	*Sacagawea*	Nat. Steel	18 Jun 2005	24 Jun 2006	27 Feb 2007
T-AKE 3	*Alan Shepard*	Nat. Steel	14 Feb 2006	6 Dec 2006	26 Jun 2007
T-AKE 4	*Richard E. Byrd*	Nat. Steel	28 Jul 2006	15 May 2007	14 Nov 2007
T-AKE 5	*Robert E. Peary*	Nat. Steel	12 Dec 2006	27 Oct 2007	5 Jun 2008
T-AKE 6	*Amelia Earhart*	Nat. Steel	29 May 2007	6 Apr 2008	—
T-AKE 7	*Carl Brashear*	Nat. Steel	2 Nov 2007	18 Sep 2008	—
T-AKE 8	*Wally Schirra*	Nat. Steel	14 Apr 2009	—	—
T-AKE 9	—	Nat. Steel	—	—	—
Displacement	35,400 tons f/l				
Dimensions	689′ (oa) × 105′6″ × 28′2″				
Machinery	1 screw; diesel-electric; hp 20 knots				
Endurance	14,000/20				
Complement	172				
Armament	none				

Notes: Fourteen to be built, to replace AE and AFS types. Named for "legendary explorers."

VEHICLE CARGO SHIPS

No.	Name	Former	Date	Reclassified	Date
AKR 7	*Comet*	LSV 7	1 Jun 1963	rec AKR 7	1 Jan 1969
AKR 8	*Taurus*	LSV 8	1 Jun 1963	rec AK 273	1 Jan 1969
AKR 9	*Sea Lift*	LSV 9	1 Jun 1963	rec AK 278	1 Jan 1969

No.	Name	Builder	Launched	Acquired	Comm.
AKR 10	*Mercury* ex-*Illinois*	Bath	21 Dec 1976	14 Apr 1980	2 Jun 1980
AKR 11	*Jupiter* ex-*Lipscomb Lykes* (14 May 1980), ex-*Arizona*	Bath	1 Nov 1975	7 May 1980	7 May 1980
Displacement	14,222 tons; 33,765 f/l; 13,158 grt				
Dimensions	684′6″(oa) × 102′ × 32′				
Machinery	2 screws; ST; 2 boilers; 37,000 SHP; 23 knots				
Endurance	10,000/23				
Complement	40				
Armament	none				

Notes: Type C7-S-95a. RO/RO vehicle carriers with side ports and stern ramp. MSC.

Service Records:

AKR 10 *Mercury* OS 1 Apr 1993. Renamed *Cape Island*, 22 Nov 1993, RRF (see p. 242).
◆Gulf War Oct 1990–Mar 1991.

AKR 11 *Jupiter* OS 26 Apr 1986. RRF 1986–1992. Renamed *Cape Intrepid*, 22 Nov 1993, RRF (see p. 242)

Figure 11.24: *USNS Sacagawea* (T-AKE 2), 2007, a new type of replenishment ship designed to replace ammunition and store ships.

Figure 11.25: *USS Chimon* (AKS 31), a converted LST.

CARGO STORES-ISSUE SHIPS

AKS 1 *Castor* Out of comm 30 Jun 1947–24 Nov 1950. Damaged in storm at sea off Yokosuka, 18 Mar 1952. Decomm 31 Oct 1968. Stricken 1 Dec 1968. BU 1969 Japan.
2★Korea K-5 K-6; 6★Vietnam Apr 1961, Sep 1963, Jul, Sep, Nov 1964–Apr 1965, Jun–Jul, Sep–Oct 1965, Apr–May, Jul–Dec 1966, Feb, Apr–May, Jul–Oct, Dec 1967–Mar, May 1968; ◆Passage to Freedom 1954, Taiwan Straits Oct–Nov 1958, Quemoy-Matsu Jan–Feb, Apr–May, Jul–Aug, Nov 1959, Jan–Feb, Apr, Jun 1960, Jan–Apr 1961, Jun–Sep, Nov 1961, Jan, Mar–Apr, Jun, Dec 1962–Jan 1963, Mar, May 1963.

AKS 4 *Pollux* Out of comm 13 Dec 1949–5 Aug 1950. Decomm 31 Dec 1968. Stricken 1 Jan 1969. BU 1969 Japan.
4★Korea K-1 K-2 K-4 K-6; 7★Vietnam Apr, Aug, Nov 1963, Aug–Sep 1964, Feb–Mar, May–Sep 1965, Nov 1965–Jan 1966, Mar–Jun 1966, Aug 1966–Jan 1967, Mar, Jun, Aug–Nov 1967, Jan–Oct 1968; ◆Taiwan Straits Sep–Dec 1958, Quemoy-Matsu 11 Feb 1961.

AKS 20 *Mercury* Decomm 28 May 1959. Stricken 1 Aug 1959. BU 1975, Brownsville.
◆Lebanon Aug–Sep 1958.

No.	Name	Former	Date
AKS 21	Belle Isle	AG 73	18 Aug 1951
AKS 22	Coasters Island	AG 74	18 Aug 1951
AKS 23	Cuttyhunk Island	AG 75	18 Aug 1951
AKS 24	Avery Island	AG 76	18 Aug 1951
AKS 25	Indian Island	AG 77	18 Aug 1951
AKS 26	Kent Island	AG 78	18 Aug 1951
AKS 27	Electron ★Korea 1951–1953	AG 146	18 Aug 1951
AKS 28	Proton ★Korea 1951–1953	AG 147	18 Aug 1951
AKS 29	Colington	AG 148	18 Aug 1951
AKS 30	League Island ★Korea 1951–1953	AG 149	18 Aug 1951
AKS 31	Chimon ★Korea	AG 150	18 Aug 1951
AKS 32	Altair	AK 257	12 Aug 1952
AKS 33	Antares	AK 258	1 Apr 1959

CARGO SHIPS AND AIRCRAFT FERRIES

No.	Name	Reclassified	Date
AKV 3	Lt. James E. Robinson	AK 274	7 May 1959
AKV 4	Pvt. Joseph F. Merrell	AK 275	7 May 1959
AKV 5	Sgt. Jack J. Pendleton	AK 276	7 May 1959

No.	Name	Builder	Launched	Acquired	In service
AKV 6	Albert M. Boe	New England	11 Jul 1945	26 Sep 1945	1 Mar 1950
AKV 7	Cardinal O'Connell	New England	11 Jun 1945	31 Aug 1945	1 Mar 1950

Displacement	5,700 tons; 11,365 f/l
Dimensions	441'6"(oa); 422' (wl) × 56'11" × 23'
Machinery	1 screw; VTE; 2,500 hp; 11 knots
Complement	254

Notes: Type EC2-S-C5. MSTS. Had kingposts instead of regular masts.

Service Records:

AKV 6 *Albert M. Boe* OS 1 Dec 1953. Stricken 11 Mar 1954, sold 1964.
Later history: Merchant *Star of Kodiak*.

AKV 7 *Cardinal O'Connell* OS 13 Jan 1954. Stricken 11 Mar 1954. Scuttled off Cape Flattery, Wash., Oct 1969.
3★Korea K-1 K-7 K-8.

No.	Name	Former
AKV 8	Kula Gulf	CVE 108
AKV 9	Cape Gloucester	CVE 109
AKV 10	Salerno Bay	CVE 110
AKV 11	Vella Gulf	CVE 111
AKV 12	Siboney	CVE 112
AKV 13	Puget Sound	CVE 113
AKV 14	Rendova	CVE 114
AKV 15	Bairoko	CVE 115
AKV 16	Badoeng Strait	CVE 116
AKV 17	Saidor	CVE 117
AKV 18	Sicily	CVE 118
AKV 19	Point Cruz	CVE 119
AKV 20	Mindoro	CVE 120
AKV 21	Rabaul	CVE 121
AKV 22	Palau	CVE 122
AKV 23	Tinian	CVE 123
AKV 24	Nehenta Bay	CVE 74
AKV 25	Hoggatt Bay	CVE 75
AKV 26	Kadashan Bay	CVE 76
AKV 27	Marcus Island	CVE 77
AKV 28	Savo Island	CVE 78
AKV 29	Rudyerd Bay	CVE 81
AKV 30	Sitkoh Bay	CVE 86
AKV 31	Takanis Bay	CVE 89
AKV 32	Lunga Point	CVE 94
AKV 33	Hollandia	CVE 97
AKV 34	Kwajalein	CVE 98
AKV 35	Bougainville	CVE 99
AKV 36	Matanikau	CVE 101
AKV 37	Commencement Bay	CVE 105
AKV 38	Block Island	CVE 106
AKV 39	Gilbert Islands	CVE 107
AKV 40	Card	CVE 11
AKV 41	Core	CVE 13
AKV 42	Breton	CVE 23
AKV 43	Croatan	CVE 25

Notes: All rec 7 May 1959, to remove ships from combatant category. AKV 40–43 activated to support Vietnam war.

LIGHT CARGO SHIPS

No.	Name	ex-Army	Builder	Completed	Acquired	Comm.
AKL 1	Camano	FS 246	Wheeler	Jun 1944	22 Feb 1947	16 Jul 1947
AKL 2	Deal	FS 263	Wheeler	Aug 1944	2 Mar 1947	3 Aug 1947
AKL 3	Elba	FS 267	Wheeler	Oct 1944	14 Mar 1947	3 Jul 1947
AKL 4	Errol	FS 274	Wheeler	Oct 1944	3 Apr 1947	9 Jul 1947

AKL 5	*Estero*	FS 275	Wheeler	Oct 1944	3 Apr 1947	5 Jul 1947
AKL 6	*Jekyl*	FS 282	Wheeler	Dec 1944	22 Feb 1947	2 May 1947
AKL 7	*Metomkin*	FS 316	Mathis	Aug 1944	28 Feb 1947	16 Aug 1947
AKL 8	*Roque*	FS 347	Kewaunee	Sep 1944	3 Apr 1947	2 May 1947
AKL 9	*Ryer*	FS 361	Sturgeon Bay	Mar 1944	3 Apr 1947	8 Jun 1947
AKL 10	*Sharps*	FS 385	Ingalls, Decatur	Oct 1944	3 Apr 1947	3 Aug 1947
AKL 11	*Torry*	FS 394	Ingalls, Decatur	Dec 1944	3 Apr 1947	—
AKL 12	*Mark*	FS 214	Higgins	Dec 1944	30 Sep 1947	2 Dec 1947
AKL 13	*Tingles*	FS 266	Wheeler	Aug 1944	30 Sep 1947	—
AKL 14	*Hewell*	FS 391	United Concrete	Jul 1944	2 Feb 1948	5 Jun 1948
AKL 15	—	FS 230	Higgins	Mar 1945	1 Mar 1950	—
AKL 16	—	FS 233	Higgins	Mar 1945	1 Mar 1950	—
AKL 17	—	FS 289	Wheeler	Feb 1945	1 Mar 1950	—
AKL 18	—	FS 174	Higgins	May 1944	1 Jul 1950	—
AKL 19	—	FS 175	Higgins	May 1944	1 Jul 1950	—
AKL 20	—	FS 193	Higgins	Aug 1944	1 Jul 1950	—
AKL 21	—	FS 259	Wheeler	Jul 1944	1 Jul 1950	—
AKL 22	—	FS 276	Wheeler	Nov 1944	1 Jul 1950	—
AKL 23	—	FS 288	Wheeler	Feb 1945	1 Jul 1950	—
AKL 24	—	FS 309	Mathis	Feb 1944	1 Jul 1950	—
AKL 25	*Banner*	FS 345	Kewaunee	Jul 1944	1 Jul 1950	—
AKL 26	—	FS 368	Sturgeon Bay	Jul 1944	1 Jul 1950	—
AKL 27	—	FS 369	Sturgeon Bay	Jul 1944	1 Jul 1950	—
AKL 28	*Brule*	FS 370	Sturgeon Bay	Jul 1944	1 Jul 1950	—
AKL 29	—	FS 371	Sturgeon Bay	Aug 1944	1 Jul 1950	—
AKL 30	—	FS 400	Ingalls, Decatur	Mar 1945	1 Jul 1950	—
AKL 31	—	FS 401	Hickinbotham	Jan 1945	1 Jul 1950	—
AKL 32	—	FS 548	United Concrete	Oct 1944	1 Jul 1950	—
AKL 33	—	FS 238	Martinolich	May 1944	1 Nov 1950	—
AKL 34	—	FS 343	Kewaunee	Jun 1944	1 Nov 1950	—
AKL 35	—	FS 383	Ingalls, Decatur	Sep 1944	1 Nov 1950	—
AKL 36	—	FS 398	Ingalls, Decatur	Feb 1945	1 Nov 1950	—
AKL 37	*Alcyone*	FS 195	Higgins	Aug 1944	8 Dec 1951	—
AKL 38	*Alhena*	FS 257	Wheeler	Jun 1944	12 Dec 1951	—
AKL 39	*Almaack*	FS 283	Wheeler	Dec 1944	12 Dec 1951	—
AKL 40	*Deimos*	FS 390	United Concrete	Jun 1944	12 Dec 1951	—
AKL 41	*Pamina*	FS 528	Calumet	Nov 1944	12 Dec 1951	—
AKL 42	*Renate*	FS 547	United Concrete	Sep 1944	12 Dec 1951	—
AKL 43	—	FS 219	Higgins	Jan 1945	1 Jan 1962	—
AKL 44	*Pueblo*	FS 344	Kewaunee	Jul 1945	12 Apr 1966	13 May 1967
AKL 45	*Palm Beach*	FS 217	Higgins	Dec 1944	18 May 1966	13 May 1967

Displacement	465 tons (AKL 33)
Dimensions	177′ (oa); 165′ (wl) × 32′9″ × 14′3″ (Higgins type: 166′3″); (AKL 33: 138′9 (wl) × 33′3 × 17′8″)
Machinery	2 screws diesel; SHP 1,000; 12 knots (AKL 33: 1 screw, diesel, SHP 875)
Complement	27

Notes: Acquired from U.S. Army. Originally classified AG 130–140, 143–145, rec 31 Mar 1949. Prior to acquisition, AKL 21 was named *Pvt. Robert T. Henry*, 25 *Capt William W. Galt*, 33 *Cpl. Henry R. Harr*, 34 *Sgt. Ellis R. Weicht*, 35 *Lt. Thomas W. Wegle*, and 36 *Cpl. John J. Pinder*. AKL 38–42 loaned to Korea. AKL 25, 44 and 45 were ELINT ships. *Brule* had a large circular structure aft.

Service notes:

AKL 1   *Camano*   Decomm, to Dept of Interior, 22 Dec 1952. Stricken 1959.
    Later history: Merchant *Star 60*, *Rio Chagres* 1984.

AKL 2   *Deal*   Decomm 8 Sep 1955. Stricken 1 Jul 1961. Sold 18 Dec 1961.
    Later history: Merchant *Don Carlos*, renamed *Olga Patricia* 1964, *Laissez-Faire* 1966, *Akuarius II* 1970, *Earl J. Conrad Jr.* 1974.
    7★Korea K-2 K-4 K-5 K-6 K-8 K-9 K-10.

AKL 3   *Elba*   to Dept of Interior 29 Jan 1952, sold 1957.
    Later history: Merchant *Triton* 1957, renamed *Morelia* 1962. Lost by grounding near San Jose del Cabo, Mexico, 6 Aug 1962.

AKL 4   *Errol*   To Dept of Interior, 29 Jan 1952. Sold 1965.
    Later history: Merchant *Palau Islander* 1965.

AKL 5   *Estero*   Decomm 22 Jan 1960. Stricken 1 Feb 1960. Sold.
    Later history: Merchant *Presidente Quirino*.
    7★Korea K-1 K-3 K-6 K-7 K-8 K-9 K-10; ◆Passage to Freedom 1954. Taiwan Straits Sep–Oct 1958.

AKL 6   *Jekyl*   Stricken 1 Nov 1957. Sold 18 May 1960.
    Later history: Merchant *Betty K. IV* 1960, renamed *Nilo*, *Hope I*, 1989.

AKL 7   *Metomkin*   To Dept of Interior 3 Aug 1951. Stricken 16 Jan 1952.

AKL 8   *Roque*   To Dept of Interior 23 Jul 1951. Stricken 29 Jan 1952.
    Later history: Merchant *Mermaid*. Foundered SE of Hawaii, 10 Aug 1982.

AKL 9   *Ryer*   Decomm 4 Aug 1955. Stricken 1 Jul 1961.
    Later history: Merchant *Ahti* 1962, renamed *Caldrill No.1* 1963, *Cuss No.1*, *West 1*, 1980.
    6★Korea K-1 K-2 K-3 K-4 K-5 K-6.

AKL 10   *Sharps*   Trfd to Korea 3 Apr 1956.
    Later history: renamed *Kun San* (AKL 908). SE1972.
    3★Korea K-6 K-7 K-8; ◆Passage to Freedom 1954.

AKL 11   *Torry*   To Dept of Interior 1952. Sold 1961.

AKL 12   *Mark*   Trfd to Taiwan, 1 Jul 1971.
    Later history: renamed *Yung Kang* (359). SE1993.
    12★Vietnam Dec 1965–Jun 1967, Jun–Dec 1968, Jun–Jul 1969, Jan–Aug, Oct 1970–Mar 1971.

AKL 13 *Tingles* OS 10 Nov 1949. Stricken 1 Apr 1959.
Later history: Merchant *Ran-Annim* 1959. BU 1982.
AKL 14 *Hewell* Decomm 15 Mar 1955. Stricken 1 Nov 1959. Sold 2 Jun 1960.
Later history: Merchant *Betty K.* 1960, renamed *Sea Princess* 1980, *Lady K.* 1984.
7★Korea K-1 K-2 K-3 K-7 K-8 K-9 K-10.
AKL 15 Stricken 1 May 1959.
Later history: Merchant *Mereghan II.*
AKL 16 Stricken 1 May 1959.
Later history: Merchant *Martha Anne* 1959, renamed *King Tower* 1982.
AKL 17 MSTS. Named *New Bedford*, 20 Nov 1961. Name canceled 26 Aug 1963. Rec **IX 308** and named *New Bedford*, Feb 1969. Torpedo test firing vessel. Stricken 4 Apr 1995.
Later history: merchant *Sea Bird.*
AKL 18 MSTS. Stricken 1 May 1959.
Later history: Merchant *Aries*, renamed *Gatun II*, *Hermosillo*, *Charlie Peterson.*
AKL 19 MSTS. Stricken 1 May 1959.
Later history: Merchant *President Laurel*, renamed *Laurel.*
AKL 20 MSTS. Stricken 1 Jul 1961.
Later history: Merchant *Star 50*, renamed *Mereghan IV* 1965.
AKL 21 MSTS. Stricken 1 May 1959.
Later history; Merchant *Kirk Star.*
AKL 22 MSTS. Stricken 1 Jan 1961.
Later history: Merchant *AKL-22.*
AKL 23 MSTS. Stricken 1 May 1959.
Later history: Merchant *AKL-23*, renamed *Chilpancingo*. Wrecked in hurricane at Isla Margarita, Baja California, 31 Aug 1967.
AKL 24 MSTS. Stricken 1959.
Later history: Merchant *President Osmena.*
AKL 25 Named *Banner*, 24 Nov 1952. Comm 24 Nov 1952. Collided with Soviet AGI *Anemometr* in Sea of Japan, 24 Jun 1966. Rec **AGER 1**, 1 Jun 1967. Decomm and stricken 14 Nov 1969. Sold 5 Jun 1970, BU Japan.
★Korea 1953; ◆Korea Jan–Mar 1968.
AKL 26 Stricken 1 Jul 1961.
Later history: Merchant *New Providence* 1961, renamed *Temac* 1964, *New Providence.*
AKL 27 Stricken 27 Apr 1966. Hulk used for salvage training. Sold 1971, BU.
AKL 28 Named *Brule*, 31 Oct 1952. Comm 31 Oct 1952. Out of comm 6 Dec 1956–1 Sep 1965. Decomm 1 Nov 1971 and trfd to Korea.
Later history: renamed *Ulsan.*
★Korea 1953; 13★Vietnam Jan 1966–Oct 1967, Apr 1968–Dec 1969, Jun 1970–Oct 1971.
AKL 29 MSTS. Stricken 1 Aug 1960.
Later history: Merchant *Menara Mas*, renamed *Johanas* 1964, *Moma* 1965, *Johanas* 1966, *King Tower* 1967. BU 1972.
AKL 30 MSTS. To Fish and Wildlife Service, 1 Jul 1961.
Later history: renamed *George B. Kelez.*
AKL 31 MSTS. To Dept of Interior, 21 Dec 1970
Later history: renamed *Robert A. Debrun* 1971.
AKL 32 Stricken 1 Jul 1961.
Later history: Merchant *Carlos Miguel*, renamed *Tangier Island* 1980.
AKL 33 Stricken 26 Apr 1958.
Later history: Merchant *Jamene* 1959, renamed *Reefer Queen*, *Blue Meridian.*
AKL 34 OS Mar 1953. Stricken 1 Oct 1958.
Later history: Merchant *AKL-34.*
AKL 35 Trfd to Korea Sep 1956.
Later history: renamed *Masan* (AKL 909). SE1972.

AKL 36 Stricken 1 Nov 1959.
Later history: Merchant *Bertha Ann*, renamed *Viceroy.*
AKL 37 Loan to Korea. Stricken 1 Feb 1960.
Later history: Merchant *Puerto Manzanillo*, renamed *Colima.*
AKL 38 Loan to Korea. Stricken 1 Feb 1960.
AKL 39 Loan to Korea. Stricken 1 Feb 1960.
AKL 40 Loan to Korea. Stricken 1 Feb 1960.
AKL 41 Loan to Korea. Stricken 1 Feb 1960.
AKL 42 Loan to Korea. Stricken 1 Feb 1960.
AKL 43 Stricken 7 Oct 1963.
Later history: Merchant *Santa Maria.*
AKL 44 *Pueblo* Rec **AGER 2**, 1 Jun 1967. Seized at sea by North Korean mtb's off east coast of North Korean, 23 Jan 1968 (1 killed). (Crew not released until 23 Dec 1968.)
Later history: Preserved as a museum at Wonsan by North Korea.
◆Korea Jan 1968.
AKL 45 *Palm Beach* Rec **AGER 3**, 2 May 1967. Stricken 1 Dec 1969. Sold May 1970.
AKL 398 *Redbud* Acquired from Coast Guard, 1949. Returned 10 Nov 1970.

OILERS

AO 22 *Cimarron* Decomm and stricken 1 Oct 1968. BU 1969.
7★Korea K-1 K-2 K-4 K-6 K-8 K-9 K-10; 4★Vietnam May–Oct 1965, Apr–Sep 1966, Apr–Sep 1967; ◆Passage to Freedom 1954, Liberia Sep–Dec 1958, Quemoy-Matsu 14 Jul 1959.
AO 24 *Platte* In collision with carrier *Kitty Hawk* off San Francisco, 16 Jun 1967. Decomm and stricken 25 Sep 1970. Sold 14 May 1971, BU.
1★Korea K-7, 1952; 8★Vietnam Feb–Aug 1965, Mar–Aug 1966, Jul 1967–Jan 1968, Sep–Dec 1968, Feb 1969, Nov 1969–Mar 1970, ◆Korea Dec 1969, Apr 1970.
AO 25 *Sabine* Out of comm 14 Feb 1955–10 Dec 1956, MSTS. OS 13 Nov 1957–14 Dec 1961. Stricken 14 Jan 1959. Reacq 1 Sep 1961. Recomm 14 Dec 1961. Decomm 20 Feb 1969. Stricken 1 Dec 1976. Sold 1 Aug 1983, BU Taiwan.
◆Cuba Jan–Mar 1962, Cuba Missile Crisis Oct–Nov 1962, Dominican Rep May–Jun 1965.
AO 26 *Salamonie* Damaged in collision with carrier *Wasp* east of San Juan, PR, 24 Mar 1967. Decomm 20 Dec 1968. Stricken 2 Sep 1969. Sold 24 Sep 1970, BU Netherlands.
◆Cuba Missile Crisis Nov 1962, Dominican Rep May–Jun 1965.
AO 27 *Kaskaskia* Out of comm 8 Apr 1955–8 Jan 1957, to MSTS. Decomm 21 Oct 1957. Stricken 2 Jan 1959. Reacq 1 Sep 1961. Recomm 6 Dec 1961. Decomm and stricken 19 Dec 1969. Sold 3 Aug 1970, BU Kaohsiung.
7★Korea K-1 K-2 K-4 K-7 K-8 K-9 K-10; ◆Cuba Missile Crisis Oct–Nov 1962, Dominican Rep Jul–Aug 1965.
AO 30 *Chemung* Out of comm 3 Jul 1950–1 Dec 1950. Decomm and stricken 18 Sep 1970. Sold 14 May 1971, BU 1971.
4★Korea K-6, K-7 K-8 K-9; 6★Vietnam Sep 1958, Dec 1960–Jan 1961, Sep–Dec 1964, Dec 1965–Mar 1966, May–Jul 1966, Jun 1967–Jan 1968, Jul 1968–Jan 1969, Oct 1969–Jan 1970; ★Taiwan Straits Sep 1958, Quemoy-Matsu Feb 1961, Korea Oct 1969, Feb–Mar 1970.
AO 32 *Guadalupe* In collision with LSD *Alamo* off Vietnam, 6 Jul 1972. Decomm and stricken 15 May 1975. Sold 16 Oct 1975, BU.
6★Korea K-2 K-4 K-6 K-7 K-8 K-9; 10★Vietnam Jan, Mar–Apr 1962, Dec 1964–May 1965, Feb–Jun 1966, Mar–Aug 1967, May–Oct 1968, Oct 1969, Aug–Oct 1970, Oct 1971–Jul 1972; ◆Taiwan Straits Nov 1958, Korea May 1968, Nov 1969.
AO 36 *Kennebec* MSTS, 1 Oct 1949. Out of comm 4 Sep 1950–11 Jan 1951, 25 Sep 1954–14 Dec 1956 and 31 Oct 1957–16 Dec 1961. Stricken 14 Jan 1959. Reacq 1 Sep 1961. Decomm 1 Apr 1970. Stricken 15 Jul 1976. Sold 1 Apr 1982, BU.

Figure 11.26: Underway replenishment at sea in the Pacific, 10 Aug 2007. *Kitty Hawk* (CV 63) and destroyer *McCampbell* (DDG 85) refuelling from oiler *John Ericsson* (T-AO 194), center.

Figure 11.27: USS *Sabine* (AO 25), a veteran oiler refitted for underway replenishment.

		7★Vietnam Aug–Sep 1964, Sep 1965–May 1966, Feb–Aug 1967, Apr–Sep 1968, Jun–Sep 1969, ◆Korea May–Jun, Oct 1969.
AO 37	*Merrimack*	MSTS, 1 Oct 1949. Out of comm 8 Feb 1950–6 Dec 1950. Decomm 20 Dec 1954. Stricken 1 Feb 1959. BU 1982 Hamburg.
AO 39	*Kankakee*	MSTS, 1 Oct 1949. Out of comm 30 Nov 1955–20 Dec 1956. Decomm 5 Nov 1957. Stricken Nov 1959. Reacq 1 Sep 1961. Recomm 29 Nov 1961. Decomm 27 Jun 1968. Stricken 1 Jun 1973. BU 1977 Brownsville, Tex.
		1★Korea K-7; ◆Cuba Missile Crisis Oct–Nov 1962, Dominican Rep May 1965.
AO 41	*Mattaponi*	MSTS, 1 Oct 1949. Out of comm 17 Apr 1950–28 Dec 1950, MSTS and 12 Oct 1954–12 Dec 1956. Decomm 11 Nov 1957. Stricken 1 Feb 1959. Reacq 1 Sep 1961. In collision with carrier *Kearsarge* off California, 5 Nov 1962. Recomm 30 Nov 1962. Decomm 30 Sep 1970. Stricken 15 Oct 1970. Sold 15 Dec 1971, BU.
		5★Vietnam Nov 1963, Feb–May 1965, Sep 1966–Mar 1967, Nov 1968–Apr 1969, Feb–Jun 1970, ◆Korea Feb, Jul 1970.
AO 42	*Monongahela*	MSTS, 1 Oct 1949. Out of comm 9 Jun 1950–9 Jan 1951, MSTS and 9 Jun 1955–28 Dec 1956, MSTS. OS 22 Aug 1957. Stricken 1 Feb 1959.
		1★Korea K-5.
AO 43	*Tappahannock*	MSTS 1 Oct 1949. Out of comm 3 Feb 1950–9 Mar 1951 and Jan 1955–12 Dec 1956 and 18 Nov 1957–31 May 1966. Damaged in collision with hospital ship *Repose* in South China Sea, 13 Jun 1967. Decomm 6 Mar 1970. Stricken 15 Jul 1976. Sold 2 Feb 1987, BU Taiwan.
		7★Vietnam Dec 1966–Jun 1967, Mar–Sep 1968, May–Aug 1969, ◆Korea Apr 1969.
AO 47	*Neches*	MSTS, 1 Oct 1949. Out of comm 10 Jul 1950–3 Jan 1951 and Jun 1955–24 Nov 1961. Collided with destroyer *Orleck* off Vietnam, 19 Mar 1970. Decomm 1970. Stricken 1 Oct 1970. Sold 15 Dec 1971, BU.
		★Vietnam Jul–Dec 1965, Jul 1966–Jan 1967, Sep–Oct, Dec 1967–Mar 1968, Sep 1968–Mar 1969, Jan–May 1970, ◆Korea Jun 1970.
AO 49	*Suamico*	Reacq 24 Jan 1948, civil crew. MSTS 1 Oct 1949, MSC. Stricken 15 Nov 1974. BU 1975 Hong Kong.
AO 50	*Tallulah*	Reacq 13 Feb 1948. MSTS 1 Oct 1949. In collision with m/v *Orion Planet* off San Pedro, Cal., 13 Feb 1955. Stricken 29 May 1975. Rec **AOT 50**, 30 Sep 1978. Stricken 31 Mar 1986. BU 1988 Taiwan.
		1★Korea.
AO 51	*Ashtabula*	Damaged by fire and explosion at Sasebo, Japan, 30 Nov 1952 (3 killed). Rebuilt 1968, new mid-section. In collision with LPD *Cleveland* off Thailand, 12 Jun 1982. Decomm 30 Sep 1982. Stricken 6 Sep 1991. Sold 25 Oct 1995. Sunk as target off San Diego, 15 Oct 2002. 4★Korea K-2 K-4 K-5 K-6; 8★Vietnam Aug–Sep 1963, Jun–Sep 1964, Aug 1965–Feb 1966, Sep 1966–Mar 1967, Jun–Nov 1969, Aug 1970–Feb 1971, Dec 1971–Jul 1972, Korea Nov–Dec 1969; ◆Quemoy-Matsu Jan–Feb 1959, Sep 1960, Evac of Vietnam 29–30 Apr 1975.
AO 52	*Cacapon*	Collided with destroyer *McKean* off Okinawa, 20 Mar 1970. Decomm and stricken 14 Aug 1973. Sold 4 Dec 1973, BU Portland, Ore. 7★Korea K-1 K-2 K-3 K-5 K-6 K-7 K-8; 8★Vietnam Mar–Jun 1965, Mar–Sep 1966, Jul 1967–Jan 1968, Aug 1968–Jan 1969, Nov 1969–Mar 1970, Apr–May 1971, Aug 1972–Mar 1973; ◆Antarctic Dec 1946–Mar 1947, Quemoy-Matsu 24 Sep 1960, Korea Oct 1969, Mar 1970, Feb 1971.
AO 53	*Caliente*	In collision with submarine tender *Nereus* off San Diego, 9 Oct 1963. Decomm and stricken 15 Dec 1973. Sold 5 Apr 1974. 4★Korea K-5 K-6 K-8 K-10; 8★Vietnam Aug 1958, Mar–May 1962, Nov 1964, Jul–Dec 1965, Mar–Jul 1968, Mar–Jul 1969, Jun–Oct 1970, Jul 1972, Feb–Mar 1973; ◆Passage to Freedom 1954.
AO 54	*Chikaskia*	MSTS, 1 Oct 1949. Out of comm 1 Oct 1949–28 Feb 1953, 7 Nov 1955–12 Dec 1956 and Dec 1958–17 Dec 1960. Stricken 1960. Reacq 1 Sep 1961. Decomm 4 Sep 1970. Stricken 1 Dec 1976. Sold 26 May 1982. 1★Korea K-10; ◆ Cuba Mar–May 1961, Cuba Missile Crisis Oct–Nov 1962.
AO 55	*Elokomin*	Collided with tug *Export* at Malta, 27 Jul 1967. Decomm and stricken 17 Mar 1970. BU ◆Cuba Apr–Jun 1961, Cuba Missile Crisis Oct–Nov 1962.

Figure 11.28: USS *Chikaskia* (AO 54).

AO 56 *Aucilla*   MSTS, 1 Oct 1949. Decomm 18 Dec 1970. Stricken 1 Dec 1976. Sold 27 Apr 1992, BU. .
★Korea 1950, 1951, 1952; ◆Lebanon Aug–Sep 1958, Dominican Rep Jun–Jul 1965.

AO 57 *Marias*   MSTS, 1 Oct 1949. Decomm 2 Oct 1973, to MSC. OS 30 Sep 1980. Decomm 15 Aug 1982. Stricken 11 Dec 1992. Sold 18 Sep 1995, BU Brownsville, Tex.
★Korea 1950; 1★Vietnam Jan–Mar 1973; ◆Lebanon Aug–Sep 1958, Cuba Missile Crisis Nov 1962.

AO 58 *Manatee*   MSTS, 1 Oct 1949. Decomm and stricken 14 Aug 1973. Sold 10 Dec 1973. BU 1974 Portland, Ore.
6★Korea K-5 K-6 K-7 K-8 K-9 K-10; 9★Vietnam Sep–Oct 1961, Jun–Sep 1964, Jul–Nov 1966, Jul–Nov 1967, Jun–ov 1968, Aug 1969–Jan 1970, Nov 1970–Mar 1971, Jun 1972–Feb 1973; ◆Taiwan Straits Aug–Sep 1958, Quemoy-Matsu 21 Jan 1961, Korea Aug 1969, Jan 1970, Oct 1970, Mar 1971.

AO 60 *Nantahala*   MSTS, 1 Oct 1949. Out of comm 1 Jun 1950–29 Dec 1950. Decomm and stricken 2 Jul 1973. used as fuel storage hulk. Sold 5 Mar 1975, BU.
◆Dominican Rep May 1965.

AO 61 *Severn*   MSTS, 1 Oct 1949. Out of comm 3 Jul 1950–29 Dec 1950. Decomm 1 Jul 1973. Stricken 1 Jul 1974. Sold 22 Jan 1975, BU Brownsville, Tex.
★Korea 1951; ◆Lebanon Jul–Aug 1958, Cuba Jun–Jul 1962.

AO 62 *Taluga*   MSTS, 1 Oct 1949. Decomm 4 May 1972, to MSC. OS 30 Sep 1980 or OS 29 Aug 1983. Stricken 21 Feb 1992. NDRF. SE.
4★Korea K-6 K-7 K-8 K-9; 12★Vietnam Mar–Apr 1962, Mar–Aug 1965, Jun 1969, Mar–Sep 1970, Aug–Sep 1971; ◆Passage to Freedom 1954, Evac of Cambodia, Apr 1975, Evac of Vietnam 29–30 Apr 1975.

AO 63 *Chipola*   MSTS, 1 Oct 1949. Out of comm 1 Aug 1955–29 Dec 1956 and 7 Nov 1957–17 Dec 1960. Stricken 1960. Reacq 1 Sep 1961. Decomm 11 Aug 1973. Stricken 14 Aug 1973. BU 1974 Portland, Ore.
★Korea 1950, 1951; 13★Vietnam Sep 1964–Jan 1965, Dec 1965–May 1966, Jun–Dec 1968, Jul–Dec 1969, Sep–Nov 1970, Jan–Mar 1971, Apr–Sep 1972; ◆Korea Jun–Jul 1969, Dec 1969–Jan 1970, Oct, Dec 1970–Jan 1971.

AO 64 *Tolovana*   MSTS, 1 Oct 1949. Out of comm . . Aug 1949–24 May 1951, to MSTS. Decomm and stricken 15 Apr 1975. Sold 16 Oct 1975, BU.
2★Korea K-6 K-7; 13★Vietnam Aug–Sep 1964, Jul–Nov 1965, Jun–Nov 1966, Nov 1967–Apr 1968, Dec 1968–Jun 1969, Mar–Jul 1970, May–Aug 1971, Oct 1972–Mar 1973; ◆Passage to Freedom 1954, Taiwan Straits Sep–Oct 1958, Korea Jan–Mar, 1 Dec 1968, Jun 1969, Jul 1970.

AO 65 *Pecos*   Reacq 30 Jan 1948. MSTS, 1 Oct 1949. Decomm and stricken 1 Oct 1974. BU 1975 Baltimore.

AO 67 *Cache*   Reacq 10 Feb 1948. MSTS, 1 Oct 1949. Stricken 6 May 1972. Rec **AOT 67**, 30 Sep 1978. Stricken 31 Mar 1986. BU 1988 Taiwan.

AO 69 *Enoree*   Out of comm 27 Mar 1947–18 Oct 1950. MSTS 30 Mar 1951. Out of comm 10 Dec 1954–10 Dec 1956. Decomm 22 Oct 1957. Stricken 1 Feb 1959. BU 1976 Brownsville, Tex.

AO 72 *Niobrara*   Out of comm 24 Sep 1946–5 Feb 1951 and 30 Nov 1954–14 Dec 1956. Decomm 12 Nov 1957. Stricken 1 Feb 1959.

AO 73 *Millicoma*   Reacq 13 Feb 1948. MSTS 1 Oct 1949. Rec **AOT 73**, 30 Sep 1978. Stricken 31 Mar 1986. BU Taiwan 1987.

AO 75 *Saugatuck*   Reacq 22 Jan 1948. MSTS, 1 Oct 1949. Rec **AOT 75**, 30 Sep 1978. Stricken 15 Feb 1995, NDRF. Sold 2 Jun 2006, BU Chesapeake, Va.

AO 76 *Schuylkill*   Reacq 30 Jan 1948. MSTS, 1 Oct 1949. Rec **AOT 76** 30 Apr 1978. Stricken 31 Mar 1986. Sold 4 Mar 1988, BU Taiwan.

AO 77 *Cossatot*   Reacq 13 Feb 1948. MSTS, 1 Oct 1949. Damaged in collision with m/v *Copper State* off Santa Barbara, Cal., 16 Jun 1968. Stricken 18 Sep 1974. Sold 2 Sep 1975, BU.

AO 78 *Chepachet*   Reacq 12 Feb 1948. MSTS, 1 Oct 1949. Stricken 13 Mar 1972. Rec **AOT 78**, 30 Apr 1978. Stricken 1 Apr 1980.

AO 79 *Cowanesque* : Reacq 18 Jan 1948. MSTS, 1 Oct 1949. Damaged in collision with m/v *Toscana* in Suez Roads, 7 Mar 1953. Went aground in Kin Bay, Okinawa, 23 Apr 1972, CTL. Stricken 1 Jun 1972. BU 1972 Kaohsiung.

Figure 11.30: *USNS Chepachet* (T-AO 78), about 1948.

Figure 11.29: *USS Severn* (AO 61), as a commissioned naval ship after 1950.

Figure 11.31: *USNS Escambia* (T-AO 80)

AO 80   *Escambia*   Reacq 26 Jan 1948. MSTS, 1 Oct 1949. Stricken 3 Oct 1957.
Later history: U.S. Army, mobile emergency power plant. BU 1971, Vietnam.

AO 81   *Kennebago*   Reacq 1 Oct 1949, MSTS. OS 27 Nov 1957–23 May 1958. Stricken 23 Jun 1959.
Later history: U.S. Army, mobile emergency power plant, Vietnam, 20 May 1966. Sold 4 Sep 1974, BU 1974 Kaohsiung.

AO 82   *Cahaba*   Reacq 5 Mar 1948. MSTS, 1 Oct 1949. Stricken 19 Dec 1955. Reacq 20 Jun 1956. Stricken 20 Jan 1958.
Later history: U.S. Army, mobile emergency power plant, Vietnam, 20 May 1966. BU 1971.

AO 83   *Mascoma*   Reacq 4 Feb 1948. MSTS, 1 Oct 1949. Stricken 18 Jun 1959. Sold 4 Nov 1966.
Later history: Merchant *Seatrain Oregon*, renamed *Transchamplain* 1967. BU 1980 Kaohsiung.

AO 84   *Ocklawaha*   Reacq 22 May 1948. To MSTS, 1 Oct 1949. Stricken 9 Jun 1959. Sold 2 Sep 1975, BU 1976 Brownsville, Tex.

AO 85   *Pamanset*   Reacq 10 Feb 1948. MSTS, 1 Oct 1949. Stricken 24 Feb 1956. Reacq 26 Jun 1956. Stricken 26 Sep 1957. Sold 3 May 1966.
Later history: Merchant *Seatrain Florida*, renamed *Florida* 1978. BU 1986, Taiwan.

AO 87   *Sebec*   Reacq 28 Apr 1950. MSTS, 1 Oct 1949. OS and Stricken 22 Dec 1955. Reacq 21 Jun 1956. Stricken 3 Sep 1957.
Later history: U.S. Army, mobile emergency power plant, Vietnam, 20 May 1966. Sold 4 Sep 1974, BU 1974 Kaohsiung.

AO 88   *Tomahawk*   Reacq 28 Feb 1948. MSTS, 1 Oct 1949. Stricken 1 Sep 1961. Sold 19 Jul 1966.
Later history: Merchant *Maine*, renamed *Seatrain Maine* 1967, *Maine* 1978. Assigned to RRF as *Maine*, 1978. (q.v.) (See p. 242)

AO 93   *Soubarissen*   Reacq 19 Feb 1948. MSTS, 1 Oct 1949. Stricken 19 Apr 1955. Reacq 6 Jul 1956. OS 30 Dec 1958. Stricken 1 Jul 1961. Sold 5 Apr 1982, BU.

AO 94   *Anacostia*   Reacq 28 Feb 1948. MSTS, 1 Oct 1949. OS and stricken 17 Dec 1957.
Later history: Merchant *Anacostia*, renamed *World Tolerance* 1963, *World Choice* 1963, *Nautilus* 1965, *Penn Ranger* 1968, *Omnium Ranger* 1973. BU 1976 Spain.

AO 95   *Caney*   Reacq 21 Feb 1948. MSTS, 1 Oct 1949. Stricken 21 May 1959.
Later history: U.S. Army, mobile emergency power plant, Vietnam, 20 May 1966. Sold 4 Sep 1974, BU 1974 Kaohsiung, Taiwan.

AO 96   *Tamalpais*   Reacq 10 Mar 1948. MSTS, 1 Oct 1949. Reinstated 28 Apr 1950. Stricken 18 Dec 1957. Sold 4 Sep 1974, BU 1974 Kaohsiung.

AO 97   *Allagash*   Decomm 21 Dec 1970. Stricken 1 Jun 1973. Sold 22 Mar 1976, BU.
◆Cuba Missile Crisis Nov–Dec 1962.

Figure 11.32: USS *Caloosahatchee* (AO 98), after being lengthened in the 1960s.

Figure 11.33: USS *Canisteo* (AO 99), November 1955, at Norfolk, Va.

AO 98   *Caloosahatchee*   In collision with LPH *Inchon* in western Mediterranean, 16 Dec 1975. Collided with destroyer *Rich* north of Virgin Islands, 12 Jul 1977. In collision with carrier *America* off Charleston, SC, 3 Dec 1980. Decomm 28 Feb 1990. Stricken 18 Jul 1994. BU 2003 UK.
◆Cuba Missile Crisis Nov–Dec 1962, Dominican Rep Sep 1965, Grenada Nov 1983.

AO 99   *Canisteo*   Decomm and stricken 2 Oct 1989. Stricken 31 Aug 1992. BU 2003, UK.
◆Antarctic 1946–47; Cuba Missile Crisis Nov–Dec 1962, Dominican Rep Aug 1965.

AO 100   *Chukawan*   In collision with carrier *Wasp* southwest of Bermuda, 20 Jan 1971. Decomm and stricken 1 Jul 1972. Sold 1 Mar 1973, BU.
◆Lebanon Aug–Sep 1958.

AO 101   *Cohocton*   Reacq 6 Mar 1948. MSTS, 1 Oct 1949. Stricken 8 Jan 1958. Sold 27 Sep 1967.
Later history: Merchant *Transoneida*, renamed *Pacific Economy* 1980. BU 1980 Kaohsiung.

Armament: 1977: 4–3″/50 guns. AO 51, 98, 99: "jumboized", 1960s, length increased to 644′, complement 370; Cargo capacity 143,000 bbls.

AO 105   *Mispillion*   Jumboized 1965–66. Decomm 26 Jul 1974, USNS. Stricken 15 Feb 1995. NDRF. SE.
8★Korea K-1 K-2 K-4 K-5 K-7 K-8 K-9 K-10; 9★Vietnam May 1964, Apr–Nov 1967, Jun–Nov 1968, Oct 1969–Feb 1970, Nov 1970–Apr 1971; ◆Taiwan Straits Jul–Sep 1958, Quemoy-Matsu Dec 1959–Jan 1960, Jun–Jul 1961, Nov 1962, Korea Aug–Sep 1969, Evac of Vietnam 29–30 Apr 1975, Mayaguez Op, 15 May 1975, Iran/Indian Ocean Jan–Mar 1979, Nov 1979–Apr 1980, Jul–Sep 1980, Jan–Mar, Jul–Sep 1981.

AO 106   *Navasota*   In collision with carrier *Princeton* off San Diego, 28 Feb 1952. Jumboized 1963–64. 3 killed assisting destroyers in collision in South China Sea, 5 Feb 1966. Decomm 13 Aug 1975, USNS. OS 2 Oct 1991. Stricken 2 Jan 1992, sold 25 Oct 1995, BU.
9★Korea K-1 K-3 K-4 K-5 K-6 K-7 K-8 K-9 K-10; 14★Vietnam Sep 1965–Apr 1966, Nov 1966–May 1967, Dec 1967–Jan, Mar–Jul 1968, Apr–Jul 1969, Jun–Nov 1970, Sep 1971–Jun 1972; ◆OpCastle 1954, Taiwan Straits Sep–Nov 1958, Korea Jan–Mar 1968, Mar, Aug 1969, Iran/Indian Ocean Feb–May, Nov 1979–May, Aug–Sep 1980, Jan–Jul 1981, Libya Jan–Feb 1986, Aug 1989, Persian Gulf Feb–Jul 1987.

AO 107   *Passumpsic*   Jumboized 1964–64. Decomm 24 Jul 1973, MSTS. Stricken 17 Dec 1991. Sold 19 Dec 1991, BU.
9★Korea K-1, K-2 K-3 K-4 K-6, K-7 K-8 K-9 K-10;10★Vietnam Apr 1963, Mar 1964, Oct–Dec 1966, Dec 1967–May 1968, Dec 1968–May 1969, Feb–Jun 1970, Apr–Aug 1971, May 1972–Feb 1973; ◆Passage to Freedom 1954, Taiwan Straits Nov 1958, Korea Jan–Mar 1968, Jun 1969, Aug 1971, Evac of Vietnam 29–30 Apr 1975, Iran/Indian Ocean

Dec 1978–Feb 1979, Dec 1979–Feb, Apr–Aug 1980, Nov 1980–Mar, Aug 1981, Gulf War Jan–Mar 1991.

AO 108 *Pawcatuck* In collision with carrier *Franklin D. Roosevelt* off Virginia, 4 Oct 1959. Jumboized 1965–66. Decomm 15 Jul 1975, MSC. OS and stricken 21 Sep 1991. NDRF. Sold 26 Aug 2005, BU Chesapeake, Va.
◆Lebanon Sep–Oct 1958, Cuba Missile Crisis Nov–Dec 1962, Dominican Rep Apr–May 1965, Lebanon Aug 1982–Jun 1983, Libya Jan–Jun 1986.

AO 109 *Waccamaw* Rec **AOR 109**, 11 Dec 1950. Conv canc, 7 May 1951, rec **AO 109**. FRAM Jan 1964. In collision with destroyer *Eugene A. Greene* in eastern Mediterranean, 18 Jan 1970. Decomm 24 Feb 1975 USNS. Collided with LSD *Fort Snelling* north of Corsica, 3 Apr 1978. Collided with carrier *Saratoga* south of Crete, 21 Nov 1978. Collision with LPH *Guadalcanal* south of Sardinia, 24 Sep 1981. Collided with LPH *Raleigh* in Mediterranean, 13 Oct 1981. OS 22 Oct 1989. Stricken 11 Oct 1991. NDRF. Sold 26 Aug 2005, BU Chesapeake, Va.
1★Vietnam Jul 1972–Jan 1973; ◆Lebanon Jul–Sep 1958, Cuba Apr 1961, Lebanon Aug–Dec 1983, Mar–May 1984.

AO 105–109 "jumboized" in 1960s: 646′ (oa) × 75′ × 35′6″; 12,840 tons, 33,987 f/l; Capacity increased to 150,000 bbls. Disarmed on transfer to MSC.

AO 110 *Conecuh* OS 24 Oct 1946. Rec **AOR 110**, 4 Sep 1952 and converted. Decomm 3 Apr 1956. Stricken 1 Jun 1960. BU 1960.

Note: Served as a replenishment ship with the fleet and this led to the development of the fast combat support ship (AOE).

AW 3 *Pasig* Out of comm Feb 1947–15 Mar 1951. Decomm 15 Jun 1955. Stricken 1 Jul 1960. Sold 16 Oct 1975, BU.
5★Korea K-5 K-6 K-7 K-8 K-9 K-10; ◆Passage to Freedom 1954.

AW 4 *Abatan* Decomm 27 Jan 1947. Stricken 1 Jul 1960. Reacq. as storage ship at Guantanamo 27 Sep 1962. Stricken 1 May 1970. Sunk as target, 10 Mar 1980.

No.	Name	Builder	Keel Laid	Launched	In service
AO 111	*Mission Buenaventura*	Marinship	29 Mar 1944	28 May 1944	18 Nov 1947
AO 112	*Mission Capistrano*	Marinship	29 Feb 1944	7 May 1944	17 Nov 1947
AO 113	*Mission Carmel*	Marinship	1 Jan 1944	28 Mar 1944	21 Oct 1947
AO 114	*Mission De Pala*	Marinship	26 Nov 1943	28 Feb 1944	22 Oct 1947
AO 115	*Mission Dolores*	Marinship	13 Feb 1944	26 Apr 1944	20 Oct 1947
AO 116	*Mission Loreto*	Marinship	27 Apr 1944	28 Jun 1944	20 Nov 1947
AO 117	*Mission Los Angeles* LD as USS *Conecuh* AO 103	Marinship	25 Apr 1945	10 Aug 1945	24 Oct 1947
AO 118	*Mission Purisima*	Marinship	10 Jun 1943	25 Aug 1943	15 Oct 1947
AO 119	*Mission San Antonio*	Marinship	15 Jan 1944	8 Apr 1944	22 Oct 1947
AO 120	*Mission San Carlos*	Marinship	1 Nov 1943	12 Feb 1944	12 Nov 1947
AO 121	*Mission San Diego*	Marinship	20 Dec 1943	24 Mar 1944	17 Oct 1947
AO 122	*Mission San Fernando*	Marinship	26 Aug 1943	25 Nov 1943	21 Oct 1947
AO 123	*Mission San Francisco* LD as USS *Contoocook* AO 104	Marinship	5 May 1945	18 Sep 1945	28 Oct 1947
AO 124	*Mission San Gabriel*	Marinship	31 Jan 1944	17 Apr 1944	14 Oct 1947
AO 125	*Mission San Jose*	Marinship	17 Jul 1943	7 Oct 1943	5 Nov 1947
AO 126	*Mission San Juan*	Marinship	30 Jul 1943	14 Oct 1943	21 Nov 1947
AO 127	*Mission San Luis Obispo*	Marinship	18 Apr 1944	18 Jun 1944	24 Oct 1947
AO 128	*Mission San Luis Rey*	Marinship	15 Oct 1943	29 Jan 1944	23 Oct 1947
AO 129	*Mission San Miguel*	Marinship	11 Aug 1943	31 Oct 1943	4 Nov 1947
AO 130	*Mission San Rafael*	Marinship	25 Sep 1943	31 Dec 1943	21 Oct 1947
AO 131	*Mission Santa Barbara*	Marinship	8 Apr 1944	8 Jun 1944	20 Oct 1947
AO 132	*Mission Santa Clara*	Marinship	15 Mar 1944	18 May 1944	5 Nov 1947
AO 133	*Mission Santa Cruz*	Marinship	26 Jun 1943	8 Sep 1943	24 Oct 1947
AO 134	*Mission Santa Ynez*	Marinship	9 Sep 1943	19 Dec 1943	22 Oct 1947
AO 135	*Mission Solano*	Marinship	8 Oct 1943	14 Jan 1944	20 Oct 1947
AO 136	*Mission Soledad*	Marinship	12 Jul 1943	24 Sep 1943	16 Oct 1947
AO 137	*Mission Santa Ana* Lchd as USS *Concho* AO 102	Marinship	18 Apr 1945	25 Jul 1945	9 Jan 1948

Displacement	5,730 tons; 22,380 f/l
Dimensions	523′6″(oa) × 68′ × 30′10″
Machinery	1 screw; turbo-electric; 10,000 SHP; 16.5 knots
Endurance	13,000/14.5
Complement	50
Armament	none

Notes: Type: T2-SE-A2 All MSTS, 1 Oct 1949.

Service Records:

AO 111 *M. Buenaventura* Stricken 1 Jul 1961; reacq 10 Nov 1961 Stricken 31 Mar 1972. Sold 26 Jun 1973.

AO 112 *M. Capistrano* Stricken 10 Jan 1955; reacq 5 Jul 1956. Rec **AG 162**, 1 Apr 1961, sound testing ship. Stricken 19 Oct 1971.
Later history: Merchant *Mission Exploration*. BU 1980, Brownsville.

AO 113 *M. Carmel* Stricken 25 Oct 1957. Sold 7 Nov 1967.
Later history: Merchant *Houston*. BU 1984 Seville.

AO 114 *M. De Pala* Stricken 15 Nov 1954; reacq 6 Jul 1956. Stricken 13 Mar 1958; reacq as **AGM 20**, 19 Sep 1964.

AO 115 *M. Dolores* Stricken 30 Mar 1955; reacq 27 Jun 1956. Stricken 19 Sep 1957.
Later history: Merchant *Tampa*. BU 1984 Castellon, Spain.

Figure 11.34: *USNS Mission Buenaventura* (T-AO 111). One of twenty-seven Mission class tankers acquired in 1947.

AO 116 *M.Loreto*   Stricken 25 Aug 1955; reacq 25 Jun 1956. Stricken 16 Jul 1959. Sold 2 Sep 1975, BU Portland, Ore.
AO 117 *M.Los Angeles* Stricken 13 Aug 1959. Sold 2 Dec 1975, BU 1976.
AO 118 *M.Purisima* Stricken 16 May 1955; reacq 26 Jun 1956. Stricken 4 Dec 1957. Hulked 1976.
★Korea 1950, 1951, 1952.
AO 119 *M.San Antonio* Stricken 22 Nov 1954. Reacq 6 Jul 1956. Stricken 16 Dec 1959. Reacq 9 Jun 1960. Stricken 11 Jan 1965.
Later history: Merchant *Transarctic*, renamed *Seatrain San Juan* 1967, *San Juan* 1978. BU 1983, Castellon.
AO 120 *M.San Carlos* Stricken 6 Nov 1957. Sold 16 May 1966.
Later history: Merchant *Seatrain Maryland*, renamed *Maryland* 1978. BU 1985.
AO 121 *M.San Diego* Stricken 30 Dec 1954. Reacq 3 Jul 1956. Stricken 16 Oct 1957. Sold 10 Nov 1966.
Later history: Merchant *Seatrain Washington*. Assigned to RRF as *Washington* 1978 (q.v.). (See p. 242)
AO 122 *M.San Fernando* Stricken 24 May 1955. Reacq 21 Jun 1956. Stricken 4 Sep 1957; reacq as **AGM 19**, 28 Sep 1964.
AO 123 *M.San Francisco* Sunk by fire and explosion after collision with m/v *Elna II* in Delaware River, 7 Mar 1957.
AO 124 *M.San Gabriel* Stricken 20 Dec 1957. Sold 24 Jun 1966.
Later history: Merchant *Delaware*, renamed *Seatrain Delaware* 1967, *Delaware* 1980. BU 1983 Castellon.
AO 125 *M.San Jose* Stricken 15 Oct 1957. Sold 24 Jun 1966.
Later history: Merchant *Ohio*, renamed *Seatrain Ohio* 1967, *Ohio* 1980. (See p. 242)
AO 126 *M.San Juan* Stricken 12 Feb 1958; Reacq as **AGM 21**, 8 Apr 1965. (See p. 242)
AO 127 *M.San Luis Obispo* Stricken 9 Nov 1954. Reacq 27 Jun 1956. Stricken 24 Sep 1957.
Later history: Merchant *Seatrain Puerto Rico*, renamed *Puerto Rico* 1978. BU 1986 Kaohsiung.
AO 128 *M.San Luis Rey* Stricken 6 May 1955. Reacq 22 Jun 1956. Stricken 19 Nov 1957. Sold 1 Feb 1972, BU 1973 Brownsville, Tex.
AO 129 *M.San Miguel* Wrecked on Laysan Reef, 775 m. northwest of Hawaii, 8 Oct 1957.
AO 130 *M.San Rafael* Ran aground in Cook Inlet, 10 May 1959. Stricken 2 Feb 1955. Reacq 20 Jun 1956. Stricken 28 Apr 1970. Sold 15 Jun 1971, BU Baltimore.
AO 131 *M.Santa Barbara* Stricken 8 Nov 1957.
Later history: Merchant *Seatrain Carolina*, renamed *Carolina* 1978. BU 1985 Kaohsiung.
4★Korea.
AO 132 *M.Santa Clara* Stricken 1 Jul 1961. Reacq 1 May 1962. Trfd to Pakistan 17 Jan 1963.
Later history: renamed *Dacca*. (A 41). SE1993.
★Korea 1950, 1951.
AO 133 *M.Santa Cruz* Stricken 23 Nov 1954. Reacq 10 Jul 1956. Stricken 15 Sep 1970. Sold 25 Jun 1971, BU Baltimore.
AO 134 *M.Santa Ynez* Rec **AOT 134** 30 Sep 1978. OS 21 Oct 1983. Stricken 1 Nov 1990. NDRF. SE.
AO 135 *M.Solano* Stricken 12 Aug 1957. Sold 26 May 1967.
Later history: Merchant *Jacksonville*. BU 1984
1★Korea K-2.
AO 136 *M.Soledad* Stricken 31 Oct 1957. Sold 4 Nov 1966.
Later history: Merchant *Seatrain California*, renamed *Transontario* 1967. BU 1979 Kaohsiung.
AO 137 *M.Santa Ana* Stricken 27 Jan 1955. Reacq 3 Jul 1956. Stricken 25 Feb 1958. Sold 2 Dec 1975, BU Terminal I.

No.	Name	Builder	Launched	In service
AO 138	*Cedar Creek* ex-*Taganrog* (1945), ex-*Cedar Creek* (1944)	Sun	15 Dec 1943	Jul 1948
AO 139	*Muir Woods* ex-*Elbrus* (1945), ex-*Muir Woods* (1945)	Swan I	9 Mar 1945	Apr 1948
AO 140	*Pioneer Valley* ex-*Krasnaia Armia* (1945), ex-*Pioneer Valley* (1944)	Swan I	6 Sep 1944	1948
AO 141	*Sappa Creek*	Alabama	15 Sep 1943	28 Apr 1948
AO 142	*Shawnee Trail* ex-*Emba II*, ex-*Pioneer Valley*	Swan I	31 May 1944	25 May 1948

Figure 11.35: USS *Hassayampa* (AO 145), fleet oiler, about 1969.

Note: Type: T2-SE-A1 All MSTS, 1 Oct 1949. Four had been on temporary lend-lease to USSR during World War II.

Service Records:
AO 138 *Cedar Creek* OS Sep 1954–1 Nov 1956. Stricken 14 Oct 1957. Sold 2 Sep 1975, BU Portland, Ore.
AO 139 *Muir Woods* Stricken 10 Jun 1959. Sold 2 Dec 1975, BU 1976.
AO 140 *Pioneer Valley* Stricken 15 Aug 1972. Sold 9 May 1973, BU Baltimore.
AO 141 *Sappa Creek* OS 7 Dec 1959. Stricken 1 Jul 1961. Sold 2 Dec 1975, BU 1975 Terminal I.
AO 142 *Shawnee Trail* OS 1 Nov 1957–20 Jan 1965. Stricken 29 Feb 1972. Sold 10 Aug 1973, BU.

No.	Name	Builder	Keel Laid	Launched	Comm.
AO 143	*Neosho*	Beth; Quincy	2 Sep 1952	10 Nov 1953	24 Sep 1954
AO 144	*Mississinewa*	NY Sbdg	4 May 1953	12 Jun 1954	18 Jan 1955
AO 145	*Hassayampa*	NY Sbdg	13 Jul 1953	12 Sep 1954	19 Apr 1955
AO 146	*Kawishiwi*	NY Sbdg	5 Oct 1953	11 Dec 1954	6 Jul 1955
AO 147	*Truckee*	NY Sbdg	21 Dec 1953	10 Mar 1955	23 Nov 1955
AO 148	*Ponchatoula*	NY Sbdg	1 Mar 1954	9 Jul 1955	12 Jan 1956

Displacement	11,600 tons; 38,000 f/l
Dimensions	655′ (oa); 640′ (wl) × 86′× 35′
Machinery	2 screws; ST; 2 B&W boilers; 28,000 SHP; 20 knots
Endurance	14,000/19
Complement	360 (USN), 129 (MSC)
Armament	2–5″/38, 6-twin 3″/50AA. *1969:* 4 twin 3″/50 *1977:* 2 twin 3″/50

Notes: AO 143, 144 and 147 fitted with helicopter platform aft. 180,000 bbls cargo. Armament removed on transfer to MSC.

Service Records:
AO 143 *Neosho* Decomm, to MSC 26 May 1978. OS 10 Aug 1992. Stricken 16 Feb 1994. NDRF. BU 2005 Brownsville.
★Cuba Missile Crisis Oct–Nov 1962, ◆Dominican Rep May–Jun 1965, Lebanon Aug–Oct 1982, Grenada Oct–Nov 1983, Libya Jan–Jun 1986, Gulf War Aug 1990, Liberia 1990.
AO 144 *Mississinewa* Collided with carrier *Saratoga* off Florida, 15 Dec 1975. Decomm, to MSC 15 Nov 1976. OS 30 Jul 1991. Stricken 16 Feb 1994, NDRF. Sold 9 Sep 2006, BU 2007 Brownsville, Tex.

◆Lebanon Jul–Sep 1958, Jul–Dec 1983, Mar–Jun 1984, Iran/Indian Ocean Nov 1980–May, Jul–Aug 1981.

AO 145 *Hassayampa* Decomm, to MSC 17 Nov 1978. OS 2 Oct 1991. Stricken 16 Feb 1994. NDRF. SE.
★Vietnam Aug 1964, May–Nov 1965, Jun–Nov 1966, Oct 1967–Apr 1968, Nov 1968–Apr 1969, Jan–May 1970, Mar–Jul 1971, Mar, Jun 1972–Jan 1973; ◆Quemoy-Matsu Jul 1958, Jul 1959, Taiwan Straits Nov–Dec 1958, Laos Apr–May 1962, Korea Apr–May 1969, Iran/Indian Ocean Apr–Jul, Oct–Dec 1980, May–Aug 1981, Libya Dec 1989, Gulf War Sep 1990–Mar 1991.

AO 146 *Kawishiwi* Collided with carrier *Lexington* south of Oahu, May 1959. In collision with LSD *Alamo*, 5 Apr 1966. Decomm, to MSC 10 Oct 1979. OS 31 Jul 1992. Stricken 7 Nov 1994, NDRF. SE.
8★Vietnam Dec 1964–Jan 1965, Dec 1965–Feb, Apr–Jun 1966, Jun–Oct 1967, Oct 1968, Jul 1969–Jan 1970, Sep–Nov 1970, Jan–Feb 1971, Feb–Sep 1972; ◆Korea Jan, Aug 1970, Evac of Vietnam 29–30 Apr 1975.

AO 147 *Truckee* Damaged in collision with carrier *Wasp* off east coast, 12 Jun 1968. Collided with carrier *Independence* in Tyrrhenian Sea, 20 Apr 1977. In collision with tender *Yellowstone* off Virginia, 22 Sep 1986. Decomm, to MSC 30 Jan 1980. OS 21 Oct 1991. Stricken 18 Jul 1994, NDRF. SE.
◆Cuba Missile Crisis Oct–Dec 1962, Lebanon Aug 1982–May 1983, Jun–Jul 1983, Gulf War Oct 1990.

AO 148 *Ponchatoula* In collision with LSD *Point Defiance* north of Hawaii, 13 Feb 1970. Damaged by boiler explosion at Pearl Harbor, 2 Nov 1976. Decomm, to MSC 5 Sep 1980. OS 1 Apr 1992. Stricken 31 Aug 1992, NDRF. SE.
12★Vietnam Apr 1959, Sep 1963, Oct 1964–Mar 1965, Sep 1966–Apr 1967, Nov 1967–May 1968, Dec 1968–Jun 1969, May–Sep 1970, Aug 1971–Jan 1972, Nov 1972–Mar 1973; ◆Taiwan Straits Sep–Oct 1958, Korea Apr–May, Sep 1970, Libya Jan 1990, Gulf War Jan–Mar 1991.

No.	Name	Builder	Keel Laid	Launched	Comm.
AO 149	*Maumee*	Sun	8 Mar 1955	16 Feb 1956	17 Dec 1956
AO 150	*Potomac*	Sun	9 Jun 1955	8 Oct 1956	30 Jan 1957
AO 151	*Shoshone*	Sun	16 Aug 1955	17 Jan 1957	15 Apr 1957
AO 152	*Yukon*	Ingalls	16 May 1955	16 Mar 1956	17 May 1957

Displacement	7,940 tons; 32,953 f/l
Dimensions	620′ (oa); 591′ (wl) × 83′6″ × 32′
Machinery	1 screw; ST; 2 boilers; 20,460 SHP; 18 knots
Endurance	18,000/18
Complement	31

Notes: Type T5-S-12a. MSTS, unarmed. Capacity 203,200 bbls.

Service Records:

AO 149 *Maumee* Rec **AOT 149**, 30 Sep 1978. OS 15 Oct 1985. RRF 1986. Stricken 13 Apr 1992, NDRF. BU Brownsville, Tex. 2007.

AO 150 *Potomac* Broke in two and sank after explosion and fire at Morehead City, NC, 26 Sep 1961. Stricken.
Later history: Salved. Stern and engines rebuilt as merchant *Shenandoah*. Reacq 1981 as **AOT 181** (see p. 217)

AO 151 *Shoshone* Rec **AOT 151**, 30 Sep 1978. OS 10 Feb 1984. RRF 1984–1994. Trfd to Office of Naval Research, 11 May 2001. NDRF. SE.

AO 152 *Yukon* Disabled by electrical fire in western Mediterranean, 6 Dec 1974. Rec **AOT 152**, 30 Sep 1978. Collided with icebreaker *Polar Sea* in Antarctic, 28 Jan 1982. RRF. OS 20 Oct 1985. RRF 1985–86. Name canc 1990. Stricken 13 Apr 1992. Sold 18 Sep 1995, BU Brownsville.

Figure 11.36: *USNS Yukon* (T-AO 152), built in 1957.

No.	Name	Builder	Launched	In service
AO 153	*Cumberland* ex-*Esso Cumberland*, ex-*Fort Cumberland*	Sun	9 May 1944	1956
AO 154	*Lynchburg* ex-*Esso Lynchburg*, ex-*Stanvac Brisbane*, ex-*Chalmette*	Swan I	20 May 1944	17 Nov 1956
AO 155	*Roanoke* ex-*Esso Roanoke*	Sun	30 Jun 1944	1956
AO 156	*Bull Run*	Sun	29 Jun 1943	22 Dec 1946
AO 157	*Paoli*	Sun	31 Oct 1944	2 Dec 1946
AO 158	*Abiqua*	Alabama	22 Sep 1943	21 Dec 1956
AO 159	*French Creek*	Sun	8 Dec 1944	28 Nov 1956
AO 160	*Logan's Fort*	Sun	30 Mar 1945	12 Dec 1956
AO 161	*Lone Jack*	Sun	21 Oct 1944	15 Jan 1957
AO 162	*Memphis* ex-*Esso Memphis*	Sun	17 Jun 1944	23 Dec 1956
AO 163	*Parkersburg* ex-*Esso Parkersburg*, ex-*Fort Cornwallis*	Sun	12 Apr 1944	1956
AO 164	*Petrolite* ex-*Hanging Rock*	Sun	13 Jan 1944	1956

Notes: Type T2-SE-A1. Acquired during Suez Crisis. MSTS

Service Records:

AO 153 *Cumberland* Stricken 1957. To Army 1966. Sold 31 Jan 1972, BU Taiwan.

AO 154 *Lynchburg* Stricken 29 Oct 1957. Sold 1969.
Later history: merchant *Marine Duval*. BU 2002 Alang.

AO 155 *Roanoke* Stricken 1957.
Later history: Merchant *Baltimore*, 1969. BU 1985 Kaohsiung.

AO 156 *Bull Run* Stricken 23 Sep 1957.
Later history: Merchant *Anchorage*, 1969. BU 1980 Brownsville.

AO 157 *Paoli* Stricken 2 Oct 1957.
Later history: Merchant *Marine Floridian*, 1966, renamed *Belofin Floridian* 1997. BU 1997 Alang.

AO 158 *Abiqua* Stricken 30 Sep 1957.
Later history: Hull split: part, merchant *Venmac I*, renamed *Intermac I*. Part: merchant *Venmac 2*. Part: merchant *Amoco Delaware*, 1970. Aft part joined to *Windsor*, renamed *Assos* 1974, *Ulrica* 1974. BU 1978 Kaohsiung.

AO 159 *French Creek* Stricken 2 Oct 1957. To Army 1966. Sold 29 Jan 1971, BU Taiwan.

AO 160 *Logan's Fort* Stricken 30 Aug 1957. To Army 1966. Sold 31 Jan 1972, BU Taiwan.

AO 161 *Lone Jack* Stricken 7 Oct 1957. To Army 1966. Sold 29 Jan 1971, BU Taiwan.

AO 162 *Memphis* Stricken 13 Sep 1960. To Army 1966. Sold 31 May 1971, BU Taiwan.

216   The Navy of the Nuclear Age, 1947–2007

AO 163 *Parkersburg*   Sold 5 Dec 1971.
     Later history: Hull split, fore part, merchant *Marine Eagle*. BU 1984. Aft part: merchant *Detsco No.3*.
AO 164 *Petrolite*   Stricken 1957.
     Later history: Hull split: aft section, merchant *Seattle*, 1969. BU 1984. Fore section, merchant *Oregon Standard*, 1969.

No.	Name	Builder	Keel Laid	Launched	In service
AO 165	*American Explorer*	Ingalls	9 Jul 1957	11 Apr 1958	27 Oct 1959

Displacement	8,400 tons; 31,300 f/l
Dimensions	615′ (oa) × 80′ × 32′
Machinery	1 screw; ST; 2 boilers; 22,000 SHP; 20 knots
Complement	47

Notes: Type T5-S-RM2a. Acquired on completion. Unarmed. Similar to *Maumee* class tankers.

Service Record: Rec **AOT 165**, 30 Sep 1978. RRF 1984–1994. NDRF. SE.
AO 166–167 Jumbo conversion of Mission class tankers canceled.

No.	Name	Builder	Keel Laid	Launched	Comm.
AO 168	*Sealift Pacific*	Todd; S. Pedro	15 Nov 1972	13 Oct 1973	14 Aug 1974
AO 169	*Sealift Arabian Sea*	Todd; S. Pedro	1 Mar 1973	26 Jan 1974	6 Feb 1975
AO 170	*Sealift China Sea*	Todd; S. Pedro	1 Oct 1973	20 Apr 1974	19 May 1975
AO 171	*Sealift Indian Ocean*	Todd; S. Pedro	1 Oct 1973	27 Jul 1974	29 Aug 1975
AO 172	*Sealift Atlantic*	Bath	Apr 1973	26 Jan 1974	26 Aug 1974
AO 173	*Sealift Mediterranean*	Bath	Mar 1973	9 Mar 1974	6 Nov 1974
AO 174	*Sealift Caribbean*	Bath	Jul 1973	8 Jun 1974	10 Feb 1975
AO 175	*Sealift Arctic*	Bath	Feb 1974	31 Aug 1974	22 May 1975
AO 176	*Sealift Antarctic*	Bath	15 Apr 1974	26 Oct 1974	1 Aug 1975

Displacement	6,487 tons; 32,000 f/l
Dimensions	587′ (oa) × 84′ × 34′4″
Machinery	1 screw; turbo diesels; 14,000 BHP; 16 knots
Endurance	12,000/16
Complement	32

Notes: Bow thruster. Built to replace WWII T2 tankers. MSTS, not armed. All rec **AOT** 30 Sep 1978. Capacity: 225,000 bbls.

Service Records:

AO 168 *Sealift Pacific*   Sold 15 Feb 1995.
     Later history: Merchant *Patty Ann* 1995. BU 2003 Alang. .
     ◆Gulf War Aug–Nov 1990.
AO 169 *Sealift Arabian Sea*   Sold 2 Mar 1995.
     Later history: Merchant *Sophil*. 1995. BU 2000 Alang.
AO 170 *Sealift China Sea*   Sold 18 Apr 1995.
     Later history: Merchant *Sant'Ambrogio*. BU 2000 Alang.
AO 171 *Sealift Indian Ocean*   Sold 2 May 1995.
     Later history: Merchant *Sant'Anna*. BU 2000 Alang.
AO 172 *Sealift Atlantic*   Sold 4 Apr 1995.
     Later history: Merchant *Mavra*. BU 2000 Alang.
AO 173 *Sealift Mediterranean*   Ran aground off Rondo Island, Indonesia, 1 Apr 1978. Sold 18 Apr 1995.
     Later history: Merchant *San Marco*. BU Alang, India, 1999.
AO 174 *Sealift Caribbean*   Sold 4 Apr 1995.
     Later history: Merchant *Santa Chiara*, Trfd to Peru (Navy), 1998, renamed *Lobitos* (ATP 159). SE2001.
AO 175 *Sealift Arctic*   Sold 4 Apr 1995.
     Later history: Merchant *Vandou*. BU 2000 Alang.
AO 176 *Sealift Antarctic*   Sold 4 Apr 1995.
     Later history: Merchant *Renata II*. BU 2002 India.

No.	Name	Builder	Keel Laid	Launched	Comm.
AO 177	*Cimarron*	Avondale	18 May 1978	28 Apr 1979	10 Jan 1981
AO 178	*Monongahela*	Avondale	15 Aug 1978	4 Aug 1979	8 Aug 1981
AO 179	*Merrimack*	Avondale	16 Jul 1979	17 May 1980	14 Nov 1981
AO 180	*Willamette*	Avondale	4 Aug 1980	18 Jul 1981	18 Dec 1982
AO 186	*Platte*	Avondale	2 Feb 1981	30 Jan 1982	16 Apr 1983

Displacement	8,210 tons; 27,500 f/l 1989: 37,866 f/l
Dimensions	591′4″(oa) × 88′ × 33′6″ *1989*: 708′4″(oa) × 83 × 33′6
Machinery	1 screw; ST; 2 boilers; 24,000 SHP; 20 knots
Complement	212
Armament	none. 1989: 2 Phalanx

Notes: "Jumboized" 1989–92 at Avondale. Capacity 120,000 bbls increased to 180,000 bbls. Helicopter deck, no hangar.

Service Records:

AO 177 *Cimarron*   Converted Jun 1990–Mar 1992. Decomm 15 Dec 1998. Stricken 3 May 1999, NDRF. SE.
     ◆Libya Nov 1987–Feb 1988, Gulf War Aug–Nov 1990, Indian Ocean May–Aug 1997.
AO 178 *Monongahela*   Converted Jan 1990–Oct 1991. Decomm and stricken 30 Sep 1999, NDRF. SE.
     ◆Lebanon Apr–Jun 1983, Libya/El Dorado Canyon Feb–May 1986, Indian Ocean Dec 1995.
AO 179 *Merrimack*   Converted Mar 1989–Dec 1990. Decomm and stricken 18 Dec 1998, NDRF. SE.
     ◆Lebanon Nov–Dec 1983, Gulf War Aug 1991–Nov 1992.
AO 180 *Willamette*   Damaged in collision with repair ship *Jason* southwest of Pearl Harbor, 10 Feb 1986. Converted Oct 1989–May 1991. Decomm and stricken 30 Apr 1999, NDRF. SE.
     ◆Persian Gulf Feb–Jul 1987, Libya Nov–Dec 1988, Liberia Oct 1993, Indian Ocean Jan–Mar 1996.
AO 186 *Platte*   In collision with frigate *Trippe* north of Puerto Rico, 19 Apr 1989. Converted Nov 1990–Sep 1992. Decomm and stricken 30 Jun 1999, NDRF. SE.
     ◆Gulf War Jan–Apr 1991.

Figure 11.37: *USNS Potomac* (T-AOT 181), 1997. With OPDS equipment on deck.

No.	Name	Builder	Launched	In service
AO 181	*Potomac* ex-*Shenandoah*, ex-*Potomac* (AO 150)	Sun	8 Oct 1956	12 Jan 1976

Displacement	7,333 tons; 34,800 f/l
Dimensions	620′ (oa) × 83′6″ × 34′
Machinery	2 screws; ST; 2 boilers; SHP 20,460; 18 knots
Complement	36

Notes: Built from stern of USS *Potomac* (AO 150) with new bow and midbody. MSC, unarmed. OPDS system.

Service Record: Rec **AOT 181** 30 Sep 1978. OS 26 Sep 1983. RRF 1984–2006. Laid up Jul 2006. NDRF. SE.

No.	Name	Builder	Launched	Acquired
AOT 182	*Columbia* ex-*Falcon Lady*	Ingalls	12 Sep 1970	1976
AOT 183	*Neches* ex-*Falcon Duchess*	Ingalls	30 Jan 1971	1976
AOT 184	*Hudson* ex-*Falcon Princess*	Ingalls	8 Jan 1972	1976
AOT 185	*Susquehanna* ex-*Falcon Countess*	Ingalls	2 Oct 1971	1976

Displacement	8,601 tons; 45,877 f/l
Dimensions	672′ (oa) × 89′ × 36′
Machinery	1 screw; ST; 2 boilers; 16.5 knots
Complement	23

Notes: All rec **AOT**, 30 Sep 1978. MSTS, unarmed. Capacity 310,000 bbls.

Service Records:

AO 182 *Columbia*   OS, Returned 1 May 1984. Stricken
   Later history: Merchant *Falcon Lady*, renamed *Mission Capistrano* 1988. (See p. 251) RPF 1988. BU 2004 U.S.
AO 183 *Neches*   OS 28 Sep 1983. Returned to owner.
   Later history: Merchant *Falcon Duchess*, renamed *Eclipse* 1984, *Falcon Duchess* 1985, *Duchess* 1992. Operated by MSC (see p. 251). BU 1997 Gadani.
AO 184 *Hudson*   OS 5 Feb 1984, Returned to owner. Stricken
   Later history: Merchant *Sea Princess*. BU 2003, *Chittagong*.
AO 185 *Susquehanna*   Returned 1 May 1984. Stricken
   Later history: Merchant *Falcon Countess* 1984. BU 1993, Alang.

No.	Name	Builder	Keel Laid	Launched	Comm.
T-AO 187	*Henry J. Kaiser*	Avondale	22 Aug 1984	5 Oct 1985	19 Dec 1986
T-AO 188	*Joshua Humphreys*	Avondale	17 Dec 1984	22 Feb 1986	3 Apr 1987
T-AO 189	*John Lenthall*	Avondale	15 Jul 1985	9 Aug 1986	25 Jun 1987
T-AO 190	*Andrew J. Higgins*	Avondale	21 Nov 1985	17 Jan 1987	22 Oct 1987
T-AO 191	*Benjamin Isherwood*	Penn Sbdg	12 Jul 1986	15 Aug 1988	—
T-AO 192	*Henry Eckford*	Penn Sbdg	22 Jan 1987	22 Jul 1989	—
T-AO 193	*Walter S. Diehl*	Avondale	7 Aug 1986	10 Oct 1987	13 Sep 1988
T-AO 194	*John Ericsson*	Avondale	13 Mar 1989	21 Apr 1990	19 Mar 1991
T-AO 195	*Leroy Grumman*	Avondale	6 Jul 1987	3 Dec 1988	2 Aug 1989
T-AO 196	*Kanawha*	Avondale	17 Jul 1989	22 Sep 1990	10 Dec 1991
T-AO 197	*Pecos*	Avondale	17 Feb 1988	23 Sep 1989	13 Jul 1990
T-AO 198	*Big Horn*	Avondale	9 Oct 1989	2 Feb 1991	21 May 1992
T-AO 199	*Tippecanoe*	Avondale	19 Nov 1990	16 May 1992	8 Feb 1993
T-AO 200	*Guadalupe*	Avondale	9 Jul 1990	15 Oct 1991	25 Sep 1992
T-AO 201	*Patuxent*	Avondale	16 Oct 1991	23 Jul 1994	21 Jun 1995
T-AO 202	*Yukon*	Avondale	15 May 1991	6 Feb 1993	25 Mar 1994
T-AO 203	*Laramie*	Avondale	28 Dec 1992	6 May 1995	5 Apr 1996
T-AO 204	*Rappahannock*	Avondale	29 Jun 1992	14 Jan 1995	7 Nov 1995

Displacement	9,500 tons; 40,700 f/l; 25,742 grt
Dimensions	677′6″(oa); 649′9″ (wl) × 97′6″ × 35′
Machinery	2 screws; diesels; 32,000 BHP; 20 knots
Endurance	6,000/20
Complement	119
Armament	none. Projected: 2–20 mm, Phalanx

Notes: AO 191–192 canc 31 Aug 1989, towed incomplete to Philadelphia NSYd and reordered from Tampa SY. This contract was cancelcd 15 Aug 1993 and the incomplete ships laid up in the James River. MSC. Helicopter deck. AO 201–204 built with double hull. Capacity 1,800,000 bbls.

Service Records:

AO 187 *Henry J. Kaiser*   OS 31 Jan 1995
   ◆Liberia 1990, Gulf War Aug 1991–Sep 1992, Iraq War 2003.
AO 188 *Joshua Humphreys*   OS 29 Jun 1996. React 23 Feb 2005. Decomm 30 Nov 2006.
   ◆Gulf War Jan–Apr 1991.

Figure 11.38: USNS *Joshua Humphreys* (T-AO 188), at Norfolk, October 1992.

Figure 11.39: USNS *Patuxent* (T-AO 201), fleet replenishment oiler, 28 Apr 2007.

AO 189 *John Lenthall*   OS 11 Nov 1996–7 Dec 1998.
♦Gulf War Apr 1991–Feb 1992.

AO 190 *Andrew J. Higgins*   OS 6 May 1996, NDRF. SE.
♦Libya Sep–Oct 1989, Gulf War Sep 1990–Sep 1992.

AO 191 *Benjamin Isherwood*   Cpl by Tampa Shipyards. Canceled 25 Oct 1993. to Marad 27 Sep 1994, laid up incomplete, 95.3% complete. Stricken 29 Dec 1997, NDRF. SE.

AO 192 *Henry Eckford*   Cpl by Tampa Shipyards. Canceled 25 Oct 1993. to Marad 4 Oct 1994, laid up incomplete, 84% complete. Stricken 29 Dec 1997, NDRF. SE.

AO 193 *Walter S. Diehl*
♦Libya May–Jun 1990, Gulf War Oct 1990–Mar 1991, Liberia Jun 1992–Jul 1993, Indian Ocean Jan–Jun 1998, Sep 2000–Mar 2001, Iraq War 2003.

AO 194 *John Ericsson*
♦Gulf War, Liberia 1990, Tsunami relief 2005.

AO 195 *Leroy Grumman*
♦Gulf War Jun 1991–May 1992, Haiti Sep–Oct 1994.

AO 196 *Kanawha*
♦Indian Ocean May–Jul, Dec 2000–Mar 2001, Iraq War 2003.

AO 197 *Pecos*   In collision with Chilean frigate *Almirante Condell*, 26 Jun 1998.
♦Gulf War Jul–Dec 1991, Liberia Mar 1993, Apr, Sep–Oct 1994, Indian Ocean Dec 1995, Jan–Mar 1997.

AO 198 *Big Horn*
♦Beirut Evac, 17–19 Jul 2006.

AO 199 *Tippecanoe*
♦Indian Ocean Aug 1997–Jan 1998, Tsunami relief 2005.

AO 200 *Guadalupe*
♦Indian Ocean Jan–May 1998.

AO 201 *Patuxent*
♦Indian Ocean Mar–Jul 1998.

AO 202 *Yukon*   Ran aground in heavy winds at Yokosuka, 8 Sep 2004.
♦Indian Ocean Dec 1995–May 1996, Mar, Jul–Aug 1997, Jun–Nov 1998.

AO 203 *Laramie*

AO 204 *Rappahannock*

GASOLINE TANKERS

AOG 1 *Patapsco*   Out of comm 29 May 1946–19 Oct 1950. Decomm 29 Jun 1955. Stricken 1 Jul 1960. Reacq 31 Aug 1965. Recomm 18 Jun 1966. Decomm 2 Sep 1969. Stricken 1 Aug 1974.
1★Korea K-7; 7★Vietnam Oct 1966–Feb 1967, Oct 1967–Apr 1968, Dec 1968–Jun 1969.
Later history: merchant fishing trawler *Arctic Storm*, 1979.

AOG 2 *Kern*   Decomm 6 Aug 1946, to Army, renamed *Y-483*. Reacq 1 Jul 1950, MSTS. OS Sep 1956. Reactiv. summer 1957. Stricken 10 Apr 1958. Sold 2 Dec 1975, BU Terminal I.

AOG 3 *Rio Grande*   Out of comm 28 Jun 1946–12 Oct 1950, MSTS. OS 6 Jan 1956. Stricken 1 Jul 1960. Sold 7 Feb 1972, BU Tacoma.
2★Korea K-8 K-9.

AOG 4 *Wabash*   to Army 29 Jul 1946, renamed *Y-484*. Reacq 1 Jul 1950, MSTS. Decomm 10 Sep 1957. Stricken 8 May 1958. NDRF. BU 2005 Brownsville.
2★Korea K-7 K-8.

AOG 5 *Susquehanna*   Decomm 15 Aug 1946, to Army, renamed *Y-485*. Stricken 23 Apr 1947. Reacq 1 Jul 1950, MSTS. Stricken 26 Mar 1959. Sold 10 Aug 1973, BU.

AOG 6 *Agawam*   Decomm 31 Jan 1957. Stricken 1 Jul 1960. Sold 16 Oct 1975, BU.

AOG 7 *Elkhorn*   Decomm 1 Jul 1972. To Taiwan 1 Jul 1972.
Later history: renamed *Hsing Lung* (515). SE2001.
1★Korea K-10, 1951, 1953; 8★Vietnam Aug–Nov 1964, Nov 1965–Mar

Figure 11.40: USS *Nespelen* (AOG 55), gasoline tanker, at sea.

1966, May–Oct 1967, Jul–Dec 1968, Sep 1969–Jan 1970; ♦Antarctic Jan–Feb 1962.

AOG 8 *Genesee*   Out of comm 14 Dec 1949–28 Jul 1950. Trfd to Chile 5 Jul 1972.
Later history: renamed *Beagle*. R1982. used as YOG. sunk as tgt 1992.
1★Korea K-7; 5★Vietnam May–Sep 1965, Jun–Oct 1966, Mar–Oct 1968.

AOG 9 *Kishwaukee*   Decomm 2 Apr 1958. Stricken 1 Jul 1960. Reacq 31 Aug 1965. Recomm 1 Sep 1966. Stricken 1 Aug 1974.
★Korea 1950–51; 7★Vietnam Dec 1966–Apr 1967, Nov 1967–May 1968.

AOG 10 *Nemasket*   Decomm 22 Sep 1959. Stricken 1 Jul 1960. NDRF. Sold 20 Sep 2005, BU 2006, Brownsville.
★Korea 1950.

AOG 11 *Tombigbee*   Out of comm 12 Dec 1949–28 Jul 1950. In collision with DE *McMorris* southeast of Honolulu, 31 Jan 1967. Decomm 7 Jul 1972. Trfd to Greece 7 Jul 1972. Stricken 15 Apr 1978.
Later history: renamed *Ariadni* (A 414). R2003
★Korea 1951–52; 9★Vietnam Mar–May 1965, Apr–Sep 1966, Oct 1967–Mar 1968, Nov 1968–May 1969, Feb–Jun 1970, Aug–Nov 1971; ♦Antarctic Jan 1963.

AOG 48 *Chehalis*   Sunk by fire and explosion at Tutuila, Samoa, 7 Oct 1949 (6 killed). Stricken 17 Oct 1949 and sold.

AOG 49 *Chestatee*   Reacq Aug 1948. MSTS Mar 1952–May 1954, Apr 1956–Sep 1957. To U.S. Air Force 16 Sep 1957. Stricken 1 Jun 1963. Sold 16 Oct 1975, BU.

AOG 50 *Chewaucan*   Stricken and trfd to Colombia 1 Jul 1975.
Later history: renamed *Tumaco* (BT7).
♦Lebanon 22 Oct 1958.

AOG 51 *Maquoketa*   Decomm 21 Feb 1947. Reacq 23 Aug 1948. MSTS. 1 Mar 1952. Decomm 18 May 1954. MSTS 14 Apr 1956. Decomm 9 Oct 1957. Stricken 12 Mar 1958. Sold 2 Dec 1975, BU Terminal I.

AOG 52 *Mattabesset*   Decomm and stricken 1 Oct 1968. BU 1969.
♦Lebanon Jul–Oct 1958.

AOG 53 *Namakagon*   Decomm 20 Sep 1957. Trfd to New Zealand 5 Oct 1962.
Later history: renamed *Endeavour* (A 184). Returned 29 Jun 1971, Trfd to Taiwan, renamed *Lung Chuan* (507). R2005.

AOG 54 *Natchaug*   Decomm 24 Jul 1959. Trfd to Greece 1 Aug 1959.
Later history: renamed *Arethousa* (A 377). R2003.
1★Korea 5.

AOG 55 *Nespelen*   Collided with m/v *Indochinois* in fog in Ambrose Channel, NY, 27 May 1948. Decomm and stricken 1 Jul 1975.
♦Antarctic Dec 1955–Feb 1956, Dec 1956–Feb 1957, Dec 1957–Feb 1958, Dec 1958–Feb 1959, Cuba Oct–Nov 1961, Cuba Missile Crisis Nov 1962.

AOG 56 *Noxubee* Decomm 6 Mar 1959. Stricken 1 Jul 1960. Reacq 23 Aug 1965. Recomm 10 Sep 1966. Damaged by mine off Quang Tri, Vietnam, 9 Sep 1969. Stricken 1 Jul 1975.
6★Vietnam Apr–Aug 1967, May–Nov 1968, Jun 1969–Jan 1970.

AOG 57 *Pecatonica* Out of comm 7 Feb 1946–24 Apr 1948. Decomm 24 Apr 1961 and trfd to Taiwan 1961
Later history: renamed *Chang Pei* (517). R2005

AOG 58 *Pinnebog* Decomm 2 May 1949. MSTS. . Mar 1952. OS Jul 1954. to MSTS 23 Apr 1956. To U.S. Air Force 16 Sep 1957. FFU.

AOG 59 *Wacissa* Stricken 23 Apr 1947. Reinstated 30 Apr 1948. MSTS. 18 Feb 1952 in svc. Went aground on Polaris Reef, Baffin Bay, 9 Oct 1952, refloated 16 Oct. OS 25 May 1954. Returned 24 May 1956. OS 16 Oct 1956. Returned 8 Apr 1957 to svc. To U.S. Air Force 16 Sep 1957, in svc with Canadian govt. Returned Stricken 1 Dec 1963. Sold 27 May 1964, BU 1965.

AOG 36 *Ontonagon* Decomm 27 Feb 1946 and trfd to Army, renamed *Y-130*. Reacq 1 Jul 1950, MSTS. To Marad 14 Dec 1954. Stricken 22 Jun 1955. IS 26 Apr 1956, MSTS. OS 25 Sep 1956. Stricken 13 Nov 1957. BU 1965 Terminal I.

AOG 68 *Peconic* Reacq, MSTS 1 Oct 1949.
Later history: Merchant *Voshell*. reacq as **Peconic**, 4 Apr 1948, MSTS. Stricken 12 Nov 1957. Sold 7 Dec 1982, BU.

No.	Name	Builder	Launched	Acquired	Comm.
AOG 76	*Tonti* ex-*Tavern*	Todd-Houston	16 May 1945	23 Aug 1945	18 May 1948
AOG 77	*Rincon* ex-*Tarland*	Todd-Houston	24 Feb 1945	5 Jun 1945	1 Jul 1950
AOG 78	*Nodaway* ex-*Belridge*, ex-*Tarcoola*	Todd-Houston	19 Feb 1945	15 May 1945	14 Aug 1950
AOG 79	*Petaluma* ex-*Raccoon Bend*, ex-*Tavispan*	Todd-Houston	3 May 1945	9 Aug 1945	14 Aug 1950
AOG 80	*Piscataqua* ex-*Cisne*, ex-*Taveta*	Todd-Houston	23 May 1945	10 Sep 1945	18 Aug 1950
Displacement	2,080 tons; 5,984 f/l				
Dimensions	325′2″(oa) × 48′2″ × 19′				
Machinery	1 screw; diesels; 1,400 BHP; 10 knots				
Endurance	5500/10				
Complement	24				

Notes: Type T1-M-BT1. Capacity 30,000 bbls. Acq by MSTS.

Service Records:

AOG 76 *Tonti* Stricken 1 Jul 1961, Trfd to Colombia.
Later history: renamed *Mamonal* (BT 62). R1975, BU.

Figure 11.41: *USNS Nodaway* (T-AOG 78), gasoline tanker.

AOG 77 *Rincon* Trfd to Korea 21 Feb 1982.
Later history: renamed *So Yang* (AO 55). R1998, BU.
2★Korea K-7 K-8; ◆Evac of Vietnam.

AOG 78 *Nodaway* OS 11 Dec 1959. Stricken 1 Jul 1961; Reacq 25 Aug 1965. OS 22 Jul 1984. RRF 1985–2006. Sold 15 Dec 2006, BU Japan.

AOG 79 *Petaluma* Trfd to Korea 21 Feb 1982.
Later history: renamed *Chin Yang/Gin Yang* (AO 56). R1997, BU South Korea.
1★Korea K-7.

AOG 80 *Piscataqua* Stricken 1 May 1974. BU 1975 Hong Kong.
3★Korea K-6 K-7 K-8; ◆Passage to Freedom 1954.

No.	Name	Builder	Keel Laid	Launched	In service
AOG 81	*Alatna*	Beth; Staten I	16 Mar 1956	16 Sep 1956	17 Jul 1957
AOG 82	*Chattahoochee*	Beth; Staten I	1 May 1956	4 Dec 1956	22 Oct 1957
Displacement	3,459 tons; 5,720 f/l				
Dimensions	302′ (oa); 285′6″ (wl) × 60′11″ × 19′				
Machinery	2 screws; diesel-electric; 4,000 BHP; 13 knots				
Endurance	5760/10				
Complement	24				
Armament	none				

Notes: Type T1-MET-24a. Built for polar operations with ice-strengthened hulls. MSTS. Rec AOT. *Alatna* had forward ice control tower removed 1968.

Service Records:

AOG 81 *Alatna* OS 8 Aug 1972, stricken. Reacq 31 Jul 1979. IS 3 Feb 1982, MSC. OS 22 Jan 1985. NDRF. RRF 1985–2006. Sold 16 Dec 2006, BU Japan.
◆Antarctic 1959, 1960, 1961.

AOG 82 *Chattahoochee* Stricken 3 May 1960; reacq Jun 1961. Stricken. Reacq 31 Jul 1979. IS 11 Jan 1982, MSC. OS 22 Jan 1985. NDRF. RRF 1985–2006. Sold 16 Dec 2006, BU Japan.
◆Antarctic 1961, 1962, 1963.

FAST COMBAT SUPPORT SHIPS

No.	Name	Builder	Keel Laid	Launched	Comm.
AOE 1	*Sacramento*	Puget Sd NSYd	30 Jun 1961	14 Sep 1963	14 Mar 1964
AOE 2	*Camden*	NY Sbdg	17 Feb 1964	29 May 1965	1 Apr 1967
AOE 3	*Seattle*	Puget Sd NSYd	1 Oct 1965	2 Mar 1968	5 Apr 1969
AOE 4	*Detroit*	Puget Sd NSYd	29 Nov 1966	21 Jun 1969	28 Mar 1970
AOE 5	—	—	—	—	—
Displacement	19,200 tons, 53,600 f/l				
Dimensions	792′9″ (oa); 770′ (wl) × 107′ × 39′4″				
Machinery	2 screws; ST; 4 boilers; 100,000 SHP; 27.5 knots				
Endurance	10,000/17				
Complement	600				
Armament	4-twin 3″/50, *1970s*: 1 Sea Sparrow launcher. *1977*: 1 Phalanx, 4-twin 3″/50 *1980s*: 1 Sea Sparrow, 2 Phalanx, 2 helicopters.				

Notes: AOE 1 and 2 used machinery built for BB 66 *Kentucky*. Combine functions of oiler, ammunition ship and store ship. Largest underway replenishment ships. Capacity 194,000 bbls. Helicopter deck aft and hangar.

Service Records:

AOE 1 *Sacramento* In collision with carrier *Abraham Lincoln* in Persian Gulf, 5 Jun 1995. Decomm 1 Oct 2004. BU 2008 Brownsville.

Figure 11.42: *USS Seattle* (AOE 3), fast combat support ship.

13★Vietnam Jan–Apr 1965, Nov 1965–Jun 1966, Dec 1966–Jun 1967, Mar–Jun 1968, Mar–Aug 1969, Mar–Aug 1970, Mar–Aug 1971, Sep 1972–Mar 1973; ◆Korea Jan–Mar 1968, Apr 1969, Iran/Indian Ocean Apr–Jul 1980, Libya Apr–Jun 1986, Gulf War Jan–Mar 1991, Liberia Dec 1992, Indian Ocean Oct 1997–Jan 1998, Aug–Sep 1999.

AOE 2 *Camden* Collided with carrier *Hancock* off Vietnam, 26 Nov 1968. In collision with destroyer *Hamner* in Gulf of Tonkin, 24 Jan 1971. Decomm and stricken 29 Sep 2005. BU 2008 Brownsville.
7★Vietnam Jul 1968–Feb 1969, Sep 1969–Mar 1970, Sep 1970–Mar 1971, Feb–Aug 1972, ◆Korea 5 Jan 1970, Iran/Indian Ocean Apr–Jun 1979, Dec 1980–Apr 1981, Persian Gulf Jun–Jul 1987, Libya Apr–May 1989, Gulf War Apr–Jul 1991, Liberia May–Jun 1994, Indian Ocean Jul–Nov 1998, Sep 2000–Jan 2001, Iraq War 2003.

AOE 3 *Seattle* Damaged in collision with tug at Norfolk, Va., 1 Feb 1982. Damaged in collision with frigate *Aylwin* in Atlantic, 11 Jun 1982. Damaged by explosion at Porto Torres, Italy, 12 Jul 1982. Decomm and stricken 22 Mar 2005. Sold 9 Apr 2005, BU Brownsville, Tex.
◆Iran/Indian Ocean Aug–Oct 1981, Lebanon Sep–Nov 1982, Jan–Apr 1986, Lebanon Jun 1984, Libya Jul–Aug 1989, Gulf War Sep 1990–Mar 1991, Indian Ocean Nov 1997–Mar 1998, Oct 1999–Mar 2000.

AOE 4 *Detroit* Collided with a tanker m/v off South Carolina, 1 Mar 1971. Damaged by explosion in stack at Newport, RI, 12 Dec 1973. Ran aground near Old Point Comfort, Va., 10 Jun 1981. Damaged by fire at Suda Bay, Crete, 9 Jan 1984. Decomm and stricken 17 Feb 2005. Sold 26 Sep 2005, BU Brownsville, Tex.
◆Iran/Indian Ocean Oct–Nov 1980, Lebanon Nov–Dec 1983, Mar 1984, Libya Mar–Jun 1986, Gulf War Aug–Sep, Nov 1990–Mar 1991, Indian Ocean Mar 1997, Nov 1998–Jan 1999.

AOE 5 Canceled 4 Nov 1968.

No.	Name	Builder	Keel Laid	Launched	Comm.
AOE 6	*Supply*	Natl Steel	24 Feb 1989	6 Oct 1990	26 Feb 1994
AOE 7	*Rainier* ex-*Paul Hamilton*	Natl Steel	31 May 1990	28 Sep 1991	1 Dec 1994
AOE 8	*Arctic*	Natl Steel	2 Dec 1991	3 Oct 1993	11 Sep 1995
AOE 9	*Conecuh*				
AOE 10	*Bridge*	Natl Steel	2 Aug 1994	24 Aug 1996	31 Mar 1998

Displacement	19,700 tons; 48,800 f/l
Dimensions	754′9 (oa); 730′ (wl) × 107′ × 39′
Machinery	2 screws; gas turbines; SHP 100,000; 26 knots
Armament	2 Bushmaster, 2 Phalanx, Sea Sparrow; removed 2001–3.
Complement	666 / civ. 235

Notes Disarmed on transfer to MSC.

Service Records:

AOE 6 *Supply* Decomm, to MSC 13 Jul 2001.
◆Indian Ocean Oct–Nov 1998, Jul–Sep 2000.
AOE 7 *Rainier* Decomm to MSC 29 Aug 2003.
◆Indian Ocean Dec 1998–Mar 1999, Jan–Feb 1997, Iraq War 2003, Tsunami relief 2005.
AOE 8 *Arctic* Decomm, to MSC 14 Jun 2002.
◆Indian Ocean Aug–Sep 1997, Jul–Sep 1999, Jul–Sep 2001, Iraq War 2003.
AOE 9 *Conecuh* construction deferred.
AOE 10 *Bridge* Decomm to MSC 24 Jun 2004.
◆Indian Ocean Feb–May 2000.

REPLENISHMENT OILERS

Note: *Conecuh* (AO 110) was rec AOR 110, 1952 (see above).

No.	Name	Builder	Keel Laid	Launched	Comm.
AOR 1	*Wichita*	Beth; Quincy	18 Jun 1966	16 Mar 1968	7 Jun 1969
AOR 2	*Milwaukee*	Beth; Quincy	29 Nov 1966	17 Jan 1969	1 Nov 1969
AOR 3	*Kansas City*	Beth; Quincy	20 Apr 1968	28 Jun 1969	6 Jun 1970
AOR 4	*Savannah*	Beth; Quincy	22 Jan 1969	23 Apr 1970	5 Dec 1970
AOR 5	*Wabash*	Beth; Quincy	21 Jan 1970	6 Feb 1971	20 Nov 1971
AOR 6	*Kalamazoo*	Beth; Quincy	28 Oct 1970	11 Nov 1972	11 Aug 1973
AOR 7	*Roanoke*	National	19 Jan 1974	7 Dec 1974	30 Oct 1976

Displacement	12,500 tons; 41,350 f/l
Dimensions	675′ (oa); 659′ (wl) × 96′ × 33′4″
Machinery	2 screws; ST; 3 Foster Wheeler boilers; 32,000 SHP; 20 knots
Endurance	10,000/17
Complement	345
Armament	2 twin 3″/50, 4–20 mmAA, 1 Sea Sparrow SAM. *1977*: 2 CIWS, 2-twin 3″/50, 1–20 mm *1980s*: 1 Sea Sparrow SAM, 2 Phalanx., 2 helicopters.

Notes: Carry petroleum and munitions. Helicopter deck aft, originally no hangar, but modified 1980s. Capacity 160,000 bbls, plus cargo. Highly successful ships.

Figure 11.43: *USNS Supply* (T-AOE 6), fast combat support ship, about 2003.

Figure 11.44: *USS Kansas City* (AOR 3), replenishment oiler, carrying both fuel and ammunition.

Service Records:

AOR 1 *Wichita* Damaged in collision with carrier *Ranger* off San Diego, 17 Jul 1983. Decomm 12 Mar 1993. Stricken 15 Feb 1995. NDRF. SE.
 4★Vietnam Jul 1970–Jan 1971, Aug–Nov 1971, Jan–Mar, Aug 1972–Feb 1973; ◆Iran/Indian Ocean Jul–Sep 1980, Libya Jan 1990.

AOR 2 *Milwaukee* Damaged in collision with m/v *Santo Prestige* while moored at Norfolk, Va., 3 Jan 1980. Decomm 27 Jan 1994. Stricken 8 Apr 1997. NDRF. SE.
 1★Vietnam Nov 1972–Feb 1973; ◆Lebanon May, Jun–Aug, Oct 1983, Libya May–Jun 1988.

AOR 3 *Kansas City* Collided with destroyer *Henry B. Wilson* at Subic Bay, 24 Feb 1975. Decomm 7 Oct 1994. Stricken 8 Apr 1997. NDRF. SE.
 3★Vietnam Jun–Nov 1971, May–Nov 1972; ◆Iran/Indian Ocean Jan, Mar–Apr 1979, Libya Sep–Nov 1987, Gulf War Jan–Apr 1991, Liberia Apr 1993.

AOR 4 *Savannah* Collided with carrier *Forrestal* in Caribbean, 9 May 1979. Decomm 28 Jul 1995. Stricken 28 Oct 1998. NDRF. SE.
 1★Vietnam May–Nov 1972; ◆Lebanon Jan 1983, Gulf War Oct 1990, Liberia 1990, Nov–Dec 1993, Haiti Sep–Oct 1994.

AOR 5 *Wabash* In collision with ammunition ship *Flint* northwest of Hawaii, 9 Jun 1976. Collided with carrier *Kitty Hawk* at Alameda, Cal., 27 Nov 1983. Decomm 30 Sep 1994. Stricken 8 Apr 1997. NDRF. SE.
 ★Vietnam Dec 1972–Mar 1973; ◆Iran/Indian Ocean Nov 1979–Jan 1980, May–Oct 1981, Libya May–Jun 1990, Gulf War Sep 1992, Liberia Dec 1992.

AOR 6 *Kalamazoo* In collision with AFS *Sylvania* off Virginia Capes, 28 Jan 1981. Decomm 16 Aug 1996. Stricken 28 Oct 1998. NDRF. SE.
 ◆Iran/Indian Ocean Aug–Oct 1980, Lebanon Dec 1982–Apr 1983, Gulf War Jan–Mar 1991.

AOR 7 *Roanoke* Went aground at Pearl Harbor, 29 Oct 1984. In collision with m/v *Mint Prosperity* at Long Beach, Cal., 2 Jul 1986. Decomm and stricken, 6 Oct 1995. NDRF. SE.
 ◆Iran/Indian Ocean Jan–May 1980, Gulf War Jul–Oct 1991.

TRANSPORTS

AP 21 *Wakefield* Decomm 15 Jun 1946. Stricken . . . 1957. BU 1964 Kearny, NJ.

AP 74 *LeJeune* Decomm 9 Feb 1948. Stricken . . Jul 1957. Sold 16 Aug 1966, BU 1966 Portland, Ore.

General Class

AP 110 *Gen. John Pope* Reacq 20 Jul 1950, MSTS. OS 14 May 1955. Reacq 17 Aug 1965, civilian crew. MSTS 1950–60, 1966–70, 1986–90.

Figure 11.45: *USNS General William Weigel* (T-AP 119).

Stricken 26 Oct 1990, NDRF. BU Brownsville, Tex. 2006.
 4★Korea K-5 K-6 K-7 K-8.

AP 111 *Gen. A.E. Anderson* MSTS, 1 Oct 1949–1958. Decomm 10 Nov 1958. Stricken 11 Dec 1958. BU 1987 Kaohsiung.
 2★Korea K-2 K-4 1951–53

AP 112 *Gen. W.A. Mann* MSTS, 1 Oct 1949. MSTS 1949–66. Stricken 1 Dec 1966. BU Taiwan 1987.
 2★Korea K-1 K-2 1951, 1952; 1★Vietnam Aug 1965.

AP 113 *Gen. H.W. Butner* MSTS, 1 Oct 1949. Decomm 28 Jan 1960. Stricken 1 Jul 1961. BU 1977 Brownsville, Tex. or Taiwan.
 2★Korea K-1 K-3 1951–52

AP 114 *Gen. William Mitchell* MSTS, 1 Oct 1949. In collision with m/v *Sirdhana* at Yokohama, 26 Nov 1960. Stricken 1 Dec 1966. Sold 1 Oct 1987, BU Taiwan.
 3★Korea K-1 K-2 K-4 1952, 1953

AP 115 *Gen. G.M. Randall* MSTS, 1 Oct 1949. Decomm 2 Jun 1961. Stricken 1 Sep 1962. Sold 8 May 1975, BU. MSTS 1949–62.
 3★Korea K-1 K-2 3

AP 116 *Gen. M.C. Meigs* Decomm 4 Mar 1946. Reacq 21 Jul 1950, civilian crew. Stricken 1 Oct 1958. Went aground and broke in two south of Cape Flattery while in tow, 9 Jan 1972. MSTS 1950–58.
 3★Korea K-8 K-9 K-10.

AP 117 *Gen. W.H. Gordon* Reacq 8 Nov 1951. Reacq May 1961. Stricken 31 Mar 1986. Sold 1987, BU Taiwan.
 3★Korea K-7 K-8 K-9; 2★Vietnam Dec 1967–Mar 1968.

AP 119 *Gen. William Weigel* Reacq 20 Jul 1950. Stricken 12 Jun 1958. Reacq 18 Aug 1965. Stricken 31 Mar 1986. MSTS 1950–58, 1965–70.
 7★Korea K-1 K-2 K-5 K-6 K-7 K-8 K-9; 1★Vietnam.

AP 176 *Gen. J.C. Breckinridge* MSTS, 1 Oct 1949. Stricken 1 Dec 1966. BU Taiwan 1987.
 4★Korea K-1 K-2 K-3 K-4 1951–52; 1★Vietnam Jul, Sep–Oct 1965.

Notes: General class, type P2-S2-R2. Armament removed. Single pole masts.

Admiral Class

AP 120 *Gen. Daniel I. Sultan* (ex-*Adm. W.S. Benson*) Reacq, 1 Mar 1950, MSTS. OS 7 Nov 1968. Stricken 9 Oct 1969. BU 1987 Kaohsiung.
 2★Korea K-1 K-2 1950, 1952, 1953; 1★Vietnam.

AP 121 *Gen. Hugh J. Gaffey* (ex-*Adm. W.L. Capps*) Reacq, 1 Mar 1950, MSTS. OS 4 Nov 1968. Stricken 9 Oct 1969. Reacq as **IX 507**, 1 Nov 1978. Stricken 29 Oct 1993. Sold 25 Oct 1995. Sunk as target 16 Jun 2000.
 ★Korea 1951–52; 1★Vietnam.

Figure 11.46: *USNS General Simon B. Buckner* (T-AP 123), a former Admiral class transport. These ships were acquired from the Army in 1950, which had taken them over in 1946 and renamed them after generals who had been killed in World War II.

AP 122   *Gen. Alexander M. Patch* (ex-*Adm. R.E. Coontz*)   Reacq 1 Mar 1950, MSTS. OS 1967. Stricken 20 Aug 1990. NDRF Sold 4 Jun 2002, BU Brownsville.
1★Vietnam.

AP 123   *Gen. Simon B. Buckner* (ex-*Adm. E.W. Eberle*)   Reacq, 1 Mar 1950, MSTS. In collision with a m/v in New York harbor, 4 Apr 1964. OS 24 Mar 1970. Stricken 20 Aug 1990. Sold 27 Jun 1997, BU Brownsville, Tex.
★Korea 1951, 1952; 1★Vietnam

AP 124   *Gen. Edwin D. Patrick* (ex-*Adm. C.F. Hughes*)   Reacq, 1 Mar 1950 MSTS. OS 30 Sep 1968. Stricken 9 Oct 1969. NDRF. BU India, 2005.
3★Korea K-1 K-2 K-5 1951, 1952.

AP 125   *Gen. Nelson M. Walker* (ex-*Adm. H.T. Mayo*)   Reacq, 1 Mar 1950, MSTS. OS 16 Feb 1957. Reacq by USN 14 Aug 1965. OS Dec 1967. Stricken 25 Jan 1981. NDRF. BU 2004 Brownsville.
3★Korea K-8 K-9 K-10 1951; 3★Vietnam

AP 126   *Gen. Maurice Rose* (ex-*Adm. Hugh Rodman*)   Reacq, 1 Mar 1950, MSTS. OS Jan 1967. Stricken 20 Aug 1990. Sold 27 Jun 1997, BU Brownsville, Tex.
1★Vietnam.

AP 127   *Gen. William O. Darby* (ex-*Adm. W.S. Sims*)   Reacq, 1 Mar 1950, MSTS. OS 1968. Stricken 9 Jan 1969. Reinst 27 Oct 1981. Rec **IX 510**, 1 Jul 1982 as accommodation ship (unnamed) at Norfolk. Stricken 26 Oct 1993. NDRF. BU 2004 Brownsville.
1★Vietnam Nov 1966–Jan 1967.

Notes: Admiral class, type P2-SE2-R1. Renamed on transfer to Army in 1946. Disarmed. Kingposts fore and aft.

General Class (C4)

AP 134   *Gen. R.L. Howze*   Decomm 1 Apr 1946, to Army. Reacq, 1 Mar 1950, MSTS. OS 31 Dec 1955. Sold 10 Apr 1968.
Later history: Merchant *Guam Bear*, renamed *New Zealand Bear* 1975, *Austral Glen* 1976, *Pacific Endeavor* 1980. BU 1980 Karachi.
5★Korea K-4 K-5 K-7 K-8 K-9; ◆Passage to Freedom 1954.

AP 135   *Gen. W.M. Black*   Decomm 28 Feb 1946, to Army. Reacq 1 Mar 1950, MSTS. OS 26 Aug 1955. Sold 13 Apr 1967.
Later history: Merchant *Green Forest*. BU 1980 Kaohsiung.
5★Korea K-5 K-6 K-7 K-8 K-9; ◆Passage to Freedom 1954

AP 137   *Gen. S.D. Sturgis*   Decomm 24 May 1946, to Army. Reacq 1 Mar 1950, MSTS. OS 28 May 1955. Sold.1967.
Later history: Merchant *Green Port*. BU 1980 Kaohsiung.

AP 138   *Gen. C.G. Morton*   Decomm 15 May 1946, to Army. Reacq 1 Mar 1950, MSTS. Stricken 29 May 1958. Sold 13 Apr 1967.

Figure 11.47: *USNS General W.G. Haan* (T-AP 158) as an Army transport in 1948.

Later history: Merchant *Green Wave*. BU 1980 Kaohsiung.
2★Korea K-2 K-4 1951, 1952.

AP 139   *Gen. R.E. Callan*   Decomm 24 May 1946, to Army. Reacq 1 Mar 1950, MSTS. Stricken 29 May 1958. To USAF 15 Jul 1961.
Later history: U.S. Air Force *Gen. H.H. Arnold* (E-2–1908). Reacq as **AGM 9**, 1 Jul 1964.

AP 140   *Gen. M.B. Stewart*   Decomm 24 May 1946, to Army. Reacq 1 Mar 1950, MSTS. OS Apr 1955. Sold 2 Aug 1967.
Later history: merchant *Albany* 1967, renamed *Mission Viking* 1974. BU 1987 Kaohsiung.

AP 141   *Gen. A.W. Greely*   Decomm 29 Mar 1946, to Army. Reacq 1 Mar 1950, MSTS. OS Mar 1955. Stricken 1 Jul 1960. Sold 10 Apr 1968.
Later history: merchant *Hawaii Bear* 1968, renamed *Austral Glade* 1975, *African Enterprise* 1980, *Caribe Enterprise* 1982. BU 1986.

AP 142   *Gen. C.H. Muir*   Decomm 18 Jun 1946, to Army. Reacq 1 Mar 1950, MSTS. OS 7 Feb 1955. Stricken 1 Jul 1960. Sold 10 Sep 1968. BU 1988.
Later history: merchant *Chicago* 1969. BU.

AP 143   *Gen. H.B. Freeman*   Decomm 4 Mar 1946, to Army. Reacq 1 Mar 1950, civilian crew. Stricken 24 Jul 1958. Sold 6 Nov 1967.
Later history: merchant *Newark* 1968. BU 1986 Kaohsiung.
2★Korea K-1 K-2 K-4 1951, 1952

AP 144   *Gen. H.F. Hodges*   Decomm 13 May 1946, to Army. Reacq 1 Mar 1950, MSTS. Sold 3 Aug 1967.
Later history: merchant *James* 1967. BU 1979 Kaohsiung.

AP 145   *Gen. Harry Taylor*   Decomm 13 Jun 1946, to Army. Reacq 1 Mar 1950, MSTS. to USAF, 15 Jul 1961.
Later history: U.S. Air Force *Gen. Hoyt S. Vandenberg* (E-2–1907). Reacq as **AGM 10**, 1 Jul 1964.

AP 146   *Gen. W.F. Hase*   Decomm 6 Jun 1946, to Army. Reacq 1 Mar 1950, MSTS. OS Jul 1954. Stricken 1 Jul 1960. Sold 16 Jul 1968.
Later history: merchant *Transidaho* 1969, renamed *Carolina* 1975, *Point Manatee* 1982. BU 1985 Brownsville, Tex.
8★Korea K-1 K-2 K-4 K-5 K-7 K-8 K-9

AP 147   *Gen. E.T. Collins*   Decomm 17 Jun 1946, to Army. Reacq 1 Mar 1950, MSTS. OS Oct 1954. Stricken 1 Jul 1960. Sold 10 Sep 1968.
Later history: merchant *New Orleans* 1969, *Guayama* 1975, *Eastern Kin* 1981. Foundered after hull cracked 1,000 m. east of Japan, 9 Jan 1982.
4★Korea K-2 K-4 K-8 K-9 1951–53.

AP 148   *Gen. M.L. Hersey*   Decomm 1 Jun 1946, to Army 6 Jun 1946. Reacq 1 Mar 1950, MSTS. Collided with m/v *Maipu* which sank, at Wesermunde, Germany, 4 Nov 1951. OS 11 Jun 1954. Stricken 1 Jul 1960. Sold 16 Jul 1968.
Later history: merchant *St. Louis* 1968. BU Taiwan 1988.
2★Korea.

AP 149 *Gen. J.H. McRae* Decomm 27 Feb 1946, to Army. Reacq 1 Mar 1950, MSTS. OS 29 Oct 1954. Sold 16 Jul 1968.
Later history: merchant *Transhawaii* 1970, *Aguadilla* 1975, *Amco Voyager* 1982, *Voyager* 1985. BU 1987 Kaohsiung.

AP 150 *Gen. M.M. Patrick* Decomm 8 Mar 1946, to Army 11 Mar 1946. Reacq 1 Mar 1950, MSTS. Sold 6 Nov 1967.
Later history: merchant *Boston* 1968. BU Taiwan 1988.
2★Korea K-1 K-2 1951, 1952

AP 151 *Gen. W.C. Langfitt* Decomm 6 Jun 1946, to Army. Reacq 1 Mar 1950, MSTS. OS 30 Sep 1957. Sold 12 Apr 1968.
Later history: merchant *Transindiana* 1969, BU 1983.

AP 153 *Gen. R.M. Blatchford* Decomm 12 Jun 1946, to Army. Reacq 1 Mar 1950, MSTS. OS Jan 1967. Stricken 9 Oct 1969. Sold 27 Jan 1969.
Later history: merchant *Stonewall Jackson* 1970, *Alex Stephens* 1973. BU 1980 Kaohsiung.
1★Vietnam

AP 154 *Gen. LeRoy Eltinge* Decomm 26 May 1946, to Army. Reacq 1 Mar 1950, MSTS. OS Jan 1967, Stricken 9 Oct 1969. Sold 27 Jan 1969.
Later history: merchant *Robert E. Lee* 1970, *Robert Toombs* 1973. BU 1980 Kaohsiung.
1★Korea K-8; 1★Vietnam Dec 1966.

AP 155 *Gen. A.W. Brewster* Decomm 10 Apr 1946, to Army. Reacq 1 Mar 1950, MSTS. OS Dec 1954. Sold 10 Sep 1968.
Later history: merchant *Philadelphia* 1968. BU Taiwan 1988.
4★Korea K-8 K-9 K-10; Passage to Freedom 1954.

AP 156 *Gen. D.E. Aultman* Decomm 15 Mar 1946, to Army. Reacq 1 Mar 1950, MSTS. Sold 6 Nov 1967.
Later history: merchant *Portland* 1968. BU 1986 Kaohsiung.

AP 157 *Gen. C.C. Ballou* Decomm 17 May 1946, to Army. Reacq 1 Mar 1950. OS . . Sep 1954. Stricken 1 Jul 1960. Sold 11 Apr 1968.
Later history: merchant *Brooklyn* 1968, renamed *Humacao* 1975, *Eastern Light* 1981. BU 1981 Kaohsiung.
3★Korea K-8 K-9 K-10.

AP 158 *Gen. W.G. Haan* Decomm 7 May 1946, to Army. Reacq 1 Mar 1950, civilian crew. OS 7 Jan 1957. Sold 6 Aug 1968.
Later history: merchant *Transoregon* 1969, *Mayaguez* 1975, *Amoco Trader* 1982, *Trader* 1985. BU 1987 Kaohsiung.

AP 159 *Gen. Stuart Heintzelman* Decomm 12 Jun 1946, to Army. Reacq 1 Mar 1950, MSTS. OS 24 Jun 1954. Stricken 1 Jul 1960. Sold 11 Apr 1968.
Later history: merchant *Mobile* 1968. BU 1984.
★Korea 1950, 1951

No.	Name	Builder	Launched	Acquired	Comm.
AP 178	*Frederick Funston* ex-APA 89	Sea-Tac; Tac.	21 Apr 1941	27 Sep 1941	1 Mar 1950
AP 179	*James O'Hara* ex-APA 90	Sea-Tac; Tac.	16 Jun 1941	30 Dec 1941	1 Mar 1950

Displacement 11,200 tons
Dimensions 492′ (oa); 465′3″ (wl) × 59′6″ × 26′6″
Machinery 1 screw; GT; SHP 8,000; 16 knots
Complement 576
Armament 1–5″/38, 2–3″/50, 8–1.1″AA guns

Notes: Type C3-S1-A3. Reacq 1950, MSTS. Troops 2,200.

Service Records:

AP 178 *Frederick Funston* Decomm 4 Apr 1946. MSTS. Stricken 1 Jul 1961, BU 1969, Portland, Ore.
1★Korea K-1 1952.

AP 179 *James O'Hara* Decomm 5 Apr 1946. MSTS Stricken 1 Jul 1961. Sold 6 Feb 1968, BU Portland, Ore.
1★Korea K-2 1951.

Figure 11.48: *USNS Henry Gibbins* (T-AP 183).

No.	Name	Builder	Launched	Acquired	Comm.
AP 180	*David C. Shanks* Lchd as *Gulfport* LD as *American Farmer*	Ingalls	27 Sep 1941	21 Oct 1942	15 Mar 1950
AP 181	*Fred C. Ainsworth* Lchd as *Pass Christian* LD as *American Shipper*	Ingalls	23 Jan 1942	20 Nov 1942	1 Mar 1950
AP 182	*George W. Goethals* Lchd as *Pascagoula* LD as *American Merchant*	Ingalls	7 Jan 1941	23 Jan 1942	1 Mar 1950
AP 183	*Henry Gibbins* Lchd as *Biloxi* LD as *American Banker*	Ingalls	23 Aug 1941	11 Sep 1942	1 Mar 1950

Displacement 10,500 tons
Dimensions 491′ (oa); 465′(wl) × 69′6″ × 26′9″
Machinery 1 screw; GT; 16.5 knots
Armament none

Notes: Type C3-IN. Troops 1,976.

Service Records:

AP 180 *David C. Shanks* MSTS. Stricken 1 Jul 1961. Sold 26 Jun 1973. BU 1973 Kaohsiung.
1★Korea K-2.

AP 181 *Fred C. Ainsworth* MSTS. Stricken 1 Jul 1961. Sold 26 Jun 1973. BU 1973 Kaohsiung.
3★Korea; ◆OpCastle 1954.

AP 182 *George W. Goethals* MSTS. Stricken 1 Jul 1961. Sold 1 Nov 1960. BU 1971 Castellon, Spain.

AP 183 *Henry Gibbins* MSTS. Stricken 28 Dec 1959.
Later history: Merchant *Empire State IV*, renamed *Bay State* 1973. Sold 3 Dec 1981, BU 1982 Kearny, NJ.

No.	Name	Builder	Launched	Acquired/In service
AP 184	*Pvt. Elden H. Johnson* ex-*Pinkney*, APH 2	Moore	4 Dec 1941	1 Mar 1950
AP 185	*Pvt. William H. Thomas* ex-*Rixey*, APH 3	Moore	30 Dec 1941	1 Mar 1950
AP 186	*Sgt. Charles E. Mower* ex-*Tryon*, APH 1	Moore	21 Oct 1941	1 Mar 1950

Displacement 9,920 tons f/l
Dimensions 450′ (oa); 420′ (wl) × 62′ × 23′6″
Machinery 1 screw; GT; 2 FW boilers; SHP 8,500; 18.2 knots
Complement 460

Notes: Reacq from Army 1950. MSTS

Figure 11.49: *USNS Pvt. Elden H. Johnson* (T-AP 184), formerly the Navy transport Pinkney.

Service Records:

AP 184 *Pvt. Elden H. Johnson* OS and stricken 27 Dec 1957. Sold 28 Sep 1970, BU 1971.

AP 185 *Pvt. William H. Thomas* OS 27 Dec 1957. Sold 28 Sep 1970, BU 1971, Taiwan.

AP 186 *Sgt. Charles E. Mower* OS 16 Jun 1954. Stricken 1 Jul 1960. Sold 3 Mar 1969, BU Portland, Ore.

No.	Name	Builder	Launched	Acquired	In service
AP 187	*Pvt. Joe P. Martinez* ex-*Stevens Victory*	Beth; Fair.	13 Apr 1945	29 May 1945	1 Mar 1950
AP 188	*Aiken Victory*	Beth; Fair.	13 Oct 1944	30 Nov 1944	21 Jul 1950
AP 189	*Lt. Raymond O. Beaudoin* ex-*Marshall Victory*	Beth; Fair.	4 Apr 1945	21 May 1945	22 Jul 1950
AP 190	*Pvt. Sadao S. Munemori* ex-*Wilson Victory*	Beth; Fair.	22 May 1945	6 Jul 1945	22 Jul 1950
AP 191	*Sgt. Howard E. Woodford* ex-*Goucher Victory*	Beth; Fair.	18 Apr 1945	2 Jun 1945	22 Jul 1950
AP 192	*Sgt. Sylvester Antolak* ex-*Stetson Victory*	Beth; Fair.	3 May 1945	16 Jun 1945	22 Jul 1950

Displacement	4,420 tons; 15,199 f/l
Dimensions	455′3″ (oa); 436′6″ (wl) × 62′ × 28′6″
Machinery	1 screw; GT; 8,500 SHP; 15.5 knots
Complement	96
Armament	none

Notes: Type VC2-S-AP2.

Service Records:

AP 187 *Pvt. Joe P. Martinez* MSTS. OS 1 Sep 1952. Stricken 8 Nov 1952. Sold 7 Oct 1971, BU Seattle.
4★Korea.

AP 188 *Aiken Victory* OS 17 Dec 1952. Stricken 12 Feb 1953. Sold 10 Aug 1971, BU Portland, Ore.
8★Korea K-1 K-2 K-3 K-45, K-6 K-7 K-8.

AP 189 *Lt. Raymond O. Beaudoin* OS 5 Nov 1952. Stricken 22 Dec 1952. Sold 20 Mar 1972, BU Taiwan.
4★Korea.

Figure 11.50: *USNS Sgt. Sylvester Antolak* (T-AP 192)

AP 190 *Pvt. Sadao S. Munemori* OS 9 Oct 1952. Stricken 6 Nov 1952. Sold 8 Dec 1969, BU 1970 Portland, Ore.
4★Korea.

AP 191 *Sgt. Howard E. Woodford* OS, stricken 4 Dec 1952. Sold 20 Mar 1972, BU Taiwan.
5★Korea K-5 K-6 K-7 K-8.

AP 192 *Sgt. Sylvester Antolak* OS 17 Sep 1952. Stricken 8 Nov 1952. Sold 8 Dec 1971, BU Seattle.
5★Korea K-1 K-2 K-4 K-5 K-6.

No.	Name	Builder	Launched	Acquired	In service
AP 193	*Marine Adder*	Kais; #3	7 Mar 1945	16 May 1945	24 Jul 1950
AP 194	*Marine Lynx*	Kais; Vanc.	9 Dec 1944	17 Jul 1945	23 Jul 1950
AP 195	*Marine Phoenix*	Kais; Vanc.	16 Dec 1944	9 Aug 1945	21 Jul 1950
AP 199	*Marine Carp*	Kais; Vanc.	6 Dec 1944	5 Jul 1945	17 Mar 1952
AP 200	*Marine Jumper*	not acquired	—	—	—
AP 201	*Marine Marlin*	not acquired	—	—	—
AP 202	*Marine Serpent*	Kais; Vanc.	30 Nov 1944	12 Jun 1945	8 May 1952

Displacement	6,710 tons; 10,210 f/l
Dimensions	522′10″ (oa); 496′7″ (wl) × 71′8″ × 30′
Machinery	1 screw; GT; 13,750 SHP; 17 knots
Complement	—
Armament	none

Notes: Type C4-S-A3. Capacity 3,485 troops. MSTS.

Service Records:

AP 193 *Marine Adder* OS, stricken 5 Jun 1958. Sold 4 Aug 1967.
Later history: Merchant *Trans-Colorado* 1967. RRF 1968 as T-AK 2005. BU 1988 Kaohsiung.
8★Korea 2, K-4 K-5 K-6 K-7 K-8 K-9 K-10; ◆Passage to Freedom 1954.

AP 194 *Marine Lynx* OS, stricken 1 May 1958.
Later history: merchant *Trans-Columbia* 1967. RRF 1968 as T-AK 2006. BU 1988 Kaohsiung.
7★Korea K-2 K-5 K-6 K-7 K-8 K-9 K-10; ◆Passage to Freedom

Figure 11.51: *USNS Marine Lynx* (T-AP 194), 1950s.

Figure 11.52: *USNS Geiger* (T-AP 197), acquired during construction.

AP 195   *Marine Phoenix*   OS, stricken 3 Nov 1958. Sold 25 Apr 1967.
Later history: merchant *Marine Phoenix* 1967, *Mohawk* 1968. BU 1979 Kaohsiung.
8★Korea K-1 K-4 K-5 K-6 K-7 K-8 K-9 K-10.

AP 199   *Marine Carp*   OS 9 Oct 1957. Stricken 11 Sep 1958. Sold 20 Jul 1967.
Later history: merchant *Green Springs* 1967. BU 1979 Kaohsiung.
1★Korea.

AP 200   *Marine Jumper*   not acquired.

AP 201   *Marine Marlin*   not acquired.

AP 202   *Marine Serpent*   OS, stricken 17 Oct 1955. Sold 16 Jul 1968.
Later history: merchant *Galveston* 1968.
3★Korea K-8 K-9 K-10; ◆Passage to Freedom 1954.

No.	Name	Builder	Keel Laid	Launched	Comm.
AP 196	*Barrett* LD as *President Jackson*	NY Sbdg	1 Jun 1949	27 Jun 1950	21 May 1952
AP 197	*Geiger* LD as *President Adams*	NY Sbdg	1 Aug 1949	9 Oct 1950	13 Sep 1952
AP 198	*Upshur* LD as *President Hayes*	NY Sbdg	30 Sep 1949	19 Jan 1951	20 Dec 1952
Displacement	11,200 tons; 17,600 f/l				
Dimensions	533′9″(oa); 499′6″ (wl) × 73′ × 27′				
Machinery	1 screw; ST; 13,500 SHP; 19 knots				
Complement	219				
Armament	none				

Notes: Type P2-S1-DN3. 1,900 troops carried. MSTS. Laid down as passenger ships, taken over during Korean War.

Service Records:

AP 196   *Barrett*   OS 1973. Stricken 1 Jul 1973. To NY Maritime Academy, 1973.
Later history: Training ship *Empire State V*. Laid up 4 Apr 1990 (as *State*), NDR BU 2007, Chesapeake, Va.
1★Korea; 3★Vietnam Apr, Jun, Nov 1968–May 1969.

AP 197   *Geiger*   Stricken 12 Feb 1980, to Mass Maritime Academy,
Later history: renamed *Bay State*. Damaged by fire off Cape Cod, 27 Dec.1981 Stricken 1 Apr 1983, BU.
1★Vietnam Jan 1967.

AP 198   *Upshur*   Damaged by fire at Brooklyn, NY, 31 Jul 1959. Stricken 2 Apr 1973; to Maine Maritime Academy.
Later history: Training ship *State of Maine*. Laid up 1990. NDRF. SE.

BARRACKS SHIPS

APB 35   *Benewah*   Out of comm 30 Aug 1946–9 Nov 1951 and 10 Mar 1956–28 Jan 1967. Mobile riverine base, Vietnam. Rec **IX 311**, 26 Feb 1971 and decomm. Stricken 1 Sep 1973. Sunk as barrier reef in Philippines, 1975.
14★Vietnam Apr 1967–Nov 1970; PUC 29 Jan–4 Mar 1968.

APB 36   *Colleton*   In service 28 Jan 1967. Mobile riverine base, Vietnam. Decomm 15 Dec 1969. Stricken 1 Jun 1973. Sold 30 Jul 1974. BU Portland, Ore.
7★Vietnam Apr 1967–Jun 1969; 2 PUC 29 Jan–4 Mar 1968, 25 Jan–19 Jun 1969.

APB 37   *Echols*   Rec **IX 504**, 1 Feb 1976. Stricken 22 Dec 1995.

APB 38   *Marlboro*   Decomm 30 Jan 1947. Stricken 1 Dec 1963. BU 1966.

APB 39   *Mercer*   Out of comm 18 Jun 1947–12 Oct 1951 and 17 Feb 1956–11 May 1968. Rec **IX 502**, 1 Nov 1975. Decomm 7 Jan 1970. Rec **APL 39**, 7 Mar 2001. Barracks ship, Sasebo, Japan.
4★Vietnam Jul–Sep 1968, Dec 1968–Aug 1969; PUC 25 Jan–5 Jul 1969.

APB 40   *Nueces*   Out of comm 30 Sep 1955–3 May 1968. Decomm 13 Mar 1970. Rec **IX 503**, 1 Nov 1975. Rec **APL 40**, 7 Mar 2001. Barracks ship, Sasebo, Japan.
4★Vietnam Jul 1968–Aug 1969. PUC 25 Jan–5 Jul 1969.

APB 41   *Wythe*   Decomm 29 May 1947. Stricken 1 May 1959. Sold 10 Sep 1959. BU.

APB 42   *Yavapai*   Decomm 3 Dec 1946. Stricken 1 May 1959.

APB 43   *Yolo*   Decomm 9 Aug 1946. Stricken 1 May 1959. Sold 1960, BU.

APB 44   *Presque Isle*   Decomm 18 Apr 1947. Stricken 1 May 1959. Trfd to Indonesia.
Later history: renamed *Teluk Ratai*

APB 45   *Blackford*   Decomm 26 Apr 1947. Stricken 1 Apr 1960. Sold 3 Aug 1960, BU.

APB 46   *Dorchester*   Decomm 16 Oct 1946. Stricken 1 Jun 1973. Sold 22 Jun 1978.
Later history: Merchant *Pacific Pride*, renamed *Alaska Packer* 1986. SE1998

APB 47   *Kingman*   Decomm 15 Jan 1947. Stricken 1 Oct 1977.

APB 48   *Vanderburgh*   Decomm 30 Jan 1947. Stricken 1 Apr 1972. Sold 15 Nov 1972, BU Portland, Ore.

APB 49   *Accomac*   Decomm 9 Aug 1946. Sold 7 Dec 1959.

APB 50   *Cameron*   Decomm 15 May 1946. Sold 1959.

Notes: Four supported joint Army-Navy riverine force in Mekong Delta in Vietnam. Complement 198, could berth 900 men.

APB 51   *DuPage*   Acquired 1951. Stricken 1 Jun 1959.
ex-*John W. Weeks*

Figure 11.53: *USNS Sgt. George D. Keathley* (T-APc 117).

Figure 11.54: *USNS Mercy* (T-AH 19) at Kupang, Timor, providing humanitarian assistance, 20 Aug 2006. The hospital ship was converted from a tanker in 1986.

COASTAL TRANSPORTS

No.	Name	Builder	Launched	Acquired & in service
APC 116	*Sgt. Jonah E. Kelley* ex-*Link Splice*	Southeastern	17 Mar 1945	1 Mar 1950
APC 117	*Sgt. George D. Keathley* ex-*Acorn Knot* LD as *Alexander R. Nininger, Jr.*	Southeastern	7 Dec 1944	1 Jul 1950
APC 118	*Sgt. Joseph E. Muller* ex-*Check Knot*	Southeastern	17 Feb 1945	1 Jul 1950
APC 119	*Pvt. Jose F. Valdez* ex-*Round Splice* LD as *Joe P. Martinez*	Butler; Dul.	27 Oct 1944	2 Sep 1950
Displacement	2,460 tons; 7,460 f/l			
Dimensions	338'8" (oa); 321'(wl) × 50' × 21'			
Machinery	1 screw; diesel; SHP 1,700; 11.5 knots			
Complement	148			
Armament	none			

Notes: Type C1-M-AV1. MSTS. Capacity 101 troops.

Service Record:

APC 116 *Sgt. Jonah E. Kelley* OS 24 Nov 1969. Stricken 28 Apr 1970. Sold 30 Oct 1972, BU.

APC 117 *Sgt. George D. Keathley* OS 11 Dec 1956. Stricken 24 Oct 1957. Reacq 1 Dec 1967 and rec **AGS 35**. OS Dec 1971. Trfd to Taiwan 29 Mar 1972.
Later history: renamed *Chiu Hwa* (AGS 398). Returned 15 Aug 1988, Sunk as target.
9★Korea

APC 118 *Sgt. Joseph E. Muller* Stricken 25 Oct 1957. Reacq 1 Dec 1962 and rec **AG 171**. Stricken 28 Apr 1970. BU 1972.
9★Korea K-1 K-2 K-4 K-5 K-6 K-7 K-8 K-9 K-10.

APC 119 *Pvt. Jose F. Valdez* Stricken 22 Dec 1959. Reacq 1 Nov 1961. Rec **AG 169**, 1 Dec 1962. Stricken 15 Aug 1976. Sold 27 Jul 1977. BU Brownsville.

HOSPITAL SHIPS

AH 12 *Haven* Out of comm 1 Jul 1947–15 Sep 1950. Decomm 30 Jun 1957, in service. OS, Stricken 1 Mar 1967.
Later history Merchant *Clendenin*, renamed *Alaskan* 1969. BU 1987 Kaohsiung, Taiwan.
8★Korea K-1 K-2 K-4 K-5 K-6 K-7 K-9 K-10; ◆Passage to Freedom 1954.

AH 13 *Benevolence* Out of comm 13 Sep 1947–21 Jul 1950. Sunk in collision with m/v *Mary Luckenbach* in San Francisco Bay while returning from sea trials, 25 Aug 1950 (23 dead).

AH 14 *Tranquillity* Decomm 26 Jul 1946. Stricken 1 Sep 1961. BU 1974 Philadelphia.

AH 15 *Consolation* Decomm 30 Dec 1955. Chartered to People to People Health Fdn, 16 Mar 1960.
Later history Merchant hospital ship *Hope*. Stricken 16 Sep 1974, BU Brownsville, Tex.
10★Korea K-1 K-2 K-3 K-4 K-5 K-6 K-7 K-8 K-9 K-10; ◆Passage to Freedom 1954.

AH 16 *Repose* Out of comm 19 Jan 1950–26 Aug 1950 in svc.-28 Oct 1946 and 21 Dec 1954–19 Oct 1965. In collision with oiler *Tappahannock* off Vietnam, 12 Jun 1967. Decomm 15 Aug 1970. Stricken 15 Mar 1974. Sold 18 Apr 1975, BU 1975.
9★Korea K-1 K-2 K-4 K-5 K-6 K-7 K-8 K-9 K-10; 10★Vietnam Feb 1966–Aug 1968, Oct 1968–Mar 1970.

AH 17 *Sanctuary* Decomm 15 Aug 1946. Stricken 1 Sep 1961. Reacq 1 Mar 1966. Recomm 15 Nov 1966. Out of comm 15 Dec 1971–18 Nov 1972. Converted to dependent support ship 1971–73. Decomm 28 Mar 1974. Stricken 16 Feb 1989, trfd to Life International Inc. Sold 21 Aug 2007.
12★Vietnam Apr 1966, Apr–Aug 1967, Dec 1967–Mar 1969, Jun 1969–May 1971.

No.	Name	Builder	Launched	In service
AH 19	*Mercy* ex-*Worth*	National Steel	19 Jul 1975	15 Dec 1986
AH 20	*Comfort* ex-*Rose City*	National Steel	12 Feb 1976	1 Dec 1987
Displacement	24,712 tons; 69,320 f/l			
Dimensions	894' (oa); 854'2" (wl) × 105'9" × 32'10"			
Machinery	1 screw; ST; 2 boilers; 24,500 SHP; 17.5 knots			
Endurance	13,400/17.5			
Complement	119 + 1,100 medical			

Notes: Former tankers, type T8–5–100b; converted by National Steel. Designed to take on casualties by helicopter. Capacity: 920+ patients.

Service Records:

AH 19 *Mercy*
◆Gulf War Sep 1990–Mar 1991, Tsunami relief 2005.

AH 20 *Comfort* Supported rescue force in New York, 12 Sep–1 Oct 2001.
◆Gulf War Aug 1990–Mar 1991, Haiti Sep–Oct 1994, Iraq War 2003.

FLOATING DRYDOCKS

Note: Some floating drydocks were named. As service craft, these are outside the scope of this book and names are provided here for information only.

AFDB 1 *Artisan*, AFDB 7 *Los Alamos*, AFDL 1 *Endeavor*, AFDL 6 *Dynamic*, AFDL 7 *Ability*, AFDL 23 *Adept*, AFDL 47 *Reliance*, AFDL 48 *Diligence*, AFDM 3 *Endurance*, AFDM 5 *Resourceful*, AFDM 6 *Competent*, AFDM 7 *Sustain*, AFDM 8 *Richland*, ARD 5 *Waterford*, ARD 7 *West Milton*, ARD 30 *San Onofre*, ARD 20 *White Sands*, ARD 22 *Windsor*, ARD 29 *Arco*, ARDM 1 *Oak Ridge*, ARDM 2 *Alamogordo*, ARDM 4 *Shippingport*.

12
FLEET TUGS

ATF 67 *Apache* Out of comm 3 Dec 1946–20 Jul 1951. Damaged by grounding off Fcheuu Island, Korea, while attempting to free grounded *LST-578*, 9 May 1952. Decomm 27 Feb 1974. Stricken 30 Mar 1974. Trfd to Taiwan 30 Jun 1974.
Later history: renamed *Ta Wan* (551). SE2001.
2★Korea K-7 K-8; 2★Vietnam Nov 1965–Mar 1966; ◆OpCastle 1954, Taiwan Straits 29 Oct 1958.

ATF 68 *Arapaho* Decomm 15 Jan 1947. Stricken 1 Jul 1961. Trfd to Argentina, 10 Jul 1961.
Later history: renamed *Comandante General Zapiola* (A 2). Went aground Nov 1971. R 1976.

ATF 69 *Chippewa* Decomm 26 Feb 1947. Stricken 1 Sep 1961. Sunk as artificial reef off Destin, Fla., 28 Feb 1990.

ATF 70 *Choctaw* Decomm 11 Mar 1947. Trfd to Colombia 31 Dec 1960.
Later history: renamed *Pedro de Heredia* (RM 72). SE2001.

ATF 71 *Hopi* Decomm 9 Dec 1955. Stricken 1 Jul 1963. Reacq for experimental purposes, 11 Jun 1986.

ATF 72 *Kiowa* Collided with destroyer *Waldron* in North Atlantic, 13 Jun 1968. Decomm 16 Oct 1972, Trfd to Dominican Republic 16 Oct 1972.

Figure 12.1: *USS Luiseno* (ATF 156), fleet tug. Later served in the Argentine Navy.

Later history: renamed *Macorix* (RM 21). Returned 5 Jun 1992, BU 1994.
◆Cuba Jan–Feb 1962, Cuba Missile Crisis Nov–Dec 1962, Dominican Rep Jun–Jul 1965.

ATF 73 *Menominee* Decomm 15 Nov 1946. Stricken 1 Nov 1959. Trfd to Indonesia 26 Jan 1961.
Later history: renamed *Rakata* (922).

ATF 74 *Pawnee* Decomm Jan 1947. Stricken 1 Sep 1962. Sold 9 Nov 1971, BU 1972 Seattle.

ATF 75 *Sioux* Out of comm 23 Apr 1947–15 Oct 1952. Decomm and trfd to Turkey 30 Oct 1972.
Later history: renamed *Gazal* (A 85/A 587). SE2001.
★Korea 1953; 8★Vietnam Jul, Sep 1965, Apr–jun 1968, Jun–Sep 1970. ◆OpCastle 1954, Korea Oct 1971,

ATF 76 *Ute* Out of comm 13 Jul 1946–14 Sep 1951. Decomm Aug 1974, to MSC. To USCG 30 Sep 1980.
Later history: USCGC *Ute* (WMEC 76). Returned 26 May 1988. Stricken 23 Jan 1989. Sunk as target 4 Aug 1991.
2★Korea K-7 K-8; 9★Vietnam Apr–Aug 1966, Aug–Dec 1967, Feb–Jun 1969, Jan, Mar–Apr 1971, Mar–May 1972; ◆Passage to Freedom 1954.

ATF 81 *Bannock* Out of comm 21 Feb 1947–11 Sep 1951. Decomm 25 Nov 1955. To Italy 3 Oct 1962.
Later history: renamed *Bannock*, renamed *CP 451* 1993. SE2001.

ATF 82 *Carib* Decomm 24 Jan 1947. Stricken 1 Jul 1963. Trfd to Colombia 15 Mar 1979.
Later history: renamed *Sebastian de Belalcazar* (RM 73). Sunk as artificial reef, 2 Sep 2004.

ATF 83 *Chickasaw* Trfd to Taiwan 5 Jan 1966.
Later history: renamed *Ta Tung* (548). R1999.
2★Korea K-9 K-10.

ATF 84 *Cree* Damaged by bomb in error while towing target off San Diego, 18 Jan 1978. Decomm and stricken 21 Apr 1978. Sunk as target 27 Aug 1978.
3★Korea K-1 K-2 K-3; ★Vietnam Feb 1965.

ATF 85 *Lipan* Decomm 31 Jul 1973, to MSC. Collided with m/v *Atlantic Prestige* in Juan de Fuca Strait, 5 Aug 1974. Trfd to USCG 30 Sep 1980.
Later history: USCGC *Lipan* (WMEC 85). Returned 9 Jun 1988. Stricken 23 Jan 1989. Sunk as target 22 Jan 1990.

4★Korea K-1 K-2 K-3 K-10; 3★Vietnam Mar–May 1965, Oct–Nov 1966, Jan–Feb 1967, Dec 1967–Mar 1968.

ATF 86 *Mataco* Decomm and stricken 1 Oct 1977. Sold 1 Apr 1979. Sank at moorings about 1992.
4★Korea K-1 K-2 K-3 K-8; 7★Vietnam Apr–Jul 1967, May–Jun, Aug 1968, Oct 1969, Jan–Feb 1970, Dec 1971; ◆Taiwan Straits Aug–Sep 1958.

ATF 87 *Moreno* Decomm 13 Aug 1946. Stricken 1 Sep 1961. Sunk as target Oct 1988.

ATF 88 *Narragansett* Decomm 21 Dec 1946. Stricken 1 Sep 1961. Trfd to Taiwan 30 Oct 1990.
Later history: renamed *Ta Feng* (555). SE2001.

ATF 90 *Pinto* Decomm 11 Jul 1946. Trfd to Peru 31 Dec 1960.
Later history: renamed *Guardian Rios* (ARA 123). SE2001.

ATF 91 *Seneca* Went aground in Hampton Roads, 11 Jan 1956. Decomm Jul 1971. Stricken 30 Oct 1985. NDRF. Sunk as target 21 Jul 2003.
◆Cuba Jan–Feb, Aug–Oct, Feb–Apr, Jul–Aug 1962, Cuba Missile Crisis Nov–Dec 1962.

ATF 92 *Tawasa* Decomm 1 Apr 1975. Stricken 15 Apr 1975. BU 1976.
2★Korea K-8 K-9; 7★Vietnam Jun–Jul 1964, Apr–Jul 1968, Apr–Aug 1969, May–Aug 1970, Feb–Mar 1972.

ATF 93 *Tekesta* Out of comm 14 Apr 1950–24 Jan 1958. IS 1958–60. Trfd to Chile 15 May 1960.
Later history: renamed *Yelcho* (AGS 64). SE1993.

ATF 94 *Yuma* Decomm 11 Nov 1955. Trfd to Pakistan 25 Mar 1959.
Later history: renamed *Madadgar* (A 42). SE1993.
2★Korea K-6 K-7.

ATF 96 *Abnaki* Collided with Soviet AGI *Gidrofon* in South China Sea, 17 Dec 1967. Decomm and stricken, 30 Sep 1978 and trfd to Mexico.
Later history: renamed *Yaqui* (A 18), renamed *Ehactl* (A 53), 1993. SE2001.
3★Korea K-5 K-6 K-7; 10★Vietnam Mar–May 1965, May–Oct 1966, Sep 1967–Jan 1968, May–Aug 1971, Oct–Dec 1972; ◆Evac of Vietnam 29–30 Apr 1975.

ATF 97 *Alsea* Decomm 15 Apr 1955. Stricken 1 Sep 1962.
Later history: merchant *Ikosiena*, 1976. BU 1996.

ATF 98 *Arikara* Decomm 1 Jul 1971 and trfd to Chile.
Later history: renamed *Sergente Aldea*.(63). SE1993.
5★Korea K-1 K-2 K-3 K-7 K-8; 4★Vietnam Aug–Dec 1966, Aug–Dec 1969, Dec 1970.

ATF 100 *Chowanoc* Decomm and stricken 1 Oct 1977, and trfd to Ecuador.
Later history: renamed *Chimborazo* (R 710/RA 70). SE2001.
1★Korea 10; 7★Vietnam Apr, Jul 1966, Oct 1968–Jan 1969, Sep 1969–Jan 1970, Apr–May 1971, Jan–Mar 1973; ◆Evac of Vietnam 29–30 Apr 1975, Mayaguez Op 15 May 1975.

ATF 101 *Cocopa* Decomm and stricken, 30 Sep 1978, and trfd to Mexico.
Later history: renamed *Seri* (A 19), renamed *Tonatiuh* (A 54), 1993.
1★Korea K-10; 4★Vietnam Jul 1962, Dec 1963, Aug–Oct 1965, Dec 1966–Mar 1967, Jul–Aug 1969, Jul–Oct 1972.
◆OpCastle 1954, Taiwan Straits Sep–Nov 1958.

ATF 102 *Hidatsa* Decomm 5 May 1948. Stricken 1 Jul 1963. Trfd to Colombia 15 Mar 1979.
Later history: renamed *Rodrigo de Bastedas* (RM 74). SE2001.

ATF 103 *Hitchiti* Out of comm 30 Apr 1948–3 Jan 1951. Decomm 30 Sep 1978 and stricken, trfd to Mexico.
Later history: renamed *Cora* (A 20), renamed *Chac* (A 55), 1993. SE2001
3★Korea K-5 K-6 K-7; 3★Vietnam Aug 1964, Dec 1965, Feb–Mar 1966, Jun–Aug 1967; ◆Taiwan Straits Nov–Dec 1958, Quemoy-Matsu Apr 1960, Apr 1963.

ATF 104 *Jicarilla* Decomm 14 Jun 1950. Stricken 1 Jul 1963. Trfd to Colombia 15 Mar 1979.
Later history: renamed *Bahia Solano* (RM 76). R1987.

ATF 105 *Moctobi* Out of comm 30 Jun 1948–8 Nov 1950. Decomm 30 Sep 1985. Stricken 28 Jan 1992. Trfd to NE Wisconsin RR Trans. Comm. 29 Dec 1997.
2★Korea K-5 K-6; 2★Vietnam Feb–May 1965, Jul–Nov 1967, Aug–Nov 1970, Mar 1973; ◆Quemoy-Matsu Nov 1959, Jul 1960, Sep 1962.

ATF 106 *Molala* Sank f/v in collision off Kaohsiung, Taiwan, 8 May 1971. Trfd to Mexico 1 Aug 1978.
Later history: renamed *Otomi* (A 17), renamed *Kukulkan* (A 52), 1993. SE2001.
3★Korea K-8 K-9 K-10; 4★Vietnam Aug–Sep 1964, Nov 1965–Jan 1966, Mar–Apr 1967, Apr–Aug 1972; ◆OpCastle 1954.

ATF 107 *Munsee* Stricken 3 Nov 1969.
Later history: Merchant *Oceanic*, renamed *Island* 1973. RR1978.
4★Vietnam Jun–Sep 1965, Dec 1967–Feb, Apr 1968.

ATF 108 *Pakana* Decomm 30 Apr 1948. Stricken 1 Jul 1963.
Later history: Bureau of Mines *Virginia City*. Sunk by gunfire, 27 May 1975.

ATF 109 *Potawatomi* Decomm 28 Apr 1948. Stricken 15 Aug 1965. Trfd to Chile 1 Sep 1962.
Later history: renamed *Janequeo* (AGS 65). Foundered in storm at Valdivia, 15 Aug 1965.

ATF 110 *Quapaw* Out of comm 30 Apr 1948–5 Dec 1950. Decomm 30 Aug 1985. Stricken 28 Jan 1992. Trfd to NE Wisconsin RR Trans. Comm. 29 Dec 1997.
2★Korea K-8 K-9; 7★Vietnam Jun–Jul, Sep 1966, Feb–Apr 1968, Mar–Apr, Jun–Jul 1969, Nov 1972; ◆Korea Jul 1971, Evac of Vietnam 29–30 Apr 1975.

ATF 111 *Sarsi* Sunk by mine off Hungnam, Korea, 27 Aug 1952 (4 killed).
2★Korea K-7 K-8.

ATF 112 *Serrano* Out of comm 31 May 1950–30 Jun 1960. Rec **AGS 24**, 15 Jun 1960. Decomm and stricken 2 Jan 1970. Sold 2 Nov 1971, BU 1972.
(as AGS) 4★Vietnam Dec 1965–May 1966, Jan–Aug 1967, Jun–Sep 1968; ◆Quemoy-Matsu May 1962, May 1963.

ATF 113 *Takelma* Decomm 30 Sep 1983. Stricken 28 Jan 1992. Trfd to Argentina 30 Sep 1993.
Later history: renamed *Suboficial Castillo* (A 11). SE2001.
2★Korea K-8 K-9; 2★Vietnam.

ATF 114 *Tawakoni* Decomm, trfd to Taiwan 1 Jun 1978.
Later history: renamed *Ta Mo* (553). SE2001.
3★Korea K-2 K-4 K-5; 4★Vietnam May 1964, Nov 1968–Feb 1969, Mar 1970; ◆OpCastle 1954, Taiwan Straits Sep–Oct 1958, Quemoy-Matsu Dec 1960, Jan 1963.

ATF 115 *Tenino* Decomm 17 May 1947. Stricken 1 Sep 1962. Reacq for experimental purposes 18 Aug 1986.

ATF 116 *Tolowa* Decomm 27 Jan 1947. Trfd to Venezuela Feb 1962.
Later history: renamed *Felipe Larrazabal* (R 11). Lost by grounding, Aug 1970.

ATF 118 *Wenatchee* Decomm 19 May 1947. Stricken 1 Sep 1962. Trfd to Taiwan 30 Oct 1990.
Later history: renamed *Ta Fang* (555).

ATF 148 *Achomawi* Decomm 10 Jun 1947. Stricken 1 Sep 1962. Sold 22 Apr 1986. Trfd to Taiwan
Later history: renamed *Ta Tu* (554). SE2001

ATF 149 *Atakapa* Out of comm 8 Nov 1946–9 Aug 1951. Decomm 1 Jul 1974, to MSC (T-ATF 149). OS 16 Aug 1981. Stricken 21 Feb 1992, NDRF. Sunk as target 25 Aug 2000.
◆Lebanon Aug 1958, Cuba Oct–Nov 1961, Mar–Aug 1962.

ATF 150 *Avoyel* Decomm 11 Jan 1947. to USCG 9 Jul 1956.
Later history: USCGC *Avoyel* (WATF 150). Decomm 30 Sep 1969 and sold.

ATF 151 *Chawasha* Decomm 30 Sep 1946. Stricken 1 Sep 1963.

ATF 152 *Cahuilla* Decomm 27 Jun 1947. Trfd to Argentina 9 Jul 1961.
Later history: renamed *Comandante General Irigoyen* (A 1). SE2001.

ATF 153 *Chilula* Decomm 8 Feb 1947. To USCG 9 Jul 1956.
Later history: USCGC *Chilula* (WATF 153).

ATF 154 *Chimariko* Decomm 31 Oct 1946. Stricken 1 Sep 1962. Sunk as target 27 Aug 1978.

ATF 155 *Cusabo* Decomm 3 Dec 1946. Trfd to Ecuador 2 Nov 1960.
Later history: renamed *Los Rios* (R 711/R101/R51/RA 71), renamed *Cayambe* 1966. SE2001.

ATF 156 *Luiseno* Stricken 1 Jul 1975 and trfd to Argentina.
Later history: renamed *Francisco de Gurruchaga* (A 3). SE2001.
◆Cuba Nov–Dec 1961, Cuba Missile Crisis Nov–Dec 1962.

ATF 157 *Nipmuc* Decomm 1 Sep 1978, Trfd to Venezuela.
Later history: renamed *Antonio Picardi* (R22). Lost by grounding, 12 Apr 1982.
◆Cuba Jan–Mar, Jun–Jul 1962, Dominican Rep Aug–Sep 1965.

ATF 158 *Mosopelea* Decomm 2 Jul 1973, to MSC. OS 30 Sep 1981. Stricken 21 Feb 1992. Sunk as target 27 Oct 1999.
◆Cuba Oct–Nov 1961, Jun–Jul 1962, Cuba Missile Crisis Oct–Nov 1962.

ATF 159 *Paiute* Out of comm 23 Aug 1985–30 Sep 1988. Decomm 7 Aug 1992. Stricken 14 Feb 1995.
◆Cuba Jul–Sep 1961, Aug–Sep 1962, Cuba Missile Crisis Oct–Nov 1962, Dominican Rep Jul–Aug 1965.

ATF 160 *Papago* Out of comm 28 Jun 1985–30 Sep 1988. Decomm 28 Jul 1992. Stricken 14 Feb 1995.
◆Cuba Jan–Feb, Oct–Dec 1961, Cuba Missile Crisis Oct–Nov 1962, Dominican Rep May 1965.

ATF 161 *Salinan* Trfd to Venezuela 1 Sep 1978.
Later history: renamed *Contralmirante Miguel Rodriguez* (R23/RA33). R2005.
◆Cuba Missile Crisis Oct–Dec 1962.

ATF 162 *Shakori* Stricken 15 Mar 1980. Trfd to Taiwan 29 Aug 1980.
Later history: renamed *Ta Tai* (563). SE2001.
1★Vietnam Jan–Feb 1966; ◆Cuba Jan–Mar 1961, Feb–Mar, Aug–Sep 1962, Cuba Missile Crisis Oct–Nov 1962, Dominican Rep May 1965.

ATF 163 *Utina* Decomm 3 Sep 1971 and trfd to Venezuela.
Later history: renamed *Felipe de Larrazabal* (R21). R1990.
◆Cuba Mar–Jul 1961, Apr–May 1962, Cuba Missile Crisis Nov–Dec 1962.

AUXILIARY TUGS (named 16 Jul 1948)

ATA 121 *Sotoyomo* Out of comm 9 Apr 1946–6 Jun 1951. Decomm 1 Jul 1961. Stricken 1 Sep 1961. Trfd to Mexico Jun 1968.
★Korea 1952–3

ATA 123 *Iuka* Decomm 26 Nov 1947. Stricken 1 Sep 1962. Sold 13 Apr 1976.
Later history: merchant *Deka Exi*. BU 1996.

Figure 12.2: *USS Accokeek* (ATA 181), auxiliary tug.

ATA 174 *Wateree* Decomm 16 Jan 1947. IS 13 Aug 1953, MSTS. OS 15 Mar 1955. Trfd to Peru 1 Nov 1961.
Later history: renamed *Unanue* (AMB 160). SE2001.

ATA 175 *Sonoma* Decomm 8 Nov 1946. Stricken 1 Sep 1962. Sold 13 Apr 1976.
Later history: merchant *Deka Epta*. BU 1989.

ATA 176 *Tonkawa* Decomm 30 Jun 1947, civilian crew. OS 8 May 1956. Stricken 1 Aug 1961; sold 5 Apr 1962.
Later history: Taiwan *Ta Sueh* (357). SE1987.

ATA 178 *Tunica* Decomm 23 Dec 1947. Stricken 1 Sep 1962. Reacq as training hulk 27 Aug 1986. Sunk as target 29 Jan 1999.

ATA 179 *Allegheny* Out of comm 10 Oct 1947–25 Jul 1949. Converted to research vessel 1952, armament and towing gear removed, hydrographic instruments added. Decomm and stricken 14 Dec 1968.
Later history: Merchant *Allegheny*, renamed *Tug Malcolm* 1980, *Matthew Beyel* 1999. SE2003.

ATA 180 Stricken 30 Mar 1948.
Later history: Merchant *Horizon*.

ATA 181 *Accokeek* Decomm 29 Jun 1972. Reacq as training hulk, Panama City, Fla., 12 May 1986. Decomm 20 Feb 1987. Stricken 31 Mar 1986. Sunk as artificial reef, date U.

ATA 182 *Unadilla* Out of comm 26 Nov 1946–3 May 1951. Decomm 22 Jul 1955. Stricken 1 Sep 1961. 13 Apr 1976 sold.
Later history: merchant *Deka Okto*. BU 1996.
2★Korea K-7 K-8.

ATA 183 *Nottoway* Decomm 22 Oct 1946. Stricken 1 Sep 1962.

ATA 184 *Kalmia* Out of comm 24 Jun 1946–5 May 1952. Trfd to Colombia 1 Jul 1971.
Later history: renamed *Bahia Utria*.

ATA 185 *Koka* Stricken 1 Sep 1971; Trfd to U.S. Samoa 3 Dec 1973.
Later history: Merchant *Talitiga*.

ATA 186 *Cahokia* Trfd to Taiwan 14 Apr 1972.
Later history: renamed *Ta Teng* (367/550). SE1987.

ATA 187 *Salish* Decomm 10 Feb 1972 and trfd to Argentina.
Later history: renamed *Alferez Sobral* (A 9).

ATA 188 *Penobscot* Stricken 28 Feb 1975.
Later history: Merchant *American Patriot*. SE1998.

ATA 189 *Reindeer* Decomm 29 Aug 1947. Stricken 1 Sep 1962. Sold 15 Nov 1974.
Later history: Merchant *Captain D.*, renamed *Captain Craig*. SE1980.

ATA 190 *Samoset* Decomm 12 Sep 1969. Trfd to Haiti 9 Aug 1971.
Later history: renamed *Henri Christophe* (MH 20). SE1993.

ATA 192 *Tillamook* . Decomm 1 Jul 1971. Trfd to Korea 9 Aug 1971.
Later history: renamed *C&GS Tan Yung*.
9★Vietnam Sep–Oct 1964, Mar–Jun, Aug–Sep, Dec 1965, Apr, Aug 1966, May–Oct 1968, Feb, Jul 1969, Nov 1970.

ATA 193 *Stallion* Out of comm 19 Sep 1946–19 Jul 1949. Decomm Oct 1969. Trfd to Dominican Republic 30 Oct 1980.
Later history: renamed *Enriquillo* (RM 22). SE2001.

ATA 194 *Bagaduce* to USCG 20 Apr 1959.
Later history: USCGC *Modoc* (WAT 194) Decomm 31 May 1979. Merchant *Modoc Pearl*.

ATA 195 *Tatnuck* Decomm 1 Jul 1971. Stricken 1 Oct 1977.
Later history: merchant *Marine Constructor* 1981, renamed *Ocean Warrior* 1993, *Tatnuck* 1999. SE2003.

ATA 196 *Mahopac* Trfd to Taiwan 1 Jul 1971.
Later history: renamed *Ta Peng* (395). SE1987.
10★Vietnam Jun–Nov 1965, Oct–Dec 1966, Jan, Apr–Jun, Sep–Oct 1967, Apr, Jul 1968, Jan, Apr–May, Sep–Oct 1969, Mar–Apr, Sep 1970.

ATA 197 *Sunnadin* Decomm 20 Nov 1969 and Stricken Sold Feb 1971.
Later history: Merchant *Kahuna*. SE1998.
3★Vietnam Nov–Dec 1965, Dec 1966–Jan, Mar 1967.

ATA 198 *Keosanqua* Decomm 25 May 1956. Stricken 1 May 1961. Trfd to Korea 2 Feb 1962.

232 The Navy of the Nuclear Age, 1947–2007

Later history: renamed *Yong Mun* (2/ATA 31). R1996.
★Korea 1951, 1952, 1953.

ATA 199 *Undaunted* Decomm 25 Aug 1947. Stricken 1 Mar 1962.
Later history: Bur.of Fisheries *Undaunted*. To U.S. Merchant Maine Academy, renamed *Kings Pointer*. Sold 1998, merchant *Undaunted*. SE2003.

ATA 201 *Challenge* Stricken 1 Sep 1962.

ATA 202 *Wampanoag* Decomm 27 Feb 1947. To USCG 25 Feb 1959.
Later history: USCGC *Comanche* (WAT 202).

ATA 203 *Navigator* Decomm 20 Oct 1946. Stricken 1 Sep 1962. Reacq as training hulk 27 Aug 1986. Sunk as target 10 Feb 2003.

ATA 204 *Wandank* Out of comm 26 Nov 1947–3 May 1952. To Dept of Interior 1 Jul 1971–22 May 1973. Stricken 1 Aug 1973 and rtnd to Trust Territories.
Later history: Merchant *Wandank*.
3★Vietnam Jan 1968, Apr–May 1969.

ATA 205 *Sciota* Decomm Jan 1947. Stricken 1 Sep 1962.

ATA 206 *Pinola* Out of comm 4 Oct 1946–10 Jan 1949. Decomm 6 Apr 1956. Stricken 1 May 1961. Trfd to Korea 1 Feb 1962.
Later history: renamed *Do Bong* (3/ATA 32). R1996.

ATA 207 *Geronimo* Decomm 19 Sep 1947. Stricken 1 Mar 1962. Loaned to Dept of Interior, 20 Sep 1962.
Later history: F&WS *Geronimo*. Trfd to Taiwan 18 Feb 1969, renamed *Chiu Lien* (AGS 563). SE1987.

ATA 208 *Sagamore* Decomm 1 Feb 1972 and trfd. to Dominican Rep 1972.
Later history: renamed *Caonabo* (RM 18). Returned 5 Jun 1992.

ATA 209 *Umpqua* Decomm 1 Jul 1971. Trfd to Colombia 1971.
Later history: renamed *Bahia Honda*. Lost by grounding, 16 Feb 1975.

ATA 210 *Catawba* Decomm. Trfd to Argentina 10 Feb 1972.
Later history: renamed *Comodoro Somellera* (A 10). Sunk in collision with tug *Suboficial Castillo* at Ushuaia, Aug 1998.
◆Iran/Indian Ocean Jun–Aug 1981, Gulf War Sep 1991, Liberia Apr–May 1993, Indian Ocean Feb–Apr 1996, Jan–Mar, Jul 1997–Jan–Mar, Jul–Sep 1998.

ATA 211 *Navajo* Decomm 10 Apr 1962. Stricken 1 May 1962. Sold 1963.
Later history: merchant *Navajo*, renamed *A.G. Navajo* 1996. SE2003.

ATA 212 *Algorma* Decomm 20 Dec 1946. Stricken 1 Sep 1962. Sold 13 Apr 1976.
Later history: merchant *Deka Ennea*, 1976, renamed *Farreda S.* 1988.

ATA 213 *Kewaydin* Decomm 30 Jun 1970. Reacq as diving and salvage training hulk, 12 May 1986. Sunk as target 3 Jun 2001.

Armament: 174: 2–20mm

No.	Former	Acquired	Fate
ATA 239	LT-532	MSTS 1 Mar 1950	Returned 1955.
ATA 240	LT-455	MSTS 1 Jul 1950	Stricken 4 Aug 1971
ATA 241	LT-60	MSTS 1 Nov 1950	Stricken 1 Sep 1961.
ATA 242	LT-132	MSTS 1 Nov 1950	Stricken 1 Sep 1961.
ATA 243	LT-646	MSTS 1 Nov 1950	Stricken 1 Sep 1961.
ATA 244	LT-156	MSTS 1 Nov 1950	Stricken 1959.

Later history: Merchant *E.A. Judd* 1959, renamed *Tyonek* 1966. Wrecked off Kodiak Island, Alaska, 1 Apr 1969.

| ATA 245 *Tuscarora* | YTB 341 | Nov 1958 | Stricken 1 Sep 1961. |

Note: ATA 239–244 acquired from U.S. Army.

No.	Name	Builder	Keel Laid	Launched	In service
T-ATF 166	*Powhatan*	Marinette	6 Jun 1978	24 Jun 1979	15 Jun 1979
T-ATF 167	*Narragansett*	Marinette	28 Nov 1978	12 May 1979	31 Oct 1979
T-ATF 168	*Catawba*	Marinette	14 Dec 1977	22 Sep 1979	23 May 1980
T-ATF 169	*Navajo*	Marinette	14 Dec 1977	20 Dec 1979	13 Jun 1980
T-ATF 170	*Mohawk*	Marinette	22 Mar 1979	5 Apr 1980	16 Oct 1980
T-ATF 171	*Sioux*	Marinette	22 Mar 1979	30 Oct 1980	12 May 1981
T-ATF 172	*Apache*	Marinette	22 Mar 1979	22 Mar 1981	30 Jul 1981

Displacement	2,000 tons; 2,260 f/l
Dimensions	240'6" (oa); 225'11" (wl) × 42' × 15'
Machinery	2 screws; diesel-electric; 4,500 BHP; 15 knots
Endurance	10,000/13
Complement	21

Notes: MSC. Not armed. Based on a commercial design, no salvage or diving equipment. Two side by side funnels.

Service Records:

ATF 166 *Powhatan* OS 10 Feb 1999 and leased to a commercial salvage firm. Stricken 5 Jun 2002. Sold 26 Feb 2008.
Later history: trfd to Naval Air Systems Command.
◆Indian Ocean Dec 1995–Feb 1996.

ATF 167 *Narragansett* OS 30 Sep 1999 and leased to a commercial salvage firm. Stricken 5 Jun 2002.
◆Iran/Indian Ocean Oct–Nov 1980, Jan–Feb, Apr–May 1981, Liberia Apr 1994.

ATF 168 *Catawba*
◆Iraq War 2003.

ATF 169 *Navajo*

ATF 170 *Mohawk* OS 16 Aug 2005.

ATF 171 *Sioux*
◆Gulf War May–Nov 1991.

ATF 172 *Apache*
◆Liberia Sep 1993–Feb 1994, Haiti Sep 1994, Indian Ocean Jan–Feb 1996.

SALVAGE AND RESCUE SHIPS

No.	Name	Builder	Keel Laid	Launched	Comm.
ATS 1	*Edenton*	Brooke Marine	28 Mar 1967	15 May 1968	23 Jan 1971
ATS 2	*Beaufort*	Brooke Marine	19 Feb 1968	20 Dec 1968	22 Jan 1972
ATS 3	*Brunswick*	Brooke Marine	27 May 1968	14 Oct 1969	19 ec 1972

Figure 12.3: *USS Edenton* (ATS 1), June 1973. A salvage tug later transferred to the Coast Guard.

Displacement	2,560 tons; 3,946 f/l
Dimensions	282′8″ (oa) × 50′ × 15′
Machinery	2 screws; diesels; 6,000 BHP; 16 knots
Complement	115
Armament	2–20 mm; 2 twin 20 mm (ATS 1)

Notes: 2 more authorized but canceled 1973. Altogether 17 were planned. Built in Great Britain.

Service Records:

ATS 1 *Edenton* Decomm 29 Mar 1996. To USCG, 18 Nov 1997. Stricken 29 Dec 1997.
Later history: USCGC *Alex Haley*, WMEC 42, 1 Jul 1999.
◆Lebanon Nov 1982, Libya Jan–Feb Apr 1986.

ATS 2 *Beaufort* Decomm 8 Mar 1996. Stricken 12 Dec 1996. Trfd to Korea, 29 Aug 1996.
Later history: renamed *Pyongtaek* (ARS 27). SE2001.
◆Gulf War Jan–May 1991.

ATS 3 *Brunswick* Decomm 8 Mar 1996. Stricken 12 Dec 1996. Trfd to Korea, 29 Aug 1996.
Later history: renamed *Kwangyang* (ARS 28). SE2001.

13
SEALIFT SHIPS

In 1949 the Military Sea Transportation Service (MSTS) was organized by the Navy to operate cargo ships, tankers, and transports. In 1950, MSTS took over operation of the ships operated by the Army. All these were civilian manned and carried the prefix USNS (U.S. Naval Ship) instead of USS; they were not commissioned naval vessels.

Other types of specialized vessels were also operated under the MSTS banner, such as surveying ships, and various types of research vessels.

In 1970, MSTS was renamed the Military Sealift Command (MSC), with the same functions. The Naval Fleet Auxiliary Force (NFAF) was created in 1972 with the transfer of the oiler *Taluga* to MSC, after a series of tests showed civilian crews could operate fleet support ships more efficiently than Navy sailors. Each year additional ships, including support vessels, are moved into the NFAF resulting in cost savings.

The Strategic Sealift Forces are composed of 1) prepositioning ships, 2) sealift ships, 3) the Ready Reserve Force, and 4) specialized ships. Sealift ships are vehicle cargo ships and similar. The Ready Reserve Force (RRF), started in 1976, is specifically structured to transport Army and Marine Corps unit equipment and initial resupply for forces deploying anywhere in the world during the critical period before adequate numbers of commercially available ships can be marshaled. The specialized ships include hospital ships, and aviation logistics ships.

Ships are designated MV for motor vessel and SS for steam ship. Ships designated USNS are government-owned ships operated by mariners employed by companies under contract to MSC. The four-digit numbers are for database and statistical use and have no operational significance. Ships with names of individuals are usually known by the last name only.

PREPOSITIONING SHIPS

A) Maritime Prepositioning Ships

The prepositioning ships are long-term charter Ro/Ro ships, chartered-barge carriers, partial containers, semisubmersible, freighters, tankers, and transport oilers stationed at distant ports to provide equipment and supplies for ground forces near to where they might be needed.

Maritime Prepositioning Ships are loaded with U.S. Marine Corps equipment and operate within a short sailing time of potential contingency sites. One squadron of MPF ships can provide all the equipment and supplies to support a U.S. Marine Expeditionary Brigade of about 15,000 personnel for 30 days. The ships are capable of off-loading at piers or offshore with special lighterage equipment. Each ship has roll-on/roll-off capability and a flight deck for helicopter operations.

In Nov 2007 these were:

MV *PFC James Anderson Jr.*	T-AK 3002	USNS *1st LT Jack Lummus*	T-AK 3011
MV *PFC William B. Baugh*	T-AK 3001	USNS *1st LT Harry L. Martin*	T-AK 3015
USNS *2nd LT John P. Bobo*	T-AK 3008	SS *PFC Eugene A. Obregon*	T-AK 3006
MV *1st LT Alex Bonnyman*	T-AK 3003	MV *PVT Franklin J. Phillips*	T-AK 3004
MV *SGT William R. Button*	T-AK 3012	SS *MAJ Stephen W. Pless*	T-AK 3007
MV *CPL Louis J. Hauge Jr.*	T-AK 3000	USNS *GYSGT Fred W. Stockham*	T-AK 3017
SS *SGT Matej Kocak*	T-AK 3005	USNS *LCPL Roy M. Wheat*	T-AK 3016
USNS *1st LT Baldomero Lopez*	T-AK 3010	USNS *PFC Dewayne T. Williams*	T-AK 3009

B) Army Prepositioned Stocks-3 (APS-3) Ships

Army Prepositioned Stocks-3 ships provide afloat prepositioning for the equipment, munitions and supplies to support U.S. Army combat units that would deploy to potential contingency sites.

The APS-3 concept of operations calls for at-sea prepositioning of combat equipment for a 2×2 heavy armored brigade (two armored and two mechanized battalions) and the 1×2 6th Brigade Afloat aboard eight (LMSRs) large Ro/Ro ships. In addition, other APS-3 ships carry cargo that supports and sustains the brigade, providing items such as water purification units, food and initial combat support equipment. The mix of cargo carried on APS-3 ships makes it possible for an armored brigade to open a theater of operations for follow-on units. Ships assigned for APS-3 in Nov 2007 were:

MV *SSG Edward A. Carter, Jr.*	T-AK 4544	USNS *Red Cloud*	T-AKR 313
USNS *Charlton*	T-AKR 314	USNS *Sisler*	T-AKR 311
USNS *Dahl*	T-AKR 312	USNS *Soderman*	T-AKR 317
MV *LTC John U. D. Page*	T-AK 4496	USNS *Watkins*	T-AKR 315
USNS *Pomeroy*	T-AKR 316	USNS *Watson*	T-AKR 310

C) Navy, Defense Logistics Agency and Air Force (NDAF) Ships as of Nov 2007:

Ships carrying U.S. Air Force munitions include:

MV *CAPT Steven L. Bennett*	T-AK 4296
MV *MAJ Bernard F Fisher*	T-AK 4396
MV *A1c William H Pitsenbarger*	T-AK 4638

Ship carrying U.S. Navy munitions:

SS *Cape Jacob*	T-AK 5029

Ship carrying Defense Logistics Agency petroleum products:

SS *Petersburg*	T-AOT 9101

Two ships, designated aviation logistics support ships, serve as intermediate maintenance facilities for U.S. Marine Corps fixed and rotary wing aircraft.

SS *Curtiss*	T-AVB 4
SS *Wright*	T-AVB 3

One ship providing transport services to the Third Marine Expeditionary Force.

MV *Westpac Express*	HSV 4676

The ships are organized into three squadrons:

MPS Squadron ONE (Mediterranean) consists of *Bobo, Wheat*.
MPS Squadron TWO (Diego Garcia) is dynamic. At present it stands at *Baugh, Bennett, Button, Carter, Kocak, Lopez, Obregon, Page, Phillips, Pitsenbarger, Williams*.
MPS Squadron THREE (Guam) is still being refined. At present it stands at *Anderson, Bonnyman, Cape Jacob, Charlton, Dahl, Fisher, Hauge, Lummus, Martin, Petersburg, Pless, Watkins, Watson, Wheeler*.

READY RESERVE FORCE

The Ready Reserve Force (RRF) program was initiated in 1976 from the Maritime Administration's National Defense Reserve Fleet (NDRF) to support the rapid worldwide deployment of U.S. military forces. It is a fleet of reserve ships maintained and crewed by the Maritime Administration, which can be activated in four to 20 days. Military Sealift Command inspects the ships and accepts them. When activated, RRF ships come under the operational control of MSC. The RRF includes roll-on/roll-off ships, lighter aboard ships, modular cargo delivery system ships, heavy lift ships, government-owned tankers and crane ships. Because of their configurations, RRF ships are uniquely capable of handling bulky, oversized military equipment.

During the Gulf War, Operations Desert Shield/Desert Storm from August 1990 through June 1992, 79 RRF vessels were activated and operated to meet military sealift requirements.

In 2003, during the wars in Afghanistan and Iraq (Operations Enduring Freedom and Iraqi Freedom), the combined strategic sealift operation provided more than 80 percent of all cargo transportation to the theater of operations. . Forty RRF vessels supported Army and Marine missions during the operations providing up to 20 percent of the total combined surge sealift capacity.

Ten of the MARAD ships were activated to aid in recovery and relief efforts in Hurricanes Katrina and Rita, the first time the ships of MARAD's Ready Reserve Force were activated at the request of the Secretary of Transportation to deal with a domestic emergency, *Cape Kennedy, Cape Knox, Cape Vincent, Diamond State, Equality State,* and *Wright,* and the first time training ships provided by MARAD to state maritime academies were pressed into service to provide food and shelter, *State of Maine, Empire State,* and *Sirius,* and also *Texas Clipper II.* They brought urgently needed supplies, including water; they provided assistance for oil spill cleanup; generated electricity, and provided 269,000 meals and 83,165 berth nights for recovery workers and evacuees.

Note: SS2007 = active Strategic Sealift April 2007.

AUXILIARY CRANE SHIPS

No.	Name	Builder	Keel laid	Launched	Completed
ACS 1	*Keystone State* ex-*President Harrison* (1984)	National Stl	23 Jan 1965	2 Oct 1965	8 May 1984
ACS 2	*Gem State* ex-*President Monroe* (1985)	National Stl	30 May 1964	22 May 1965	31 Oct 1985
ACS 3	*Grand Canyon State* ex-*President Polk* (1985)	National Stl	20 Mar 1964	23 Jan 1965	12 Dec 1986

Displacement	28,660 tons f/l; 17,128 grt
Dimensions	668'6"(oa); 632'11" (wl) × 76'2" × 33
Machinery	1 screw; steam turbines; SHP 19,250; 20 knots
Endurance	13,000/20
Complement	64

Notes: C6-S-MA1QD. Converted 1983–84.

Service Records:

ACS 1	*Keystone State*	RRF 1984–2007 SE.
ACS 2	*Gem State*	RRF 1985–2007 SE.
ACS 3	*Grand Canyon State*	RRF 1986–2007 SE.

Figure 13.1: USNS *Gopher State* (T-ACS 4), auxiliary crane ship, converted in 1987.

No.	Name	Builder	Keel laid	Launched	Completed
ACS 4	*Gopher State* ex-*Export Leader* (1987)	Bath	26 Jul 1971	8 Jul 1972	12 Oct 1987
ACS 5	*Flickertail State* ex-*Lightning* (1987)	Bath	27 Nov 1967	11 May 1968	9 Feb 1988
ACS 6	*Cornhusker State* ex-*Stag Hound* (1987)	Bath	14 Feb 1967	2 Nov 1968	12 Apr 1988
Displacement	13,900 tons; 26,670 tons f/l;				
Dimensions	609'8"(oa); 581'8"(wl) × 91'2" × 30				
Machinery	1 screw; steam turbines; SHP 17,500; 20 knots				
Endurance	9,340/20				
Complement	52				

Notes: C5-S-MA73C. Prefix SS.

Service Records:

ACS 4   *Gopher State*   RRF 1987–2007 SE. ◆Gulf War. Based at Diego Garcia, 1999. Iraq War 2002–3.

ACS 5   *Flickertail State*   RRF 1988–2007 SE. ◆Gulf War. Supported Marines, Haiti, Mar 2004.

ACS 6   *Cornhusker State*   RRF 1988–2007 SE. ◆Gulf War, Iraq War 2002–3.

No.	Name	Builder	Keel laid	Launched	Completed
ACS 7	*Diamond State* ex-*President Truman* (1988), ex-*Japan Mail* (1975)	Todd; S.Pedro	22 Nov 1960	8 Aug 1961	15 Dec 1988
ACS 8	*Equality State* ex-*American Builder* (1989), ex-*Philippine Mail* (1985), ex-*Santa Rosa* (1983) ex-*President Roosevelt* (1983), ex-*Washington Mail* (1975)	Todd; S.Pedro	6 Jul 1960	11 May 1961	24 May 1989
Displacement	15,138 tons lt; 31,498 f/l; 15,518 grt				
Dimensions	667'10" (oa); 632'11" (wl) × 76' × 33'2"				
Machinery	1 screw; 2 steam turbines; SHP 22,000; 20 knots				
Endurance	14,000/20				
Complement					

Notes: C6-S-MA1XB. Lengthened and converted.

Service Records:

ACS 7   *Diamond State*   RRF 1988–2006. Gulf War. LU 28 Jul 2006. NDRF. SE.

ACS 8   *Equality State*   RRF 1989–2006. Gulf War. LU Jul 2006. NDRF. SE.

No.	Name	Builder	Keel laid	Launched	Completed
T-ACS 9	*Green Mountain State* ex-*American Altair* (1990), ex-*Mormacaltair* (1983)	Ingalls	2 Dec 1963	20 Aug 1964	24 Sep 1990
T-ACS 10	*Beaver State* ex-*American Draco* (1997), ex-*Mormacdraco* (1983)	Ingalls	13 Apr 1964	14 Jan 1965	4 May 1997
T-ACS 11	(*American Banker*) ex-*Santa Paula* (1985), ex-*President Eisenhower* (1983), ex-*Philippine Mail* (1975)	Todd; S.Pedro		6 Jan 1962	
T-ACS 12					
Displacement	11,714 tons; 22,900 tons f/l; 14,000 grt				
Dimensions	665'9" (oa); 634'10"(wl) × 75'1" × 31'6"				
Machinery	1 screw; steam turbines; SHP 19,000; 21 knots				
Endurance	17,000/20				
Complement	64				

Notes: C6-S-MA60D. Conversion of ACS 10–12 canceled but ACS 10 was resumed later.

Service Records:

ACS 9   *Green Mountain State*   RRF 1990–2006. LU Jul 2006. NDRF. SE.

ACS 10   *Beaver State*   conversion canc 12 Jan 1990, to Marad 9 Apr 1990. Conversion resumed 1992. RRF 1997–2006. LU Jul 2006 NDRF. SE.

ACS 11   canceled. NDRF. Sold 2004, BU Brownsville.

ACS 12   canceled

HOSPITAL SHIPS (see p. 226)

AH 19	*Mercy*	SS2007
AH 20	*Comfort*	SS2007

AVIATION BASE SHIPS (see p. 169)

AVB 3	*Wright*	ex-*Young America* RRF 1997–2007. SE. SS2007.
AVB 4	*Curtiss*	ex-*Great Republic* RRF 1997–2007. SE. SS2007.

CONTAINER SHIPS

No.	Name	Builder	Launched	In service
T-AK 9205	*Strong Virginian* ex-*St. Magnus* (1992), ex-*Jolly Indaco* (1986), ex-*St. Magnus* (1985)	Bremer Vulkan	16 Dec 1983	Jul 1992
Displacement	29,000 tons f/l; 16,169 grt			
Dimensions	475'8" (oa) × 105' × 29'6"			
Machinery	2 screws; diesel; 16.5 knots			
Complement				

Notes: Prefix MV. Fitted to carry 500-bed portable military hospital. Can carry four Army LCUs.

Service Record: Based at Diego Garcia 30 Sep 1998. Deleted Aug 2002. Returned to owner.

    Later history: Merchant *Virginian*, 2003.

No.	Name	Builder	Launched	In service
T-AKR 9718	Lt. Col. Calvin P. Titus	Blohm & Voss	25 Jan 1975	31 Mar 1994
	ex-*Albert Maersk* (1995), ex-*Adrian Maersk* (1984)			
T-AKR 9966	SP5 Eric G. Gibson	Blohm & Voss	12 Dec 1975	31 Mar 1994
	ex-*Adrian Maersk* (1994), ex-*Axel Maersk* (1984)			
Displacement	50,000 tons f/l; 40,640 grt			
Dimensions	784'10" (oa) × 100'3" × 37'9"			
Machinery	1 screw; diesels; 31.800 hp; 21 knots			
Complement	22			

Notes: Chartered for five years. Replaced by two new vessels with the same names, 1999.
Service Records:
T-AKR 9718 *Titus*   Deleted 2 Apr 1999.
    Later history: Merchant *Maersk Arizona*, 1999. .
T-AKR 9966 *Gibson*   Deleted 9 Jul 1999.
    Later history: Merchant *Maersk Alaska*, 1999, then *Jolly Nero*, 2006.

No.	Name	Builder	Launched	Acquired	In service
T-AK 4638	A1C William H. Pitsenbarger	Atlantique	3 Sep 1983	1 Mar 2001	12 Dec 2001
	ex-*Therese Delmas* (2001)				
Displacement	31,986 tons f/l; 30,750 grt				
Dimensions	622' (oa); 575'6" (wl) × 106' × 37'6"				
Machinery	1 screw; diesel; 13,800 bhp; 17.5 knots				
Complement	23				

Notes: Container ship. Prefix MV. Carries USAF munitions.
Service Record: ◆Iraq War 2003. SS2007.

No.	Name	Builder	Launched	In service
T-AK 4396	Maj. Bernard F. Fisher	Odense	21 Dec 1984	9 Sep 1999
	ex-*Sea Fox* (1999), ex-*American Hawaii* (1987), ex-*Sea Fox*			
T-AK 5091	SP5 Eric G. Gibson	Odense	5 Oct 1984	7 Jul 1999
	ex-*Lykes Adventurer* (1999), ex-*Sea Wolf* (1998), ex-*American North Carolina* (1987), ex-*Sea Wolf* (1984)			
T-AK 5089	LTC. Calvin P. Titus	Odense	11 Jul 1985	1 Jun 1999
	ex-*Sea Lion* (1999), ex-*American Michigan* (1987), ex-*Sea Witch* (1985)			
Displacement	48,000 tons f/l; 34,318 grt			
Dimensions	652' (oa); 611'6" (wl) × 106' × 34'			
Machinery	1 screw; diesel; 23,030 bhp; 19 knots			
Complement	21			

Notes: Prefix MV. RoRo, stern door/ramp. *Gibson* and *Titus* replaced two older vessels with same names, T-AK 4398 & 4397. *Fisher* carries USAF munitions.
Service Records:
T-AK 4396 *Fisher*   ◆Iraq War 2003. SS2007.
T-AK 5091 *Gibson*   LU 1 Aug 2003.
T-AK 5089 *Titus*   LU 1 Jun 2003.

No.	Name	Builder	Launched	Acquired	In service
T-AK 4296	Capt. Stephen L. Bennett	Samsung	Aug 1984	21 May 1997	19 Nov 1997
	ex-*Sea Pride* (1997), ex-*Martha II* (1996), ex-*TNT Express* (1991)				
Displacement	59,207 tons f/l; 29,223 grt				
Dimensions	687' (oa); 656' (wl) × 99'9" × 37'6"				
Machinery	1 screw; diesel; 16,320 hp; 18.35 knots				
Complement	26				

Notes: Container ship, converted at Bender Sbdg, Mobile. Prefix MV. Carries USAF munitions.
Service Record: Iraq War 2003. At Diego Garcia 2006. SS2007.

No.	Name	Builder	Launched	In service
AK	Sagamore	Yardimci, Tuzla	1996	—
	ex-*Mint Arrow* (1997), ex-*Fas Red Sea II* (1996)			
Displacement	3,837 grt			
Dimensions	330'6" (oa); 308'6" (wl) × 52'6" × 20'3"			
Macinery	1 screw; diesel; 13 knots			
Complement	15			

Note: Small self-loading container ship. Operates in Indian Ocean. Prefix MV NDRF. SE.

No.	Name	Builder	Launched	In service
T-AK 4729	American Tern	Neptun	16 Feb 1990	26 Dec 2002
	ex-*Kariba* (2002), ex-*Kota Agung* (2000), ex-*Lykes Flyer* (2000), ex-*Torm Africa* (1997), ex-*Kariba* (1996), ex-*Serenity* (1996)			
Displacement	8,650 tons; 17,350 tons f/l; 52,898 f/l			
Dimensions	521' (oa) × 76' × 33'			
Machinery	1 screw; diesel; bhp; 16 knots			
Complement	21			

Notes: Container ship. Fitted for icebreaking. Provides supplies for McMurdo Sound, Antarctica.

MARITIME PREPOSITIONING SHIPS

No.	Name	Builder	Keel laid	Launched	In Service
T-AKR 310	Watson	National Stl	23 May 1996	26 Jul 1997	23 Jun 1998
T-AKR 311	Sisler	National Stl	15 Apr 1997	28 Feb 1998	1 Dec 1998
T-AKR 312	Dahl	National Stl	12 Nov 1997	2 Oct 1998	13 Jul 1999
T-AKR 313	Red Cloud	National Stl	29 Jun 1998	7 Aug 1999	18 Jan 2000
T-AKR 314	Charlton	National Stl	19 Jun 1999	11 Dec 1999	23 May 2000
T-AKR 315	Watkins	National Stl	24 Aug 1999	28 Jul 2000	12 Apr 2001
T-AKR 316	Pomeroy	National Stl	25 Apr 2000	10 Mar 2001	14 Aug 2001
T-AKR 317	Soderman	National Stl	31 Oct 2000	26 Apr 2002	24 Sep 2002
Displacement	62,968 tons f/l; 29,000 lt				
Dimensions	951'5" (oa); 889'9" (wl) × 105'9" × 34'				
Machinery	2 screws; gas turbines; 64,000 SHP; 24 knots				
Endurance	12,700/24				
Complement	30				

Notes: Ro/Ro Ships. Prefix USNS. Operated by Maersk Line. Similar to *Bob Hope* class with gas turbines. Two side vehicle-cargo ports, stern ramp. Capacity, 394,000 square feet of vehicle cargo space. These ships carry Army munitions.
Service Records:
T-AKR 310 *Watson*   ◆Iraq War 2003. SS2007.
T-AKR 311 *Sisler*   Damaged by fire in drydock at South Boston, Mass., 10 Aug 2007. SS2007.
T-AKR 312 *Dahl*   ◆Iraq War 2003. SS2007.
T-AKR 313 *Red Cloud*   SS2007.
T-AKR 314 *Charlton*   SS2007.
T-AKR 315 *Watkins*   ◆Iraq War 2003. SS2007.
T-AKR 316 *Pomeroy*   SS2007.
T-AKR 317 *Soderman*   SS2007.

Sealift Ships 239

Figure 13.2: *USNS Bob Hope* (T-AKR 300), large, medium-speed roll-on/roll-off ship in Souda Bay, Crete, 20 Jan 2004. Named for the legendary American entertainer who worked to raise morale of U.S. troops for over fifty years.

Figure 13.3: *USNS Benavidez* (T-AKR 306), a Large, Medium-Speed Roll-on/Roll-off Ship, docked in Souda Bay, Crete, 6 Jan 2004.

No.	Name	Builder	Keel Laid	Launched	In Service
T-AKR 300	*Bob Hope*	Avondale	29 May 1995	27 Mar 1997	18 Nov 1998
T-AKR 301	*Fisher*	Avondale	15 Apr 1996	21 Oct 1997	4 Aug 1999
T-AKR 302	*Seay*	Avondale	14 Mar 1997	25 Jun 1998	28 Mar 2000
T-AKR 303	*Mendonca*	Avondale	3 Nov 1997	10 Apr 1999	30 Jan 2001
T-AKR 304	*Pililaau*	Avondale	29 Jun 1998	28 Jan 2000	24 Jul 2001
T-AKR 305	*Brittin*	Avondale	3 May 1999	21 Oct 2000	11 Jul 2002
T-AKR 306	*Benavidez*	Avondale	15 Dec 1999	21 Jul 2001	10 Sep 2003
Displacement	34,408 tons; 62,069 tons f/l				
Dimensions	950′ (oa); 889′9″ (wl) × 105′10″ × 34′8″				
Machinery	2 screws; diesel; 65,160 bhp; 24 knots				
Endurance	13,800/24				
Complement	35				

Notes: Ro/Ro ships. Prefix USNS. Operated by Maersk Line. Two side vehicle ports, stern ramp.

Service Records:

T-AKR 300 *Bob Hope*   SS2007.
     ◆Indian Ocean Feb–May 2000, Iraq War 2003.

Figure 13.4: *M/V SGT William R. Button* (T-AK 3012), 2000. A container Ro-Ro ship, became USNS in 2006.

T-AKR 301 *Fisher*   SS2007.
T-AKR 302 *Seay*   SS2007.
T-AKR 303 *Mendonca*   SS2007.
T-AKR 304 *Pililaau*   SS2007.
     ◆Iraq War 2003.
T-AKR 305 *Brittin*   SS2007.
     ◆Iraq War 2003.
T-AKR 306 *Benavidez*   SS2007.

T-AK 3017 *GySgt Fred W. Stockham*   (see *Soderman* (AKR 199), p. 240)

No.	Name	Builder	Launched	Acquired
T-AK 3008	*2nd Lt. John P. Bobo*	Gen. Dyn; Quincy	19 Jan 1985	14 Feb 1985
T-AK 3009	*PFC Dewayne T. Williams*	Gen. Dyn; Quincy	18 May 1985	6 Jun 1985
T-AK 3010	*1st Lt. Baldomero Lopez*	Gen. Dyn; Quincy	26 Oct 1985	20 Nov 1985
T-AK 3011	*1st Lt. Jack Lummus*	Gen. Dyn; Quincy	22 Feb 1986	6 Mar 1986
T-AK 3012	*Sgt. William R. Button*	Gen. Dyn; Quincy	17 May 1986	22 May 1986
Displacement	19,588 tons; 40,846 tons f/l, 44,543 grt			
Dimensions	673′ (oa); 652′9″ (wl) × 105′6″ × 29′6″			
Machinery	1 screw; 2 diesels; 26,400 bhp; 16.8 knots			
Endurance	12,840/18			
Complement	55			

Notes: Type C8-M-MA134j. Built for the purpose MPS ships. Container Ro/Ro Ships; helicopter platform aft, bow thruster. Prefix MV; purchased 17 Jan 2006 and redesignated. USNS. Operated by Overseas Marine Corp. Capacity: 1,605,000 gallons plus 162,500 square feet of vehicle deck space.

Service Records:

T-AK 3008 *Bobo*   Ran aground in Gulf of Cadiz, 6 Nov 1997. ◆Iraq War 2003. SS2007.
T-AK 3009 *Williams*   SS2007.
T-AK 3010 *Lopez*   SS2007.
T-AK 3011 *Lummus*   ◆Tsunami relief. SS2007.
T-AK 3012 *Button*   SS2007.

No.	Name	Builder	Launched	Acquired	In Service
T-AK 3005	Sgt. Matej Kocak ex-*John B. Waterman* (1983)	Sun	14 Mar 1981	15 Dec 1982	3 Oct 1984
T-AK 3006	PFC Eugene A. Obregon ex-*Thomas Heyward* (1983) (L by Penn SY)	Sun	15 May 1982	1 Feb 1983	15 Jan 1985
T-AK 3007	Maj. Stephen W. Pless ex-*Charles Carroll* (1984)	Gen. Dyn; Quincy	24 Oct 1982	15 May 1983	1 May 1985

Displacement	26,125 tons; 48,754 tons f/l, 25,426 grt
Dimensions	821′ (oa); 770′4″ (wl) × 105′6″ × 32′2″
Machinery	1 screw; 2 steam turbines; 30,000 SHP; 20 knots
Endurance	13,000/20
Complement	60

Notes: Type C7-S-133a. Prefix SS. RoRo ships, converted by National Stl with a 126′ mid-section added during conversion. Helicopter platform aft, bulbous bow, stern door/ramp. Capacity 1,544,000 gallons of bulk fuels and 152,524 square feet for vehicle cargo.

Service Records:

T-AK 3005	Kocak	◆Iraq War 2003. SS2007.
T-AK 3006	Obregon	◆Iraq War 2003. SS2007.
T-AK 3007	Pless	◆Iraq War 2003, Tsunami relief. SS2007.

No.	Name	Builder	Converted by	Launched	Acquired	In service
T-AK 3000	Cpl. Louis J. Hauge Jr. ex-*Estelle Maersk* (1984)	Odense	Sparrows Pt	3 Aug 1979	3 Jan 1983	7 Sep 1984
T-AK 3001	PFC William B. Baugh ex-*Eleo Maersk* (1984)	Odense	Beaumont	8 Dec 1978	17 Jan 1983	29 Oct 1984
T-AK 3002	PFC James Anderson Jr. ex-*Emma Maersk* (1984)	Odense	Sparrows Pt	23 Mar 1979	28 Oct 1983	26 Mar 1985
T-AK 3003	1st Lt. Alexander Bonnyman Jr. ex-*Emilie Maersk* (1984)	Odense	Beaumont	3 Aug 1979	30 Jan 1984	26 Sep 1985
T-AK 3004	Pvt. Harry Fisher ex-*Evelyn Maersk* (1984)	Odense	Sparrows Pt	12 Oct 1979	2 Apr 1984	12 Sep 1985

Displacement	23,365 lt; 46,552 tons f/l; 38,411 grt
Dimensions	755′6″ (oa); 705′ (wl) × 90′6″ × 33′10″
Machinery	1 screw; diesel; 16,800 bhp; 17.5 knots
Endurance	10,800/17.5
Complement	34

Notes: Container Ro/Ro Ships. Chartered, operated by Maersk Line; prefix MV. Converted by Bethlehem to MPS 1985, *Hauge*, *Anderson*, and *Fisher* at Sparrows Pt, and *Baugh* and *Bonnyman* at Beaumont, Texas. A mid-section of 157′6″ added during conversion. Helicopter platform aft, bulbous bow. Capacity: 1,283,000 gallons of bulk fuels and 120,080 square feet of vehicle storage space.

Service Records:

T-AK 3000	Hauge	◆Iraq War 2003. Tsunami relief. SS2007.
T-AK 3001	Baugh	◆Iraq War 2003. SS2007.
T-AK 3002	Anderson	◆Iraq War 2003. Tsunami relief. SS2007.
T-AK 3003	Bonnyman	Renamed *1st Lt. Alex Bonnyman Jr.*, 4 Mar 1986. SS2007. ◆Iraq War 2003, Tsunami relief.
T-AK 3004	Fisher	Renamed *Pvt. Franklin J. Phillips*, 1991. SS2007. ◆Iraq War 2003.

Figure 13.5: SS *GySgt Fred W. Stockham* (T-AK 3017), Marine Corps prepositioning ship.

No.	Name	Builder	Launched	Acquired	In service
T-AKR 295	Shughart ex-*Sgt 1st Randall D. Shughart*, ex-*Laura Maersk* (1996)	Odense	9 Jul 1980	7 May 1996	—
T-AKR 297	Yano ex-*Sgt 1st Rodney J.T. Yano*, ex-*Leise Maersk* (1996)	Odense	19 Sep 1980	8 Feb 1997	—
T-AKR 299	Soderman ex-*PFC William A. Soderman*, ex-*Lica Maersk* (1997)	Odense	20 Mar 1981	11 Nov 1997	1998

Displacement	33,971 tons; 54,298 tons f/l; 43,325 grt (*Stockham*: 54,298 f/l, 32,589 lt)
Dimensions	906′9″ (oa); 850′7″ (wl) × 105′7″ × 34′10″
Machinery	1 screw; diesel; 46,653 bhp; 24 knots
Endurance	12,200/24
Complement	35

Notes: Ro/Ro Ships. Prefix USNS. Operated by Bay Ship Management Co. Converted by National Steel. Intended to carry equipment for an Army armor task force. Four side ramps, stern ramp, helicopter landing pad aft. *Soderman* converted to Marine Corps prepositioning ship and renamed 2001.

T-AKR 295 Shughart ◆Iraq War 2003. SS2007.
T-AKR 297 Yano Collided with frigate *Vandegrift* at San Diego, 25 Feb 1996. ◆Iraq War 2003. SS2007.
T-AKR 299 Soderman o/s for conversion, 2000–01. Renamed *GySgt Fred W. Stockham* & rec **T-AK 3017**, 1 Mar 2001. ◆Iraq War 2003. SS2007.

No.	Name	Builder	Launched	In service
T-AKR 296	Gordon ex-*MSgt Gary I. Gordon*, ex-*Jutlandia* (1993)	Burmeister	22 Sep 1972	23 Aug 1996
T-AKR 298	Gilliland ex-*Cpl Charles I. Gilliland*, ex-*Selandia* (1993)	Burmeister	20 Apr 1972	24 May 1997

Displacement	33,163 tons; 55,422 tons f/l; 54,035 grt
Dimensions	954′ (oa); 894′6″ (wl) × 105′10″ × 35′9″
Machinery	3 screws; diesel; 78,6000 bhp; 24 knots
Endurance	12,000/24
Complement	95

Notes: Ro/Ro Ships. Prefix USNS. Converted by Newport News 1993, lengthened in Korea 1984. Names shortened.

Figure 13.6: *USNS LCPL Roy M. Wheat* (T-AK 3016), in service in 2003.

Service Records:

T-AKR 296 *Gordon* ◆Iraq War 2003. SS2007.
T-AKR 298 *Gilliland* Broke loose during storm while under conversion at Newport News and collided with destroyer *Deyo*, Jun 1996. ◆Iraq War 2003. SS2007.

No.	Name	Builder	Launched	In service
T-AK 3016	*LCpl Roy M. Wheat* ex-*Bazaliya* (1997), ex-*Vladimir Vaslayev* (1996)	Chernomorskiy	1987	7 Nov 2003
Displacement	50,570 tons; f/l; 32,264 grt			
Dimensions	863'4"(oa); 787'2"(wl) × 98'4" × 35'1"			
Machinery	2 screws; 2 gas turbines; 46,000 SHP; 22 knots			
Endurance	40,000/26.5			
Complement	42			

Notes: Ro/Ro Ship. Prefix USNS. Ice strengthened. Converted by Bender Sbdg, Mobile., midbody of 120' added & new turbines installed.

Service Record: SS2007

No.	Name	Builder	Launched	Reacquired
T-AK 323	*Merlin* ex-*American Merlin* (T-AK 9302), ex-*Utrillo* (1992), ex-*CGM Utrillo* (1987)	La Ciotat	1 Oct 1977	Sep 2002
Displacement	26,378 tons; lt, 40,357 f/l; 26,409 grt			
Dimensions	670'(oa) × 87' × 34'6'			
Machinery	1 screw; diesel; 23,400 hp; 16 knots			
Complement	19			

Notes: Container-Ro/Ro ship for carrying USAF munitions. Prefix MV. Bulbous bow. At Diego Garcia to 2001.

Renamed **TSgt. John A. Chapman**, 8 Apr 2005. Deleted 10 Sep 2007.
Later history: Merchant

No.	Name	Builder	Launched	In service
T-AK 3015	*1st Lt Harry L. Martin* ex-*Tarago* (2000), ex-*Nosac Cedar* (1994), ex-*CGM Rabelais* (1993), ex-*Rabelais* (1989), ex-*Liliooet* (1988)	Bremer Vulkan	30 Nov 1978	21 Apr 2000
Displacement	19,586 tons; lt, 51,531 tons; f/l; 39,441 grt			
Dimensions	754' (oa); 688'11" (wl) × 105'9" × 33'8"			
Machinery	1 screw; diesel; 25,700 bhp; 17 knots			
Endurance	16,000/17			
Complement	36			

Notes: Ro/Ro Ship. Prefix USNS. Converted by Atlantic Drydock Co., Jacksonville, Fla. Stern ramp. Carries Air Force ammunition.

Figure 13.7: *USNS 1st Lt Harry L. Martin* (T-AK 3015), carries Air Force ammunition.

Figure 13.8: *M/V SSG Edward A. Carter Jr.* (T-AK 4544), a container ship, carries army munitions.

Service Record: ◆ Iraq War 2003; Tsunami relief. SS2007

No.	Name	Builder	Launched	In service
T-AK 4496	*LTC John U.D. Page* ex-*American Utah* (2000), ex-*Newark Bay* (2000), ex-*Utah* (1988), ex-*Irene D.* (1988), ex-*American Utah* (1987)	Daewoo	Jul 1985	1 Mar 2001
T-AK 4544	*SSG Edward A. Carter, Jr.* ex-*Sealand Oregon* (2001), ex-*OOCL Innovation* (2000), ex-*Nedlloyd Hudson* (1993), ex-*Nebraska* (1988), ex-*Susan C.* (1988), ex-*American Nebraska* (1987)	Daewoo	30 Dec 1984	13 Jun 2001
Displacement	74,500 tons; f/l; 57,075 grt			
Dimensions	949'9"(oa); 915'(wl) × 105'6" × 35'			
Machinery	1 screw; diesel; 28,000 bhp; 18 knots			
Complement	22			

Notes: Container ships. Converted by Norfolk SB & DD Co. Prefix MV. Carry Army munitions, replacing ammunition carriers *Green Valley*, *Green Harbour* and *Jeb Stuart*.

Service Records:

T-AK 4496 *Page*   ◆ Iraq War 2003. SS2007.
T-AK 4544 *Carter*   ◆ Iraq War 2003. SS2007.

No.	Name	Builder	Launched	In service
T-AK W9519	*Baffin Strait* ex-T-AK 9519, ex-*Steamers Future*, ex-*STL Future*, ex-*Mekong Star*, ex-*Eagle Faith*	Wuhu	1997	2005
Displacement	8,299 tons; 4,276 grt			
Dimensions	330′ × 53′ × 21′			
Machinery	1 screw, diesel, 13 knots			
Complement	13			

Notes: Chartered, replaced *Sagamore*.

VEHICLE CARGO SHIPS

No.	Name	Builder	Launched	Acquired	In service
AKR 287	*Algol* ex-*Sea-Land Exchange*	Rotterdam	22 Sep 1972	13 Oct 1981	19 Jun 1984
AKR 288	*Bellatrix* ex-*Sea-Land Trade*	Rheinstal	30 Sep 1972	13 Oct 1981	10 Sep 1984
AKR 289	*Denebola* ex-*Sea-Land Resource*	Rotterdam	10 May 1973	27 Oct 1981	10 Sep 1985
AKR 290	*Pollux* ex-*Sea-Land Market*	Weser	18 May 1975	16 Nov 1981	31 Mar 1986
AKR 291	*Altair* ex-*Sea-Land Finance*	Rheinstal	28 Apr 1973	3 Jan 1982	13 Nov 1985
AKR 292	*Regulus* ex-*Sea-Land Commerce*	Weser	18 Dec 1972	10 Nov 1981	28 Aug 1985
AKR 293	*Capella* ex-*Sea-Land McLean*	Rotterdam	9 Sep 1971	16 Apr 1982	1 Jul 1984
AKR 294	*Antares* ex-*Sea-Land Galloway*	Weser	13 May 1972	16 Apr 1982	12 Jul 1984
Displacement	31,000 tons; 55,425 f/l				
Dimensions	946′2″(oa); 893′(wl) × 105′6″ × 36′8″				
Machinery	2 screws; ST; 2 boilers; 120,000 SHP; 33 knots				
Endurance	12,200/27				
Complement	45				

Notes: High speed merchant ships acquired and converted to Roll-on/Roll-off capability. Prefix USNS, changed to SS, 1 Oct 2007. Helicopter landing deck amidships. AK 289–291 rec AKR, 10 Sep 1982. AK 292–294 rec AKR, 1 Nov 1983. SL7 class. Trfd to RRF, 1 Oct 2008.

Service Record:

AKR 287 *Algol*   ◆Gulf War Oct 1990-Apr 1991, Iraq War 2003. SS2007.

Figure 13.9: *USNS Antares* (T-AKR 294), at Antwerp, January 1986. One of a class of eight converted to Ro-Ro capability in 1982.

AKR 288	*Bellatrix*	◆Gulf War Sep 1990–Mar 1991. SS2007.
AKR 289	*Denebola*	◆Gulf War Oct 1990–Mar 1991. SS2007.
AKR 290	*Pollux*	◆Gulf War Oct 1990–Mar 1991. SS2007.
AKR 291	*Altair*	◆Gulf War Sep 1990–Mar 1991, Iraq War 2003. SS2007.
AKR 292	*Regulus*	◆Gulf War Oct 1990–Mar 1991. SS2007.
AKR 293	*Capella*	◆Gulf War Sep 1990–Apr 1991, Iraq War 2003. SS2007.
AKR 294	*Antares*	Had engine breakdown, Aug 1990, and was towed into a Spanish port. ◆Gulf War. SS2007.

No.	Name	Builder	Launched	Acquired	In service
T-AKR 10	*Cape Island* ex-*USNS Mercury* (1993), ex-*Illinois* (1980)	Bath	21 Dec 1976	22 Nov 1993	Nov 1993
T-AKR 11	*Cape Intrepid* ex-*USNS Jupiter* (1994), ex-*Lipscomb Lykes* (1980), ex-*Arizona* (1979)	Bath	1 Nov 1975		Apr 1986
T-AKR 5062	*Cape Isabel* ex-*Charles Lykes* (1986), ex-*Nevada* (1979)	Bath	15 May 1976		Jun 1986
T-AKR 5076	*Cape Inscription* ex-*Tyson Lykes* (1988), ex-*Maine* (1979)	Bath	24 May 1975	2 Sep 1987	Sep 1987
Displacement	33,765 tons; f/l; 23,382 grt (*Island* 13,155 grt)				
Dimensions	684′9″ (oa); 639′10″ (wl) × 102′ × 32′1″				
Machinery	2 screws; steam turbines; 37,000 SHP; 24 knots				
Endurance	10000/23				
Complement	36				

Notes: Type C7-S-95a. Prefix SS. Ro/Ro vehicle carriers with side ports and stern ramp (10 & 11) (see p. 206); others quarter stern door.

Service Record:

T-AKR 10 *Cape Island* RRF 1993–2007. Iraq War 2002-3. SE SS2007.
T-AKR 11 *Cape Intrepid* RRF 1986–1992 (as *Jupiter*), 1993–2007 SE SS2007. ◆Gulf War (as *Jupiter*), Iraq War 2002-3.
T-AKR 5062 *Cape Isabel* RRF 1987–2007 SE. ◆Gulf War, Iraq War 2002-3. SS2007.
T-AKR 5076 *Cape Inscription* RRF 1987–2007 SE. ◆Gulf War, Iraq War 2002-3. SS2007.

AKR 7 *Comet*   RRF 1986–2005. Gulf War NDRF. SE. (See p. 204).
AKR 9 *Meteor* RRF 1985–2005. Gulf War NDRF. SE. (See p. 205).

No.	Name	Builder	Launched	In service
T-AK 5021	*Maine* ex-*Seatrain Maine* (1977), (forward) ex-*Ohio*, ex-*Mission San Jose* (AO 125) (cargo) ex-*Mercury*, ex-*Mission San Juan* (AO 126) (aft) ex-*Maine*, ex-*Tomahawk* (AO 88)	Marinship	10 Aug 1943	Jun 1979
T-AK 5020	*Washington* ex-*Seatrain Washington* (1977), (forward) ex-*Tomahawk* (AO 88) (cargo) ex-*Mission San Jose* (AO 125) (aft) ex-*Mission San Diego* (AO 121)	Marinship	29 Mar 1944	Feb 1978
Displacement	21,240 & 21,177 tons; f/l; 8,025 grt			
Dimensions	559′7″ (oa); 538′11″ (wl) × 67′11″ × 27′			
Machinery	1 screw; steam turbine; 10,000 SHP; 16.5 knots			
Endurance	12000/16			
Complement	27			

Notes: Originally built as tankers (T2-SE-A2), and converted to carry railway cars. Rebuilt from sections of three different ships.

Service Records:

T-AK 5021 *Maine* RRF 1984–1991. ◆Gulf War 13 Sep 1990. LU 12 Jun 1991, NDRF. SE.
T-AK 5020 *Washington* RRF 1984–1991. ◆Gulf War 29 Aug 1990. LU 12 Jun 1991, NDRF. BU 2001.

No.	Name	Builder	Launched	In service
T-AKR 5077	*Cape Lambert* ex-*Federal Lakes* (1988), ex-*Avon Forest* (1985)	Port Weller	19 Apr 1973	Nov 1987
T-AKR 5078	*Cape Lobos* ex-*Federal Seaway* (1988), ex-*Laurentian Forest* (1986), ex-*Grand Encounter* (1985), ex-*Laurentian Forest* (1980)	Port Weller	23 Apr 1972	14 Mar 1988
Displacement	30,375 tons; f/l, 12,000 tons; lt; 22,286 grt			
Dimensions	681′10″ (oa); 621′6″ (wl) × 75′2″ × 30′2″			
Machinery	2 screws; diesels; 18,000 hp; 19 knots			
Endurance	6000/17			
Complement	27			

Notes: Former newsprint carriers. Prefix MV. RoRo cargo, bulbous bow, side doors and ramps. Ice strengthened.

Service Records:

T-AKR 5077 *Cape Lambert*   RRF 1987–2006. ◆Gulf War, Iraq War 2002–3. LU Jul 2006 NDRF. SE.

T-AKR 5078 *Cape Lobos*   RRF 1988–2006. ◆Gulf War, Iraq War 2002–3. LU Jul 2006 NDRF. SE.

No.	Name	Builder	Launched	Acquired	In service
T-AKR 5069	*Cape Edmont* ex-*Parralla* (1986)	Eriksbergs	20 Aug 1970	10 Apr 1987	Apr 1987
Displacement	32,543 tons; f/l; 12,000 lt; 12,902 grt				
Dimensions	652′11″ (oa); 602′6″ (wl) × 94′ × 30′10″				
Machinery	1 screw; diesels; 25,920 hp; 20.7 knots				
Endurance	20000/17				
Complement	31				

Notes: Prefix: MV. Quarter stern door/ramp; bulbous bow.

Service Record: *Cape Edmont*. RRF 1987–2007 SE. ◆Gulf War 24 Aug 1990, Iraq War 2002–3. SS2007.

No.	Name	Builder	Launched	In service
T-AKR 5067	*Cape Henry* ex-*Barber Priam* (1986)	Mitsubishi	17 Nov 1978	28 Sep 1986
T-AKR 5068	*Cape Horn* ex-*Barber Tonsberg* (1986)	Kaldnes	31 Jan 1979	10 Dec 1986
T-AKR 5066	*Cape Hudson* ex-*Barber Taif* (1986)	Tangen	20 Sep 1978	30 Oct 1986
Displacement	15,000 tons; lt; 51,836 f/l; 37,815 grt			
Dimensions	749′6″ (oa); 693′9″ (wl) × 105′10″ × 35′5″			
Machinery	1 screw; diesel; 17,288 hp; 21 knots			
Endurance	24300/17			
Complement	28/34			

Notes: Prefix MV. Angled stern door, bulbous bow. RoRo cargo. Details vary.

Service Records:

T-AKR 5067 *Cape Henry*   RRF 1987–2007. SE ◆Gulf War, active at Diego Garcia, Iraq War 2002–3. SS2007.

T-AKR 5068 *Cape Horn*   RRF 1987–2007. SE ◆Gulf War, at Diego Garcia. Damaged by engine room fire at sea 800 miles. east of Hawaii, 31 Mar 2002 (2 killed), Rtnd to svc 1 Jul 2002. Iraq War 2002–3. SS2007.

T-AKR 5066 *Cape Hudson*   RRF 1987–2007. SE ◆Gulf War, active at Diego Garcia, Iraq War 2002–3. SS2007.

No.	Name	Builder	Launched	Acquired	In service
T-AKR 5054	*Cape Decision* ex-*Tombarra* (1985)	Eriksbergs	29 Mar 1973	15 Oct 1985	Oct 1985
T-AKR 5055	*Cape Diamond* ex-*Tricolor* (1985)	Dunkerque	18 Mar 1972	15 Oct 1985	Oct 1985
T-AKR 5052	*Cape Douglas* ex-*Lalandia* (1985)	Eriksbergs	27 Sep 1972	15 Nov 1985	Nov 1985
T-AKR 5053	*Cape Domingo* ex-*Tarago* (1985)	Dunkerque	7 Oct 1972	30 Oct 1985	Oct 1985
T-AKR 5051	*Cape Ducato* ex-*Barranduna* (1985)	Eriksbergs	15 Mar 1972	5 Dec 1985	Dec 1985
Displacement	13,220 lt; 35,173 tons; f/l; 24,437 grt				
Dimensions	680′3″ (oa); 633′10″ (wl) × 97′ × 31′6″				
Machinery	1 screw; diesels; 27,000 bhp; 22 knots				
Endurance	19000/18				
Complement	27				

Notes: Prefix MV. RoRo cargo, quarter stern door/ramp; bulbous bow.

Service Records:

T-AKR 5054 *Cape Decision*   RRF 1985–2007 SE. ◆Gulf War, active at Diego Garcia. Iraq War 2002–3. SS2007.

T-AKR 5055 *Cape Diamond*   RRF 1985–2007 SE ◆Gulf War, Iraq War 2002–3. SS2007.

T-AKR 5053 *Cape Domingo*   RRF 1985–2007 SE ◆Gulf War, Iraq War 2002–3. SS2007.

T-AKR 5052 *Cape Douglas*   RRF 1985–2007 SE. ◆Gulf War, active at Diego Garcia. Iraq War 2002–3. SS2007.

T-AKR 5051 *Cape Ducato*   RRF 1987–2007 SE. ◆Gulf War, Iraq War 2002–3. SS2007.

No.	Name	Builder	Launched	In service
T-AKR 9673	*American Condor* ex-*Zenit Express* (1984), ex-*Kuwait Express* (1983)	Kockums	24 Jan 1981	—
T-AK 2044	*American Eagle* ex-*Zenit Eagle* (1986), ex-*Finneagle* (1983)	Kockums	29 Nov 1980	1994
T-AKR 9672	*American Falcon* ex-*Zenit Falcon* (1986), ex-*Finnclipper* (1983)	Kockums	24 Oct 1981	—
Displacement	13,166 lt, (2044); 32.799 tons; f/l; 15,636 grt			
Dimensions	635′3″ (oa); 593′ (wl) × 91′10″ × 29′6″			
Machinery	2 screws; diesel; 21,230 hp; 22 knots			
Endurance	16000/19			
Complement	21			

Notes: Bridge forward, twin funnels aft. RoRo, stern door/ramp.

Service Record:

T-AKR 9673 *American Condor*   Deleted 1993.
  Later history: Merchant *Stena Porter* 1994, *Tor Scandia* 1998, *Eurocargo Europa* 2006.

T-AK 2044 *American Eagle*   Purchased Dec 1992. Renamed *Cape Orlando* 12 Sep 1994. RRF 1994–2007 SE. Iraq War 2002–3. SS2007.

T-AKR 9672 *American Falcon*   Deleted 1993.
  Later history: Merchant *Stena Partner* 1994, *Tor Flandria* 1998, *Eurocargo Africa* 2006.

No.	Name	Builder	Launched	Acquired	In service
T-AKR 1001	*Adm. William M. Callaghan*	Sun	17 Oct 1967	30 Jun 1987	19 Dec 1967
Displacement	13,161 lt; 26,537 tons; f/l; 24,171 grt				
Dimensions	694′3″ (oa) × 92′ × 29′				
Machinery	2 screws; gas turbines; 50,000 SHP' 26 knots				
Endurance	6000/25				
Complement	33				

Notes: Built for the Navy but chartered; purchased 1986. First all-gas-turbine ship built for USN. Bulbous bow, stern door/ramp. Engines replaced 1977. Prefix GTS.

Service Record: *Callaghan* RRF 1987–2007 SE. ◆Gulf War, Iraq War 2002–3. SS2007.

No.	Name	Builder	Launched	In service
T-AKR 9666	*Cape Vincent* ex-*Taabo Italia* (1993), ex-*Merzario Italia* (1991)	Fincantieri	28 Mar 1984	19 Aug 1994
T-AKR 9701	*Cape Victory* ex-*Merzario Britannia* (1993)	Fincantieri	24 Sep 1984	2 Sep 1994
Displacement	28,215 tons; f/l; 22,423 grt			
Dimensions	631'9" (oa); 566'9"(wl) × 87' × 27'9"			
Machinery	1 screw; diesel; 11,850 bhp; 16 knots			
Endurance	21000/16			
Complement	25			

Notes: Roll-on roll-off (Ro-Ro) container ship. Bulbous bow. Prefix MV.

Service Records:

T-AKR 9666 *Cape Vincent* RRF 1994–2007 SE. Iraq War 2002–3. SS2007.
T-AKR 9701 *Cape Victory* RRF 1994–2007 SE. Iraq War 2002–3. SS2007.

No.	Name	Builder	Launched	In service
T-AKR 9961	*Cape Washington* ex-*Hual Transporter* (1993)	Gdynia	1981	5 Apr 1994
T-AKR 9962	*Cape Wrath* ex-*Hual Trader* (1993), ex-*Hoegh Trader* (1982)	Gdynia	1981	30 Sep 1994
Displacement	22,145 lt; 53,500 tons; f/l, 22,820 grt			
Dimensions	697'4" (oa); 642' (wl) × 105'11" × 38'2"			
Machinery	1 screw; diesel; 17,400 hp; 17 knots			
Complement	27			

Notes: Prefix MV.

Service Records:

T-AKR 9961 *Cape Washington* RRF 1994–2007 SE. active at Diego Garcia. Iraq War 2002–3. SS2007.
T-AKR 9962 *Cape Wrath* RRF 1994–2007 SE. Iraq War 2002–3. SS2007.

No.	Name	Builder	Launched	In service
T-AKR 9960	*Cape Race* ex-*Stena America* (1993), ex-*G & C Admiral* (1993), ex-*Seaspeed America* (1987)	Kawasaki	15 Mar 1977	11 Sep 1994
T-AKR 9679	*Cape Ray* ex-*Saudi Makkah* (1993), ex-*Seaspeed Asia* (1981)	Kawasaki	1977	17 Dec 1994
T-AKR 9678	*Cape Rise* ex-*Saudi Riyadh* (1993), ex-*Seaspeed Arabia* (1981)	Kawasaki	29 Oct 1976	15 Nov 1994
Displacement	32,054 tons; 14,825 grt			
Dimensions	647'10" (oa) × 105'10" × 32'10"; 197.5oa 180bp × 32.2			
Machinery	1 screw; diesel; 28,000 bhp, 19.75 knots			
Complement	—			

Notes: Ro-Ro Cargo, bulbous bow. Stern door/ramp, superstructure forward. Prefix MV.

Service Record:

T-AKR 9960 *Cape Race* RRF 1994–2007 SE. 1 Feb 1996, Joint Venture. Iraq War 2002–3. SS2007.
T-AKR 9679 *Cape Ray* RRF 1994–2007 SE. Iraq War 2002–3. SS2007.
T-AKR 9678 *Cape Rise* RRF 1994–2007 SE. 1 Feb 1996, Joint Venture. Iraq War 2002–3. SS2007.

Figure 13.10: *MV Cape Vincent*, Ro-Ro vehicle transport, at anchor in Souda Bay, Crete, 2 Mar 2003.

No.	Name	Builder	Launched	In service
T-AKR 113	*Cape Taylor* ex-*Thekwini* (1993), ex-*ASL Cygnus* (1992), ex-*Cygnus* (1989), ex-*Rabenfels* (1981)	Sasebo	31 Mar 1977	27 Jul 1994
T-AKR 112	*Cape Texas* ex-*USNS Lyra* (1993), ex-*Reichenfels* (1981)	Howaldt	16 Jun 1977	19 Aug 1994
T-AKR 9711	*Cape Trinity* ex-*Santos* (1993), ex-*Canadian Forest* (1991), ex-*Santos* (1990), ex-*Radbod* (1987), ex-*Norefjord* (1982), ex-*Rheinfels* (1981)	Howaldt	Dec 1977	21 Nov 1994
Displacement	9,687 tons; lt; 26,455 f/l; 12,159, 13,098 & 14,174 grt (resp)			
Dimensions	627'10" (oa); 583'10"(wl) × 89'3" × 28'2", (*Cape Texas*, 634'2" (oa)			
Machinery	1 screw; diesels; 18,980 bhp; 20.5 knots			
Complement	49			

Notes: Prefix MV.

Service Records:

T-AKR 113 *Cape Taylor* RRF 1994–2007 SE. Iraq War 2002–3. SS2007.
T-AKR 112 *Cape Texas* RRF 1994–2007 SE. Iraq War 2002–3. SS2007.
T-AKR 9711 *Cape Trinity* RRF 1994–2007 SE. Iraq War 2002–3. SS2007.

No.	Name	Builder	Launched	In service
AK 9670	*Strong Texan* ex-*Dock Express Texas* (1989), ex-*Happy Runner* (1984)	Arnhem	22 Oct 1976	—
Displacement	5,454 tons; f/l; 1,382 grt			
Dimensions	268'4" (oa); 244'1" (wl) × 51'6" × 18'3"			
Machinery	2 screws; diesels; 2,500 bhp; 12 knots			
Complement	27			

Notes: Heavy-lift cargo ship. Ro-Ro, stern door/ramp.
Service Record: *Strong Texan*: Deleted after 2000.
Later history: Merchant *Perge* 2003

No.	Name	Builder	Launched	In service
T-AKR 9301	*American Merlin* ex-*CGM Utrillo* (1992), ex-*Utrillo* (1987)	LaCiotat	Jun 1977	30 Sep 1993
T-AKR 9302	*Buffalo Soldier* ex-*CGM Monet* (1992), ex-*Monet* (1987)	La Ciotat	Jun 1977	30 Sep 1993
Displacement	36,000 tons; f/l; 24,409 grt			
Dimensions	669'7" (oa); 639'11" (wl) × 87'1" × 35'3"			
Machinery	1 screw; diesel; 23,400 bhp; 19 knots			
Complement	—			

Notes: Prefix MV. RoRo, quarter stern/door ramp. *Buffalo Soldier* replaced by *Pitsenbarger*, 2001.

Sealift Ships   245

Service Records:

T-AKR 9301 *American Merlin*   Deleted 30 Sep 1998. Reacq as **Merlin** (T-AK 323) 2003. (see p. 241).

T-AKR 9302 *Buffalo Soldier*   Deleted Jul 2001.
  Later history: merchant *Global Patriot*, 2005.

No.	Name	Builder	Launched	In service
T-AKR 5083	*Cape Kennedy*	Tsurumi	17 Oct 1978	11 Jun 1996
	ex-*Nedlloyd Rosario* (1996), ex-*Rosario* (1988), ex-*Nedlloyd Rosario* (1986)			
T-AKR 5082	*Cape Knox*	Tsurumi	24 Jun 1978	15 Jul 1996
	ex-*Nedlloyd Rouen* (1996), ex-*Rouen* (1988), ex-*Nedlloyd Rouen* (1986)			
Displacement	36,450 tons; f/l; 21,144 grt			
Dimensions	695'8" (oa); × 105'11" × 35'2"			
Machinery	1 screw; diesel; 25,400 bhp; 19 knots			
Complement	—			

Notes: RoRo, stern door/ramp.

T-AKR 5083 *Cape Kennedy*   RRF 1996–2007 SE. Iraq War 2002–3. SS2007.
T-AKR 5082 *Cape Knox*   RRF 1996–2007 SE Iraq War 2002–3. SS2007.

BARGE CARRYING SHIPS

No.	Name	Builder	Launched	In service
T-AK 9651	*American Kestrel*	Avondale	May 1972	1989
	ex-*Lash Pacfico* (1989)			
T-AK 5073	*Cape Farewell*	Avondale	Jan 1973	2 Apr 1987
	ex-*American Mar* (1987), ex-*Delta Mar* (1986)			
T-AK 5070	*Cape Flattery*	Avondale	19 May 1973	14 May 1987
	ex-*Delta Norte* (1987)			
T-AK 1015	*Green Island*	Avondale	Oct 1974	17 Sep 1982
	ex-*George Wythe* (1984), ex-*Green Island* (1980)			
T-AK 2049	*Green Valley*	Avondale	Jun 1974	Feb 1984
	ex-*Button Gwinnett* (1984), ex-*Green Valley* (1980)			
Displacement	62,314 tons; f/l; 29,508 grt; 28,487 (*Green Island, Valley*), 26,406 (*Am.Kestrel*)			
Dimensions	893'4" (oa); 797'2" (wl) × 100' × 40'10"			
Machinery	1 screw; steam turbines; 32,000 SHP; 22.75 knots			
Endurance	15000/22			
Complement	29			

Notes: Type C9-S-81d. Prefix SS. LASH ships. Barge carriers, bulbous bow. Two large travelling cranes. *Delta Sud*, to be named *Cape Fear*, not acquired after her machinery was damaged during conversion. *Green Valley* used as Army ammunition prepositioning ship.

Service Records:

T-AK 9651 *American Kestrel*   Deleted 1995.
  Later history: Merchant *Belofin Kestrel*, 1995. BU 1995, Alang, India.
T-AK 5073 *Cape Farewell*   RRF 1987–2007. SE ◆Gulf War 20 Aug 1990. SS2007.
T-AK 5070 *Cape Flattery*   RRF 1987–2007. SE ◆Gulf War 19 Aug 1990. LU 2006. SS2007.
T-AK 1015 *Green Island*   Deleted. BU 2002, Alang, India.
T-AK 2049 *Green Valley*   Deleted 2001. BU 2001, Chittagong.

No.	Name	Builder	Launched	In service
T-AKR 5063	*Cape May*	Gen. Dyn Quincy	27 Feb 1972	21 Jul 1986
	ex-*Almeria Lykes* (1986)			
T-AKR 5064	*Cape Mendocino*	Gen. Dyn Quincy	Aug 1971	15 Oct 1986
	ex-*Doctor Lykes* (1986)			
T-AKR 5065	*Cape Mohican*	Gen. Dyn Quincy	23 Sep 1972	22 Aug 1986
	ex-*Tillie Lykes* (1986)			
Displacement	57,290 tons; f/l; 21,667 grt			
Dimensions	873'9" (oa); 721'6" (wl) × 105'10" × 39'1"			
Machinery	1 screw; 2 steam turbines; 36,000 SHP; 20.5 knots			
Endurance	14300/19.25			
Complement	40			

Notes: Type C8-S-82a. LASH type. Heavy-load barge carriers. Stern door.

Service Records:

T-AKR 5063 *Cape May*   RRF 1986–2007 SE. ◆Gulf War 22 Aug 1990,. SS2007.
T-AKR 5064 *Cape Mendocino*   RRF 1986–2004. ◆Gulf War. Deleted 1 Jul 2004. NDRF. SE.
T-AKR 5065 *Cape Mohican*   RRF 1986–2007 SE. ◆Gulf War 21 Aug 1990. SS2007.

LASH SHIPS

No.	Name	Builder	Launched	Acquired	In service
T-AK 2046	*American Veteran*	Avondale	29 Jul 1972	1 Feb 1984	Apr 1984
	ex-*Austral Moon* (1984), ex-*Australia Bear* (1976), ex-*Philippine Bear* (1975)				
T-AK 5061	*Austral Lightning*	Avondale	Feb 1971	1 Apr 1985	May 1985
	ex-*Lash Espana* (1976)				
T-AK 5071	*Cape Florida*	Avondale	10 Oct 1970	13 Feb 1987	Feb 1987
	ex-*American Caribe* (1987) ex-*Delta Caribe* (1986), ex-*LASH Turkiye* (1978)				
T-AK 2064	*Green Harbour*	Avondale	20 Jul 1974		Oct 1981
	ex-*William Hooper* (1984), ex-*Green Harbour* (1980)				
T-AKR 1192	*Lash Atlantico*	Avondale	9 Mar 1972	—	—
Displacement	44,606 tons; f/l; 26,456 grt; 28,487 grt (*Green Harbour*)				
Dimensions	819'10" (oa); 723'10" (wl) × 100' × 40'6"				
Machinery	1 screw; steam turbine; 32,000 SHP; 22.5 knots				
Endurance	13,000/22.5				
Complement	32 & 27				

Notes: Type C8-S-81b. 1st two converted from LASH barge carriers to combination barge/container ships. Two large travelling cranes.

Service Records:

T-AK 2046 *American Veteran*   Chartered 27 Oct 1981. Renamed *Austral Rainbow* (T-AKR 1005). Deleted Feb 2000. BU 1995 Alang, India.
T-AK 5061 *Austral Lightning*   Chartered 6 Oct 1981 as **T-AK 1004**. RRF 1985–2006 ◆Gulf War 17 Nov 1990. Renamed *Cape Fear* (T-AK 5061). LU Jul 2006. NDRF. SE.
T-AK 5071 *Cape Florida*   RRF 1987–2006. ◆Gulf War. LU 27 Jul 2006. NDRF. SE.
T-AK 2064 *Green Harbour*   Deleted 2001. BU Chittagong 2001.
T-AKR 1192 *Lash Atlantico*   Deleted. BU 1996, Alang, India.

No.	Name	Builder	Launched	In service
T-AK 9204	*Jeb Stuart*	Sumitomo	1970	Jul 1992
	ex-*Atlantic Forest* (1992)			
Displacement	65,000 tons; f/l; 33,221 grt			
Dimensions	857'4" (oa) × 106'10" × 39'9"; 261.4oa 235.2bp × 32.5			
Machinery	1 screw; diesel; 26,000 bhp; 18 knots			
Endurance	25,920/18			
Complement	24			

Notes: LASH ship. Prefix MV.

Service Record: MPS. Deleted 2001. BU 2001, Alang, India.

CARGO SHIPS

No.	Name	Builder	Launched	In service
T-AK 2062	*American Cormorant* ex-*Ferncarrier* (1985), ex-*Kollbris* (1982)	Eriksbergs	30 May 1975	Oct 1985

Displacement	38,571 tons; 47,500 tons; 70,692 f/l; 10,195 grt.
Dimensions	738'2" (oa) × 135' × 32'8"
Machinery	1 screw; diesel; 25,000 bhp; 16 knots
Endurance	27,000/16
Complement	19

Notes: Semi-submersible, ultra-heavy lift ship, converted from tanker, 1982, lengthened. Prefix MV, chartered.

Service Record: MPS. Deleted 30 Sep 2002.
    Later history: Merchant *Asian Atlas*, 2005.

No.	Name	Builder	Launched	In service
T-AK 9720	*Galveston Bay* ex-*Mallory Lykes* (1986)	Avondale	5 Oct 1965	1986

Displacement	14,081 grt
Dimensions	665'9" (oa); 634'10" (wl) × 75'1" × 31'6"
Machinery	1 screw; steam turbines; 19,000 SHP; 21 knots
Complement	—

Notes: Type C6-S-60c.

Service Record: Renamed *Galveston Bay* (**T-AK 9720**), 1986. Deleted 1997. NDRF 12/98 (as *Mallory Lykes*) T-AK 2037
    Later history: Merchant *Pioneer P*. 1997. BU Alang 1997.

No.	Name	Builder	Launched	In service
T-AK 1014	*Cape Nome* ex-*Rapid* (1988), ex-*American Rapid* (1984), ex-*Red Jacket* (1982), ex-*Mormacstar* (1970)	Ingalls	11 Apr 1969	7 Dec 1987
T-AK 1013	*Rover* ex-*American Rover* (1983), ex-*Defiance* (1982), ex-*Mormacsea* (1970)	Ingalls	19 Oct 1968	1987

Displacement	27,980 tons; f/l; 11,757 grt
Dimensions	601'6" (oa); 559'10" (wl) × 90' × 34'
Machinery	1 screw; 2 steam turbines; 30,000 SHP; 23.6 knots
Complement	27 & 37

Notes: Type C5-S-78a. Bulbous bow. RoRo ships.

Service Records:

T-AK 1014 *Cape Nome*   RRF 1987–2004. ◆Gulf War 29 Aug 1990. Deleted 1 Sep 2004. NDRF. SE.
T-AK 1013 *Rover*   Orig chartered as *Defiance*. Deleted BU 1993, Alang, India.

No.	Name	Builder	Launched	In service
T-AK 851	*Cleveland* ex-*President Cleveland* (1989), ex-*American Mail* (1978)	Newport News	3 May 1969	1989
T-AK 5051	*Cape Gibson* ex-*President Jackson* (1988), ex-*Indian Mail* (1978)	Newport News	27 Jul 1968	1 Apr 1988 Acq 15 Mar 1988
T-AK 2039	*Cape Girardeau* ex-*President Adams* (1988), ex-*Alaskan Mail* (1978)	Newport News	16 Apr 1968	12 Apr 1988 Acq 15 Mar 1988

Figure 13.11: *SS Cape Girardeau* (T-AK 2039) steaming in the Pacific, 16 Jul 2004.

Displacement	31,995 tons; f/l; 15,949 grt
Dimensions	604'10" (oa); 582'4" (wl) × 82'2" × 35'
Machinery	1 screw; steam turbines; 24,000 SHP; 21 knots
Endurance	14000/21
Complement	36

Notes: Type C5-S-75a.

Service Record:

T-AK 851 *Cleveland*   Deleted.
T-AK 5051 *Cape Gibson*   RRF 1988–2007. SE. ◆Gulf War, Iraq War 2002–3. SS2007.
T-AK 2039 *Cape Girardeau*   Acq 23 May 1983 as *President Adams*. RRF 1988–2007. SE ◆Gulf War 26 Sep 1990. SS2007.

No.	Name	Builder	Launched	In service
T-AK 9123	*John Lykes*	Ingalls	16 Apr 1960	—
T-AK 9808	*Joseph Lykes*	Ingalls	16 Nov 1959	—
T-AK 9838	*Leslie Lykes*	Sparrows Pt	20 Jul 1961	—
T-AK 9783	*Nancy Lykes*	Sparrows Pt	12 Apr 1961	—

Displacement	11,591 grt
Dimensions	592'6" (oa); 567'6" (bp) × 69' × 30'
Machinery	1 screw; steam turbine; 9,900 SHP; 17 knots
Endurance	18800/16
Complement	32

Notes: Type C5-S-37e. Additional section added amidships 1972.

Service Records:

T-AK 9123 *John Lykes*   Deleted. BU 1995, Alang.
T-AK 9808 *Joseph Lykes*   Deleted.
    Later history: conv to barge 1992, renamed *Lykes Innovator*. BU 1996 Mexico.
T-AK 9838 *Leslie Lykes*   Deleted. BU 1995, Alang.
T-AK 9783 *Nancy Lykes*   Deleted. BU 1993, Kaohsiung.

No.	Name	Builder	Launched	In service
T-AK 1011	*American Monarch* ex-*Wyoming* (1981)	Avondale	1969	—
T-AK 1009	*American Spartan* ex-*Michigan* (1981)	Avondale	1969	Mar 1982
T-AK 1003	*American Spitfire* ex-*Spitfire* (1981)	Avondale	1969	Oct 1981
T-AK 1008	*American Titan* ex-*Colorado* (1981)	Avondale	19 Sep 1968	Mar 1982
T-AK 1010	*American Trojan* ex-*Santa Victoria* (1989), ex-*Montana* (1981)	Avondale	6 Apr 1968	Jan 1981

Displacement 21,617 tons f/l; 13,053 grt
Dimensions 578′10″ (oa); 544′4″ (wl) × 82′ × 32′6″
Machinery 1 screw; steam turbines; 16,000 SHP; 23 knots
Endurance 12,000/23
Complement 29

Notes: Type C4-S-69b. Self-loading container ship. Chartered. Prefix SS.

Service Record:

T-AK 1011 *Monarch* Deleted. BU 1991 Alang.
T-AK 1009 *Spartan* Flooded engine room off Diego Garcia 15 Dec 1982. Deleted. BU 1983 Kaohsiung.
T-AK 1003 *Spitfire* Deleted. BU 1991 Alang.
T-AK 1008 *Titan* Deleted BU. 1991 Alang.
T-AK 1010 *Trojan* Deleted 1989.
   Later history: Merchant *Santa Victoria* 1989, BU 1991, Alang.

No.	Name	Builder	Launched	In service
T-AK 5060	*Cape Blanco* ex-*Mason Lykes* (1986)	Avondale	10 Jul 1965	Jul 1985
T-AK 5059	*Cape Bon* ex-*Velma Lykes* (1986)	Avondale	16 Jul 1966	Jul 1985 acq 26 Jun 1985
T-AK 5058	*Cape Borda* ex-*Howell Lykes* (1986)	Avondale	16 Apr 1966	Apr 1985 acq 25 Apr 1985
T-AK 5057	*Cape Bover* ex-*Frederick Lykes* (1986)	Avondale	12 Feb 1966	Apr 1985 acq 1 Apr 1985
T-AK 5056	*Cape Breton* ex-*Dolly Turman* (1986)	Avondale	4 Jun 1966	May 1985 acq 1 May 1985
T-AK 2040	*Elizabeth Lykes*	Avondale	31 Oct 1964	1983
T-AK 2043	*Letitia Lykes*	Avondale	26 Oct 1966	1983
T-AK 2048	*Louise Lykes*	Avondale	5 Sep 1964	—
T-AK 9636	*Ruth Lykes*	Avondale	9 Jan 1965	—
T-AK 2045	*Tampa Bay* ex-*Stella Lykes* (1986)	Avondale	18 Dec 1965	—

Displacement 21,840 tons f/l; 10,723 grt, 7,424 grt (Eliz.L & other Lykes)
Dimensions 539′10″ (oa) × 76′ × 32′8″
Machinery 1 screw; 2 steam turbines; 15,500 SHP; 21 knots
Endurance 20,000/20
Complement 38

Notes: Type C4-S-66a. *Letitia Lykes* carried a 1,000-bed field hospital. This type has twin funnels abreast.

Service Record:

T-AK 5060 *Cape Blanco* RRF 1985–2002. ◆Gulf War 9 Dec 1990. LU 19 Dec 2002. NDRF. SE.
T-AK 5059 *Cape Bon* RRF 1985–2000. ◆Gulf War 10 Dec 1990, Deleted 1 Oct 2000 Converted to Mass. Maritime Academy TS, Jan 2001, renamed **Enterprise** (T-AP 1003), 25 Oct 2002.
T-AK 5058 *Cape Borda* RRF 1985–2003. ◆Gulf War 26 Aug 1990, LU 28 Apr 2003. NDRF. SE.
T-AK 5057 *Cape Bover* RRF 1985–2003. ◆Gulf War 9 Dec 1990, LU 28 Apr 2003. NDRF. SE.
T-AK 5056 *Cape Breton* RRF 1985–2002. ◆Gulf War 29 Aug 1990, LU 29 Dec 2002. NDRF. SE.
T-AK 2040 *Elizabeth Lykes* Deleted. BU 1995 Alang.
T-AK 2043 *Letitia Lykes* Deleted 1994. BU 1994, Alang, India.
T-AK 2048 *Louise Lykes* Deleted. BU 1995 Alang (as *Louise*).
T-AK 9636 *Ruth Lykes* Deleted. BU 1994 Alang (as *Ruth*).
T-AK 2045 *Tampa Bay* Deleted 1994. BU 1996, Alang (as *Tampa*).

No.	Name	Builder	Launched	In service
AK 5030	*Santa Barbara* ex-*Delta Bolivia* (1980), ex-*Santa Barbara* (1978)	Sun	14 Sep 1966	1984
AK 5031	*Santa Clara*	Sun	Jan 1966	1984
AK 5032	*Santa Cruz* ex-*Delta Ecuador* (1980) ex-*Santa Cruz* (1978)	Sun	9 Nov 1965	1984
AK 5033	*Santa Elena* ex-*Delta Panama*, ex-*Santa Elena*	Sun	6 Jul 1966	1984
AK 5034	*Santa Isabel* ex-*Delta Peru*, ex-*Santa Isabel*	Sun	9 Mar 1967	1984
AK 5035	*Santa Lucia* ex-*Delta Venezuela*, ex-*Santa Lucia*	Sun	26 Aug 1965	1984

Displacement 9,313 grt
Dimensions 170.69 (oa); 163 (bp) × 24.85 × 9.3
Machinery 1 screw; ST; 15,500 SHP; 20 knots
Complement —

Notes: Type C4-S-65a.

AK 5030 *Santa Barbara* RRF 1984–1988. Deleted 15 Apr 1988.
   Later history: Merchant *Santa Barbara II*, 1990. BU 1990 Alang.
AK 5031 *Santa Clara* RRF 1984–1988. Deleted 29 Apr 1988. NDRF.
AK 5032 *Santa Cruz* RRF 1984–1988. Deleted. NDRF. BU 2004 Brownsville.
AK 5033 *Santa Elena* RRF 1984–1988. Deleted 31 May 1988. NDRF. BU 2003, USA.
AK 5034 *Santa Isabel* RRF 1984–1988. Deleted 15 Jun 1988. NDRF. BU 2004, Brownsville.
AK 5035 *Santa Lucia* RRF 1984–1988. Deleted 30 Jun 1988. NDRF.

No.	Name	Builder	Launched	In service
AK 2051	*Santa Adela* ex-*Delta Africa* (1980), ex-*Prudential Oceanjet* (1978)	Sparrows Pt	2 Dec 1965	1982
AK 2047	*Santa Juana* ex-*Delta America* (1980), ex-*Prudential Seajet* (1978)	Sparrows Pt	2 Sep 1965	1982

Notes: Type C4-S-64b.

AK 2051 *Santa Adela* Deleted. BU 1991 Alang
AK 2047 *Santa Juana* Deleted. BU 1991 Alang

No.	Name	Builder	Launched	In service
T-AK 5012	*Cape Alava* ex-*Comet* (1980), ex-*African Comet* (1980)	Ingalls	24 Mar 1962	Apr 1980 reAcq 11 Jan 1991
T-AK 5010	*Cape Alexander* ex-*Meteor* (1980), ex-*African Meteor* (1980)	Ingalls	7 Jul 1962	Apr 1980
T-AK 5009	*Cape Ann* ex-*Mercury* (1980), ex-*African Mercury* (1980)	Ingalls	12 May 1962	Mar 1980
T-AK 5011	*Cape Archway* ex-*Neptune* (1980), ex-*African Neptune* (1980)	Ingalls	15 Sep 1962	Apr 1980
T-AK 5013	*Cape Avinof* ex-*Sun* (1980), ex-*African Sun* (1980)	Ingalls	8 Dec 1962	Apr 1980 Reacq 29 Jan 1991
T-AK 2034	*Dawn* ex-*African Dawn* (1980)	Ingalls	16 Dec 1962	1980

Displacement 18,560 tons f/l; 11,309 grt
Dimensions 571′10″ (oa); 540′11″ (wl) × 75′2″ × 30′10″
Machinery 1 screw; steam turbines; 18,150 shp; 21.5 knots
Endurance 13,300/20
Complement 32

Notes: Type C4-S-58a. Miramar says Cape Alexander was ex-Afr. Mercury & Cape Ann was Afr. Meteor.

Service Records:

T-AK 5009 *Cape Ann*   RRF 1984–2002. ◆Gulf War, LU 19 Dec 2002. NDRF. SE.

T-AK 5010 *Cape Alexander*   RRF 1984–2003. ◆Gulf War, LU 31 Mar 2003. NDRF. SE.

T-AK 5011 *Cape Archway*   RRF 1984–2002. ◆Gulf War, LU 19 Dec 2002. NDRF. SE.

T-AK 5012 *Cape Alava*   RRF 1984–2000. ◆Gulf War, LU 1 Oct 2000. NDRF. SE.

T-AK 5013 *Cape Avinof*   RRF 1984–2003. LU 31 Mar 2003. NDRF. SE.

T-AK 2034 *Dawn*   NDRF. SE.

No.	Name	Builder	Launched	In service
T-AK 2016	*Pioneer Commander* ex-*American Commander* (1967)	Quincy	20 Dec 1962	Jun 1982
T-AK 2018	*Pioneer Contractor* ex-*American Contractor* (1966)	Quincy	22 Mar 1963	Sep 1981
T-AK 2019	*Pioneer Crusader* ex-*American Crusader* (1967)	Quincy	30 Jul 1963	Sep 1981
T-AK 2011	*American Champion*	Newport News	14 Dec 1962	2 Jun 1980

Displacement	21,053 tons f/l; 11,105 grt
Dimensions	560′11″ (oa); 529′10″ (bp) × 75′1″ × 32′2″
Machinery	1 screw; steam turbines; 22,500 shp; 23.1 knots
Endurance	12,000/21
Complement	43

Notes: Type C4-S-57a.

Service Records:

T-AK 2016 *Pioneer Commander*   RRF 1984–2000. LU 1 Oct 2000. NDRF. SE.

T-AK 2018 *Pioneer Contractor*   RRF 1984–2000. LU 1 Oct 2000. NDRF. SE.

T-AK 2019 *Pioneer Crusader*   RRF 1984–1998. LU 7 May 1998. NDRF. SE.

T-AK 2011 *American Champion*   Chartered 30 Sep 1982. BU 1987. Kaohsiung

No.	Name	Builder	Launched	In service
T-AK 5029	*California* ex-*Santa Rita* (1980), ex-*California* (1974)	Newport News	28 Jul 1961	Dec 1980
T-AK 5022	*Santa Ana* ex-*C.E. Dant* (1974)	National Stl	18 Aug 1962	May 1980 re acq 10 Jan 1991
T-AK 5075	*Cape Johnson* ex-*Mormacsaga* (1988), ex-*American Saga* (1985), ex-*Mormacsaga* (1983), ex-*M.M. Dant* (1977)	National Stl	5 May 1962	Jun 1988 acq 29 Feb 1988
T-AK 5077	*Cape Juby* ex-*Mormacsea* (1988), ex-*American Sea* (1985), ex-*Mormacsea* (1983), ex-*Hawaii* (1977)	National Stl	9 Feb 1962	Jul 1988 acq 13 Jul 1988

Displacement	22,629 tons; 9,345 grt
Dimensions	565′ (oa); 528′5″ (wl) × 76′ × 32′
Machinery	1 screw; steam turbines; 19,250 shp; 20.75 knots
Endurance	12,599/20
Complement	20/75

Notes: Type C4-S-1u. Prefix SS. *Cape Jacob* carries USN munitions.

Service Records:

T-AK 5029 *California*   RRF 1984–2007 SE. ◆Gulf War (as *California*). Renamed *Cape Jacob*, 1993. Iraq War 2002–3. SE 2007.

T-AK 5022 *Santa Ana*   RRF 1984–2004. ◆Gulf War (as *Santa Ana*). Renamed *Cape John*, 1993. Iraq War 2002–3. NDRF. SE.

Figure 13.12: SS *Cape John* (T-AK 5022), cargo ship in the Arabian Gulf, 25 Apr 2003. A CH-46 *Sea Knight* helicopter is picking up ammunition.

T-AK 5075 *Cape Johnson*   RRF 1988–2004. ◆Gulf War, Iraq War 2002–3. LU 1 Jul 2004. NDRF. SE.

T-AK 5077 *Cape Juby*   RRF 1988–2004. ◆Gulf War. LU 1 Jul 2004. NDRF. SE.

No.	Name	Builder	Launched	In service
T-AK 5049	*Del Monte* ex-*Delta Brasil* (1980)	Ingalls	12 Dec 1967	Jul 1984
T-AK 5050	*Del Valle* ex-*Delta Uruguay* (1980)	Ingalls	15 Jun 1968	Jul 1984
T-AK 5026	*Del Viento* ex-*Delta Mexico* (1980)	Ingalls	5 Oct 1968	Apr 1984

Displacement	19,285 tons f/l; 7,146 /10,396 grt
Dimensions	521′10″ (oa) × 69′10″ × 30′10″
Machinery	1 screw; steam turbines; 14,250 shp; 20 knots
Endurance	13,600/18.6
Complement	31/36

Notes: Type C3-S-76a. Bulbous bows.

Service Record:

T-AK 5026 *Del Viento*   RRF 1984–1994. LU 7 Oct 1994. NDRF. SE.

T-AK 5049 *Del Monte*   RRF 1984–1994. ◆Gulf War. LU 1 Apr 1994. NDRF. SE.

T-AK 5050 *Del Valle*   RRF 1984–1994. ◆Gulf War. LU 7 Oct 1994. NDRF. SE.

No.	Name	Builder	Launched	In service
T-AK 5008	*Banner* ex-*Export Banner* (1982)	National Stl	17 Dec 1960	Jan 1983
T-AK 2032	*Bay* ex-*Export Bay* (1980)	National Stl	8 Apr 1961	—
T-AK 2031	*Builder* ex-*Export Builder* (1980)	National Stl	12 Aug 1961	—
T-AK 2033	*Buyer* ex-*Export Buyer* (1980)	National Stl	25 Nov 1961	29 Feb 1988
T-AK 5019	*Courier* ex-*Export Courier* (1981)	Sun	5 Apr 1962	Aug 1983

Displacement	19,400 tons f/l; 10,659 grt
Dimensions	493′ (oa); 469′11″ (wl) × 73′ × 30′6″
Machinery	1 screw; steam turbines; 13,750 shp; 20 knots
Complement	32

Notes: Type C3-S-46a.

Service Records:

T-AK 5008 *Banner* RRF 1984–2000. ◆Gulf War. LU 1 Oct 2000. NDRF. SE.
T-AK 2032 *Bay* Deleted. NDRF. SE.
T-AK 2031 *Builder* Deleted. NDRF. 12/98.
T-AK 2033 *Buyer* RRF 1989–1994. ◆Gulf War. LU 7 Oct 1994. NDRF. SE.
T-AK 5019 *Courier* RRF 1984–1999. ◆Gulf War. LU 1 Oct 1999.

No.	Name	Builder	Launched	In service
T-AK 5005	*Adventurer* ex-*Export Adventurer* (1980)	NY Sbdg	9 Jul 1960	Feb 1980
T-AK 5008	*Agent* ex-*Export Agent* (1980)	National Stl	30 Jan 1960	Feb 1980
T-AK 5006	*Aide* ex-*Export Aide* (1980)	National Stl	4 Jun 1960	Apr 1980
T-AK 5007	*Ambassador* ex-*Export Ambassador* (1981)	NY Sbdg	23 Apr 1960	Dec 1980

Displacement	15,750 tons f/l; 7.848 grt
Dimensions	492′11″ (oa); 469′8″ (bp) × 73′ × 27′11″
Machinery	1 screw; steam turbine; 13,750 shp; 19 knots
Endurance	12,000/18.5
Complement	32

Notes: Type C3-S-38a.

Service Record:

T-AK 5005 *Adventurer* RRF 1984–1994. LU 7 Oct 1994. NDRF. SE.
T-AK 5008 *Agent* RRF 1984–1994. ◆Gulf War. LU 7 Oct 1994. NDRF. SE.
T-AK 5006 *Aide* RRF 1984–1994. LU 7 Oct 1994. NDRF. SE.
T-AK 5007 *Ambassador* RRF 1984–1994. ◆Gulf War. LU 7 Oct 1994. NDRF. SE.

No.	Name	Builder	Launched	In service
T-AK 5044	*Gulf Banker*	Avondale	5 Oct 1963	Nov 1984
T-AK 5045	*Gulf Farmer*	Avondale	3 Aug 1963	Nov 1984
T-AK 5046	*Gulf Merchant*	Avondale	16 May 1964	Nov 1984
T-AK 2035	*Gulf Shipper*	Avondale	15 Feb 1964	Aug 1984
T-AK 2036	*Gulf Trader*	Avondale	28 Dec 1963	Nov 1984

Displacement	17,210 tons f/l; 6,399 or 8,970 grt
Dimensions	494′8″ (oa) × 69′2″ × 30′2″
Machinery	1 screw; steam turbines; 11,000 shp; 18.75 knots
Complement	30/36

Notes: Type C3-S-37d.

Service Records:

T-AK 5044 *Gulf Banker* RRF 1985–2000. ◆Gulf War. LU 1 Oct 2000. NDRF. SE.
T-AK 5045 *Gulf Farmer* RRF 1985–1998. LU 7 May 1998. NDRF. SE.
T-AK 5046 *Gulf Merchant* RRF 1985–1998. LU 7 May 1998. NDRF. SE.
T-AK 2035 *Gulf Shipper* RRF 1985–1998. LU 7 May 1998. NDRF. SE.
T-AK 2036 *Gulf Trader* RRF 1985–2000. ◆Gulf War. LU 1 Oct 2000. NDRF. SE.

No.	Name	Builder	Launched	In service
T-AK 5040	*Cape Canaveral* ex-*Allison Lykes* (1985)	Avondale	11 May 1963	Aug 1984 reacq 2 Feb 1991
T-AK 5037	*Cape Canso* ex-*Aimee Lykes* (1985)	Avondale	13 Oct 1962	Aug 1984
T-AK 5042	*Cape Carthage* ex-*Margaret Lykes* (1985)	Avondale	9 Mar 1963	Sep 1984
T-AK 5043	*Cape Catoche* ex-*Christopher Lykes* (1985)	Avondale	22 Dec 1962	Nov 1984
T-AK 5036	*Cape Chalmers* ex-*Adabelle Lykes* (1986)	Sparrows Pt	6 Dec 1962	Nov 1984
T-AK 5038	*Cape Charles* ex-*Charlotte Lykes* (1986)	Sparrows Pt	16 May 1963	Nov 1984
T-AK 5039	*Cape Clear* ex-*Mayo Lykes* (1986)	Sparrows Pt	14 Aug 1963	Nov 1984
T-AK 5041	*Cape Cod* ex-*Sheldon Lykes* (1986)	Sparrows Pt	11 Jul 1962	Nov 1984

Displacement	18,560 tons f/l; 9,296 grt
Dimensions	494′9″ (oa) × 69′2″ × 32′
Machinery	1 screw; steam turbines; 11,000 shp; 18.75 knots
Endurance	18,300/17.7
Complement	30/37

Notes: Type C3-S-37c. These ships were first in service under their original merchant names.

Service Records:

T-AK 5040 *Cape Canaveral* RRF 1984–1994. LU 7 Oct 1994. Deleted. 17 Jun 1997. NDRF. SE.
T-AK 5037 *Cape Canso* RRF 1984–1994. ◆Gulf War. LU 1 Apr 1994. NDRF. SE.
T-AK 5042 *Cape Carthage* RRF 1984–1998. ◆Gulf War. LU 7 May 1998. NDRF. SE.
T-AK 5043 *Cape Catoche* RRF 1985–1994. ◆Gulf War. LU 7 Oct 1994. NDRF. SE.
T-AK 5036 *Cape Chalmers* RRF 1985–2000. LU 1 Oct 2000. NDRF. SE.
T-AK 5038 *Cape Charles* RRF 1985–1992. ◆Gulf War. LU 8 Dec 1992. NDRF. SE.
T-AK 5039 *Cape Clear* RRF 1984–1996. ◆Gulf War. LU 4 Dec 1996. NDRF. SE.
T-AK 5041 *Cape Cod* RRF 1985–2000. ◆Gulf War. LU 1 Oct 2000. NDRF. SE.

No.	Name	Builder	Launched	In service
T-AK 5074	*Cape* ex-*Mormaccape* (1983)	Todd; S.Pedro	6 Jun 1960	15 Feb 1987
T-AK 5016	*Lake* ex-*Mormaclake* (1977)	Sun	5 Jan 1961	Mar 1977
T-AK 5017	*Pride* ex-*Mormacpride* (1977)	Sun	1 Feb 1960	Feb 1977
T-AK 5018	*Scan* ex-*Mormacscan* (1977)	Sun	21 Mar 1961	Feb 1977

Displacement	18,365 tons f/l
Dimensions	485′11″ (oa); 457′10″ (wl) × 68′ × 28′6″
Machinery	1 screw; steam turbine; 11,000 shp; 19 knots
Endurance	14,000/18
Complement	50

Notes: Type C3-S-33a. *Northern Light* & *Southern Cross* (AK 284–285) are of same class (p. 205).

Service Records:

T-AK 5074 *Cape* RRF 1987–2000. Renamed *Cape Catawba*, 1989. ◆Gulf War. LU 1 Oct 2000. NDRF. SE.
T-AK 5016 *Lake* RRF 1984–2000. ◆Gulf War, LU 1 Oct 2000. NDRF SE.
T-AK 5017 *Pride* RRF 1984–1994. ◆Gulf War, LU 1994. NDRF SE.
T-AK 5018 *Scan* RRF 1984–2000. LU 1 Oct 2000. NDRF BU 2008 Brownsville.

No.	Name	Builder	Launched	In service
T-AK 9652	Advantage	Tsurumi	27 Apr 1977	Oct 1988
	ex-*Tacna II* (1988), ex-*Thermopylae* (1985),			
	ex-*Als Confidence* (1984), ex-*Barber Thermopylae* (1984)			
	ex-*Thermopylae* (1981)			
Displacement	27,750 tons f/l; 18,296 grt			
Dimensions	560′11″ (oa); 542′6″ (wl) × 86′6″ × 32′9″			
Machinery	1 screw; diesel; 14,000 BHP; 17.5 knots			
Complement	22			

Notes: Ammunition ship for the Air Force.

Service Record: Deleted 1994.

No.	Name	Builder	Launched	In service
T-AK 9653	Noble Star	Kaldnes	11 Mar 1977	31 Dec 1988
	ex-*Concordia Star* (1985), ex-*Hoegh Star* (1984),			
	ex-*Costa Atlantica* (1983), ex-*Costa Mediterranea* (1981),			
	ex-*Concordia Star* (1982)			
Displacement	24,000 tons f/l; 16,840 grt			
Dimensions	562′3″ (oa); 534′8″ (wl) × 83′5″ × 34′7″			
Machinery	1 screw; diesel; 13,100 hp; 17.5 knots			
Complement	17.5			

Notes: Carries Navy field hospital. PPF.

Service Record: ◆Gulf War. Deleted before 2004.

No.	Name	Builder	Launched	In service
T-AK 9655	Green Ridge	Howaldt	12 Jan 1979	—
	ex-*Woerman Mercur* (1988), ex-*Sloman Mercur* (1984),			
	ex-*Carol Mercur* (1980), ex-*Sloman Mercur* (1979)			
T-AK 2050	Green Wave	Howaldt	10 Jan 1980	—
	ex-*Woerman Mira* (1984), ex-*Sloman Mira* (1984)			
Displacement	5,169 tons;. 18,178 tons f/l, 5,805 grt			
Dimensions	507′ (oa); 479′1″ (wl) × 69′9″ × 24′6″			
Machinery	1 screw; diesels; 10,000 BHP; 18 knots			
Endurance	14,400/17			
Complement	22			

Notes: Prefix MV. Bulbous bow, ice strengthened. Similar ships. *Green Ridge* chartered to support fleet hospital afloat.

Service Records:

T-AK 9655 *Green Ridge*   PPS. Deleted 13 Aug 2001.
    Later history: Merchant *Lautan Arafura*, 2001.
T-AK 2050 *Green Wave*   Deleted Mar 2003.
    Later history: Merchant *Al Mansourah*, 2003.

No.	Name	Builder	Launched	In service
—	Maersk Constellation	Odense	2 Feb 1980	30 Nov 1988
T-AK 2053	ex-*Elisabeth Maersk* (1988), ex-*C.R. Marseille* (1988),			
	ex-*Elisabeth Maersk* (1987)			
Displacement	11,717 tons, 32,242 f/l, 20,529 grt			
Dimensions	598′ (oa); 551′9″ (wl) × 90′ × 32′			
Machinery	1 screw; diesels; 15,960 BHP; 18 knots			
Complement	21			

Notes: Prefix MV. RoRo, bulbous bow, stern door/ramp

Service Record: Deleted before 1995.

No.	Name	Builder	Launched	In service
—	Lincoln	Beth; S.Fran.	29 Aug 1960	1980
	ex-*President Lincoln*			
—	President	Beth; S.Fran.	20 Dec 1960	1980
	ex-*President Tyler*, L as *President Roosevelt*			
Displacement	13,233 grt			
Dimensions	171.8 (oa); 161.1 (wl) × 23.3 ×			
Machinery	1 screw; diesel; 20 knots			

Notes: Type C4-S-1q
Lincoln RRF 1984. NDRF. SE.
President RRF 1984–1985 NDRF. SE.

AK 2005   *Transcolorado*   ex-*Marine Adder*   BU 1988   see p. 224   SE1984.
AK 2006   *Transcolumbia*   ex-*Marine Lynx*   BU 1988   see p. 224   SE1984.
Note: Type C4-S-B1

AK 1808   *Hattiesburg Victory*   RRF 1986–1988. deleted 15 Jul 1988. NDRF. BU 2001.
AK 1809   *American Victory*   RRF 1986–1988. deleted 31 Mar 1988. NDRF. 12/98.
AK 5001   *Catawba Victory*   RRF 1984–1987. deleted 4 May 1987. NDRF. 12/98 SE2001.
Note: Type VC2-S-AP2

T-AKR 9716   *Strong American*

TRANSPORT OILERS/TANKERS

No.	Name	Builder	Launched	In service
T-AOT 1004	Courier	Todd	24 Apr 1976	3 Dec 1981
	ex-*Zapata Courier* (1981)			
T-AOT 1001	Patriot	Todd; S.Pedro	11 Jan 1975	9 Sep 1982
	ex-*Zapata Patriot* (1981)			
T-AOT 1002	Ranger	Todd; S.Pedro	17 May 1975	16 Oct 1981
	ex-*Zapata Ranger* (1981)			
T-AOT 1003	Rover	Todd; S.Pedro	8 Nov 1975	1 Jan 1982
	ex-*Ogden River* (1981), ex-*Zapata Rover*			
T-AOT 1007	American Courier	Beth; Quincy	16 Sep 1962	5 Jun 1980
Displacement	35,100 tons d/w; 21,572 grt			
Dimensions	710′7″ (oa) × 84′ × 37′			
Machinery	1 screw; diesel; 14,000 hp; 16 knots			
Complement	27			

Notes: Type T6-S-98a Capacity 308,000 bbls.

Service Records:

T-AOT 1004 *Courier*   ◆Gulf War 9 Jan 1991. LU 1 Oct 2000. NDRF.
    Later history: Merchant *Couri* 2003. BU 2003 Alang.
T-AOT 1001 *Patriot*   Deleted about 1995c.
    Later history: Damaged by fire off Pasir Gudang, 22 Jul 2002, CTL. BU Bombay 2003.
T-AOT 1002 *Ranger*   Deleted about 1995c.
    Later history: Merchant *Kathryn Sea* 1996, *W.S. Challenger*, 1998, *Warmseas Challenger* 1999. BU 2003 Alang.
T-AOT 1003 *Rover*   Deleted about 1995c.
    Later history: Merchant *Rove*, 2004. BU 2004 China.
T-AOT 1007 *American Courier*   Chartered 30 Sep 1982. Rec **T-AO 2015**. BU 1985 Algeciras.

No.	Name	Builder	Launched	In service
T-AOT 1121	Gus W. Darnell L as Ocean Champion	American; Tampa	10 Aug 1985	11 Sep 1985
T-AOT 1125	Lawrence H. Gianella LD as Ocean Star	American; Tampa	19 Apr 1986	22 Apr 1986
T-AOT 1122	Paul Buck ex-Ocean Champion	American; Tampa	1 Jun 1985	11 Sep 1985
T-AOT 1124	Richard G. Matthieson ex-Ocean Spirit	American; Tampa	15 Feb 1986	18 Feb 1986
T-AOT 1123	Samuel L. Cobb ex-Ocean Triumph	American; Tampa	2 Nov 1985	15 Nov 1985

Displacement	39,624 tons f/l; 19,937 grt, 21,471grt (Gianella, Buck)
Dimensions	615′ (oa); 587′6″(wl) × 90′ × 34′
Machinery	1 screw; diesel; 15,300 BHP; 16 knots
Endurance	12000/12
Complement	24

Notes: Modified T5 design tankers. Built for naval service, but chartered. Forward sections built by Avondale. Ice-strengthened hulls. Capacity 240,000 bbls. Prefix SS; all (except Darnell) purch by MSC, 15 Jan 2003 and redesignated USNS.

Service Records:

T-AOT 1121 Gus W. Darnell   Deleted 10 Sep 2005.
T-AOT 1125 Lawrence H. Gianella   SS2007.
T-AOT 1122 Paul Buck   SS2007.
T-AOT 1124 Richard G. Matthieson   SS2007.
T-AOT 1123 Samuel L. Cobb   SS2007.

AOT 165 American Explorer,   (see p. 216) RRF 1984–1993. NDRF. SE.

No.	Name	Builder	Launched	In service
T-AOT 5084	Chesapeake ex-Hess Voyager (1980)	Sparrows Pt	18 Aug 1964	20 Jul 1991
T-AOT 9101	Petersburg ex-Sinclair Texas (1981)	Sparrows Pt	2 Apr 1963	1 Aug 1991

Displacement	14,977 tons, 48,993 f/l; 27,015 & 27,469 grt
Dimensions	736′2″ (oa); 704′10″(wl) × 102′10″ × 39′9″
Machinery	1 screw; steam turbines; SHP 15,000; 15 knots
Complement	38

Notes: Both fitted with Offshore Petroleum Discharge System (OPDS). Prefix SS.

Service Records:

T-AOT 5084 Chesapeake   RRF 1991–2007 SE. ◆Iraq War 2002–3. SS2007.
T-AOT 9101 Petersburg   RRF 1991–2007. SE Iraq War 2002–3. LU2007.

No.	Name	Builder	Launched	Acquired	In service
T-AOT 5083	Mount Vernon ex-Mount Vernon Victory (1989)	Beth Quincy	27 Oct 1960	31 Mar 1990	Mar 1990
T-AOT 5076	Mount Washington	Beth Quincy	20 Sep 1963	30 Sep 1989	Oct 1989

Displacement	65,800 tons f/l; 27,797 grt
Dimensions	736′2″ (oa) × 102′10″ × 40′3″
Machinery	1 screw; steam turbines; 21,500 SHP; 17.5 knots
Complement	38

Notes:
Service Records:

T-AOT 5083 Mount Vernon   RRF 1990–1994. LU 7 Oct 1994. NDRF. SE.
T-AOT 5076 Mount Washington   RRF 1989–2005. LU NDRF. SE.

Figure 13.13: SS Chesapeake (T-AOT 5084), fitted with Offshore Petroleum Discharge System, notice equipment and machinery on deck.

No.	Name	Builder	Launched	Acquired	In service
T-AOT 5075	American Osprey ex-Gulfprince (1982)	Sparrows Pt	3 Dec 1957	3 Jun 1987	Jun 1987

Displacement	44,840 tons f/l; 20,143 grt
Dimensions	660′11″ (oa) × 89′11″ × 36′1″
Machinery	1 screw; steam turbines; 15,000 SHP; 17 knots
Endurance	14,000/17
Complement	30

Notes: Converted by Alabama DD. Prefix SS.

Service Record: American Osprey RRF 1987–2000. ◆Gulf War, at Diego Garcia. LU 1 Apr 2000. NDRF. SE.

No.	Name	Builder	Launched	In service
T-AOT 5005	Mission Capistrano ex-Falcon Lady (1988), ex-USS Columbia (AOT 182) (1984), ex-Falcon Lady (1976)	Ingalls	12 Sep 1970	29 Feb 1988
T-AOT	Duchess ex-Falcon Duchess, ex-Eclipse, ex-USS Neches (AOT 183), ex-Falcon Duchess	Ingalls	30 Jan 1971	1992

Displacement	45,877 tons f/l; 20,751 grt
Dimensions	672′2″ (oa) × 89′2″ × 36′3″
Machinery	1 screw; diesel; 16,000 hp; 16.5 knots
Complement	23

Notes: Falcon class oilers acquired for Ready Reserve. (See p. 217)

Service Records:

T-AOT 5005 Mission Capistrano   RRF 1988–2004. LU 1 Jul 2004. BU 2004. U.S. NDRF. SE.
T-AOT   Duchess   BU 1997 Gadani.

No.	Name	Builder	Launched	In service
T-AO 9659	Omi Champion ex-Ogden Champion (1985), ex-Penn Champion (1974)	Sparrows Ptr	9 Jul 1969	—
T-AOT 1203	Overseas Alice	Sparrows Pt	22 Feb 1968	6 Oct 1982
T-AOT 1204	Overseas Valdez ex-Overseas Audrey (1971)	Sparrows Pt	23 Apr 1968	Aug 1982
T-AOT 1205	Overseas Vivian	Sparrows Pt	15 Aug 1968	14 Nov 1982

Displacement	46,273 tons f/l; 20,879 grt
Dimensions	660' (oa) × 90'2" × 36'8"
Machinery	1 screw; 2 steam turbines; 15,000 SHP; 16.25 knots
Endurance	13,000/16
Complement	27

Notes: Chartered to MCS. All rtnd about 1995.

Service Records:

T-AOT 1203 *Overseas Alice*   Deleted BU 1996 Alang.
T-AOT 1204 *Overseas Valdez*   Deleted BU 1997 Alang.
T-AOT 1205 *Overseas Vivian*   Deleted BU 2001 Alang, India.
T-AO 9659 *Omi Champion*   Deleted renamed *Champion* 1994. BU 1999, Alang.

No.	Name	Builder	Launched	Acquired	In service
T-AOT 1012	*Mission Buenaventura* ex-*Spirit of Liberty* (1989)	Sparrows Pt	14 Jun 1968	9 Oct 1987	Oct 1987

Displacement	46,243 tons f/l; 20,947 grt
Dimensions	660' (oa); 629'11" (wl) × 90'2" × 38'3"
Machinery	1 screw; steam turbines; 15,000 SHP; 16.5 knots
Endurance	12,000/16.5
Complement	27

Service record: *Mission Buenaventura* RRF 1987–2004. LU 1 Jul 2004. NDRF. SE.

No.	Name	Builder	Launched	In service
AOT 1201	*New York Sun*	Sun	22 Sep 1979.	1985
AOT 1202	*Texas Trader* ex-*Philadelphia Sun*	Sun	1981	1997

Displacement	20,391 & 17,491 grt resp
Dimensions	612' (oa); 580' (wl) × 90'2" × 36'9"
Machinery	1 screw; diesel; 14,400 bph; 15 knots
Complement	—

Notes: Type T2-SE-A1.

AOT 1201 *New York Sun*   Renamed *Allegiance*. Deleted 1997.
   Later history: Merchant *Allegi* 2007. BU 2007 Chittagong.
AOT 1202 *Philadelphia Sun*   Renamed *Perserverance* 1997. Deleted 1999.
   Later history: Merchant *France* 2007. BU 2007 Chittagong.

No.	Name	Builder	Launched	In service
T-AOG 9687	*Bluetank Starlet* ex-*Asalimi-5* (1990), ex-*Shuko Maru No.1* (1979)	Mie SY	1971	—

Displacement	1991 grt
Dimensions	297'6" (oa); 275'7" (bp) × 44'4" × 20'
Machinery	1 screw; diesel; 2,400 bhp; 15 knots

Service Record: Chartered.
   Later history: Merchant *Star I* 1995, *Persi* 1998, BU Bombay 2003.

No.	Name	Builder	Launched	In service
T-AOG 9622	*Bravado*	Fosen	1977	—

Displacement	5,995 tons f/l; 2,110 grt
Dimensions	304'6" (oa) × 47'11" × 22'
Machinery	1 screw; diesel; 2,800 hp; 12.5 knots
Complement	16

Notes: Coastal tanker, chartered. Capacity 28,000 bbls.

Service Record: Deleted about 1994.
   Later history: Merchant *Ditte Theresa* 1996, renamed *Santa Maria* 2006.

No.	Name	Builder	Launched	In service
T-AO 9657	*Newbridge* ex-*Christian F. Reinauer*, ex-*N.W. Gokey* (1971)	Bushey	1947	—

Displacement	1,488 grt
Dimensions	243' (oa) × 40'2" × 16
Machinery	1 screw; diesel; 1,200 bhp; 12 knots
Complement	—

Notes: Coastal tanker.

Service Record: Deleted.
   Later history: renamed *Bobbi J.* (1988), *Jax Fuel* (1994), *Stella D.* (1994).

No.	Name	Builder	Launched	In service
T-AOT 1209	*Falcon Champion*	Bath	10 Sep 1983	19 Jan 1984
T-AOT 1208	*Falcon Leader*	Bath	26 Feb 1983	18 Aug 1983

Displacement	36,522 tons f/l; 17,735 grt
Dimensions	666'2" (oa) × 84' × 31'6"
Machinery	1 screw; diesels; 14,500 hp; 16 knots
Endurance	27,000/16
Complement	28

Notes: Type T6-M-136a. Built for MSC. Capacity 225,000 bbls.

Service Records:

T-AOT 1209 *Falcon Champion*   Deleted Jan 1989.
   Later history: Ren. *Asphalt Commander*, 1996.
T-AOT 1208 *Falcon Leader*   Deleted Aug 1988. NDRF. Sold Jun 2001. RR2006.
   Later history: Merchant *Sabine Eagle* 1992, *Seabrook* 2005.

No.	Name	Builder	Launched	In service
T-AOT 94A	*Valiant* ex-*Seta* (1991), ex-*Chimborazo* (1990), ex-*Thomona* (1979)	Kleven	May 1973	1991

Displacement	10,600 tons f/l; 4,415 grt
Dimensions	396' (oa) × 52'7" × 22'8"
Machinery	1 screw; diesel; 4,200 bhp; 13.5 knots
Complement	—

Notes: Coastal tanker. Prefix MV.

Service Record: Deleted.
   Merchant *Titan Venus* 2001.

No.	Name	Builder	Launched	In service
T-AG 5001	*VADM K.R. Wheeler*	—	2007	20 Sep 2007

Displacement	
Dimensions	348'5" × 70' × 27'6"
Machinery	16 knots
Complement	26

Notes: Acquired on five-year charter. Prefix MV. Funnels and bridge forward, OPDS.

No.	Name	Builder	Launched	In service
AOT	*Montauk* ex-*Bitten Theresa* (2001)	Tuzla Gerni, Tuzla	1999	—

Displacement	3,457 tons
Dimensions	357'11" (oa); 326'8" (wl) × 52'6" × 18'7"
Machinery	1 screw; 1 diesel; 2,665 bhp; 12 knots
Complement	13

Notes: Small shallow-draft tanker. Prefix MV.

Sealift Ships 253

Figure 13.14: *MV VADM K.R. Wheeler* (T-AG 5001). A stern view of the OPDS ship, 2007.

TRANSPORTS

No.	Name	Builder	Launched	In service
T-AP 1000	*Patriot State* ex-*Santa Mercedes* (1984)	Sparrows Pt	30 Jul 1963	4 Mar 1986

Displacement	20,500 tons f/l; 11,188 grt
Dimensions	544'11" (oa) × 79'2" × 29'
Machinery	2 screws; steam turbines; 19,800 SHP; 20 knots
Complement	33

Notes: S5-S-MA49c. Massachusetts state training ship.

Service Record: *Patriot State* RRF 1985–1999. OS 31Dec 1998. Active at Buzzards Bay, Mass., 1996. NDRF. SE.

No.	Name	Builder	Launched	In service
T-AP 1001	*Empire State VI*	Newport News	16 Sep 1961	14 Oct 1988 acq 3 Jan 1990
	ex-*Cape Junction*, ex-*Mormactide* (1989), ex-*Oregon* (1977)			

Displacement	22,629 tons f/l; 12,304 grt
Dimensions	564'11" (oa) × 78'2" × 31'7"
Machinery	1 screw; steam turbines; 17,500 SHP; 20 knots
Complement	—

Notes: New York State Maritime Academy training ship.

Service Record: *Empire State*. RRF 1990–2004. Active, Ft Schuyler, NY, 1996. LU 1 Sep 2004 NDRF. SE.

T-AP 1002 *Golden Bear* added 5 Apr 1999. RRF 1999–2007 SE.
T-AP 1003 *Enterprise* RRF 2004. ex-*Cape Bon* (25 Oct 2002) NDRF. SE.

RANGE SUPPORT SHIPS

No.	Name	Builder	Launched	In service
T-AGDS 9642	*Seacor Clipper* ex-*Nicor Clipper* (1990)	Moss Point	20 Apr 1982	6 May 1987

Displacement	424 grt
Dimensions	253'11" (oa) × 44' × 13'
Machinery	2 screws; diesel; 6,000 bhp; 10 knots
Complement	—

Notes: Range support ship. RoRo cargo/tug.

Service Record: Chartered 1987–1997. Rechartered 1999. Deleted 2002.
Later history: Merchant *Elsa Leigh* 2002.

No.	Name	Builder	Launched	In service
—	*SeaMark III*	Bushey	1958	—

Displacement	550 tons f/l; 198 grt
Dimensions	150' (oa) × 50' × 9'3"
Machinery	1 screw; diesel; 1,800 bhp
Complement	4

Notes: Small cargo ship/tug used to support space tracking facilities in the Caribbean.

SUBMARINE SUPPORT VESSELS

No.	Name	Built	Acquired	GRT	Dimensions	Speed (knots)
SSV 4499	*C-Commando*	1997	Feb 1997	2,053 grt	220' × 56' × 16'5	11
MV 9999	*Carolyn Chouest*	1977	Jan 1994	2,543 grt	238' × 52' × 15'	12
AGDS 9642	*Cory Chouest* ex-*Far Clipper* (1987), ex-*Tender Clipper* (1986)	1974	Mar 1997	1,689 grt	266' × 59'6" × 14'	11
MV 4225	*Dolores Chouest*	1978	Dec 1978	294 grt	240' × 40' × 12'	13
MV	*Kellie Chouest*	1996	Feb 1996	2,786 grt	310' × 52' × 15'	13
MV	*Laney Chouest*	1985	1985	497 grt	234' × 50' × 14'	16
—	*Margaret B. Chouest*	1995	Nov 1995	—	320' × 60' × 19'	—

Notes: All chartered to USN. *Carolyn*, *Kellie* and *Dolores* are deep submergence support tenders for *NR-1* and other submersibles. *C-Commando* is support ship for ASDS. *Cory* is an acoustic research ship, has catamaran hull, operational in Hawaii area.
Builder: North American; Larose, La.; Utstein Hatlo, Ulsteinvik (*Cory*).

Service Records:
SSV 4499 *C-Commando* Based at Pearl Harbor.
MV 9999 *Carolyn Chouest* Based at Groton, Conn.
MV *Kellie Chouest* Based at San Diego.

MV 4225 *Dolores Chouest* Based at Norfolk.
MV *Laney Chouest* Deleted 30 Sep 1998. RTO.
  Later history: Merchant *Seaway Legend* 1998, *Acergy* 2006.
Cory Chouest: Based in Hawaii.
Margaret B. Chouest Support ship at Diego Garcia. Deleted 1993.

14
UNITED STATES COAST GUARD

Transferred from the Treasury Department to the Department of Transportation, 1 May 1967, and then to the Department of Homeland Security, 1 Mar 2003.

The principal peacetime missions of the Coast Guard are enforcement of laws and treaties, including enforcement of customs and immigration laws (including prevention of smuggling and narcotics), port safety, environmental protection, merchant marine safety, aids to navigation (lighthouses), search and rescue, and recreational boating safety. Since 2001 port security and anti-terrorism activities have required particular attention. Despite its vital domestic role in national security, Coast Guard units have been sent overseas, to Vietnam, and later to the Persian Gulf.

All Coast Guard ships are termed "cutters," and are generally identified by length. Coast Guard designations are derived from Navy designations with the prefix W. In 1966, a major redesignation was carried out. In 2004, a new series of designations was developed. Most cutters are painted white, and buoy tenders and tugs black. A blue and red stripe with the Coast Guard shield was painted on all ships starting April 1967.

CUTTERS IN SERVICE, 1947

WPG 319 *Champlain*   Recomm canceled. Sold 25 Mar 1948, BU.
WPG 321 *Itasca*   Recomm canceled. Sold 4 Oct 1950, BU
WPG 163 *Mocoma*   Recomm 20 Mar 1947. Went aground south of Fowey Rocks near Miami, 27 Mar 1950. Decomm 8 May 1950. Sold 15 Jul 1955.
WPG 164 *Sebec*   Recomm and renamed *Tampa*, 27 May 1947. Decomm 10 Aug 1954. Sold 16 Feb 1959.
WPG 79 *Onondaga*   Decomm 24 Jul 1947. Sold 7 Dec 1954, BU
WPG 80 *Tahoma*   Decomm 24 Oct 1947. Rec **WAGE 10**, 1 May 1952, examination vessel in Chesapeake Bay. Decomm 5 Junl 1953. Sold 17 Oct 1955.
     Later history: Merchant *Steers M.K.* SE1963.

Note: As examination vessel, *Tahoma* was painted yellow with the word "GUARD" in black painted on both sides.

Treasury Class

WPG 31 *Bibb*   Rescued 69 people from flying boat *Bermuda Sky Queen* which was forced to land in mid-Atlantic west of Bermuda, 14 Oct 1947. Decomm 30 Sep 1984. Sunk as artificial reef off Key Largo, Fla., Nov 1987.
     ★Vietnam Jul 1968–Feb 1969; PUC.
WPG 32 *Campbell*   Decomm 1 Apr 1982. Sunk as target off Hawaii, 29 Nov 1984.
     ★Vietnam Jan–Jul 1968.
WPG 33 *Duane*   Damaged by grounding in Hog Island Channel, 3 Aug 1971. Decomm 1 Aug 1985. Sunk as artificial reef near Key Largo, Fla., 27 Nov 1987.
     ★Vietnam Jan–Jul 1968.
WPG 35 *Ingham*   Sllightly damaged by fire, 10 May 1965. Decomm 27 May 1988.
     Later history: Museum at Patriots Point, SC.
     ★Vietnam Aug 1968–Feb 1969; 2 PUC.

Figure 14.1: *USCGC Bibb* (WPG 31), Treasury class cutter, 1950s.

WPG 36 *Spencer* Engineering training school 23 Jan 1974. Decomm 15 Dec 1980. Sold 8 Oct 1981, BU.
★Vietnam Feb–Sep 1969; PUC.
WPG 37 *Taney* Decomm 7 Dec 1986.
Later history: Museum at Baltimore, Md.
1★Korea 1951, 1952; ★Vietnam May–Sep 1969, Jan 1970.

Notes: Armament: 1946, 1–5″/38, 1 twin 40 mm, 8–20 mm, hedgehog (*Bibb, Spencer, Taney* only 2–20 mm); 1966 40 mm & 20 mm replaced by TT. Rec **WHEC**, 1 May 1966.

Owasco Class

WPG 39 *Owasco* Out of comm 1951–15 Aug 1955. Decomm 27 Jun 1973. Sold 7 Oct 1974, BU 1977.
★Vietnam Aug 1968–Mar 1969.
WPG 40 *Winnebago* Ran aground entering Pearl Harbor, 26 Mar 1962. Decomm 27 Feb 1973. Sold 7 Oct 1974, BU 1977.
1★Korea Dec 1951–Jan 1952, May–Jun 1952, Aug 1953; ★Vietnam Nov 1968–Jun 1969; PUC.
WPG 41 *Chautauqua* Damaged by fire at San Francisco, 20 Jan 1967. Decomm 1 Aug 1973. Sold, BU.
1★Korea 1952.
WPG 42 *Sebago* Out of comm 31 Oct 1949–17 Dec 1952. Decomm 29 Feb 1972. Sold 14 Apr 1972, BU.
★Vietnam Mar–Nov 1969.
WPG 43 *Iroquois* Went aground on reef off Midway, 29 Jun 1954, refloated 1 Jul. Decomm 13 Jan 1965. Sold 1 Jun 1965.
1★Korea 1951, 1952.
WPG 44 *Wachusett* Decomm 30 Aug 1973. Sold 18 Nov 1974, BU.
1★Korea Mar 1951, Feb 1952, Apr–May 1953; ★Vietnam Dec 1968–Apr 1969; 2 PUC.
WPG 64 *Escanaba* Engine disabled at sea off Virginia Beach, 19 Jan 1969. Decomm 28 Jun 1973. Sold 16 Jan 1974, BU Camden, NJ.
1★Korea 1951, 1952.
WPG 65 *Winona* Decomm 31 May 1974. Sold 1980, BU.
1★Korea 1951, 1952; ★Vietnam Feb–Oct 1968.
WPG 66 *Klamath* Decomm 1 May 1973. Sold 18 Nov 1974, BU.
1★Korea 1951–1953; ★Vietnam Jul–Sep 1969, Jan–Apr 1970.
WPG 67 *Minnetonka* Decomm 31 May 1974. BU 1974.
1★Korea 1952; ★Vietnam Jan–Sep 1968.
WPG 68 *Androscoggin* Out of comm 31 Oct 1949–8 May 1950. Decomm 27 Feb 1973. Sold 7 Oct 1974, BU.

Figure 14.2: *USCGC Escanaba* (WPG 64), Owasco class gunboat type cutter.

★Vietnam Dec 1967–Jul 1968; ◆Cuba May 1961, Cuba Missile Crisis Oct–Dec 1962.
WPG 69 *Mendota* Decomm 1 Nov 1973.
★Vietnam Mar–Oct 1969; PUC.
WPG 70 *Pontchartrain* Rescued all passengers from ditched airliner 1100 miles east of Honolulu, 16 Oct 1956. Decomm 19 Oct 1973.
1★Korea Mar 1952, Jul–Aug 1952, Jan–Mar 1953; ★Vietnam Mar–Nov 1970.

Note: Rec **WHEC**, 1 May 1966.

HIGH ENDURANCE CUTTERS

No.	ex-AVP	Acquired	Comm	Decomm
WAVP 370 *Casco*	12	1949	19 Apr 1949	21 Mar 1969
WAVP 371 *Mackinac*	13	21 Apr 1949	11 May 1949	28 Dec 1967
WAVP 372 *Humboldt*	21	Jan 1949	29 Mar 1949	30 Sep 1969
WAVP 373 *Matagorda*	22	7 Mar 1949	8 Jun 1949	1 Jan 1968
WAVP 374 *Absecon*	23	5 Jan 1949	May 1949	9 May 1972
WAVP 375 *Chincoteague*	24	7 Mar 1949	7 Mar 1949	21 Jun 1972
WAVP 376 *Coos Bay*	25	5 Jan 1949	4 May 1949	1 Sep 1966
WAVP 377 *Rockaway*	29	24 Dec 1948	24 Dec 1948	29 Jan 1972

Rec **WAGO 377**, 1965. Rec **WOLE 377**, 23 Sep 1971.

WAVP 378 *Half Moon*	26	Sep 1948	30 Jul 1948	15 Jul 1969

★Vietnam Jun–Dec 1967.

WAVP 379 *Unimak*	31	14 Sep 1948	3 Jan 1949	29 Apr 1988

Out of comm 31 May 1975–Aug 1977. Rec **WTR**, 28 Nov 1969–1977.

WAVP 380 *Yakutat*	32	31 Aug 1948	23 Nov 1948	1 Jan 1971

★Vietnam May–Dec 1967, Jun–Aug, Oct–Dec 1970; ◆Cuba Apr–May 1961.

WAVP 381 *Barataria*	33	Sep 1948	1 Aug 1949	29 Aug 1969

Damaged by engine room explosion off Unimak Island, Alaska, 24 Mar 1968.
★Vietnam May–Dec 1967; ◆Cuba Jan 1961.

WAVP 382 *Bering Strait*	34	14 Sep 1948	14 Dec 1948	1 Jan 1971

★Korea Dec 1951–Feb 1952, Jan–Feb 1954; ★Vietnam May 1967–Feb 1968, Jun–Aug, Nov–Dec 1970.

WAVP 383 *Castle Rock*	35	16 Sep 1948	18 Dec 1948	21 Dec 1971

★Vietnam Jul–Aug, Oct–Nov 1971.

WAVP 384 *Cook Inlet*	36	20 Sep 1948	15 Jan 1949	21 Dec 1971

★Vietnam Jul–Dec 1971; ◆Cuba Missile Crisis, Oct–Dec 1962.

WAVP 385 *Dexter*	11	19 Jul 1946	20 Sep 1946	18 Jan 1968

Out of comm 17 Dec 1952–30 Jun 1958. Sunk as target 1968.

WAVP 386 *McCulloch*	56	27 May 1946	25 Nov 1946	21 Jun 1972

Later history: Trfd to Vietnam, renamed *Ngo Kuyen*. Trfd to Philippines 1976, renamed *Gregorio de Pilar* (PS 8). R1990

WAVP 387 *Gresham*	57	26 Jun 1946	26 Jun 1946	25 Apr 1973

Out of comm Sep 1969–Jan 1970. Rec **WAGW 387**, 27 Feb 1970. Sold 25 Oct 1973, BU Rotterdam.
1★Korea Jan 1953; ★Vietnam May 1967–Jan 1968.

Notes: Rec **WHEC**, 1 May 1966. 370–384 loaned by USN, 385–387 transferred. Armament: 1–5″/38 gun. Balloon shelter added aft. For complete details, see pp. 168–9.

Hamilton Class

No.	Name	Builder	Keel Laid	Launched	Comm.
WHEC 715	*Hamilton*	Avondale	4 Jan 1965	18 Dec 1965	20 Feb 1967
WHEC 716	*Dallas*	Avondale	7 Feb 1966	1 Oct 1966	26 Oct 1967
WHEC 717	*Mellon*	Avondale	25 Jul 1966	11 Feb 1967	22 Dec 1967
WHEC 718	*Chase*	Avondale	15 Oct 1966	20 May 1967	1 Mar 1968
WHEC 719	*Boutwell*	Avondale	3 Dec 1966	17 Jun 1967	24 Jun 1968

WHEC 720	*Sherman*	Avondale	13 Feb 1967	23 Sep 1967	23 Aug 1968
WHEC 721	*Gallatin*	Avondale	17 Apr 1967	18 Nov 1967	20 Dec 1968
WHEC 722	*Morgenthau*	Avondale	17 Jul 1947	10 Feb 1968	14 Feb 1969
WHEC 723	*Rush*	Avondale	23 Oct 1967	16 Nov 1968	3 Jul 1969
WHEC 724	*Munro*	Avondale	18 Feb 1970	5 Dec 1970	27 Sep 1971
WHEC 725	*Jarvis*	Avondale	9 Sep 1970	24 Apr 1971	30 Dec 1971
WHEC 726	*Midgett*	Avondale	5 Apr 1971	4 Sep 1971	30 Mar 1972

Displacement	2,716 tons; 3,050 f/l
Dimensions	378′2″ (oa); 350′ (wl) × 42′9″ × 14′
Machinery	2 screws; CODOG; 2 gas turbines; 28,000 SHP 2 diesel; 7,200 bhp; 29 knots
Endurance	14,000/11 diesel; 2,400/29 GT
Complement	178
Armament	1–5″/38 gun, 1–3″/62, 1–20 mm Phalanx, Harpoon SSM
	1988–92: 1–76 mm/62, 2 Bushmaster, 1 Phalanx

Notes: 36 originally planned. Designed to operate as frigates in wartime. Retractable bow propeller for close maneuvering. Projected with DASH. Helicopter hangar, aluminum superstructure. ASW upgrade 1967–87; FRAM modernization 1988–92. ASW weapons removed 1992.

Service Records:

WHEC 715 *Hamilton*
★Vietnam Oct 1969–May 1970.

Figure 14.3: *USCGC Absecon* (WHEC 374), August 1971. A former Navy seaplane tender. (Kludas)

Figure 14.4: *USCGC Sherman* (WHEC 720), high endurance cutter about 1970 before FRAM refit.

Figure 14.5: *USCGC Gallatin* (WHEC 721), about 1995. High endurance cutter. Notice helicopter hangar and pad, Phalanx CIWS aft, and new gun forward.

WHEC 716 *Dallas*
★Vietnam Oct 1969–May 1970; ◆Persian Gulf 2003.
WHEC 717 *Mellon*
★Vietnam Feb–Jun 1970.
WHEC 718 *Chase* Damaged by engine room fire off Boston, 8 May 1985.
★Vietnam Nov 1969–May 1970; ◆Grenada Oct–Nov 1983, Indian Ocean May–Jun 1998.
WHEC 719 *Boutwell* Rescued 500 people from burning cruise ship *Prinsendam* in Gulf of Alaska, 1980.
◆Persian Gulf 2003.
WHEC 720 *Sherman*
★Vietnam May–Aug, Oct–Nov 1970.
WHEC 721 *Gallatin*
WHEC 722 *Morgenthau*
★Vietnam Dec 1970–Jul 1971.
WHEC 723 *Rush*
★Vietnam Nov 1970–Jun 1971.
WHEC 724 *Munro*
◆Tsunami relief 2005.
WHEC 725 *Jarvis* Went aground near Iliuliuk Bay, 15 Nov 1972.
WHEC 726 *Midgett*
◆Indian Ocean Aug–Sep 1999.

MARITIME SECURITY CUTTERS

No.	Name	Builder	Keel Laid	Launched	Comm.
WMSL 750	*Bertholf*	Ingalls	29 Mar 2005	29 Sep 2006	4 Aug 2008
WMSL 751	*Waesche*	Ingalls	11 Sep 2006	12 Jul 2008	—
WMSL 752	*Hamilton*	National	—	—	—

Displacement	3,206 tons; 4,112 f/l
Dimensions	421′5″ (oa); 390′ (wl) × 54′ × 21′7″
Machinery	2 screws; CODAG; 1 GT; 30,565 hp 2 diesel; 19,310 bhp; 28 knots
Endurance	12,000
Complement	150
Armament	1–57 mm/70, 1 Phalanx, helicopters

Notes: Designed as successor to the *Hamilton* class, for oceanic operations. Twin helicopter hangars. Originally designated National Security Cutters.

MEDIUM SECURITY CUTTERS

No.	Name	Builder	Keel Laid	Launched	Comm.
WMSM 915	—	—	—	—	—

Displacement	2,922 tons
Dimensions	341′ (oa) × 54′
Machinery	2 screws; diesel; 23 knots
Endurance	9,000
Complement	95
Armament	1–57 mm 1 h/c

Notes: Designed as successor to the *Bear* and *Reliance* classes, for oceanic operations. Stern ramp for interceptor boats.

Figure 14.6: *USCGC Bertholf* (WMSL, 750), the first of the new maritime security cutters, 2007.

MEDIUM ENDURANCE CUTTERS

No.	Name	ex-	Acq from USN	Fate
WMEC 76	*Ute*	ATF 76	30 Sep 1980	Stricken and rtnd to USN 26 May 1988. Sunk as target.
WMEC 85	*Lipan*	ATF 85	30 Sep 1980	Decomm 31 Mar 1988. R2tnd to USN 9 Jun 1988
WMEC 150	*Avoyel*	ATF 150	9 Jul 1956	Decomm 30 Sep 1969. Sold.
WMEC 153	*Chilula*	ATF 153	9 Jul 1956	Decomm 19 Jun and rtnd to USN 27 Jun 1991.
WMEC 165	*Cherokee*	ATF 66	29 Jun 1946	Decomm 30 Jan 1990. Stricken and rtnd to USN 28 Feb 1991. Sunk as target 1993.
WMEC 166	*Tamaroa* ex-*Zuni*	ATF 95	29 Jun 1946	Decomm 1 Feb 1994. Sank in drydock when crewmember opened valves, New York, 14 Mar 1963; salved. Trfd to Intrepid Museum 28 Feb 1994

Later history: Museum at Richmond, Va.

No.	Name	ex-	Acq from USN	Fate
WMEC 194	*Modoc* ex-*Bagaduce*	ATA 194	20 Apr 1959	Decomm 31 May 1979.

Later history: merchant *Modoc Pearl*. SE2004

No.	Name	ex-	Acq from USN	Fate
WMEC 202	*Comanche* ex-*Wampanoag*	ATA 202	25 Feb 1959	Decomm 30 Jan 1980.
WMEC 6	*Escape*	ARS 6	4 Dec 1980	Decomm 29 Jun 1995.
WAT/WAGO 167	*Acushnet* ex-*Shackle*	ARS 9	29 Jun 1946	Rec WMEC 167, 1978
WAT/WMEC 168	*Yocona* ex-*Seize*	ARS 26	28 Jun 1946	Decomm 14 Jun 1996. Sunk as target off Guam, 20 Jun 2006.

Notes: Acquired from USN. Former fleet tugs or salvage vessels. Rec WMEC, or WAGO (*Acushnet*), 1 May 1966.

Figure 14.7: *USCGC Tamaroa* (WMEC 166). The former Navy tug *Zuni* as medium endurance cutter.

Figure 14.8: *USCGC Active* (WMEC 618), medium edurance cutter, about 1970.

Reliance Class

No.	Name	Builder	Keel Laid	Launched	Comm.
WMEC 615	*Reliance*	Todd; Hosuton	29 Sep 1962	25 May 1963	20 Jun 1964
WMEC 616	*Diligence*	Todd; Houston	29 Aug 1962	20 Jul 1963	26 Aug 1964
WMEC 617	*Vigilant*	Todd; Houston	1 Jan 1963	23 Dec 1963	3 Oct 1964
WMEC 618	*Active*	Christy	29 Jun 1964	31 Jul 1965	30 Sep 1966
WMEC 619	*Confidence*	Curtis Bay	4 Aug 1964	8 May 1965	19 Feb 1966
WMEC 620	*Resolute*	Curtis Bay	17 May 1965	30 Apr 1966	5 Dec 1966
WMEC 621	*Valiant*	Amer; Lorain	28 Feb 1966	14 Jan 1967	7 Apr 1967
WMEC 622	*Courageous*	Amer; Lorain	14 Mar 1966	18 Mar 1967	6 Jun 1967
WMEC 623	*Steadfast*	Amer; Lorain	2 May 1966	24 Jun 1967	25 Sep 1968
WMEC 624	*Dauntless*	Amer; Lorain	24 Oct 1966	21 Oct 1967	10 Jun 1968
WMEC 625	*Venturous*	Amer; Lorain	14 Nov 1966	11 Nov 1967	16 Aug 1968
WMEC 626	*Dependable*	Amer; Lorain	13 Feb 1967	10 Jun 1967	5 Jan 1969
WMEC 627	*Vigorous*	Amer; Lorain	10 Nov 1967	4 May 1968	2 May 1969
WMEC 628	*Durable*	Curtis Bay	1 Jul 1966	29 Apr 1967	8 Dec 1967
WMEC 629	*Decisive*	Curtis Bay	29 Apr 1967	14 Dec 1967	23 Aug 1968
WMEC 630	*Alert*	Curtis Bay	5 Jan 68/25 Nov 1967	19 Oct 1968	4 Aug 1969
Displacement	950 tons; 1,007 f/l				
Dimensions	210′6″ (oa); 200′ (wl) × 34′ × 10′6″				
Machinery	2 screws; diesel; BHP 5,000; 18 knots				
Endurance	2,700/18				
Complement	74				
Armament	1–3″/50, replaced by 1 Bushmaster (1987–94)				

Notes: WPC rec WMEC, 1 May 1966. Modernized 1984–96. 615–619 modernized 1986–90, re-engined, stack added.

Service Records:

WMEC 615 *Reliance*   Rec **WTR 615**, Jun 1975. Rec **WMEC 615**, 16 Aug 1982.
WMEC 616 *Diligence*
WMEC 617 *Vigilant*
WMEC 618 *Active*
WMEC 619 *Confidence*
WMEC 620 *Resolute*   Slightly damaged in collision with cutter *Avoyel* south of San Francisco, 10 Jan 1968. Decomm 13 Sep 1996, SLEP.
WMEC 621 *Valiant*
WMEC 622 *Courageous*   Decomm and stricken 27 Sep 2001. Trfd to Sri Lanka 24 Jun 2004.
    Later history: renamed *Samadura* (P 621).
WMEC 623 *Steadfast*
WMEC 624 *Dauntless*
WMEC 625 *Venturous*
WMEC 626 *Dependable*
WMEC 627 *Vigorous*

Figure 14.9: *USCGC Harriet Lane* (WMEC 903), medium endurance cutter, "Famous" class.

WMEC 628 *Durable*   Decomm and stricken 20 Sep 2001. Trfd to Colombia 3 Sep 2003.
    Later history: renamed *Valle del Cauca* (44).
WMEC 629 *Decisive*   Seized Soviet trawler *Taras Shevchenko* 130 miles off Nantucket for violating 200-mile limit, 10 Apr 1977. Recomm 19 Apr 1999, after SLEP.
WMEC 630 *Alert*

Bear Class

No.	Name	Builder	Keel Laid	Launched	Comm.
WMEC 901	*Bear*	Tacoma	24 Aug 1979	25 Sep 1980	4 Feb 1983
WMEC 902	*Tampa*	Tacoma	12 Apr 1980	19 Mar 1981	16 Mar 1984
WMEC 903	*Harriet Lane*	Tacoma	15 Oct 1980	6 Feb 1982	20 Sep 1984
WMEC 904	*Northland*	Tacoma	9 Apr 1981	7 May 1982	17 Dec 1984
WMEC 905	*Spencer* ex-*Seneca* (30 Sep 1981)	Derecktor	26 Jun 1982	17 Apr 1984	28 Jun 1986
WMEC 906	*Seneca* ex-*Escanaba* or ex-*Pickering* (30 Sep 1981)	Derecktor	16 Sep 1982	17 Apr 1984	4 May 1987
WMEC 907	*Escanaba* ex-*Tahoma*	Derecktor	1 Apr 1983	2 Jun 1985	27 Aug 1987
WMEC 908	*Tahoma* ex-*Spencer* or ex-*Legare* (30 Sep 1981)	Derecktor	28 Jun 1983	2 Jun 1985	6 Apr 1987
WMEC 909	*Campbell* ex-*Argus* (30 Sep 1981)	Derecktor	10 Aug 1984	29 Apr 1986	19 Aug 1988
WMEC 910	*Thetis* ex-*Tahoma* (30 Sep 1981)	Derecktor	24 Aug 1984	29 Apr 1986	30 Jun 1989
WMEC 911	*Forward* ex-*Erie* (30 Sep 1981)	Derecktor	11 Jul 1986	18 Aug 1987	4 Aug 1989
WMEC 912	*Legare* ex-*McCulloch* (30 Sep 1981)	Derecktor	11 Jul 1986	18 Aug 1987	4 Aug 1989
WMEC 913	*Mohawk* ex-*Ewing* (30 Sep 1981)	Derecktor	18 Jun 1987	18 May 1988	20 Mar 1990
Displacement	1,200 tons; 1,820 tons f/l				
Dimensions	270′ (oa); 255′ (wl) × 38′ × 14′				
Machinery	2 screws; geared diesel; 7,200 bhp; 19.5 knots				
Endurance	3,850/19.5				
Complement	100				
Armament	1–76 mm AA, 1 helicopter				

Notes: Multipurpose cutters, low speed. Reputed to be poor sea boats. Officially known as the Famous Class.

260   The Navy of the Nuclear Age, 1947–2007

Service Records:
WMEC 901 *Bear*
WMEC 902 *Tampa*
WMEC 903 *Harriet Lane*
WMEC 904 *Northland*
WMEC 905 *Spencer*
WMEC 906 *Seneca*
WMEC 907 *Escanaba*
WMEC 908 *Tahoma*
WMEC 909 *Campbell*
WMEC 910 *Thetis*
WMEC 911 *Forward*
WMEC 912 *Legare*
WMEC 913 *Mohawk*

WMEC 38 *Storis*   see WAGL, p.270.

No.	Name	Builder	Keel Laid	Launched	Commd
WMEC 39	*Alex Haley* ex-*Edenton* (ATS 1)	Brooke Marine	28 Mar 1967	15 May 1968	10 Jul 1999

Displacement	2,650 tons; 3,200 f/l
Dimensions	288'8" (oa); 264' (wl) × 50' × 15'2"
Machinery	2 screws; diesel; 6,800 bhp; 16 knots
Endurance	10,000/13
Complement	99
Armament	2 Bushmaster, 1 helicopter

Notes: Former salvage tug transferred from USN 18 Nov 1997. Re-engined and rearmed, helicopter hangar added. Station: Kodiak, Alaska.

DESTROYER ESCORTS

No.	Name	ex-USN	to USCG	Returned to USN	
WDE 422	*Newell*	DE 322	20 Jul 1951	31 Mar 1954	1★Korea 1952
WDE 424	*Falgout*	DE 324	24 Aug 1951	21 May 1954	1★Korea 1952
WDE 425	*Lowe*	DE 325	20 Jul 1951	1 Jun 1954	1★Korea 1952
WDE 428	*Finch*	DE 328	24 Aug 1951	23 Aug 1954	1★Korea 1952
WDE 433	*Koiner*	DE 331	20 Jun 1951	19 May 1954	1★Korea 1952
WDE 434	*Forster*	DE 334	20 Jun 1951	25 May 1954	1★Korea 1952
WDE 482	*Ramsden*	DE 382	28 Mar 1952	10 Apr 1954	1★Korea 1953
WDE 485	*Richey*	DE 385	1 Dec 1952	Jun 1954	★Korea Aug–Nov 1953
WDE 487	*Vance*	DE 387	15 May 1952	16 Jun 1954	—
WDE 488	*Lansing*	DE 388	15 Jun 1952	29 Mar 1954	—
WDE 489	*Durant*	DE 389	15 May 1952	16 Jun 1954	Korea Nov 1953
WDE 491	*Chambers*	DE 391	11 Jun 1952	30 Jul 1954	—

Loaned from USN. Weather balloon shelter added aft of funnel. All stationed in Pacific.

PATROL VESSELS

WSC 125 *Active*   Laid up 1947–50. Decomm 2 Apr 1962. Sold 6 Sep 1963.
  Later history: Merchant *Haida*, 19.. *Mercy Ship*. SE1992
WSC 126 *Agassiz*   Decomm 13 Oct 1969. Trfd to USMMA.16 Oct 1969
  Later history: Merchant *Agassiz*. se1980 (USMMA, TS 16 Oct 69)
WSC 127 *Alert*   Decomm 10 Jan 1969. Sold 28 Oct 1969.
  Later history: Merchant *Alert*. SE1992.

Figure 14.10: USCGC *Durant* (WDE 489). Twelve destroyer escorts served in the Coast Guard 1951–54.

Figure 14.11: USCGC *Ewing* (WSC 137), 125-foot patrol vessel.

WSC 129 *Bonham*   Decomm 20 Apr 1959. Sold 30 Dec 1959.
  Later history: Merchant *Polar Star*. SE1992.
WSC 130 *Boutwell*   Port Isabel & Brownsville, Tex. Decomm 7 May 1963. Sold 16 May 1964.
  Later history: Merchant *State Bell*, renamed *Amoco Rebel* 1972, *Activa* 1979. SE1998.
WSC 131 *Cahoone*   Mount Edgecumbe, Alaska 1946; Galveston 1954. Decomm 11 Mar 1968. Sold 12 Dec 1968.
WSC 132 *Cartigan*   New York 1947; Galveston 1950; Panama City, Fla. 1953. Decomm 12 Oct 1968. Sold 9 Apr 1969.
  Later history: Merchant *Cartigan*. Abandoned 2004.
WSC 133 *Colfax*   Laid up 1948–51. Cape May, NJ. Decomm 9 Nov 1954. Sold 5 Jan 1956.
  Later history: Merchant *Colfax*, renamed *Cape Charles*. SE1980.
WSC 134 *Crawford*   Decomm 15 Aug 1947. Trfd to Woods Hole Inst. 28 Nov 1955.
  Later history: Merchant *Crawford*.
WSC 135 *Diligence*   San Pedro, Cal. Decomm 30 Sep 1961. Sold 30 Jan 1963, BU.
WSC 136 *Dix*   Decomm 13 Jan 1948. Sold 16 Jun 1948.
  Later history: Merchant *Valkyrie*.

WSC 137 *Ewing* — Laid up 1947–48. Decomm 23 Jun 1967. Sold 23 Jan 1969.
WSC 138 *Faunce* — Decomm 13 Jan 1948. Sold 16 Jun 1948.
   Later history: Merchant tug *Humble AC-2*, renamed *Myra White* 1961, *Vitow II* 1964, *Anastasia* 1975.
WSC 139 *Frederick Lee* — Decomm 15 Dec 1964. Sold 19 May 1966.
   Later history: Merchant *Virgil E.*, renamed *Taurus*. SE1992.
WSC 140 *General Greene* — Went aground in gale on Cape Cod, Mar 1960. Decomm and trfd to Newburyport, Mass., 15 Nov 1968.
   Later history: museum at Newburyport, Mass.
WSC 141 *Harriet Lane* — Decomm 29 Apr 1946. Sold 16 Jun 1948.
   Later history: Merchant *Humble AC-4*, renamed *Snipe*, *Roy-Von* 1973. SE1974.
WSC 143 *Kimball* — Laid up 1947–50. Ketchikan, Alaska 1950; Brownsville, Tex. 1958. Decomm 31 Dec 1968. Sold 24 Feb 1970.
WSC 144 *Legare* — Brownsville, Tex.; New Bedford, Mass.; Freeport, Mass. Decomm 5 Mar 1968. Sold 29 Nov 1968.
   Later history: Merchant *Kathryn*. SE1974.
WSC 145 *Marion* — Norfolk, Va. Decomm 15 Feb 1962. Sold 8 Mar 1963.
   Later history: Merchant *Top Cat*, renamed *Jupiter*.
WSC 146 *McLane* — Brownsville, Tex. Decomm 31 Dec 1968. Sold 14 Nov 1969.
   Later history: Merchant *Manatra II*. Abandoned 1987, but restored as museum ship, Muskegon, Mich. 1993.
WSC 147 *Morris* — San Pedro, Cal. Decomm 7 Aug 1970. Trfd to Sea Scouts, 5 Nov 1971.
   Later history: Merchant *Dauntless*.
WSC 148 *Nemaha* — Decomm 21 Jul 1947. Sold 14 Jun 1948.
   Later history: Merchant *Nemaha*, renamed *Sea Monarch II* 1952, *Le Roi* 1958, *International Tug* 1968, *Emerson I Den Den* SE1998.
WSC 150 *Reliance* — Decomm 8 Aug 1947. Sold 16 Jun 1948.
WSC 151 *Rush* — Decomm 21 Aug 1947. Sold 6 Jul 1948.
   Later history: Merchant tug *Humble AC-1*, 1964 *Vitow I*. SE1974.
WSC 152 *Tiger* — Decomm 12 Nov 1947. Sold 14 Jun 1948.
   Later history: Merchant *Tiger*, renamed *Cherokee*, *Polar Merchant* 1976. SE1992.
WSC 153 *Travis* — Port Everglades, Fla. Decomm 5 Jun 1962. Sold 15 Nov 1962.
   Later history: Merchant *State Chief*, renamed *Amoco Renegade* 1974, *Amalaka* 1976, *Lake Calvese* 1986. SE1998.
   ◆Cuba Jan–Jun 1961.
WSC 154 *Vigilant* — Decomm 9 Nov 1954. Sold 3 Jan 1956.
   Later history: Merchant *Vigilant*, renamed *Bunker Hill*. SE1974.
WSC 156 *Yeaton* — New London, Conn. Decomm 18 Jul 1969. Sold 16 Jul 1970.
   Later history: Merchant *Johnson*.
WSC 157 *Cuyahoga* — To USN (YX 21), 29 May 1933. Rec AG 26, 30 Nov 1937. Returned to USCG, 17 May 1941. **WIX 157** Sunk in collision with m/v *Santa Cruz II* off Smith Point, Va., 20 Oct 1978 (11 dead). Raised and sunk as artificial reef, 20 Mar 1979.

Note: Armament 1960: 1–40 mm gun

WPC 100 *Argo* — Decomm 30 Oct 1948. Sold 2 Nov 1955.
   Later history: Merchant *Circle Line XII*. SE1980.
WPC 101 *Ariadne* — Laid up 1946–1949. Decomm 23 Dec 1968. Sold 26 Sep 1969.
   ◆Cuba Missile Crisis Oct–Dec 1962.
WPC 102 *Atalanta* — Decomm 1 Aug 1950. Sold 7 Dec 1954.
   Later history: Merchant *Atalanta*. SE1980.
WPC 103 *Aurora* — Decomm 17 Jan 1968. Sold 16 Dec 1968.
   Later history: Merchant *Aurora*. SE1998.
   ◆Cuba Oct–Dec 1962, Dominican Rep May 1965.
WPC 104 *Calypso* — Decomm 25 Jul 1948. Sold 2 Nov 1955.
   Later history: Merchant *Circle Line XI*.
WPC 105 *Cyane* — Decomm 1 Aug 1950. Sold 7 Dec 1954.
   Later history: Merchant *Can Am*, renamed *Ruby E.* 1965. Sunk as fish reef at Mission Bay, Cal., 18 Jul 1989.
WPC 106 *Daphne* — Decomm 29 Nov 1946. Sold 7 Dec 1954.
   Later history: Merchant *Daphne*, renamed *Alaska Venture*, *Daphne*. SE1974–80.
WPC 107 *Dione* — Laid up 1947–51. Freeport, Tex. Decomm 8 Feb 1963. Sold 24 Feb 1964.
   Later history: Merchant *Big Trouble*, renamed *Delta I*, *Al Rashid* 1972. SE1992.
WPC 108 *Galatea* — Decomm 15 Mar 1948. Sold to Dominican Republic, 1 Jul 1948.
   Later history: renamed *Restauración* (P104/P206). SE1987.
WPC 109 *Hermes* — Decomm 2 Nov 1948. Sold 16 May 1958, BU Oakland, Cal.
WPC 110 *Icarus* — Decomm 21 Oct 1946. Sold to Dominican Republic, 1 Jul 1948.
   Later history: renamed *Independencia* (P105/P204). SE1987.
WPC 111 *Nemesis* — St. Petersburg, Fla. Decomm 20 Nov 1964. Sold 2 Feb 1966 BU (conv to restaurant).
   ◆Cuba Jan–Oct 1961, Cuba Missile Crisis Oct–Dec 1962.
WPC 112 *Nike* — Gulfport, Miss. Decomm 5 Nov 1964. Sold 9 May 1966.
   Later history: Merchant *Circle Line XVI*. SE1980.
WPC 113 *Pandora* — Decomm 1 May 1959. Sold 4 Nov 1959.
WPC 114 *Perseus* — San Diego. Decomm 26 Jun 1959. Sold 4 Nov 1959.
   Later history: Merchant *Circle Line XV*. SE1980.
WPC 115 *Thetis* — Decomm 1 Jul 1947. Sold to Dominican Republic, 1 Jul 1948.
   Later history: renamed *Rafael Atoa* (P106), then *Libertad*. (P205). SE1987.
WPC 116 *Triton* — Gulf of Mexico. Decomm 12 Jan 1967. Sold 16 Jan 1969.
   Later history: Merchant *Circle Line XVII*. SE1980.

No.	Name	former	trfd	fate
WPC 120	*Jackson*	PCER 858	28 Feb 1946	Decomm 24 Jul 1947
WPC 121	*Bedloe*	PCER 860	18 Sep 1946	Decomm 17 Jul 1947, sold 23 Dec 1947

Notes: Acquired from USN, sold because of shortage of personnel.

PATROL BOATS

Former USN submarine chasers acquired as air rescue boats:

No.	Name	ex-USN	Acquired	No.	Name	ex-USN	Acquired
WAVR 411	Air Avocet	SC-453	20 Nov 1945	WAVR 447	Air Penguin	SC-1010	6 Dec 1945
WAVR 412	Air Brant	SC-499	11 Oct 1945	WAVR 448	Air Petrel	SC-1013	23 Oct 1945
WAVR 413	Air Cardinal	SC-511	11 Oct 1945	WAVR 449	Air Pheasant	SC-1015	11 Oct 1945
WAVR 414	Air Condor	SC-512	24 Oct 1945	WAVR 450	Air Phoebe	SC-1016	23 Oct 1945
WAVR 415	Air Cormorant	SC-536	19 Feb 1946	WAVR 451	Air Pigeon	SC-1017	30 Oct 1945
WAVR 416	Air Crow	SC-539	4 Dec 1945	WAVR 452	Air Piper	SC-1022	9 Oct 1945
WAVR 417	Air Curlew	SC-540	11 Oct 1945	WAVR 453	Air Plover	SC-1023	23 Oct 1945
WAVR 418	Air Drake	SC-541	30 Oct 1945	WAVR 454	Air Puffin	SC-1027	10 Dec 1945
WAVR 419	Air Eider	SC-635	8 Oct 1945	WAVR 455	Air Quail	SC-1028	8 Jan 1946
WAVR 420	Air Egret	SC-642	24 Jan 1946	WAVR 456	Air Raven	SC-1032	29 Nov 1945
WAVR 421	Air Falcon	SC-653	30 Oct 1945	WAVR 457	Air Redwing	SC-1033	4 Dec 1945
WAVR 422	Air Finch	SC-656	17 Jan 1946	WAVR 458	Air Robin	SC-1037	16 Jan 1946
WAVR 423	Air Gannet	SC-659	5 Dec 1945	WAVR 459	Air Rook	SC-1038	25 Jan 1946
WAVR 424	Air Goose	SC-662	23 Oct 1945	WAVR 460	Air Ruff	SC-1054	21 Feb 1946
WAVR 425	Air Graylag	SC-665	tfr canceled	WAVR 461	Air Sheldrake	SC-1055	27 Nov 1945
WAVR 426	Air Grebe	SC-670	19 Mar 1946	WAVR 462	Air Shrike	SC-1062	23 Oct 1945
WAVR 427	Air Gull	SC-672	11 Oct 1945	WAVR 463	Air Skimmer	SC-1063	23 Oct 1945
WAVR 428	Air Hawk	SC-682	23 Oct 1945	WAVR 464	Air Skylark	SC-1064	30 Oct 1945
WAVR 429	Air Heron	SC-684	12 Jan 1946	WAVR 465	Air Snipe	SC-1068	28 Feb 1946
WAVR 430	Air Ibis	SC-710	11 Oct 1945	WAVR 466	Air Sparrow	SC-1069	6 Dec 1945
WAVR 431	Air Jay	SC-711	9 Oct 1945	WAVR 467	Air Starling	SC-1070	4 Dec 1945
WAVR 432	Air Kestrel	SC-714	1 Dec 1945	WAVR 468	Air Stork	SC-1296	11 Oct 1945
WAVR 433	Air Killdeer	SC-715	9 Jan 1946	WAVR 469	Air Swallow	SC-1297	23 Oct 1945
WAVR 434	Air Lapwing	SC-717	30 Oct 1945	WAVR 470	Air Swan	SC 1339	15 Nov 1945
WAVR 435	Air Linnet	SC-753	1 Dec 1945	WAVR 471	Air Swift	SC 1340	30 Oct 1945
WAVR 436	Air Loon	SC-758	24 Jan 1946	WAVR 472	Air Tanager	SC 1347	21 Nov 1945
WAVR 437	Air Mallard	SC-772	7 Dec 1945	WAVR 473	Air Teal	SC 1348	30 Oct 1945
WAVR 438	Air Martin	SC-775	27 Mar 1946	WAVR 474	Air Tern	SC 1355	23 Oct 1945
WAVR 439	Air Merlin	SC-985	30 Oct 1945	WAVR 475	Air Thrush	SC 1356	9 Oct 1945
WAVR 440	Air Oriole	SC-987	11 Oct 1945	WAVR 476	Air Toucan	SC 1357	24 Oct 1945
WAVR 441	Air Owl	SC-988	11 Oct 1945	WAVR 477	Air Warbler	SC 1362	8 Feb 1946
WAVR 442	Air Parrakeet	SC-989	30 Oct 1945	WAVR 478	Air Waxwing	SC 1367	10 Jan 1946
WAVR 443	Air Parrot	SC-996	30 Oct 1945	WAVR 479	Air Willet	SC 1369	7 Feb 1946
WAVR 444	Air Partridge	SC-1003	20 Nov 1945	WAVR 480	Air Wren	SC 1373	30 Jan 1946
WAVR 445	Air Peacock	SC-1004	3 Dec 1945	WAVR 481	Air Scaup	SC-1307	12 Feb 1946
WAVR 446	Air Pelican	SC-1009	3 Dec 1945	WAVR 482	Air Scooter	SC 1329	7 Feb 1946

95-Foot Class (Cape class)

No.	Name	Completed	Fate
W-95300	Cape Small	17 Jul 1953	Trfd to Marshall Islands 13 Apr 1987, renamed *Ionmeto 2*. R1992
W-95301	Cape Coral	21 Sep 1953	Stricken 1987
W-95302	Cape Higgon	14 Oct 1953	Trfd to Uruguay 5 Jan 1990; renamed *Colonia* (P10); SE2001
W-95303	Cape Upright	2 Jul 1953	Trfd to Bahamas 30 Jun 1989; renamed *David Tucker* (P 07); R1995
W-95304 (i)			Trfd to Ethiopia, *PC-11*; Lost Apr 1977
W-95304	Cape Gull	8 Jun 1953	Decomm 15 May 1986; scuttled 1989
W-95305	Cape Hatteras	28 Jul 1953	Decomm 14 Mar 1991; trfd to Mexico, renamed *Cabo Catoche* (P 44), SE2001
W-95306	Cape George	10 Aug 1953	Decomm 3 Sep 1989; trfd to Palau 10 Jun 1990, tfr canc FFU
W-95307	Cape Current	24 Aug 1953	Decomm 1 May 1989; trfd to Bahamas, 30 Jun 1989, renamed *Austin Smith* (P 08); R1995 ◆Cuba Oct–Dec 1962.
W-95308	Cape Strait	10 Sep 1953	Decomm 21 Jan 1983
W-95309	Cape Carter	7 Dec 1953	Decomm 19 Jan 1990; trfd to Mexico 2 Mar 1990, renamed *Jalisco*, renamed *Cabo Corrientes* (P 42); SE2001
W-95310 (i)			Trfd to Ethiopia, *PC-12*
W-95310	Cape Wash	15 Dec 1953	Decomm 1 Jun 1987, to USN, ren. *Venture*, patrol boat; SE2005
W-95311	Cape Hedge	21 Dec 1953	Decomm 7 Jan 1987; to USN, ren. *Vanguard*; trfd to Mexico 27 Apr 1990, renamed *Nayarit*, renamed *Cabo Corzo* (P 43); SE2001.
W-95312	Cape Knox	13 Jun 1955	Decomm 10 Feb 1989 ◆Cuba Oct–Dec 1962.
W-95313	Cape Morgan	5 Jul 1955	Trfd to Bahamas 20 Oct 1989, renamed *Fort Fincastle* (P 11); R1999 ◆Cuba Jan 1961–Oct 1962, Cuba missile crisis Oct–Dec 1962.
W-95314	Cape Fairweather	18 Jul 1955	Decomm 4 Mar 1986 ◆Cuba missile crisis Oct–Dec 1962.
W-95315	—	1 Aug 1955	Trfd to Haiti 26 Feb 1956, renamed *Vertières*, renamed *La Crète à Pierrot*.

Figure 14.12: *USCGC Cape Fox* (WPB 95316), 95-foot patrol boat.

W-95316	*Cape Fox*	22 Aug 1955	Trfd to Bahamas 30 Jun 1989, renamed *San Salvador II* (P 10); R1999
W-95317	*Cape Jellison*	7 Sep 1955	Decomm 12 Dec 1986; trfd to Sea Scouts 1993.
W-95318	*Cape Newagen*	26 Sep 1955	Stricken; trfd to Mexico 1982
W-95319	*Cape Romain*	11 Oct 1955	Decomm 11 Aug 1989; to USN; stricken 1993
W-95320	*Cape Starr*	15 Aug 1956	Decomm 16 Jan 1987
W-95321	*Cape Cross*	20 Aug 1958	Decomm 20 Mar 1990; trfd to Micronesia 30 Mar 1990, renamed *Paluwlap*
W-95322	*Cape Horn*	3 Sep 1958	Decomm 25 Jan 1990; trfd to Uruguay 5 Jan 1990, renamed *Rio Negro* (P11); SE2001
W-95323	*Cape Darby*	3 Oct 1958	Trfd to Korea 24 Mar 1969, renamed *PB–11*; R1984 ◆Cuba Jan 1961–Oct 1962, Cuba missile crisis Oct–Dec 1962.
W-95324	*Cape Shoalwater*	9 Dec 1958	Trfd to Bahamas 30 Jun 1989, renamed *Fenrick Sturrup* (P 06); R1995 ◆Cuba Jan 1961–Oct 1962, Cuba missile crisis Oct–Dec 1962
W-95325	*Cape Florida*	28 Oct 1958	Trfd to Korea 13 Nov 1968, renamed *PB-7*; lost 1971
W-95326	*Cape Corwin*	14 Nov 1958	Decomm 6 Apr 1990; trfd to Micronesia 30 Sep 1990, renamed *Constitution*
W-95327	*Cape Porpoise*	21 Nov 1958	Trfd to Korea 13 Nov 1968, renamed *PB-8*; R1984
W-95328	*Cape Henlopen*	5 Dec 1958	Trfd to Costa Rica 28 Sep 1989, renamed *Astronauta Franklin Chang* (SP 951); SE 2001
W-95329	*Cape Kiwanda*	28 Apr 1959	Trfd to Korea 24 Mar 1969, renamed *PB-12*; R1984
W-95330	*Cape Falcon*	12 May 1959	Trfd to Korea 13 Nov 1968, renamed *PB-9*; R1984
W-95331	*Cape Trinity*	26 May 1959	Trfd to Korea 13 Nov 1968, renamed *PB-10*; R1984 ◆Cuba Jan 1961–Oct 1962, Cuba missile crisis Oct–Dec 1962
W-95332	*Cape York*	9 Jun 1959	Trfd to Bahamas 30 Jun 1989, renamed *Edward William* (P 08); R1995
W-95333	*Cape Rosier*	23 Jun 1959	Trfd to Korea 24 Sep 1968, renamed *PB-3*; R1984
W-95334	*Cape Sable*	7 Jul 1959	Trfd to Korea 24 Sep 1968, renamed *PB-5*; R1984
W-95335	*Cape Providence*	21 Jul 1959	Trfd to Korea 24 Sep 1968, renamed *PB-6*; R1984

Displacement	105 tons; 321–335: 98 tons
Dimensions	95′ (oa) × 19′ × 5′
Machinery	2 screws; diesel; BHP 2,200; 20 knots
Endurance	2,600/9 (95300–311), 3,000/9 (95312–320), 1,500/8 (95321–335)
Complement	14
Armament	300–311: 2–20 mm. 312–320: 1–40 mm 321–335: 1–20 mm

Notes: Intended for harbor patrol and coastal ASW. Four built for Iran. Named Jan 1964. Built by Curtis Bay. Modernized 1977–80, new engines, electronics.

82-Foot Class (Point Class)

No.	Name	Completed	Fate
W-82301	*Point Caution*	5 Oct 1960	Trfd to Vietnam 29 Apr 1970, renamed *Nguyen An* (HQ716); SE1972
			★Vietnam Jul 1965–Apr 1970. PUC
W-82302	*Point Hope*	5 Oct 1960	Trfd to Costa Rica 3 May 1991, renamed *Colonel Alfonso Monje* (SP 281); SE2001
W-82303	*Point Young*	26 Oct 1960	Trfd to Vietnam 16 Mar 1970, renamed *Tran Lo*, (HQ714); SE1972
			★Vietnam Oct 1965–Jul 1969.
W-82304	*Point League*	9 Nov 1960	Trfd to Vietnam 16 May 1969, renamed *Le Phuoc Duc* (HQ701), renamed *Le Van Nga*; SE1972
			★Vietnam Jun 1966–May 1969.
W-82305	*Point Partridge*	23 Nov 1960	Trfd to Vietnam 27 Mar 1970, renamed *Bui Viet Thanh* (HQ715); SE1972
			★Vietnam Feb 1966–Mar 1970.
W-82306	*Point Jefferson*	7 Dec 1960	Trfd to Vietnam 21 Feb 1970, renamed *LeDgoc An* (HQ712); SE1972
			★Vietnam Feb 1966–Feb 1970.
W-82307	*Point Glover*	7 Dec 1960	Trfd to Vietnam 14 Feb 1970, renamed *Dao Van Danh* (HQ711); SE1972
			★Vietnam Aug 1965–Feb 1969. PUC
W-82308	*Point White*	18 Feb 1961	Trfd to Vietnam 12 Jan 1970, renamed *Le Dinh Hang* (HQ708); SE1972
			★Vietnam Mar 1966–Jan 1970. PUC (2)
W-82309	*Point Arden*	1 Feb 1961	Trfd to Vietnam 14 Feb 1970, renamed *Pham Nguc Chau* (HQ710); SE1972
			★Vietnam Jul 1965–Feb 1970. PUC
W-82310	*Point Garnet*	15 Mar 1961	Trfd to Vietnam 16 May 1969, renamed *Le Van Nea* (HQ700); renamed *Le Phuoc Dui* SE1972
			★Vietnam Aug 1965–May 1969.
W-82311	*Point Verde*	15 Mar 1961	Trfd to Mexico 12 Jun 1991, renamed *Punto Morro* (P 60); SE2001
W-82312	*Point Swift*	22 Mar 1961	Decomm 30 Mar 1995.
W-82313	*Point Slocum*	12 Apr 1961	Trfd to Vietnam 11 Dec 1969, renamed *Nguyen Ngoc Thach* (HQ706)
			◆Cuba missile crisis Oct–Dec 1962, Vietnam Feb 1966–Dec 1969.
W-82314	*Point Thatcher*	13 Sep 1961	Decomm 13 Mar 1992, training

W-82315	*Point Clear*	25 Apr 1961	Trfd to Vietnam 15 Sep 1969, renamed *Huynh Van Duc* (HQ702)
	★Vietnam Aug 1965–Sep 1969.		
W-82316	*Point Mast*	10 May 1961	Trfd to Vietnam 15 Jun 1970, renamed *Ho Dang La* (HQ721)
	★Vietnam Aug 1965–Jun 1970. PUC (2)		
W-82317	*Point Comfort*	24 Mar 1961	Trfd to Vietnam 17 Nov 1969, renamed *Dao Thuc* (HQ704)
	★Vietnam Aug 1965–Nov 1969. PUC		
W-82318	*Point Herron*	14 Jun 1961	Trfd to Mexico 21 Jun 1991, renamed *Punta Nastun* (P 61). SE2001
W-82319	*Point Orient*	28 Jun 1961	Trfd to Vietnam 14 Jul 1970, renamed *Nguyen Kim Hung* (HQ723)
	★Vietnam Jul 1965–Jul 1970. PUC		
W-82320	*Point Kennedy*	19 Jul 1961	Trfd to Vietnam 16 Mar 1970, renamed *Huynh Van Ngan* (HQ713)
	★Cuba missile crisis Oct–Dec 1962, Vietnam Feb 1966–Mar 1970.		
W-82321	*Point Lomas*	9 Aug 1961	Trfd to Vietnam 26 May 1970, renamed *Van Dien* (HQ718)
	★Vietnam Feb 1966–May 1970. PUC		
W-82322	*Point Hudson*	30 Aug 1961	Trfd to Vietnam 11 Dec 1969, renamed *Dan Van Hoanh* (HQ707)
	★Vietnam Feb 1966–Dec 1969.		
W-82323	*Point Grace*	27 Sep 1961	Trfd to Vietnam 15 Jun 1970, renamed *Dam Thoai*, (HQ720)
	★Vietnam Feb 1966–Jun 1970. PUC (2)		
W-82324	*Point Grey*	11 Oct 1961	Trfd to Vietnam 14 Jul 1970, renamed *Nuy Bo*, (HQ722), *Huynh Bo*
	★Vietnam Aug 1965–Jul 1970.		
W-82325	*Point Dume*	1 Nov 1961	Trfd to Vietnam 14 Feb 1970, renamed *Truong Tru Yen*, (HQ709), *Thuong Tien*
	★Vietnam Jul 1965–Feb 1970. PUC		
W-82326	*Point Cypress*	22 Nov 1961	Trfd to Vietnam 15 Aug 1970, renamed *Ho Day* (HQ725)
	★Vietnam Feb 1966–Aug 1970. PUC (2)		
W-82327	*Point Banks*	13 Dec 1961	Trfd to Vietnam 26 May 1970, renamed *Ngo Van Quyen* (HQ719)
	★Vietnam Mar–Apr 1967.		
W-82328	*Point Gammon*	31 Jan 1962	Trfd to Vietnam 11 Nov 1969, renamed *Nguyen Dao* (HQ703)
	★Vietnam Jul 1965–Nov 1969. PUC		
W-82329	*Point Welcome*	14 Feb 1962	Trfd to Vietnam 29 Apr 1970, renamed *Nguyen Han* (HQ717); damaged in error by US aircraft off DMZ, Vietnam, 12 Aug 1966 (2 killed)
	★Vietnam Jul 1965–Apr 1970.		
W-82330	*Point Ellis*	28 Feb 1962	Trfd to Vietnam 9 Dec 1969, renamed *Le Ngoc Thanh* (HQ705)
	★Vietnam Jul 1965–Dec 1969. PUC		
W-82331	*Point Marone*	14 Mar 1962	Trfd to Vietnam 15 Aug 1970, renamed *Truong Ba* (HQ724)
	★Vietnam Aug 1965–Aug 1970. PUC (2)		
W-82332	*Point Roberts*	6 Jun 1962	Decomm Feb 1992
W-82333	*Point Highland*	27 Jun 1962	Decomm 14 Jul 2001; trfd to Trinidad and Tobago, renamed *Bacolet Point* (CG 10)

Figure 14.13: *CGC Point Gammon* (WPB 82328), 82-foot patrol boat, in Vietnam grey. She was transferred to Vietnam in 1969.

W-82334	*Point Ledge*	18 Jul 1962	Went aground at Charlotte Amalie, VI, during hurricane, 16 Sep 1995; stricken 30 Aug 1998; trfd to Venezuela, renamed *Albatros* (PG 33); SE2001
W-82335	*Point Countess*	8 Aug 1962	Decomm 29 Jun 2000; trfd to Georgia, renamed *Tsotne Dadiani*
W-82336	*Point Glass*	29 Aug 1962	Decomm 9 Apr 2001 and trfd to NOAA
W-82337	*Point Divide*	19 Sep 1962	Decomm 30 Mar 1995; to Washington Academy
W-82338	*Point Bridge*	10 Oct 1962	Decomm 28 Sep 2001 and tfrd to Costa Rica, renamed *Pancho Carrasco* (82-4)
W-82339	*Point Chico*	29 Oct 1962	Decomm 14 Jun 2001 and trfd to Costa Rica, renamed *Juan Rafael Mora* (82-3)
W-82340	*Point Batan*	21 Nov 1962	Decomm 17 Sep 1999; trfd to Dominican Republic 1 Oct 1999, renamed *Aries*
W-82341	*Point Lookout*	12 Dec 1962	Decomm 24 Mar 1994; scuttled as reef 1997.
W-82342	*Point Baker*	30 Oct 1963	Decomm 12 Feb 2002 and trfd to Georgia, renamed *Niko Nikoladze*, ren. *Gen. Mazniashvili*
W-82343	*Point Wells*	30 Nov 1963	Decomm 13 Oct 2000 and trfd to Colombia, renamed *Cabo Manglares*
W-82344	*Point Estero*	11 Dec 1963	Decomm 8 Feb 2001 and trfd to Colombia, renamed *Cabo Tiboun* (143)
W-82345	*Point Judith*	26 Jul 1966	Decomm, trfd to Venezuela 20 Dec 1991, renamed *Alcatraz* (PG 32) SE2001
W-82346	*Point Arena*	26 Aug 1966	Decomm 30 Mar 1995
W-82347	*Point Bonita*	12 Sep 1966	Decomm 14 Nov 2000. Trfd to Trinidad and Tobago, renamed *Galera Point*
W-82348	*Point Barrow*	4 Oct 1966	Decomm, Trfd to Panama 7 Jun 1991, renamed *Tres de Noviembre* (P 204); SE2001
W-82349	*Point Spencer*	20 Oct 1966	Damaged by fire SW of Galveston, Tex., 28 May 1998; decomm 12 Dec 2000; trfd to Dominican Republic, renamed *Sirius*

W-82350	*Point Franklin*	14 Nov 1966	Trfd to Venezuela 23 Jun 1998, renamed *Pelicano* (PG 34); SE2001
W-82351	*Point Bennett*	19 Dec 1966	Decomm 12 Feb 1999 and trfd to Trinidad and Tobago, renamed *Corozal Point*
W-82352	*Point Sal*	5 Dec 1966	Decomm 24 May 2001 and trfd to Colombia, 29 May 2001, renamed *Cabo de la Vela* (144)
W-82353	*Point Monroe*	27 Dec 1966	Decomm 19 Aug 2001 and trfd to NOAA
W-82354	*Point Evans*	10 Jan 1967	Decomm 16 Nov 1999; trfd to Philippines 16 Nov 1999
W-82355	*Point Hannon*	23 Jan 1967	Decomm 11 Jan 2001 and trfd to Panama, renamed *Cinco de Noviembre*
W-82356	*Point Francis*	3 Feb 1967	Decomm 9 Mar 1999. Trfd to Panama 21 Apr 1999, renamed *10 de Noviembre* (P 207); SE2001
W-82357	*Point Huron*	17 Feb 1967	Decomm 21 Apr 1999; trfd to Panama 21 Apr 1999, renamed *28 de Noviembre* (P 206); SE2001
W-82358	*Point Stuart*	17 Mar 1967	Decomm 3 May 2001 and trfd to El Salvador, 12 May 2001, renamed *GC-12*
W-82359	*Point Steele*	26 Apr 1967	Decomm 9 Jul 1998; trfd to Antigua, renamed *Hermitage* (P 03); SE2001
W-82360	*Point Winslow*	3 Mar 1967	Decomm 22 Sep 2000; trfd to Panama, renamed *Cuatro de Noviembre*
W-82361	*Point Charles*	15 May 1967	Decomm 13 Dec 1991; trfd to Texas A&M Univ; 1991
W-82362	*Point Brown*	30 Mar 1967	Decomm 30 Sep 1991; trfd to Kingsborough Comm. College, NY
W-82363	*Point Nowell*	13 Jun 1967	Decomm 19 Oct 1999 and trfd to Jamaica, renamed *Savanna Point*
W-82364	*Point Whitehorn*	13 Jul 1967	Decomm 30 Mar 1995; scuttled as reef 1997
W-82365	*Point Turner*	14 Apr 1967	Decomm 3 Apr 1998; trfd to St. Lucia, renamed *Alphonse Reynolds*
W-82366	*Point Lobos*	29 May 1967	Decomm 13 Oct 2001 and trfd to NOAA
W-82367	*Point Knoll*	27 Jun 1967	Decomm 11 Sep 1991; trfd to Venezuela, renamed *Petrel* (PG 31); SE2001
W-82368	*Point Warde*	14 Aug 1967	Decomm 30 Jun 2000; trfd to Colombia, renamed *Cabo Corrientes*
W-82369	*Point Heyer*	2 Aug 1967	Decomm 11 Dec 1998; trfd to Trinidad and Tobago 12 Feb 1999, renamed *Crown Point*
W-82370	*Point Richmond*	25 Aug 1967	Decomm 30 Sep 1997; trfd to Ecuador 22 Aug 1997, renamed *24 de Mayo*; SE2001
W-82371	*Point Barnes*	21 Apr 1970	Decomm 12 Jan 2000; trfd to Jamaica, renamed *Belmont Point*
W-82372	*Point Brower*	21 Apr 1970	Decomm 12 Sep 2001; trfd to Azerbaijan, 28 Jan 2003, renamed *S-201*
W-82373	*Point Camden*	4 May 1970	Decomm 10 Dec 1999; trfd to Costa Rica 12 Dec 1999, renamed *Santa Maria* (SP 822)
W-82374	*Point Carrew*	18 May 1970	Decomm 22 Aug 2000; trfd to Argentina, renamed *Rio Santiago*
W-82375	*Point Doran*	1 Jun 1970	Decomm 22 Mar 2001 and trfd to Philippines, renamed *Brigadier Abraham Campo* (PG 396)
W-82376	*Point Harris*	22 Jun 1970	Stricken 12 Apr 1992; damaged in hurricane at Kauai, Hawaii, 11 Sep 1992
W-82377	*Point Hobart*	13 Jul 1970	Decomm 8 Jul 1999, trfd to Argentina 12 Jul 1999, renamed *Punta Mogotes*
W-82378	*Point Jackson*	3 Aug 1970	Decomm 30 May 2000; trfd to Turkmenistan, renamed *Merjen*
W-82379	*Point Martin*	20 Aug 1970	Decomm 24 Aug 1999; trfd to Dominican Republic 1 Oct 1999, renamed *Antares*

Displacement	67–69 tons
Dimensions	82′10″ (oa) × 17′2″ × 5′9″
Machinery	2 screws; diesel; 1,600 BHP; 23.5 knots
Complement	10
Armament	MG

Notes: Built between 1960 and 1970 at Curtis Bay, except 82345–349 by Martinac. Designed for port security and search-and-rescue. Named Jan 1964.

Island Class

No.	Name	Builder	Launched	Comm.
WPB 1301	*Farallon*	Bollinger	27 Aug 1985	15 Nov 1985
WPB 1302	*Manitou*	Bollinger	9 Oct 1985	24 Jan 1986
	Decomm 19 Jul 2004 for conversion. Decomm 17 Apr 2007			
WPB 1303	*Matagorda*	Bollinger	15 Dec 1985	25 Apr 1986
	Decomm 23 Jan 2003 for conversion, recomm 5 Mar 2004. Decomm 17 Apr 2007			
WPB 1304	*Maui*	Bollinger	13 Jan 1985	22 Mar 1986
	◆Persian Gulf Jul 2004–			
WPB 1305	*Monhegan*	Bollinger	15 Feb 1985	16 Jun 1986
	Decomm 7 Jan 2004 for conversion, recomm 4 Oct 2005. Decomm 17 Apr 2007			
WPB 1306	*Nunivak*	Bollinger	15 Mar 1986	4 Jul 1986
	Decomm 2 Mar 2004 for conversion, recomm 15 Feb 2005. Decomm 17 Apr 2007			
WPB 1307	*Ocracoke*	Bollinger	12 Apr 1986	4 Aug 1986
WPB 1308	*Vashon*	Bollinger	10 May 1986	15 Aug 1986
	Decomm 19 Apr 2004 for conversion, recomm 9 Mar 2005. Decomm 17 Apr 2007			
WPB 1309	*Aquidneck*	Bollinger	14 Jun 1986	26 Sep 1986
	◆Persian Gulf 2003			
WPB 1310	*Mustang*	Bollinger	11 Jul 1986	29 Aug 1986
WPB 1311	*Naushon*	Bollinger	22 Aug 1986	3 Oct 1986
WPB 1312	*Sanibel*	Bollinger	3 Oct 1986	14 Nov 1986
WPB 1313	*Edisto*	Bollinger	21 Nov 1986	7 Jan 1987
WPB 1314	*Sapelo*	Bollinger	8 Jan 1987	24 Feb 1987
WPB 1315	*Matinicus*	Bollinger	26 Feb 1987	16 Apr 1987
WPB 1316	*Nantucket*	Bollinger	17 Apr 1987	4 Jun 1987
WPB 1317	*Attu*	Bollinger	4 Dec 1987	9 May 1988
	Decomm 2003 for conversion, recomm 2 Aug 2004. Decomm 17 Apr 2007			
WPB 1318	*Baranof*	Bollinger	15 Jan 1988	20 May 1988
	◆Persian Gulf 2003			
WPB 1319	*Chandeleur*	Bollinger	19 Feb 1988	8 Jun 1988
WPB 1320	*Chincoteague*	Bollinger	25 Mar 1988	8 Aug 1988
WPB 1321	*Cushing*	Bollinger	29 Apr 1988	8 Aug 1988
WPB 1322	*Cuttyhunk*	Bollinger	3 Jun 1988	15 Oct 1988
WPB 1323	*Drummond*	Bollinger	8 Jul 1988	19 Oct 1988

Figure 14.14: USCGC *Cuttyhunk* (WPB, 1322), Island class patrol boat, 7 Aug 2003.

WPB	Name	Builder		
WPB 1324	Key Largo ex-*Largo*	Bollinger	12 Aug 1988	24 Dec 1988
WPB 1325	Metompkin	Bollinger	16 Sep 1988	12 Jan 1989
	Decomm 9 Jun 2003 for conversion, recomm 14 May 2004. Decomm 17 Apr 2007			
WPB 1326	Monomoy ◆Persian Gulf Jul 2004–	Bollinger	21 Oct 1988	16 Dec 1988
WPB 1327	Orcas	Bollinger	25 Nov 1988	14 Apr 1989
WPB 1328	Padre	Bollinger	6 Jan 1989	24 Feb 1989
	Decomm 2003 for conversion, recomm 7 Jun 2004. Decomm 17 Apr 2007			
WPB 1329	Sitkinak	Bollinger	10 Feb 1989	31 Mar 1989
WPB 1330	Tybee	Bollinger	17 Mar 1989	9 May 1989
WPB 1331	Washington	Bollinger	21 Apr 1989	9 Jun 1989
WPB 1332	Wrangell ◆Persian Gulf 2003	Bollinger	26 May 1989	24 Jun 1989
WPB 1333	Adak ◆Persian Gulf 2003	Bollinger	30 Jun 1989	27 Nov 1989
WPB 1334	Liberty	Bollinger	4 Aug 1989	22 Sep 1989
WPB 1335	Anacapa	Bollinger	8 Sep 1989	13 Jan 1990
WPB 1336	Kiska	Bollinger	13 Oct 1989	1 Dec 1989
WPB 1337	Assateague	Bollinger	17 Nov 1989	15 Jun 1990
WPB 1338	Grand Isle ex-*Amelia Island* (Feb 1991)	Bollinger	—	19 Apr 1991
WPB 1339	Key Biscayne ex-*Annette Island* (Feb 1991)	Bollinger	—	27 Apr 1991
WPB 1340	Jefferson Island ex-*Bainbridge Island* (Feb 1991)	Bollinger	—	16 Aug 1991
WPB 1341	Kodiak Island ex-*Block Island* (Feb 1991)	Bollinger	9 Feb 1991	21 Jun 1991
	Damaged by engine room fire off Alabama, 3 Oct 1996			
WPB 1342	Long Island ex-*Galveston Island* (Feb 1991)	Bollinger	19 Mar 1991	27 Aug 1991
WPB 1343	Bainbridge Island ex-*Grand Isle* (Feb 1991)	Bollinger	19 Apr 1991	14 Jun 1991
WPB 1344	Block Island ex-*Isle Royale* (Feb 1991)	Bollinger	—	22 Nov 1991
WPB 1345	Staten Island ex-*Jefferson Island* (Feb 1991)	Bollinger	—	1 Oct 1991
WPB 1346	Roanoke Island ex-*Key Biscayne* (Feb 1991)	Bollinger	—	5 Nov 1991
WPB 1347	Pea Island ex-*Kodiak Island* (Feb 1991)	Bollinger	6 Sep 1991	14 Jan 1992
WPB 1348	Knight Island	Bollinger	—	10 Dec 1991
WPB 1349	Galveston Island ex-*Long Island* (Feb 1991)	Bollinger	15 Nov 1991	25 Feb 1992

Displacement	141 tons; 165 f/l
Dimensions	110′ (oa) × 21′ × 7′4″ (123′ modernized units)
Machinery	2 shafts; diesel; BHP 6,200; 28 knots
Endurance	900/30; 2700/12
Complement	16
Armament	1–20 mm gun, replaced by 1 Bushmaster

Notes: Built for offshore surveillance and search-and-rescue operations. Steel hull with aluminum deck and superstructure. Modernization of whole class by Bollinger was planned, including lengthening of hull by 13 feet, but program stopped at eight units. *Matagorda*, *Metomkin*, *Padre*, and *Attu* modernized 2003, and *Nunivak*, *Vashon*, *Monhegan*, and *Manitou* in 2004. Next four were to be *Nantucket*, *Chandeleur*, *Matinicus* and *Ocracoke*, but program was suspended because of cracking in hulls. The converted boats were taken out of service 2006.

Heritage Class

No.	Name	Builder	Keel Laid	Launched	Comm.
WPB 1400	Leopold	Curtis Bay	27 Aug 1990	—	—
WPB 1401	—	Curtis Bay	—	—	—

Displacement	157 tons fl
Dimensions	118′ (oa) × 22′6″ × 8′4″
Machinery	2 screws; diesel; 30 knots
Endurance	720/30
Complement	17
Armament	1–20 mm

Note: suspended 25 Nov 1991. 95 units were planned to replace Cape and Point class patrol boats. Canceled because of changes in missions needed. 40 percent complete.

MARINE PROTECTOR CLASS

WPB	Name	Comm.	WPB	Name	Comm.
87301	Barracuda	7 Apr 1998	87311	Cobia	8 Sep 1999
87302	Hammerhead	29 Jul 1998	87312	Hawksbill	6 Oct 1999
87303	Mako	9 Sep 1998	87313	Cormorant	3 Nov 1999
87304	Marlin	2 Dec 1998	87314	Finback	1 Dec 1999
87305	Stingray	13 Jan 1999	87315	Amberjack	29 Dec 1999
87306	Dorado	24 Feb 1999	87316	Kittiwake	26 Jan 2000
87307	Osprey	7 Apr 1999	87317	Blackfin	23 Feb 2000
87308	Chinook	19 May 1999	87318	Bluefin	22 Mar 2000
87309	Albacore	30 Jun 1999	87319	Yellowfin	19 Apr 2000
87310	Tarpon	11 Aug 1999	87320	Manta	17 May 2000

United States Coast Guard

87321	*Coho*	14 Jun 2000		87349	*Shearwater*	7 Aug 2002
87322	*Kingfisher*	12 Jul 2000		87350	*Petrel*	4 Sep 2002
87323	*Seahawk*	9 Aug 2000		87351	—	tfrd to Malta 13 Nov 2002, ren P-1
87324	*Steelhead*	6 Sep 2000		87352	*Sea Lion*	13 Nov 2003
87325	*Beluga*	4 Oct 2000		87353	*Skipjack*	17 Dec 2003
87326	*Blacktip*	1 Nov 2000		87354	*Dolphin*	14 Jan 2004
87327	*Pelican*	24 Nov 2000		87355	*Hawk*	11 Feb 2004
87328	*Ridley*	27 Dec 2000		87356	*Sailfish*	10 Mar 2004
87329	*Cochino*	24 Jan 2001		87357	*Sawfish*	7 Apr 2004
87330	*Man-o-War*	21 Feb 2001		87358	*Swordfish*	23 Jul 2005
87331	*Moray*	21 Mar 2001		87359	*Tiger Shark*	11 Jul 2005
87332	*Razorbill*	18 Apr 2001		87360	*Blue Shark*	16 Aug 2005
87333	*Adelie*	16 May 2001		87361	*Sea Horse*	1 Jun 2005
87334	*Gannet*	13 Jun 2001		87362	*Sea Otter*	29 Jun 2005
87335	*Narwhal*	11 Jul 2001		87363	*Manatee*	27 Jul 2005
87336	*Sturgeon*	8 Aug 2001		87364	*Ahi* ex-*Diamondback*	24 Aug 2005
87337	*Sockeye*	5 Sep 2001		87365	*Pike*	21 Sep 2005
87338	*Ibis*	3 Oct 2001			ex-*Alligator* ex-*Piranha*	
87339	*Pompano*	31 Oct 2001		87366	*Terrapin*	23 March 2006
87340	*Halibut*	28 Nov 2001			ex-*Crocodile* ex-*Skate*	
87341	*Bonito*	2 Jan 2002		87367	*Sea Dragon*	31 Oct 2007
87342	*Shrike*	23 Jan 2002		87368	*Sea Devil*	6 Feb 2008
87343	*Tern*	20 Feb 2002		87369	*Snapper*	13 Aug 2008
87344	*Heron*	20 Mar 2002		87370	*Diamondback*	17 Sep 2008
87345	*Wahoo*	17 Apr 2002		87371	*Reef Shark*	22 Oct 2008
87346	*Flying Fish*	15 May 2002		87372	*Crocodile*	26 Nov 2008
87347	*Haddock*	12 Jun 2002		87373	*Sea Dog*	—
87348	*Brant*	10 Jul 2002		87374	*Sea Fox*	—

Displacement 89.5 tons f/l
Dimensions 87′ (oa); 80′10″ (wl) × 19′6″ × 5′8″
Machinery 2 screws; diesel; 1,500 BHP; 25 knots
Complement 10
Armament 2 MG

Notes: "Protector" class. Replacement for 82-foot type (Point class). All built by Bollinger.

Acquired from USN:	former	Acquired	Comm
WPC 12	*Cyclone*	PC 1	29 Jan 2000	never
WPC 2	*Tempest*	PC 2	10 Oct 2005	6 Dec 2005
WPC 4	*Monsoon*	PC 4	8 Oct 2004	—
WPC 8	*Zephyr*	PC 8	8 Oct 2004	—
WPC 13	*Shamal*	PC 13	29 Sep 2004	6 Dec 2004
WPC 14	*Tornado*	PC 14	6 Dec 2004	6 Dec 2004

Notes: *Cyclone* returned to USN for transfer to Philippines. *Thunderbolt* (PC 12) served in USCG Mar–Jul 2000 to determine feasibility of Coast Guard operating these ships. Acquired for homeland defense operations after 2001. *Zephyr* and *Monsoon* returned to USN, 22 Aug 2008.

Figure 14.15: *USCGC Shamal* (WPC 13). Navy patrol boat transferred in 2004.

SURFACE EFFECTS SHIPS

No.	Name	Builder	Launched	Comm
WSES 1	*Dorado*	Bell-Halter	Dec 1978	18 Jun 1981

Displacement 128 tons; 162 tons f/l
Dimensions 110′ (oa); 97′(wl) × 39′ × 7′ or 4′6″ (on cushion)
Machinery 2 screws; 2 diesel; 3,600 hp; 33 knots
Complement 18

Borrowed from USN. Lengthened 1982 by 50′. Returned to USN 24 Sep 1982, rec IX 515, 11 May 1987.

No.	Name	Builder	Comm.	Decomm
WSES 2	*Sea Hawk*	Bell Halter	17 Nov 1982	28 Jan 1994
WSES 3	*Shearwater*	Bell Halter	17 Nov 1982	28 Jan 1994
WSES 4	*Petrel*	Bell Halter	8 Jul 1983	28 Jan 1994

Displacement: 110 tons; 150 f/l
Dimensions: 109′1″ (oa) × 39′ × 5′6″ (on cushion), 8′2″ (off)
Machinery: 2 screws; diesels; 3,600 BHP; 15 knots / 2 fans; diesels; 890 BHP; 33 knots max
Complement: 17
Armament: 2 MG

Notes: Acquired for drug-enforcement role, but returned to USN.

WPBH 1 *Flagstaff* Ex-PGH 1. In svc 29 Sep 1976–30 Sep 1978 (see p. 129) Tested at Wood's Hole, Mass.
WMEH 1 *High Point* Ex-PCH 1. In svc 2 Mar 1977–30 Sep 1978. (See p. 129)

Figure 14.16: *USCGC Southwind* (WAGB 280), icebreaker, about 1970. Notice helicopter hangar aft.

Figure 14.17: *USCGC Northwind* (WAGB 282), about 1980. Notice raised funnel.

Figure 14.18: *USCGC Polar Star* (WAGB 10). One of two large cutters built to replace the *Wind* class. Icebreaker hulls are painted red.

ICEBREAKERS

WAG 83 *Mackinaw*   Great Lakes. Rec **WAGB 83**, 1 May 1966. Decomm and stricken 6 Jun 2006.
Later history: Museum at Mackinaw City, Mich.

WAGB 278 *Northwind*   Trfd to USSR 26 Feb 1944–19 Dec 1951, renamed *Severni Veter*. Returned as USS *Northwind* (AGB 5). Renamed *Staten Island* (AGB 5), 15 Apr 1952. Returned to USCG and renamed **Staten Island**, **WAGB 278**, 1 Feb 1966. Damaged when she struck uncharted rock north of Mawson Station, Antarctica, 28 Feb 1971. Decomm 15 Nov 1974. Sold 14 May 1975, BU.

WAGB 279 *Eastwind*   Severely damaged in collision with tanker *Gulfstream* off Barnegat, NJ, 20 Jan 1949 (10 killed). Decomm 13 Dec 1968. Sold 31 Jul 1972, BU 1976 Kearny, NJ.
◆Antarctic 1955–56, 1960, 1961, 1962, 1963.

WAGB 280 *Southwind*   Trfd to USSR 23 Mar 1945–28 Dec 1949, renamed *Kapitan Belusov*. Returned and renamed USS *Atka* (AGB 3), 28 Apr 1950. Returned to USCG and renamed **Southwind**, 18 Jan 1967. Stricken 31 May 1974. Sold 14 Jan 1976.

WAGB 281 *Westwind*   Trfd to USSR 21 Feb 1945–19 Dec 1951, renamed *Severni Polius*. Returned as AGB 6, renamed **Westwind**. Decomm 29 Feb 1988. BU 1988 Taiwan.
◆Antarctic 1957–58.

WAGB 282 *Northwind*   Decomm 20 Jan 1989. Sold 18 May 1998, BU Brownsville, Tex.
◆Antarctic 1947, 1957, 1959.

Notes: Wind class: 278, 280 and 281 loaned to Soviet Union as lend-lease, returned and placed in service with USN. Bow propeller removed. Helicopter platform and hangar added. *Northwind* and *Westwind* had funnel raised. All guns removed 1969–70.

WAG 38 *Storis*   Rec **WAGB 38**, 1 May 1966. Rec **WMEC 38**, 1 Jul 1972; converted to medium cutter. First foreign military vessel to visit Petropavlovsk, Kamchatka, since 1854, 1992. Decomm 8 Feb 2007. NDRF Nov 2007.

Notes: Armament 1972: 1–3″/50, 2 MG; 2006: 1–25mm gun, 2MG. Acquired from USN.

WAGB 283 *Burton Island*   Ex-AGB 1. Comm 15 Dec 1966. Decomm 9 May 1978. Sold 7 Oct 1980, BU 1982. Operation Deep Freeze, 1967–1978.

WAGB 284 *Edisto*   Ex-AGB 2. Comm 20 Oct 1965. Collided with cargo ship *Mizar* in Arctic, 6 Oct 1972. Decomm 15 Nov 1974. Sold 29 Sep 1977, BU Baltimore.

Note: Both modified with helicopter hangar and deck, and *Burton Island* had raised forward superstructure.

WAGB 4 *Glacier*   Ex-AGB 4. 30 Jun 1966. Decomm 17 Jun 1987; 3 Oct 1991 to Marad. NDRF Nov 2007.
Later history: to be trfd to The Glacier Society, renamed *Glacier GB4*.

Polar Class

No.	Name	Builder	Keel Laid	Launched	Comm.
WAGB 10	*Polar Star*	Lockheed	—	17 Nov 1973	19 Jan 1976
WAGB 11	*Polar Sea*	Lockheed	—	25 Jun 1975	23 Feb 1978

Displacement	10,430 tons; 13,623 f/l
Dimensions	399′10″ (oa); 337′2″ (wl) × 83′6″ × 33′6″
Machinery	3 screws; CODOG; diesels; gas turbines; 78,000 BHP; 18 knots
Endurance	18,000/18
Complement	138
Armament	2 MG. 2 helicopters

Notes: Hangar and flight deck aft. Have had engineering problems.

Figure 14.19: *USCGC Healy* (WAGB 20). Arctic research and suport ship.

Figure 14.20: *USCGC Calumet* (WYT 86), 1949.

Figure 14.21: *USCGC Sauk* (WYT 99), July 1975.

Service Record:
WAGB 10 *Polar Star*
WAGB 11 *Polar Sea*   In collision with oiler *Yukon* in Antarctic, 28 Jan 1982.

No.	Name	Builder	Keel Laid	Launched	Comm.
WAGB 20	*Healy*	Avondale	16 Sep 1996	15 Nov 1997	21 Aug 2000

Displacement	16,400 tons f/l
Dimensions	419'10" (oa); 397'8" (wl) × 82' × 29'6"
Machinery	2 screws; diesel-electric; 46,000 BHP; 17 knots
Armament	2 MG; 2 h/c
Complement	110

Notes: Arctic support and research ship. Original design revised, ship reduced in size and power.

No.	Name	Builder	Keel Laid	Launched	Comm.
WLBB 30	*Mackinaw*	Marinette	9 Feb 2004	6 Apr 2005	10 Jun 2006

Displacement	3,500 tons
Dimensions	240' (oa) × 58'6" × 16'
Machinery	1 screw; diesel; 9,119 shp; 15 knots
Endurance	4,000/12
Complement	55

Replaced old *Mackinaw* (WAGB 83). Great Lakes.

ICEBREAKING TUGS

WYT 60   *Manitou*   New York. Decomm 19 Nov 1980.
     Later history: Merchant *Manitou*. SE2003.
WYT 61   *Kaw*   Sault Ste. Marie, Mich.; Cleveland 1951. Decomm 22 Jun 1989.
     Later history: Merchant *Kaw*, renamed *Roger Stahl* 1997. SE2003
WYT 71   *Apalachee*   Baltimore, Md.; Portland, Me. (1984). Stricken 10 Apr 1986.
WYT 72   *Yankton*   Portland, Me. Decomm 28 Sep 1984.
WYT 73   *Mohican*   New York; Portsmouth, Va. 1976. Decomm 26 Jun 1986.
WYT 86   *Calumet*   San Francisco. Decomm 29 Sep 1967. Sold 25 Nov 1968.
     Later history: Merchant *Calumet*. SE1998.
WYT 87   *Hudson*   New Orleans; Brownsville, Tex. 1958; Norfolk, Va. 1962. Decomm 11 Nov 1968. Trfd to Northwestern College, 8 Jul 1970.
     Later history: Merchant *Hudson*. SE1974.
WYT 88   *Navesink*   New York. Decomm 30 Oct 1968. Sold 21 May 1970.
     Later history: Merchant *Sherman IX*. SE1974.
WYT 89   *Tuckahoe*   New York. Decomm 14 Nov 1968. Trfd to Dept of HEW, 16 Apr 1969.
     Later history: Merchant *W. Dallas Herring* (Dept of HEW), renamed *Tuckahoe, J. Edward Slatten*. SE1980.
WYT 90   *Arundel*   Chicago, Ill., Buffalo, NY (1980). Decomm 30 Apr 1982.
WYT 91   *Mahoning*   New York. Struck submerged wreck in Arthur Kill, NY, 8 Nov 1972. Decomm 1 Oct 1984.
WYT 92   *Naugatuck*   Seattle; Sault Ste. Marie, Mich. 1955. Decomm 15 Jan 1979.
WYT 93   *Raritan*   Portsmouth, Va.; Milwaukee 1963; Grand Haven, Mich., 1973; New York 1980. Decomm 14 May 1988.
WYT 96   *Chinook*   Decomm 1 Jul 1986.
WYT 97   *Ojibwa*   Boston; Buffalo 1954. Decomm 6 May 1980. Sold 22 Dec 1980.
WYT 98   *Snohomish*   Rockland, Me. Struck submerged object and damaged in Penobscot River, 13 Jan 1984. Decomm 4 Apr 1986.

Figure 14.22: *USCGC Mobile Bay* (WYT 103), icebreaking tug, stationed in the Great Lakes.

WYT 99 *Sauk* New York; Gloucester City, NJ, 1965; New York 1968. Struck rock and sank in Hudson River, 4 Jan 1962; salved. Decomm 30 Apr 1985. Sold.
Later history: converted to 2-mast schooner, 2000.

Katmai Bay Class

No.	Name	Builder	Keel Laid	Launched	Comm.
WTGB 101	*Katmai Bay*	Tacoma	7 Nov 1977	8 Apr 1978	8 Jan 1979
WTGB 102	*Bristol Bay*	Tacoma	13 Feb 1978	22 Jul 1978	5 Apr 1979
WTGB 103	*Mobile Bay*	Tacoma	13 Feb 1978	11 Nov 1978	6 May 1979
WTGB 104	*Biscayne Bay*	Tacoma	29 Aug 1978	3 Feb 1979	8 Dec 1979
WTGB 105	*Neah Bay*	Tacoma	6 Aug 1979	2 Feb 1980	18 Aug 1980
WTGB 106	*Morro Bay*	Tacoma	6 Aug 1979	11 Jul 1980	25 Jan 1981
WTGB 107	*Penobscot Bay*	Bay City	24 Jul 1983	27 Jul 1984	4 Sep 1984
WTGB 108	*Thunder Bay*	Tacoma	20 Jul 1984	15 Aug 1985	29 Dec 1985
WTGB 109	*Sturgeon Bay*	Bay City	9 Jul 1986	12 Sep 1987	20 Aug 1988
WTGB 110	*Curtis Bay*	—	—	—	—
Displacement	662 tons f/l				
Dimensions	140′ (oa) × 37′8″ × 12′6″				
Machinery	1 screw; diesel-electric; 2,500 BHP; 14.7 knots				
Endurance	4,000/12				
Complement	17				
Armament	2 MG				

Notes: WYTM rec WTGB, 5 Feb 1979 or on completion.

Service Records:
WTGB 101 *Katmai Bay* Sault Ste. Marie, Mich.
WTGB 102 *Bristol Bay* Detroit, Mich.
WTGB 103 *Mobile Bay* Sturgeon Bay, Wis.
WTGB 104 *Biscayne Bay* St. Ignace, Mich.
WTGB 105 *Neah Bay* Cleveland, Ohio.
WTGB 106 *Morro Bay* Out of comm 28 Sep 1998–Sep 2001. Training ship, Coast Guard Academy. New London, Conn.
WTGB 107 *Penobscot Bay* Bayonne, NJ.
WTGB 108 *Thunder Bay* Rockland, Me.
WTGB 109 *Sturgeon Bay* Bayonne, NJ.
WTGB 110 *Curtis Bay* Canceled.

Figure 14.23: *USCGC Arbutus* (WAGL 203), lighthouse tender.

LIGHTHOUSE TENDERS/BUOY TENDERS

Note: WAGL rec as indicated, 1 Jan 1965.

WAGL/WAG 38 *Storis* Rec **WAGB 38**, 1 May 1966. Rec **WMEC 38**, 1 Jul 1972. Stationed in Alaska and Arctic.
WAGL/WLM 203 *Arbutus* St. George, NY. Decomm 27 Mar 1967. Sold 24 Mar 1969.
WAGL 205 *Beech* St. George, NY. Decomm 23 Jan 1963. Sold 28 Aug 1964.
WAGL 207 *Cedar* Kodiak, Alaska. Decomm 29 Jun 1950. Sold 27 Jun 1955.
WAGL/WLI 208 *Columbine* San Francisco. Decomm 8 Oct 1965. Sold 29 Jun 1967.
WAGL/WLM 212 *Fir* Decomm 1 Oct 1991. NDRF December 1998.
Later history: Museum, Sacramento, Cal. 2002.

Note: Reengined to diesel 1951.

WAGL 215 *Hawthorn* New London, Conn. Decomm 24 Jul 1964. Sold 29 Nov 1965, BU
WAGL 217 *Hemlock* Ketchikan, Alaska. Decomm 17 Jun 1958. Sold 2 Aug 1961.
Later history: Merchant barge *Hemlock*. SE1980.
WAGL/WLI 219 *Hickory* St. George, NY. Decomm 10 Jan 1967. Sold 28 Apr 1969.
Later history: Merchant *Hickory*. SE1980.
WAGL/WLM 220 *Hollyhock* Sturgeon Bay, Wis., Detroit 1959, Miami 1962. Decomm 31 Mar 1982.
Later history: Merchant *Good News Mission Ship*. Sunk as artificial reef off Pompano Beach, Fla., 1990.

Note: Reengined to diesel 1954.

WAGL 223 *Althea* Fort Pierce, Fla. Decomm 10 Nov 1962. Sold 26 Nov 1963.
Later history: Merchant *Little Red*. Foundered in Mississippi River, 23 Oct 1966.
WAGL 224 *Juniper* St. Petersburg, Fla. Decomm 15 Jul 1975. Sold Dec 1975.
Later history: Merchant *Juniper*. SE1998.

WAGL/WLM 227 *Lilac*   Gloucester, NJ. Decomm 3 Feb 1972. Stricken 6 Jun 1972.
   Later history: Donated to Harry Lundeberg Seafarers Intl Union Seamanship School, Baltimore, Md. Sold 2004 as museum in New York, NY.
WAGL/WLI 228 *Linden*   Washington, NC; Portsmouth, Va. 1953; St. George NY 1963. . Went aground near Portsmouth, Va., 10 Feb 1955. Decomm 29 May 1969. Sold 22 May 1970.
   Later history: Merchant *Venture*. SE1974.
WAGL/WLI 234 *Maple*   Ogdensburg, NY; Detroit 1958. Decomm 1 Jun 1973.
   Later history: To USN 8 Aug 1973. Trfd to EPA 1974, renamed *Roger W. Simons*. OS 1995.
WAGL/WLM 237 *Mistletoe*   Portsmouth, Va. Decomm 15 Aug 1968. Sold 14 Aug 1969.
WAGL/WLI 238 *Narcissus*   Portsmouth, Va. Sold to Guiana 5 May 1971
   Later history: renamed *Maripa*.
WAGL/WLM 239 *Oak*   New York. Decomm 6 Nov 1964. To Smithsonian Inst., 3 Mar 1967.
WAGL 161 *Phlox*   Sold 20 Jan 1949.
   Later history: merchant *Salvor*, renamed *Big Red*. Lost 1970.
WAGL 246 *Spruce*   Trfd to USC&GS, 17 May 1950.
WAGL/WLI 248 *Tamarack*   Sault Ste. Marie, Mich. Decomm 27 Oct 1970. Sold 2 Aug 1971.
   Later history: Merchant *Tamarack*. SE1974.
WAGL 250 *Violet*   Baltimore. Decomm 2 Jan 1962. Sold 8 Mar 1963.
WAGL/WLM 252 *Walnut*   Honolulu; Miami 1955; San Pedro, Cal. 1967. Collided with m/v *American Leader*, 1 Sep 1965. Decomm 31 Mar 1982. Trfd to Honduras, 1 Jul 1982. (converted to diesel 1954)
   Later history: renamed *Yojoa* (FNH 252). SE2001.
WAGL/WLI 254 *Wistaria*   Baltimore. Decomm 7 Oct 1966. Sold 6 Dec 1968.
WAGL/WLI 255 *Zinnia*   Gloucester City, NJ; New York 1967; New Orleans 1969. Decomm 14 Jan 1972. Stricken 1 Mar 1972, trfd to USAF.
WAGL 256 *Birch*   St. Petersburg, Fla. Decomm 24 Feb 1963. Sold 30 Jul 1964.
WAGL/WLI 257 *Bluebonnet*   Decomm 18 Jan 1965. Sold 19 May 1966.
   Later history: Merchant *Tiffany*. SE1998.
WAGL/WLIC 258 *Cherry*   WLIC Decomm 1 Dec 1964. Sold to Surinam, 20 May 1965.
WAGL/WLIC 288 *Dahlia*   Decomm 9 Oct 1964. Sold to Surinam, 20 May 1965.
WAGL/WLI 260 *Elm*   **WLI 72260**. Decomm 30 Jul 1969. Stricken 19 Jun 1972.
WAGL/WLI 261 *Jasmine*   New Orleans. Decomm 18 Jan 1965. Sold 19 May 1966.
   Later history: Merchant *Cape Romanzoff*. SE1980.
WAGL 263 *Myrtle*   Galveston. Decomm 8 Feb 1963. Sold 19 May 1964.
WAGL 265 *Palmetto*   Charleston, SC. Decomm 23 May 1958. Sold 13 Apr 1959
WAGL 266 *Poinciana*   Miami. Decomm 17 Aug 1962. Sold 26 Nov 1963.
   Later history: Merchant *Red's Baby*.
WAGL 267 *Rhododendron*   Seattle. Decomm 20 Aug 1958. To State of Washington, 20 Apr 1959.
   Later history: Merchant *Can-Do*. Sank off Anchor Point, Alaska, 25 Nov 1966.
WAGL 367 *Blackrock*   Decomm 24 Aug 1954. Trfd to Haiti 2 Nov 1955.
   Later history: renamed *Amiral Killick* (GC 7). SE1962.
WAGL 408 *Aster*   Seattle, Wash. Decomm 15 Aug 1962. Sold 1963.
WAGL 409 *Thistle*   Ketchikan, Alaska. Decomm 1 Aug 1957. Sold 25 Mar 1958.
   Later history: Merchant *WPC Victor*.

Balsam Class (all WLB, 1 Jan 1965)

WAGL/WLB 406 *Acacia*   Grand Haven, Mich. Decomm and stricken 7 Jun 2006.
   Later history: To be a museum, Chicago, Ill.
WAGL/WLB 62 *Balsam*   Alaska 1958. Decomm 6 Mar 1975. Sold 13 Sep 1977.
   Later history: merchant *Baranof*.
WAGL/WLB 388 *Basswood*   Stricken 4 Sep 1998. Sold 24 Nov 2000. Vietnam Oct 1967–May 1972.
WAGL/WLB 389 *Bittersweet*   Alaska; Woods Hole, Mass. 1976. Decomm 18 Aug 1997. Trfd to Estonia 5 Sep 1997.
   Later history: renamed *Valvas*. (PVL 109). SE2001.
WAGL/WLB 390 *Blackhaw*   Honolulu 1954; Sangley Point, Philippines 1967–71; San Francisco. Decomm and stricken 26 Feb 1993. Sunk as target 1997.
   ★Vietnam Mar 1968–Mar 1971.
WAGL/WLB 391 *Blackthorn*   Sunk in collision with tkr m/v *Texas Capricorn* in Tampa Bay, 28 Jan 1980 (27 lost). Raised and sunk as artificial reef, 30 Jul 1981.
WAGL/WLB 392 *Bramble*   Detroit, Mich.; Port Huron, Mich. 1975; Caribbean 1986–87; Port Huron. Decomm 22 May 2003.
   Later history: Museum, Port Huron, Mich.
WAGL/WLB 306 *Buttonwood*   SLEP 1991. Decomm 28 Jun 2001. Trfd to Dominican Republic 30 Jun 2001.
   Later history: renamed *Almirante Didiez Burgos* (C 457).
WAGL/WLB 270 *Cactus*   Rec **WAGO 270**, 30 Apr 1967. Rec **WAGL/WLB 270**, 1969. Went aground at Grays Harbor, Wash., 29 Sep 1971. Decomm 22 Nov 1971. Sold 9 Oct 1973. BU Tacoma 1994.
WAGL/WLB 300 *Citrus*   Ketchikan; Coos Bay 1982. Rec **WMEC 300**, Feb 1980. Rammed by m/v *Pacific Star* which was scuttled southwest of San Diego when stopped for drug search, 1 Jan 1985. Trfr to Mexico canc 28 Aug 1994. Decomm 1 Sep 1994. Trfd to Dominican Republic, 16 Sep 1995.
   Later history: renamed *Almirante Juan Alejandro Acosta* (C 456). SE2001.
WAGL/WLB 292 *Clover*   Alaska; Eugene, Ore. Rec **WMEC** 1990 Decomm 1 Jun 1990. Sunk as target 26 Jun 1990.
WAGL/WLB 301 *Conifer*   Rebuilt, reengined 1983. Decomm 23 Jun 2000.
WAGL/WLB 277 *Cowslip*   Portland, Me. Decomm 23 Mar 1973 and sold.
   Later history: Merchant *Cowslip*. Repurchased as **Cowslip (WLB 277)**, 19 Jan 1981. Recomm 9 Nov 1981. SLEP 1983–84. Decomm 1 Nov 2002. Trfd to Nigeria, 23 Jan 2003, renamed *Ologbo* (A 502).
WAGL/WLB 295 *Evergreen*   Damaged by fire, 23 Dec 1968. Rec **WAGO 295**, Feb 1973. Rec **WMEC**, 1 May 1982. Decomm 13 Jun 1990. Sunk as target 25 Nov 1992.
WAGL/WLB 393 *Firebush*   St. George, NY; Kodiak, Alaska 1979. In collision with m/v *Hickory Knoll* at Baltimore, 17 Jul 1973. Decomm 30 Jun 2003 and trfd to Nigeria.
   Later history: renamed *Nwamba* (A 503).
WAGL/WLB 290 *Gentian*   Stricken 1 Jun 1998. Reinstated 1 Apr 1999 as **WIX 290**. Caribbean support tender. Decomm 1 Jun 1998. Recomm 27 Sep 1999. Decomm and stricken 23 Jun 2006. Trfd to Colombia 15 Oct 2007.
   Later history: renamed *San Andres*.
WAGL/WLB 394 *Hornbeam*   Damaged in collision with m/v *Docelago* off Nantucket, 24 May 1972. Decomm 30 Sep 1999.
WAGL/WLB 395 *Iris*   Galveston, Tex.; Astoria, Ore. 1972. Beached at Aransas Pass, Tex. after being holed during dragging operation, 19 Oct 1957. Damaged by engine room fire off Oregon, 24 Apr 1980. Decomm 20 Jun 1995. NDRF Dec 1998.

Figure 14.24: *USCGC Firebush* (WLB 393).

WAGL/WLB 297 *Ironwood*   Monterey, Cal.; Guam 1950; Honolulu 1954; Homer, Alaska 1969; Adak 1975; Kodiak 1979. Decomm 6 Oct 2000. ★Korea Nov 1951–May 1954; ★Vietnam Jul–Aug 1967.

WAGL/WLB 291 *Laurel*   Rockland, Me.; Ketchikan 1975; San Pedro, Cal., 1983; Mayport, Fla. 1993. Decomm 10 Dec 1999.

WAGL/WLB 302 *Madrona*   Portsmouth, Va.; Charleston, SC, 1984. Decomm 12 Apr 2002 and trfd to El Salvador.
   Later history: renamed *Manuel Jose Arce* (BL 01).

WAGL/WLB 396 *Mallow*   Astoria, Ore.; Honolulu 1965; Guam 1967; Honolulu 1975. Decomm 24 May 1997.

WAGL/WLB 397 *Mariposa*   St. Georges, NY; New London, Conn. 1973; Detroit 1974; Seattle 1991. Decomm 17 Mar 2000. Acq by USN 17 Apr 2000 as non-operational TS.

WAGL/WLB 305 *Mesquite*   Sault Ste. Marie, Mich.; Galveston 1980; Duluth 1985; Charlesvois, Mich. 1989. Ran aground on reef off Escanaba, Mich., 10 Apr 1964. Lost by grounding off Keweenaw Point, Lake Superior, 4 Dec 1989. Hulk sunk in Keystone Bay, 14 Jul 1990. ◆Grenada.

WAGL/WLB 308 *Papaw*   Miami; Charleston, SC 1954; Galveston 1991. Decomm 23 Jul 1999.

WAGL/WLB 307 *Planetree*   Guam; Honolulu 1954; Juneau, Alaska 1974; Ketchikan 1985. Decomm 19 Mar 1999. Nov 2007.
   ★Korea May–Jul 1954; ★Vietnam Apr 1966–Apr 1967.

WAGL/WLB 398 *Redbud*   Loan to USN, 25 Mar 1949. Returned 20 Nov 1970.
   Later history: Trfd to Philippines 1 Mar 1972, renamed *Kalinga* (TK89/AG 89) SE2001.

WAGL/WLB 399 *Sagebrush*   San Juan, PR. Decomm 26 Apr 1988. Scuttled 28 Apr 1988.
   ◆Cuba missile crisis Oct–Dec 1962, Dominican Rep Feb 1966.

WAGL/WLB 400 *Salvia*   Mobile, Ala. In collision with dredge *Duplex* in Mobile Channel, 9 Feb 1964. Decomm 4 Oct 1991.
   Later history: Salvage training ship for USN, Little Creek, Va.

WAGL/WLB 401 *Sassafras*   Cape May, NJ; New York 1978; Honolulu 1981, then Guam. Went aground in Hudson River, 12 Jan 1969. Decomm and trfd to Nigeria 30 Oct 2003.
   Later history: renamed *Obula* (A 504).

WAGL/WLB 402 *Sedge*   Kodiak, Alaska, 1950; Cordova, Alaska 1957; Homer, Alaska 1974. Decomm 15 Nov 2002. Trfd to Nigeria 21 Dec 2002.
   Later history: renamed *Kyanwa* (A 501).

WAGL/WLB 296 *Sorrel*   Boston; Sitka, Alaska 1954; Seward, Alaska 1965; Cordova, Alaska 1973; New York 1976. Decomm 28 Jun 1996.

WAGL/WLB 403 *Spar*   Woods Hole, Mass.; Bristol, RI, 1951. Undersea charting expedition in northern Atlantic, 1966. Boston, 1967; South Portland, Me. 1973. Decomm 28 Feb 1997.

WAGL/WLB 406 *Sundew*   Great Lakes. Decomm 27 May 2004.

WAGL/WLB 405 *Sweetbrier*   Juneau, Alaska. Decomm 27 Aug 2001. Trfd to Ghana, 26 Oct 2001.
   Later history: renamed *Bonsu*.

WAGL/WLB 309 *Sweetgum*   Mayport, Fla. Decomm 15 Feb 2002 and trfd to Panama.
   Later history: renamed *Independencia* (401).

WAGL/WLB 303 *Tupelo*   Toledo, Ohio; Astoria, Ore. 1969. Decomm 30 Sep 1975. Sold 13 Sep 1977.
   Later history: Merchant *Courageous*. SE2003.

WAGL/WLB 289 *Woodbine*   Lake Michigan. Decomm 15 Feb 1972. Stricken 9 Jun 1972.
   Later history: Merchant *Woodbine*. SE2003.

WAGL/WLB 407 *Woodrush*   Decomm 28 Apr 2001. Trfd to Ghana, 4 May 2001.
   Later history: renamed *Anzone*.

Number	Name	Builder	Launched	Acquired
WAGL/WLB 328	*Magnolia* ex-USS *Barricade* ACM 3 ex-*Col. John P. Story*	Marietta	16 Jul 1942	28 Jun 1946
WAGL/WLB 329	*Ivy* ex-USS *Barbican* ACM 5 ex-*Col. George Armistead*	Marietta	18 Aug 1942	12 Jun 1946
WAGL/WLB 330	*Jonquil* ex-USS *Bastion* ACM 6 ex-*Col. Henry J. Hunt*	Marietta	2 Dec 1941	18 Jun 1946
WAGL/WLB 331	*Heather* ex-USS *Obstructor* ACM 7 ex-*Lt. William J. Sylvester*	Marietta	24 Mar 1942	28 Jun 1946
WAGL/WLB 332	*Willow* ex-USS *Picket* ACM 8 ex-*Gen. Henry Knox*	Marietta	1941	24 Jun 1946
WARC 333	*Yamacraw* ex-USS *Trapper* ACM 9 ex-*Maj. Gen. Arthur Murray*	Marietta	15 Aug 1942	20 Jun 1946
Displacement	1,320 tons fl			
Dimensions	188′2″ (oa); 168′8″ (wl) × 37′ × 12′6″			
Machinery	2 screws; Skinner Unaflow; 2 CE boilers; 1,200 SHP; 12.5 knots			
Armament	none			
Complement	52			

Notes: WLB, 1 Jan 1965. Former Army mine planters acquired by USN in 1944–45. *Yamacraw* was a cable layer.

Service Record:

WAGL 328 *Magnolia*   San Francisco; Astoria, Ore. 1965; Decomm 13 Aug 1971. Sold 15 Nov 1972.
   Later history: Merchant *Galaxy*. Sank after fire and explosion, 2 Oct 2002.

WAGL 329 *Ivy*   Miami; Portland, Ore. 1951. Decomm 26 Nov 1969. Sold Nov 1970.
   Later history: Merchant *Balboa* 1970, renamed *El Cid* 1980.

WAGL 330 *Jonquil*   Portsmouth, Va. Decomm 15 Sep 1969. Sold 6 May 1970, BU 1970, Bordentown, NJ.

WAGL 331 *Heather*   San Pedro, Cal. Decomm 15 Dec 1967. To Seattle Comm. College 12 Apr 1968.

WAGL 332 *Willow*   San Juan, PR; San Francisco 1950. Decomm 10 Oct 1969. Sold 28 Jul 1971.
   Later history: Merchant *Royal Alaskan* 1972.

WARC 333 *Yamacraw*   Returned to USN 17 Apr 1959. Stricken 1 Jul 1965.

No.	Name	Builder	Launched	Comm.
WLM 540	*White Sumac*	Niagara SB	14 Jun 1943	19 Sep 1947
WLM 541	*White Alder*	Niagara SB	30 Jun 1943	19 Sep 1947
WLM 542	*White Bush*	Basalt	5 Feb 1944	1 Nov 1947
WLM 543	*White Holly*	Basalt	8 Apr 1944	1 Dec 1947
WLM 544	*White Sage*	Erie Concrete	9 Jun 1943	9 Aug 1947
WLM 545	*White Heath*	Erie Concrete	21 Jul 1943	9 Aug 1947
WLM 546	*White Lupine*	Erie Concrete	28 Jul 1943	5 Sep 1947
WLM 547	*White Pine*	Erie Concrete	28 Aug 1943	3 Aug 1947
Displacement	435 tons; 600 f/l			
Dimensions	133′ (oa) × 31′ × 9′			
Machinery	2 screws; diesel; 600 BHP; 9.8 knots			
Complement	23			

Notes: ex-YF lighters, acquired from USN 1947. Modernized 1974, re-engined.

Service Records:

WAGL/WLM 540 *White Sumac*   Key West, Fla. Decomm 9 Jul 1999. Trfd to Dominican Republic 1 Aug 2002.
   Later history: renamed *Capotillo* (BA 2).
WAGL/WLM 541 *White Alder*   Sunk in collision with m/v *Helena* near White Castle, La., 7 Dec 1968 (17 lost).
WAGL/WLM 542 *White Bush*   Astoria, Ore. Decomm 16 Sep 1985. Sunk as target off southern California, 17 Jun 2004.
WAGL/WLM 543 *White Holly*   Seattle; New Orleans 1971. Decomm 8 Jul 1998.
WAGL/WLM 544 *White Sage*   Bristol, RI & Woods Hole, Mass. Decomm 28 Jun 1996.
WAGL/WLM 545 *White Heath*   Boston. Decomm 31 Mar 1998. Trfd to Tunisia 10 Jun 1998.
   Later history: renamed *Tabarka*
WAGL/WLM 546 *White Lupine*   Lake Ontario; Rockland, Me. 1967. Decomm 28 Feb 1998. Trfd to Tunisia 10 Jun 1998.
   Later history: renamed *Turquenness*.
WAGL/WLM 547 *White Pine*   Memphis, Tenn.; Mobile 1976. Decomm 29 Jun 1999. Trfd to Dominican Republic.
   Later history: renamed *Tortuguero* (RA 1). SE2001.

No.	Name	Builder	Launched	Comm.
WLM 685	*Red Wood*	Curtis Bay	4 Apr 1964	6 Aug 1964
WLM 686	*Red Beech*	Curtis Bay	6 Jun 1964	20 Nov 1964
WLM 687	*Red Birch*	Curtis Bay	19 Feb 1965	7 Jun 1965
WLM 688	*Red Cedar*	Curtis Bay	1 Aug 1970	18 Dec 1970
WLM 689	*Red Oak*	Curtis Bay	19 Jun 1971	10 Dec 1971
Displacement	371 tons; 525 f/l			
Dimensions	157 (oa) × 33 × 6			
Machinery	2 screws; diesel; 1,800 BHP; 12.8 knots			
Complement	31			

Notes: Unarmed. Hulls strengthened for light icebreaking.

Service Record:

WLM 685 *Red Wood*   New London, Conn.; Philadelphia 1996. Decomm 1 Jun 1999. Trfd to Argentina 13 Sep 1999.
   Later history: renamed *Ciudad de Rosario* (Q 62).
WLM 686 *Red Beech*   New York. Decomm 18 Jun 1997. Sunk as artificial reef off Ocean City, Md., 10 Jun 2000.
WLM 687 *Red Birch*   San Francisco; Baltimore 1976. Decomm 9 Jun 1998. Trfd to Argentina 10 Jun 1998.
   Later history: renamed *Punta Alta* (Q 12).

Figure 14.25: *USCGC Red Beech* (WAGL 686), lighthouse tender in New York harbor, about 1968.

WLM 688 *Red Cedar*   Portsmouth, Va. Decomm 30 Mar 1999 and trfd to Argentina, 30 Apr 1999.
   Later history: renamed *Ciudad de Zarate* (Q 61).
WLM 689 *Red Oak*   Gloucester City, NJ. Decomm 28 Mar 1996. Scuttled 1999.

Juniper Class

No.	Name	Builder	Launched	Comm.	Station
WLB 201	*Juniper*	Marinette	24 Jun 1995	3 Jul 1996	Newport, RI
WLB 202	*Willow*	Marinette	15 Jun 1996	10 Apr 1997	Newport, RI
WLB 203	*Kukui*	Marinette	3 May 1997	1 Jan 1998	Honolulu
WLB 204	*Elm*	Marinette	24 Jan 1998	29 Jun 1998	Atlantic Beach, NC
WLB 205	*Walnut*	Marinette	22 Aug 1998	22 Feb 1999	Honolulu
WLB 206	*Spar* ex-*Dogwood* (2000)	Marinette	12 Aug 2000	3 Aug 2001	Kodiak, Alaska
WLB 207	*Maple*	Marinette	16 Dec 2000	19 Oct 2001	Sitka, Alaska
WLB 208	*Aspen*	Marinette	21 Apr 2001	24 Jan 2002	San Francisco
WLB 209	*Sycamore*	Marinette	28 Jul 2001	3 Jul 2002	Cordova, Alaska
WLB 210	*Cypress*	Marinette	27 Oct 2001	11 Oct 2002	Mobile, Ala.
WLB 211	*Oak*	Marinette	26 Jan 2002	7 Mar 2003	Charleston, SC
WLB 212	*Hickory*	Marinette	11 May 2002	3 Jul 2003	Homer, Alaska
WLB 213	*Fir*	Marinette	18 Aug 2002	8 Nov 2003	Astoria, Ore.
WLB 214	*Hollyhock*	Marinette	25 Jan 2003	30 Apr 2004	Port Huron, Mich.
WLB 215	*Sequoia*	Marinette	23 Aug 2003	15 Oct 2004	Apra, Guam
WLB 216	*Alder*	Marinette	7 Feb 2004	10 Jun 2005	Duluth, Minn.
Displacement	2,000 tons f/l				
Dimensions	225′ (oa); 206′ (wl) × 46′ × 13′				
Machinery	1 screw; diesel; 6,200 BHP; 15 knots				
Range	6,000/15				
Complement	40				

Notes: Built to replace *Balsam* Class.

Service Notes:

WLB 214 *Hollyhock*   In collision with m/v *Stewart J. Cort* on St. Mary's River, Mich., 25 Mar 2004.

Keeper Class

No.	Name	Builder	Keel Laid	Launched	Comm.	Station
WLM 551	*Ida Lewis*	Marinette	Aug 1994	14 Oct 1995	11 Apr 1997	Newport, RI
WLM 552	*Katherine Walker*	Marinette	—	14 Sep 1996	1 Nov 1997	Bayonne, NJ
WLM 553	*Abbie Burgess* ex-*Abigail Burgess*	Marinette	30 Sep 1996	5 Apr 1997	31 Jul 1998	Rockland, Me.
WLM 554	*Marcus Hanna*	Marinette	—	23 Aug 1997	19 May 1998	S.Portland, Me.
WLM 555	*James Rankin*	Marinette	—	25 Apr 1998	1 May 1999	Baltimore, Md.
WLM 556	*Joshua Appleby*	Marinette	—	8 Aug 1998	7 May 1999	St. Petersburg, Fla.
WLM 557	*Frank Drew*	Marinette	—	5 Dec 1998	5 Apr 2000	Portsmouth, Va.
WLM 558	*Anthony Petit*	Marinette	—	30 Jan 1999	18 May 2000	Ketchikan, Alaska
WLM 559	*Barbara Mabrity*	Marinette	—	27 Mar 1998	20 Nov 1999	Mobile, Ala.
WLM 560	*William Tate*	Marinette	—	8 May 1999	3 Jun 2000	Philadelphia
WLM 561	*Harry Claiborne*	Marinette	—	10 Jun 1999	28 Mar 2000	Galveston, Tex.
WLM 562	*Maria Bray*	Marinette	—	28 Aug 1999	26 Jul 2000	Atlantic Beach, Fla.
WLM 563	*Henry Blake*	Marinette	12 Jan 1999	20 Nov 1999	12 Oct 2000	Everett, Wash.
WLM 564	*George Cobb*	Marinette	9 Mar 1999	18 Dec 1999	27 Oct 2000	San Pedro, Cal.

Displacement:	845 tons f/l
Dimensions	175′ (oa); 155′ (wl) × 36′ × 7′11″
Machinery	diesel; 1,710 BHP; 12 knots
Complement	18

Notes: Coastal buoy tenders. Named after famous lighthouse keepers. Z-drive Azimuth thruster propulsion units, designed to rotate independently 360-degrees, replace standard rudder and propeller.

Figure 14.26: *USCGC Elm* (WLB 204), large buoy tender.

BUOY TENDERS (RIVER) 1947

Cosmos Class (WLI)

WAGL 293	*Cosmos*	St. Petersburg, Fla. Decomm 16 Aug 1985.
WAGL 294	*Barberry*	Portsmouth, Va. Decomm 1 Sep 1970. Sold 23 Feb 1971.
	Later history: Merchant *J. Millard Tawes*. SE1980.	
WAGL 298	*Rambler*	Charleston, SC.
WAGL 299	*Brier*	Brunswick, Ga.; Atlantic City, NJ 1965. In collision with f/v *Two Brothers Second* in Creighton Narrows, Ga., 17 Mar 1962. Decomm 9 Nov 1967. To USN, IX 307, 10 Mar 1969.
WAGL 313	*Bluebell*	Portland, Ore.
WAGL 315	*Smilax*	Atlantic Beach, NC.
WAGL 316	*Primrose*	**WLR** 316. Decomm 15 Jul 1999.
WAGL 317	*Verbena*	North Carolina. Decomm 1 Sep 1977. Sold Feb 1978.
	Later history: Merchant *Nancy Lee*. Sunk as artificial reef off Cape Lookout, NC, Jan 1989.	

Clematis Class

WAGL 286	*Clematis*	Galveston. **WLI 74286**. Decomm 17 Oct 1976. To TVA Feb 1977
WAGL 287	*Shadbush*	Mobile, Ala.; New Orleans 1967; Galveston 1975. **WLI 74287**. Decomm 24 Feb 1976. Sold Oct 1976
WAGL/WLR 259	*Dogwood*	Lower Mississippi River. Decomm 11 Aug 1989.
WAGL/WLR 304	*Fern*	Decomm 1 Sep 1971. Sold 19 Jun 1972.
WAGL/WLR 63	*Forsythia*	Allegheny and Ohio Rivers; Memphis 1963. Decomm 12 Aug 1977.
WAGL/WLR 285	*Foxglove*	St. Louis, Mo. Decomm 8 Jul 1977. sold.
	Later history: Merchant *Foxglove*, renamed *Harvey*, then *Maranatha*.	
WAGL 213	*Goldenrod*	Decomm 26 May 1973. Stricken 26 Sep 1973, trfd to NSF.
WAGL/WLR 310	*Lantana*	Mississippi and Ohio Rivers. Rec **WLR 80310**. Decomm 27 Oct 1991.
WAGL/WLR 264	*Oleander*	Peoria, Ill.; Kansas City, Mo. 1950; Point Pleasant, W.Va. 1961. Rec **WLR 73264**. Decomm 31 Jul 1977.
WAGL 241	*Poplar*	Decomm 17 Jun 1973. Stricken 26 Sep 1973.
WAGL/WLIC 268	*Sycamore*	Decomm 30 Jun 1977.
WAGL/WLR 311	*Sumac*	Decomm 9 Jul 1999.
	Later history: Marine Learning Inst., St. Louis, Mo.	
WAGL 251	*Wakerobin*	Sold to War Dept (Engineers), 20 Apr 1955.

WLI 641	*Azalea*	Curtis Bay	1958	—
WLI 642	*Buckthorn*	Mobile Ship Repair	comm 17 Jul 1964	Sault Ste. Marie, Mich.

Displacement	188 tons
Dimensions	100′ (oa) × 24′ × 4′
Machinery	2 screws; diesels; 600 BHP; 11.9 knots
Complement	15

WLIC 800	*Pamlico*	Curtis Bay	11 Aug 1976
WLIC 801	*Hudson*	Curtis Bay	14 Oct 1976
WLIC 802	*Kennebec*	Curtis Bay	6 Apr 1977
WLIC 803	*Saginaw*	Curtis Bay	22 Sep 1977
Displacement	413 tons		
Dimensions	160′ (oa) × 30′ × 4′		
Machinery	2 screws; diesels; 1,000 BHP; 10 knots		
Complement	14		

Notes: (Tenders and tugs below 100′ not listed)

MISCELLANEOUS VESSELS

Cargo Ships 1947

WAK 169 *Nettle*   Kwajalein, Guam, Cavite, 1953. Trfd to Philippines 9 Jan 1968
   Later history: renamed *Limasawa* (TK 79/AE 79). SE2001.
   ★Vietnam May 1966–Jun 1967.
WAK 170 *Trillium*   Honolulu. Decomm 15 Nov 1950. Trfd to Korea 7 Jul 1955.
   Later history: renamed *Mokpo* (AKL 907). SE1972.
WAK 185 *Unalga*   Decomm 19 Jan 1950.
   Later history: Merchant *Tipton*, renamed *Sea Alaska*.
WAK 186 *Kukui*   Honolulu. Provided logistic support for LORAN stations in Pacific. In collision with m/v *Myonki Maru No. 25* off Yokosuka, Japan, 24 Jun 1970. Decomm and trfd to Philippines 1 Mar 1972.
   Later history: renamed *Mactan* (TK 90/AC 90). SE2001.
   ★Korea May 1953.
WAK 246 *Spruce*   Decomm 6 Jan 1950. Trfd to C&GS, 17 May 1950.

No.	Name	Builder	Launched	Comm
WAGR 410	*Courier*	Froemming	23 Mar 1945	15 Feb 1952
	ex-*Coastal Messenger*, ex-*Doddridge* (AK 176)			
Displacement	5,650 tons f/l			
Dimensions	338′9″ (oa) × 50′4″ × 17′3″			
Machinery	1 screw; diesel; 1,700 SHP; 10.5 knots			
Complement	94			

Notes: Six ships were originally planned. WAGR 411–415 would have been named *Messenger, Envoy, Harbinger, Interpreter,* and *Ariel.*

In comm 15 Feb 1952 to 25 Aug 1964, as relay station for Voice of America in eastern Mediterranean. Recomm 30 Apr 1966, rec **WTR 410**. Decomm 1972.

No.	Name	Builder	Launched	Comm
WHEO 701	*Joseph Henry*	—	—	—
Displacement	3,400 tons			
Dimensions	374′ (oa) × 48′6″ × 17′			
Machinery	1 screw; ST; 10,000 SHP; 16 knots			
Complement	140			

Notes: Oceanographic research ship. Never ordered. Funding stopped after creation of NOAA 1965.

Figure 14.27: *USCGC Courier* (WAG 410), off Rhodes, 1959, serving as a relay station for Voice of America broadcasts.

Training Vessels

No.	Name	Builder	Launched	Acquired
WIX 327	*Eagle*	Blohm & Voss	13 Jun 1936	15 May 1946
	ex-*Horst Wessel*			
Displacement	1,634 tons; 1,816 f/l			
Dimensions	295′ (oa); 231′ (wl) × 39′2″ × 17′			
Machinery	1 screw; aux. Diesels; 740 BHP; 10.5 knots			
Complement	65 (+ 195 cadets)			

Notes: Former German sail training ship seized after World War II. Three-mast bark, steel hull. Two sisterships went to Brazil and the Soviet Union.

No.	Name	Formerly	Acquired	Decomm	Station
WTR 885	*Tanager*	MSF 385	4 Oct 1963	1 Feb 1972	Yorktown, Va.; Alameda, Cal.
WTR 899	*Lamar*	PCE 899	29 Jul 1964	30 Sep 1969	Monterey, Cal.
WTR 379	*Unimak* (see p. 256)	—	—	—	—
WIX 157	*Cuyahoga* (see p. 261)	—	—	—	—

Figure 14.28: *USCGC Tanager* (WTR 885), former Navy minesweeper acquired as training ship, 1963.

15
NATIONAL OCEANIC AND ATMOSPHERIC ADMINISTRATION (NOAA)

Until 1965 NOAA was called the Coast and Geodetic Survey (C&GS). In about 1970, a new numbering system was instituted with classes determined by "horsepower tonnage." A three digit number in which the first digit indicates the "horsepower tonnage" or the sum of the shaft horsepower plus gross tonnage, with prefix for Research (R) or Survey (S).

IN SERVICE, 1947

No.	Name	Built	Fate
—	Hydrographer	1928	Sold 1967
OSS 28	Explorer	1940	Sold 1968
OSS 30	Pathfinder	1942	Sold 1972
ASV 79	Lester Jones	1940	Sold 1967
—	George D. Cowie	1933	Sold 1962
ASV 83	Wainwright	1942	Sold 1967
ASV 82	Hilgard	1942	Sold 1961
—	Sosbee	1945	Sold 1961

ACQUIRED FROM USN 1945–46

No.	Name	Former	Fate
OSS 31	Pioneer	AVP 27 (AGP 7)	Sold 1966, BU Terminal I
—	Bowie	PCS-1405	Decomm 1 Feb 1967
—	Derickson	PCS-1458 (AGS 6)	Sold 1954
—	Hodgson	PCS-1450	Trfd to Korea, Mar 1968, renamed Suro 3
—	Bowen	SC-1361	Sold 1957
—	Parker	SC-1277	Sold 1957
—	Stirni	SC-1358	Sold 1957

Figure 15.1: *USC&GSS Explorer* (OSS 28)

No.	Name	Builder	Built	Acq	Dimensions	Fate
—	*Scott*	Thornycroft	1950	1955	73′ × 15.6′ × 5′	sold 1961
ASV 89	*Marmer* ex-*Walter Wyman* (PHS) (29 May 1957)	Spedden	1932	1957	100.7′ × 22′ × 10′	sold 1968

Old	New	Name	Builder	Launched	Comm.
OSS 1	R101	*Oceanographer*	Aerojet	18 Apr 1964	13 Jul 1966
OSS 2	R102	*Discoverer*	Aerojet	29 Oct 1964	29 Apr 1967

Displacement	3,959 tons
Dimensions	303′4″ (oa) × 52′ × 18′6″
Machinery	2 screws; diesel-electric; 5,000 BHP; 18 knots
Endurance	12,250/15
Complement	92

Notes: Type S2-MET-MA62a.

Service Records
R 101   *Oceanographer*   Decomm 1996.
R 102   *Discoverer*   Decomm 16 Aug 1996.

Old	New	Name	Builder	Launched	Comm.
OSS 3	R103	*Researcher*	Amer; Toledo	5 Oct 1968	8 Oct 1970

Displacement	2,875 tons
Dimensions	278′3″ (oa) × 51′ × 16′4″
Machinery	2 screws; diesel; 3,200 BHP; 16 knots
Endurance	9,700/13
Complement	66

Notes: Type S2-MT-MA74a.

Service Record: renamed *Malcolm Baldrige*, 5 Mar 1988. Decomm 23 Aug 1996. Sold 1999.

    Later history: merchant research vessel *Ushuaia*.

No.	Name	Builder	Keel Laid	Launched	Comm.
R104	*Ronald H. Brown* ex-*Researcher* (1996)	Halter	21 Feb 1995	30 May 1996	19 Jul 1997

Displacement	2,100 tons; 3,250 f/l
Dimensions	274′ (oa) × 52′ × 17′
Machinery	2 screws; diesel-electric; 6,000 SHP; 15 knots
Complement	60

Notes: Built as AGOR 26. Largest vessel in NOAA fleet when completed.

No.	Name	Former	ex-USS	Acquired	Comm.
R330	*McArthur*	AGOS 7	*Indomitable*	9 Dec 2002	20 May 2003
R333	*Ka'imimoana*	AGOS 15	*Titan*	31 Aug 1993	26 Apr 1996
R334	*Hi'ialakai*	AGOS 3	*Vindicator*	30 Oct 2001	3 Sep 2004
R335	*Oscar Elton Sette*	AGOS 13	*Adventurous*	5 Jun 1992	22 Jan 2003
R336	*Gordon Gunter*	AGOS 18	*Relentless*	17 Mar 1993	28 Aug 1998
R339	*Okeanos Explorer*	AGOS 16	*Capable*	13 Sep 2004	13 Aug 2008
R—	—	AGOS 9	*Assertive*	1 Sep 2002	

Displacement	2,328 tons f/l; 1,486 grt
Dimensions	224′ (oa) × 43′ × 16′
Machinery	2 screws; diesel-electric; 3,200 bhp; 11 knots
Complement	35

Notes: Former Navy oceanographic surveillance ships.

Figure 15.2: NOAA ship *Malcolm Baldrige* (R 103), at Wellington, New Zealand, Mar 1990. Originally commissioned as *Researcher*.

Figure 15.3: NOAA ship *Ronald H. Brown* (R. 104), the largest NOAA vessel when built.

Service Records
R 330   *McArthur*   Seattle.
R 333   *Ka'imimoana*   Honolulu.
R 334   *Hi'ialakai*   Hawaii.
R 335   *Sette*   Honolulu.
R 336   *Gunter*   Pascagoula.
R 339   *Okeanos Explorer*   Quonset, RI.

No.	Name	Builder	Launched	Comm.
S222	*Thomas Jefferson* ex-*Littlehales* (T-AGS 52)	Halter	14 Feb 1991	8 Jul 2003

Displacement	2,000 tons; 1,466 grt
Dimensions	208′2″ (oa); 190′ (wl) × 45′ × 14′
Machinery	1 screw; diesel; 2,550 BPH; 16 knots
Complement	36

Notes: Norfolk

No.		Name	Builder	Launched	Comm.
OSS 32	S132	Surveyor	National Stl	25 Apr 1958	30 Apr 1960

Displacement	3,150 tons
Dimensions	292'4" (oa) × 46' × 18'
Machinery	1 screw; ST; 2 boilers; 3,200 SHP; 16 knots
Endurance	8,000/12
Complement	120

Notes: Type S2-S-RM28a. Helicopter platform added aft.

Service Record: Decomm 1995.

No.		Name	Builder	Launched	Comm.
CSS 30	S330	McArthur	Norfolk SB	15 Nov 1965	15 Dec 1966
CSS 31	S331	Davidson	Norfolk SB	7 May 1966	10 Mar 1967

Displacement	995 tons
Dimensions	175' (oa) × 38' × 11'6"
Machinery	2 screws; diesel; 1,600 BHP; 13 knots
Endurance	6,000/12
Complement	40

Notes: Type S1-MT1-MA70a.

Service Records

S 330	McArthur	Stricken 20 May 2003.
S 331	Davidson	Stricken 1997.

No.	Name	Builder	Keel Laid	Launched	Comm.
R224	Oscar Dyson	Halter	18 Apr 2002	17 Oct 2003	28 May 2005
R225	Henry B. Bigelow	Halter	21 May 2004	8 Jul 2005	16 Jul 2007
R226	Pisces	Halter	23 Jun 2006	19 Dec 2007	—
R227	Bell M. Shimada	Halter	15 Jun 2007	—	—

Displacement	1,840 tons; 2,479 f/l
Dimensions	208'7" (oa) × 48'11" × 19'5"
Machinery	1 screw; diesel-electric; 2,440 BHP; 14 knots
Complement	39

Notes: Fisheries survey vessels.

Service Record

R 224	Dyson	Kodiak.
R 225	Bigelow	Northeast U.S.
R 226	Pisces.	
R 227	Shimada	

Acquired from U.S. Coast Guard

Former	Name	Date	Notes
WPB 82336	Point Glass	9 Apr 2001	By Flower Garden Banks National Marine Sanctuary. Decomm 2006.
WPB 82353	Point Monroe	19 Aug 2001	—
WPB 82366	Point Lobos	13 Oct 2001	—

No.		Name	Builder	Launched	Comm.
MSS 20	S220	Fairweather	Aerojet	8 Mar 1967	2 Oct 1968
MSS 21	S221	Rainier	Aerojet	10 Mar 1967	2 Oct 1968
MSS 22	S222	Mount Mitchell	Aerojet	21 Nov 1966	23 Mar 1968

Displacement	1,798 tons; 1,591 grt
Dimensions	231' (oa) × 42' × 13'10"
Machinery	2 screws; diesel; 2,400 BHP; 14.5 knots
Endurance	5,800/11
Complement	58

Notes: Type S1-MT-MA72a.

Service Record

S 220	Fairweather	Stricken 1989. Recomm 18 Aug 2004. Ketchikan.
S 221	Rainier	Seattle.
S 222	Mount Mitchell	Stricken 1995.

No.		Name	Builder	Launched	Comm.
ASV 90	S590	Rude	Jakobson	17 Aug 1966	29 Mar 1967
ASV 91	S591	Heck	Jakobson	1 Nov 1966	29 Mar 1967

Displacement	220 tons fl
Dimensions	90' (oa) × 22' × 7'2"
Machinery	2 screws; diesels; 800 BHP; 9 knots
Endurance	650/9
Complement	11

Notes: S1-MT-MA71a

Service Records

ASV 90	Rude	Decomm 25 Mar 2008
ASV 91	Heck	Stricken 1995.

Old	No.	Name	Builder	Launched	Comm.
CSS 28	S328	Peirce	Marietta	15 Oct 1962	6 May 1963
CSS 29	S329	Whiting	Marietta	20 Nov 1962	8 Jul 1963

Displacement	760 tons
Dimensions	164' (oa) × 33' × 10'
Machinery	2 screws; diesel; 1,600 BHP; 12.5 knots
Endurance	5,700/12
Complement	40

Notes: Type S1-MT-59a.

Service Records

CSS 328	Peirce TS	tfrd to New York City, 1993, renamed Elizabeth A. Fisher,
CSS 329	Whiting	Stricken 2 May 2003.

Figure 15.4: *USC7GSS Peirce* (CSS 28).

No.	Name	Builder	Launched	Comm.
ASV 92 S492	Ferrel	Zeigler	4 Apr 1968	4 Jun 1968
Displacement	363 tons			
Dimensions	133'3" (oa) × 32' × 7'			
Machinery	2 screws; diesel; 750 BHP; 10.6 knots			
Endurance	1,600/8			
Complement	16			

Notes: Type S1-MT-MA83a.

Service Record: Stricken 21 Nov 2002.

No.	Name	Builder	Launched	Comm.
R223	Miller Freeman	Amer; Lorain	1967	1974
Displacement	1,920 tons f/l; 1,515 grt			
Dimensions	216'6" (oa) × 41' × 20'			
Machinery	1 screw; diesel; 2,150 BHP; 12 knots			
Endurance	8,900/12			
Complement	40			

Notes: Fisheries research ship.

Service Record: Laid up 1968–74. Struck submerged reef and damaged off Kodiak Island, 1 Apr 2004. Seattle.

No.	Name	Builder	Launched	Comm.
R332	Oregon II	Ingalls	Feb 1967	17 Mar 1977
Displacement	952 tons f/l; 703 grt			
Dimensions	170' (oa) × 34' × 14'			
Machinery	1 screw; diesels; 1,600 BHP; 12 knots			
Endurance	8,900/12			
Complement	31			

Notes: Fisheries research ship.

Service Record: Pascagoula.

No.	Name	Builder	Launched	Comm.
R342	Albatross IV	Southern	19 Apr 1962	May 1963
Displacement	1,089 tons f/l; 1,115 grt			
Dimensions	187' (oa) × 33' × 16'			
Machinery	1 Kort nozzle; diesels; 1,130 BHP; 10 knots			
Endurance	3,800/10			
Complement	36			

Notes: Fisheries research ship. Stern-ramp trawler.

Service Record: Woods Hole, Mass.

No.	Name	Builder	Launched	Comm.
R352	Nancy Foster ex-Agate Pass (YTT 12)	McDermott	6 Sep 1990	10 May 2004
Displacement	1,000 tons; 1,200 f/l			
Dimensions	186'6" (oa); 176'6" (wl) × 40' × 10'6"			
Machinery	2 all-azimuth drives; diesel-electric; 1,250 SHP; 11 knots			
Complement	37			

Notes: Built by USN as torpedo trials craft but laid up on completion. Norfolk.

No.	Name	Builder	Launched	Comm.
R443	Townsend Cromwell	McDermott	1963	1963
Displacement	652 tons f/l			
Dimensions	163' (oa) × 33' × 12'10"			
Machinery	2 screws; diesels; 800 BHP; 10 knots			
Endurance	7,200/10			
Complement	28			

Notes: Acquired by NOAA in 1975. Fisheries research ship.

Service Record: Decomm 10 Oct 2002. Trfd to American Samoa.

No.	Name	Builder	Launched	Comm.
R444	David Starr Jordan	Christy	19 Dec 1964	8 Jan 1966
Displacement	993 tons f/l; 873 grt			
Dimensions	170'10" (oa) × 36'9" × 15'9"			
Machinery	2 screws; diesels; 1,086 BHP; 11.5 knots			
Endurance	8,560/11.5			
Complement	32			

Notes: Built for the Bureau of Commercial Fisheries; acquired by NOAA in 1987. Helicopter deck aft.

Service Record: La Jolla, Cal.

No.	Name	Builder	Launched	Comm.
R445	Delaware II	S.Portland	Dec 1967	12 Mar 1975
Displacement	897 tons f/l; 610 grt			
Dimensions	155' (oa) × 30' × 14'9"			
Machinery	1 screw; diesel; 1,230 BHP; 11 knots			
Endurance	6,300/11			
Complement	25			

Service Record: Woods Hole, Mass.

No.	Name	Builder	Launched	Comm.
R446	Chapman	Bender	1979	1980
Displacement	520 tons f/l			
Dimensions	127' (oa) × 29'10" × 14'			
Machinery	1 screw; diesel; 1,250 BHP; 19 knots			
Endurance	3,000/9			
Complement	18			

Service Record: Decomm 2 Jun 1998.

No.	Name	Builder	Launched	Comm.
R552	John N. Cobb	Western	16 Jan 1950	18 Feb 1950
Displacement	250 tons f/l; 185 grt			
Dimensions	93' (oa) × 26' × 11'			
Machinery	1 screw; diesel; 325 BHP; 9 knots			
Endurance	2,800/9			
Complement	13			

Notes: Wood hull, trawler type. Transferred from Fish & Wildlife Service, 1 Jul 1972.

Service Record: Decomm 13 Aug 2008. Seattle.

Old	No.	Name	Built	Acq	Builder	Tons	Length	Fate
FRV 51	R551	Oregon	1946			373	100′	Stricken 1972
		Spruce	1945	1950	Higgins	935	176′	
		ex-Spruce WAK 246, ex-FS 222						
ARV 80	R680	Virginia Key	1952			90	65′	
	R441	George B. Kelez	1945	1970	Ingalls; Dec.	936	176′6″	Sold 1982
		ex-AKL 30, ex-FS 400						
—	R663	Murre II	1943	1987	Martinolich	295	86 × 26′9″ × 7′6″	Sold 1991
—	R693	Shenahon		1953	Mo.Valley	98		LU 1996

ENVIRONMENTAL PROTECTION AGENCY

Peter Wise Lake Guardian, 850 tons, built 1981, length 180′, acquired 1988, SE.

Name	Formerly	Acquired	Disposition
Peter W. Anderson	PG 86 Antelope	1978	SE
Rachel Carson	PG 88 Crockett	1977	OS 1982
Roger R. Simons	WAGL 234 Maple	1974	sold 1989

NATIONAL SCIENCE FOUNDATION

Name	Displacement	Built	Disposition
Nathaniel B. Palmer	6800	1991	SE
Polar Duke	1645	1983	OS 1997
Laurence M. Gould	2755	1997	SE

Note: All designed for polar operations. *Palmer* and *Gould* built by Edison Chouest Offshore Inc., Galliano, Louisiana.

PRINCIPAL SHIP BUILDERS

Aerojet	Aerojet-General Corp., Jacksonville, Fla.
Alabama DD	Alabama Dry Dock and Shipbuilding Co., Mobile, Ala.
Amer; Lorain	American Shipbuilding Co., Lorain, Ohio
Amer; Toledo	American Shipbuilding Co., Toledo, Ohio
Amyot	Felix Amyot, Cherbourg, France
Ansaldo	Societa per Azioni Ansaldo, Genoa-Sestri, Italy
Arnhem	Arnhemische Schps. Maats., Arnhem, Netherlands
ASMAR	Asmar S.A., Talcahuano, Chile
Astoria	Astoria Marine Construction Co., Astoria, Ore.
Atlantique	Chantiers de l'Atlantique, St. Nazaire, France
Austal	Austal USA, Mobile, Ala.
Avondale	Avondale Shipyards Inc, Avondale, La.
Basalt	Basalt Rock Co., Napa, Cal.
Bath	Bath Iron Works Corp., Bath, Me.
Bay City	Bay City Marine Co., Tacoma, Wash.
Bazan	Bazan Empresa Nacional de Construcciones Navales Militares, El Ferrol and Cartagena, Spain
Bell-Halter	Bell-Halter Inc., New Orleans, La.
Bellingham	Bellingham Shipyards Co., Bellingham, Wash.
Berg	Berg Shipbuilding Co., Seattle, Wash.
Beth; Fair	Bethlehem Fairfield Shipyard, Inc., Baltimore, Md.
Beth; Quincy	Bethlehem Shipbuilding Corp., Quincy, Mass.
Beth; S.Fran.	Bethlehem Steel Co., San Francisco, Cal.
Beth; Staten I	Bethlehem Steel Co., Staten Island, NY
Blohm & Voss	Blohm & Voss, Hamburg, Germany
Boeing	Boeing Co., Seattle, Wash.
Bollinger	Bollinger Shipyards, Lockport, La.
Boston NSYd	Boston Naval Shipyard, Boston, Mass.
Breda	Cantiere Navale Breda, Venice, Italy
Bremer Vulkan	Bremer Vulkan Schiffbau & Maschinenfabrik, Vegesack, Germany
Brooke Marine	Brooke Marine, Ltd., Lowestoft, England
Broward	Broward Marine, Dania Beach, Fort Lauderdale, Fla.
Burger	Burger Boat Co., Manitowoc, Wis.
Burmeister	Burmeister & Wain, Copenhagen, Denmark
Bushey	Ira S. Bushey & Sons, Inc., Brooklyn, NY
Butler; Duluth	Walter Butler Shipbuilders Inc., Duluth, Minn.
Calship	California Shipbuilding Corp., Terminal Island, Los Angeles, Cal.
Calumet	Calumet Shipyard & Dry Dock Co., Chicago, Ill.

Castellammare	Cantiere Navale Castellamare di Stabia (Italcantieri), Naples, Italy
Chernomorskiy	"Chernomorskiy" Shipyard, Nikolayev, Ukraine
Christy	Christy Corp., Sturgeon Bay, Wis.
Colberg	Colberg Boat Works, Stockton, Stockton, Cal.
Cons; Wilm	Consolidated Steel Corp., Wilmington, Los Angeles, Cal.
Consolidated	Consolidated Shipbuilding Corp., Morris Heights, New York, NY
Copenhagen	Royal Dockyard, Copenhagen, Denmark
CRDA	Cantiere Riuniti dell'Adriatico, Trieste, Italy
CUF SY (Lisbon	CUF Shipyard, Lisbon, Portugal
Curtis Bay	Coast Guard Yard, Curtis Bay, Md.
Daewoo	Daewoo SB & Heavy Machinery Ltd, Okpo, South Korea
De Noord	Van der Giessen-de-Noord N.V. (formerly Werf de Noord), Alblasserdam, Netherlands
Defoe	Defoe Shipbuilding Co., Bay City, Mich.
Derecktor	Robert E. Derecktor, Middletown, R.I.
Dorchester	Dorchester Shipbuilding Corp., Dorchester, NJ
DTCN	Directions Techniques Des Constructions Naval, Cherbourg, France
Dubigeon	S.A. des Anciens Chantiers Dubigeon, Nantes, France
Dunkerque	Chantiers de France-Dunkerque, Dunkerque, France
Electric Boat	Electric Boat Co., Groton, Conn.
Erie Concrete	Erie Concrete & Steel Supply Co., Erie, Pa.
Eriksbergs	Eriksbergs M/V A/B, Goteborg, Sweden
Fairfield	Fairfield Shipbuilding & Engineering Co., Glasgow, Scotland (now Upper Clyde)
Fincantieri	Fincantieri-Cant. Nav. Italiani S.p.A., Genoa, Italy
Fosen	Fosen M.V., Fevag
Froemming	Froemming Bros., Inc., Milwaukee, Wis.
Fulton	Fulton Shipyard Co., Antioch, Cal.
Gdynia	Stocznia im. "Komuny Paryskiej", Gdynia, Poland
Georgia Sbdg	Georgia Shipbuilding, Savannah, Ga
Gen. Dyn; Quincy	General Dynamics, Quincy, Mass.
General; Boston	General Shipbuilding and Engineering Works, Boston, MA
Gibbs	Gibbs Corp., Jacksonville, Fla.
Grebe	Henry C. Grebe & Co., Chicago, Ill.
Grumman	Grumman Aircraft Engineering Corp., Stuart, Fla.
Gulf	Gulf Shipbuilding Corp., Mobile, Ala.
Gunderson	Gunderson Marine Inc., Portland, Ore.
Gusto	N.V.Werf Gusto, Schiedam, Netherlands
Halter	Halter Marine Services, New Orleans, La. & Moss Point, Miss.
Harbor	Harbor Boat Building Co., Terminal Island, Cal.
Helsingor	Helsingör Skibsvaerft, Helsingør, Denmark
Hickinbotham	Hickinbotham Bros., Stockton, Cal.
Higgins	Higgins Industries, Inc., New Orleans, La.
Hiltebrant	Hiltebrant Ddrydock Co., Kingston, NY
Hodgdon	Hodgdon Bros., Goudy & Stevens, East Boothbay, Me.
Howaldt	Howaldswerke-Deutsche Werft A.G., Kiel, Germany
Incat Tasmania	Incat, Hobart, Tasmania, Australia
Ingalls	Ingalls Shipbuilding Co., Pascagoula, Miss.
Ingalls; Decatur	Ingalls Shipbuilding Co., Decatur, Ala.
Intermarine	Intermarine USA, Savannah, Ga.
Jakobson	Jacobson Shipyard, Oyster Bay, NY
Jones; Brun	J.A. Jones Construction Co., Brunswick, Ga.
Jones; PC	J.A. Jones Construction Co., Panama City, Fla.
Kais; Vanc	Kaiser Co., Vancouver, Wash.
Kaiser #4	Kaiser Co., Richmond Yard No.4, Richmond, Cal.
Kaldnes	Kaldnes M/V A/S, Tönsberg, Norway
Kawasaki	Kawasaki Heavy Ind. Ltd., Sakaide, Japan
Kewaunee	Kewaunee Shipbuilding & Engineering Co.l, Kewaunee, Wis.
Kleven	Kleven M/V A/S, Ulsteinvik, Norway
Kneass	George W. Kneass Co., San Francisco, Cal.
Kockums	Kockums AB, Malmö, Sweden

Kroger	Krögerwerft, Rendsburg, Germany
La Ciotat	Chantiers Navals de La Ciotat, La Ciotat, France
Lake Union	Lake Union Dry Dock Co., Inc. Seattle, Wash.
LD Smith	Leatham D. Smith Ship Building Co., Sturgeon Bay, Wis. (Later Christy)
Levingston	Levingston Ship Building Co., Orange, Tex.
Lisnave	Estaleiros Navais de Lisboa Lisnave, Lisbon, Portugal
Lockheed	Lockheed Shipbuilding and Construction, Seattle, Wash.
Loire	Ateliers et Chantiers de la Loire, St. Nazaire, France
Luders	Luders Marine Construction Co., Stamford, Conn.
M.M. Davis	M.M. Davis & Sons, Inc., Solomons, Md.
Mare I NSYd	Mare Island Naval Shipyard, Vallejo, Cal.
Marietta	Marietta Manufacturing Co., Point Pleasant, W.Va.
Marinette	Marinette Marine Corp., Marinette, Wis.
Marinship	Marinship Corp., Sausalito, Cal.
Martinac	J.M. Martinac SB Corp., Tacoma, Wash.
Martinolich	Martinolich SB Co., San Diego, Cal.
Maryland Sbdg	Maryland SB & DD Co., Baltimore, Md.
Mathis	John H. Mathis Co., Camden, NJ
McCloskey	McCloskey & Co., Tampa, Fla.
McDermott	McDermott Inc., Amelia, La.
Mediteranee	Constructions Navales et Industrielles de la Mediteranée, La Seyne, France
Mie SY	Mie Zosen, Yokohama, Japan
Mitsubishi	Mitsubishi Heavy Industries Ltd, Nagasaki and Kobe, Japan
Mondego	Estaleiros Navals do Mondego, Figueira da Foz, Portugal
Moore	Moore Dry Dock Co., Oakland, Cal.
Moss Point	Moss Point Marine, Inc., Escatawpa, Miss.
National Stl	National Steel & SB Co., San Diego, Cal.
Neptun	Neptun Schiffswerft, Rostock, Germany
Nevins	Henry B. Nevins, Inc., City Island, NY
New York NSYd	New York Naval Shipyard, Brooklyn, NY
New England	New England Shipbulding Corp., South Portland, Me.
Newport News	Newport News Shipbuilding & Dry Dock Corp., Newport News, Va.
Niagara SB	Niagara Shipbuilding Corp., Buffalo, NY
Niestern	Gebr. Niestern Scheepswerven, Deflzijl, Netherlands
Norfolk SB	Norfolk Shipbuilding and Drydock Co., Norfolk, Va.
Norfolk NSYd	Norfolk Naval Shipyard, Portsmouth, Va.
Normand	Chantiers & Ateliers Augustin Normand, Le Havre, France (later A.& C. du Havre)
Normandie	Chantiers de Normandie, Rouen, France
North American, Larose	North American Shipbuilding Co., Larose, La.
NY Sbdg	New York Shipbuilding Co., Camden, NJ
Northwest	Northwest Marine Iron Works, Portland, Ore.
Odense	Odense Staalskibsvaerft A/S, Lindo, Odense, Denmark
Oregon	Oregon Shipbuilding Co., Portland, Ore.
Pacific	Pacific Boatbuilding Co., Tacoma, Wash.
Penhoet	Chantiers et Ateliers de Saint Nazaire (Penhoët), St. Nazaire, France
Penn SY	Pennsylvania Shipyards, Inc., Beaumont, Tex.
Penn Sbdg	Pennsylvania Shipbuilding, Chester, Pa. (Formerly Sun)
Permanente 2	Permanente Metals Corp., Yard No. 2, Richmond, Cal.
Peterson	Peterson Builders, Sturgeon Bay, Wis.
Phila. NSYd	Philadelphia Naval Shipyard, Philadelphia, Pa.
Port Weller	Port Weller Dry Docks Ltd, St. Catherines, Ont.
Portsmouth NSYd	Portsmouth Naval Shipyard, Portsmouth, NH
Puget Sd Brdg	Puget Sound Bridge & Dredging Co., Seattle, Wash.
Puget Sd NSYd	Puget Sound Naval Shipyard, Bremerton, Wash.
Pusey & Jones	Pusey & Jones Corp., Wilmington, Del.
Quincy Adams	Quincy Adams Yacht Yard, Inc., Quincy, Mass.
Rheinstal	Nordseewerke Rheinstahl, Emden, Germany
Rio de Janeiro	Arsenal da Marinha, Rio de Janeiro, Brazil
Rotterdam	RotterdamscheDroogdok Mij., Rotterdam, Netherlands

S.Portland	South Portland Shipbuilding Corp., South Portland, Me.
Sample	Frank L. Sample, Jr., Boothbay Harbor, Me.
Samsung	Samsung Shipbuilding Co., Koje, South Korea
San Fran. NSYd	San Francisco Naval Ship Yard, San Francisco, Cal.
Sasebo	Sasebo Heavy Industries Co. Ltd, Sasebo
Sea-Tac; Tac	Seattle-Tacoma Shipbulding Corp., Tacoma, Wash.
Seattle Sbdg	Seattle Shipbuilding & Dry Dock Co., Seattle, Wash.
Seine	Ateliers et Chantiers de la Seine Maritime, Le Trait, France
Sewart Seacraft	Sewart Seacraft Inc., Berwick, La.
Sima, Callao	Sima, Callao, Peru
Smit	N.V. Machinefabriek en Scheepswerf van P. Smit, Jr., Rotterdam, Netherlands
South Coast	South Coast Co., Newport Beach, Cal.
Southeastern	Southeastern Shipbuilding Corp., Savannah, Ga.
Southern	Southern Shipyard Corp., Newport News, Va.
Sparrows Pt	Bethlehem Steel Co. Inc., Sparrows Point, Md.
Stephen Bros	Stephen Brothers Inc., Stockton, Cal.
Stowman	Stowman Shipyards, Inc., Dorchester, NJ
Sturgeon Bay	Sturgeon Bay Shipbuilding & Dry Dock Co., Sturgeon Bay, Wis.
Sumitomo	Sumitomo SB & Mchry Co. Ltd, Uraga SY, Yokosuka
Sun	Sun Shipbuilding & Dry Dock Co., Chester, Pa.
Swan I	Kaiser Co. Inc., Swan Island Yard, Portland, Ore.
Swan Hunter	Swan Hunter & Wigham Richardson, Wallsend-on-Tyne, England
Tacoma Boat	Tacoma Boat Building Co., Tacoma, Wash.
Tampa	Tampa SB Co, Inc., Tampa, Fla.
Tampa Marine	Tampa Marine Corp., Tampa, Fla.
Tangen	Tangen Verft A/S, Kragerö, Norway
Tirreno	Cantieri del Tirreno, Ancona, Italy
Todd; Houston	Todd Houston Shipbuilding Corp., Houston, Tex.
Todd; S.Pedro	Todd Shipyards Corp., San Pedro, Los Angeles, Cal.
Todd; Seattle	Todd Shipyards, Seattle, Wash.
Trumpy	John Trumpy & Sons, Annapolis, Md.
Tsurumi	Nippon Kokan K.K., Tsurumi
Tuzla Gerni, Tuzla	Tuzla Gemi Endustrisi A.S., Tuzla, Turkey
United Concrete	United Concrete Pipe Corp., Long Beach, Cal.
Upper Clyde	Upper Clyde Shipbuilders, Glasgow, Scotland
Viana do Castelho	Est. Navais de Viana do Castelo, Viana do Castelo, Portugal
Weser	A.G. Weser, Bremen, Germany
Western	Western Boatbuilding Co., Tacoma, Wash.
Wheeler	Wheeler S.B. Corp., Whitestone, Long Island, NY
Willemsoord	Rijkswerf Willemsoord, Netherlands
Wilmington Bt	Wilmington Boat Works, Inc., Wilmington, Cal.
Wilton	Wilton-Fijenoord Dok-en Werf Maats., Schiedam, Netherlands
Wuhu	Wuhu Shipbuilding Corporation, Wuhu, China
Yardimci, Tuzla	Yardimci Gemi A.S., Tuzla, Turkey
Zeigler	Zeigler Shipyard, Jennings, La.

SELECTED BIBLIOGRAPHY

SERIAL PUBLICATIONS

Merchant Vessels of the United States (various from 1870)
Record, American Bureau of Shipping (various from 1870)
Warship International (International Naval Research Organization)
Combat Fleets of the World
Jane's Fighting Ships
Schell, *Register of Merchant Ships* completed in (1890 to 1939)
Lloyds' Register of Shipping
Lloyds' Register of American Yachts
U.S. Navy, *Ships' Data U.S. Naval Vessels*, 1945, 1949
Ships and Aircraft of the U.S. Fleet, 1939–2004
Marine News (World Ship Society)

BOOKS

Alden, John D. *The Fleet Submarine in the U.S. Navy.* Annapolis, Md.: Naval Institute Press, 1979.

Bauer, K. Jack & Roberts, Stephen S. *Register of Ships of the U.S. Navy, 1775–1990: Major Combatants.* New York: Greenport, Conn. 1991.

Cagle, Malcolm W. & Manson, Frank A. *The Sea War in Korea.* Annapolis, Md.: United States Naval Institute, 1957.

Cooney, David M. *A Chronology of the United States Navy: 1775–1965.* New York, N.Y.: Franklin Watts, Inc., 1965.

Fahey, James C. *The Ships and Aircraft of the United States Fleet.* New York: Ships and Aircraft, 1939–1958.

Friedman, Norman. *U.S. Battleships: An Illustrated Design History.* Annapolis, Md.: Naval Institute Press, 1985.

Friedman, Norman. *U.S. Cruisers: An Illustrated Design History.* Annapolis, Md.: Naval Institute Press, 1984.

Friedman, Norman. *U.S. Destroyers: An Illustrated Design History.* Annapolis, Md.: Naval Institute Press, 1982.

Friedman, Norman. *U.S. Small Combatants.* Annapolis, Md.: Naval Institute Press, 1987.

Polmar, Norman. *The Ships and Aircraft of the United States Fleet* (various editions).

Raven, Alan. *Fletcher-Class Destroyers.* Annapolis, Md.: Naval Institute Press, 1989.

Scheina, Robert L. *U.S. Coast Guard Cutters & Craft, 1946–1990.* Annapolis, Md.: Naval Institute Press, 1990.

Sontag, Sheila & Drew, Christopher. *Blind Man's Bluff: the Untold Story of American Submarine Espionage.* New York: Public Affairs, 1998.

U.S. Navy. *Dictionary of American Naval Fighting Ships*, 8 vols. Washington, D.C.: Naval Historical Center, Department of the Navy, 1959–81.

U.S. Navy and Marine Corps Awards Manual (NavPers 15,790 Revised 1953), Published by Bureau of Naval Personnel, Department of the Navy, Washington, DC.

Winkler, David F. *Cold War at Sea.* Annapolis, Md.: Naval Institute Press, 2000.

Terzibaschitsch, Stefan. *Das FRAM-Modernisierungsprogramm Der U.S. Navy.* Munchen: J.F. Lehmanns Verlag.

Websites
www.destroyers.org
www.navsource.org
Miramar Ship Index (http://www.miramarshipindex.org.nz/)

INDEX

THE NAVY OF THE NUCLEAR AGE
PLAN OF THE BOOK

Introduction	vii
Explanation of Data	xi
Abbreviations	xiii
US Navy Type Designations	xv
US Naval Ordnance, 1947–2007	xix
Biography – William J. Jurens	xxix
Chronology, 1947–2007	xxxi

1. Aircraft Carriers — 1
   - a. Carriers on the Navy List — 2
   - b. Escort Carriers — 10
2. Submarines — 13
   - a. Submarines on the Navy List — 14
   - b. Nuclear Attack Submarines — 25
   - b. Strategic Missile Submarines — 33
3. Battleships — 37
4. Cruisers — 39
   - a. Cruisers on the Navy List — 39
   - a. Guided Missile Cruisers — 42
   - b. Command Ships — 44
   - c. Frigates/Cruisers — 45
5. Destroyers — 53
   - a. Destroyers on the Navy List — 54
   - b. Escort Destroyers — 69
   - a. Guided Missile Destroyers — 73
6. Escorts/Frigates — 79
   - a. Destroyer Escorts on the Navy List — 79
   - a. Escorts — 87
   - b. Frigates — 89
   - c. Missile Frigates — 92
7. Amphibious Ships — 97
   - a. Amphibious Assault Ships — 97
   - b. Amphibious Transport Docks — 100
   - c. Littoral Combat Ships — 102
   - d. Dock Landing Ships — 102
   - e. Tank Landing Ships — 105
   - f. Rocket Ships — 115
   - g. Amphibious Command Ships — 117
   - h. Amphibious Cargo Ships — 119
   - i. Attack Transports — 121
   - j. High Speed Transports — 124
8. Patrol Combatants — 127
   - a. Gunboats — 127
   - b. Frigates — 128
   - c. Hydrofoils — 129
   - d. Patrol Vessels — 131
   - e. Patrol Motor Gunboats — 137
   - f. Fast Patrol Boats — 139
9. Mine Warfare Ships — 141
   - a. Minelayers — 141
   - b. Minesweepers — 143
   - c. Mine Countermeasures Ships — 151
   - d. Coastal Minesweepers — 151
   - e. Inshore Minesweepers — 161
10. Tenders — 163
    - a. Destroyer Tenders — 163
    - b. Submarine Tenders — 165
    - c. Submarine Rescue Vessels — 166
    - d. Seaplane Tenders — 167
    - e. Repair Ships — 170
    - f. Cable Repairing Ships — 173
    - f. Salvage Vessels — 174
    - g. Miscellaneous Auxiliaries — 175
    - h. Icebreakers — 179
    - i. Intelligence Collectors — 180
    - j. Missile Range Instrumentation Ships — 181
    - k. Oceanographic Surveillance Ships — 183
    - l. Radar Picket Ships — 185
    - m. Surveying Ships — 186
    - n. Oceanographic Research Ships — 189
    - o. Net Laying Ships — 190
    - p. Unclassified Vessels — 192
11. Transports and Supply Ships — 195
    - a. Ammunition Ships — 195
    - b. Store Ships — 197
    - c. Combat Store Ships — 199
    - d. Cargo Ships — 200

e. Dry Cargo Ships 206
f. Vehicle Cargo Ships 206
g. Cargo Stores-issue Ships 207
h. Light Cargo Ships 207
i. Oilers 209
j. Gasoline Tankers 218
k. Fast Combat Support Ships 219
l. Replenishment Oilers 220
m. Transports 221
n. Barracks Ships 225
o. Hospital Ships 226
12. Fleet Tugs 229
a. Auxiliary Tugs 231
b. Salvage and Rescue Ships 232
13. Sealift Ships 235
a. Auxiliary Crane Ships 236
b. Container Ships 237
c. Maritime Prepositioning Ships 238
d. Vehicle Cargo Ships 242
e. Lash Ships 245
f. Cargo Ships 246
g. Transport Oilers/ Tankers 250
h. Transports 253
i. Support Ships 253
14. U.S. Coast Guard 255
a. High Endurance Cutters 256
b. Maritime Security Cutters 257
c. Medium Endurance Cutters 258
d. Patrol Vessels 260
e. Patrol Boats 262
f. Surface Effects Ships 267
g. Icebreakers 268
h. Icebreaking Tugs 269
i. Lighthouse Tenders/ Buoy Tenders 270
j. Miscellaneous Vessels 275
15. NOAA 277
Principal Ship Builders 283
Selected Bibliography 287
Plan of the Book 289
Index 291

INDEX FOR VOL. 5
THE NAVY OF THE NUCLEAR AGE 1947–2007

1st Lt. Alex Bonnyman Jr., AK 3003, 240
1st Lt. Alexander Bonnyman Jr., AK 3003, 240
1st Lt. Baldomero Lopez, AK 3010, 239
1st Lt. Harry L. Martin, AK 3015, 241
1st Lt. Jack Lummus, AK 3011, 239
2nd Lt. John P. Bobo, AK 3008, 239

A1C William H. Pitsenbarger, AK 4638, 238
Abatan, AW 4, 213
Abbie Burgess, WLM 553, 274
Abbot, DD 629, 58
Abercrombie, DE 343, 84
Ability, MSO 519, 150
Ability, AFDL 7, 227
Abingdon, PC 1237, 133
Abiqua, AO 158, 215
Able, AGOS 20, 185
Abnaki, ATF 96, 230
Abraham Lincoln, CVN 72, 8
Abraham Lincoln, SSBN 602, 33
Absecon, AVP 23, 168; WAVP/ WHEC 374, 256
Acacia, WAGL/WLB 406, 271
Acadia, AD 42, 164
Accentor, AMCU 15, 160

Accokeek, ATA 181, 231
Accomac, APB 49, 225
Achelous, ARL 1, 171
Achernar, AKA 53, 119
Achomawi, ATF 148, 230
Acme, MSO 508, 150
Acree, DE 167, 81
Active, WMEC 618, 259
Active, WSC 125, 260
Acushnet, WAT/WAGO/WMEC 167, 258
Adak, WPB 1333, 266
Adams, DM/MMD 27, 141
Addison County, LST 31, 105
Adelie, WPB 87333, 267
Adelphi, AG 181, 177
Adept, AFDL 23, 227
Adirondack, AGC 15, 118
Adm. William M. Callaghan, AKR 1001, 243
Adonis, ARL 4, 171
Adria, AF 30, 197
Adroit, MSO 509, 150
Advance, MSO 510, 150
Advantage, AK 9652, 250
Adventurer, AK 5005, 249
Adventurous, AGOS 13, 183
Aegir, AS 23, 165
Aeolus, ARC 3, 173
Affray, MSO 511, 150
Agassiz, WSC 126, 260
Agawam, AOG 6, 218
Agenor, ARL 3, 171

Agent, AK 5008, 249
Agerholm, DD 826, 65
Aggressive, MSO 422, 147
Agile, MSO 421, 147
Ahi, WPB 87364, 267
Ahrens, DE 575, 79
Aide, AK 5006, 249
Aiken Victory, AP 188, 224
Ainsworth, DE/FF 1090, 90
Air Avocet, WAVR 411, 262
Air Brant, WAVR 412, 262
Air Cardinal, WAVR 413, 262
Air Condor, WAVR 414, 262
Air Cormorant, WAVR 415, 262
Air Crow, WAVR 416, 262
Air Curlew, WAVR 417, 262
Air Drake, WAVR 418, 262
Air Egret, WAVR 420, 262
Air Eider, WAVR 419, 262
Air Falcon, WAVR 421, 262
Air Finch, WAVR 422, 262
Air Gannet, WAVR 423, 262
Air Goose, WAVR 424, 262
Air Graylag, WAVR 425, 262
Air Grebe, WAVR 426, 262
Air Gull, WAVR 427, 262
Air Hawk, WAVR 428, 262
Air Heron, WAVR 429, 262
Air Ibis, WAVR 430, 262
Air Jay, WAVR 431, 262
Air Kestrel, WAVR 432, 262
Air Killdeer, WAVR 433, 262
Air Lapwing, WAVR 434, 262

Air Linnet, WAVR 435, 262
Air Loon, WAVR 436, 262
Air Mallard, WAVR 437, 262
Air Martin, WAVR 438, 262
Air Merlin, WAVR 439, 262
Air Oriole, WAVR 440, 262
Air Owl, WAVR 441, 262
Air Parrakeet, WAVR 442, 262
Air Parrot, WAVR 443, 262
Air Partridge, WAVR 444, 262
Air Peacock, WAVR 445, 262
Air Pelican, WAVR 446, 262
Air Penguin, WAVR 447, 262
Air Petrel, WAVR 448, 262
Air Pheasant, WAVR 449, 262
Air Phoebe, WAVR 450, 262
Air Pigeon, WAVR 451, 262
Air Piper, WAVR 452, 262
Air Plover, WAVR 453, 262
Air Puffin, WAVR 454, 262
Air Quail, WAVR 455, 262
Air Raven, WAVR 456, 262
Air Redwing, WAVR 457, 262
Air Robin, WAVR 458, 262
Air Rook, WAVR 459, 262
Air Ruff, WAVR 460, 262
Air Scaup, WAVR 481, 262
Air Scooter, WAVR 482, 262
Air Sheldrake, WAVR 461, 262
Air Shrike, WAVR 462, 262
Air Skimmer, WAVR 463, 262
Air Skylark, WAVR 464, 262
Air Snipe, WAVR 465, 262
Air Sparrow, WAVR 466, 262
Air Starling, WAVR 467, 262
Air Stork, WAVR 468, 262
Air Swallow, WAVR 469, 262
Air Swan, WAVR 470, 262
Air Swift, WAVR 471, 262
Air Tanager, WAVR 472, 262
Air Teal, WAVR 473, 262
Air Tern, WAVR 474, 262
Air Thrush, WAVR 475, 262
Air Toucan, WAVR 476, 262
Air Warbler, WAVR 477, 262
Air Waxwing, WAVR 478, 262
Air Willet, WAVR 479, 262
Air Wren, WAVR 480, 262
Ajax, AR 6, 170
Akutan, AE 13, 196
Alabama, SSBN 731, 36
Alabama, BB 60, 37
Alacrity, MSO 520, 150; AG 520, 178

Alameda County, LST 32, 105; AVB 1, 169
Alamo, LSD 33, 103
Alamogordo, ARDM 2, 227
Alan Shepard, AKE 3, 206
Alaska, SSBN 732, 36
Alaska, CB 1, 39
Alatna, AOG 81, 219
Albacore, AGSS 569, 22
Albacore, WPB 87309, 266
Albany, SSN 753, 31
Albany, CA 123, 40; CG 10, 43
Albatross, AMS 1, 151
Albatross, MSC 289, 159
Albatross IV, R 342, 280
Albemarle, AV 5, 167
Albert David, DE/FF 1050, 89
Albert J. Myer, ARC 6, 173
Albert M. Boe, AKV 6, 207
Albert T. Harris, DE 447, 86
Albert W. Grant, DD 649, 58
Albuquerque, SSN 706, 30
Albuquerque, PF 7, 128
Alchiba, AK 261, 203
Alcona, AK 157, 201
Alcor, AK 259, 201
Alcyone, AKL 37, 208
Aldebaran, AF 10, 197
Alder, WLB 216, 273
Alert, WMEC 630, 259
Alert, WSC 127, 260
Alex Haley, WMEC 39, 260
Alexander Hamilton, SSBN 617, 35
Alexander J. Luke, DE 577, 79; DER 577, 86
Alexandria, SSN 757, 31
Alfred A. Cunningham, DD 752, 62
Algol, AKA/LKA 54, 119
Algol, AKR 287, 242
Algorab, AK 262, 203
Algorma, ATA 212, 232
Alhena, AKL 38, 208
Allagash, AO 97, 212
Allegheny, ATA 179, 231
Allen M. Sumner, DD 692, 60
Allentown, PF 52, 129
Almaack, AKL 39, 208
Aloe, AN 6, 191
Alsea, ATF 97, 230
Alshain, AKA 55, 119
Alstede, AF 48, 198
Altair, AK 257, 201; AKS 32, 207
Altair, AKR 291, 242
Altamaha, CVE/CVHE 18, 10

Althea, WAGL 223, 270
Alturas, PC 602, 132
Altus, PC 568, 132
Aludra, AF 55, 198
Alvin C. Cockrell, DE 366, 85
Ambassador, AK 5007, 249
Amberjack, SS 522, 21
Amberjack, WPB 87315, 266
Amelia Earhart, AKE 6, 206
America, CVA/CV 65, 7
America, LHA 6, 99
American Champion, AK 2011, 248
American Condor, AKR 9673, 243
American Cormorant, AK 2062, 246
American Courier, AOT 1007, 250
American Eagle, AK 2044, 243
American Explorer, AO 165, 216
American Explorer, AOT 165, 251
American Falcon, AKR 9672, 243
American Kestrel, AK 9651, 245
American Mariner, AGM 12, 182
American Merlin, AKR 9301, 244
American Monarch, AK 1011, 246
American Osprey, AOT 5075, 251
American Spartan, AK 1009, 246
American Spitfire, AK 1003, 246
American Tern, AK 4729, 238
American Titan, AK 1008, 246
American Trojan, AK 1010, 246
American Veteran, AK 2046, 245
American Victory, AK 1809, 250
Amesbury, APD 46, 124
Amherst, PCER 853, 134
Amick, DE 168, 81
Ammen, DD 527, 56
Ampere, ADG 11, 190
Amphion, AR 13, 170
Amphitrite, ARL 29, 172
Amsterdam, CL 101, 42
Amycus, ARL 2, 171
Anacapa, WPB 1335, 266
Anacortes, PC 1569, 134
Anacostia, AO 94, 212
Anchorage, LPD 23, 102
Anchorage, LSD 36, 104
Andalusia, PC 1173, 133
Andrew J. Higgins, AO 190, 217
Andrew Jackson, SSBN 619, 35
Andrews, PC 606, 132
Andromeda, AKA 15, 119
Androscoggin, WPG/WHEC 68, 256
Angler, SS/AGSS/IXSS 240, 15; SSK 240, 23
Annapolis, SSN 760, 31

Annapolis, AGMR 1, 183
Anoka, PC 571, 132
Antares, AK 258, 201; AKS 33, 207
Antares, AKR 294, 242
Antelope, PG 86, 127
Anthedon, AS 24, 165
Anthony, DD 515, 56; DDE 515, 69
Anthony Petit, WLM 558, 274
Antietam, CV/CVS 36, 3
Antietam, CG 54, 50
Antigo, PC 470, 131
Antioch, AG 180, 177
Antrim, FFG 20, 93
Anzio, CVE/CVHE 57, 10
Anzio, CG 68, 51
Apache, ATF 67, 229
Apache, ATF 172, 232
Apalachee, WYT 71, 269
Apollo, AS 25, 165
Appalachian, AGC 1, 117
Aquarius, AK 263, 203
Aquidneck, WPB 1309, 265
Aquila, PHM 4, 130
Arapaho, ATF 68, 229
Arbutus, WAGL/WLM 203, 270
Arcadia, AD 23, 164
Arcata, PC 601, 132
Archerfish, SS/AGSS 311, 16
Archerfish, SSN 678, 29
Arco, ARD 29, 227
Arctic, AOE 8, 220
Arcturus, AF 52, 198; see *Golden Eagle*
Ardent, AM/MSF 340, 144
Ardent, MCM 10, 151
Arenac, APA 128, 122
Arequipa, AF 31, 197
Argo, WPC 100, 261
Argonaut, SS 475, 21
Ariadne, WPC 101, 261
Aries, PHM 5, 130
Arikara, ATF 98, 230
Aristaeus, ARB 1, 171
Arkansas, CGN 41, 50
Arleigh Burke, DDG 51, 76
Arlington, LPD 24, 102
Arlington, AGMR 2, 183
Armistead Rust, AGS 9, 186
Armstrong County, LST 57, 106
Arneb, AKA/LKA 56, 119
Arnold J. Isbell, DD 869, 67
Arthur L. Bristol, APD 97, 125
Arthur Middleton, APA 25, 121
Arthur W. Radford, DD 968, 71
Artisan, AFDB 1, 227

Arundel, WYT 90, 269
Ash, AN 7, 191
Asheboro, PC 822, 132
Asheville, SSN 758, 31
Asheville, PG 84, 127
Ashland, LSD 1, 102
Ashland, LSD 48, 105
Ashtabula, AO 51, 210
Askari, ARL 30, 172
Aspen, WLB 208, 273
Aspro, SS/AGSS 309, 16
Aspro, SSN 658, 28
Assateague, WPB 1337, 266
Assertive, AGOS 9, 183
Assurance, MSO 521, 150; AG 521, 178
Assurance, AGOS 5, 183
Aster, WAGL 408, 271
Asterion, AF 63, 199
Astoria, CL 90, 41
Atakapa, ATF 149, 230
Atalanta, WPC 102, 261
Atchison County, LST 60, 106
Atherton, DE 169, 81
Atka, AGB 3, 179
Atlanta, SSN 712, 30
Atlanta, CL 104, 42; IX 304, 192
Atlantis, AGOR 25, 190
Atlas, ARL 7, 171
Attu, WPB 1317, 265
Atule, SS/AGSS 403, 20
Aubrey Fitch, FFG 34, 94
Auburn, AGC 10, 118
Aucilla, AO 56, 211
Audacious, AGOS 11, 183
Augusta, SSN 710, 30
Augusta, CA 31, 39
Auk, AM/MSF 57, 143
Aulick, DD 569, 57
Ault, DD 698, 60
Aurora, WPC 103, 261
Austin, LPD 4, 101
Austral Lightning AK 5061/AK 1004. 245
Austral Rainbow AKR 1005. 245, see *American Veteran*
Avenge, MSO 423, 147
Avenger, MCM 1, 151
Aventinus, ARVE 3, 172
Avery Island, AG 76, 175; AKS 24, 207
Avocet, AMCU/MHC 16, 160
Avoyel, ATF 150, 230; WMEC 150, 258
Aylwin, DE/FF 1081, 90
Azalea, WLI 641, 274

Bache, DD 470, 55; DDE 470, 69
Badger, DE/FF 1071, 90
Badoeng Strait, CVE/CVU 116, 11; AKV 16, 207
Baffin Strait AK W9519, 242
Bagaduce, ATA 194, 231
Bagley, DE/FF 1069, 90
Bailey, DD 492, 54
Bainbridge, DLGN/CGN 25, 47
Bainbridge, DDG 96, 78
Bainbridge Island, WPB 1343, 266
Bairoko, CVE/CVU 115, 11; AKV 15, 207
Baker, DE 190, 81
Balao, SS/AGSS 285, 16
Bald Eagle, AF 50, 198
Balduck, APD/LPR 132, 126
Baldwin, DD 624, 55
Balsam, WAGL/WLB 62, 271
Baltimore, SSN 704, 30
Baltimore, CA 68, 39
Bamberg County, LST 209, 106
Bancroft, DD 598, 54
Bang, SS 385, 19
Bangust, DE 739, 81
Banner, AGER 1, 179; AKL 25, 208
Banner, AK 5008, 248
Banning, PCE 886, 134
Bannock, ATF 81, 229
Baranof, WPB 1318, 265
Barataria, AVP 33, 168; WAVP/WHEC 381, 256
Barb, SS 220, 14
Barb, SSN 596, 27
Barbara Mabrity, WLM 559, 274
Barbel, SS 580, 23
Barber, APD 57, 124
Barbero, SS 317, 17; SSG 317, 24; ASSA 317, 25
Barberry, WAGL/WLI 294, 274
Barbet, AMS 41, 151
Barbey, DE/FF 1088, 90
Barbour County, LST 1195, 114
Barnegat, AVP 10, 168
Barnes, CVE/CVHE 20, 10
Barney, DDG 6, 73
Barnstable County, LST 1197, 114
Barnwell, APA 132, 122
Baron, DE 166, 81
Barr, APD 39, 124
Barracuda, SSK 1, 24; SST 3, 25
Barracuda, WPB 87301, 266
Barrett, AP 196, 225
Barry, DD 933, 70

Barry, DDG 52, 76
Bartlett, AGOR 13, 189
Barton, DD 722, 61
Bashaw, SS/AGSS 241, 15; SSK 241, 23
Basilan, AG 68, 175
Basilone, DD 824, 65; DDE 824, 69
Bass, SSK 2, 24; SS 551, 21
Bassett, APD 73, 125
Basswood, WAGL/WLB 388, 271
Bataan, CVL 29, 5; AVT 4, 169
Bataan, LHD 5, 99
Batesburg, PCE 903, 135
Batfish, SS/AGSS 310, 16
Batfish, SSN 681, 29
Bath, PF 55, 129
Baton Rouge, SSN 689, 30
Bauer, DE 1025, 87
Bausell, DD 845, 66
Bay, AK 2032, 248
Bay Lander, IX 514, 193
Baya, SS/AGSS 318, 17
Bayfield, APA 33, 122
Bayonne, PF 21, 128
Beacon, PG 99, 127
Beale, DD 471, 55; DDE 471
Bear, WMEC 901, 259
Bearss, DD 654, 58
Beatty, DD 756, 62
Beaufort, ATS 2, 232
Beaufort, PCS 1387, 135
Beaver State, ACS 10, 237
Becuna, SS/AGSS 319, 17
Bedloe, WPC 121, 261
Beech, WAGL 205, 270
Beeville, PC 617, 132
Begor, APD/LPR 127, 126
Bel Air, PC 1191, 133
Belet, APD 109, 125
Belknap, DLG/CG 26, 48
Bell, DD 587, 58
Bell M. Shimada, R 227, 279
Bellatrix, AKA 3, 119
Bellatrix, AF 62, 198
Bellatrix, AKR 288, 242
Belle Grove, LSD 2, 103
Belle Isle, AKS 21, 207; AG 73, 175
Belleau Wood, CVL 24, 5
Belleau Wood, LHA 3, 99
Bellerophon, ARL 31, 172
Belmont, AG 167, 178; AGTR 4, 180
Beltrami, AK 162, 201
Beluga, WPB 87325, 267
Benavidez, AKR 306, 239

Benevolence, AH 13, 226
Benewah, IX 311, 192; APB 35, 225
Benfold, DDG 65, 76
Benham, DD 796, 60
Benicia, PG 96, 127
Benjamin Franklin, SSBN 640, 35
Benjamin Isherwood, AO 191, 217
Benjamin Stoddert, DDG 22, 73
Benner, DD 807, 64; DDR 807, 69
Bennett, DD 473, 55
Bennington, CV/CVS 20, 3
Bennion, DD 662, 58
Benson, DD 421, 54
Benton County, LST 263, 106
Benzie County, LST 266, 106
Bergall, SS 320, 17
Bergall, SSN 667, 28
Bering Strait, AVP 34, 168
Bering Strait, WAVP/WHEC 382, 256
Berkeley, DDG 15, 73
Berkeley County, LST 279, 106
Berkshire County, LST 288, 106
Bernalillo County, LST 306, 106
Bertholf, WMSL 750, 257
Bessemer, AG 186, 177
Besugo, SS/AGSS 321, 17
Betelgeuse, AK 260, 201
Bethany, PC 620, 132
Beverly W. Reid, APD/LPR 119, 126
Bexar, APA/LPA 237, 123
Bibb, WPG/WHEC 31, 255
Biddle, DLG/CG 34, 48
Biddle, DDG 5, 73
Big Black River, LSMR/LFR 401, 115
Big Horn, AO 198, 217
Big Horn River, LSMR 402, 115
Bigelow, DD 942, 70
Billfish, SS/AGSS 286, 16
Billfish, SSN 676, 29
Biloxi, CL 80, 41
Birch, WAGL 256, 271
Birmingham, SSN 695, 30
Birmingham, CL 62, 41
Bisbee, PF 46, 129
Biscayne Bay, WTGB 104, 270
Bittern, MHC 43, 161
Bittersweet, WAGL/WLB 389, 271
Bivin, DE 536, 86
Black, DD 666, 59
Black Warrior River, LSMR/LFR 404, 116
Blackbird, AMCU/MHC 11, 160
Blackfin, SS 322, 18
Blackfin, WPB 87317, 266

Blackfish, SS 221, 14
Blackford, APB 45, 225
Blackhaw, WAGL/WLB 390, 271
Blackhawk, MHC 58, 161
Blackrock, WAGL 367, 271
Blackstone River, LSMR 403, 116
Blackthorn, WAGL/WLB 391, 271
Blacktip, WPB 87326, 267
Blair, DE 147, 82; DER 147, 86
Blakely, DE/FF 1072, 90
Blanco County, LST 344, 106
Blandy, DD 943, 70
Bledsoe County, LST 356, 106
Blenny, SS/AGSS 324, 18
Blessman, APD 48, 124
Block Island, CVE/CVU 106, 11; LPH 1, 97; AKV 38, 207
Block Island, WPB 1344, 266
Blower, SS 325, 18
Blue, DD 744, 61
Blue Jacket, AF 51, 198
Blue Jay, AMCU/MHC 17, 160
Blue Ridge, AGC 2, 117
Blue Ridge, LCC 19, 118
Blue Shark, WPB 87360, 267
Blueback, SS 326, 18
Blueback, SS 581, 23
Bluebell, WAGL/WLI 313, 274
Bluebird, MSC 121, 156
Bluebird, ASR 19, 166
Bluebonnet, WAGL/WLI 257, 271
Bluefin, WPB 87318, 266
Bluefish, SS 222, 14
Bluefish, SSN 675, 28
Bluegill, SS/AGSS 242, 15; SSK 242, 23
Bluetank Starlet, AOG 9687, 252
Bluffton, PC 461, 131
Boarfish, SS 327, 18
Bob Hope, AKR 300, 239
Bobolink, AMS 2, 151; AMCU/MHC 44, 160
Bogue, CVE/CVHE 9, 10
Boise, SSN 764, 31
Boise, CL 47, 41
Bold, MSO 424, 147
Bold, AGOS 12, 183
Bollinger, APA 234, 123
Bolster, ARS 38, 175
Bon Homme Richard, CV 31, 3
Bondia, AF 42, 198
Bonefish, SS 582, 23
Bonham, WSC 129, 260
Bonhomme Richard, LHD 6, 99

Bonita, SSK 3, 24; SS 552, 21
Bonito, WPB 87341, 267
Boone, FFG 28, 94
Boone County, LST 389, 106
Booth, DE 170, 81
Bordelon, DD 881, 68; DDR 881, 69
Borie, DD 704, 61
Borum, DE 790, 80
Boston, SSN 703, 30
Boston, CA 69, 39; CAG 1, 42
Bostwick, DE 103, 80
Botetourt, APA 136, 122
Bottineau, APA 235, 123
Bougainville, CVE/CVU 100, 11; AKV 35, 207
Boulder, LST 1190, 114
Boutwell, WHEC 719, 256
Boutwell, WSC 130, 260
Bowditch, AGS 21, 187
Bowditch, AGS 62, 189
Bowen, DE/FF 1079, 90
Bowen NOAA, 277
Bowers, APD 40, 124
Bowfin, SS/AGSS/IXSS 287, 16
Bowie NOAA, 277
Bowman County, LST 391, 106
Boxer, CV/CVS 21, 3; LPH 4, 97
Boxer, LHD 4, 99
Boxwood, AN 8, 191
Boyd, DD 544, 57
Boyle, DD 600, 54
Bradford, DD 545, 57
Bradley, DE/FF 1041, 89
Bradley County, LST 400, 106
Braine, DD 630, 58
Bramble, WAGL/WLB 392, 271
Brambling, AMS 42, 151
Branch County, LST 482, 106
Brant, AMS 43, 151
Brant, WPB 87348, 267
Brattleboro, PCER 852, 134
Bravado, AOG 9622, 252
Bray, APD 139, 126
Bream, SS/AGSS 243, 15; SSK 243, 23
Breeman, DE 104, 80
Bremerton, SSN 698, 30
Bremerton, CA 130, 40
Breton, CVE/CVHE/CVU 23, 10; AKV 42, 207
Brewster County, LST 483, 106
Brewton, DE/FF 1086, 90
Briareus, AR 12, 170
Bridge, AOE 10, 220

Bridget, DE 1024, 87
Brier, IX 307, 192; WAGL/WLI 299, 274
Bright, DE 747, 81
Brill, SS 330, 18
Brinkley Bass, DD 887, 68
Briscoe, DD 977, 71
Brister, DE 327, 83; DER 327, 86
Bristol, DD 857, 63
Bristol Bay, WTGB 102, 270
Bristol County, LST 1198, 114
Brittin, AKR 305, 239
Broadbill, AM/MSF 58, 143
Broadkill River, LSMR/LFR 405, 116
Brock, APD 93, 125
Bronstein, DE 189, 81
Bronstein, DE/FF 1037, 89
Bronx, APA 236, 123
Brooke, DEG/FFG 1, 92
Brookings, APA 140, 122
Brooklyn, CL 40, 41
Brough, DE 148, 82
Brown, DD 546, 57
Brownson, DD 868, 67
Bruce C. Heezen, AGS 64, 189
Brule, AKL 28, 208
Brumby, DE/FF 1044, 89
Brunswick, ATS 3, 232
Brush, DD 745, 61
Bryant, DD 665, 59
Bryce Canyon, AD 36, 164
Buchanan, DD 484, 54
Buchanan, DDG 14, 73
Buchanan County, LST 504, 106
Buck, DD 761, 62
Buckeye, AN 13, 191
Buckley, DE 51, 79; DER 51, 86
Buckthorn, AN 14, 191
Buckthorn, WLI 642, 274
Buffalo, SSN 715, 30
Buffalo Soldier, AKR 9302, 244
Bugara, SS/AGSS 331, 18
Builder, AK 2031, 248
Bulkeley, DDG 84, 78
Bull, APD 78, 125
Bull Run, AO 156, 215
Bullard, DD 660, 58
Bulloch County, LST 509, 106
Bulwark, MSO 425, 147
Bumper, SS 333, 18
Bunch, APD 79, 125
Buncombe County, LST 510, 106
Bunker Hill, CV/CVS 17, 3; AVT 9, 169

Bunker Hill, CG 52, 50
Bunting, AMS 3, 151
Bunting, AMCU/MHC 45, 160
Burdo, APD 133, 126
Burias, AG 69, 175
Burke, APD 65, 125
Burleson, APA 67, 122
Burlington, PF 51, 129
Burnett County, LST 512, 106
Burns, DD 588, 58
Burrfish, SS 312, 16; SSR 312, 25
Burrows, DE 105, 80
Burton Island, AG 88/AGB 1, 179; WAGB 283, 268
Bushnell, AS 15, 165
Butte, AE 27, 197
Butternut, AN 9, 191
Buttonwood, WAGL/WLB 306, 271
Buyer, AK 2033, 248

Cabezon, SS/AGSS 334, 18
Cabildo, LSD 16, 103
Cable, ARS 19, 174
Cabot, CVL 28, 5; AVT 3, 169
Cabrilla, SS/AGSS 288, 16
Cacapon, AO 52, 210
Cache, AO/AOT 67, 211
Cactus, WAGL/WLB/WAGO 270, 271
Caddo Parish, LST 515, 106
Cadiz, PC 1081, 132
Cadmus, AR 14, 170
Cahaba, AO 82, 212
Cahokia, ATA 186, 231
Cahoone, WSC 131, 260
Cahuilla, ATF 152, 230
Caiman, SS 323, 18
Calaveras County, LST 516, 106
Calcaterra, DE 390, 83; DER 390, 87
Caldwell, DD 605, 54
Calhoun County, LST 519, 106
Caliente, AO 53, 210
California, DLGN/CGN 36, 49
California, AK 5029, 248
California, SSN 781, 33
Callaghan, DDG 994, 76
Callao, IX 205, 192
Caloosahatchee, AO 98, 212
Calumet, WYT 86, 269
Calvert, APA 32, 121
Calypso, WPC 104, 261
Camanche, ACM/MMA 11, 141
Camano, AKL 1, 207
Cambria, APA 36, 122

Camden, AOE 2, 219
Cameron, APB 50, 225
Camp, DE 251, 82; DER 251, 86
Campbell, WPG/WHEC 32, 255
Campbell, WMEC 909, 259
Canadian River, LSMR 406, 116
Canandaigua, PC 1246, 133
Canastota, PC 1135, 133
Canberra, CA 70, 39; CAG 2, 42
Caney, AO 95, 212
Canisteo, AO 99, 212
Canon, PG 90, 127
Canonicus, ACM/MMA 12, 141
Canopus, AS 34, 166
Capable, AGOS 16, 183
Cape, MSI 2, 161
Cape, AK 5074, 249
Cape Alava, AK 5012, 247
Cape Alexander AK 5010. 247
Cape Ann, AK 5009, 247
Cape Archway, AK 5011, 247
Cape Avinof, AK 5013, 247
Cape Blanco, AK 5060, 247
Cape Bon, AK 5059, 247
Cape Borda, AK 5058, 247
Cape Bover, AK 5057, 247
Cape Breton, AK 5056, 247
Cape Canaveral, AK 5040, 249
Cape Canso, AK 5037, 249
Cape Carter, WPB 95309, 262
Cape Carthage, AK 5042, 249
Cape Catawba, AK 5074, 249; see *Cape*
Cape Catoche, AK 5043, 249
Cape Chalmers, AK 5036, 249
Cape Charles, AK 5038, 249
Cape Clear, AK 5039, 249
Cape Cod, AD 43, 164
Cape Cod, AK 5041, 249
Cape Coral, WPB 95301, 262
Cape Corwin, WPB 95326, 263
Cape Cross, WPB 95321, 263
Cape Current, WPB 95307, 262
Cape Darby, WPB 95323, 263
Cape Decision, AKR 5054, 243
Cape Diamond, AKR 5055, 243
Cape Domingo, AKR 5053, 243
Cape Douglas, AKR 5052, 243
Cape Ducato, AKR 5051, 243
Cape Edmont, AKR 5069, 243
Cape Esperance, CVE/CVU 88, 11
Cape Fairweather, WPB 95314, 262
Cape Falcon, WPB 95330, 263
Cape Farewell, AK 5073, 245

Cape Fear, AK 5061, 245; see *Austral Lightning*
Cape Flattery, AK 5070, 245
Cape Florida, AK 5071, 245
Cape Florida, WPB 95325, 263
Cape Fox, WPB 95316, 263
Cape George, WPB 95306, 262
Cape Gibson, AK 5051, 246
Cape Girardeau, AK 2039, 246
Cape Gloucester, CVE/CVHE 109, 11; AKV 9, 207
Cape Gull, WPB 95304, 262
Cape Hatteras, WPB 95305, 262
Cape Hedge, WPB 95311, 262
Cape Henlopen, WPB 95328, 263
Cape Henry, AKR 5067, 243
Cape Higgon, WPB 95302, 262
Cape Horn, AKR 5068, 243
Cape Horn, WPB 95322, 263
Cape Hudson, AKR 5066, 243
Cape Inscription, AKR 5076, 242
Cape Intrepid, AKR 11, 242
Cape Isabel, AKR 5062, 242
Cape Island, AKR 10, 242
Cape Jellison, WPB 95317, 263
Cape Johnson, AK 5075, 248
Cape Juby, AK 5077, 248
Cape Kennedy, AKR 5083, 245
Cape Kiwanda, WPB 95329, 263
Cape Knox, AKR 5082, 245
Cape Knox, WPB 95312, 262
Cape Lambert, AKR 5077, 243
Cape Lobos, AKR 5078, 243
Cape May, AKR 5063, 245
Cape May, County LST 521, 107
Cape Mendocino, AKR 5064, 245
Cape Mohican, AKR 5065, 245
Cape Morgan, WPB 95313, 262
Cape Newagen, WPB 95318, 263
Cape Nome, AK 1014, 246
Cape Orlando, AKR 2044, 243; see *American Eagle*
Cape Porpoise, WPB 95327, 263
Cape Providence, WPB 95335, 263
Cape Race, AKR 9960, 244
Cape Ray, AKR 9979, 244
Cape Rise, AKR 9678, 244
Cape Romain, WPB 95319, 263
Cape Rosier, WPB 95333, 263
Cape Sable, WPB 95334, 263
Cape Shoalwater, WPB 95324, 263
Cape Small, WPB 95300, 262
Cape St. George, CG 71, 51
Cape Starr, WPB 95320, 263

Cape Strait, WPB 95308, 262
Cape Taylor, AKR 113, 244
Cape Texas, AKR 112, 244
Cape Trinity, AKR 9711, 244
Cape Trinity, WPB 95331, 263
Cape Upright, WPB 95303, 262
Cape Victory, AKR 9701, 244
Cape Vincent, AKR 9666, 244
Cape Wash, WPB 95310, 262
Cape Washington, AKR 9961, 244
Cape Wrath, AKR 9962, 244
Cape York, WPB 95332, 263
Capella, AKR 293, 242
Caperton, DD 650, 58
Capitaine, SS/AGSS 336, 18
Capodanno, DE/FF 1093, 90
Capps, DD 550, 57
Capricornus, AKA/LKA 57, 119
Capt. Arlo L. Olson, AK 245, 202
Capt. Stephen L. Bennett, AK 4296, 238
Carbonero, SS/AGSS 337, 18
Card, CVE/CVHE/CVU 11, 10; AKV 40, 207
Cardinal, AMS 4, 151
Cardinal, MSH 1, 161
Cardinal, MHC 60, 161
Cardinal O'Connell, AKV 7, 207
Carib, ATF 82, 229
Carl Brashear, AKE 7, 206
Carl Vinson, CVN 70, 8
Carlinville, PC 1120, 133
Carmi, PC 466, 131
Carmick, DD 493, 54; DMS 33, 143
Carney, DDG 64, 76
Caroline County, LST 525, 107
Carolyn Chouest, MV 9999, 253
Caron, DD 970, 71
Carp, SS/AGSS/IXSS 338, 18
Carpellotti, APD 136, 126
Carpenter, DD/DDK 825, 65; DDE 825, 69
Carr, FFG 52, 94
Carroll, DE 171, 81
Carronade, IFS 1/LFR 1, 117
Carson City, PF 50, 129
Carter, DE 112, 80
Carter Hall, LSD 3, 103
Carter Hall, LSD 50, 105
Carthage, AG 185, 177
Cartigan, WSC 132, 260
Casa Grande, LSD 13, 103
Cascade, AD 16, 163
Casco, AVP 12, 168; WAVP/ WHEC 370, 256

Casimir Pulaski, SSBN 633, 35
Cassia County, LST 527, 107
Cassin Young, DD 793, 59
Castle, DD 720, 63
Castle Rock, AVP 35, 168
Castle Rock, WAVP/WHEC 383, 256
Castor, AKS 1, 207
Catahoula County, LST 528, 107
Catalpa, AN 10, 191
Catamount, LSD 17, 103
Catawba, ATA 210, 232
Catawba, ATF 168, 232
Catawba Victory, AK 5001, 250
Cates, DE 763, 81
Catfish, SS 339, 18
Catoctin, AGC 5, 118
Catskill, MCS 1, 142
Cavalier, APA 37, 122
Cavalla, SS/AGSS 244, 15; SSK 244, 23
Cavalla, SSN 684, 29
Cavallaro, APD 128, 126
Cayuga, LST 1186, 114
Cayuga County, LST 529, 107
C-Commando, SSV 4499, 253
Cebu, ARG 6, 170
Cecil J. Doyle, DE 368, 85
Cedar, WAGL 207, 270
Cedar Creek, AO 138, 214
Centaurus, AK 264, 203
Cepheus, AK 265, 203
Cero, SS/AGSS 225, 14
Chadron, PC 564, 131
Chafee, DDG 90, 78
Chaffinch, AMCU/MHC 18, 160
Chain, ARS 20, 174
Challenge, ATA 201, 232
Chambers, DE 391, 83; DER 391, 87; WDE 491, 260
Champion, AM/MSF 314, 144
Champion, MCM 4, 151
Champlain, WPG 319, 255
Champlin, DD 601, 54
Chancellorsville, CG 62, 50
Chandeleur, AV 10, 167
Chandeleur, WPB 1319, 265
Chandler, DDG 996, 76
Change, AM/MSF 159, 145
Chanticleer, ASR 7, 166
Chapman, R 446, 280
Chara, AKA 58, 119; AE 31, 197
Chariton River, LSMR 407, 116
Charles Ausburne, DD 570, 57
Charles Berry, DE 1035, 88

Charles Carroll, APA 28, 121
Charles E. Brannon, DE 446, 86
Charles F. Adams, DDG 2, 73
Charles F. Hughes, DD 428, 54
Charles H. Davis, AGOR 5, 189
Charles H. Roan, DD 853, 66
Charles J. Badger, DD 657, 58
Charles J. Kimmel, DE 584, 84
Charles Lawrence, APD 37, 124
Charles P. Cecil, DD 835, 65; DDR 835, 69
Charles R. Ware, DD 865, 67
Charles River, LSMR 408, 116
Charles S. Sperry, DD 697, 60
Charleston, LKA 113, 121
Charlotte, SSN 766, 31
Charlottesville, PF 25, 128
Charlton, AKR 314, 238
Charr, SS/AGSS/IXSS 328, 18
Charrette, DD 581, 57
Chase, WHEC 718, 256
Chase County, LST 532, 107
Chatelain, DE 149, 82
Chattahoochee, AOG 82, 219
Chatterer, AMS 40, 151
Chauncey, DD 667, 59
Chautauqua, WPG/WHEC 41, 256
Chauvenet, AGS 29, 188
Chawasha, ATF 151, 230
Cheboygan County, LST 533, 107
Chehalis, PG 94, 127
Chehalis, AOG 48, 218
Chelan County, LST 542, 107
Chemung, AO 30, 209
Chenango, CVE/CVHE 28, 10
Chepachet, AO/AOT 78, 211
Cherokee, WMEC 165, 258
Cherry, WAGL/WLIC 258, 271
Chesapeake, AOT 5084, 251
Chestatee, AOG 49, 218
Chester, CA 27, 39
Chester T. O'Brien, DE 421, 85
Chesterfield County, LST 551, 107
Chestnut, AN 11, 191
Chevalier, DD 805, 64; DDR 805, 69
Chewaucan, AOG 50, 218
Chewink, AMCU/MHC 19, 160
Cheyenne, SSN 773, 31
Cheyenne, AG 174, 176
Chicago, SSN 721, 30
Chicago, CA 136, 40
Chicago, CG 11, 43
Chickadee, AM/MSF 59, 143
Chickasaw, ATF 83, 229

Chicot, AK 170, 201
Chief, AM/MSF 315, 144
Chief, MCM 12, 151
Chikaskia, AO 54, 210
Chilton, APA/LPA 38, 122
Chilula, ATF 153, 231
Chilula, WMEC 153, 258
Chimaera, ARL 33, 172
Chimango, AMCU/MHC 20, 160
Chimariko, ATF 154, 231
Chimon, AG 150, 177; AKS 31, 207
Chincoteague, AVP 24, 168; WAVP/WHEC 375, 256
Chincoteague, WPB 1320, 265
Chinook, PC 9, 136
Chinook, WPB 87308, 266
Chinook, WYT 96, 269
Chipola, AO 63, 211
Chippewa, ATF 69, 229
Chittenden County, LST 561, 107
Chivo, SS 341, 18
Chloris, ARVA 4, 172
Choctaw, ATF 70, 229
Chopper, SS/AGSS/IXSS 342, 18
Chosin, CG 65, 51
Chourre, ARV 1, 171
Chowanoc, ATF 100, 230
Chub, SS 329, 18
Chukawan, AO 100, 212
Chung-Hoon, DDG 93, 78
Churchill County, LST 583, 107
Cimarron, AO 22, 209
Cimarron, AO 177, 216
Cinchona, AN 12, 191
Cincinnati, SSN 693, 30
Citrus, WAGL/WLB 300, 271
City of Corpus Christi, SSN 705, 30
Clamagore, SS 343, 18
Clamour, AM/MSF 160, 145
Clamp, ARS 33, 175
Clarence K. Bronson, DD 668, 59
Clarence L. Evans, DE 113, 81
Clarion River, LSMR/LFR 409, 116
Clark, FFG 11, 93
Clark Fork River, LSMR 410, 116
Clarke County, LST 601, 107
Clarksburg, AG 183, 177
Claud Jones, DE 1033, 88
Claude V. Ricketts, DDG 5, 74, see *Biddle*
Claxton, DD 571, 57
Clearwater County, LST 602, 107
Clematis, WAGL 286/WLI 74286, 274
Clemson, AG 184, 177
Cleveland, CL 55, 41

Cleveland, LPD 7, 101
Cleveland, AK 851, 246
Clifton Sprague, FFG 16, 93
Climax, AM/MSF 161, 145
Clinton, APA 144, 122
Clover, WAGL/WLB 292, 271
Clytie, AS 26, 165
Coastal Crusader, AGM 16, 182; AGS 36, 187
Coastal Sentry, AGM 15, 182
Coasters Harbor, AG 74, 175; AKS 22, 207
Coates, DE 685, 84
Cobbler, SS 344, 18
Cobia, SS/AGSS 245, 15
Cobia, WPB 87311, 266
Cochino, SS 345, 18
Cochino, WPB 87329, 267
Cochrane, DDG 21, 73
Cockatoo, AMCU/MHC 21, 160
Cockrill, DE 398, 83
Coconino County, LST 603, 107
Cocopa, ATF 101, 230
Cod, SS/AGSS/IXSS 224, 14
Cofer, APD 62, 125
Coffman, DE 191, 81
Coghlan, DD 606, 54
Cogswell, DD 651, 58
Coho, WPB 87321, 267
Cohocton, AO 101, 212
Cohoes, AN/ANL 78, 191
Col. William J. O'Brien, AK 246, 202
Colahan, DD 658, 58
Cole, DDG 67, 76
Colfax, WSC 133, 260
Colington, AG 148, 177; AKS 29, 207
Colleton, APB 36, 225
Collett, DD 730, 61
Colonial, LSD 18, 103
Colorado, BB 45, 37
Columbia, SSN 771, 31
Columbia, CL 56, 41
Columbia, AO/AOT 182, 217
Columbine, WAGL/WLI 208, 270
Columbus, SSN 762, 31
Columbus, CA 74, 40; CG 12, 43
Comanche, WMEC 202, 258
Comet, AK 269/LSV 7/AKR 7, 204, 206, 242
Comfort, AH 20, 226, 237
Commencement Bay, CVE/CVHE 105, 11; AKV 37, 207
Compass Island, AG 153, 176
Compel, AM/MSF 162, 145

Competent, AM/MSF 316, 144
Competent, AFDM 6, 227
Compton, DD 705, 61
Comstock, LSD 19, 103
Comstock, LSD 45, 104
Comte de Grasse, DD 974, 71
Concise, AM/MSF 163, 145
Concord, AFS 5, 199
Condor, AMS 5, 151
Cone, DD 866, 67
Conecuh, AO/AOR 110, 213
Conecuh, AOE 9, 220
Confidence, WMEC 619, 259
Conflict, MSO 426, 147
Conger, SS/AGSS 477, 21
Conifer, WAGL/WLB 301, 271
Conklin, DE 439, 85
Conneaut, PCS 1444, 135
Connecticut, SSN 22, 32
Conner, DD 582, 57
Connole, DE/FF 1056, 90
Connolly, DE 1073, 90
Conolly, DD 979, 71
Conquest, MSO 488, 147
Conserver, ARS 39, 175
Consolation, AH 15, 226
Constant, MSO 427, 147
Constellation, CVA/CV 64, 7
Constellation, IX 20, 192
Constitution, ex-IX 21, 192
Contender, AGOS 2, 183
Control, AM/MSF 164, 145
Converse, DD 509, 56
Conway, DD 507, 56; DDE 507, 69
Cony, DD 508, 56; DDE 508, 69
Conyngham, DDG 17, 73
Cook, DE/FF 1083, 90
Cook, APD/LPR 130, 126
Cook Inlet, AVP 36, 168; WAVP/WHEC 384, 256
Coolbaugh, DE 217, 79
Cooner, DE 172, 81
Coontz, DLG 9, 45; DDG 40, 75
Cooperstown, PC 484, 131
Coos Bay, AVP 25, 168; WAVP/WHEC 376, 256
Copahee, CVE/CVHE 12, 10
Copeland, FFG 25, 93
Coral Sea, CVB/CVA/CV 43, 5
Corbesier, DE 438, 85
Cordele, PC 1125, 133
Corduba, AF 32, 197
Core, CVE/CVHE/CVU 13, 10; AKV 41, 207

Corinth, PC 1547, 134
Cormorant, MSC 122, 156
Cormorant, MHC 57, 161
Cormorant, WPB 87313, 266
Cornhusker State, ACS 6, 237
Coronado, LPD 11, 101; AGF 11, 119
Coronado, PF 38, 128
Coronis, ARL 10, 171
Corporal, SS 346, 18
Corpus Christi, SSN 705, 30
Corpus Christi Bay, ARVH 1, 172
Corregidor, CVE/CVU 58, 10
Corry, DD 817, 64; DDR 817, 69
Corsair, SS/AGSS 435, 21
Corson, AVP 37, 168
Cosmos, WAGL/WLI 293, 274
Cossatot, AO 77, 211
Cotinga, AMCU/MHC 22, 160
Cotton, DD 669, 59
Coucal, ASR 8, 166
Counsel, AM/MSF 165, 145
Courageous, WMEC 622, 259
Courier, AK 5019, 248
Courier, AOT 1004, 250
Courier, WAGR 246, 275
Courlan, AMS 44, 151
Courser, AMS 6, 151
Courtney, DE 1021, 87
Cove, MSI 1, 161
Cowanesque, AO 79, 211
Cowell, DD 547, 57
Cowie, DD 632, 55; DMS 39, 143
Cowpens, CVL 25, 5; AVT 1, 169
Cowpens, CG 63, 51
Cowslip, WAGL/WLB 277, 271
Cpl. Louis J. Hauge Jr., AK 3000, 240
Crag, AM/MSF 214, 145
Crawford, WSC 134, 260
Cread, APD 88, 125
Creddock, AM/MSF 356, 146
Cree, ATF 84, 229
Creon, ARL 11, 171
Crescent City, APA 21, 121
Crestview, PCE 895, 135
Crevalle, SS/AGSS 291, 16
Croaker, SS/AGSS/IXSS 246, 15; SSK 246, 23
Croatan, CVE/CVHE/CVU 25, 10; AKV 43, 207
Crockett, APA 148, 122
Crockett, PG 88, 127
Crocodile, WPB 87372, 267
Crommelin, FFG 37, 94
Cromwell, DE 1014, 87

Cronin, DE 704, 80; DEC 704, 87
Crook County, LST 611, 107
Crosley, APD 87, 125
Cross, DE 448, 86
Crossbill, AMS 45, 151
Crow, AMS 7, 151
Cruise, AM/MSF 215, 145
Cubera, SS/AGSS 347, 18
Culebra Island, ARG 7, 170
Culpeper, PC 1240, 133
Cumberland, AO 153, 215
Cumberland River, LSMR 411, 116
Cumberland Sound, AV 17, 168
Curb, ARS 21, 174
Curlew, AMS 8, 151
Current, ARS 22, 174
Currier, DE 700, 80
Currituck, AV 7, 167
Curry County, LST 685, 108
Curtis Wilbur, DDG 54, 76
Curtiss, AV 4, 167
Curtiss, AVB 4, 169, 237
Curtiss Bay, WTGB 110, 270
Curts, FFG 38, 94
Cusabo, ATF 155, 231
Cushing, DD 797, 60
Cushing, DD 985, 72
Cushing, WPB 1321, 265
Cusk, SS/AGSS 348, 19; SSG 348, 24
Cutlass, SS 478, 21
Cuttyhunk, WPB 1322, 265
Cuttyhunk Island, AG 75, 175; AKS 23, 207
Cuyahoga, WSC/WIX 157, 261, 275
Cyane, WPC 105, 261
Cyclone, PC 1, 136; WPC 12, 267
Cypress, WLB 210, 273

Da Nang, LHA 5, 99; see *Peleliu*
Dace, SS 247, 15
Dace, SSN 607, 27
Daedalus, ARL 35, 172
Dahl, AKR 312, 238
Dahlgren, DLG 12, 45; DDG 43, 75
Dahlia, WAGL/WLIC 288, 271
Dale, DLG/CG 19, 46
Dale W. Peterson, DE 337, 83
Dalhart, PC 619, 132
Dallas, SSN 700, 30
Dallas, WHEC 716, 256
Dalton Victory, AK 256, 201
Daly, DD 519, 56
Damato, DD 871, 67; DDE 871, 69
Damon M. Cummings, DE 643, 80

Dane, APA 238, 123
Dania, PCE 870, 134
Daniel, DE 335, 83
Daniel A. Joy, DE 585, 84
Daniel Boone, SSBN 629, 35
Daniel T. Griffin, APD 38, 124
Daniel Webster, SSBN 626, 35
Daphne, WPC 106, 261
Darby, DE 218, 79
Darter, SS 576, 23
Dash, MSO 428, 147
Dashiell, DD 659, 58
Dauntless, WMEC 624, 259
David C. Shanks, AP 180, 223
David R. Ray, DD 971, 71
David Starr Jordan, R 444, 280
David W. Taylor, DD 551, 57
Davidson, DE/FF 1045, 89
Davidson, CSS 31/S 331, 279
Daviess County, LST 692, 108
Davis, DD 937, 70
Davison, DD 618, 54; DMS 37, 143
Dawn, AK 2034, 247
Day, DE 225, 84
Dayton, CL 105, 42
De Haven, DD 727, 61
De Kalb County, LST 715, 108
De Long, DE 684, 84
De Soto County, LST 1171, 113
De Steiguer, AGOR 12, 189
De Wert, FFG 45, 94
Deal, AKL 2, 207
Dealey, DE 1006, 87
Decatur, DD 936, 70; DDG 31, 75
Decatur, DDG 73, 77
Decisive, WMEC 629, 259
Defender, MCM 2, 151
Defense, AM/MSF 317, 144
Defiance, PG 95, 127
Deft, AM 216, 145
Deimos, AKL 40, 208
Del Monte, AK 5049, 248
Del Valle, AK 5050, 248
Del Viento, AK 5026, 248
Delaware II, R 445, 280
Deliver, ARS 23, 174
Delta, AR 9, 170
Demeter, ARB 10, 171
Denebola, AF 56, 199
Denebola, AKR 289, 242
Dennis, DE 405, 85
Dennis J. Buckley, DD 808, 64; DDR 808, 69
Density, AM/MSF 218, 145

Dentuda, SS/AGSS 335, 18
Denver, CL 58, 41
Denver, LPD 9, 101
Dependable, WMEC 626, 259
Deperm, ADG 10, 190
Derickson NOAA, 277
Des Moines, CA 134, 40
Des Plaines River, LSMR/LFR 412, 116
Design, AM/MSF 219, 145
Detector, MSO 429, 147
Detroit, AOE 4, 219
Deuel, APA 160, 122
Devastator, AM/MSF 318, 144
Devastator, MCM 6, 151
Device, AM/MSF 220, 145
Devilfish, SS/AGSS 292, 16
Dewey, DLG 14, 46; DDG 45, 76
Dewey, DDG 105, 78
Dexter, WAVP/WHEC 385, 256
Dextrous, AM/MSF 341, 144
Dextrous, MCM 11, 151
Deyo, DD 989, 72
Diablo, SS/AGSS 479, 21
Diachenko, APD/LPR 123, 126
Diamond Head, AE 19, 197
Diamond State, ACS 7, 237
Diamondback, WPB 87370, 267
Diligence, AFDL 48, 227
Diligence, WMEC 616, 259
Diligence, WSC 135, 260
Diodon, SS 349, 19
Diomedes, ARB 11, 171
Dione, WPC 107, 261
Dionysus, AR 21, 170
Diphda, AKA 59, 119
Diploma, AM/MSF 221, 145
Dipper, AM/MSF 357, 146
Direct, MSO 430, 147
Discoverer, OSS 2/R 102, 278
Diver, ARS 5, 174
Dix, WSC 136, 260
Dixie, AD 14, 163
Dixon, AS 37, 166
Dodge County, LST 722, 108
Dogfish, SS 350, 19
Doggett County, LST 689, 108
Dogwood, WAGL/WLR 259, 274
Dolores Chouest, MV 4255, 253
Dolphin, AGSS 555, 23
Dolphin, WPB 87354, 267
Dominant, MSO 431, 147
Don O. Woods, APD 118, 126
Donald B. Beary, DE/FF 1085, 90

Index 299

Donald Cook, DDG 75, 77
Donald W. Wolf, APD 129, 126
Donner, LSD 20, 103
Dorado, WPB 87306, 266
Dorado, WSES 1, 267
Doran, DD 634, 55; DMS 41, 143
Dorchester, APB 46, 225
Dortch, DD 670, 59
Douglas, PG 100, 127
Douglas A. Munro, DE 422, 85
Douglas County, LST 731, 108
Douglas H. Fox, DD 779, 62
Douglas L. Howard, DE 138, 82
Dour, AM/MSF 223, 145
Downes, DE/FF 1070, 90
Doyle, DD 494, 54; DMS 34, 143
Doyle, FFG 39, 94
Doyle C. Barnes, DE 353, 84
Dragonet, SS 293, 16
Drum, SS/AGSS 228, 14
Drum, SSN 677, 29
Drummond, WPB 1323, 265
Duane, WPG/WHEC 33, 255
Dubuque, LPD 8, 101
Duchess AOT , 251
Dufilho, DE 423, 85
Dukes County, LST 735, 108
Duluth, CL 87, 41
Duluth, LPD 6, 101
Duncan, DD 874, 67; DDR 874, 69
Duncan, FFG 10, 93
Dunlin, AMCU 23, 160
Dunn County, LST 742, 108
DuPage, APB 51, 225
DuPont, DD 941, 70
Durable, WMEC 628, 259
Durango, PC 1260, 134
Durant, DE 389, 83; DER 389, 87; WDE 489, 260
Durham, LKA 114, 121
Durik, DE 666, 80
Dutton, AGS 8, 186
Dutton, AGS 22, 187
Duval County, LST 758, 108
Duxbury Bay, AVP 38, 168
Dwight D. Eisenhower, CVN 69, 8
Dyess, DD 880, 68; DDR 880, 69
Dynamic, MSO 432, 147
Dynamic, AFDL 6, 227
Dyson, DD 572, 57

Eager, AM/MSF 224, 145
Eagle, WIX 327, 275
Earheart, APD 113, 126

Earl K. Olsen, DE 765, 81
Earl V. Johnson, DE 702, 80
Earle, DD 635, 55; DMS 42, 143
Earle B. Hall, APD 107, 125
Eastwind, IX 234, 192
Eastwind, WAGB 279, 268
Eaton, DD 510, 56
Eberle, DD 430, 54
Ebert, DE 768, 81
Ebony, AN 15, 191
Echols, IX 504, 192; APB 37, 225
Eddy County, LST 759, 108
Edenton, PC 1077, 132
Edenton, ATS 1, 232
Edgecombe, APA 164, 122
Edison, DD 439, 54
Edisto, AG 89/AGB 2, 179; WAGB 284, 268
Edisto, WPB 1313, 265
Edmonds, DE 406, 85
Edsall, DE 129, 81
Edson, DD 946, 70
Edward H. Allen, DE 531, 86
Edward McDonnell, DE/FF 1043, 89
Edwards, DD 619, 54
Edwin A. Howard, DE 346, 84
Effective, AGOS 21, 185
Egeria, ARL 8, 171
Egret, AMS 46, 151
Eichenberger, DE 202, 79
Eisenhower, CVN 69, 8
Eisner, DE 192, 81
El Paso, LKA 117, 121
Elba, AKL 3, 207
Elder, AN 20, 191
Eldorado, AGC/LCC 11, 118
Eldridge, DE 173, 81
Electra, AKA 4, 119
Electron, AG 146, 177; AKS 27, 207
Elizabeth Lykes, AK 2040, 247
Elk River, LSMR 501, 116
Elk River, IX 501, 192
Elkhorn, AOG 7, 218
Elkins, PC 1216, 133
Elliot, DD 967, 71
Ellyson, DD 454, 54; DMS 19, 143
Elm, WAGL/WLI 260, 271
Elm, WLB 204, 273
Elmer Montgomery, DE/FF 1082, 90
Elokomin, AO 55, 210
Elrod, FFG 55, 94
Elsmere, PCS 1413, 135
Eltanin, AK 270, 204
Elusive, MSO 433, 147; see *Engage*

Ely, PCE 880, 134
Embattle, MSO 434, 147
Emory S. Land, AS 39, 166
Empire State VI, AP 1001, 253
Endeavor, AFDL 1, 227
Endicott, DD 495, 54; DMS 35, 143
Endurance, MSO 435, 147
Endurance, AFDM 3, 227
Endymion, ARL 9, 171
Energy, MSO 436, 147
Engage, MSO 433, 147
England, DLG/CG 22, 46
English, DD 696, 60
Enhance, MSO 437, 147
Enoree, AO 69, 211
Enright, APD 66, 125
Entemedor, SS 340, 18
Enterprise, CV/CVA/CVS 6, 2
Enterprise, CVAN/CVN 65, 8
Enterprise, AP 1004, 253
Epperson, DD 719, 63; DDE 719, 69
Epping Forest, LSD 4, 103; MCS 7, 142
Equality State, ACS 8, 237
Erben, DD 631, 58
Ericsson, DD 440, 54
Ernest G. Small, DD 838, 65; DDR 838, 69
Errol, AKL 4, 207
Escalante River, LSMR 502, 116
Escambia, AO 80, 212
Escanaba, WPG/WHEC 64, 256
Escanaba, WMEC 907, 259
Escape, ARS 6, 174; WMEC 6, 258
Escondido, PC 1169, 133
Esmeraldo County, LST 761, 108
Essex, CV/CVA/CVS 9, 2
Essex, LHD 2, 99
Esteem, MSO 438, 147
Estero, AKL 5, 208
Estes, AGC/LCC 12, 118
Estocin, FFG 15, 93
Ethan Allen, SSBN/SSN 608, 34
Etlah, AN 79, 191
Eucalyptus, AN 16, 191
Eugene A. Greene, DD 711, 63; DDR 711, 69
Eugene E. Elmore, DE 686, 84
Eunice, PCE 846, 134
Euryale, AS 22, 165
Evans, DE 1023, 87
Evansville, PF 70, 129
Everett, PF 8, 128
Everett F. Larson, DD 830, 65; DDR 830, 69

Everglades, AD 24, 164
Evergreen, WAGL/WLB 295, 271
Eversole, DD 789, 64
Ewing, WSC 137, 261
Excel, MSO 439, 147
Excultant, MSO 441, 147
Execute, AM/MSF 232, 145
Exploit, MSO 440, 147
Explorer, OSS 28, 277

Fabius, ARVE 5, 172
Facility, AM/MSF 233, 145
Fahrion, FFG 22, 93
Fairfax County, LST 1193, 114
Fairview, PCER 850, 134
Fairweather, MSS 20/S 220, 279
Falcon, MSC 190, 156
Falcon, MHC 59, 161
Falcon Champion, AOT 1209, 252
Falcon Leader, AOT 1208, 252
Falgout, DE 324, 83; DER 324, 86; WDE 424, 260
Fall River, CA 131, 40
Fanning, DE/FF 1076, 90
Fanshaw Bay, CVE/CVHE 70, 10
Farallon, WPB 1301, 265
Farenholt, DD 491, 54
Fargo, CL 106, 42
Faribault, AK 179, 201
Farmington, PCE 894, 135
Farquhar, DE 139, 82
Farragut, DLG 6, 45; DDG 37, 75
Farragut, DDG 99, 78
Faunce, WSC 138, 261
Fearless, MSO 442, 147
Fechteler, DD 870, 67; DDR 870, 69
Fentress, AK 180, 201
Fern, WAGL/WLR 304, 274
Ferrel, ASV 92/S 492, 280
Fessenden, DE 142, 82; DER 142, 86
Fidelity, MSO 443, 147
Fieberling, DE 640, 80
Fife, DD 991, 72
Finback, SS 230, 14
Finback, SSN 670, 28
Finback, WPB 87314, 266
Finch, DE 328, 83; DER 328, 86; WDE 428, 260
Fir, WAGL/WLM 212, 270
Fir, WLB 213, 273
Firebolt, PC 10, 136
Firebush, WAGL/WLB 393, 271
Firecrest, AMS 10, 151
Firedrake, AE 14, 196

Firm, MSO 444, 147
Fisher, AKR 301, 239
Fiske, DD 842, 66; DDR 842, 69
Fitch, DD 462, 54; DMS 25, 143
Fitzgerald, DDG 62, 76
Flagstaff, PGH 1, 129; WPBH 1, 267
Flagstaff, AGM 21, 182
Flaherty, DE 135, 82
Flambeau River, LSMR 503, 116
Flamingo, AMS 1, 151
Flasher, SS 249, 15
Flasher, SSN 613, 27
Flatley, FFG 21, 93
Fletcher, DD 445, 55; DDE 445, 69
Fletcher, DD 992, 72
Flicker, AMS 9, 151
Flickertail State, ACS 5, 237
Flint, CL 97, 41
Flint, AE 32, 197
Florida, SSBN/SSGN 728, 36
Florikan, ASR 9, 166
Flounder, SS 251, 15
Floyd B. Parks, DD 884, 68
Floyd County, LST 762, 108
Floyds Bay, AVP 40, 168
Flyer, AG 178, 177
Flying Fish, SS/AGSS 229, 14
Flying Fish, SSN 673, 28
Flying Fish, WPB 87346, 267
Fogg, DE 57, 79; DER 57, 86
Fomalhaut, AE 20, 197; AK 22, 200
Foote, DD 511, 56
Force, MSO 445, 147
Ford, FFG 54, 94
Ford County, LST 772, 108
Foreman, DE 633, 80
Formoe, DE 509, 86
Forrest Royal, DD 872, 67
Forrest Sherman, DD 931, 70
Forrest Sherman, DDG 98, 78
Forrestal, CVA/CV 59, 6; AVT 59, 169
Forster, DE 334, 83; DER 334, 87; WDE 434, 260
Forsythia, WAGL/WLR 63, 274
Fort Fisher, LSD 40, 104
Fort Mandan, LSD 21, 103
Fort Marion, LSD 22, 103
Fort McHenry, LSD 43, 104
Fort Snelling, LSD 30, 103
Fortify, MSO 446, 147
Forward, WMEC 911, 259
Foss, DE 59, 79
Fowler, DE 222, 79
Fox, DLG/CG 33, 48

Foxglove:, WAGL/WLR 285, 274
Frament, APD 77, 125
Francis Hammond, DE/FF 1067, 90
Francis M. Robinson, DE 220, 79
Francis Marion, APA/LPA 249, 124
Francis Scott Key, SSBN 657, 35
Francovich, APD 116, 126
Frank Cable, AS 40, 166
Frank Drew, WLM 557, 274
Frank E. Evans, DD 754, 62
Frank Knox, DD 742, 63; DDR 742, 69
Frankford, DD 497, 54
Franklin, CV/CVS 13, 2; AVT 8, 169
Franklin D. Roosevelt, CVB/CVA/CV 42, 4
Franks, DD 554, 57
Frazier, DD 607, 54
Fred C. Ainsworth, AP 181, 223
Fred T. Berry, DD 858, 66; DDE 858, 69
Frederick, LST 1184, 114
Frederick Funston, AP 178, 223
Frederick Lee, WSC 139, 261
Fredonia, PC 1174, 133
Freedom, LCS 1, 102
Freedom, IX 43, 192
Fremont, APA/LPA 44, 122
French, DE 367, 85
French Creek, AO 159, 215
Fresno, CL 121, 41
Fresno, LST 1182, 114
Frigate Bird, MSC 191, 156
Frontier, AD 25, 164
Frost, DE 144, 82
Frostburg, PC 785, 132
Frybarger, DE 705, 80; DEC 705, 87
Fullam, DD 474, 55
Fulmar, AMS 47, 151
Fulton, AS 11, 165
Furman, AK 280, 205
Furse, DD 882, 68; DDR 882, 69

Gabilan, SS 252, 15
Gadwall, AM/MSF 362, 146
Gage, APA 168, 122
Gainard, DD 706, 61
Galatea, WPC 108, 261
Galena, PC 1136, 133
Galilea, AKN 6, 201
Gallant, MSO 489, 147
Gallatin, WHEC 721, 257
Gallery, FFG 26, 93
Gallipolis, PC 778, 132

Gallup, PG 85, 127
Gallup, PF 47, 129
Galveston, CL 93, 42; CLG 3, 42
Galveston Bay, AK 9720, 246
Galveston Island, WPB 1349, 266
Gandy, DE 764, 81
Gannet, MSC 290, 159
Gannet, WPB 87334, 267
Gansevoort, DD 608, 54
Gantner, APD 42, 124
Gar, SS 206, 14
Garcia, DE/FF 1040, 89
Gardiners Bay, AVP 39, 168
Garfield County, LST 784, 108
Garfield Thomas, DE 193, 81
Garland, AM/MSF 238, 145
Garnett County, AGP 786, 185; LST 786, 108
Gary, FFG 51, 94
Gary Chouest, AGDS 9642, 253
Gatch, DE 1026, 87; see *Hooper*
Gatling, DD 671, 59
Gato, SS 212, 14
Gato, SSN 615, 27
Gayety, AM/MSF 239, 145
Gear, ARS 34, 175
Gearing, DD 710, 63
Geiger, AP 197, 225
Gem State, ACS 2, 236
Gemini, PHM 6, 130
Gen. A.E. Anderson, AP 111, 221
Gen. A.W. Brewster, AP 155, 223
Gen. A.W. Greely, AP 141, 222
Gen. Alexander M. Patch, AP 122, 222
Gen. C.C. Ballou, AP 157, 223
Gen. C.G. Morton, AP 138, 222
Gen. C.H. Muir, AP 142, 222
Gen. D.E. Aultman, AP 156, 223
Gen. Daniel I. Sultan, AP 120, 221
Gen. E.T. Collins, AP 147, 222
Gen. Edwin D. Patrick, AP 124, 222
Gen. G.M. Randall, AP 115, 221
Gen. H.B. Freeman, AP 143, 222
Gen. H.F. Hodges, AP 144, 222
Gen. H.H. Arnold, AGM 9, 182
Gen. H.W. Butner AP 113. 221
Gen. Harry Taylor, AP 145, 222
Gen. Hoyt S. Vandenberg, AGM 10, 182
Gen. Hugh J. Gaffey, IX 507, 193; AP 121, 221
Gen. J.C. Breckinridge, AP 176, 221
Gen. J.H. McRae, AP 149, 223
Gen. John Pope, AP 110, 221
Gen. LeRoy Eltinge, AP 154, 223

Gen. M.B. Stewart, AP 140, 222
Gen. M.C. Meigs, AP 116, 221
Gen. M.L. Hersey, AP 148, 222
Gen. M.M. Patrick, AP 150, 223
Gen. Maurice Rose, AP 126, 222
Gen. Nelson M. Walker, AP 125, 222
Gen. R.E. Callan, AP 139, 222
Gen. R.L. Howze, AP 134, 222
Gen. R.M. Blatchford, AP 153, 223
Gen. S.D. Sturgis, AP 137, 222
Gen. Simon B. Buckner, AP 123, 222
Gen. Stuart Heintzelman, AP 159, 223
Gen. W.A. Mann, AP 112, 221
Gen. W.C. Langfitt, AP 151, 223
Gen. W.F. Hase, AP 146, 222
Gen. W.G. Haan, AP 158, 223
Gen. W.H. Gordon, AP 117, 221
Gen. W.M. Black, AP 135, 222
Gen. William Mitchell, AP 114, 221
Gen. William O. Darby, AP 127, 222
Gen. William Weigel, AP 118, 221
Gendreau, DE 639, 80
General Greene, WSC 140, 261
Genesee AOG 8. 218
Gentian, WAGL/WLB 290, 271
Gentry, DE 349, 84
George, DE 697, 80
George A. Johnson, DE 583, 84
George B. Kelez NOAA, 281
George Bancroft, SSBN 643, 35
George C. Marshall, SSBN 654, 35
George Clymer, APA 27, 121
George Cobb, WLM 564, 274
George D. Cowie ASV, 277
George E. Davis, DE 357, 84
George H.W. Bush, CVN 77, 8
George K. Mackenzie, DD 836, 65
George Phillip, FFG 12, 93
George W. Goethals, AP 182, 223
George W. Ingram, APD 43, 124
George Washington, CVN 73, 8
George Washington, SSBN/SSN 598, 33
George Washington Carver, SSBN 656, 35
Georgetown, AG 165, 178; AGTR 2, 180
Georgia, SSBN/SSGN 729, 36
Gerald R. Ford, CVN 78, 9
Germantown, LSD 42, 104
Geronimo, ATA 207, 232
Gettysburg, CG 64, 51
Gettysburg, PCE 904, 135
Gherardi, DD 637, 55; DMS 30, 143

Gibson County, LST 794, 108
Gila River, LSMR 504, 116
Gilbert Islands, CVE/CVU 107, 11
Gilbert Islands, AKV 39, 207
Gillespie, DD 609, 54
Gillette, DE 681, 80
Gilligan, DE 508, 86
Gilliland, AKR 298, 240
Gilmer, PC 565, 131
Glacier, AGB 4, 179; WAGB 4, 268
Gladiator, AM/MSF 319, 144
Gladiator, MCM 9, 151
Gleaves, DD 423, 54
Glenard P. Liscomb, SSN 685, 30
Glendale, PF 36, 128
Glennon, DD 840, 66
Glenolden, PC 782, 132
Glenwood, PC 1140, 133
Glomar Explorer, AG 193, 178
Gloucester, PF 22, 128
Glover, AGDE/AGFF 1, 179; AG 163, 178; FF 1098, 92
Glynn, APA 239, 123
Goldcrest, AMCU/MHC 24, 160
Golden Bear, AP 1002, 253
Golden Eagle, AF 52, 198
Goldenrod, WAGL 213, 274
Goldfinch, AMS 12, 151
Goldsborough, DDG 20, 73
Gonzalez, DDG 66, 76
Goodrich, DD 831, 65; DDR 831, 69
Gopher State, ACS 4, 237
Gordius, ARL 36, 172
Gordon, AKR 296, 240
Gordon Gunter, R 336, 278
Gosport, IX 517, 193
Goss, DE 444, 85
Gosselin, APD 126, 126
Grackle, AMS 13, 151
Grady, DE 445, 85
Graffias, AF 29, 197
Grafton, PCS 1431, 135
Graham County, LST 1176, 113; AGP 1176, 185
Grainger, AK 184, 201
Grampus, SS 523, 21
Grand Canyon, AD 28, 164; AR 24, 170
Grand Canyon State, ACS 3, 236
Grand Isle, WPB 1338, 266
Grand Rapids, PG 98, 127
Grand River, LSMR 505, 116
Grant County, LST 1174, 113
Grapple, ARS 7, 174

Grapple, ARS 53, 175
Grasp, ARS 24, 174
Grasp, ARS 51, 175
Gravely, DDG 107, 78
Gray, DE/FF 1054, 90
Grayback, SS/SSG 574, 24; APSS/LPSS 574, 24
Graylag, AM/MSF 364, 146
Grayling, SSN 646, 28
Grayson, DD 435, 54
Great Sitkin, AE 17, 196
Green Bay, LPD 20, 102
Green Bay, PG 101, 127
Green Harbour, AK 2064, 245
Green Island, AK 1015, 245
Green Mountain State, ACS 9, 237
Green Ridge, AK 9655, 250
Green River, LSMR 506, 116
Green Valley, AK 2049, 245
Green Wave, AK 2050, 250
Greenbrier River, LSMR 507, 116
Greencastle, PC 1119, 133
Greeneville, SSN 772, 31
Greenfish, SS 351, 19
Greenlet, ASR 10, 166
Greenling, SS 213, 14
Greenling, SSN 614, 27
Greenville Victory, AK 237, 201
Greenwich Bay, AVP 41, 168
Greenwood, DE 679, 80
Greer County, LST 799, 108
Gregory, DD 802, 60
Grenadier, SS 525, 21
Gresham, WAVP/WHEC 387, 256
Gridley, DLG/CG 21, 46
Gridley, DDG 101, 78
Griffin, AS 13, 165
Grimes, APA 172, 122
Grinnell, PC 1230, 133
Grommet Reefer, AF 53, 198
Grosbeak, AMS 14, 151
Grosse-Pointe, PC 1546, 134
Groton, SSN 694, 30
Groton, PCE 900, 135
Grouper, SS/AGSS 214, 14; SSK 214, 23
Grouse, AMS 15, 151
Growler, SSG 577, 24
Guadalcanal, CVE/CVU 60, 10
Guadalcanal LPH 7, 97
Guadalupe, AO 32, 209
Guadalupe, AO 200, 217
Guam, CB 2, 39
Guam, LPH 9, 97

Guardfish, SS 217, 14
Guardfish, SSN 612, 27
Guardian, MCM 5, 151
Guardian, AGR 1, 185
Guavina, SS/AGSS 362, 19; SSO/AOSS 362, 25
Gudgeon, SS/AGSS 567, 22
Guest, DD 472, 55
Guide, MSO 447, 147
Guitarro, SS 363, 19
Guitarro, SSN 665, 28
Gulf Banker, AK 5044, 249
Gulf Farmer, AK 5045, 249
Gulf Merchant, AK 5046, 249
Gulf Shipper, AK 2035, 249
Gulf Trader, AK 2036, 249
Gull, AMS 16, 151; AMCU/MHC 46, 160
Gunason, DE 795, 80
Gunnel, SS 253, 15
Gunnison River, LSMR 508, 116
Gunston Hall, LSD 5, 103
Gunston Hall, LSD 44, 104
Gurke, DD 783, 64
Gurnard, SS 254, 15
Gurnard, SSN 662, 28
Gus W. Darnell, AOT 1121, 251
Gustafson, DE 182, 81
Guymon, PC 1177, 133
Gwin, DM/MMD 33, 141
Gyatt, DD 712, 63; DDG 1, 73
Gypsy, ARSD 1, 172
Gyre, AGOR 21, 190
GySgt Fred W. Stockham, AK 3017, 239, 240, see Soderman

H.H. Hess, AGS 38, 188
Haas, DE 424, 85
Hackleback, SS/AGSS 295, 16
Haddo, SSN 604, 27
Haddo, SS 255, 15
Haddock, SS 231, 14
Haddock, SSN 621, 27
Haddock, WPB 87347, 267
Hailey, DD 556, 57
Haines, APD 84, 125
Haiti Victory, AK 238, 201
Hake, SS/AGSS 256, 15
Hale, DD 642, 58
Haleakala, AE 25, 197
Half Moon, AVP 26, 168; EAVP/WHEC 378, 256
Halfbeak, SS 352, 19
Halford, DD 480, 56

Halibut, SSGN 587, 27
Halibut, WPB 87340, 267
Hall, DD 583, 58
Halsey, DLG/CG 23, 46
Halsey, DDG 97, 78
Halsey Powell, DD 686, 59
Halyburton, FFG 40, 94
Hambleton, DD 455, 54; DMS 20, 143
Hamilton, WHEC 715, 256
Hamilton, WMSL 752, 257
Hamilton County, LST 802, 108
Hamlin, AV 15, 168
Hammann, DE 131, 81
Hammerberg, DE 1015, 87
Hammerhead, SS 364, 19
Hammerhead, SSN 663, 28
Hammerhead, WPB 87302, 266
Hamner, DD 718, 63
Hampden County, LST 803, 108
Hampshire County, LST 819, 108
Hampton, SSN 767, 31
Hampton, PCS 1386, 135
Hamul, AD 20, 163
Hanazuki, DD 934, 71
Hancock, CV/CVS 19, 3
Hanford, PC 1142, 133
Hank, DD 702, 60
Hanna, DE 449, 86
Hanson, DD 832, 65; DDR 832, 69
Haraden, DD 585, 58
Harder, SS 568, 22
Hardhead, SS 365, 19
Harkness, AGS 12, 186; AMCU/MHC 12, 160
Harkness, AGS 32, 188
Harlan County, LST 1196, 114
Harlan R. Dickson, DD 708, 61
Harlequin, AM/MSF 365, 146
Harmon, DE 678, 80
Harnett County, LST 821, 108; AGP 821, 185
Harold E. Holt, DE/FF 1074, 90
Harold J. Ellison, DD 864, 67
Harpers Ferry, LSD 49, 105
Harrier, AM/MSF 366, 147
Harriet Lane, WMEC 903, 259
Harriet Lane, WSC 141, 261
Harris County, LST 822, 108
Harrison, DD 573, 57
Harry Claiborne, WLM 561, 274
Harry E. Hubbard, DD 748, 61
Harry E. Yarnell, DLG/CG 17, 46
Harry F. Bauer, DM/MMD 26, 141
Harry L. Corl, APD 108, 125

Harry L. Glucksman, MSS 1, 162
Harry R. Kenyon, DE 683, 80
Harry S. Truman, CVN 75, 8
Harry W. Hill, DD 986, 72
Hart, DD 594, 58
Hartford, SSN 768, 31
Hartley, DE 1029, 87
Harveson, DE 316, 82; DER 316, 86
Harwood, DD 861, 67; DDE 861, 69
Hassayampa, AO 145, 214
Hattiesburg Victory, AK 1808, 250
Haven, AH 12, 226
Haverfield, DE 393, 83; DER 393, 87
Haverford, AG 179, 177
Havre, PCE 877, 134
Hawaii, SSN 776, 33
Hawaii, CB 3, 39; CBC 1, 39
Hawes, FFG 53, 94
Hawk, AMS 17, 151
Hawk, WPB 87355, 267
Hawkbill, SS 366, 19
Hawkbill, SSN 666, 28
Hawkins, DD 873, 67; DDR 873, 69
Hawksbill, WPB 87312, 266
Hawthorn, WAGL 215, 270
Hayes, AG 195, 178
Hayes, AGOR 16, 190
Hayler, DD 997, 72
Haynsworth, DD 700, 60
Hayter, APD 80, 125
Hazard, AM/MSF 240, 145
Hazel, AN 29, 191
Hazelwood, DD 531, 56
Healy, DD 672, 59
Healy, WAGB 20, 269
Heather, WAGL/WLB 331, 272
Heck, ASV 91/S 591, 279
Hector, AR 7, 170
Heed, AM/MSF 100, 143
Heermann, DD 532, 56
Helena, SSN 725, 30
Helena, CA 75, 40
Helios, ARB 12, 171
Hemlock, WAGL 217, 270
Hemminger, DE 746, 81
Henderson, DD 785, 64
Henley, DD 762, 62
Hennepin, AK 187, 201
Henrico, APA/LPA 45, 122
Henry A. Wiley, DM/MMD 29, 141
Henry B. Bigelow, R 225, 279
Henry B. Wilson, DDG 7, 73
Henry Blake, WLM 563, 274
Henry Clay, SSBN 625, 35

Henry County, LST 824, 109
Henry Eckford, AO 192, 217
Henry Gibbins, AP 183, 223
Henry J. Kaiser, AO 187, 217
Henry L. Stimson, SSBN 655, 35
Henry M. Jackson, SSBN 730, 36
Henry W. Tucker, DD 875, 67; DDR 875, 69
Henson, AGS 63, 189
Hepburn, DE/FF 1055, 90
Herald, AM/MSF 101, 143
Herbert C. Jones, DE 137, 82
Herbert J. Thomas, DD 833, 65; DDR 833, 69
Hercules, PHM 2, 130
Herkimer, AK 188, 201
Hermes, WPC 109, 261
Hermitage, LSD 34, 103
Herndon, DD 638, 55
Heron, AMS 18, 151; MHC 52, 161
Heron, WPB 87344, 267
Hewell, AG 145, 177; AKL 14, 208
Hewitt, DD 966, 71
Heyliger, DE 510, 86
Heywood L. Edwards, DD 663, 58
Hickman County, LST 825, 109
Hickory, WAGL/WLI 219, 270
Hickory, WLB 212, 273
Hickox, DD 673, 59
Hidatsa, ATF 102, 230
Higbee, DD 806, 64; DDR 806, 69
Higgins, DDG 76, 77
High Point, PCH 1, 129; WMEH 1, 267
Highland Light, IX 48, 192
Hi'ialakai, R 334, 278
Hilarity, AM/MSF 241, 145
Hilary P. Jones, DD 427, 54
Hilbert, DE 742, 81
Hilgard, ASV 82, 277
Hill, DE 141, 82
Hillsborough County, LST 827, 109
Hillsdale County, LST 835, 109
Hissem, DE 400, 84; DER 400, 87
Hitchiti, ATF 103, 230
Hobby, DD 610, 54
Hobson, DD 464, 54
Hobson, DMS 26, 143
Hodges, DE 231, 84
Hodgson NOAA, 277
Hoe, SS 258, 15
Hoel, DDG 13, 73
Hoggatt Bay, CVE/CVU 75, 10
Hoggatt Bay, AKV 25, 207

Hoist, ARS 40, 175
Holder, DD 819, 64; DDE 819, 69
Holland, AS 32, 165
Holland, ARG 18, 171
Hollandia, CVE/CVU 97, 11; AKV 33, 207
Hollidaysburg, PCS 1385, 135
Hollis, APD/LPR 86, 125
Hollister, DD 788, 64
Holly, AN 19, 191
Hollyhock, WAGL/WLM 220, 270
Hollyhock, WLB 214, 273
Holmes County, LST 836, 109
Holston River, LSMR 509, 116
Holt, DE 706, 84
Holton, DE 703, 80
Honesdale, PC 566, 132
Honolulu, SSN 718, 30
Honolulu, CL 48, 41
Hooper, DE 1026, 87
Hooper Island, ARG 17, 171
Hopewell, DD 681, 59
Hopi, ATF 71, 229
Hopper, DDG 70, 77
Hopping, APD 51, 124
Hoquiam, PF 5, 128
Horace A. Bass, APD/LPR 124, 126
Hornbeam, WAGL/WLB 394, 271
Hornbill, AMS 19, 151
Horne, DLG/CG 30, 48
Hornet, CV/CVS 12, 2
Houghton, PC 588, 132
Houston, SSN 713, 30
Houston, CL 81, 41
Howard, DDG 83, 78
Howard D. Crow, DE 252, 82
Howard F. Clark, DE 533, 86
Howard W. Gilmore, AS 16, 165
Howorth, DD 592, 58
HSV-XI, IX 532, 193
Hubbard, APD 53, 124
Hudson, DD 475, 55
Hudson, AO/AOT 184, 217
Hudson, WYT 87, 269
Hudson, WLIC 801, 275
Hue City, CG 66, 51
Hugh Purvis, DD 709, 61
Hull, DD 945, 70
Humboldt, AVP 21, 168
Humboldt, WAVP/WHEC 372, 256
Hummer, AMS 20, 151
Hummingbird, MSC 192, 156
Hunley, AS 31, 165

Hunt, DD 674, 59
Hunter Marshall, APD 112, 126
Hunterdon County, LST 838, 109; AGP 838, 185
Hunting, AG 335, 178
Huntington, CL 107, 42
Huntsville, AGM 7, 181
Hurricane, PC 3, 136
Hurst, DE 250, 82
Huse, DE 145, 82
Hyades, AF 28, 197
Hydrographer OSS, 277
Hyman, DD 732, 61
Hyman G. Rickover, SSN 709, 30

Ibis, WPB 87338, 267
Icarus, WPC 110, 261
Icefish, SS 367, 19
Ida Lewis, WLM 551, 274
Illusive, MSO 448, 147
Impeccable, AM/MSF 320, 144
Impeccable, AGOS 23, 185
Impervious, MSO 449, 147
Implicit, AM 246, 145
Implicit, MSO 455, 147
Inaugural, AM/MSF 242, 145
Inch, DE 146, 82
Inchon, LPH 12, 97; MCS 12, 142
Incredible, AM/MSF 249, 145
Independence, CVL 22, 5
Independence, CVA/CV 62, 6
Independence, LCS 2, 102
Indian Island, AG 77, 175; AKS 25, 207
Indiana, BB 58, 37
Indianapolis, SSN 697, 30
Indomitable, AGOS 7, 183
Indra, ARL 37, 172
Inflict, MSO 456, 147
Ingersoll, DD 652, 58
Ingersoll, DD 990, 72
Ingham, WPG/WHEC 35, 255
Ingraham, DD 694, 60
Ingraham, FFG 61, 94
Instill, AM/MSF 252, 145
Integrity, AGOS 24, 185
Interceptor, AGR 8, 185
Interdictor, AGR 13, 185
Interpreter, AGR 14, 185
Interrupter, AGR 15, 185
Intrepid, CV/CVS 11, 2
Intrigue, AM/MSF 253, 145
Invade, AM/MSF 254, 145
Investigator, AGR 9, 185

Invincible, AGM 24, 183; AGOS 10, 183
Iowa, BB 61, 37
Ipswich, PC 1186, 133
Ira Jeffery, APD 44, 124
Iredell County, LST 839, 109
Irex, SS/AGSS 482, 21
Iris, WAGL/WLB 395, 271
Iron County, LST 840, 109
Ironwood, WAGL/WLB 297, 272
Iroquois, WPG 43, 256
Irwin, DD 794, 59
Isherwood, DD 520, 56
Isle Royale, AD 29, 164
Itasca, WPG 321, 255
Iuka, ATA 123, 231
Ivy, WAGL/WLB 329, 272
Iwo Jima, LPH 2, 97
Iwo Jima, LHD 7, 99
Izard, DD 589, 58

J. Douglas Blackwood, DE 219, 79
J. Richard Ward, DE 243, 82
J.R.Y. Blakely, DE 140, 82
Jacamar, AMCU/MHC 25, 160
Jacana, MSC 193, 156
Jaccard, DE 355, 84
Jack, SS 259, 15
Jack, SSN 605, 27
Jack C. Robinson, APD 72, 125
Jack Miller, DE 410, 85
Jack W. Wilke, DE 800, 80
Jack Williams, FFG 24, 93
Jackdaw, AMS 21, 151
Jackson, WPC 120, 261
Jacksonville, SSN 699, 30
Jacob Jones, DE 130, 81
Jallao, SS 368, 19
James C. Owens, DD 776, 62
James E. Craig, DE 201, 79
James E. Kyes, DD 787, 64
James E. Williams, DDG 95, 78
James K. Polk, SSBN 645, 35
James M. Gilliss, AGS 13, 186; AMCU/MHC 13, 160
James M. Gilliss, AGOR 4, 189
James Madison, SSBN 627, 35
James Miller, DD 535, 56, *see Miller*
James Monroe, SSBN 622, 35
James O'Hara, AP 179, 223
James Rankin, WLM 555, 274
James River, LSMR 510, 116
Jamestown, AG 166, 178; AGTR 3, 180
Janssen, DE 396, 83

Jarrett, FFG 33, 94
Jarvis, DD 799, 60
Jasmine, WAGL/WLI 261, 271
Jason, AR 8/ARH 1, 170
Jason Dunham, DDG 109, 78
Jasper, PC 486, 131
Jeb Stuart, AK 9204, 245
Jeffers, DD 621, 54; DMS 27, 143
Jefferson City, SSN 759, 31
Jefferson County, LST 845, 109
Jefferson Island, WPB 1340, 266
Jekyl, AKL 6, 208
Jenkins, DD 447, 55; DDE 447, 69
Jenks, DE 665, 80
Jennings County, LST 846, 109
Jerome County, LST 848, 109
Jesse L. Brown, DE/FF 1089, 90
Jesse L. Taylor, FFG 50, 94
Jesse Rutherford, DE 347, 84
Jicarilla, ATF 104, 230
Jimmy Carter, SSN 23, 32
Jobb, DE 707, 84
John A. Bole, DD 755, 62
John A. Moore, FFG 19, 93
John Adams, SSBN 620, 35
John Blish, AGS 10, 186
John C. Butler, DE 339, 84
John C. Calhoun, SSBN 630, 35
John C. Stennis, CVN 74, 8
John D. Henley, DD 553, 57
John Day River, LSMR 511, 116
John Ericsson, AO 194, 217
John F. Kennedy, CVA/CV 67, 7
John Hancock, DD 981, 71
John Hood, DD 655, 58
John King, DDG 3, 73
John L. Hall, FFG 32, 94
John L. Williamson, DE 370, 85
John Lenthall, AO 189, 217
John Lykes, AK 9123, 246
John Marshall, SSBN/SSN 611, 34
John McDonnell, AGS 51, 188
John N. Cobb, R 552, 280
John P. Gray, APD 74, 125
John Paul Jones, DD 932, 70; DDG 32, 75
John Paul Jones, DDG 53, 76
John Q. Roberts, APD 94, 125
John R. Craig, DD 885, 68
John R. Perry, DE 1034, 88
John R. Pierce, DD 753, 62
John Rodgers, DD 574, 57
John Rodgers, DD 983, 72

John S. McCain, DL 3, 45; DDG 36, 75
John S. McCain, DDG 56, 76
John W. Thomason, DD 760, 62
John W. Weeks, DD 701, 60
John Willis, DE 1027, 87
John Young, DD 973, 71
Johnnie Hutrchins, DE 360, 85
Johnson County, LST 849, 109
Johnston, DD 821, 65
Johnstown, AGM 20, 182
Jonas Ingram, DD 938, 70
Jonquil, WAGL/WLB 330, 272
Joseph E. Campbell, APD 49, 124
Joseph E. Connolly, DE 450, 86
Joseph Henry, WHEO 701, 275
Joseph Hewes, DE/FF 1078, 90
Joseph K. Taussig, DE 1030, 87
Joseph Lykes, AK 9808, 246
Joseph M. Auman, APD 117, 126
Joseph P. Kennedy Jr., DD 850, 66
Joseph Strauss, DDG 16, 73
Josephus Daniels, DLG/CG 27, 48
Joshua Appleby, WLM 556, 274
Joshua Humphreys, AO 188, 217
Josiah Willard Gibbs, AGOR 1, 189
Jouett, DLG/CG 29, 48
Joyce, DE 317, 82; DER 317, 86
Jubilant, AM/MSF 255, 146
Julius A. Furer, DEG/FFG 6, 92
Julius A. Raven, APD 110, 125
Juneau, CL 119, 41
Juneau, LPD 10, 101
Juniata County, LST 850, 109
Juniper, WAGL 224, 270
Juniper, WLB 201, 273
Jupiter, AVS 8, 169
Jupiter, AKR 11, 206

K-1, SSK 1, 24
K-2, SSK 2, 24
K-3, SSK 3, 24
Kadashan Bay, CVE/CVU 76, 10
Kadashan Bay, AKV 26, 207
Ka'imimoana, R 333, 278
Kalamazoo, AOR 6, 220
Kalk, DD 611, 54
Kalmia, ATA 184, 231
Kamehameha, SSBN/SSN 642, 35
Kanawha, AO 196, 217
Kane, AGS 27, 187
Kane County, LST 853, 109
Kankakee, AO 39, 210
Kansas City, AOR 3, 220

Karin, AF 33, 197
Kasaan Bay, CVE/CVU 69, 10
Kaskaskia, AO 27, 209
Katherine Walker, WLM 552, 274
Katmai Bay, WTGB 101, 270
Kauffman, FFG 59, 94
Kaw, WYT 61, 269
Kawishiwi, AO 146, 214
Kearny, DD 432, 54
Kearsarge, CV/CVS 33, 3
Kearsarge, LHD 3, 99
Keith, DE 241, 82
Kellar, AGS 25, 187
Kellie Chouest AG, 253
Kelso, PC 1170, 133
Kemper County, LST 854, 109
Kendall C. Campbell, DE 443, 85
Kendrick, DD 612, 54
Kennebago, AO 81, 212
Kennebec, AO 36, 209
Kennebec, WLIC 802, 275
Kenneth D. Bailey, DD 713, 63; DDR 713, 69
Kenneth M. Willett, DE 354, 84
Kenneth Whiting, AV 14, 168
Kent County, LST 855, 109
Kent Island, AG 78, 176; AKS 26, 207
Kentucky, SSBN 737, 36
Kentucky, BB 66, 38
Keosanqua, ATA 198, 231
Kephart, APD 61, 125
Keppler, DD 765, 63; DDE 765, 69
Kermit Roosevelt, ARG 16, 170
Kern, AOG 2, 218
Kerrville, PC 597, 132
Kershaw, APA 176, 122
Kerstin, AF 34, 198
Kestrel, AMCU/MHC 26, 160
Kewaunee, PC 1178, 133
Kewaydin, ATA 213, 232
Key, DE 348, 84
Key Biscayne, WPB 1339, 266
Key Largo, WPB 1324, 266
Key West, SSN 722, 30
Keystone State, ACS 1, 236
Kidd, DD 661, 58
Kidd, DDG 993, 76
Kidd, DDG 100, 78
Kilauea, AE 26, 197
Kildeer, AMCU 27, 160
Killen, DD 593, 58
Kilo Moana, AGOR 26, 190
Kimball, WSC 143, 261

Kimberly, DD 521, 56
King, DLG 10, 45; DDG 41, 75
King County, LST 857, 109; AG 157, 177
Kingbird, MSC 194, 156
Kingfish, SS 234, 15
Kingfisher, MHC 56, 161
Kingfisher, WPB 87322, 267
Kingman, APB 47, 225
Kingsport, AG 164, 177
Kingsport Victory, AK 239, 201
Kinkaid, DD 965, 71
Kinzer, APD 91, 125
Kiowa, ATF 72, 229
Kirk, DE/FF 1087, 90
Kirkpatrick, DE 318, 82; DER 318, 86
Kirwin, APD/LPR 90, 125
Kishwaukee, AOG 9, 218
Kiska, AE 35, 197
Kiska, WPB 1336, 266
Kite, AMS 22, 151
Kittery, PC 1201, 133
Kittiwake, ASR 13, 166
Kittiwake, WPB 87316, 266
Kitty Hawk, CVA/CV 63, 7
Klakring, FFG 42, 94
Klamath, WPG/WHEC 66, 256
Kleinsmith, APD 134, 126
Kline, APD 120, 126
Klondike, AD 22, 164; AR 22, 170
Knapp, DD 653, 58
Knave, AM/MSF 256, 146
Knight, DD 633, 55; DMS 40, 143
Knight Island, WPB 1348, 266
Knorr, AGOR 15, 190
Knox, DE/FF 1052, 90
Knudson, APD/LPR 101, 125
Kodiak, LSM 161, 115
Kodiak Island, WPB 1341, 266
Koelsch, DE/FF 1049, 89
Koiner, DE 331, 83; DER 331, 86
Koiner, WDE 433, 260
Koka, ATA 185, 231
Kraken, SS 370, 19
Kretchmer, DE 329, 83; DER 329, 86
Krishna, ARL 38, 172
Kukui, WLB 203, 273
Kukui, WAK 186, 275
Kula Gulf, CVE/CVU 108, 11; AKV 8, 207
Kwajalein, CVE/CVU 98, 11; AKV 34, 207
Kyne, DE 744, 81

L. Mendel Rivers, SSN 686, 29
L.Y. Spear, AS 36, 166
La Jolla, SSN 701, 30
La Moure County, LST 883, 109
La Moure County, LST 1194, 114
La Prade, DE 409, 85
La Salle, LPD 3, 100; AGF 3, 119
La Vallette, DD 448, 55
Laboon, DDG 58, 76
Laertes, AR 20, 170
Lafayette, SSBN 616, 35
Lafayette County, LST 859, 109
Laffey, DD 724, 61
Lake, AK 5016, 249
Lake Champlain, CVA/CVS 39, 4
Lake Champlain, CG 57, 50
Lake County, LST 880, 109
Lake Erie, CG 70, 51
Lakeland, LSM 373, 115
Lamar, PCE 899, 135; WTR 899, 275
Lamoille River, LSMR/LFR 512, 116
Lamons, DE 743, 81
Lamprey, SS 372, 19
Lancetfish, SS 296, 16
Laney Chouest AG, 253
Langley, CVL 27, 5
Laning, APD/LPR 55, 124
Lansdale, DD 766, 64
Lansdowne, DD 486, 54
Lansing, DE 388, 83; DER 388, 87; WDE 488, 260
Lantana, WAGL/WLR 310/WLR 80310, 274
Lapeer, PC 1138, 133
Lapon, SS 260, 15
Lapon, SSN 661, 28
Lapwing, AMS 48, 151
Laramie, AO 203, 217
Laramie River, LSMR/LFR 513, 116
Larchmont, PC 487, 131
Lardner, DD 487, 54
Lark, AMS 23, 151
Lash Atlantico, AKR 1192, 245
Lassen, DDG 82, 78
Lassen, AE 3, 195
Latimer, APA 152, 122
Latona, AF 35, 198
Laub, DD 613, 54
Laurel, WAGL/WLB 291, 272
Laurentia, AF 44, 198
Laurinburg, PC 1212, 133
Lavaca, APA 180, 122
Lawrence, DDG 4, 73
Lawrence C. Taylor, DE 415, 85

Lawrence County, LST 887, 109
Lawrence H. Gianella, AOT 1125, 251
Lawrence M. Gould NSF, 281
Laws, DD 558, 57
Laysan Island, ARST 1, 172
LCpl Roy M. Wheat, AK 3016, 241
Le Ray Wilson, DE 414, 85
Leader, MSO 490, 147
League Island, AG 149, 177; AKS 30, 207
Leahy, DLG/CG 16, 46
Leary, DD 879, 68; DDR 879, 69
Lee County, LST 888, 109
Lee Fox, APD 45, 124
Leftwich, DD 984, 72
Legare, WMEC 912, 259
Legare, WSC 144, 261
Lejeune, AP 74, 221
Leland E. Thomas, DE 420, 85
Lenawee, APA 195, 122
Lenoir, PC 582, 132
Leo, AKA 60, 119
Leonard F. Mason, DD 852, 66
Leopold, WPB 1400, 266
Leroy Grumman, AO 195, 217
Leslie L.B. Knox, DE 580, 84
Leslie Lykes, AK 9838, 246
Lester, DE 1022, 87
Lester Jones, ASV 79, 277
Letitia Lykes, AK 2043, 247
Levy, DE 162, 81
Lewis, DE 535, 86
Lewis and Clark, SSBN 644, 35
Lewis and Clark, AKE 1, 206
Lewis B. Puller, FFG 23, 93
Lewis Hancock, DD 675, 59
Lexington, CV/CVA/CVS/CVT 16, 3; AVT 16, 169
Leyte, CV/CVA/CVS 32, 3; AVT 10, 169
Leyte Gulf, CG 55, 50
Liberty, AG 168, 178; AGTR 5, 180
Liberty, WPB 1334, 266
Libra, AKA/LKA 12, 119
Liddle, APD 60, 125
Lilac, WAGL/WLM 227, 271
Limpkin, MSC 195, 156
Lincoln AK, 250
Lincoln County, LST 898, 109
Linden, WAGL/WLI 228, 271
Lindenwald, LSD 6, 103
Lindsey, DM/MMD 32, 141
Ling, SS/AGSS/IXSS 297, 16
Linn County, LST 900, 109

Linnet, AMS 24, 151
Lioba, AF 36, 198
Lionfish, SS/AGSS 298, 16
Lipan, ATF 85, 229; WMEC 85, 258
Litchfield County, LST 901, 109
Little Rock, CL 92, 41; CLG/CG 4, 42
Littlehales, AGS 7, 186
Littlehales, AGSc 15, 186
Littlehales, AGS 52, 188
Livermore, DD 429, 54
Lizardfish, SS 373, 19
Lloyd, APD 63, 125
Lloyd E. Acree, DE 356, 84
Lloyd Thomas, DD 764, 63; DDE 764, 69
Locator, AGR 6, 185
Lockwood, DE/FF 1064, 90
Locust, AN 22, 191
Lodestone, ADG 8, 190
Loeser, DE 680, 80
Lofberg, DD 759, 62
Logan, APA 196, 122
Logan's Fort, AO 160, 215
Loggerhead, SS/AGSS 374, 19
Lone Jack, AO 161, 215
Long, DE/FF 1060, 90
Long Beach, CGN 9, 42
Long Beach, PF 34, 128
Long Island, WPB 1342, 266
Longspur, AMCU/MHC 28, 160
Longview, AGM 3, 181
Lookout, AGR 2, 185
Lorain County, LST 1177, 113
Lorikeet, AMS 49, 151
Los Alamos, AFDB 7, 227
Los Angeles, SSN 688, 30
Los Angeles, CA 135, 40
Louden, PC 1213, 133
Lough, DE 586, 84
Louise Lykes, AK 2048, 247
Louisiana, SSBN 743, 36
Louisville, SSN 724, 30
Louisville, CA 28, 39
Lovelace, DE 198, 79
Lowe, DE 325, 83; DER 325, 86; WDE 425, 260
Lowry, DD 770, 62
Loy, APD 56, 124
Loyal, AGOS 22, 185
Loyalty, MSO 457, 147
Lt. Col. Calvin P. Titus, AKR 9718, 238
Lt. George W.G. Boyce, AK 251, 201
Lt. James E. Robinson, AKV 3/AK 274, 201, 207; AG 170, 178

Lt. Raymond O. Beaudoin, AP 189, 224
Lt. Robert Craig, AK 252, 201
LTC Calvin P. Titus, AK 5089, 238
LTC John U.D. Page, AK 4496, 241
Lubbock, APA 197, 122
Luce, DLG 7, 45; DDG 38, 75
Lucid, MSO 458, 147
Ludington, PC 1079, 132
Ludlow, DD 438, 54
Luiseno, ATF 156, 231
Lunga Point, CVE/CVU 94, 11; AKV 32, 207
Luzerne County, LST 902, 109
Luzon, ARG 2, 170
Lyman County, LST 903, 109
Lyman K. Swenson, DD 729, 61
Lynch, AGOR 7, 189
Lynchburg, AO 154, 215
Lynde McCormick, DDG 8, 73
Lynn, AG 182, 177
Lyon County, LST 904, 109

Macabi, SS 375, 19
MacDonough, DLG 8, 45; DDG 39, 75
Machias, PF 53, 129
Mack, DE 358, 84
Mackenzie, DD 614, 54
Mackerel, SST 1, 25
Mackinac, AVP 13, 168; WAVP/WHEC 371, 256
Mackinac, WAG/WAGB 83, 268
Mackinaw, WAGB 30, 269
Macomb, DD 458, 54; DMS 22, 143
Macon, CA 132, 40
Maddox, DD 731, 61
Madera County, LST 905, 109
Madison, DD 425, 54
Madrona, WAGL/WLB 302, 272
Maersk Constellation, AK 2053, 250
Magnet, ADG 9, 190
Magnolia, WAGL/WLB 328, 272
Magoffin, APA 199, 122
Magpie, AMS 25, 151
Magpie, AMCU/MHC 29, 160
Mahan, DLG 11, 45; DDG 42, 75
Mahan, DDG 72, 77
Mahlon S. Tisdale, FFG 27, 93
Mahnomen County, LST 912, 109
Mahoning, WYT 91, 269
Mahoning County, LST 914, 110
Mahopac, ATA 196, 231
Maine, SSBN 741, 36
Maine, AK 5021, 242

Mainstay, AM/MSF 261, 146
Maj. Bernard F. Fisher, AK 4396, 238
Maj. Stephen W. Pless, AK 3007, 240
Major, DE 796, 80
Makassar Strait, CVE/CVU 91, 11
Makin Island, LHD 8, 99
Mako, WPB 87303, 266
Malabar, AF 37, 198
Malcolm Baldrige, R 103, 278; see Researcher
Mallard, AMCU/MHC 30, 160
Mallow, WAGL/WLB 396, 272
Malone, PC 553, 131
Maloy, DE/EDE 791, 80
Malvern, PC 580, 132
Manatee, AO 58, 211
Manatee, WPB 87363, 267
Manayunk, AN 81, 192
Manchester, CL 83, 41
Mango, AN 24, 191
Manila Bay, CVE/CVU 61, 10
Manitou, WPB 1302, 265
Manitou, WYT 60, 269
Manitowoc, LST 1180, 114
Manley, DD 940, 70
Manning, DE 199, 79
Man-o-War, WPB 87330, 267
Mansfield, DD 728, 61
Manta, SS/AGSS 299, 16
Manta, WPB 87320, 266
Manville, PC 581, 132
Mapiro, SS 376, 19
Maple, WAGL/WLI 234, 271
Maple, WLB 207, 273
Maquoketa, AOG 51, 218
Marathon, PG 89, 127
Marchand, DE 249, 82
Marcus Hanna, WLM 554, 274
Marcus Island, CVE/CVHE 77, 10; AKV 27, 207
Marfa, PCE 842, 134
Margaret B. Chouest AG, 253
Maria Bray, WLM 562, 274
Mariano G. Vallejo, SSBN 658, 35
Marias, AO 57, 211
Maricopa County, LST 938, 110
Marietta, AN 82, 192
Marine Adder, AP 193, 224
Marine Carp, AP 199, 224
Marine Fiddler, AK 267, 203
Marine Jumper, AP 200, 224
Marine Lynx, AP 194, 224
Marine Marlin, AP 201, 224
Marine Phoenix, AP 195, 224

Marine Serpent, AP 202, 224
Marinette County, LST 953, 110
Marion, WSC 145, 261
Marion County, LST 975, 110
Mariposa:, WAGL/WLB 397, 272
Mark, AG 143, 177; AKL 12, 208
Markab, AD 21, 163; AR 23, 170
Marlboro, APB 38, 225
Marlin, SST 2, 25
Marlin, WPB 87304, 266
Marmer, ASV 89, 278
Marquette, AKA 95, 120
Mars, AFS 1, 199
Marsh, DE 699, 80
Marshall, DD 676, 59
Marshfield, AK 282, 205
Martin H. Ray, DE 338, 83
Martinez, PC 1244, 133
Mary Sears, AGS 65, 189
Maryland, SSBN 738, 36
Maryland, BB 46, 37
Marysville, PCER 857, 134
Mascoma, AO 83, 212
Mason, DDG 87, 78
Massachusetts, BB 59, 37
Massey, DD 778, 62
Mataco, ATF 86, 230
Matagorda, AVP 22, 168; WAVP/WHEC 373, 256
Matagorda, WPB 1303, 265
Matanikau, CVE/CVU 101, 11; AKV 36, 207
Mathews, AKA 96, 120
Matinicus, WPB 1315, 265
Mattabasset, AOG 52, 218
Mattaponi, AO 41, 210
Maui, ARG 8, 170
Maui, WPB 1304, 265
Maumee, AO/AOT 149, 215
Mauna Kea, AE 22, 197
Mauna Loa, AE 8, 196
Maurice J. Manuel, DE 351, 84
Maurice River, LSMR 514, 116
Maury, AGS 16, 186
Maury, AGS 39, 188
Mayfield, PC 1196, 133
Maynard, PC 780, 132
Mayo, DD 422, 54
Mazama, AE 9, 196
McArthur, R 330, 278
McArthur, CSS 30/S 330, 279
McCaffery, DD 860, 67; DDE 860, 69
McCalla, DD 488, 54
McCampbell, DDG 85, 78

McCandless, DE/FF 1084, 90
McClelland, DE 750, 81
McCloy, DE/FF 1038, 89
McClusky, FFG 41, 94
McConnell, DE 163, 81
McCook, DD 496, 54; DMS 36, 143
McCord, DD 534, 56
McCoy Reynolds, DE 440, 85
McCracken, APA 198, 122
McCulloch, WAVP/WHEC 386, 256
McDermut, DD 677, 59
McDougal, AG 126, 176
McFaul, DDG 74, 77
McGinty, DE 365, 85
McGowan, DD 678, 59
McInerney, FFG 8, 93
McKean, DD 784, 64; DDR 784, 69
McKee, DD 575, 57
McKee, AS 41, 166
McLanahan, DD 615, 54
McLane, WSC 146, 261
McMinnville, PCS 1401, 135
McMorris, DE 1036, 88
McNair, DD 679, 59
McNulty, DE 581, 84
Meade, DD 602, 54
Meadowlark, MSC 196, 156
Mechanicsburg, PC 779, 132
Medina, PC 1209, 133
Medregal, SS/AGSS 480, 21
Medrick, AMCU 31, 160
Meeker County, LST 980, 110
Megara, ARVA 6, 172
Mellette, APA 156, 122
Mellon, WHEC 717, 256
Melville, AGOR 14, 190
Melvin, DD 680, 59
Melvin R. Nawman, DE 416, 85
Melvin Shields, DE/FF 1066, 90
Memphis, SSN 691, 30
Memphis, AO 162, 215
Menard, APA 201, 122
Mender, ARSD 2, 172
Mendonca, AKR 303, 239
Mendota, WPG/WHEC 69, 256
Menelaus, ARL 13, 171
Menges, DE 320, 82
Menhaden, SS 377, 19
Menifee, APA 202, 122
Menominee, ATF 73, 229
Merapi, AF 38, 198
Mercer, APB 39, 225; IX 502, 192
Mercury, AGM 21, 182
Mercury, AKR 10, 206

Mercury, AKS 20, 207
Mercy, AH 19, 226, 237
Meredith, DD 890, 68
Merganser, AMS 26, 151; AMCU/MHC 47, 160
Meriwether, APA 203, 122
Merlin, AK 323, 241
Mero, SS 378, 19
Merrick, AKA/LKA 97, 120
Merrill, DD 976, 71
Merrill, DE 392, 83
Merrimack, AO 37, 210
Merrimack, AO 179, 216
Mertz, DD 691, 59
Mervine, DD 489, 54; DMS 31, 143
Mesa Verde, LPD 19, 102
Mesquite:, WAGL/WLB 305, 272
Metcalfe, DD 595, 58
Meteor, AKR 9, 205; see *Sea Lift;* 242
Metivier, DE 582, 84
Metomkin, AKL 7, 208
Metompkin, WPB 1325, 266
Metropolis, PC 589, 132
Metuchen, PC 781, 132
Meyerkord, DE/FF 1058, 90
Miami, SSN 755, 31
Miami, CL 89, 41
Miantonomah, ACM/MMA 13, 141
Michael Murphy, DDG 112, 78
Michelson, AGS 23, 187
Michigan, SSBN/SSGN 727, 36
Micka, DE 176, 81
Midas, ARB 5, 171
Middlesex County, LST 983, 110
Midgett, WHEC 725, 257
Midway, CVB/CVA/CV 41, 4
Mifflin, APA 207, 122
Milford, AG 187, 177
Milius, DDG 69, 77
Millard County, LST 987, 110
Milledgeville, PC 1263, 134
Miller, DD 535, 56
Miller, DE/FF 1091, 90
Miller Freeman, R 223, 280
Millicoma, AO/AOT 73, 211
Mills, DE 383, 83; DER 383, 87
Milwaukee, AOR 2, 220
Mimosa, AN 26, 191
Minah, AMCU/MHC 14, 160
Mindanao, ARG 3, 170
Minden, PC 1176, 133
Mindoro, CVE/CVU 120, 11
Mindoro, AKV 20, 207
Mineral County, LST 988, 110

Mingo, SS 261, 15
Minivet, AMCU 32, 160
Minneapolis, CA 36, 39
Minneapolis-Saint Paul, SSN 708, 30
Minnesota, SSN 783, 33
Minnetonka, WPG/WHEC 67, 256
Minos, ARL 14, 171
Minotaur, ARL 15, 171
Mirfak, AK 271, 204
Mispillion, AO 105, 212
Mission Bay, CVE/CVU 59, 10
Mission Buenaventura AO 111. 213
Mission Buenaventura, AOT 1012, 252
Mission Capistrano, AO 112, 213; AG 162, 177
Mission Capistrano, AOT 5005, 251
Mission Carmel, AO 113, 213
Mission De Pala, AO 114, 213
Mission Dolores, AO 115, 213
Mission Loreto, AO 116, 213
Mission Los Angeles, AO 117, 213
Mission Purisima, AO 118, 213
Mission San Antonio, AO 119, 213
Mission San Carlos, AO 120, 213
Mission San Diego, AO 121, 213
Mission San Fernando, AO 122, 213
Mission San Francisco, AO 123, 213
Mission San Gabriel, AO 124, 213
Mission San Jose, AO 125, 213
Mission San Juan, AO 126, 213
Mission San Luis Obispo, AO 127, 213
Mission San Luis Rey, AO 128, 213
Mission San Miguel, AO 129, 213
Mission San Rafael, AO 130, 213
Mission Santa Ana, AO 137, 213
Mission Santa Barbara, AO 131, 213
Mission Santa Clara, AO 132, 213
Mission Santa Cruz, AO 133, 213
Mission Santa Ynez, AO/AOT 134, 213
Mission Solano, AO 135, 213
Mission Soledad, AO 136, 213
Mississinewa, AO 144, 214
Mississippi, BB 41, 37
Mississippi, CGN 40, 50
Mississippi, AG 128, 176
Mississippi, SSN 782, 33
Missoula, APA 211, 123
Missouri, BB 63, 38
Missouri, SSN 780, 33
Mistletoe, WAGL/WLM 237, 271
Mitscher, DL 2, 45; DDG 35, 75
Mitscher, DDG 57, 76
Mizar, AK 272, 204

Moale, DD 693, 60
Moana Wave, AGOR 22, 190
Mobile, CL 63, 41
Mobile, LKA 115, 121
Mobile Bay, CG 53, 50
Mobile Bay, WTGB 103, 270
Mocking Bird, AMS 27, 151
Mocoma, WPG 163, 255
Moctobi, ATF 105, 230
Modoc, WMEC 194, 258
Mohawk, ATF 170, 232
Mohawk, WMEC 913, 259
Mohican, WYT 73, 269
Moinester, DE/FF 1097, 90
Molala, ATF 106, 230
Momsen, DDG 92, 78
Mona Island, ARG 9, 170
Monadnock, ACM/MMA 14, 141
Monhegan, WPB 1305, 265
Monitor, MCS 5, 142
Monmouth County, LST 1032, 110
Monomoy, WPB 1326, 266
Monongahela, AO 42, 210
Monongahela, AO 178, 216
Monroe County, LST 1038, 110
Monrovia, APA 31, 121
Monsoon, PC 4, 136; WPC 4, 267
Monssen, DD 798, 60
Montague, AKA 98, 120
Montauk AOT, 252
Monterey, CVL 26, 5; AVT 2, 169
Monterey, CG 61, 50
Montgomery County, LST 1041, 110
Monticello, LSD 35, 103
Montpelier, SSN 765, 31
Montpelier, CL 57, 41
Montrose, APA/LPA 212, 123
Moore, DE 240, 82
Moosbrugger, DD 980, 71
Moray, SS/AGSS 300, 16
Moray, WPB 87331, 267
Moreno, ATF 87, 230
Morgan County, LST 1048, 110
Morgenthau, WHEC 722, 257
Morris, PC 1179, 133
Morris, WSC 147, 261
Morro Bay, WTGB 106, 270
Morton, DD 948, 70
Mosley, DE 321, 82
Mosopelea, ATF 158, 231
Motive, AM/MSF 102, 144
Mount Baker, AE 4, 195
Mount Baker, AE 34, 197
Mount Hood, AE 29, 197

Mount Katmai, AE 16, 196
Mount McKinley, AGC/LCC 7, 118
Mount Mitchell, MSS 22/S 222, 279
Mount Olympus, AGC 8, 118
Mount Vernon, LSD 39, 104
Mount Vernon, AOT 5083, 251
Mount Washington, AOT 5076, 251
Mount Whitney, LCC 20, 118
Mountrail, APA/LPA 213, 123
Muir, DE 770, 81
Muir Woods, AO 139, 214
Mulberry, AN 27, 191
Muliphen, AKA/LKA 61, 119
Mullany, DD 528, 56
Mullinix, DD 944, 70
Munda, CVE/CVU 104, 11
Munising, PC 1228, 133
Munro, WHEC 724, 257
Munsee, ATF 107, 230
Murphy, DD 603, 54
Murray, DD 576, 57; DDE 576, 69
Murre II NOAA, 281
Murrelet, AM/MSF 372, 144
Muscle Shoals, AGM 19, 182
Muskallunge, SS 262, 15
Muskingum, AK 198, 201
Muskogee, PF 49, 129
Mustang, WPB 1310, 265
Mustin, DDG 89, 78
Myers, APD 105, 125
Myles C. Fox, DD 829, 65; DDR 829, 69
Myrmidon, ARL 16, 171
Myrtle, WAGL 263, 271

Nahant, AN 83, 192
Naifeh, DE 352, 84
Namakagon, AOG 53, 218
Nancy Foster, R 352, 280
Nancy Lykes, AK 9783, 246
Nansemond County, LST 1064, 110
Nantahala, AO 60, 211
Nantucket, WPB 1316, 265
Narcissus, WAGL/WLI 238, 271
Narragansett, ATF 88, 230
Narragansett, ATF 167, 232
Narwhal, SSN 671, 29
Narwhal, WPB 87335, 267
Nashawena, AG 142, 176
Nashville, CL 43, 41
Nashville, LPD 13, 101
Nassau, CVE/CVHE 16, 10
Nassau, LHA 4, 99
Natchaug, AOG 54, 218

Nathan Hale, SSBN 623, 35
Nathanael Greene, SSBN 636, 35
Nathaniel B. Palmer NSF, 281
Natoma Bay, CVE/CVU 62, 10
Natrona, APA 214, 123
Naubuc, AN 84, 192
Naugatuck, WYT 92, 269
Nausett, ACM/MMA 15, 141
Naushon, WPB 1311, 265
Nautilus, SSN 571, 25
Navajo, ATA 211, 232
Navajo, ATF 169, 232
Navarro, APA/LPA 215, 123
Navasota, AO 106, 212
Navesink, WYT 88, 269
Navigator, ATA 203, 232
Neah Bay, WTGB 105, 270
Neal A. Scott, DE 769, 81
Nebraska, SSBN 739, 36
Neches, AO 47, 210
Neches, AO/AOT 183, 217
Nehenta Bay, CVE/CVU 74, 10; AKV 24, 207
Nelson, DD 623, 54
Nemaha, WSC 148, 261
Nemasket, AOG 10, 218
Nemesis, WPC 111, 261
Neodesha, IX 540, 193
Neosho, AO 143, 214
Neptune, ARC 2, 173
Nereus, AS 17, 165
Neshoba, APA 216, 123
Nespelen, AOG 55, 218
Nettle, WAK 169, 275
Neuendorf, DE 200, 79
Neunzer, DE 150, 82
Nevada, SSBN 733, 36
New, DD 818, 64; DDE 818, 69
New Bedford, IX 308, 192
New Hampshire, SSN 778, 33
New Haven, CLK 2, 45
New Jersey, BB 62, 37
New Kent, APA 217, 123
New London County, LST 1066, 110
New Mexico, SSN 779, 33
New Orleans, CA 32, 39
New Orleans, LPH 11, 97
New Orleans, LPD 18, 102
New York, LPD 21, 102
New York City, SSN 696, 30
New York Sun, AOT 1201, 252
Newbridge, AO 9657, 252
Newell, DE 322, 83; DER 322, 86; WDE 422, 260

Newman, APD 59, 124
Newman K. Perry, DD 883, 68; DDR 883, 69
Newport, LST 1179, 114
Newport, PF 27, 128
Newport News, SSN 750, 30
Newport News, CA 148, 40
Niagara Falls, AFS 3, 199
Niblack, DD 424, 54
Nicholas, DD 449, 55; DDE 449, 69
Nicholas, FFG 47, 94
Nicholson, DD 442, 54
Nicholson, DD 982, 71
Nields, DD 616, 54
Nightingale, AMS 50, 151
Nike, WPC 112, 261
Nimble, AM 266, 146
Nimble, MSO 459, 147
Nimitz, CVN 68, 8
Niobrara, AO 72, 211
Nipmuc, ATF 157, 231
Nitro, AE 23, 197
Nitze, DDG 94, 78
Noa, DD 841, 66
Noble, APA 218, 123
Noble Star, AK 9653, 250
Nodaway, AOG 78, 219
Norfolk, SSN 714, 30
Norfolk, CLK/DL 1, 45
Norman Scott, DD 690, 59
Normandy, CG 60, 50
Norris, DD 859, 66; DDE 859, 69
North Carolina, SSN 777, 33
North Carolina, BB 55, 37
North Dakota, SSN 784, 33
Northampton, CLC/CC 1, 44
Northern Light, AK 284, 205
Northland, WMEC 904, 259
Northwind, WAGB 278, 268
Northwind, WAGB 282, 268
Norton Sound, AV 11/AVM 1, 167
Norwalk, AK 279, 205
Notable, MSO 460, 147
Nottoway, ATA 183, 231
Noxubee, AOG 56, 219
Nueces, APB 40, 225; IX 503, 192
Numitor, ARL 17, 171
Nunivak, WPB 1306, 265
Nuthatch, AM/MSF 60, 143
Nutmeg, AN 33, 191
Nye County, LST 1067, 110

Oahu, ARG 5, 170
Oak, WAGL/WLM 239, 271

Oak, WLB 211, 273
Oak Hill, LSD 7, 103
Oak Hill, LSD 51, 105
Oak Ridge, ARDM 1, 227
Oakland, CL 95, 41
O'Bannon, DD 450, 55; DDE 450, 69
O'Bannon, DD 987, 72
Oberlin, PC 560, 131
Oberon, AKA 14, 119
O'Brien, DD 725, 61
O'Brien, DD 975, 71
Observation Island, AG 154, 176; AGM 23, 183
Observer, MSO 461, 147
O'Callahan, DE/FF 1051, 89
Oceanographer, OSS 1/R 101, 278
Oceanside, LSM 175, 115
Oceanus, ARB 2, 171
Ocklawaha, AO 84, 212
Ocracoke, WPB 1307, 265
Odax, SS 484, 21
Odum, APD 71, 125
O'Flaherty, DE 340, 84
Ogden, LPD 5, 101
Ogden, PF 39, 128
Oglethorpe, AKA 100, 120
O'Hare, DD 889, 68; DDR 889, 69
Ohio, SSBN/SSGN 726, 36
Ojibwa, WYT 97, 269
Okaloosa, APA 219, 123
O'Kane, DDG 77, 77
Okanogan, APA/LPA 220, 123
Okeanos Explorer, R 339, 278
Okinawa, LPH 3, 97
Oklahoma City, SSN 723, 30
Oklahoma City, CL 91, 41; CLG/CG 5, 42
Oldendorf, DD 972, 71
Oleander, WAGL/WLR 264/WLR 73264, 274
Oliver Hazard Perry, FFG 7, 93
Oliver Mitchell, DE 417, 85
Olmsted, APA 188, 122
Olney, PC 1172, 133
Olympia, SSN 717, 30
Olympia, IX 40, 192
Omaha, SSN 692, 30
Omi Champion, AO 9659, 251
Oneida, APA 221, 123
O'Neill, DE 188, 81
Oneota, AN 85, 192
Onondaga, WPG 79, 255
Onslow, AVP 48, 168
Ontonagon, AOG 36, 219

Opponent, AM/MSF 269, 146
Opportune, ARS 41, 175
Oracle, AM/MSF 103, 144
Orange County, LST 1068, 110
Orca, AVP 49, 168
Orca, IX 508, 193
Orcas, WPB 1327, 266
Ordronaux, DD 617, 54
Oregon, FRV 51/R 551, 281
Oregon City, CA 122, 40
Oregon II, R 332, 280
O'Reilly, DE 330, 83
Oriole, AMCU/MHC 33, 160
Oriole, MHC 55, 161
Orion, AS 18, 165
Oriskany, CV/CVA 34, 3
Orleans Parish, LST 1069, 110; MCS 6, 142
Orleck, DD 886, 68
Ortolan, AMCU/MHC 34, 160
Ortolan, ASR 22, 167
Osage, MCS 3, 142
Osberg, DE 538, 86
Oscar Austin, DDG 79, 78
Oscar Dyson, R 224, 279
Oscar Elton Sette, R 335, 278
Osmus, DE 701, 80
Osprey, AMS 28, 151
Osprey, MHC 51, 161
Osprey, WPB 87307, 266
Osterhaus, DE 164, 81
Ostrich, AMS 29, 151
Oswald, DE 767, 81
Otter, DE 210, 79
Otterstetter, DE 244, 82; DER 244, 86
Ouachita County, LST 1071, 110
Ouellet, DE/FF 1077, 90
Outagamie County, LST 1073, 110
Outpost, AGR 10, 185
Overseas Alice, AOT 1203, 251
Overseas Valdez, AOT 1204, 251
Overseas Vivian, AOT 1205, 251
Overton County, LST 1074, 111
Owasco, WPG/WHEC 39, 256
Owen, DD 536, 56
Owl, AMCU/MHC 35, 160
Owyhee River, LSMR/LFR 515, 116
Oxford, AG 159, 177; AGTR 1, 180
Oyster Bay, AVP 28, 168
Ozark, MCS 2, 142
Ozbourn, DD 846, 66

Paddle, SS 263, 15
Padre, WPB 1328, 266

Page County, LST 1076, 111
Paiute, ATF 159, 231
Pakana, ATF 108, 230
Palau, CVE/CVU 122, 11; AKV 22, 207
Palawan, ARG 10, 170
Palm, AN 28, 191
Palm Beach, AGER 3, 180; AKL 45, 208
Palmetto, WAGL 265, 271
Palmyra, ARST 3, 172
Pamanset, AO 85, 212
Pamina, AKL 41, 208
Pamlico, WLIC 800, 275
Pampanito, SS/AGSS 383, 19
Panamint, AGC 13, 118
Pandemus, ARL 18, 171
Pandora, WPC 113, 261
Paoli, AO 157, 215
Papago, ATF 160, 231
Papaw, WAGL/WLB 308, 272
Paragould, PC 465, 131
Parche, SS/AGSS 384, 19
Parche, SSN 683, 29
Pargo, SS 264, 15
Pargo, SSN 660, 28
Paricutin, AE 18, 197
Park County, LST 1077, 111
Parker, DD 604, 54
Parker NOAA, 277
Parkersburg, AO 163, 215
Parks, DE 165, 81
Parle, DE 708, 84
Parrakeet, AMS 30, 151
Parrot, MSC 197, 156
Parsons, DD 949, 70; DDG 33, 75
Partridge, AMS 31, 151; AMCU 36, 160
Pasadena, SSN 752, 31
Pasadena, CL 65, 41
Pascagoula, PCE 874, 134
Pasco, PF 6, 128
Pasig, AW 3, 213
Passaconaway, AN 86, 192
Passaic, AN 87, 192
Passumpsic, AO 107, 212
Patapsco, AOG 1, 218
Patchogue, PC 586, 132
Pathfinder, AGS 60, 189
Pathfinder, OSS 30, 277
Patrick Henry, SSBN/SSN 599, 33
Patriot, MCM 7, 151
Patriot, AOT 1001, 250
Patriot State, AP 1000, 253

Patroclus, ARL 19, 171
Patterson, DE/FF 1061, 90
Patuxent, AO 201, 217
Paul, DE/FF 1080, 90
Paul Buck, AOT 1122, 251
Paul F. Foster, DD/EDD 964, 71
Paul G. Baker, DE 642, 80
Paul Hamilton, DD 590, 58
Paul Hamilton, DDG 60, 76
Paul Revere, APA/LPA 248, 124
Pavlic, APD 70, 125
Pawcatuck, AO 108, 213
Pawnee, ATF 74, 229
Payette County, LST 1079, 111
Pea Island, WPB 1347, 266
Peacock, MSC 198, 156
Pearl Harbor, LSD 52, 105
Pearl River, LSMR 516, 116
Pecatonica, AOG 57, 219
Pecos, AO 65, 211
Pecos, AO 197, 217
Pee Dee River, LSMR 517, 116
Pegasus, PHM 1, 130
Peiffer DE 588. 84
Peirce, CSS 28/S 328, 279
Peleliu, LHA 5, 99
Pelias, AS 14, 165
Pelican, AMS 32, 151
Pelican, MHC 53, 161
Pelican, WPB 87327, 267
Pembina, AK 200, 201
Pender County, LST 1080, 111
Penguin, ASR 12, 166
Pennsylvania, SSBN 735, 36
Penobscot, ATA 188, 231
Penobscot Bay, WTGB 107, 270
Pensacola, LSD 38, 104
Pentheus, ARL 20, 171
Peoria, LST 1183, 114
Perch, SS/IX22 313, 16; SSP/ASSP/APSS/LPSS 313, 16
Peregrine, AM/MSF 373, 144; AG 176, 178
Perkins, DD 877, 68; DDR 877, 69
Permit, SS 178, 14
Permit, SSN 594, 27
Perry, DD 844, 66
Perseus, AF 64, 199
Perseus, WPC 114, 261
Persistent, MSO 491, 147
Persistent, AGOS 6, 183
Petaluma, AOG 79, 219
Peter W. Anderson EPA, 281
Peter Wise Lake Guardian EPA, 281

Petersburg, AOT 9101, 251
Peterson, DD 969, 71
Peterson, DE 152, 82
Peto, SS 265, 15
Petoskey, PC 569, 132
Petrel, ASR 14, 166
Petrel, WPB 87350, 267
Petrel, WSES 4, 267
Petrof Bay, CVE/CVU 80, 10
Petrolilte, AO 164, 215
Pettit, DE 253, 82
PFC Dewayne T. Williams, AK 3009, 239
PFC Eugene A. Obregon, AK 3006, 240
PFC James Anderson Jr., AK 3002, 240
PFC William B. Baugh, AK 3001, 240
Phantom, AM 273, 146
Phaon, ARB 3, 171
Pharris, DE/FF 1094, 90
Pheasant, AM/MSF 61, 143
Philadelphia, SSN 690, 30
Philadelphia, CL 41, 41
Philip, DD 498, 56; DDE 498, 69
Philippine Sea, CV/CVS 47, 4; AVT 11, 169
Philippine Sea, CG 58, 50
Phlox, WAGL 61, 271
Phoebe, MSC 199, 156
Phoenix, SSN 702, 30
Phoenix, CL 46, 41
Phoenix, AG 172, 177
Pickaway, APA/LPA 222, 123
Pickerel, SS 524, 21
Picket, AGR 7, 185
Picking, DD 685, 59
Pictor, AF 54, 198
Picuda, SS 382, 19
Piedmont, AD 17, 163
Pierre, PC 1141, 133
Pigeon, AM/MSF 374, 144
Pigeon, ASR 21, 167
Pike, SS 173, 14
Pike, WPB 87365, 267
Pikeville, PC 776, 132
Pililaau, AKR 304, 239
Pillsbury, DE 133, 82; DER 133, 86
Pilot, AM/MSF 104, 144
Pima County, LST 1081, 111
Pinckney, DDG 91, 78
Pine Island, AV 12, 167
Pinnacle, AM 274, 146
Pinnacle, MSO 462, 147
Pinnebog, AOG 58, 219
Pinola, ATA 206, 232

Pintado, SS/AGSS 387, 19
Pintado, SSN 672, 28
Pinto, ATF 90, 230
Pioneer, AM/MSF 105, 144
Pioneer, OSS 31, 277
Pioneer Commander, AK 2016, 248
Pioneer Contractor, AK 2018, 248
Pioneer Crusader, AK 2019, 248
Pioneer Valley, AO 140, 214
Pipefish, SS/AGSS 388, 19
Piper, SS/AGSS 409, 20
Piranha SS/AGSS389, 19
Pirate, AM 275, 146
Piscataqua, AOG 80, 219
Pisces, R 226, 279
Pit River, LSMR 518, 116
Pitkin County, LST 1082, 111
Pittsburgh, SSN 720, 30
Pittsburgh, CA 72, 40
Pivot, AM 276, 146
Pivot, MSO 463, 147
Placerville, PC 1087, 132
Plaice, SS 390, 19
Plainview, AGEH 1, 180
Planetree, WAGL/WLB 307, 272
Platte, AO 24, 209
Platte, AO 181, 216
Pledge, AM 277, 146
Pledge, MSO 492, 147
Plover, AMS 33, 151
Pluck, MSO 464, 147
Plumas County, LST 1083, 111
Plunger, SS 179, 14
Plunger, SSN 595, 27
Plunkett, DD 431, 54
Plymouth Rock, LSD 29, 103
Pochard, AM/MSF 375, 144
Pocomoke, AV 9, 167
Pocono, AGC/LCC 16, 118
Pogy, SS 266, 15
Pogy, SSN 647, 28
Poinciana, WAGL 266, 271
Point Arden, WPB 82309, 263
Point Arena, WPB 82346, 264
Point Baker, WPB 82342, 264
Point Banks, WPB 82327, 264
Point Barnes, WPB 82371, 265
Point Barrow, AKD 1, 206
Point Barrow, WPB 82348, 264
Point Batan, WPB 82340, 264
Point Bennett, WPB 82351, 265
Point Bonita, WPB 82347, 264
Point Bridge, WPB 82338, 264
Point Brower, WPB 82372, 265

Point Brown, WPB 82362, 265
Point Camden, WPB 82373, 265
Point Carrew, WPB 82374, 265
Point Caution, WPB 82301, 263
Point Charles, WPB 82361, 265
Point Chico, WPB 82339, 264
Point Clear, WPB 82315, 264
Point Comfort, WPB 82317, 264
Point Countess, WPB 82335, 264
Point Cruz, CVE/CVU 119, 11;
  AKV 19, 207
Point Cypress, WPB 82326, 264
Point Defiance, LSD 31, 103
Point Divide, WPB 82337, 264
Point Doran, WPB 82375, 265
Point Dume, WPB 82325, 264
Point Ellis, WPB 82330, 264
Point Estero, WPB 82344, 264
Point Evans, WPB 82354, 265
Point Francis, WPB 82356, 265
Point Franklin, WPB 82350, 265
Point Gammon, WPB 82328, 264
Point Garnet, WPB 82310, 263
Point Glass, WPB 82336, 264;
  NOAA 279
Point Glover, WPB 82307, 263
Point Grace, WPB 82323, 264
Point Grey, WPB 82324, 264
Point Hannon, WPB 82355, 265
Point Harris, WPB 82376, 265
Point Herron, WPB 82318, 264
Point Heyer, WPB 82369, 265
Point Highland, WPB 82333, 264
Point Hobart, WPB 82377, 265
Point Hope, WPB 82302, 263
Point Hudson, WPB 82322, 264
Point Huron, WPB 82357, 265
Point Jackson, WPB 82378, 265
Point Jefferson, WPB 82306, 263
Point Judith, WPB 82345, 264
Point Kennedy, WPB 82320, 264
Point Knoll, WPB 82367, 265
Point League, WPB 82304, 263
Point Ledge, WPB 82334, 264
Point Lobos, WPB 82366, 265;
  NOAA, 279
Point Loma, AGDS 2, 179
Point Lomas, WPB 82321, 264
Point Lookout, WPB 82341, 264
Point Marone, WPB 82331, 264
Point Martin, WPB 82379, 265
Point Mast, WPB 82316, 264
Point Monroe, WPB 82353, 265,
  NOAA, 279

Point Nowell, WPB 82363, 265
Point Orient, WPB 82319, 264
Point Partridge, WPB 82305, 263
Point Richmond, WPB 82370, 265
Point Roberts, WPB 82332, 264
Point Sal, WPB 82352, 265
Point Slocum, WPB 82313, 263
Point Spencer, WPB 82349, 264
Point Steele, WPB 82359, 265
Point Stuart, WPB 82358, 265
Point Swift, WPB 82312, 263
Point Thatcher, WPB 82314, 264
Point Turner, WPB 82365, 265
Point Verde, WPB 82311, 263
Point Warde, WPB 82368, 265
Point Welcome, WPB 82329, 264
Point Wells, WPB 82343, 264
Point White, WPB 82308, 263
Point Whitehorn, WPB 82364, 265
Point Winslow, WPB 82360, 265
Point Young, WPB 82303, 263
Polar Duke NSF, 281
Polar Sea, WAGB 11, 268
Polar Star, WAGB 10, 268
Polaris, AF 11, 197
Polk County, LST 1084, 111
Pollack, SSN 603, 27
Pollux, AKS 4, 207
Pollux, AKR 290, 242
Pomeroy, AKR 316, 238
Pomfret, SS 391, 19
Pomodon, SS 486, 21
Pompano, WPB 87339, 267
Pompon, SS 267, 15; SSR 267, 25
Ponce, LPD 15, 101
Ponchatoula, AO 148, 214
Pontchartrain, WPG/WHEC 70, 256
Poole, DE 151, 82
Pope, DE 134, 82
Poplar, WAGL 241, 274
Porpoise, SS 172, 14
Port Clinton, PC 1242, 133
Port Royal, CG 73, 51
Portage, PCE 902, 135
Porter, DDG 78, 77
Porter, DD 800, 60
Porterfield, DD 682, 59
Portland, CA 33, 39
Portland, LSD 37, 104
Portsmouth, SSN 707, 30
Portsmouth, CL 102, 42
Portunus, ARC 1, 173
Poseidon, ARL 12, 171
Potawatomi, ATF 109, 230

Potomac, AO 150, 215
Potomac, AO/AOT 181, 217
Potter County, LST 1086, 111
Poughkeepsie, PF 26, 128
Powder River, LSMR 519, 116
Power, DD 839, 66
Powhatan, ATF 166, 232
Prairie, AD 15, 163
Prairie State, IX 15, 192
Pratt, DE 363, 85
Preble, DLG 15, 46; DDG 46, 76
Preble, DDG 88, 78
Prescott, PCS 1423, 135
Preserver, ARS 8, 174
President AK, 250
President Adams, APA 19, 121
President Hayes, APA 20, 121
President Jackson, APA 18, 121
Presley, DE 371, 85
Presque Isle, APB 44, 225
Prestige, MSO 465, 147
Preston, DD 795, 59
Prevail, AM 107, 144; AGS 20, 187
Prevail, AGOS 8, 183; IX 537, 193
Price, DE 332, 83; DER 332, 86
Prichett, DD 561, 57
Pride, DE 323, 83
Pride, AK 5017, 249
Prime, MSO 466, 147
Primrose, WAGL/WLI/WLR 316, 274
Prince William, CVE/CVHE 31, 10
Princeton, CV/CVS 37, 3; LPH 5, 97
Princeton, CG 59, 50
Procyon, AF 61, 198
Proserpine, ARL 21, 171
Protector, AGR 11, 185
Proteus, AS 19, 165
Proton, AG 147, 177; AKS 28, 207
Providence, SSN 719, 30
Providence, CL 82, 41; CLG/CG 6, 43
Provo, AG 173, 176
Prowess, AM/MSF 280, 146; IX 305, 192
Ptarmigan, AM/MSF 376, 144
Pueblo, AGER 2, 180; AKL 44, 208
Puffer, SS 268, 15
Puffer, SSN 662, 28
Puget Sound, CVE/CVHE 113, 11; AKV 13, 207
Puget Sound, AD 38, 164
Pulaski County, LST 1088, 111
Purdy, DD 734, 61

Puritan, ACM/MMA 16, 141
Pursuit, AM 108, 144; AGS 17, 187
Putnam, DD 757, 62
Pvt. Elden H. Johnson, AP 184, 223
Pvt. Francis X. McGraw, AK 241, 201
Pvt. Frank J. Petrarca, AK 250, 203
Pvt. Franklin J. Phillips, AK 3004, 240
Pvt. Harry Fisher, AK 3004, 240
Pvt. Joe E. Mann, AK 253, 201
Pvt. Joe P. Martinez, AP 187, 224
Pvt. John F. Thorson, AK 247, 202
Pvt. John R. Towle, AK 240, 201
Pvt. Jose F. Valdez, AG 169, 178; AKV 4/AK 275, 201
Pvt. Joseph F. Merrell, AKV 4, 207; AK 275, 202
Pvt. Leonard C. Brostrom, AK 255, 203
Pvt. Sadao S. Munemori, AP 190, 224
Pvt. William H. Thomas, AP 185, 223
Pyro, AE 24, 197

Quail, AM/MSF 377, 145
Quapaw, ATF 110, 230
Queenfish, SS/AGSS 393, 19
Queenfish, SSN 661, 28
Quick, DD 490, 54; DMS 32, 143
Quillback, SS 424, 20
Quincy, CA 71, 39
Quirinus, ARL 39, 172

Rabaul, CVE/CVHE 121, 11; AKV 21, 207
Raby, DE 698, 80; DEC 698, 87
Raccoon River, LSMR 520, 116
Rachel Carson EPA, 281
Racine, LST 1191, 114
Radcliffe, AG 188, 177
Radford, DD 446, 55; DDE 446, 69
Rail, AMCU/MHC 37, 160
Rainier, AE 5, 195
Rainier, AOE 7, 220
Rainier, MSS 21/S 221, 279
Rainy River, LSMR 521, 116
Raleigh, LPD 1, 100
Ramage, DDG 61, 76
Rambler, WAGL/WLI 298, 274
Ramsden, DE 382, 83; DER 382, 87; WDE 482, 260
Ramsey, DEG/FFG 2, 92
Randall, APA 224, 123
Randolph, CV/CVS 15, 2
Range Recoverer, AG 161, 177; AGM 2, 181
Range Sentinel, AGM 22, 182

Range Tracker, AG 160, 177; AGM 1, 181
Ranger, CVA/CV 61, 6
Ranger, AOT 1002, 250
Rankin, AKA/LKA 103, 120
Ransom, AM/MSF 283, 146
Rappahannock, AO 204, 217
Raritan, LSM 540, 115
Raritan, WYT 93, 269
Rasher, SS/AGSS/IXSS 269, 15; SSR 269, 25
Rathburne, DE/FF 1057, 90
Raton, SS/AGSS 270, 15; SSR 270, 25
Raven, AM/MSF 55, 143
Raven, MHC 61, 161
Rawlins, APA 226, 123
Ray, SS 271, 15; SSR 271, 25
Ray, SSN 663, 28
Ray K. Edwards, APD 96, 125
Raymon W. Herndon, APD 121, 126
Raymond, DE 341, 84
Razorback, SS 394, 19
Razorbill, WPB 87332, 267
Ready, PG 87, 127
Reaper, MSO 467, 147
Reasoner, DE/FF 1063, 90
Rebel, AM/MSF 284, 146
Reclaimer, ARS 42, 175
Recovery, ARS 43, 175
Recruit, AM/MSF 285, 146
Red Beech, WLM 686, 273
Red Birch, WLM 687, 273
Red Cedar, WLM 688, 273
Red Cloud, AKR 313, 238
Red Oak, WLM 689, 273
Red River, LSMR/LFR 522, 116
Red Wood, WLM 685, 273
Redbud, WAGL/WLB 398, 272
Redfin, SS/AGSS 272, 15; SSR 272, 25
Redfish, SS/AGSS 395, 20
Redfish, SSN 680, 29
Redhead, AMS 34, 151; AMCU/MHC 48, 160
Rednour, APD 102, 125
Redpoll, AMS 57, 151
Redstart, AM/MSF 378, 145
Redstone, AGM 20, 182
Redwing, MSC 200, 156
Redwood, AN 30, 191
Reedbird, AMS 51, 151
Reef Shark, WPB 87371, 267
Reeves, DLG/CG 24, 46

Reeves, APD 52, 124
Reform, AM 286, 146
Refresh, AM 287, 146
Register, APD 92, 125
Regulus, AF 57, 199
Regulus, AKR 292, 242
Rehoboth, AVP 50, 168; AGS 50, 187
Reid, FFG 30, 94
Reign, AM/MSF 288, 146
Reina Mercedes, IX 25, 192
Reindeer, ATA 189, 231
Relentless, AGOS 18, 183
Reliance, AFDL 47, 227
Reliance, WMEC/WTR 615, 259
Reliance, WSC 150, 261
Remey, DD 688, 59
Remora, SS 487, 21
Renate, AKL 42, 208
Rendova, CVE/CVU 114, 11; AKV 14, 207
Reno, CL 96, 41
Renshaw, DD 499, 56; DDE 499, 69
Rentz, FFG 46, 94
Renville, APA 227, 123
Report, AM/MSF 289, 146
Repose, AH 16, 226
Republican River, LSMR 523, 116
Requin, SS/AGSS 481, 21; SSR 481, 25
Requisite, AM 109, 144; AGS 18, 187
Researcher, OSS 3/R 103, 278
Resolute, WMEC 620, 259
Resourceful, AFDM 5, 227
Reuben James, DE 153, 79; DER 153, 86
Reuben James, FFG 57, 94
Revenge, AM/MSF 110, 144
Rexburg, PCER 855, 134
Rhea, AMS 52, 151
Rhode Island, SSBN 730, 36
Rhode Island, SSBN 740, 36
Rhodes, DE 384, 83; DER 384, 87
Rhododendron, WAGL 267, 271
Rice County, LST 1089, 111
Rich, DD 820, 65; DDE 820, 69
Richard B. Anderson, DD 786, 64
Richard B. Russell, SSN 687, 29
Richard E. Byrd, DDG 23, 74
Richard E. Byrd, AKE 4, 206
Richard E. Kraus, DD 849, 66; AG 151, 177
Richard G. Matthieson, AOT 1124, 251
Richard L. Page, DEG/FFG 5, 92
Richard M. Rowell, DE 403, 85

Richard P. Leary, DD 664, 58
Richard S. Bull, DE 402, 85
Richard S. Edwards, DD 950, 70
Richard W. Suesens, DE 342, 84
Richey, DE 385, 83; WDE 485, 260
Richfield, AGM 4, 181
Richland AFDM 8. 227
Richmond K. Turner, DLG/CG 20, 46
Ricketts, DE 254, 82
Riddle, DE 185, 81
Ridgway, PC 1193, 133
Ridley, WPB 87328, 267
Rigel, AF 58, 199
Riley, DE 579, 84
Rincon, AOG 77, 219
Rinehart, DE 196, 81
Ringgold, DD 500, 56
Ringness, APD/LPR 100, 125
Rio Grande, AOG 3, 218
Ripley, PC 808, 132
Rival, MSO 468, 147
Riverhead, PC 567, 132
Rizzi, DE 537, 86
Roanoke, CL 145, 42
Roanoke, AO 155, 215
Roanoke, AOR 7, 220
Roanoke Island, WPB 1346, 266
Roark, DE/FF 1053, 90
Robert A. Owens, DD/DDK 827, 65; DDE 827, 69
Robert Brazier, DE 345, 84
Robert D. Conrad, AGOR 3, 189
Robert E. Lee, SSBN/SSN 601, 33
Robert E. Peary, DE 132, 82
Robert E. Peary, DE/FF 1073, 90
Robert E. Peary, AKE 5, 206
Robert F. Keller, DE 419, 85
Robert G. Bradley, FFG 49, 94
Robert H. McCard, DD 822, 65
Robert H. Smith, DM/MMD 23, 141
Robert I. Paine, DE 578, 80
Robert K. Huntington, DD 781, 62
Robert L. Paine, DER 578, 86
Robert L. Wilson, DD 847, 66; DDE 847, 69
Roberts, DE 749, 81
Robin, AMS 53, 151
Robin, MHC 54, 161
Robinson, DD 562, 57
Robison, DDG 12, 73
Rochester, CA 124, 40
Rock, SS/AGSS 274, 15; SSR 274, 25

Rockaway, AVP 29, 168; WAVP/ WHEC/ WAGO/WOLE 377, 256
Rockbridge, APA 228, 123
Rockford, PF 48, 129
Rockingham, APA 229, 123
Rockville, PCER 851, 134
Rockwall, APA 230, 123
Rocky Mount, AGC 3, 117
Rodman, DD 456, 54; DMS 21, 143
Rodney M. Davis, FFG 60, 94
Roger R. Simons EPA, 281
Roger Revelle, AGOR 24, 190
Rogers, DD 876, 67; DDR 876, 69
Rogers Blood, APD 115, 126
Rolette, AKA 99, 120
Rolf, DE 362, 85
Rolla, PC 483, 131
Rollins, AG 189, 177
Rombach, DE 364, 85
Romulus, ARL 22, 171
Ronald H. Brown, R 104, 278
Ronald Reagan, CVN 76, 8
Roncador, SS/AGSS/IXSS 301, 16
Ronquil, SS 396, 20
Rooks, DD 804, 60
Roosevelt, DDG 80, 78
Roque, AKL 8, 208
Rose Knot, AGM 14, 182
Roselle, AM/MSF 379, 145
Rosewood, AN 31, 191
Ross, DD 563, 57
Ross, DDG 71, 77
Rover, AK 1013, 246
Rover, AOT 1003, 250
Rowan, DD 782, 64
Rowe, DD 564, 57
Roy O. Hale, DE 336, 83; DER 336, 87
Royono, IX 235, 192
Ruchamkin, APD/LPR 89, 125
Rudderow, DE 224, 84
Ruddy, AM/MSF 380, 145
Rude, ASV 90/S 590, 279
Rudyerd Bay, CVE/CVU 81, 10; AKV 29, 207
Ruff, AMS 54, 151
Runels, APD 85, 125
Runner, SS/AGSS/IXSS 476, 21
Rupertus, DD 851, 66
Rush, WHEC 723, 257
Rush, WSC 151, 261
Rushmore, LSD 14, 103
Rushmore, LSD 47, 105

Russell, DDG 59, 76
Russell County, LST 1090, 111
Ruth Lykes, AK 9636, 247
Rutland, APA 192, 122
Ryer, AKL 9, 208

S.P. Lee, AG 192, 178; AGS 31, 187
Sabalo, SS 302, 16
Sabine, AO 25, 209
Sablefish, SS/AGSS 303, 16
Sacagawea, AKE 2, 206
Sacramento, AOE 1, 219
Safeguard, ARS 25, 174
Safeguard, ARS 50, 175
Sagacity, MSO 469, 147
Sagadahoc County, LST 1091, 111
Sagamore, ATA 208, 232
Sagamore AK, 238
Sage, AM/MSF 111, 144
Sagebrush, WAGL/WLB 399, 272
Saginaw, LST 1188, 114
Saginaw, WLIC 803, 275
Saginaw Bay, CVE/CVHE 82, 10
Sagitta, AK 87, 200
Saidor, CVE/CVHE 117, 11; AKV 17, 207
Sailfish, SSR/SS 572, 25
Sailfish, WPB 87356, 267
St. Clair County, LST 1096, 111
St. Croix River, LSMR 524, 116
St. Francis River, LSMR/LFR 525, 116
St. George, AV 16, 168
St. Johns River, LSMR 526, 117
St. Joseph River, LSMR 527, 117
St. Louis, CL 49, 41
St. Louis, LKA 116, 121
St. Mary's River, LSMR 528, 117
St. Paul, CA 73, 40
St. Regis River, LSMR 529, 117
Saipan, CVL 48, 5; CC 3, 44; AVT 6, 169
Saipan, LHA 2, 99
Salamonie, AO 26, 209
Salem, CA 139, 40
Salerno Bay, CVE/CVU 110, 11; AKV 10, 207
Salinan, ATF 161, 231
Saline County, LST 1101, 111
Salisbury Sound, AV 13, 167
Salish, ATA 187, 231
Salmon, SSR/SS 573, 25
Salmon Falls River, LSMR 530, 117
Salt Lake City, SSN 716, 30
Saluda, IX 87, 192

Salute, MSO 470, 147
Salvager, ARSD 3, 172
Salvia, WAGL/WLB 400, 272
Salvor, ARS 52, 175
Sam Houston, SSBN/SSN 609, 34
Sam Rayburn, SSBN 635, 35
Samar, ARG 11, 170
Samoset, ATA 190, 231
Sampan Hitch, AGM 18, 182
Sample, DE/FF 1048, 89
Sampson, DDG 10, 73
Sampson, DDG 102, 78
Samuel B. Roberts, DD 823, 65
Samuel B. Roberts, FFG 58, 94
Samuel Chase, APA 26, 121
Samuel Eliot Morison, FFG 13, 93
Samuel Gompers, AD 37, 164
Samuel L. Cobb, AOT 1123, 251
Samuel N. Moore, DD 747, 61
Samuel S. Miles, DE 183, 81
San Antonio, LPD 17, 102
San Bernardino, LST 1189, 114
San Bernardino County, LST 1110, 111
San Carlos, AVP 51, 168
San Diego, CL 53, 41
San Diego, LPD 22, 102
San Diego, AFS 6, 199
San Francisco, SSN 711, 30
San Francisco, CA 38, 39
San Jacinto, CVL 30, 5; AVT 5, 169
San Jacinto, CG 56, 50
San Joaquin County, LST 1122, 111
San Jose, AFS 7, 199
San Juan, SSN 751, 31
San Juan, CL 54, 41
San Marcos, LSD 25, 103
San Onofre, ARD 30, 227
San Pablo, AVP 30, 168; AGS 30, 187
San Pedro, PF 37, 128
San Saba, APA 232, 123
Sanborn, APA 193, 122
Sanctuary, AH 17, 226
Sand Lance, SS 381, 19
Sand Lance, SSN 660, 28
Sandalwood, AN 32, 191
Sanderling, AMS 35, 151
Sanderling, AMCU/MHC 49, 160
Sandoval, APA/LPA 194, 122
Sandpiper, AMCU/MHC 38, 160
Sands, AGOR 6, 189
Sandusky, PF 54, 129
Sangay, AE 10, 196
Sanibel, WPB 1312, 265
Santa Adela, AK 2051, 247

Santa Ana, AK 5022, 248
Santa Barbara, AE 28, 197
Santa Barbara, AK 5030, 247
Santa Clara, AK 5031, 247
Santa Cruz, AK 5032, 247
Santa Elena, AK 5033, 247
Santa Fe, SSN 763, 31
Santa Fe, CL 60, 41
Santa Isabel, AK 5034, 247
Santa Juana, AK 2047, 247
Santa Lucia, AK 5035, 247
Santee, CVE/CVHE 29, 10
Sapelo, WPB 1314, 265
Sappa Creek, AO 141, 214
Sarasota, APA 204, 122
Saratoga, CVA/CV 60, 6
Sarda, SS/AGSS 488, 21
Sargent Bay, CVE/CVU 83, 10
Sargo, SSN 583, 26
Sarpedon, ARB 7, 171
Sarsfield, DD 837, 65
Sarsi, ATF 111, 230
Sassafras, WAGL/WLB 401, 272
Satterlee, DD 626, 55
Saturn, AFS 10, 200
Satyr, ARL 23, 171
Saufley, DD/EDD 465, 55; DDE/EDDE 465, 69
Saugatuck, AO/AOT 75, 211
Saugus, MCS 4, 142
Sauk, WYT 99, 270
Sausalito, PF 4, 128
Savage, DE 386, 83; DER 386, 87
Savannah, AOR 4, 220
Savannah, CL 42, 41
Savo Island, CVE/CVU 78, 10; AKV 28, 207
Sawfish, SS 276, 15
Sawfish, WPB 87357, 267
Scabbardfish, SS 397, 20
Scamp, SSN 588, 26
Scan, AK 5018, 249
Scanner, AGR 5, 185
Schenectady, LST 1185, 114
Schmitt, APD 76, 125
Schofield, DEG/FFG 3, 92
Schroeder, DD 501, 56
Schuyler Otis Bland, AK 277, 204
Schuylkill, AO/AOT 76, 211
Sciota, ATA 205, 232
Scorpion, SSN 589, 26
Scoter, AM/MSF 381, 145
Scott, DDG 995, 76
Scott, DE 214, 79

316 Index

Scott ASV, 278
Scout, AM/MSF 296, 146
Scranton, SSN 756, 31
Scribner, APD 122, 126
Scrimmage, AM/MSF 297, 146
Scroggins, DE 799, 80
Scuffle, AM/MSF 298, 146
Sculpin, SSN 590, 26
Scurry, AM/MSF 304, 146
Sea Cat, SS/AGSS 399, 20
Sea Devil, SS/AGSS 400, 20
Sea Devil, SSN 664, 28
Sea Devil, WPB 87368, 267
Sea Dog, SS/AGSS 401, 20
Sea Dog, WPB 87373, 267
Sea Dragon, WPB 87367, 267
Sea Fighter, FSF 1, 194
Sea Flyer, IX 515, 193
Sea Fox, SS 402, 20
Sea Fox, WPB 87374, 267
Sea Hawk, WSES 2, 267
Sea Horse, WPB 87361, 267
Sea Leopard, SS 483, 21
Sea Lift, AK 278/LSV 9/AKR 9, 205; AKR 9, 206
Sea Lion, IX 506, 192
Sea Lion, WPB 87352, 267
Sea Otter, WPB 87362, 267
Sea Owl, SS/AGSS 405, 20
Sea Poacher SS/AGSS406, 20
Sea Robin, SS 407, 20
Sea Shadow, IX 529, 193
Seacor Clipper, AGDS 9642, 253
Seadragon, SSN 584, 26
Seagull, AMS 55, 151
Seahawk, WPB 87323, 267
Seahorse, SS/AGSS 304, 16
Seahorse, SSN 669, 28
Seal, SS 183, 14
Sealift Antarctic, AO/AOT 176, 216
Sealift Arabian Sea, AO/AOT 169, 216
Sealift Arctic, AO/AOT 175, 216
Sealift Atlantic, AO/AOT 172, 216
Sealift Caribbean, AO/AOT 174, 216
Sealift China Sea, AO/AOT 170, 216
Sealift Indian Ocean, AO/AOT 171, 216
Sealift Mediterranean, AO/AOT 173, 216
Sealift Pacific, AO/AOT 168, 216
Sealion, SS 315, 16; SSP/ASSP/APSS/LPSS 315, 16
Seaman, DD 791, 64
SeaMark III AG, 253

Searcher, AGR 4, 185
Seattle, AOE 3, 219
Seawolf, SSN 575, 26
Seawolf, SSN 21, 32
Seay, AKR 302, 239
Sebago, WPG/WHEC 42, 256
Sebec, AO 87, 212
Sebec, WPG 164, 255
Sedge, WAGL/WLB 402, 272
Sedgwick County, LST 1123, 111
Seer, AM/MSF 112, 144
Segundo, SS 398, 20
Sellers, DDG 11, 73
Sellstrom, DE 255, 82; DER 255, 86
Seminole, AKA/LKA 104, 120
Semmes, DDG 18, 73
Seneca, ATF 91, 230
Seneca, WMEC 906, 259
Sennet, SS 408, 20
Sentinel, AMCU/MHC 39, 160
Sentry, AM/MSF 299, 146
Sentry, MCM 3, 151
Sequoia, AG 23, 175
Sequoia, WLB 215, 273
Serene, AM/MSF 300, 146
Serpens, AK 266, 203
Serrano, AGS 24, 187; ATF 112, 230
Severn, AO 61, 211
Seymour D. Owens, DD 767, 64
Sgt. Andrew Miller, AK 242, 201
Sgt. Archer T. Gammon, AK 243, 201
Sgt. Charles E. Mower, AP 186, 223
Sgt. Curtis E. Shoup, AG 175, 177
Sgt. George D. Keathley, AGS 35, 187; APC 117, 226
Sgt. George Peterson, AK 248, 202
Sgt. Howard E. Woodford, AP 191, 224
Sgt. Jack J. Pendleton, AKV 5/AK 276, 201; AKV 5, 207
Sgt. Jonah E. Kelley, APC 116, 226
Sgt. Joseph E. Muller, APC 118, 226; AG 171, 178
Sgt. Matej Kocak, AK 3005, 240
Sgt. Morris E. Crain, AK 244, 201
Sgt. Sylvester Antolak, AP 192, 224
Sgt. Truman Kimbro, AK 254, 201
Sgt. William R. Button, AK 3012, 239
Shad, SS 235, 15
Shadbush, WAGL 287/WLI 74287, 274
Shadwell, LSD 15, 103
Shakamaxon, AN 88, 192
Shakori, ATF 162, 231
Shamal, PC 13, 136; WPC 13, 267

Shamrock Bay, CVE/CVU 84, 10
Shangri-La, CV/CVS 38, 3
Shannon, DM/MMD 25, 141
Shark, SSN 591, 26
Sharps, AKL 10, 208
Shasta, AE 6, 195
Shasta, AE 33, 197
Shawnee Trail, AO 142, 214
Shea, DM/MMD 30, 141
Shearwater, AMCU 40, 160
Shearwater, AG 177, 175
Shearwater, WPB 87349, 267
Shearwater, WSES 3, 267
Sheldrake, AM 62, 143; AGS 19, 187
Shelikof, AVP 52, 168
Shelter, AM/MSF 301, 146
Shelton, DD 790, 64
Shenahon NOAA, 281
Shenandoah, AD 26, 164
Shenandoah, AD 44, 164
Sherburne, APA 205, 122
Sherman, WHEC 720, 257
Shields, DD 596, 58
Shiloh, CG 67, 51
Shipley Bay, CVE/CVHE 85, 10
Shippingport, ARDM 4, 227
Short Splice, AK 249, 203
Shoshone, AO/AOT 151, 215
Shoup, DDG 86, 78
Shoveler, AM/MSF 382, 145
Shreveport, LPD 12, 101
Shrike, MSC 201, 157
Shrike, MHC 62, 161
Shrike, WPB 87342, 267
Shughart, AKR 295, 240
Sibley, APA 206, 122
Siboney, CVE/CVU 112, 11; AKV 12, 207
Sicily, CVE/CVU 118, 11; AKV 18, 207
Sides, FFG 14, 93
Sierra, AD 18, 163
Signet, AM/MSF 302, 146
Sigourney, DD 643, 58
Sigsbee, DD 502, 56
Silas Bent, AGS 26, 187
Silversides, SS/AGSS 236, 15
Silversides, SSN 679, 29
Silverstein, DE 534, 86
Simon Bolivar, SSBN 641, 35
Simon Lake, AS 33, 166
Simon Newcomb, AGS 14, 186
Simpson, FFG 56, 94
Sims, APD 50, 124

Sioux, ATF 75, 229
Sioux, ATF 171, 232
Sirago, SS 485, 21
Sirius, AF 60, 198
Sirius, AFS 8, 200
Sirocco, PC 6, 136
Siskin, AMS 58, 151
Sisler, AKR 311, 238
Sitkinak, WPB 1329, 266
Sitkoh Bay, CVE/CVU 86, 10; AKV 30, 207
Skagit, AKA/LKA 105, 120
Skate, SSN 578, 26
Skill, MSO 471, 147
Skimmer, AMCU/MHC 41, 160
Skipjack, SSN 585, 26
Skipjack, WPB 87353, 267
Skirmish, AM/MSF 303, 146
Skowhegan, PCE 843, 134
Skylark, ASR 20, 166
Skywatcher, AGR 3, 185
Slater, DE 766, 81
Sloat, DE 245, 82
Smalley, DD 565, 57
Smilax, WAGL/WLI 315, 274
Smoky Hill River, LSMR/LFR 531, 117
Smyrna River, LSMR 532, 117
Snake River, LSMR 533, 117
Snapper, WPB 87369, 267
Snatch, ARS 27, 174
Snohomish, WYT 98, 269
Snohomish County, LST 1126, 111
Snook, SSN 592, 26
Snowden, DE 246, 82
Snyder, DE 745, 81
Sockeye, WPB 87337, 267
Soderman, AKR 317, 238
Soderman, AKR 299, 240
Solano County, LST 1128, 111
Soley, DD 707, 61
Solvay, PC 603, 132
Somers, DD 947, 70; DDG 34, 75
Somerset, LPD 25, 102
Somerset, PCE 892, 134
Somersworth, PCER 849, 134
Somervell County, LST 1129, 111
Sonoma, ATA 175, 231
Sorrel, WAGL/WLB 296, 272
Sosbee ASV, 277
Sotoyomo, ATA 121, 231
Soubarissen, AO 93, 212
South Carolina, DLGN/CGN 37, 49
South Dakota, BB 57, 37

Southerland, DD 743, 63; DDR 743, 69
Southern Cross, AK 285, 205
Southwind, WAGB 280, 268
SP5 Eric G. Gibson, AKR 9966, 238
SP5 Eric G. Gibson, AK 5091, 238
Spadefish, SS/AGSS 411, 20
Spadefish, SSN 668, 28
Spangenberg, DE 223, 79; DER 223, 86
Spangler, DE 696, 80
Spar, WAGL/WLB 403, 272
Spar, WLB 206, 273
Sparrow, AMCU 42, 160
Spartanburg County, LST 1192, 114
Spear, AM/MSF 322, 144
Specter, AM/MSF 306, 146
Speed, AM/MSF 116, 144
Spencer, WPG/WHEC 36, 256
Spencer, WMEC 905, 259
Sperry, AS 12, 165
Sphinx, ARL 24, 171
Spica, AFS 9, 200
Spiegel Grove, LSD 32, 103
Spikefish, SS/AGSS 404, 20
Spinax, SS/AGSS 489, 21; SSR 489, 25
Spindrift, IX 49, 192
Spokane, CL 120, 41; AG 191, 178
Spoonbill, MSC 202, 157
Spot, SS 413, 20
Sprig, AM/MSF 384, 145
Springer, SS 414, 20
Springfield, SSN 761, 31
Springfield, CL 66, 41; CLG/CG 7, 43
Sproston, DD 577, 57; DDE 577, 69
Spruance, DD 963, 71
Spruance, DDG 111, 78
Spruce, WAGL 246, 271; WAK 246, 275
Spruce NOAA, 281
Squall, PC 7, 136
SSG Edward A. Carter Jr., AK 4544, 241
Staff, AM/MSF 114, 144
Stafford, DE 411, 85
Stafford County, LST 1142, 112
Stallion, ATA 193, 231
Stalwart, MSO 493, 147
Stalwart, AGOS 1, 183
Stanly, DD 478, 55
Stanton, DE 247, 82
Stark, FFG 31, 94
Stark County, LST 1134, 111

Starling, AM/MSF 64, 143
Staten Island, AGB 5, 179; WAGB 278, 268; see *Northwind*
Staten Island, WPB 1345, 266
Staunch, AM/MSF 307, 146
Steadfast WMEC 623., 259
Steady, AM/MSF 118, 144
Steamer Bay, CVE/CVHE 87, 11
Steelhead, SS 280, 15
Steelhead, WPB 87324, 267
Stein, DE/FF 1065, 90
Steinaker, DD 863, 67; DDR 863, 69
Stembel, DD 644, 58
Stentor, ARL 26, 171
Stephen Potter, DD 538, 56
Stephen W. Groves, FFG 29, 94
Sterett, DLG/CG 31, 48
Sterett, DDG 104, 78
Sterlet, SS 392, 19
Stern, DE 187, 81
Stetham, DDG 63, 76
Steuben County, LST 1138, 111
Stevens, DD 479, 55
Stevenson, DD 645, 55
Stewart, DE 238, 82
Stickell, DD 888, 68; DDR 888, 69
Stickleback, SS 415, 20
Stingray, WPB 87305, 266
Stirni NOAA, 277
Stockdale, DDG 106, 78
Stockdale, DE 399, 84
Stockham, DD 683, 59
Stockton, DD 646, 55
Stoddard, DD 566, 57
Stone County, LST 1141, 111
Stonewall Jackson, SSBN 634, 35
Storis, WAG/WAGB 38/WMEC 38, 268; WAGL 38, 270
Stormes, DD 780, 62
Stout, DDG 55, 76
Strategy, AM/MSF 308, 146
Straub, DE 181, 81
Straus, DE 408, 85
Strength, AM/MSF 309, 146
Stribling, DD 867, 67
Strickland, DE 333, 83; DER 333, 86
Strive, AM/MSF 117, 144
Strong, DD 758, 62
Strong American, AKR 9716, 250
Strong Texan, AK 9670, 244
Strong Virginian, AK 9205, 237
Stump, DD 978, 71
Sturdy, MSO 494, 147
Sturgeon, SSN 637, 28

Sturgeon, WPB 87336, 267
Sturgeon Bay, WTGB 109, 270
Sturtevant, DE 239, 82; DER 239, 86
Suamico, AO 49, 210
Sublette County, LST 1144, 112
Success, AM/MSF 310, 146
Suffolk County, LST 1173, 113
Suisun, AVP 53, 169
Sumac, WAGL/WLR 311, 274
Summit County, LST 1146, 112
Sumner, AGS 61, 189
Sumner County, LST 1148, 112
Sumter, LST 1181, 114
Sunbird, ASR 15, 166
Suncook, AN 80, 192
Sundew:, WAGL/WLB 406, 272
Sunfish, SS 281, 15
Sunfish, SSN 659, 28
Sunnadin, ATA 197, 231
Sunnyvale, AGM 5, 181
Superior, AM/MSF 311, 146
Supply, AOE 6, 220
Surfbird, AM/MSF 383, 145; ADG 383, 190
Suribachi, AE 21, 197
Surprise, PG 97, 127
Surveyor, OSS 32/S 132, 279
Susanville, PC 1149, 133
Susquehanna, AO/AOT 185, 217
Susquehanna, AOG 5, 218
Sussex, AK 213, 201
Sustain, AM/MSF 119, 144
Sustain, AFDM 7, 227
Sutter County, LST 1150, 112
Sutton, DE 771, 81
Suwannee CVE/CVHE 27 , 10
Swallow, AMS 36, 151
Swan, AMS 37, 151
Swanson, DD 443, 54
Swasey, DE 248, 82
Sway, AM/MSF 120, 144
Swearer, DE 186, 81
Sweetbrier:, WAGL/WLB 405, 272
Sweetgum, WAGL/WLB 309, 272
Sweetwater County, LST 1152, 112
Swenning, DE 394, 83
Swerve, MSO 495, 147
Swift, AM/MSF 122, 144
Swift, HSV 2, 193
Sword Knot, AGM 13, 182
Swordfish, SSN 579, 26
Swordfish, WPB 87358, 267
Sycamore, WLB 209, 273
Sycamore, WAGL/WLIC 268, 274

Sylvania, AFS 2, 199
Symbol, AM/MSF 123, 144

T-1, SST 1, 25
T-2, SST 2, 25
T-35, DD 935, 71
Tabberer, DE 418, 85
Tacoma, PG 92, 127
Tacoma, PF 3, 128
Taconic, AGC/LCC 17, 118
Tahoma, WPG 80/WAGE 10, 255
Tahoma, WMEC 908, 259
Takanis Bay, CVE/CVU 89, 11; AKV 31, 207
Takelma, ATF 113, 230
Talbot, DEG/FFG 4, 92
Talbot County, LST 1153, 112
Talladega, APA/LPA 208, 123
Tallahatchie County, LST 1154, 112; AVB 2, 169
Tallulah, AO/AOT 50, 210
Taluga, AO 62, 211
Tamalpais, AO 96, 212
Tamarack, WAGL/WLI 248, 271
Tamaroa, WMEC 166, 258
Tambor, SS 198, 14
Tampa, WMEC 902, 259
Tampa Bay, AK 2045, 247
Tanager, AM/MSF 385, 145; WTR 385, 275
Taney, WPG/WHEC 37, 256
Tang, SS/AGSS 563, 22
Tangier, AV 8, 167
Tanner, AGS 15, 186
Tanner, AGS 40, 188
Tappahannock, AO 43, 210
Tarawa, CV/CVS 40, 4; AVT 12, 169
Tarawa, LHA 1, 99
Tarpon, SS 175, 14
Tarpon, WPB 87310, 266
Tarrytown, PC 1252, 133
Tatnuck, ATA 195, 231
Tattnall, DDG 19, 73
Tatum, APD 81, 125
Taurus, PHM 3, 130
Taurus, AK 273/LSV 8/AKR 8, 204, 206
Taussig, DD 746, 61
Tautog, SS 199, 14
Tautog, SSN 639, 28
Tawakoni, ATF 114, 230
Tawasa, ATF 92, 230
Taylor, DD 468, 55; DDE 468, 69
Tazewell, APA 209, 123

Teaberry, AN 34, 191
Teak, AN 35, 191
Tecumseh, SSBN 628, 35
Tekesta, ATF 93, 230
Telamon, ARB 8, 171
Telfair, APA 210, 123
Tempest, PC 2, 136; WPC 2, 267
Tenacious, AGOS 17, 183
Tench, SS/AGSS 417, 20
Tenino, ATF 115, 230
Tennessee, SSBN 734, 36
Tercel, AM/MSF 386, 145
Tern, WPB 87343, 267
Terrapin, WPB 87366, 267
Terrebonne Parish, LST 1156, 112
Terrell County, LST 1157, 112
Terror, CM 5/MMF 5, 141
Terry, DD 513, 56
Teton, AGC 14, 118
Texas, SSN 775, 33
Texas, CGN 39, 50
Texas Trader, AOT 1202, 252
Thach, FFG 43, 94
Thaddeus Porter, DE 369, 85
Thames River, LSMR 534, 117
The Sullivans, DD 537, 56
The Sullivans, DDG 68, 77
Theodore E. Chandler, DD 717, 63
Theodore Roosevelt, CVN 71, 8
Theodore Roosevelt, SSBN 600, 33
Thetis, WMEC 910, 259
Thetis, WPC 115, 261
Thetis Bay, CVE/CVU 90, 11; CVHA 1, 11; LPH 6, 97
Thistle, WAGL 409, 271
Thomas, DE 102, 80
Thomas A. Edison, SSBN/SSN 610, 34
Thomas E. Fraser, DM/MMD 24, 141
Thomas F. Nickel, DE 587, 84
Thomas G. Hart, DE/FF 1092, 90
Thomas G. Thompson, AGOR 9, 189
Thomas G. Thompson, AGOR 23, 190
Thomas J. Gary, DE 326, 83; DER 326, 86
Thomas Jefferson, SSBN/SSN 618, 34
Thomas Jefferson, APA 30, 121
Thomas Jefferson, S 222, 278
Thomas S. Gates, CG 51, 50
Thomas Washington, AGOR 10, 189
Thomason, DE 203, 79
Thomaston, LSD 28, 103
Thompson, DMS 38, 143; DD 627, 55
Thor, ARC 4, 173

Thorn, DD 647, 55
Thorn, DD 988, 72
Thornback, SS 418, 20
Thornhill, DE 195, 81
Thrasher, MSC 203, 157
Threadfin, SS 410, 20
Threat, AM/MSF 124, 144
Thresher, SSN 593, 27
Thrush, MSC 204, 157
Thuban, AKA/LKA 19, 119
Thunder Bay, WTGB 108, 270
Thunderbolt, PC 12, 136
Ticonderoga, CV/CVS 14, 2
Ticonderoga, CG 47, 50
Tidewater, AD 31, 164
Tiger, WSC 152, 261
Tiger Shark, WPB 87359, 267
Tigrone, SS/AGSS 419, 20; SSR 419, 25
Tilefish, SS 307, 16
Tillamook, ATA 192, 231
Tillman, DD 641, 55
Tills, DE 748, 81
Timbalier, AVP 54, 169
Timber Hitch, AGM 17, 182
Timmerman, DD 828, 65; EAG/AG 152, 177
Tingey, DD 539, 56
Tingles, AG 144, 177; AKL 13, 208
Tinian, CVE/CVU 123, 11; AKV 23, 207
Tinosa, SS 283, 16
Tinosa, SSN 606, 27
Tinsman, DE 589, 84
Tioga County, LST 1158, 112
Tippecanoe, AO 199, 217
Tipton, PC 1231, 133
Tirante, SS 420, 20
Tiru, SS 416, 20
Titan, AGOS 15, 183
Titania, AKA 13, 119
Token, AM/MSF 126, 144
Toledo, SSN 769, 31
Toledo, CA 133, 40
Tollberg, APD 103, 125
Tolman, DM/MMD 28, 141
Tolovana, AO 64, 211
Tolowa, ATF 116, 230
Tom Green County, LST 1159, 112
Tomahawk, AO 88, 212
Tombigbee, AOG 11, 218
Tomich, DE 242, 82
Tonawanda, AN 89, 192
Tonkawa, ATA 176, 231

Tonti, AOG 76, 219
Tooele, PC 572, 132
Topeka, SSN 754, 31
Topeka, CL 67, 41; CLG 8, 43
Tornado, PC 14, 136; WPC 14, 267
Toro, SS/AGSS 422, 20
Torry, AKL 11, 208
Torsk, SS/AGSS 423, 20
Tortuga, LSD 26, 103
Tortuga, LSD 46, 105
Toucan, AM/MSF 387, 145
Towanda, PC 592, 132
Towers, DDG 9, 73
Towhee, AM/MSF 388, 145; AGS 28, 187
Townsend Cromwell, R 443, 280
Tracer, AGR 15, 186; see *Interrupter*
Tranquillity, AH 14, 226
Transcolorado, AK 2005, 250
Transcolumbia, AK 2006, 250
Trathen, DD 530, 56
Traverse County, LST 1160, 112
Travis, WSC 153, 261
Traw, DE 350, 84
Trenton, LPD 14, 101
Trepang, SS/AGSS 412, 20
Trepang, SSN 674, 28
Trigger, SS 564, 22
Trillium, WAK 170, 275
Tringa, ASR 16, 166
Trinity River, LSMR 535, 117
Tripoli, CVE/CVU 64, 10
Tripoli, LPH 10, 97
Trippe, DE/FF 1075, 90
Triton, SSRN 586, 26
Triton, WPC 116, 261
Triumph, AM/MSF 323, 144
Triumph, AGOS 4, 183
Trout, SS 566, 22
Truckee, AO 147, 214
Truett, DE/FF 1095, 90
Trumpeter, DE 180, 81
Trumpetfish, SS 425, 21
Trutta, SS 421, 20
Truxtun, DLGN/CGN 35, 49
Truxtun, DDG 103, 78
Truxtun, APD 98, 125
TSgt John A. Chapman, AK 323, 241; see *Merlin*
Tuckahoe, WYT 89, 269
Tucson, SSN 770, 31
Tucson, CL 98, 41
Tucumcari, PGH 2, 129
Tulare, AKA/LKA 112, 120

Tullibee, SSN 597, 27
Tumult, AM/MSF 127, 144
Tunica, ATA 178, 231
Tunny, SS/ 282, 16; SSG 282, 24; APSS/LPSS 282, 24
Tunny, SSN 682, 29
Tunxis, AN 90, 192
Tupelo, WAGL/WLB 303, 272
Turkey, AMS 56, 151
Turner, DD 834, 65; DDR 834, 69
Turner Joy, DD 951, 70
Tuscaloosa, CA 37, 39
Tuscaloosa, LST 1187, 114
Tusk, SS 426, 21
Tutuila, ARG 4, 170
Tweedy, DE 532, 86
Twin Falls, AGM 11, 181; AGS 37, 187
Twining, DD 540, 56
Tybee, WPB 1330, 266
Typhon, ARL 28, 171
Typhoon, PC 5, 136

Uhlmann, DD 687, 59
Ukiah, PC 1251, 133
Ulvert M. Moore, DE 442, 85
Ulysses, ARB 9, 171
Ulysses S. Grant, SSBN 631, 35
Umpqua, ATA 209, 232
Unadilla, ATA 182, 231
Unalga, WAK 185, 275
Undaunted, ATA 199, 232
Underwood, FFG 36, 94
Unicorn, SS 436, 21
Unimak, AVP 31, 168; WAVP/WHEC/WTR 379, 256, 275
Union, AKA/LKA 106, 120
United States, CVA 58, 5
United States, CVN 75, 8
Upham, APD 99, 125
Upshur, AP 198, 225
Ute, ATF 76, 229; WMEC 76, 258
Utina, ATF 163, 231
Uvalde, AKA 88, 119

VADM K.R. Wheeler, AG 5001, 252
Valcour, AGF 1, 119; AVP 55, 169
Valdez, DE/FF 1096, 90
Valentine, AF 47, 198
Valiant AOT 94A, 252
Valiant, WMEC 621, 259
Valley Forge, CV/CVS 45, 4; LPH 8, 97
Valley Forge, CG 50, 50
Valor, MSO 472, 147

Valve, ARS 28, 174
Vamarie, IX 47, 192
Vammen, DE 644, 80
Van Valkenburgh, DD 656, 58
Van Voorhis, DE 1028, 87
Vance, DE 387, 83; DER 387, 87; WDE 487, 260
Vancouver, LPD 2, 100
Vandalia, PC 1175, 133
Vandegrift, FFG 48, 94
Vanderburgh, APB 48, 225
Vandivier, DE 540, 86; DER 540, 87
Vanguard, AG 194, 178; AGM 19, 182
Varian, DE 798, 80
Vashon, WPB 1308, 265
Vega, AF 59, 199
Vega, AK 286, 205
Vela, AK 89, 201
Vella Gulf, CVE/CVHE 111, 11; AKV 11, 207
Vella Gulf, CG 72, 51
Velocity, AM/MSF 128, 144
Vent, ARS 29, 175
Venture, MSO 496, 147
Venturous, WMEC 625, 259
Verbena, WAGL/WLI 317, 274
Verdin, AMS 38, 151
Vermilion, AKA/LKA 107, 120
Vernon County, LST 1161, 112
Vesole, DD 878, 68; DDR 878, 69
Vesuvius, AE 15, 196
Vicksburg, CL 86, 41
Vicksburg, CG 69, 51
Victoria, AK 281, 205
Victorious, AGOS 19, 185
Vigil, AGR 12, 185
Vigilance, AM/MSF 324, 144
Vigilant, WMEC 617, 259
Vigilant, WSC 154, 261
Vigor, MSO 473, 147
Vigorous, WMEC 627, 259
Viking, ARS 1, 174
Vincennes, CL 64, 41
Vincennes, CG 49, 50
Vindicator, AGOS 3, 183
Violet, WAGL 250, 271
Vireo, MSC 205, 157
Virginia, SSN 774, 33
Virginia, CGN 38, 50
Virginia Key, ARV 80/R 680, 281
Virgo, AKA 20, 119; AE 30, 197
Vital, MSO 474, 147
Voge, DE/FF 1047, 89
Vogelgesang, DD 862, 67

Volador, SS 490, 21
Von Steuben, SSBN 632, 35
Vreeland, DE/FF 1068, 90
Vulcan, AR 5, 170

W.S. Sims, DE/FF 1059, 90
Wabash, AOG 4, 218
Wabash, AOR 5, 220
Waccamaw, AO/AOR 109, 213
Wachusett, WPG/WHEC 44, 256
Wacissa, AOG 59, 219
Waddell, DDG 24, 74
Wadleigh, DD 689, 59
Wadsworth, DD 516, 56
Wadsworth, FFG 9, 93
Waesche, WMSL 751, 257
Wagner, DE 539, 86; DER 539, 87
Wahkiakum County, LST 1162, 112
Wahoo, SS 565, 22
Wahoo, WPB 87345, 267
Wainwright, DLG/CG 28, 48
Wainwright, ASV 83, 277
Wakefield, AP 21, 221
Wakerobin, WAGL 251, 274
Waldo County, LST 1163, 112
Waldron, DD 699, 60
Walke, DD 723, 61
Walker, DD 517, 56; DDE 517, 69
Wallace L. Lind, DD 703, 60
Waller, DD 466, 55; DDE 466, 69
Wally Schirra, AKE 8, 206
Walnut, WAGL/WLM 252, 271
Walnut, WLB 205, 273
Walrus, SS 437, 21
Walsh, APD 111, 126
Walter B. Cobb, APD 106, 125
Walter C. Wann, DE 412, 85
Walter S. Diehl, AO 193, 217
Walter S. Gorka, APD 114, 126
Walter X. Young, APD 131, 126
Walton, DE 361, 85
Walworth County, LST 1164, 112
Wampanoag, ATA 202, 232
Wandank, ATA 204, 232
Wantuck, APD 125, 126
Wapakoneta, PC 579, 132
Warbler, MSC 206, 157
Warrick, AKA 89, 119
Warrington, DD 843, 66
Warrior, MCM 8, 151
Wasatch, AGC 9, 118
Washburn, AKA/LKA 108, 120
Washington, BB 56, 37
Washington, AK 5020, 242

Washington, WPB 1331, 266
Washoe County, LST 1165, 112
Washtenaw County, LST 1166, 112; MSS 2, 162
Wasp, CV/CVS 18, 3
Wasp, LHD 1, 99
Watchman, AGR 16, 185
Wateree, ATA 174, 231
Waterford, ARD 5, 227
Waterman, DE 740, 81
Waters, AGS 45, 188
Watertown, AGM 6, 181
Watkins, AKR 315, 238
Watson, AKR 310, 238
Watts, DD 567, 57
Wauseon, PC 1229, 133
Waverly, PC 1225, 133
Waxbill, AMS 39, 151; AMCU/MHC 50, 160
Waxsaw, AN 91, 192
Waxwing, AM/MSF 389, 145
Wayne E. Meyer, DDG 108, 78
Waynesburg, PC 777, 132
Weatherford, PC 618, 132
Weaver, DE 741, 81
Weber, APD 75, 125
Webster, ARV 2, 171
Webster, AG 190, 177
Wedderburn, DD 684, 59
Weeden, DE 797, 80
Weiss, APD/LPR 135, 126
Welch, PG 93, 127
Welch, PC 817, 132
Welles, DD 628, 55
Wenatchee, ATF 118, 230
Wesson, DE 184, 81
West Milton, ARD 7, 227
West Virginia, SSBN 736, 36
West Virginia, BB 48, 37
Westchester County, LST 1167, 112
Westerly, PC 1198, 133
Westpac Express, HSV 4676, 193
Westwind, AGB 6, 179; WAGB 281, 268
Wexford County, LST 1168, 112
Whale, SS 239, 15
Whale, SSN 638, 28
Wheatear, AM/MSF 390, 145
Wheeling, AGM 8, 181
Whetstone, LSD 27, 103
Whidbey, AG 141, 175
Whidbey Island, LSD 41, 104
Whipple, DE/FF 1062, 90
Whippoorwill, MSC 207, 157

Whirlwind, PC 11, 136
White Alder, WLM 541, 273
White Bush, WLM 542, 273; IX 542, 193
White Heath WLM 545 , 273
White Holly, WLM 543, 273
White Lupine, WLM 546, 273
White Marsh, LSD 8, 103
White Pine, WLM 547, 273
White Plains, CVE/CVU 66, 10
White Plains, AFS 4, 199
White River, LSMR/LFR 536, 117
White Sage, WLM 544, 273
White Sands, AGDS 1, 179
White Sands, ARD 20, 227
White Sumac, WLM 540, 273
Whitehall, PCER 856, 134
Whitehurst, DE 634, 80
Whiteside, AKA 90, 119
Whitewood, AG 129, 176
Whitfield County, LST 1169, 112
Whiting, CSS 29/S 329, 279
Whitley, AKA 91, 120
Wichita, CA 45, 39
Wichita, AOR 1, 220
Wickes, DD 578, 57
Widgeon, MSC 208, 157
Wildwood, PC 1181, 133
Wiley, DD 597, 58
Wilhoite, DE 397, 8; DER 397, 87
Wilkes, AGS 33, 187
Wilkes, DD 441, 54
Wilkes-Barre, CL 103, 42
Wilkinson, DL 5, 45
Will Rogers, SSBN 659, 35
Willamette, AO 180, 216
Willard Keith, DD 775, 62
William C. Cole, DE 641, 80
William C. Lane, DD 763, 63
William H. Bates, SSN 680, 29
William H. Standley, DLG/CG 32, 48
William J J J. Pattison, APD 104, 125
William M. Hobby, APD 95, 125
William M. Wood, DD 715, 63; DDR 715, 69
William P. Lawrence, DDG 110, 78

William R. Rush, DD 714, 63; DDR 714, 69
William Seiverling, DE 441, 85
William T. Powell, DE 213, 79; DER 213, 86
William Tate, WLM 560, 274
William V. Pratt, DLG 13, 45; DDG 44, 76
Williams, DE 372, 85
Williamsburg, AGC 369, 118
Willis, DE 395, 83
Willis A. Lee, DL 4, 45
Willmarth, DE 638, 80
Willow, WAGL/WLB 332, 272
Willow, WLB 202, 273
Wiltsie, DD 716, 63
Winder, PCS 1376, 135
Windham Bay, CVE/CVU 92, 11
Windham County, LST 1170, 112
Windlass, ARSD 4, 172
Windsor, ARD 22, 227
Wingfield, DE 194, 81
Winnebago, WPG/WHEC 40, 256
Winnemucca, PC 1145, 133
Winona, WPG/WHEC, 65, 256
Winslow, AG 127, 176
Winston, AKA/LKA 94, 120
Winston S. Churchill, DDG 81, 78
Wisconsin, BB 64, 38
Wiseman, DE 667, 80
Wistaria, WAGL/WLI 254, 271
Witek, DD/EDD 848, 66
Wood County, LST 1178, 113
Woodbine:, WAGL/WLB 289, 272
Woodpecker, MSC 209, 157
Woodrow R. Thompson, DD 721, 63
Woodrow Wilson, SSBN 624, 35
Woodrush, WAGL/WLB 407, 272
Woodson, DE 359, 85
Woodstock, PC 1180, 133
Woodworth, DD 460, 54
Woolsey, DD 437, 54
Worcester, CL 144, 42
Worden, DLG/CG 18, 46
Worland, PCE 845, 134
Worthington, PC 1137, 133
Worthy AGOS 14. 183
Wrangell, AE 12, 196

Wrangell, WPB 1332, 266
Wren, DD 568, 57
Wright, CVL 49, 5; CC 2, 44; AVT 7, 169
Wright, AVB 3, 169, 237
Wyandot, AKA 92, 120; AK 283, 205
Wyman, AGS 34, 187
Wyoming, SSBN 742, 36
Wythe, APB 41, 225

X-1 X-1, 23
Xanthus, AR 19, 170

Yakutat, AVP 32, 168; WAVP/WHEC 380, 256
Yamacraw, ARC 5, 173; WARC 333, 272
Yancey, AKA/LKA 93, 120
Yankton, WYT 72, 269
Yano, AKR 296, 240
Yarnall, DD 541, 56
Yavapai, APB 42, 225
Yazoo, AN 92, 192
Yeaton, WSC 156, 261
Yellowfin, WPB 87319, 266
Yellowstone, AD 27, 164
Yellowstone, AD 41, 164
Yocona, WAT/WMEC 168, 258
Yokes, APD 69, 125
Yolo, APB 43, 225
York County, LST 1175, 113
Yorktown, CVA/CVS 10, 2
Yorktown, CG 48, 50
Yosemite, AD 19, 163
Young, DD 580, 57
Yukon, AO/AOT 152, 215
Yukon, AO 202, 217
Yuma, ATF 94, 230

Z-39, DD 939, 71
Zeal, AM/MSF 131, 144
Zelima, AF 49, 198
Zellars, DD 777, 62
Zephyr, PC 8, 136; WPC 8, 267
Zeus, ARB 4, 171
Zeus, ARC 7, 173
Zinnia, WAGL/WLI 255, 271
Zumwalt, DDG 1000, 78